Criminal Law, Second Edition
Steven I. Friedland, Catherine L. Carpenter,
Kami N. Chavis, and Catherine Arcabascio

Current Issues in Constitutional Litigation, Third Edition
Sarah E. Ricks and Evelyn M. Tenenbaum

Employment Discrimination, Third Edition
Sandra F. Sperino and Jarod S. Gonzalez

Energy Law
Joshua P. Fershee

Evidence, Second Edition
Pavel Wonsowicz

International Business Transactions
Amy Deen Westbrook

International Women's Rights, Equality, and Justice
Christine M. Venter

The Lawyer's Practice
Kris Franklin

Professional Responsibility
Barbara Glesner Fines

Property
Alicia Kelly and Nancy Knauer

Sales, Second Edition
Edith R. Warkentine

Secured Transactions
Edith R. Warkentine and Jerome A. Grossman

Torts
Paula J. Manning

Workers' Compensation Law, Second Edition
Michael C. Duff

Your Brain and Law School
Marybeth Herald

Current Issues in Constitutional Litigation

A Context and Practice Casebook

THIRD EDITION

Sarah E. Ricks
Distinguished Clinical Professor of Law
Rutgers Law School

Evelyn M. Tenenbaum
Professor of Law
Albany Law School

Carolina Academic Press
Durham, North Carolina

ISBN 978-1-5310-1918-1
e-ISBN 978-1-5310-1919-8
LCCN 2020932499

Carolina Academic Press
700 Kent Street
Durham, NC 27701
Telephone (919) 489-7486
Fax (919) 493-5668
www.cap-press.com

Printed in the United States of America

To Tom, Kate, and Charlie, with love
and in memory of Jack Lee Young (1981–2013)

—Sarah Ricks, Philadelphia, Pennsylvania

To Howard, Joanna, and Karen, with love

—Evelyn Tenenbaum, Albany, New York

Carolina Academic Press Context and Practice Series

Michael Hunter Schwartz
Series Editor

Administrative Law, Second Edition
Richard Henry Seamon

Advanced Torts, Second Edition
Alex B. Long and Meredith J. Duncan

Animal Law—New Perspectives on Teaching Traditional Law
Kathy Hessler, Joyce Tischler, Pamela Hart, and Sonia S. Waisman

Antitrust Law
Steven Semeraro

Civil Procedure, Second Edition
Gerald F. Hess, Theresa M. Beiner, and Scott R. Bauries

Civil Procedure for All States
Benjamin V. Madison, III

Complex Litigation
James M. Underwood

Constitutional Law, Second Edition
David Schwartz and Lori Ringhand

A Context and Practice Global Case File:
An Intersex Athlete's Constitutional Challenge,
Hastings v. USATF, IAAF, and IOC
Olivia M. Farrar

A Context and Practice Global Case File:
***Rossi v. Bryce*, An International Embryo and Surrogacy Dispute**
Olivia M. Farrar

A Context and Practice Global Case File:
***Thorpe v. Lightfoot*, A Mother's International Hague Petition**
for the Return of Her Child
Olivia M. Farrar

Contracts, Third Edition
Michael Hunter Schwartz and Adrian J. Walters

Current Issues in Constitutional Litigation

Contents

Table of Cases

What's Past Is Prologue: Foreword to Third Edition by Aderson Bellegarde François[1]

In the winter of 1907, Albert Martin Kales, an 1899 graduate of Harvard Law School and professor at Northwestern University Law School, published an article in the Harvard Law Review titled "The Next Step in the Evolution of the Casebook."[2] In it, Professor Kales argued that "the comparative merits of the casebook and the text-book methods of teaching law are no longer an issue in legal education," that casebooks "have driven the text-book out of existence as a means of education," and that the time had come to ask "what is to be the next step in their evolution?"[3] In Professor Kales' view, for all of their virtues, casebooks had one fatal flaw: by focusing exclusively on important English and national cases they did not afford sufficient flexibility to the law teacher who wished to instruct students on how the law of local jurisdictions fits into the national scheme.

In the spring of 2007, Professor Matthew Bodie published an article in the *Journal of Legal Education* titled "The Future of the Casebook: An Argument for an Open-Source Approach."[4] In it, Professor Bodie argued that "ever since Christopher Langdell devised the first compilation to teach his students using the case method, law professors have relied on casebooks to provide the substantive basis for their courses," that "the casebook is, quite simply, the written centerpiece of legal education," but that "despite its privileged position, the casebook as we know it is probably on its way to extinction."[5] In Professor Bodie's view, for all of their virtues, the fatal flaw of most casebooks is that, by relying on a fixed set of bound cases they do not afford law teachers sufficient flexibility to customize the materials in the book to fit their teaching styles, the demands of their courses, and the needs of their students.

1. A version of this essay was published in The Law Teacher (Fall 2011) at 26. Since then, the author has joined the faculty of Georgetown Law School as Professor of Law & Director, Institute for Public Representation Civil Rights Law Clinic.

2. Albert Martin Kales, *The Next Step in the Evolution of the Casebook*, 2 Harv. L. Rev. 92 (1907).

3. *Id.*

4. Matthew Bodie, *The Future of the Casebook: An Argument for an Open-Source Approach*, 57 J. Legal Educ. 10 (2007).

5. *Id.*

At the time Professor Kales published his call for the next evolutionary step in the development of the casebook, the case method had been in widespread use for barely thirty-five years,[6] there were only sixty-one published casebooks in circulation,[7] and it would be at least another year before West Publishing company established a national casebook market with the launch of the American Casebook Series.[8] In the intervening century between Professor Kales' call for its evolution and Professor Bodie's warning of its extinction, the casebook has been in a near constant state of change. Indeed, a year after he first distributed the introductory bound collection of cases to his Harvard students, Langdell himself began to edit it, not only adding and expunging cases but also eventually including commentaries that had been absent in the very first iterations of the book.[9] It sometimes seems as though the casebook has been in a constant state of flux ever since.

Perhaps the reason law teachers seem to be endlessly tinkering with the format of the casebook is that, as a teaching tool, the casebook is not terribly well suited for the case method. Strictly understood, the case method rests on the idea that the goal of law teaching is not to impart legal knowledge but to introduce legal reasoning. As Professor Peggy Cooper Davis recently showed, while it has long been the accepted view that Langdell's case method is overly rigid and formalistic in its insistence that law is a science and that legal reasoning, when subjected to scientific methods, can lead to the right answers, there is, in fact, nothing in Langdell's published works, letters and other collected papers that supports the claim that he was concerned about imparting knowledge so that students arrived at the right answers.[10] Rather, the case method and its accompanying Socratic dialogue was first and foremost an attempt at "giving students the chance to learn in the way that psychologists increasingly say that both children and adults learn best: by working collaboratively and at the growing edge of their abilities—at times sharing and applying collaborators' knowledge and methods, at times gaining new knowledge and developing new methods."[11] The problem is that a relatively short time after the case method was widely adopted, casebook authors increasingly began to organize and format their volumes to achieve maximum coverage of particular legal subjects.[12] That transformation of the casebook into a tool for coverage was based on a failure to recognize that, in Langdell's view, "science or not, law poses hard questions that can't be, or at least haven't been, resolved with certainty." As such, "the notion that the courses offered should include everything a

---

6. Russell L. Weaver, *Langdell's Legacy: Living with the Case Method*, 36 VILL. L. REV. 517, 520–21 (1991).

7. Douglas W. Lind, *An Economic Analysis of Early Casebook Publishing*, 96 LAW LIBR. J. 95, 103–04 (2004).

8. *Id.* at 107.

9. Steve Shepard, *Casebooks, Commentaries, and Curmudgeons: An Introductory History of Law in the Lecture Hall*, 82 IOWA L. REV. 547, 600–01 (1997).

10. Peggy Cooper Davis, *Desegregating Legal Education*, 26 GA. ST. L. REV. 1271, 1281 (2010).

11. *Id.* at 1289.

12. *See generally*, Shepard, *Casebooks, Commentaries*, 82 IOWA L. REV. 547.

student need know, that he need consider or will consider that is not gone over in class, is a mistaken one."[13]

Of all the non-core upper-level law school courses, perhaps none is as prone to the mistaken notion that "courses should include everything students need to know," and none is as ill equipped to keep that dubious promise, than the typical civil rights course. I speak from personal experience, being both the supervising attorney for the Civil Rights Clinic at Howard University School of Law and a professor of several upper level civil rights and constitutional law seminars.

So, it is particularly heartening to now have a casebook from Professor Sarah Ricks and her collaborator Professor Evelyn Tenenbaum that offers a vision of civil rights litigation teaching, not as a survey of the body of constitutional provisions, judicial decisions, legislative enactments, and regulatory regimes that make up federal civil rights law, but as a meditation on whether and how Congress, the courts, and American society have kept or broken faith with the constitutional ideal of respect for human rights and equality. Using mostly—though not exclusively—prison and police litigation, focusing on selected legislation, cases, briefs, and social developments, and relying on a set of interlocking questions and problems for discussion, Professor Ricks demonstrates that, particularly when it comes to civil rights litigation, "law professors should worry less about details and ramifications, and should concentrate more on method, technique, vocabulary, approach, arts, and the other things that go to make up a lawyer who will be adequately qualified to dig into problems,—for the most part, problems the details of which we could not possibly teach him now no matter how hard we tried."[14]

Professor Ricks' decision to use civil rights law to teach the fundamental indeterminacy of legal reasoning and the intellectual versatility of legal practice is perhaps best demonstrated not just by the relatively small number of cases she has culled from the vast body of civil rights precedent, but by her decision to place federal district and circuit court rather than Supreme Court opinions at the center of her book. Indeed, it is no exaggeration to suggest that Supreme Court precedent is the least important feature of the book. This choice is made abundantly clear in the introductory chapter on § 1983, more than two-thirds of which Ricks devotes to a discussion of the social milieu of the reconstruction Era, the rise of the Ku Klux Klan, and first-hand testimony of victims of Klan violence. Only after providing this background does Ricks make any mention of the Supreme Court's decision of *Monroe v. Pape*,[15] which is credited with reviving § 1983 as a viable civil rights tool after it had fallen into disuse following the Supreme Court's evisceration of the Reconstruction civil rights statues of 1866, 1870, 1871 and 1875.

13. Roscoe Pound, *Book Review*, 4 ILL. L. REV. 150 (1909).

14. Erwin Griswold, *Some Thoughts About Legal Education Today*, in FRONTIERS IN LAW AND LEGAL EDUCATION 77 (1961).

15. 365 U.S. 167 (1961).

Where one would normally expect a recapitulation of Supreme Court precedent, Professor Ricks offers attorneys' interviews and briefs as a way of making evident the indispensable role advocates play in the development of civil rights law. The relegation of the Supreme Court as a distant overseer is, like so many decisions in this beautifully written book, an attempt to take back the casebook to its true origins: as a tool to teach not knowledge but reasoning, not details but techniques, not doctrine but method.

Of course, Professor Ricks' casebook is not the first or the only one to supplement cases with historical materials, scholarly discussions, workbook problems, or even practice documents. Many, if not most, casebooks nowadays do the same thing in one fashion or another. However, in many casebooks, these supplemental materials are yet another means of increasing coverage of the substantive doctrinal law students need to know—the idea being that, to fully cover, say, federal employment discrimination law, it is necessary for students to know the historical circumstances of the passage of Title VII of Civil Rights Act of 1964. What makes Professor Ricks' casebook different in an important respect is that the historical and practice materials are not there to supplement coverage of doctrine but to provide a structure for students to address "the complex and contradictory interplay of a formalistic deference to authority and an indeterminacy that allows the law to respond to notions of justice and efficiency."[16]

My years of serving both as a civil rights clinician and a doctrinal professor of constitutional law have taught me that the most difficult issues students encounter are almost never about doctrine. Rather, far more challenging are questions such as: How do you choose between advancing a new theory of a claim, knowing you will likely face a skeptical, if not hostile, judicial audience, or rehearsing the more conventional argument that does nothing to advance the law? How do you rhetorically frame your case in a way that the court is predisposed to understand, accept and respect, while at the same time telling a story that rings true to a client who spent years trying to just get someone to listen? Why, if we are being honest, do so many pro bono civil rights litigants seem at first (or even second) blush a little mentally disturbed? Did the psychological pressure of spending years fighting a losing battle against social forces bent on destroying them eventually extract a psychic cost now made manifest through their unshakable conviction that their pro bono attorney is secretly conspiring against them? Or is the fact that they took on the fight in the first place itself evidence of a less than fully developed sense of self-preservation because most of us supposedly rational folks would not be so quick to tilt at the windmills of the system by, say, trying, as did James Meredith, to singlehandedly racially integrate the University of Mississippi? Or is it really us advocates, ever the products of the legal status quo even while challenging it, who are afflicted with a skewed perspective for being too quick to reduce every question of justice and fairness into a legal issue?

No Supreme Court case I am aware of holds the answer to these questions. But, without explicitly framing her book as a historical and cultural critique of American

16. Davis, *Desegregating Legal Education*, 26 Ga. St. L. Rev. at 1289.

civil rights law, Professor Ricks has, in fact, offered a trenchant account of how civil rights law is a catalogue of public morality and a registry of social consciousness; how any civil rights doctrine, whether significant or minor, whether honored or abused, reveals something about the people who adopted it and the ideas they profess to hold dear; and how civil rights litigation is not merely (or indeed mainly) a contest over the technical requirements of judicial, legislative and administrative rules but a reflection of American society's ideas of justice, fairness, power, equality and democracy.

But above all this: Professor Ricks has managed to accomplish in this textbook, with prose at once clearheaded and lyrical, in a format at once straightforward and complex, and with materials at once conventional and unexpected, the difficult and seemingly contradictory task of pointing the way to the future of the casebook while at the same time proving herself a true intellectual heir to Langdell's original vision of the case method.

Aderson Bellegarde François
Professor of Law & Director,
Institute for Public Representation Civil Rights Law Clinic
Georgetown Law School
Washington, DC December 2019
(originally published in 2011)

Foreword to Second Edition by Rebecca E. Zietlow

Professor Ricks and Professor Tenenbaum's CURRENT ISSUES IN CONSTITUTIONAL LITIGATION is an excellent, innovative textbook. It is both a comprehensive treatment of the substantive material and an effective tool for teaching practical skills to law students. As law students increasingly demand practical skills courses, some professors fear that they will be required to sacrifice coverage of substantive law. This textbook shows that it is not necessary to make such a choice. The innovative means in which the material is presented motivates students to learn the substantive law in even greater scope and depth than a conventional lecture class. The material is presented through appellate decisions, jury instructions, and other sources that practicing lawyers use. This material is accessible to students, and it more closely resembles the practice of law than the conventional presentation of only Supreme Court cases. The book also presents contextual information, which enables students to understand the issues covered in a sophisticated fashion. Students become engaged in the subjects presented, and this also motivates them to learn more.

The strongest aspect of CURRENT ISSUES IN CONSTITUTIONAL LITIGATION is the inclusion of simulation exercises. The students enjoy the exercises and take on the responsibility of teaching the material to other students as they engage in the simulations. Thus the students take ownership of the learning process, and have a great time as well. Many of my students have told me that they wish that there were more classes like this one in law school. I agree.

Rebecca E. Zietlow
Charles W. Fornoff Professor of Law and Values
University of Toledo College of Law
January 2015

Foreword to Second Edition by Michael P. O'Connor

CURRENT ISSUES IN CONSTITUTIONAL LITIGATION: A CONTEXT AND PRACTICE CASEBOOK is far and away the best book available today to teach, and for your students to learn, constitutional litigation. Before using this text, I had used several other books to teach civil rights litigation courses. None of the other texts compared favorably with that produced by Ricks and Tenenbaum. The cases are well chosen and go beyond the standard Supreme Court offerings, providing students with examples of how the law is interpreted and developed by litigators in the lower courts.

But the additional materials are what make this text stand apart as a "Context and Practice Casebook." The law practice simulations allow students to access this material in a manner that bridges the divide between doctrinal and clinical education, while the supplemental materials permit professors to engage students with various learning modalities.

No book I have used has been so uniformly praised by my students (100% favorable ratings). The interviews, background reports and excerpts of briefs allow students to grasp the critical development of both the law and the litigation strategies used by practitioners to shape the law in the trenches.

CURRENT ISSUES IN CONSTITUTIONAL LITIGATION engages students across the spectrum, from those taking the class because it fits their schedules to those who intend to pursue careers in civil rights litigation. It is that rare casebook that can help you make a difference in your students' career choices and, ultimately, their lives. It helps you to bring alive the stories of the people behind these cases, both the litigants and the litigators. By making the litigation real and accessible, students embrace it. Through that embrace, the next generation of civil rights litigators is born, and the struggle to safeguard and expand constitutional protections continues.

Michael P. O'Connor
University of La Verne College of Law
January 2015

Foreword to First Edition by David Rudovsky

This new casebook admirably fills a significant need in the teaching of the complex and dynamic issues in the area of constitutional litigation. For many years, law teachers of this increasingly important topic have either had to generate their own materials or choose among some few standard casebooks. Now, Professor Ricks has authored a new and quite different casebook that provides far more than the usual cases, comments and questions.

Professor Ricks approaches the constitutional and statutory materials from several perspectives: doctrinal development, legislative responses, litigation decisions, and practical considerations that inform the litigation and decision making in this area. Included in each substantive chapter are the social and political contexts of the constitutional issues, leading Supreme Court and Circuit Court opinions, excerpts from oral arguments on major cases in the Supreme Court, legislative initiatives, expert reports, jury instructions, representative pleadings, and even interviews with leading civil rights litigators. Students are provided with the full range of materials from the files of litigators to the decisions by the courts.

As an example, the chapter on prisoner rights litigation includes the leading cases and the development of controlling doctrine, but also provides a rich mix of materials from litigation files, investigative reports from public interest organizations, and legislative hearings that bear on the major issues. Professor Ricks also provides thoughtful questions and innovative simulations that will encourage students to think through these problems from the perspectives of the lawyers, inmates, prison officials, judges, and legislators.

The world of constitutional litigation is far broader than case law. Professor Ricks has captured the multi-dimensional aspects of this field of law and has produced a casebook that will greatly enhance teaching, learning and practice of constitutional litigation.

David Rudovsky
Kairys, Rudovsky, Messing & Feinberg
University of Pennsylvania Law School
Philadelphia, Pennsylvania
August 2010

Foreword to First Edition by Karen Blum

For years I've been putting together my own materials to teach a course on Police Misconduct Litigation. The course takes a practical approach and gets the students involved in working on real cases with attorneys, from both the plaintiffs' and defense bar, who are experienced in the area of section 1983 litigation. There has been no casebook that provides students with the opportunity to see how all the facets of a case come together.

Sarah Ricks has created an incredibly useful, contextually-based casebook that tells the story of constitutional litigation from many different perspectives. Students go behind the scenes and come to understand litigation from reading not only case law, but from examining briefs, oral arguments, pleadings, and expert opinions.

Chapter Six explores Fourth Amendment standards and Police Misconduct. The Chapter begins with facts and statistics about a police officer's job, the typical job requirements, salaries, and training. This is important information for students to have when they are reading cases that evaluate the reasonableness of a police officer's conduct. Following the key cases of *Tennessee v. Garner* and *Graham v. Connor*, the Chapter includes sample jury instructions and verdict forms for excessive force cases. An excessive force "dog-bite" case is followed from complaint to verdict, giving the students insight into how multiple claims and defendants may be reduced as the case proceeds, with the ultimate disposition of the case turning on a single issue in a single claim with respect to a single officer. Students are invited to think about the time and expense of litigation and the economic pressures to reject a settlement that would not compensate for the investment of time expended by plaintiff's counsel. The coverage of *Scott v. Harris* includes excerpts from the oral argument and an amicus brief submitted by the National Police Accountability Project. A post-*Scott* Circuit decision provides a window for exploration of how *Scott* is being applied and whether it establishes a "*per se*" rule for the use of deadly force in cases involving motor vehicle chases.

For professors and students who want more from legal education than the unadorned case-method approach can provide, Professor Ricks has compiled a set of materials that brings the case law to life. Teaching and learning about constitutional litigation will be a much richer experience thanks to her efforts.

Karen M. Blum
Professor of Law
Suffolk University Law School
Boston, Massachusetts
August 2010

Series Editor's Preface

Welcome to a new type of casebook. Designed by leading experts in law school teaching and learning, Context and Practice casebooks assist law professors and their students to work together to learn, minimize stress, and prepare for the rigors and joys of practicing law. **Student learning and preparation for law practice are the guiding ethics of these books.**

Why would we depart from the tried and true? Why have we abandoned the legal education model by which we were trained? Because legal education can and must improve.

In Spring 2007, the Carnegie Foundation published *Educating Lawyers: Preparation for the Practice of Law* and the Clinical Legal Education Association published *Best Practices for Legal Education*. Both works reflect in-depth efforts to assess the effectiveness of modern legal education, and both conclude that legal education, as presently practiced, falls quite short of what it can and should be. Both works criticize law professors' rigid adherence to a single teaching technique, the inadequacies of law school assessment mechanisms, and the dearth of law school instruction aimed at teaching law practice skills and inculcating professional values. Finally, the authors of both books express concern that legal education may be harming law students. Recent studies show that law students, in comparison to all other graduate students, have the highest levels of depression, anxiety and substance abuse.

The problems with traditional law school instruction begin with the textbooks law teachers use. Law professors cannot implement *Educating Lawyers* and *Best Practices* using texts designed for the traditional model of legal education. Moreover, even though our understanding of how people learn has grown exponentially in the past 100 years, no law school text to date even purports to have been designed with educational research in mind.

The Context and Practice Series is an effort to offer a genuine alternative. Grounded in learning theory and instructional design and written with *Educating Lawyers* and *Best Practices* in mind, Context and Practice casebooks make it easy for law professors to change.

I welcome reactions, criticisms, and suggestions; my e-mail address is mschwartz@pacific.edu. Knowing the author(s) of these books, I know they, too, would appreciate your input; we share a common commitment to student learning. In fact, students, if your professor cares enough about your learning to have adopted this book, I bet s/he would welcome your input, too!

Michael Hunter Schwartz, Series Designer and Editor
Consultant, Institute for Law Teaching and Learning
Dean and Professor of Law, McGeorge School of Law,
University of the Pacific

Acknowledgments for First, Second, and Third Editions

Thank you to Michael Hunter Schwartz and Gerry Hess for creating and editing the Context and Practice Series, and for energetic and thoughtful guidance along the way.

Professors who assign the casebook generously have shared suggestions for this Third Edition. In particular, thank you to the Honorable John A. Gibney, Jr., United States District Judge for the Eastern District of Virginia, Barry N. Kramer, and Rebecca Zietlow for offering valuable comments. Law professors who teach and write about civil rights, federal courts, and constitutional law generously gave constructive feedback on much of this material in earlier drafts. Thank you to Karen Blum, Aderson Francois, Sally Goldfarb, Earl Maltz, Joan Meier, Andrea Mooney, Mike O'Connor, David Rudovsky, Richard Saphire, Allan Stein, and Penny Venetis. Thank you to Harriet Katz and David Nadvorney for encouragement and for sharing their teaching expertise, and to Mary Kay Ricks for sharing her historical expertise. I learned a great deal from the thorough vetting and insightful comments of active civil rights practitioners Elise Bruhl, Craig Gottlieb, and Jane Istvan, and federal court litigator Tom Dolgenos. Thank you to the many civil rights lawyers who allowed me to include interviews with them.

For inspiration and guidance on how to shape these ideas into a book, thank you to my current and former colleagues, Bob Williams, Beth Hillman, John Beckerman, Earl Maltz, and colleagues at other schools, Joan Malmud Rocklin, Susan Wawrose, and especially Tom Cobb.

Several groups gave me constructive feedback on presentations of earlier drafts of portions of these materials. Thank you to Lynda Dodd and participants in a City University of New York civil rights writers' workshop, to the Association of Legal Writing Directors Scholars Forum (Marquette Law School, Milwaukee WI); the Delaware Valley Legal Writing Consortium (Temple Law School, Philadelphia PA); the Women's Studies Senior Seminar (Rutgers-Camden College, Camden, N.J.); and the Rutgers-Camden Clinical Faculty Scholarship Colloquium. Thank you to Hays Butler and John Joergensen for library research guidance. Thanks especially to Evelyn Tenenbaum for her thoughtful comments on every single chapter.

All of the Rutgers Law School students and University of Pennsylvania Law School students who enrolled in *Current Issues in Civil Rights Litigation* and in *Civil Rights* between 2004 and 2019 contributed to shaping this book. I am grateful to them for their flexibility and willingness to work with these materials as they evolved. Several

Rutgers students made particularly valuable contributions: Alison Anderson, Lucille Bongiovanni, Patrick Castaneda, Erin Carroll, Shanon Chant, Jessica Corbett, Jacqueline Corsentino, Ashley Cunliffe, Shlomo Cytryn, Elizabeth D'Ancona, Jacqueline Dilks, Nick Ferrara, Jason Fortenberry, Angie Gambone, Carl Goldfarb, Morgan Humphrey, Bryce Hurst, Alison Keating, Kathleen Kelliher, Aryn Keyel, Yoshi Kumara, Brad Kushner, Valerie Manos, Carl Minniti, Brian Morrison, Arthur Murphy, Amanda Nordstrom, Julie Paull, Amy Pearl, Peter Colonna Romano, Alex Rubenstein, Marie Saraceni, Kristofer Scarpa, Meha Siyam, Peregrin Sorter, Geoff Stark, Lisa Szymanski, Alyson Tomljenovic, Cody Valdez, Christy Whitfield, Catie Williams, Lynda Yamamoto, Diane Yandach, and Jack Lee Young. Thank you to Jason Fortenberry for creating the companion website for the book.

Thank you to Rutgers Law School and University of Pennsylvania Law School for financial support. I am grateful to Rutgers Law Co-Dean Kim Mutcherson and former Dean Ray Solomon for their support of my scholarship.

Thank you to my husband, Tom Dolgenos, for talking through these ideas and for unflagging support, and to my children, Kate and Charlie, for sharing their mother's attention and time with this project.

At Carolina Academic Press, Evelyn and I are grateful to Linda Lacy, Scott Sipe, and Tim Colton for enthusiasm and patient guidance, and to Keith Sipe and Rachael Meier for their efforts and support. Evelyn Tenenbaum adds thanks and appreciation for their assistance to Michael Pape, Patrick Collins, Chelsea Cerutti, Ashley Behan, Jonathan Gillerman, and Chitra Anbalagan, to Dean Thomas F. Guernsey and Associate Dean James T. Gathii for their support of her scholarship, and to Albany Law School for financial support. For the third edition, Evelyn would like to thank Stephanie Reighart for her invaluable research assistance, editing suggestions, and photographs, and Theresa Colbert for her invaluable assistance with the manuscript. She would also like to thank Dean Alicia Ouellette and Director of Faculty Research and Scholarship Christian Sundquist for their support of her scholarship.

Current Issues in Constitutional Litigation

Chapter One

Historical Context and Introduction to Modern 42 U.S.C. § 1983

A. Introduction

This book focuses on current issues in constitutional litigation. It includes practical materials for you to learn the basic constitutional and statutory doctrines necessary to litigate common current constitutional cases, those arising under the 4th, 8th, and 14th Amendments to the Constitution, and under the 1st Amendment in prisons.

Unlike most constitutional law casebooks, this book focuses on doctrinal development in the federal circuits. The Supreme Court supervises the federal circuits and resolves circuit splits but there is tension between the Supreme Court's supervisory role and the size of its docket relative to the circuit dockets. While the Supreme Court now decides fewer than 100 cases on the merits per year, the federal courts of appeals decide more than 30,000 cases on the merits. Realistically, then, for most litigants, the decisions of the federal circuit courts are final.

This book has several themes. The Supreme Court has not yet decided many of the issues in this area, and different approaches are percolating in the circuits. Even when the Supreme Court has decided an issue, the Court's language is just the beginning of doctrinal development in the federal courts. Doctrine develops by application to different situations and therefore the lower federal courts, administrators, legislators, and attorneys each play important roles in shaping doctrine. Debates about what these doctrines mean are not only academic. Plaintiff's lawyers, defense lawyers, courts, local government administrators and others apply this law every day.

To illustrate all of the above, the book includes Supreme Court decisions and federal circuit court decisions demonstrating differing applications of Supreme Court doctrine and emerging circuit splits; documents illustrating how doctrine develops in the federal courts, such as model jury instructions, appellate oral arguments, appellate briefs, pleadings, and expert reports; and documents and exercises illustrating how statutory changes are made, such as testimony to legislative bodies and Congressional reports.

In addition, the book includes a series of realistic law practice simulations to allow you to creatively explore the roles of attorneys in shaping and applying legal doctrine. To help you grasp the difficult choices faced by those responsible for ensuring government compliance with constitutional standards, the book includes background information about the lives of prison guards, police, and social workers. The book includes short interviews with civil rights attorneys. In addition, to help remind us of the human faces behind the legal doctrines, the book includes statements made directly by people affected by these legal doctrines, without the intermediary of a lawyer.

B. Translating the Results of the Civil War into Law

Before turning to the current state of the law, it is useful to briefly sketch the historical background for the statute that is used to litigate current constitutional cases, 42 U.S.C. § 1983. Congress enacted the statute in 1871, during the Reconstruction era following the Civil War. The statute, which was the first part of the six-section Ku Klux Klan Act, was intended to provide a federal remedy for deprivations of federal rights. Section 1983 now provides:

> Every person who, under color of any statute, ordinance, regulation, custom, or usage, of any State or Territory or the District of Columbia, subjects, or causes to be subjected, any citizen of the United States or other person within the jurisdiction thereof to the deprivation of any rights, privileges, or immunities secured by the Constitution and laws, shall be liable to the party injured in an action at law, suit in equity, or other proper proceeding for redress, except that in any action brought against a judicial officer for an act or omission taken in such officer's judicial capacity, injunctive relief shall not be granted unless a declaratory decree was violated or declaratory relief was unavailable. For the purposes of this section, any Act of Congress applicable exclusively to the District of Columbia shall be considered to be a statute of the District of Columbia.

The Civil War ended in 1865. The decade that followed, the Reconstruction period, was the political revolution that attempted to restructure the legal system to reflect the results of the war. The federal government attempted to define the post-war roles of the newly freed slaves and the post-war relationship between the federal and state governments. The Reconstruction Amendments to the United States Constitution are the Thirteenth Amendment, ratified in 1865, which freed the slaves; the Fourteenth Amendment, ratified in 1868; and the Fifteenth Amendment, ratified in 1870, which protected the right to vote "regardless of race, color, or previous condition of servitude."[1]

---

1. While not a majority view, at least one scholar argues that "[t]he Framers of the Fourteenth Amendment ... intended to alter the system of federalism, transferring the role of protecting individual

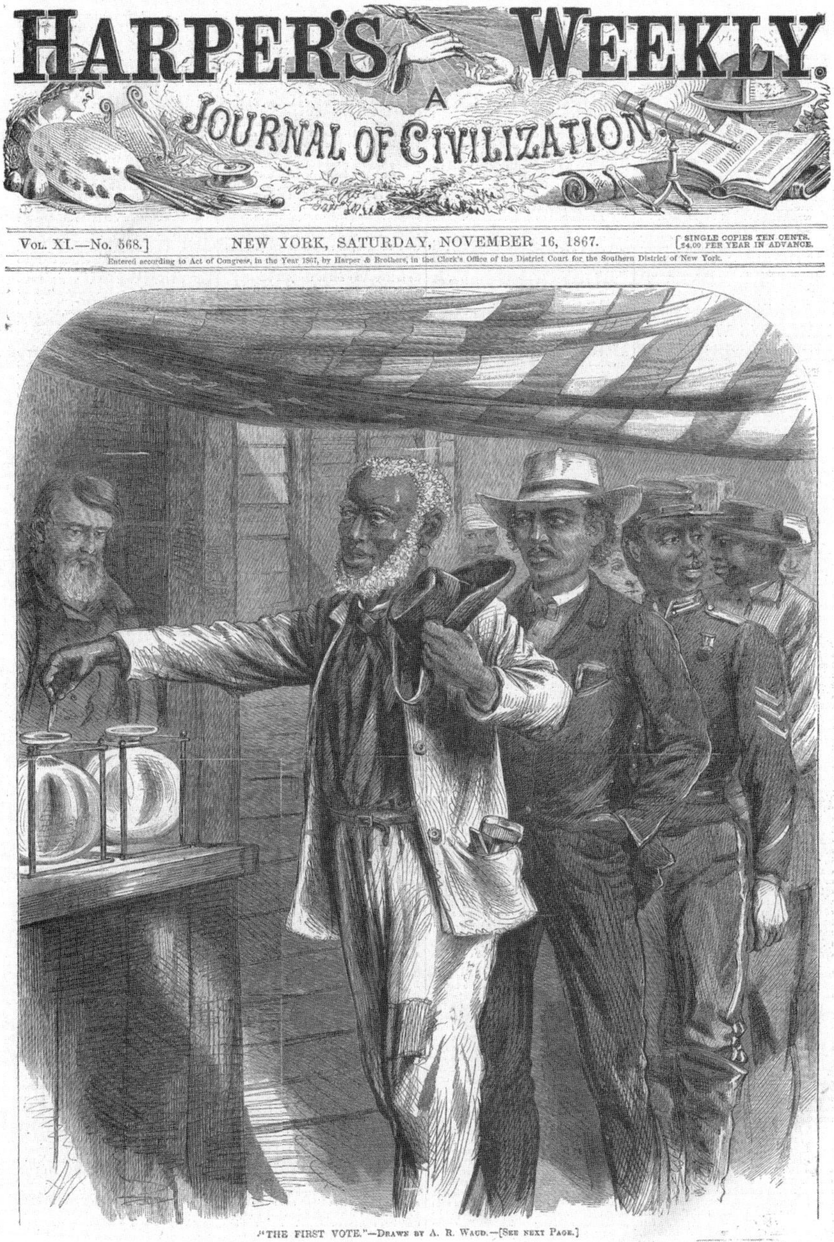

During Reconstruction, African-American men voted and were elected to political office. A *Harper's Weekly* cover illustration of African-Americans at the polling place showed men from different walks of life—a freedman, a man in a fine suit, a sol-

---

rights from the states to the federal government." Rebecca E. Zietlow, Enforcing Equality: Congress, The Constitution, and the Protection of Individual Rights 54–55 (N.Y.U. Press 2006).

dier—all in line to vote.[2] African-American men ran for and were elected to public office. Professor Eric Foner elaborates: "Although whites generally retained political control, the fact that well over six hundred blacks, the majority former slaves, served as legislators represented a stunning change in American politics.... The spectacle of former slaves representing the low-country rice kingdom or the domain of Natchez cotton nabobs epitomized the political revolution wrought by Reconstruction."[3] In South Carolina, "[t]hroughout Reconstruction, [African-Americans] comprised a majority of the House of Representatives, controlled its key committees, and, beginning in 1872, elected black speakers. In 1874, blacks gained a majority in the state senate as well."[4] The potential political clout of the African-Americans can be appreciated from their numbers. For example, in 1870 the black population of South Carolina was 416,000 while the white population was 290,000; "blacks formed a majority in twenty of the state's thirty-one counties."[5]

C. Resistance in Former Confederate States

Former Confederates violently resisted the societal and political changes caused by the Union's victory in the Civil War. "Emancipation, and then the appearance of black federal troops in the conquered South, had been offense enough; when, under the terms of congressional Reconstruction, men of color began to vote, win elections, and wield political authority, the patience of Southerners was pushed to its limit."[6] Beginning around 1866, white resisters organized themselves into groups, such as the Ku Klux Klan, to terrorize the newly freed slaves and freedman, often in nighttime raids on their houses, armed with guns, knives, whips, nooses, and fire, and often in disguise. The Klan targeted community and political leaders, their families, and their white Republican supporters.

A Congressional report published in 1872 summarized the Tennessee origin and spread of the Ku Klux Klan and its political purposes:

> It was composed of the late rebel soldiers as opposed to Union men; of democrats as opposed to the white and negro republicans in the Union Leagues; of those who resisted as against those who sustained [the] Governor['s] efforts to maintain order and preserve peace.... Starting in Tennessee, it had rapidly spread into adjoining States and ... had manifested itself by its acts, to a greater or less extent, in every one of the late insurrectionary States as early

2. "The First Vote," engraving based on a sketch by Alfred R. Waud, *Harper's Weekly*, November 16, 1867, *available at* http://objectofhistory.org/objects/extendedtour/votingmachine/?order=2.

3. Eric Foner, A Short History of Reconstruction 151 (Harper Perennial 1990).

4. *Id. See also* Philip Dray, Capitol Men: The Epic Story of Reconstruction Through the Lives of the First Black Congressmen (Houghton Mifflin Co. 2008). For a comprehensive history, *see* Eric Foner, Reconstruction: America's Unfinished Revolution, 1863–1877 (Harper Perennial 1988).

5. Dray, *supra* note 4, at 79.

6. *Id.* at ix.

> as during the summer and fall of 1868.... Coming into existence after the thirteenth amendment to the Constitution was adopted, it visited its vengeance in Tennessee upon the negro and the Union man whose acts had liberated him. The reconstruction acts, being another step to secure national safety, were met with increased bitterness.... When the fourteenth amendment was proposed, conferring citizenship and its rights and privileges upon the negro, and imposing disabilities to hold office upon those who had already disregarded the obligations of office, the contest became still more bitter.... The adoption of the fifteenth amendment, having made the ballot secure against the spirit which opposed the thirteenth, and rejected, as far as it could, the fourteenth amendment, presented the colored man clothed with freedom, citizenship, and the ballot. The organization of 1866 [the Klan], animated by the spirit and composed of the material already mentioned, had developed in the opposite direction, and in 1870 and 1871, it [committed violent acts against those who sought to prosecute] "the murderers of colored men"[; against those opposed to the Klan; against those who] "exercis[ed] political rights"[; and against teachers of African-American children. The Klan] "destroyed school-houses and drove away school-teachers"[and] "in all the States examined into, it committed murders, whippings, and outrages"] ... [W]hatever may have been its original intent or the avowed design with which men were seduced into it, [the Klan] has become a political organization whose purpose ... is to put the democratic party up and the radical party down, to oppose the [13th, 14th, and 15th] amendments to the Constitution [and] to have a white man's government.... The race so recently emancipated, against which banishment or serfdom is thus decreed, but which has been clothed by the Government with the rights and responsibilities of citizenship, ought not to be, and we feel assured will not be left hereafter without protection against the hostilities and sufferings it has endured in the past, as long as the legal and constitutional powers of the Government are adequate to afford it....

Report of the Joint Select Committee to Inquire into the Condition of Affairs in the Late Insurrectionary States, 42d Congress, 2d Session, Report No. 41, Vol. 1, at 8299 (1872).

D. Section 1983 as a Congressional Response to Klan Resistance

According to Professor Marshall S. Shapo, the Reconstruction-era legislators who enacted the Ku Klux Klan Act, of which § 1983 was one part, "were concerned about a widespread outbreak of violence, principally fostered by an organization of marauders.... [and] exacerbated by the relative inaction of state and local governments. A reading of the entire debates compels the conclusion that the statute was aimed at a situation which bordered on anarchy."[7] The Supreme Court summarized the historical conditions that led Congress to enact legislation to protect the new federal rights of citizens:

> The specific historical catalyst for the Civil Rights Act of 1871 was the campaign of violence and deception in the South, fomented by the Ku Klux Klan, which was denying decent citizens their civil and political rights.... The debates on the Act chronicle the alarming insecurity of life, liberty, and property in the Southern States, and the refuge that local authorities extended to the authors of these outrageous incidents.... By providing a remedy for the violation of constitutional rights, Congress hoped to restore peace and justice to the region through the subtle power of civil enforcement.

Wilson v. Garcia, 471 U.S. 261, 276–77 (1985). Professor Foner explains that the Ku Klux Klan Act as a whole "for the first time designated certain crimes committed by citizens as offenses punishable under federal law. Conspiracies to deprive citizens of the right to vote, hold office, serve on juries, and enjoy the equal protection of the laws, could now, if states failed to act effectively against them, be prosecuted by federal district attorneys, and even lead to military intervention and the suspension of habeas corpus."[8]

The Supreme Court has reasoned that Congress intended the section of the Act now codified as 42 U.S.C. § 1983 to be a vehicle to permit individual citizens to protect their new federal rights from violations by state and local government:

> Section 1983 opened the federal courts to private citizens, offering a uniquely federal remedy against incursions under the claimed authority of state law upon rights secured by the Constitution and laws of the Nation.... Congress clearly conceived that it was altering the relationship between the States and the Nation with respect to the protection of federally created rights; it was concerned that state instrumentalities could not protect those rights; it realized that state officers might, in fact, be antipathetic to the vindication of those rights; and it believed that these failings extended to the state courts.... The very purpose of Section 1983 was to interpose the federal courts between the States and the people, as guardians of the people's federal rights—to protect the people from unconstitutional action under color of state law.

Mitchum v. Foster, 407 U.S. 225, 239–242 (1972).

To help you appreciate the roles of individual attorneys in shaping the law, this book contains several interviews with civil rights attorneys. Below is a profile of the United States Attorney General who initiated federal prosecutions of Klan members.

---

7. Marshall S. Shapo, *Constitutional Tort:* Monroe v. Pape, *and the Frontiers Beyond*, 60 Nw. U. L. Rev. 277, 280 (1965).

8. Foner, Reconstruction: America's Unfinished Revolution, *supra* note 4, at 454–55.

Profile of Amos T. Akerman

Amos T. Akerman was a former Confederate who served as Attorney General in the Grant Administration. Akerman was born in New Hampshire, and moved to the South after graduating from Dartmouth in 1842, settling in Georgia.[9] Before the war, Akerman purchased a 300-acre farm "which he worked himself, along with a small 'force' of slaves."[10] During the Civil War, Akerman served in the Confederate government.[11] He joined the Republican Party after the war,[12] and participated in framing Georgia's new constitution in 1867–68,[13] resolving "to let Confederate ideas rule us no longer [and] to discard the doctrines of states' rights and slavery."[14]

President Ulysses Grant appointed Akerman to be U.S. Attorney General in mid-1870. Akerman made prosecution of members of the Ku Klux Klan

9. Dray, *supra* note 4, at 78.

10. *Id.* at 92.

11. Robert J. Kaczorowski, The Politics of Judicial Interpretation: The Federal Courts, Department of Justice and Civil Rights, 1866–1876, 79 (N.Y.: Oceana Publ'n, Inc. 1985).

12. *Id.* at 80.

13. Dray, *supra* note 4, *at* 92.

14. William S. McFeely, Amos T. Akerman: The Lawyer and Racial Justice, *in* Region, Race, and Reconstruction: Essays in Honor of C. Vann Woodward 402 (J. Morgan Kousser & James M. McPherson eds., N.Y.: Oxford Univ. Press, 1982) (quoting letter from Akerman to George W. Heidy, Aug. 22, 1876).

a priority of the newly-formed Justice Department. In lieu of increasing federal troops in the South—which had fallen to 6,000 in 1869, from 12,000 in 1868—"Akerman wanted instead to use the federal courts to pursue Klansman as vicious criminals, isolating them from Southern society. The legal teeth for such an approach would be provided by pending legislation that would become known as Ku Klux Klan Act."[15] Choosing to combat Klan violence using the criminal justice system instead of federal troops, the Justice Department began in 1871 to prosecute hundreds of accused Klansmen, "[d]espite a limited budget, difficulties in securing evidence, the reluctance of some victims to testify, and the fact that defendants employed talented and experienced lawyers to oppose the overworked district attorneys...."[16] Most of the 1,193 cases brought in 1871 were in Alabama, Mississippi, North and South Carolina, and Tennessee, with a conviction or confession rate as high as 75% in North Carolina and as low as 48% in South Carolina.[17] President Grant declared a "condition of lawlessness" in parts of South Carolina, suspended the writ of *habeas corpus*, and sent federal troops to occupy the region;[18] about 2,000 Klansman fled the state.[19] Historian Philip Dray posits that Akerman "was perhaps the lone high-ranking federal official who knew what it was to live in fear of the Klan, for he had a wife and several children still residing in Georgia."[20]

By the end of 1871, the Attorney General decided the federal judiciary was overwhelmed by the volume of prosecutions in South Carolina and shifted strategy to selectively prosecute socially influential ring leaders.[21] "Personally directing the government's legal strategy, the Attorney General allowed those who confessed and identified the organization's leaders to escape without punishment, while trying a few dozen of the worst offenders *before predominantly black juries.* Most of those indicted eventually pleaded guilty and received prison sentences.... Akerman embarked on a personal crusade to make known the full horror of Southern violence, lecturing in the North and unsettling Cabinet meetings with accounts of Klan atrocities.... [Secretary of State Hamilton Fish complained] that [Akerman] had the Klan 'on the brain.... It has got to be a bore to listen twice a week to this thing.'"[22] In part because advisors to President Grant thought Akerman focused too much on prosecuting the Klan and in part because Akerman had alienated powerful

15. Dray, *supra* note 4, at 94.

16. Foner, *supra* note 3, at 196.

17. Kaczorowski, *supra* note 11, at 87–88.

18. *Id.* at 88; Foner, *supra* note 3, at 196; Foner, Reconstruction: America's Unfinished Revolution, *supra* note 4, at 457–58.

19. Foner, Reconstruction: America's Unfinished Revolution, *supra* note 4, at 458.

20. Dray, *supra* note 4, at 93.

21. Kaczorowski, *supra* note 11, at 90.

22. Foner, *supra* note 3, at 196–97 (emphasis added); Foner, Reconstruction: America's Unfinished Revolution, *supra* note 4, at 458.

railroad interests,[23] Attorney General Akerman resigned in the midst of the trials, in December 1871.[24] Philip Dray summarizes his impact: "In his eighteen months on the job Akerman had set the new Justice Department in motion, stirred Northern concern about Southern violence, and led a fruitful campaign to vanquish the Ku Klux Klan. Although his successor ... would largely continue Akerman's policies, not for another century would the federal government have a leading law enforcement officer similarly willing to vigorously prosecute civil rights violations in the South."[25]

E. Testimony of Survivors

Shortly after Congress enacted the Ku Klux Klan Act, a Joint Committee of the House and Senate began hearings on conditions in the former Confederate states, including incidents of Klan violence.[26] "Committee members fanned out across the South to hear evidence of Klan outrages ... ranging from voter intimidation to whippings and murder. The report revealed a clear pattern of white brutality and made novel use of the raw, unfiltered voices of Southern freedman taken in recorded testimony."[27] While the hearings took place after § 1983 was enacted, the testimony of the survivors excerpted below helps to understand the historical conditions that motivated the legislation.

Note that the first three witnesses quoted below were elected members of the state governments of Georgia, Mississippi, and South Carolina. They were members of the Republican party, the same political party as the sitting President. The fourth witness was a member of the United States military charged with investigating Klan violence in South Carolina.

23. Dray, *supra* note 4, at 100.

24. Foner, Reconstruction: America's Unfinished Revolution, *supra* note 4, at 458.

25. Dray, *supra* note 4, at 100.

26. On March 10, 1871, a Senate committee reported on their investigation of "crimes and outrages of a political character" in North Carolina and suggested similar investigations in other states. Report of the Joint Select Committee to Inquire into the Condition of Affairs in the Late Insurrectionary States, 42d Congress, 2d Session, Report No. 41, Vol. 1, at 1 (1872). On March 23, 1871, President Ulysses Grant sent Congress a message (quoted in its entirety in *Monroe*) seeking "legislation to secure life, liberty, and property, and the enforcement of law in all parts of the United States" and on April 20, 1871, the statute including the predecessor to § 1983 was passed. *Id.* "Before the passage of that act," a Joint Committee was appointed to inquire into the safety of life and property of citizens in "the late insurrectionary States." *Id.* In 1872, the Joint Committee published thirteen volumes of testimony.

27. Dray, *supra* note 4, at 89.

Report of the Joint Select Committee to Inquire into the Condition of Affairs in the Late Insurrectionary States

(Washington, Government Printing Office 1872)

Testimony by Abram Colby, a member of the Georgia legislature:

> On the 29th of October 1869, they broke my door open, took me out of bed, took me to the woods and whipped me three hours or more and left me for dead. They said to me, 'Do you think you will ever vote another damned [R]adical [Republican] ticket?' I said, 'I will not tell you a lie.' I supposed they would kill me anyhow....
>
> Q: What is the character of those men who were engaged in whipping you?
>
> A: Some are first-class men in our town. One is a lawyer, one a doctor, and some are farmers.... They said I had voted for Grant and had carried the Negroes against them. About two days before they whipped me they offered me $5000 to go with them and said they would pay me $2500 in cash if I would let another man go to the legislature in my place. I told them I would not do it if they would give me all the county was worth....
>
> Q: How long before you recovered from the effects of this treatment?
>
> A: I have never got over it yet. They broke something inside me. I cannot do any work now though I always made my living before in the barbershop, hauling wood, [etc.].
>
> Q: You spoke about being elected to the next legislature?
>
> A: Yes, sir, but they run me off during the election. They swore they would kill me if I sta[yed]. The Saturday night before the election I went to church. When I got home they just peppered the house with shot and bullets.
>
> ...
>
> No man can make a free speech in my county I do not believe it can be done anywhere in Georgia.
>
> Q: You say no man can do it?
>
> A: I mean no Republican, either white or colored.

Testimony of Robert Gleeds, formerly enslaved and state senator in Mississippi, explaining the goals of the Ku Klux Klan to the Congressional committee:

> We believe it had two objects. One was political, and the other was to hold the black man in subjection to the white man and to have white supremacy in the South. A paper published in Alabama said in plain words "We must kill or drive away the leading Negroes and only let the humble and submissive remain." That was in 1868. I was down there canvassing and read the paper and saved the copy. I spoke of it often—the idea of a party being buildup on the principle of the open slaughter of human beings. And it was well car-

ried out in Tuscaloosa County and in Pickens County. You will find but three colored men at that time who would dare speak openly of Republican principles, except where a great many colored people lived. Since then it has been a great deal worse.[28]

Testimony of Samuel Nuckles, a legislator from South Carolina:

I am a refugee from Union County.... I have been threatened with the Ku Klux. You see I am a member of the house of representatives.... [The legislature] took a recess for the Christmas holidays. I aimed to go home and went as far as Union village and two of my boys met me and told me not to go home for they threatened to kill me if I did. I have been here [Columbia] ever since. Three of my boys were run off on account of the Ku Klux. They [the Klan] became bitter against me because I went to Washington as one of the committee on account of the whippings and outrages in my county. On the day of election I was at Gowdey's polling precinct. A gentleman named Bill Byars got mad because the election was conducted so promptly by Henry Owens.

Q: Conducted so what?

A: So promptly so nicely you know having carried off so smoothly. Twelve white men would come in and vote, and then twelve colored men. They would keep anyone from pestering the voters as they went in, colored or white. Mr. Byars was standing talking to me and he said, "Nuckles, I'll bet you $500 that in two years from today there'll not be a colored man voting in the town." I said, "How do you know?" He says, "You'll know by waiting." He was only mad because the voting was going so, for after awhile the white men voting gave out and the colored men still kept up by twelves and consequently we beat them that day by two hundred and fifty votes. A very short time after that Mr. Owens was killed. There are a great many refugees here. They do not want to go back unless something is done. The Republican party is scattered and beaten and run out. They have on leaders up there. That is the report that has been sent to us several times, that if we submit and vote the Democratic ticket we can stay there. But we do not propose to do that.

Q: How old are you?

A: I am about 57 years old. I can read a little and write my name. I first took that up here some years back. I never was at school.

Q: You were a slave?

A: Yes, sir; a hard-down slave. I was born and bred in Union County and I have been in no place I like better, but it has become so I can't live there, and it seems that I am hardly living here.[29]

---

28. Testimony *reprinted in* THE TROUBLE THEY SEEN: THE STORY OF RECONSTRUCTION IN THE WORDS OF AFRICAN AMERICANS, at 366 (Dorothy Sterling, ed., Da Capo Press 1994).

29. *Id.* at 377–78.

Testimony of Lewis Merrill, Major Seventh Calvary

While the below testimony concerns events post-dating the enactment of § 1983, it is useful to grasp the extent of the influence of the Ku Klux Klan in certain counties. Lewis Merrill, Major Seventh Calvary, Adjutant General, Department of the South, was an official sent by the federal government to investigate Klan violence in South Carolina. His report concerns events between September 17, 1871 and January 8, 1872:

> In my previous reports I have repeatedly expressed the opinion that the local civil authorities were powerless to cope with the strength of the Ku-Klux conspiracy, even if willing to make the attempt, and I have been compelled to believe that the desire to make the attempt was entirely wanting.... The pretense that it was impossible to detect the criminals was transparent, as I have been able, with very limited means at my command, to trace numbers of the crimes....
>
> It is alleged by [local authorities] in excuse for this course, that no formal complaints were made by the victims of these outrages. While this was true, it was the result of the listlessness and indifference with which these complaints come to be received when made, and the fact that no complaint had ever brought redress....
>
> Whatever doubts I have entertained of the willful connivance of the civil authorities at these crimes, were entirely dissipated by the facts of the session of the civil court in September. These completely demonstrated the truth of my assertion that the courts were not only unable to prevent these outrages, but were unwilling to try to do so.[30]
>
> ...
>
> [After detailing the failure of local criminal justice authorities to investigate or seriously consider punishment for Klan violence in September 1871] The whole conduct of their duty was so broad a farce, that it was very distasteful to be forced in contact with it, and present developments show it to have been the most ghastly mockery of justice that it is possible to conceive.
>
> If any other evidence were needed of the fact, that the body of the local civil authorities[31] is either in complicity with the Ku-Klux conspiracy, or intimidated by it, it is to be found in the fact ... that at least three of the justices of the peace ... have been members of the Ku-Klux, and that at least one-third of the white members of the grand and petit juries, at the last term of court, were members, and among the number some who were officers of high grade in the order, and at least two of the number having been accessory to Ku-Klux murders.

30. Joint Select Committee to Inquire into the Condition of Affairs in the Late Insurrectionary States, 42d Congress, 2d Session, Report No. 41 (Washington, Government Printing Office 1872), Vol. 5, at 1600.

31. *Id.* at 1601.

In view of this, it is small wonder that eleven murders, and more than six hundred cases of whipping, and other brutal outrages by the Ku-Klux, have to this day gone unnoticed ... so far as any serious effort of the local authorities has been concerned.

[Since Major Merrill lacked the means to "meet the secret power of the Ku-Klux, rightly called by themselves the *Invisible Empire*, for a more absolute and tyrannical control of than they held over the whole people where they existed has never been exercised by human power," he reported his findings to the Attorney General of the United States.]

[The Attorney General, upon considering Major Merrill's evidence and other evidence of Klan violence was] convinced ... that the worst reports which had been heretofore made of the power and of the infernal purpose and conduct of the order fell far short of the facts. It has since become evident that what at that time would ... have been deemed the wildest exaggeration, falls short of the truth.

The warning proclamation and the proclamation suspending the writ of *habeas corpus* followed close upon the report of the Attorney General of the facts ... [M]any of the Ku-Klux leaders ... with the cowardice which has characterized all their infamous crimes, fled, leaving their poorer followers and ignorant dupes to stand sponsors for the crimes of which they had been the chief authors and instigators.

Two days after the telegraphic notification of the suspension of the writ of *habeas corpus* ... I began effecting the arrest of such persons as we had evidence to show were guilty of crime ... The troops were so disposed that a large number of arrests were effected simultaneously over the county.... The rank and file were bewildered and demoralized. Looking about for their chiefs and counselors, and finding that, to get orders or advice, they must go to them in jail or follow their flight, they recognized the fact that the game was up, that the organization was broken, and all over the country they betook themselves to flight or came in and surrendered."

...

Those arrested and those who have surrendered are of every social grade, from the highest to the lowest, including representatives of all the liberal professions, even ministers of the gospel.[32]

...

A large part, even of the membership of the order, is of persons who would have recoiled from personal participation in such crimes, and there are many who sought membership solely to protect themselves against violence threatened for entertaining and expressing sentiments condemnatory of its acts and purposes.

32. *Id.* at 1602.

In short, the conspiracy may be stated to have practically included the whole white community within the ages when active participation in public affairs was possible. Those who were no sworn members were greatly in the minority, and were of only three classes; such as applauded and approved the purposes of the organization without being willing to join its ranks, to approve its grosser crimes, or to take the chances for punishment for being accessory to them; second, such as sympathized with its objects, but feebly objected to its crimes ... ; and third, and by far the smallest class, those who had no sympathy with its objects, or anything but condemnation for its acts, but who had come to learn that security from personal indignity required silence.

The number of persons whose arrest was ordered, but who were known at that time to have fled, is about fifty, and includes many of the leading and most criminal conspirators.[33] ... [About 40–50 others have fled, although no serious charges were then pending but evidence since discovered would likely convict them of "grave crimes."]

Up to and including December 31, 1871, 195 persons in all have been arrested by the military and placed in confinement.... Arrests, surrenders, and flights of persons, against whom accusation upon probable cause is made, aggregate about eight hundred; of these an appreciable proportion are below the voting age.... The total white voters of the county is about twenty-three hundred, of whom a small majority live in that part of the county from which most of the surrenders have come.

From these facts, I think the number of sworn members of the organization in the whole county is underestimated when placed at eighteen hundred.

Such a state of facts show that, at the time of the suspension of the writ, York County was, in point of fact, an armed camp, and that it was not for want of power to do it, but because the flight of the leaders made organized resistance hopeless, that danger of this kind was not encountered.... I am convinced, too, that the moral effect of the suspension of the writ had much to do with the complete collapse of the organization.

Of the 195 persons who have ... been in custody of the military ... : fifty were admitted to bail ... forty were similarly admitted to bail on personal recognizance ... seventy-nine were transferred to the custody of the United States marshal [because their positions in the Klan or the gravity of the crimes created risks of organized resistance or witness intimidation].[34]

The impossibility of procuring intelligent white men to assist in the arrests, the desire to avoid temptation to resistance by using negroes, and the absence of knowledge of the personal appearance of the persons sought, combined

33. *Id.* at 1603.

34. *Id.* at 1604.

to make the duty of arresting them unusually difficult for the officers and men engaged.

The total number who were arrested, charged with violation of law ... was 169; of these, there have been arraigned before the court and tried, 5, (all of whom were found guilty;) arraigned and pleaded guilty by confession in open court, 12; indicted and not yet arraigned 118; indictments still pending, (the mass of business before the court making it impossible to reach their cases at this term,) 14; arrested and confessions and used as State's evidence, 20.

In concluding this report it is proper for me to say, that in York County the Ku-Klux organization, as such, is completely crushed. Its leaders have fled, or been arrested; and they are now either undergoing sentence or awaiting the investigation of their cases before a civil court.

...

These social leaders have a most uncompromising hostility to the citizenship of the negro, and have never yet recognized his right to fair and just treatment, or to the[35] equal protection of the law, and their hostility extends to all who maintain his rights and politically fraternize with him.

These men have ruled Northwest South Carolina with a rod of iron. The good men of the community have been overborne and silenced by the secret but powerful influence brought to bear on them from all sides by the Ku-Klux organization, until all law was defied with perfect impunity; judges, juries, and magistrates alike conniving at the crimes, or being in complicity with the conspiracy.

...

The cause of Ku-Kluxism lies in the dissatisfaction of the white leaders with the results of the war, and in their determination to nullify these, as far as possible; a dissatisfaction chiefly growing out of the citizenship and enfranchisement of the negro and his refusal to be controlled toward their political views.

...

[Now that "more thoughtful men of York County" are freed from "the thralldom of the Ku-Klux"] ... [t]o secure this end they must be protected in their efforts by the moral influence of the presence of troops for the present, and until they become strong enough to hold their own against the bad influence that still surrounds them.... [While withdrawal of federal troops is desirable] I must also invite careful attention to the necessity for being sure that respect for law is firmly re-established, and its just administration certain and unmolested, before the aid of the military arm of the Government is withdrawn.[36]

35. *Id.* at 1605.
36. *Id.* at 1606.

According to the 1872 Congressional Report, the Klan was "a political organization whose purpose" was to oppose the 13th, 14th and 15th Amendments, the constitutional changes that attempted to translate the results of the Civil War into law. Similarly, Captain Merrill believed the Klan was opposed to "the results of the war," chiefly "the citizenship and enfranchisement of the negro."

A very different view of Klan motives is presented in the classic novel *Gone With the Wind*, written after the demise of Reconstruction and at a time when laws restricting the conduct of African-Americans were once again in place:

> It was the large number of outrages on women and the ever-present fear for the safety of their wives and daughters that drove Southern men to cold and trembling fury and caused the Ku Klux Klan to spring up overnight. And it was against this nocturnal organization that the newspapers of the North cried out most loudly, never realizing the tragic necessity that brought it into being. The North wanted every member of the Ku Klux hunted down and hanged, because they had dared take the punishment of crime into their own hands at a time when the ordinary processes of law and order had been overthrown by the invaders.[37]

For further discussion

1. According to Major Merrill's testimony, what roles did judges have in the Ku Klux Klan conspiracy in York County, South Carolina in 1871? Try to keep that in mind in reading Absolute Immunity in Chapter 9.

2. For an overview of the Reconstruction era with text by historian Eric Foner, visit http://www.digitalhistory.uh.edu/era.cfm?eraid=8&smtid=1.

3. Following the demise of Reconstruction, Southern states imposed "Jim Crow" laws, which were in place for the many decades before the beginning of the modern civil rights movement:

> The Reconstruction years, which began at the end of the Civil War, witnessed a temporary realignment of political forces, in which black [male] citizens were able to vote and were elected to local and national offices. But by 1877, the North proved incapable of stopping southern white resistance and pulled out its troops. Reconstruction, which had already proven weak in many areas of the Deep South, collapsed. In the 1890s, poll taxes and literacy tests succeeded in disenfranchising all but a handful of southern blacks ... In place of slavery came 'Jim Crow' laws that governed almost every aspect of life for Black Americans living below the Mason-Dixon line.

Henry Hampton & Steve Fayer, VOICES OF FREEDOM: AN ORAL HISTORY OF THE CIVIL RIGHTS MOVEMENT FROM THE 1950S THROUGH THE 1980S, xi (Bantam Books, N.Y. 1990); *see* Richard Hofstadter & Beatrice K. Hofstadter, GREAT ISSUES IN AMER-

---

37. Margaret Mitchell, GONE WITH THE WIND, 656 (The MacMillan Co. N.Y. 1936).

ICAN HISTORY: FROM RECONSTRUCTION TO THE PRESENT DAY, 1864–1981, Vol. 3, 437–38 (Random House, N.Y. 1982) ("[s]uch devices as the poll tax and literacy tests as well as white intimidation ... for decades all but barred Southern blacks from voting"; "Through the early 1960s, outside the South, a growing national consensus came to recognize that laws discriminating against blacks—Jim Crow laws—offended the American ideal of equality before the law. Only the central government had the capacity to abolish Jim Crow").[38]

4. *Lynching as a tool of social control.* The federal government withdrew troops from the South in 1877, effectively ending Reconstruction. But violence against African Americans continued. Recently, the Equal Justice Initiative "documented 4084 racial terror lynchings in twelve Southern states between the end of Reconstruction in 1877 and 1950.... [and] 300 racial terror lynchings in other states during this time period."[39] According to the Equal Justice Initiative, "[t]error lynchings fueled the mass migration of millions of black people from the South into urban ghettos in the North and West throughout the first half of the twentieth century. Lynching created a fearful environment where racial subordination and segregation was maintained with limited resistance for decades."[40]

Among "the first Americans to understand lynching was a form of caste oppression and to recognize that it would have to be exposed to be destroyed" was Ida B. Wells,[41] the African-American author and political activist. Wells, born enslaved in Mississippi,[42] exposed lynching to American and British audiences through her writing and public speeches.[43] Wells came to consider lynching "[a]n excuse to get rid of Negroes who were acquiring wealth and property and thus keep the race terrorized...."[44] Despite a white Memphis mob threatening her life and destroying her newspaper's office in 1892, Wells continued her writing and speaking tours from New York.[45] In a preface to her 1892 study of lynching, Frederick Douglass wrote: "if American moral sensibility were not hardened by persistent infliction of outrage and crime against colored people, a scream of horror, shame and indignation would rise to Heaven wherever your pamphlet shall be read."[46]

---

38. In 1939, the Department of Justice established a Civil Rights Section and began to enforce the Reconstruction statutes. For discussion of those efforts, *see* Robert K. Carr, FEDERAL PROTECTION OF CIVIL RIGHTS: QUEST FOR A SWORD (Cornell Univ. Press, Ithaca, N.Y. 1947) and Risa Goluboff, THE LOST PROMISE OF CIVIL RIGHTS (Harvard Univ. Press, Cambridge, Mass. 2007).

39. Equal Justice Initiative, *Lynching in America: Confronting the Legacy of Racial Terror*, Key Finding 1, (3d Ed. 2017) https://lynchinginamerica.eji.org/report/.

40. *Id.* at Introduction; *id.* at Key Finding 4.

41. Philip Dray, AT THE HANDS OF PERSONS UNKNOWN: THE LYNCHING OF BLACK AMERICA 54 (Modern Library 2003).

42. Ida B. Wells, CRUSADE FOR JUSTICE: THE AUTOBIOGRAPHY OF IDA B. WELLS xiv (Univ. Chicago Press 1970).

43. *Id.* at xviii–xxii.

44. *Id.* at 64.

45. *Id.* at xiii, xviii–xxii, xxv–xxvi, 61–67; Dray, AT THE HANDS OF PERSONS UNKNOWN, *supra* note 41, at 65.

46. Dray, *supra* note 41, at 67.

IDA B. WELLS.

In 1928, Wells began her autobiography because "our race has little of its own that is definite or authentic" about the "storm and stress immediately after the Civil War, of the Ku Klux Klan, of ballot-box stuffing, wholesale murders of Negroes who tried to exercise their new-found rights as free men and citizens."[47] In her autobiography, CRUSADE FOR JUSTICE, Wells wrote that in fighting against lynching, she often confronted the myth that "Negro men are despoilers of the virtue of white women."[48] Her response: "First: That all the machinery of law and politics is in the hands of those who commit the lynching; … and that it is only wealthy white men whom the law fails to reach … Second: Hundreds of Negroes including women and children are lynched for trivial offenses … and that the law refused to punish the murderers because it is not considered a crime to kill a Negro … Third: Many of the cases of 'Assault' are simply adulteries between white women and colored men."[49]

5. *The only successful coup in the United States?* On November 10, 1898, white supremacists violently overthrew the elected government of Wilmington, North Carolina. The riot was not spontaneous, concluded the 2009 North Carolina historical commission report.[50] Rather, the study concluded, an "influential body of white businessmen … led the campaign that resulted in the violence and overthrow of municipal government."[51] "Armed whites under the leadership of the city's white elite used the

---

47. Wells, *supra* note 42, at 4.

48. *Id.* at 136.

49. *Id.* at 137.

50. LeRae Sikes Umfleet, A DAY OF BLOOD: THE 1898 WILMINGTON RACE RIOT, xix (N. Carolina Off. of Archives and History 2009).

51. *Id.* at xviii.

Alexander Manly

threat of paramilitary forces to remove from office Wilmington's duly elected, biracial city government."[52]

Republican-Populist alliance (Fusion)

Blacks outnumbered whites in Wilmington, "held considerable political power," including elected and appointed public positions, and "figured centrally in Wilmington's business life."[53] In North Carolina, a coalition of working class whites and Republicans, "the preponderance of whom were African-Americans," won both North Carolina state legislative houses in 1894.[54] They enacted new laws that encouraged black voting and, in 1896, "mainly due to black voting ... won every statewide race in North Carolina," including Governor.[55]

White supremacy campaign and riot

"The racial massacre in Wilmington almost certainly would not have occurred without the statewide white supremacy campaign of 1898," which included public speeches and news stories that "pilloried blacks in the most sinister manner, with

---

52. Melton McLaurin, *Racial Violence in Wilmington, 1898*, Moving Forward Together: A Community Remembers 1898 (2008) 11.

53. H. Leon Prather, Sr., *We Have Taken a City*, DEMOCRACY BETRAYED 16–18 (Univ. N. Carolina Press 1998).

54. Prather, *supra* note 53, at 18 ("Populists placed class interests above racial solidarity and formed a working alliance with the Republicans"); *id.*

55. *Id.* at 19; Andrea Meryl Kirshenbaum, *"The Vampire that Hovers Over North Carolina": Gender, White Supremacy, and the Wilmington Race Riot of 1898*, 4 Southern Cultures 7 (Fall 1998).

ugly cartoons cunningly drawn to provoke white racial fears."[56] For months before the November 1898 coup, "white leadership in Wilmington" developed plans "for instigating violence ... implement[ed] a strategy to quell that violence, and to call the affair a riot ... rather than what it actually was—a planned insurrection."[57] White supremacists weaponized an August 1898 editorial by African American newspaper owner Alexander Manly, in which he denied the myth of the black male rapist and called on whites to " 'teach your men purity' " because it was " 'no worse for a black man to be intimate with a white woman, than for a white man to be intimate with a colored woman.' "[58] Manly's editorial "gave the party of white supremacy all the political cover it could require for its conspiracy to seize power in Wilmington."[59]

On November 9, 1898, white citizens gathered as Alfred M. Waddell announced a "White Declaration of Independence."[60] The Declaration asserted that the Constitution "did not anticipate the enfranchisement" of African-Americans, that "we will no longer be ruled, and will never again be ruled by men of African origin," nor tolerate interracial political alliances.[61] The Declaration concluded that Manly's editorial was "so vile and slanderous" that in most communities it would "have resulted in the lynching" of the editor, called for Manly's paper to be closed, and Manly "banished" from Wilmington.[62]

The following morning, Waddell "lined up about 500 men" in rows of four, and marched on Wilmington streets to Manly's newspaper office.[63] The group grew to about 2000.[64] Waddell led the mob to destroy Manly's newspaper and burn the building.[65] "Once the [newspaper] office was destroyed, Wilmington descended into a state of panic ... The majority of the violence and bloodshed took place in Brooklyn, the traditionally African-American neighborhood.[66] After a white man was wounded, whites "retaliated by aiming for any blacks who came within sight and firing in unison into a group of black men, killing another five or six of them."[67]

Wilmington businesses had purchased a machine gun for the Wilmington Light Infantry and the naval militia also deployed a rapid-firing gun on city streets.[68] "The

56. Prather, *supra* note 53, at 20–21.

57. Umfleet, *supra* note 50, at xviii.

58. *Id.* at 64; Prather, *supra* note 53, at 23.

59. Prather, *supra* note 53, at 24.

60. Umfleet, *supra* note 50, at 73–74.

61. *Id.* at 76–77 (quoting the Declaration).

62. *Id.* at 77 (quoting the Declaration).

63. Prather, *supra* note 53, at 31.

64. *Id.* at 32.

65. *Id.*

66. Umfleet, *supra* note 50, at 86–87; *id.* ("first shots between whites and blacks were fired ... as armed white men returned from the fire to their neighborhoods").

67. *Id.* at 93.

68. *Id.* at 96, 98; Prather, *supra* note 53, *at* 28 ("leaders of the white supremacy movement spent the staggering sum of $1,200 to purchase a new, rapid-firing Gatling gun").

rapid fire guns were used not only to intimidate black men on the streets but ... [also to] target[] all the [African American] churches and force[] ministers to open their doors to searches by whites."[69] Red Shirts, "a terrorist wing of the Democratic Party," backed the militias.[70] Waddell claimed about 20 African-Americans were killed, but death toll estimates vary, as some victims were secretly buried.[71] Hundreds of African Americans fled Wilmington to hide in nearby woods, cemeteries, and swamps.[72]

Overthrow of Wilmington's elected government

As the riot continued, the upper-class white businessmen moved to overthrow Wilmington's government. Coup leaders used the riot as a "smokescreen for their violent and revolutionary seizure of power from the legally elected Fusionist [Republican-Populist] government."[73] Coup leaders, aided by "one hundred to two hundred armed men in the corridors of city hall" and violence in the streets, pressured Wilmington's mayor and other city government officials to resign, and they did.[74] The entire police department was forced to resign "so that it could be taken over by white Democrats."[75] Waddell, leader of the mob who destroyed Manley's newspaper, became the new Mayor.[76]

The coup leaders gave the new Mayor Waddell "a list of prominent Republicans, both white and black, who must be banished from Wilmington."[77] They targeted three groups for banishment. "First were the African American leaders who were vocal supporters of full participation in government by blacks and open opponents of the white supremacy campaign. Second were African American businessmen and entrepreneurs whose financial successes were galling to the white upper and working classes. Third were white Republicans who benefited from African American voting support."[78] The new government backed its banishment orders with force. For example, "soldiers with fixed bayonets ... walked six of the most prominent of the black Republicans who had not already fled town" to be loaded on a guarded train, with orders to never return.[79]

The 1898 riot, coup, and banishment campaign had a profound impact. In 2009, the North Carolina historical commission concluded that the change in Wilmington's government "completely terminated black participation in city and county government until the advent of the civil rights era."[80] Moreover:

---

69. Umfleet, *supra* note 50, at 99.
70. Prather, *supra* note 53, at 25; *id.* at 33.
71. *Id.* at 35.
72. Umfleet, *supra* note 50, at 101–02.
73. Prather, *supra* note 53, at 36.
74. Umfleet, *supra* note 50, at 104.
75. Prather, *supra* note 53, at 37.
76. Umfleet, *supra* note 50, at 104.
77. Prather, *supra* note 53, at 37.
78. Umfleet, *supra* note 50, at 106.
79. Prather, *supra* note 53, at 37.
80. Umfleet, *supra* note 50, at xviii.

> the 1898 political campaign ... proved to be a catalyst for the state: Jim Crow legislation and the subjugation of African Americans was the result throughout North Carolina. Because Wilmington rioters were able to murder blacks in daylight and overthrow a legitimately elected Republican government without penalty or federal intervention, everyone in the state, regardless of race, knew that the white-supremacy campaign was triumphant on all fronts.[81]

6. *The Second Ku Klux Klan.* The U.S. Supreme Court summarized the resurgence of the Ku Klux Klan in the early part of the 20th century:

> By the end of Reconstruction in 1877, the first Klan no longer existed ... The genesis of the second Klan began in 1905, with the publication of Thomas Dixon's THE CLANSMEN: AN HISTORICAL ROMANCE OF THE KU KLUX KLAN. Dixon's book was a sympathetic portrait of the first Klan, depicting the Klan as a group of heroes "saving" the South from blacks and the "horrors" of Reconstruction ... D.W. Griffith turned Dixon's book into the movie *The Birth of a Nation* in 1915.... Soon thereafter, in November 1915, the second Klan began ... The new Klan's ideology did not differ much from that of the first Klan. As one Klan publication emphasized, "We avow the distinction between [the] races, ... and we shall ever be true to the faithful maintenance of White Supremacy and will strenuously oppose any compromise thereof in any and all things." [W. Wade, THE FIERY CROSS: THE KU KLUX KLAN IN AMERICA 147–148 (1987)] (internal quotation marks omitted). Violence was also an elemental part of this new Klan. By September 1921, the *New York World* newspaper documented 152 acts of Klan violence, including 4 murders, 41 floggings, and 27 tar-and-featherings. Wade 160.
>
> ...
>
> The decision of this Court in *Brown v. Board of Education,* 347 U.S. 483 (1954), along with the civil rights movement of the 1950's and 1960's, sparked another outbreak of Klan violence. These acts of violence included bombings, beatings, shootings, stabbings, and mutilations. See, e.g., Chalmers[, HOODED AMERICANISM: THE HISTORY OF THE KU KLUX KLAN 349–350 (1980)]; Wade 302–303. Members of the Klan burned crosses on the lawns of those associated with the civil rights movement, assaulted the Freedom Riders, bombed churches, and murdered blacks as well as whites whom the Klan viewed as sympathetic toward the civil rights movement.

Virginia v. Black, 538 U.S. 343, 353–56 (2003).

7. Since the focus of this book is 42 U.S.C. § 1983 litigation, and the statute rarely was invoked before 1961, the Chapter will skip forward in time.

---

81. Umfleet, *supra* note 50, at xviii–xix.

F. Brief Introduction to Modern 42 U.S.C. § 1983

Section 1983 authorizes a court to grant relief when a plaintiff's federally protected rights have been violated by a state or local official or other person who acted under color of state law. The statute does not create substantive rights but is a vehicle for remedying violations of rights that are established elsewhere, either in the federal constitution or federal laws.

Yet § 1983 was not a frequently litigated statute before 1961. In its first fifty years, the statute generated only 21 cases. *See Crawford-El v. Britton*, 523 U.S. 574, 611 (1998) (Scalia, J., dissenting). By 1981, however, there were 15,639 § 1983 suits filed, representing "over 8.6% of the total federal district court civil docket." *Patsy v. Board of Regents of the State of Florida*, 457 U.S. 496, 534 (1982) (Powell, J., dissenting). "By 1985 not counting prisoner petitions, the number was over 17,000, and by 1992 the number was over 20,000."[82] While not limited to § 1983 cases, recent federal judicial business statistics reflect that 41,741 "civil rights" cases were filed in the twelve month period ending September 30, 2018, and that an additional 18,842 prisoners' civil rights cases and 9,708 prison condition cases were filed during that same year.[83] Supreme Court Justice Samuel Alito has stated that, even since the recent enactment of a federal statute to limit civil rights claims by prisoners:

> prisoner civil rights and prison conditions cases still account for an outsized share of filings: From 2000 through 2005, such cases represented between 8.3% and 9.8% of the new filings in the federal district courts, or on average about one new prisoner case every other week for each of the nearly 1000 active and senior district judges across the country.

Woodford v. Ngo, 548 U.S. 81, 94 n.4 (2006).

There are several causes for the huge growth in the federal court § 1983 docket since 1961. First, in 1961, in *Monroe v. Pape*,[84] the Supreme Court broadly construed § 1983 by holding that it provided a remedy for violations of federal constitutional rights even if the conduct complained of also violated state law and created a state law cause of action. Second, in 1976, Congress enacted the Civil Rights Attorneys Fees Act, which authorized an award of attorneys fees to parties who prevail in actions brought under various statutes including § 1983. This fee-shifting statute for prevailing plaintiffs created an incentive for attorneys to enforce federal rights under § 1983. Third, in 1978, in *Monell v. Dept. of Social Services of the City of New York*,[85] the

82. *See* William W. Schwarzer & Russell R. Wheeler, *On the Federalization of Civil and Criminal Justice*, 23 Stetson L. Rev. 651, 697 (1994).

83. Table C-2A, *U.S. District Courts—Civil Cases Commenced by Nature of Suit, During the 12-Month Periods Ending September 30, 20014 Through 2018, available at* https://www.uscourts.gov/sites/default/files/data_tables/jb_c2a_0930.2018.pdf.

84. 365 U.S. 167 (1961).

85. 436 U.S. 658 (1978).

Supreme Court held that municipalities are subject to § 1983 liability when the violation of federal rights is caused by enforcement of a municipal policy or custom. The availability of damages from local governments created a potential "deep pocket," encouraging lawsuits against municipal defendants. More general causes of the increase in § 1983 litigation since 1961 are the increase in the prison population[86] and perhaps the increased litigiousness of Americans.

Before reading *Monroe*, consider the differing views of several federal judges on the significance of *Monroe*, the attorney fee statute, and their impact on the current federal civil rights docket:

> *Justice Antonin Scalia*
>
> The § 1983 that was created by *Monroe* "bears scant resemblance to what Congress enacted almost a century earlier.... *Monroe* changed a statute that had generated only 21 cases in the first 50 years of its existence into one that pours into the federal courts tens of thousands of suits each year, and engages this Court in a losing struggle to prevent the Constitution from degenerating into a general tort law."[87]
>
> *Judge Ruggiero Aldisert (3d Cir.)*
>
> "the Court resuscitated, if not resurrected ... § 1983" in *Monroe* and "[s]ince that day, this federal remedial statute has been successfully utilized to correct tens of thousands of civil rights violations of all description, in high school classrooms to maximum security wings of state prisons. Section 1983 has been a major force in protecting the individual from countless abuses by the city, county, and state. We have become a more civilized society because of the protections it affords those under police arrest or confined to penal institutions."[88]
>
> *Justice Lewis Powell*
>
> Section 1983 is "a statute that already has burst its historical bounds," is "no longer is confined to deprivations of individual rights as intended in 1871," and "has become a major vehicle for general litigation in the federal courts by individuals and corporations."[89]
>
> *Judge Richard Posner (7th Cir.)*
>
> "the pressure to transform state common law torts into federal constitutional torts comes from the immunities and damage ceilings that states frequently impose on suits against their public officials ... from a sense that state judges

86. Anthony Amsterdam, *Verbatim*, 31-MAY Champion 51 (May 2007) ("In 1974, there were fewer than 280,000 people in prison in America. By 2004, the number was more than 2.1 million").

87. *Crawford-El v. Britton*, 523 U.S. 574, 611 (1998) (Scalia, J., dissenting).

88. *Hernandez v. Denton*, 861 F.2d 1421, 1428 (9th Cir. 1988) (Aldisert, J., concurring and dissenting) (sitting by designation on 9th Circuit), *cert. granted and vacated*, 493 U.S. 801 (1989).

89. *Parratt v. Taylor*, 451 U.S. 527, 553–554 and n.13 (1981) (Powell, J., concurring in judgment), *overruled by Daniels v. Williams*, 474 U.S. 327 (1986).

are sometimes unsympathetic to suits against the state, and from the availability of attorney's fees awards in civil rights suits under 42 U.S.C. § 1988."[90]

Judge Alvin Krenzler (N.D. Ohio)

"from 1871 through 1961, there were very few cases brought under the statute ... Since *Monroe*, there have been thousands of reported and unreported § 1983 cases, and the only thing that is consistent about them is their inconsistency. Law school professors have been having a field day analyzing the courts' decisions ... [t]here are almost as many law review articles discussing § 1983 decisions as there are reported cases."[91]

Judge Abner Mikva (D.C. Cir.)

"While Section 1983 has reaped its share of criticism for encouraging federal intervention in local affairs, it remains on the books as the workhorse of civil rights litigation."[92]

Questions to guide reading of *Monroe*

1. Does *Monroe* primarily address constitutional or statutory language? How does the Supreme Court frame the legal question concerning the individual police defendants?
2. Why did the individual defendants argue that their acts were not "under color of" law?
3. What does *Monroe* identify as the three main purposes of § 1983?
4. Why does *Monroe* say it is "no answer" to an injured plaintiff that a state law remedy exists for the injury?
5. Since *Classic* and *Screws* were criminal cases, why are they relevant to how "color of law" should be construed under § 1983?
6. What evidence does the majority point to in support of its view that Congress had acquiesced in earlier constructions of "under color of" statutory language? Does the concurrence agree on this point?
7. Does § 1983 require that the deprivation of rights be intentional on the part of the defendant?
8. Recall Mr. Colby's excerpted testimony to the Joint Committee. Was his situation in any way similar to that confronted by the Monroe family? How do you think the factual background that precipitated the enactment of § 1983 might have influenced the majority in *Monroe*, if at all?
9. How do you think Justice Harlan might have responded to Justice Scalia's earlier-quoted criticism of *Monroe*?

---

90. *Spencer v. Lee*, 864 F.2d 1376, 1382 (7th Cir. 1989), *cert. denied*, 494 U.S. 1016 (1990).
91. *Eaton v. City of Solon*, 598 F.Supp. 1505, 1509 (N.D. Ohio 1984).
92. *Morgan v. District of Columbia*, 824 F.2d 1049, 1056 (D.C. Cir. 1987).

10. According to *Monroe*, is the City of Chicago a "person" under § 1983?
11. According to Justice Frankfurter's dissent, what kinds of cases other than those complying with state statutes did Congress intend to reach through § 1983?
12. How would you respond to Justice Frankfurter's concern that the *Monroe* construction of § 1983 would transform it into a way to regulate the daily business of every local police officer and clerk?

Monroe v. Pape

365 U.S. 167 (1961)

Mr. Justice DOUGLAS delivered the opinion of the Court.

This case presents important questions concerning the construction of [42 U.S.C. § 1983].... The complaint alleges that 13 Chicago police officers broke into petitioners' home in the early morning, routed them from bed, made them stand naked in the living room, and ransacked every room, emptying drawers and ripping mattress covers. It further alleges that Mr. Monroe was then taken to the police station and detained on 'open' charges for 10 hours, while he was interrogated about a two-day-old murder, that he was not taken before a magistrate, though one was accessible, that he was not permitted to call his family or attorney, that he was subsequently released without criminal charges being preferred against him. It is alleged that the officers had no search warrant and no arrest warrant and that they acted 'under color of the statutes, ordinances, regulations, customs and usages' of Illinois and of the City of Chicago....

I.

Petitioners claim that the invasion of their home and the subsequent search without a warrant and the arrest and detention of Mr. Monroe without a warrant and without arraignment constituted a deprivation of their 'rights, privileges, or immunities secured by the Constitution' within the meaning of [§ 1983]. It has been said that when 18 U.S.C. § 241 made criminal a conspiracy "to injure, oppress, threaten, or intimidate any citizen in the free exercise or enjoyment of any right or privilege secured to him by the Constitution," it embraced only rights that an individual has by reason of his relation to the central government, not to state governments.... But the history of the section of the Civil Rights Act presently involved does not permit such a narrow interpretation. Section [1983] came onto the books as § 1 of the Ku Klux Act of April 20, 1871.... It was one of the means whereby Congress exercised the power vested in it by § 5 of the Fourteenth Amendment to enforce the provisions of that Amendment.

...

So far petitioners are on solid ground. For the guarantee against unreasonable searches and seizures contained in the Fourth Amendment has been made applicable to the States by reason of the Due Process Clause of the Fourteenth Amendment....

II.

There can be no doubt at least since *Ex parte Virginia*, 100 U.S. 339, 346–347 (1880) ... that Congress has the power to enforce provisions of the Fourteenth Amendment against those who carry a badge of authority of a State and represent it in some capacity, whether they act in accordance with their authority or misuse it. *See Home Tel. & Tel. Co. v. City of Los Angeles*, 227 U.S. 278, 287–296 (1913).... The question with which we now deal is the narrower one of whether Congress, in enacting [§ 1983], meant to give a remedy to parties deprived of constitutional rights, privileges and immunities by an official's abuse of his position. *Cf. Williams v. United States*, 341 U.S. 97 (1951); *Screws v. United States*, 325 U.S. 91 (1945); *United States v. Classic*, 313 U.S. 299 (1941).... We conclude that it did so intend.

It is argued that 'under color of' enumerated state authority excludes acts of an official or policeman who can show no authority under state law, state custom, or state usage to do what he did. In this case it is said that these policemen, in breaking into petitioners' apartment, violated the Constitution and laws of Illinois. It is pointed out that under Illinois law a simple remedy is offered for that violation and that, so far as it appears, the courts of Illinois are available to give petitioners that full redress which the common law affords for violence done to a person; and it is earnestly argued that no 'statute, ordinance, regulation, custom or usage' of Illinois bars that redress.

The Ku Klux Act grew out of a message sent to Congress by President Grant on March 23, 1871, reading:

> 'A condition of affairs now exists in some States of the Union rendering life and property insecure and the carrying of the mails and the collection of the revenue dangerous. The proof that such a condition of affairs exists in some localities is now before the Senate. That the power to correct these evils is beyond the control of State authorities I do not doubt; that the power of the Executive of the United States, acting within the limits of existing laws, is sufficient for present emergencies is not clear. Therefore, I urgently recommend such legislation as in the judgment of Congress shall effectually secure life, liberty, and property, and the enforcement of law in all parts of the United States. * * *'[7]

The legislation—in particular the section with which we are now concerned—had several purposes. There are threads of many thoughts running through the debates. One who reads them in their entirety sees that the present section had three main aims. First, it might, of course, override certain kinds of state laws.... Second, it provided a remedy where state law was inadequate.... But the purposes were much broader. The third aim was to provide a federal remedy where the state remedy, though adequate in theory, was not available in practice....

This Act of April 20, 1871, sometimes called "the third 'force bill,'" was passed by a Congress that had the Klan 'particularly in mind.' The debates are replete with ref-

7. Cong. Globe, 42d Cong., 1st Sess., p. 244.

erences to the lawless conditions existing in the South in 1871. There was available to the Congress during these debates a report, nearly 600 pages in length, dealing with the activities of the Klan and the inability of the state governments to cope with it.... It was not the unavailability of state remedies but the failure of certain States to enforce the laws with an equal hand that furnished the powerful momentum behind this 'force bill.'

...

The debates were long and extensive. It is abundantly clear that one reason the legislation was passed was to afford a federal right in federal courts because, by reason of prejudice, passion, neglect, intolerance or otherwise, state laws might not be enforced and the claims of citizens to the enjoyment of rights, privileges, and immunities guaranteed by the Fourteenth Amendment might be denied by the state agencies.

...

But Section 1—the section with which we are here concerned—was not changed as respects any feature with which we are presently concerned. The words 'under color of' law were in the legislation from the beginning to the end. The changes hailed by the opposition—indeed the history of the evolution of § 2 much relied upon now—are utterly irrelevant to the problem before us, *viz.*, the meaning of 'under color of' law.... Opponents of the Act, however, did not fail to note that by virtue of Section 1 federal courts would sit in judgment on the misdeeds of state officers. Proponents of the Act, on the other hand, were aware of the extension of federal power contemplated by every section of the Act. They found justification, however, for this extension....

...

Although the legislation was enacted because of the conditions that existed in the South at that time, it is cast in general language and is as applicable to Illinois as it is to the States whose names were mentioned over and again in the debates. It is no answer that the State has a law which if enforced would give relief. The federal remedy is supplementary to the state remedy, and the latter need not be first sought and refused before the federal one is invoked. Hence the fact that Illinois by its constitution and laws outlaws unreasonable searches and seizures is no barrier to the present suit in the federal court.

We had before us in *United States v. Classic* ... 18 U.S.C.A. § 242, which provides a criminal punishment for anyone who 'under color of any law, statute, ordinance, regulation, or custom' subjects any inhabitant of a State to the deprivation of 'any rights, privileges, or immunities secured or protected by the Constitution or laws of the United States.' ... The right involved in the *Classic* case was the right of voters in a primary to have their votes counted. The laws of Louisiana required the defendants 'to count the ballots, to record the result of the count, and to certify the result of the election.' *United States v. Classic, supra*, 313 U.S. 325–326. But according to the indictment they did not perform their duty. In an opinion written by Mr. Justice (later Chief Justice) Stone, in which Mr. Justice Roberts, Mr. Justice Reed, and Mr. Justice Frankfurter joined, the Court ruled, 'Misuse of power, possessed by virtue of state law and made possible only because the wrongdoer is clothed with the authority of state law, is action taken 'under color of' state law.' *Id.*, 313 U.S. 326.... There was a dissenting opinion; but the ruling as to the meaning of 'under color of' state law was not questioned.

That view of the meaning of the words 'under color of' state law, 18 U.S.C.A. § 242, was reaffirmed in *Screws v. United States*, *supra*, 325 U.S. 108–113. The acts there complained of were committed by state officers in performance of their duties, *viz.*, making an arrest effective. It was urged there, as it is here, that 'under color of' state law should not be construed to duplicate in federal law what was an offense under state law. *Id.*, 325 U.S. 138–149, 157–161 (dissenting opinion). It was said there, as it is here, that the ruling in the *Classic* case as to the meaning of 'under color of' state law was not in focus and was ill-advised. *Id.*, 325 U.S. 146–147 (dissenting opinion). It was argued there, as it is here, that 'under color of' state law included only action taken by officials pursuant to state law. *Id.*, 325 U.S. 141–146 (dissenting opinion). We rejected that view. *Id.*, 325 U.S. 110–113, 114–117 (concurring opinion). We stated: 'The construction given [18 U.S.C.A. s 242] in the *Classic* case formulated a rule of law which has become the basis of federal enforcement in this important field. The rule adopted in that case was formulated after mature consideration. It should be good for more than one day only.... The *Classic* case was not the product of hasty action or inadvertence. It was not out of line with the cases which preceded. It was designed to fashion the governing rule of law in this important field. We are not dealing with constitutional interpretations which throughout the history of the Court have wisely remained flexible and subject to frequent re-examination. The meaning which the *Classic* case gave to the phrase 'under color of any law' involved only a construction of the statute. Hence if it states a rule undesirable in its consequences, Congress can change it. We add only to the instability and uncertainty of the law if we revise the meaning of ... 18 U.S.C.A. § 242 to meet the exigencies of each case coming before us.' *Id.*, 325 U.S. 112–113.

We adhered to that view in *Williams v. United States*, *supra*, 341 U.S. 99.

Mr. Shellabarger, reporting out the bill which became the Ku Klux Act, said of the provision with which we now deal: 'The model for it will be found in the second section of the act of April 9, 1866, known as the 'civil rights act.' * * * This section of this bill, on the same state of facts, not only provides a civil remedy for persons whose former condition may have been that of slaves, but also to all people where, under color of State law, they or any of them may be deprived of rights * * *.'[32]

Thus, it is beyond doubt that this phrase should be accorded the same construction in both statutes—in [§ 1983] and in 18 U.S.C.A. § 242.

Since the *Screws* and *Williams* decisions, Congress has had several pieces of civil rights legislation before it. [In civil rights legislation considered or enacted in 1956, 1957, and 1960, no congressional committee reports challenged the Supreme Court's prior constructions of "under color of" law.] If the results of our construction of 'under color of' law were as horrendous as now claimed, if they were as disruptive of our federal scheme as now urged, if they were such an unwarranted invasion of

32. Cong. Globe, 42d Cong., 1st Sess., App. 68.

States' rights as pretended, surely the voice of the opposition would have been heard in those [Congressional] Committee reports. Their silence and the new uses to which 'under color of' law have recently been given reinforce our conclusion that our prior decisions were correct on this matter of construction.

We conclude that the meaning given 'under color of' law in the *Classic* case and in the *Screws* and *Williams* cases was the correct one; and we adhere to it.

In the *Screws* case we dealt with a statute that imposed criminal penalties for acts 'wilfully' done. We construed that word in its setting to mean the doing of an act with 'a specific intent to deprive a person of a federal right.' 325 U.S. at 103.... We do not think that gloss should be placed on [§ 1983] which we have here. The word 'wilfully' does not appear in [§ 1983]. Moreover, [§ 1983] provides a civil remedy, while in the *Screws* case we dealt with a criminal law challenged on the ground of vagueness. Section [1983] should be read against the background of tort liability that makes a man responsible for the natural consequences of his actions. So far, then, the complaint states a cause of action. There remains to consider only a defense peculiar to the City of Chicago.

III.

The City of Chicago asserts that it is not liable under [§ 1983]. We do not stop to explore the whole range of questions tendered us on this issue at oral argument and in the briefs. For we are of the opinion that Congress did not undertake to bring municipal corporations within the ambit of [§ 1983].

When the bill that became the Act of April 20, 1871, was being debated in the Senate, Senator Sherman of Ohio proposed an amendment which would have made 'the inhabitants of the county, city, or parish' in which certain acts of violence occurred liable 'to pay full compensation' to the person damaged or his widow or legal representative. [The House refused to adopt the Sherman Amendment.]

The objection to the Sherman amendment ... was that 'the House had solemnly decided that in their judgment Congress had no constitutional power to impose any obligation upon county and town organizations, the mere instrumentality for the administration of state law.' The question of constitutional power of Congress to impose civil liability on municipalities was vigorously debated with powerful arguments advanced in the affirmative.[46]

Much reliance is placed on the Act of February 25, 1871 ... entitled 'An Act prescribing the Form of the enacting and resolving Clauses of Acts and Resolutions of Congress, and Rules for the Construction thereof.' Section 2 of this Act provides that 'the word 'person' may extend and be applied to bodies politic and corporate.' It should be noted, however, that this definition is merely an allowable, not a mandatory, one. It is said that doubts should be resolved in favor of municipal liability because private remedies against officers for illegal searches and seizures are conspicuously ineffective, and because municipal liability will not only afford plaintiffs responsible

---

46. *See* especially the comments of Senator Sherman. *Id.*, 820–821.

defendants but cause those defendants to eradicate abuses that exist at the police level. We do not reach those policy considerations. Nor do we reach the constitutional question whether Congress has the power to make municipalities liable for acts of its officers that violate the civil rights of individuals.

The response of the Congress to the proposal to make municipalities liable for certain actions being brought within federal purview by the Act of April 20, 1871, was so antagonistic that we cannot believe that the word 'person' was used in this particular Act to include them. Accordingly we hold that the motion to dismiss the complaint against the City of Chicago was properly granted. But since the complaint should not have been dismissed against the officials the judgment must be and is reversed. Reversed.

Mr. Justice HARLAN, whom Mr. Justice STEWART joins, concurring.

Were this case here as one of first impression, I would find the 'under color of any statute' issue very close indeed. However, in *Classic* and *Screws* this Court considered a substantially identical statutory phrase to have a meaning which, unless we now retreat from it, requires that issue to go for the petitioners here.

From my point of view, the policy of *stare decisis*, as it should be applied in matters of statutory construction and, to a lesser extent, the indications of congressional acceptance of this Court's earlier interpretation, require that it appear beyond doubt from the legislative history of the 1871 statute that *Classic* and *Screws* misapprehended the meaning of the controlling provision, before a departure from what was decided in those cases would be justified. Since I can find no such justifying indication in that legislative history, I join the opinion of the Court. However, what has been written on both sides of the matter makes some additional observations appropriate.

Those aspects of Congress' purpose which are quite clear in the earlier congressional debates, as quoted by my Brothers DOUGLAS and FRANKFURTER in turn, seem to me to be inherently ambiguous when applied to the case of an isolated abuse of state authority by an official. One can agree with the Court's opinion that: 'It is abundantly clear that one reason the legislation was passed was to afford a federal right in federal courts because, by reason of prejudice, passion, neglect, intolerance or otherwise, state laws might not be enforced and the claims of citizens to the enjoyment of rights, privileges, and immunities guaranteed by the Fourteenth Amendment might be denied by the state agencies * * *' Without being certain that Congress meant to deal with anything other than abuses so recurrent as to amount to 'custom, or usage.' One can agree with my Brother FRANKFURTER, in dissent, that Congress had no intention of taking over the whole field of ordinary state torts and crimes, without being certain that the enacting Congress would not have regarded actions by an official, made possible by his position, as far more serious than an ordinary state tort, and therefore as a matter of federal concern. If attention is directed at the rare specific references to isolated abuses of state authority, one finds them neither so clear nor so disproportionately divided between favoring the positions of the majority or the dissent as to make either position seem plainly correct.

...

Mr. Justice FRANKFURTER, dissenting except insofar as the Court holds that this action cannot be maintained against the City of Chicago.

Abstractly stated, this case concerns a matter of statutory construction.... Again abstractly stated, this matter of statutory construction is one upon which the Court has already passed. But it has done so under circumstances and in settings that negative those considerations of social policy upon which the doctrine of *stare decisis*, calling for the controlling application of prior statutory construction, rests.

...

III.

We must determine what Congress meant by 'under color' of enumerated state authority. [Summarizing earlier applications of 'under color of']

...

A sharp change from this uniform application of seventy years was made in [*United States v. Classic*, 313 U.S. 299 (1941)], but without acknowledgment or indication of awareness of the revolutionary turnabout from what had been established practice.... (I joined in this opinion without having made an independent examination of the legislative history of the relevant legislation or of the authorities drawn upon for the *Classic* construction. Acquiescence so founded does not preclude the responsible recognition of error disclosed by subsequent study.)

...

[A]lthough this Court has three times found that conduct of state officials which is forbidden by state law may be 'under color' of state law for purposes of the Civil Rights Acts, it is accurate to say that that question has never received here the consideration which its importance merits.... Neither *Classic* nor *Screws* nor *Williams* warrants refusal now to take account of those [legislative] debates and the illumination they afford.

...

IV.

This case squarely presents the question whether the intrusion of a city policeman for which that policeman can show no such authority at state law as could be successfully interposed in defense to a state-law action against him, is nonetheless to be regarded as 'under color' of state authority within the meaning of [§ 1983]. Respondents, in breaking into the Monroe apartment, violated the laws of the State of Illinois. Illinois law appears to offer a civil remedy for unlawful searches; petitioners do not claim that none is available.... Did the enactment by Congress of § 1 of the Ku Klux Act of 1871 encompass such a situation?

That section, it has been noted, was patterned on the similar criminal provision of § 2, Act of April 9, 1866. The earlier Act had as its primary object the effective nullification of the Black Codes, those statutes of the Southern legislatures which had so burdened and disqualified the Negro as to make his emancipation appear illusory. The Act had been vetoed by President Johnson....

...

Insofar as the Court undertakes to demonstrate—as the bulk of its opinion seems to do—that [§ 1983] was meant to reach some instances of action not specifically authorized by the avowed, apparent, written law inscribed in the statute books of the States, the argument knocks at an open door. No one would or could, deny this, for by its express terms the statute comprehends deprivations of federal rights under color of any 'statute, ordinance, regulation, *custom, or usage*' of a State. (Emphasis added.) The question is, what class of cases other than those involving state statute law were meant to be reached. And, with respect to this question, the Court's conclusion is undermined by the very portions of the legislative debates which it cites. For surely the misconduct of individual municipal police officers, subject to the effective oversight of appropriate state administrative and judicial authorities, presents a situation which differs *toto coelo* from one [intended by the examples provided in the legislative history].... These statements indicate that Congress—made keenly aware by the post-bellum conditions in the South that States through their authorities could sanction offenses against the individual by settled practice which established state law as truly as written codes—designed [§ 1983] to reach, as well, official conduct which, because engaged in 'permanently and as a rule,' or 'systematically,' came through acceptance by law-administering officers to constitute 'custom, or usage' having the cast of law.... They do not indicate an attempt to reach, nor does the statute by its terms include, instances of acts in defiance of state law and which no settled state practice, no systematic pattern of official action or inaction, no 'custom, or usage, of any State,' insulates from effective and adequate reparation by the State's authorities.

Rather, all the evidence converges to the conclusion that Congress by [§ 1983] created a civil liability enforceable in the federal courts only in instances of injury for which redress was barred in the state courts because some 'statute, ordinance, regulation, custom, or usage' sanctioned the grievance complained of. This purpose, manifested even by the so-called 'Radical' Reconstruction Congress in 1871, accords with the presuppositions of our federal system. The jurisdiction which Article III of the Constitution conferred on the national judiciary reflected the assumption that the state courts, not the federal courts, would remain the primary guardians of that fundamental security of person and property which the long evolution of the common law had secured to one individual as against other individuals. The Fourteenth Amendment did not alter this basic aspect of our federalism.

...

[I]n the present case petitioners argue that the wrongs done them were committed not by individuals but by the police as state officials. There are two senses in which this might be true. It might be true if petitioners alleged that the redress which state courts offer them against the respondents is different than that which those courts would offer against other individuals, guilty of the same conduct, who were not the police. This is not alleged. It might also be true merely because the respondents are the police—because they are clothed with an appearance of official authority which is in itself a factor of significance in dealings between individuals. Certainly the nighttime intrusion of the man with a star and a police revolver is a different phenomenon than the night-time intrusion of a burglar. The aura of power which a show of authority carries with it has been created by state government. For this reason the national legislature, exercising its power to implement the Fourteenth Amendment, might well attribute responsibility for the intrusion to the State and legislate to protect against such intrusion. The pretense of authority alone might seem to Congress sufficient basis for creating an exception to the ordinary rule that it is to the state tribunals that individuals within a State must look for redress against other individuals within that State. The same pretense of authority might suffice to sustain congressional legislation creating the exception. But until Congress has declared its purpose to shift the ordinary distribution of judicial power for the determination of causes between co-citizens of a State, this Court should not make the shift. Congress has not in [§ 1983] manifested that intention.

...

Of course, these last considerations would be irrelevant to our duty if Congress had demonstrably meant to reach by [§ 1983] activities like those of respondents in this case. But where it appears that Congress plainly did not have that understanding, respect for principles which this Court has long regarded as critical to the most effective functioning of our federalism should avoid extension of a statute beyond its manifest area of operation into applications which invite conflict with the administration of local policies. Such an extension makes the extreme limits of federal constitutional power a law to regulate the quotidian business of every traffic policeman, every registrar of elections, every city inspector or investigator, every clerk in every municipal licensing bureau in this country. The text of the statute, reinforced by its history, precludes such a reading.

...

We cannot expect to create an effective means of protection for human liberties by torturing an 1871 statute to meet the problems of 1960.

...

'Under color' of law meant by authority of law in the nineteenth century. No judicial sympathy, however strong, for needs now felt can give the phrase—a phrase which occurs in a statute, not in a constitution—any different meaning in the twentieth.

...

If a plaintiff can show that defendant is acting pursuant to the specific terms of a state statute or of a municipal ordinance, [§ 1983] will apply.... If he can show that defendant's conduct is within the range of executive discretion in the enforcement of a state statute, or municipal ordinance, [§ 1983] will apply.... Beyond these cases will lie the admittedly more difficult ones in which he seeks to show some "'custom or usage' which has become common law."

...

For further discussion

1. Police went to the Monroe apartment because Mary Saisi had identified a mugshot photo of Mr. Monroe as the likely murderer of her husband. In fact, Mary Saisi had conspired with her boyfriend to murder her husband, and both Mrs. Saisi and her boyfriend went to prison for the murder. For an excellent explanation of the factual background of the case, *see* Myriam E. Gilles, *Police, Race and Crime in 1950s Chicago: Monroe v. Pape as Legal Noir* in Civil Rights Stories (Myriam Gilles and Risa Goluboff, eds., Foundation 2007).

2. Professor Alan Chen summarized the many ways that, since *Monroe*, the Supreme Court has reduced the availability of § 1983 damages actions, including:

- Expanding the concept of qualified immunity (discussed in Chapter 11 of this book)
- Heightening the pleading standards for § 1983 plaintiffs because of the difficulty of pleading constitutional violations under the Supreme Court's decision in *Iqbal* (Chapters 10 and 12)
- Not permitting due process claims based on a liberty interest in reputation unless the plaintiff is at the same time deprived of another legal right (Chapter 8)
- Limiting the ability of plaintiffs to obtain attorneys fees (Chapter 10).

Alan K. Chen, *Rosy Pictures and Renegade Officials: The Slow Death of Monroe v. Pape*, 78 U.M.K.C. L. Rev. 889, 910–16 (2010).

Questions to guide reading of *Monell*

1. The *Monell* majority overruled *Monroe*'s holding that local governments are not "persons" who may be defendants under § 1983. What evidence in the legislative history of § 1983 did the *Monell* majority cite in support of its view that "any person" includes municipalities?
2. According to *Monell*, did Congress mean for local governments to be held liable for their officially adopted policies?
3. According to *Monell*, did Congress intend for local governments to be held liable for constitutional deprivations caused by a municipal custom—even if there had been no formal, official approval of that custom?
4. Under *Monell*, why shouldn't a municipality be held liable for a constitutional violation solely because it is the employer of the wrongdoer?
5. Consider Justice Frankfurter's dissent in *Monroe* while reading *Monell*. Does *Monell* appear to adopt a standard for municipal liability that was proposed by the dissent in *Monroe* for personal liability—liability only when an act is done in obedience to local law or in conformity with a systematic practice of violations? Why do you think the theory that was not accepted for personal liability was adopted by the Court in the context of municipal liability?

Monell v. Dept. of Social Services of the City of New York

436 U.S. 658 (1978)

Mr. Justice BRENNAN delivered the opinion of the Court.

Petitioners, a class of female employees of the Department of Social Services and of the Board of Education of the city of New York, commenced this action under 42 U.S.C. § 1983 in July 1971. The gravamen of the complaint was that the Board and the Department had as a matter of official policy compelled pregnant employees to take unpaid leaves of absence before such leaves were required for medical reasons.

...

We granted *certiorari* ... to consider

> "Whether local governmental officials and/or local independent school boards are 'persons' within the meaning of 42 U.S.C. § 1983 when equitable relief in the nature of back pay is sought against them in their official capacities?"....

[W]e now overrule *Monroe v. Pape* ... insofar as it holds that local governments are wholly immune from suit under § 1983.[7]

I

In *Monroe v. Pape*, we held that "Congress did not undertake to bring municipal corporations within the ambit of [§ 1983]." 365 U.S., at 187. The sole basis for this conclusion was an inference drawn from Congress' rejection of the "Sherman amendment" to the bill which became the Civil Rights Act of 1871 ... the precursor of § 1983. The Amendment would have held a municipal corporation liable for damage done to the person or property of its inhabitants by private persons "riotously and tumultuously assembled." Cong. Globe, 42d Cong., 1st Sess., 749 (1871) (hereinafter Globe). Although the Sherman amendment did not seek to amend § 1 of the Act, which is now § 1983, and although the nature of the obligation created by that amendment was vastly different from that created by § 1, the Court nonetheless concluded in *Monroe* that Congress must have meant to exclude municipal corporations from the coverage of § 1 because " 'the House [in voting against the Sherman amendment] had solemnly decided that in their judgment Congress had no constitutional power to impose any *obligation* upon county and town organizations, the mere instrumentality for the administration of state law.' " 365 U.S., at 190 (emphasis added), quoting Globe 804 (Rep. Poland). This statement, we thought, showed that Congress doubted its "constitutional power ... to impose *civil liability* on municipalities," 365 U.S., at 190 (emphasis added), and that such doubt would have extended to any type of civil liability.

A fresh analysis of the debate on the Civil Rights Act of 1871, and particularly of the case law which each side mustered in its support, shows, however, that *Monroe*

7. However, we do uphold *Monroe v. Pape*, insofar as it holds that the doctrine of *respondeat superior* is not a basis for rendering municipalities liable under § 1983 for the constitutional torts of their employees. *See* Part II, *infra*.

incorrectly equated the "obligation" of which Representative Poland spoke with "civil liability."

A. An Overview

There are three distinct stages in the legislative consideration of the bill which became the Civil Rights Act of 1871. On March 28, 1871, Representative Shellabarger, acting for a House select committee, reported H.R. 320, a bill "to enforce the provisions of the fourteenth amendment to the Constitution of the United States, and for other purposes." H.R. 320 contained four sections. Section 1, now codified as 42 U.S.C. § 1983, was the subject of only limited debate and was passed without amendment. Sections 2 through 4 dealt primarily with the "other purpose" of suppressing Ku Klux Klan violence in the Southern States. The wisdom and constitutionality of these sections—not § 1, now § 1983—were the subject of almost all congressional debate and each of these sections was amended. The House finished its initial debates on H.R. 320 on April 7, 1871, and one week later the Senate also voted out a bill. Again, debate on § 1 of the bill was limited and that section was passed as introduced.

Immediately prior to the vote on H.R. 320 in the Senate, Senator Sherman introduced his amendment. This was not an amendment to § 1 of the bill, but was to be added as § 7 at the end of the bill. Under the Senate rules, no discussion of the amendment was allowed and, although attempts were made to amend the amendment, it was passed as introduced. In this form, the amendment did not place liability on municipal corporations, but made any inhabitant of a municipality liable for damage inflicted by persons "riotously and tumultuously assembled."

The House refused to acquiesce in a number of amendments made by the Senate, including the Sherman amendment, and the respective versions of H.R. 320 were therefore sent to a conference committee. Section 1 of the bill, however, was not a subject of this conference since, as noted, it was passed verbatim as introduced in both Houses of Congress.

On April 18, 1871, the first conference committee completed its work on H.R. 320. The main features of the conference committee draft of the Sherman amendment were these: First, a cause of action was given to persons injured by

> "any persons riotously and tumultuously assembled together ... with intent to deprive any person of any right conferred upon him by the Constitution and laws of the United States, or to deter him or punish him for exercising such right, or by reason of his race, color, or previous condition of servitude...."

Second, the bill provided that the action would be against the county, city, or parish in which the riot had occurred and that it could be maintained by either the person injured or his legal representative. Third, unlike the amendment as proposed, the conference substitute made the government defendant liable on the judgment if it was not satisfied against individual defendants who had committed the violence. If a municipality were liable, the judgment against it could be collected

> "by execution, attachment, mandamus, garnishment, or any other proceeding in aid of execution or applicable to the enforcement of judgments against municipal corporations; and such judgment [would become] a lien as well upon all moneys in the treasury of such county, city, or parish, as upon the other property thereof."

In the ensuing debate on the first conference report, which was the first debate of any kind on the Sherman amendment, Senator Sherman explained that the purpose of his amendment was to enlist the aid of persons of property in the enforcement of the civil rights laws by making their property "responsible" for Ku Klux Klan damage.

...

The first conference substitute passed the Senate but was rejected by the House....

Because the House rejected the first conference report a second conference was called and it duly issued its report. The second conference substitute for the Sherman amendment abandoned municipal liability and, instead, made "any person or persons having knowledge [that a conspiracy to violate civil rights was afoot], and having power to prevent or aid in preventing the same," who did not attempt to stop the same, liable to any person injured by the conspiracy. The amendment in this form was adopted by both Houses of Congress and is now codified as 42 U.S.C. § 1986.

The meaning of the legislative history sketched above can most readily be developed by first considering the debate on the report of the first conference committee. This debate shows conclusively that the constitutional objections raised against the Sherman amendment—on which our holding in *Monroe* was based—would not have prohibited congressional creation of a civil remedy against state municipal corporations that infringed federal rights. Because § 1 of the Civil Rights Act does not state expressly that municipal corporations come within its ambit, it is finally necessary to interpret § 1 to confirm that such corporations were indeed intended to be included within the "persons" to whom that section applies.

B. Debate on the First Conference Report

... Proponents of the Sherman amendment did not, however, discuss in detail the argument in favor of its constitutionality. Nonetheless, it is possible to piece together such an argument from the debates....

House opponents of the Sherman amendment—whose views are particularly important since only the House voted down the amendment—did not dispute Shellabarger's claim that the Fourteenth Amendment created a federal right to protection, ... but they argued that the local units of government upon which the amendment fastened liability were not obligated to keep the peace at state law and further that the Federal Government could not constitutionally require local governments to create police forces, whether this requirement was levied directly, or indirectly by imposing damages for breach of the peace on municipalities. The most complete statement of this position is that of Representative Blair:

> "The proposition known as the Sherman amendment ... is entirely new. It is altogether without a precedent in this country.... That amendment claims the power in the General Government to go into the States of this Union and lay such obligations as it may please upon the municipalities, which are the creations of the States alone...." ... [H]ere it is proposed, not to carry into effect an obligation which rests upon the municipality, but to create that obligation, and that is the provision I am unable to assent to...."

[We] conclude that opponents of the Sherman amendment found it unconstitutional substantially because of the reasons stated by Representative Blair....

There was ample support for Blair's view that the Sherman amendment, by putting municipalities to the Hobson's choice of keeping the peace or paying civil damages, attempted to impose obligations on municipalities by indirection that could not be imposed directly, thereby threatening to "destroy the government of the States." Globe 795.

If municipal liability under § 1 of the Civil Rights Act of 1871 created a similar Hobson's choice, we might conclude, as *Monroe* did, that Congress could not have intended municipalities to be among the "persons" to which that section applied. But this is not the case.

First, opponents expressly distinguished between imposing an obligation to keep the peace and merely imposing civil liability for damages on a municipality that was obligated by state law to keep the peace, but which had not in violation of the Fourteenth Amendment.

...

Second, the doctrine of dual sovereignty apparently put no limit on the power of federal courts to enforce the Constitution against municipalities that violated it.... § 1 of the Civil Rights Act simply conferred jurisdiction on the federal courts to enforce § 1 of the Fourteenth Amendment....

C. Debate on § 1 of the Civil Rights Bill

From the foregoing discussion, it is readily apparent that nothing said in debate on the Sherman amendment would have prevented holding a municipality liable under § 1 of the Civil Rights Act for its own violations of the Fourteenth Amendment. The question remains, however, whether the general language describing those to be liable under § 1—"any person"—covers more than natural persons. An examination of the debate on § 1 and application of appropriate rules of construction show unequivocally that § 1 was intended to cover legal as well as natural persons.

...

The sentiments expressed in Representative Shellabarger's opening speech were echoed by Senator Edmunds ... :

> "The first section is one that I believe nobody objects to, as defining the rights secured by the Constitution of the United States when they are assailed by any State law or under color of any State law, and it is merely carrying

> out the principles of the civil rights bill [of 1866], which have since become a part of the Constitution." Globe 568.

... And he agreed that the bill "secure[d] the rights of white men as much as of colored men." *Id.*, at 696.

In both Houses, statements of the supporters of § 1 corroborated that Congress, in enacting § 1, intended to give a broad remedy for violations of federally protected civil rights. Moreover, since municipalities through their official acts could, equally with natural persons, create the harms intended to be remedied by § 1, and, further, since Congress intended § 1 to be broadly construed, there is no reason to suppose that municipal corporations would have been excluded from the sweep of § 1.... One need not rely on this inference alone, however, for the debates show that Members of Congress understood "persons" to include municipal corporations.

...

In addition, by 1871, it was well understood that corporations should be treated as natural persons for virtually all purposes of constitutional and statutory analysis....

...

That the "usual" meaning of the word "person" would extend to municipal corporations is also evidenced by an Act of Congress which had been passed only months before the Civil Rights Act was passed. This Act provided that "in all acts hereafter passed ... the word 'person' may extend and be applied to bodies politic and corporate ... unless the context shows that such words were intended to be used in a more limited sense." ...

Municipal corporations in 1871 were included within the phrase "bodies politic and corporate" and, accordingly, the "plain meaning" of § 1 is that local government bodies were to be included within the ambit of the persons who could be sued under § 1 of the Civil Rights Act.

Our analysis of the legislative history of the Civil Rights Act of 1871 compels the conclusion that Congress did intend municipalities and other local government units to be included among those persons to whom § 1983 applies. Local governing bodies,[55] therefore, can be sued directly under § 1983 for monetary, declaratory, or injunctive relief where, as here, the action that is alleged to be unconstitutional implements or executes a policy statement, ordinance, regulation, or decision officially adopted and promulgated by that body's officers. Moreover, although the touchstone of the § 1983 action against a government body is an allegation that official policy is responsible for a deprivation of rights protected by the Constitution, local governments, like

---

55. Since official-capacity suits generally represent only another way of pleading an action against an entity of which an officer is an agent—at least where Eleventh Amendment considerations do not control analysis—our holding today that local governments can be sued under § 1983 necessarily decides that local government officials sued in their official capacities are "persons" under § 1983 in those cases in which, as here, a local government would be suable in its own name.

every other § 1983 "person," by the very terms of the statute, may be sued for constitutional deprivations visited pursuant to governmental "custom" even though such a custom has not received formal approval through the body's official decisionmaking channels. As Mr. Justice Harlan, writing for the Court, said in *Adickes v. S. H. Kress & Co.*, 398 U.S. 144, 167–168 (1970): "Congress included customs and usages [in § 1983] because of the persistent and widespread discriminatory practices of state officials.... Although not authorized by written law, such practices of state officials could well be so permanent and well settled as to constitute a 'custom or usage' with the force of law."

On the other hand, the language of § 1983, read against the background of the same legislative history, compels the conclusion that Congress did not intend municipalities to be held liable unless action pursuant to official municipal policy of some nature caused a constitutional tort. In particular, we conclude that a municipality cannot be held liable solely because it employs a tortfeasor—or, in other words, a municipality cannot be held liable under § 1983 on a *respondeat superior* theory.

We begin with the language of § 1983 as originally passed:

> "*[A]ny person who*, under color of any law, statute, ordinance, regulation, custom, or usage of any State, *shall subject, or cause to be subjected*, any person ... to the deprivation of any rights, privileges, or immunities secured by the Constitution of the United States, shall, any such law, statute, ordinance, regulation, custom, or usage of the State to the contrary notwithstanding, be liable to the party injured in any action at law, suit in equity, or other proper proceeding for redress...."

17 Stat. 13. (emphasis added).

The italicized language plainly imposes liability on a government that, under color of some official policy, "causes" an employee to violate another's constitutional rights. At the same time, that language cannot be easily read to impose liability vicariously on governing bodies solely on the basis of the existence of an employer-employee relationship with a tortfeasor. Indeed, the fact that Congress did specifically provide that A's tort became B's liability if B "caused" A to subject another to a tort suggests that Congress did not intend § 1983 liability to attach where such causation was absent....

Equally important, creation of a federal law of *respondeat superior* would have raised all the constitutional problems associated with the obligation to keep the peace, an obligation Congress chose not to impose because it thought imposition of such an obligation unconstitutional.

...

We conclude, therefore, that a local government may not be sued under § 1983 for an injury inflicted solely by its employees or agents. Instead, it is when execution of a government's policy or custom, whether made by its lawmakers or by those whose edicts or acts may fairly be said to represent official policy, inflicts the injury that the government as an entity is responsible under § 1983. Since this case unquestionably involves official policy as the moving force of the constitutional violation found by the District Court, we must reverse the judgment below.

...

III

Although we have stated that *stare decisis* has more force in statutory analysis than in constitutional adjudication because, in the former situation, Congress can correct our mistakes through legislation ... we have never applied *stare decisis* mechanically to prohibit overruling our earlier decisions determining the meaning of statutes.

...

First, *Monroe v. Pape*, insofar as it completely immunizes municipalities from suit under § 1983, was a departure from prior practice.... Moreover, the constitutional defect that led to the rejection of the Sherman amendment would not have distinguished between municipalities and school boards, each of which is an instrumentality of state administration.... For this reason, our cases ... holding school boards liable in § 1983 actions are inconsistent with *Monroe*....

...

Second, the principle of blanket immunity established in *Monroe* cannot be cabined short of school boards. Yet such an extension would itself be inconsistent with recent expressions of congressional intent. In the wake of our decisions, Congress not only has shown no hostility to federal-court decisions against school boards, but it has indeed rejected efforts to strip the federal courts of jurisdiction over school boards....

...

Third, municipalities can assert no reliance claim which can support an absolute immunity ... Finally, even under the most stringent test for the propriety of overruling a statutory decision proposed by Mr. Justice Harlan in *Monroe*—"that it appear beyond doubt from the legislative history of the 1871 statute that [*Monroe*] misapprehended the meaning of the [section]," 365 U.S., at 192 (concurring opinion)—the overruling of *Monroe* insofar as it holds that local governments are not "persons" who may be defendants in § 1983 suits is clearly proper. It is simply beyond doubt that, under the 1871 Congress' view of the law, were § 1983 liability unconstitutional as to local governments, it would have been equally unconstitutional as to state officers. Yet everyone—proponents and opponents alike—knew § 1983 would be applied to state officers and nonetheless stated that § 1983 was constitutional. And, moreover, there can be no doubt that § 1 of the Civil Rights Act was intended to provide a remedy, to be broadly construed, against all forms of official violation of federally protected rights. Therefore, absent a clear statement in the legislative history supporting the conclusion that § 1 was not to apply to the official acts of a municipal corporation—which simply is not present—there is no justification for excluding municipalities from the "persons" covered by § 1.

For reasons stated above, therefore, we hold that *stare decisis* does not bar our overruling of *Monroe* insofar as it is inconsistent with Parts I and II of this opinion.

...

Mr. Justice REHNQUIST, with whom THE CHIEF JUSTICE joins, dissenting.

Seventeen years ago, in *Monroe v. Pape*, 365 U.S. 167 (1961), this Court held that the 42d Congress did not intend to subject a municipal corporation to liability as a "person" within the meaning of 42 U.S.C. § 1983. Since then, the Congress has remained silent, but this Court has reaffirmed that holding on at least three separate occasions ... Today, the Court abandons this long and consistent line of precedents, offering in justification only an elaborate canvass of the same legislative history which was before the Court in 1961. Because I cannot agree that this Court is "free to disregard these precedents," which have been "considered maturely and recently" by this Court ... I am compelled to dissent.

I

As this Court has repeatedly recognized ... considerations of *stare decisis* are at their strongest when this Court confronts its previous constructions of legislation. In all cases, private parties shape their conduct according to this Court's settled construction of the law, but the Congress is at liberty to correct our mistakes of statutory construction, unlike our constitutional interpretations, whenever it sees fit.

...

The Court's assertion that municipalities have no right to act "on an assumption that they can violate constitutional rights indefinitely," is simply beside the point. Since *Monroe*, municipalities have had the right to expect that they would not be held liable retroactively for their officers' failure to predict this Court's recognition of new constitutional rights. No doubt innumerable municipal insurance policies and indemnity ordinances have been founded on this assumption, which is wholly justifiable under established principles of stare decisis. To obliterate those legitimate expectations without more compelling justifications than those advanced by the Court is a significant departure from our prior practice.

...

III

The decision in *Monroe v. Pape* was the fountainhead of the torrent of civil rights litigation of the last 17 years. Using § 1983 as a vehicle, the courts have articulated new and previously unforeseeable interpretations of the Fourteenth Amendment. At the same time, the doctrine of municipal immunity enunciated in *Monroe* has protected municipalities and their limited treasuries from the consequences of their officials' failure to predict the course of this Court's constitutional jurisprudence. None of the Members of this Court can foresee the practical consequences of today's removal of that protection. Only the Congress, which has the benefit of the advice of every segment of this diverse Nation, is equipped to consider the results of such a drastic change in the law. It seems all but inevitable that it will find it necessary to do so after today's decision.

...

For further discussion

1. Justice Rehnquist suggests in his dissent that Congress might want to overrule the majority's construction of § 1983. If you were asked to draft language amending § 1983 to accomplish that result, what language would you propose?

2. Suppose you represent a city. A newspaper reports that a police officer shot a New Year's Eve partygoer because the man fired celebratory shots in the air. The man's attorney is quoted as saying "the shooter's actions are the result of policies and procedures by the city" and that "the police department has failed to promptly and thoroughly investigate and evaluate police shootings in the past." In a phone call to the Mayor to explain the possible legal significance of the attorney's comments, what would you say?

3. Section 1983 applies to state and local officials. As the Supreme Court explained in footnote 55 of *Monell*, claims against state governments are also governed by the 11th Amendment, the subject of Chapter 15. Federal officials also can be sued for violating constitutional rights. In *Bivens v. Six Unknown Fed. Narcotics Agents*, 403 U.S. 388 (1971), the Supreme Court "'established that the victims of a constitutional violation by a federal agent have a right to recover damages against the official in federal court despite the absence of any statute conferring such a right.'" *Hartman v. Moore*, 547 U.S. 250, 255 n. 2 (2006) (further citation omitted). "Though more limited in some respects ... a *Bivens* action is the federal analog to suits brought against state officials under ... 42 U.S.C. § 1983." This book does not explore *Bivens* actions.

4. This Chapter has briefly sketched the historical context for enacting § 1983 and briefly introduced the modern conceptions of individual and local government liability under § 1983. The next several chapters explore specific constitutional rights that § 1983 can be used to protect.

Chapter Two

Eighth Amendment Prisoner Litigation

Office of the Clerk
UNITED STATES COURT OF APPEALS
FOR THE TWELFTH CIRCUIT

Re: *Miller v. Tappan & Ludwig*
Appeal No. 20-0414

Dear Counsel:

The Court hereby informs counsel for Appellant Miller, an inmate, and counsel for Appellees Correctional Officers Tappan and Ludwig, that oral argument will take place in the above-captioned appeal in Courtroom A. Because the application of *Farmer v. Brennan* is a question of first impression in this Circuit, the Court requests that the parties be prepared to discuss that decision in detail at oral argument.

Sincerely,

Kate Dolgenos
Brief Specialist

A. Chapter Overview

The 8th Amendment prohibits cruel and unusual punishment of a person convicted of a crime. This Chapter includes factual background about the jobs of correctional officers and the conditions of inmates, including prison health care, prison violence, and prison rape. It includes a legislative response to the problem of prison rape.

The Chapter begins with the Supreme Court's establishment in *Estelle* that the 8th Amendment's ban on cruel and unusual punishment prohibits "deliberate indifference" to serious medical needs of convicted prisoners. The same deliberate indifference standard applies to other conditions of confinement claims, such as overcrowding (*Wilson*). *Farmer* further defined "deliberate indifference" to mean that the defendant subjectively appreciated the risk of harm to the plaintiff and deliberately disregarded it. Claims based on medical care or other conditions of confinement have both an objective element and a subjective element. Plaintiff must allege facts showing both (1) an "objective" element, that the injury or medical need is "sufficiently serious" to be the basis of an 8th Amendment violation and (2) a "subjective" element, that the prison official acted "with a sufficiently culpable state of mind" (*Estelle*, *Wilson*, *Farmer*).

Should the same deliberate indifference standard apply to prison officials' use of force to quell a prison riot? *Whitley* answered "no," instead requiring plaintiffs to meet the higher threshold of force applied "maliciously and sadistically for the very purpose of causing harm." In *Hudson*, the Supreme Court extended the *Whitley* "malicious and sadistic" standard to all 8th Amendment claims based on prison security. While plaintiffs have a higher burden for the subjective element in prison security cases than they do for the subjective element in prison health or condition cases, plaintiffs have a lesser burden for the objective element. For 8th Amendment claims based on correctional officers' use of force to restore prison security, plaintiffs do not need to allege a serious injury (*Hudson*) or even a *de minimis* injury (*Wilkins*). Rather, the Supreme Court has held that for prison use of force cases, the primary focus is on the subjective element: "[T]he 'core judicial inquiry,' [is] not whether a certain quantum of injury was sustained, but rather 'whether force was applied in a good-faith effort to maintain or restore discipline, or maliciously and sadistically to cause harm.'' *Wilkins v. Gaddy*, 559 U.S. 34, 37 (2010) (further citation omitted).

To appreciate how the federal courts have fleshed out the *Farmer* deliberate indifference standard, this Chapter includes circuit court model jury instructions and includes applications of that standard in the context of violence inflicted by other prisoners (*Giroux*), including by prison gang members (*Miller* and *Rodriguez*).

Note that the Prison Litigation Reform Act of 1996 imposed procedural requirements and other limitations on prison litigation and is addressed separately in Chapter 10.

The Eighth Amendment provides: Excessive bail shall not be required, nor excessive fines imposed, nor cruel and unusual punishments inflicted.

B. Factual Context

American jails and prisons hold more than 2 million people, about one-fifth of the world's penal population.[1] The United States has "the highest prison population rate—that is, the number of prisoners per 100,000 of the national population" at

1. Of the 10.74 million people held in penal institutions throughout the world, either as pre-trial detainees/remand prisoners or as convicted and sentenced inmates, "more than 2.1 million prisoners [are] in the United States...." Roy Walmsley, *World Prison Population List* (12th Ed., data as of Sept. 2018) at 2, available at http://www.prisonstudies.org/sites/default/files/resources/downloads/wppl_12.pdf.

655 per 100,000, followed by El Salvador (604). By contrast, "more than half of all countries and territories (53%) have rates below 150 per 100,000."[2]

In 2019, the Prison Policy Initiative reported that "[t]he American criminal justice system holds almost 2.3 million people in 1,719 state prisons, 109 federal prisons, 1,772 juvenile correctional facilities, 3,163 local jails [and other institutions]."[3] The U.S. incarcerated population was not always that large. "In just two decades—between 1987 and 2007—America's incarcerated population nearly tripled [to 2.4 million]."[4]

The Eighth Amendment governs each inmate's conditions of confinement. Prisoner lawsuits are a substantial portion of the federal docket. Recall Justice Samuel Alito's comment in Chapter 1, that prisoner civil rights and prison conditions cases "represented between 8.3% and 9.8% of the new filings in the federal district courts" between 2000 and 2005. Inmate claims against prison or jail officials based on use of excessive force by guards, on inmate-on-inmate violence, and on prison health care are all governed by Eighth Amendment standards.

Prison and jail guards occupy the same space as inmates for much of every day. Guards suffer higher than normal rates of heart attacks, ulcers, hypertension, depression, and divorce.[5] Correction officer turnover averages 16% annually—more where the pay is lower.[6] "Directors of systems remain on the job for no more than three years on average, and their rapid turnover destabilizes entire systems."[7] In testimony before the Vera Institute's Commission on Safety and Abuse in America's Prisons, a New Jersey corrections official stated that the suicide rate for corrections officers was 39% higher than that of other professions; that corrections officers had the second highest mortality rate of all occupations; and that their average life expectancy was only age 58.[8] Writing about his undercover experience as a New York correctional officer, an investigative journalist recalled being fascinated by a display at the corrections academy of "inmate weapons: a sharpened piece of Plexiglas, a filed down serving spoon, a metal spike." Ted Conover, NEWJACK (Vintage 2001) at 13.

To learn more about life in prison for both the guards and the inmates, visit the website of the Vera Institute of Justice, Commission on Safety and Abuse in America's

---

2. *Id.*

3. Wendy Sawyer and Peter Wagner, MASS INCARCERATION: THE WHOLE PIE 2019, p. 1 (March 2019), https://www.prisonpolicy.org/reports/pie2019.html.

4. NAT'L. PRISON RAPE ELIMINATION COMM'N, NATIONAL PRISON RAPE ELIMINATION COMMISSION REPORT 43 (2009), https://www.ncjrs.gov/pdffiles1/226680.pdf.

5. Brian Dawe, *PTSD, Depression, Suicide & Divorce are Highest Among Correctional Officers*, AMOR UP NOW, (May 21, 2018), https://armorupnow.org/2018/05/21/ptsd-depression-suicide-divorce-are-highest-among-correctional-officers/.

6. VERA INST. OF JUST., CONFRONTING CONFINEMENT: A REPORT OF THE COMMISSION ON SAFETY AND ABUSE IN AMERICA'S PRISONS 15 (2006), http://www.vera.org/pubs/confronting-confinement.

7. *Id.*

8. William Hepner, M.Ed., Opening Remarks to the Vera Inst. of Just., Comm'n on Safety and Abuse in America's Prisons 204–209 (November 1, 2005) (transcript available at https://storage.googleapis.com/vera-web-assets/inline-downloads/Hearing-3-Day-1.pdf).

Prisons, http://www.prisoncommission.org/, or read an inmate's reflections on a typical day.[9] Try to visit a local jail or prison or watch a documentary about prison life.

For a sense of what life is like for correctional officers, consider the following excerpt from a magazine profile of several guards in a medium-to-high security prison in California, most of whom did not plan a corrections career but were looking for "decent pay, job security, and benefits":[10]

> One of the most dangerous assignments is the Administrative Segregation Unit [where inmates are placed for disciplinary reasons and sometimes for their own protection].... "It's like a jail within a jail. I mean, these inmates get personal. Talking about your family, talking about, you know, your mother, your spouse. They try to assault you by trying to stab you or slice you when you approach the cell[," said Lt. Ray Marrero, a public information officer].
>
> ...
>
> Officer Estrella ... is assigned to the Investigative Services Unit. "I'm an institutional gang investigator at this institution. I specialize in the gangs, all disruptive groups and/or prison gangs validated by the Department of Corrections: the Mexican Mafia, the Black Guerilla Family, the Aryan Brotherhood, the Nazi Lowriders, the Nuestra Familia.... The majority of them are the Skinheads that come out of the East County area of San Diego...." Estrella ... has a tool for retrieving inmates' weapons found in the yard. "We don't want to put our hands on them," he said. "They're either bloody or they've got drugs on them. There are syringes that the inmates manufacture or tattoo guns with hepatitis A through Z."
>
> ...
>
> Most correctional officers ... carry pepper spray, a personal alarm, a side-handle baton, and a whistle.... [Officer Estrella said] "At this institution the use of the spray is ... almost an everyday occurrence."
>
> ...[Officer Murillo, a female corrections officer said,] "It's really stressful when you first start, because you really haven't established a rapport with the inmates and they're always, constantly, trying you out. They're always testing you. They'll approach you and they'll bark at you and if you say 'No,' they'll bark at you, hoping that you're going to back off and give them what they want."
>
> "It also happens when there is a brand-new inmate and he'll try you," she said.... "You can't back off, because if you back off, you show them fear.

9. For example, *see*, Jerry Metcalf, *A Day in the Life of a Prisoner*, The Marshall Project (July 12, 2018), https://www.themarshallproject.org/2018/07/12/a-day-in-the-life-of-a-prisoner; Trevor, *A Day in the Life of a Prisoner*, Pacific Standard (July 14, 2015), https://psmag.com/news/a-day-in-the-life-of-a-prisoner.

10. Shari McCullough, *Commitment*, San Diego Reader (Mar. 24, 2005), http://www.sandiegoreader.com/news/2005/mar/24/committment/.

Then it's worse—it's really bad, because the other inmates are watching you. They're always watching how you react. If they see that you are scared, you're going to have more inmates doing the same thing."

...

"We had one officer in the kitchen—female staff—who ... got hit with batteries in a sock. She retired. Her head was shattered and smashed in...."

...

Murillo has been assaulted herself ... "I ... got stuck with a needle from a tattoo gun," she added. "The tattoo gun was stored in an inappropriate area, and when I went looking for a pen I poked myself with a needle. I never found out ... if it had been used, so I had to go through the treatment and getting tested.... I didn't catch any hepatitis or AIDS or anything. But it was a tremendous stress on my family.... I went and I saw a psychiatrist over it."

...

"Every time we have to run to an alarm you feel like it's going to be real, or you respond to a fight or something happening right in front of you, you have to act," said Murillo.... "Your heart just pounds a hundred miles per hour. Your body just goes through tremendous shock, because afterwards everything just hurts. All my muscles hurt.... That happens at least once or twice a week," she continued.

...

With the high incidence of hepatitis and AIDS in California prisons, bodily fluids, a weapon that's readily available to inmates, have become deadly. "They make these concoctions of urine and feces and try to throw it at you, try to hit you in your face," said Marrero. "I can't tell you about the potential for communicable diseases with hepatitis, AIDS, and everything else. That's a very common, common thing that happens.... We have to ... get [officers] treated medically, immediately.... No one wants to bring these diseases home to their family."

Inmates also manufacture weapons inside [the prison]. Cavazos explained: "We try not to leave any kind of Styrofoam cups around—they make weapons out of that. They melt it down.... They make weapons out of the wires from the fencing. Ink pens.... They're very creative." ... Wagner elaborated[:] "They can melt plastic down and make weapons. They can utilize a toothbrush—what they do is take a razor blade from regular disposable razors, they'll take that blade out, they'll tape it to the toothbrush, make a handle.... They'll sharpen it inside their cell by scraping it against the wall.... Any kind of plastic, a big piece of plastic, they'll just keep doing it till it's a point."

...

> Marrero said that as soon as he gets home, he takes a shower, "because I smell like the prison, you know. There's a distinct prison smell that sticks on you, and you need to wash that off. You're constantly washing your hands during the course of the day, even though you're wearing gloves whenever you're patting down inmates...."[11]

With these conditions in mind, consider the following examples of employment ads for corrections jobs. In 2019, the Nebraska Department of Correction advertised a starting pay of $18.43 per hour, plus medical, vacation, tuition, and retirement benefits, and required a high school diploma or equivalent, with a preference for both English and Spanish skills.[12] A Minnesota Sheriff's Office advertised a corrections officer position paying up to $22.91 per hour, and requiring a high school diploma or GED plus two years work experience in a role requiring interaction with others and computer skills.[13] In addition to "interpersonal skill to build rapport with inmates as a means of ... limiting aggression," candidates should expect to intervene in inmate disputes, use physical restraint when necessary, and screen incoming inmates to determine whether they need immediate medical attention or pose a threat to others.[14] A Florida corrections officer position supervising inmate road crews working on construction, maintenance, or emergency response projects required an equivalent to a high school diploma and a year's experience in construction or agriculture, plus knowledge of firearms and other skills, and warned job-holders may be subjected to "fumes," "blood and other bodily fluids," and "intense noises."

C. Prison Health Care

Inmates suffer from the same medical and dental problems that afflict non-inmates, but inmates also suffer from some health problems more frequently than non-inmates. A study published in 2017 reported that "37% of prisoners and 44% of jail inmates had been told in the past by a mental health professional that they had a mental disorder."[15] Similarly, an earlier Department of Justice study reported that more than half of all prison and jail inmates had a mental health problem, including 705,600 inmates in State prisons, 78,800 in Federal prisons, and 479,900 in local jails.[16] Female

11. *Id.*

12. *Corrections Corporal—NCCW*, Government Jobs, https://www.governmentjobs.com/jobs/2492982-0/corrections-corporal-nccw?keyword=corrections&daysPosted=7&pagetype=searchPage. (last visited July 13, 2019).

13. *Correctional Officers*, Government Jobs, https://www.governmentjobs.com/jobs/2492101-0/correctional-officer?page=6&keyword=corrections&daysPosted=7&pagetype=searchPage. (last visited July 13, 2019).

14. *Id.*

15. Jennifer Bronson & Marcus Berzofsky, Bureau of Just. Stat., Special Report: Indicators of Mental Health Problems Reported by Prisoners and Jail Inmates, 2011–12, 1 (2017).

16. Doris J. James & Lauren E. Glaze, Bureau of Just. Stat., Special Report: Mental Health Problems of Prison and Jail Inmates 1 (2006), http://bjs.ojp.usdoj.gov/content/pub/pdf/mhppji.pdf. Congress assessed this percentage much lower in the legislative findings of the Prison Rape Elimination

inmates had higher rates of mental health problems than male inmates (state prisons: 73% of females and 55% of males; local jails: 75% of females and 63% of males).[17] Mental health issues are related to drug abuse: about three-fourths of those who had a mental health problem met criteria for substance dependence or abuse.[18]

"High rates of disease ... among prisoners, coupled with inadequate funding for correctional health care, endanger prisoners, staff, and the public.... Left untreated, staph infections and diseases such as tuberculosis, hepatitis C, and HIV directly affect our families, neighborhoods, and communities."[19]

In 2015, about 17,000 people with HIV were in state and federal prisons.[20] The prevalence of HIV is higher among prisoners than among the general population.[21] "The higher prevalence of HIV, chronic hepatitis B, and chronic hepatitis C infection within correctional facilities can partially be explained by the higher percentage of inmates with a history of injection drug abuse" and the association of injection drug use with high risk sexual activity.[22] The states of New York, Florida, and Louisiana have higher rates of inmates living with HIV.[23] Correctional officers must balance security concerns with keeping inmates' medical conditions private:

> Escorting inmates to get medications, visit a doctor, or go to the infirmary is a security issue and may strain correctional staff resources. These same elements of care may make it difficult to keep the inmate's infection status confidential. If it becomes known, the inmate may be ostracized and harassed by staff or other inmates.[24]

Act. *See* Prison Rape Elimination Act of 2003 § 102(3), 42 U.S.C. § 15601(3) (2006) ("As many as 16 percent of inmates in State prisons and jails, and 7 percent of Federal inmates, suffer from mental illness.").

17. JAMES & GLAZE, *supra* note 17, at 1.

18. *Id.*

19. VERA INST. OF JUST., CONFRONTING CONFINEMENT: A REPORT OF THE COMMISSION ON SAFETY AND ABUSE IN AMERICA'S PRISONS 13 (2006), http://www.vera.org/pubs/confronting-confinement.

20. Rebecca G. Kinney & Lara B. Strick, *HIV and Corrections, Overview of U.S. Correctional System*, NAT'L HIV CURRICULUM (Sept. 5, 2018), https://www.hiv.uw.edu/go/key-populations/hiv-corrections/core-concept/all. Rebecca G. Kinney & Lara B. Strick, *HIV and Corrections, Overview of U.S. Correctional System*, NAT'L HIV CURRICULUM (Sept. 5, 2018), https://www.hiv.uw.edu/go/key-populations/hiv-corrections/core-concept/all. HIV is a virus that attacks cells that help the body fight infection; AIDS is the late stage of HIV infections that occurs when the HIV infection progresses to such an extent as to severely limit the body's ability to fight infection. When treated with antiretroviral therapy, the virus is unable to replicate. In the U.S., most people with HIV do not develop AIDS as a result of anti-viral therapy. For additional information, *see* HIV Basics, hiv.gov/hiv-basics.

21. *Id.*

22. *Id.*; *see* 33 U.S.C. § 30301(7) (2017) ("Infection rates for other sexually transmitted diseases, tuberculosis, and hepatitis B and C are also far greater for prisoners than for the American population as a whole").

23. Kinney & Strick, *supra* note 21.

24. U.S. DEP'T OF HEALTH & HUM. SERVS., IDU/HIV PREVENTION: PROVIDING SERVICES TO INMATES LIVING WITH HIV 2 (August 2001), http://www.cdc.gov/idu/facts/cj-hiv.pdf.

HIV infection is also a housing issue. Most state/federal systems house inmates with HIV (non-AIDS) and inmates with AIDS in the general population with no restrictions.[25] In city/county systems, 75% of inmates with HIV (non-AIDS) and 27% for those with AIDS are housed in the general population with no restrictions.[26] By contrast, until 2013 (South Carolina), 2012 (Alabama), and 2010 (Mississippi), some corrections systems housed HIV-infected inmates in separate facilities.[27]

The Centers for Disease Control and Prevention (CDC) recommends that HIV prevention education in prisons address male-male sex (whether consensual, in exchange for money or goods, or by rape), address tattooing, and address injection drug use.[28] Very few prisons (Mississippi, Vermont) and jails (Los Angeles, New York, Philadelphia, San Francisco, and the District of Columbia) provide condoms to inmates;[29] in 2014, California joined Vermont in making condoms available throughout its state prisons without onerous restrictions.[30] The CDC also recommends weighing the following patient characteristics before beginning medical treatment:

- will the inmate choose and be able to adhere to the regimen?
- will the inmate's drug addiction interfere?

---

25. THEODORE M. HAMMETT, SOFIA KENNEDY, & SARAH KUCK, NATIONAL SURVEY OF INFECTIOUS DISEASES IN CORRECTIONAL FACILITIES: HIV AND SEXUALLY TRANSMITTED DISEASES 2, 16 (2007), http://www.ncjrs.gov/pdffiles1/nij/grants/217736.pdf.

26. *Id.*

27. U.S. Dep't of Health & Hum. Servs., Ctrs. for Disease Control & Prevention, *HIV Transmission Among Male Inmates in a State Prison System—Georgia, 1992–2005*, 55 MORBIDITY & MORTALITY WKLY. REP. 421, 425 (April 21, 2006), http://www.cdc.gov/mmwr/PDF/wk/mm5515.pdf. According to the American Civil Liberties website, Mississippi decided in March 2010 to terminate its segregation of HIV-positive inmates. *See* Suzanne Ito, *Mississippi Ends Draconian Segregation Policy Against Prisoners with HIV*, ACLU: Speak Freely (Mar. 17, 2010, 3:12 PM), http://www.aclu.org/blog/prisoners-rights/mississippi-ends-draconian-segregation-policy-against-prisoners-hiv; *see also*, Press Release, Am. Civ. Lib. Union, Decision ACLU Lawsuit Paves Way for HIV Prisoners to Have Access to Services, Classes and Trainings Available to Other Prisoners (Dec. 21, 2012) (announcing an end to a similar policy in Alabama), https://www.aclu.org/prisoners-rights/judge-orders-alabama-stop-segregation-hiv-prisoners-alabama; Press Release, Am. Civ. Lib. Union, Announcement Marks Culmination of Quarter-Century ACLU Campaign to End Discriminatory and Arbitrary Practice (July 10, 2013) (announcing that South Carolina would end its HIV segregation policy), https://www.aclu.org/prisoners-rights/south-carolina-becomes-final-state-end-segregation-prisoners-hiv.

28. U.S. Dep't of Health & Hum. Servs., Ctrs. for Disease Control & Prevention, *HIV Transmission Among Male Inmates in a State Prison System—Georgia, 1992–2005*, 55 MORBIDITY & MORTALITY WKLY. REP., 421, 423 (April 21, 2006), available at http://www.cdc.gov/mmwr/PDF/wk/mm5515.pdf.

29. *Id.*; Babak Moazen *et al.*, *Availability, Coverage and Barriers Towards Condom Provision in Prisons: A Review of the Evidence*, 13 (2019) (Vermont, Los Angeles, Philadelphia, and New York are among the few U.S. systems that provide condoms), https://www.researchgate.net/publication/330543762_Availability_Coverage_and_Barriers_Towards_Condom_Provision_in_Prisons_A_Review_of_the_Evidence.

30. George Lavender, *Condoms in the Clink*, AL JAZEERA AMERICA, http://america.aljazeera.com/articles/2014/11/6/california-condomsinprison.html (Nov. 6, 2014).

- does the inmate have viral hepatitis or other infectious, mental illness, or chronic health conditions; if so, will this diminish the effectiveness of therapy?[31]

Ronald Day, an inmate and peer educator for the Prisoners for AIDS Counseling and Education Program at a New York prison, explained that, in his view, "prison is a microcosm of the larger society" and that "the problems with HIV/AIDS in prison seem to parallel those in the community."[32] Mr. Day explained: "[S]ome HIVers contend that the care they receive swings like a pendulum from reasonable to grossly inadequate, depending usually on the health care provider or their placement in a particular facility. Indeed, the medical department is known for its ineptness and its indifference to prisoners' medical needs. On the other hand, however, we sometimes transfer blame, such as for a death, serious ailment, or late diagnosis of a terminal illness, to the medical department unjustifiably. Clearly, we have only ourselves to blame when we neglect our healthcare and compound this problem by continuing to engage in risky behaviors. Although prison officials have care, custody, and control over our bodies, this doesn't mean that we should abdicate responsibility for our physical and mental well being ... [S]ince we are a marginalized group, not much interest is paid to the problems of prisoners, as if dodging them will make them disappear and prevent them from resurfacing in the community."[33]

"The rampant spread of Hepatitis C in this country's penal system will not remain confined to those imprisoned. Ninety percent of the nation's incarcerated will be released back into the community, representing a healthcare crisis that cannot be ignored.... Unchecked in prison, hepatitis C threatens the world outside."[34]

"The most dangerous thing coming out of prison these days may be something most convicts don't even know they have: hepatitis C.... [B]y some estimates, around 40 percent of the 2.2 million in jail and prison are infected, compared with just 2 percent of the general population. Eventually, when they are released, medical experts predict they will be a crushing burden on the health care system ... [and] will be carriers, spreading the disease."[35] Hepatitis C is linked to infected needles used for drugs and tattoos.[36] Treatment for Hepatitis C exists. While the treatment cost is dramatically lower now than in 2017, when it cost about $70,000 per patient, even at the lower

---

31. U.S. Dep't of Health & Hum. Servs., IDU/HIV Prevention: Providing Services to Inmates Living with HIV 2 (August 2001), http://www.cdc.gov/idu/facts/cj-hiv.pdf.

32. Ronald F. Day, *HIV/AIDS in Prison: Crisis of the Confined*, The Body: Body Positive, (Oct. 1, 2004), https://www.thebody.com/article/hiv-aids-prison-crisis-confined.

33. *Id.*

34. Martha Mendoza, *A Pending Healthcare Crisis: HCV in U.S. Prisons,* Hepatitis Central, (March 14, 2007), http://www.hepatitis-central.com/mt/archives/2007/03/hcv_in_us_priso.html.

35. *Id.*; Turgay Ayer *et al*, *Prioritizing Hepatitis C Treatment in U.S. Prisons*, 67 Operations Research 853, 854 (2019) (Hepatitis C virus is ten times higher inside correctional systems than among the general population).

36. Mendoza, *supra* note 35.

current price of $25,000 per patient, treating 10% of infected inmates could cost several billion dollars.[37] "'It's a hard sell to convince taxpayers why additional resources should be spent on the health care of the incarcerated when there are a lot of people who aren't incarcerated who don't have adequate health care,' said Dr. Joseph Bick, chief medical officer at the California Medical Facility at Vacaville."[38]

For further discussion

Did anything in this factual background cause you to question your own assumptions or surprise you? What dilemmas do you think lawyers representing prisoners might have to face and resolve? What dilemmas do you think lawyers representing corrections officers might have to face and resolve? What was the most important thing you learned from this reading?

Questions to guide reading of *Estelle*

1. How does Justice Marshall connect the obligation to provide medical care to the text of the 8th Amendment? According to *Estelle,* how did early Supreme Court decisions read the 8th Amendment, and how have more recent cases read the 8th Amendment? In a dissent from a different decision in this Chapter, Justice Thomas criticized *Estelle* as having "loosed the Eighth Amendment from its historical moorings." Do you agree?
2. Why does the government have an obligation to provide medical care to prisoners?
3. The standard *Estelle* announced to measure a prisoner's claim that medical treatment violates the 8th Amendment "cruel and unusual punishments" clause has both an objective element and a subjective element. What are they? What are the three ways for a prisoner to prevail on an 8th Amendment denial of medical treatment claim?
4. Why did *Estelle* hold that negligent failure to provide adequate medical care does not constitute an 8th Amendment violation? Does a prison doctor's decision to choose a simpler and less effective treatment constitute deliberate indifference?
5. Based on *Estelle*, what arguments would you expect counsel for prisons to make in 12(b)(6) motions to dismiss medical treatment claims by prisoners?
6. What role do you think counsel to a prison should play? Should the role have a proactive, educational aspect? Or is it primarily reactive?

---

37. Anne Spaulding & Jagpreet Chhatwal, *Nominal Pricing Can Help Jails and Prisons Treat Hepatitis C Without Breaking the Bank*, STAT: FIRST OPINION (Jan. 9, 2019), https://www.statnews.com/2019/01/09/nominal-pricing-prisons-jails-treat-hepatitis-c/.

38. Mendoza, *supra* note 35.

Estelle v. Gamble

429 U.S. 97 (1976)

Mr. Justice MARSHALL delivered the opinion of the Court.

Respondent J. W. Gamble, an inmate of the Texas Department of Corrections, was injured on November 9, 1973, while performing a prison work assignment. On February 11, 1974, he instituted this civil rights action under 42 U.S.C. § 1983, complaining of the treatment he received after the injury....

Because the complaint was dismissed for failure to state a claim, we must take as true its handwritten, *pro se* allegations.... According to the complaint, Gamble was injured on November 9, 1973, when a bale of cotton fell on him while he was unloading a truck. He continued to work but after four hours he became stiff and was granted a pass to the unit hospital. At the hospital a medical assistant, "Captain" Blunt, checked him for a hernia and sent him back to his cell. Within two hours the pain became so intense that Gamble returned to the hospital where he was given pain pills by an inmate nurse and then was examined by a doctor. The following day, Gamble saw a Dr. Astone who diagnosed the injury as a lower back strain, prescribed Zactirin (a pain reliever) and Robaxin (a muscle relaxant), and placed respondent on "cell-pass, cell-feed" status for two days, allowing him to remain in his cell at all times except for showers. On November 12, Gamble again saw Dr. Astone who continued the medication and cell-pass, cell-feed for another seven days. He also ordered that respondent be moved from an upper to a lower bunk for one week, but the prison authorities did not comply with that directive. The following week, Gamble returned to Dr. Astone. The doctor continued the muscle relaxant but prescribed a new pain reliever, Febridyne, and placed respondent on cell-pass for seven days, permitting him to remain in his cell except for meals and showers. On November 26, respondent again saw Dr. Astone, who put respondent back on the original pain reliever for five days and continued the cell-pass for another week.

On December 3, despite Gamble's statement that his back hurt as much as it had the first day, Dr. Astone took him off cell-pass, thereby certifying him to be capable of light work. At the same time, Dr. Astone prescribed Febridyne for seven days. Gamble then went to a Major Muddox and told him that he was in too much pain to work. Muddox had respondent moved to "administrative segregation." On December 5, Gamble was taken before the prison disciplinary committee, apparently because of his refusal to work. When the committee heard his complaint of back pain and high blood pressure, it directed that he be seen by another doctor.

On December 6, respondent saw petitioner Gray, who performed a urinalysis, blood test, and blood pressure measurement. Dr. Gray prescribed the drug Ser-Ap-Es for the high blood pressure and more Febridyne for the back pain. The following week respondent again saw Dr. Gray, who continued the Ser-Ap-Es for an additional 30 days. The prescription was not filled for four days, however, because the staff lost it. Respondent went to the unit hospital twice more in December; both times he was seen by Captain Blunt, who prescribed Tiognolos (described as a muscle relaxant). For all of December, respondent remained in administrative segregation.

In early January, Gamble was told on two occasions that he would be sent to the "farm" if he did not return to work. He refused, nonetheless, claiming to be in too much pain. On January 7, 1974, he requested to go on sick call for his back pain and migraine headaches. After an initial refusal, he saw Captain Blunt who prescribed sodium salicylate (a pain reliever) for seven days and Ser-Ap-Es for 30 days. Respondent returned to Captain Blunt on January 17 and January 25, and received renewals of the pain reliever prescription both times. Throughout the month, respondent was kept in administrative segregation.

On January 31, Gamble was brought before the prison disciplinary committee for his refusal to work in early January. He told the committee that he could not work because of his severe back pain and his high blood pressure. Captain Blunt testified that Gamble was in "first class" medical condition. The committee, with no further medical examination or testimony, placed respondent in solitary confinement.

Four days later, on February 4, at 8 a.m., respondent asked to see a doctor for chest pains and "blank outs." It was not until 7:30 that night that a medical assistant examined him and ordered him hospitalized. The following day a Dr. Heaton performed an electrocardiogram; one day later respondent was placed on Quinidine for treatment of irregular cardiac rhythm and moved to administrative segregation. On February 7, respondent again experienced pain in his chest, left arm, and back and asked to see a doctor. The guards refused. He asked again the next day. The guards again refused. Finally, on February 9, he was allowed to see Dr. Heaton, who ordered the Quinidine continued for three more days. On February 11, he swore out his complaint.

II.

The gravamen of respondent's § 1983 complaint is that petitioners have subjected him to cruel and unusual punishment in violation of the Eighth Amendment.... The history of the constitutional prohibition of "cruel and unusual punishments" has been recounted at length in prior opinions of the Court and need not be repeated here.... It suffices to note that the primary concern of the drafters was to proscribe "torture(s)" and other "barbar(ous)" methods of punishment.... Accordingly, this Court first applied the Eighth Amendment by comparing challenged methods of execution to concededly inhuman techniques of punishment. *See Wilkerson v. Utah*, 99 U.S. 130, 136 (1879) ("[I]t is safe to affirm that punishments of torture ... and all others in the same line of unnecessary cruelty, are forbidden by that amendment ..."); *In re Kemmler*, 136 U.S. 436, 447 (1890) ("Punishments are cruel when they involve torture or a lingering death ...").

Our more recent cases, however, have held that the Amendment proscribes more than physically barbarous punishments.... The Amendment embodies "broad and idealistic concepts of dignity, civilized standards, humanity, and decency...," ... against which we must evaluate penal measures. Thus, we have held repugnant to the Eighth Amendment punishments which are incompatible with "the evolving standards of decency that mark the progress of a maturing society," or which "involve the unnecessary and wanton infliction of pain"....

These elementary principles establish the government's obligation to provide medical care for those whom it is punishing by incarceration. An inmate must rely on prison authorities to treat his medical needs; if the authorities fail to do so, those needs will not be met. In the worst cases, such a failure may actually produce physical "torture or a lingering death," *In re Kemmler, supra*, the evils of most immediate concern to the drafters of the Amendment. In less serious cases, denial of medical care may result in pain and suffering which no one suggests would serve any penological purpose.... The infliction of such unnecessary suffering is inconsistent with contemporary standards of decency as manifested in modern legislation[8] codifying the common-law view that "it is but just that the public be required to care for the prisoner, who cannot by reason of the deprivation of his liberty, care for himself."

We therefore conclude that deliberate indifference to serious medical needs of prisoners constitutes the "unnecessary and wanton infliction of pain," ... proscribed by the Eighth Amendment. This is true whether the indifference is manifested by prison doctors in their response to the prisoner's needs[10] or by prison guards in intentionally denying or delaying access to medical care or intentionally interfering with the treatment once prescribed. Regardless of how evidenced, deliberate indifference to a prisoner's serious illness or injury states a cause of action under 1983.

This conclusion does not mean, however, that every claim by a prisoner that he has not received adequate medical treatment states a violation of the Eighth Amendment. An accident, although it may produce added anguish, is not on that basis alone to be characterized as wanton infliction of unnecessary pain. In *Louisiana ex rel. Francis v. Resweber*, 329 U.S. 459 (1947), for example, the Court concluded that it was not unconstitutional to force a prisoner to undergo a second effort to electrocute him after a mechanical malfunction had thwarted the first attempt. Writing for the plurality, Mr. Justice Reed reasoned that the second execution would not violate the Eighth Amendment because the first attempt was an "unforeseeable accident." *Id.*, at 464.... Mr. Justice Frankfurter's concurrence, based solely on the Due Process Clause of the Fourteenth Amendment, concluded that since the first attempt had failed because of "an innocent misadventure," *id.*, at 470, the second would not be "'repugnant

8. *See, e.g.*, [canvassing state statutes and referencing state regulations which specify standards of medical care for prisoners].

10. *See, e.g.*, *Williams v. Vincent*, 508 F.2d 541 (C.A.2 1974) (doctor's choosing the "easier and less efficacious treatment" of throwing away the prisoner's ear and stitching the stump may be attributable to "deliberate indifference ... rather than an exercise of professional judgment"); *Thomas v. Pate*, 493 F.2d 151, 158 (C.A.7), *cert. denied*, 419 U.S. 879 (1974) (injection of penicillin with knowledge that prisoner was allergic, and refusal of doctor to treat allergic reaction); *Jones v. Lockhart*, 484 F.2d 1192 (C.A.8 1973) (refusal of paramedic to provide treatment); *Martinez v. Mancusi*, 443 F.2d 921 (C.A.2 1970), *cert. denied*, 401 U.S. 983 (1971) (prison physician refuses to administer the prescribed pain killer and renders leg surgery unsuccessful by requiring prisoner to stand despite contrary instructions of surgeon).

to the conscience of mankind,'" *id.*, at 471, quoting *Palko v. Connecticut*, 302 U.S. 319, 323 (1937).[13]

Similarly, in the medical context, an inadvertent failure to provide adequate medical care cannot be said to constitute "an unnecessary and wanton infliction of pain" or to be "repugnant to the conscience of mankind." Thus, a complaint that a physician has been negligent in diagnosing or treating a medical condition does not state a valid claim of medical mistreatment under the Eighth Amendment. Medical malpractice does not become a constitutional violation merely because the victim is a prisoner. In order to state a cognizable claim, a prisoner must allege acts or omissions sufficiently harmful to evidence deliberate indifference to serious medical needs. It is only such indifference that can offend "evolving standards of decency" in violation of the Eighth Amendment.

III.

Against this backdrop, we now consider whether respondent's complaint states a cognizable § 1983 claim. The handwritten *pro se* document is to be liberally construed.... Even applying these liberal standards, however, Gamble's claims against Dr. Gray, both in his capacity as treating physician and as medical director of the Corrections Department, are not cognizable under § 1983. Gamble was seen by medical personnel on 17 occasions spanning a 3-month period: by Dr. Astone five times; by Dr. Gray twice; by Dr. Heaton three times; by an unidentified doctor and inmate nurse on the day of the injury; and by medical assistant Blunt six times. They treated his back injury, high blood pressure, and heart problems. Gamble has disclaimed any objection to the treatment provided for his high blood pressure and his heart problem; his complaint is "based solely on the lack of diagnosis and inadequate treatment of his back injury." ... The doctors diagnosed his injury as a lower back strain and treated it with bed rest, muscle relaxants and pain relievers. Respondent contends that more should have been done by way of diagnosis and treatment, and suggests a number of options that were not pursued.... The Court of Appeals agreed, stating: "Certainly an x-ray of (Gamble's) lower back might have been in order and other tests conducted that would have led to appropriate diagnosis and treatment for the daily pain and suffering he was experiencing." [*Gamble v. Estelle*,] 516 F.2d [937,] 941 [(5th Cir. 1975)]. But the question whether an X-ray or additional diagnostic techniques or forms of treatment is indicated is a classic example of a matter for medical judgment. A medical decision not to order an X-ray, or like measures, does not represent cruel and unusual punishment. At most it is medical malpractice, and as such the proper forum is the state court under the Texas Tort Claims Act.[15]

...

---

13. He noted, however, that "a series of abortive attempts" or "a single, cruelly willful attempt" would present a different case. 329 U.S., at 471....

15. Tex.Rev.Civ.Stat., art. 6252-19, § 3 (Supp. 1976). Petitioners assured the Court at argument that this statute can be used by prisoners to assert malpractice claims....

Mr. Justice STEVENS, dissenting.

Most of what is said in the Court's opinion is entirely consistent with the way the lower federal courts have been processing claims that the medical treatment of prison inmates is so inadequate as to constitute the cruel and unusual punishment prohibited by the Eighth Amendment. I have no serious disagreement with the way this area of the law has developed thus far, or with the probable impact of this opinion. Nevertheless ... I am unable to join it.... [in part because], it describes the State's duty to provide adequate medical care to prisoners in ambiguous terms which incorrectly relate to the subjective motivation of persons accused of violating the Eighth Amendment rather than to the standard of care required by the Constitution.

...

Exercise 2-A: Applying *Estelle* at the 12(b)(6) stage

You are a law clerk to a trial court judge deciding a 12(b)(6) motion to dismiss the plaintiff's complaint. The defendant prison officials moved to dismiss solely on the basis that the Complaint does not allege a serious medical need. Without reaching the issue of "deliberate indifference," consider the following in deciding what recommendation to make to the Judge.

- Do the facts below sufficiently allege the objective element of an 8th Amendment medical need claim?
- Focus on the first two nurses, Nurse Weldon and Nurse Quintana
- What facts are relevant to evaluating the "serious medical need"? Are the facts relevant to the objective element of the 8th Amendment medical treatment claim only facts about the prisoner's symptoms at the time of the prison employee's actions? Or should the alleged harm to the plaintiff—here, pain and eventually a heart attack—satisfy the objective serious medical need?
- Where a delay in treatment results in severe pain, should that satisfy the "serious medical need" standard?
- Would it make a difference if the Complaint were filed *pro se*?

Ms. Mata was incarcerated. During the evening of October 29, 2000, she sought medical attention because she was experiencing severe chest pain. Ms. Mata reported her chest pain to Nurse Weldon, who responded there was nothing she could do because the infirmary was closed. She told Ms. Mata to return to sick call at the infirmary the following morning.

Ms. Mata returned to the infirmary, as advised, on the morning of October 30. She informed Nurse Quintana of her continuing chest pain. Ms. Mata reported her chest pain as "eight" on a scale from "zero to ten," with ten being the worst pain a patient can imagine and zero being no pain at all. Nurse Quintana performed a nursing assessment including an electrocardiogram

(EKG). Nurse Quintana read the EKG as normal and gave Ms. Mata a permission slip to allow her to miss work and other prison-related assignments for the day. Ms. Mata claims that her pain persisted throughout the day, causing her to report it to several guards, but she did not return to the infirmary again that day.

The next morning, at 6:00 a.m. on October 31, Ms. Mata returned to the infirmary. [Nurse C] administered a second EKG and told Ms. Mata it was normal, although it is undisputed that this EKG showed changes from the one performed the prior day. [Nurse D] arrived at the infirmary shortly after the evaluation ... performed an independent assessment and informed Ms. Mata that she suffered from a chest lining inflammation. [Nurse D] also read the second EKG as normal, and she forwarded the EKG printout to a doctor for review. The physician ordered [Nurse D] to send Ms. Mata immediately to the hospital. [Nurse D] instructed Ms. Mata to return to her housing unit and change into "full greens" for the trip to the hospital. Ms. Mata did as she was told, walking approximately two blocks up hill, changing her clothes, and then walking back to the main facility. She was then transported to a hospital emergency room in Pueblo, Colorado.

At the hospital, it was determined that Ms. Mata had suffered a heart attack. Heart surgery was performed the same day but it was unsuccessful. Ms. Mata suffered permanent and irreversible damage to her heart and sustained a permanent disability.

Ms. Mata filed this action against the four prison nurses from whom she sought treatment, asserting that their failure to provide her adequate medical care violated the 8th Amendment.

For further discussion

1. The Supreme Court held in *Helling v. McKinney*, 509 U.S. 25 (1993) that an inmate had sufficiently alleged a claim based on the future harm posed by exposure to secondhand smoke: "[the inmate] states a cause of action under the Eighth Amendment by alleging that [correctional officers] have, with deliberate indifference, exposed him to levels of [environmental tobacco smoke] that pose an unreasonable risk of serious damage to his future health." *Id.* at 35.

2. Consider the health conditions for the correctional staff. For example, even though inmates and prison staff occupy the same space, a jail employee and his wife who developed staph infections because of the same filthy conditions that violated the 8th Amendment rights of the inmates were denied recovery, because the Constitution does not require that the government provide a safe working environment for employees. *Kaucher v. County of Bucks*, 455 F.3d 418 (3d Cir. 2006). For the inmate suit, *see Keller v. County of Bucks*, No. 03-4017, 2005 WL 675831, at *1 (E.D. Pa. Mar. 22, 2005), *aff'd* 209 Fed. Appx. 201 (3d Cir. Dec. 22, 2006). Do those results seem fair?

3. Recall that the factual background in this Chapter referenced a new treatment for Hepatitis C. At least one federal court has held that failing to treat prisoners with the new Hepatitis C antivirals violates the Eighth Amendment. In *Stafford v. Carter*, the trial court held prisoners infected with Hepatitis C had objectively serious medical needs, and prison administrators were deliberately indifferent to the substantial risk Hepatitis C posed to prisoner health. 2018 WL 4361639 at *20 (S.D. Ind. Sept. 13, 2018) (finding that "chronic HCV is a curable disease, and the only effective treatment—[Direct-Acting Antiviral oral medications]—can cure it within eight to twelve weeks").

D. Violence in Prison

1. The Vera Institute of Justice convened a Commission on Safety and Abuse in America's Prisons to hold hearings and publish a comprehensive report documenting issues confronting jails and prisons. Among their findings was the presence of violence: "Corrections officers told the Commission about a near-constant fear of being assaulted. Former prisoners recounted gang violence, rape, beatings by officers, and in one large jail, a pattern of illegal and humiliating strip-searches. Former Florida Warden Ron McAndrew described small groups of officers operating as 'goon squads' to abuse prisoners and intimidate other staff."[2] Similarly, after spending months undercover as a New York corrections officer and trainee, investigative journalist Ted Conover learned that the "most stressful scenario" a corrections officer could face is being held hostage, "a complete turning of the tables between officer and inmate—payback time to the highest degree." Trainees learned to watch for warning signs of a prison disturbance, such as "inmates wearing heavy clothes (often with magazines or newspapers tucked underneath, to deflect knife thrusts) in warm weather, inmates who were normally well behaved trying to get [locked into their cells] so they wouldn't have to mix with the general population." Ted Conover, NEWJACK (Vintage 2001) at 51–52.

The below excerpt is from testimony by Ronald Kaschak to the Vera Commission. Mr. Kaschak worked for an Ohio County Sheriff's Department for six years, until June 2004, when he resigned after pleading guilty to criminal charges for his role in beating an inmate. In reading his statement, consider the pressures on a corrections officer to comply with a supervisor's order to assault an inmate who has assaulted another guard and to refuse either to report the guards' assault or to testify against them. Does Mr. Kaschak's perspective shed light on the "blue line of silence" that some consider an obstacle to proving wrongdoing by law enforcement? As counsel for a prison or for prisoners, would the possibility of a "blue line" of silence among law enforcement influence your litigation decisions?

---

2. VERA INST. OF JUST., CONFRONTING CONFINEMENT: A REPORT OF THE COMMISSION ON SAFETY AND ABUSE IN AMERICA'S PRISONS, 11–12 (2006), http://www.vera.org/pubs/confronting-confinement.

Statement by Ronald Kaschak to the Commission on Safety and Abuse in America's Prisons

(November 1, 2005)[3]

On December 28, 2001, there was an incident that occurred that has changed my life forever.... I received a signal 7 on my radio [indicating] a fight between inmates.... After the inmates were locked down in their cells is when we had learned that an inmate had assaulted a female deputy.... [She] pointed out Tawhon Easterly as the inmate who struck her.... Two other deputies went into inmate Easterly's cell and escorted him downstairs. These two deputies, along with 5 other deputies, and the corporal who was my supervisor took the inmate into the gym.... I learned later that ... they were beating him.

After they were done in the gym with the inmate, they ... placed him into his cell.... I was sitting in ... the office, with Sergeant Blue. Sergeant Blue had told me that Major Orange had called down and asked him, "Why the fuck is inmate Easterly not in the hospital!" ... [T]he phone rang again. It was Major Orange. When Sergeant Blue hung up the phone, he said Major Orange wants inmate Easterly in the hospital for striking one of his deputies. Sergeant Blue then gave myself, Deputy Yellow, Green, and Purple a strict order, from Major Orange, to go upstairs and move inmate Easterly into "the hole" and take care of him.

At this point, the other deputies and myself went to his cell and instructed the Deputy to open Easterly's door. Deputies Yellow and Green went into the inmate's cell and escorted him out while another deputy and myself walked behind them.... [I]n the hallway ... Deputies Yellow and Green took inmate Easterly to the floor while Deputy Purple and myself each held one of his legs down. Deputies Yellow and Green started punching inmate Easterly and I delivered 3 knee strikes to his legs.... The other three deputies continued to beat Easterly. This continued for around another minute.... Deputy Yellow and Green then stripped him of his clothes and drug him through the pod to his cell. Deputy Purple and myself stayed in the hallway. While the other two placed him in his cell, Deputy Yellow yelled, "This is what happens when you hit a female deputy." ... [N]o reports of the incident were written, until September 2002....

[In August 2002, Mr. Kaschak interviewed for a police department position and, when he refused to answer whether he had ever struck a person while on duty, the police department requested a follow-up interview.] When I went back up to the station, I told them about the incident. I never thought twice about it then since the person administering the [polygraph], I have known my whole life....

[T]he Austintown Police Department [told me] they were sending a letter to Sheriff Grey stating what I had told them during the polygraph. A few weeks later, Major

3. Ronald Kaschak, Statement to the Vera Institute of Justice, Commission on Safety and Abuse in America's Prisons, (Nov. 1, 2005) (transcript pp. 58–66 available at http://www.vera.org/commission-safety-and-abuse-americas-prisons-public-hearing-3).

Orange ... the one who ordered the assault on the prisoner [called me into his office.] ... He ... stated, "What the fuck am I supposed to do now that this is public record?" He was [waving] the letter from the Austintown Police Department.... [H]e told me to write a report about the incident and when I was done writing the report he was going to arrest me for assault.... He began yelling, I am giving you a direct order to write a report. I again stated that I won't write a report without [union] representation. At this point, the Major called Sergeant Silver into the office. When she arrived, Major Orange said that I was being placed on administrative leave. He proceeded to take my gun, badge, access card and magazines. Sergeant Silver said I had to write a report or the Major could fire me. Major Orange then asked me one more time to write a report and at this time I agreed to write one.

In this report, I falsified it so I would not implicate Major Orange. I said the inmate became aggressive so we had to use force to get him under control. I also never mentioned the Major's name in my report. When I got done with the report, I took it over to his office and handed it to him. The Major then read the report and handed me back my gun, badge, access card and magazines. He then stated not to worry about anything, that it was over and to go back to work.

[Federal prosecutors investigated and pursued the incident.] In March of 2004, I made the toughest decision I ever had to make. I made a plea agreement with the government. I agreed to cross the blue-line and to testify against the other cops. They were more to me than just my coworkers, they were also my friends. Many of them were at my wedding.... [T]hey were people I trusted who would have my back if I were ever in trouble. Now I was about to send these people that I called my friends to prison....

[B]ecause of me not thinking for myself, I lost my whole career and my dream.... I lost my career, my house and a lot of my friends because I agreed to become a government witness and testify against other cops.... When a supervisor gives you a direct order, you either obey it or you get fired.... I hope you never have to be in the situation where a superior has lost perspective about why they are a police officer and gives a command that abuses their power. Remember you still have a choice [to walk away] though, so please don't make the same mistake I made.... [Note: Mr. Karashak was sentenced to probation. Mr. Easterly settled his civil lawsuit for $65,000.]

2. In 2014, a Federal Bureau of Investigation agent was commended for her role in exposing civil rights violations and corruption in Alabama's prisons.

> There was never any dispute that Rocrast Mack, a 24-year-old serving time on drug charges in a state prison in Alabama, died at the hands of corrections officers in 2010. What wasn't immediately clear was how and why the inmate sustained a lethal beating ... Mack was beaten in three separate prison locations over a 40-minute period. He died the next day from his injuries. Guards claimed Mack was fighting them throughout the ordeal and sustained his fatal injuries in a fall ...
>
> "The injuries that caused Mack's death did not match up with the story the corrections officers were telling," said [FBI Special Agent Susan] Hanson....

What did emerge was a portrait of a corrupt prison environment led by a heavy-handed guard—Lt. Michael Smith. Smith, the main subject in the investigation, held sway over corrections officers and inmates alike. A few guards privately acknowledged that Smith's history of intimidation could eventually land him in hot water. For Hanson, who conducted hundreds of interviews over nearly three years, the key to cracking the case was to find a sympathetic guard whose conscience carried more weight than his fear of Smith.

"It really was working with one of the officers, spending a lot of time with him, and telling him that the story just doesn't make sense. It cannot have happened that way," Hanson said. The guard implicated Smith but never broke ranks from the original narrative—that their use of force was justified.

To build her case, Hanson [had investigators take] extensive photographs from witnesses' vantage points that could support or refute their claims [and create visuals of where each of the assaults occurred]. "That's where she was able to start separating fact from fiction[." The FBI created] ... an interactive blueprint of the prison that showed everyone's precise locations during the beatings. In the end, the evidence revealed how a cadre of guards, led by Smith, struck and kicked Mack so severely he died—and then conspired to cover it up.

"It was very helpful during trial," said Hanson. Four officers were convicted [in 2013] on civil rights, obstruction of justice, and conspiracy charges and received prison terms—including Smith, who was sentenced to 30 years. Hanson ... said the case is still heartbreaking to her because Mack was in the care of officials who had been bestowed a public trust.[4]

Questions to guide reading of *Whitley*

1. Did the majority assume any facts in the way it framed the issue?
2. Plaintiff wanted the deliberate indifference standard to apply to his claim that prison officials violated his 8th Amendment right to be free from cruel and unusual punishment. But *Whitley* held that the general 8th Amendment standard of "unnecessary and wanton infliction of pain" applies differently in different contexts—that there is more than one 8th Amendment standard. Why was "deliberate indifference" appropriate in *Estelle* but not in the different factual context of the prison riot in *Whitley*? Keep the conceptual framework of *Whitley* in mind when you read *Lewis*, a 14th Amendment substantive due process case in Chapter 3.
3. What test did *Whitley* instead hold is appropriate for prison security measures taken to quell prison situations (like a riot) that pose significant risks for

4. Federal Bureau of Investigation, *Agent Exposes Civil Rights Crimes in Alabama Prison*, News: Stories (Oct. 17, 2014), http://www.fbi.gov/news/stories/2014/october/agent-exposes-civil-rights-crimes-in-alabama-prison/agent-exposes-civil-rights-crimes-in-alabama-prison.

the safety of inmates and prison staff? What factors did *Whitley* identify as relevant in deciding whether that test has been met?

4. What policy arguments did *Whitley* identify in support of the "malicious and sadistic for the very purpose of causing harm" standard? Does deference to the "considered" choices of administrators seem incongruous in the context of decisions made in haste? Why or why not?
5. Why did *Whitley* hold there was no jury question presented? Does the standard as applied by *Whitley* seem to be more deferential than as originally announced?
6. Under *Whitley*, what do you think expert testimony would have to show in order to create a jury question?
7. Why did the dissent call the *Whitley* majority internally inconsistent? Why did it argue that the majority decision usurped the jury function?

Whitley v. Albers

475 U.S. 312 (1986)

Justice O'CONNOR delivered the opinion of the Court.

This case requires us to decide what standard governs a prison inmate's claim that prison officials subjected him to cruel and unusual punishment by shooting him during the course of their attempt to quell a prison riot.

I

At the time he was injured, respondent Gerald Albers was confined in cellblock "A" of the Oregon State Penitentiary. Cellblock "A" consists of two tiers of barred cells housing some 200 inmates. The two tiers are connected by a stairway that offers the only practical way to move from one tier to another.

At about 8:30 on the evening of June 27, 1980, several inmates were found intoxicated at the prison annex. Prison guards attempted to move the intoxicated prisoners, some of whom resisted, to the penitentiary's isolation and segregation facility. This incident could be seen from the cell windows in cellblock "A," and some of the onlookers became agitated because they thought that the guards were using unnecessary force. Acting on instructions from their superiors, Officers Kemper and Fitts, who were on duty in cellblock "A," ordered the prisoners to return to their cells. The order was not obeyed. Several inmates confronted the two officers, who were standing in the open area of the lower tier. One inmate, Richard Klenk, jumped from the second tier and assaulted Officer Kemper. Kemper escaped but Officer Fitts was taken hostage. Klenk and other inmates then began breaking furniture and milling about.

Upon being informed of the disturbance, petitioner Harol Whitley, the prison security manager, entered cellblock "A" and spoke with Klenk. Captain Whitley agreed to permit four residents of cellblock "A" to view the inmates who had been taken to segregation earlier. These emissaries reported back that the prisoners in segregation were intoxicated but unharmed. Nonetheless, the disturbance in cellblock "A" continued.

Whitley returned to the cellblock and confirmed that Fitts was not harmed. Shortly thereafter, Fitts was moved from an office on the lower tier to cell 201 on the upper tier, and Klenk demanded that media representatives be brought into the cellblock. In the course of the negotiations, Klenk, who was armed with a homemade knife, informed Whitley that one inmate had already been killed and other deaths would follow. In fact, an inmate had been beaten but not killed by other prisoners.

Captain Whitley left the cellblock to organize an assault squad. When Whitley returned to cellblock "A," he was taken to see Fitts in cell 201. Several inmates assured Whitley that they would protect Fitts from harm, but Klenk threatened to kill the hostage if an attempt was made to lead an assault. Klenk and at least some other inmates were aware that guards had assembled outside the cellblock and that shotguns had been issued. Meanwhile, respondent had left his cell on the upper tier to see if elderly prisoners housed on the lower tier could be moved out of harm's way in the event that tear gas was used. Respondent testified that he asked Whitley for the key to the row of cells housing the elderly prisoners, and Whitley indicated that he would return with the key. Whitley denied that he spoke to respondent at any time during the disturbance.

Whitley next consulted with his superiors, petitioners Cupp, the prison Superintendent, and Kenney, the Assistant Superintendent. They agreed that forceful intervention was necessary to protect the life of the hostage and the safety of the inmates who were not rioting, and ruled out tear gas as an unworkable alternative. Cupp ordered Whitley to take a squad armed with shotguns into cellblock "A."

Whitley gave the final orders to the assault team, which was assembled in the area outside cellblock "A." Petitioner Kennicott and two other officers armed with shotguns were to follow Whitley, who was unarmed, over the barricade the inmates had constructed at the cellblock entrance. A second group of officers, without firearms, would be behind them. Whitley ordered Kennicott to fire a warning shot as he crossed the barricade. He also ordered Kennicott to shoot low at any prisoners climbing the stairs toward cell 201, since they could pose a threat to the safety of the hostage or to Whitley himself, who would be climbing the stairs in an attempt to free the hostage in cell 201.

At about 10:30 p.m., Whitley reappeared just outside the barricade. By this time, about a half hour had elapsed since the earlier breaking of furniture, and the noise level in the cellblock had noticeably diminished. Respondent, who was standing at the bottom of the stairway, asked about the key. Whitley replied "No," clambered over the barricade, yelled "shoot the bastards," and ran toward the stairs after Klenk, who had been standing in the open areaway along with a number of other inmates. Kennicott fired a warning shot into the wall opposite the cellblock entrance as he followed Whitley over the barricade. He then fired a second shot that struck a post near the stairway. Meanwhile, Whitley chased Klenk up the stairs, and shortly thereafter respondent started up the stairs. Kennicott fired a third shot that struck respondent in the left knee. Another inmate was shot on the stairs and several others on the lower tier were wounded by gunshot. The inmates in cell 201 prevented Klenk from entering, and Whitley subdued Klenk at the cell door, freeing the hostage.

As a result of the incident, respondent sustained severe damage to his left leg and mental and emotional distress. He subsequently commenced this action pursuant to 42 U.S.C. § 1983, alleging that petitioners deprived him of his rights under the Eighth ... Amendment[].... Many of the facts were stipulated ... but both sides also presented testimony from witnesses to the disturbance and the rescue attempt, as well as from expert witnesses with backgrounds in prison discipline and security. At the conclusion of trial, the District Judge directed a verdict for petitioners ... [T]he Ninth Circuit reversed in part and affirmed in part.... We granted certiorari ... and now reverse.

II

The language of the Eighth Amendment, "[e]xcessive bail shall not be required, nor excessive fines imposed, nor cruel and unusual punishments inflicted," manifests "an intention to limit the power of those entrusted with the criminal-law function of government." *Ingraham v. Wright*, 430 U.S. 651, 664 (1977). The Cruel and Unusual Punishments Clause "was designed to protect those convicted of crimes," *ibid.*, and consequently the Clause applies "only after the State has complied with the constitutional guarantees traditionally associated with criminal prosecutions." *Id.*, at 671, n. 40. See also *Revere v. Massachusetts General Hospital*, 463 U.S. 239, 244, (1983); *Bell v. Wolfish*, 441 U.S. 520, 535, n. 16 (1979). An express intent to inflict unnecessary pain is not required, *Estelle v. Gamble*, 429 U.S. 97, 104 (1976) ("deliberate indifference" to a prisoner's serious medical needs is cruel and unusual punishment), and harsh "conditions of confinement" may constitute cruel and unusual punishment unless such conditions "are part of the penalty that criminal offenders pay for their offenses against society." *Rhodes v. Chapman*, 452 U.S. 337, 347 (1981).

Not every governmental action affecting the interests or well-being of a prisoner is subject to Eighth Amendment scrutiny, however. "After incarceration, only the 'unnecessary and wanton infliction of pain'... constitutes cruel and unusual punishment forbidden by the Eighth Amendment." *Ingraham v. Wright*, *supra*, 430 U.S., at 670 (quoting *Estelle v. Gamble*, *supra*, 429 U.S., at 103) (citations omitted). To be cruel and unusual punishment, conduct that does not purport to be punishment at all must involve more than ordinary lack of due care for the prisoner's interests or safety. This reading of the Clause underlies our decision in *Estelle v. Gamble*, *supra*, at 105–106, which held that a prison physician's "negligen[ce] in diagnosing or treating a medical condition" did not suffice to make out a claim of cruel and unusual punishment. It is obduracy and wantonness, not inadvertence or error in good faith, that characterize the conduct prohibited by the Cruel and Unusual Punishments Clause, whether that conduct occurs in connection with establishing conditions of confinement, supplying medical needs, or restoring official control over a tumultuous cellblock. The infliction of pain in the course of a prison security measure, therefore, does not amount to cruel and unusual punishment simply because it may appear in retrospect that the degree of force authorized or applied for security purposes was unreasonable, and hence unnecessary in the strict sense.

The general requirement that an Eighth Amendment claimant allege and prove the unnecessary and wanton infliction of pain should also be applied with due regard for differences in the kind of conduct against which an Eighth Amendment objection is lodged. The deliberate indifference standard articulated in *Estelle* was appropriate in the context presented in that case because the State's responsibility to attend to the medical needs of prisoners does not ordinarily clash with other equally important governmental responsibilities. Consequently, "deliberate indifference to a prisoner's serious illness or injury," *Estelle*, *supra*, at 105, can typically be established or disproved without the necessity of balancing competing institutional concerns for the safety of prison staff or other inmates. But, in making and carrying out decisions involving the use of force to restore order in the face of a prison disturbance, prison officials undoubtedly must take into account the very real threats the unrest presents to inmates and prison officials alike, in addition to the possible harms to inmates against whom force might be used. As we said in *Hudson v. Palmer*, 468 U.S. 517, 526–527 (1984), prison administrators are charged with the responsibility of ensuring the safety of the prison staff, administrative personnel, and visitors, as well as the "obligation to take reasonable measures to guarantee the safety of the inmates themselves." In this setting, a deliberate indifference standard does not adequately capture the importance of such competing obligations, or convey the appropriate hesitancy to critique in hindsight decisions necessarily made in haste, under pressure, and frequently without the luxury of a second chance.

Where a prison security measure is undertaken to resolve a disturbance, such as occurred in this case, that indisputably poses significant risks to the safety of inmates and prison staff, we think the question whether the measure taken inflicted unnecessary and wanton pain and suffering ultimately turns on "whether force was applied in a good faith effort to maintain or restore discipline or maliciously and sadistically for the very purpose of causing harm." *Johnson v. Glick*, 481 F.2d 1028, 1033 (CA2) (Friendly, J.), *cert. denied*, 414 U.S. 1033 (1973). As the District Judge correctly perceived, "such factors as the need for the application of force, the relationship between the need and the amount of force that was used, [and] the extent of injury inflicted," 481 F.2d, at 1033, are relevant to that ultimate determination ... From such considerations inferences may be drawn as to whether the use of force could plausibly have been thought necessary, or instead evinced such wantonness with respect to the unjustified infliction of harm as is tantamount to a knowing willingness that it occur.... But equally relevant are such factors as the extent of the threat to the safety of staff and inmates, as reasonably perceived by the responsible officials on the basis of the facts known to them, and any efforts made to temper the severity of a forceful response.

When the "ever-present potential for violent confrontation and conflagration," *Jones v. North Carolina Prisoners' Labor Union, Inc.*, 433 U.S. 119, 132 (1977), ripens into actual unrest and conflict, the admonition that "a prison's internal security is peculiarly a matter normally left to the discretion of prison administrators," *Rhodes v. Chapman*, *supra*, 452 U.S., at 349, n. 14, carries special weight. "Prison administrators ... should be accorded wide-ranging deference in the adoption and execution of policies and practices that in their judgment are needed to preserve internal order and discipline and to maintain institutional security." *Bell v. Wolfish*, 441 U.S., at 547. That deference extends to a prison security measure taken in response to an actual confrontation with riotous inmates, just as it does to prophylactic or preventive measures intended to reduce the incidence of these or any other breaches of prison discipline. It does not insulate from review actions taken in bad faith and for no legitimate purpose, but it requires that neither judge nor jury freely substitute their judgment for that of officials who have made a considered choice. Accordingly, in ruling on a motion for a directed verdict in a case such as this, courts must determine whether the evidence goes beyond a mere dispute over the reasonableness of a particular use of force or the existence of arguably superior alternatives. Unless it appears that the evidence, viewed in the light most favorable to the plaintiff, will support a reliable inference of wantonness in the infliction of pain under the standard we have described, the case should not go to the jury.

III

Since this case comes to us from a decision of the Court of Appeals reversing the District Court's directed verdict for petitioners, we evaluate the facts in the light most favorable to respondent. The Court of Appeals believed that testimony that the disturbance was subsiding at the time the assault was made, and the conflicting expert testimony as to whether the force used was excessive, were enough to allow a jury to find that respondent's Eighth Amendment rights were violated. We think the Court of Appeals effectively collapsed the distinction between mere negligence and wanton conduct that we find implicit in the Eighth Amendment. Only if ordinary errors of judgment could make out an Eighth Amendment claim would this evidence create a jury question.

To begin with, although the evidence could be taken to show that the general disturbance had quieted down, a guard was still held hostage, Klenk was armed and threatening, several other inmates were armed with homemade clubs, numerous inmates remained outside their cells, and the cellblock remained in the control of the inmates. The situation remained dangerous and volatile. As respondent concedes, at the time he was shot "an officer's safety was in question and ... an inmate was armed and dangerous." Prison officials had no way of knowing what direction matters would take if they continued to negotiate or did nothing, but they had ample reason to believe that these options presented unacceptable risks.

Respondent's expert testimony is likewise unavailing. One of respondent's experts opined that petitioners gave inadequate consideration to less forceful means of intervention, and that the use of deadly force under the circumstances was not necessary to "prevent imminent danger" to the hostage guard or other inmates. Respondent's second expert testified that prison officials were "possibly a little hasty in using the firepower" on the inmates. At most, this evidence, which was controverted by petitioners' experts, establishes that prison officials arguably erred in judgment when they decided on a plan that employed potentially deadly force. It falls far short of a showing that there was no plausible basis for the officials' belief that this degree of force was necessary. Indeed, any such conclusion would run counter to common sense, in light of the risks to the life of the hostage and the safety of inmates that demonstrably persisted notwithstanding repeated attempts to defuse the situation. An expert's after-the-fact opinion that danger was not "imminent" in no way establishes that there was no danger, or that a conclusion by the officers that it was imminent would have been wholly unreasonable.

Once the basic design of the plan was in place, moreover, it is apparent why any inmate running up the stairs after Captain Whitley, or interfering with his progress towards the hostage, could reasonably be thought to present a threat to the success of the rescue attempt and to Whitley—particularly after a warning shot was fired. A sizable group of inmates, in defiance of the cell-in order and in apparent support of Klenk, continued to stand in the open area on the lower tier. Respondent testified that this was not "an organized group," and that he saw no inmates armed with clubs in that area. But the fact remains that the officials had no way of knowing which members of that group of inmates had joined with Klenk in destroying furniture, breaking glass, seizing the hostage, and setting up the barricade, and they certainly had reason to believe that some members of this group might intervene in support of Klenk. It was perhaps also foreseeable that one or more of these inmates would run up the stairs after the shooting started in order to return to their cells. But there would be neither means nor time to inquire into the reasons why each inmate acted as he did. Consequently, the order to shoot, qualified as it was by an instruction to shoot low, falls short of commanding the infliction of pain in a wanton and unnecessary fashion.

As petitioners' own experts conceded, a verbal warning would have been desirable, in addition to a warning shot, if circumstances permitted it to be given without undue risk. While a jury might conclude that this omission was unreasonable, we think that an inference of wantonness could not properly be drawn. First, some warning was given in the form of the first shot fired by Officer Kennicott. Second, the prison officials could have believed in good faith that such a warning might endanger the success of the security measure because of the risk that it would have allowed one or more inmates to climb the stairs before they could be stopped. The failure to provide for verbal warnings is thus not so insupportable as to be wanton. Accordingly, a jury could not properly find that this omission, coupled with the order to shoot, offended the Eighth Amendment.

To be sure, the plan was not adapted to take into account the appearance of respondent on the scene, and, on the facts as we must take them, Whitley was aware that respondent was present on the first tier for benign reasons. Conceivably, Whitley could have added a proviso exempting respondent from his order to shoot any prisoner climbing the stairs. But such an oversight simply does not rise to the level of an Eighth Amendment violation. Officials cannot realistically be expected to consider every contingency or minimize every risk, and it was far from inevitable that respondent would react as he did. Whitley was about to risk his life in an effort to rescue the hostage, and he was understandably focusing on the orders essential to the success of the plan. His failure to make special provision for respondent may have been unfortunate, but is hardly behavior from which a wanton willingness to inflict unjustified suffering on respondent can be inferred.

Once it is established that the order to shoot low at anyone climbing the stairs after a warning shot was not wanton, respondent's burden in showing that the actual shooting constituted the wanton and unnecessary infliction of pain is an extremely heavy one. Accepting that respondent could not have sought safety in a cell on the lower tier, the fact remains that had respondent thrown himself to the floor he would not have been shot at. Instead, after the warning shot was fired, he attempted to return to his cell by running up the stairs behind Whitley. That is equivocal conduct. While respondent had not been actively involved in the riot and indeed had attempted to help matters, there is no indication that Officer Kennicott knew this, nor any claim that he acted vindictively or in retaliation. Respondent testified that as he started to run up the stairs he "froze" when he looked to his left and saw Kennicott, and that "we locked eyes." Kennicott testified that he saw several inmates running up the stairs, that he thought they were pursuing Whitley, and that he fired at their legs. To the extent that this testimony is conflicting, we resolve the conflict in respondent's favor by assuming that Kennicott shot at respondent rather than at the inmates as a group. But this does not establish that Kennicott shot respondent knowing it was unnecessary to do so. Kennicott had some basis for believing that respondent constituted a threat to the hostage and to Whitley, and had at most a few seconds in which to react. He was also under orders to respond to such a perceived threat in precisely the manner he did. Under these circumstances, the actual shooting was part and parcel of a good-faith effort to restore prison security. As such, it did not violate respondent's Eighth Amendment right to be free from cruel and unusual punishments.

...

The judgment of the Court of Appeals is Reversed.

Justice MARSHALL, with whom Justice BRENNAN, Justice BLACKMUN, and Justice STEVENS join, dissenting.

I share the majority's concern that prison officials be permitted to respond reasonably to inmate disturbances without unwarranted fear of liability. I agree that the threshold for establishing a constitutional violation under these circumstances is high. I do not agree, however, that the contested existence of a "riot" in the prison lessens the constraints imposed on prison authorities by the Eighth Amendment.

The majority has erred, I believe, both in developing its legal analysis and in employing it. First, the especially onerous standard the Court has devised for determining whether a prisoner injured during a prison disturbance has been subjected to cruel and unusual punishment is incorrect and not justified by precedent. That standard is particularly inappropriate because courts deciding whether to apply it must resolve a preliminary issue of fact that will often be disputed and properly left to the jury. Finally, the Court has applied its test improperly to the facts of this case. For these reasons, I must respectfully dissent.

I

The Court properly begins by acknowledging that, for a prisoner attempting to prove a violation of the Eighth Amendment, "[a]n express intent to inflict unnecessary pain is not required, *Estelle v. Gamble*, 429 U.S. 97, 104 (1976)." Rather, our cases have established that the "unnecessary and wanton" infliction of pain on prisoners constitutes cruel and unusual punishment prohibited by the Eighth Amendment, even in the absence of intent to harm. *Ibid.*; see also *Ingraham v. Wright*, 430 U.S. 651, 670 (1977).... Having correctly articulated the teaching of our cases on this issue, however, the majority inexplicably arrives at the conclusion that a constitutional violation in the context of a prison uprising can be established only if force was used "maliciously and sadistically for the very purpose of causing harm," ... thus requiring the very "express intent to inflict unnecessary pain" that it had properly disavowed....

The Court imposes its heightened version of the "unnecessary and wanton" standard only when the injury occurred in the course of a "disturbance" that "poses significant risks,".... But those very questions—whether a disturbance existed and whether it posed a risk—are likely to be hotly contested. It is inappropriate, to say the least, to condition the choice of a legal standard, the purpose of which is to determine whether to send a constitutional claim to the jury, upon the court's resolution of factual disputes that in many cases should themselves be resolved by the jury.

The correct standard for identifying a violation of the Eighth Amendment under our cases is clearly the "unnecessary and wanton" standard, which establishes a high hurdle to be overcome by a prisoner seeking relief for a constitutional violation. The full circumstances of the plaintiff's injury, including whether it was inflicted during an attempt to quell a riot and whether there was a reasonable apprehension of danger, should be considered by the factfinder in determining whether that standard is satisfied in a particular case. There is simply no justification for creating a distinct and more onerous burden for the plaintiff to meet merely because the judge believes that the injury at issue was caused during a disturbance that "pose[d] significant risks to the safety of inmates and prison staff,".... Determination of whether there was such a disturbance or risk, when disputed, should be made by the jury when it resolves disputed facts, not by the court in its role as arbiter of law....

II

The Court properly begins its application of the law by reciting the principle that the facts must be viewed in the light most favorable to respondent, who won a reversal of a directed verdict below.... If, under any reasonable interpretation of the facts, a jury could have found the "unnecessary and wanton" standard to be met, then the directed verdict was improper. The majority opinion, however, resolves factual disputes in the record in petitioners' favor and discounts much of respondent's theory of the case. This it is not entitled to do.

The majority pays short shrift to respondent's significant contention that the disturbance had quieted down by the time the lethal force was employed ... Respondent presented substantial testimony to show that the disturbance had subsided; that only one prisoner, Klenk, remained in any way disruptive; and that even Klenk had calmed down enough at that point to admit that he had " 'gone too far.' " The majority asserts that "a guard was still held hostage, Klenk was armed and threatening, several other inmates were armed with homemade clubs, numerous inmates remained outside their cells, and ... [t]he situation remained dangerous and volatile." Respondent's evidence, however, indicated that the guard was not, in fact, in danger. He had been put into a cell by several inmates to prevent Klenk from harming him. Captain Whitley had been to see the guard, and had observed that the inmates protecting him from Klenk were not armed and had promised to keep Klenk out. According to respondent's evidence, moreover, no other inmates were assisting Klenk in any way when the riot squad was called in; they were simply "milling around," waiting for Klenk to be taken into custody, or for orders to return to their cells. Respondent's evidence tended to show not that the "situation remained dangerous and volatile," but, on the contrary, that it was calm. Although the Court sees fit to emphasize repeatedly "the risks to the life of the hostage and the safety of inmates that demonstrably persisted notwithstanding repeated attempts to defuse the situation," I can only point out that respondent bitterly disputed that any such risk to guards or inmates had persisted. The Court just does not believe his story.

The Court's treatment of the expert testimony is equally insensitive to its obligation to resolve all disputes in favor of respondent. Respondent's experts testified that the use of deadly force under these circumstances was not justified by any necessity to prevent imminent danger to the officers or the inmates; that the force used was excessive; and that even if deadly force had been justified, it would have been unreasonable to unleash such force without a clear warning to allow nonparticipating inmates to return to their cells. Insofar as expert testimony can ever be useful to show that prison authorities engaged in the "unnecessary and wanton" infliction of pain, even though it will always amount to "after-the-fact opinion" regarding the circumstances of the injury, respondent's expert evidence contributed to the creation of a factual issue.

The majority characterizes the petitioners' error in using deadly force where it was not justified as an "oversight." This is an endorsement of petitioners' rendition of the facts. As portrayed by respondent's evidence, the "error" was made in cold blood. Respondent's involvement started when, at the request of one of the inmates, he approached petitioner Whitley, who was talking to Klenk, to ask if Whitley would supply a key to a gate so that the elderly and sick patients in so-called "medical cells" near the area of disturbance could be removed before any tear gas was used. Captain Whitley said that he would go and get the key, and left the cellblock ... In two or three minutes, Whitley returned. Respondent went to the door of the cellblock, and asked

Whitley if he had brought the key. Whitley responded "'No,'" turned his head back and yelled: "'Let's go, let's go. Shoot the bastards!'"

Respondent, afraid, ran from his position by the door and headed for the stairs, the only route back to his cell. He caught some movement out of the corner of his eye, looked in its direction, and saw petitioner Kennicott. According to respondent: "'I froze. I looked at him; we locked eyes, then I looked down and seen the shotgun in his hand, then I seen the flash, and the next thing I know I was sitting down, grabbing my leg.'" Losing a great deal of blood, respondent crawled up the stairs and fell on his face, trying to get out of range of the shotguns. After about 10 minutes, an officer grabbed respondent by the hair and dragged him downstairs. As he lay there, another officer came and stood over respondent and shoved the barrel of a gun or gas pistol into respondent's face. Respondent was left lying and bleeding profusely for approximately 10 or 15 more minutes, and was then taken to the prison hospital. He suffered very severe injury. Meanwhile, Klenk had been subdued with no resistance by Whitley, who was unarmed.

Other testimony showed that, although most of the inmates assembled in the area were clearly not participating in the misconduct, they received no warning, instructions, or opportunity to leave the area and return to their cells before the officers started shooting. Neither respondent nor any other inmate attempted to impede the officers as they entered the cellblock. The officers were described as "wild," "agitated, excited," not in full control of their emotions. One officer, prior to entering Cellblock "A," told the others to "'shoot their asses off, and if Klenk gets in the way, kill him.'" At the time of this assault, the cellblock was described as "quiet."

If a jury credited respondent's testimony and that of his witnesses, it would have believed that there was only one inmate who was temporarily out of control, Klenk—"scared," and "high,"—and ready to give up. The disturbance in the block had lasted only 15 or 20 minutes when it subsided, and there appeared to be no lasting danger to anyone. Respondent was shot while he stood motionless on the stairs, and was left to bleed for a perilously long time before receiving any assistance.

III

Part III of the Court's opinion falls far short of a rendition of the events in the light most favorable to respondent. In that light, the facts present a very close question as to whether the prison officials' infliction of pain on respondent could be said to display the level of wantonness necessary to make out a constitutional violation. At the very least, it is clear that fair-minded people could differ on the response to that question, and that is all it takes to preclude a directed verdict.

The majority suggests that the existence of more appropriate alternative measures for controlling prison disturbances is irrelevant to the constitutional inquiry, but surely it cannot mean what it appears to say. For if prison officials were to drop a bomb on a cellblock in order to halt a fistfight between two inmates, for example, I feel confident that the Court would have difficulty concluding, as a matter of law, that such an action was not sufficiently wanton to present a jury question, even though concededly taken in an effort to restore order in the prison. Thus, the question of wantonness in the context of prison disorder, as with other claims of mistreatment under the Eighth Amendment, is a matter of degree. And it is precisely in cases like this one, when shading the facts one way or the other can result in different legal conclusions, that a jury should be permitted to do its job. Properly instructed, a jury would take into account the petitioners' legitimate need to protect security, the extent of the danger presented, and the reasonableness of force used, in assessing liability. Moreover, the jury would know that a prisoner's burden is a heavy one, if he is to establish an Eighth Amendment violation under these circumstances. Whether respondent was able to meet that burden here is a question for the jury. From the Court's usurpation of the jury's function, I dissent. I would affirm the judgment of the Court of Appeals.

8th Amendment Threshold Fault Inquiry

Cruel & unusual punishment = unnecessary & wanton infliction of pain

Deliberate indifference

Estelle v. Gamble

- to serious medical needs
- no competing interests

Malicious and sadistic use of force for the purpose of causing harm

Whitley v. Albers

- force during prison disturbance balances threat to targeted inmates, other inmates, prison officials, visitors
- decisions made in haste, under pressure, without luxury of second chance

Where would *Wilson, Hudson,* and *Farmer* appear on this chart?
Does *Farmer* add to the meaning of "deliberate indifference"?

For further discussion

1. What standard should govern claims based on prison conditions, such as overcrowding—the *Whitley* "malicious and sadistic" standard or the *Estelle* "deliberate indifference" standard? In an opinion by Justice Scalia in *Wilson v. Seiter*, 501 U.S. 294 (1991), the Court answered that it was the latter—the deliberate indifference standard—that governed. There, Ohio inmate Pearly Wilson alleged that prison officials had violated his 8th Amendment rights because of prison overcrowding, excessive noise, inadequate heating and cooling, improper ventilation, unclean restrooms, unsanitary food preparation, housing with mentally and physically ill inmates, and other allegations. The Court held:

> *Whitley* teaches that, assuming the conduct is harmful enough to satisfy the objective component of an Eighth Amendment claim ... whether it can be

> characterized as "wanton" depends upon the constraints facing the official. From that standpoint, we see no significant distinction between claims alleging inadequate medical care and those alleging inadequate "conditions of confinement." Indeed, the medical care a prisoner receives is just as much a "condition" of his confinement as the food he is fed, the clothes he is issued, the temperature he is subjected to in his cell, and the protection he is afforded against other inmates. There is no indication that, as a general matter, the actions of prison officials with respect to these nonmedical conditions are taken under materially different constraints than their actions with respect to medical conditions. Thus..., "[w]hether one characterizes the treatment received by [the prisoner] as inhumane conditions of confinement, failure to attend to his medical needs, or a combination of both, it is appropriate to apply the 'deliberate indifference' standard articulated in *Estelle*."

Wilson, 501 U.S. at 303. (Chapter 7 explains that the circuits do not agree on what legal standard should govern prison condition claims by pretrial detainees (14th Amendment), as opposed to such claims by convicted prisoners (8th Amendment)).

2. Should the "malicious and sadistic" standard be limited to prison riot situations? The Supreme Court answered "no" in *Hudson v. McMillian*, 503 U.S. 1, 7 (1992), extending the *Whitley* standard outside the context of a prison riot to all claims that correctional officers used excessive force. *Hudson* further held that "the use of excessive physical force against a prisoner may constitute cruel and unusual punishment [even] when the inmate does not suffer serious injury." *Id.* Therefore, the Court simultaneously imposed a high burden on plaintiffs for the subjective element of the 8th Amendment claim but lowered the burden for the objective element, holding that for excessive force claims, plaintiff need not allege the "serious" injury that is required for medical care and other 8th Amendment conditions of confinement claims. The lesser objective standard is sufficient because "[w]hen prison officials maliciously and sadistically use force to cause harm," "contemporary standards of decency always are violated ... whether or not significant injury is evident. Otherwise, the Eighth Amendment would permit any physical punishment, no matter how diabolic or inhuman, inflicting less than some arbitrary quantity of injury." *Hudson*, 503 U.S. at 9.

3. In *Wilkins v. Gaddy*, 559 U.S. 34 (2010) (*per curiam*), the Supreme Court reversed a Fourth Circuit decision for misapplying *Hudson's* lowered objective injury standard, holding the Fourth Circuit's requirement that a prisoner allege more than "*de minimis*" injuries was "at odds with *Hudson's* direction to decide excessive force claims based on the nature of the force rather than the extent of the injury." *Id.* at 34. The Fourth Circuit affirmed the dismissal of the complaint for failure to state a claim. The Supreme Court summarized the factual allegations:

> According to the complaint, [corrections officer] Gaddy, apparently angered by Wilkins' request for a grievance form, "snatched [Wilkins] off the ground and slammed him onto the concrete floor." Gaddy "then proceeded to punch, kick, knee and choke [Wilkins] until another officer had to physically remove him from [Wilkins]." Wilkins further alleged that, "[a]s a result of the excessive

> force used by [Gaddy], [he] sustained multiple physical injuries including a bruised heel, lower back pain, increased blood pressure, as well as migraine headaches and dizziness" and "psychological trauma and mental anguish including depression, panic attacks and nightmares of the assault."

Id. at 35. *Wilkins* summarized *Hudson* as having "rejected the notion that 'significant injury' is a threshold requirement for stating an excessive force claim. The 'core judicial inquiry,' [in *Hudson*] was not whether a certain quantum of injury was sustained, but rather 'whether force was applied in a good-faith effort to maintain or restore discipline, or maliciously and sadistically to cause harm.' *Wilkins*, *id.* at 37 (quoting *Hudson*, 503 U.S. at 7). While an inmate "who complains of a 'push or shove' that causes no discernible injury almost certainly fails to state a valid excessive force claim," *id.* at 38 (further citation omitted), and the prohibition of cruel and unusual punishments "necessarily excludes from constitutional recognition *de minimis* uses of physical force, provided that the use of force is not of a sort repugnant to the conscience of mankind," *id.* at 37–38 (further citation omitted), the Supreme Court held in *Wilkins* that "[i]njury and force ... are only imperfectly correlated, and it is the latter that ultimately counts." *Id.* at 38.

Wilkins held that *Hudson* did not "merely serve to lower the injury threshold for excessive force claims from 'significant' to 'non-de minimis'—whatever those ill-defined terms might mean. Instead, [*Hudson*] aimed to shift the 'core judicial inquiry' from the extent of the injury to the nature of the force—specifically, whether it was nontrivial and 'was applied ... maliciously and sadistically to cause harm.'" *Id.* at 39 (quoting *Hudson*, 503 U.S. at 7). In *Wilkins*, the Court noted that most Circuits to consider the issue had rejected the Fourth Circuit's *de minimis* injury requirement, *id.* at 39, n. 2 (citing, *e.g.*, *Wright v. Goord*, 554 F.3d 255, 269–270 (2d Cir. 2009) ("[O]ur Court has reversed summary dismissals of Eighth Amendment claims of excessive force even where the plaintiff's evidence of injury was slight.... [T]he absence of any significant injury to [the plaintiff] does not end the Eighth Amendment inquiry, for our standards of decency are violated even in the absence of such injury if the defendant's use of force was malicious or sadistic")).

Wilkins held the extent of the plaintiff's injury is "one factor that may suggest 'whether the use of force could plausibly have been thought necessary' in a particular situation," *Wilkins*, *id.* at 37 (quoting *Whitley*, 475 U.S. at 321), "may also provide some indication of the amount of force applied," *id.* at 37, and is relevant evidence in assessing damages. *Id.* But *Wilkins* also reaffirmed *Hudson*'s ruling that "not 'every malevolent touch by a prison guard gives rise to a federal cause of action.'" *Id.* (quoting *Hudson*, 503 U.S. at 9). Did *Wilkins* do away with the objective element in prisoner use of force cases? If not, after *Wilkins*, how would you describe the legal significance of the plaintiff's injury and what plaintiff must prove?

4. *Wilkins* abrogated a line of Fourth Circuit decisions that had required more than *de minimis* injury, decisions issued as early as 1994—sixteen years before *Wilkins*. Should plaintiffs whose claims were dismissed between 1994–2010 for failure to allege or prove more than *de minimis* injury have any recourse, since the Supreme Court

found that the Fourth Circuit had misapplied *Hudson* for all those years? Why do you think the Supreme Court did not correct this misinterpretation before 2010? Keep this example in mind as you consider other examples of the Supreme Court's refusal to exercise its supervisory powers over the lower federal courts.

5. Can a correctional officer's sexual abuse of an inmate violate the Eighth Amendment? The Third Circuit said yes, drawing on the framework for excessive force claims. *See Ricks v. Shover*, 891 F.3d 468, 477–78 (3d Cir. 2018) (objectively serious sexual contact includes "sexualized fondling, coerced sexual activity, combinations of ongoing harassment and abuse, and exchanges of sexual activity for special treatment or to avoid discipline").

Exercise 2-B

You are a summer associate for a law firm deciding whether to represent an inmate *pro bono*. From notes of an interview with the inmate, you understand the inmate alleges that a correctional officer violated the inmate's 8th Amendment rights by subjecting him to excessive force. The inmate alleges that the correctional officer was angry because the inmate requested a grievance form. The inmate alleges that the correctional officer took out his Taser, held it close to the inmate and pressed it against his chest for several minutes, threatening to use it on the inmate, told the inmate how dangerous a Taser to the chest would be at close range, but ultimately did not use the Taser. The inmate was scared, was slightly bruised where the Taser was pressed into his chest, and has had recurring nightmares about the incident but did not need medical treatment.

Should the law firm represent the prisoner? What facts must be pled to support each element of the claim? Before meeting with the supervising attorney to make a recommendation, is there specific additional information you would like to have from the inmate? Are there legal questions you would like to research?

Exercise 2-C

Review the factual scenario in Exercise 2-B. With that factual scenario in mind, review the Model Jury Instructions below. Predict whether the facts could state an 8th Amendment claim in a district court within the Third Circuit. Predict whether the facts could state a claim in a district court within the Fifth Circuit. If the results are different, does that seem fair?

Exercise 2-D

Background on jury instructions

Before a federal jury begins to deliberate, the district court judge instructs the jury on the relevant law. The jury instructions are often lengthy documents, in excess of thirty pages, and are written in the first person because they are the judge's words to the jury. The judge (usually with help from law clerks) writes the instructions, reads them out loud to the jury, and sometimes allows the jury to bring a copy of the instructions into the jury room. Jury instructions in an individual case are tailored to the evidence in that case and communicate the current law of the jurisdiction where the jury sits. They are usually based on published model jury instructions, specific instructions requested by the opposing attorneys in pre-trial written submissions, and the court's own research. The instructions often are finalized after an adversarial oral conference with counsel. Alleged errors in jury instructions frequently are the basis for appeal.

Law Practice Simulation

Before comparing the below Model Jury Instructions from the Third Circuit and Fifth Circuit, suppose you have been appointed to a panel of distinguished attorneys charged with drafting a model jury instruction for district courts within the Twelfth Circuit to use when instructing juries on Section 1983 excessive force claims by convicted prisoners.

Some on the panel advocate the adoption of the Third Circuit's model instructions, which require plaintiff to prove physical pain or intense fear or emotional pain but do not require proof of significant physical injury and do not explicitly require the jury's deference to prison officials' judgment concerning appropriate use of force. Some on the panel wish to adopt the Fifth Circuit's model jury instruction. Others are concerned about the effect of the Supreme Court's decision in *Wilkins*. The Twelfth Circuit judges who chair the jury instruction panel will make the final decision of what instructions to adopt.

Third Circuit Model Jury Instruction for an Eighth Amendment Excessive Force Claim, with comments[5]

4.10 Section 1983—Excessive Force—Convicted Prisoner

. . .

In order to establish [his/her] claim for violation of the Eighth Amendment, [plaintiff] must prove that [defendant] used force against [him/her]

5. The Third Circuit's Model Jury Instructions for civil cases, Chapter 4: Instructions for Civil Rights Claims Under Section 1983 (July 2019), are available at https://www.ca3.uscourts.gov/model-

maliciously, for the purpose of causing harm, rather than in a good faith effort to maintain or restore discipline. It is not enough to show that, in hindsight, the amount of force seems unreasonable; the plaintiff must show that the defendant used force maliciously, for the purpose of causing harm. When I use the word "maliciously," I mean intentionally injuring another, without just cause or reason, and doing so with excessive cruelty or a delight in cruelty. [Plaintiff] must also prove that [defendant's] use of force caused some [harm] [physical injury] to [him/her].

In deciding whether [plaintiff] has proven this claim, you should consider [whether [defendant] used force against [plaintiff],] whether there was a need for the application of force, and the relationship between that need for force, if any, and the amount of force applied. In considering whether there was a need for force, you should consider all the relevant facts and circumstances that [defendant] reasonably believed to be true at the time of the encounter. Such circumstances can include whether [defendant] reasonably perceived a threat to the safety of staff or inmates, and if so, the extent of that threat. In addition, you should consider whether [defendant] made any efforts to temper the severity of the force [he/she] used.

You should also consider [whether [plaintiff] was physically injured and the extent of such injury] [the extent of [plaintiff's] injuries]. But a use of force can violate the Eighth Amendment even if it does not cause significant injury. Although the extent of any injuries to [plaintiff] may help you assess whether a use of force was legitimate, a malicious and sadistic use of force violates the Eighth Amendment even if it produces no significant physical injury.

Comment

...

<u>Content of the Eighth Amendment standard for excessive force</u>.... "[W]henever prison officials stand accused of using excessive physical force in violation of the Cruel and Unusual Punishments Clause," the issue is "whether force was applied in a good faith effort to maintain or restore discipline, or maliciously and sadistically to cause harm." *Hudson v. McMillian*, 503 U.S. 1, 6–7 (1992). The Court has stressed that prison officials' decisions are entitled to deference; although this deference "does not insulate from review actions taken in bad faith and for no legitimate purpose, ... it requires that neither judge nor jury freely substitute their judgment for that of officials who have made a considered choice." *Whitley*, 475 U.S. at 322.

The factors relevant to the jury's inquiry include "the need for the application of force, the relationship between the need and the amount of force that was used, [and] the extent of injury inflicted," *Whitley*, 475 U.S. at

civil-jury-table-contents-and-instructions (Reporter Catherine T. Struve). The instructions for Excessive Force—Convicted Prisoner appear on pages 125–30.

321...." But equally relevant are such factors as the extent of the threat to the safety of staff and inmates, as reasonably perceived by the responsible officials on the basis of the facts known to them, and any efforts made to temper the severity of a forceful response." *Id.*...

In assessing the use of force, "the extent of injury suffered by [the] inmate is one factor," but a plaintiff can establish an Eighth Amendment excessive force claim even without showing "serious injury." *Hudson*, 503 U.S. at 7; *see also Wilkins v. Gaddy*, 130 S. Ct. 1175, 1177, 1178 (2010) (per curiam) (rejecting Fourth Circuit's requirement of "a showing of significant injury in order to state an excessive force claim," and reiterating "*Hudson*'s direction to decide excessive force claims based on the nature of the force rather than the extent of the injury"). "When prison officials maliciously and sadistically use force to cause harm, contemporary standards of decency always are violated.... This is true whether or not significant injury is evident." *Id.* at 9. Although "the Eighth Amendment does not protect an inmate against an objectively *de minimis* use of force,.... *de minimis* injuries do not necessarily establish *de minimis* force." *Smith v. Mensinger*, 293 F.3d 641, 648–49 (3d Cir. 2002). "[T]he degree of injury is relevant for any Eighth Amendment analysis, [but] there is no fixed minimum quantum of injury that a prisoner must prove that he suffered through objective or independent evidence in order to state a claim for wanton and excessive force." *Brooks v. Kyler*, 204 F.3d 102, 104 (3d Cir. 2000). "Although the extent of an injury provides a means of assessing the legitimacy and scope of the force, the focus always remains on the force used (the blows)." *Id.* at 108.

In *Young v. Martin*, 801 F.3d 172 (3d Cir. 2015), the court of appeals held that there was a genuine dispute of material fact as to whether prison guards violated the Eighth Amendment by securing a mentally ill prisoner in a four-point restraint chair, naked, for fourteen hours. The court concluded that a reasonable jury could find that prison officials subjected him to a substantial risk of physical harm and unnecessary pain, given the tightness of the restraints, the length of time restrained, his nakedness, the cold air blowing on him, and his inability to hold his own weight once released.

Other sets of model instructions include a requirement that plaintiff suffered harm as a result of the defendant's use of force. *See, e.g.*, Fifth Circuit (Civil) Instruction ... The model also includes this requirement, although there does not appear to be Third Circuit caselaw that specifically addresses whether harm in general (as distinct from physical injury) is an element of an Eighth Amendment excessive force claim. Assuming that the plaintiff must prove some harm, proof of physical injury clearly suffices. In the light of the Supreme Court's indication that the Eighth Amendment is designed to protect against torture, *see Hudson*, 503 U.S. at 9, proof of physical pain or intense fear or emotional pain should also suffice, even absent significant physical injury.

...

Some sets of model instructions state explicitly that the jury must give deference to prison officials' judgments concerning the appropriateness of force in a given situation. *See* Fifth Circuit (Civil) Instruction ... However, in *Douglas v. Owens*, 50 F.3d 1226 (3d Cir. 1995), the district court gave an instruction that omitted any explicit mention of deference, *see id.* at 1232 n.13 (quoting instruction), and the Court of Appeals held the instruction "was proper and adequate under the facts of this case" because the district court's reference to "force ... applied in a good faith effort to maintain or restore discipline" indicated to the jury that the defendants should not necessarily be held liable merely because they used force that "is later determined to have been unnecessary," *id.* at 1233.

Fifth Circuit's Model Jury Instruction for Eighth Amendment Excessive Force Claims[6]

10.7A EIGHTH AMENDMENT (EXCESSIVE FORCE)

Plaintiff [name] claims that Defendant [name] violated [his/her] Eighth Amendment right to be protected from excessive and unnecessary force.

The Eighth Amendment to the Constitution of the United States protects inmates like Plaintiff [name] from cruel and unusual punishment.

To recover damages for this alleged constitutional violation, Plaintiff [name] must prove by a preponderance of the evidence that:

1. Defendant [name] used excessive force against [him/her]; and
2. Plaintiff [name] suffered some harm as a result of Defendant [name]'s use of force.

Whether a use of force against a prison inmate is excessive depends on whether the force was applied in a good-faith effort to maintain or restore discipline, or whether it was done maliciously or sadistically to cause harm. If the force was used maliciously or sadistically for the purpose of harming Plaintiff [name], then it was excessive.

To act "maliciously" means to intentionally do a wrongful act without just cause or excuse, with an intent to inflict injury, or under circumstances that show an evil intent. To act "sadistically" means to inflict pain on the person for one's own pleasure.

In deciding whether the force used was excessive, you must give prison officials wide-ranging deference in the adoption and execution of policies and practices that in their judgment are needed to preserve internal order and discipline and to maintain internal security in the prison. In making

---

6. The Fifth Circuit's Model Jury Instructions for civil cases are available at http://www.lb5.uscourts.gov/juryinstructions/ (Oct. 2016). Instructions for Eighth Amendment (Excessive Force) appear as Chapter 10.7A.

this determination, you may consider the following nonexclusive factors: (1) the extent of the injury suffered; (2) the need for the application of force; (3) the relationship between the need and the amount of force used; (4) the threat reasonably perceived by the responsible officials; and (5) any efforts made to temper the severity of a forceful response.

In considering the second element—harm—not every malevolent, harmful, or injurious touch by a prison guard gives rise to a claim under federal law. But an inmate like Plaintiff [name] need not show significant injury to establish a constitutional violation.

Even a slight use of force, under certain circumstances, may be so repugnant to the conscience of mankind that a claim may exist. The extent of injury an inmate suffers is one factor that may suggest whether the use of the force could reasonably have been thought necessary in the particular situation.

...

For further discussion

Unlike the 8th Amendment, which is phrased in broad, general language and prohibits the government from falling beneath a level of care to prisoners, "cruel and unusual punishment," the South African Constitution imposes specific obligations to affirmatively provide a level of care to prisoners, "human dignity." The South African Constitution provides:

35. Arrested, detained and accused persons

(2) Everyone who is detained, including every sentenced prisoner, has the right—

...

e. to conditions of detention that are consistent with human dignity, including at least exercise and the provision, at state expense, of adequate accommodation, nutrition, reading material and medical treatment; and

f. to communicate with, and be visited by, that person's—

i. spouse or partner;

ii. next of kin;

iii. chosen religious counsellor; and

iv. chosen medical practitioner.[7]

Are there benefits to having a Constitution phrased in broad terms, such as the 8th Amendment? Are there benefits to having a Constitution guarantee specific rights, such as the South African guarantee that prisoners be provided "adequate accommodation, nutrition, reading material and medical treatment"? Are there disadvantages

7. S. Afr. Const., 1996.

to either approach? Can you think of benefits or disadvantages to having a Constitution that sets a floor (cruel and unusual punishment) as opposed to an affirmative duty (human dignity and specific guarantees)?

E. Prison Rape

Questions to guide reading of *Farmer* Oral Argument

1. What relief did Farmer seek in this suit? What relief did Farmer seek in an earlier suit against different prison officials?
2. Can you articulate the difference between negligence and the standard advocated by the plaintiff inmate?
3. What does the Seventh Circuit's choice not to write an opinion in this case suggest about the importance the Circuit accorded the case?
4. If you were counsel to a prison considering where to house a transgender inmate, what guidance would you give your client?

Oral Argument before U.S. Supreme Court in *Farmer v. Brennan*[8]

January 12, 1994

Oral Argument of Elizabeth Alexander on behalf of Dee Farmer

MS. ALEXANDER: Mr. Chief Justice, and may it please the Court: The petitioner in this case is a transsexual. She is a young, nonviolent prisoner of feminine appearance and demeanor. Prior to her incarceration, she had undergone silicone breast injections and unsuccessful surgery to remove her testicles. She alleges that she was raped approximately 10 days after her placement in general population at the Terre Haute Penitentiary. Rape is one of the most painful and humiliating things that—

QUESTION: Would you—would you preface your remarks by telling us where the petitioner is now located and under what circumstances, and also telling us precisely what relief it is that you are presently seeking?

MS. ALEXANDER: Yes, Your Honor. The petitioner is currently confined at FCI Florence in Florence, Colorado. This is a medium security facility. She is in general population at that medium security facility.

8. Transcript of Oral Argument, *Farmer v. Brennan*, 511 U.S. 825 (1994) (No. 92-7247).

QUESTION: And what relief is it precisely that is being sought here?

MS. ALEXANDER: She is seeking two things. She is seeking damages from the respondents. She is also seeking—

QUESTION: From the individual respondents?

MS. ALEXANDER: Yes, Your Honor. She—

QUESTION: None of whom were involved in her placement at Terre Haute?

MS. ALEXANDER: Your Honor, we would argue that they—that their actions did cause that placement, and I will—I will get to that.

QUESTION: All right.

MS. ALEXANDER: She is also seeking an injunction to prevent her return to a penitentiary....

QUESTION: An injunction to prevent her from being moved to a different facility?

MS. ALEXANDER: Not to a different facility, to—to another penitentiary such as Terre Haute.

...

QUESTION: The petitioner is in the general population at the current facility?

MS. ALEXANDER: Yes, Your Honor.

...

QUESTION: Is the incidence of rape higher at maximum— ... The more secure the prison, the higher the incidence of rape, or in medium security facilities?

MS. ALEXANDER: Justice Ginsburg, I don't believe that there can be any generalization. What is a level of violence is not—not so—doesn't so much turn on the security designation of the facility as a particular atmosphere and practices at that facility.

QUESTION: In terms of the injunctive relief that you're seeking, though, I don't comprehend why Farmer is more at risk in a maximum-security facility than at a medium security facility.

MS. ALEXANDER: The allegation in this case is that the primary risk came from the fact that violent individuals were allowed to have access to her in the general population at Terre Haute. It is—it is—the confinement of violent other prisoners that she pointed to as a risk to her, and that within 10 days of her placement in general population at Terre Haute materialized in her rape.

QUESTION: And yet she did—did want to be in the general population, because when she was at Lewisburg didn't she object to being in administrative detention?

Ms. Alexander: I would submit that she wanted a safe placement. She wanted—she would have preferred that safe placement to have been in general population. But what—what—certainly, she did not want to be raped. She wanted a safe placement. She has a disagreement with prison officials at Lewisburg as to what that safe placement would be. The Federal court agreed, in that case, with the prison officials that the only safe placement was in segregation, not in general population at the penitentiary.

Question: Well, isn't it a part of your case, just to follow this line of questioning, that the maximum-security prisons are the most dangerous because they have the most dangerous people, or is that not your case?

Ms. Alexander: Is it not the argument. The argument is what is a dangerous facility has to do with a number of factors, the characteristics of the prisoner—in this case this was a prisoner who was at extraordinarily unusual risk—and the characteristics of the facility, the particular facility.

If in a facility with very violent offenders, inappropriate and inadequate steps are taken to protect the prisoners, that is a facility in which there is extraordinarily high risk of what happened to this petitioner. That is within 10 days of her placement, her rape.

Question: So then the Government doesn't make an error if it selects a—a maximum security prison, necessarily.

Ms. Alexander: Not necessarily. Petitioner—

Question: And it doesn't make an error if it puts the person in the general population, necessarily.

Ms. Alexander: Whether—not necessarily. It would depend on the characteristics of the prisoner and the characteristics of general population in that facility. Petitioner asks for an opportunity to prove that this placement in the general population at Terre Haute violated the Eighth Amendment because it was obvious to respondents that petitioner was at an unreasonable risk.

What does obvious risk mean in the context of this case? Suppose we were making a list of people who would be at obvious risk of sexual assault if placed in a high security male prison. Women would be at the top of the list, surely, and the risk is so obvious that we cannot imagine a prison deciding to confine women in general population at a male high security facility. But also near the top of the list would be someone who had the appearance and demeanor of a woman, a transsexual like petitioner.

. . .

QUESTION: How about a young man with a slight build, youthful 18, 19-year-old, slender male.

MS. ALEXANDER: There—one could easily imagine a number of facilities in which a person as described by Your Honor would be at obvious and unreasonable risk in general population.

...

QUESTION: ... [O]n the Government's theory, the official has got to draw the conclusion which you say should be inferred by any reasonable person from the obviousness of the risk, whereas under your standard you don't have to prove that the conclusion was actually drawn, you simply have to prove knowledge of the facts that made it obvious.

MS. ALEXANDER: That's right.... Petitioner argues that deliberate indifference exists when a risk of serious and likely harm was either known or obvious to the defendants, defendants had the ability to forestall the harm but defendants nonetheless failed to act. And like respondent's standard—again to clarify—this standard requires a demonstration that the defendants knew the underlying facts that rendered the risk obvious. Unlike respondent's standard, it does not require proof that the defendants recognized an obvious risk when they saw it.

This is a rights standard because inherent in the affirmative duty that prison officials owe to protect the safety of those in their care is at least, at least a duty to know what is obvious to anyone in their position.

QUESTION: Well, doesn't your standard come pretty close to being just negligence?

MS. ALEXANDER: No, Your Honor....

QUESTION: [B]ut you really water it down, it seems to me, in your application. You say that simply awareness of an obvious risk is enough, that one—the fact finder need not further infer that their—that the person was deliberately indifferent to the risk. Well, why is that any different from negligence?

MS. ALEXANDER: Your Honor, it's not simply obvious risk. It is when an obvious risk exists that the prison official had the ability to fix and then in that situation did not fix. This is not a negligence standard....

QUESTION: But we're—we're talking about a very aspect of liability, or state of mind basically. And the Government says you may infer deliberate indifference from the obviousness of a risk. You say you don't even have to do that; simply knowledge of the obviousness of risk, without any inference by the fact finder, is enough. And

I honestly don't see why that's much different than negligent—than the state of mind required for negligent injury.

...

QUESTION: Isn't there a subjective element to deliberate indifference?

MS. ALEXANDER: Yes. And the subjective element has to—has to do with the fact that always the facts are viewed from the perspective of the defendant. But I do agree with the first part of Justice Scalia's question. I agree that the Court has always treated deliberate indifference as one standard, the same standard. And that standard in *Wilson* says "deliberate indifference as articulated in *Estelle*."

...

QUESTION: ... Are there any individual defendants here who were officers or officials at Terre Haute?

MS. ALEXANDER: The warden at Terre Haute, Your Honor. And this is—this is also the respondent who, in the Lewisburg case that was referred to earlier in questioning, had filed a declaration that led to the Federal court finding that it was—that of course it's unsafe to put a transsexual in general population at this penitentiary.

QUESTION: Now, in the prior litigation when this prisoner wanted to be taken out of solitary and put in the general population, the Bureau of Prisons took the position that the prisoner was too high risk to do that?

MS. ALEXANDER: Yes, Your Honor. And they said—and the Bureau of Prisons was successful in Federal Court because the Federal Court found that—that the decision of the officials that this transsexual should not be in general population was an appropriate decision for the officials to make.

QUESTION: And does that position and knowledge, is that attributable now to the warden at Terre Haute, in your view?

MS. ALEXANDER: I would say that that means that there was actual knowledge on the part of this respondents. Of course ... this additional information about actual knowledge wasn't available to the trial court....

QUESTION: Why wasn't it available?

MS. ALEXANDER: Because the petitioner ... who was proceeding without counsel, didn't put that information in.

QUESTION: I see.

...

MS. ALEXANDER: ... I want to turn to another point ... : respondents' attempt to defend their standard by arguing that this case is about the wide latitude that prison officials must have in running prisons, and in particular in making housing decisions.

The concerns respondents raise about the complexities of decisions of prison staff are not wrong, but they're not central to this case. The respondents' claim here is that they lacked actual knowledge of an unreasonable risk to the petitioner. According to the transfer documents in the record, respondents didn't even consider petitioner's transsexuality when they placed her in general population in a penitentiary, even though the most distinctive fact about this petitioner is her transsexual status.

You can't claim to have considered a risk you also say you didn't know about, thus respondents' denial of actual knowledge of the unreasonable risk logically precludes them from claiming that the placement was based on a reasoned judgment. Thus this isn't a case about deference, it's a case about the proper standard under the Eighth Amendment.

. . .

QUESTION: Suppose—suppose this—Farmer had said at Terre Haute, as Farmer did at Lewisburg, I want to be in the general population, and then this horrible event occurred, would she still have a 1983 case?

MS. ALEXANDER: Yes, Your Honor. There might be some circumstances in which the fact that the plaintiff essentially represented that there wasn't an unreasonable risk would render an otherwise obvious risk not obvious, but if the risk was obvious, then we ought to think about who has the better information on that. It's—certainly the prison officials know—knew far more about what general population was like at Terre Haute than did the petitioner.

And so it's—it's the wrong concept to think of taking from the prison officials, who have the information, the duty and giving it to prisoners who don't have the duty and also who don't have the information. Because that—the notice—the requirement that you warn prison officials that is so frequent in the Seventh Circuit, either the warning's superfluous in that they already have the information or you're required to warn them about something that you don't know as a prison[er], something they're in the better position to—to address.

. . .

Oral Argument of Paul Bender [on behalf of the prison respondents]

[Deputy Solicitor General, Department of Justice]

. . .

MR. BENDER: ... The Court said that it took the case to deal with this subjective/objective issue, and that's what I would like to address.... I think it's important in thinking about this, to think first about what deliberate indifference means. Everybody agrees that that's the standard, deliberate indifference. I think there are at least two factors in deliberate indifference, and it's important not to get them confused with each other.

In a situation like this where you're talking about protecting an inmate from attacks by other inmates, deliberate indifference has one element of the prison official's knowledge of the risk. There's did the prison official know, or if you take the objective approach, should the prison official have known that there was, in fact, a risk? That's the first element. Then there's a second element; knowing about a certain risk—and there are lots of risks in prison—was the prison official deliberately indifferent to that risk.

We take the position, as did the Seventh Circuit, that on the first of those elements the Court has already decided—and if it hadn't it should decide now—that it is a subjective standard. You cannot be deliberately indifferent to a risk unless you know about the risk. And that is the position that we urge you to adopt.

QUESTION: Now, Mr. Bender, on that point do you accept the model penal code definition of knowledge?

...

MR. BENDER: Well, I think what the model penal code definition is referring to is what's often called the ostrich situation, the head-in-the-sand situation, that if there's a—if there is a high probability and you stop yourself from making a conclusion, you turn away from it, that that can also be dealt with as actual knowledge. But otherwise, I think you need to have actual knowledge. Just the fact—

QUESTION: Well, then I'm not sure you do then agree with the—with the model penal code. It seems to me the model penal—it's one thing to say you can infer from knowledge of the risk that you knew about it, or that you had the necessary subjective standard. But to say there's simply a high prob—that you knew there was a high probability, it seems to me it would fall a good deal short of ultimately inferring actual intent.

...

MR. BENDER: Well, that's what—that's where I think we can get confused between the first issue and the second. If you're aware of a high probability of risk, it seems to me you are aware of a risk. And then the question is were you deliberately indifferent to the risk that you were aware of, and those are two different questions. It's not enough to show, in a deliberate indifference case, that the prison officials were aware that there was a dangerous situation. You've also got to show that they were deliberately indifferent to that dangerous situation.

QUESTION: But is it your position that the finder of fact must infer that they actually knew of the risk?

MR. BENDER: Yes, that they knew of the danger, right.

QUESTION: That you could infer it from knowledge of other—other facts.

MR. BENDER: Right. We believe that you can make such a finding based on circumstantial evidence, but the finding must be—if you have a jury, you should tell the jury that they—in order to find there's a violation of the Eighth Amendment, you have to find that the defendant knew of the risk—

QUESTION: Then I suggest you don't really agree with the model penal code.

...

MR. BENDER: ... I think the confusing thing is we're dealing here with risks to begin with, and so we're dealing with probabilities, and you've got to be aware of the probability.

QUESTION: In other words, the probability is a—is, in effect, an inference. I mean there are facts and there are inferences from them. The risk is an inference which you draw from the facts, and you're saying you've got to prove that they drew the inference. *I.e.*, in the model penal code's terms, you've got to prove that they understood the high probability that these facts implied. That—isn't that what you're saying?

...

MR. BENDER: Yes, I think so. Otherwise it's hard to say that you're deliberate indifferent to it, if you don't know about it....

QUESTION: If you're a bad logician, you may have a defense.

MR. BENDER: You may have a defense to a—to an Eighth Amendment claim. You may not have a defense to a negligence claim. And it's really important to understand here that there's also a possibility of bringing a Tort Claims Act suit for negligence.

...

MR. BENDER: ... the Seventh Circuit never wrote an opinion in this case....

...

MR. BENDER: I should say, in that connection, that the Government's position in this case is a position that is—is forged from a variety of interests that we have. The Government interests are certainly in defending officials of the Bureau of Prisons against unjustifiable and incorrect suits of violations of the Eighth Amendment. But the Government also plays a role in suing prisons for unconstitutional prison conditions, and I think it's important that we bear both of those things in mind.

And, for example, in trying to remedy unconstitutional prison conditions, I don't think that we should be required to show that the people who are running those institutions should be treated as criminals. That's not—that just may—it seems to me is too heavy a burden. I think—

QUESTION: What is the second part of your charge? The first part is actual knowledge of the risk.

MR. BENDER: Of the risk.

QUESTION: But once you have actual knowledge of the risk, then what?

MR. BENDER: Then you have to be deliberately indifferent to the risk, which means that there has to be something that you could do readily to avoid the risk, and you have to have made a decision not to do that even though it was something that could easily have been done. That's the indifferent part of it, and the—and the deliberate indifferent part of it is that you are aware that there's something you could do and that you don't do anything to deal with it.

Now that's very hard to quantify, and I think that's where the obviousness comes into it, and I think that's one of the confusions. There if you—there you could say if it is obvious that something should be done and this person didn't do it, that might amount to deliberate indifference. Obvious in the sense that there's something that can be done to alleviate the risk and that action isn't taken.

QUESTION: Mr. Bender, we've talked in—trying to phrase in general terms without being concrete about the particular allegations ... [Your adversary's brief] points to a Bureau of Prisons report in 1986 which, quote, stated that petitioner would be subject to a great deal of sexual pressure because of her youth and feminine appearance. Now, is that a sufficient knowledge of the risk that's at stake in this case?

...

MR. BENDER: No, because the risk has to be a very serious risk, a very severe risk of very serious harm. Otherwise every prison official in the country would be violating the Eighth Amendment at every moment. There's always a risk in every prison of something happening.

...

I think there has to be a very great likelihood that the person is in danger. Sexual pressure seems to me an awfully vague term to refer to that. It would be better—it would be an allegation that's closer to liability in this case if it was subject to a considerable risk of being attacked. And it has to be a considerable risk of being attacked, not just a small risk. And that is, again, a very hard part of the standard to quantify, but it's important to realize that it's got to be more than the normal risks in prison.

And, also, people who are young and effeminate have to be housed somewhere in an institution. You—I don't think it's fair to them to say that they always have to be kept in a solitary confinement situation. The Bureau of Prisons likes to have people in the general population, and the fact that there is a small danger that a person will be attacked in the general population does not seem to me to—

QUESTION: Well isn't it fairly generally known that the danger is not really small, just throughout the prison system? Don't you start from a predicate of very substantial danger throughout the system?

MR. BENDER: No, I don't think that's—I don't think that's true, at least with the Federal prison system. The—the statistics that I've seen, which are published statistics from 1989, indicates that the number of assaults of any kind, including sexual assaults but other assaults as well, in the Federal prison system in 1989 in general was about 1 percent of the population, a little bit less than 1 percent of the population.

That does not suggest to me that throughout the system there is a considerable risk. Interestingly enough as well, the statistics for the institution to which the petitioner was transferred, Terre Haute, the statistics of assault—assaultive occasions there during that year are exactly the same, almost exactly the same percentage, slightly less 1—less than 1 percent. There may be some institutions at some times where there is a much greater risk, and I don't mean to denigrate a 1 percent risk.

QUESTION: What do you mean by 1 percent? 1 percent of all of the prisoners were involved in an assault?

MR. BENDER: Were assaulted.

...

QUESTION: —Presumably there are occasionally these incidents that don't surface.

MR. BENDER: Right.... And the position of the respondents here is that the four respondents who were responsible for sending the petitioner to Terre Haute only sent the petitioner to Terre Haute as a—as an institution. They knew that when he got to Terre Haute he would be put in a segregated situation, administrative detention, for purposes of evaluation, and that the officials there would know what the situation was in Terre Haute at the time, and would know about his transsexualism and his history in prison previously, and that they would then make a decision, based on their—their based judgment, about whether it was safe to put him in the general population.

And it's not at all certain that they would make a judgment to put him in the general population. When he was at Lewisburg, which was the first institution he landed at, he was never put in the general population. And therefore you cannot say on this record that there could be enough evidence to survive a summary judgment motion that these—that these defendants had the knowledge of the risk.

Because even if you were to assume that there was a substantial risk in the general population at Terre Haute—and there's not any basis for that either given the statistics I've just mentioned. Even if you were to assume that, there's no inevitability that the petitioner is going to go into the general population at Terre Haute. He could stay in segregation for a substantial time and then be moved to another institution.

...

Rebuttal argument of Elizabeth Alexander

Thank you, Your Honor. When the Government refers to the record, of course they're referring to a record that we had no opportunity to develop with regard to the risk at Terre Haute. But I would submit, even bearing that in mind, that whatever the general risk, if it's 1 percent, of assault per year in Terre Haute, that wasn't this petitioner's risk of assault. This petitioner was at a—at an extraordinarily high and unusual risk in comparison to the background risk.

...

And this also points out to something that is, I think, one of the real practical problems, and one of the things that's wrong with the Government's proposed standard. In this case what is it that the—that the respondents didn't know about this petitioner? Presumably they would—they would—the record seems to indicate, and at least it is alleged that they knew she was a transsexual.

...

Questions to guide reading of *Farmer*

1. Both parties argued that "deliberate indifference" should mean "recklessness." What did *Farmer* identify as the difference between the two arguments? What practical consequences might there have been if the Supreme Court had adopted the prisoner's proffered test instead of the standard advocated by the correction officials?
2. Does the defendant have to have acted or failed to act believing that the inmate would be hurt? Why did *Farmer* state that prison officials won't be motivated to be ignorant of obvious risks? Do you agree?

3. Can a prison defendant be deliberately indifferent if he knew of an obvious, substantial risk to a prisoner but didn't know the identity of the ultimate attacker?
4. Even if a risk is obvious, what circumstances did *Farmer* sketch out for how defendants can still prevail?
5. The 8th Amendment test has an objective element and a subjective element. What are they? Is the concept of a "reasonable" response by the defendant an objective inquiry?
6. Do you think *Farmer* emphasized the role of a factfinder and how a jury should be instructed (*e.g*, footnote 8)? If so, does that suggest that the majority in *Farmer* thought "deliberate indifference" cases often would reach a jury for factfinding?
7. How does *Farmer* tie the subjective appreciation of risk of harm to the text of the 8th Amendment prohibition on cruel and unusual punishment?
8. In his dissent, Justice Thomas argued that the 8th Amendment should not apply to "prison conditions not imposed as part of a sentence" and that *Estelle* should be overruled. What are some practical consequences of that view, if other Justices were to adopt it?

Farmer v. Brennan

511 U.S. 825 (1994)

Justice SOUTER delivered the opinion of the Court.

A prison official's "deliberate indifference" to a substantial risk of serious harm to an inmate violates the Eighth Amendment. *See* ... *Estelle v. Gamble*, 429 U.S. 97 (1976). This case requires us to define the term "deliberate indifference," as we do by requiring a showing that the official was subjectively aware of the risk.

I

The dispute before us stems from a civil suit brought by petitioner, Dee Farmer, alleging that respondents, federal prison officials, violated the Eighth Amendment by their deliberate indifference to petitioner's safety. Petitioner, who is serving a federal sentence for credit card fraud, has been diagnosed by medical personnel of the Bureau of Prisons as a transsexual, one who has "[a] rare psychiatric disorder in which a person feels persistently uncomfortable about his or her anatomical sex," and who typically seeks medical treatment, including hormonal therapy and surgery, to bring about a permanent sex change.... For several years before being convicted and sentenced in 1986 at the age of 18, petitioner, who is biologically male, wore women's clothing (as petitioner did at the 1986 trial), underwent estrogen therapy, received silicone breast implants, and submitted to unsuccessful "black market" testicle-removal surgery.... Petitioner's precise appearance in prison is unclear from the record before us, but petitioner claims to have continued hormonal treatment while incarcerated by using drugs smuggled into prison, and apparently wears clothing in a feminine manner, as by displaying a shirt "off one shoulder[.]" The parties agree that petitioner "projects feminine characteristics." ...

The practice of federal prison authorities is to incarcerate preoperative transsexuals with prisoners of like biological sex ... and over time authorities housed petitioner in several federal facilities, sometimes in the general male prison population but more often in segregation. While there is no dispute that petitioner was segregated at least several times because of violations of prison rules, neither is it disputed that in at least one penitentiary petitioner was segregated because of safety concerns....

On March 9, 1989, petitioner was transferred for disciplinary reasons from the Federal Correctional Institute in Oxford, Wisconsin (FCI-Oxford), to the United States Penitentiary in Terre Haute, Indiana (USP-Terre Haute). Though the record before us is unclear about the security designations of the two prisons in 1989, penitentiaries are typically higher security facilities that house more troublesome prisoners than federal correctional institutes.... After an initial stay in administrative segregation, petitioner was placed in the USP-Terre Haute general population. Petitioner voiced no objection to any prison official about the transfer to the penitentiary or to placement in its general population. Within two weeks, according to petitioner's allegations, petitioner was beaten and raped by another inmate in petitioner's cell. Several days later, after petitioner claims to have reported the incident, officials returned petitioner to segregation to await, according to respondents, a hearing about petitioner's HIV-positive status.

Acting without counsel, petitioner then filed a *Bivens* complaint, alleging a violation of the Eighth Amendment. See *Bivens v. Six Unknown Fed. Narcotics Agents*, 403 U.S. 388 (1971).... As defendants, petitioner named respondents: [federal prison officials]. [T]he complaint alleged that respondents either transferred petitioner to USP-Terre Haute or placed petitioner in its general population despite knowledge that the penitentiary had a violent environment and a history of inmate assaults, and despite knowledge that petitioner, as a transsexual who "projects feminine characteristics," would be particularly vulnerable to sexual attack by some USP-Terre Haute inmates. This allegedly amounted to a deliberately indifferent failure to protect petitioner's safety, and thus to a violation of petitioner's Eighth Amendment rights.... [The district court granted summary judgment to prison officials, without ruling on plaintiff's outstanding discovery motions]. [T]he United States Court of Appeals for the Seventh Circuit summarily affirmed without opinion. We granted certiorari ... because Courts of Appeals had adopted inconsistent tests for "deliberate indifference."....

II.A

The Constitution "does not mandate comfortable prisons," ... but neither does it permit inhumane ones, and it is now settled that "the treatment a prisoner receives in prison and the conditions under which he is confined are subject to scrutiny under the Eighth Amendment." ... In its prohibition of "cruel and unusual punishments," the Eighth Amendment places restraints on prison officials, who may not, for example, use excessive physical force against prisoners.... The Amendment also imposes duties on these officials, who must provide humane conditions of confinement; prison officials must ensure that inmates receive adequate food, clothing, shelter, and medical care, and must "take reasonable measures to guarantee the safety of the inmates," ... *Estelle*, 429 U.S., at 103. Cf. *DeShaney v. Winnebago County Dept. of Social Servs.*, 489 U.S. 189, 198–199 (1989).

In particular, as the lower courts have uniformly held, and as we have assumed, "prison officials have a duty ... to protect prisoners from violence at the hands of other prisoners." ... Having incarcerated "persons [with] demonstrated proclivit[ies] for antisocial criminal, and often violent, conduct," ... having stripped them of virtually every means of self-protection and foreclosed their access to outside aid, the government and its officials are not free to let the state of nature take its course. Cf. *DeShaney*, *supra*, 489 U.S., at 199–200; *Estelle*, *supra*, 429 U.S., at 103–104. Prison conditions may be "restrictive and even harsh," ... but gratuitously allowing the beating or rape of one prisoner by another serves no "legitimate penological objectiv[e]," ... any more than it squares with "'evolving standards of decency,'" *Estelle*, *supra*, 429 U.S., at 102.... Being violently assaulted in prison is simply not "part of the penalty that criminal offenders pay for their offenses against society." *Rhodes v. Chapman*, 452 U.S. 337, 347 (1981).

It is not, however, every injury suffered by one prisoner at the hands of another that translates into constitutional liability for prison officials responsible for the victim's safety. Our cases have held that a prison official violates the Eighth Amendment only when two requirements are met. First, the deprivation alleged must be, objectively, "sufficiently serious," ... a prison official's act or omission must result in the denial of "the minimal civilized measure of life's necessities,".... For a claim (like the one here) based on a failure to prevent harm, the inmate must show that he is incarcerated under conditions posing a substantial risk of serious harm....[3]

The second requirement follows from the principle that "only the unnecessary and wanton infliction of pain implicates the Eighth Amendment." ... To violate the Cruel and Unusual Punishments Clause, a prison official must have a "sufficiently culpable state of mind." ... In prison-conditions cases that state of mind is one of "deliberate indifference" to inmate health or safety, ... *Estelle*, *supra*, 429 U.S., at 106, a standard the parties agree governs the claim in this case. The parties disagree, however, on the proper test for deliberate indifference, which we must therefore undertake to define.

B.1

Although we have never paused to explain the meaning of the term "deliberate indifference," the case law is instructive. The term first appeared in the United States Reports in *Estelle v. Gamble*, 429 U.S., at 104, and its use there shows that deliberate indifference describes a state of mind more blameworthy than negligence. In considering the inmate's claim in *Estelle* that inadequate prison medical care violated the Cruel and Unusual Punishments Clause, we distinguished "deliberate indifference to serious medical needs of prisoners," *ibid.*, from "negligen[ce] in diagnosing or treating

3. At what point a risk of inmate assault becomes sufficiently substantial for Eighth Amendment purposes is a question this case does not present, and we do not address it.

a medical condition," *id.*, at 106, holding that only the former violates the Clause. We have since read *Estelle* for the proposition that Eighth Amendment liability requires "more than ordinary lack of due care for the prisoner's interests or safety." *Whitley v. Albers*, 475 U.S. 312, 319 (1986).

While *Estelle* establishes that deliberate indifference entails something more than mere negligence, the cases are also clear that it is satisfied by something less than acts or omissions for the very purpose of causing harm or with knowledge that harm will result. That point underlies the ruling that "application of the deliberate indifference standard is inappropriate" in one class of prison cases: when "officials stand accused of using excessive physical force." ... see also *Whitley*, *supra*, 475 U.S., at 320. In such situations, where the decisions of prison officials are typically made " 'in haste, under pressure, and frequently without the luxury of a second chance,' " *Hudson v. McMillian*, *supra*, 503 U.S., at 6 (quoting *Whitley*, *supra*, 475 U.S., at 320), an Eighth Amendment claimant must show more than "indifference," deliberate or otherwise. The claimant must show that officials applied force "maliciously and sadistically for the very purpose of causing harm," 503 U.S., at 6 (internal quotation marks and citations omitted), or, as the Court also put it, that officials used force with "a knowing willingness that [harm] occur," *id.*, at 7 (internal quotation marks and citation omitted). This standard of purposeful or knowing conduct is not, however, necessary to satisfy the mens rea requirement of deliberate indifference for claims challenging conditions of confinement; "the very high state of mind prescribed by *Whitley* does not apply to prison conditions cases." *Wilson*, *supra*, 501 U.S., at 302–303.

With deliberate indifference lying somewhere between the poles of negligence at one end and purpose or knowledge at the other, the Courts of Appeals have routinely equated deliberate indifference with recklessness.... It is, indeed, fair to say that acting or failing to act with deliberate indifference to a substantial risk of serious harm to a prisoner is the equivalent of recklessly disregarding that risk.

That does not, however, fully answer the pending question about the level of culpability deliberate indifference entails, for the term recklessness is not self-defining. The civil law generally calls a person reckless who acts or (if the person has a duty to act) fails to act in the face of an unjustifiably high risk of harm that is either known or so obvious that it should be known. See Prosser and Keeton § 34, pp. 213–214; Restatement (Second) of Torts § 500 (1965). The criminal law, however, generally permits a finding of recklessness only when a person disregards a risk of harm of which he is aware. See R. Perkins & R. Boyce, Criminal Law 850–851 (3d ed. 1982); J. Hall, General Principles of Criminal Law 115–116, 120, 128 (2d ed. 1960) (hereinafter Hall); American Law Institute, Model Penal Code § 2.02(2)(c), and Comment 3 (1985).... The standards proposed by the parties in this case track the two approaches (though the parties do not put it that way): petitioner asks us to define deliberate indifference as what we have called civil-law recklessness, and respondents urge us to adopt an approach consistent with recklessness in the criminal law.

We reject petitioner's invitation to adopt an objective test for deliberate indifference. We hold instead that a prison official cannot be found liable under the Eighth Amendment for denying an inmate humane conditions of confinement unless the official knows of and disregards an excessive risk to inmate health or safety; the official must both be aware of facts from which the inference could be drawn that a substantial risk of serious harm exists, and he must also draw the inference.... The Eighth Amendment does not outlaw cruel and unusual "conditions"; it outlaws cruel and unusual "punishments." An act or omission unaccompanied by knowledge of a significant risk of harm might well be something society wishes to discourage, and if harm does result society might well wish to assure compensation. The common law reflects such concerns when it imposes tort liability on a purely objective basis.... But an official's failure to alleviate a significant risk that he should have perceived but did not, while no cause for commendation, cannot under our cases be condemned as the infliction of punishment.

In *Wilson v. Seiter*, we rejected a reading of the Eighth Amendment that would allow liability to be imposed on prison officials solely because of the presence of objectively inhumane prison conditions. See 501 U.S., at 299–302. As we explained there, our "cases mandate inquiry into a prison official's state of mind when it is claimed that the official has inflicted cruel and unusual punishment." *Id.*, at 299. Although "state of mind," like "intent," is an ambiguous term that can encompass objectively defined levels of blameworthiness, see 1 W. LaFave & A. Scott, Substantive Criminal Law §§ 3.4, 3.5, pp. 296–300, 313–314 (1986) (hereinafter LaFave & Scott)..., it was no accident that we said in *Wilson* and repeated in later cases that Eighth Amendment suits against prison officials must satisfy a "subjective" requirement. See *Wilson*, *supra*, 501 U.S., at 298.... It is true, as petitioner points out, that *Wilson* cited with approval Court of Appeals decisions applying an objective test for deliberate indifference to claims based on prison officials' failure to prevent inmate assaults. See 501 U.S., at 303 [citations omitted]. But *Wilson* cited those cases for the proposition that the deliberate indifference standard applies to all prison-conditions claims, not to undo its holding that the Eighth Amendment has a "subjective component." 501 U.S., at 298. Petitioner's purely objective test for deliberate indifference is simply incompatible with *Wilson*'s holding.

To be sure, the reasons for focusing on what a defendant's mental attitude actually was (or is), rather than what it should have been (or should be), differ in the Eighth Amendment context from that of the criminal law. Here, a subjective approach isolates those who inflict punishment; there, it isolates those against whom punishment should be inflicted. But the result is the same: to act recklessly in either setting a person must "consciously disregar[d]" a substantial risk of serious harm. Model Penal Code § 2.02(2)(c).

At oral argument, the Deputy Solicitor General advised against frank adoption of a criminal-law *mens rea* requirement, contending that it could encourage triers of fact to find Eighth Amendment liability only if they concluded that prison officials acted like criminals ... We think this concern is misdirected. *Bivens* actions against federal prison officials (and their 42 U.S.C. § 1983 counterparts against state officials) are civil in character, and a court should no more allude to the criminal law when enforcing the Cruel and Unusual Punishments Clause than when applying the Free Speech and Press Clauses, where we have also adopted a subjective approach to recklessness.... That said, subjective recklessness as used in the criminal law is a familiar and workable standard that is consistent with the Cruel and Unusual Punishments Clause as interpreted in our cases, and we adopt it as the test for "deliberate indifference" under the Eighth Amendment.

2

Our decision that Eighth Amendment liability requires consciousness of a risk is thus based on the Constitution and our cases, not merely on a parsing of the phrase "deliberate indifference." ...

We are no more persuaded by petitioner's argument that, without an objective test for deliberate indifference, prison officials will be free to ignore obvious dangers to inmates. Under the test we adopt today, an Eighth Amendment claimant need not show that a prison official acted or failed to act believing that harm actually would befall an inmate; it is enough that the official acted or failed to act despite his knowledge of a substantial risk of serious harm.... We doubt that a subjective approach will present prison officials with any serious motivation "to take refuge in the zone between 'ignorance of obvious risks' and 'actual knowledge of risks.'" Brief for Petitioner 27. Whether a prison official had the requisite knowledge of a substantial risk is a question of fact subject to demonstration in the usual ways, including inference from circumstantial evidence ... and a factfinder may conclude that a prison official knew of a substantial risk from the very fact that the risk was obvious. Cf. LaFave & Scott § 3.7, p. 335 ("[I]f the risk is obvious, so that a reasonable man would realize it, we might well infer that [the defendant] did in fact realize it; but the inference cannot be conclusive, for we know that people are not always conscious of what reasonable people would be conscious of"). For example, if an Eighth Amendment plaintiff presents evidence showing that a substantial risk of inmate attacks was "longstanding, pervasive, well-documented, or expressly noted by prison officials in the past, and the circumstances suggest that the defendant-official being sued had been exposed to information concerning the risk and thus 'must have known' about it, then such evidence could be sufficient to permit a trier of fact to find that the defendant-official had actual knowledge of the risk." Brief for Respondents 22.[8]

---

8. While the obviousness of a risk is not conclusive and a prison official may show that the obvious escaped him ... he would not escape liability if the evidence showed that he merely refused to verify underlying facts that he strongly suspected to be true, or declined to confirm inferences of risk that he strongly suspected to exist (as when a prison official is aware of a high probability of facts indicating that one prisoner has planned an attack on another but resists opportunities to obtain final confirmation; or when a prison official knows that some diseases are communicable and that a single needle is being used to administer flu shots to prisoners but refuses to listen to a subordinate who he strongly suspects will attempt to explain the associated risk of transmitting disease). When instructing juries in deliberate indifference cases with such issues of proof, courts should be careful to ensure that the requirement of subjective culpability is not lost. It is not enough merely to find that a reasonable

Nor may a prison official escape liability for deliberate indifference by showing that, while he was aware of an obvious, substantial risk to inmate safety, he did not know that the complainant was especially likely to be assaulted by the specific prisoner who eventually committed the assault. The question under the Eighth Amendment is whether prison officials, acting with deliberate indifference, exposed a prisoner to a sufficiently substantial "risk of serious damage to his future health," ... and it does not matter whether the risk comes from a single source or multiple sources, any more than it matters whether a prisoner faces an excessive risk of attack for reasons personal to him or because all prisoners in his situation face such a risk. See Brief for Respondents 15 (stating that a prisoner can establish exposure to a sufficiently serious risk of harm" by showing that he belongs to an identifiable group of prisoners who are frequently singled out for violent attack by other inmates"). If, for example, prison officials were aware that inmate "rape was so common and uncontrolled that some potential victims dared not sleep [but] instead ... would leave their beds and spend the night clinging to the bars nearest the guards' station," ... it would obviously be irrelevant to liability that the officials could not guess beforehand precisely who would attack whom. *Cf. Helling*, *supra*, 509 U.S., at 33 (observing that the Eighth Amendment requires a remedy for exposure of inmates to "infectious maladies" such as hepatitis and venereal disease "even though the possible infection might not affect all of those exposed")....

Because, however, prison officials who lacked knowledge of a risk cannot be said to have inflicted punishment, it remains open to the officials to prove that they were unaware even of an obvious risk to inmate health or safety. That a trier of fact may infer knowledge from the obvious, in other words, does not mean that it must do so. Prison officials charged with deliberate indifference might show, for example, that they did not know of the underlying facts indicating a sufficiently substantial danger and that they were therefore unaware of a danger, or that they knew the underlying facts but believed (albeit unsoundly) that the risk to which the facts gave rise was insubstantial or nonexistent.

In addition, prison officials who actually knew of a substantial risk to inmate health or safety may be found free from liability if they responded reasonably to the risk, even if the harm ultimately was not averted. A prison official's duty under the Eighth Amendment is to ensure "reasonable safety," ... a standard that incorporates due regard for prison officials' "unenviable task of keeping dangerous men in safe custody under humane conditions,".... Whether one puts it in terms of duty or deliberate indifference, prison officials who act reasonably cannot be found liable under the Cruel and Unusual Punishments Clause.

We address, finally, petitioner's argument that a subjective deliberate indifference test will unjustly require prisoners to suffer physical injury before obtaining court-ordered correction of objectively inhumane prison conditions. "It would," indeed,

---

person would have known, or that the defendant should have known, and juries should be instructed accordingly.

"be odd to deny an injunction to inmates who plainly proved an unsafe, life-threatening condition in their prison on the ground that nothing yet had happened to them." ... But nothing in the test we adopt today clashes with that common sense. Petitioner's argument is flawed for the simple reason that "[o]ne does not have to await the consummation of threatened injury to obtain preventive relief." ... Consistently with this principle, a subjective approach to deliberate indifference does not require a prisoner seeking "a remedy for unsafe conditions [to] await a tragic event [such as an] actua[l] assaul[t] before obtaining relief." *Helling*, *supra*, at 33–34.

...

Accordingly, we reject petitioner's arguments and hold that a prison official may be held liable under the Eighth Amendment for denying humane conditions of confinement only if he knows that inmates face a substantial risk of serious harm and disregards that risk by failing to take reasonable measures to abate it.

III. A

Against this backdrop, we consider whether the District Court's disposition of petitioner's complaint, summarily affirmed without briefing by the Court of Appeals for the Seventh Circuit, comports with Eighth Amendment principles. We conclude that the appropriate course is to remand.

...

The summary judgment record does not so clearly establish respondents' entitlement to judgment as a matter of law on the issue of subjective knowledge that we can simply assume the absence of error below. For example, in papers filed in opposition to respondents' summary-judgment motion, petitioner pointed to respondents' admission that petitioner is a "non-violent" transsexual who, because of petitioner's "youth and feminine appearance" is "likely to experience a great deal of sexual pressure" in prison.... And petitioner recounted a statement by one of the respondents, then warden of the penitentiary in Lewisburg, Pennsylvania, who told petitioner that there was "a high probability that [petitioner] could not safely function at USP-Lewisburg," *id.*, at 109, an incident confirmed in a published District Court opinion.

...

[W]e think it proper to remand for reconsideration of petitioner's Rule 56(f) motion and, whether additional discovery is permitted or not, for application of the Eighth Amendment principles explained above.[10].... The judgment of the Court of Appeals is vacated, and the case is remanded for further proceedings consistent with this opinion.

---

10. The District Court's opinion is open to the reading that it required not only advance notification of a substantial risk of assault, but also advance notification of a substantial risk of assault posed by a particular fellow prisoner. See App. 124 (referring to "a specific threat to [a prisoner's] safety"). The Eighth Amendment, however, imposes no such requirement....

Justice BLACKMUN, concurring.

I agree with Justice STEVENS that inhumane prison conditions violate the Eighth Amendment even if no prison official has an improper, subjective state of mind. This Court's holding in *Wilson v. Seiter*, 501 U.S. 294 (1991), to the effect that barbaric prison conditions may be beyond the reach of the Eighth Amendment if no prison official can be deemed individually culpable, in my view is insupportable in principle and is inconsistent with our precedents interpreting the Cruel and Unusual Punishments Clause. Whether the Constitution has been violated "should turn on the character of the punishment rather than the motivation of the individual who inflicted it." *Estelle v. Gamble*, 429 U.S. 97, 116 (1976) (STEVENS, J., dissenting). *Wilson v. Seiter* should be overruled.

Although I do not go along with the Court's reliance on *Wilson* in defining the "deliberate indifference" standard, I join the Court's opinion, because it creates no new obstacles for prison inmates to overcome, and it sends a clear message to prison officials that their affirmative duty under the Constitution to provide for the safety of inmates is not to be taken lightly. Under the Court's decision today, prison officials may be held liable for failure to remedy a risk so obvious and substantial that the officials must have known about it, and prisoners need not "'await a tragic event [such as an] actua[l] assaul[t] before obtaining relief[.]'" [quoting majority].

Homosexual rape or other violence among prison inmates serves absolutely no penological purpose.... The horrors experienced by many young inmates, particularly those who, like petitioner, are convicted of nonviolent offenses, border on the unimaginable. Prison rape not only threatens the lives of those who fall prey to their aggressors, but is potentially devastating to the human spirit. Shame, depression, and a shattering loss of self-esteem accompany the perpetual terror the victim thereafter must endure.... Unable to fend for himself without the protection of prison officials, the victim finds himself at the mercy of larger, stronger, and ruthless inmates. Although formally sentenced to a term of incarceration, many inmates discover that their punishment, even for nonviolent offenses like credit card fraud or tax evasion, degenerates into a reign of terror unmitigated by the protection supposedly afforded by prison officials....

The fact that our prisons are badly overcrowded and understaffed may well explain many of the shortcomings of our penal systems. But our Constitution sets minimal standards governing the administration of punishment in this country, ... and thus it is no answer to the complaints of the brutalized inmate that the resources are unavailable to protect him from what, in reality, is nothing less than torture....

...

Wilson's myopic focus on the intentions of prison officials is also mistaken. Where a legislature refuses to fund a prison adequately, the resulting barbaric conditions should not be immune from constitutional scrutiny simply because no prison official acted culpably. *Wilson* failed to recognize that "state-sanctioned punishment consists not so much of specific acts attributable to individual state officials, but more of a cumulative agglomeration of action (and inaction) on an institutional level." ... The responsibility for subminimal conditions in any prison inevitably is diffuse, and often borne, at least in part, by the legislature. Yet, regardless of what state actor or institution caused the harm and with what intent, the experience of the inmate is the same. A punishment is simply no less cruel or unusual because its harm is unintended. In view of this obvious fact, there is no reason to believe that, in adopting the Eighth Amendment, the Framers intended to prohibit cruel and unusual punishments only when they were inflicted intentionally....

The Cruel and Unusual Punishments Clause was not adopted to protect prison officials with arguably benign intentions from lawsuits. The Eighth Amendment guarantees each prisoner that reasonable measures will be taken to ensure his safety. Where a prisoner can prove that no such reasonable steps were taken and, as a result, he experienced severe pain or suffering without any penological justification, the Eighth Amendment is violated regardless of whether there is an easily identifiable wrongdoer with poor intentions.

...

Justice THOMAS, concurring in the judgment.

Prisons are necessarily dangerous places; they house society's most antisocial and violent people in close proximity with one another. Regrettably, "[s]ome level of brutality and sexual aggression among [prisoners] is inevitable no matter what the guards do ... unless all prisoners are locked in their cells 24 hours a day and sedated." [citing 7th Circuit opinion]. Today, in an attempt to rectify such unfortunate conditions, the Court further refines the "National Code of Prison Regulation," otherwise known as the Cruel and Unusual Punishments Clause. *Hudson v. McMillian*, 503 U.S. 1, 28 (1992) (THOMAS, J., dissenting).

I adhere to my belief, expressed in *Hudson* and *Helling v. McKinney*, 509 U.S. 25 (1993) (THOMAS, J., dissenting), that "judges or juries—but not jailers—impose 'punishment.'" *Id.*, at 40. "[P]unishment," from the time of the Founding through the present day, "has always meant a 'fine, penalty, or confinement inflicted upon a person by the authority of the law and the judgment and sentence of a court, for some crime or offense committed by him.'" *Id.*, at 38 (quoting Black's Law Dictionary 1234 (6th ed. 1990)).... Conditions of confinement are not punishment in any recognized sense of the term, unless imposed as part of a sentence. *See Helling*, *supra*, at 42 (THOMAS, J., dissenting). As an original matter, therefore, this case would be an easy one for me: Because the unfortunate attack that befell petitioner was not part of his sentence, it did not constitute "punishment" under the Eighth Amendment.

[H]owever, we do not write on a clean slate. Beginning with *Estelle v. Gamble*, 429 U.S. 97 (1976), the Court's prison condition jurisprudence has been guided, not by the text of the Constitution, but rather by "evolving standards of decency that mark the progress of a maturing society." *Id.*, at 102 (internal quotation marks omitted).... I continue to doubt the legitimacy of that mode of constitutional decisionmaking, the logical result of which, in this context, is to transform federal judges into superintendents of prison conditions nationwide.... Although *Estelle* loosed the Eighth Amendment from its historical moorings, the Court is now unwilling to accept the full consequences of its decision and therefore resorts to the "subjective" (state of mind) component of post-*Estelle* Eighth Amendment analysis in an attempt to contain what might otherwise be unbounded liability for prison officials under the Cruel and Unusual Punishments Clause....

Although I disagree with the constitutional predicate of the Court's analysis, I share the Court's view that petitioner's theory of liability—that a prison official can be held liable for risks to prisoner safety of which he was ignorant but should have known—fails under even "a straightforward application of *Estelle*." *Helling*, *supra*, 509 U.S., at 42 (THOMAS, J., dissenting). In adopting the "deliberate indifference" standard for challenges to prison conditions, *Estelle* held that mere "inadverten[ce]" or "negligen[ce]" does not violate the Eighth Amendment. 429 U.S., at 105–106.... Petitioner's suggested "should have known" standard is nothing but a negligence standard, as the Court's discussion implicitly assumes.... Thus, even under *Estelle*, petitioner's theory of liability necessarily fails.

...

Even though the Court takes a step in the right direction by adopting a restrictive definition of deliberate indifference, I cannot join the Court's opinion. For the reasons expressed more fully in my dissenting opinions in *Hudson* and *Helling*, I remain unwilling to subscribe to the view, adopted by *ipse dixit* in *Estelle*, that the Eighth Amendment regulates prison conditions not imposed as part of a sentence. Indeed, "[w]ere the issue squarely presented, ... I might vote to overrule *Estelle*." *Helling*, 509 U.S., at 42 (THOMAS, J., dissenting).... For these reasons, I concur in the Court's judgment. In doing so, however, I remain hopeful that in a proper case the Court will reconsider *Estelle* in light of the constitutional text and history.

For further discussion

If you were counsel to a prison, where would you recommend that transgender inmates be housed? Dee Farmer sued prison officials once for housing her with men and once for housing her in administrative segregation. Is the answer to house her with women? County jail officials in Maine who housed Cheyenne Lamson, a transgender inmate, with female inmates were sued for doing so—by a female inmate. In *Crosby v. Reynolds*, 763 F.Supp. 666 (D. Me. 1991), the court granted the government officials qualified immunity, reasoning:

> The Jail officials here were confronted with a situation that had no perfect answer. Lamson did not want to be segregated; it was physically and psychologically unsafe to place Lamson with males; and, as it turned out, some female inmates such as the plaintiff objected to Lamson being housed with them.

Id. at 669–70.

Exercise 2-E: Applying *Farmer* at the 12(b)(6) Stage

Do the factual allegations below state an 8th Amendment claim?

- What arguments could defendant Dr. Garcia make in support of a 12(b)(6) motion?
- Is the injury objectively serious?
- Was Dr. Garcia subjectively deliberately indifferent to the safety of plaintiff?
- What responses could plaintiff make?

Facts

Plaintiff Jackey Bond, a state inmate at Stateville Correctional Center, acting *pro se*, sued various physicians and prison officials under 42 U.S.C. § 1983, alleging deliberate indifference to his medical needs in violation of his Eighth Amendment rights....

When Mr. Bond was first transferred to Stateville ... he complained of back and throat pain that went untreated by other defendants not party to this motion. [Several months later], he saw an ear, nose and throat (E.N.T.) specialist who found two cysts on his vocal chords and indicated that he was regurgitating acid from his stomach that was eating away at the lining in his throat. The E.N.T. specialist prescribed Tagamet for Mr. Bond and suggested that he see a gastroenterologist if his acid reflux problem did not improve. Mr. Bond also saw a "voice specialist" who likewise recommended seeing a gastroenterologist, because until the acid reflux problem was solved, there was nothing he could do for Mr. Bond's throat.

[Several months later], Mr. Bond was transferred to Pinckneyville Correctional Center. While there, Mr. Bond saw Dr. Garcia. Mr. Bond alleges that Dr. Garcia failed to respond to his requests for treatment and ignored the recommendations of the E.N.T. and voice specialists at Stateville that Mr. Bond see a gastroenterologist. Mr. Bond alleges that Dr. Garcia told him he would simply have to live with the cysts, acid reflux, and back pain for the rest of his life. Mr. Bond alleges that his throat condition worsened, and that he can hardly swallow or talk.

To guide reading of interview with plaintiff's counsel

This is an interview with Elizabeth Alexander, former Director of the American Civil Liberties Union (ACLU) National Prison Project and plaintiff's counsel for two Supreme Court decisions in this Chapter, *Wilson* and *Farmer*. In reading the interview, consider what motivations can sustain a lawyer's choice of career. Consider what role extrinsic rewards and intrinsic motivations might play in influencing your own career path.

Interview with Elizabeth Alexander

Q: What initially drew you to prisoner rights litigation?

A: When I moved to Madison, Wisconsin in 1973 when my husband started teaching, I was seven months pregnant. At the time, that was not helpful in job interviewing. I got a part-time job in the clinic of the University of Wisconsin Law School, where my husband was teaching. I supervised law students providing services to prisoners and mental patients in state facilities. Under the law school's contract with the state, we could not file actions regarding conditions of confinement in the facilities. I came to be outraged at the physical conditions and emotional abuse of the patients at the maximum security mental hospital where I was assigned, so when a job opened up that involved litigating conditions of confinement in the state's prisons, I leaped at the opportunity and have been involved in conditions of confinement litigation ever since.

Q: Why has it been a rewarding career?

A: I am concerned about the power imbalance and inherent potential of abuse when someone is incarcerated, particularly because of the lack of effective oversight. I enjoy litigation and this gives me the assurance that the work I do is also morally sound.

Q: What do you think is the most pressing issue currently confronting jail and prison administrators?

A: The gross overuse of the criminal justice sanction. The U.S. has the highest rate of incarceration in the entire world and holds almost one-quarter of the world's prisoners. If all the prisoners and jail detainees were in one city, it would be the fourth largest city in the country. The fundamental cause of our infatuation with incarceration is race: we would not tolerate this system if it applied to whites and blacks in the same manner. Economic and social disparities among ethnic groups are worsened by this disproportionate imprisonment, because those coming out of prison are permanently in large part exiled from the economic and political system.

Q: Dee Farmer sued once for being housed in administrative segregation and once for being housed in the general male population. Is there a solution to housing pre-operative transgender inmates that you would recommend?

A: The decision should be made on a case-by-case basis with a presumption for assigning the prisoner to his or her chosen gender, with continuation of treatment to maintain secondary sexual characteristics of the chosen gender.

Q: In your long litigation career, do you have a favorite case? Why is it your favorite?

A: Ironically, my favorite case is not a prison case. When you win a prison case, you may have removed the constitutional violations, but it is still a soul-killing prison. Before I went into conditions of confinement litigation, my first year out of law school in 1971, I spent a year preparing an urban renewal case for trial in the South End of Dearborn, Michigan, where [the city was planning to] tear down a multi-ethnic neighborhood that was growing increasingly Middle Eastern. Ultimately, as a result of the lawsuit, the city abandoned its quest. Homeowners got payments and the city built new amenities in the neighborhood. I went back to the South End several years ago and was overjoyed to see the vibrant community, better than ever, that now thrives in the South End. It is now the largest Middle Eastern community in the country. I am very proud of having a role, in league with the community itself, in saving it.

Q: Do you have any guidance for students thinking of representing prisoners? For students thinking of defending civil rights claims against government officials?

A: Just one piece of general advice: do not jump to the conclusion that your client is telling the truth and also do not assume that your client is lying. Equally important, never assume that the government is telling the truth.[2]

F. Legislative Reaction to the Problem of Prison Rape

Nearly a decade after *Farmer*, Congress enacted the Prison Rape Elimination Act of 2003, Pub. L. No. 108-79, 117 Stat. 972 (codified at 42 U.S.C. § 15601 et seq. (2006)). Congress made the following findings:

> [E]xperts have conservatively estimated that at least 13 percent of the inmates in the United States have been sexually assaulted in prison. Many inmates have suffered repeated assaults. Under this estimate, nearly 200,000 inmates now incarcerated have been or will be the victims of prison rape. The total number of inmates who have been sexually assaulted in the past 20 years likely exceeds 1,000,000.
>
> (3) Inmates with mental illness are at increased risk of sexual victimization. America's jails and prisons house more mentally ill individuals than all of the Nation's psychiatric hospitals combined....

---

2. Email from Elizabeth Alexander to Sarah Ricks (Nov. 27, 2007).

(4) Young first-time offenders are at increased risk of sexual victimization. Juveniles are 5 times more likely to be sexually assaulted in adult rather than juvenile facilities—often within the first 48 hours of incarceration.

(5) Most prison staff are not adequately trained or prepared to prevent, report, or treat inmate sexual assaults.

...

(7) ... Prison rape undermines the public health by contributing to the spread of [HIV/AIDS, sexually transmitted diseases, tuberculosis, and hepatitis B and C] and often giving a potential death sentence to its victims.

...

(10) Prison rape increases the level of homicides and other violence against inmates and staff, and the risk of insurrections and riots.

(11) Victims of prison rape suffer severe physical and psychological effects that hinder their ability to integrate into the community and maintain stable employment upon their release from prison. They are thus more likely to become homeless and/or require government assistance.

...

(14) The high incidence of prison rape undermines the effectiveness and efficiency of United States Government expenditures through grant programs such as those dealing with health care; mental health care; disease prevention; crime prevention, investigation, and prosecution; prison construction, maintenance, and operation; race relations; poverty; unemployment and homelessness.... [because it]:

...

(B) increases the levels of violence, directed at inmates and at staff, within prisons;

(C) increases health care expenditures, both inside and outside of prison systems, and reduces the effectiveness of disease prevention programs by substantially increasing the incidence and spread of HIV, AIDS, tuberculosis, hepatitis B and C, and other diseases;

(D) increases mental health care expenditures, both inside and outside of prison systems, by substantially increasing the rate of post-traumatic stress disorder, depression, suicide, and the exacerbation of existing mental illnesses among current and former inmates;

(E) increases the risks of recidivism, civil strife, and violent crime by individuals who have been brutalized by prison rape....

The Prison Rape Elimination Act created a national Commission to study the incidence of sexual abuse in correctional facilities and to develop standards for correctional facilities nationwide to move toward eliminating prison rape. Below is an excerpt from the Commission's report.

Questions to guide reading of the Prison Rape Report

1. According to the Commission, why is prison overcrowding linked to sexual abuse?
2. According to testimony before the Commission, why are some corrections officials supportive of court oversight of prisons?
3. According to testimony by rape survivors, what are some of the disincentives to complain about sexual abuse to correctional officials?

The Prison Rape Elimination Commission Report

(June 23, 2009)[3]

FACING THE NUMBERS

Dramatic increases in the prisoner population over the past 20 years are due more to legislative changes than to increases in crime rates. The "war on drugs" that began in the 1980s and continued over the last two decades resulted in new policies requiring incarceration for drug-related offenses that previously involved primarily probation or diversion. Coupled with mandatory-minimum sentences, many more people were incarcerated and for longer periods of time. The "three-strikes" laws, introduced in 1993, mandated sentences from 15 years to life in prison for persons convicted of three crimes. As of 2008, nearly half of the States had some form of a "three-strikes" law, although the criteria for applying the law vary across jurisdictions....

Along with the rapidly increasing number of people incarcerated, the demographics of those individuals have changed in ways that have flooded facilities with individuals who are especially vulnerable to sexual abuse. The number of incarcerated adult women increased by 757 percent from 1977 to 2007. Legislative changes in 45 States since 1992 also made it easier to incarcerate juveniles with adults....

HARD TO HEAL

... Sexual abuse experienced in any environment commonly invokes shock, numbness, withdrawal, and denial. Almost all victims of an invasive or violent sexual assault develop some symptoms of posttraumatic stress disorder (PTSD) in the weeks after the attack. These include numbing, intrusive thoughts, nightmares, insomnia, flashbacks during which the victim vividly re-experiences the event, outbursts of anger or irritability, and panic attacks. For some victims, PTSD symptoms resolve several months after the incident; for others, PTSD becomes chronic....

...

3. Nat'l. Prison Rape Elimination Comm'n, National Prison Rape Elimination Commission Report (2009), https://www.ncjrs.gov/pdffiles1/226680.pdf.

The closed nature of correctional facilities can lead to especially devastating effects for sexual abuse victims. In confinement, victims cannot hide from or escape their perpetrators; they are trapped with their assailant unless corrections officials intervene. The constant threat of subsequent abuse and physical proximity to danger are likely to increase the risk of developing PTSD and other aftereffects. The consequences of sexual abuse may be worse for those who are young, have a past history of sexual abuse, or have a preexisting mental illness....

ZERO TOLERANCE "WITH TEETH"

[A culture of zero tolerance for sexual abuse, means that s]taff and incarcerated individuals understand what constitutes sexual abuse, know penalties exist for perpetration by prisoners or staff, and believe management will treat all incidents seriously.... Staff also know that there are penalties for simply standing by when sexual abuse is occurring and for non-reporting, whether the abuse is perpetrated by prisoners or other staff....

Zero-tolerance policies prohibit *any* sexual contact between staff, volunteers, or contractors and incarcerated individuals. Moreover, all forms of forced or coercive sexual contact occurring among incarcerated persons will be fully investigated, sanctioned (if authority to do so exists), and referred for prosecution if the prohibited conduct violates State criminal laws.

"TURNED OUT" OR TRAUMATIZED

T.J. Parsell was raped for the first time in 1978 when he entered Riverside Correctional Facility in Ionia, Michigan. His experience illustrates how being known as a victim literally attracts predators. "I hoped no one would find out about it, but as I walked the yard in a daze, other inmates pointed and laughed," he told the Commission. "Once an inmate has been turned out, he's considered a target wherever he goes." According to Robert Dumond, a researcher and clinician with expertise in prison sexual abuse, the culture inside men's correctional facilities makes it extremely difficult for prisoners to change such perceptions, even over time....

Even if survivors are not branded as easy targets, the emotional scars of being previously sexually abused—either inside the facility or previously in the community—can create a vulnerability to future abuse. Sexual abuse prior to incarceration appears to be much more common among incarcerated women than men. Studies found that from 31 to 59 percent of incarcerated women reported being sexually abused as children, and 23 to 53 percent reported experiencing sexual abuse as adults. The Bureau of Justice Statistics also found that incarcerated mentally ill prisoners were more than twice as likely to have a history of prior sexual abuse as the general incarcerated population. Past victimization may contribute to feelings of helplessness in the face of danger and inhibit victims' ability to seek protection....

Peddle v. Sawyer documents how a male corrections officer in a Federal women's prison in Danbury, Connecticut, sexually assaulted a prisoner, Sharon Peddle, whose case file described a history of sexual abuse and vulnerability to being manipulated by men she viewed as authority figures. The officer, who had been investigated several times for sexually abusing other prisoners, read Peddle's case file without authorization. He then sexually assaulted her regularly throughout 1995 and 1996 and threatened to have her transferred to another facility, away from her family members, if she told anyone or refused to submit to him. Other officers were aware of the abuse, and some even helped to facilitate it. A fellow officer in the housing unit would call Peddle out of her cell and leave her with the abusive officer in an area where they would not be observed. Even after she was reassigned to a special mental health unit for victims of chronic abuse, the officer followed her. He arranged to be reassigned to the unit and "regularly woke Ms. Peddle and took her to the TV room or stairwell where he compelled her to submit to oral and vaginal sex." After more than a year of raping Peddle, the officer was arrested and pled guilty to six counts of sexual abuse.

PROTECTION NOT SEGREGATION

...

The Commission's standards allow facilities to segregate victims or potential victims of sexual abuse only as a last resort. The standard permits facilities to place individuals in protective custody, especially if they request it, but only on a short-term basis.... When prisoners at high risk of victimization cannot be safely housed anywhere other than in segregation, the Commission suggests that facilities consider a transfer to another facility. The Commission discourages the creation of specialized units for vulnerable groups, and the standard specifically prohibits housing assignments based solely on a person's sexual orientation, gender identity, or genital status because this practice can lead to labeling that is both demoralizing and dangerous....

THE RISKS OF CROWDING

...

Crowding is both a risk factor—environmental rather than personal—and a real barrier to carving out safe spaces for vulnerable prisoners. In 2007, 19 States and the Federal system were operating at more than 100 percent of their highest capacity....

Forced to accommodate a larger prisoner population than most facilities were designed to house, administrators have taken drastic measures. Cells designed for one person now hold two, with double-celling now the norm in many facilities, significantly increasing the opportunities for sexual abuse. Many corrections administrators make use of any unoccupied space as housing. Facilities convert day rooms, cafeterias, classrooms, storage areas, and basements into makeshift dormitories, with intrinsic risk for abuse and supervision challenges.... As a facility's population expands, prisoners also have fewer or no opportunities to participate in education and job training. Idleness and the stress of living in crowded conditions lead to conflict....

WHEN PROTECTION REQUIRES COURT INTERVENTION

...

Corrections officials themselves have told us that they rely in part on litigation to command the resources they need to protect prisoners from sexual abuse. In her testimony before a House Judiciary Subcommittee, former Warden of San Quentin State Prison and former head of the California Department of Corrections and Rehabilitation Jeanne Woodford said, "Any good prison administrator should not fear the involvement of the courts. From my experience over the last 30 years as a corrections official, I have come to understand the importance of court oversight. The courts have been especially crucial during recent years, as California's prison population has exploded, and prison officials have been faced with the daunting task of running outdated and severely overcrowded facilities.... All of this court intervention has been necessary because of my state's unwillingness to provide the Department with the resources it requires. These lawsuits have helped the state make dramatic improvements to its deeply flawed prison system."

...

Garrett Cunningham was raped in the prison laundry by the officer charged with supervising his work.... Cunningham testified that, "When I screamed from the terrible pain, [the officer] told me to shut up.... After it was over, I was dazed. He took me to the shower in handcuffs, turned on the water and put me under it. I was crying under the shower and saw blood running down my legs."

Afterward, the officer warned Cunningham that if he reported what happened he would have him transferred to a rougher unit where prison gang members would rape him repeatedly. He told Cunningham that prison officials were his friends and would do nothing. Cunningham was too frightened to file a grievance. As he testified before a House Judiciary Subcommittee, "At first, I didn't dare tell anyone about the rape.... [To begin the process of exhausting the facility's administrative remedies] I would have had to file a first prison grievance within 15 days.... I had no idea, at that point, that I was even required to file a grievance in order to bring a lawsuit. Even if I had known, during those first 15 days, my only thoughts were about suicide and ... how to get myself into a safe place ... so I would not be raped again." ...

"For me, I have found no justice," Cunningham told members of the Subcommittee. "Because I didn't file a grievance with the friends of [the assailant] within 15 days of being raped by him, I was forever barred from filing a lawsuit about it in Federal court. My hope is that Congress will acknowledge the realities of prison life, which makes 'exhausting administrative remedies' under the [Prison Litigation Reform Act] impossible at times."

PROTECTION FROM RETALIATION

Necole Brown was sexually abused over the course of 5 years by a corrections officer she first encountered in a Michigan State prison in 1996 who stalked and victimized her even while she was on parole. In her testimony to the Commission, she recalled that the officer "constantly threatened me, that if I told anybody, he would make sure that I would either be punished by being sent to administrative seg[regation] or that I would lose my privileges such as the phone, visits with my family and friends, and even that I would not be allowed to leave the prison ... He had the ability to write me up for so-called misconduct any time he wanted ... [T]he more tickets I got, the more good time I lost, meaning the release on parole would be delayed. I felt like I had to do the things that he asked me to do so I could survive in prison and to be able to come home." When Brown finally reported the abuse and sought help from an attorney, the retaliation grew worse and involved other staff. "Correctional officers would interrupt my attorney visits, withhold my mail, search me or try to degrade me in front of other people for no reason."

Victims of sexual abuse are silenced by threats as well as by actions taken against them, and some are punished when they do speak out. Retaliation by staff can include unwarranted disciplinary action, unfavorable changes in housing and work assignments, and threats of violence against the victim or even the victim's family.... An incarcerated person who reports sexual abuse perpetrated by another prisoner also risks retaliation, which can range from violence, to being shunned by other prisoners, to being falsely reported for breaking facility rules.

...

The culture of the correctional environment can make staff and offenders fearful of reporting. In *Baron v. Hickey*, a correctional officer reported misconduct that he observed in his facility in 2003. As a result, his tires were slashed, he was called a "rat," and coworkers threatened him. He complained more than 30 times to leadership and ultimately resigned. He filed suit against the agency for these retaliatory actions and was awarded $500,000 in damages.

...

ANALYZING THE EVIDENCE

In situations where one prisoner has allegedly abused another prisoner ... [d]istinguishing between consensual and nonconsensual sex in an environment in which sex is traded for protection or comfort is difficult, especially absent physical injury and witnesses.... Although consensual sex may be a reality in correctional facilities for women as well as for men, when confronted with an allegation of abuse between prisoners, investigators must not erroneously or prematurely conclude that the encounter was not forced.

For further discussion

1. Testimony before the Commission included the observation that workplace culture in hierarchical organizations like correctional facilities is established "from the top down," which suggests the importance of holding supervisors responsible if they condone, acquiesce in, or are indifferent to the sexual abuse of inmates. While *respondeat superior* liability is prohibited by § 1983, courts long have recognized supervisory liability under § 1983. Yet the Supreme Court has called into question the continued existence of supervisory liability under § 1983, *Ashcroft v. Iqbal*, 556 U.S. 662 (2009). Supervisory liability is explored further in Chapter 12.

2. As explained earlier in this Chapter, Dee Farmer sued correctional officials for segregating Farmer in protective custody and then sued different correctional officials for housing Farmer in the general population. In the excerpt above, the Prison Rape Elimination Commission discourages use of segregation except as a temporary measure, discourages the creation of specialized units for vulnerable groups, and counsels against housing based on sexual orientation or gender identity. Does the Commission report change your view of where correctional administrators should house sexually vulnerable prisoners?

3. The Commission Report states that it is difficult to distinguish consensual from nonconsensual sex because in correctional facilities, "sex is traded for protection." For correctional administrators, is there tension between the duty to protect the health of the inmates by, for example, distributing condoms in male correctional facilities, and the duty to detect and punish sexual abuse?

4. Garrett Cunningham, one of the rape survivors quoted by the Commission Report, also testified before the Vera Institute of Justice. Transcript of his Vera Institute testimony and the testimony of others is available online.[4] To read the testimony of other survivors of prison rape, please visit the "Survivor Stories" page at the Just Detention International website.[5]

5. In the above excerpt, rape survivor Garrett Cunningham testified that in the weeks following his rape by a correctional officer, he did not file a grievance with prison officials in part because he was traumatized, in part because of threats of retaliation by the rapist, and in part because of his ignorance of the necessity of filing a prison grievance in order to later file a federal lawsuit, called an exhaustion requirement. Consider Mr. Cunningham's situation when reading about the exhaustion requirement of the Prison Litigation Reform Act, examined in Chapter 10.

6. In May 2012, pursuant to the Prison Rape Elimination Act, the Justice Department released administrative regulations to prevent, detect, and respond to sexual abuse in prison. The Justice Department described the regulations as the first federal effort to set standards to protect inmates in adult prisons and jails, lockups, community confinement facilities, and juvenile facilities at the federal, state, and local levels. While the final rule is binding on the Federal Bureau of Prisons, states that do not comply with the standards are subject to a reduction in federal funds they would otherwise receive for prisons. Below are excerpts from the Justice Department's summary of the new requirements.

Prevent: To prevent sexual abuse, the standards require, among other things, that facilities:

...

4. *See* Vera Inst. of Just., *Accounts of Life in Prison*, https://storage.googleapis.com/vera-web-assets/inline-downloads/Hearing-1-Accounts-of-Life-in-Prison.pdf (last visited July 13, 2019).

5. *See Survivor Stories*, Just Detention Int'l., https://justdetention.org/story/ (last visited July 10, 2019).

- Screen inmates for risk of being sexually abused or sexually abusive, and use screening information to inform housing, bed, work, education and program assignments;
- Develop and document a staffing plan that provides for adequate levels of staffing and, where applicable, video monitoring;
- Train employees on their responsibilities in preventing, recognizing and responding to sexual abuse;
- Perform background checks on prospective employees and not hire abusers;
- Prevent juveniles from being housed with adult inmates or having unsupervised contact with adult inmates in common spaces;
- Ban cross-gender pat-down searches of female inmates in prisons and jails and of both male and female residents of juvenile facilities;
- Incorporate unique vulnerabilities of lesbian, gay, bisexual, transgender, intersex and gender nonconforming inmates into training and screening protocols;
- Enable inmates to shower, perform bodily functions and change clothing without improper viewing by staff of the opposite gender;
- Restrict the use of solitary confinement as a means of protecting vulnerable inmates; and
- Enter into or renew contracts only with outside entities that agree to comply with the standards.

Detect: To detect sexual abuse, the standards require, among other things, that facilities:

- Make inmates aware of facility policies and inform them of how to report sexual abuse;
- Provide multiple channels for inmates to report sexual abuse, including by contacting an outside entity, and allow inmates to report abuse anonymously upon request;
- Provide a method for staff and other third parties to report abuse on behalf of an inmate;
- Develop policies to prevent and detect any retaliation against those who report sexual abuse or cooperate with investigations; and
- Ensure effective communication about facility policies and how to report sexual abuse with inmates with disabilities and inmates who are limited English proficient;

Respond: To respond to sexual abuse, the standards require, among other things, that facilities:

- Provide timely and appropriate medical and mental health care to victims of sexual abuse;

- Where available, provide access to victim advocates from rape crisis centers for emotional support services related to sexual abuse;
- Establish an evidence protocol to preserve evidence following an incident and offer victims no-cost access to forensic medical examinations;
- Investigate all allegations of sexual abuse promptly and thoroughly, and deem allegations substantiated if supported by a preponderance of the evidence;
- Discipline staff and inmate assailants appropriately, with termination as the presumptive disciplinary sanction for staff who commit sexual abuse;
- Allow inmates a full and fair opportunity to file grievances regarding sexual abuse so as to preserve their ability to seek judicial redress after exhausting administrative remedies; and
- Maintain records of incidents of abuse and use those records to inform future prevention planning.

See Dept. of Justice, *Justice Department Releases Final Rule to Prevent, Detect and Respond to Prison Rape* (May 17, 2012), *available at* http://www.justice.gov/opa/pr/2012/May/12-ag-635.html. The rule is available at: www.ojp.usdoj.gov/programs/pdfs/prea_final_rule.pdf.

G. Development of Doctrine in the Circuits: Applying the *Farmer* Standard to a Factual Record

---

Questions to guide reading of *Giroux*

1. Note that the district court approved the findings of a magistrate judge. What role do magistrate judges have in the federal court system?
2. Why did the First Circuit hold that Hartley could have had actual knowledge of a substantial risk of harm to Plaintiff even though he did not know the identity of the person who posed a threat to Plaintiff? How does *Farmer* support that reasoning?
3. Why did the First Circuit hold that Hartley's failure to act could constitute deliberate indifference to Plaintiff's safety?

Giroux v. Somerset County

178 F.3d 28 (1st Cir. 1999)

LIPEZ, Circuit Judge.

Shawn Giroux, a former inmate at the Somerset County Jail, brought suit pursuant to 42 U.S.C. § 1983 against one prison employee (Sergeant Hartley) ... after he was assaulted by another inmate. Giroux alleges a violation of the Eighth Amendment prohibition of "cruel and unusual punishments"....

I. A. Facts

... Giroux was incarcerated in the Somerset County Jail in September 1995. On September 19, 1995, Deputy Doug Manson informed Giroux that a detective from the Somerset County Sheriff's Department wanted to speak with Giroux. Manson escorted Giroux from his cell to meet with the detective. Robert Tucker, an inmate with whom Giroux shared a common day room,[2] threatened Giroux in the presence of Manson upon hearing that Giroux was going to meet with the detective. Robert Tucker apparently thought that Giroux was going to be asked for information about Tucker. After meeting with the detective, Giroux was escorted to a new cell; his belongings had been collected and moved for him. Although no reason for Giroux's September 19th cell change is reflected in the jail's records, it is a fair inference that Giroux was relocated in response to Robert Tucker's threats.

The next day, September 20, 1995, Robert Tucker again threatened Giroux as he was taken past Robert Tucker's cell on his way to breakfast. While at breakfast, Scott Tucker, Robert Tucker's brother, sat down at a table with Giroux and communicated a veiled threat to Giroux and two other inmates, Tony St. Pierre and Wayne Curtis, telling them that they were lucky that his brother Robert Tucker was "on the other side of the glass" or "on the opposite side of the window" (referring to the fact that they were separated from Robert Tucker during breakfast). Following breakfast on September 20th, Scott Tucker and other inmates who Giroux believed were in association with Robert and Scott Tucker passed by Giroux's cell and threatened Giroux, telling him "you're dead."

Later that day Giroux and fellow inmates St. Pierre and Curtis met with Jail Administrator Judith Thornton and, according to Giroux, requested protective custody due to the Tucker brothers' threats.[3] Although Thornton testified in her deposition that she has no recollection of such a meeting, jail records indicate that Giroux was placed on cell feed status on September 20, 1995, and Giroux is listed in jail records as being on cell feed status again on September 21, 1995. There is no policy in the record governing the use of cell feed status to protect inmates. Nevertheless, every employee deposed testified to the practice of using cell feeding as a protective device. Indeed, according to that testimony, the only reasons for an inmate to be placed on cell feed status are (1) health related or (2) as a form of protective custody from other inmates. Jail employees, including co-defendant and shift supervisor Sergeant Fred Hartley, testified that the inmate roster should have indicated the reason for

---

2. Cells in the jail accommodate two inmates. Each cell is connected to one other cell by a day room which is shared by all four inmates.

3. The defendants claimed, and continue to argue here, that prisoners may only request protective custody in writing and that no prisoner may be placed in protective custody without such a written request, absent extenuating circumstances. In contrast, the jail's D-243 policy covering "Special Management Inmates" simply refers to inmates in protective custody "at the request of the inmates or the jail staff." We need not determine whether Giroux formally requested protective custody because there is ample evidence from which a jury could conclude that he was, in fact, granted a form of protective custody.

Giroux's cell feed status. Although no reason for cell feeding Giroux is recorded in the jail's records, it is a fair inference that he was being cell fed because of threats against him.

Co-defendant Sergeant Fred Hartley was the shift supervisor on the evening and night of September 21, 1995. Giroux and eight or nine other inmates participated in the jail's visitation period that evening. After Giroux had been in the common visiting room for some time,[4] Scott Tucker was brought into the same visitation room. The record does not establish who escorted Giroux and Scott Tucker into the visitation room. According to policy, all the prisoners are subjected to a strip search after participating in visitation and before being returned to their cells. The inmates wait for this search in a holding cell in which they are under observation through a plexiglass window. No prison guards are physically present. After an argument began between Scott Tucker and another inmate in the holding cell, the other inmate was escorted out of the holding cell. Immediately thereafter, Scott Tucker began an argument with Giroux, and they exchanged words. Scott Tucker then physically assaulted Giroux, causing a broken nose, torn shoulder ligaments, and a head laceration which required stitches to close. Because Hartley was close by, distributing medication to other inmates, he was the first person to break up the fight between Scott Tucker and Giroux.

...

The district court, adopting the findings and conclusions of the magistrate judge, held that the evidence that Sergeant Hartley had violated Giroux's Eighth Amendment rights was insufficient and granted all defendants a summary judgment on the § 1983 claims. Although acknowledging a fair inference that Sergeant Hartley knew that Giroux was on cell feed status, the court noted that the Eighth Amendment requires an actual, subjective appreciation of a risk of harm in order to hold prison officials liable under the Cruel and Unusual Punishments Clause of the Eighth Amendment, and that Giroux had "presented no facts that Hartley knew of the threats to [Giroux's] life, or that those threats were made by an inmate who was in the holding cell with [Giroux]."

...

II.A. The Cruel and Unusual Punishments Clause of the Eighth Amendment

The Eighth Amendment prohibits "cruel and unusual punishments," and "it is now settled that 'the treatment a prisoner receives in prison and the conditions under which he is confined are subject to scrutiny under the Eighth Amendment.'" *Farmer v. Brennan*, 511 U.S. 825, 832 (1994) (quoting *Helling v. McKinney*, 509 U.S. 25, 31 (1993)). Prison officials have a duty to "provide humane conditions of confinement; prison officials must ensure that inmates receive adequate food, clothing, shelter, and medical care, and must 'take reasonable measures to guarantee the safety of the inmates.'" *Id.* (quoting *Hudson v. Palmer*, 468 U.S. 517, 526–27 (1984)). That duty

4. There was conflicting testimony as to whether a prisoner on cell feed status should be in a group visitation room with other inmates. There is no jail policy on this point in the record.

has its origins in the forced dependency of inmates: "Having incarcerated persons with demonstrated proclivities for antisocial criminal, and often violent, conduct, having stripped them of virtually every means of self-protection and foreclosed their access to outside aid, the government and its officials are not free to let the state of nature take its course." *Id.* at 833 (internal quotations and brackets omitted). Therefore, under the Eighth Amendment, "prison officials have a duty ... to protect prisoners from violence at the hands of other prisoners." *Id.*...

However, not every injury suffered by a prisoner at the hands of a fellow inmate gives rise to an Eighth Amendment claim. In order for a prison-conditions complaint[8] to state a violation of the Eighth Amendment, two requirements must be met. First, the alleged deprivation of adequate conditions must be objectively serious, *i.e.*, "the inmate must show that he is incarcerated under conditions posing a substantial risk of serious harm." *Id.* at 834. Second, the official involved must have had "a sufficiently culpable state of mind," *Wilson v. Seiter*, 501 U.S. 294, 299 (1991), described as "deliberate indifference" to inmate health or safety. *Farmer*, 511 U.S. at 834.[9] In this context, "deliberate indifference" means that "a prison official cannot be found liable under the Eighth Amendment for denying an inmate humane conditions of confinement unless the official knows of and disregards an excessive risk to inmate health or safety." *Id.* at 837. This standard, requiring an actual, subjective appreciation of risk, has been likened to the standard for determining criminal recklessness. *See id.* at 839–40 (holding that "subjective recklessness as used in the criminal law is a familiar and workable standard that is consistent with the Cruel and Unusual Punishments Clause as interpreted in our cases, and we adopt it as the test for 'deliberate indifference' under the Eighth Amendment"); *see also id.* at 837–38 (citing to Model Penal Code § 2.02(2)(c) and noting that criminal recklessness requires a person to "consciously disregar[d] a substantial risk of serious harm"). While the Supreme Court has admonished the lower courts to "be careful to ensure that the requirement of subjective culpability is not lost," *id.* at 843 n. 8, "[w]hether a prison official had the requisite knowledge of a substantial risk is a question of fact subject to demonstration in the usual ways, including inference from circumstantial evidence, and a factfinder may conclude that a prison official knew of a substantial risk from the very fact that the risk was obvious." *Id.* at 842 (internal citation omitted). Even if prison officials know of a substantial risk to inmate health or safety but fail to prevent the harm, they "may be found free

---

8. *See Farmer*, 511 U.S. at 832; *Wilson v. Seiter*, 501 U.S. 294, 303 (1991) (characterizing "the protection [a prisoner] is afforded against other inmates" as a "condition of confinement").

9. We are aware that the cases have used the term "wantonness" to describe the culpability required for an Eighth Amendment violation. *See Farmer*, 511 U.S. at 834; *Wilson*, 501 U.S. at 303. However, as *Wilson* makes clear, whether an official's acts can be considered "wanton" is a contextual inquiry, depending on the type of claim and the constraints facing the official. *Wilson*, 501 U.S. at 303; *see also Hudson v. McMillian*, 503 U.S. 1, 5 (1992) ("What is necessary to establish an 'unnecessary and wanton infliction of pain' ... varies according to the nature of the alleged [Eighth Amendment] violation.") (quoting *Whitley v. Albers*, 475 U.S. 312, 320 (1986)). *Farmer* is the controlling precedent for the type of conditions-of-confinement claim at issue in this case and we therefore use the "deliberate indifference" standard as therein articulated. *See Farmer*, 511 U.S. at 835–44.

from liability if they respond reasonably to the risk." *Id.* at 844. With these standards in mind, we turn to the claim against Sergeant Hartley.

B. Sergeant Hartley

In assessing the claim against Sergeant Hartley, we must determine whether a reasonable juror, on the basis of the summary judgment record, could conclude that Hartley "kn[ew] that [Giroux] face[d] a substantial risk of serious harm and disregard[ed] that risk by failing to take reasonable measures to abate it." *Farmer*, 511 U.S. at 847. Consistent with the magistrate judge's recommendation, the district court assumed that a substantial risk of serious harm had been shown but concluded that there was insufficient evidence to support an inference of Hartley's actual knowledge of the risk, and granted a summary judgment....

1. Knowledge of a Substantial Risk of Serious Harm

According to Hartley's own testimony, cell feed status indicated either that the prisoner had a health problem or that the prisoner was in protective custody. Hartley also testified that one of his responsibilities as shift supervisor was to review the cell block assignment roster each day at the start of his shift. A juror could reasonably conclude, therefore, that Hartley performed this obligatory administrative task on September 21, 1995, thus alerting him at the very least to the fact that Giroux was on cell feed status, and that one of the two explanations for that cell feed status involved the risk that Giroux could be harmed by another inmate. As *Farmer* instructs, Hartley did not have to know the identity of the particular person threatening Giroux in order to have actual knowledge of the risk. *See Farmer*, 511 U.S. at 843 ("[A] prison official [may not] escape liability for deliberate indifference by showing that, while he was aware of an obvious, substantial risk to inmate safety, he did not know that the complainant was especially likely to be assaulted by the specific prisoner who eventually committed the assault."). If Hartley understood that there was a high probability of a danger to Giroux, he would not escape liability if the evidence showed that he merely ... declined to confirm inferences of risk that he strongly suspected to exist (as when a prison official is aware of a high probability of facts indicating that one prisoner has planned an attack on another but resists opportunities to obtain final confirmation ...). *Id.* at 843 n. 8. In our view, the summary judgment record supports the inference that Hartley was aware of a high probability that Giroux was vulnerable to attack from another inmate but took no action despite that awareness.

2. Deliberate Indifference to the Known Risk

The next inquiry, then, is whether Hartley's inaction in the face of the known risk evinced the culpability required for an Eighth Amendment violation. Prison officials "who actually knew of a substantial risk to inmate health or safety may be found free from liability if they responded reasonably to the risk, even if the harm ultimately was not averted." *Id.* at 844.

The record discloses no circumstances that constrained Hartley from responding reasonably to protect Giroux: no time pressure, no lack of resources, no competing concerns whatsoever. *See, e.g., id.* at 835 (distinguishing claims alleging excessive use of force by prison guards because in that context the alleged actions of prison officials are generally taken "in haste, under pressure, and frequently without the luxury of a second chance") (quoting *Hudson v. McMillian*, 503 U.S. 1, 6 (1992)). Hartley acknowledged that he was obliged to find out the reason for cell feed status when the cell block assignment roster did not contain that information, but he claimed that this information was for his own edification and that he had no responsibility, as shift supervisor, to disseminate that information to the subordinates on his shift. Other prison employees, including two subordinates who were working the night Giroux was attacked by Tucker, testified that it was the responsibility of the shift supervisor to tell them about any inmates who were being cell fed for protective purposes when such protective purposes were not listed on the inmate roster.

On this record, therefore, there is a genuine and material factual dispute about the scope of Hartley's responsibility as shift supervisor. In resolving that dispute, a reasonable juror could find that it was Hartley's responsibility as shift supervisor to confirm the basis for the cell feeding of each inmate in cell feed status and to alert the employees on his shift to that basis, in order to reasonably protect the inmates in his custody. A juror could find that Hartley's abdication of his responsibility, in the face of such a known danger to Giroux's safety, was a reckless dereliction of duty rising to the level of Eighth Amendment deliberate indifference. "When a supervisory official is placed on actual notice of a prisoner's need for physical protection or medical care, administrative negligence can rise to the level of deliberate indifference to or reckless disregard for a prisoner's safety." [citation omitted]. The court erred in ruling that the summary judgment record could not support a finding that Hartley was deliberately indifferent to Giroux's safety.

...

Questions to guide reading of *Miller*

Miller is the basis for Simulation 1.

1. Why did the Seventh Circuit find it significant that no defendants knew that Grandberry posed a threat to Miller?
2. Did *Miller* suggest that a prison official cannot be deliberately indifferent if he or she did not know that the victim was especially likely to be assaulted by the specific prisoner who committed the assault? If so, is there tension between the reasoning in *Miller* and *Farmer*?
3. Both the First Circuit in *Giroux* and the Seventh Circuit in *Miller* applied *Farmer* in the context of a prisoner who was first threatened by a group of other inmates and then assaulted by one of the members of that inmate group. Can you reconcile their holdings?
4. Do *Miller* and *Giroux* agree on what makes a risk obvious?
5. What strategies do lawyers use to address conflicting authority?

6. Why do you think the Seventh Circuit chose to issue this as a non-precedential opinion?

Miller v. McBride

64 Fed. Appx. 558 (7th Cir. 2003)

Before COFFEY, RIPPLE, and DIANE P. WOOD, Circuit Judges.

A dispute over a missing book escalated into a bloody fight between two inmates at an Indiana prison. One of the inmates, Paul Eugene Miller, was injured during the fight and subsequently sued prison officials under 42 U.S.C. § 1983 for failing to protect him from other prisoners, particularly those in the notorious Gangster Disciples gang.... On May 13, 1997, while serving time at the Westville Correctional Center (WCC) in northern Indiana, Mr. Miller informed prison staff that he had been threatened by several Gangster Disciples (whom he identified by name) and requested housing in the protective custody dormitory. The record does not reflect why the gang members threatened Mr. Miller. His case manager at WCC, Ms. Susan Tappan, transferred him to protective custody that same day. In the same request, Mr. Miller also asked to be housed in a single cell (protective custody was comprised of an open dorm area with no cells), but Ms. Tappan informed him that WCC did not have any.

On September 21 or 22, prisoner J. Grandberry, an alleged member of the Gangster Disciples but not one of those that Mr. Miller had named in his earlier request, was transferred into the same protective custody dorm. Other prisoners quickly alerted Mr. Miller that Grandberry had been inquiring as to his whereabouts. Once again, the record does not reflect why Grandberry was looking for Mr. Miller, but Mr. Miller speculates that Grandberry intended to carry out a "hit" on him, ordered by either the Gangster Disciples or prison staff.

Upon returning to the dorm on September 23, Mr. Miller discovered that one of his books was missing. Another prisoner told Mr. Miller that he had earlier seen Grandberry carrying something away from Mr. Miller's bed. Mr. Miller then confronted Grandberry and asked him whether he had taken the book. Mr. Miller, testifying at his deposition, stated that he did not first tell a staff member about the missing book because he did not expect a fight. But an argument between the two ensued, and Grandberry punched Mr. Miller in the face several times. Another prisoner intervened and started fighting with Grandberry, drawing several other prisoners into the fray. Mr. Miller stated that "as far as I'm concerned, it's done and over with" and started walking away from the fight.... But Grandberry came up behind him and hit him over the head with a padlock. During the fight, there was no prison guard monitoring the floor because Officer Thomas Ludwig, the guard assigned to the protective custody dorm that day, had left the dorm shortly before the fight without securing a relief officer. After Mr. Miller was later treated for his injury, he learned that the blow had ruptured his eardrum.

For reasons that the record does not make clear, Ms. Tappan transferred Mr. Miller three weeks later from protective custody to another dorm. Within 30 minutes of

Mr. Miller's arrival in this new dorm, unidentified gang members surrounded him. Prison staff immediately transferred him back to protective custody. But Ms. Tappan, concluding that there was not enough substantiating documentation to keep him in protective custody, transferred him sometime after that back into the general population, and eventually to another prison. Mr. Miller filed with Daniel McBride, superintendent of WCC, two grievances about the transfers out of protective custody and his injuries from the fight, but Superintendent McBride denied both grievances.

Mr. Miller thereafter filed in district court this § 1983 suit alleging that McBride, Tappan, and Ludwig failed to heed his requests for protective custody and failed to protect him from other prisoners, ultimately resulting in his being injured during the fight with Grandberry. Mr. Miller further alleged that the defendants, in retaliation for his filing several lawsuits, intentionally placed Grandberry in the same dorm, knowing that Grandberry would likely attack him. The district court granted summary judgment for the defendants, concluding that Mr. Miller failed to establish that the defendants exhibited deliberate indifference to his safety....

The central question in this case is whether the fight and Mr. Miller's various housing placements are enough to raise a triable issue on whether any of the defendants exhibited deliberate indifference to Mr. Miller's safety, amounting to cruel and unusual punishment under the Eighth Amendment. Prison officials have a duty to protect prisoners from other prisoners, but this does not mean that the Eighth Amendment is implicated every time a prisoner harms another. *Farmer v. Brennan*, 511 U.S. 825, 833–34 (1994). Rather, to survive summary judgment, Mr. Miller must show that he was incarcerated under conditions posing a "substantial risk of serious harm" and that the defendants acted with deliberate indifference to that danger. *Id.* at 834. It is the latter question of deliberate indifference that is at issue here, because we can assume that Mr. Miller's injury, or the risk of being attacked by a Gangster Disciple in a similar fashion, was sufficiently serious.

A prison official may be found deliberately indifferent only if he "knows of and disregards an excessive risk to inmate health or safety; the official must both be aware of facts from which the inference could be drawn that a substantial risk of serious harm exists, and he must also draw the inference." *Id.* at 837. Ordinary, or even gross, negligence is not enough to establish liability. *Washington v. LaPorte County Sheriff's Dep't*, 306 F.3d 515, 518 (7th Cir. 2002). And officials who actually know of a substantial risk to inmate safety are free from liability if they respond reasonably to the risk, even if the harm ultimately is not averted. *Peate v. McCann*, 294 F.3d 879, 882 (7th Cir. 2002). Furthermore, a supervisor cannot be held liable unless he was personally involved in the wrongful conduct, either by participating in or causing the alleged constitutional violation....

We begin our analysis with Mr. Miller's various placements in prison housing. When he requested protective custody because of threats from named Gangster Disciples, Ms. Tappan responded reasonably by immediately transferring him to protective custody. Although Mr. Miller may have wished to be transferred to a facility with single cells or to have remained in protective custody later after his fight with Grandberry, courts afford prison administrators—in this case Ms. Tappan and Superintendent McBride—great discretion in deciding where to place prisoners....

As for the fight with Grandberry, there is no evidence that any of the defendants knew that Grandberry posed a threat to Mr. Miller. Mr. Miller did not alert any staff members to the potential danger upon learning that Grandberry had asked about him nor did he inform staff that he intended to confront Grandberry about the missing book. *See Washington*, 306 F.3d at 518 (officials cannot have actual knowledge of risk unless prisoner reports trouble); *cf. Case v. Ahitow*, 301 F.3d 605, 607 (7th Cir. 2002) (summary judgment precluded where plaintiff notified prison staff about threats from another prisoner). Although Mr. Miller had reported threats from other Gangster Disciples (and assuming that prison staff even knew that Grandberry was affiliated with the Gangster Disciples), the defendants could not be expected to know that Grandberry in particular posed a threat to Mr. Miller, as he had never identified Grandberry as an antagonist in the past. *See Peate*, 294 F.3d at 883 (staff cannot be expected to predict fights without any knowledge of "bad blood" between prisoners); *Lewis v. Richards*, 107 F.3d 549, 554 (7th Cir. 1997) (officials had no way of knowing that plaintiff was in heightened peril when he did not report new threats from different gang members). In fact, Mr. Miller admitted during his deposition that even he did not expect a fight with Grandberry. Although it was almost certainly negligent for Officer Ludwig to leave the dorm without securing a replacement monitor, even gross negligence is not enough to establish constitutional liability. *Washington*, 306 F.3d at 518. And Superintendent McBride cannot be liable for Mr. Miller's injuries from the fight because he lacked personal involvement in the incident; he was not involved in either the decision to transfer Mr. Miller to that dorm in May or the day-to-day operations of the unit.... Finally, there is absolutely no evidence that any of the defendants, or any other prison officials for that matter, arranged for Grandberry to attack Mr. Miller in retaliation for filing lawsuits. *Cf. Case*, 301 F.3d at 606–07 (discussing evidence of guard offering to cover for prisoner who planned to attack another prisoner). We conclude, as did the district court, that Mr. Miller has not shown that the defendants were deliberately indifferent to his safety....

Questions to guide reading of *Rodriquez*

1. Why did the Eleventh Circuit hold that a reasonable juror could find that Kugler knew "facts indicating a sufficiently substantial danger" and thus actually knew that Rodriguez faced a substantial risk of serious harm?
2. Why did the Eleventh Circuit hold that the concerns expressed by Rodriguez were specific enough to put Johnson on actual notice of a risk of harm?
3. Why did the Eleventh Circuit find that a corrections official could be deliberately indifferent even though he did not know Plaintiff was likely to be assaulted by the particular person who assaulted him?
4. Like the plaintiffs in *Giroux* and *Miller*, Rodriguez faced threats from a group. Can you reconcile the holdings in *Miller* and *Rodriguez*?

5. Why did the Eleventh Circuit hold that Rodriguez could demonstrate a causal connection between Rodriguez's injury and the actions of Kugler and Johnson, even though they did not have final authority to order Rodriguez's release from protective custody?
6. If the dissent's view of causation had prevailed, when would a low-level correctional officer be liable for failing to prevent an inmate-on-inmate attack? What incentives for correctional officer behavior would that have created?
7. If you represented the correctional officers, what next steps would you recommend upon receiving this decision? What other considerations might you weigh?

Rodriguez v. Secretary for Dept. of Corrections

508 F.3d 611 (11th Cir. 2007)

ANDERSON, Circuit Judge.

Appellant Miguel V. Rodriguez, a Florida prisoner, filed this § 1983 suit against two prison officials, Appellees Raymond Kugler and Charles Johnson, alleging that they violated his Eighth Amendment right to be free from cruel and unusual punishment. Specifically, Rodriguez says that while he was being held in administrative segregation, he informed Kugler and Johnson that members of his former gang had threatened to kill him upon his release into the general prison population. He therefore asked Kugler and Johnson to place him in protective custody or, alternatively, to transfer him from the prison. Rodriguez says that despite being confronted with the information of the death threats and his requests for protection, Kugler and Johnson recommended that he be released into the general population. Mere hours after reentering the general population, Rodriguez was violently assaulted—stabbed in the back and chest with a shank—by Arnold Cleveland, a member of the Latin Kings. Rodriguez says that Kugler's and Johnson's failure to take reasonable steps aimed at preventing the attack, the threat of which each was subjectively aware, violated the Eighth Amendment under *Farmer v. Brennan*, 511 U.S. 825 (1994).

...

I. Facts

... In 2002, Rodriguez was an inmate at the Everglades Correctional Institution (ECI) in Miami, Florida. Raymond Kugler was the Assistant Warden for Operations at ECI and, in that capacity, shared responsibility for prison security. Charles Johnson was the Colonel of ECI and was, in that capacity, the chief of prison security.

During the winter of 2002, Rodriguez was under "close management," which in ECI parlance means that he was segregated from the general prison population for security purposes. Rodriguez had been in close management since January 2001 because of an ongoing investigation of gang activity at ECI and because he had assaulted a fellow inmate while in the [general population]. On at least one previous occasion,

Rodriguez had been placed in close management in response to his request that the prison provide him protection.

While under close management in early 2002, Rodriguez "learned that gang members at ECI wanted to kill [him]." Those who wanted to kill him were members of his former gang, the Latin Kings, which had a particularly strong presence at ECI. They wanted to kill Rodriguez as retribution for his having renounced his membership. On at least two occasions while under close management, Rodriguez verbally told Kugler "of the threat made against my life" by members of his former gang and "asked [Kugler] that I be transferred to another correctional institution for my protection." Rodriguez's transfer request was "in addition to requesting that [I] be placed in protective custody."[4] *Id.* Kugler took no action with respect to Rodriguez's allegations or his requests for protection.

Rodriguez also spoke to Johnson on a number of occasions regarding the threats on his life. According to his trial testimony, Rodriguez, beginning in March 2002, told Johnson "[t]hat I was afraid for my life and that I didn't want to go out to the [general population] and that he should give me protection and give me a transfer" from ECI.... Rodriguez specifically informed Johnson that his life had been threatened by members of the Latin Kings. Rodriguez explained to Johnson why he was scared of the Latin King members at ECI, stating that "they would shout at me, telling me that they were going to kill me." *Id.* at 139. One of Rodriguez's fellow inmates, Antania Tyrone Flowers, testified at trial to a conversation that he overheard between Rodriguez and Johnson. In that conversation, Rodriguez asked Johnson for protection from the gang members in the [general population] and, specifically, that he be transferred to another prison. According to Flowers, Johnson responded that "he was going to look into it and ... get with the classification officer..., and he'd let [Rodriguez] know what they [were] going to do about that." ... Johnson, however, did not "look into" anything, did not "get with" anyone, and did not otherwise tell anyone about Rodriguez's safety concerns. Nor did he act on those concerns himself, something he was authorized to do.

In addition to verbally expressing his security concerns to Kugler and Johnson, Rodriguez also filed with ECI a written form, known as an Inmate Request form, dated February 18, 2002, in which he stated: "I have a problem with another inmate in this compound. I want you to tell me my status here where I am. I submitted a request for protection. I want to know ... whether you are going to give me a transfer." The February 18 Inmate Request form, submitted while Rodriguez was still under close management, was addressed to both the "Warden" and the "Asst. Warden."[5] *Id.* Ro-

4. Kugler says he does not recall having any conversations with Rodriguez.

5. As the Assistant Warden for Operations, including security, Kugler concedes that he would ordinarily have received a security-related Inmate Request form like Rodriguez's.... He denies, however, having seen the Inmate Request form submitted by Rodriguez any time prior to this lawsuit.... As the Colonel of ECI, and thus the chief of security, Johnson likewise concedes that "if it [an Inmate Request form] addressed a security concern, [the prison employee who translated it] would have forwarded it to me." ... Like Kugler, Johnson denies that he ever saw Rodriguez's Inmate Request form prior to this lawsuit....

driguez received a response from someone at ECI, communicated on the bottom of the Inmate Request form itself, before the attack occurred. ECI's response acknowledged an ongoing investigation into gang activity among the prison population.

Submitting an Inmate Request form is not the only way a prisoner at ECI may bring a security concern to the attention of the appropriate officials. Johnson, who (like Kugler) had frequent face-to-face contact with inmates at ECI, testified in his deposition that inmates may also bring their security concerns directly to ECI officials through informal conversation. ECI officials knew what to do when faced with such concerns because ECI had in place an established protocol for dealing with situations in which a prisoner reports that he fears his life is in jeopardy. According to Johnson, the protocol is triggered as follows:

> [If an inmate] comes to me and state[s] that he is in fear for his life, I am going to make him stand right there and I'm going to call the shift supervisor and explain to the shift supervisor, "This inmate stated he's in fear for his life, please place him in administrative confinement until we do a protective management review."....

Johnson explained that a "protective management review" entails having a sergeant "go and investigate" the inmate's claims. Such a review requires that the sergeant "get all the statements from everybody" that the inmate says he is having trouble with. *Id.* Once that process is complete, according to Johnson, if the prisoner's safety concerns are substantiated, the appropriate prison officials "get[ ] together and we normally recommend he [the complaining inmate] be transferred from the institution." No protective management review was ever initiated in response to the safety concerns expressed by Rodriguez.

On April 3, 2002, a Classification Review meeting was held to determine whether Rodriguez was ready to be released from close management back into the general population. Such meetings are convened periodically for inmates under close management, and there is nothing in the record to indicate that the April 3 meeting was scheduled in response to Rodriguez's complaints. Present at this meeting were Rodriguez, Kugler, Johnson, and a classification officer. Kugler and Johnson, along with the classification officer, formed a three-person team tasked with the responsibility of making a recommendation to another group of individuals—a "classification team"—regarding an inmate's suitability for release from close management. The classification team was the body empowered to make final decisions about whether to release an inmate from close management. Neither Kugler nor Johnson had final authority (either individually or jointly) to order Rodriguez's release from close management. They do not, however, dispute that either one of them could have recommended to the classification team that Rodriguez be held in protective custody while the threats on his life were investigated—*e.g.*, by a "protective management review"—or that he be transferred to another institution. Nor do they dispute the fact that each of them had independent authority to initiate a protective management review. Instead of pursuing any of these alternatives, Kugler and Johnson ignored Rodriguez's repeated requests for protection and recommended to the classification team that he be released into the [general population].

During the April 3 meeting, Rodriguez again told Kugler that he believed his life was in danger and requested that he be transferred to another institution for protection.[7] Kugler ignored Rodriguez's request and told him that he was being recommended for release to the [general population] and that "he had to make any request for transfer from the [general population]."[8] *Id.* During the meeting, Kugler told Rodriguez that if he did not comply with the order to return to the [general population], Kugler would "give [him] a disciplinary report and continue him on [close management] status."[9] At the conclusion of the April 3 meeting, Rodriguez was recommended for release from close management and was released six days later on April 9 at 6:00 p.m.

On the morning of April 10, 2002, only hours after having been transferred to the compound, Rodriguez was stabbed in the back and chest with a shank by Arnold Cleveland, an "enforcer"[10] of the Latin Kings.

III. Discussion

The Eighth Amendment imposes a duty on prison officials "to protect prisoners from violence at the hands of other prisoners." *Farmer*, 511 U.S. at 833.... A prison official violates the Eighth Amendment when he actually (subjectively) knows that an inmate is facing a substantial[12] risk of serious harm, yet disregards that known risk by failing to respond to it in an (objectively) reasonable manner. *See Farmer*, 511 U.S. at 829, 837, 844. As with any other claim brought under § 1983, to succeed, the inmate must demonstrate a causal connection between the prison official's conduct and the Eighth Amendment violation.

With regard to the subjective component of the Eighth Amendment claim, the Court in *Farmer* held that the prison "official must both be aware of facts from which the inference could be drawn that a substantial risk of serious harm exists, and he must also draw the inference." 511 U.S. at 837. The Court also held: "Whether a prison official had the requisite knowledge of a substantial risk is a *question of fact* subject to demonstration in the usual ways, including inference from circumstantial evidence." *Id.* at 842 (emphasis added). A prison official cannot avoid liability under the Eighth Amendment "by showing that ... he did not know the complainant was

7. Kugler denies that Rodriguez raised any security-related concerns at the April 3 meeting.

8. Kugler denies this.

9. Kugler denies this.

10. The role of an "enforcer" is to exact physical retribution on those who repudiate their gang membership.

12. Because the Court's task in *Farmer* was only "to define the term 'deliberate indifference,'" the Court expressly declined to address "at what point a risk of inmate assault becomes *sufficiently substantial* for Eighth Amendment purposes." 511 U.S. at 829, 834 n. 3 (emphasis added). Neither Kugler nor Johnson argues that the risk of harm facing Rodriguez was insufficiently substantial for Eighth Amendment purposes. In the context of this case, we conclude that the gang-related threats made on Rodriguez's life, which were explicitly reported to prison officials, present a substantial enough risk of harm to trigger a prison official's Eighth Amendment duty to act; that is, to take some steps to investigate the likelihood that the reported threat will materialize and to take some steps aimed at reducing the likelihood of the risk.

especially likely to be assaulted by the *specific prisoner* who eventually committed the assault." *Id.* at 843 (emphasis added). This is because "[t]he question under the Eighth Amendment is whether prison officials, acting with deliberate indifference, exposed a prisoner to a sufficiently substantial 'risk of serious damage to his future health.'" *Id.* (quoting *Helling v. McKinney*, 509 U.S. 25, 35 (1993)).

The Court in *Farmer* identified three ways that prison officials might avoid Eighth Amendment liability. Officials might show: (1) "that they did not know of the underlying facts indicating a sufficiently substantial danger and that they were therefore unaware of a danger"; (2) "that they knew the underlying facts but believed (albeit unsoundly) that the risk to which the facts gave rise was insubstantial or nonexistent"; or (3) that "they responded reasonably to the risk, even if the harm ultimately was not averted." 511 U.S. at 844.

A. Summary Judgment to Kugler

1. Did Kugler Actually Know Rodriguez Faced a Substantial Risk of Serious Harm?

... Rodriguez argues that the district court erred in granting summary judgment to Kugler because there is evidence in the record from which a reasonable juror could find that Kugler actually knew that Rodriguez faced a substantial risk of serious harm from his former gang members. Specifically, Rodriguez says, the summary-judgment record viewed in the light most favorable to him demonstrates that: (1) he verbally informed Kugler on at least two occasions that his life had been threatened by members of his former gang and that, to avoid injury, he needed either to be transferred to another prison or to be placed in protective custody at ECI; and that (2) he, by means of the written Inmate Request form, informed Kugler that he feared for his safety in the [general population] and requested a transfer from ECI. This, Rodriguez says, is enough evidence of subjective knowledge to get his claim to a jury. We agree.

Rodriguez submitted a declaration in opposition to Kugler's summary-judgment motion in which he stated that "While in Close Management ('CM') at ECI prior to the April 10, 2002 stabbing incident, I learned that gang members at ECI wanted to kill me." ... Viewed in the light most favorable to Rodriguez, this evidence gives rise to an inference that he received threats on his life, from members of his former gang, prior to the stabbing. Rodriguez stated in his declaration that "verbally on at least two separate occasions [prior to the April 10 stabbing]" "I informed [Kugler] ... of the threat made against my life and asked that I be transferred to another correctional institution for my protection." ... Again, viewed in the light most favorable to Rodriguez, the reasonable inference created by this evidence is that the threat of which Rodriguez twice informed Kugler was the gang-related threat referenced in the preceding paragraph of his declaration, the threat we can infer from Rodriguez's knowledge that "gang members at ECI wanted to kill [him]." ...

With regard to Rodriguez's verbal complaints, Kugler said in his deposition that he did not remember having any conversation with Rodriguez in which Rodriguez mentioned the threats to his life or his need for a transfer or protective custody. Kugler's denial flatly contradicts Rodriguez's allegations. Besides denying that such conversations ever took place, Kugler also challenges the sufficiency of Rodriguez's declaration on the ground that it does not "furnish any specifics as to who was posing the alleged threats." … Kugler's challenge to the declaration in this respect is without merit, however, as confirmed by the Supreme Court in *Farmer*: "Nor may a prison official escape liability for deliberate indifference by showing that … he did not know that the complainant was especially likely to be assaulted by the specific prisoner who eventually committed the assault." 511 U.S. at 843.… We conclude that Rodriguez's declaration testimony, coupled with Kugler's inability to recall any security-related conversations with Rodriguez, is sufficient to create a genuine issue of material fact about whether Kugler had subjective knowledge that Rodriguez faced a substantial risk of serious harm.

With regard to the submission of Rodriguez's February 18, 2002, Inmate Request Form—in which he stated that he had "a problem with another inmate in this compound," that he had "submitted a request for protection," and that he "want[ed] to know … whether you are going to give me a transfer"—Kugler testified in his deposition that, although he would ordinarily have received a security-related Inmate Request form like Rodriguez's, he never saw the one submitted by Rodriguez. Kugler's testimony that he would ordinarily have received such a form, coupled with his express denial that he received the one submitted on February 18, leads us to conclude that there is a genuine issue of material fact about whether Kugler was aware of the Inmate Request form prior to the attack. This dispute of fact, in turn, is relevant to the question whether Kugler had subjective knowledge that Rodriguez faced a substantial risk of serious harm.[15]

2. Did Kugler Respond Reasonably to the Known Risk?

"[P]rison officials who actually knew of a substantial risk to inmate health or safety may be found free from liability if they responded reasonably to the risk, even if the harm ultimately was not averted." *Farmer*, 511 U.S. at 844. More succinctly, "prison officials who act reasonably cannot be found liable under the Cruel and Unusual Punishments Clause." *Id.* at 845.…

Rodriguez argues on appeal that Kugler responded to the threatened risk of harm in an objectively unreasonable manner. But the district court, given that it granted summary judgment to Kugler solely on the basis that Kugler lacked subjective knowledge of the risk, stopped short of addressing this question.… Because it is not necessary for us to do so, we decline to address the objective component of Rodriguez's

---

15. Standing alone, the dispute over whether Kugler received the Inmate Request form probably would not suffice to create a genuine issue of fact about Kugler's subjective knowledge of a substantial risk of serious harm and thus would not have precluded summary judgment in Kugler's favor. That is because, even if Kugler did receive it, the form does not contain much about the nature of the anticipated risk. Rather, it vaguely states that "I have a problem with another inmate in this compound" and "[have made a] request for protection." But when the information contained in the form is considered in conjunction with Rodriguez's declaration testimony that he verbally informed Kugler at least twice of the gang-related threats to his life, then Kugler's denial about receiving the Inmate Request form becomes more important to the inquiry of Kugler's subjective knowledge.

Eighth Amendment claim. We accordingly leave to the district court on remand the task of considering this issue in the first instance.

3. Did Kugler Cause Rodriguez's Injury?

In granting summary judgment to Kugler, the district court did not consider whether Kugler caused the Eighth Amendment violation.... On appeal, however, Kugler asks us to affirm the district court's judgment on the ground that he did not cause the violation. For the reasons stated below with respect to Johnson, we reject Kugler's argument because the record contains evidence from which a reasonable juror could find a causal connection between Kugler's actions and the Eighth Amendment violation.

B. Judgment as a Matter of Law to Johnson

1. Did Johnson Actually Know Rodriguez Faced a Substantial Risk of Harm?

Johnson argues that he did not actually know that Rodriguez faced a substantial risk of serious harm. Johnson says that Rodriguez's complaints were too vague to trigger his Eighth Amendment duty to act. The evidence Rodriguez presented at trial, however, tells a different story. That evidence is sufficient to permit a reasonable juror to find that Johnson actually knew that Rodriguez faced a substantial risk of serious harm....

Rodriguez testified at trial that he first spoke with Johnson about his fear of being released into the [general population] on March 28. On that date, Rodriguez told Johnson "[t]hat I was afraid for my life and that I didn't want to go out to the [general population] and that he should give me protection and give me a transfer" to another institution. Rodriguez spoke to Johnson again at the April 3 Classification Review meeting. At that meeting Rodriguez "told the colonel that I didn't want to be released to the [general population] because ... I was afraid that other inmates would attack me, that I wanted for him to give me a protection and a transfer." On at least one occasion, Rodriguez specifically told Johnson that some member or members of the Latin Kings had issued a death threat against him. Rodriguez "told him [Johnson] that I was a ... retired gang member and that the Latin Kings wanted to attack me because I didn't want to continue being a Latin King, and that that was one of the reasons why I wanted protection at Everglades, because there were an excess amount of members of that gang in there." Rodriguez told Johnson that "all the members were sending me messages ... [and] [w]hen I went past, they would shout at me, telling me they were going to kill me."

Johnson argues that no reasonable juror could conclude from this evidence that Rodriguez communicated to Johnson "specific facts from which an inference could be drawn that a substantial risk of serious harm exists." We disagree....

Here ... Rodriguez told Johnson the following specific information: (1) that he was a former Latin King who decided to renounce his membership; (2) that members of the Latin Kings had threatened to kill him when he returned to the [general population] in retaliation for his renunciation; (3) that the [general population] at ECI was heavily populated with Latin Kings; and (4) that, in order to prevent an attempt on his life, he needed either to be transferred to another institution or to be placed in protective custody....

2. Did Johnson Respond Reasonably to the Known Risk?

... Rodriguez argues on appeal that Johnson responded to the threatened risk of harm in an objectively unreasonable manner. But (as in the case of Kugler) the district court did not address this question, given that it granted judgment as a matter of law to Johnson solely on the basis that Johnson did not cause the Eighth Amendment violation.... Because it is not necessary for us to do so, we decline to address the objective component of Rodriguez's Eighth Amendment claim. We accordingly leave to the district court on remand the task of considering this issue in the first instance.

3. Did Johnson Cause Rodriguez's Injury?

The district court granted Johnson judgment as a matter of law solely on the basis of its determination that Johnson did not cause the Eighth Amendment violation. Johnson could not have caused the violation, the district court reasoned, because he did not have final authority at the April 3 meeting to order Rodriguez's release from close management. That lack of authority was dispositive of the issue, the district court concluded, because it was Rodriguez's release from close management that "caused" him to be in the general population where he could be attacked by Arnold Cleveland.... We disagree with the district court's narrow view of causation because it is inconsistent with our precedents in this context....

For purposes of determining whether Johnson caused the Eighth Amendment violation and Rodriguez's subsequent injury, the "critical" question is whether Johnson was "in a position to take steps that could have averted the stabbing incident ... but, through [deliberate] indifference, failed to do so." To determine whether Johnson caused Rodriguez's injury, we look at his "duties, discretion and means." [relying on 11th Circuit precedent].

Here, the record evidence is sufficient to permit a reasonable juror to find that the "necessary causal link" has been established.

First, there is no doubt that Johnson, the chief of security at ECI, had the means substantially to improve Rodriguez's safety. Kugler testified ... that if an inmate voiced a life-threatening security concern to him, he was fully authorized to set in motion procedures to place the inmate in immediate administrative confinement and initiate a protective management review aimed at eliminating the risk of harm. That course of action "could have averted," ... the life-threatening risk of harm facing Rodriguez because it could have resulted in Rodriguez's transfer from ECI....

Second, a reasonable juror could conclude from the evidence that Johnson "knew that the actions he undertook would be insufficient to provide [the inmate] with reasonable protection from violence.".... The evidence in this case supports such an inference because the only action Johnson took in response to Rodriguez's requests for protection was to recommend that Rodriguez be returned to the compound—where he would have no protection at all from the Latin Kings who had threatened his life.

Third, the fact that ECI had an established protocol for handling an inmate's life-threatening security concerns—immediate administrative segregation, combined with a thorough protective management review—demonstrates that Johnson had "other means [ ] available to him which he nevertheless disregarded," ... and that those means were means that "could have averted," ... the substantial risk of serious harm facing Rodriguez.

We are satisfied that the evidence in this case is sufficient to permit a reasonable juror to find the "necessary causal link" between Johnson's actions and Rodriguez's injury. [Our causation analysis, and the conclusion we reach, is fully applicable to Kugler.] Because we are unable to say that "there [was] no legally sufficient evidentiary basis for a reasonable juror to find for [Rodriguez]" on the issue of causation, Fed.R.Civ.P. 50(a), we must vacate the judgment as a matter of law entered in favor of Johnson.[20]

COX, Circuit Judge, dissenting.

I respectfully dissent from the court's opinion because Miguel Rodriguez failed to present any evidence from which a reasonable jury could conclude that the conduct of Colonel Johnson or Assistant Warden Kugler caused his injury. I would therefore affirm the district court's decision to grant summary judgment in favor of Kugler and judgment as a matter of law in favor of Johnson....

[I]nstead of requiring some proof of an affirmative causal connection, as our precedent requires, the court holds that Rodriguez need only demonstrate that Johnson or Kugler failed to take steps [that] *could have* averted the stabbing. The court fails to consider whether the classification team gave any weight to Johnson's or Kugler's recommendation that Rodriguez be released to the general prison population, a point on which Rodriguez has offered no evidence. Thus, the inquiry should end here. "The causal relation does not exist when the continuum between Defendant's

---

20. The dissent points out that Johnson and Kugler had the authority to make only recommendations with respect to placement and classification decisions, which decisions rest with the state classification team. However, we respectfully submit that proof of causation in this case does not turn on the ultimate placement or classification decision with respect to Rodriguez. There was evidence in this case that both Johnson and Kugler, acting alone and independently, had the authority to trigger the "protective management review protocol," which would result in immediate administrative confinement, pending the appropriate investigation and ultimate decision by the state classification team. There was also evidence that Rodriguez was stabbed only hours after being transferred to the general population. Thus, we conclude that a reasonable jury could find that the stabbing at issue in this case would not have occurred if either Johnson or Kugler had acted on the alleged warnings, and caused Rodriguez to be placed in immediate protective confinement pending investigation. Whether Rodriguez would have faced a similar danger upon his ultimate release into the general population, if that were the ultimate decision of the state classification team, is a matter for another day and another case. Unlike the dissent ... we believe that a reasonable jury could conclude that it is more likely than not that Rodriguez' injury would have been avoided had either Johnson or Kugler followed the protocol.

action and the ultimate harm is occupied by the conduct of deliberative and autonomous decision-makers." *Dixon v. Burke County*, 303 F.3d 1271, 1275 (11th Cir. 2002). The state classification team's decision—as deliberate and autonomous decision-makers—to release Rodriguez to the general prison population broke the continuum of causation between Johnson's and Kugler's recommendation and Rodriguez's injury....

Ignoring ... basic principles of causation, the court [also] holds that a reasonable jury could find that Johnson or Kugler caused Rodriguez's injury, since either or both of them could have placed Rodriguez in [temporary] administrative confinement while the state classification team conducted a protective management review to determine if his classification should change.... Rodriguez simply has made no showing that a recommendation for a protective management review would have prevented his ultimate release into the general prison population and his subsequent injury.... What the court terms "a matter for another day and another case" is actually the precise question before us today: has Rodriguez demonstrated that Johnson's or Kugler's failure to order temporary administrative confinement was the legal cause of his injury? The answer is no.

To buttress its holding that Johnson and Kugler had "power to control prisoner placement," the court relies on the Supreme Court case of *Farmer v. Brennan*, 511 U.S. 825 (1994). In *Farmer*, the defendants argued that they had no power to control placement of the plaintiff, an inmate who had recently been transferred to an out-of-state prison. However, an affidavit from one defendant admitted that the plaintiff was placed in administrative segregation at the out-of-state prison pursuant to a "request" from their office. On this evidence, the Supreme Court concluded that "the record gives at least a suggestion" that the defendants could control prison placement at the out-of-state facility. *Id.* at 850. The court analogizes *Farmer* to this case, holding that the causation element is satisfied since Johnson and Kugler could have "requested" that a protective management review be conducted and thus had "power to control prisoner placement." We cannot speculate as to what would—or might—have happened if Johnson or Kugler had requested a protective management review. Further, nothing in *Farmer* indicates that the type of administrative segregation involved in that case was in any way akin to the temporary administrative segregation of the kind we have here.

For further discussion

1. Note that Kugler and Johnson did not argue that they "knew the underlying facts but believed (albeit unsoundly) that the risk ... was insubstantial or nonexistent" or that they "responded reasonably to the risk," two additional defenses available to prison officials.

2. Plaintiff Miguel Rodriguez was represented *pro bono* before the Eleventh Circuit by Paul Avron of Berger Singerman in Boca Raton, Florida, who reported that there was a trial on remand after the Eleventh Circuit's decision and that the plaintiff lost. Settlement negotiations before the trial did not succeed. He said: "Based on the facts as I understand them, I truly believe Mr. Rodriguez should have been physically iso-

lated somewhere—at minimum, he should have been transferred to another prison." Mr. Rodriguez is in prison for the rest of his life. Telephone interview, Philadelphia, Pennsylvania (Dec. 23, 2008).

3. *Giroux*, *Miller* and *Rodriguez* all applied the *Farmer* standard to situations where inmates who faced danger from other inmates were separated from the general population for their own protection. Protection is not the only reason for segregating certain inmates; some inmates are separated for punitive reasons. Recall that at the beginning of this Chapter a corrections officer described a separate unit within the prison where inmates would be sent for punishment, "like a jail within a jail." While not at all typical, consider the particularly punitive detention facility in a midwestern American prison, graphically described in this excerpt from *Gillis v. Litscher*, 468 F.3d 488 (7th Cir. 2006) (opinion by Evans, Circuit Judge):

> Stripped naked in a small prison cell with nothing except a toilet; forced to sleep on a concrete floor or slab; denied any human contact; fed nothing but "nutri-loaf"; and given just a modicum of toilet paper—four squares—only a few times. Although this might sound like a stay at a Soviet gulag in the 1930s, it is, according to the claims in this case, Wisconsin in 2002. Whether these conditions are, as a matter of law, only "uncomfortable, but not unconstitutional" as the State contends, is the issue we consider in this case.
>
> Nathan Gillis ... was a prisoner at the Wisconsin [prison] ... dubbed the "Supermax," ... Wisconsin's highest security prison. It is an all-segregation facility, designed to house recalcitrant inmates.
>
> ...
>
> Gillis arrived at Supermax on February 15, 2002. Within 2 weeks of his arrival he was placed in the [Behavioral Modification Program, "BMP"] for an infraction of what he sees as a relatively minor rule. The rule requires that inmates sleep with their heads toward the back of the cell (and the toilet). Gillis slept with his head toward the front of the cell and on occasion covered his head. He says that the rule was not being uniformly enforced and that some inmates did not follow the rule because it forced them to lie with their heads next to the toilet. The defendants ... argue that compliance with the rule is necessary so guards can see an inmate's head through a small window on the cell door. If the guards cannot see the head of the inmate, they cannot determine his condition. Defendants also say that they began to enforce the rule on February 22, 2002, which is about a week before the BMP was imposed on Gillis.... [I]t was for this infraction that Gillis was placed in the BMP. The BMP is a program designed to force difficult inmates to conform to the rules. The memo Gillis received upon being placed in the program is as follows:
>
> Stage One: You will be placed on stage one for a period of three days. All property will be removed from your cell during this time and you will receive nutri-loaf for meals.

Stage Two: Upon completion of three days in stage one with appropriate behavior the Unit Manager may initiate stage two. Stage two will be in effect for 7 days. In stage two your in-cell property will be limited to a segregation smock. You will receive regular meals. In stage two you will receive hygiene items two times per day and will receive showers on regular shower days. Upon completion of day 7 in stage two with appropriate behavior, the Unit Manager may deactivate the plan.

> * Any inappropriate behavior, as described above, will result in being placed on day one of stage one.
>
> * Security restrictions may also alter this plan and will continue after deactivation of plan.
>
> * This plan will be in effect for a period of six months and will be activated when you display inappropriate behavior as explained above.
>
> * The Unit Manager may modify this plan at any time.

... After successful completion of the 3 days at stage one, Gillis would have been eligible to move to stage two, but he was continued in stage one for 2 more days because ... of very bad, but possibly unrelated behavior—smearing blood and feces around his cell. The defendants say such behavior is related to the rule because guards cannot see through a feces-covered window. After 5 days, Gillis moved on to stage two, where he stayed for 7 more days.

In stage one, Gillis was deprived of nearly all human contact and sensory stimuli. He had no property in his cell and no privileges. He was stark naked and had no mattress or other bedding. He slept naked on the concrete floor or on the concrete slab that is the bed. He tried to sleep next to a heat vent, but the air from the vent was cool. He says he was so cold that he had to walk around his small cell some 14 hours a day trying to stay warm. He claims he developed sores on his feet from pacing and on his body from sleeping on the concrete and that his request for soap to clean his sores was denied. Defendants dispute that Gillis had to walk to keep warm. They say the temperature in the cell was always 70 degrees or above, apparently in their view a temperature at which people sleep comfortably without pajamas or bedding.

Gillis was fed nutri-loaf—basically a ground-up block of food. He was denied mail, visitors, phone privileges, canteen items, writing materials, and use of the law library. There is a dispute of fact over the amount of toilet paper he received. He says he received it on only five occasions during the entire time he was in the BMP, and then it was four squares at a time. The defendants say he received toilet paper on request.

When he was placed in stage two, he was given what is called a sleeveless "seg smock," which is a one-piece item of clothing much like a poncho which covers a person from chest to below the groin. It is worn without underwear.

Gillis also began to receive regular meals in styrofoam containers and a toothbrush and toothpaste, but no soap. He was finally allowed to shower 9 days into his ordeal. He was not given bedding or a mattress.

The program had an adverse effect on Gillis's mental stability. He heard voices telling him that "these people were trying to kill" him. He suffered panic attacks, with palpitations, shortness of breath, and a feeling that he was going to die. He became suicidal. He inflicted wounds on his body and wrote the words "help me" in blood on the walls of his cell. When a guard noticed the wounds and called the health services unit, Gillis was transferred to a different cell, where he further injured himself and began smearing feces on his cell walls and on the window. He was placed on clinical observation, but the conditions of his confinement did not change.

...

To prevail on his Eighth Amendment claim, Gillis must show that the BMP imposed conditions which denied him "the minimal civilized measure of life's necessities." *Rhodes v. Chapman*, 452 U.S. 337, 347 (1981); *see also Wilson v. Seiter*, 501 U.S. 294 (1991).

...

Under the amendment, life's necessities include shelter and heat ... as well as hygiene items.... A lack of heat, clothing, or sanitation can violate the Eighth Amendment. [citing cases from the Seventh, Eighth, and Tenth circuits].... Some conditions of confinement may establish an Eighth Amendment violation in combination when each alone would not do so. This is true when the deprivations have a mutually enforcing effect which produces the deprivation of a single, identifiable human need, such as food or warmth, for example "a low cell temperature at night combined with a failure to issue blankets." *Wilson v. Seiter*, 501 U.S. 294, 304 (1991).... Because of competing facts and inferences in this case, whether Gillis was denied the "minimal civilized measure of life's necessities" cannot be determined on summary judgment ... As always in conditions of confinement cases, we are reluctant to interfere with the administration of the prisons.... But our reluctance does not mean we can avoid our obligation to carefully evaluate constitutional claims, such as this one.

...

Guide to Law Practice Simulation 1

Description

This is an appellate oral argument before the fictional Twelfth Circuit based on the facts of *Miller v. McBride.* Assume the application of *Farmer v. Brennan* is a question of first impression in the Twelfth Circuit. Two students represent the plaintiff prisoner. Two students represent the defendant prison officials Tappan and Ludwig (McBride is not a defendant). One student is a judge on the Twelfth Circuit.

To prepare, consider issues such as:

- Under *Farmer*, can a defendant be liable if he did not know the underlying facts indicating danger? Or if she knew underlying facts concerning the risk—but did not draw the inference?
- Is a risk obvious any time a person in protective custody is attacked—because defendants must have known that a person in protective custody was at risk?
- Should courts treat prison gang members as a single entity?
- Under *Farmer*, can a defendant be deliberately indifferent if the defendant declined to confirm inferences of risk—like the probability of a future attack?
- Under *Farmer*, can a defendant be liable if he was aware of a risk but did not know the identity of the specific prisoner who would assault the plaintiff?
- Can the Seventh Circuit's decision in *Miller* be reconciled with *Giroux* and *Rodriguez*?

Purpose

- Better understand 8th Amendment deliberate indifference standard by comparing variations in how it was applied in *Farmer*, *Giroux*, *Miller*, *Rodriguez*
- Explore how attorneys shape 8th Amendment deliberate indifference doctrine by simulating the roles of attorneys and a judge in applying doctrine to real facts (the *Miller* facts)
- Prepare for law practice either by persuasively advocating client's legal position and responding to questions or by identifying ambiguities in doctrine or in its application to facts and posing questions to advocates
- There is no need to do any research—the relevant cases are in the casebook. You can rely on the Seventh Circuit decision in *Miller* as non-binding, foreign authority

Structure

- Appellants—Question and answer with Judge (8 minutes)
- Appellees—Question and answer with Judge (8 minutes)
- After 15 minutes, questioning will open up to the entire class
- Both Appellants and Appellees—Question and Answer with Judge and rest of class (15 minutes)
- Please prepare a question for every simulation, even if you are not one of the students playing a role.

- To ensure full class participation, and as a courtesy to your fellow students, please close your laptops during law practice simulations.

Practice Pointer

Research must be as efficient as possible. In practice, whether the lawyer is defense counsel billing by the hour or project or plaintiff's counsel advancing the costs of the litigation, the lawyer must consider the cost of legal research. One way to reduce legal research costs is to rely on secondary sources that can quickly lead the lawyer to sources of binding law. Government lawyers also must be concerned about making efficient use of research time because, like most lawyers, they juggle multiple demands on their time and often work with little support staff.

Before searching online for particular cases, consider reviewing some of the following published resources to learn the vocabulary of the field, to identify current debates, and to collect citations to binding current authority. The focused treatise by Michael Avery, David Rudovsky, Karen Blum & Jennifer Laurin, POLICE MISCONDUCT: LAW AND LITIGATION (3d ed. Clark Boardman 2014 & Oct. 2018 Supp.), and the more comprehensive treatises by Sheldon Nahmod, CIVIL RIGHTS AND CIVIL LIBERTIES LITIGATION: THE LAW OF SECTION 1983 (4th ed., West 2014 & Sept. 2018 Supp.); and by Martin A. Schwartz, SECTION 1983 LITIGATION: CLAIMS AND DEFENSES (4th ed., Wolters Kluwer 2018), all available on WestlawEdge, each have excellent explanations of 8th Amendment concepts and current citations. Other very helpful treatises include Ivan E. Bodensteiner & Rosalie Berger Levinson, STATE AND LOCAL GOVERNMENT CIVIL RIGHTS LIABILITY (2019), available on WestlawEdge; Martin A. Schwartz & Kathryn R. Urbonya, SECTION 1983 LITIGATION (2d ed., Federal Judicial Center 2008), *available on* WestlawEdge as FJC: Section 1983 Litigation; and Joseph G. Cook & John L. Sobieski, Jr., CIVIL RIGHTS ACTIONS (Matthew Bender & Co. 2019) (multi-volume), available on Lexis Advance and Lexis database Civil Rights Actions.

Federal model jury instructions—some of which are included in this Chapter—can help you efficiently identify current 8th Amendment issues and locate recent citations to binding law. Model jury instructions often are available for free on the federal circuit court websites. Other sources that are helpful for the same reasons are practice guides and legal encyclopedias. *See, e.g.*, Fay Stender and Ronald M. Sinoway, *Prisoners' Rights Litigation*, 22 AM. JUR. TRIALS 1 (updated May 2019); James L. Buchwalter, *Cause of Action for Prison's Failure to Protect Inmate from Assault*, 33 Causes of Action 2d 605 (updated July 2019); and Edward J. Hanlon, *Proof of Unconstitutional Prison Conditions*, 24 Am. Jur. Proof of Facts 3d 467 (updated June 2019).

American Law Reports articles provide useful summaries of particular 8th Amendment topics and citations to relevant cases, organized by jurisdiction with new cases added weekly. *See, e.g.*, Robin Cheryl Miller, Annotation, *Federal constitutional and statutory claims by HIV-positive inmates as to medical treatment or conditions of confinement*, 162 A.L.R. Fed. 181 (2000, updated weekly).

All of the above sources may be available through electronic databases, depending on your employer's subscriptions. In addition, you can identify current issues and citations by searching the briefs filed recently in the relevant jurisdiction that are available in the WestlawEdge or Lexis brief banks. Once you have located relevant, binding authority, be sure to update those sources via Shepard's on Lexis Advance or KeyCite on WestlawEdge to confirm their accuracy and to locate additional, more recent authority.

For all prison litigation, it is important to research the procedural requirements and other relevant provisions of the Prison Litigation Reform Act of 1996, a statute discussed in Chapter 10.

In Memory of Jack Lee Young (1981–2013), Advocate for Prisoners

Jack had been a staff attorney for the Plattsburgh office of Prisoners' Legal Services of New York for only one year when he died at age 32.

But already, "Jack had become a true and effective prisoner advocate," wrote Michael Cassidy, Managing Attorney for the office. Mr. Cassidy wrote: "Jack brought real help and compassion to countless individuals, many of whom were more desperate, more broken, and more alone than most people who do not do this work can ever truly appreciate. Individuals who were cast out by society, thrown and locked away, out of sight and out of mind, and so easily reviled and de-humanized by both the society that had condemned them and many of those charged with their custody." Jack successfully helped ensure that prisoners "in need of medical care and mental health care received the services they required and that the law demanded," Cassidy wrote. "He helped secure the release of prisoners who had been wrongfully placed in the unbelievably harsh and inhumane conditions of solitary confinement." Jack's rewards, Cassidy wrote, were "the victories he obtained, all the more sweet and satisfying due to their unfortunate rarity," "the many heart-felt appreciations he regularly received from clients for all that he did for them," and the knowledge that he had "helped give voice to those often deprived of any voice."

Jack graduated from Rutgers School of Law-Camden in 2009, took the Civil Rights Litigation class based on this book in 2008, and was a research assistant for the first edition of this book.

When Jack died, he was preparing to file a 42 U.S.C. § 1983 due process claim on behalf of a prisoner placed in solitary confinement for six months and was also investigating several officer use of force cases that may have violated the Eighth Amendment. Jack was particularly interested in the rights of transgender prisoners and took the lead in Prisoner Legal Services' role in an amicus brief to the First Circuit concerning discrimination against a transgender prisoner.

Jack's excitement to be embarking on a career of advocacy for prisoners is suggested by an email he sent to Professor Ricks just a year before he died:

> *So happy to let you know that I just accepted a position with Prisoners' Legal Services of New York in Plattsburgh. The job at PLS is doing exactly what I want. This work has literally been a dream of mine since I was in your constitutional litigation course in law school. Thank you so much for sharing your passion with that class, it's literally been life-changing for me.*
>
> *Now I just have to figure out how to actually be a lawyer and how to live on very little money (with lots of vacation days!). Wish me luck!*
>
> *Best,*
>
> *Jack*

Chapter Three

Fourteenth Amendment Substantive Due Process: Part One

> "[N]or shall any State deprive any person of life, liberty, or property, without due process of law"

A. Chapter Overview

For an individual to state a due process claim, the individual must have been deprived of life, liberty, or property. In the absence of a protected interest, there cannot be either a procedural or a substantive due process claim.

Procedural due process claims allege that the government deprived the person of a protected interest in life, liberty, or property by failing to abide by certain procedural steps to ensure that the deprivation is fair. By contrast, substantive due process claims allege that the government action that deprived the person of a protected interest in life, liberty, or property, is prohibited, regardless of the procedural steps that might have been followed.

"'[T]he touchstone of due process is protection of the individual against arbitrary action of government,' *Wolff v. McDonnell*, 418 U.S. 539, 558 (1974), whether the fault lies in a denial of fundamental procedural fairness, *see, e.g.*, *Fuentes v. Shevin*, 407 U.S. 67, 82 (1972) (the procedural due process guarantee protects against 'arbitrary takings'), or in the exercise of power without any reasonable justification in the service of a legitimate governmental objective, *see, e.g.*, *Daniels v. Williams*, 474 U.S. [327,] 331 (1986) (the substantive due process guarantee protects against government power arbitrarily and oppressively exercised)." *County of Sacramento v. Lewis*, 523 U.S. 833, 845–6 (1998). For a substantive due process claim based on abuse of executive power, the action must be "clearly unjustified by any legitimate objective" of government. *Lewis*, 523 U.S. at 840.

Challenges to government action specifically authorized by legislation or rules are analyzed differently than the claims examined in this Chapter. *E.g.*, *Washington v. Glucksberg*, 521 U.S. 702 (1997) (challenge to statute concerning physician-assisted suicide analyzed under rational basis test); *Planned Parenthood v. Casey*, 505 U.S. 833 (1992) (challenge to statute concerning abortion analyzed under undue burden test).

This Chapter concerns substantive due process challenges to executive actions that were not specifically authorized by legislation or rules. Not every loss of life, liberty, or property constitutes a "deprivation" of due process. The Supreme Court in *Daniels* held that negligent conduct by state officials does not deprive a person of life, liberty, or property under the 14th Amendment Due Process Clause. While negligence is not enough, what state of mind requirement *is* sufficient for a state official's conduct to "deprive" a person of due process? In the context of a police car chase, in separate briefs to the Supreme Court in *Lewis*, local governments argued that a police officer's conduct should not violate due process unless the officials' state of mind "shocked the conscience," while bystanders accidentally injured by police chases advocated for a deliberate indifference standard (Amici Briefs). The Supreme Court held in *Lewis* that executive action violates substantive due process only when it is "arbitrary or conscience shocking in a constitutional sense" (*Lewis*), a legal standard that encompasses a spectrum of fault ranging from a minimum of "something more than negligence" to "intent to cause harm." What standard applies depends on the factual context. This Chapter includes a chart illustrating the *Lewis* spectrum of fault.

Lewis requires a court analyzing a substantive due process challenge to executive action to (1) decide the threshold issue of what standard "shocks the conscience" in that particular factual context and then (2) decide what facts plaintiff must allege and prove with respect to defendant's state of mind. The federal circuits have struggled to apply *Lewis* in contexts other than police chases. This Chapter includes circuit court applications of the *Lewis* "conscience shocking" standard(s) to alleged deprivations of liberty (*Ziccardi*) and property (*Eichenlaub*).

Questions to guide reading of *Daniels*

1. Under *Daniels* and *Parratt*, does § 1983 have any state-of-mind requirement independent of whatever is necessary to show a violation of the underlying constitutional right? What holding of *Parratt* did *Daniels* overrule?
2. What did *Daniels* identify as the intended goals of the 14th Amendment Due Process Clause? According to *Daniels*, what is the relationship between federal constitutional law and state tort law?
3. Plaintiff in *Daniels* argued that requiring Plaintiffs to allege something more than negligence would raise serious concerns about what "more" than negligence would be required. Would the higher standard be intent? Or recklessness? Or gross negligence? The Plaintiff also argued that those words did not have clear meanings and would be difficult to apply. Why did *Daniels* reject those arguments?

4. After *Daniels*, what argument do you think governmental defendants to physical injury claims under the 14th Amendment Due Process Clause are very likely to make?

Daniels v. Williams

474 U.S. 327 (1986)

Justice REHNQUIST delivered the opinion of the Court.

In *Parratt v. Taylor*, 451 U.S. 527 (1981), a state prisoner sued under 42 U.S.C. § 1983, claiming that prison officials had negligently deprived him of his property without due process of law. After deciding that § 1983 contains no independent state-of-mind requirement, we concluded that although petitioner had been "deprived" of property within the meaning of the Due Process Clause of the Fourteenth Amendment, the State's postdeprivation tort remedy provided the process that was due. Petitioner's claim in this case, which also rests on an alleged Fourteenth Amendment "deprivation" caused by the negligent conduct of a prison official, leads us to reconsider our statement in *Parratt* that "the alleged loss, even though negligently caused, amounted to a deprivation." *Id.*, at 536–537.... We conclude that the Due Process Clause is simply not implicated by a negligent act of an official causing unintended loss of or injury to life, liberty, or property.

In this § 1983 action, petitioner seeks to recover damages for back and ankle injuries allegedly sustained when he fell on a prison stairway. He claims that, while an inmate at the city jail in Richmond, Virginia, he slipped on a pillow negligently left on the stairs by respondent, a correctional deputy stationed at the jail. Respondent's negligence, the argument runs, "deprived" petitioner of his "liberty" interest in freedom from bodily injury, *see Ingraham v. Wright*, 430 U.S. 651, 673 (1977); because respondent maintains that he is entitled to the defense of sovereign immunity in a state tort suit, petitioner is without an "adequate" state remedy.... Accordingly, the deprivation of liberty was without "due process of law."

...

In *Parratt v. Taylor*, we granted certiorari, as we had twice before, "to decide whether mere negligence will support a claim for relief under § 1983." 451 U.S., at 532.... After examining the language, legislative history, and prior interpretations of the statute, we concluded that § 1983, unlike its criminal counterpart, 18 U.S.C. § 242, contains no state-of-mind requirement independent of that necessary to state a violation of the underlying constitutional right. *Id.*, at 534–535.... We adhere to that conclusion.

But in any given § 1983 suit, the plaintiff must still prove a violation of the underlying constitutional right; and depending on the right, merely negligent conduct may not be enough to state a claim. *See, e.g.... Estelle v. Gamble*, 429 U.S. 97, 105 (1976) ("deliberate indifference" to prisoner's serious illness or injury sufficient to constitute cruel and unusual punishment under the Eighth Amendment).

In *Parratt*, before concluding that Nebraska's tort remedy provided all the process that was due, we said that the loss of the prisoner's hobby kit, "even though negligently caused, amounted to a deprivation [under the Due Process Clause]." 451 U.S., at 536–537. Justice Powell, concurring in the result, criticized the majority for "pass[ing] over" this important question of the state of mind required to constitute a "deprivation" of property. *Id.*, at 547. He argued that negligent acts by state officials, though causing loss of property, are not actionable under the Due Process Clause. To Justice Powell, mere negligence could not "wor[k] a deprivation in the *constitutional sense*." *Id.*, at 548, (emphasis in original). Not only does the word "deprive" in the Due Process Clause connote more than a negligent act, but we should not "open the federal courts to lawsuits where there has been no affirmative abuse of power." *Id.*, at 548–549.... Upon reflection, we agree and overrule *Parratt* to the extent that it states that mere lack of due care by a state official may "deprive" an individual of life, liberty, or property under the Fourteenth Amendment.

The Due Process Clause of the Fourteenth Amendment provides: "[N]or shall any State deprive any person of life, liberty, or property, without due process of law." Historically, this guarantee of due process has been applied to *deliberate* decisions of government officials to deprive a person of life, liberty, or property. *E.g.*... *Rochin v. California*, 342 U.S. 165 (1952) (stomach pumping) ... *Ingraham v. Wright*, 430 U.S. 651 (1977) (paddling student); *Hudson v. Palmer*, 468 U.S. 517 (1984) (intentional destruction of inmate's property). No decision of this Court before *Parratt* supported the view that negligent conduct by a state official, even though causing injury, constitutes a deprivation under the Due Process Clause. This history reflects the traditional and common-sense notion that the Due Process Clause ... was " 'intended to secure the individual from the arbitrary exercise of the powers of government,' " ... *See also Wolff v. McDonnell*, 418 U.S. 539, 558 (1974) ("The touchstone of due process is protection of the individual against arbitrary action of government").... By requiring the government to follow appropriate procedures when its agents decide to "deprive any person of life, liberty, or property," the Due Process Clause promotes fairness in such decisions. And by barring certain government actions regardless of the fairness of the procedures used to implement them, *e.g.*, *Rochin*, *supra*, it serves to prevent governmental power from being "used for purposes of oppression["]....

We think that the actions of prison custodians in leaving a pillow on the prison stairs, or mislaying an inmate's property, are quite remote from the concerns just discussed. Far from an abuse of power, lack of due care suggests no more than a failure to measure up to the conduct of a reasonable person. To hold that injury caused by such conduct is a deprivation within the meaning of the Fourteenth Amendment would trivialize the centuries-old principle of due process of law.

The Fourteenth Amendment is a part of a Constitution generally designed to allocate governing authority among the Branches of the Federal Government and between that Government and the States, and to secure certain individual rights against both State and Federal Government. When dealing with a claim that such a document creates a right in prisoners to sue a government official because he negligently created an unsafe condition in the prison, we bear in mind Chief Justice Marshall's admonition that "we must never forget, that it is a *constitution* we are expounding," *McCulloch v.*

Maryland, 4 Wheat. (17 U.S.) 316, 407 (1819) (emphasis in original). Our Constitution deals with the large concerns of the governors and the governed, but it does not purport to supplant traditional tort law in laying down rules of conduct to regulate liability for injuries that attend living together in society. We have previously rejected reasoning that " 'would make of the Fourteenth Amendment a font of tort law to be superimposed upon whatever systems may already be administered by the States,' " *Paul v. Davis*, 424 U.S. 693, 701 (1976), quoted in *Parratt v. Taylor*, 451 U.S., at 544....

The only tie between the facts of this case and anything governmental in nature is the fact that respondent was a sheriff's deputy at the Richmond city jail and petitioner was an inmate confined in that jail. But while the Due Process Clause of the Fourteenth Amendment obviously speaks to some facets of this relationship ... we do not believe its protections are triggered by lack of due care by prison officials. "Medical malpractice does not become a constitutional violation merely because the victim is a prisoner," *Estelle v. Gamble*, 429 U.S. 97, 106 (1976), and "false imprisonment does not become a violation of the Fourteenth Amendment merely because the defendant is a state official." *Baker v. McCollan*, 443 U.S. 137, 146 (1979). Where a government official's act causing injury to life, liberty, or property is merely negligent, "no procedure for compensation is *constitutionally* required." *Parratt*, *supra*, 451 U.S., at 548 (Powell, J., concurring in result) (emphasis added)....

That injuries inflicted by governmental negligence are not addressed by the United States Constitution is not to say that they may not raise significant legal concerns and lead to the creation of protectible legal interests. The enactment of tort claim statutes, for example, reflects the view that injuries caused by such negligence should generally be redressed.... It is no reflection on either the breadth of the United States Constitution or the importance of traditional tort law to say that they do not address the same concerns.

In support of his claim that negligent conduct can give rise to a due process "deprivation," petitioner makes several arguments, none of which we find persuasive. He states, for example, that "it is almost certain that some negligence claims are within § 1983," and cites as an example the failure of a State to comply with the procedural requirements of *Wolff v. McDonnell*, *supra*, before depriving an inmate of good-time credit. We think the relevant action of the prison officials in that situation is their deliberate decision to deprive the inmate of good-time credit, not their hypothetically negligent failure to accord him the procedural protections of the Due Process Clause. But we need not rule out the possibility that there are other constitutional provisions that would be violated by mere lack of care in order to hold, as we do, that such conduct does not implicate the Due Process Clause of the Fourteenth Amendment.

Petitioner also suggests that artful litigants, undeterred by a requirement that they plead more than mere negligence, will often be able to allege sufficient facts to support a claim of intentional deprivation. In the instant case, for example, petitioner notes that he could have alleged that the pillow was left on the stairs with the intention of harming him. This invitation to "artful" pleading, petitioner contends, would engender sticky (and needless) disputes over what is fairly pleaded. What's more, requiring complainants to allege something more than negligence would raise serious questions about what "more" than negligence—intent, recklessness or "gross negligence"—is required,[3] and indeed about what these elusive terms mean.... But even if accurate, petitioner's observations do not carry the day. In the first place, many branches of the law abound in nice distinctions that may be troublesome but have been thought nonetheless necessary: "I do not think we need trouble ourselves with the thought that my view depends upon differences of degree. The whole law does so as soon as it is civilized." ... (Holmes, J., partially concurring). More important, the difference between one end of the spectrum—negligence—and the other—intent—is abundantly clear. *See* O. Holmes, *The Common Law* 3 (1923). In any event, we decline to trivialize the Due Process Clause in an effort to simplify constitutional litigation.

...

Petitioner alleges that he was injured by the negligence of respondent, a custodial official at the city jail. Whatever other provisions of state law or general jurisprudence he may rightly invoke, the Fourteenth Amendment to the United States Constitution does not afford him a remedy.

Questions to guide reading of Amici Brief

Below are two "friend of the court" briefs filed in *Lewis*, the next Supreme Court case in this Chapter. *Lewis* concerned a police car chase that ended in a fatal accident. You may want to read the facts of *Lewis* before reading the Amici briefs.

1. Why do you think Amici local and state governments advocated a 4th instead of a 14th Amendment analysis?
2. Focusing on the 14th Amendment substantive due process argument, what constitutional principles from *Daniels* did the government Amici invoke?
3. Can you tell what 14th Amendment legal standard the government Amici were advocating that the Supreme Court adopt? After reading *Lewis*, do you think the brief used "shock the conscience" in the same way the Supreme Court used that term in *Lewis*?
4. What role for state law regulation of police chases did the brief advocate? How would the government Amici respond to the claim made in the STOPP

---

3. Despite his claim about what he might have pleaded, petitioner concedes that respondent was at most negligent. Accordingly, this case affords us no occasion to consider whether something less than intentional conduct, such as recklessness or "gross negligence," is enough to trigger the protections of the Due Process Clause.

Amicus brief that follows that "the police vehicle remains the last unregulated weapon in a police officer's arsenal"?

Amici Curiae Brief of Local and State Government Organizations in *Lewis*

1997 WL 458770 (Aug. 8, 1997)

Brief of The National Association of Counties, U.S. Conference of Mayors, National League of Cities, National Governors' Association, Council of State Governments, International City/County Management Association, and International Municipal Lawyers Association. By Charles Rothfeld, Mayer, Brown & Platt, and Richard Ruda, State and Local Legal Center, Washington D.C.

INTEREST OF THE AMICI CURIAE

Amici are organizations whose members include state, county, and municipal governments and officials throughout the United States. They have a compelling interest in the issues presented in this case: whether and by what standard a state law enforcement official who engages in a vehicular pursuit resulting in injury to the fleeing suspect may be held liable under the Fourteenth Amendment for a violation of substantive due process where the injury to the suspect was accidental or unintentional.

...

SUMMARY OF ARGUMENT

A. [The Fourth Amendment Defines the Process that is Due to an Individual During a Police Pursuit and There Was No Fourth Amendment Violation in this Case]

The court of appeals was incorrect in concluding that respondents have presented a cognizable substantive due process claim.... [It]t is the Fourth Amendment that defines the process due an individual who is the subject of a police pursuit. *Graham v. Connor*, 490 U.S. 386, 395 (1989). And "[w]here a particular amendment 'provides an explicit textual source of constitutional protection' against a particular sort of government behavior, 'that Amendment, not the more generalized notion of 'substantive due process,' must be the guide to analyzing these claims.'" *Albright v. Oliver*, 510 U.S. 266, 273 (1994) (plurality opinion) (citation omitted). Appropriately analyzed under the Fourth Amendment, there was no constitutional violation in this case.

B. [Unintended or Accidental Injuries are Not Actionable as a Violation of Substantive Due Process]

If due process analysis is not wholly displaced in this case by the Fourth Amendment, the court of appeals applied an incorrect substantive due process standard in holding that recklessness may give rise to a constitutional violation. In fact, the Due Process Clause is concerned with "*deliberate* decisions of government officials to deny a person life, liberty, or property." *Daniels v. Williams*, 474 U.S. 327, 331 (1986) (emphasis in original). This conclusion flows from the language, history, and purpose of the Clause, which was designed to prevent governmental power from being used for purposes of oppression. The Ninth Circuit's recklessness standard is inconsistent with this understanding. Moreover, substantive due process comes into play only when the challenged governmental action was so brutal or offensive that it "shocks the conscience." *Rochin v. California*, 342 U.S. 165, 172 (1952). Reckless conduct does not meet that exacting standard.

C. [The Regulation of Police Pursuits is Appropriately Left to the States and Local Governments]

Addressing the consequences of reckless or negligent police conduct is appropriately left to state tort law. In setting the limits on liability in this area, a host of considerations go into balancing the interests of injured parties on the one hand and the needs of effective law enforcement on the other. Tort law is well-adapted to striking that balance. And many States provide for liability on the part of the officer or his employer when such pursuits result in injury. Moreover, most States and localities have adopted policies regulating high-speed vehicular pursuits. In these circumstances, the relevant choices are best made "by locally elected representatives, and not by federal judges interpreting the basic charter of Government for the entire country." *Collins v. City of Harker Heights*, 503 U.S. 115, 129 (1992).

ARGUMENT

A POLICE PURSUIT RESULTING IN UNINTENDED INJURY IS NOT ACTIONABLE UNDER THE DUE PROCESS CLAUSE

...

B. Unintended Or Accidental Injuries are Not Actionable as a Violation of Substantive Due Process

1. The Ninth Circuit['s] ... approach would recognize a substantive due process violation even where the injury was merely accidental. Such a radical expansion of substantive due process has no support in the text or history of the Due Process Clause, or in this Court's precedents interpreting the provision.

"As a general matter, the Court has always been reluctant to expand the concept of substantive due process because guideposts for responsible decisionmaking in this unchartered area are scarce and open-ended." *Collins*, 503 U.S. at 115. Instead, the Court has been faithful to the central purpose of the provision: "[t]he Due Process Clause of the Fourteenth Amendment was intended to prevent government from abusing [its] power, or employing it as an instrument of oppression." *Ibid.* (citations and internal quotation marks omitted). *See Albright*, 510 U.S. at 271–272 (plurality opinion) (noting limited circumstances in which the Court has applied protections of substantive due process). Although this Court has not had "occasion to consider whether something less than intentional conduct, such as recklessness or 'gross negligence,' is enough to trigger the protections of the Due Process Clause" (*Daniels*, 474 U.S. at 334 n. 3), the principles established by this Court support the requirement of intentional conduct to prove violations of due process ... *See Parratt v. Taylor*, 451 U.S. 527, 548 (1981) (Powell, J., concurring in result) ("A 'deprivation' connotes an intentional act denying something to someone, or, at the very least, a deliberate decision not to act to prevent a loss."). The constitutional text thus suggests that an unintended loss of life, liberty, or property simply is not cognizable under the Due Process Clause.

...

"[I]n the substantive due process analysis, it is the State's *affirmative act of restraining the individual's freedom to act on his own behalf*—through incarceration, institutionalization, or other similar restraint of personal liberty—which is the 'deprivation of liberty' triggering the protections of the Due Process Clause * * *." *DeShaney v. Winnebago County Dep't of Social Servs.*, 489 U.S. 189, 200 (1989) (emphasis added).

The Court's decisions have been consistent in applying this understanding, repeatedly rejecting attempts to transform the Due Process Clause into a residuary provision protecting individuals from unsafe conditions created or left uncorrected by the State. In *Daniels*, for example, the Court made clear that "the Due Process Clause is simply not implicated by a *negligent* act of an official causing unintended loss of or injury to life, liberty, or property." 474 U.S. at 328 (emphasis in original). Similarly, the Court held in *DeShaney* that the Due Process Clause is not implicated when the State fails to provide care or adequate protective services to an individual who is not within its custody. *See* 489 U.S. at 194. While recognizing the natural impulse "to find a way for [the injured parties] to receive adequate compensation for the grievous harm inflicted upon them," the Court concluded that, absent an affirmative act by the State, the State's duty of care was a matter to be redressed by state tort law, not the Constitution. *Id.* at 202–203.

Likewise, in *Collins* the Court rejected the argument that a city's "deliberate indifference" to the safety of one of its employees who died by asphyxia during the course of his employment "was arbitrary government action that must 'shock the conscience.'" 503 U.S. at 126. Because the "deliberate indifference" claim was "analogous to a fairly typical state-law tort claim," it was a matter to be addressed by the States and municipalities, "rather than by federal judges interpreting the basic charter of Government for the entire country." *Id.* at 128–129.

Against this background, the Ninth Circuit's holding ultimately is flawed because it has no foundation in constitutional principle. After all, this Court rejected the contention that negligent acts by government officials violate due process because such an expansive reading of the Clause has no relationship to the purpose of restraining governmental "oppression." *See Daniels*, 474 U.S. at 330–333. And while reckless conduct may present a greater danger of injury than does negligence, that difference likewise is not relevant to the purposes of the Due Process Clause. Of course, actions that are reckless may appropriately be actionable in tort. The Constitution, however,

> deals with the large concerns of governors and the governed, but it does not purport to supplant traditional tort law in laying down rules of conduct to regulate liability for injuries that attend living together in society. [The Court] ha[s] previously rejected reasoning that "would make of the Fourteenth Amendment a font of tort law to be superimposed upon whatever systems may already be administered by the States[.]"

Daniels, 474 U.S. at 332 (citations omitted). And "[i]t is no reflection on either the United States Constitution or the importance of traditional tort law to say that they do not address the same concerns." *Id.* at 333. *See Collins*, 503 U.S. at 129.

Contrary to the court of appeals' conclusion, the State thus does not "deprive" the fleeing individual or the general public of any due process right simply by initiating and then continuing a high-speed police pursuit. There of course is no "deprivation" of life or liberty in the pursuit itself, even if the pursuit is initiated and continued in reckless disregard for the pursued individual's safety; during the course of the pursuit, the fleeing individual is not restrained by any affirmative act of the State.[7] The deprivation occurs, if at all, when there is an affirmative act by the State that vitiates the individual's liberty. And in this case, there was no such affirmative act by the State because Officer Smith "did not intend to hit Lewis with his patrol car." Lewis's restraint from movement and loss of life were accidental and thus do not constitute a "deprivation" of due process.

Recognizing a deprivation of due process in these circumstances would work an unprecedented expansion of substantive due process, conferring a cause of action upon individuals who have not been restrained in their liberty by an affirmative act of the State. *Cf. DeShaney*, 489 U.S. at 198–200 (distinguishing cases in which duty of care was imposed on State for individuals within its custody). Such a precedent potentially would expose all sorts of state conduct to constitutional scrutiny, such as the State's unsafe maintenance of its roadways or water supply, its use of asbestos in its buildings, or its contamination of the air with pollutants in a manner that is claimed to be reckless. The Fourteenth Amendment was not meant to address these sorts of dangers "that attend living together in society." *Daniels*, 474 U.S. at 332.

2. The decision below also is flawed for a second, related reason. Obviously, not all intentional deprivations of life, liberty, or property deny the affected individual due process; a constitutional violation occurs only when the government's conduct is so "brutal" or "offensive" that it "shocks the conscience." ... [T]he Court has consistently applied the "shocks the conscience" standard to substantive due process claims involving allegedly arbitrary deprivations of life or liberty by individual government officials acting apart from a specific statutory or regulatory scheme ... In the Court's most recent consideration of such a substantive due process claim, it likewise held that a city's alleged conduct in failing to provide a safe working environment to its employees did not state a claim under the Fourteenth Amendment because the conduct could not "properly be characterized as arbitrary, or conscience shocking, in the constitutional sense." *Collins*, 503 U.S. at 128....

The Ninth Circuit's deliberate indifference or recklessness standard cannot be reconciled with these decisions: it would permit violations of substantive due process

7. For instance, a fleeing suspect who is pursued by law enforcement officials but eludes capture surely could not have been deprived of life or liberty during the pursuit, even if the law enforcement officials initiated and continued the pursuit in reckless disregard for the suspect's safety. *Cf. Tennessee v. Garner*, 471 U.S. 1, 31 (1985) (O'Connor, J., dissenting) (expressing skepticism about "allow[ing] criminal suspects who successfully escape to return later with § 1983 claims against officers who used, albeit unsuccessfully, deadly force in their futile attempt to capture the fleeing suspect").

without any determination that the alleged conduct was "brutal," "offensive," or "shocking to the conscience." ... The deliberate indifference standard thus ignores "our Nation's history, legal traditions, and practices," which provide "crucial guideposts for responsible decisionmaking" in the due process analysis....

Indeed, in only one area has the Court adopted a standard of deliberate indifference as the measure of evaluating the constitutionality of state conduct. In *Estelle v. Gamble*, 429 U.S. 97, 104 (1976), the Court considered an Eighth Amendment claim of cruel and unusual punishment in the context of a prisoner's failure to receive medical treatment. This Court held "that deliberate indifference to serious medical needs of prisoners constitutes the 'unnecessary and wanton infliction of pain,' proscribed by the Eighth Amendment." *Ibid.* (citation omitted). This standard was appropriate for evaluating the State's failure to provide medical care to prisoners within its custody "because the State's responsibility to attend to the medical needs of prisoners does not ordinarily clash with other equally important governmental responsibilities" and because medical care generally did not involve situations requiring split-second decisions. *Whitley v. Albers*, 475 U.S. 312, 320 (1986).

In *Whitley*, however, the Court rejected the application of the "deliberate indifference" standard in evaluating a prisoner's claim that prison officials subjected him to cruel and unusual punishment by shooting him in the course of their attempt to quell a prison riot. The Court reasoned that "a deliberate indifference standard does not adequately capture the importance of such competing obligations, or convey the appropriate hesitancy to critique in hindsight decisions necessarily made in haste, under pressure, and frequently without the luxury of a second chance." *Ibid.*

The same holds true for police pursuits. The State has important obligations to enforce the law, to apprehend suspects, to investigate suspicious conduct, and to prevent fleeing suspects from endangering others or themselves. Typically, as was true in this case, whether to initiate and then to continue a pursuit requires snap decisions: the law enforcement officer must act in great "haste [and] under pressure, and frequently without the luxury of a second chance." *Whitley*, 475 U.S. at 320. *See Graham*, 490 U.S. at 397. The entire pursuit in this case, for example, lasted all of 75 seconds. To adopt a "deliberate indifference" standard to evaluate this conduct would undervalue the importance of the State's obligations in law enforcement and would invite wholesale second-guessing of decisions that must be made under considerable pressure.

Questions to guide reading of Amicus Brief

1. Note how many people were killed as a result of police car chases between 1991–95 and how many people were killed during the same period as a result of firearm-related justified homicides.
2. In Miami, what were the main reasons for high-speed pursuits between 1990–94? What were the most common results? Is it fair to argue that the penalty for running a stop sign was injury or death?

3. Does this brief's invocation of the concept of "the constitutionalization of tort law" echo a theme in *Daniels*?

Amicus Brief of Solutions to the Tragedies of Police Pursuits in Lewis

1997 WL 907568 (Oct. 1, 1997) by Andrew C. Clarke, Memphis, Tennessee

SUMMARY OF ARGUMENT

The police vehicle is the last unregulated weapon in a police officer's arsenal. Each year thousands of people are injured and killed during the course of high speed pursuits. While many injuries occur to the driver of the fleeing vehicle, many totally innocent third parties are injured and killed during the course of high speed pursuits.... [M]any criminologists believe that more people are killed each year during the course of high-speed pursuits than any other police activity, including firearms. Given that thousands of people are injured and killed during the course of high speed chases each year, Amicus submits that police pursuits should be restricted by the substantive due process component of the Fourteenth Amendment and that officers should not be given unbridled discretion with respect to the instigation, continuation and termination of pursuits.

... [T]here is a conflict among the Circuits regarding the proper standard to be employed in substantive due process police chase cases: 1) "shocks the conscience" and 2) "deliberate indifference" or "reckless disregard." Amicus submits that the "shocks the conscience" standard is undefinable and will not serve to provide either law enforcement or the public with a meaningful standard from which they can take steps to reduce the number of tragedies from police pursuits.

Amicus submits that the "deliberate indifference" or "reckless disregard" standard governing other law enforcement actions will provide both law enforcement and the public with a familiar standard from which to formulate training and policies to reduce the number of injuries or deaths stemming from pursuits. Imposing liability for violating a victim's substantive due process rights under a "deliberate indifference" or "reckless disregard" standard will not result in a constitutionalization of tort law. This standard would only seek to hold an officer liable for injuries to a victim resulting from a pursuit when an officer consciously disregards a known danger to a victim or class of victims during the course of a pursuit.

ARGUMENT

I. WHETHER A POLICE OFFICER WHO DISPLAYS DELIBERATE INDIFFERENCE TO OR RECKLESS DISREGARD OF THE RISKS OF A HIGH-SPEED PURSUIT TO THE PUBLIC IS LIABLE FOR INJURIES PROXIMATELY CAUSED TO THE SUSPECT AND/OR INNOCENT THIRD PARTY FOR VIOLATING THE VICTIM'S SUBSTANTIVE DUE PROCESS RIGHTS.

On May 3, 1988, John Basaman was driving home from a day trip to Philadelphia along with his wife and children. As he entered a controlled intersection in Evesham

Township, N.J., his car was struck by a man being chased by the police [for a minor traffic offense]. His wife and infant son were killed and his two year old son was critically injured. The Basaman family lived not more than a mile from us.

Just three days later, on May 8, 1988, Erin Walsh, a neighbor and schoolmate of my daughter's, was coming home from her job at a handicapped facility. A man being chased by the police [again, for a minor traffic offense] crossed into her lane and collided head-on with her car. Tragically, not only was Erin killed, but her mother, who was travelling in the car directly behind her daughter's, witnessed the entire scene. Understandably, the community was outraged that three totally innocent people had been killed, three others had suffered injuries and that two families had been devastated within a few days.

...

Many noted criminologists and police officers have opined that the most deadly weapon in the police officer's arsenal is a police vehicle. A police vehicle or vehicle fleeing from the police travelling at sixty miles per hour has a greater potential for harm than a bullet from a gun. Despite the vast number of persons injured and killed each year from police pursuits, the police vehicle remains the last unregulated weapon in a police officer's arsenal.

...

From 1991–1995, there were 1727 pursuit-related deaths and [according to Federal Bureau of Investigation statistics on police use of firearms] 2063 firearm-related deaths.... [I]n 1995, the number of pursuit-related deaths exceeds the number of justifiable homicides committed by law enforcement even though the figures regarding pursuits are neither complete nor final.

...

Miami and Metro-Dade Studies

[I]n Dade County, Florida.... for the years 1990–1994 [, t]he [police pursuit] results are as follows:

1. 1,049 high-speed pursuits were initiated;
2. 448 (45%) were initiated for traffic offenses;
3. 45 (4%) were initiated as a result of a broadcast stating "be on the lookout" for a suspect vehicle;
4. 334 (35%) were initiated for suspected felony offenses;
5. 157 (16%) were initiated because of a suspect vehicle;
6. 55 (0.05%) were initiated for unknown reasons;
7. 428 (41%) of pursuits resulted in collisions;
8. 257 (20%) of pursuits resulted in injuries;
9. 10 (3%) of pursuits lasted less than one minute;
10. 37 (10%) of pursuits lasted 2–4 minutes;

11. 206 (59%) of pursuits lasted 5–10 minutes;

12. 99 (28%) of pursuits lasted 11 or more minutes.

... [I]n 1992, the Metro-Dade Police Department changed its pursuit policy from a judgmental policy, one in which the officer makes most of the operational decisions during a pursuit, to a restrictive policy which limits pursuits to known violent felons. This change in policy resulted in a drastic reduction of pursuits from 279 in 1992 to 51 in 1993....

[James Auten studied 700 police pursuits in Illinois] ... With respect to pursuits for traffic offenses, Auten opined:

> "For at least 46 people that ultimate penalty for running a stop sign, speeding, failure to yield, improper passing, etc., was an injury or death. That's ridiculous! If public safety is in fact the ultimate goal, then it seems rather obvious that pursuits initiated for this reason should be eliminated."

...

[A] police officer's most valuable tool in diminishing the risks that a pursuit poses to the public is to discontinue the chase....

Questions to guide reading of *Lewis*

Lewis is included also in Chapter 6, for its relevance to the 4th Amendment, and in Chapter 11, for its relevance to qualified immunity.

1. On what issue did the Supreme Court grant certiorari? What standard did *Lewis* adopt?
2. Is the Supreme Court eager to expand the concept of substantive due process? What does *Lewis* identify as core goals of due process, and particularly of substantive due process?
3. *Lewis* held that due process does not impose liability whenever somebody cloaked with state authority causes harm. Why can't negligent conduct violate substantive due process?
4. *Lewis* adopted a "shocks the conscience" standard for all substantive due process claims of executive abuse of power. For a substantive due process claim of executive abuse of power, what level of culpability is most likely to be considered conscience-shocking?
5. *Lewis* held that the middle range of culpability—more than negligence but less than intentional conduct, such as recklessness or deliberate indifference—can sometimes be egregious enough to be conscience-shocking. Why might this standard be difficult to apply? As a practical matter, how might a lawyer determine the meanings of those phrases?
6. Why did *Lewis* analogize sudden police chases (under the Due Process Clause) to prison responses to prison riots (an 8th Amendment analysis)?

Why did *Lewis* reject the analogy of sudden police chases to prison officials' medical treatment for inmates and therefore reject the corresponding "deliberate indifference" standard for police chases?

7. Why did the motorcycle passenger in *Lewis* fail to state a substantive due process claim? Is it likely a plaintiff will ever satisfy the *Lewis* standard?
8. Compare and contrast the threshold fault standard for 8th Amendment claims in *Whitley/Farmer* with the threshold fault standard for 14th Amendment substantive due process claims in *Lewis*. Both fault standards are visually represented in charts in this book, in Chapter 2 and in this Chapter.
9. Do you think the Supreme Court intended the "shocks the conscience" standard to apply to executive conduct outside of the context of police car chases?

County of Sacramento v. Lewis

523 U.S. 833 (1998)

Justice SOUTER delivered the opinion of the Court.

The issue in this case is whether a police officer violates the Fourteenth Amendment's guarantee of substantive due process by causing death through deliberate or reckless indifference to life in a high-speed automobile chase aimed at apprehending a suspected offender. We answer no, and hold that in such circumstances only a purpose to cause harm unrelated to the legitimate object of arrest will satisfy the element of arbitrary conduct shocking to the conscience, necessary for a due process violation.

I

On May 22, 1990, at approximately 8:30 p.m., petitioner James Everett Smith, a Sacramento County sheriff's deputy, along with another officer, Murray Stapp, responded to a call to break up a fight. Upon returning to his patrol car, Stapp saw a motorcycle approaching at high speed. It was operated by 18-year-old Brian Willard and carried Philip Lewis, respondents' 16-year-old decedent, as a passenger. Neither boy had anything to do with the fight that prompted the call to the police.

Stapp turned on his overhead rotating lights, yelled to the boys to stop, and pulled his patrol car closer to Smith's, attempting to pen the motorcycle in. Instead of pulling over in response to Stapp's warning lights and commands, Willard slowly maneuvered the motorcycle between the two police cars and sped off. Smith immediately switched on his own emergency lights and siren, made a quick turn, and began pursuit at high speed. For 75 seconds over a course of 1.3 miles in a residential neighborhood, the motorcycle wove in and out of oncoming traffic, forcing two cars and a bicycle to swerve off the road. The motorcycle and patrol car reached speeds up to 100 miles an hour, with Smith following at a distance as short as 100 feet; at that speed, his car would have required 650 feet to stop.

The chase ended after the motorcycle tipped over as Willard tried a sharp left turn. By the time Smith slammed on his brakes, Willard was out of the way, but Lewis was not. The patrol car skidded into him at 40 miles an hour, propelling him some 70 feet down the road and inflicting massive injuries. Lewis was pronounced dead at the scene.

Respondents, Philip Lewis's parents and the representatives of his estate, brought this action under [42 U.S.C. § 1983] against petitioner[] ... Deputy Smith, alleging a deprivation of Philip Lewis's Fourteenth Amendment substantive due process right to life.... [T]he Court of Appeals reversed the summary judgment in favor of Smith and remanded for trial.

We granted certiorari ... to resolve a conflict among the Circuits over the standard of culpability on the part of a law enforcement officer for violating substantive due process in a pursuit case. Compare [*Lewis v. Sacramento County*,] 98 F.3d [434], 441[(9th Cir. 1996)] ("deliberate indifference" or "reckless disregard"), with *Evans v. Avery*, 100 F.3d 1033, 1038 (C.A.1 1996) ("shocks the conscience"), *cert. denied*, 520 U.S. 1210 (1997) [and precedents from 10th, 3rd, 4th, 5th Circuits] (same). We now reverse.

II

Our prior cases have held the provision that "[n]o State shall ... deprive any person of life, liberty, or property, without due process of law," U.S. Const., Amdt. 14, § 1, to "guarante[e] more than fair process," *Washington v. Glucksberg*, 521 U.S. 702, 719 (1997), and to cover a substantive sphere as well, "barring certain government actions regardless of the fairness of the procedures used to implement them," *Daniels v. Williams*, 474 U.S. 327, 331 (1986).... The allegation here that Lewis was deprived of his right to life in violation of substantive due process amounts to such a claim, that under the circumstances described earlier, Smith's actions in causing Lewis's death were an abuse of executive power so clearly unjustified by any legitimate objective of law enforcement as to be barred by the Fourteenth Amendment. *Cf. Collins v. Harker Heights*, 503 U.S. 115, 126 (1992) (noting that the Due Process Clause was intended to prevent government officials " ' "from abusing [their] power, or employing it as an instrument of oppression" ' ") (quoting *DeShaney v. Winnebago County Dept. of Social Servs.*, 489 U.S. 189, 196 (1989)....

Leaving aside the question of qualified immunity, which formed the basis for the District Court's dismissal of their case,[5] respondents face two principal objections to their claim. The first is that its subject is necessarily governed by a more definite provision of the Constitution (to the exclusion of any possible application of substantive due process); the second, that in any event the allegations are insufficient to state a substantive due process violation through executive abuse of power. Respondents can meet the first objection, but not the second.

A

Because we have "always been reluctant to expand the concept of substantive due process," *Collins v. Harker Heights*, *supra*, at 125 ... we held in *Graham v. Connor*,

---

5. [*Note: This footnote is included in Chapter 11, Qualified Immunity.*]

490 U.S. 386 (1989), that "[w]here a particular Amendment provides an explicit textual source of constitutional protection against a particular sort of government behavior, that Amendment, not the more generalized notion of substantive due process, must be the guide for analyzing these claims." *Albright v. Oliver*, 510 U.S. 266, 273 (1994)....

> [*Note: The Court held the claim was properly analyzed under substantive due process, not under the Fourth Amendment. This portion of the decision will be assigned in the Fourth Amendment reading.*]

...

B

Since the time of our early explanations of due process, we have understood the core of the concept to be protection against arbitrary action.... We have emphasized time and again that "[t]he touchstone of due process is protection of the individual against arbitrary action of government," *Wolff v. McDonnell*, 418 U.S. 539, 558 (1974), whether the fault lies in a denial of fundamental procedural fairness, *see, e.g.*, *Fuentes v. Shevin*, 407 U.S. 67, 82 (1972) (the procedural due process guarantee protects against 'arbitrary takings'), or in the exercise of power without any reasonable justification in the service of a legitimate governmental objective, *see, e.g.*, *Daniels v. Williams*, 474 U.S., at 331 ... (the substantive due process guarantee protects against government power arbitrarily and oppressively exercised). While due process protection in the substantive sense limits what the government may do in both its legislative ... and its executive capacities ... criteria to identify what is fatally arbitrary differ depending on whether it is legislation or a specific act of a governmental officer that is at issue.

Our cases dealing with abusive executive action have repeatedly emphasized that only the most egregious official conduct can be said to be "arbitrary in the constitutional sense," *Collins v. Harker Heights*, 503 U.S., at 129 ... thereby recognizing the point made in different circumstances by Chief Justice Marshall, "'that it is a *constitution* we are expounding,'" *Daniels v. Williams*.... Thus, in *Collins v. Harker Heights*, for example, we said that the Due Process Clause was intended to prevent government officials "'"from abusing [their] power, or employing it as an instrument of oppression."'" 503 U.S., at 126 (quoting *DeShaney v. Winnebago County Dept. of Social Servs.*, 489 U.S., at 196....

To this end, for half a century now we have spoken of the cognizable level of executive abuse of power as that which shocks the conscience. We first put the test this way in *Rochin v. California*, *supra*, at 172–173, where we found the forced pumping of a suspect's stomach enough to offend due process as conduct "that shocks the conscience" and violates the "decencies of civilized conduct." In the intervening years we have repeatedly adhered to *Rochin*'s benchmark. *See, e.g.*.... *Whitley v. Albers*, 475 U.S. 312, 327 (1986).... Most recently, in *Collins v. Harker Heights* ... we said again that the substantive component of the Due Process Clause is violated by executive action only when it "can properly be characterized as arbitrary, or conscience shocking, in a constitutional sense." While the measure of what is conscience shocking is no calibrated yard stick, it does, as Judge Friendly put it, "poin[t] the way." *Johnson v. Glick*, 481 F.2d 1028, 1033 (C.A.2), *cert. denied*, 414 U.S. 1033 (1973).

It should not be surprising that the constitutional concept of conscience shocking duplicates no traditional category of common-law fault, but rather points clearly away from liability, or clearly toward it, only at the ends of the tort law's spectrum of culpability. Thus, we have made it clear that the due process guarantee does not entail a body of constitutional law imposing liability whenever someone cloaked with state authority causes harm. In *Paul v. Davis*, 424 U.S. 693, 701 (1976), for example, we explained that the Fourteenth Amendment is not a "font of tort law to be superimposed upon whatever systems may already be administered by the States," and in *Daniels v. Williams*, 474 U.S., at 332 we reaffirmed the point that "[o]ur Constitution deals with the large concerns of the governors and the governed, but it does not purport to supplant traditional tort law in laying down rules of conduct to regulate liability for injuries that attend living together in society." We have accordingly rejected the lowest common denominator of customary tort liability as any mark of sufficiently shocking conduct, and have held that the Constitution does not guarantee due care on the part of state officials; liability for negligently inflicted harm is categorically beneath the threshold of constitutional due process. *See id.*, at 328.... It is, on the contrary, behavior at the other end of the culpability spectrum that would most probably support a substantive due process claim; conduct intended to injure in some way unjustifiable by any government interest is the sort of official action most likely to rise to the conscience-shocking level. *See Daniels v. Williams*, 474 U.S., at 331 ("Historically, this guarantee of due process has been applied to *deliberate* decisions of government officials to deprive a person of life, liberty, or property" (emphasis in original)).

Whether the point of the conscience shocking is reached when injuries are produced with culpability falling within the middle range, following from something more than negligence but "less than intentional conduct, such as recklessness or 'gross negligence,'" *id.*, at 334, n. 3 is a matter for closer calls. To be sure, we have expressly recognized the possibility that some official acts in this range may be actionable under the Fourteenth Amendment, *ibid.*, and our cases have compelled recognition that such conduct is egregious enough to state a substantive due process claim in at least one instance. We held in *City of Revere v. Massachusetts Gen. Hospital*, 463 U.S. 239 (1983), that "the due process rights of a [pretrial detainee] are at least as great as the Eighth Amendment protections available to a convicted prisoner." *Id.*, at 244.... Since it may suffice for Eighth Amendment liability that prison officials were deliberately indifferent to the medical needs of their prisoners, *see Estelle v. Gamble*, 429 U.S. 97, 104 (1976), it follows that such deliberately indifferent conduct must also be enough to satisfy the fault requirement for due process claims based on the medical needs of someone jailed while awaiting trial....

Rules of due process are not, however, subject to mechanical application in unfamiliar territory. Deliberate indifference that shocks in one environment may not be so patently egregious in another, and our concern with preserving the constitutional proportions of substantive due process demands an exact analysis of circumstances before any abuse of power is condemned as conscience shocking.

Thus, attention to the markedly different circumstances of normal pretrial custody and high-speed law enforcement chases shows why the deliberate indifference that shocks in the one case is less egregious in the other (even assuming that it makes sense to speak of indifference as deliberate in the case of sudden pursuit). As the very term "deliberate indifference" implies, the standard is sensibly employed only when actual deliberation is practical, *see Whitley v. Albers*, 475 U.S., at 320 … and in the custodial situation of a prison, forethought about an inmate's welfare is not only feasible but obligatory under a regime that incapacitates a prisoner to exercise ordinary responsibility for his own welfare.

…

Nor does any substantial countervailing interest excuse the State from making provision for the decent care and protection of those it locks up; "the State's responsibility to attend to the medical needs of prisoners [or detainees] does not ordinarily clash with other equally important governmental responsibilities." *Whitley v. Albers*, *supra*, at 320.

But just as the description of the custodial prison situation shows how deliberate indifference can rise to a constitutionally shocking level, so too does it suggest why indifference may well not be enough for liability in the different circumstances of a case like this one. We have, indeed, found that deliberate indifference does not suffice for constitutional liability (albeit under the Eighth Amendment) even in prison circumstances when a prisoner's claim arises not from normal custody but from response to a violent disturbance. Our analysis is instructive here:

> "[I]n making and carrying out decisions involving the use of force to restore order in the face of a prison disturbance, prison officials undoubtedly must take into account the very real threats the unrest presents to inmates and prison officials alike, in addition to the possible harms to inmates against whom force might be used.… In this setting, a deliberate indifference standard does not adequately capture the importance of such competing obligations, or convey the appropriate hesitancy to critique in hindsight decisions necessarily made in haste, under pressure, and frequently without the luxury of a second chance."

Whitley v. Albers, 475 U.S., at 320.…

We accordingly held that a much higher standard of fault than deliberate indifference has to be shown for officer liability in a prison riot. In those circumstances, liability should turn on "whether force was applied in a good faith effort to maintain or restore discipline or maliciously and sadistically for the very purpose of causing harm." *Id.*, at 320–321 (internal quotation marks omitted). The analogy to sudden police chases (under the Due Process Clause) would be hard to avoid.

Like prison officials facing a riot, the police on an occasion calling for fast action have obligations that tend to tug against each other. Their duty is to restore and maintain lawful order, while not exacerbating disorder more than necessary to do their jobs. They are supposed to act decisively and to show restraint at the same moment, and their decisions have to be made "in haste, under pressure, and frequently without the luxury of a second chance." *Id.*, at 320.... A police officer deciding whether to give chase must balance on one hand the need to stop a suspect and show that flight from the law is no way to freedom, and, on the other, the high-speed threat to all those within stopping range, be they suspects, their passengers, other drivers, or bystanders.

To recognize a substantive due process violation in these circumstances when only midlevel fault has been shown would be to forget that liability for deliberate indifference to inmate welfare rests upon the luxury enjoyed by prison officials of having time to make unhurried judgments, upon the chance for repeated reflection, largely uncomplicated by the pulls of competing obligations. When such extended opportunities to do better are teamed with protracted failure even to care, indifference is truly shocking. But when unforeseen circumstances demand an officer's instant judgment, even precipitate recklessness fails to inch close enough to harmful purpose to spark the shock that implicates "the large concerns of the governors and the governed." *Daniels v. Williams*, 474 U.S., at 332. Just as a purpose to cause harm is needed for Eighth Amendment liability in a riot case, so it ought to be needed for due process liability in a pursuit case. Accordingly, we hold that high-speed chases with no intent to harm suspects physically or to worsen their legal plight do not give rise to liability under the Fourteenth Amendment, redressible by an action under § 1983.

The fault claimed on Smith's part in this case accordingly fails to meet the shocks-the-conscience test. In the count charging him with liability under § 1983, respondents' complaint alleges a variety of culpable states of mind: ... "recklessness, gross negligence and conscious disregard for [Lewis's] safety," *id.*, at 13, ¶ 18, and "oppression, fraud and malice," *ibid.*... The Court of Appeals understood the claim to be one of deliberate indifference to Lewis's survival, which it treated as equivalent to one of reckless disregard for life. We agree with this reading of respondents' allegations, but consequently part company from the Court of Appeals, which found them sufficient to state a substantive due process claim.[14]

Smith was faced with a course of lawless behavior for which the police were not to blame. They had done nothing to cause Willard's high-speed driving in the first place, nothing to excuse his flouting of the commonly understood law enforcement authority to control traffic, and nothing (beyond a refusal to call off the chase) to encourage him to race through traffic at breakneck speed forcing other drivers out of their travel lanes. Willard's outrageous behavior was practically instantaneous, and so was Smith's instinctive response. While prudence would have repressed the reaction, the officer's instinct was to do his job as a law enforcement officer, not to induce Willard's lawlessness, or to terrorize, cause harm, or kill. Prudence, that is,

14. To say that due process is not offended by the police conduct described here is not, of course, to imply anything about its appropriate treatment under state law.

was subject to countervailing enforcement considerations, and while Smith exaggerated their demands, there is no reason to believe that they were tainted by an improper or malicious motive on his part.

Regardless whether Smith's behavior offended the reasonableness held up by tort law or the balance struck in law enforcement's own codes of sound practice, it does not shock the conscience, and petitioners are not called upon to answer for it under § 1983.... [Reversed].

Justice SCALIA, with whom Justice THOMAS joins, concurring in the judgment.

... I would reverse the judgment of the Ninth Circuit, not on the ground that petitioners have failed to shock my still, soft voice within, but on the ground that respondents offer no textual or historical support for their alleged due process right. Accordingly, I concur in the judgment of the Court.

For further discussion

1. Is it difficult for plaintiffs to satisfy the *Lewis* standard? In a concurrence written eleven years after *Lewis*, a Sixth Circuit judge wrote:

> Neither side has cited any case, from any circuit or district court, in which an officer's actions in a police chase have ultimately been found to shock the conscience, nor are we aware of any such case. [Several district courts have denied summary judgment in police-pursuit cases on the basis that a jury could find that the officer's conduct shocked the conscience, but all of those courts have been reversed on appeal.] As a result, although *Lewis* established in 1998 that an officer's conduct in a police chase could theoretically shock the conscience, there have been no examples of what specific kinds of conduct rise to that level.

Jones v. Byrnes, 585 F.3d 971, 978 n.4 (6th Cir. 2009) (Martin, J., concurring).

2. Note that municipal liability was not before the Supreme Court in *Lewis*.

Exercise 3-A

Imagine yourself in the situation of an attorney briefing a substantive due process case immediately after *Lewis* was decided in 1998. Would *Lewis* be relevant outside the police chase context? If you represented a social worker alleged to have violated a mother's substantive due process rights by temporarily removing the mother's child from her custody because of evidence of child abuse, would you argue that *Lewis* should apply? How? Keep this hypothetical in mind when reading *Ziccardi*, a Third Circuit application of *Lewis* authored by now-Supreme Court Justice Samuel Alito and the next case in this Chapter.

B. Development of Doctrine in the Circuits: Applying *Lewis* to Liberty Interests

To state a due process claim, a plaintiff must allege the deprivation of a protected interest in life, liberty, or property. This section concerns liberty interests. The federal circuit decision below concerns a substantive due process claim based on the alleged deprivation of plaintiff's liberty interest in his bodily integrity when he was rendered quadriplegic by treatment by paramedics. (*Ziccardi*). The circuit's analysis is based on circuit precedent concerning a mother's liberty interest in raising her minor children, which she alleged was violated by a social worker obtaining temporary custody of her children as part of a child abuse investigation (*Miller*). The scope of the parental liberty interest is explored in more depth in Chapter 13.

Questions to guide reading of *Ziccardi*

1. *Ziccardi* relies on *Miller*, an earlier Third Circuit application of *Lewis*. In *Miller*, what level of fault did the Third Circuit hold would "shock the conscience" in the context of a social worker's removal of a child from his mother's custody?
2. *Lewis* recognized that the 14th Amendment substantive due process standards may vary depending upon the factual context. Why do you think *Ziccardi* had trouble understanding and applying *Lewis* and *Miller*?
3. What standard did *Ziccardi* ultimately hold should apply to paramedics who cause injury to a person they were summoned to rescue? Why do you think the court relied on the meaning of "deliberate indifference" as that term is applied in the 8th Amendment context? What standard had the paramedics advocated before the district court in *Ziccardi*?
4. After reviewing the circuit court opinion in *Ziccardi*, what advice would you give to the City defendants if they were your clients? What advice would you give to Plaintiff, if he were your client?

Ziccardi v. City of Philadelphia

288 F.3d 57 (3d Cir. 2002)

ALITO, Circuit Judge.

... The action was filed by James Smith, now deceased, against two Philadelphia Fire Department paramedics and the city. Smith alleged that the paramedics rendered him a quadriplegic by lifting him after he had fallen from a wall and sustained spinal injury. He claimed that the actions of the paramedics violated his rights under the Due Process Clause of the Fourteenth Amendment.

I.

In the early morning hours of May 16, 1998, after a night of drinking, James Smith, then 24 years old ... sat down on the wall in front of [his aunt's] house and eventually fell asleep.... He apparently fell from the wall and dropped about eight feet to the sidewalk below.... [Two] Philadelphia Fire Department paramedics, responded to a 911 call placed by a neighbor. According to ... a neighbor, [w]hen the paramedics approached Smith, they asked him what his name was and what was wrong.... He said: "I'm hurt. I hurt my head." ... Smith repeated several times that he had hurt his neck.... One of the paramedics said: "[G]et up. Are you drunk?" and "[G]et up or we're going to call the police." ... Smith responded, "I can't get up." ... After nudging Smith a few times and again asking him to get up, the paramedics each grabbed one of Smith's arms and "snatched him up and threw each arm over their shoulders and dr[agged] him to the ... stretcher," which they had removed from the ambulance and placed in the street ... [The neighbor] said that the paramedics "snatched up" Smith "pretty hard" and that after they did so his head jerked back.... [In her] words, Smith "sort of got real limp after that, like everything started hanging on him," and he did not move his arms or legs thereafter....

...

The paramedics then laid him down, got the stretcher, put him on the stretcher, and transported him to a hospital.... When Smith reached the hospital, the doctors recognized the seriousness of his condition and stabilized his neck by putting him in a hard collar and placing him on a board.... He was diagnosed with permanent quadriplegia.... A physician who treated Smith at the hospital stated:

> It is a medical certainty that [the paramedics] should have immobilized his cervical spine prior to moving him. To have, instead, lifted him by his arms and then by his shoulders and legs is unconscionable. It is my opinion within a reasonable degree of medical certainty, that Mr. Smith's quadriplegia is directly attributable to the actions of the paramedics.

...

II.

... [The paramedics argue that] the plaintiff was required to show that they had "actual knowledge" that he had suffered a serious spinal injury and that they nevertheless moved him "with actual deliberate indifference to his safety" [and] that even proof of "actual deliberate indifference" may not suffice [because] under our decision in *Miller v. City of Philadelphia*, 174 F.3d 368 (3d Cir. 1999), "a state of mind that approaches 'an intent to harm' plaintiff is required to prove a constitutional violation in the instant context."

...

IV. A.

The appellants' remaining argument is that even "subjective deliberate indifference" is not enough ... [Their] position [is] that something more than subjective deliberate indifference but less than actual intent to harm is required. Relying on a phrase in *Miller*, they contend that the requisite intent is "gross negligence or arbitrariness that indeed 'shocks the conscience.'" *Miller*, 174 F.3d at 375–76 ...

B.

The intent needed to support a substantive due process claim is a question that has long troubled our court.... The Supreme Court most recently discussed this issue in *County of Sacramento v. Lewis*, 523 U.S. 833 (1998), a police chase case. After noting that "'[t]he touchstone of due process is protection of the individual against arbitrary action of government,'" *id.* at 845 ... the Court added that "the cognizable level of executive abuse of power" is "that which shocks the conscience." *Id.* at 846....

...

We have applied *Lewis* in several subsequent cases. In *Miller*, on which the appellants rely, a mother and her children claimed that a social worker violated their substantive due process rights by taking actions that led to an emergency *ex parte* order removing the children from the mother's custody due to suspected child abuse. *Miller*, 174 F.3d at 370–71. Noting that "a social worker acting to separate parent and child ... rarely will have the luxury of proceeding in a deliberate fashion," we held that "the standard of culpability for substantive due process purposes must exceed both negligence and deliberate indifference, and reach a level of gross negligence or arbitrariness that indeed 'shocks the conscience.'" *Id.* at 375–76.

...

C.

The [paramedics'] current argument—that Smith is required to prove something more than subjective deliberate indifference but less than an intent to harm—was never raised in the district court. Instead, the [paramedics] argued in the district court that an intent to harm is needed. They maintained that the intent-to-harm standard adopted in *Lewis* should apply and stated: "Paramedics are similarly situated to pursuing police officers and their actions should be held to the same consci[ence] shocking standard. They make decisions in haste, under pressure, and without the luxury of a second chance." [We now address] whether *Miller* requires proof of more than subjective deliberate indifference....

We agree with the appellants that *Miller*, which is of course binding on us, mandates at least something more than subjective deliberate indifference as that term is defined in *Farmer v. Brennan*, 511 U.S. 825 (1994).... *Miller* is important here for at least two reasons. First, the lead plaintiff in *Miller* (the mother)—like Smith in this case ... was not in a situation analogous to institutionalization, but the court nevertheless held that an actual intent to harm was not needed to support the due process claim. *Miller*, 174 F.3d at 375–76. Second, *Miller*'s reason for holding that more than deliberate indifference had to be shown—the social worker's need to act without "the luxury of proceeding in a deliberate fashion," *id.* at 375—seems equally applicable here. While the record in the present case does not suggest that the appellants had any particular need to move Smith quickly—for example, he was not in a dangerous location and did not appear to have any other medical problems requiring prompt movement—the social worker in *Miller* similarly does not appear to have had a need to make a split-second decision. What the *Miller* court seems to have had in mind was the need for the social worker to act in a matter of hours or minutes. Nevertheless, the *Miller* court held that the nature of the situation faced by the social worker mandated proof of something more than subjective deliberate indifference, and this holding seems to require the application of a similar standard here.

We must thus attempt to determine exactly what *Miller* required. The [paramedics] have seized upon the phrase "a level of gross negligence or arbitrariness that indeed 'shocks the conscience.'" *Id.* at 375–76. The *Miller* court used this phrase as one part of its explanation of the ground for affirming a grant of summary judgment for the social worker, and we do not think that the phrase was intended as a precise articulation of the governing legal standard.[6]

So what did *Miller* require? We can approach an answer by noting what *Miller* did not demand. As noted, *Miller* expressly stated that the defendant social worker need not have acted with the purpose of causing the relevant harm, namely, removal of the children without good cause. *Id.* at 375. Nor did *Miller* suggest that the defendant had to have known that this harm was practically certain to result.... On the other hand, *Miller* demanded something more than deliberate indifference, which requires (in the sense applicable here) that a person consciously disregard "a substantial risk of serious harm." *Farmer*, 511 U.S. at 836.... *Miller* thus appears to have demanded proof of something less than knowledge that the harm was practically certain but more than knowledge that there was a substantial risk that the harm would occur. A simple way of putting this is that *Miller* mandated proof that the defendant was aware of more than a substantial risk—let us say a great risk—that there was no good cause for the removal of the children.

...

In summary, then, we understand *Miller* to require in a case such as the one before us, proof that the defendants consciously disregarded, not just a substantial risk, but a great risk that serious harm would result if, knowing Smith was seriously injured, they moved Smith without support for his back and neck. On remand in the present case, we believe that the district court should apply this standard and instruct the jury accordingly if one is empanelled.

---

6. The phrase is not well suited for that purpose. "[A]rbitrariness" is a general requirement for a substantive due process violation, *see Lewis*, 523 U.S. at 846 ... not a specification of a precise degree of intent. And "gross negligence" is a lower level of intent than even tort-law recklessness, which is, in turn, lower than criminal-law recklessness or subjective deliberate indifference. *Id.* at 849....

Illustration of *Lewis* threshold spectrum of fault inquiry

Shocks the conscience

Standard for all substantive due process claims based on executive conduct.
Spectrum of fault from "more than negligence" to "intent to harm"

Does not Shock the Conscience		**Shocks the Conscience**
Negligence does not shock the conscience; it is "categorically beneath" due process	Something more than negligence but less than intentional conduct—can shock the conscience Depends on: 1) whether there is time to deliberate 2) whether there are interests that must be weighed with the Plaintiff's competing interests 3) more culpability is required to shock the conscience if pressurized situation, little time for reflection, or if balancing competing interests	Intent to harm—"inten[t] to injure in some way unjustifiable by any governmental interest" most likely would shock the conscience

For further discussion

1. Using the above spectrum of fault chart as a guide to the standard of fault necessary to prove a substantive due process claim based on executive conduct, where would you chart the facts of *Lewis*, *Ziccardi*, and *Daniels*?

2. Where would you chart a claim alleging that a city employee, while driving the city's van to provide transportation to handicapped citizens, looked down at his phone to send a text message, did not notice a stop sign, and hit a pedestrian in the crosswalk? Where would you place a claim alleging that the same city driver of the handicapped transportation vehicle drove a woman confined in a wheelchair to a remote location and sexually assaulted her?

3. Where would you chart a claim alleging that, over several months, the city officials responsible for approving real estate development plans repeatedly rejected a developer's plan, despite the developer's several alterations in the plan to satisfy the

city's various objections, because the city officials considered the developer a "troublemaker" and threatened to "sever" his attorney's head?

4. Keep the last example in mind as you read the next section on the development of legal doctrine in the federal circuit courts, which addresses how to apply *Lewis* to property interests.

C. Development of Doctrine in the Circuits: Applying *Lewis* to property interests

As noted, to state a due process claim, a plaintiff must allege the deprivation of a protected interest in life, liberty, or property. The certiorari briefs below concern a substantive due process claim based on the deprivation of plaintiff's real property. These briefs are also included to illustrate the difference between a brief on the merits and a brief arguing that the Supreme Court should exercise its discretionary authority to accept a case. Petitions for certiorari are the subjects of Simulations in Chapter 4 and Chapter 11. Bear in mind that not all property is entitled to substantive due process protection, a subject explored in Chapter 8 (Procedural Due Process) (summarizing cases where procedural, but not substantive, due process protected property interests such as property interest in public employment).

Questions to guide reading of *Eichenlaub* briefs

1. Why does the petitioner assert that there is a split in the circuits about whether the *Lewis* "shocks the conscience" standard applies to all substantive due process claims involving executive action?
2. Why does the responding brief argue that the circuit split identified by petitioner does not exist?
3. Do you think there is a clear difference between the legal standards "shocks the conscience" and "arbitrary" or "irrational"? If so, what is it?
4. In practice, should an attorney be cautious about how another attorney surveys the views of various circuits? Or even how a judge summarizes a circuit survey? Why?

Petition for Certiorari in *Eichenlaub v. Township of Indiana*

2007 WL 1835543 (June 25, 2007)

By Gerri L. Sperling, Metz Lewis L.L.C., Pittsburgh, PA; Catherine E. Stetson, Christopher T. Handman, Dominic F. Perella, Hogan & Hartson L.L.P., Washington, D.C.

QUESTION PRESENTED

In *County of Sacramento v. Lewis*, 523 U.S. 833 (1998), this Court held that a police officer engaged in a high-speed pursuit does not violate the Fourteenth Amendment's guarantee of substantive due process unless his actions "shock the conscience." The courts of appeals are deeply divided over the following question:

Whether—as the Third Circuit below held, in accord with the Tenth, Eleventh, and D.C. Circuits—all substantive-due-process claims involving executive action are subject to the "shocks the conscience" standard, or whether—as the First, Second, Fourth, Fifth, Sixth, Seventh, and Ninth Circuits have held—only certain types of executive action are subject to that standard.

...

INTRODUCTION

This case concerns an important question of constitutional law: whether the "shocks the conscience" test applies to all substantive-due-process claims involving executive action, or only to a certain subset. In *County of Sacramento v. Lewis*, 523 U.S. 833 (1998), this Court "granted certiorari to resolve a conflict among the Circuits over the standard of culpability on the part of a law enforcement officer for violating substantive due process in a pursuit case." *Id.* at 839 (citation omitted). The Court held that the correct test for these sorts of cases is whether the police action "shocks the conscience." *Id.* at 847. Since *Lewis*, the federal courts of appeals have divided seven-to-four over whether "shocks the conscience" likewise provides the substantive-due-process "standard of culpability" for all executive officers in all contexts.

This case squarely presents that question. The Eichenlaubs, petitioners here, were embroiled in a land-use dispute with government officials in Indiana Township, Pennsylvania. As the dispute dragged on, these officials subjected the Eichenlaubs to egregious treatment, including baseless civil citations and a colossal retroactive "mid-year" property-tax assessment that changed the existing $6,800 bill into one for more than $68,000. Armed with evidence that this treatment was retaliatory, the Eichenlaubs filed suit under 42 U.S.C. § 1983, alleging that the Township's actions were driven by an "improper motive" and therefore violated the Fourteenth Amendment's substantive-due-process guarantee.

...

STATEMENT OF THE CASE

1. ... The Eichenlaubs own two parcels of property in [the Township]. Beginning in the mid-1990s, the Eichenlaubs sought the Township's permission to develop one parcel for residential use and to grade portions of the other parcel for use as a container nursery for their landscaping business.

But the Township refused, leveling a number of meritless and arbitrary objections to the Eichenlaubs' proposals. For example, respondent Jeffrey Curti informed the Eichenlaubs that they could not build homes on the first parcel unless they obtained both a grading permit and approval for a revised subdivision plan under the Township's current subdivision ordinance.... Under protest, they applied for and received a grading permit, hired an engineering firm, and then submitted a revised subdivision plan. The Township still refused to approve the Eichenlaubs' plans ... The Eichenlaubs repeatedly revised their plan to conform to the Board[of Supervisors'] wishes and the Board repeatedly denied the plan anyway.... Finally ... the Board voted to conditionally approve the yet-again-revised plan.... The Eichenlaubs [saw the many conditions not applied to other Township property owners and therefore] withdrew their plan application.

2. ... Displeased with the Eichenlaubs for having criticized and publicized the Township's arbitrary actions, the Township launched a series of attacks against them. The most egregious example involved the Eichenlaubs' taxes. In early 2001, property owned by the Eichenlaubs ... had received a collective assessment of $6,800.... But in October of the same year, the Eichenlaubs received notice of a retroactive assessment change, upping the tax bill ... tenfold, to $68,000. Through discovery, the Eichenlaubs learned that the Township employee responsible for this stunning turnabout was the girlfriend of ... the Township manager who long had been embroiled in the Eichenlaubs' land-use dispute.... [Other] retaliation the Eichenlaubs alleged.... [included] onerous subdivision requirements ... unannounced inspections of the Eichenlaubs' property and ... baseless citations.... In March 2001, the Board obstructed the Eichenlaubs' ability to develop their land by refusing to sign off on documents allowing utility companies to serve their property ... this decision was made behind closed doors and never subjected to a public vote.... These abuses of authority were further livened by comments ranging from revealing to vicious: One Township official, for example, derided David Eichenlaub as a "troublemaker," ... and referred to the Eichenlaubs' attorney in graphically vulgar terms, stating, among other things, that he wanted to "sever" the attorney's head....

...

REASONS FOR GRANTING THE WRIT

I. THE COURTS OF APPEALS ARE DEEPLY DIVIDED OVER WHETHER THE "SHOCKS THE CONSCIENCE" STANDARD APPLIES TO ALL SUBSTANTIVE-DUE-PROCESS CLAIMS INVOLVING EXECUTIVE ACTION.

The Third Circuit's decision in this case exacerbates an entrenched circuit split on a question federal courts regularly face: whether the "shocks the conscience" standard applies across the board to all executive action, or just to certain types of executive action. The Third Circuit below held that it applies universally to all executive action, joining the Tenth, Eleventh, and District of Columbia Circuits in embracing that categorical rule. But at least seven other circuits—the First, Second, Fourth, Fifth, Sixth, Seventh, and Ninth—have recognized and applied other yardsticks when evaluating certain types of executive action.

...

2. ... Four other circuits—the Second, Fourth, Fifth, and Sixth—have adopted an approach to substantive-due-process claims that squarely conflicts with the categorical approach adopted by the Third Circuit: They apply the "shocks the conscience" test to some claims of executive action but not to others.

The Second Circuit, for example ... has applied an entirely different standard to several categories of executive-action substantive-due-process cases. In the land-use context, for instance, the court held ... that "[i]n order to prove that their right to substantive due process was violated" by government refusal to grant a given land-use permit or certificate, plaintiffs "must show (1) that they had a valid property interest in the certificate *** and (2) that the Town infringed that interest in an arbitrary or irrational manner." *O'Mara v. Town of Wappinger*, 485 F.3d 693, 700 (2d Cir. 2007)....

The Fourth, Fifth, and Sixth Circuits take the same basic approach as the Second, which is to say each applies "shocks the conscience" to some types of executive action, but another test for other types of executive action. Thus, the Fourth Circuit has consistently held that a substantive-due-process violation in the land-use context requires a showing "(1) that [plaintiff] had property or a property interest; (2) that the state deprived [it] of this property or property interest; and (3) that the state's action falls so far beyond the outer limits of legitimate governmental action that no process could cure the deficiency." *Tri County Paving, Inc. v. Ashe County*, 281 F.3d 430, 440 (4th Cir. 2002)....

Similarly, the Fifth and Sixth Circuits apply a rational-basis test when evaluating substantive-due-process claims in the land-use context. *See Simi Inv. Co., Inc. v. Harris County*, 236 F.3d 240, 250–251 (5th Cir. 2000) ("[W] e must ask next whether this denial is rationally related to a legitimate governmental interest."), *cert. denied*, 534 U.S. 1022 (2001) ... *Brody v. City of Mason*, 250 F.3d 432 (6th Cir. 2001). In *Brody*, for example, the Sixth Circuit ruled that "to sustain a substantive due process claim, in the context of zoning administrative action, 'a plaintiff must show that the state administrative agency has been guilty of 'arbitrary and capricious action' in the strict sense, meaning 'that there is no rational basis for the *** [administrative] decision.'" *Id.* at 438 (quoting *Pearson v. City of Grand Blanc*, 961 F.2d 1211, 1221 (6th Cir. 1992))....

3. Although seven circuits have adopted a rule that conflicts with the Third Circuit's rule below, three other circuits—the Tenth, Eleventh, and District of Columbia Circuits—have embraced the Third Circuit's approach. *See, e.g., Camuglia v. City of Albuquerque*, 448 F.3d 1214, 1222 (10th Cir. 2006) (applying *Lewis* rubric in context of restaurant inspections); *Tinker v. Beasley*, 429 F.3d 1324, 1327 (11th Cir. 2005) (requiring substantive-due-process claimant to meet both Lewis test ...); *Fraternal Order of Police Dep't of Corrs. Labor Comm. v. Williams*, 375 F.3d 1141, 1145 (D.C. Cir. 2004) (applying *Lewis*). These circuits have, in other words, applied "shocks the conscience" across the board and have done so on the understanding that the test is a "general rule" governing executive-action cases. *Nix v. Franklin County Sch. Dist.*, 311 F.3d 1373, 1375 (11th Cir. 2002) (applying "shocks the conscience" to the case of a high school student who died during an in-school accident), *cert. denied*, 538 U.S. 946 (2003). The Eighth Circuit, for its part, apparently labors under an intra-circuit split: It has applied a rationality test in certain land-use cases, *see Iowa Coal Min. Co. v. Monroe County*, 257 F.3d 846, 853 (8th Cir. 2001), while in other cases of the same type it has applied the "shocks the conscience" formulation, *see Koscielsld v. City of Minneapolis*, 435 F.3d 898, 902 (8th Cir. 2006).

...

II. THE THIRD CIRCUIT'S RULE CONFLICTS WITH THIS COURT'S PRECEDENTS.

... Nothing in *Lewis* suggests—much less holds—that "shocks the conscience" is to be applied across the board to every type of executive action when evaluating a substantive-due-process claim. To the contrary, the Court in *Lewis* carefully followed its established practice of limiting the "shocks the conscience" test to executive actions that actually implicate police conduct. Thus, the Court clarified that it had granted certiorari "to resolve a conflict among the Circuits over the standard of culpability *on the part of a law enforcement officer* for violating substantive due process in a pursuit case." 523 U.S. at 839 (emphases added). And confirming that it intended no radical revision to existing precedent, the Court emphasized that the narrow "issue in th[e] case is whether a police officer violates the Fourteenth Amendment's guarantee of substantive due process by causing death through deliberate or reckless indifference to life in a high-speed automobile chase aimed at apprehending a suspected offender," or whether the officer is liable in that event only if he engages in conduct that "shock[s] the conscience." *Id.* at 836....

In light of this language, many of the federal appeals courts read *Lewis* as limited to the specific type of executive action at issue there and its close analogs. [citing Seventh and Second Circuit decisions].

...

[E]xtending "shocks the conscience" beyond its traditional sphere distorts the substantive-due-process inquiry ... [The circuit court] rejected the Eichenlaubs' substantive-due-process claim in part because "there [was] no allegation of corruption or self-dealing" against the Township officials. But there is no reason why punitive and baseless government actions against a landowner should be actionable if taken for reasons of greed, but not if taken for reasons of revenge or other ill motives.... Such actions are, in a word, arbitrary. Yet the "shocks the conscience" test will capture some and not others, because it relies on a court's subjective sense of outrage to determine whether or not an abuse is actionable.

...

Brief in Opposition to Certiorari in *Eichenlaub v. Township of Indiana*

2007 WL 2115672 (July 20, 2007)

By Charles W. Craven, Marshall, Dennehey, Warner, Coleman & Goggin, Philadelphia, PA

REASONS FOR DENYING THE PETITION

...

[T]he petition's arguments fail to appreciate that the *Lewis* standard equates "shocks the conscience" with "most egregious" and "arbitrary in the constitutional sense," and uses those terms interchangeably.... [T]he Court's opinion in *Lewis* expressly draws that that equation. In that opinion, the Court observed that "the core of the concept" of due process is "protection against arbitrary action" and that "only the most egregious official conduct can be said to be 'arbitrary in the constitutional sense.'" [*County of Sacramento v.*] *Lewis* ... 523 U.S. at 845–846 (citation omitted). After noting its long history of speaking of "the cognizable level of executive abuse of power as that which shocks the conscience," the Court noted that, in *Collins v. Harker Heights,* 503 U.S. 115, 128 (1992), it "said again that the substantive component of the Due Process Clause is violated by executive action only when it 'can properly be characterized as arbitrary, or conscience shocking, in a constitutional sense.'" *Lewis, supra,* 523 U.S. at 846, 847.

...

IV. CURRENT CASE LAW PROVIDES NO SUPPORT FOR THE PETITION'S "IMPROPER MOTIVE" STANDARD OR ITS CIRCUIT CENSUS

...

Moreover, current case law refutes petitioners' specter of an "exacerbate[d]," "entrenched," "intractable," "intensified," "deep," "seven-to-four" conflict among the circuits, confusion among the lower courts, and a "glaring lack of uniformity throughout the Nation".... As the following circuit review demonstrates, the petition's census must be completely realigned, and that realignment reveals no need for intervention by this Court.

FIRST CIRCUIT.... [I]n *Mongeau v. City of Marlborough,* [492 F.3d 14 (1st Cir. 2007), *cert. denied,* ___ U.S. ___, 128 S.Ct. 898 (2008),] a land-use case, the First Circuit reconfirmed that "a plaintiff may prevail on a substantive due process claim only if the defendant has engaged in behavior that 'shocks the conscience,'".... In addition, *Mongeau* noted that the First Circuit has "stated with 'a regularity bordering on the monotonous' that to be liable for a violation of substantive due process rights, a defendant must have engaged in behavior that is 'conscience-shocking,'" and that the court has "repeatedly affirmed the use of this standard in the context of challenges to land use decisions." *Mongeau,* ___ F.3d at ___ (2007 U.S. App. LEXIS 14812, p. 7).... Given the above, the First Circuit must be realigned with the Third, Tenth, Eleventh and D.C. Circuits.

SECOND CIRCUIT. The petition asserts that the Second Circuit applies "an entirely different standard," under which the court first determines whether the claimant has a valid property interest in the permit or certificate, and then whether the executive acted in an "arbitrary or irrational manner." ... [A]rbitrary or irrational executive action in the land use context obtains "only when government acts with 'no legitimate reason for its decision.'" *Crowley v. Courville*, 76 F.3d 47, 52 (2nd Cir. 1996). As noted above, that standard is hardly "entirely different" from the "shocks the conscience" standard.

Furthermore, in *O'Connor v. Pierson*, 426 F.3d 187, 203 (2nd Cir. 2005) ... the Second Circuit squarely recognized that *Lewis* "set the bar higher for challenges to executive action," and that "'only the most egregious official conduct,' conduct that 'shocks the conscience,' will subject the government to liability for a substantive due process violation based on executive action." The court also recognized that *Lewis* swept broadly beyond prison riots and high-speed police chases. *O'Connor*, 426 F.3d at 204 (*Lewis* "did not distinguish between different types of substantive due process claims, so 'constitutionally arbitrary' action for purposes of a property-based substantive due process claim is action that shocks the conscience.").

In addition, less than 10 months after *Lewis* was filed, the Second Circuit quickly applied the "shocks the conscience test" to a land use claim and underscored the limited role that substantive due process and the federal courts had in state land use cases in *Natale v. Town of Ridgefield*, 170 F.3d 258, 262–263 (2nd Cir. 1999).... Given the above, the Second Circuit must be realigned with the First, Third, Tenth, Eleventh and D.C. Circuits.

FOURTH CIRCUIT. The Fourth Circuit must also be realigned to join the First, Second, Third, Tenth, Eleventh and D.C. Circuits.

Shortly after *Lewis* was filed, the Fourth Circuit recognized in *Hawkins v. Freeman*, 195 F.3d 732, 738 (4th Cir. 1999) that "Courts now considering any claim of substantive due process violation must look for principal guidance to" *Lewis* ... and that, under *Lewis*, "the issue of fatal arbitrariness should be addressed as a 'threshold question,' asking whether the challenged conduct was 'so egregious, so outrageous, that it may fairly be said to shock the contemporary conscience.'" Two years later, in *Young v. City of Mt. Ranier*, 238 F.3d 567, 574 (4th Cir. 2001), the court noted the continued broad applicability of the *Lewis* standard stating, "Broadly speaking, the substantive due process provision of the Fourteenth Amendment protects against egregious, arbitrary governmental conduct. *See County of Sacramento v. Lewis*, 523 U.S. 833, 845–46 (1998). Only governmental conduct that "shocks the conscience" is actionable as a violation of the Fourteenth Amendment." More recently, in *United States v. Al-Hamdi*, 356 F.3d 564, 574 (4th Cir. 2004), the court reconfirmed that "[a]n executive act can violate substantive due process only when the act shocks the conscience. *County of Sacramento v. Lewis*, 523 U.S. 833, 846 (1998)."

The tripartite test partially quoted by the petition from *Tri-County Paving, Inc. v. Ashe County*, 281 F.3d 430 (4th Cir. 2002), does not represent a departure from the high standard set by *Lewis*. That test requires a property claimant to "demonstrate: '(1) that [it] had property or a property interest; (2) that the state deprived [it] of this property or property interest; and (3) that the state's action falls so far beyond the outer limits of legitimate governmental action that no process could cure the deficiency.'" *Id.* at 440 (citation omitted). The test was formulated, because "[s]ubstantive due process protections 'run only to state action so arbitrary and irrational, so unjustified by any circumstance or governmental interest, as to be literally incapable of avoidance by any pre-deprivation procedural protections or of adequate rectification by any post-deprivation state remedies.'" *Id.* (citation omitted). That formulation hardly undermines *Lewis*.

FIFTH CIRCUIT. The Fifth Circuit has not repudiated its decision rendered shortly after *Lewis* in *Morris v. Dearborne*, 181 F.3d 657, 668 (5th Cir. 1999). In *Morris*, which involved a teacher's fabrication of sexual abuse against a student's father, the court recognized and applied the "shocks the conscience" standard, and alternatively expressed that standard as conduct "so egregious, so outrageous, that it may fairly be said to shock the contemporary conscience" or as "abusive, irrational or malicious abuse of government power that shocks the conscience."

The petition relies on *Simi Investment Co. Inc. v. Harris County Texas*, 236 F.3d 240 (5th Cir. 2000), to position the Fifth Circuit. Yet, that case does not deviate from *Lewis*, because the Court of Appeals recognized "that reliance on substantive due process must be taken with the 'utmost care,'" and it expressly limited its "holding to the type of blatant governmental interference with property rights that is now before us." *Id.* at 249.

Moreover, the petition ignores *Conroe Creosoting Co. v. Montgomery County Texas*, 249 F.3d 337 (5th Cir. 2001) ... a land-use dispute, the Fifth Circuit explicitly noted that "Courts generally examine due process challenges to executive action by asking 'whether the behavior of the governmental officer is so egregious, so outrageous, that it may fairly be said to shock the contemporary conscience.'" *Id.* at 341 (citation omitted). Consequently, the Fifth Circuit must be placed with the First, Second, Third, Fourth, Tenth, Eleventh and D.C. Circuits.

SIXTH CIRCUIT. The petition's circuit census must also be corrected to include the Sixth Circuit with the First, Second, Third, Fourth, Fifth, Tenth, Eleventh and D.C. Circuits.

Brody v. City of Mason, 250 F.3d 432 (6th Cir. 2001) stated that, in a land-use case, "a plaintiff must show that the state administrative agency has been guilty of 'arbitrary and capricious action' in the strict sense, meaning 'that there is no rational basis for the ... [administrative] decision,'" and recognized that "[t]his requires a very strong showing. 'The administrative action will withstand substantive due process attack unless it "'is not supportable on any rational basis'" or is "'willful and unreasoning action, without consideration and in disregard of the facts or circumstances of the case.'" *Id.* at 438 (citations omitted). But, as noted above with respect to other "strict sense" or "constitutional sense" cases, that standard does not differ from the *Lewis* standard.

Moreover, two more recent cases underscore that the Sixth Circuit follows the *Lewis* standard. In *Banks v. City of Whitehall*, 344 F.3d 550, 554–555 (6th Cir. 2003) (citations omitted), a land-use case, the court rejected a substantive due process claim, because "the conduct of Whitehall officials in enforcing those codes and regulations was neither 'arbitrary' nor 'conscience-shocking' in the constitutional sense." Likewise, in *Schroder v. City of Fort Thomas*, 412 F.3d 724, 730–731 (6th Cir. 2005), the court explained that "our cases stress that, where a plaintiff claims that a non-custodial substantive due process violation has occurred because of the government's deliberate indifference, something more must be shown—a something that we have variously described as 'callous[] disregard [for] the risk of injury,' or action 'in an arbitrary manner that 'shocks the conscience' or that indicates an[] intent to injure.'"

SEVENTH CIRCUIT. Like the First, Second, Fourth, Fifth, and Sixth Circuits, the Seventh Circuit must also be realigned with the Third, Tenth, Eleventh and D.C. Circuits.

...

See, *Christensen v. County of Boone*, 483 F.3d 454, 462 n. 2 ([7th Cir.] 2007) ("When, as in the present case, a plaintiff complains of abusive executive action, this "conscience shocking" test determines liability.... *See County of Sacramento v. Lewis*, 523 U.S. 833, 846–47 (1997) (clarifying this distinction)."); *Montgomery v. Stefaniak*, 410 F.3d 933, 939 (7th Cir. 2005) (wrongful discharge claim) ("'The scope of substantive due process, however, is very limited and protects plaintiffs only against arbitrary government action that "shocks the conscience.' ...").

EIGHTH CIRCUIT. Although placing the Eighth Circuit with the Third, Tenth and D.C. Circuits, the petition mistakenly understated that support by positing an internal division in the Eighth Circuit between the "truly irrational" test and the "shocks the conscience" test. (Pet. 19.) However ... *Koscielski v. City of Minneapolis*, 435 F.3d 898 (8th Cir. 2006), actually disproves the alleged internal split, because that case draws a clear equation between the "truly irrational" test and the "shocks the conscience" test. The same equation was noted by the *en banc* court in *Singleton v. Cecil*, 176 F.3d 419, 425 n. 7 (8th Cir. 1999).

...

NINTH CIRCUIT ...

Squaw Valley [*Development Co. v. Goldberg*, 375 F.3d 936, 949–950 (9th Cir. 2004)] illustrates that the Ninth Circuit recognizes that "[t]he touchstone of due process is protection of the individual against arbitrary action of government," and that "[t]he substantive component of the Due Process Clause 'forbids the government from depriving a person of life, liberty, or property in such a way that "shocks the conscience" or "interferes with rights implicit in the concept of ordered liberty." *Squaw Valley*, 375 F.3d at 948. The case also demonstrates that, even though one defendant "harbor[ed] actual 'hostility' and 'antagonism' toward" the property owner and had no factual support for his claim that the owner failed to comply with regulations, *id.* at 947, and even though the defendants subjected the owner to "selective and overzealous enforcement" and "to a tyrannical regime of regulatory abuse designed to drive the resort out of business," the owner did not have an actionable claim under the Fourteenth or the Fifth Amendments. *Id.* at 948.

. . .

The petition should be denied, because the case law does not ... demonstrate a division among the circuit courts to support their call for this Court's intervention.

For further discussion

1. The Supreme Court denied certiorari in *Eichenlaub* in 2007.

2. A denial of certiorari does not mean that the federal circuit court decision was right or wrong, does not mean that the asserted circuit split does not exist, and does not mean that the issues addressed in the petition for certiorari are not important. Petitions for certiorari have a slim chance of being granted. Most are denied because the U.S. Supreme Court has a discretionary docket and cannot hear the vast majority of cases it is requested to hear. For example, of the 6,315 certiorari petitions filed in 2017–18, the Court agreed to hear 69 arguments; of the 6,305 certiorari petitions filed in 2016–17, the Court agreed to hear 71 arguments.[1] While the number of cases decided by the Supreme Court is fairly consistent over recent years, that number is lower than in decades past. "Between the mid-1980s and the late 1990s, the number of decisions with full, signed opinions dropped from 140 per term to 80."[2] The drop in the number of cases decided by the Supreme Court is not a consequence of fewer petitions for certiorari; on the contrary, the nearly 8,000 petitions filed in 2001 "represented an 87 percent increase over the average of 4,227 in the 1982–1986 terms."[3] The federal circuit courts, which do not have a discretionary docket but hear appeals as of right, have a far larger docket. For example, the federal circuit courts terminated 29,738 appeals on the merits in the one-year period ending September 30, 2019.[4]

3. Consider the consequences of these statistics for practicing attorneys. Is the size of the federal appellate docket relative to the size of the Supreme Court docket relevant in making recommendations to clients? As a practical matter, are the decisions of the federal circuit courts most likely the last word for your client's case? Should that affect your client's decision to take an appeal to the federal circuit courts? How could the number of certiorari petitions *filed* compared to the number of certiorari petitions *granted* be relevant in making recommendations to a client contemplating the offer or acceptance of a settlement agreement during the pendency of a federal circuit appeal? Should it affect the decision to settle before briefing or argument of the appeal

---

1. Roberts, C.J., *2018 Year-End Report on the Federal Judiciary*, 12 (Dec. 31, 2018), https://www.supremecourt.gov/publicinfo/year-end/2018year-endreport.pdf.

2. Lawrence Baum, The Supreme Court 105 (8th ed. 2004).

3. *Id.* at 104.

4. Table B-5, U.S. Courts of Appeals—Decisions in Cases Terminated on the Merits By Circuit and Nature of Proceeding During the 12-Month Period Ending September 30, 2019, http://www.uscourts.gov/sites/default/files/data_tables/jb_b5_0930.2019.pdf

in the federal circuit court? Or to settle after hearing the circuit court's concerns at oral argument, if the case is selected for oral argument? Keep in mind that many circuit court cases are not selected for oral argument but are decided by the court on the briefs alone. How could the number of certiorari petitions *filed* compared to the number of certiorari petitions *granted* be relevant in making recommendations to a client contemplating the offer or acceptance of a settlement agreement after an adverse circuit court ruling? How should it be relevant in making recommendations to a client contemplating whether to file a petition for certiorari? Simulations in Chapter 4 and Chapter 11 concern petitions for certiorari.

4. More generally, do you think the number of certiorari petitions filed compared to the number of certiorari petitions granted has any significance to federal circuit judges issuing decisions? Or any relevance to the Supreme Court's role as supervisor of the federal circuit courts?

5. This book contains many federal circuit court decisions, which is unusual for a law school casebook. Can you identify some of the motivations for including circuit court decisions?

Chapter Four

Substantive Due Process (Part Two) — Two Exceptions to the General Rule of *DeShaney*: State-Created Danger and Special Relationship

A. Chapter Overview

This Chapter concerns the general rule of *DeShaney v. Winnebago County Dept. of Social Services*, 489 U.S. 189 (1989), that the state owes no duty to protect a person from harm inflicted by private actors. This Chapter also explores two exceptions to that general rule.

Under the state-created danger exception to *DeShaney*, the state can be liable if the state created the opportunity for the infliction of private harm or rendered the plaintiff more vulnerable to private harm. What factual circumstances might qualify as a state-created danger? The Supreme Court has not yet expressly adopted this exception and the circuits vary in their approaches. While one circuit held that a police officer could be liable for creating the danger that a drunken woman would not arrive home safely where the officer stopped an inebriated couple on the street on a winter night and allowed the husband to leave (*Kneipp*), another circuit held that a police officer could not be held liable for creating the danger that plaintiff would be shot where the officer loaned a gun to a confidential informant who had a dispute with plaintiff, a rival drug dealer, and the confidential informant shot plaintiff (*McClendon*). As the Supreme Court has not yet expressly adopted — or rejected — the state-created danger exception to *DeShaney*, you may be one of the lawyers who helps to shape a national rule

The special relationship doctrine is a second exception to *DeShaney's* general rule that the government does not protect against private violence. If the state affirmatively exercises its power to restrain an individual's liberty so that the individual cannot care for him or herself, the state then must ensure the individual's safety. *DeShaney* provided the examples of incarceration or institutionalization as "restraints on personal liberty" sufficient to trigger the protection of substantive due process. Are there factual situations sufficiently analogous to incarceration or institutionalization that they also should give rise to an affirmative duty to protect under substantive due process? This Chapter examines situations found sufficiently and insufficiently analogous to incarceration or institutionalization to qualify for substantive due process protection (public day school in *Patel*, public residential school for the deaf in *Walton*, foster care and situations similar to foster care in *Nicini*).

The relationship of the general rule of *DeShaney* and the two exceptions to that general rule may be visualized like this:

General rule of *DeShaney*

Failure to protect an individual against private violence does not violate 14th Amendment substantive due process

Two Exceptions

1 **Special relationship**

- Involuntary custody
- Affirmative duty to protect does not arise from knowledge of plight but from limits the state has placed on person "to act on his own behalf—through incarceration, institutionalization, or other similar restraint of personal liberty."

2 **State-created danger**

"While the state may have been aware of the dangers that Joshua faced in the free world, it played no part in their creation, nor did it do anything to render him any more vulnerable to them."

DeShaney was a failed § 1983 claim against a social worker who did not prevent a father's physical abuse of his child. This Chapter concludes by canvassing alternatives to constitutional civil litigation for addressing the problem of child protective service workers who fail to prevent harm to children by the dangerous adults in those children's lives.

B. Factual Context

Before reading the Supreme Court's decision in *DeShaney*, consider the challenging jobs of licensed social workers and other social services employees who work with families who may neglect or abuse their children. Child and family social workers "protect vulnerable children[,] ... help families find housing or services, ... intervene when children are in danger of neglect or abuse. Some help arrange adoptions, locate foster families, or work to reunite families."[1] In 2016, there were approximately 317,600 "child, family, and school" social workers in the U.S. labor market.[2] Entry-level jobs usually require a bachelor's degree in social work; some allow a major in a related field.[3] Employment information about caseworkers who investigate allegations of child abuse and neglect is not as easily available. The median annual wage for child, family, and school social workers was $46,270 in 2018,[4] while the median annual wage for mental health and substance abuse social workers was $44,840.[5]

In thinking about the demands of the work, consider the following examples of employment ads for child protective service workers. For a job investigating cases of suspected abuse, neglect, or abandonment, the state government of Florida advertised a starting salary of $39,600 plus benefits and required a college degree, with a preference for a bachelor's or master's degree in social work.[6] A local government in Virginia advertised a job investigating suspected child abuse and neglect that required the applicant to have knowledge of "investigating and interviewing techniques," the abilities "to investigate high risk cases; testify in court proceedings;" "analyze case information to make sound judgments within the framework of existing laws"; "respond to the client's emotions" and "work in stressful situations and maintain diplomacy."[7] The Texas state government advertised for child protective services investigators to determine "if abuse or neglect happened," to assess the risk of future abuse or neglect, which may require removing a child from the family; to "respond[] quickly in crisis situations" that "can be dangerous"; to prepare reports; to talk "frankly and objectively with families about matters they may consider personal and private, such as ... sex abuse, and personal relationships"; to communicate with schools, police, and attor-

---

1. Bureau of Labor Statistics, U.S. Dep't of Labor, *Occupational Outlook Handbook, 2019 Edition*, "Social Workers: What They Do," https://www.bls.gov/ooh/community-and-social-service/social-workers.htm#tab-2.

2. Bureau of Labor Statistics, U.S. Dep't of Labor, *Occupational Outlook Handbook, 2019 Edition*, "Social Workers: Job Outlook," https://www.bls.gov/ooh/community-and-social-service/social-workers.htm#tab-6.

3. Bureau of Labor Statistics, U.S. Dep't of Labor, *Occupational Outlook Handbook, 2019 Edition*, "Social Workers: How to Become One," https://www.bls.gov/ooh/community-and-social-service/social-workers.htm#tab-4.

4. Bureau of Labor Statistics, U.S. Dep't of Labor, *Occupational Outlook Handbook, 2019 Edition*, "Social Workers: Pay," https://www.bls.gov/ooh/community-and-social-service/social-workers.htm#tab-5.

5. *Id.*

6. State of Florida, *Advertisement for Child Protective Investigator, Madison, Florida*, Indeed (July 2019) https://www.indeed.com/viewjob?jk=6f4158caab9bb068&tk=1dg066ibph1ki802&from=serp&vjs=3.

7. Virginia Dep't of Social Services—Local, *Advertisement for Family Services Specialist, Shenandoah Valley, Virginia*, Indeed (July 2019), https://www.indeed.com/viewjob?jk=0db4818f4f38a226&tk=1dfupncm30gf8002&from=serp&vjs=3 (requiring Bachelor's in human services or in any field plus two years relevant experience).

neys; to testify in court; all while "[w]ork[ing] under constant deadlines that require prioritizing tasks and ... work[ing] flexible hours."[8]

While social workers earn more than child protective service positions, they also have higher education requirements. For example, Catholic Guardian Services in Bronx, New York advertised for a Social Work Supervisor to interview, hire, evaluate, and train family support workers and required a Master's Degree in Social Work, fluency in Spanish, ability to respect the rights of "those with differing cultural, racial, sexual or ethnic identities," for a salary of $55–60,000, plus benefits.[9] Los Angeles County, California advertised for a child welfare worker with either a master's degree in social work or counseling or a bachelor's plus social work experience.[10] The job required the social worker to investigate allegations of child abuse, work with law enforcement to remove children from abusive environments, review criminal histories to assess fitness of adults living in a household, prepare for court testimony and cross-examination, and be on-call nights and weekends to provide emergency services.[11] The job required the social worker to "defus[e] ... hostile or high-stress situation[s]," while clearly communicating information to "a variety of individuals" about "civil rights, legal rights and responsibilities, and other numerous issues in accordance with Federal and California State laws and regulations and Department policies and procedures related to confidentiality by explaining information in a patient and clear manner."[12]

Below is a profile of the work and employees of the Stamford office of the Connecticut Department of Children and Families ("D.C.F."):

"Turnover in the office is constant and quick. 'I've seen someone leave a Post-it on her computer, "I quit," and never come back,' Ilia Morrows, a 29-year-old who has spent four years with the department, said. It wasn't only the acute awareness that a child could be killed if you made the wrong decision—and that it could be you being named on the local TV news. It wasn't only everyone's knowledge of the summer before last: three deaths—a 14-year-old's suicide; an infant's suffocation, possibly accidental but definitely suspicious; a toddler's baking to death in the back

8. Texas Dep't. of Family and Protective Services, *Child Protective Service Case Worker Trainee*, Indeed (July 17, 2019) https://www.indeed.com/viewjob?jk=5c06ab228c4b80b9&tk=1dfurdblq2808003&from=serp&vjs=3.

9. Catholic Guardian Services, *Advertisement for Social Work Supervisor*, Indeed (July 2019) https://www.indeed.com/viewjob?cmp=Catholic-Guardian-Services&t=Social+Work+Supervisor&jk=49dfe5e13f77b031&sjdu=Azw5ooPpE40j9fx-_jN2J-OdHObW2oHaRc6RRao_qIRNvx7vYzxs8N6p_O1auzsfDCXWIWlIMgEqHr2BMUz9AQ&tk=1dg01rla0huki802&adid=303568709&pub=4a1b367933fd867b19b072952f68dceb&vjs=3.

10. County of Los Angeles, *Advertisement for Children's Social Worker II Position*, Governmentjobs.com (May 2, 2016), https://www.governmentjobs.com/careers/lacounty/jobs/1364304/childrens-social-worker-ii?utm_campaign=google_jobs_apply&utm_source=google_jobs_apply&utm_medium=organic.

11. *Id.*

12. *Id.*

of a car—two in families under the watch of the Stamford office, the third in a family that had just moved to Stamford after being investigated and cleared by another D.C.F. office. It wasn't only the knowledge of 7-year-old Nixzmary Brown, who had recently been allowed to remain with her family by New York City's child-welfare system and was reportedly beaten to death by her stepfather. It was also the extreme authority, the burden of holding it, of wielding it, the prerogative to enter a family's home and split it apart. 'It's almost hard to comprehend that we have that ability,' Morrows said. 'It's so huge.'

The staff is made up of investigators and treatment workers, with investigators handling the initial unannounced knock on the door after a report of abuse or neglect comes into the state's hot line. Investigators have up to 45 days to decide whether to take a kid into D.C.F. custody, or to leave him at home but compel the family to accept the department's long-term help, or to deem a report unsubstantiated and let the case go. During this time they can enter the house again and again and interview school nurses and neighbors, anyone who might know how well or terribly a child is being cared for. To take control of a child for longer than four days, the department needs a judge's approval, but if a social worker senses that a child is at immediate risk, a supervisor's signature on a form known as a '96-hour hold' will let her walk away with that boy, that girl or all the children in the house.

[Annette] Johnson is in the treatment unit, which inherits cases from investigations and focuses not only on the protracted evaluation of families but also on guiding and, ideally, strengthening them so that children don't have to be removed or so that those who have been seized can be returned.... A treatment worker might send an abusive father to group counseling for men who batter, a mother ... to a hospital program for substance abusers, a child to individual therapy, all with private providers under contract with D.C.F. But to be part of the treatment unit does not mean that you don't take kids. Morrows, who is now in investigations, told me that during her first year with D.C.F., in another office, she had a treatment case with a family whose three children—an 11-year-old girl and boys who were 9 and 8—suddenly confided that their father, an alcoholic, was coming home drunk, waking them and forcing them to kneel on rice or punching them in the stomach. If they doubled over from his blow, he commanded them to stand bent that way for long periods until he allowed them to straighten.

"You can't do this, you can't take my babies!" Morrows remembered the mother pleading, collapsed in agony on the floor, when Morrows tried to invoke a 96-hour hold after the father refused to move out of the home and the mother would not leave with the kids. "Do something!" the mother screamed at her husband. Outside the apartment, neighbors gathered in the hallway of the run-down complex—ominously, Morrows said, because D.C.F. is a known and not very welcome agency in the city's poor neighborhoods. Slightly built and self-restrained, she waited. On her cellphone with her office, she was told that the police were on their way. But now, amid the mother's sobbing, the kids told Morrows they would not go, that everything they'd said was a lie. The police, when at last they arrived, had to grab the children, lifting them in their arms. Two of the kids clung to the frame of the front door with both hands as they were carried out. The cops had to pry at their fingers, wrestle their bodies through.

'I almost started giggling hysterically,' Morrows said, describing how she nearly broke down. 'I really wanted to sit on the floor with Mom and cry.' Then she recalled her feelings hours later, in the aftermath of what had been her first removal: 'I was shocked at what my job is, at the career choice that I had made. I went home thinking, How do I have this power? In this state, in this country, the government can come in and take your kids. Tell you you're unfit to take care of your kids. It was earth-shattering to me. It rocks you to your core.'"[13]

For further discussion

1. For more background, try to watch a documentary about the jobs of child protective service workers and social workers, such as a 2005 PBS Frontline series called "Failure to Protect," available from PBS Video, www.pbs.org.

2. You may also learn more about incidents of child abuse or civil suits arising from child abuse investigations from following local news. For example, New Jersey settled a suit for $7.5 million "over a botched child welfare case in which a 7-year-old boy's ... mummified remains were found in the basement of a Newark apartment" rented by the boy's cousin, who later pleaded guilty to criminal charges, and another cousin who admitted he killed the child.[14] While the state's child welfare agency had investigated abuse complaints involving Faheem Williams, the agency had closed the file about a year before his corpse was found; the state paid $1 million to the estate of Faheem Williams and $6.5 million to two of his siblings, who had been found "emaciated" in a room adjacent to where the body was discovered.[15]

3. Once child protective service workers or social workers determine there is a need for government intervention, there is not uniform agreement on what form intervention should take. "Two distinct camps in the world of child welfare each insist it has the better approach. One camp leans toward removing children from their homes and placing them in foster care. The other camp favors keeping children in their homes and correcting underlying problems, such as drug abuse.... [Richard Gelles, a professor of Child Welfare and Family Violence at the University of Pennsylvania] said he believes the family-preservation model does not work. 'It's a profound disagreement and one in which I believe the scientific evidence is firmly on my side,' he said.... The family-preservation model, championed by the National Coalition

---

13. Daniel Bergner, *The Case of Marie and Her Sons*, N.Y. Times Magazine, July 23, 2006, at 31–32, *available at* http://www.nytimes.com/2006/07/23/magazine/23welfare.html.

14. Associated Press, *N.J. to pay $7.5 million settlement in boy's death*, Phila. Inquirer, Nov. 12, 2006.

15. *Id.*

for Child Protection Reform and the Annie E. Casey Foundation ... sees hope in keeping families intact by enlisting assistance from other family members and offering services from drug counseling to parenting training."[16]

4. Some programs attempt to move children from foster care into permanent homes with grandparents or other relatives and name the relatives as guardians. "States struggling to fill a void left by parents lost to drug addiction, AIDS and incarceration are increasingly using such programs to deal with the rising costs of foster care ... States like the programs because they are cheaper than foster homes, which require more oversight. Child welfare advocates like them, too, because they are more permanent. Critics say the programs are a new form of welfare and potentially more costly than advocates claim ... Foster care costs up to $80,000 per child per year.... In Washington ... foster parents receive nearly $800 per month per child, whereas the only public resource available to a caregiver outside the foster care system is welfare, at roughly $239 a month.... Critics say states should not pay relatives to do what is their responsibility to do anyway ..."[17]

5. Consider the role of the social worker or child protective service worker assigned to make decisions about child abuse, child neglect, when or whether to remove a child from a parent's care for a medical examination or to require services or to terminate parental rights. Lawyers may represent the local governments at every stage. Lawyers may also represent some of the family members under scrutiny. What are some professional dilemmas faced by lawyers representing the local governments? Are their interests the same as the abused or neglected child? What dilemmas do you think lawyers representing abused or neglected children might have to face and resolve? Are their interests always adverse to the interests of the parents/custodians? These issues are further explored in Chapter 9, in the context of absolute or qualified immunity for social workers.

C. The General Rule of *DeShaney*

Questions to guide reading of *DeShaney* oral argument

Below is the Supreme Court oral argument in *DeShaney*, the next case in the Chapter. You may want to read the facts of *DeShaney* before reading the oral argument.

1. What was the petitioner's "enmeshment" theory? Why does one Justice suggest that petitioner's theory, if adopted, would deter local governments from undertaking child abuse programs?

---

16. Mitch Lipka, *A 'tug-of-war' at N.J. child-care agency*, PHILA. INQUIRER, Dec. 28, 2003.

17. Ian Urbina, *With Parents Absent, Trying to Keep Child Care in the Family*, N.Y. TIMES, July 23, 2006.

2. Why did the government respondents contend that petitioner's theory was an attempt to circumvent the state action requirement?
3. What was the government respondents' view of the potential for liability if Joshua had been placed in foster care?
4. As you read the transcript, consider the quality of the oral arguments.

Supreme Court oral argument in *DeShaney*

Oral Argument of DONALD JAMES SULLIVAN on Behalf of Petitioners

MR.SULLIVAN: Mr. Chief Justice, and may it please the Court:

We are here contending today not for a broad constitutional mandate to the states to do all good things to all people, nor do we contend for a broad constitutional duty to prevent all harm or all sadness, nor do we contend for a broad constitutional duty to protect all children in all cases.

...

We do suggest that there is one and only one exquisitely narrow circumstance where there is an affirmative duty. I would suggest that there are two primary elements to the one and only one circumstance for which we argue.

The first is the existence of a child/parent relationship. The other is what I term enmeshment, intricate intimacy, enmeshment of the agents of the state in a particular circumstance which would have three characteristics: the first, an extreme danger to a particular individual child; the second, abundant actual knowledge on the part of the agents of the state; and the third, an actual undertaking by the state to protect the child.

...

QUESTION: Well, why don't we start with the language of the Fourteenth Amendment which says that a state shall not—what does it state—deprive any person of life, liberty or property without due process of law.

MR. SULLIVAN: Yes, sir.

QUESTION: Now, certainly we've held in many cases that the state may not deprive someone of life, but we've never held that that provision protects in the constitutional sense a private—a private attack on another person.

MR. SULLIVAN: I agree with that, Mr. Chief Justice. And I would further agree that in the—in the context in which prior to today that question has been addressed by the Court, I agree that that's the correct holding. For example, if you were to hold otherwise, then the police department would have an obligation to prevent the mugging and a whole host of things that are simply unworkable and are not to be found in the Constitution.

. . .

QUESTION: Well, the only—the only cases in which the Court has found an affirmative duty on the part of the state to provide basic services is in a setting like a prison or a state institution where the state has already deprived the individual of the individual's liberty and institutionalized them.

. . .

MR. SULLIVAN: . . . I think that's what the notion of enmeshment—and that's not a phrase that I'm aware the Court has used. . . .

QUESTION: If—if your theory were to be accepted, it seems to me it would have a real deterrent effect on state child abuse programs. Why would a state want to undertake a child abuse program at all if they face liability if they guess wrong? I can't—I think you're asking the Court to take a step that is perhaps quite unwarranted and quite dangerous.

MR. SULLIVAN: . . . But this Court relatively recently decided *Daniels* and decided *Davidson*, and I think solves that problem entirely because . . . under those cases that even if we guess wrong, we are safe from liability. . . . [E]ven if you're negligent, it's okay in a 1983 setting. . . . [U]nder the existing holdings of this Court, which I do not ask the Court to change, we've already said to the child protection agency it's okay to guess wrong. It's okay if you make a mistake. And that has to be. I think government can't function without that—

. . .

QUESTION: Would your case be any different if you had none of this history but a very stupid social worker who went in and saw lots of evidence of child abuse and failed to remove the child from the home immediately?

. . .

QUESTION: My question is if you just have those stark facts, a social worker visits a home, sees the child that a reasonable social worker should have known was in extreme danger—

MR. SULLIVAN: Yes.

QUESTION: —and fails to remove the child, has the state committed a constitutional violation?

MR. SULLIVAN: In an appropriate fact setting, yes, I believe so.

QUESTION: Well, I've given you the facts. The answer is yes.

...

Question: What is magical about the fact that the citizen, here the child, is in threat from—from his father rather than from someone else? Suppose a case worker goes in and finds an elderly person starving. Why wouldn't there be a similar obligation on the part of the state? Why wouldn't you—you find the state liable for depriving this person of life if the person dies because the state did not provide food? Why wouldn't that—

Mr. Sullivan: ... The Constitution is interposed in the relationship between the child and its—and its parent.

...

It's interposed, more precisely, when the—when the state says we suspect there might be a problem for this child. We're going to terminate your rights. At that point there's no question but what the parent's constitutional rights in the relationship are recognized, both his substantive rights to his possession of his child and his procedural rights to have witnesses and hearings....

Question: But that's a—that's a limitation on the state—those cases. They say the state can't do certain things. You're trying to turn that around and say that arising out of that same relationship is a duty on the state.

...

Oral Argument of MARK J. MINGO on behalf of the Respondents

Mr. Mingo: Thank you, Mr. Chief Justice. May it please the Court:

We believe this case involves an attempt by the Petitioners to transform the private wrongdoing of a natural father into state action for purposes of invoking the Fourteenth Amendment. The primary issue presented is whether a county's failure to prevent the infliction of harm by a third party upon a person at liberty constitutes a due process violation of the Fourteenth Amendment.

We believe that there was no state deprivation of a constitutionally protected right for three main reasons. First, the Fourteenth Amendment's concept of liberty does not include a right to basic protective services from the state. Secondly, there is no state action in a constitutional sense which caused a deprivation in this case. Third, we believe that the actions of the social worker did not evince the state of mind necessary to invoke the Fourteenth Amendment.

...

MR. MINGO: ... The Fourteenth Amendment has been viewed by this Court as imposing no constitutional duty upon the states to provide substantive services to its citizens. The Court also has held that if the state chooses to provide some form of protective services, the Fourteenth Amendment does not tell the state how far they must go in providing those services.

QUESTION: Mr. Mingo, if this child had been in foster care placed by the state or the county, would there be potential liability?

MR. MINGO: Justice O'Connor, in that instance, we believe there may well be potential liability because in that case we have, at least arguably, state action in the sense that the state took a child out of his natural surroundings, arguably put him in state-controlled surroundings and thereby increased the risk of harm to that child. In that instance, I believe we may well have a case somewhat analogous to the prison setting and perhaps more analogous to the mental institution setting that was present in *Youngberg v. Romeo*.

...

QUESTION: Why wasn't that what happened in January of 1983 when they returned the child? ...

MR. MINGO: In January of 1983—

QUESTION: Because they had custody of the child for a few days.

MR. MINGO: —the hospital had custody of the child because of the fact that the juvenile court—not the social workers, not the Department of Social Services, but Wisconsin juvenile court—through its intake worker placed the child in the temporary custody of a hospital.

QUESTION: All right. And assume, having done that, the hospital now learns if we return the child to his father, the father has the knife and is about [to] abuse the child, do you say the state can go ahead and return the child?

MR. MINGO: Although that is certainly not the case before this Court, in that instance, I believe from a constitutional standpoint only a county or a department of social services could return the child without facing constitutional liability.

QUESTION: Even with knowledge that there's—even with knowledge of extreme danger and almost certain serious abuse of this kind?

MR. MINGO: Even with that knowledge, Your Honor.

QUESTION: Well, why is that different then from the foster home case that Justice O'Connor asked you about?

Mr. Mingo: In the foster home setting, we have the state taking a child away from his natural surroundings, putting him in another set of surroundings, which are state controlled, state operated—

. . .

Question: . . . Supposing the juvenile court is given evidence that if you return the child to the home, the child will be seriously abused forthwith? . . . Would the state be liable if it went ahead and returned the child?

. . .

Mr. Mingo: I don't believe in that instance we would have state action because we have not done anything to increase the risk of harm to that child, whereas in Justice O'Connor's example, we certainly can be said to have increased the risk of harm to the child because we took that child away from his or her natural surroundings and put that child into an arguably more dangerous set of surroundings. And we believe that's what triggers state action.

Question: What if you don't give it back to the father, but you give it back to—to the wrong person? You give it back to some . . . some mad criminal who has just been released from a mental institution knowing or you ought to know that this is not the—not the father. Would the state have any liability in those circumstances?

Mr. Mingo: Justice Scalia, I believe in that set of circumstances there well may be liable—liability because we have state action—

Question: So, what you're saying is what makes a difference is whether you're just returning him to the status he was in before you took over the temporary custody. Is that—is that the difference?

Mr. Mingo: I believe that the important factor to be looked at is whether or not the state action can fairly be said to have increased the risk of harm to that child. If the answer to that threshold question is yes, then I believe we have state action in a constitutional sense.

Question: Increased it from what? From what it was before the state took custody or from what it was when the state had custody?

Mr. Mingo: From what it was before the state interjected and took custody.

Question: Which is more important than the abuse to poor Joshua?

Mr. Mingo: We're not saying it's more important, but the parents certainly have a constitutionally protected right which must be observed by the social worker.

Question: Poor Joshua.

. . .

Question: And under your theory, I take it if two policemen see a rape and watch it just for their own amusement, no violation of the Constitution.

MR. MINGO: We would concede that there is no constitutional violation in that particular case ... In this case it is undisputed by both sides that there was no direct deprivation or direct infliction of harm upon the Petitioners nor was the Petitioner in the custody of the state at the time of the alleged wrongdoing.

In order to circumvent the—the state action or constitutional deprivation requirement, counsel has proposed in their brief a special relationship theory which today they appear to call an enmeshment theory. No matter what it is, this theory would hold states liable wherever they have expressed a desire to afford protection to an individual and where they have some generalized knowledge of the victim's plight. We submit that such a theory has no support in the language of the Fourteenth Amendment, no support in Section 1983, nor does it have any support in any prior decision of this Court.

What their theory would do is open up local governments to massive new areas of exposure precisely because of the fact that the states, if we were to accept Petitioners' theory, become liable for the acts of private wrongdoers. There are numerous governmental agencies other than social services departments which seek to afford some degree of protection to the public. Certainly police departments, fire departments, emergency ambulance services fall into that very same category. It seems to us that if Petitioners are to prevail in these types of cases, the effect will be to greatly expand the financial drain on local governments thereby making the very services that Petitioners claim they wish to encourage less available to the public as a whole.

...

For further discussion

1. Plaintiff's counsel in *DeShaney* announced his candidacy for political office after the Supreme Court granted certiorari but before the argument. Lynda G. Dodd, *DeShaney v. Winnebago County: Governmental Neglect and the Blessings of Liberty*, CIVIL RIGHTS STORIES (Foundation 2008, Myriam E. Gilles and Risa L. Goluboff, eds.) 203. A member of the plaintiff's litigation team wanted to invite experienced appellate attorneys from the American Civil Liberties Union Children's Rights Project to argue before the Supreme Court but plaintiff's counsel was unwilling to relinquish his role, even though the election was less than a week after the Supreme Court argument. *Id.* at 202–03. Joshua Deshaney's mother was frustrated by her lawyers, and even wrote to Chief Justice Rehnquist seeking to have her lawyers replaced. *Id.*

2. Should local counsel step aside for experienced national advocacy organizations? Or for lawyers with experience before the Supreme Court? If so, when—after certiorari has been granted? Or earlier, when the decision to seek certiorari is made?

3. Supreme Court litigation is increasingly handled by specialists, not the lawyers who originally represent the client. The New York Times reported that in 1980 only 6% of Supreme Court cases were litigated by lawyers who specialize in Supreme Court litigation. But in 2007–08, that had increased to 50% of the Supreme Court docket. Adam Liptak, *Specialists' Help at Court Can Come With a Catch*, N.Y. Times (Oct. 9, 2010). In 2014, Reuters reported that, among clients represented by private counsel, a group of 66 lawyers, "far less than 1 percent of lawyers who filed appeals to the Supreme Court ... were involved in 43 percent of the cases the high court chose to decide from 2004 through 2012." Joan Biskupic, Janet Roberts, and John Shiffman, *At America's court of last resort, a handful of lawyers now dominates the docket*, Reuters Investigates (Dec. 8, 2014).

4. What are some consequences of an increasingly specialized group of lawyers who represent clients before the Supreme Court? Is it possible some have their own professional goals apart from obtaining the best results for their clients?

Questions to guide reading of *DeShaney*

1. What was petitioner's claim against the government social workers and local officials?
2. According to *DeShaney*, why doesn't the Due Process Clause require the state to protect life, liberty or property against private action?
3. According to *DeShaney*, under what limited circumstances does the state have a duty of care toward certain individuals (a "special relationship")? Why?
4. Why didn't the state have a "special relationship" or any constitutional duty to protect Joshua DeShaney?
5. Why do you think *DeShaney* referenced the potential existence of a state tort law remedy for Plaintiff?
6. Did *DeShaney* suggest in footnote 9 that incarceration or institutionalization may be analogous to other government relationships with individuals?
7. Justice Brennan's dissent suggested that, by setting up a government child protection program, Wisconsin relieved others of any sense of obligation to do more than report child abuse and that that state intervention created a special relationship with Joshua. Do you agree? If the broader theory of liability that Justice Brennan advocated had been adopted, would that have created any incentive for local governments to reduce services to abused children?
8. After *DeShaney*, what arguments do you expect government defendants to make?
9. What arguments do you expect plaintiffs to make to avoid *DeShaney's* general rule that the state owes no duty to protect against private violence?

DeShaney v. Winnebago County Dept. of Social Services

489 U.S. 189 (1989)

Chief Justice REHNQUIST delivered the opinion of the Court.

Petitioner is a boy who was beaten and permanently injured by his father, with whom he lived. Respondents are social workers and other local officials who received complaints that petitioner was being abused by his father and had reason to believe that this was the case, but nonetheless did not act to remove petitioner from his father's custody. Petitioner sued respondents claiming that their failure to act deprived him of his liberty in violation of the Due Process Clause of the Fourteenth Amendment to the United States Constitution. We hold that it did not.

I

The facts of this case are undeniably tragic. Petitioner Joshua DeShaney was born in 1979. In 1980, a Wyoming court granted his parents a divorce and awarded custody of Joshua to his father, Randy DeShaney. The father shortly thereafter moved to … Winnebago County, Wisconsin, taking the infant Joshua with him [, remarried and divorced again.]

The Winnebago County authorities first learned that Joshua DeShaney might be a victim of child abuse in January 1982, when his father's second wife complained to the police, at the time of their divorce, that he had previously "hit the boy causing marks and [was] a prime case for child abuse." … The Winnebago County Department of Social Services (DSS) interviewed the father, but he denied the accusations, and DSS did not pursue them further. In January 1983, Joshua was admitted to a local hospital with multiple bruises and abrasions. The examining physician suspected child abuse and notified DSS, which immediately obtained an order from a Wisconsin juvenile court placing Joshua in the temporary custody of the hospital. Three days later, the county convened an ad hoc "Child Protection Team"—consisting of a pediatrician, a psychologist, a police detective, the county's lawyer, several DSS caseworkers, and various hospital personnel—to consider Joshua's situation. At this meeting, the Team decided that there was insufficient evidence of child abuse to retain Joshua in the custody of the court. The Team did, however, decide to recommend several measures to protect Joshua, including enrolling him in a preschool program, providing his father with certain counseling services, and encouraging his father's girlfriend to move out of the home. Randy DeShaney entered into a voluntary agreement with DSS in which he promised to cooperate with them in accomplishing these goals.

Based on the recommendation of the Child Protection Team, the juvenile court dismissed the child protection case and returned Joshua to the custody of his father. A month later, emergency room personnel called the DSS caseworker handling Joshua's case to report that he had once again been treated for suspicious injuries. The caseworker concluded that there was no basis for action. For the next six months, the caseworker made monthly visits to the DeShaney home, during which she observed a number of suspicious injuries on Joshua's head; she also noticed that he had not been enrolled in school, and that the girlfriend had not moved out. The caseworker dutifully recorded these incidents in her files, along with her continuing suspicions that someone in the DeShaney household was physically abusing Joshua, but she did nothing more. In November 1983, the emergency room notified DSS that Joshua had been treated once again for injuries that they believed to be caused by child abuse. On the caseworker's next two visits to the DeShaney home, she was told that Joshua was too ill to see her. Still DSS took no action.

In March 1984, Randy DeShaney beat 4-year-old Joshua so severely that he fell into a life-threatening coma. Emergency brain surgery revealed a series of hemorrhages caused by traumatic injuries to the head inflicted over a long period of time. Joshua did not die, but he suffered brain damage so severe that he is expected to spend the rest of his life confined to an institution for the profoundly retarded. Randy DeShaney was subsequently tried and convicted of child abuse.

Joshua and his mother brought this action under 42 U.S.C. § 1983 in the United States District Court for the Eastern District of Wisconsin against respondents Winnebago County, DSS, and various individual employees of DSS. The complaint alleged that respondents had deprived Joshua of his liberty without due process of law, in violation of his rights under the Fourteenth Amendment, by failing to intervene to protect him against a risk of violence at his father's hands of which they knew or should have known.

. . .

II

. . . Petitioners contend that the State deprived Joshua of his liberty interest in "free[dom] from . . . unjustified intrusions on personal security," . . . by failing to provide him with adequate protection against his father's violence. The claim is one invoking the substantive rather than the procedural component of the Due Process Clause; petitioners do not claim that the State denied Joshua protection without according him appropriate procedural safeguards . . . but that it was categorically obligated to protect him in these circumstances. . . .

But nothing in the language of the Due Process Clause itself requires the State to protect the life, liberty, and property of its citizens against invasion by private actors. The Clause is phrased as a limitation on the State's power to act, not as a guarantee of certain minimal levels of safety and security. It forbids the State itself to deprive individuals of life, liberty, or property without "due process of law," but its language cannot fairly be extended to impose an affirmative obligation on the State to ensure that those interests do not come to harm through other means. Nor does history support such an expansive reading of the constitutional text. Like its counterpart in the Fifth Amendment, the Due Process Clause of the Fourteenth Amendment was intended to prevent government "from abusing [its] power, or employing it as an instrument of oppression," *Davidson v. Cannon, supra*, 474 U.S., at 348; *see also Daniels v. Williams, supra*, 474 U.S., at 331 (" "to secure the individual from the arbitrary exercise of the powers of government,'" " and "to prevent governmental power from being 'used for purposes of oppression' ") (internal citations omitted); *Parratt v. Taylor*, 451 U.S. 527, 549 (1981) (Powell, J., concurring in result) (to prevent the "affirmative abuse of power"). Its purpose was to protect the people from the State, not to ensure that the State protected them from each other. The Framers were content to leave the extent of governmental obligation in the latter area to the democratic political processes.

Consistent with these principles, our cases have recognized that the Due Process Clauses generally confer no affirmative right to governmental aid, even where such aid may be necessary to secure life, liberty, or property interests of which the government itself may not deprive the individual. *See, e.g., Harris v. McRae*, 448 U.S. 297, 317–318 (1980) (no obligation to fund abortions or other medical services) (discussing Due Process Clause of Fifth Amendment); *Lindsey v. Normet*, 405 U.S. 56, 74 (1972) (no obligation to provide adequate housing) (discussing Due Process Clause of Fourteenth Amendment).... As we said in *Harris v. McRae*: "Although the liberty protected by the Due Process Clause affords protection against unwarranted *government* interference..., it does not confer an entitlement to such [governmental aid] as may be necessary to realize all the advantages of that freedom." 448 U.S., at 317–318 (emphasis added). If the Due Process Clause does not require the State to provide its citizens with particular protective services, it follows that the State cannot be held liable under the Clause for injuries that could have been averted had it chosen to provide them. As a general matter, then, we conclude that a State's failure to protect an individual against private violence simply does not constitute a violation of the Due Process Clause.

Petitioners contend, however, that even if the Due Process Clause imposes no affirmative obligation on the State to provide the general public with adequate protective services, such a duty may arise out of certain "special relationships" created or assumed by the State with respect to particular individuals.... Petitioners argue that such a "special relationship" existed here because the State knew that Joshua faced a special danger of abuse at his father's hands, and specifically proclaimed, by word and by deed, its intention to protect him against that danger.... Having actually undertaken to protect Joshua from this danger—which petitioners concede the State played no part in creating—the State acquired an affirmative "duty," enforceable through the Due Process Clause, to do so in a reasonably competent fashion. Its failure to discharge that duty, so the argument goes, was an abuse of governmental power that so "shocks the conscience," *Rochin v. California*, 342 U.S. 165, 172 (1952), as to constitute a substantive due process violation....[4]

Several of the Courts of Appeals have read this language as implying that once the State learns that a third party poses a special danger to an identified victim, and indicates its willingness to protect the victim against that danger, a "special relationship" arises between State and victim, giving rise to an affirmative duty, enforceable through the Due Process Clause, to render adequate protection....

We reject this argument. It is true that in certain limited circumstances the Constitution imposes upon the State affirmative duties of care and protection with respect to particular individuals. In *Estelle v. Gamble*, 429 U.S. 97 (1976), we recognized that the Eighth Amendment's prohibition against cruel and unusual punishment, made applicable to the States through the Fourteenth Amendment's Due Process Clause ... requires the State to provide adequate medical care to incarcerated prisoners. 429 U.S., at 103–104 ... We reasoned that because the prisoner is unable "'by reason of the deprivation of his liberty [to] care for himself,'" it is only "'just'" that the State be required to care for him....

In *Youngberg v. Romeo*, 457 U.S. 307 (1982), we extended this analysis beyond the Eighth Amendment setting,[6] holding that the substantive component of the Fourteenth Amendment's Due Process Clause requires the State to provide involuntarily committed mental patients with such services as are necessary to ensure their "reasonable safety" from themselves and others. *Id.*, at 314–325; *see id.*, at 315, 324 (dicta indicating that the State is also obligated to provide such individuals with "adequate food, shelter, clothing, and medical care"). As we explained: "If it is cruel and unusual punishment to hold convicted criminals in unsafe conditions, it must be unconstitutional [under the Due Process Clause] to confine the involuntarily committed—

---

4. The genesis of this notion appears to lie in a statement in our opinion in *Martinez v. California*, 444 U.S. 277 (1980). In that case, we were asked to decide, *inter alia*, whether state officials could be held liable under the Due Process Clause of the Fourteenth Amendment for the death of a private citizen at the hands of a parolee. Rather than squarely confronting the question presented here—whether the Due Process Clause imposed upon the State an affirmative duty to protect—we affirmed the dismissal of the claim on the narrower ground that the causal connection between the state officials' decision to release the parolee from prison and the murder was too attenuated to establish a "deprivation" of constitutional rights within the meaning of § 1983. *Id.*, at 284–285.... But we went on to say:

> "[T]he parole board was not aware that appellants' decedent, as distinguished from the public at large, faced any special danger. We need not and do not decide that a parole officer could never be deemed to 'deprive' someone of life by action taken in connection with the release of a prisoner on parole. But we do hold that at least under the particular circumstances of this parole decision, appellants' decedent's death is too remote a consequence of the parole officers' action to hold them responsible under the federal civil rights law." *Id.*, at 285 (footnote omitted).

6. The Eighth Amendment applies "only after the State has complied with the constitutional guarantees traditionally associated with criminal prosecutions.... [T]he State does not acquire the power to punish with which the Eighth Amendment is concerned until after it has secured a formal adjudication of guilt in accordance with due process of law." *Ingraham v. Wright*, 430 U.S. 651, 671–672, n. 40 (1977)....

who may not be punished at all—in unsafe conditions." *Id.*, at 315–316; *see also Revere v. Massachusetts General Hospital*, 463 U.S. 239, 244 (1983) (holding that the Due Process Clause requires the responsible government or governmental agency to provide medical care to suspects in police custody who have been injured while being apprehended by the police).

But these cases afford petitioners no help. Taken together, they stand only for the proposition that when the State takes a person into its custody and holds him there against his will, the Constitution imposes upon it a corresponding duty to assume some responsibility for his safety and general well-being. *See Youngberg v. Romeo, supra*, 457 U.S., at 317 ("When a person is institutionalized—and wholly dependent on the State[,] ... a duty to provide certain services and care does exist"). The rationale for this principle is simple enough: when the State by the affirmative exercise of its power so restrains an individual's liberty that it renders him unable to care for himself, and at the same time fails to provide for his basic human needs—*e.g.*, food, clothing, shelter, medical care, and reasonable safety—it transgresses the substantive limits on state action set by the Eighth Amendment and the Due Process Clause. *See Estelle v. Gamble, supra*, 429 U.S., at 103–104; *Youngberg v. Romeo, supra*, 457 U.S., at 315–316.... The affirmative duty to protect arises not from the State's knowledge of the individual's predicament or from its expressions of intent to help him, but from the limitation which it has imposed on his freedom to act on his own behalf. *See Estelle v. Gamble, supra*, 429 U.S., at 103 ("An inmate must rely on prison authorities to treat his medical needs; if the authorities fail to do so, those needs will not be met"). In the substantive due process analysis, it is the State's affirmative act of restraining the individual's freedom to act on his own behalf—through incarceration, institutionalization, or other similar restraint of personal liberty—which is the "deprivation of liberty" triggering the protections of the Due Process Clause, not its failure to act to protect his liberty interests against harms inflicted by other means.

The *Estelle-Youngberg* analysis simply has no applicability in the present case. Petitioners concede that the harms Joshua suffered occurred not while he was in the State's custody, but while he was in the custody of his natural father, who was in no sense a state actor.[9] While the State may have been aware of the dangers that Joshua faced in the free world, it played no part in their creation, nor did it do anything to render him any more vulnerable to them. That the State once took temporary custody of Joshua does not alter the analysis, for when it returned him to his father's custody, it placed him in no worse position than that in which he would have been had it not acted at all; the State does not become the permanent guarantor of an individual's

9. ... Had the State by the affirmative exercise of its power removed Joshua from free society and placed him in a foster home operated by its agents, we might have a situation sufficiently analogous to incarceration or institutionalization to give rise to an affirmative duty to protect. Indeed, several Courts of Appeals have held, by analogy to *Estelle* and *Youngberg*, that the State may be held liable under the Due Process Clause for failing to protect children in foster homes from mistreatment at the hands of their foster parents.... We express no view on the validity of this analogy, however, as it is not before us in the present case.

safety by having once offered him shelter. Under these circumstances, the State had no constitutional duty to protect Joshua.

It may well be that, by voluntarily undertaking to protect Joshua against a danger it concededly played no part in creating, the State acquired a duty under state tort law to provide him with adequate protection against that danger. *See* Restatement (Second) of Torts § 323 (1965) (one who undertakes to render services to another may in some circumstances be held liable for doing so in a negligent fashion); *see generally* W. Keeton, D. Dobbs, R. Keeton, & D. Owen, Prosser and Keeton on the Law of Torts § 56 (5th ed. 1984) (discussing "special relationships" which may give rise to affirmative duties to act under the common law of tort). But the claim here is based on the Due Process Clause of the Fourteenth Amendment, which, as we have said many times, does not transform every tort committed by a state actor into a constitutional violation. *See Daniels v. Williams*, 474 U.S., at 335–336.... A State may, through its courts and legislatures, impose such affirmative duties of care and protection upon its agents as it wishes. But not "all common-law duties owed by government actors were ... constitutionalized by the Fourteenth Amendment." *Daniels v. Williams, supra*, 474 U.S., at 335.... Because, as explained above, the State had no constitutional duty to protect Joshua against his father's violence, its failure to do so—though calamitous in hindsight—simply does not constitute a violation of the Due Process Clause.

Judges and lawyers, like other humans, are moved by natural sympathy in a case like this to find a way for Joshua and his mother to receive adequate compensation for the grievous harm inflicted upon them. But before yielding to that impulse, it is well to remember once again that the harm was inflicted not by the State of Wisconsin, but by Joshua's father. The most that can be said of the state functionaries in this case is that they stood by and did nothing when suspicious circumstances dictated a more active role for them. In defense of them it must also be said that had they moved too soon to take custody of the son away from the father, they would likely have been met with charges of improperly intruding into the parent-child relationship, charges based on the same Due Process Clause that forms the basis for the present charge of failure to provide adequate protection.

The people of Wisconsin may well prefer a system of liability which would place upon the State and its officials the responsibility for failure to act in situations such as the present one. They may create such a system, if they do not have it already, by changing the tort law of the State in accordance with the regular lawmaking process. But they should not have it thrust upon them by this Court's expansion of the Due Process Clause of the Fourteenth Amendment.

Justice BRENNAN, with whom Justice MARSHALL and Justice BLACKMUN join, dissenting.

... It may well be, as the Court decides ... that the Due Process Clause as construed by our prior cases creates no general right to basic governmental services.... [But n]o one ... has asked the Court to proclaim that, as a general matter, the Constitution safeguards positive as well as negative liberties.

... In a constitutional setting that distinguishes sharply between action and inaction, one's characterization of the misconduct alleged under § 1983 may effectively decide the case. Thus, by leading off with a discussion (and rejection) of the idea that the Constitution imposes on the States an affirmative duty to take basic care of their citizens, the Court foreshadows—perhaps even preordains—its conclusion that no duty existed even on the specific facts before us....

The Court's baseline is the absence of positive rights in the Constitution and a concomitant suspicion of any claim that seems to depend on such rights. From this perspective, the DeShaneys' claim is first and foremost about inaction (the failure, here, of respondents to take steps to protect Joshua), and only tangentially about action (the establishment of a state program specifically designed to help children like Joshua)....

I would begin from the opposite direction. I would focus first on the action that Wisconsin has taken with respect to Joshua and children like him, rather than on the actions that the State failed to take. Such a method is not new to this Court. Both *Estelle v. Gamble*, 429 U.S. 97 (1976), and *Youngberg v. Romeo*, 457 U.S. 307 (1982), began by emphasizing that the States had confined J.W. Gamble to prison and Nicholas Romeo to a psychiatric hospital. This initial action rendered these people helpless to help themselves or to seek help from persons unconnected to the government. *See Estelle, supra*, 429 U.S. at 104 ("[I]t is but just that the public be required to care for the prisoner, who cannot by reason of the deprivation of his liberty, care for himself")....

...

Moreover, to the Court, the only fact that seems to count as an "affirmative act of restraining the individual's freedom to act on his own behalf" is direct physical control. *Ante* (listing only "incarceration, institutionalization, [and] other similar restraint of personal liberty" in describing relevant "affirmative acts"). I would not, however, give *Youngberg* and *Estelle* such a stingy scope. I would recognize, as the Court apparently cannot, that "the State's knowledge of [an] individual's predicament [and] its expressions of intent to help him" can amount to a "limitation ... on his freedom to act on his own behalf" or to obtain help from others ... [and] that a State may be found complicit in an injury even if it did not create the situation that caused the harm.

...

To put the point more directly, these cases signal that a State's prior actions may be decisive in analyzing the constitutional significance of its inaction. I thus would locate the DeShaneys' claims within the framework of cases like *Youngberg* and *Estelle* ... by considering the actions that Wisconsin took with respect to Joshua.

Wisconsin has established a child-welfare system specifically designed to help children like Joshua. Wisconsin law places upon the local departments of social services such as respondent (DSS or Department) a duty to investigate reported instances of child abuse.... In this way, Wisconsin law invites—indeed, directs—citizens and other governmental entities to depend on local departments of social services such as respondent to protect children from abuse.

The specific facts before us bear out this view of Wisconsin's system of protecting children. Each time someone voiced a suspicion that Joshua was being abused, that information was relayed to the Department for investigation and possible action.

...

In these circumstances, a private citizen, or even a person working in a government agency other than DSS, would doubtless feel that her job was done as soon as she had reported her suspicions of child abuse to DSS. Through its child-welfare program, in other words, the State of Wisconsin has relieved ordinary citizens and governmental bodies other than the Department of any sense of obligation to do anything more than report their suspicions of child abuse to DSS.... It simply belies reality, therefore, to contend that the State "stood by and did nothing" with respect to Joshua. Through its child-protection program, the State actively intervened in Joshua's life and, by virtue of this intervention, acquired ever more certain knowledge that Joshua was in grave danger. These circumstances, in my view, plant this case solidly within the tradition of cases like *Youngberg* and *Estelle*.

...

As the Court today reminds us, "the Due Process Clause of the Fourteenth Amendment was intended to prevent government 'from abusing [its] power, or employing it as an instrument of oppression.'".... My disagreement with the Court arises from its failure to see that inaction can be every bit as abusive of power as action, that oppression can result when a State undertakes a vital duty and then ignores it. Today's opinion construes the Due Process Clause to permit a State to displace private sources of protection and then, at the critical moment, to shrug its shoulders and turn away from the harm that it has promised to try to prevent. Because I cannot agree that our Constitution is indifferent to such indifference, I respectfully dissent.

Justice BLACKMUN, dissenting.

... As Justice BRENNAN demonstrates, the facts here involve not mere passivity, but active state intervention in the life of Joshua DeShaney—intervention that triggered a fundamental duty to aid the boy once the State learned of the severe danger to which he was exposed.

The Court fails to recognize this duty because it attempts to draw a sharp and rigid line between action and inaction. But such formalistic reasoning has no place in the interpretation of the broad and stirring Clauses of the Fourteenth Amendment.

...

Poor Joshua! Victim of repeated attacks by an irresponsible, bullying, cowardly, and intemperate father, and abandoned by respondents who placed him in a dangerous predicament and who knew or learned what was going on, and yet did essentially nothing except, as the Court revealingly observes ... "dutifully recorded these incidents in [their] files." It is a sad commentary upon American life, and constitutional principles—so full of late of patriotic fervor and proud proclamations about "liberty and justice for all"—that this child, Joshua DeShaney, now is assigned to live out the remainder of his life profoundly retarded. Joshua and his mother, as petitioners here, deserve—but now are denied by this Court—the opportunity to have the facts of their case considered in the light of the constitutional protection that 42 U.S.C. § 1983 is meant to provide.

For further discussion

1. Justice Harry Blackmun wrote in an unusually personal voice in his *DeShaney* dissent, calling the beaten boy "Poor Joshua!". Why do you think Justice Blackmun chose that phrase? What does his choice of language suggest about his attitude toward the majority opinion, and perhaps more generally toward the institutional decision making process of the Supreme Court? *See* Linda Greenhouse, BECOMING JUSTICE BLACKMUN: HARRY BLACKMUN'S SUPREME COURT JOURNEY 232 (Times Books 2005).

2. Section 1983 claims alleging violations of the parent's liberty interest in the care, custody, and control of minor children frequently are litigated when state actors, such as caseworkers or social workers, investigate allegations of child abuse or neglect, *Miller v. City of Philadelphia*, 174 F.3d 368 (3d Cir. 1999) (summarized in this Chapter), remove children from their parents' custody, *id.* at 371, refuse to return children to their parents' custody, *e.g., Ernst v. Child and Youth Services of Chester County*, 108 F.3d 486 (3d Cir.), *cert. denied*, 522 U.S. 850 (1997) (excerpted in Chapter 9 Absolute Immunity), or seek to terminate parental rights to a child. The parental liberty interest may be protected by procedural due process, *e.g., Miller*, 174 F.2d at 372, or substantive due process, *id.* at 374, or both. *Id.* at 372–74.

3. *DeShaney* left open the possibility that the Due Process Clause could be violated by harm inflicted by a private person if the state created the danger that caused the harm. *DeShaney* stated: "While the State may have been aware of the dangers that Joshua faced in the free world, it played no part in their creation, nor did it do anything to render him any more vulnerable to them." Courts have relied on this suggestion of an exception to *DeShaney's* general rule to recognize the "state-created danger" theory of substantive due process liability. The "state-created danger" theory is explored below.

4. To grasp how the general rule of *DeShaney* fits with the "state-created danger" and "special relationship" exceptions to that general rule, it may help to visualize the relationship. See Chart in Section A of this Chapter.

D. Development of Doctrine in the Circuits: State-Created Danger Exception to *DeShaney*

Questions to guide reading of *Kneipp*

Kneipp is the basis for Simulation 2.

1. What legal test did *Kneipp* adopt for applying the state-created danger theory?
2. What evidence did *Kneipp* hold was sufficient for a jury to find in favor of Plaintiff on each of the four prongs of the test?
3. In his dissent in *DeShaney*, Justice Brennan reasoned that, in a constitutional setting that distinguished sharply between action and inaction, the characterization of the misconduct could decide the case. Do you agree? Is it easy to differentiate affirmative from passive conduct? Or to recast one as the other?
4. Note that *Kneipp* was decided before *Lewis*, the Supreme Court decision discussed in Chapter 3. Why is *Kneipp's* holding that the "shock the conscience" standard is limited to police chases overruled by *Lewis*?
5. If you represented the defendant, what advice would you give your client upon receiving this decision?

Kneipp v. Tedder

95 F.3d 1199 (3d Cir. 1996)

MANSMANN, Circuit Judge.

In a civil rights complaint brought against ... City of Philadelphia ... police officers, the parents and legal guardians of Samantha Kneipp allege that late one January evening when Kneipp, in an obvious state of severe inebriation, was attempting to return on foot to her nearby apartment, the police officers stopped her and sent her on alone.

We hold that, if proven, the facts alleged will sustain a prima facie case of a violation of Kneipp's Fourteenth Amendment substantive due process right and her liberty interest in personal security under the theory that city police officers increased the risk of harm to Kneipp which ultimately resulted in the severe damages she sustained. In so holding, we adopt the "state-created danger" theory as a viable mechanism for establishing a constitutional violation under 42 U.S.C. § 1983....

I.

The events leading to the tragedy that befell Samantha Kneipp began in the late evening of January 23, 1993. Samantha and her husband Joseph were returning on foot from a night of drinking at a tavern in Bucks County, Pennsylvania.[2] According to Joseph, Samantha was visibly intoxicated—she smelled of urine, staggered when she walked and, at times, was unable to walk without assistance. Joseph testified that he had to carry Samantha a portion of the way home.

The distance between the tavern and the Kneipps' home was approximately one mile. Shortly after midnight, now January 24, 1993, Philadelphia Police Officer Wesley Tedder stopped the Kneipps for causing a disturbance on the highway.[3] At this point, the Kneipps were only one-third of a block from their home. Unable to stand by herself, Samantha was leaning on Officer Tedder's car.[4] Officer Tedder questioned Samantha and Joseph separately; he stated in his deposition that he smelled alcohol on Samantha and found both of them to be intoxicated. He gave Samantha instructions to go stand somewhere, which she did not follow.[5] Joseph told Officer Tedder that he just wanted to get his wife into their apartment.

Shortly after Officer Tedder stopped the Kneipps, three other police officers arrived separately at the scene and positioned themselves across the street from Officer Tedder.[6] Joseph left Officer Tedder and crossed over to the other side of the street where the police cars were situated. Joseph told one of the officers that he had a babysitter watching his son and that he was supposed to be home by now. Joseph then asked the officer if he could go home, to which the officer replied, "Yeah, sure." When Joseph left to walk home, Samantha was leaning on the front of a police car in the presence of several police officers. Joseph testified that he assumed that because Samantha was drunk, the police officers were going to take her either to the hospital or to the police station. His thoughts at the time were that Samantha should not be

2. Joseph testified at his deposition that when he left for work at 9:00 a.m. that morning, there had been two quarts of beer in the refrigerator; however, when he got home from work, they were gone. He assumed that Samantha had consumed the beer that afternoon, thus necessitating their excursion to the tavern in the evening. Samantha is an alcoholic and had recently spent a week in a detoxification facility.

3. The Kneipps were quarreling over Samantha's desire to continue drinking—she wanted Joseph to buy her a six pack of beer and take it home, but he refused. Because of this, Samantha was refusing to go home.

4. Dr. Richard Saferstein, a forensic scientist, projected that Samantha's blood alcohol level at the time she was detained by Officer Tedder would have been approximately .25%, assuming she had not consumed any alcohol after she left the tavern. At this level, according to Dr. Saferstein, Samantha would have "serious incapacitation of muscular coordination, critical judgment, normal perception, and cognitive functions."

5. Officer Tedder stated in his deposition that he told them to "either knock it off or go in the house or [he] was going to take him in for intoxication."

6. One officer, Francis Healy, arrived sometime between 12:10 a.m. and 12:13 a.m. In his deposition, Officer Healy testified that when he arrived at the scene, he observed Samantha and Officer Tedder engaged in a discussion, and Tedder was telling her what to do; he did not see Joseph anywhere. Officer Healy heard Tedder tell Samantha to go home, and she turned around and started walking to what he believed to be her house. At about the same time, Officer Healy was "waived off" by Tedder and he departed at approximately 12:20 a.m.

left alone in her inebriated state and that the police officers would take care of her,[7] so he proceeded home without her. Officer Tedder, however, sent Samantha home alone;[9] she never reached her apartment building.

When his wife did not return to their apartment, Joseph went out to look for her. He saw a police car parked in a Sunoco station not far from his apartment building. As Joseph approached the car, he discovered Officer Tedder inside, and asked him if he had locked up Samantha or had taken her to the hospital. According to Joseph, Officer Tedder told him "to get out of here before he locked [him] up." Because of a previous experience with the Philadelphia police, Joseph took Officer Tedder's remark seriously and left. Joseph decided to continue looking for Samantha, and as he proceeded in the direction of a neighborhood convenience store, he thought he saw someone resembling Samantha, dressed in similar clothing, getting into an orange car. Because of Samantha's previous infidelity, Joseph thought that if it were Samantha, she was cheating on him again and would return when she was done. Joseph was never certain, however, that the woman he saw entering the car was Samantha. Joseph decided to forego his search and returned home.

At approximately 1:51 a.m., Officer Francis Healy responded to a radio call reporting that an individual was found unconscious at the bottom of an embankment next to a parking lot at the shopping plaza across the street from the Kneipps' home. The unconscious individual was Samantha Kneipp. Joseph was awakened around 4:00 a.m. by Officer Healy, who informed him that Samantha had fallen and was in the hospital.

---

7. A reasonable jury could believe that Joseph was correct in assuming that the police would take care of Samantha given his need to get home and care for their son. For example, when the police told Mr. Kneipp that he could go home (in response to his question), it was implicit that the police were going to take care of Mrs. Kneipp. The police were aware that Mrs. Kneipp was sufficiently intoxicated to need assistance. Given the circumstances, what could "Can I leave?" mean other than "Will you take care of my wife so I can leave?" Mr. Kneipp was not under arrest and the only thing preventing him from leaving was the need to take care of his wife. Why would he ask for permission to leave other than to indicate that he expected the police to take care of his wife? And when the police said "you can leave," that reasonably implied that they would take care of his wife. This affirmative action on the part of the police led Mr. Kneipp to leave his wife unattended, something he alleges he otherwise would not have done.

9. The Police Department Incident Report completed by Officer Tedder regarding his encounter with the Kneipps on January 24, 1993 at 12:01 a.m. indicated: "Above intoxicated and causing disturbance on Hwy. Adjusted. Sent Home." Based on this statement and the testimony of other witnesses, we believe reasonable jurors could infer that Officer Tedder sent Samantha home alone. Nonetheless, whether or not Officer Tedder actually sent Samantha home is not critical to our decision since the danger was created when Samantha was separated from her private source of rescue and subsequently abandoned by the police.

As a result of her exposure to the cold,[14] Samantha suffered hypothermia, which caused a condition known as anoxia. Consequently, the anoxia resulted in permanent brain damage impairing many basic body functions.[16]

...

II.

... Here, Samantha Kneipp's legal guardians have alleged that the ... police officers violated Samantha's right to substantive due process guaranteed by the Fourteenth Amendment. In *DeShaney v. Winnebago Co. Dep't of Social Serv.*, 489 U.S. 189, 197 (1989), the Supreme Court considered whether the due process clause of the Fourteenth Amendment imposed upon the state an affirmative duty to protect an individual against private violence where a special relationship exists between the state and the private individual. The Court found that the special relationship which would impose affirmative duties of care and protection on the state existed only in certain limited circumstances, such as when the state takes a person into its custody and holds him there against his will. *Id.* at 199–201. The Court explained:

> In the substantive due process analysis, it is the State's affirmative act of restraining the individual's freedom to act on his own behalf—through incarceration, institutionalization, or other similar restraint of personal liberty—which is the "deprivation of liberty" triggering the protections of the Due Process Clause, not its failure to act to protect his liberty interests against harms inflicted by other means.

Id. at 200 (footnote omitted). Applying this principle to the facts in *DeShaney*, the Court did not find a due process violation as the harms suffered by the child occurred while he was in the custody of his father, not in the state's custody. *Id.* at 201.

In the case before us, we agree with the district court that the special relationship required by *DeShaney* did not exist between Samantha and the police officers ... In *DeShaney*, the Supreme Court left open the possibility that a constitutional violation might have occurred despite the absence of a special relationship when it stated: "While the State may have been aware of the dangers that Joshua faced in the free world, it played no part in their creation, nor did it do anything to render him any more vulnerable to them." *Id.* at 201. Several of our sister courts of appeals have cited this comment by the Court as support for utilizing a state-created danger theory to establish a constitutional claim under 42 U.S.C. § 1983. *See Uhlrig v. Harder*, 64 F.3d 567, 572 n.7 (10th Cir. 1995), *cert. denied*, 516 U.S. 1118 (1996); *Dwares v. City of*

---

14. The temperature reading at 11:50 p.m. on January 23, 1993 in the vicinity where Samantha was found unconscious was 34 degrees Fahrenheit.

16. The brain damage sustained by Samantha reduced her level of functioning to an extremely low level, in that she is now unable to swallow and must be fed by a feeding tube inserted into her stomach; she is virtually blind; she cannot walk or sit upright; her oral communication is dysarthric; and she suffers from bowel and bladder incontinence. Despite these physical problems, Samantha is projected to live an average life expectancy....

New York, 985 F.2d 94, 99 (2d Cir. 1993); *Reed v. Gardner*, 986 F.2d 1122, 1125 (7th Cir.), *cert. denied*, 510 U.S. 947 (1993); *Freeman v. Ferguson*, 911 F.2d 52, 55 (8th Cir. 1990). Moreover, two other courts of appeals, in decisions predating *DeShaney*, recognized the state-created danger theory as a basis for establishing a constitutional claim under section 1983. *See Cornelius v. Town of Highland Lake*, 880 F.2d 348 (11th Cir. 1989), *cert. denied*, 494 U.S. 1066 (1990); *Wood v. Ostrander*, 879 F.2d 583 (9th Cir. 1989), *cert. denied*, 498 U.S. 938 (1990) ... Until now, we have not, however, been presented with the appropriate factual background to support a finding that state actors created a danger which deprived an individual of her Fourteenth Amendment right to substantive due process. Samantha Kneipp's case presents the right set of facts which, if believed, would trigger the application of the state-created danger theory. We turn first to our previous decisions in this area.

In the 1990 case of *Brown v. Grabowski*, [922 F.2d 1097, 1114–16 (3d Cir. 1990), *cert. denied*, 501 U.S. 1218 (1991)], Deborah Evans had been abducted and murdered by her former live-in boyfriend, Clifton McKenzie. Prior to the abduction, McKenzie had held Evans hostage for three days, during which he repeatedly threatened and sexually assaulted her. Although Evans and her family reported this information to the local police, criminal charges were never filed. Shortly thereafter, Evans was abducted and imprisoned in the trunk of her car where she froze to death. The personal representative of Evans' estate filed a civil rights complaint against the borough and employees of the police department alleging, inter alia, that Detective Grabowski, in failing to file criminal charges against McKenzie and in failing to inform Evans of her right as a victim of domestic violence to obtain a restraining order against McKenzie, violated her constitutional rights to due process and of access to the civil and criminal courts.

The plaintiff in *Brown* relied upon *Wood v. Ostrander*, 879 F.2d 583 (9th Cir. 1989) ... in support of her argument that the state-created danger theory was a viable basis for imposing constitutional liability under section 1983. In *Wood*, a police officer stranded the female passenger of a drunk driver along the side of the road in a high-crime area at 2:30 a.m. While undertaking the five mile walk to her home, the passenger accepted a ride from a stranger who took her to a secluded area and raped her. The Court of Appeals for the Ninth Circuit held that the plaintiff had raised a triable issue of fact as to whether the police officer "'affirmatively placed [her] in a position of danger.'" 879 F.2d at 589–90 (citation omitted). The court further held that the plaintiff was distinguishable from the general public and, therefore, the police had a duty to offer her some degree of peace and safety. *Id.* at 590 (citing *White v. Rochford*, 592 F.2d 381, 384 & n. 6 (7th Cir. 1979)).

...

We found *Wood* ... distinguishable from the facts in *Brown* ... [because the plaintiff in *Brown*] failed to offer any evidence that the police officers acted [affirmatively] to create or to exacerbate the danger that the former boyfriend posed to the victim. 922 F.2d at 1116. The plaintiff demonstrated only that Detective Grabowski failed to advise the victim of her right to seek a protective order. *Id.* Thus, we concluded in

Brown that the plaintiff had failed to establish a cognizable constitutional claim under section 1983.

In 1992, sitting in banc, we considered the state-created danger theory in *D.R. by L.R. v. Middle Bucks Area Vo. Tech. School*, 972 F.2d 1364 (3d Cir. 1992). There two female students at a public high school alleged that they were physically, verbally and sexually molested by male students in a unisex bathroom and in a darkroom, which were parts of the graphic arts classroom. The students' parents brought a civil rights action against the school district and several school officials and employees, alleging that the defendants created the danger that resulted in a violation of the plaintiffs' constitutional rights. In support of this claim, plaintiffs argued that the school defendants "'created a climate which facilitated sexual and physical abuse of students'" and, having thrust plaintiffs into this situation, "were obligated to protect them from violations of their personal bodily integrity by other students who were also under defendants' control." *Id.* at 1373.

In *D.R.*, we recognized that the state-created danger theory had been utilized by several courts of appeals to find a constitutional violation under section 1983 in non-custodial settings. *Id.* We read the post-*DeShaney* decisions to frame the inquiry as "whether the state actors involved affirmatively acted to create plaintiff's danger, or to render him or her more vulnerable to it." *Id.* (citation omitted). We continued that "[l]iability under the state created danger theory is predicated upon the states' affirmative acts which work to plaintiffs' detriments in terms of exposure to danger." *Id.* at 1374. We quoted the following comment from the Court of Appeals for the Seventh Circuit:

> We do not want to pretend that the line between action and inaction, between inflicting and failing to prevent the infliction of harm, is clearer than it is. If the state puts a man in a position of danger from private persons and then fails to protect him, it will not be heard to say that its role was merely passive; it is as much an active tortfeasor as if it had thrown him into a snake pit.

Id. (quoting *Bowers v. DeVito*, 686 F.2d 616, 618 (7th Cir. 1982)).

We concluded in *D.R.* that the facts presented did not show that the defendants created the students' danger, increased their risk of harm, or made them more vulnerable to the assaults. *Id.* Moreover, we found the state-created danger line of cases to be factually distinguishable in a critical respect: in the cases where the courts imposed a constitutional duty based on a state-created danger, the state had affirmatively acted to create the danger. *Id.* In *D.R.*, we found that the harm to the students resulted solely from the acts of private individuals, and not from the type of intermingling between state conduct and private violence that imposed liability in *Wood*.... *Id.* at 1375. The acts or omissions of the school defendants in *D.R.*, we concluded, did not rise to the level of affirmative action required to impose liability under the state-created danger theory.

In the 1994 case of *Fagan v. City of Vineland*, 22 F.3d 1296 (3d Cir. 1994) (*in banc*) ... the plaintiffs claimed their constitutional rights to substantive due process were violated when police officers recklessly conducted a high speed pursuit in violation of the Attorney General's guidelines. We held that the appropriate standard to be applied in police pursuit cases involving an alleged violation of substantive due process is the "shocks the conscience" test.... [but we] believe that the ... shocks the conscience standard is limited to police pursuit cases, and accordingly, we are not bound to follow that standard in the case before us.

In the 1995 case of *Mark v. Borough of Hatboro*, we suggested a test for applying the state-created danger theory. We found that cases predicating constitutional liability on a state-created danger theory have four common elements:

> (1) the harm ultimately caused was foreseeable and fairly direct; (2) the state actor acted in willful disregard for the safety of the plaintiff; (3) there existed some relationship between the state and the plaintiff; (4) the state actors used their authority to create an opportunity that otherwise would not have existed for the third party's crime to occur.

51 F.3d at 1152. We further noted that "[t]he cases where the state-created danger theory was applied were based on discrete, grossly reckless acts committed by the state or state actors using their peculiar positions as state actors, leaving a discrete plaintiff vulnerable to foreseeable injury." *Id.* at 1153. Those courts which have recognized the state-created danger theory have employed a deliberate indifference standard.[21] *Id.* at 1152 (quoting *Johnson v. Dallas Independent School Dist.*, 38 F.3d 198, 201 (5th Cir. 1994), *cert. denied*, 514 U.S. 1017 (1995); *Wood*, 879 F.2d at 588 ...).

...

III.

We begin by applying the four common elements we set forth in *Mark* for the state-created danger theory. First, the injuries to Samantha were foreseeable—Dr. Saferstein stated in his report that at a blood alcohol level of .25%, Samantha's muscular coordination was seriously impaired. Joseph's testimony as to how he had to help his wife walk, even carry her at times, also tends to show that Samantha's ability to walk was impaired. A reasonable trier of fact could conclude that in Samantha's state of intoxication, she would be more likely to fall and injure herself if left unescorted than someone who was not inebriated. Based on the facts and inferences most favorable to the legal guardians, we hold that a reasonable jury could find that the harm likely to befall Samantha if separated from Joseph while in a highly intoxicated state in cold weather was indeed foreseeable.

Second, we find the plaintiffs have adduced sufficient evidence to raise a material issue as to whether Officer Tedder acted in willful disregard for Samantha's safety. The plaintiffs presented evidence regarding Samantha's level of intoxication and impairment; by Officer Tedder's own testimony, he admitted that he knew Samantha

21. In the past, we have declined to distinguish terms such as "deliberate indifference," "reckless indifference," "gross negligence," or "reckless disregard" in the context of a violation of substantive due process under the Fourteenth Amendment....

was drunk. Moreover, Tedder's statement that he sent Samantha and Joseph home together is contradicted by the testimony of Joseph, Officer Healy and Tina Leone.

We also believe the legal guardians have proved the third element—a relationship between the state and the person injured (here Officer Tedder and Samantha and Joseph Kneipp) during which the state places the victim in danger of a foreseeable injury.[22] *Mark*, 51 F.3d at 1153. Here it is alleged that Officer Tedder, exercising his powers as a police officer, placed Samantha in danger of foreseeable injury when he sent her home unescorted in a visibly intoxicated state in cold weather. A reasonable jury could find that Officer Tedder exerted sufficient control over Samantha to meet the relationship requirement.

Finally, there is sufficient evidence in the summary judgment record to show that Officer Tedder and the other police officers used their authority as police officers to create a dangerous situation or to make Samantha more vulnerable to danger had they not intervened. The conduct of the police, in allowing Joseph to go home alone and in detaining Samantha, and then sending her home unescorted in a seriously intoxicated state in cold weather, made Samantha more vulnerable to harm. It is conceivable that, but for the intervention of the police, Joseph would have continued to escort his wife back to their apartment where she would have been safe. A jury could find that Samantha was in a worse position after the police intervened than she would have been if they had not done so. As a result of the affirmative acts of the police officers, the danger or risk of injury to Samantha was greatly increased. Thus, we believe that a reasonable jury could find that the fourth and final requirement of *Mark* was satisfied here.

We find additional support for our position in the courts of appeals' decisions previously cited. *See Reed v. Gardner*, 986 F.2d at 1127 (police officer who removed a sober driver and left behind a passenger whom he knew to be drunk with the keys to the car was subject to liability under 42 U.S.C. § 1983); *Freeman v. Ferguson*, 911 F.2d at 54 (police chief, by interfering with police officers' enforcement of restraining order, created the danger which resulted in the victims' deaths and thus deprived victims of their constitutional rights); *White v. Rochford*, 592 F.2d at 385 (police officers who arrested uncle for drag racing and left minor children alone in abandoned car on the side of a busy, limited-access highway in cold weather had deprived children of their constitutional rights to personal security where the abandonment resulted in physical and emotional injury to the children).

In contrast to the above cited authority stands the *en banc* decision of the United States Court of Appeals for the Eighth Circuit in *Gregory v. City of Rogers, Arkansas*, 974 F.2d 1006 (8th Cir. 1992), *cert. denied*, 507 U.S. 913 (1993). In that case, the

---

22. We view the "state-created danger" relationship to be different than the "special relationship" required by *DeShaney* to impose liability under section 1983. The relationship requirement under the state-created danger theory contemplates some contact such that the plaintiff was a foreseeable victim of a defendant's acts in a tort sense. The special relationship in *DeShaney*, on the other hand, has a custodial element to it—the state must affirmatively act to restrain an individual's freedom to act on his or her own behalf either through incarceration, institutionalization, or some other comparable limit of personal liberty. 489 U.S. at 200.

plaintiffs brought a civil rights action against the municipality and one of its police officers on the basis that defendants had a duty to provide for the safety of the passengers of a drinking group after the police arrested their designated driver on an outstanding warrant. After detaining the designated driver along the road for several minutes, the police allowed the designated driver to drive the car to the police station. The intoxicated passengers remained in the car, which was parked in front of the police station, while the designated driver cleared up the outstanding warrant inside the station with the police. After waiting approximately thirty minutes, one of the intoxicated passengers, the owner of the car, drove the car away and subsequently was involved in a one-car accident, killing himself and seriously injuring his passenger. Plaintiffs contended that the police officer actively placed the passengers in danger by permitting them to stay in the car unattended while waiting for the designated driver at the police station "'in spite of their obviously intoxicated condition.'" *Id.* at 1009–10.

In *Gregory*, the plaintiffs' argument turned on whether the police officer knew or should have known the passengers were intoxicated. The court of appeals found that the plaintiffs failed to submit sufficient evidence which would lead a reasonable trier of fact to conclude that the police officer knew or should have known that the passengers were intoxicated and unfit to drive, and thus, upheld the district court's grant of summary judgment. The court of appeals, however, did not end its analysis there. It went on to say that even if the police officers knew the passengers were intoxicated, a reasonable jury could not find that the police officer affirmatively placed the passengers in danger by leaving them unattended in the car at the station. *Id.* at 1011. The court explained that it was the designated driver who placed the passengers in danger by leaving the keys in the car when he went into the police station. *Id.* at 1012. To impose a duty on the police to take affirmative action to protect the passengers, the court held, would circumvent the general rule that plaintiffs do not have a constitutional right to be protected by the police against harm inflicted by third persons. *Id.* (citing ... *DeShaney*, 489 U.S. at 195–96).

Gregory, however, is distinguishable from this case in two respects. First the court of appeals in *Gregory* found that the police officer did not know that the passengers were intoxicated—neither the testimony of the witnesses, nor the behavior of the two passengers observed during the traffic stop on the roadway indicated they were intoxicated. In contrast here, Officer Tedder admitted that he knew Samantha was drunk at the time he was questioning her, and Samantha was observed staggering, walking and standing with difficulty, requiring that she lean on parked cars or be carried by her husband.

The second distinction is who created the danger—in *Gregory*, the court found that the third party created the danger by leaving the keys in the car; in the case before us, the police officers intervened to cut off Samantha's private source of protection by giving Joseph permission to go home alone, thereby increasing the danger that Samantha would suffer harm in her visibly intoxicated state when they abandoned her. The affirmative acts of the police officers here created a dangerous situation, requiring that they take additional measures to ensure Samantha's safety. That they failed to take the appropriate measures, knowing that Samantha was severely intoxicated, shows that the police officers acted with reckless disregard for her safety. On the other hand, the conduct of the police officer in *Gregory* did not rise to a level of recklessness. He did not know the passengers were drunk; nor did he take any affirmative action to create the dangerous situation—leaving the keys in the car. Put another way, the passengers in *Gregory* were never abandoned; all they had to do was remain in the safety of the car and await the return of their driver. Samantha, however, was isolated from her husband and then abandoned by the police.

Questions to guide reading of *McClendon*

McClendon also is included in Chapter 11, for its relevance to qualified immunity.

1. How did the majority summarize the Plaintiff's theory of substantive due process (state-created danger) liability against the individual detective?
2. What language in *DeShaney* did the majority recognize as the basis for the state-created danger theory adopted by other Circuits?
3. What did the majority glean from the variety of tests for state-created danger that have been adopted by Circuits other than the Fifth Circuit? How did the majority integrate *Lewis* into state-created-danger doctrine? Do you agree with that reading of *Lewis*?
4. Why did the majority hold that there was no evidence that Detective Carney acted more than negligently?
5. According to Judge Parker's dissent, what are the key elements of the state-created danger theory? Why would Judge Parker have held that the record was enough to create a jury question on each element? What is your reaction to the dissent's description of the majority's intentions in deciding the state-created danger claim as it did?

McClendon v. City of Columbia

305 F.3d 314 (5th Cir. 2002), *cert. denied*, 537 U.S. 1232 (2003)

PER CURIAM.

[This opinion is joined by Chief Judge King and Circuit Judges Jolly, Higginbotham, Davis, Jones, Smith, Barksdale, Benavides, Stewart, Dennis and Clement]

I. FACTUAL AND PROCEDURAL BACKGROUND

[On appeal from summary judgment to the Defendant, we view the facts in the light most favorable to Plaintiff. In July 1993, defendant Detective James Carney loaned a gun to Kevin Loftin, an informant for the Columbia Police Department, to enable Loftin to protect himself from plaintiff Peter McClendon. Loftin subsequently used the gun to shoot McClendon.]

Between May of 1992 and December of 1993, [Detective Carney paid Loftin] to serve as an informant for the Columbia Police Department. Loftin assisted Detective Carney and the [police] with drug enforcement investigations. During the week prior to July 12, 1993, Loftin spoke to Detective Carney about a conflict that had developed between Loftin and McClendon. Specifically, Loftin feared that McClendon might retaliate against Loftin for supplying a gun to an individual who subsequently shot McClendon's friend. Loftin told Detective Carney that McClendon was "fixing to try [Loftin]," and that the situation between the two men was at a "boiling point." Upon hearing about the situation, Detective Carney loaned Loftin a handgun so that Loftin could protect himself from McClendon. This handgun, which Detective Carney retrieved from his desk drawer, was apparently seized by the [police] as evidence in an unrelated investigation.

On the evening of July 12, 1993, McClendon and Loftin encountered each other (apparently by chance) at the Hendrix Street Apartments, where Loftin was staying. An altercation ensued, and Loftin shot McClendon in the face with the handgun that Loftin had obtained from Detective Carney. McClendon is now permanently blind as a result of the incident.

...

McClendon claims that Detective Carney violated McClendon's right to bodily integrity under the substantive component of the *Due Process Clause of the Fourteenth Amendment* because Carney's affirmative misconduct enhanced the risk of harm to McClendon.[5] Specifically, McClendon argues: (1) that Detective Carney knowingly and affirmatively created a dangerous situation by providing Loftin with a gun; (2) that Detective Carney failed to take any reasonable steps to diffuse the danger; and (3) that Detective Carney abused his authority by creating an opportunity for Loftin to harm McClendon that would not otherwise have existed.

...

III. DID DETECTIVE CARNEY'S CONDUCT VIOLATE AN ACTUAL CONSTITUTIONAL RIGHT?

... Ordinarily, a state official has no constitutional duty to protect an individual from private violence. *See DeShaney v. Winnebago County Dep't of Soc. Servs.*, 489 U.S. 189, 197 (1989) (holding that, as a general matter, a state's "failure to protect an individual against private violence simply does not constitute a violation of the Due Process Clause"). In *DeShaney*, however, the Court clarified that this general rule is not absolute: "in certain limited circumstances the Constitution imposes upon the State affirmative duties of care and protection with respect to particular individuals." *Id.* at 198. When the state, through the affirmative exercise of its powers, acts to restrain an individual's freedom to act on his own behalf "through incarceration, institutionalization, or other similar restraint of personal liberty," the state creates a

5. ... This court has recognized a substantive due process right to be free from state-occasioned damage to a person's bodily integrity in certain contexts....

"special relationship" between the individual and the state which imposes upon the state a constitutional duty to protect that individual from dangers, including, in certain circumstances, private violence. *Id.* at 200.

A number of courts have read ... *DeShaney* to suggest a second exception to the general rule against state liability for private violence. *DeShaney* involved a § 1983 action brought on behalf of a child against state social workers. The child, who suffered serious injuries as a result of parental abuse, alleged that the social workers had violated his substantive due process rights because they were aware of the probability of abuse and failed to intervene to protect him or remove him from his father's home. *Id.* at 191. In rejecting this claim on the ground that there was no "special relationship" between the child and the state, the Supreme Court also noted that, "[w]hile the State may have been aware of the dangers that [the child] faced in the free world, *it played no part in their creation, nor did it do anything to render him any more vulnerable to them.*" *Id.* at 201 (emphasis added). Many of our sister circuits have read this language to suggest that state officials can have a duty to protect an individual from injuries inflicted by a third party if the state actor played an affirmative role in creating or exacerbating a dangerous situation that led to the individual's injury. Those courts accepting some version of this "state-created danger" theory have applied the exception in a variety of factual contexts,[6] and have adopted a variety

6. *See, e.g.*, *Butera v. District of Columbia*, 235 F.3d 637, 651 (D.C. Cir. 2001) (adopting the state-created danger theory, but rejecting a § 1983 claim brought against a police department and individual officers on behalf of an individual who was shot while working as an undercover operative for the department); *Kallstrom v. City of Columbus*, 136 F.3d 1055, 1066–67 (6th Cir. 1998) (adopting the state-created danger theory in the context of a § 1983 claim brought by undercover police officers alleging that city officials released personal information from their personnel files to the drug conspirators that the officers were investigating); *Kneipp v. Tedder*, 95 F.3d 1199, 1201, 1208 (3d Cir. 1996) (adopting the state-created danger theory in the context of a § 1983 claim brought against a city and police officers on behalf of a woman who suffered brain damage when the officers allegedly left her alone to walk home on a cold night while she was intoxicated); *Uhlrig v. Harder*, 64 F.3d 567, 572 (10th Cir. 1995) (accepting the state-created danger theory, but rejecting a § 1983 claim brought against state mental health officials on behalf of an activity therapist who was killed by a mental hospital patient); *Reed v. Gardner*, 986 F.2d 1122, 1125 (7th Cir. 1993) (adopting the state-created danger theory in the context of a § 1983 claim brought by motorists who were injured in an automobile collision with an allegedly drunk driver against police officers who had previously failed to arrest the driver); *Dwares v. City of New York*, 985 F.2d 94, 98–99 (2d Cir. 1993) (adopting the state-created danger theory in the context of a § 1983 claim brought by demonstrators against police officers who allegedly conspired to permit a group of "skinheads" to assault the demonstrators with impunity); *Freeman v. Ferguson*, 911 F.2d 52, 54–55 (8th Cir. 1990) (adopting the state-created danger theory in the context of a § 1983 claim brought on behalf of a woman killed by her estranged husband against a police chief who allegedly directed his officers to ignore her pleas for police assistance); *Cornelius v. Town of Highland Lake*, 880 F.2d 348, 356 (11th Cir. 1989) (overruled on other grounds by *White v. Lemacks*, 183 F.3d 1253, 1256 (11th Cir. 1999)) (adopting the state-created danger theory in the context of a § 1983 claim brought against town and prison officials by a town clerk who was abducted and terrorized by prison inmates assigned to a community work program); *Wood v. Ostrander*, 879 F.2d 583, 590 (9th Cir. 1989) (adopting the state-created danger theory in the context of a § 1983 claim brought against police officers by the passenger of an impounded vehicle who was raped after officers allegedly abandoned her on the side of the road).

of tests in expounding the theory.[7] While this court has recognized the validity of the "special relationship" exception to the general *DeShaney* rule that state officials have no constitutional duty to protect individuals from private violence, *see, e.g., Walton v. Alexander*, 44 F.3d 1297, 1299 (5th Cir. 1995), we have not yet determined whether a state official has a similar duty to protect individuals from state-created dangers....

Regardless of the theory of liability that a plaintiff is pursuing, in order to state a viable substantive due process claim the plaintiff must demonstrate that the state official acted with culpability beyond mere negligence. The Supreme Court's discussions of abusive executive action have repeatedly emphasized that "only the most egregious official conduct can be said to be arbitrary in the constitutional sense." *County of Sacramento v. Lewis*, 523 U.S. 833, 846 (1998) (quoting *Collins*, 503 U.S. at 129) (internal quotations omitted). The Court has "spoken of the cognizable level of executive abuse of power as that which shocks the conscience." *Id.* In elaborating on "the constitutional concept of conscience shocking," the Court has "made it clear that the due process guarantee does not entail a body of constitutional law imposing liability whenever someone cloaked with state authority causes harm." *Id.* at 848. "[L]iability for negligently inflicted harm is categorically beneath the threshold of constitutional due process." *Id.*

Consistent with these principles, courts applying both the "special relationship" exception to the *DeShaney* rule and the "state-created danger" exception to the *DeShaney* rule have generally required plaintiffs to demonstrate (or, at the motion-to-dismiss stage, to allege) that the defendant state official at a minimum acted with

---

7. *See, e.g., Kallstrom*, 136 F.3d at 1066 ("Liability under the state-created-danger theory is predicated upon affirmative acts by the state which either create or increase the risk that an individual will be exposed to private acts of violence.... [W]e require plaintiffs alleging a constitutional tort under § 1983 to show special danger in the absence of a special relationship between the state and either the victim or the private tortfeasor. The victim faces special danger where the state's actions place the victim specifically at risk, as distinguished from a risk that affects the public at large."); *Kneipp*, 95 F.3d at 1208 ("[C]ases predicating constitutional liability on a state-created danger theory have four common elements: (1) the harm ultimately caused was foreseeable and fairly direct; (2) the state actor acted in willful disregard for the safety of the plaintiff; (3) there existed some relationship between the state and the plaintiff; (4) the state actors used their authority to create an opportunity that otherwise would not have existed for the third party's crime to occur.") (quoting *Mark v. Borough of Hatboro*, 51 F.3d 1137, 1152 (3d Cir. 1995)) (internal quotations omitted); Uhlrig, 64 F.3d at 574 ("Plaintiff must demonstrate that (1)[he] was a member of a limited and specifically definable group; (2) Defendants' conduct put [him] and the other members of that group at substantial risk of serious, immediate and proximate harm; (3) the risk was obvious or known; (4) Defendants acted recklessly in conscious disregard of that risk; and (5) such conduct, when viewed in total, is conscience shocking."); *Reed*, 986 F.2d at 1126 ("[P]laintiffs ... may state claims for civil rights violations if they allege state action that creates, or substantially contributes to the creation of, a danger or renders citizens more vulnerable to a danger than they otherwise would have been."); *Freeman*, 911 F.2d at 55 ("[A] constitutional duty to protect an individual against private violence may exist in a non-custodial setting if the state has taken affirmative action which increased the individual's danger of, or vulnerability to, such violence beyond the level it would have been absent state action.").

deliberate indifference toward the plaintiff.[8] *See, e.g., Butera v. District of Columbia*, 235 F.3d 637, 652 (D.C. Cir. 2001) (state-created danger); *Nicini v. Morra*, 212 F.3d 798, 810 (3d Cir. 2000) (special relationship); *Huffman v. County of Los Angeles*, 147 F.3d 1054, 1059 (9th Cir. 1998) (state-created danger).

Our examination of the summary judgment record reveals (in accordance with the conclusion of the district court) that McClendon has not adduced any evidence suggesting that Detective Carney acted with anything other than ordinary negligence in the instant case. While Detective Carney was informed that McClendon potentially posed a threat to Loftin's safety, there is no indication that Detective Carney was aware that Loftin had any violent intentions toward McClendon. Indeed, Loftin had no criminal history and had a longstanding, positive working relationship with Detective Carney as a confidential informant. Moreover, given that Detective Carney had no reason to anticipate that Loftin and McClendon would have a chance encounter at the Hendrix Street Apartments, Detective Carney could not have predicted that Loftin would have the opportunity to assault McClendon with the gun that Detective Carney loaned Loftin for self-protection. Thus, while Detective Carney's actions in providing Loftin with a gun were certainly inadvisable, there is no evidence in the record suggesting that he acted with knowledge that his conduct would pose a threat to McClendon's safety. Under these circumstances, no rational trier of fact could find that Detective Carney acted with any level of culpability beyond mere negligence.

Thus, under the facts established by the summary judgment record, viewed in the light most favorable to McClendon, there is no violation by Detective Carney of McClendon's substantive due process rights. Negligent infliction of harm by a state actor does not rise to the level of a substantive due process violation, regardless of whether the plaintiff's injury was inflicted directly by a state actor or by a third party ... [McClendon has not demonstrated] the violation of an actual constitutional right [and we affirm summary judgment for] Detective Carney....

PARKER, Circuit Judge, joined by WIENER and DeMOSS, Circuit Judges, dissenting.

What would a reasonable person think would happen if a police officer in the course of his employment takes a pistol from the evidence locker or from his desk and gives it to a gang member with a history of drug involvement who needs it for a confrontation with a drug dealer? Any reasonable person would conclude that the state created or enhanced a dangerous situation when the officer gave the pistol to the gang member. There is no dispute that the gang member, Kevin Loftin, used the pistol provided by Detective Carney to shoot the drug dealer, McClendon.

---

8. To act with deliberate indifference, a state actor must "know [ ] of and disregard[ ] an excessive risk to [the victim's] health or safety." *Ewolski v. City of Brunswick*, 287 F.3d 492, 513 (6th Cir. 2002) (quoting *Farmer v. Brennan*, 511 U.S. 825, 837 (1994)) (internal quotations omitted). The state actor's actual knowledge is critical to the inquiry. A state actor's failure to alleviate "a significant risk that he should have perceived but did not," while "no cause for commendation," does not rise to the level of deliberate indifference. *Farmer*, 511 U.S. at 837.

So how does one read the majority opinion, particularly in light of the fact that the majority does not reject the state-created danger theory outright? The only way to explain the majority opinion is that it clearly reflects a court that aspires to be the only circuit in the country to reject the state-created danger theory but cannot bring itself to admit it. Instead, the Court has embarked on a ten-year course of back-door rejection by assuming arguendo that the theory is viable and then finding that the victim has just not made the case. Far better it would be if this Circuit wants to embrace the extreme position of being the only circuit to reject the theory to simply say so.

...

I. IS THE STATE-CREATED DANGER THEORY A VIABLE THEORY IN THIS CIRCUIT?

The majority's Achilles' heel is its unwillingness to either adopt or reject the state-created danger theory as the law of the Circuit. Over the last ten years, at least seven state-created danger cases have arrived in our Circuit, but we have never taken a position on whether the state-created danger theory is a valid one, choosing instead to duck the issue. We simply stated in each case (without explicitly adopting or rejecting the theory) that the evidence is insufficient to raise a genuine issue of material fact concerning one or more of the elements that comprise the theory. Our methodological approach—assuming arguendo for the purposes of each case that the state-created danger theory is a valid one but never explicitly rejecting or adopting it—cannot be defended and leaves this area of circuit law in a perpetual state of confusion.

...

[T]he linchpin for concluding that a substantive due process violation can be made out under the state-created danger theory is the "affirmative conduct" requirement. The "affirmative conduct" requirement prevents the state from being held liable for acts of omission. Similarly, the theory's requirements that the state actor must know that his actions endanger a specific individual and that a direct causal connection must exist between the state actor's conduct which increases the danger and the actual injury itself[6] are commensurate with the Supreme Court's recognition that the Due Process Clause "is phrased as a limitation on the State's power to act, not as a guarantee of certain minimal levels of safety and security." *DeShaney v. Winnebago County Department of Social Services*, 489 U.S. 189, 195 (1989).[7]

---

6. *See Kneipp v. Tedder*, 95 F.3d 1199, 1208 (3rd Cir. 1996) (the harm ultimately caused by the state-created danger must be foreseeable and fairly direct).

7. In the case at bar, the "affirmative action" element, "knowledge" element, and "causation" element are satisfied. First, Detective Carney knew that Loftin intended to use the gun in any altercation with McClendon. Thus, he had actual knowledge that McClendon was at substantial risk of injury. Second, Detective Carney engaged in affirmative conduct because he gave Loftin a deadly weapon which Loftin could use to shoot McClendon. Third, there is a direct causal connection between the injury suffered and the affirmative conduct. Detective Carney created the danger that McClendon would be shot in the face by giving Loftin the gun. If Carney had not given Loftin the gun, Loftin would only have had his bare fists to use as weapons in any potential altercation with McClendon. Thus, but for Carney giving Loftin the gun, Loftin likely could not have caused McClendon to suffer such severe injuries.

...

Consequently, the state-created danger theory is overwhelmingly accepted in today's federal jurisprudence. In the face of such overwhelming authority, the majority cowers. It does not have the courage to be the only federal circuit court of appeals in the nation to explicitly reject the state-created danger theory even though that is clearly what it wants to do. Although the majority refuses to take the road less traveled in a principled albeit unpopular way, it is perfectly willing to accomplish its objectives through subterfuge. The majority knows only too well how to play the game. If the Circuit never rules on whether this is a viable theory, the Circuit makes it exceedingly difficult for the district courts to rule that the Circuit law in state-created danger cases is "clearly established" for purposes of a qualified immunity analysis. Thus, state actors who engage in behavior that falls within the confines of the "state-created danger" theory will always escape liability under the majority's view no matter how egregious their behavior. That is an insidious approach to the law and I reject it outright.

The Circuit should quit hiding the ball from the public and make a decision one way or the other. It has refused. [In refusing to make this decision, the majority attempts to create the illusion that no Circuit split exists in hopes of avoiding Supreme Court scrutiny.] However, I favor adopting, as has the rest of the country, the state-created danger theory as a viable mechanism for obtaining Section 1983 relief in this Circuit.

...

A. Carney's actions constitute deliberate indifference

... Because Detective Carney had plenty of time to "deliberate" as to whether he could properly give Loftin the gun, McClendon is only required to prove that Detective Carney acted with deliberate indifference. For two main reasons, I find that McClendon has produced sufficient evidence from which a rational trier of fact could not avoid concluding that Carney acted with deliberate indifference to McClendon's substantive due process right.

First, McClendon gave Loftin a gun at a time when he knew the dispute between McClendon and Loftin was "at a boiling point." Detective Carney knew that Loftin wanted the gun because he desired to use it as a weapon in any altercation with McClendon. He knew that Loftin and McClendon were likely to meet at some point in time. It is true that he had no specific knowledge that they would see each other at the Hendrix Street Apartments on the night in question. However, this fact is largely irrelevant to our analysis. The "knowledge" inquiry under a deliberate indifferent analysis does not require such a level of specificity. Clearly, Detective Carney had actual knowledge that Loftin and McClendon would likely have an altercation and that violence would almost certainly ensue between the two ... What does the majority think Loftin intended to do with the gun provided to him by Detective Carney—place it on his wall as a souvenir? Of course not, gang members who ask for guns typically have violent intentions as any competent police officer knows. The majority implies that Detective Carney was not aware that Loftin had any violent intentions towards McClendon because Detective Carney merely "loaned" the gun to Loftin for self-protection. However, the majority's suggestion that Detective Carney believed that Loftin only intended to use the gun for self-protection belies common sense and is not a fact which a rational jury would be required to accept as true ...

In short, Loftin is a gang member who serves as a confidential informant because he is involved in the drug scene. McClendon is a drug dealer. Any officer with enough sense to be entrusted with a gun knows that if he gives a gun to a gang member with a history of drug involvement who is anticipating a confrontation with a drug dealer, there is a strong likelihood that should an altercation arise the gang member will use that gun to shoot the drug dealer, with or without provocation [A reasonable officer would recognize that this action would create a danger which could result in violating McClendon's constitutional rights.]

Second, Detective Carney took property held by the City of Columbia (i.e., the gun) and gave it to a confidential informant. The majority characterizes this act as "inadvisable" or perhaps "negligent." I characterize the act as criminal.

...

Questions to guide reading of *Butera*

Butera also is included in Chapter 11, for its relevance to qualified immunity, and in Chapter 13, for its relevance to the scope of the parental liberty interest.

1. After canvassing the circuits that have adopted the state-created danger/state endangerment theory, what does *Butera* hold is a "key requirement" for constitutional liability?
2. In *Butera*, the D.C. Circuit adopted the state-created danger/endangerment theory. How does the Court summarize this theory of liability?
3. How does *Butera* integrate *Lewis* into its adoption of the state-created danger theory?
4. Why does *Butera* hold that the appropriate fault standard for the state-created danger claim there was "deliberate indifference"?

Butera v. District of Columbia

235 F.3d 637 (D.C. Cir. 2001)

ROGERS, Circuit Judge.

This appeal arises from the tragic death of 31-year-old Eric Butera while he served as an undercover operative for the Metropolitan Police Department of the District of Columbia.

...

On November 16, 1997, Eric Butera telephoned ... Police ... to provide information about the highly publicized triple homicide at the Starbucks coffee shop.... He told

Detective Anthony Patterson ... that [twice] while he was purchasing or using crack cocaine at a ... housing complex in Southwest Washington, D.C., he overheard someone talking about the Starbucks murders ... Eric Butera told Detective [Anthony] Patterson that he had come forward with this information because "he was no longer taking drugs, he was attempting to get his life in order and he wanted to do the right thing." ...

[The police] officers decided to stage an undercover drug purchase at the house where Eric Butera had overheard the conversation and seen the drugs and firearms ... Eric Butera agreed [to assist and to help the operation resemble his previous visits to the house] ...

Eric Butera told them that usually he would enter and exit through the back door of the house, and that the entire transaction generally took "anywhere from one minute to ten minutes, maybe fifteen minutes." Eric Butera and the officers agreed to follow this same pattern, with one exception: Eric Butera would exit through the front door and meet the officers at a pre-arranged location ... They supplied him with $80 in marked twenty dollar bills to make the drug purchase.

Detective [Anthony] Brigidini drove Eric Butera to the house around 9:20 p.m., and watched as Eric Butera approached the back door. As Eric Butera knocked on the door, Detective Brigidini drove away and parked approximately one hundred fifty feet from the house ... Detective Brigidini also intended to place himself in a position where he could see the front of the house (from which he expected Eric Butera to emerge) and the rear opening of the walkway behind the house; from his location, however, he was unable to see the back of the house. Meanwhile, Detective Patterson and Sergeant [Nicholas] Breul parked their car, with their windows down, in a location that enabled them to see only part of the back alley of the housing complex.[1] As a result, none of the officers was in a position to see (or otherwise monitor) Eric Butera when he attempted to enter the house.

After approximately fifteen minutes had passed since Eric Butera approached the house, Detective Brigidini, who had not seen Eric Butera, notified Sergeant Breul and Detective Patterson that he was becoming uneasy [and circled the streets in his car] to look for him.... Sergeant Breul and Detective Patterson also began to look for Eric Butera. Approximately thirty minutes after Detective Brigidini dropped off Eric Butera, uniformed police officers ... appeared at the scene ... responding to a "911" call by a civilian reporting an unconscious person in the rear walkway of the house where Detective Brigidini had left Eric Butera ...

Because the officers had left Eric Butera at the rear of the house, they were unaware that he had never gained entry; rather, Eric Butera was accosted by three men, who robbed and stomped him to death in the alley behind the house.

---

1. At that time, Sergeant Breul joked to Detective Patterson that they should keep the windows down so they could "hear any gunshots or screams."

. . .

[At trial, the jury awarded the following damages:

Compensatory Damages	
Survival Act Claim	$462,000
Wrongful Death Act Claim	$68,000
Civil Rights Claim of Eric Butera	$36,000,000
Civil Rights Claim of Terry Butera	$34,000,000
Punitive Damages	
Against the District of Columbia	$27,000,000
Against the four Officers	$570,000
($142,000 for each officer)]	

. . .

II. A. State Endangerment.

As a general matter, a State's failure to protect an individual from private violence, even in the face of a known danger, "does not constitute a violation of the Due Process Clause." *DeShaney v. Winnebago County Dep't of Soc. Servs.*, 489 U.S. 189, 197 (1989).... The Due Process Clause, the Supreme Court has emphasized, is "phrased as a limitation on the State's power to act, not as a guarantee of certain minimal levels of safety and security." *DeShaney*, 489 U.S. at 195. Thus, the Due Process Clause "generally confer[s] no affirmative right to governmental aid, even where such aid may be necessary to secure life, liberty, or protect property interests of which the government itself may not deprive the individual." *Id.* at 196. It followed in *DeShaney* that the State was not constitutionally liable for the permanent brain damage to a child who was beaten severely by his father, notwithstanding evidence that the State was aware of the child's physical abuse yet failed to remove the child from his father's custody. *See id.* at 202.

Despite this general rule, the *DeShaney* Court acknowledged that, in "certain limited circumstances[,] the Constitution imposes upon the State affirmative duties of care and protection with respect to particular individuals." *Id.* at 198. One such circumstance, the Court stated, arises when the State "takes a person into its custody and holds him there against his will," hence depriving him of liberty. *Id.* at 199–200; *see also Youngberg v. Romeo*, 457 U.S. 307, 317 (1982); *Estelle v. Gamble*, 429 U.S. 97, 103–04 (1976)....[9]

. . .

9. In *Estelle*, the Supreme Court held that the cruel and unusual punishment clause of the Eighth Amendment obliges the State to provide medical care to prisoners. *See* 429 U.S. at 103–04. *Youngberg* extended this obligation as a matter of substantive due process to mental patients who were involuntarily committed. *See* 457 U.S. at 315–16. In Revere, the Supreme Court held that the Due Process Clause also requires the State to provide medical care to persons who were injured while being apprehended by the police. *See* 463 U.S. at 244.

In addition to custody, the *DeShaney* Court left open the possibility that, under a second set of circumstances, the State could be liable for harm inflicted to an individual by third parties. In explaining the absence of constitutional liability for the child's physical abuse by his father, the Court stated:

> While the State may have been aware of the dangers that Joshua faced in the free world, it played no part in their creation, nor did it do anything to render him more vulnerable to them.

DeShaney, 489 U.S. at 201. All circuit courts of appeals, except this circuit, have by now relied on this passage in *DeShaney* to acknowledge that there may be possible constitutional liability under § 1983 "where the state creates a dangerous situation or renders citizens more vulnerable to danger."[10] *Reed v. Gardner*, 986 F.2d 1122, 1125 (7th Cir. 1993), *cert. denied*, 510 U.S. 947 (1993). In *Reed*, police officers arrested a presumably sober driver and left behind an obviously intoxicated passenger, who subsequently drove the car and was involved in a collision with the victims. The Seventh Circuit held that the victims of the collision stated a substantive due process claim because "[p]olice officers who remove sober drivers and leave behind drunk passengers with keys may be said to create a danger." *Id.* at 1125. Similarly, in *Wood*, a police officer arrested a drunk driver at 2:30 a.m. and impounded his vehicle, leaving the driver's female passenger by the side of the road in a high-crime area. The passenger, who was five miles from her home, accepted a ride from a stranger, who raped her. *See* 879 F.2d at 586. The Ninth Circuit held that the passenger had "raised a triable issue of fact as to whether [the police officer] affirmatively placed [her] in a position of danger." *Id.* at 589–90 (citation omitted). Additionally, in *Kallstrom v. City of Columbus*, 136 F.3d 1055 (6th Cir. 1998), city officials released personal information from the files of undercover police officers (including names, addresses, and telephone numbers of the officers and their families) to defense counsel for the alleged drug conspirators whom the officers had investigated. The Sixth Circuit held that "the City's actions placed the officers and their family members in 'special danger' by substantially increasing the likelihood that a private actor would deprive them of their liberty interest in personal security." *Id.* at 1067.

The circuit courts have adopted the State endangerment concept in a range of fact patterns concerning alleged misconduct by State officials. Regardless of the conduct at issue, however, the circuits have held that a key requirement for constitutional liability is affirmative conduct by the State to increase or create the danger that results in harm to the individual. No constitutional liability exists where the State actors "had no hand in creating a danger but [simply] 'stood by and did nothing when suspicious circumstances dictated a more active role for them.'" *Reed*, 986 F.2d at 1125 (quoting *DeShaney*, 489 U.S. at 203); *see also Kallstrom*, 136 F.3d at 1066; *Armijo v. Wagon Mound Public Schools*, 159 F.3d 1253, 1262–63 (10th Cir. 1998); *Frances-Colon v. Ramirez*, 107 F.3d 62, 64 (1st Cir. 1997); *Estate of Stevens v. City of Green Bay*, 105 F.3d 1169, 1176–77 (7th Cir. 1997); *Johnson v. Dallas Indep. Sch. Distr.*, 38

10. [Citing cases from First–Eleventh Circuits.]

F.3d 198, 201 (5th Cir. 1994); *Dwares v. City of New York*, 985 F.2d 94, 99 (2d Cir. 1993); *Gregory v. City of Rogers*, 974 F.2d 1006, 1010 (8th Cir. 1992) (*en banc*); *L.W. v. Grubbs*, 974 F.2d 119, 121 (9th Cir. 1992). Absent such affirmative conduct by the State to endanger an individual, courts have rejected liability under a State endangerment concept. *See, e.g., S.S. v. McMullen*, 225 F.3d 960, 962 (8th Cir. 2000) (*en banc*); *Stevens v. Umsted*, 131 F.3d 697, 705 (7th Cir. 1997).

Unlike other circuit courts of appeals, this court has never been presented with a State endangerment claim; rather, it has only addressed the first *DeShaney* exception—custody ...

The development of the State endangerment concept by the circuit court of appeals is consistent with the notion, implied in *DeShaney*, that something less than physical custody may suffice to present a substantive due process claim. We join the other circuits in holding that, under the State endangerment concept, an individual can assert a substantive due process right to protection by the District of Columbia from third-party violence when District of Columbia officials affirmatively act to increase or create the danger that ultimately results in the individual's harm. In so doing, we are "mindful of the caution we must exercise in expanding the liberty interests protected by substantive due process," *Harbury* [*v. Deutch*], 233 F.3d [596,] 605 [D.C. Cir. 2000)] (citing and quoting *Collins v. City of Harker Heights*, 503 U.S. 115, 125 (1992)), but conclude that the circuits' exposition of the concept has mitigated some of the general concerns about the lack of guideposts; to that extent, the court is hardly "break[ing] new ground in this field." *Collins*, 503 U.S. at 125.

To assert a substantive due process violation, however, the plaintiff must also show that the District of Columbia's conduct was "so egregious, so outrageous, that it may fairly be said to shock the contemporary conscience." [*Lewis*], 523 U.S. at 847 n.8. This stringent requirement exists to differentiate substantive due process, which is intended only to protect against arbitrary government action, from local tort law. *See id.* at 845–46, 848–49; *Daniels v. Williams*, 474 U.S. 327, 331 (1986) ... *see also Paul v. Davis*, 424 U.S. 693, 701 (1976). Hence, while it may be possible under District of Columbia tort law for a plaintiff to obtain a remedy by proving mere negligence or failure to exercise due care, this "lowest common denominator of customary tort liability" is "categorically beneath the threshold of constitutional due process." [*Lewis*], 523 U.S. at 848–49.

> It is, on the contrary, behavior at the other end of the culpability spectrum that would most probably support a substantive due process claim; conduct intended to injure in some way unjustifiable by any government interest is the sort of official action most likely to rise to the conscience-shocking level.

Id. at 849. Hence, in [*Lewis*], in the context of a highspeed chase by police officers that accidentally killed a fleeing motorcyclist, the Supreme Court held that the plaintiff must satisfy the higher "intent to harm" standard to prove that the officers' behavior was conscience-shocking. *See id.* at 854.

The Supreme Court in [*Lewis*] acknowledged, however, that in some circumstances the "point of the conscience shocking" can be reached by proving "something more than negligence but 'less than intentional conduct, such as recklessness or gross negligence.'" *Id.* at 849 (citation omitted). While such proof "is a matter for closer calls," *id.*, this lower threshold, the Supreme Court has instructed, is appropriate in circumstances where the State has a heightened obligation toward the individual. For example, where the State has taken a person into custody, it "so restrains [his] liberty that it renders him unable to care for himself"; therefore, the "Constitution imposes upon [the State] a corresponding duty to assume some responsibility for his safety and general well-being." *Id.* at 851 (quoting *DeShaney*, 489 U.S. at 199–200). Further, where an individual is in State custody, prison officials have "the luxury ... of ... time to make unhurried judgments, upon the chance for repeated reflection, largely uncomplicated by the pulls of competing obligations." *Id.* at 853. Because of these special circumstances, a State official's deliberate indifference in the context of state custody can be "truly shocking." *Id.*

As in the context of State custody, the State also owes a duty of protection when its agents create or increase the danger to an individual. Like prison officials who are charged with overseeing an inmate's welfare, State officials who create or enhance danger to citizens may also be in a position where "actual deliberation is practical." *Id.* at 851. In the instant case, the officers had the opportunity to plan the undercover operation with care. In view of the officers' duty to protect Eric Butera, he may prove that the officers' treatment of him in connection with the attempted undercover drug buy "shocked the conscience" by meeting the lower threshold of "deliberate indifference."

For further discussion

Consider a state-created danger claim in the different context of a police conspiracy to avoid arresting a husband for domestic violence. Several weeks prior to her murder, Veronica Williams filed assault charges against her husband, Cleaven Williams. Baltimore Police Officer Daniel Lioi withheld the warrant for Cleaven Williams' arrest from the domestic violence unit responsible for serving it. Further, Lioi warned Cleaven about the warrant and texted him advice on how to avoid capture. When Cleaven arrived at police headquarters, Lioi refused to arrest him, falsely claiming that the warrant could not be found. Three days later, Veronica Williams successfully petitioned for a protective order against her husband, Cleaven Williams. As Veronica was leaving the courthouse, Cleaven stabbed Veronica, who was pregnant with the couple's fourth child. Within a few days, Veronica suffered a miscarriage and died. Cleaven Williams is incarcerated for her murder.

Veronica Williams' family alleged that Lioi violated arrest warrant procedures because of his prior relationship with Cleaven Williams and thereby enabled Cleaven to be free at the time he killed his wife, Veronica. In holding plaintiffs stated a state-created danger claim, the Fourth Circuit relied in part on *Butera* for the concept that the state must act affirmatively to increase the danger, not simply stand by and do nothing. Lioi's conduct was "far more than a mere passive failure to act" because "Lioi conspired with Cleaven Williams to help Williams avoid being arrested. Lioi actively interfered with the execution of the warrant by not only failing to turn the warrant over to the proper unit with the [Baltimore Police] responsible for its execution, but also by warning Mr. Williams and giving him advice about how to avoid service of the warrant. Furthermore, Lioi lied to avoid service of the arrest warrant by falsely contending that it could not be found ... Lioi's alleged affirmative acts with his co-conspirator, Cleaven Williams, to avoid arrest directly enabled Mr. Williams to perpetrate the harm to Mrs. Williams." *Robinson v. Lioi*, 536 F. App'x 340, 340–46 (4th Cir. 2013).

Questions to guide reading of law review article

1. According to the article, between 1997–2003, there was doctrinal divergence between the Third Circuit's published binding state-created danger decisions and the circuit's unpublished, non-binding decisions. How did they diverge on the mental culpability standard?
2. According to the article, what were some of the practical ramifications of doctrinal inconsistency between the precedential and non-precedential decisions for state-created danger litigants and district courts deciding their cases?

The Perils of Unpublished Non-Precedential Federal Appellate Opinions: A Case Study of the Substantive Due Process State-Created Danger Doctrine in One Circuit

81 Wash. L. Rev. 217, 235–49 (2006)
by Sarah E. Ricks

III. THE PREVALENCE OF "UNPUBLISHED," NON-PRECEDENTIAL THIRD CIRCUIT STATE-CREATED DANGER DECISIONS

The state-created danger theory of substantive due process liability is a frequently invoked constitutional theory litigated under 42 U.S.C. § 1983. The theory is an exception to the general rule set forth by the Supreme Court in *DeShaney v. Winnebago County Department of Social Services* that a state is not constitutionally obligated to protect its citizens from the violent acts of private persons. Under the state-created danger exception, state actors may be held liable for private violence when the state actors create the risk of the privately inflicted harm. State-created danger claims are litigated in a wide variety of factual contexts. For example, claims may be brought against state actors such as police, public school officials, emergency medical technicians, or security guards for increasing the risk of harm suffered by a plaintiff, even though the state actors did not themselves inflict the harm. While the Supreme Court has not directly ruled on the validity of the state-created danger theory, this exception to the general rule of *DeShaney* is now widely accepted by the federal courts as establishing a substantive due process claim.

Since 1996, when the Third Circuit first adopted the state-created danger theory, district courts within the circuit have issued more than eighty state-created danger decisions. Despite such volume in the district courts, the Third Circuit itself published only one precedential state-created danger decision in the seven-year period following its adoption of the state-created danger theory. A single precedent in seven years does not reflect the total number of Third Circuit dispositions of state-created danger appeals between 1996 and 2003. That number is likely known only by the Circuit itself, since the Third Circuit's non-precedential opinions issued before January 2002 were not released to West or Lexis and are not searchable in electronic form. An informal survey of Third Circuit opinions reveals that in the fifty-three months from July 1998 to December 2002 alone, the Third Circuit issued at least thirteen non-precedential opinions addressing state-created danger claims. Despite evidence that state-created danger is a frequently litigated constitutional doctrine invoked in a wide variety of factual settings, and despite at least thirteen opportunities to do otherwise, the Third Circuit declined to issue any precedent on the doctrine for the six years between 1997 and 2003.

IV. THE DIVERGENCE BETWEEN PUBLISHED BINDING PRECEDENT AND "UNPUBLISHED," NON-PRECEDENTIAL THIRD CIRCUIT STATE-CREATED DANGER OPINIONS: FOUR EXAMPLES

This Part compares the divergent binding and non-precedential opinions applying the state-created danger doctrine within the Third Circuit. The comparison demonstrates that the risks of non-precedential opinions are real. During the six-year interval between binding state-created danger decisions, the Third Circuit created inconsistent non-precedential opinions on the identical legal theory. This Part examines the following four doctrinal divergences in Third Circuit precedential and non-precedential state-created danger decisions: (1) inconsistent mental culpability standards; (2) inconsistent analysis of derivative claims by family members; (3) inconsistent state action requirements; and (4) inconsistent municipal liability standards.

A. Example One: State of Mind Requirement

If non-precedential opinions simply apply established law, then the mental culpability standards applied in the Third Circuit's precedential and non-precedential state-created danger decisions should be identical. They are not. Rather, non-precedential opinions recognized a Supreme Court-mandated doctrinal shift in the state of mind requirement for state-created danger years before Third Circuit precedent did. The non-precedential opinions issued between the Third Circuit's precedential decisions—that is, between 1997 and 2003—demonstrate that this was a confused area of the law, where Third Circuit judges were struggling to articulate the doctrinal ramifications of the Supreme Court's decision in *County of Sacramento v. Lewis* for the Third Circuit state-created danger test. Further, since 2003, the Third Circuit precedential state-created danger decisions reveal ongoing doctrinal disagreement about "the vexing problem" of the correct mental culpability standard in "this elusive area of the law," suggesting that this doctrine even now remains insufficiently settled for routine application. Finally, the Third Circuit's refusal until 2003 to grapple in a precedential opinion with the doctrinal implications of the Supreme Court's *Lewis* decision left district courts and litigants uncertain about the binding law, which likely encouraged litigation and discouraged settlement.

1. Under the Third Circuit's Pre-*Lewis* Precedent, the State of Mind Requirement for a State-Created Danger Claim Was "Willful Disregard/Deliberate Indifference"

Before the Supreme Court's decision in *Lewis*, Third Circuit precedent permitted government actors to be held liable for creating a danger if they "willfully disregarded" the safety of the plaintiff. In *Kneipp v. Tedder*, the Third Circuit adopted the state-created danger theory and applied a four-part test:

(1) the harm ultimately caused was foreseeable and fairly direct;

(2) the state actor acted in willful disregard for the safety of the plaintiff;

(3) there existed some relationship between the state and the plaintiff; and

(4) the state actors used their authority to create an opportunity that otherwise would not have existed for the third party's crime to occur.

The Third Circuit adopted a single fault standard for all state-created danger claims—"willful disregard," which it equated with "deliberate indifference"—and specifically rejected the "shocks the conscience" standard. In the seven years between the adoption of the theory (in 1996) and 2003, the Third Circuit issued only one state-created danger precedent. That opinion applied the "willful disregard for the safety of the plaintiff" standard, again equating it with "deliberate indifference."

2. The Supreme Court Subsequently Held that All Substantive Due Process Claims Must Shock the Conscience

After the Third Circuit adopted the state-created danger theory in 1996, the Supreme Court announced a new analytic framework to determine the mental culpability standard for all substantive due process claims arising from executive action, of which state-created danger is a subset. In *Lewis*, the Supreme Court held that the threshold question is what fault standard along the continuum from deliberate indifference to intent to harm will "shock the conscience": "[T]he cognizable level of executive abuse of power [is] that which shocks the conscience."

"Shocks the conscience" is a not a single standard. Rather, it encompasses a spectrum of fault from more than negligence to intent to harm. According to the Supreme Court, whether fault will be conscience-shocking in the "middle range, following from something more than negligence but 'less than intentional conduct,'" depends upon the factual context, including (1) whether the state actor has time to deliberate and (2) whether the state actor must weigh interests that compete with the plaintiff's. More culpability is required to shock the conscience if the state actor was acting in a pressurized situation, with little time for reflection, or if the state actor was balancing competing legitimate interests—such as a pursuing police officer's balancing of the risks of the chase against the risks of permitting the suspect to escape. The Supreme Court recognized that it had held "deliberate indifference" to shock the conscience only in the context of medical care for prisoners, where the state actors had "the luxury" of "time to make unhurried judgments, upon the chance for repeated reflection, largely uncomplicated by the pulls of competing obligations."[18]

3. Divergence Between Precedential and Non-Precedential Third Circuit State-Created Danger State of Mind Requirements Between 1997 and 2003

The Third Circuit entered no precedential state-created danger decisions between 1997 and 2003. During those years, while the Circuit's precedents required only "willful disregard" and expressly rejected the "shocks the conscience" standard, several Third Circuit panels issued non-precedential opinions either casting doubt on the continued doctrinal viability of the Third Circuit's state-of-mind requirement or explicitly holding that aspect of its doctrine to have been narrowed by the intervening Supreme Court endorsement of the "shocks the conscience" analytic framework for all substantive due process claims. Inexplicably, the Third Circuit twice chose non-precedential decisions to announce this change in state-created danger doctrine, bypassing the opportunity to clarify the doctrinal confusion.

Meanwhile, compounding the doctrinal confusion, other Third Circuit non-precedential opinions applied the binding "willful disregard/deliberate indifference" standard, but without wrestling with *Lewis's* threshold inquiry into what fault level would "shock the conscience," or with *Lewis's* acknowledgment that courts had held "deliberate indifference" to violate substantive due process only where there is an opportunity to deliberate and an absence of competing interests—in the custodial context of prison medical care.

4. Precedential Acknowledgement that *Lewis* Changed the State-Created Danger Doctrine

The Third Circuit broke its years of precedential silence on the state-created danger doctrine by issuing three precedential decisions in a single month of 2003. While the different opinions did not speak in unison about the ramifications of *Lewis* for state-created danger analysis, all three precedents agreed that the Third Circuit's doctrine had been superseded by the Supreme Court's *Lewis* decision five years earlier—the doctrinal shift first articulated in non-precedential opinions at least as early as 2001. The first precedent clarified "the vexing problem" of "the appropriate lens through which we must view actions in the state-created danger context" by establishing that the *Lewis* "shocks the conscience" standard governed a claim against emergency medical technicians. In a second precedent, the Third Circuit again recognized the doctrinal shift "in this elusive area of the law" mandated by the Supreme Court in *Lewis* five years earlier, by clarifying that the Third Circuit already had read the shocks the conscience framework both (1) to encompass degrees of wrongfulness ranging from deliberate indifference to intent to harm, depending on the factual circumstances, and (2) to be the framework for all substantive due process cases arising from executive action.

Within weeks, the Third Circuit issued a third precedential opinion, again recognizing what the non-precedential opinions had articulated years earlier: "[O]ur sum-

18. A chart illustrating the spectrum of fault under the *Lewis* "shocks the conscience" standard appears in Chapter Three.

mary of the law regarding state created dangers in [1996] needs to be updated to reflect the Supreme Court's subsequent decision in [*Lewis*]." In a one-judge opinion with a concurrence in the judgment, Judge Walter K. Stapleton fleshed out the doctrinal shifts already suggested in non-precedential opinions:

> (1) the *Lewis* "shocks the conscience" analytic framework applies to all substantive due process claims involving executive action, "and we must, of course, apply it" to state-created danger;
>
> (2) shocks the conscience is not a single standard but describes a range of conduct from deliberate indifference to intent to harm, depending on the factual context; and
>
> (3) five years earlier, *Lewis's* shocks the conscience analytic method had superseded the Third Circuit's blanket willful disregard standard for state-created danger claims.

Even though the fault standard was not dispositive, Judge Stapleton sought to guide future courts and litigants by carefully explaining the analytical method *Lewis* prescribed to determine the applicable fault standard. That thoughtful guidance could have been undertaken three years earlier by at least two Third Circuit panels which similarly had found the precise fault standard not dispositive, but chose to issue non-precedential opinions, thus perpetuating the doctrinal ambiguity.

5. Practical Consequences of Doctrinal Inconsistency for District Courts and Litigants

The Third Circuit's belated precedential adherence to Supreme Court doctrine is inconsistent with the appellate function. The Third Circuit's refusal until 2003 to wrestle in precedent with the doctrinal ramifications of *Lewis* on state-created danger left district courts and litigants within the Third Circuit uncertain as to whether the single "willful disregard" standard had survived the Supreme Court's 1998 endorsement of the shocks the conscience spectrum-of-fault framework. Many district courts concluded that the *Lewis* "shocks the conscience" standard superseded Third Circuit precedent. One relied on the Third Circuit's non-precedential endorsement of "shocks the conscience" as "not entitled to precedential effect" but "instructive." Another district court emphasized the importance of resolving the doctrinal implications of *Lewis*. Despite that evidence of a need for appellate guidance, the Third Circuit nevertheless chose to affirm the district court's judgment in a non-precedential opinion—an appellate opinion that purported to alter binding law. Even after the Third Circuit's two non-precedential opinions purporting to update the state-of-mind requirement to "shocks the conscience"—decisions that certainly should have been precedential—district courts were not sure whether to follow the "willful disregard" standard of Third Circuit precedent, as some did, or instead apply a standard different from Circuit precedent, as others did. Doctrinal divergence between precedential and non-precedential decisions undermined the predictive value of precedent, resulting in litigant uncertainty about litigation strategy and settlement value. For example, in one case where settlement negotiations terminated based on the plaintiff's reading of Third Circuit state-created danger precedent, the Third Circuit went on to reject the plaintiff's claim in a non-precedential opinion that characterized the claim as "border[ing] on frivolity."

The doctrinal ambiguity perpetuated by the Third Circuit's refusal to issue precedential state-created danger decisions likely encouraged litigation and discouraged settlement, thus undercutting the efficiency rationale for non-precedential opinions. In 2004, a Third Circuit judge candidly acknowledged that the doctrinal uncertainty following *Lewis*, which the Third Circuit now recognizes as having substantially narrowed state-created danger, likely encouraged plaintiffs to characterize state tort claims as constitutional violations: "[T]he most important of the recent modifications" to the circuit's state-created danger precedent involved the Supreme Court's imposition of the shocks the conscience standard:

> [I]t is no longer enough that [the state actor] has acted in "willful disregard" of the plaintiff's safety.... [T]he substitution of "shocks the conscience" for willful disregard is a significant limitation. In this context, our continued adherence to *Kneipp* [Third Circuit precedent], if only in name, colors plaintiffs' perception of their burden and tempts them to allege constitutional violations where none exist.

During the Third Circuit's six-year precedential silence, the appellate court repeatedly chastised plaintiffs for alleging state-created dangers on facts that should have been alleged in tort. In 2002, for example, a non-precedential opinion not only refused to reach the issue of whether *Lewis* raised the Third Circuit's lower fault standard to a shocks the conscience standard, as the district court had held, but rebuked plaintiffs for believing they had a constitutional claim at all: "We are faced in this appeal with another case in which plaintiffs have tried to transmute their state-law claims into constitutional torts." But given the divergence between precedential and non-precedential opinions and the Third Circuit's refusal to publish its many rejections of state-created danger claims, plaintiffs' error may not have been careless lawyering but, rather, evidence of a need for appellate guidance.[19]

Exercise 4-A

The vast majority of federal appellate opinions—approximately 88%—are non-precedential.[20] According to the above article, some of the non-precedential state-created danger opinions noted the doctrinal changes re-

19. Federal Rule of Appellate Procedure Rule 32.1 was amended in 2006 to permit citation of non-precedential opinions issued after January 1, 2007. While many circuits had limited or prohibited citation of non-precedential opinions before the rule change, the Third Circuit had permitted citation of non-precedential opinions even before the national rule change.

20. Administrative Office of the U.S. Courts, U.S. Courts of Appeals—Type of Opinion or Order Filed in Cases Terminated on the Merits, by Circuit, During the 12-Month Period Ending September 30, 2018, Table B-12, https://www.uscourts.gov/sites/default/files/data_tables/jb_b12_0930.2018.pdf.

quired by *Lewis* years before the precedential opinions did. What are some of the consequences of the existence of non-precedential opinions for litigation strategy? Should a careful litigant cite non-precedential opinions in any of the following circumstances:

- in arguments to the authoring circuit court?
- in arguments to the district courts bound by the authoring circuit?
- in settlement negotiations with opposing counsel?
- in making recommendations to clients?

Exercise 4-B

The below Model Jury Instructions were published in July 2019. The instructions reflect that, 20 years after the Supreme Court decided *Lewis*, courts and litigants were still wrestling with the consequences of *Lewis* on the state-of-mind requirement of the state-created danger doctrine. Does that surprise you?

Consider that jury instructions are intended to be plain language explanations of the law that will be readily grasped by a group of lay people. Do you think a jury will readily grasp the meaning of the second element of the state-created danger doctrine, the state of mind requirement? Do you think a jury will readily grasp how to apply that legal standard to the facts proved at trial? How would you explain these instructions to your client?

Are the below Model Jury Instructions on the second element of the state-created danger doctrine, the state-of-mind requirement, consistent with your understanding of the spectrum of fault in *Lewis*? Do the Model Jury Instructions adequately account for the existence of competing interests in determining the level of fault necessary? If you were an attorney assigned to review Third Circuit model jury instructions for consistency with Supreme Court doctrine, would you recommend that the second element of the state-created danger instruction be amended? If so, why?

Model Civil Jury Instructions for Third Circuit

4.14 Section 1983—State-Created Danger (2019) (Second Element)

...

Second: [Defendant] acted with [conscious disregard of a great risk of serious harm] [deliberate indifference].

...

[[**For cases in which the requisite level of culpability is subjective deliberate indifference:**] The second of these four elements requires [plaintiff] to show that [defendant] acted with deliberate indifference. To show that [defendant] was deliberately indifferent, [plaintiff] must show that [defendant] knew that there was a substantial risk of a serious harm to [plaintiff], and that [defendant] disregarded that risk by failing to take reasonable measures to address it. [Plaintiff] must show that [defendant] actually knew of the risk. If [plaintiff] proves that the risk of harm was obvious, you are entitled to infer from the obviousness of the risk that [defendant] knew of the risk. [However, [defendant] claims that even if there was an obvious risk, [he/she] was unaware of that risk. If you find that [defendant] was unaware of the risk,[21] then you must find that [he/she] was not deliberately indifferent.]]

[**For cases in which the requisite level of culpability is objective deliberate indifference:**] The second of these four elements requires [plaintiff] to show that [defendant] acted with deliberate indifference. To show that [defendant] was deliberately indifferent, [plaintiff] must show that [defendant] knew or should have known that there was a substantial risk of a serious harm to [plaintiff], and that [defendant] disregarded that risk by failing to take reasonable measures to address it.

[[**For cases in which the requisite level of culpability is conscious disregard of a great risk of serious harm:**] The second of these four elements requires [plaintiff] to show that [defendant] acted with conscious disregard of a great risk of serious harm. It is not enough to show that [defendant] was careless or reckless. On the other hand, [plaintiff] need not show that [defendant] acted with the purpose of causing harm. Rather, [plaintiff] must show that [defendant] knew there was a great risk of serious harm, and that [defendant] consciously disregarded that risk.]

...

Comment

...

The second element.... In *County of Sacramento v. Lewis*, 523 U.S. 833 (1998), the Supreme Court held that a "shocks the conscience test" governs substantive due process claims arising from high-speed chases, and that in the context of a high-speed chase that test requires "a purpose to cause harm." *Id.* at 854. The Court of Appeals has since made clear that state-created danger claims require "a degree of culpability that shocks the conscience." *Bright v. Westmoreland County*, 443 F.3d 276, 281 (3d Cir. 2006).[22] *See also Morrow v. Balaski*, 719 F.3d 160 (3d Cir. 2013) (*en banc*)

21. It is unclear who has the burden of proof with respect to a defendant's claim of lack of awareness of an obvious risk....

22. *See also Marasco*, 318 F.3d at 507 (noting that *Miller v. City of Philadelphia*, 174 F.3d 368, 374–75 (3d Cir. 1999) "suggested that the 'shocks the conscience' standard [applies] to all substantive due process cases"); *Schieber v. City of Philadelphia*, 320 F.3d 409, 419 (3d Cir. 2003) (opinion of Stapleton, J.) ("[N]egligence is not enough to shock the conscience under any circumstances. . . . [M]ore culpability is required to shock the conscience to the extent that state actors are required to act promptly and under pressure. Moreover, the same is true to the extent the responsibilities of the state actors require a judgment between competing, legitimate interests."); *id.* at 423 (reversing denial of summary judgment to police officers sued by parents who alleged their daughter was murdered after officers responded to 911 call but failed to enter daughter's apartment, "[b]ecause the record would not support a finding of more than negligence on the part of" the officers)....

(stating the second element as "a state actor acted with a degree of culpability that shocks the conscience"); *Mann v. Palmerton Area School District*, 872 F.3d 165, 171–72 (3d Cir. 2017) (same, and holding that a "coach may be held liable where the coach requires a player, showing signs of a concussion, to continue to be exposed to violent hits"); *cf. Spady v. Bethlehem Area Sch. Dist.*, 800 F.3d 633, 638 (3d Cir. 2015) (reciting the elements from pre-1998 cases, including that "the state actor acted in willful disregard for the safety of the plaintiff").

However, "the precise degree of wrongfulness required to reach the conscienceshocking level depends on the circumstances of a particular case." *Marasco*, 318 F.3d at 508. "The level of culpability required to shock the conscience increases as the time state actors have to deliberate decreases." *Sanford v. Stiles*, 456 F.3d 298, 309 (3d Cir. 2006); *see also, e.g., Walter v. Pike County, Pa.*, 544 F.3d 182, 192–93 (3d Cir. 2008).

As the court explained in *Haberle v. Troxell*, 885 F.3d 170 (3d Cir. 2018):

> The required degree of culpability varies based on the "the circumstances of each case," and, in particular, on the time pressure under "which the government actor[ ] had to respond...." *Phillips v. Cty. of Allegheny*, 515 F.3d 224, 240 (3d Cir. 2008). Split-second decisions taking place in a "hyperpressurized environment," usually do not shock the conscience unless they are done with "an intent to cause harm." *Sanford*, 456 F.3d at 309. At the other end of the continuum, actions taken after time for "unhurried judgments" and careful deliberation may shock the conscience if done with deliberate indifference. *Id.* (quoting *Lewis*, 523 U.S. at 853). In the middle are actions taken under "hurried deliberation." *Id.* at 310. Such situations involve decisions that need to be made "in a matter of hours or minutes." *Ziccardi v. City of Philadelphia*, 288 F.3d 57, 65 (3d Cir. 2002). If that standard applies, then an officer's actions may shock the conscience if they reveal a conscious disregard of "a great risk of serious harm rather than a substantial risk." *Sanford*, 456 F.3d at 310.

Haberle, 885 F.3d at 177. *See also Sauers v. Borough of Nesquehoning*, 905 F.3d 711, 717 (3d Cir. 2018) ("Our case law establishes three distinct categories of culpability depending on how much time a police officer has to make a decision.").

The classic example of a hyperpressurized situation is the high-speed car chase of a fleeing suspect....

For examples at the other end of the continuum, where there is time for unhurried judgments, *see, e.g., L.R. v. School District of Philadelphia*, 836 F.3d 235, 246 (3d Cir. 2016) (holding that "the appropriate culpability standard here is deliberate indifference, since there is nothing to indicate that [defendant] faced circumstances requiring him to make a quick decision"); *Marasco*, 318 F.3d at 508 (stating that "in the custodial situation of a prison, where forethought about an inmate's welfare is possible, deliberate indifference to a prisoner's medical needs may be sufficiently shocking").[23]

Older decisions described the intermediate standard as "gross negligence or arbitrariness that shocks the conscience." *Marasco*, 318 F.3d at 509. But the court of appeals recognized that this phrasing "is not well suited" to convey the nature of the standard, *Ziccardi v. City of Philadelphia*, 288 F.3d 57, 66 n.6 (3d Cir. 2002), and explained that the intermediate standard requires a showing that a defendant "consciously disregarded, not just a substantial risk, but a great risk that serious harm would result." *Id.* at 66; *see also Sanford*, 456 F.3d at 310 (holding that "the relevant question is whether the officer consciously disregarded a great risk of harm").[24]

The court of appeals has "been clear in recent years that the level of culpability required to shock the conscience when an officer has time for hurried deliberation is 'a conscious disregard of a great risk of serious harm.'" *Sauers*, 905 F.3d at 717 n.6. Accordingly, the Instruction uses this phrasing rather than refer to "gross negligence or arbitrariness that shocks the conscience."

Sauers also announced that "Police officers now have fair warning that their conduct when engaged in a high speed pursuit will be subject to the full body of our state-created danger case law." *Id.* at 723. In particular, where there is no compelling justification for a high speed pursuit, and an officer has time to consider whether to do so, constitutional liability can arise from "a conscious disregard of a great risk of serious harm," *id.*, the standard between intent to harm and deliberate indifference that is applicable "when an officer has time for hurried deliberation." *Id.* at 717. *Sauers*

23. In *Phillips*, Michalski was suspended and then fired from his job as a 911 dispatcher. After his suspension, two of his former dispatcher colleagues gave him information that would help him to locate Phillips (Michalski's exgirlfriend's new boyfriend). After being fired, Michalski told his former colleagues that he had nothing to live for and that his exgirlfriend and Phillips would "pay for putting him in his present situation." The dispatchers failed to contact Phillips, the exgirlfriend, or the police departments of the areas in which those two people were located. Michalski then shot and killed his exgirlfriend, her sister, and Phillips. *Phillips*, 515 F.3d at 228–29. The court of appeals held that the deliberate indifference standard applied to the dispatchers because they "had no information which would have placed them in a 'hyperpressurized environment.'" *Id.* at 241.

24. Despite stating the standard as one involving conscious disregard, the *Sanford* court also noted in the next sentence—and apparently with respect to the same point on the shocks-the-conscience spectrum—that "it is possible that actual knowledge of the risk may not be necessary where the risk is 'obvious.'" *Sanford*, 456 F.3d at 310. Earlier in its opinion (as mentioned in the footnote following this one), the *Sanford* court discussed a similar point in connection with the deliberate indifference standard, *see id.* at 309 & n.13.

See also Rivas v. City of Passaic, 365 F.3d 181, 184, 196 (3d Cir. 2004) (holding that emergency medical technicians "who responded to an emergency in an apartment where a middleaged man was experiencing a seizure" would be held to have violated substantive due process only if they "consciously disregard[ed] a substantial risk that [the man] would be seriously harmed by their actions") *id.* at 196 (stating that this test would be met if the EMTs had falsely told police officers that the man was violent and had failed to tell the police officers that the man was suffering a seizure); *cf. Brown v. Commonwealth of Pennsylvania*, 318 F.3d 473, 481 (3d Cir. 2003) (holding that "EMTs who attempted to arrive at the scene of the incident as rapidly as they could" did not behave in a way that shocks the conscience).

distinguished *County of Sacramento v. Lewis*, 523 U.S. 833 (1998), so that the intent-to-harm standard set in *Lewis* applies when officers are responding to emergencies or making split-second decisions to pursue fleeing suspects—but not when there is no compelling justification for an officer to engage in high-speed pursuit and the officer has time to consider whether to engage in such inherently risky behavior. *See also Haberle v. Troxell*, 885 F.3d 170 (3d Cir. 2018) (holding that this intermediate standard applied where a person with suicidal tendencies had stolen a deadly weapon (so this was not a time for casual deliberation) but a few hours had passed and there was no indication of escalation (so instantaneous action was not required)).

Sauers concluded that the conduct alleged—making a U-turn and driving recklessly at speeds over 100 miles per hour to pursue a non-fleeing motorist who had committed a minor traffic offense, resulting in the death of a passenger in a unrelated vehicle—met this standard. By contrast, *Haberle* concluded that an officer's decision to "immediately knock [on the apartment door of a suicidal person who had stolen a deadly weapon] while other officers counseled waiting manifests only a disagreement over how to manage a risk, not a disregard of it," 885 F.3d at 177–78, even though suicide resulted immediately.

. . .

In *L.R. v. School District of Philadelphia*, 836 F.3d 235, 245 (3d Cir. 2016), the court of appeals stated that a teacher who released a kindergartener to a stranger "knew, or should have known, about the risk of his actions." In *Kedra v. Schroeter*, 876 F.3d 424, 439 (3d Cir. 2017), the court of appeals read this passage from *L.R.* as adopting the objective standard. Thus the current standard in the circuit appears to be the objective standard.

Kedra, however, did not apply the objective standard to the defendant in that case, because the objective standard had not been clearly established at the time of the conduct involved in that case. It nevertheless concluded that the allegations of the complaint were "more than sufficient to state a claim for a state-created danger based on actual knowledge of a substantial risk of serious harm—the subjective theory of deliberate indifference that was then-clearly established." 876 F.3d at 444. Accordingly, there are cases, such as *Kedra*, that may go to a jury on the subjective standard, because the underlying events occurred before the objective standard became clearly established.

Kedra involved a police officer who was training other officers in firearm safety but failed to perform safety checks. As a result, he failed to realize that the gun he was demonstrating was loaded, and pointed that gun at a fellow officer and pulled the trigger, killing him. Applying the subjective standard, the court of appeals explained that it had "regularly relied on the obviousness of risk as a permissible and highly relevant basis from which to infer actual knowledge—even directing in our Model Civil Jury Instructions that, in assessing deliberate indifference for state-created danger claims, a jury is 'entitled to infer from the obviousness of the risk that [the state actor] knew of the risk.' Third Circuit Model Civil Jury Instructions § 4.14 (Mar. 2017)." *Kedra v. Schroeter*, 876 F.3d 424, 442 (3d Cir. 2017). Accordingly, the court concluded that the allegations of the complaint permitted the inference that the defendant officer "acted with actual knowledge of a substantial risk of lethal harm—that is, knowledge that gives rise to a degree of culpability that shocks the conscience under the then-clearly established actual knowledge theory of deliberate indifference." *Id.* at 448 (internal quotation marks and citations omitted); *see also id.* at 446–47 (stating that "the subjective knowledge test requires knowledge only of the substantial risk of serious harm, not of the certainty of that harm").

...

For further discussion

Kristopher Kime was killed on the street during a crowded Seattle Mardi Gras celebration when young men randomly attacked people in the crowd. While police were present on the periphery of the crowd, they did not intervene. Review the below facts and settlement terms of the state-created danger claim by the family of Mr. Kime against the City of Seattle and read the interview of the plaintiffs' counsel, Karen Koehler. Why do you think the non-monetary terms of the settlement were important to the Kime family? Do you think non-monetary terms might be useful in settling many claims? How do you think an attorney can determine whether non-monetary settlement terms are important to a client?

"No Greater Love Hath Man Than This, That A Man Lay Down His Life For His Friends ..." February 20, 2001, Kristopher Randal Kime, Age 20

Man killed at Mardi Gras was trying to help woman
(Seattle Times, March 2, 2001)
Ian Ith & Nancy Bartley, contrbns. by Nicole Brodeur

Kristopher Kime never knew what hit him. Jostling with close friends in the increasingly violent crowd at Mardi Gras in Pioneer Square on [February 27–28, 2001], he saw a young woman knocked to the pavement by a group of violent attackers. He bent over to help her to her feet, fearing she would be trampled.

That's when someone from behind smashed a bottle into the back of Kime's head. He crumpled to the pavement, unconscious. Several attackers set upon him wildly, kicking him in the head before moving on. Kime's family and friends say he was murdered amid the mayhem of Fat Tuesday.

...

"[F]ighting was breaking out everywhere," [Kime's friend] said. "I saw a girl being pulled around by her hair until she was knocked down, and somebody was kicking her. It was disgusting, a whole group of people beating up one person." Kime tried to help. [His 2 female friends] tried to help someone else ... [Hearing hysterical screams, one] pushed through the crowd and looked down ... [S]he didn't recognize the unconscious man lying in the street. Then someone turned him over and propped up his head. It was Kime....

But the melee made it impossible for an aid crew to get to the scene. It was 1 a.m.... the height of the Mardi Gras frenzy. Police later said they were being assaulted by the crowd, which was catapulting bottles and other debris at them. The fire department said it couldn't respond directly to rescue Kime because the scene couldn't be secured by police.

[We picked him up and moved him at 1:15 a.m., said Kime's friend.] A few off-duty firefighters arrived and helped carry Kime to a nearby police car. A police sergeant drove Kime to the Seattle Fire Department headquarters.... Then an ambulance took him to Harborview Medical Center. It was 1:44 a.m., according to police reports. [Doctors pronounced Kime dead the next day.]

Chief stands by standby tactic
(Seattle Times, March 2, 2001)
Anne Koch with Jim Brunner, Mike Carter & Christine Clarridge

Although grieved by the violence and destruction he saw Tuesday night in Pioneer Square, Seattle Police Chief Gil Kerlikowske defends his decision to wait until crowds thinned to send officers in to clear the streets.

The Mardi Gras chaos left one person dead, one seriously injured, many hurt and thousands of dollars of property damaged.

[Seventy-two people were injured "in the melee," and 22 arrested.] "I think we moved in at the proper time given the size of that crowd, the mob mentality that existed and what I saw," Kerlikowske said at a news conference yesterday. "And I take responsibility, and I stand by that decision." ...

As many as 350 officers were stationed around Pioneer Square late Tuesday and early Wednesday, but police didn't go in to clear the mobs until after 1 a.m., after bands of violent youths had beaten, kicked and robbed other crowd members, turned over cars and smashed store windows....

[The police] guild president, said he has heard from many officers stationed on the street that night who felt frustrated and helpless standing on the sidelines.

"Police officers are sworn to do a duty, and they want to do that," he said. "When they're held back, they're not able to do what they got into the job to do."

[The police chief said] "I don't know of a single police tactic that exists to be able to insert officers into the middle of a mob.... We brought a number of people out. We were able to rescue people. We were able to make over 21 arrests on the periphery."

Furthermore, the chief said, in some cases it would have caused more disruption and violence than had already occurred if police had fought their way through the crowd.

But ... a bicycle officer who worked Tuesday night, said he was sickened by having to remain on the fringe of the violence and had serious problems with the leadership's decision to hang back ...

"I saw at least three violent felony assaults. The universal reaction (from officers there) was one of frustration and anguish. And I mean acute anguish."

[He] said criticism in the media and by others of the force demonstrated by police [in an earlier incident] may have influenced the decision by top police officials to be more passive Tuesday night ..."I really felt like (police leaders) were reluctant for a variety of reasons to use the equipment they assembled."

One commander, who asked not to be identified, agreed: ... "It would be easy to conclude, based on what I saw and heard, that there was an unnecessary delay in getting officers deployed." ...

Despite criticism, Kerlikowske has won praise from the police guild for taking immediate responsibility for the event....

The City of Seattle paid $1.75 million to Kristopher Kime's family in a settlement that also included a private meeting with Police Chief Gil Kerlikowske, an annual $2,500 scholarship to a young adult under 21 who has demonstrated self-sacrifice or compassion, notice of public safety meetings, and installation of a plaque honoring Mr. Kime in a public square.[1]

1. If you were drafting the state-created danger allegations of the Kime Complaint, what facts could you allege to overcome *DeShaney's* admonition that government officials are not liable if they simply "stood by and did nothing when suspicious circumstances dictated a more active role for them"? What state-of-mind requirement would be consistent with *Lewis*? What allegations would be necessary to satisfy that state-of-mind requirement? If you were drafting a motion to dismiss the Kime complaint, what arguments would you make?

2. Anne Peyton Bryant was skating through New York's Central Park at 6 p.m. in June, 2000, as a parade was breaking up. Suddenly, a mob of men doused her with water and beer, threw her to the ground, and began groping her body. The mob chanted,

1. Associated Press, *City reaches settlement with family of Mardi Gras victim*, SEATTLEPI (Aug. 13, 2002), https://www.seattlepi.com/news/article/City-reaches-settlement-with-family-of-Mardi-Gras-1093531.php.

"go, go, go," and was so thick that she could not see the sky. As the mob turned its attention to other women, Ms. Bryant said she ran to a police officer on a scooter, then three more, pleading for help. She was ignored. At a nearby precinct house, she was told to come back and make a report when she had calmed down, she said. Ms. Bryant sued the city for failing to heed her cries for help. After six years, on the eve of trial, the city agreed to pay her $125,000. Ms. Bryan's settlement was the last of 22 with women who alleged they were attacked during the same parade. Ms. Bryant's ordeal inspired her to change careers and attend New York Law School, with hopes of handling cases involving violence against women. Her law practice focuses on divorce and fulfilled her goal because, "sadly, far too many divorces cases involve violence against women."[2]

3. Contrast the different outcome of a Philadelphia case. During an annual outdoor event "in which fraternities and sororities gather in Philadelphia for partying and revelry," plaintiff JoEllyn Jones alleged several males pulled her from a car, tore off her clothes, sexually assaulted her, and stole her money; she further alleged that two police officers assigned to crowd control in the area observed the assault but refused to attempt to stop the assault or to arrest the men, even though plaintiff pointed them out. *Jones v. City of Philadelphia*, 185 F.Supp.2d 413, 414 (E.D. Pa. 2001). The district court granted a 12(b)(6) motion to dismiss the state-created danger claim because the complaint did not contain any facts that the state actors used their authority to create an opportunity that otherwise would not have existed for the private violence to occur. *Id.* at 417.

Interview with Karen K. Koehler, Plaintiffs' Counsel in *Kime*[3]

Q: How did you come to represent the Kime family?

A: They interviewed a number of lawyers who felt they did not have a good case, but I felt that there was a terrible wrong and that I would do whatever I had to in order to make it right.

Q: How did you reach such interesting settlement terms?

A: We talked extensively with his whole family—grandparents, siblings, step-mom, half-brother, sister. Even though the parents are divorced, they united for the effort. Because this wasn't the typical accident case, what we talked about was that it wasn't just about money, even though the civil justice system compensates victims with money. We wanted to make sure that he did not die in vain and that his life and the mistakes made that night would not fade away. The non-monetary aspects were equally the focus, and we spent as much time negotiating these other things as the money.

---

2. *See* Anemona Hartocollis, *Victim of Post-Parade Sex Attack Settles Suit Over Police Indifference*, N.Y. Times (Mar. 17, 2006), https://www.nytimes.com/2006/03/17/nyregion/victim-of-postparade-sex-attack-settles-suit-over-police.html?searchResultPosition=1; email to Sarah Ricks, Camden, New Jersey (Oct. 14, 2014).

3. Telephone Interview by Peregrin Sorter, Camden, New Jersey (Spring 2007).

The reason for the difficulty with the plaque is that [Seattle's] Pioneer Square is on the historic register and it is governed by a historic board. The city said we couldn't do it unless the board approved, and that the board wouldn't likely do it because it was morbid. You know, people coming to Pioneer Square and reading a plaque about someone dying there. They were proposing several other locations for the site of the plaque. It's almost funny, they had us spinning around over other locations, they wanted it everywhere except where he was killed. Every year since this has happened his family goes there and lights a vigil. His mother just emailed me and told me when they would be going this year. The plaque is there forever, this was the biggest condition and the most concrete one.

Q: Do you think that the City was willing to settle with the Kime family in part because of political pressure due to negative press?

A: Yes. The City was scared of litigating the facts in regards to Kris Kime. They stood by while he was killed. If I were the City, I wouldn't want to litigate these facts. Cases with these facts beg for justice and can make for law adverse to the interests of the City.

Q: Any advice for law students interested in a civil rights law practice?

A: Yes, you should become a member of Public Justice, the American Civil Liberties Union, and the American Constitution Society.

Consider the creative terms of the settlement, how the attorney communicated with her clients to determine their goals, and how non-monetary terms were useful in achieving the clients' goals. For more on creative settlement terms, *see* Brent T. White, *Say You're Sorry: Court-Ordered Apologies as a Civil Rights Remedy*, 91 Cornell L. Rev. 1261, 1408–10 (2006) (proposing apology as a partial remedy, identifying who should make the apology and the public or private forum for the apology as factors to consider, and emphasizing the need for other remedies); Brent T. White, *Saving Face: The Benefits of Not Saying I'm Sorry*, 72 Law & Contemp. Problems 261 (2009) (identifying the limits of apology as a remedy but advocating that courts consider compelled apologies from government officials when useful to "restore the dignity of the injured person or group"); City of Philadelphia Press Release (Nov. 19, 2018) (two African-American men arrested while waiting for a business associate at a Philadelphia Starbucks settled their litigation against the City in return for an apology, $1, plus $200,000 for an entrepreneurial program for Philadelphia high schools).

Guide to Law Practice Simulation 2

Description

This is an interoffice debate among the attorneys representing the defendant police Officer Tedder on whether to seek certiorari from the fictional Twelfth Circuit to the U.S. Supreme Court on the state-created danger issue only. While the simulation is based on the facts of *Kneipp v. Tedder*, 95 F.3d 1199 (3d Cir. 1996), the relevant circuit is the fictional Twelfth Circuit. The state-created danger doctrine has not been litigated in the Twelfth Circuit since *Kneipp*. All students represent the police officer. Two students are junior, in-house counsel who do not think the client should petition for certiorari. Two students are private counsel who do think the client should seek certiorari and would like to represent the client, for a fee. One student is the in-house senior counsel who will decide whether or not to recommend petitioning for certiorari to the client.

For information on the rules governing the grant of a petition for certiorari, please review Rule 10 of the Rules of the Supreme Court of the United States, which provides:

> Considerations Governing Review on Certiorari
>
> Review on a writ of certiorari is not a matter of right, but of judicial discretion. A petition for a writ of certiorari will be granted only for compelling reasons. The following, although neither controlling nor fully measuring the Court's discretion, indicate the character of the reasons the Court considers:
>
> (a) a United States court of appeals has entered a decision in conflict with the decision of another United States court of appeals on the same important matter; has decided an important federal question in a way that conflicts with a decision by a state court of last resort; or has so far departed from the accepted and usual course of judicial proceedings, or sanctioned such a departure by a lower court, as to call for an exercise of this Court's supervisory power;
>
> . . .
>
> (c) a state court or a United States court of appeals has decided an important question of federal law that has not been, but should be, settled by this Court, or has decided an important federal question in a way that conflicts with relevant decisions of this Court.
>
> A petition for a writ of certiorari is rarely granted when the asserted error consists of erroneous factual findings or the misapplication of a properly stated rule of law.

To prepare, consider issues such as:

- Which parts of Supreme Court Rule 10 may be relevant?
- What level of mental culpability in these circumstances would shock the conscience?
- Is *Kneipp* consistent with *DeShaney*? With *McClendon*? With *Butera*?
- What are the benefits of seeking Supreme Court intervention? What are the risks?
- What other practical considerations should inform litigation decisions?

Purpose

- Better understand 14th Amendment general rule of *DeShaney*
- Better understand 14th Amendment state-created danger doctrine by talking through legal test and comparing variations in how circuits apply it, including *Kneipp*, *McClendon*, and *Butera*, and explanation of the doctrine within those cases
- Explore attorney roles in shaping 14th Amendment doctrine by simulating roles of attorneys applying doctrine to real facts (the *Kneipp* facts)
- Learn distinction between grounds for petition for certiorari and a brief on the merits
- Prepare for law practice by discussing practical considerations underlying litigation decisions, such as cost, likelihood of certiorari being granted, political consequences for clients such as a police department and elected city officials
- Prepare for law practice by either persuasively advocating legal position and responding to questions or by identifying ambiguities in doctrine or in its application to facts and posing questions to advocates
- There is no need to do any research—the relevant cases are in the casebook. You can rely on the Third Circuit decision in *Kneipp* as foreign authority.

Structure

- Outside counsel advocating that the client seek certiorari—Question and Answer with senior in-house counsel (8 minutes)
- Junior in-house, advocating that the client not seek certiorari—Question and Answer with senior in-house counsel (8 minutes)
- After about 15 minutes, questioning will be opened up to the entire class
- Both sides—Question and Answer with senior in-house counsel and rest of class (15 minutes)
- Please prepare a question for every simulation, even if you are not one of the students playing a role.
- To ensure full class participation, and as a courtesy to your fellow students, please close your laptops during law practice simulations.

For further discussion

After evaluating arguments similar to those in Law Practice Simulation 2, lawyers for plaintiffs in *Reat v. Rodriguez*, including Erwin Chemerinsky, now Dean of Berkeley Law School, filed a petition for certiorari on a state-created danger claim in 2016. In *Reat*, a driver and his three passengers were physically assaulted by a group of men. The driver and passengers escaped, drove to safety, called 911, and were instructed to return to the scene of the confrontation to await police and medical assistance. After following those instructions, their assailants returned and murdered passenger Jimma Reat. Plaintiffs sued the 911 operator. Plaintiffs claimed the 911 operator created the danger to Mr. Reat because he did "'play[]' a 'part in creating' and rendering an individual 'more vulnerable' to the danger" of being shot. Petition for Certiorari in *Reat v. Rodriguez,* No. 16-643, 2016 WL 6803676 (Nov. 10, 2016) at *2 (citing *DeShaney*).

Petitioners argued:

> This case meets the [Supreme] Court's criteria for granting certiorari. Since 1989, the majority of Courts of Appeals have agreed that a state actor may be liable for action that creates or increases danger to an individual under *DeShaney*. But they have adopted increasingly divergent tests for "state created danger" claims and are irreconcilably divided on the question presented here—whether the plaintiff must *also* show that the state action imposed limitations on the person's freedom to act on his own behalf. In this [case, a] 911 operator sent victims of a hate crime back into danger by refusing to send the police to their apartment complex, to where they had safely fled, and instead directed them to drive back to the crime scene, park their car on the side of the road, flash their hazard lights, and wait for the police—which he never sent. While parked, their assailants found them, shooting and killing Jimma Reat in front of his family.
>
> The Tenth Circuit sided with the Fourth and Fifth Circuits in holding that the state actor must "limit[] in some way the liberty of a citizen to act on his own behalf" to bring a ... state created danger claim.... The Second, Sixth, Seventh, Eighth, and Ninth Circuits, have all held to the contrary, explicitly rejecting any such freedom restriction requirement for the doctrine to apply—and instead allowing liability when the state's conduct creates or increases danger, without respect to the plaintiff's liberty.
>
> By requiring a freedom limitation relationship, the minority approach of the Tenth, Fourth and Fifth Circuits renders any distinct danger creation exception toothless, a holding that effectively (and dangerously) immunizes all government conduct in this area absent custody or physical control. As these courts and legal scholars have pointed out in rejecting the minority view, "[s]uch a requirement decisively curbs any operative state-created danger theory" by "instead impos[ing] a special relationship prerequisite." Christopher M. Eisenhauer, *Police Action and The State-Created Danger Doctrine: A Proposed Uniform Test,* 120 Penn St. L. Rev. 893, 902 (2016)....
>
> Courts of Appeals openly recognize this substantive circuit split. *See Butera v. District of Columbia,* 235 F.3d 637, 654 (D.C. Cir. 2001) (noting the "lack of clarity in the law of the circuits", which are "inconsistent in their elaborations" of danger creation claims); ... *McClendon v. City of Columbia,* 258 F.3d 432 (5th Cir. 2001) (noting the "variety of tests" in the circuits).

Id. at *2–*4. The Supreme Court denied certiorari in 2017; *see* Petition for Certiorari in *Schroeter v. Kedra,* No. 17-1204, 2018 WL 1110433, at *6 (Feb. 23, 2018), *cert. de-*

nied, ___ U.S. ___, 138 S.Ct. 1990 (2018) (while "[a]t least eight sister circuits" recognize the state-created danger theory, the Supreme Court "has yet to adopt the standard for culpability in this type of case").

E. Development of Doctrine in the Circuits: Special Relationship Exception to *DeShaney*

There is a second exception to the general principle of *DeShaney* that the state is not liable under substantive due process for harm inflicted by a private person. *Deshaney* held that the government can be liable for privately inflicted harm if the government had entered into a "special relationship" with the plaintiff. *DeShaney* held that "it is the State's affirmative act of restraining the individual's freedom to act on his own behalf—through incarceration, institutionalization, or other similar restraint of personal liberty—which is the 'deprivation of liberty' triggering the protections of the Due Process Clause...." What factual situations did the Court intend to include in "other similar restraint on personal liberty"? What makes a government's restraint of a person sufficiently similar to incarceration or involuntary commitment to qualify for substantive due process protection? The following cases consider the special relationship exception to *DeShaney's* general rule that the government is not obligated to protect its citizens against private acts of violence.

Questions to guide reading of *Patel*

1. Why did the Ninth Circuit reject the plaintiff's attempt to analogize public school day students to incarcerated prisoners or to involuntarily committed mental patients?
2. For the purposes of applying the "special relationship" exception to *DeShaney*, why did the Ninth Circuit hold the individualized education plan for the student was not relevant?
3. If you represented the public school, how would you summarize *Patel* in a conversation with your client? In light of the holding of *Patel*, what advice might you give your client?

Patel v. Kent School District

648 F.3d 965 (9th Cir. 2011)

TALLMAN, Circuit Judge.

A.H., a developmentally disabled high-school student, had several sexual encounters with another developmentally disabled student in a school bathroom. Her mother alleges these encounters were the result of the school's failure to properly supervise A.H.... A.H. is a former student at Kentridge High School (KHS) in the Kent School District (Kent, Washington). Her mother is plaintiff-appellant Madhuri Patel....

During the relevant time, A.H.'s disabilities affected her day-to-day life in various ways. She was sometimes unable to complete basic tasks like holding her eating utensils correctly, blowing her nose, and zipping her clothes. Socially, A.H. had difficulty maintaining an appropriate physical distance from other people, refraining from talking about personal or embarrassing things, and conveying an age-appropriate understanding of etiquette.... In [May] 2006, A.H.'s freshman year ... KHS established an Individualized Education Plan (IEP) for A.H. A.H. was put in a self-contained classroom taught by defendant-appellee Francine Wilhelm, a special-education teacher. The school invoked a "no contact" order to prevent any further physical contact between A.H. and other students. School staff were required to escort A.H. to Wilhelm's classroom when she arrived in the morning, to any classes outside Wilhelm's classroom, and to the bus at the end of the day....

The incidents leading directly to this lawsuit occurred [in] spring 2007.... [T]hat semester Wilhelm had been allowing A.H. (then age sixteen) to go on her own to a bathroom immediately adjacent to Wilhelm's classroom. At least five times during these unsupervised trips to the bathroom, A.H. had sex with a boy named Matt, another developmentally disabled student in Wilhelm's class. A counselor determined the sex might be "consensual" even though both students were developmentally disabled. Despite her recognition that the IEP called for constant supervision, Wilhelm believed allowing A.H. to use the bathroom on her own as a sophomore was an important step in fostering her development[.] ... Wilhelm did not know A.H. was having sex with Matt in the bathroom, but she was aware the two potentially had some type of relationship.... Wilhelm also relayed this information to Patel via email....

[About two months] later, Wilhelm saw Matt leave her classroom just a few seconds after A.H. had gone to the bathroom. Wilhelm "raced out of the room," called to A.H. from outside the bathroom, and escorted her back to class. Wilhelm said A.H. was "very angry" with Wilhelm for "interfering with her." At the school's direction, Wilhelm again emailed Patel to explain the incident.... After receiving the email, Patel asked her daughter whether she was having a relationship with another student. A.H. admitted she and Matt had sex in the bathroom at least twice.... Patel sent two emails to KHS, one to Wilhelm and one to [the] Principal.... These emails disclosed A.H.'s sexual relationship with Matt and expressed Patel's anger about the situation.... Patel's email to [the] Principal ... also revealed for the first time that, contrary to the results of the school's previous investigation, [a year earlier] A.H. and [a different boy] had sex in a different school bathroom during her freshman year. Patel's email ambiguously claimed school officials knew this all along.... But as the district court correctly noted, there was no evidence school officials knew that A.H. had sex at school her freshman year until Patel told them so in these spring 2007 emails....

Patel removed A.H. from [the school]. She reported the sexual encounters to the King County Sheriff's Department. The sheriff's office took a statement from Matt, who admitted he "had sexual relations with [A.H.] at least five times." ...

III

... Although Patel may still have viable state-law claims against the defendants, her § 1983 claim against Wilhelm fails as a matter of law. *Cf. DeShaney v. Winnebago Cnty. Dep't of Soc. Servs.*, 489 U.S. 189, 202 (1989) ("[T]he Fourteenth Amendment ... does not transform every tort committed by a state actor into a constitutional violation.")....

[T]he Fourteenth Amendment's Due Process Clause generally does not confer any affirmative right to governmental aid, even where such aid may be necessary to secure life, liberty, or property interests. *DeShaney*, 489 U.S. at 196. As a corollary, the Fourteenth Amendment typically "does not impose a duty on [the state] to protect individuals from third parties." *Morgan v. Gonzales*, 495 F.3d 1084, 1093 (9th Cir.2007). There are two exceptions to this rule: (1) when a "special relationship" exists between the plaintiff and the state (the special-relationship exception), *DeShaney*, 489 U.S. at 198–202; and (2) ... the state-created danger exception.... If either exception applies, a state's omission or failure to protect may give rise to a § 1983 claim.

Because Patel's § 1983 claim is based on an omission by Wilhelm—her alleged failure to properly supervise A.H.—Patel can establish a due process violation only if one of these two exceptions applies....

A

We begin with the special-relationship exception. The Supreme Court formally established this exception in *DeShaney*, 489 U.S. at 198–202. The exception applies when a state "takes a person into its custody and holds him there against his will." *Id.* at 199–200. The types of custody triggering the exception are "incarceration, institutionalization, or other similar restraint of personal liberty." *Id.* at 200. When a person is placed in these types of custody, we allow due process claims against the state for a fairly simple reason: a state cannot restrain a person's liberty without also assuming some responsibility for the person's safety and well-being. *Id.* at 199–200.

Under this exception, the state's constitutional duty arises "not from the State's knowledge of the individual's predicament or from its expressions of intent to help him, but from the limitation which [the State] has imposed on his freedom." *Id.* at 200. In other words, the person's substantive due process rights are triggered when the state restrains his liberty, not when he suffers harm caused by the actions of third parties. *Id.* at 195, 200.

The special-relationship exception does not apply when a state fails to protect a person who is not in custody. *See id.* at 195–202. In *DeShaney*, for instance, a four-year-old boy was brutally and repeatedly beaten by his father. *Id.* at 191–93.... The Supreme Court rejected the boy's § 1983 due process claim, holding the special-relationship exception did not apply because the boy was in the custody of his father, not the state. *Id.* at 201. Even though the state had extensive information strongly suggesting abuse, the boy's due process rights were not triggered because he was not in state custody. *Id.* at 200–02.

...

Although we have not yet applied *DeShaney* to the context of compulsory school attendance ... [a]t least seven circuits have held that compulsory school attendance alone is insufficient to invoke the special-relationship exception. [citing authority from 1st, 5th, 6th, 10th, 8th, 3d, and 7th Circuits]. Our sister circuits have reasoned that, unlike incarceration or institutionalization, compulsory school attendance does not restrict a student's liberty such that neither the student nor the parents can attend to the student's basic needs.... Even when school attendance is mandatory, the parents—not the state—remain the student's primary caretakers.... Going a step further, most of these circuits have expressly held that combining in loco parentis duties with compulsory school attendance still does not create a "special relationship." ... These decisions have emphasized that a state-law obligation does not necessarily create a duty of care under the Fourteenth Amendment.... Applying this bedrock principle, our sister circuits uniformly hold that requiring school attendance does not sufficiently restrict a student's liberty under *DeShaney* to transform the school's in loco parentis duties into a constitutional obligation....

We find particularly instructive the Third Circuit's analysis [in *D.R. v. Middle Bucks Area Vocational Tech. Sch.*, 972 F.2d 1364, 1366–67 (3d Cir. 1992) (*en banc*)]. In that case, one plaintiff was a female student with communicative disabilities. *Id.* at 1366 n. 5. She claimed multiple male students sexually molested her in a unisex school bathroom and a darkroom. *Id.* at 1366.... Affirming dismissal of the § 1983 claim, the Third Circuit refused to apply the special-relationship exception. *Id.* at 1373. The court emphasized that, despite compulsory school attendance and in loco parentis status, the student remained in the custody of her parents, not the school. *Id.* at 1370–72. She went home every night, and her parents had the authority at all times to put her in a different school or educate her at home. *Id.* Thus, the school's authority did not "create the type of physical custody necessary to bring it within [*DeShaney*]." *Id.* at 1372.

While we certainly have sympathy for Patel's position as a concerned and caring parent, we decline to depart from this persuasive authority. Compulsory school attendance and in loco parentis status do not create "custody" under the strict standard of *DeShaney*. Like the schoolchildren in the cases cited above, A.H.'s freedom was not restrained by KHS in a manner akin to "incarceration" or "institutionalization." *See DeShaney*, 489 U.S. at 200. A.H. did not live at school; she lived at home with her mother. Although she was statutorily required to attend school somewhere, her mother could have removed her from KHS at any time, and in fact did so.... These facts preclude a custodial relationship.

To the extent Patel argues we should distinguish this case because the IEP obligated KHS to guard against A.H.'s special vulnerabilities, *DeShaney* suggests otherwise. In the case of a minor child, custody does not exist until the state has so restrained the child's liberty that the parents cannot care for the child's basic needs. *See DeShaney*, 489 U.S. at 199–201. A tailored educational program for a disabled student does not meet this threshold. *Middle Bucks*, 972 F.2d at 1371–72. KHS's agreement to provide enhanced supervision did not prevent Patel from caring for A.H.'s basic needs. Patel always remained A.H.'s primary caretaker.... Under *DeShaney*, we are concerned only with whether KHS so restrained A.H.'s liberty that it rendered Patel "*unable* to care for [her]." *See* 489 U.S. at 200 (emphasis added). It did not.

...

For further discussion

1. The Ninth Circuit in *Patel* relied heavily on *D.R. v. Middle Bucks*, a Third Circuit special relationship decision that analyzed similar facts. In *D.R.*, the Third Circuit left open the possibility that foster care could qualify as a special relationship because, unlike mandatory school attendance, foster care could be sufficiently analogous to "incarceration, institutionalization, or similar restraint on liberty." While foster care was not the subject of *D.R.*, the Third Circuit reasoned: "[S]ome courts have imposed a constitutional duty to protect foster children by analogy to involuntarily institutionalized individuals.... A relationship between the state and foster children arises out of the state's affirmative act in finding the children and placing them with state-approved families.... By so doing, the state assumes an important continuing, if not immediate, responsibility for the child's well-being. In addition, the child's placement renders him or her dependent upon the state, through the foster family, to meet the child's basic needs.... Students, on the other hand, do not depend upon the schools to provide for their basic human needs.... Even during the school day, however, parents or others remain a child's primary caretakers and decisionmakers." *D.R. v. Middle Bucks Area Vocational Tech. Sch.*, 972 F.2d 1364, 1372 (3d Cir. 1992) (*en banc*).

2. Do you think foster care should qualify for the special relationship exception to the general rule of *DeShaney*? Keep your view in mind when reading *Nicini*, which appears later in this Chapter.

Questions to guide reading of *Walton*

1. What was Plaintiff's claim against the school superintendent? What was Plaintiff's argument for why there was a "special relationship" between the state and the residential students at the school?
2. How did the majority summarize the narrow circumstances that give rise to a "special relationship"? The majority acknowledged *DeShaney's* language that a state's affirmative restraint on an individual's liberty, "through incarceration, institutionalization, *or other similar restraint of personal liberty*" is what gives rise to a special relationship. What key fact did the majority require in order to recognize a special relationship analogous to jail or institutionalization? Why did the majority reject Plaintiff's argument that he was in a special relationship with the school for the deaf, analogous to jail or institutionalization?
3. Instead of focusing on whether Plaintiff was voluntarily in state custody, how would the concurrence have framed the issue presented?

4. Both the majority and the concurrence recognized that *DeShaney* left open the possibility a special relationship could be created by a state's restraint of personal liberty "similar" to jail or institutionalization. Why did the concurrence argue that the majority read that language too narrowly?
5. Instead of focusing on whether Plaintiff was voluntarily in state custody, as the majority did, what did the concurrence argue should be the focus of the special relationship analysis? What factors would it weigh? Why would the concurrence have recognized a special relationship between the school and Plaintiff?
6. Are you more persuaded by the majority or the concurrence?

Walton v. Alexander

44 F.3d 1297 (5th Cir. 1995)

JOLLY, Circuit Judge.

[N]othing in the language of the Due Process Clause itself requires the State to protect the life, liberty, and property of its citizens against invasion by private actors. The Clause is phrased as a limitation on the State's power to act, not as a guarantee of certain minimal levels of safety and security. It forbids the State itself to deprive individuals of life, liberty, or property without 'due process of law,' but its language cannot fairly be extended to impose an affirmative obligation on the State to ensure that those interests do not come to harm through other means. Nor does history support such an expansive reading of the constitutional text. Like its counterpart in the Fifth Amendment, the Due Process Clause of the Fourteenth Amendment was intended to prevent government "from abusing [its] power, or employing it as an instrument of oppression."[1]

Christopher Walton was not harmed by the acts of the state or by a state actor; Christopher Walton was harmed by the acts of a private party. He was harmed while attending a state institution, the Mississippi School for the Deaf, as a resident student. He was twice sexually molested by a fellow classmate. He sued the superintendent of the Mississippi School for the Deaf, Alma Alexander, under 42 U.S.C. § 1983. He alleged that the state violated his substantive due process right to bodily integrity under the Fourteenth Amendment because Alexander failed to take appropriate steps to protect him from these sexual assaults by a fellow student.... Although we agree that a very narrow class of persons who stand in a "special relationship" with the state enjoys a clearly established constitutional right to some degree of state protection from known threats of harm by private actors, this "special relationship" only arises when a person is involuntarily confined or otherwise restrained against his will pursuant to a governmental order or by the affirmative exercise of state power. This relationship does not arise solely because the state exercises custodial control over an individual such as is the case when a person voluntarily resides in a state facility.

---

1. *DeShaney v. Winnebago County Dep't. of Social Servs.*, 489 U.S. 189, 198–99 (1989).

Consequently, we conclude that because no "special relationship" existed between the state and Walton, Superintendent Alexander owed Walton no constitutional duty of protection from harm inflicted upon him at the instance of his classmate …

I

During 1987–1988, the Mississippi School for the Deaf (the "School") was one of several state supported institutions available throughout the state to deaf children. Local school districts were obligated to provide deaf educational facilities if more than five deaf students were located within the district. In addition to public facilities, there were private deaf institutions in Mississippi. Deaf children were free to attend either a public or private facility located in Mississippi. Once choosing to attend the Mississippi School for the Deaf, however, those students residing on campus were under the twenty-four hour custody of the School and subjected to strict rules concerning what they were allowed to do and when they could come and go. School employees maintained close supervision over these students and reported any misconduct to the school superintendent.

Christopher Walton was a resident student attending the School during 1987–1988. During the latter part of 1987, a fellow classmate sexually assaulted Walton. This incident was reported to school officials, including defendant Alexander. Alexander filed a report with the Mississippi Department of Public Welfare. Pursuant to the School's policies, both the School and the Mississippi Department of Public Welfare conducted an investigation of the assault. After notifying the parents of both children, the School provided counselling for each child and suspended both children for three days.

Upon return from suspension, the two students were placed in separate dormitories. Budgetary constraints, however, forced the school to close one of the two male dormitories in 1988. Consequently, the boys were again housed in the same building. Walton was assigned a separate unit with a private bathroom, designed to keep him out of the bathrooms with the other male students. Walton, unfortunately, was assaulted a second time by the same classmate. Alexander was not informed of this second assault.

…

II

The central issue we address today is whether the state created a "special relationship" with Walton, as a resident student under its custodial care, so that it owed some duty—arising under the Due Process Clause of the Fourteenth Amendment to the United States Constitution—to protect Walton's bodily integrity from third party non-state actors. We conclude that, as a matter of law, it did not.

…

In examining Walton's claims, it is important to keep in mind that "section 1983 imposes liability for violations of rights protected by the Constitution, not for violations of duties of care arising out of tort law." [citing Fifth Circuit].… Walton's claim arises under the substantive, rather than the procedural component of the Due Process Clause. This component "protects individual liberty against 'certain government actions regardless of the fairness of the procedures used to implement them.'" *Collins v. City of Harker Heights*, 503 U.S. 115, 125 (1992) (quoting *Daniels v. Williams*, 474 U.S. 327, 331 (1986)). We have held that "[t]he right to be free of state-occasioned damage to a person's bodily integrity is protected by the fourteenth amendment guarantee of due process." [citing Fifth Circuit] ... We have not, however, extended this right to encompass harm inflicted on a person by a private actor outside the context of involuntary confinement.

The Due Process Clause confers protection to the general public against unwarranted governmental interference, but it does not confer an entitlement to governmental aid as may be necessary to realize the advantages of liberty guaranteed by the Clause. *DeShaney v. Winnebago County Dep't. of Social Servs.*, 489 U.S. 189, 196 (1989). In certain limited situations, however, the Supreme Court has recognized that the Constitution may impose on the state a special duty of care owed to certain restricted classes of persons. *See Estelle v. Gamble*, 429 U.S. 97, 103–04 (1976), *cert. denied*, 434 U.S. 974 (1977); *Youngberg v. Romeo*, 457 U.S. 307, 315–16 (1982). This duty generally arises when the state deprives a citizen of his liberty so that he is unable to care for himself. *Id.* In *Estelle*, a state prisoner sued prison officials for failing to provide him with adequate medical care in violation of the Eighth Amendment's prohibition against "cruel and unusual punishment." *Estelle*, 429 U.S. at 101–02. The Court agreed that the Eighth Amendment, made applicable to the states through the Fourteenth Amendment, imposed upon prison officials a duty to provide prisoners with medical care. *Id.* at 103–04. The Court held that this duty arose because the prisoners were incarcerated and were deprived of their liberty so that in certain respects they were unable to care for themselves. *Id.* at 103–04.

In *Youngberg*, the Court similarly found a duty of protection owed under the substantive component of the Due Process Clause of the Fourteenth Amendment. *Youngberg*, 457 U.S. at 315–25. The Court held that when persons are involuntarily committed to a mental institution and, thus, completely dependent on the state, the state has a duty to provide such patients with certain services and care as are necessary for their "reasonable safety" from themselves and others. *Id.* at 315–25. The Court reasoned that if the Eighth Amendment prohibited prison officials from holding prisoners in unsafe conditions, then certainly the Fourteenth Amendment prohibited involuntarily committed mental patients from being held in unsafe conditions. *Id.* at 315–16.

Thus, with *Estelle* and *Youngberg* as precedential background, the Court approached the question presented in *DeShaney*, 489 U.S. 189 (1989)—whether the substantive component of the due process clause imposes on the state a duty of protection to non-incarcerated and non-institutionalized persons from the harmful acts of non-state actors.... Referring to *Estelle* and *Youngberg*, the Court acknowledged that "when the State takes a person into its custody and holds him there against his will, the Constitution imposes upon it a corresponding duty to assume some responsibility for his safekeeping and general well-being." *Id.*, 489 U.S. at 199–200. The Court further explained that when the state so restrains an individual's liberty that he is unable to act for himself, and "at the same time fails to provide for his basic human needs—

e.g., food, clothing, shelter, medical care, and reasonable safety—it transgresses the substantive limits on state action set by ... the Due Process Clause." *Id.* at 200. This duty to protect, the Court found, arises not because of the state's knowledge of the individual's situation, but from the limitation the state imposed on his freedom to act on his own behalf. *Id.* The Court thus reached its holding that the state's affirmative restraint on an individual's liberty, "through incarceration, institutionalization, or other similar restraint of personal liberty," not its failure to act, is the compulsion required to create a "special relationship" and invoke the protection of the Due Process Clause. *DeShaney*, 489 U.S. at 200. The Court, thus, found that because Joshua's injuries occurred while in the custody of his father and not while in the custody of the DSS, the state had no constitutional duty to protect him. *Id.* at 210. The Court did observe, however, that if the state by its affirmative exercise of power had taken Joshua out of his home and placed him in a foster home operated by state agents, then a relationship might be created sufficiently analogous to institutionalization or incarceration so that a duty to protect would arise. *Id.* at 210 n.9.

Since *DeShaney* was decided by the Supreme Court, we have followed its language strictly and have held consistently that only when the state, by its affirmative exercise of power, has custody over an individual involuntarily or against his will does a "special relationship" exist between the individual and the state.

...

Recurring throughout [Fifth Circuit] cases that we have decided since *DeShaney* is the iteration of the principle that if the person claiming the right of state protection is voluntarily within the care or custody of a state agency, he has no substantive due process right to the state's protection from harm inflicted by third party non-state actors. We thus conclude that *DeShaney* stands for the proposition that the state creates a "special relationship" with a person only when the person is involuntarily taken into state custody and held against his will through the affirmative power of the state; otherwise, the state has no duty arising under the Constitution to protect its citizens against harm by private actors.

C

We turn now to consider whether Walton is entitled to claim constitutional protection against the acts of his classmate. Walton argues that a "special relationship" existed between the state and the resident students in Alexander's charge, which imposed upon Alexander a constitutional duty to protect Walton from his fellow classmate's sexual assault. Walton argues that this "special relationship" arose because he lost a substantial measure of his freedom to act because of the significant custodial component present in the regimen of the residential school, which caused him to become dependent on the School for his basic needs. As a resident, Walton slept at the School and took his meals at the School. The School strictly regulated when Walton could come and when he could go. Furthermore, the School severely restricted the conditions under which he could leave the campus. For the most part, the School determined his daily schedule of duties, classes, and activities when he was on campus. Walton alludes to the point that *DeShaney's* "special relationship" is created by "similar restraint of personal liberty" as that experienced by prisoners and involuntarily committed mental patients, and argues that his residence at the School, placed him under this type of "similar restraint of personal liberty." Thus, he argues that *DeShaney* requires recognition of a "special relationship" between the state and himself.

The record will support the factual contentions asserted by Walton. It is also true, as Walton argues, that *DeShaney* holds that due process is implicated when the state affirmatively restrains a person's liberty "through incarceration, institutionalization, or other similar restraint." *DeShaney*, 489 U.S. at 200. Still further, we can agree that Walton forfeited a portion of his autonomy when he became a resident of the School.

But far more important for our purposes today, the record also reflects that Walton attended the school through his own free will (or that of his parents) without any coercion by the state. Although Walton's freedom was curtailed, it was he who voluntarily subjected himself to the rules and supervision of the School officials. Walton's willful relinquishment of a small fraction of liberty simply is not comparable to that measure of almost total deprivation experienced by a prisoner or involuntarily committed mental patient. Nor do the facts establish that the state, through its affirmative acts, held Walton at the School involuntarily and against his will. To the contrary, the record shows that Walton attended this school voluntarily with the option of leaving at will, an option that was never withdrawn. We therefore cannot agree that Walton's status as a resident student places him within the narrow class of persons who are entitled to claim from the state a constitutional duty of protection from harm at the hands of private parties.

We think it is important to apply *DeShaney* as it is written. *DeShaney* emphasizes—as we emphasize at the very outset of this opinion—that extending the Due Process Clause to impose on the state the obligation to defend and to pay for the acts of non-state third parties is a burden not supported by the text or history of the Clause, nor by general principles of constitutional jurisprudence. Such an expansion of the state's liability for acts of third parties only can make constitutional sense—that is, holding a government accountable and liable for its official actions—when the state has effectively taken the plaintiff's liberty under terms that provide no realistic means of voluntarily terminating the state's custody and which thus deprives the plaintiff of the ability or opportunity to provide for his own care and safety. It is under such extreme circumstances that the state itself, by its affirmative act and pursuant to its own will, has effectively used its power to force a "special relationship," with respect to which it assumes a certain liability. In short, this "special relationship" does not arise solely because the state exercises custodial control over an individual when a person voluntarily resides in a state facility under its custodial rules. Consequently, we hold that no "special relationship" existed between Walton and Alexander. Since Alexander had no constitutional duty to protect Walton against his classmate's violence, the allegations that she failed to do so simply do not state a violation of the Due Process Clause.

...

In sum, we hold that a "special relationship" arises between a person and the state only when this person is involuntarily confined against his will through the affirmative exercise of state power. Absent this "special relationship," the state has no duty to protect nor liability from failing to protect a person under the due process clause of the Fourteenth Amendment from violence at the hands of a private actor ...[7]

PARKER, Circuit Judge, with whom POLITZ, Chief Judge and STEWART, Circuit Judge, join, concurring specially.

The notion that individuals have a fundamental substantive due process right to bodily integrity is beyond debate. It is also clear that the State[1] owes no general affirmative duty to its citizens to ensure that their rights do not come to harm by other means. What is not so clear is how the Court should resolve the tension often created by the violation of the individual right to bodily integrity by non-state actors under circumstances where the State's role is not strictly a passive one. The constitutional analysis in such circumstances should focus on the role of the State to determine whether a duty exists.

When the role of the State is such that an individual's liberty is limited by state action through incarceration or commitment to a state institution, a corresponding duty is created to assume responsibility for the safety and well-being of the person committed. Christopher Walton, a hearing-impaired minor, was not incarcerated or committed to an institution by the State of Mississippi, but neither was the State a passive player in the facts and circumstances that led to the violation of his bodily integrity. He resided in a state-controlled environment created by the State at the Mississippi School for the Deaf where Ms. Alma Alexander presided as superintendent.

Instead of examining the role of the State in this case, the majority has focused on the role of Christopher Walton's parents in choosing to enroll him in Ms. Alexander's school. Finding their action to be voluntary, the majority announces a bright line rule that represents an extreme constitutional viewpoint. The Court's holding is based on an erroneous reading of the Supreme Court's guidance in *DeShaney*, and draws an arbitrary, illogical, and formalistic line between those persons who are entitled to constitutional protection from the State's deliberate indifference to their safety and those who are not.

I cannot agree with the conclusion that the State had absolutely no duty to residential students of the Mississippi School for the Deaf to provide at least some level of protection from assault by other students. I would nonetheless reverse the denial of De-

---

7. We find no need to respond to the familiar arguments raised by the special concurrence. As we have made clear in this opinion, state tort laws are available for, and are the appropriate remedy for redress for the sorts of wrong suffered by Walton at the hands of his fellow student, a private actor who was no agent of the state.

1. The term "State" refers to state and local governmental entities and their agents. *DeShaney v. Winnebago County Dept. of Social Services*, 489 U.S. 189, 195 n.1 (1989).

fendant Alexander's Motion for Summary Judgment because there was no evidence that she was deliberately indifferent to Christopher Walton's safety, and thus there was no showing that the defendant breached the appropriate constitutional standard.

I.

The question presented in this case is whether the State by accepting custody of Walton and exercising extensive control over his day-to-day activities established such a "special relationship" with Walton as to give rise to an affirmative duty to protect him from injury by other students. Walton's assailant was not a state actor; he was another student. However, under the special relationship theory, it is the State's affirmative act of restraining an individual's freedom to act on his own behalf that is the deprivation of liberty triggering the protection of the Due Process Clause. Therefore, what this Court should do is determine whether, under the circumstances, the State sufficiently restrained Walton's personal liberty to trigger the corresponding duty to assume some level of responsibility for his safety and well-being.

The Supreme Court has recognized such a duty in the context of incarceration and involuntary commitment.[4] A duty of protection has also been recognized [by the Tenth and Eleventh Circuits] in cases where a child is involuntarily placed in a foster home. On the other hand, in *DeShaney* the Court found that the county department of social services had no duty to protect a child who was harmed by, and while in the custody of, his natural father.

The plaintiffs in *DeShaney* argued that the rationale of *Estelle* and *Youngberg*, should apply. In distinguishing these precedents, the Court noted that "[t]aken together [these cases] stand only for the proposition that when the State takes a person into its custody and holds him there against his will, the Constitution imposes upon it a corresponding duty to assume some responsibility for his safety and general well-being." Apparently focusing on this characterization of *Estelle* and *Youngberg*, the majority holds that a special relationship can exist between the State and a person "only when the person is involuntarily taken into state custody and held against his will through the affirmative power of the state[.]"

The majority gives the *DeShaney* holding a broad effect by defining the question presented this way: "whether the substantive component of the due process clause imposes on the state a duty of protection to non-incarcerated and non-institutionalized persons from the harmful acts of non-state actors." However, it is clear that the *DeShaney* court did not foreclose "special relationships" in all cases of non-incarcerated and non-institutionalized persons.

Although *Estelle* and *Youngberg* both involved persons who were taken into custody "involuntarily," the Court [in *DeShaney*] explained that the requisite deprivation could occur through "incarceration, institutionalization, or other similar restraint of personal liberty." The precise type of restraint that will create a corresponding affirmative duty was not spelled-out in *DeShaney*, but it seems clear that "similar re-

4. *See Youngberg v. Romeo*, 457 U.S. 307 (1982); *Estelle v. Gamble*, 429 U.S. 97 (1976).

straint of personal liberty" means that there may be circumstances other than those in *Estelle* and *Youngberg* that give rise to a constitutional duty to protect.

The majority's holding that custody must be "involuntary" and "against [a person's] will" is so restrictive that it precludes any type of custody short of incarceration or institutionalization giving rise to the duty of protection. In effect, the majority has confined the duty of protection to the circumstances found in *Estelle* and *Youngberg*. Such a narrow application of this duty clearly was not contemplated in *DeShaney*.

II.

... This Court's previous opinions have recognized that a special relationship is created when the State "so restrains an individual's liberty that it renders him unable to care for himself." This standard does not limit the affirmative duty of protection to cases where a person is taken into custody "involuntarily," and, instead, is more appropriately read to focus on the conditions of the particular custodial relationship.... In addition, *Leffall v. Dallas Independent School Dist.*[, 28 F.3d 521 (5th Cir. 1994),] provides the majority no support. In *Leffall*, a student was killed by random gunfire in the high school parking lot after a school dance. In holding that the school had no duty to provide for the student's safety, this Court noted that *Leffall* did not involve a school for the disabled or a boarding school with twenty-four hour custody of its students, and therefore did not involve the same level of custodial control found in *Walton*. [*Id.* at 529.] Thus, our previous decisions do not support the bright-line rule adopted today by the majority.

...

III.

By requiring that the State take a person into custody involuntarily before gaining a duty to protect that person, the majority has arbitrarily limited due process rights in a way that cannot accurately reflect the nature of the custodial control actually exercised by the State. Rather than simply asking whether a person entered state custody "voluntarily," we should examine the nature of the custodial relationship that existed between the State and the plaintiff.

Under the majority's rule, the State could treat differently a foster child whose parents admit they cannot properly care for the child and willingly turn the child over to foster care from a child who is taken from unwilling parents. The same distinction would exist between voluntarily and involuntarily committed mental patients, even though their circumstances following commitment would show identical levels of state control, and thus identical restraint of personal liberty. The question is not so much how the individual got into state custody, but to what extent the State exercises dominion and control over that individual.

Commentators have been critical of "involuntariness" as a threshold requirement in the context of the custodial control exercised in public schools. For example, Professor Karen Blum has stated that

> [a]ny insistence that a legal compulsion to attend school be present before an affirmative duty to protect is recognized would result in the drawing of

> irrational and arbitrary classifications defining the circumstances and situations in which students are afforded constitutional protection. The key to the duty owed should be the state's assumption of responsibility for the care and control of students while they are physically present in a state-created and controlled environment.[19]

Even in the context of a regular public school, teachers and school officials exercise extensive control over the activities of the children in their custody, and during the school-day those same officials are in the exclusive position to provide for the protection of those children. As one member of this Court recently observed, "[t]o suggest that parents somehow are in a better position than the schools to protect their children from the ravages of weapons smuggled onto campus during the school day is cruelly irrational. To hope that students who are unarmed can protect themselves from the depredation of armed criminals in their midst is ridiculous." [*Johnson v. Dallas Independent School Dist.*, 38 F.3d 198, 203 n.7 (5th Cir. 1994).]

Instead of asking whether a person was taken into custody involuntarily, we should consider several factors to determine whether a special relationship exists in a particular case: 1) the authority and discretion state actors have to control the environment and the behavior of the individuals in their custody, 2) the responsibilities assumed by the State, 3) the extent to which an individual in state custody must rely on the State to provide for his or her basic needs, and 4) the degree of control actually exercised by the State in a given situation.

The majority concedes that Walton lived at the School for the Deaf five days a week. In fact, the School controlled when he went to bed and when he awoke, and where he slept in relation to other students. The School controlled when and where he ate his meals and even what he ate. The School decided when he went to class and when he could recreate. The School also strictly regulated when and under what conditions Walton could come and go.

It is certain that Walton depended on school officials to provide for his basic needs while he was in their custody. A child with Walton's handicap would be particularly dependent on the adults with whom he resided. In other words, if the School did not provide for his basic needs while he was in its functional custody, those needs would go unmet.

There can be no doubt that extensive control measures were required in the context of a residential facility for the deaf. Nor can there be any doubt that the School had the authority and discretion to exercise control and restraint over the activities of the students in its custody. By the same token, however, the State necessarily assumed some responsibility for the students' safety and general well-being when it accepted them into its custody and imposed restraints on their ability to act on their own behalf. Under these circumstances, the control exercised by the School and the re-

---

19. Karen M. Blum, *DeShaney: Custody, Creation of Danger, and Culpability*, 27 Loy. L.A. L.Rev. 435, 450 (1994)....

straints imposed on Walton's personal liberty were sufficient to meet the *DeShaney* threshold. Yet, because Walton was not seized by the State and forced to attend the residential school against his will, the majority holds that the School had no duty with respect to Walton's safety and well-being.

IV.

The majority's zeal to ensure that those state actors entrusted with the responsibility to care for and protect our most vulnerable citizens may do so with constitutional impunity—regardless of their conduct—produces a result that surely must appear absurd to the average citizen. Under the holding of this opinion, law abiding, tax paying citizens who, because they may be simply obeying the compulsory attendance laws or because they have no other economic choice, deliver a child to the care, custody and control of the State, do so at their own risk. At the same time, those who find themselves in the care, custody and control of the State because they are criminals are wrapped in the protective cloak of the constitution.

For further discussion

Note the procedural posture of *Walton*. Alexander took an interlocutory appeal from the denial of qualified immunity. An interlocutory appeal is an appeal taken before final judgment is entered in the lawsuit and is available only in limited circumstances. This is a common procedural mechanism for seeking appellate review of qualified immunity. Because the doctrine insulates government defendants from litigation unless the plaintiff establishes that the defendant violated a constitutional right that was clearly established at the time of the alleged incident, a government defendant usually can immediately appeal the district court's denial of qualified immunity. *Harlow v. Fitzgerald*, 457 U.S. 800, 818–19 (1982); *Mitchell v. Forsyth*, 472 U.S. 511, 528–29 (1985). *See* Chapter 11.

Questions to guide reading of *Nicini*

1. What dicta from *DeShaney* did *Nicini* rely on to frame the issue of what factual circumstances might create a "special relationship"?
2. Why did *Nicini* hold that foster care is analogous to prisoners and institutionalized persons? Why did *Nicini* recognize that the analogy between foster care and institutionalized persons isn't perfect?
3. Did *Nicini* and *Walton* accord different significance to the voluntariness of placement with the state? Why did *Nicini* nevertheless hold the Plaintiff's placement created a "special relationship"? Are you persuaded by the analogy of the placement in *Nicini* to traditional foster care?
4. Based on your reading of *Walton*, how do you think the Fifth Circuit would have analyzed the *Nicini* facts? How would the *Walton* dissent have analyzed the *Nicini* facts?

5. Assume you represent a local government agency similar to the Division of Youth and Family services in *Nicini*. Assume *Nicini* is binding in your jurisdiction. Would you make any recommendations to your client based on *Nicini*?

Nicini v. Morra

212 F.3d 798 (3d Cir. 2000)

SLOVITER, Circuit Judge.

Anthony Nicini, Jr., filed suit under 42 U.S.C. § 1983 and state tort law against Frank Cyrus, a Family Services Specialist with the New Jersey Department of Human Services, Division of Youth and Family Services ("DYFS"), and other defendants, alleging they violated his constitutional rights because he was abused by the person with whom he was staying while in DYFS custody.

I. FACTS

In February 1990, fifteen-year-old Anthony Nicini, Jr., was admitted to the [hospital] after an apparent suicide attempt. DYFS became involved when [the hospital] notified it of Nicini's allegations that his father had physically abused him. Two DYFS caseworkers responded to [the hospital], and Nicini told them that he was afraid of his father, who "punches a lot" and "always hits with closed fist." Nicini also said that he had attempted suicide before. DYFS notified the prosecutor's office of Nicini's allegations and assisted his mother in obtaining a temporary restraining order against Nicini's father. DYFS also assigned caseworker Frank Cyrus to Nicini's case.

Nicini continued to have difficulty at home and in school. According to a DYFS report dated September 27, 1990, Nicini slashed his wrists that month in an apparent suicide attempt and thereafter left home after an argument with his mother. The report states that Nicini "has no where to go and needs placement." DYFS was informed on October 9, 1990, that Nicini was not at school and that he had previously told the assistant principal that he would not return home. On October 10, 1990, DYFS received a call from the police in Cherry Hill, New Jersey, that Nicini had been located and that he had repeated his refusal to return home and again stated that his father was abusive. That same day, a DYFS caseworker contacted Nicini's mother, who said that she did not want Nicini to return home, and his father, who could not identify any relatives with whom Nicini could stay. Nicini's father came to DYFS to sign a foster care placement agreement.[2]

DYFS placed Nicini in the foster home of Dennis Armento but Nicini ran away on or before November 2, 1990. After Nicini was located, his aunt, Catherine Livingston, agreed to DYFS's request that Nicini stay with her. On or before December 31, 1990, Nicini ran away once again. Livingston had apparently become ill and DYFS

---

2. Although the parties have not educated us as to the meaning of this agreement, it appears that "[a] child may come into the custody of [DYFS] and be placed in foster care pursuant to either a voluntary-placement agreement or a court order." ...

arranged for Nicini to stay with Bonnie Nicini, another aunt. Cyrus then arranged that Nicini be evaluated by a psychiatrist, Dr. Charles Trigiani. Dr. Trigiani was unsure after Nicini's first appointment on January 3, 1991, whether Nicini required inpatient psychiatric care but agreed to recommend Nicini's evaluation at [the hospital]. On January 10, 1991, Cyrus informed Nicini's mother of Dr. Trigiani's recommendation and requested that she bring Nicini to [the hospital].

What happened thereafter is not clear from the record or the appendices submitted with the parties' briefs, but apparently Nicini was not admitted to [the hospital] at that time. However, a DYFS report dated January 30, 1991 notes that Nicini was at [the] Hospital with an infected hand and might require admission to treat the infection. Bonnie Nicini reportedly stated that the plan was to hospitalize Nicini for depression. The report also states that when the hospital sought consent from Nicini's mother for his treatment, she refused and claimed he was in DYFS custody. At some point thereafter, Nicini was transferred to [the hospital's] psychiatric unit for evaluation. On February 5, 1991, DYFS learned that Nicini had run away from the psychiatric unit after [the hospital] recommended the possibility of admitting Nicini to treat his depression.

Nicini ran to the home of Edward and Dolores Morra in Cherry Hill, New Jersey. Nicini's older brother Danny had gone to school with their children and had stayed with them while experiencing similar family problems. On February 9, 1991, the police notified DYFS that they had located Nicini at the Morra home. According to a DYFS incident report, Nicini had been taken to [the hospital] but was "ready for discharge." A DYFS caseworker (not Cyrus) contacted Catherine Livingston, who stated that she had known Nicini was at the Morra home and that she would not permit him to return to her home. The caseworker then spoke to Nicini's father, who expressed his belief that the Morras were "not [a] good placement but [who] *agreed to weekend placement*." (emphasis in original). After being given the option of taking Nicini home or locating a relative with whom Nicini could stay, Nicini's father told the caseworker to speak to Livingston. She, of course, had already refused to take Nicini back.

The caseworker then permitted Nicini, who "was refusing to go anywhere else," to return to the Morra home that day, Saturday, February 9, 1991. The incident report states that "Frank Cyrus will contact[the Morras] on Monday [February 11]."

Between February 9, 1991 and February 28, 1991, Cyrus visited Nicini twice at the Morra home. He also had telephone contacts with Nicini and the Morras. Cyrus's first visit was apparently on Monday, February 11, 1991 (expert report). It was Cyrus's overall impression that "everything was positive," and that everything "point[ed] towards [Nicini] doing well there and becoming stabilized and progressing.... Additionally, a counselor from an outreach center visited Nicini once a week at the Morra home. During that same time period, Cyrus performed a perpetrator ("PERP") check on the Morras, which would have revealed any criminal record of sexual abuse in the state of New Jersey, including any reports of such abuse to DYFS. The PERP check revealed nothing.

Cyrus interviewed the Morras during a home visit. He did not remember asking whether they had ever had any contact with any law enforcement agency but he recalled asking Edward Morra if anything would prevent him from becoming a foster parent, and Morra replied in the negative.

On February 28, 1991, Nicini appeared at a hearing before the Honorable Vincent D. Segal in the Family Part of the Chancery Division of the Superior Court of New Jersey. Although the record does not make clear the purpose of the hearing, the proceedings were apparently related both to certain criminal conduct by Nicini and to where he should be placed. As a result of the hearing, Judge Segal sentenced Nicini to two years probation and also concluded that Nicini should remain with the Morras.

Cyrus was present and testified at the hearing along with Nicini, Nicini's mother, and Catherine Livingston, Nicini's aunt. Also present were the Assistant Prosecutor for Camden County, New Jersey, and Ronald DeSimone, an attorney representing Nicini. Cyrus informed the court of Nicini's prior placements and that Nicini:

> is currently with a friend and the family, the Morra family. He's not with a foster family. Tony was with the foster family initially, Mr. Dennis Armento, and he left the home unofficially.... Tony found his way to the Morras, who I guess was a friend of his. The Morras indicated they would—they knew him, they liked him and they wouldn't mind him staying there. He's been there now for a couple of weeks. They have indicated that he's doing very well there, no problems. But that is not an official foster home, that's an unofficial home.

In response to the court's query whether the Morras would qualify as para-foster parents, Cyrus stated:

> Yes they would, your Honor. We've—so far the only thing I've done is a perp check, perpetrator check, and there's nothing that's come up. There's no—nothing we've seen in terms of any problem with the law. Although I think, and Mrs. Nicini can speak for herself, I think she has some objections about it on a full time basis. But the family seems to show an interest towards Tony, they have said they wouldn't mind keeping him—keeping him on a temporary basis. He has been stable since he's been with them. But like I say that's—right now they are not an official foster family, although I'm sure they would—they would apply for para-foster custody if the parents are willing to let them.

When Judge Segal asked Nicini's mother for her comments, she stated as to the Morras:

> [T]hey have harbored my oldest son on several occasions when he had taken off.... I don't know them personally, only—only what I had heard. My oldest daughter knows—goes to school with kids that are friends with Eric Morra, their son, which I believe is 16 or 17, and I've been told that he's into drugs. I don't know if it's true or not, but it's just what I've heard. I don't know, something just seems strange about these people, why they would—if they don't know Tony, why they would even take him in.

Nicini's attorney suggested to the court, in light of these concerns, that Nicini "should also be monitored for drugs periodically and—and maybe something should be looked in with this Morra family, in light of what Mrs. Nicini had said I think maybe a closer investigation on whether or not that's an appropriate placement...."

Nicini's own testimony regarding his stay with the Morras was positive. After recounting the difficulties he experienced with his parents and with his prior placements, Nicini described his relationship with the Morras:

> I don't love them or anything, but they're people I can talk to. I mean ever since I been there almost every night I've been up talking to Mr. Morra, his name is Ed. I've been up most of the time talking to him about how I feel about my parents and the way I've been living and how I've been treated and all.

Nicini also told Judge Segal that the Morras were tutoring him until he was re-enrolled in school.

Judge Segal then summarized the history of physical abuse at the hands of Nicini's father and summarized a report prepared by Nicini's outreach counselor (not Cyrus), which stated that Nicini was no longer suicidal and had made a "fine adjustment to the location where he's presently located." Judge Segal ruled that Nicini would "come[] under the care and supervision" of DYFS, that he would remain with the Morras "for so long as [DYFS] thinks that's an appropriate placement," and that "[u]nder no circumstances is [DYFS] to return the boy to the home of his parents without the authority of the Court[.]" Judge Segal specifically declined to order drug monitoring despite the request of Nicini's attorney because there was no indication that drugs were involved in the matter.

The record is once again sparse regarding the time period after the February 28, 1991 Family Court hearing. On March 11, 1991, less than two weeks after the hearing, Cyrus forwarded to the Morras an application to become para-foster parents. The para-foster application process, as summarized in Cyrus's letter to the Morras, requires completion of an application form, a financial statement, an authorization for release of information, a police reference form, and an agreement between the state of New Jersey, DYFS, and the foster parent. The applicant must also schedule a visit to DYFS for fingerprinting, and DYFS conducts a Home Study Evaluation. The applicant's fingerprints are used to conduct a National Crime Institute Check (NCIC). The Morras never returned the application, and, as we know from hindsight, there was no opportunity for Cyrus to follow up.

On March 15, 1991, four days after Cyrus sent the application to the Morras, Nicini fled the Morra home. He later told investigators that since the second or third day of his arrival there, Edward Morra had been providing him with drugs and alcohol and assaulting him sexually. Further investigation revealed that Edward Morra had been convicted in New York in 1975 for corrupting the morals of a minor and for distribution of controlled substances to minors. In March 1994, following the events described here, Edward Morra was convicted in New Jersey of sexual assault and is currently serving a forty-year state prison term with a period of parole ineligibility of twenty years.

...

NICINI'S SECTION 1983 CLAIM

Nicini's section 1983 claim rests on the Due Process Clause of the Fourteenth Amendment. He invokes the substantive component of due process, which "protects individual liberty against 'certain government actions regardless of the fairness of the procedures used to implement them.'" *Collins v. City of Harker Heights, Tex.*, 503 U.S. 115, 125 (1992) (quoting *Daniels v. Williams*, 474 U.S. 327, 331 (1986)). Specifically, Nicini alleges that Cyrus ... deprived him of "the right to be free from the infliction of unnecessary pain or abuse ... and the fundamental right to physical safety." ... [Cyrus] contends, however, that Nicini has not established a constitutional violation because "[t]here is no way that Mr. Cyrus should or could have known about the tragic events that would occur at the Morra home."

A.

As a general proposition, a state's failure to protect an individual against private violence does not constitute a violation of due process. *DeShaney*, 489 U.S. at 202.... However, the Court recognized that "in certain limited circumstances the Constitution imposes upon the State affirmative duties of care and protection with respect to particular individuals." *Id.* at 198. As examples of situations in which the state has such a duty, the Court cited its decision in *Estelle v. Gamble*, 429 U.S. 97 (1976), which held that the Eighth Amendment's prohibition against cruel and unusual punishment required the state "to provide adequate medical care to incarcerated prisoners," *DeShaney*, 489 U.S. at 198, and *Youngberg v. Romeo*, 457 U.S. 307 (1982), which held that substantive due process "requires the State to provide involuntarily committed mental patients with such services as are necessary to ensure their 'reasonable safety' from themselves and others," *DeShaney*, 489 U.S. at 199 (citation omitted).

The state's affirmative "dut[y] of care and protection," *id.* at 198, in those cases stemmed "not from the State's knowledge of the individual's predicament or from its expressions of intent to help him, but from the limitation which it has imposed on his freedom to act on his own behalf." *Id.* at 200. In holding that the state did not have such a "special relationship" with Joshua DeShaney, the Court explained that "[w]hile the State may have been aware of the dangers that Joshua faced in the free world, it played no part in their creation, nor did it do anything to render him any more vulnerable to them." *Id.* at 201.

Of particular significance to the matter before us, the Court also suggested that "[h]ad the State by the affirmative exercise of its power removed Joshua from free society and placed him in a foster home operated by its agents, we might have a situation sufficiently analogous to incarceration or institutionalization to give rise to an affirmative duty to protect." *Id.* at 201 n.9....

After *DeShaney*, many of our sister courts of appeals held that foster children have a substantive due process right to be free from harm at the hands of state-regulated foster parents. *See, e.g., Lintz v. Skipski*, 25 F.3d 304, 305 (6th Cir. 1994); *Norfleet v. Arkansas Dep't of Human Servs.*, 989 F.2d 289, 293 (8th Cir. 1993); *Yvonne L. v. New Mexico Dep't of Human Servs.*, 959 F.2d 883, 891–93 (10th Cir. 1992); *K.H. v. Morgan*, 914 F.2d 846, 848–49 (7th Cir. 1990). These courts have accepted the analogy between persons the state places in foster care and those it incarcerates or institutionalizes. *See, e.g., K.H.*, 914 F.2d at 849 ("Once the state assumes custody of a person, it owes him a rudimentary duty of safekeeping...."); *Yvonne L.*, 959 F.2d at 891–93 (discussing and approving cases imposing liability in foster care context).

We have suggested, although never directly held, that state actors owe a duty to children placed in foster care. In *D.R.*, 972 F.2d at 1368–73, we held that a public high school student who was allegedly sexually molested by other students during school hours could not maintain a claim against school officials based on a "special relationship" theory. We held that public high school students were not comparable to prisoners or the involuntarily committed because "parents remain the [students'] primary caretakers," *id.* at 1371, and because students "may turn to persons unrelated to the state for help on a daily basis," *id.* at 1372. We also noted that this court has principally read *DeShaney* as "setting out a test of physical custody." *Id.* at 1370.

...

In *D.R.*, we recognized that "some courts have imposed a constitutional duty to protect foster children by analogy to involuntarily institutionalized individuals," 972 F.2d at 1372, and stated, albeit in *dictum*:

> A relationship between the state and foster children arises out of the state's affirmative act in finding the children and placing them with state-approved families. By so doing, the state assumes an important continuing, if not immediate, responsibility for the child's well-being. In addition, the child's placement renders him or her dependent upon the state, through the foster family, to meet the child's basic needs.

Id. (citations omitted)....

We find our discussion in *D.R.* and the numerous decisions of the other courts of appeals on this issue persuasive. Foster children, like the incarcerated or the involuntarily committed, are "placed ... in a custodial environment ... [and are] unable to seek alternative living arrangements." *Taylor v. Ledbetter*, 818 F.2d 791, 795 (11th Cir. 1987) (*en banc*). We now hold that when the state places a child in state-regulated foster care, the state has entered into a special relationship with that child which imposes upon it certain affirmative duties. The failure to perform such duties can give rise, under sufficiently culpable circumstances, to liability under section 1983.

We recognize that the analogy between foster children on the one hand and prisoners and institutionalized persons on the other is incomplete. For example, foster children, especially older ones, enjoy a greater degree of freedom and are more likely to be able to take steps to ensure their own safety. Nonetheless, any distinctions between children placed in foster care and the prisoners at issue in *Estelle* or the institutionalized mentally retarded persons at issue in *Youngberg* are matters of degree rather than of kind. *See Norfleet*, 989 F.2d at 292 (although there is a closer relationship between the state and prisoners than between the state and foster children, "the situations are sufficiently analogous"). In each of these cases the state, by affirmative act, renders the individual substantially "dependent upon the state ... to meet [his or her] basic needs." *D.R.*, 972 F.2d at 1372.

We are aware that Nicini came to stay with the Morras on his own initiative and that the Morras were not officially approved by the state as either foster or para-foster parents. However, Cyrus does not contest that Nicini was in DYFS custody throughout the relevant period. Furthermore, the record is replete with evidence that Nicini was substantially dependent upon DYFS and that DYFS acquiesced in Nicini's stay at the Morra home. At least by October 10, 1990, when Nicini's father signed a foster care placement agreement, DYFS was able to arrange for his foster placement. At some point, the Superior Court of New Jersey awarded custody of Nicini to DYFS and DHS. Nicini was thereafter placed on several occasions with DYFS-approved foster parents and with relatives. It also appears that after the police located Nicini at the Morra home and took him to [the hospital], DYFS returned him to their home over the objections of his aunt and his father.[8] Under these facts, we believe Nicini's situation is sufficiently analogous to a foster care placement to fall within the "special relationship" exception to *DeShaney*.

"Para-foster" care is not defined in the statute or regulations governing DYFS. The current regulations, however, refer to "para care," defined as "a service involving the placement of a child in a private family home by anyone other than DYFS, and which DYFS approves for payment after an approval process is completed." ... Unlike foster parents, para-foster parents are "approved by DYFS for the income maintenance and services to [a] particular child and not for the placement of other foster children." *Id.* Nicini does not suggest that DYFS was precluded from approving his stay with the Morras if they were neither foster parents or para-foster parents.

B.

Having established that Nicini has alleged a protected interest and a sufficient relationship with the state to state a cause of action under section 1983, we turn to the District Court's determination that summary judgment was appropriate because Cyrus's actions did not amount to a violation of Nicini's constitutional rights. We must first determine what level of conduct is egregious enough to amount to a constitutional violation and, then, whether there is sufficient evidence that Cyrus's conduct rose to that level.

8. Livingston seems to have objected on the ground that Nicini "was a sick boy who needed hospitalization." The DYFS incident report that documents the objection of Nicini's father does not contain the basis for his objection (he apparently testified at his deposition that he informed a DYFS caseworker named Diana Smith of his belief that the Morra home was a "haven for runaway juveniles," but it clearly states that he agreed to weekend placement with the Morras. The same report states that DYFS had "custody of Anthony through court order."

We begin with the decision in *County of Sacramento v. Lewis*, 523 U.S. 833 (1998) [which] emphasized that "'[t]he touchstone of due process is protection of the individual against arbitrary action of government.'" *Lewis*, 523 U.S. at 845.... Mere negligence is never sufficient for substantive due process liability. *See Daniels v. Williams*, 474 U.S. 327 (1986). Under *Lewis*, substantive due process liability attaches only to executive action that is "so ill-conceived or malicious that it 'shocks the conscience.'" *Miller v. City of Philadelphia*, 174 F.3d 368, 375 (3d Cir. 1999) (quoting *Lewis*, 523 U.S. at 846).

...

Lewis therefore makes clear that a plaintiff seeking to establish a constitutional violation must demonstrate that the official's conduct "shocks the conscience" in the particular setting in which that conduct occurred. In some circumstances, conduct that is deliberately indifferent will shock the conscience. Indeed, in the foster care context, most of the courts of appeals have applied the deliberate indifference standard, although they have defined that standard in slightly different ways. *See, e.g., White v. Chambliss*, 112 F.3d 731, 737 (4th Cir. 1997) (liability if defendant was "plainly placed on notice of a danger and chose to ignore the danger"); *Taylor*, 818 F.2d at 796 (foster child must show "actual knowledge of abuse or that agency personnel deliberately failed to learn what was occurring in the foster home"); *Doe v. New York City Dep't of Soc. Servs.*, 649 F.2d 134, 145 (2d Cir. 1981) (deliberate indifference "cannot exist absent some knowledge triggering an affirmative duty to act.... Defendants may be held liable [for] ... deliberate indifference to a known injury, a known risk, or a specific duty").

In *Miller*, we evaluated the actions of a social worker who after receiving allegations of abuse separated a child from her natural parent under a standard that "exceed[ed] ... deliberate indifference." *Miller*, 174 F.3d at 375. We held that the worker would be liable only if his conduct reached "a level of gross negligence or arbitrariness that indeed shocks the conscience." *Id.* at 375–76 (quotation omitted). We also stressed that although "a social worker acting to separate parent and child does not usually act in the hyperpressurized environment of a prison riot or a high speed chase..., he or she rarely will have the luxury of proceeding in a deliberate fashion." *Id.* at 375. Cyrus, unlike the social worker in *Miller*, had time "to make unhurried judgments" in investigating whether to permit Nicini to remain with the Morras. *Lewis*, 523 U.S. at 853. In the context of this case, we agree that Cyrus's actions in investigating the Morra home should be judged under the deliberate indifference standard.

In *Farmer v. Brennan*, 511 U.S. 825 (1994), the Court clarified the deliberate indifference standard applicable in suits challenging prison conditions under the Eighth Amendment. It adopted a subjective standard of liability consistent with recklessness as that term is defined in criminal law. The Court held that "a prison official cannot be found liable ... unless the official knows of and disregards an excessive risk to inmate health and safety; the official must both be aware of facts from which the inference could be drawn that a substantial risk of serious harm exists, and he must also draw the inference." *Id.* at 837.

This case does not require us to determine whether an official's failure to act in light of a risk of which the official should have known, as opposed to failure to act in light of an actually known risk, constitutes deliberately indifferent conduct in this setting.[10] We will assume arguendo that Nicini's proposed standard of "should have known" is applicable. Nevertheless, as *Lewis* makes clear, the relevant inquiry is whether the defendant's conduct "shocks the conscience."

Under the circumstances of this case, we cannot agree that Cyrus's conduct meets that standard. To the contrary, we conclude that Cyrus's conduct in investigating the Morras amounted, at most, to negligence. For the same reason, we need not consider whether failure to perform a specific duty can ever amount to deliberate indifference, *see Taylor*, 818 F.2d at 797; *Doe*, 649 F.2d at 145, as there is no evidence that Cyrus failed to perform any required duty.

C.

...

On appeal, Nicini contends that the District Court too narrowly construed Cyrus's responsibility by looking to whether Cyrus knew or suspected that Morra had a history of abusing children rather than whether Cyrus knew or suspected that the placement was unsafe ... In his affidavit, Cyrus stated:

> The DYFS policies and procedures required that I conduct a perpretrator [sic] "PERP" check with the DYFS Central Registry when a child ends up at a home which is not a DYFS placement. I conducted one. The PERP check revealed no criminal information regarding the Morras. DYFS can not access National Crime Institute Check ("NCIC") ... nor a State criminal background check.

Nicini does not argue that Cyrus failed to act in accordance with applicable DYFS policy and procedure.

To establish Cyrus's liability, Nicini offered only the report of Dr. Atkins, the psychologist he proffered as an expert, that Cyrus should have done more than was re-

10. We recognize that the deliberate indifference standard applicable in *Farmer* to challenges to prison conditions does not necessarily apply to the substantive due process claims of a foster child. *See City of Revere v. Massachusetts Gen. Hosp.*, 463 U.S. 239, 244 (1983) (pretrial detainees entitled under due process to "at least as great" protection as is afforded convicted prisoners under the Eighth Amendment); *Spencer v. Knapheide Truck Equip. Co.*, 183 F.3d 902, 906–07 (8th Cir. 1999) (declining to decide whether pretrial detainee's claim should be judged by *Farmer's* subjective deliberate indifference standard or by objective standard); *cf. Boring v. Kozakiewicz*, 833 F.2d 468, 472 (3d Cir. 1987) (suggesting that "[t]o apply the Eighth Amendment standard to mentally retarded persons would be little short of barbarous"). Nevertheless, we note that after *Farmer* the courts of appeals have shown a tendency to apply a purely subjective deliberate indifference standard outside the Eighth Amendment context. *See, e.g., Gant v. Wallingford Bd. of Educ.*, 195 F.3d 134, 141 n. 6 (2d Cir. 1999) (rejecting "should have known" standard in due process action challenging conduct of school officials and other defendants in responding to complaints of racial harassment against student); *Qian v. Kautz*, 168 F.3d 949, 955–56 (7th Cir. 1999) (detainee's due process claims judged by *Farmer* standard); *Hare v. City of Corinth, Miss.*, 74 F.3d 633, 648 (5th Cir. 1996) (same).

quired of him by DYFS's practices and procedures. The relevant portion of that report states:

> In light of the information available to Frank Cyrus at the time of his investigation of the Morra household, particularly the criminal record of Morra which was a matter of public record and which could have been obtained by an appropriate national police record search with the permission of Morra being required by Cyrus prior to placement, it is the opinion of this clinician that this investigation was conducted with total indifference to all available facts that were clearly material to any social worker who would be called upon to make such a placement.

As is evident, Dr. Atkins believed that Cyrus should have undertaken a national police search (which the psychologist recognized required Morra's consent) even though the Morras were not applicants to become an official DYFS foster family or para-foster family. Dr. Atkins never explained how Cyrus could have performed what the psychologist termed the "appropriate national police record search" without Morra's cooperation and never responded to Cyrus's sworn statement that he could not access the National Crime Information Center.

Unable to point to a state requirement or a DYFS policy or procedure violated by Cyrus, Nicini argues that Cyrus nonetheless should have been on notice that a more detailed investigation of the Morras was required. As to the period from the date DYFS learned where Nicini was, February 9, 1991, and the date of the Family Court hearing that approved Nicini's temporary placement status, February 28, 1991, the record reveals consistent monitoring and oversight by Cyrus and DYFS. On February 9, Nicini was located at the Morra home and, after being taken to [the hospital], "was refusing to go anywhere else" than back to the Morra home. On that day, a DYFS caseworker visited with the Morras and made detailed notes about the condition of the home and the Morra family's willingness "to help Tony." Cyrus visited Nicini twice during the following nineteen days and also made contact by telephone during that period. An outreach counselor also visited Nicini once a week and filed a report that supported Cyrus's testimony at the February 28 hearing that Nicini appeared to be doing well there.

Nicini did not tell Cyrus of the sexual assaults during the visits Cyrus made with him or during the phone conversations Cyrus made to him while he was at the Morra home, although the assaults began within two or three days of Nicini's arrival there. Nicini, albeit a minor, was not of such tender years that he was unable to communicate this information. He was fifteen years old and had left an earlier placement to find the Morras on his own. Significantly, although Nicini testified at the February 28, 1991 hearing he did not inform the court of the assaults. Nor, apparently, did he inform his attorney, who likewise mentioned nothing of the assaults at the hearing. Thus, the record reveals little from which Cyrus could have inferred that Nicini faced a "substantial risk of serious harm." *Farmer*, 511 U.S. at 837.

...

Nicini argues that Cyrus should have elicited alcohol and substance abuse through a urine analysis. But Nicini completely ignores the fact that the judge heard Mrs. Nicini's objections and expressly declined to require drug monitoring as requested by Nicini's attorney because there was "no indication that drugs are involved in this matter." The judge then approved placement of Nicini at the Morra home, specifically holding that Nicini would "come[ ] under the care and supervision" of DYFS and that he would remain at the Morras as long as DYFS thought it "appropriate." Nicini points to nothing else in the post-hearing period that should have put Cyrus or DYFS on notice that continued placement with the Morras was inappropriate.

In her vigorous dissent, our colleague would have us second-guess Cyrus's actions from hindsight. That is not our task. Nor is it called for in the circumstances of this case. The dissent relies heavily on the report by Dr. Atkins to assert that despite his compliance with DYFS policies Cyrus should be liable for failing to engage in a "heightened level of inquiry, interview and investigation." But Dr. Atkins, who never interviewed the persons involved, focuses "particularly" on Cyrus's failure to obtain Morra's consent to a criminal background check without pointing to specific facts from which Cyrus should have inferred that such a check was necessary. The fact that Nicini's "problems went well beyond those of the average troubled juvenile" under DYFS care and supervision, furnished Cyrus no clue about the appropriateness *vel non* of the Morra home as a placement. Given that the only reason Cyrus had to question the appropriateness of the Morra home was the suspicions of Nicini's mother and father, Nicini's insistence on remaining at the Morra home, and Cyrus's first-hand impression that Nicini was "doing well there," an impression corroborated by Nicini's TRIS worker and by Nicini himself at the hearing before Judge Segal, a jury could not permissibly conclude that Cyrus's investigation was so inadequate as to manifest deliberate indifference to Nicini's rights.

Nor are we persuaded by the cases cited by the dissent in which other courts determined a jury could reasonably find deliberate indifference because the facts in those cases are not analogous to those in this case. It may be dramatic to attempt to analogize Cyrus to a caseworker who "allow[s] a child to starve before his eyes," ... but, so far as the record reveals, there was nothing "before [Cyrus's] eyes" that suggested that Nicini faced a substantial risk of serious harm. To the contrary, Nicini's TRIS worker confirmed that while at the Morra home Nicini was no longer suicidal, no longer depressed, and appeared to be adjusting well.

The evidence adduced by Nicini, even when interpreted most favorably to him, not only falls short of the demanding standard for deliberate indifference set forth in *Farmer*, it also fails to establish that Cyrus was more than negligent, if it even establishes that.

Child Protective Service Workers Walk a Constitutional Tightrope

Plaintiff claims social worker intervened too soon

Mother claimed social worker removed children from her custody on insufficient evidence and without adequate process (14th Amendment procedural and substantive due process)[1]

Child claimed social workers directed forcible removal of himself, then a minor, based on 3 complaints of alleged neglect (4th Amendment)[2]

Parents and children claimed social workers removed children without a court order or evidence that the children were in immediate danger (4th Amendment)[3]

1. Miller v. City of Philadelphia, 174 F.3d 368 (3d Cir. 1999).
2. Brokaw v. Mercer, 235 F.3d 1000 (7th Cir. 2000).
3. Gates v. Texas Dep't of Protective & Reg. Servs., 537 F.3d 404 (5th Cir. 2008).

Plaintiff claims social worker intervened too late

Mother claimed social worker failed to take action in the face of evidence that custodial father was abusing child (14th Amendment substantive due process)[1]

Child's estate claimed social worker failed to investigate suspicious behavior by parent who adopted child from state's custody (14th Amendment substantive due process, special relationship doctrine)[2]

1. Deshaney v. Winnebago County Dep't of Soc. Servs., 489 U.S. 189 (1989).
2. Johnson ex. rel. Estate of Cano v. Holmes, 455 F.3d 1133 (10th Cir. 2006).

Exercise 4-C

You are a lawyer for a local government agency responsible for child protective services. The head of the agency is a Mayoral appointee and a social worker. He believes in maximum flexibility in structuring living arrangements for children who, as a result of agency action, are no longer living with their families. To help these children overcome their histories of neglect or abuse, he believes in allowing the child a say in deciding where to be placed, whether the placement is with a government-approved foster parent, a member of the child's family, or a friend of the child. *Nicini* was decided this morning and is binding in your jurisdiction. The head of the agency just called you to ask what *Nicini* means for the agency's decisions about placing children who cannot stay with their parents in their own homes. How will you answer?

For further discussion

DeShaney only rejected a federal substantive due process claim against the social worker. Even in the absence of a federal constitutional claim, there are other ways to sanction a caseworker or social worker who does not adequately perform his or her duties and there are other legal remedies.

State tort law remedies

The Court in *DeShaney* specifically recognized the possibility that state law tort remedies could be pursued against the social worker—if permitted under that state's statute waiving sovereign immunity from suit with respect to tort claims brought against state and local employees.

Employment sanctions

A government employee who fails to perform assigned duties can be fired, suspended, or demoted, subject to procedural due process requirements and any union or contractual restrictions. *See* Chapter 8 (procedural due process rights of public employees).

Criminal prosecution

This is an example of an extreme remedy. The Philadelphia District Attorney's Office took the perhaps unprecedented step of criminally prosecuting social workers who were ostensibly providing a child with services in the home, yet did not intervene as the mother slowly starved the child to death. Below is an excerpt from the Report of the Grand Jury on its criminal indictment of social workers who, like the social workers in *DeShaney*, failed to take action to protect a child under their watch.

In re County Investigating Grand Jury XXII

In the Court of Common Pleas First Judicial District of Pennsylvania, Criminal Trial Division, Lynne Abraham, District Attorney. Misc. No. 0003211-2007, C-5, Report of the Grand Jury (2008).

We almost wish this had been a whodunit.

But we know who did it. The real question was: How could they?

How could parents have been so unloving? How could professionals have been so indifferent? And most of all, how could the Philadelphia Department of Human Services—the giant, expensive safety net we have set up to protect the children of uncaring or incompetent parents—have been so uncaring and incompetent?

Danieal (pronounced "Danielle") Kelly was a 14-year-old girl who was starved to death. When she died she weighed 42 pounds. That is the average weight for a child of five. Danieal had cerebral palsy, which impaired her physical and intellectual development. But that wasn't the reason she died. Her mother simply stopped feeding her enough to live.

At one time, under the care of her stepmother and compassionate teachers, she was a happy, smiling, singing, student....

Left to their own devices, however, neither her father nor her mother bothered to bring Danieal to school, or to a doctor, or even outside for air. Eventually, concerned relatives and friends contacted DHS. Everything should have changed for Danieal then. But nothing did—even as more neglect reports came into the agency, even as social workers (supposedly) investigated and responded, even as Danieal lost more than half of her body weight, even as she was left lying alone on a bed in a dark room, unable to move, with bed sores so deep and rotted that they went down to the bone.

Employees of DHS [the Department of Human Services] and the private agency it hired were, when they bothered to show up at all, literally on the other side of the door. But they rarely if ever went inside. The biggest flurry of activity occurred only after Danieal died—when supervisors and staff scrambled to manufacture records in an effort to make it look like they had been doing something.

Certainly the person most directly responsible for the death of this child was her own mother, with the father not much better. But, despicable as the parents were, they were not that remarkable: there are people like that in the world. That is why DHS—and the private company hired by DHS, which called itself "MultiEthnic Behavioral Health"—exist. Yet these agencies, whose sole function is supposed to be protecting children from such parents, passed up almost every opportunity, over a period of years, to save Danieal.

As a result, we are recommending charges against not only the parents, but also several employees of DHS and its outside agency. These employees should be prosecuted for endangering Danieal by failing to fulfill their legal duties of care, and for attempting to cover up their inaction through record tampering and perjury. We also recommend charging several friends of Danieal's mother for lying to us under oath in an effort to hide Mrs. Kelly's mistreatment of her daughter.

We realize that complaints about DHS have been heard before. But no one inside the system has been prosecuted, despite a long string of deaths of children under DHS's protection. We are hoping that appropriate criminal charges ... may help illustrate the depth of the problems, and help finally to fix them.

...

<u>Julius Murray: Involuntary Manslaughter, Endangering the Welfare of Children, Recklessly Endangering Another Person</u>

...

From the time he took over her case in April 2006, it was Julius Murray's duty to make sure that Danieal received medical attention, schooling, and services for her disability. At a minimum, he was required ... to visit the family's home twice a week and verify that the children were safe.

The evidence presented to the Grand Jury, however, makes clear that Murray very seldom visited the house. Andrea Kelly told a newspaper reporter that he had not been there all summer and that he had her sign blank forms declaring he had made visits when he had not.... The condition of Danieal's body alone proved that he could not have checked on the child's safety for several weeks, if ever.

Among his duties, Murray was also supposed to make sure that Danieal saw a doctor, but he never did that either. The record—even MultiEthnic's own file—is devoid of any indication of effort made or service provided to the Kelly family by Murray. His fraudulent nonperformance of a job on which a little girl's life depended easily meets the 'reckless or grossly negligent manner' standard necessary for involuntary manslaughter. Andrea Kelly was able to starve her daughter over a period of months only because Murray did not do his job.

The same evidence supports charging Murray with recklessly endangering another person. That crime is established if the [social] worker performed the tasks assigned to him recklessly and if he thereby placed Danieal in danger of death or serious bodily injury. Murray's failure to make required visits to check on Danieal's safety surely constituted recklessness. And Danieal's death is indisputable proof that his reckless conduct placed her in danger.

The evidence also establishes the offense of endangering the welfare of a child. Murray had a duty, imposed by contract and by Pennsylvania's child protective service laws, to shield Danieal from neglect. From the simple fact that she had been accepted for services by DHS, he knew that she was at risk of neglect by her mother. That the Kelly family was assigned to receive the highest level of [social] services meant that the risk was great and that frequent visits were necessary for the children's protection. Yet Murray falsified visitation records rather than check on the children....

Mickal Kamuvaka: Involuntary Manslaughter, Endangering the Welfare of Children, Recklessly Endangering Another Person, Perjury

...

Kamuvaka testified under oath that Murray visited Danieal's family twice a week and documented these contacts on progress notes as mandated. She said that she reviewed these progress notes every week, that she reviewed them, and that they were then placed in the family's case file. This is plainly false. The evidence presented established that almost all of the progress notes purporting to represent visits by Murray were fabricated on August 4, 2006....

...

The evidence before the Grand Jury showed that no one at MultiEthnic monitored the Kelly children's medical care; that no one alerted DHS when visits were not made for weeks, if not months at a time; and that no one held monthly case reviews.

...

That Kamuvaka was complicit in her caseworkers' fraudulent nonperformance was confirmed by her actions after Danieal died. She apparently was not horrified when she found on August 4 that the Kelly file documented at most a couple of home visits by Murray. She did not fire the employee or even reprimand him. Instead, she called in [others] to help make up a false file.... Kamuvaka's failure to perform her duties in this case easily constituted recklessness and gross negligence, and Danieal's death was a direct result.... By not asking for progress notes, or conducting monthly case reviews, she allowed [Murray] to shirk the vitally important home visits to check on the safety of the Kelly children. And this allowed Andrea Kelly the unsupervised time needed to kill her daughter by starvation and neglect.

...

Dana Poindexter: Endangering the Welfare of Children, Recklessly Endangering Another Person, Perjury

...

As an intake social worker, it was his duty to investigate the four separate reports that came into DHS's hotline alleging that Danieal was being neglected. He was obligated to speak to the people making the reports, visit the family, talk to the parents and children, inspect the home, investigate the substance of the reports, and assess the risk to Danieal and her siblings. Because the allegations included medical neglect and failure to attend school, Poindexter needed to contact doctors and school officials. By law, his investigation had to be completed within 60 days of a report. At that time he was to either close the case or recommend that DHS accept the family for services.

Poindexter was well aware of his duty. He had been a social worker for 12 years when the first report about Danieal Kelly came to him in August 2003. [Further, in] July 2003, a month before he received the first neglect report about Danieal, Poindexter was reprimanded and suspended when a three-week-old baby died shortly after he failed to check on the safety of the baby's family.

...

So the question becomes: Were his efforts so lame or meager that they could not reasonably be expected to protect the child's physical or psychological welfare? The answer is crushingly clear. Poindexter's "efforts" were less than meager. He did not complete a single investigation or risk assessment. Nearly three years after the first report about the Kelly children was assigned to him, all of the reports were simply declared "unsubstantiated" or "unable to complete," even though the neglect alleged—no medical care, no services, and no school—was patently true. He failed to do the paperwork either to close Danieal's case or to accept the family for services as he should have. As a result, her case languished in his cubicle without action. Indeed, his file on the family was buried at the bottom of a filing cabinet-sized box, beneath food wrappers and unopened envelopes relating to other children's cases.

Between August 2003 and April 2005, Poindexter received four reports that Danieal was being neglected. These came on top of the 2002 report about the Kelly family that was assigned to Poindexter ... The reports from May 2004, June 2004, and April 2005 all alleged that Danieal was not receiving medical care, services, or schooling. They also reported her general neglect and mistreatment—being left alone in her bed or stroller, screaming and not being cleaned. Had Poindexter bothered to investigate the April 2005 report alone, he would have found that Danieal had not been in school for over four years and that she had not had medical treatment or services for her disability at least since she moved back to Philadelphia in 2003.

For two and a half years, Poindexter did *nothing* to try to protect Danieal ... Poindexter did not have to save Danieal himself. All he had to do was fill out the paperwork necessary to recommend the Kelly family for services. He could even have passed his paperwork on to someone who might care about mistreated, disabled children—instead of hoarding it in his cubicle amid trash and unopened letters, thereby assuring that no one else would secure services for Danieal ... By sitting on the Kelly file, he compounded the danger to Danieal by obstructing others from intervening on her behalf.

For further discussion

1. Do you think the threat of criminal sanctions against social workers or child protective service workers who do not adequately protect vulnerable children from dangers within the children's homes is good social policy? Why or why not?

2. Mr. Murray pleaded guilty and Ms. Kamuvaka and Mr. Poindexter were found guilty of criminal charges.

Practice Pointer

To efficiently determine the current status of substantive due process protections for liberty or property interests in your client's jurisdiction, it is helpful to begin by consulting sources that summarize the topic. Before searching online for specific decisions, consider reviewing secondary sources to learn the vocabulary of the topic, to identify current issues, and to collect current citations. Beginning your research with secondary sources can significantly reduce your research time and increase your efficiency. Review the Practice Pointer that concludes Chapter 2 for suggestions of helpful treatises that focus on constitutional litigation.

Many *American Law Reports* articles summarize particular constitutional topics and provide practical suggestions and citations to relevant cases, organized by jurisdiction. *See, e.g.*, Joseph M. Pellicciotti, Annotation, *"State-Created Danger," or Similar Theory, As Basis for Civil Rights Action Under 42 U.S.C.A. § 1983*, 159 A.L.R. Fed. 37 (2000 and updated weekly). Legal encyclopedias can be helpful for the same reasons, although their treatment is less in-depth. *See, e.g.*, George Blum, et al., *Differing protections of procedural and substantive due process*, 16B Am. Jur. 2d Constitutional Law § 953 (updated May 2019).

Because substantive due process affords protection against a wide range of governmental action and the analysis differs depending on the factual context, it is most helpful to your client to rely on decisions analyzing the same claim your client is pursuing or defending and in factually analogous circumstances. Many secondary sources address particular substantive due process claims. *See, e.g.*, Michael Avery, David Rudovsky, Karen Blum & Jennifer Laurin, *Failure to provide police protection—General principles*, Police Misconduct: Law and Litigation § 2:36 (updated Oct. 2018); Michael E. Withey & Karen Koehler, *Cause of Action for State-Created Danger Under 42 U.S.C.A. § 1983*, 21 Causes of Action 2d 175 (updated July 2019). In addition, many secondary sources address substantive due process doctrine as applied in specific factual contexts. *See, e.g.*, Mark S. Dennison, *Zoning: Proof of Wrongful Land Use Regulation Pursuant to Section 1983*, 30 Am. Jur. Proof of Facts 3d 503 (updated June 2019); Ronna Greff Schneider, *Defining Property and Liberty Interests of Students—Goss. v. Lopez*, 1 Education Law § 3:6 (updated March 2018); Brian W. Blaesser & Alan C. Weinstein, *The Entitlement Requirement—Substantive Due Process*, Federal Land Use Law & Litigation § 2:5 (updated Oct. 2018); Anne M. Payne, *Establishing Personal Liability of Public School Teacher for Injuries or Damage to Student Resulting from Harassment or Bullying of Student by Teacher*, 109 Am. Jur. Proof of Facts 3d 105 (2009 and updated June 2019).

Other sources that can help you efficiently identify current issues and locate recent citations to binding law are continuing legal education materials. Federal model jury instructions are useful for the same reasons and are often available on federal circuit court websites.

All of the above sources may be available through electronic databases, depending on your employer's subscriptions. In addition, you can identify current issues and citations by searching the briefs filed recently in the relevant jurisdiction that are available in the Westlaw Edge and Lexis Advance brief banks. Once you have located relevant, binding authority, update those sources via Shepard's on Lexis Advance or KeyCite on Westlaw Edge to confirm their accuracy and to locate additional, more recent authority.

Chapter Five

42 U.S.C. § 1983 Action under Color of Law

A. Chapter Overview

In *Monroe v. Pape*, 365 U.S. 167 (1961) (Chapter 1), the Supreme Court held that 42 U.S.C. § 1983 action "under color of" state law includes both action pursuant to local law and action in violation of local law. *Monroe* vastly expanded the scope of § 1983 liability because it held that for many claims the availability of a state law remedy did not preclude the availability of a § 1983 remedy.

This Chapter further explores the meaning of action "under color of law." The "color of law" inquiry is most straightforward when a public employee is sued for acts the employee took while exercising the employee's public responsibilities. Generally, employment by a state or local government is enough to hold the defendant to be a state actor (*West*), even if the defendant is not a full-time employee but is instead a part-time contractor (*West*). The "color of law" inquiry is more complex when a state or local government employee is off-duty and acts for private reasons. The federal circuit courts have held that off-duty officials can still act under color of law. While the Supreme Court has not yet ruled on the issue, the materials in this Chapter illustrate that the circuits have identified various factors to be weighed in determining whether an off-duty state or local government employee is acting on behalf of the state or is acting as a private person (*Barna*, *Martinez*, *Anderson*, federal jury instructions).

The absence of a national rule for determining when a police officer's violent acts are state action or are instead private action can lead to inconsistent results. While state-law remedies—such as employee discipline or criminal prosecution—involve separate issues, for § 1983 purposes, it is significant whether the officer was a private citizen or a state actor at the time of the conduct. If the officer was a private actor, it is less likely that a government will pay damages for harm inflicted by the officer, because the conduct had nothing to with the police officer's job.

The Supreme Court may one day announce a national rule to determine when personally motivated violence by a police officer is action "under color of law." You may be one of the lawyers who helps to craft a national rule.

Questions to guide reading of *West*

1. If a person is employed by the state (or local government), will that generally be sufficient to consider that person's conduct "under color of" state law? Even if the person is abusing his/her government power (*Monroe*)?
2. Why did *West* reject the analogy of prison doctors to public defenders, who were held not to act under color of state law in *Polk*?
3. *West* held that the doctor's conduct was "fairly attributable to the state" and therefore was action under color of state law for Section 1983 purposes. Why?

West v. Atkins

487 U.S. 42 (1988)

Justice BLACKMUN delivered the opinion of the Court.

This case presents the question whether a physician who is under contract with the State to provide medical services to inmates at a state-prison hospital on a part-time basis acts "under color of state law," within the meaning of 42 U.S.C. § 1983, when he treats an inmate.

I

Petitioner, Quincy West, tore his left Achilles tendon in 1983 while playing volleyball at [the North Carolina] state prison in which he was incarcerated.... [West was sent to] Central Prison Hospital, the acute-care medical facility operated by the State for its more than 17,500 inmates. Central Prison Hospital has one full-time staff physician, and obtains additional medical assistance under "Contracts for Professional Services" between the State and area physicians.

Respondent, Samuel Atkins, M.D., a private physician, provided orthopedic services to inmates pursuant to one such contract. Under it, Doctor Atkins was paid approximately $52,000 annually to operate two "clinics" each week at Central Prison Hospital, with additional amounts for surgery. Over a period of several months, he treated West's injury by placing his leg in a series of casts. West alleges that although the doctor acknowledged that surgery would be necessary, he refused to schedule it, and that he eventually discharged West while his ankle was still swollen and painful, and his movement still impeded. Because West was a prisoner in "close custody," he was not free to employ or elect to see a different physician of his own choosing.

Pursuant to 42 U.S.C. § 1983, West, proceeding *pro se*, commenced this action against Doctor Atkins ... for violation of his Eighth Amendment right to be free from cruel and unusual punishment. West alleged that Atkins was deliberately indifferent to his serious medical needs, by failing to provide adequate treatment....

II

To state a claim under § 1983, a plaintiff must allege the violation of a right secured by the Constitution and laws of the United States, and must show that the alleged deprivation was committed by a person acting under color of state law. *Parratt v. Taylor*, 451 U.S. 527, 535 (1981) (overruled in part on other grounds, *Daniels v. Williams*, 474 U.S. 327, 330–331 (1986)).... The only issue before us is whether petitioner has established the second essential element—that respondent acted under color of state law in treating West's injury.

A

The traditional definition of acting under color of state law requires that the defendant in a § 1983 action have exercised power "possessed by virtue of state law and made possible only because the wrongdoer is clothed with the authority of state law." *United States v. Classic*, 313 U.S. 299, 326 (1941). *Accord*, *Monroe v. Pape*, 365 U.S. 167, 187 (1961) (adopting *Classic* standard for purposes of § 1983) (overruled in part on other grounds, *Monell v. New York City Dept. of Social Services*, 436 U.S. 658, 695–701 (1978)).... In *Lugar v. Edmondson Oil Co.*, 457 U.S. 922 (1982), the Court made clear that if a defendant's conduct satisfies the state-action requirement of the Fourteenth Amendment, "that conduct [is] also action under color of state law and will support a suit under § 1983." *Id.*, 457 U.S., at 935.... In such circumstances, the defendant's alleged infringement of the plaintiff's federal rights is "fairly attributable to the State." *Lugar*, 457 U.S., at 937.

To constitute state action, "the deprivation must be caused by the exercise of some right or privilege created by the State ... or by a person for whom the State is responsible," and "the party charged with the deprivation must be a person who may fairly be said to be a state actor." *Ibid.* "[S]tate employment is generally sufficient to render the defendant a state actor." *Id.*, at 936, n. 18; *see id.*, at 937. It is firmly established that a defendant in a § 1983 suit acts under color of state law when he abuses the position given to him by the State. *See Monroe v. Pape*, 365 U.S., at 172.... Thus, generally, a public employee acts under color of state law while acting in his official capacity or while exercising his responsibilities pursuant to state law. *See, e.g., Parratt v. Taylor*, 451 U.S., at 535–536....

Indeed, *Polk County v. Dodson* ... is the only case in which this Court has determined that a person who is employed by the State and who is sued under § 1983 for abusing his position in the performance of his assigned tasks was not acting under color of state law.... [There t]he Court accordingly concluded that when representing an indigent defendant in a state criminal proceeding, the public defender does not act under color of state law for purposes of § 1983 because he "is not acting on behalf of the State; he is the State's adversary." [454 U.S. 312,] 323, n. 13 [(1981)]....

B

...

In contrast to the public defender, Doctor Atkins' professional and ethical obligation to make independent medical judgments did not set him in conflict with the State and other prison authorities. Indeed, his relationship with other prison authorities was cooperative.... We thus find the proffered analogy between respondent and the public defender in *Polk County* unpersuasive.

[T]he Court of Appeals ... misread *Polk County* as establishing the general principle that professionals do not act under color of state law when they act in their professional capacities.... To the extent this Court in *Polk County* relied on the fact that the public defender is a "professional" in concluding that he was not engaged in state action, the case turned on the particular professional obligation of the criminal defense attorney to be an adversary of the State, not on the independence and integrity generally applicable to professionals as a class. Indeed, the Court of Appeals' reading would be inconsistent with cases, decided before and since *Polk County*, in which this Court either has identified professionals as state actors ... or has assumed that professionals are state actors in § 1983 suits, *see, e.g., Estelle v. Gamble*, 429 U.S. 97 (1976) (medical director of state prison who was also the treating physician).... Defendants are not removed from the purview of § 1983 simply because they are professionals acting in accordance with professional discretion and judgment.

...

C

We now make explicit what was implicit in our holding in *Estelle*: Respondent, as a physician employed by North Carolina to provide medical services to state prison inmates, acted under color of state law for purposes of § 1983 when undertaking his duties in treating petitioner's injury. Such conduct is fairly attributable to the State.

The Court recognized in *Estelle*: "An inmate must rely on prison authorities to treat his medical needs; if the authorities fail to do so, those needs will not be met." 429 U.S., at 103. In light of this, the Court held that the State has a constitutional obligation, under the Eighth Amendment, to provide adequate medical care to those whom it has incarcerated. *Id.*, at 104.... North Carolina employs physicians, such as respondent, and defers to their professional judgment, in order to fulfill this obligation. By virtue of this relationship, effected by state law, Doctor Atkins is authorized and obliged to treat prison inmates, such as West. He does so "clothed with the authority of state law." *United States v. Classic*, 313 U.S., at 326. He is "a person who may fairly be said to be a state actor." *Lugar v. Edmondson Oil Co.*, 457 U.S. at 937. It is only those physicians authorized by the State to whom the inmate may turn. Under state law, the only medical care West could receive for his injury was that provided by the State. If Doctor Atkins misused his power by demonstrating deliberate indifference to West's serious medical needs, the resultant deprivation was caused, in the sense relevant for state-action inquiry, by the State's exercise of its right to punish West by incarceration and to deny him a venue independent of the State to obtain needed medical care.

The fact that the State employed respondent pursuant to a contractual arrangement that did not generate the same benefits or obligations applicable to other "state employees" does not alter the analysis. It is the physician's function within the state system, not the precise terms of his employment, that determines whether his actions can fairly be attributed to the State.... Contracting out prison medical care does not relieve the State of its constitutional duty to provide adequate medical treatment to those in its custody, and it does not deprive the State's prisoners of the means to vindicate their Eighth Amendment rights.[14] The State bore an affirmative obligation to provide adequate medical care to West; the State delegated that function to respondent Atkins; and respondent voluntarily assumed that obligation by contract.

Nor does the fact that Doctor Atkins' employment contract did not require him to work exclusively for the prison make him any less a state actor than if he performed those duties as a full-time, permanent member of the state prison medical staff. It is the physician's function while working for the State, not the amount of time he spends in performance of those duties or the fact that he may be employed by others to perform similar duties, that determines whether he is acting under color of state law.[15] ... Doctor Atkins must be considered to be a state actor.... [W]e conclude that respondent's delivery of medical treatment to West was state action fairly attributable to the State, and that respondent therefore acted under color of state law for purposes of § 1983.

...

For further discussion

1. For background on privately operated prisons, *see* Richard Frankel, *Regulating Privatized Government Through § 1983*, 76 U. Chi. L. Rev. 1449 (2009) (arguing for *respondeat superior* liability on private § 1983 defendants even if public § 1983 defendants remain exempt); Richard Frankel, *The Failure of Analogy in Conceptualizing Private Entity Liability Under Section 1983*, 78 UMKC L. Rev. 967 (2010). As noted in Chapter 1, in *Minneci v. Pollard*, 565 U.S. 118, 131 (2012), the Supreme Court held that federal prisoners could not sue private prison guards in a *Bivens* action for violating their constitutional rights "where that conduct is of a kind that typically falls within the scope of traditional state tort law...."

2. State action is a constitutional concept and color of law is a statutory concept. Yet as a practical matter of litigation, the concepts are treated as the same. *Lugar v. Edmondson Oil Co.*, 457 U.S. 922, 929 (1982) ("[I]t is clear that in a § 1983 action brought against a state official, the statutory requirement of action 'under color of state law' and the 'state action' requirement of the Fourteenth Amendment are identical."); *see Rendell-Baker v. Kohn*, 457 U.S. 830, 838 (1982) ("[i]n cases under § 1983, 'under color' of law has consistently been treated as the same thing as the 'state action' required under the Fourteenth Amendment.") (quoting *United States v. Price*, 383

---

14. As the dissent in the Court of Appeals explained, if this were the basis for delimiting § 1983 liability, "the state will be free to contract out all services which it is constitutionally obligated to provide and leave its citizens with no means for vindication of those rights, whose protection has been delegated to 'private' actors, when they have been denied." [citation omitted].

15. Contrary to respondent's intimations, the fact that a state employee's role parallels one in the private sector is not, by itself, reason to conclude that the former is not acting under color of state law in performing his duties. "If an individual is possessed of state authority and purports to act under that authority, his action is state action. It is irrelevant that he might have taken the same action had he acted in a purely private capacity...." *Griffin v. Maryland*, 378 U.S. 130, 135 (1964)....

U.S. 787, 794 n.7 (1966))). If a party's conduct meets the requirements for state action, the same acts also qualify as actions taken "under color of state law" for purposes of § 1983. *Lugar*, 457 U.S. at 935; *Am. Mfrs. Mut. Ins. Co. v. Sullivan*, 526 U.S. 40, 49–50 (1999) (linking the color-of-law element of 42 U.S.C. § 1983 to the underlying state-action requirement of the Fourteenth Amendment, and holding that both exclude from their reach "merely private conduct, no matter how discriminatory or wrongful") (internal quotation marks and citation omitted); *Focus on the Family v. Pinellas Suncoast Transit Authority*, 344 F.3d 1263, 1276 n.4 (11th Cir. 2003) ("For simplicity's sake, we refer to this as § 1983's 'state action' requirement.").

B. Development of Doctrine in the Circuits

The Supreme Court has not defined at what point a government employee ceases to represent the state but the circuits have held that off-duty officials can still act "under color of law." The following cases illustrate different circuit approaches to the question of when conduct of government employees *ceases to be* action under color of law. Before reading the cases, consider these examples of personally motivated violence by law enforcement officers, whether on or off-duty:

- in Texas, an off-duty deputy sheriff lured his wife's former boyfriend to his home, beat him, inserted his service revolver in the boyfriend's mouth, said, "I'll kill you. I'm a cop. I can," then—in his squad car—followed the boyfriend's car to the town's border;[1]
- in Louisiana, a police chief assaulted his sister-in-law on the premises of the police station while arguing with her over family and political matters.[2]

And consider these examples of conduct that appears to be personally motivated violence by law enforcement officers:

- in Colorado, an off-duty Sheriff's Deputy, who was out of uniform and on his way home from work in his personal car, shot and killed a man riding in a pickup truck during a fight that broke out on the off-ramp;[3]
- in New York, according to criminal charges, an off-duty police officer shot his girlfriend in the face with his service-issued Glock 9-mm handgun, killing her. The District Attorney said, "A young woman is murdered. A New York City police officer is charged with her death. However, the sad reality is that this was, in essence, a domestic violence incident that occurs all too frequently and illus-

---

1. *U.S. v. Tarpley*, 945 F.2d 806 (5th Cir. 1991), *cert. denied*, 504 U.S. 917 (1992).
2. *Delacambre v. Delacambre*, 635 F.2d 407 (5th Cir. 1981).
3. Jeff Francis, *Off-Duty Officer Shoots and Kills Man in Argument* (Nov. 14, 2007, 12:00PM), https://coloradocommunitymedia.com/stories/off-duty-officer-shoots-kills-man-in-argument,109522; *see* Robert Garrison, *Affidavit: Off-duty Colorado corrections officer shot, killed neighbor over fireworks dispute* (July 8, 2019, 3:47PM), https://www.thedenverchannel.com/news/crime/affidavit-off-duty-colorado-corrections-officer-shot-killed-neighbor-over-fireworks-dispute.

trates that police officers are not immune from social problems that are endemic in our society."[4]

Consider also how armed off-duty police officers can help protect the public. For example:

- in Utah, just before Valentine's Day, an off-duty police officer at a mall with his wife shot and killed a heavily armed gunman who had come to the mall intending to shoot random shoppers. The gunman already had killed five shoppers and wounded four others;[5]
- in Pennsylvania, an off-duty officer drew his weapon and tackled a man in the midst of robbing a convenience store cash register.[6]

Questions to guide reading of *Barna*

1. Is "under color of" state law limited to employees who are exercising actual authority? What were some of the reasons the court held that the off-duty officers exercised no "actual authority"?
2. Can an off-duty police officer act under color of state law? What are some examples?
3. Does *Barna* suggest whether personally motivated violence can ever be action under color of law?
4. What were some of the reasons the court held the officers exercised no "purported authority"?
5. Why was the officer's use of the nightstick insufficient to satisfy the test for action under color of law? Would you have ruled the same way?

Barna v. City of Perth Amboy

42 F.3d 809 (3d Cir. 1994)

STAPLETON, Circuit Judge.

Louis and Theresa Barna ("Mr. and Mrs. Barna") sued [police officers and the City of Perth Amboy] for violations of their constitutional rights stemming from an alleged assault.... We conclude that judgment as a matter of law was proper on Mr. Barna's assault-based claim because the evidence could not support a finding that the officers were acting under color of state law.

---

4. *Off-Duty NYPD Cop Charged with Murder of Girlfriend*, North Country Gazette (May 11, 2007), http://www.northcountrygazette.org/news/2007/05/11/cop_shoot/.

5. *Off-Duty Officer First to Engage Trolley Square Shooter*, KSL.com (Feb. 13, 2007, 3:00PM), http://www.ksl.com/index.php?nid=148&sid=890580.

6. *See* YouTube video on the companion website for this book, http://constitutionallitigation.rutgers.edu/ (select "Resources" and select top video, "Philadelphia Police Officer Off-Duty").

...

I.

The relevant facts as established by the plaintiffs' presentation of their case at trial are as follows. On the evening of December 21, 1990, Louis and Theresa Barna went to dinner with Mrs. Barna's sister, Mary Haelson ("Aunt Mary"), and Mrs. Barna's mother. After dinner, and after taking Mrs. Barna's mother home, Mr. and Mrs. Barna and Aunt Mary went to a bar. Mr. and Mrs. Barna each consumed significant quantities of alcohol during the evening.

The Barnas and Aunt Mary left the bar to return to the Barnas' home. On the way, they stopped at a Christmas tree business owned by a longtime friend of Mrs. Barna's family, Bobby DeHane. Mr. and Mrs. Barna were also in this line of business and Mrs. Barna was angry at Mr. DeHane, believing that earlier in the day he had reported electrical code violations at the Barnas' Christmas tree lot to a government agency. Mrs. Barna got out of the car and unsuccessfully sought out DeHane in order to confront him. Aunt Mary coaxed her back into the car.

DeHane's Christmas tree lot was across the street from another bar. Coincidentally, Perth Amboy Police Officers Paul Otterbine ("Otterbine") and Richard Echevarria ("Echevarria") were outside that bar in Officer Echevarria's truck. Officer Otterbine is the brother of Mrs. Barna and Aunt Mary. Although the officers were off-duty and not in uniform, they were armed with their service revolvers and with their police-issue "PR-24" nightsticks. Otterbine noticed his mother's car, and saw his two sisters and Mr. Barna. Aunt Mary signaled to her brother that Mr. and Mrs. Barna were drunk and wanted to damage the Dehane property and asked Otterbine to follow her home. Otterbine explained to his partner that there was a problem with Mr. and Mrs. Barna and asked Echevarria to accompany him. The two officers, in Echevarria's truck, then followed Mr. and Mrs. Barna and Aunt Mary back to the Barnas' home.

At the Barnas' home, Aunt Mary attempted to leave with her sister, Dena Otterbine, who had been babysitting the Barnas' children. Mr. Barna testified that, when he saw his sisters-in-law pulling away in their car, he signaled for them to stop by standing in the path of their car and waving his arms. Aunt Mary, who was driving, stopped the car. Mr. Barna testified that he then went to the side of the car, knelt down to speak with Aunt Mary through the driver's side window, and asked her to stay with Mrs. Barna and the children while he went out. Instead, Aunt Mary drove slowly away, dragging Mr. Barna who was holding onto the driver's side door. Aunt Mary stopped the car after dragging Mr. Barna fifty or sixty feet.

Officer Otterbine, who apparently witnessed this, began yelling at Mr. Barna and accused him of hitting his sister, Aunt Mary. Mr. Barna argued with Officers Otterbine and Echevarria, telling them: "Look, you guys are out of your jurisdiction. Just get out of here, go home, this is none of your concern." ... Echevarria then responded: "Jurisdiction? I'll show you jurisdiction." ... Echevarria and Otterbine then attacked Mr. Barna and beat him up. Mr. Barna testified that he was largely passive during the fight, and that at one point Officer Otterbine used his nightstick to place Mr. Barna in a chokehold....

After beating up Mr. Barna, Officers Otterbine and Echevarria left Mr. Barna on the sidewalk and returned to Echevarria's truck. They attempted to leave the scene, but Mrs. Barna prevented their departure. She slapped her brother in the mouth and told the two officers not to go anywhere.

> [Events quickly escalated when Mr. Barna pointed a gun at the officers, who then drew their weapons. Mr. Barna then retrieved a 12-gauge shotgun from his house and audibly shuffled it, then locked himself in the house; after back-up police were called, both Barnas were arrested.]

...

At trial, the Barnas called fourteen witnesses over five days. At the close of the Barnas' case, [the district court granted judgment for defendants as a matter of law pursuant to Fed. R. Civ. P. 50(a).] ... [T]he district court explained, correctly in our view, that the events of that evening should be viewed as comprising two distinct incidents: (1) a "family altercation" between the officers and Mr. Barna; and (2) the officers' response to Mr. Barna's brandishing of firearms following their attempt to leave. The court found that the evidence viewed in the light most favorable to the plaintiffs could not support a claim under 42 U.S.C. § 1983 because, as to the first event, the officers' actions were not performed under color of state law....

II.

...

"To state a claim under § 1983, a plaintiff must allege the violation of a right secured by the Constitution and laws of the United States, and must show that the alleged deprivation was committed by a person acting under color of state law." *West v. Atkins*, 487 U.S. 42, 48 (1988).

A. Assault Under Color of State Law

"The traditional definition of acting under color of state law requires that the defendant in a § 1983 action have exercised power 'possessed by virtue of state law and made possible only because the wrongdoer is clothed with the authority of state law.'" *West v. Atkins*, 487 U.S. 42, 49 (1988) (quoting *United States v. Classic*, 313 U.S. 299, 326 (1941)). Accordingly, acts of a state or local employee in her official capacity will generally be found to have occurred under color of state law. *Id.*; *Flagg Bros. v. Brooks*, 436 U.S. 149, 157 n. 5 (1978). This will be so whether the complained of conduct was in furtherance of the state's goals or constituted an abuse of official power. *West*, 487 U.S. at 49–50; *Monroe v. Pape*, 365 U.S. 167, 184–87 (1961), *overruled in part on other grounds, Monell v. Department of Social Services*, 436 U.S. 658 (1978). "It is firmly established that a defendant in a section 1983 suit acts under color of state law when he abuses the position given to him by the State." *West*, 487 U.S. at 49; *Screws v. United States*, 325 U.S. 91, 111 (1945) ("Acts of [police] officers who undertake to perform their official duties are included whether they hew to the line of their authority or overstep it.").

"It is [also] clear that under 'color' of law means under 'pretense' of law." *Screws*, 325 U.S. at 111. Thus, one who is without actual authority, but who purports to act according to official power, may also act under color of state law. In *Griffin v. Maryland*, the Supreme Court held that a deputy sheriff employed by a private park operator acted under color of state law when he ordered the plaintiff to leave the park, escorted him off the premises, and arrested him for criminal trespass. *Griffin v. Maryland*, 378 U.S. 130, 135 (1964) (analyzing state action necessary for a claim under the Equal Protection Clause of the Fourteenth Amendment). While the deputy sheriff was in actuality acting as a private security guard and as agent of the park operator rather than as agent of the state, he "wore a sheriff's badge and consistently identified himself as a deputy sheriff rather than as an employee of the park," and consequently "purported to exercise the authority of a deputy sheriff." *Id.* at 135.[9] The Court concluded that the privately employed deputy sheriff had been acting as a state actor, stating:

> If an individual is possessed of state authority and purports to act under that authority, his action is state action. It is irrelevant that he might have taken the same action had he acted in a purely private capacity.

Id.

In this same vein, off-duty police officers who purport to exercise official authority will generally be found to have acted under color of state law. Manifestations of such pretended authority may include flashing a badge, identifying oneself as a police officer, placing an individual under arrest, or intervening in a dispute involving others pursuant to a duty imposed by police department regulations. *See, e.g.*, *Rivera v. La Porte*, 896 F.2d 691, 696 (2d Cir. 1990) (identification as a peace officer, arrest of plaintiff, and use of police car); *Lusby v. T.G. & Y. Stores, Inc.*, 749 F.2d 1423 (10th Cir. 1984) (flashing of police badge and identification as police officer working as security guard), *vacated on other grounds*, 474 U.S. 805 (1985), *adhered to on remand*, 796 F.2d 1307 (10th Cir.), *cert. denied*, 479 U.S. 884 (1986); *Stengel v. Belcher*, 522 F.2d 438, 441 (6th Cir. 1975), *cert. dismissed*, 429 U.S. 118 (1976) (intervening in barroom brawl).

On the other hand, a police officer's purely private acts which are not furthered by any actual or purported state authority are not acts under color of state law. *See Delcambre v. Delcambre*, 635 F.2d 407, 408 (5th Cir. 1981) (holding that alleged assault by on-duty police chief at police station did not occur under color of state law because altercation with the plaintiff, defendant's sister-in-law, arose out of a personal dispute and defendant neither arrested nor threatened to arrest the plaintiff); *see also D.T. v. Independent School Dist. No. 16*, 894 F.2d 1176 (10th Cir.) (finding sexual molestation

---

9. Under a local ordinance, the county sheriff could deputize individuals who were employed to act as private security personnel. The individuals would be appointed as "special deputy sheriffs," and although they were paid by and acted as agents for the company or individual on whose account the appointment was made, they "ha[d] the same power and authority as deputy sheriffs possess within the area to which they are appointed." *Griffin*, 378 U.S. at 132 n. 1.

of students by public school teacher/coach that occurred on an excursion unconnected to school activities during school vacation period when teacher was not employed by the school district did not occur under color of state law), *cert. denied*, 498 U.S. 879 (1990). While a police-officer's use of a state-issue weapon in the pursuit of private activities will have "furthered" the § 1983 violation in a literal sense, courts generally require additional indicia of state authority to conclude that the officer acted under color of state law. *Compare Bonsignore v. City of New York*, 683 F.2d 635 (2d Cir. 1982) (holding that officer who used police handgun to shoot his wife and then commit suicide did not act under color of state law even though he was required to carry the police gun at all times) *with Stengel v. Belcher*, 522 F.2d at 441 (finding evidence supported determination of "under color" where off-duty officer intervened in barroom brawl as required by relevant police department regulations); *United States v. Tarpley*, 945 F.2d 806, 809 (5th Cir. 1991) (finding requirement under color of state law met where off-duty deputy sheriff assaulted wife's alleged ex-lover in a private vendetta but identified self as police officer, used service revolver, and intimated that he could use police authority to get away with the paramour's murder), *cert. denied*, 504 U.S. 917 (1992).

In this case, Officers Otterbine and Echevarria were off duty when the altercation with Mr. Barna occurred, and the evidence indicates that the underlying nature of their dispute was personal. The evidence would not support a finding that the officers were acting with actual police authority during the altercation. Nor would it support a finding that they purported to be acting with police authority.

While the fact that they were off duty is not dispositive of whether the officers were exercising actual police authority, there was no evidence to indicate that the officers were on official police business. First, the officers were literally "out of their official jurisdiction." [Under New Jersey statute] ... a police officer may act in his or her official capacity outside of this jurisdiction under only two circumstances: (1) when in hot pursuit of a person whom the officer believes to have committed a crime ... or (2) when making an arrest anywhere in the state for a crime committed in the officer's presence.... Officers Otterbine and Echevarria, who were Perth Amboy police officers, thus could not have been acting with official authority under the facts of this case when they allegedly assaulted Mr. Barna at his home in the *Town of Woodbridge*. *See Rambo v. Daley*, 851 F. Supp. 1222, 1224 (N.D. Ill.1994) (recognizing police officers had no actual authority to conduct arrest in neighboring state and analyzing further to determine whether officers acted with purported authority)....

Otterbine decided to follow the Barnas to their home at the request of a relative and asked his partner, with whom he was sharing a social evening, to accompany him. The altercation began when Officer Otterbine accused Mr. Barna of hitting the officer's sister, Aunt Mary. His partner then intervened to support him and, at the end of the fracas, the two officers attempted to leave. The officers had not been called to the scene to conduct official police business, nor were they in pursuit of Mr. Barna on the belief that he had already committed a crime. Finally, the fact that they attempted to leave after the assault establishes that the officers were not trying to arrest

Mr. Barna at the time they assaulted him. Thus, there was no evidence to support a finding that the officers were clothed with actual state authority during the initial phase of the altercation, prior to Mr. Barna's brandishing of firearms.

This situation is thus unlike that in *Black v. Stephens*, 662 F.2d 181 (3d Cir. 1981), *cert. denied*, 455 U.S. 1008 (1982), where we concluded that an on-duty police officer may act under color of state law when he performs official duties that arose in a quasi-personal context. In *Black*, the plaintiff brought a § 1983 claim against a police officer in connection with an arrest and prosecution that arose out of a traffic incident involving the plaintiff's and the officer's vehicles. We found sufficient indicia of state authority to uphold the denial of judgment notwithstanding the verdict because the police officer was an on-duty (although plain-clothed) detective, he wore a police academy windbreaker, and he had initiated contact with the plaintiff on the belief that the plaintiff's actions warranted official investigation. *Black v. Stephens*, 662 F.2d at 188. Here there was no evidence that the alleged assault occurred as a result of official police concerns; on the contrary, the evidence indicates that the assault arose out of the officer's familial and personal concerns.

Turning to the issue of whether the officers purported to be acting with state authority when they followed the Barnas home and accosted Mr. Barna, we also find no evidence supporting the Barnas' position. The officers did not identify themselves as police officers, they did not indicate that they were acting on official police business, and importantly, they did not attempt to arrest Mr. Barna, or otherwise invoke their police authority, during the initial phase of the altercation.

The only arguable connections between the officers' alleged assault of Mr. Barna and the use of police authority are: (1) Echevarria's comment, "I'll show you jurisdiction," made in response to Mr. Barna's statement that the officers were out of their jurisdiction, and (2) evidence that Echevarria used a state-issue "PR-24" nightstick to hold Mr. Barna during the assault—a weapon that Officer Echevarria could only legally carry in New Jersey because of his position as a police officer. We believe Officer Echevarria's comment regarding the officers' "jurisdiction" is too ambiguous to be of significant value on the issue of state authority. As noted, the officers were in fact out of their police jurisdiction. Instead of indicating that Echevarria intended to exercise official police authority, the comment could just as likely have been meant to convey that Echevarria intended, despite the lack of any real or purported authority, to put Mr. Barna in his place.

The use of a police-issue nightstick is undoubtedly the Barnas' strongest support for the view that the officers were acting under color of state law during the alleged assault. The nightstick was an objective indicia of police authority, and Echevarria was legally entitled to possess it only because of his position as a police officer. At the time it was used, however, Echevarria did not have actual authority to use the nightstick, since, by [state statute], an officer may only carry the weapon while on duty or while traveling to or from an authorized place of police duty. Nor, under the circumstances of this case, do we view the use of the nightstick to hold Mr. Barna during the assault as an assertion by Echevarria of official authority. In short, we believe the unauthorized use of a police-issue nightstick is simply not enough to color this clearly personal family dispute with the imprimatur of state authority.[11]

To hold otherwise would create a federal cause of action out of any unauthorized use of a police-issue weapon, without regard to whether there are any additional circumstances to indicate that the officer was exercising actual or purported police authority. We do not understand the under color requirement of § 1983 to be satisfied by such a tenuous connection to state authority. *See Bonsignore v. City of New York*, 683 F.2d 635 (2d Cir. 1982) (holding that officer who used police handgun to shoot his wife and then commit suicide did not act under color of state law even though he was required to carry the police gun at all times); *cf. Rivera v. La Porte*, 896 F.2d 691 (2d Cir. 1990) (finding assault occurred under color of state law when officer used service revolver to beat plaintiff and then arrested plaintiff for events giving rise to the assault). The district court properly granted judgment as a matter of law in favor of Officers Otterbine and Echevarria on the assault-based claim because a jury could not reasonably find that the assault occurred under color of state law.

...

Off-duty police can act under color of law:

- either by exercising actual authority or purported authority
- either path can lead to the result, acting under color of law

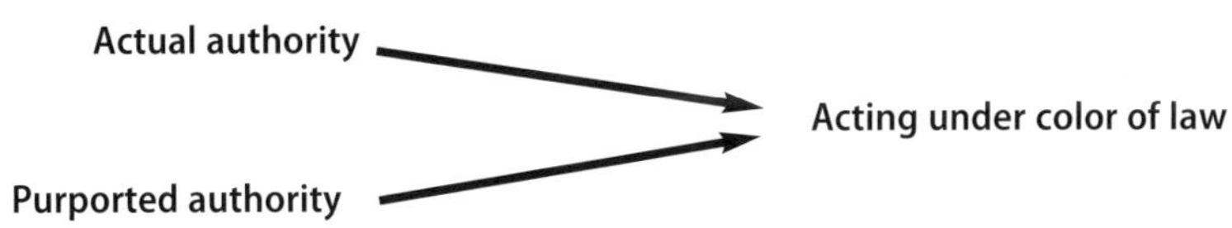

Questions to guide reading of *Martinez*

Martinez is the basis for Simulation 3.

1. *Martinez* holds that not every action by a police officer is attributable to the state. What are some of the general rules that *Martinez* identifies for weighing whether a police officer's conduct is action under color of law?

---

11. ... [T]he county's official policy [that] its police officers are police twenty-four hours a day ... is insufficient indicia of state authority under the circumstances of this case. At most, the existence of such a policy might have the effect of authorizing official police action (such as an arrest) conducted by an off-duty police officer. In such a situation, the policy might be probative of "under color" action if the defendant officer allegedly violated the plaintiff's rights while engaging in activities normally associated with the police function. *See, e.g.*, *Stengel v. Belcher*, 522 F.2d 438, 441 (6th Cir. 1975) (finding indicia of "under color" element where off-duty officer intervened in barroom brawl and used state-issue weapon pursuant to police policy), *cert. dismissed*, 429 U.S. 118 (1976).

2. What are some of the facts that *Martinez* identifies as significant but not dispositive of the color of law issue?
3. Why does *Martinez* hold that Valentin's shooting of his fellow police officer was not action under color of law?
4. According to *Martinez*, can a police officer's privately motivated use of a police-issued weapon ever constitute action under color of law? Note and comment on the majority's reliance on *Barna*. Is the majority's reading of *Barna* consistent with your reading of *Barna*?
5. What reasons does the dissent list for why it would have held that Valentin *did* act under color of law in harassing Martinez?
6. Why did the dissent emphasize its rejection of the majority's suggestion that Valentin might not have been acting under color of state law *even* if Martinez had been a civilian?

Martinez v. Colon

54 F.3d 980 (1st Cir.), *cert. denied*, 516 U.S. 987 (1995)

SELYA, Circuit Judge.

...

In the early morning hours of May 26, 1988, [Martinez], a youthful member of Puerto Rico's police force, drove to the [Precinct.] Though Martinez was not scheduled to begin his shift until 4:00 a.m., he arrived early, pursuant to local custom, in order to procure his post assignment. Martinez alleges that he was on duty from the moment he arrived—even before his shift began—because from that point forward he was subject to the shift commander's orders.

Upon Martinez' arrival, a fellow officer who was on duty at the time, Angel Valentin Corali (Valentin), approached Martinez' car and called him "pretty boy" ("papito lindo"). When Martinez alighted, Valentin drew his service revolver, pointed it at Martinez' stomach, cocked the hammer, placed his finger on the trigger, and inquired if Martinez was afraid. Valentin then disarmed the weapon, and Martinez hurried inside the station, first telling Valentin: "Don't horse around with that because you will kill me."

Shortly after this fracas had occurred, Valentin accosted Martinez in the radio room, inserted his finger into a small hole in Martinez' undershirt, and ripped it. Once again, Martinez walked away from Valentin. He then changed into his uniform, entered the waiting room, and reported to his shift supervisor, defendant-appellee Juan Trinidad Marrero (Trinidad).

Soon thereafter, Valentin reappeared, pointed his revolver at Martinez' genitals, cocked the hammer, and, with his finger on the trigger, threatened to "blow away" Martinez' penis (asking him, somewhat rhetorically, if he was scared). When Valentin lowered the weapon, Martinez immediately moved away from him. Within minutes

Valentin again approached Martinez, cocked the revolver, aimed it at Martinez' groin, and resumed his taunting. The revolver accidentally discharged, maiming Martinez.

The first encounter took place in the precinct's parking lot and the rest transpired inside the police station. According to Martinez, roughly twenty minutes elapsed from start to finish. All parties agree that the shooting, which occurred before the 4:00 a.m. shift change, was unintentional.

B. Travel of the Case.

On May 22, 1989, Martinez filed suit in federal district court against ... Rafael Colon Pizarro (Colon), Luis A. Velez Rentas (Velez), and Trinidad (collectively, "the officers" or "the defendants"). Invoking 42 U.S.C. § 1983 and premising jurisdiction on the existence of a federal question, *see* 28 U.S.C. § 1331 (1988), he alleged that his rights had been abridged in that each defendant owed him a duty to intervene and protect him from readily discernible harm at the hands of a fellow officer, but each defendant breached this duty by subsequent inaction. [Claims against Valentin were not before the court in this appeal.]

...

III. ANALYSIS

There are two essential elements of an action under section 1983: "(i) that the conduct complained of has been committed under color of state law, and (ii) that this conduct worked a denial of rights secured by the Constitution or laws of the United States." ... *accord West v. Atkins*, 487 U.S. 42, 48 (1988); *Daniels v. Williams*, 474 U.S. 327, 330–31 (1986). Of course, the reference to "state law" cannot be taken literally, for Puerto Rico enjoys the functional equivalent of statehood in regard to section 1983 and, thus, state law includes Puerto Rico law....

For purposes of this appeal, the defendants do not contest the plaintiff's allegation that, at all relevant times, the defendants were on duty and acting under color of state law.... [O]ur inquiry [is] whether the facts, taken most congenially to the plaintiff, can support a finding that the defendants violated a right secured to the plaintiff... by the Constitution....

A. The Duty to Intervene.

Plaintiff pins his hopes principally on a claim that the defendants' failure to protect him from the imminent peril posed by Valentin abridged his right to substantive due process. The touchstone of the law in this area is the Supreme Court's opinion in *DeShaney*.... Chief Justice Rehnquist, writing for the majority, explained that the Due Process Clause ordinarily does not require the state to protect an individual's life, limb, or property against the marauding of third parties not acting to the state's behoof. *See* [*DeShaney*, 489 U.S.] at 196. Consequently, "a State's failure to protect an individual against private violence simply does not constitute a violation of the Due Process Clause." *Id.* at 197.

Although the *DeShaney* Court left open the possibility of certain circumscribed exceptions to the general rule of nonliability, Martinez makes no effort to slide within them. He does not argue that he was in the custody of the state, *see id.* at 198–200 (discussing right to protection arising in favor of incarcerated prisoners and involuntarily committed mental patients), or that he was in its "functional custody," *see id.* at 201 n. 9 (discussing possible existence of situations analogous to incarceration or institutionalization), or that the state made him more vulnerable to Valentin's actions, *see id.* at 201. Rather, Martinez contends that *DeShaney* is altogether inapposite.

To the extent that this contention is based simply and solely on the fact that, unlike in *DeShaney*, the defendants here are police officers, not social workers, we reject it. Of course, police officers *sometimes* have an affirmative duty to intervene that is enforceable under the Due Process Clause. For example, "[a]n officer who is present at the scene [of an arrest] and who fails to take reasonable steps to protect the victim of another officer's use of excessive force can be held liable under section 1983 for his nonfeasance," provided that he had a "realistic opportunity" to prevent the other officer's actions. *Gaudreault v. Municipality of Salem*, 923 F.2d 203, 207 n. 3 (1st Cir. 1990), *cert. denied*, 500 U.S. 956 (1991); *accord O'Neill v. Krzeminski*, 839 F.2d 9, 11–12 (2d Cir. 1988). But this line of cases does not, as plaintiff importunes, carve out an exception to the *DeShaney* rule. Instead, such cases escape the rule because the aggressor is acting under color of his public office.

...

We cannot imagine a more paradigmatic exercise of state authority than the processes of handcuffing, detaining, and interrogating a citizen. *Gaudreault* and *O'Neill*, then, are cases in which the aggressor is acting under color of state law. The *DeShaney* rule—which addresses the "State's failure to protect an individual against *private* violence," *DeShaney*, 489 U.S. at 197 (emphasis supplied)—is not implicated in such cases because the violence in question is not private but "public," *i.e.*, attributable to state action.

Private violence—even private violence engaged in by one who happens to work for the state—has different legal ramifications than violence attributable to state action.

...

Translated to the police milieu, these cases mean that when an on-duty police officer witnesses violence, the existence *vel non* of a constitutional duty to intervene will most often hinge on whether he is witnessing private violence or violence attributable to state action. It remains to be seen how and where the line that separates one from the other should be drawn.

B. Private Action.

In attempting to distinguish private violence from violence attributable to state action for purposes of applying the *DeShaney* rule, courts must beware simplistic solutions. To be sure, violence is attributable to state action if the perpetrator is acting under color of state law ... but that is a virtual tautology. Furthermore, the construct—"acting under color of state law"—rarely depends on any single, easily determinable fact, such as a policeman's garb, *see, e.g.*, *Stengel v. Belcher*, 522 F.2d 438,

441 (6th Cir. 1975) (explaining that whether a police officer is "in or out of uniform is not controlling"), *cert. dismissed*, 429 U.S. 118 (1976), duty status, *see, e.g., Pitchell v. Callan*, 13 F.3d 545, 548 (2d Cir. 1994) (explaining that "whether an officer was on or off duty when the challenged incident occurred" is not dispositive); *Stengel*, 522 F.2d at 441 (same), or whereabouts, *see, e.g., Delcambre v. Delcambre*, 635 F.2d 407, 408 (5th Cir. 1981) (*per curiam*) (holding that a police chief's assault on a private citizen was not conduct under color of law even though it occurred at police headquarters). Nor does "acting under color of state law" depend on whether an officer stays strictly within the line of duty, or oversteps it. *See Monroe v. Pape*, 365 U.S. 167, 172 (1961); *Screws v. United States*, 325 U.S. 91 (1945). For instance, a police officer who exercises, but misuses or exceeds, his lawfully possessed authority is generally thought to be acting under color of law. *See, e.g., Gibson v. City of Chicago*, 910 F.2d 1510, 1518 (7th Cir. 1990).

The point is that segregating private action from state action calls for a more sophisticated analysis. In general, section 1983 is not implicated unless a state actor's conduct occurs in the course of performing an actual or apparent duty of his office, or unless the conduct is such that the actor could not have behaved in that way but for the authority of his office. Thus, whether a police officer is acting under color of state law turns on the nature and circumstances of the officer's conduct and the relationship of that conduct to the performance of his official duties. *See Pickrel v. City of Springfield*, 45 F.3d 1115, 1118 (7th Cir. 1995).

We think this focus follows inexorably from *West*, where the Court wrote that "[t]he traditional definition of acting under color of state law requires that the defendant ... have exercised power 'possessed by virtue of state law and made possible only because the wrongdoer is clothed with the authority of state law.'" *West*, 487 U.S. at 49 (quoting *United States v. Classic*, 313 U.S. 299, 326 (1941)). Hence, a person acts under color of state law "when he abuses the position given to him by the State." *Id.* at 50. The key determinant is whether the actor, at the time in question, purposes to act in an official capacity or to exercise official responsibilities pursuant to state law. *See id.*

Logically, then, not every action undertaken by a person who happens to be a police officer is attributable to the state. Though "under 'color' of law means under 'pretense' of law," even so, the acts of state officials "in the ambit of their personal pursuits" are not state action. *Screws*, 325 U.S. at 111; *see also Gibson*, 910 F.2d at 1518. Accordingly, a policeman's private conduct, outside the line of duty and unaided by any indicia of actual or ostensible state authority, is not conduct occurring under color of state law. *See Barna v. City of Perth Amboy*, 42 F.3d 809, 816 (3d Cir. 1994); *United States v. Tarpley*, 945 F.2d 806, 809 (5th Cir. 1991), *cert. denied*, 504 U.S. 917 (1992); *Dang Vang v. Vang Xiong X. Toyed*, 944 F.2d 476, 479 (9th Cir. 1991).... Even though "acting under color of law" includes "acting under pretense of law" for purposes of a state action analysis, there can be no pretense if the challenged conduct is not related in some meaningful way either to the officer's governmental status or to the performance of his duties.

C. Separating Wheat from Chaff.

Explicating the standard for segregating private action from action attributable to the state does not complete our task. Since the private conduct of police officers does not constitute action attributable to the state and, therefore, does not give rise to section 1983 liability under *DeShaney* or otherwise, we must determine whether Valentin, at the time and place in question, was engaged in purely personal pursuits or, conversely, whether he was acting under color of state law. To do so, we must assess the nature of his conduct in light of the totality of surrounding circumstances. *See Pitchell*, 13 F.3d at 548....

Here, the record is transpicuously clear that throughout the course of Martinez' ordeal Valentin did not exercise, or purport to exercise, any power (real or pretended) possessed by virtue of state law. To the contrary, Valentin was bent on a singularly personal frolic: tormenting an acquaintance.[5] Though on duty and in uniform, Valentin's status as a police officer simply did not enter into his benighted harassment of his fellow officer. Hazing of this sort, though reprehensible, is not action under color or pretense of law.

Nor can it be said that Valentin's actions were in any meaningful way related either to his official status or to the performance of his police duties. In this regard, the case bears a resemblance to *Delcambre*. There, the Fifth Circuit ruled that the plaintiff, who had been assaulted on the premises of the municipal police station by her brother-in-law, the police chief, had no cognizable claim under 42 U.S.C. § 1983. *See Delcambre*, 635 F.2d at 408. The assault arose out of a family squabble, and the court found that the police chief, though on duty, "was not acting under color of law as required for liability under [section 1983]." *Id.*

To be sure, Valentin shot Martinez with his service revolver, and in that sense it might be argued that the shooting was made possible by Valentin's status as a police officer. *See Cassady v. Tackett*, 938 F.2d 693, 695 (6th Cir. 1991) (concluding that, in "allegedly flourishing and threatening to use his gun" against a coworker, the defendant acted under color of state law because he "had authority or power to carry the gun in the jail only because he was [the county's] elected jailer")....

[We do] not embrace [this argument]. We do not think it is reasonable to hold that *every* use of a policeman's gun, even in the course of purely personal pursuits, creates a cause of action under section 1983. Instead, we are of the view that the context in which a service revolver is used, not just the mere fact of its use, must be consulted to determine the constitutional relevance of the officer's conduct. Consequently, "[w]hile a police officer's use of a state-issue weapon in the pursuit of private activities will have 'furthered' the § 1983 violation in a literal sense," a court needs "additional indicia of state authority to conclude that the officer acted under color of state law." *Barna*, 42 F.3d at 817–18 (holding that "unauthorized use of a police-issue nightstick

5. To use the plaintiff's spoken characterization, Valentin was "hors[ing] around"; or, as plaintiff put it in his second amended complaint, "playing 'Russian roulette' with another man's genitalia."

is simply not enough to color [a] clearly personal family dispute with the imprimatur of state authority").

Here, plaintiff has not produced any evidence tending to show that his tormentor, when brandishing the firearm, was exercising or purporting to exercise police power.[6] In the absence of any additional indicia of state action, we believe that the unauthorized use of a government-issue weapon is too attenuated a link to hold together a section 1983 claim. *See Barna*, 42 F.3d at 818–19 … *see also Bonsignore v. City of N.Y.*, 683 F.2d 635, 638–39 (2d Cir. 1982) (holding that a police officer who wounded his wife and killed himself using a gun which he was authorized to carry because of his status as an officer "was not acting under color of state law since his actions were not 'committed in the performance of any actual or pretended duty,' but were performed 'in the ambit of [his] personal pursuits'") (quoting *Screws*, 325 U.S. at 111 …).

…

IV. CONCLUSION

We need go no further. Because the defendants' failure to intervene and protect the plaintiff against Valentin's private actions, though regrettable, cannot be said to have violated rights secured to the plaintiff by the United States Constitution, *see DeShaney*, 489 U.S. at 196–97, the district court did not err in summarily disposing of the federal claims….[12]

BOWNES, Senior Circuit Judge, dissenting.

…

[T]he majority's factual recitation … is not a full-bodied portrayal of what happened.

I.

Plaintiff, Martinez, was a young (age twenty) and comparatively new member of the Puerto Rico Police Force. On the day of the events giving rise to this case, he arrived at the police station sufficiently early to be given his duty assignment. Martinez

---

6. Had Martinez been a civilian rather than a fellow officer, the significance of Valentin's uniform and weapon for purposes of the color-of-law determination might well have been greater. *See, e.g., Jones v. Gutschenritter*, 909 F.2d 1208, 1212–13 (8th Cir. 1990) (observing that the presence of a uniformed and armed police officer may reasonably cause a civilian to refrain from taking action to protect his rights). But when the victim is himself a fellow officer and the particular interaction between the two officers is of a distinctively personal nature, it can generally be assumed that the aggressor's official trappings, without more, will not lead the victim to believe that the aggressor is acting with the imprimatur of the state and, in turn, to forgo exercising his legal rights. The facts in this case are congruent with this hypothesis. The campaign of terror that Valentin mounted was patently personal in nature, and Martinez unquestionably realized as much; indeed, there was not the slightest indication that Valentin's conduct was undertaken pursuant to the authority of his office. Plainly, the fact that Martinez walked away numerous times shows that he was not "so intimidated" by Valentin's status as a policeman "as to cause him to refrain from exercising his legal right[s]." *Id.* at 1212.

12. Of course, the dismissal operates without prejudice to whatever rights plaintiff may have to prosecute the pendent claims in the courts of Puerto Rico.

parked his car in the police parking lot. He got out of his car and started towards the police station to get his orders for the day. There were four other police officers in the lot: the defendants—Colon, Vélez and Trinidad—and Valentin, who is not a defendant. As the majority acknowledges, the defendants were, at all relevant times, on duty as police officers and acting under color of state law. The three defendants observed the events that took place in the parking lot and the police station and heard Valentin's denigrating remarks to Martinez. None of the defendants asked Valentin to stop his verbal and physical assaults against Martinez. To put it starkly, they stood by and watched without protest Valentin "blow away" Martinez's penis.

As Martinez walked across the parking lot, Valentin said to the defendants, "Here comes Pretty Boy." Valentin then accosted Martinez, drew his service revolver, pointed it directly at Martinez's genital area, cocked it, put his finger on the trigger, asked Martinez if he was afraid, and then lowered the revolver. Martinez told Valentin: "Don't horse around with that because you will kill me." Martinez then proceeded into the station house. A short time later Valentin again confronted Martinez; this time he pushed his finger through a hole in Martinez's undershirt and ripped the shirt open. The record does not disclose whether any words were spoken at this juncture. Martinez put his police uniform on and reported to his shift supervisor, defendant Trinidad.

A short time later Valentin again assaulted Martinez. This assault was similar to the first confrontation, but with an ominous threat. This time Valentin pushed the muzzle of his loaded and cocked revolver into the front of Martinez's pants and threatened to "blow away" Martinez's penis. Valentin then asked Martinez if he was scared. After Valentin withdrew the weapon, Martinez moved away from him.

A short time later, within minutes, Valentin again accosted Martinez. He loaded and cocked his revolver and then inserted it into the front of Martinez's pants while continuing to verbally abuse him. The charade ended when Valentin's revolver discharged. Valentin's prior threat became a reality; Martinez's penis was in fact blown away and he was rendered permanently impotent.

The majority calls the shooting accidental and says, "All parties agree that the shooting ... was unintentional." Whether the shooting was accidental or not, it can be concluded, based on Valentin's words and actions, that it was an accident that was bound to happen. What Valentin did makes Russian roulette seem like a parlor game.

II.

The majority's central holding is premised on a ruling that Valentin was not acting under color of state law. In my view, the facts taken in the light most favorable to plaintiff establish that Valentin was acting under color of state law.

As the majority points out: " '[T]he traditional definition of acting under color of state law requires that the defendant have exercised power possessed by virtue of state law and made possible only because the wrongdoer is clothed with the authority of the state.' " *Ante* at 986 (quoting *West v. Atkins*, 487 U.S. 42, 49 (1988)) (ellipses and internal quotation marks omitted). Simply stated, "a person acts under color of state law 'when he abuses the position given him by the State.'" *Id.* (quoting *West*, 487 U.S. at 50). I think that Valentin exercised power possessed by virtue of Puerto Rico law and made possible only because he was clothed with the authority of Puerto Rico, and that he abused that power.

Even if I disregard the obvious—that Valentin was in uniform, on duty, in the police station, and used his service revolver to commit the tort (all of which militate heavily in favor of a finding that Valentin abused his position as a police officer)—I believe that Valentin's status as a police officer was the only reason the defendants took no action. If Valentin had been a private citizen and had been tormenting Martinez in the same manner, the bystander officers certainly would have intervened. The record gives rise to a reasonable inference that Valentin's police-officer status led the bystander officers to conclude that: (1) Valentin was not mentally unbalanced to the point that he might actually shoot Martinez, but a stable person only engaged in harassment or horseplay; and (2) Valentin was skilled enough with firearms to be allowed to engage in this sort of stupidity. Consequently, the record gives rise to an inference that Valentin's police-officer status was a *sine qua non* of the bystander officers' non-intervention. In my view, this inference establishes that Valentin was acting under color of state law.

The majority suggests that Martinez's status as a police officer somehow reduced the likelihood that Martinez perceived Valentin to be acting with the imprimatur of the Commonwealth ... I believe the opposite conclusion is at least as likely to be true. After the bystander officers (including Trinidad, who had supervisory authority) failed to intervene during the initial rounds of abuse by Valentin, Martinez could well have concluded that this type of hazing of young officers was standard fare in the ... Precinct. Therefore, Martinez could well have believed that the Commonwealth acquiesced in Valentin's actions.

Because Valentin was acting under color of state law, I think it pellucid that *DeShaney* does not bar this suit. At most, *DeShaney* precludes civil rights actions against state actors under the Due Process Clause for failing to protect an individual against private violence. See 489 U.S. at 197.

...

The majority concedes that Valentin's use of his service revolver might arguably bring his actions within the color of state law ... This is then rejected ... [I disagree because] [f]airly construed, Martinez's argument that Valentin's status as an on-duty police officer made him a state actor incorporates the argument that Valentin used the indicia and tools of his trade (including his service revolver) to carry out the shooting. For me, this is more than enough to allow us to consider Valentin's use of his service revolver as a factor in determining whether he was a state actor.

...

Finally, I think it important to refute the majority's suggestion that Valentin might not have been acting under color of state law even if Martinez had been a civilian. *Ante* at ... n. 6 ("Had Martinez been a civilian rather than a fellow officer, the significance of Valentin's uniform and weapon for purposes of the color-of-law determination *might well have been* greater.") (emphasis supplied). I find the suggestion remarkable. If a civilian had suffered the abuse Martinez experienced at the hands of an *on-duty, uniformed police officer using his service revolver in front of other officers in a police station*, well-settled precedent would dictate a finding that the civilian was victimized under color of state law. We should not even hint that this may not be so.

...

IV.

Police officers are entrusted with great powers—including the privileged use of force—for the very purpose of preventing lawless violence. When an officer abuses those powers in front of his peers, he in effect presumes their tacit acquiescence, if not outright approval. In this situation, the other officers have a constitutional duty to intervene. I therefore respectfully dissent.

Questions to guide reading of *Anderson*

1. According to *Anderson*, what are the three critical requirements for an off-duty law enforcement officer to be held to be acting under color of state law?
2. What key facts did *Anderson* identify as satisfying the first two elements? The third element?
3. In your opinion, is there a substantive difference between the factors/totality of the circumstances test articulated in *Barna* and the three-element test articulated in *Anderson*?
4. If you were a plaintiff's lawyer, would you prefer one over the other? Why?

Anderson v. Warner

451 F.3d 1063 (9th Cir. 2006)

FLETCHER, Circuit Judge.

In this § 1983 suit, Thomas Anderson appeals from the district court's grant of summary judgment to individual defendant Charles Warner.... [Anderson contends that Warner assaulted him while acting under color of state law. We reverse summary judgment].

I. Background

On the morning of July 30, 2001, Anderson and Warner were slowly driving their own vehicles toward the Redwood Valley Parade. Anderson was momentarily distracted and accidentally rear-ended Warner's vintage pickup truck. Warner got out of his truck, went back to Anderson's vehicle, opened Anderson's door, and began hitting Anderson in the face and neck. Warner's wife, who had been a passenger, also got out of the truck. A probation officer and friend of Warner, Thomas Cropp, was driving the vehicle in front of Warner. Cropp got out of his vehicle and came back to join Warner and his wife. At the time of the assault, Warner was employed by the

Mendocino County Sheriff's Department as the jail commander. On the day of the assault, Warner was off duty and out of uniform.

Recounting the assault in his declaration, Anderson stated:

> I heard someone yell t[o] call the police and then a woman I later learned was Mr. Warner's wife yelled, "he is a cop". I then said to Mr. Warner, "You're a cop?" and something to the effect that this was another Rodney King. He replied that he was and I heard him tell witnesses he was a cop and to stay back. I also heard a person who I now know is named Thomas Cropp tell people he was a probation officer and that this was police business. He told people to move on. Mr. Warner did not contradict him.

In his deposition, Anderson recounted that he had briefly been rendered unconscious by the assault. He then described what he saw after he regained consciousness:

> Well, what happened after I came to, I sat up and noticed Mr. Warner and this other guy and this lady holding their hands up, telling the crowd to disperse—that it's a police matter, and that Warner was an officer[.]

"This other guy," described by Anderson as having gray hair and a "small gray beard," was Thomas Cropp. "This lady" was Warner's wife. The deposition continued:

> Q: Tell me what you heard the man with gray hair and a beard say?
>
> A [by Anderson]: I heard him say that for the crowd to disperse.
>
> Q: Did he use the word "disperse"?
>
> A: Yes.
>
> Q: What were his actual words if you can remember?
>
> A: He was just telling the crowd to back up, to disperse, this is police business.
>
> ...
>
> Q: Now did you also hear some other person make some comment ...?
>
> A: Yes.
>
> Q: Who was that?
>
> A: This big woman on the right-hand side of Mr. Warner, on the right-hand side of the crowd. And she was saying that he was a cop.
>
> Q: What do you recall her actual words to be?
>
> A: "He's a cop. Let him alone. Look what he did to his truck."

Later in the deposition, Anderson stated that fire department personnel came to the scene:

> Mr. Warner looked and seen that the fire department was running down the road. He went—he slid back behind my seat and held my head, and he was telling me ... that he was a police officer, not to say anything, that he'll fix it. He'll work it out.

Tony Maples was a witness to the assault. He provided a sworn declaration to which he attached a transcript of a taped interview with the police after the event. Maples stated in the interview:

> I yelled "Somebody call the cops[.]" And [the lady in the red shirt] goes, "He is a cop". And I went, "Oh my gosh" ... and then ... I started yelling, "Then what is he doing this for?" ... And the lady goes, "Well look at his—look what that guy did to my—did to his truck. Let him be—let him hit him."

Ginerva Chandler, another witness, provided a sworn declaration to which she attached a transcript of her taped interview with the police. She stated that she had passed the scene of the accident on her bicycle:

> And we could hear them yelling and we assumed the guy in [Anderson's car] was hurt and they were going to try and get him out of the car.... And then what I heard was a woman yelling, you'll have to excuse the language, "Fucking caused the accident," and then yelling, "He's a cop. He's a cop," and we saw them reaching in the car to get the gentleman in the car out and we just kept rolling.

...

III. Discussion

...

Section 1983 does not create any substantive rights, but is instead a vehicle by which plaintiffs can bring federal constitutional and statutory challenges to actions by state and local officials ... "The purpose of § 1983 is to deter state actors from using the badge of their authority to deprive individuals of their federally guaranteed rights." *McDade v. West*, 223 F.3d 1135, 1139 (9th Cir. 2000)....

A. Warner

Anderson claims that Warner violated § 1983 when he invoked his law enforcement status in order to keep others from interfering with the assault. To state a claim under § 1983, a plaintiff must both (1) allege the deprivation of a right secured by the federal Constitution or statutory law, and (2) allege that the deprivation was committed by a person acting under color of state law. *West v. Atkins*, 487 U.S. 42, 48 (1988). Our focus is on the second requirement.

At the time of the assault, Warner was an employee of the Mendocino County Sheriff's Department. He was the county jail commander with the rank of lieutenant. Earlier in his career, as a lower-ranking officer, Warner had frequently worn a uniform while on duty. In his position as jail commander, he rarely wore a uniform even while on duty. Warner was entitled, by virtue of his position, to carry a gun while performing his duties in the jail and while transporting prisoners outside the jail. He was not entitled to carry a gun while off duty.

As a county jail commander, Warner's status under California law was that of a "custodial officer." Under California [statute], "a custodial officer is a public officer, not a peace officer, employed by a law enforcement agency [of a county] ... who has the authority and responsibility for maintaining custody of prisoners...." [C]ustodial officers may make warrantless arrests only while on duty....

Warner did not have the status of "peace officer" under California law.... [P]eace officers may make warrantless arrests "whenever the officer or employee has reasonable cause to believe that the person to be arrested has committed a misdemeanor in the presence of the officer or employee that is a violation of a statute or ordinance that the officer or employee has the duty to enforce."

A police report in the record summarizes an interview between Warner and an investigating police officer. Warner is reported to have said that he acted because he thought Anderson was trying to "flee the scene of the accident," and that he "punched" Anderson "about two times." Warner argues that, as a custodial officer, he had no authority to try and prevent Anderson from leaving the scene of the accident or to issue commands to the crowd that had gathered at the scene.

...

[Warner] argues that because he was a "custodial officer" rather than a "peace officer," he could not have been acting under color of state law within the meaning of § 1983 when he assaulted Anderson. He contends that he could not have been abusing his authority, and hence acting under of color of state law, because the scope of his authority did not extend to the acts he committed. We disagree with Warner's contention that he was not acting under color of state law.

There is no "rigid formula" for determining whether a state or local law official is acting under color of state law...." State employment is generally sufficient to render the defendant a state actor," *Atkins*, 487 U.S. at 48 (internal quotations and alterations omitted), but "whether a[n] ... officer is acting under color of state law turns on the nature and circumstances of the officer's conduct and the relationship of that conduct to the performance of his official duties." *Martinez v. Colon*, 54 F.3d 980, 986 (1st Cir. 1995). "Misuse of power, possessed by virtue of state law and possible only because the wrongdoer is clothed with the authority of state law, is action taken 'under the color' of state law." *United States v. Classic*, 313 U.S. 299, 326 (1941). "It is firmly established that a defendant in a § 1983 suit acts under color of state law when he abuses the position given to him by the State." *Atkins*, 487 U.S. at 49–50.

We hold that Warner was acting under color of state law when he invoked his law enforcement status to keep bystanders from interfering with his assault on Anderson. In the circumstances of this case, there are three critical requirements that must be satisfied. First, the defendant's action must have been "performed while the officer is acting, purporting, or pretending to act in the performance of his or her official duties." *McDade*, 223 F.3d at 1140. Second, the officer's pretense of acting in the performance of his duties must have had the purpose and effect of influencing the behavior of others. *See Van Ort v. Estate of Stanewich*, 92 F.3d 831, 839–40 (9th Cir. 1996) (finding no color of state law because the victim had not opened the door based on defendant's status as a police officer). Third, the challenged conduct must be "related in some meaningful way either to the officer's governmental status or to the performance of his duties." *Martinez*, 54 F.3d at 987.

We consider the first two requirements together: (1) the defendant must have pretended to act in the performance of his official duties, (2) with the purpose and effect of influencing the behavior of others. Viewing the evidence in Anderson's favor, it is clear both that Warner pretended to act in performance of his official duties, and that his actions had the purpose and effect of discouraging bystanders from interfering. Anderson stated in his declaration that "I heard [Warner] tell witnesses he was a cop and to stay back." In his deposition, he stated that after he regained consciousness, he "noticed Mr. Warner and this other guy and this lady holding their hands up, telling the crowd to disperse—that it's a police matter, and that Warner was an officer." Further, it is reasonably clear from the statements of witnesses Maples and Chandler that Warner's statements had the effect of influencing the behavior of others. For example, when Chandler heard that Warner was a "cop," she did not get off her bicycle, but rather "just kept rolling."

The third requirement is that Warner's conduct must be sufficiently related "either to the officer's governmental status or to the performance of his official duties." *Martinez*, 54 F.3d at 987. This requirement cannot mean that an officer must have been acting within the scope of his authority in order for him to have been acting under color of state law. If that were true, no § 1983 suit could ever succeed, for the premise of a successful suit is that the officer acted illegally—that is, outside the scope of his authority. Instead, the requirement must mean only that the challenged conduct must have a sufficiently close relationship to the officer's "governmental status" or to "the performance of his duties."

In the context of this case, this third requirement means that Warner must have used "the badge of [his] authority" to deprive an individual of his rights, *McDade*, 223 F.3d at 1139, by invoking his "governmental status" to influence the behavior of those around him. A key aspect of this requirement is that the officer must have invoked his actual status. For example, a law enforcement officer employed by the Sheriff's Office who says, "I am a cop, stand back" is invoking his governmental status. By contrast, a janitor employed by the Sheriff's Office who says the same thing is not invoking his governmental status—for the simple reason that he is not, in fact, a "cop."

We hold that Warner invoked his "governmental status" within the meaning of this requirement. According to Anderson, Warner said that he was a "cop" and told the bystanders to stay back. "Cop" is a generic, non-technical term. It can, of course, refer to a "peace officer" under California law. But it can also encompass and refer to Warner's status as a "custodial officer." If Warner had been a janitor in the county jail, his statement that he was a "cop" would not have been enough to render his conduct under color of law, for the term "cop" would have been a clearly inaccurate characterization of his status. But Warner was, instead, a lieutenant in the Mendocino County Sheriff's Department and the commander of the county jail. "Cop" is a sufficiently capacious term to include that status.

We therefore conclude that when Warner told the bystanders that he was a "cop" and ordered them to stay back, he was acting under color of state law. "Misuse of power, possessed by virtue of state law and made possible only because the wrongdoer is clothed with the authority of state law, is action taken 'under color of' state law." *Classic*, 313 U.S. at 326.

...

Jury Instructions

Contrast the differing approaches taken by the Eighth Circuit and the Third Circuit on how to instruct the jury on "color of law." Which do you think would be more useful to a jury?

A. Eighth Circuit Model Civil Jury Instruction

4.20 DEFINITION: COLOR OF STATE LAW (42 U.S.C. § 1983)

Acts are done under color of law when a person acts or [falsely appears] [falsely claims] [purports] to act in the performance of official duties under any state, county or municipal law, ordinance or regulation.

Committee Comments

See Monroe v. Pape, 365 U.S. 167 (1961), *overruled in part, Monell v. Department of Social Services*, 436 U.S. 658 (1978); *Screws v. United States*, 325 U.S. 91 (1945); *United States v. Classic*, 313 U.S. 299 (1941) [further citation omitted]. The court should, if possible, rule on the record whether the conduct of the defendant, if it occurred as claimed by the plaintiff, constitutes acts under color of state (county, municipal) law and should not instruct the jury on this issue. In most cases, the color of state law issue is not challenged and the jury need not be instructed on it. If it must be instructed, this instruction should normally be sufficient.[7]

B. Third Circuit Model Civil Jury Instruction[8]

Chapter 4. Instructions for Civil Rights Claims under Section 1983

4.4.2 Section 1983—Action under Color of State Law—Determining When an Official Acted under Color of State Law

Model

[Defendant] is an official of [the state of ______] [the county of ______] [the city of ______]. However, [defendant] alleges that during the events at

---

7. Manual of Model Civil Jury Instructions, 8th Cir. Civil Jury Instr. § 4.20 (2019), in Westlaw database FEDCIV-JI8C 4.20.

8. Catherine T. Struve, Reporter, 3d Cir. Civil Jury Instr. § 4.4.2 (July 2019), http://www.ca3.uscourts.gov/ (select "Model Jury Instructions," select "Model Civil Jury Table of Contents and Instructions").

issue in this lawsuit, [defendant] was acting as a private individual, rather than acting under color of state law.

For an act to be under color of state law, the person doing the act must have been doing it while clothed with the authority of the state, by which I mean using or misusing the authority of the state. You should consider the nature of the act, and the circumstances under which it occurred, to determine whether it was under color of state law.

The circumstances that you should consider include:

- [*Using bullet points, list any factors discussed in the Comment below, and any other relevant factors, that are warranted by the evidence.*]

You must consider all of the circumstances and determine whether [plaintiff] has proved, by a preponderance of the evidence, that [defendant] acted under color of state law.

Comment

"[S]tate employment is generally sufficient to render the defendant a state actor." *Lugar v. Edmondson Oil Co., Inc.*, 457 U.S. 922, 935 n.18 (1982) [footnote omitted]. In some cases, however, a government employee defendant may claim not to have acted under color of state law. Instruction 4.4.2 directs the jury to determine, based on the circumstances,[27] whether such a defendant was acting under color of state law [footnote omitted].

Various factors may contribute to the conclusion concerning the presence or absence of action under color of state law.[29] The court should list any relevant factors in Instruction 4.4.2. In the case of a police officer defendant, factors could include:

- Whether the defendant was on duty.[30] This factor is relevant but not determinative. An off-duty officer who purports to exercise official authority acts under color of state law.[31] Conversely, an officer who is pursuing purely private motives, in an interaction unconnected with his or her official duties, and who does not purport to exercise official authority does not act under color of state law.[32]
- Whether police department regulations provide that officers are on duty at all times.[33]
- Whether the defendant was acting for work-related reasons. However, the fact that a defendant acts for personal reasons does not necessarily prevent a finding that the defendant is acting under color of state law. A defendant who pursues a personal goal, but who uses governmental authority to do so, acts ... under color of state law.[34]
- Whether the defendant's actions were related to his or her job as a police officer.[35]
- Whether the events took place within the geographic area covered by the defendant's police department.[36]

- Whether the defendant identified himself or herself as a police officer.[37]
- Whether the defendant was wearing police clothing.[38]
- Whether the defendant showed a badge.[39]
- Whether the defendant used or was carrying a weapon issued by the police department.[40]
- Whether the defendant used a police car or other police equipment.[41]
- Whether the defendant used his or her official position to exert influence or physical control over the plaintiff.
- Whether the defendant purported to place someone under arrest.[42]

In a case involving a non-police officer defendant, factors could include:

- Whether the defendant was on duty.[43] This factor is relevant but not determinative. An off-duty official who purports to exercise official authority acts under color of state law.[44] Conversely, an official who is pursuing purely private motives, in an interaction unconnected with his or her official duties, and who does not purport to exercise official authority does not act under color of state law.[45]
- Whether the defendant was acting for work-related reasons. However, the fact that a defendant acts for personal reasons does not necessarily prevent a finding that the defendant is acting under color of state law. A defendant who pursues a personal goal, but who uses governmental authority to do so, acts under color of state law.[46]
- Whether the defendant's actions were related to his or her job as a government official.[47]
- Whether the events took place within the geographic area covered by the defendant's department.[48]
- Whether the defendant identified himself or herself as a government official.[49]
- Whether the defendant was wearing official clothing.[50]
- Whether the defendant showed a badge.[51]
- Whether the defendant used his or her official position to exert influence over the plaintiff.

Footnotes

27. The court should take care not to narrow the jury's focus; the jury should be instructed to consider all relevant circumstances. *See Harvey v. Plains Twp. Police Dep't*, 635 F.3d 606, 608 (3d Cir. 2011) (remanding for new trial due to erroneous verdict form and explaining that "[a]ction under color of state law must be addressed after considering the totality of the circumstances and cannot be limited to a single factual question").

29. *Compare, e.g., Barna v. City of Perth Amboy*, 42 F.3d 809, 816–17 (3d Cir. 1994) (off-duty, non-uniformed officers with police-issue weapons did not act under color of law in altercation with brother-in-law of one of the officers; officers were outside the geographic

scope of their jurisdiction, and altercation started when officer accused his brother-in-law of hitting his sister, after which officer's partner joined the fight, after which both officers tried to leave) *with Black v. Stephens*, 662 F.2d 181, 188 (3d Cir. 1981) (police officer acted under color of law in altercation that began with a dispute over a traffic incident; "he was on duty as a member of the Allentown Police force, dressed in a police academy windbreaker and ... he investigated the Blacks' vehicle because he thought the driver was either intoxicated or in need of help"); *see also Paul v. Davis*, 424 U.S. 693, 717 (1976) (Brennan, J., joined by Marshall, J., and in relevant part by White, J., dissenting) ("[A]n off-duty policeman's discipline of his own children, for example, would not constitute conduct 'under color of' law.").

30. "[G]enerally, a public employee acts under color of state law while acting in his official capacity or while exercising his responsibilities pursuant to state law." *West*, 487 U.S. at 50.

31. "[O]ff-duty police officers who flash a badge or otherwise purport to exercise official authority generally act under color of law." *Bonenberger v. Plymouth Tp.*, 132 F.3d 20, 24 (3d Cir. 1997).

32. "[N]ot all torts committed by state employees constitute state action, even if committed while on duty. For instance, a state employee who pursues purely private motives and whose interaction with the victim is unconnected with his execution of official duties does not act under color of law." *Bonenberger*, 132 F.3d at 24.

33. *See Torres v. Cruz*, 1995 WL 373006, at *4 (D.N.J. Aug. 24, 1992) (holding that it was relevant to question of action under color of state law that police manual "states that although the officers will be assigned active duty hours, 'all members shall be considered on duty at all times and shall act promptly, at any time, their services are required or requested'").

34. *See Basista v. Weir*, 340 F.2d 74, 80–81 (3d Cir. 1965) ("Assuming arguendo that Scalese's actions were in fact motivated by personal animosity that does not and cannot place him or his acts outside the scope of Section 1983 if he vented his ill feeling towards Basista ... under color of a policeman's badge.").

35. "Manifestations of ... pretended [official] authority may include flashing a badge, identifying oneself as a police officer, placing an individual under arrest, or intervening in a dispute involving others pursuant to a duty imposed by police department regulations." *Barna v. City of Perth Amboy*, 42 F.3d 809, 816 (3d Cir. 1994).

36. *See id.* at 816–17.

37. *See Griffin v. Maryland*, 378 U.S. 130, 135 (1964).

38. *See Abraham v. Raso*, 183 F.3d 279, 287 (3d Cir. 1999).

39. *See Bonenberger*, 132 F.3d at 24.

40. "While a police-officer's use of a state-issue weapon in the pursuit of private activities will have 'furthered' the § 1983 violation in a literal sense, courts generally require additional indicia of state authority to conclude that the officer acted under color of state law." *Barna*, 42 F.3d at 817; *see also id.* at 818 (holding that "the unauthorized use of a police-issue night-stick is simply not enough to color this clearly personal family dispute with the imprimatur of state authority").

41. *Rodriguez v. City of Paterson*, 1995 WL 363710, at *3 (D.N.J. June 13, 1995) (fact that defendant was equipped with police radio was relevant to question of action under color of state law).

42. *See Griffin*, 378 U.S. at 135 (holding that the defendant, "in ordering the petitioners to leave the park and in arresting and instituting prosecutions against them—purported to exercise the authority of a deputy sheriff. He wore a sheriff's badge and consistently identified himself as a deputy sheriff rather than as an employee of the park"); *Abraham*, 183 F.3d at 287 ("[E]ven though Raso was working off duty as a security guard, she was acting

under color of state law: she was wearing a police uniform, ordered Abraham repeatedly to stop, and sought to arrest him.").

43. *West*, 487 U.S. at 50.

44. *Bonenberger*, 132 F.3d at 24.

45. *Bonenberger*, 132 F.3d at 24.

46. *Basista*, 340 F.2d at 80–81.

47. *Barna v. City of Perth Amboy*, 42 F.3d 809, 816 (3d Cir. 1994). *See also Galena v. Leone*, 638 F.3d 186, 197 (3d Cir. 2011) (citing *Barna* and stating that "there is no doubt that Leone was acting under color of state law when, in his official capacity as chairperson of the Council, he ordered the deputy sheriff to escort Galena from the Council meeting").

48. *See id.* at 816–17.

49. *See Griffin*, 378 U.S. at 135.

50. *See Abraham*, 183 F.3d at 287.

51. *See Bonenberger*, 132 F.3d at 24.

Exercise 5-A

When does an off-duty police officer act under color of law?

- Based on your reading of *Barna, Martinez, Anderson,* and the circuit jury instructions, what factors are weighed in evaluating whether an off-duty police officer acted "under color of" law?
- In the chart below, at the two ends of the spectrum are the easy cases: clearly private action on the left and clearly action under color of law on the right. In the blank middle area in the chart, write down some of the factors you think courts or juries rely on in determining if an off-duty police officer's conduct was action under color of law.

Developing a Factual Record

One of the skills lawyers must develop is the ability to determine what kind of facts will help prove a claim or a defense. The lawyer must then plan how to investigate the facts and locate evidence to satisfy the relevant legal standard. This book has several exercises designed to help you develop fact investigation skills. For Exercise

5-A, you synthesized legal standards from multiple sources. For exercise 5-B, you will plan questions to ask a client to elicit factual information to satisfy that legal standard—facts to prove that an off-duty police officer acted "under color of law."

Developing Questions for a Client Interview

Lawyers decide the steps needed to accomplish the client's goals, while the client makes the ultimate decisions (whether to litigate or to settle, for example). To best represent the client, the lawyer wants to learn both what the client wants (money, public vindication) and why (I want money because I have to pay the rent; I want public vindication because I was wronged).

For the lawyer to fully understand the client's problem, goals, and reasons for those goals, one step is to interview the client.[9] The attorney's purposes in interviewing the client also include learning what the client knows about the facts, reducing the client's anxiety, forming the attorney client relationship, and explaining the attorney's procedures to the client. The lawyer's objectives at the interview are listening, exploring, and strategizing, rather than "solving the problem."

The client's goals in a client interview are to tell his or her story (in a confidential setting) and to be heard. The client's goals also include getting advice, assistance, perspective; understanding the process; and developing a good working relationship.

During the interview, lawyers let the client do most of the talking, try to build rapport, and try to be conscious of when and how often they interrupt a client. Lawyers use active listening techniques such as reframing what the client is explaining ("so as I understand it you feel, want, need") both to move the conversation along and to make sure the lawyer is learning all relevant information from the client. Like a funnel, a client interview typically begins with open-ended questions ("tell me what happened," "what would you like to see happen"), then moves to narrower questions to elicit detail. As the client speaks, the lawyer might take notes about specific topics to revisit and explore in greater detail, rather than derailing the conversation by narrowing the topic too quickly.

Once the client has told the story fully, the lawyer typically will ask questions about each specific topic that needs revisiting. For each particular topic to revisit, the lawyer again starts with broad questions, then narrows the focus. The lawyer determines the source of the client's knowledge and typically exhausts the client's memory on a topic before moving to the next topic.

Exercise 5-B concerns the narrowly focused phase of the client interview. For Exercise 5-B, you will focus on drafting questions to elicit details related only to one specific topic, whether the off-duty police officer acted under color of law.

---

9. This brief introduction to client interviewing is based on Richard Neumann & Stefan Krieger, Essential Lawyering Skills: Interviewing, Counseling, Negotiation, and Persuasive Fact Analysis (4th ed. 2011).

Exercise 5-B

Visit the companion website for this book, http://constitutionallitigation.rutgers.edu/, select "Resources," and scroll down to the bottom (7th) video. Or Search YouTube for the bar surveillance video of an off-duty Chicago police officer attacking a female bartender. Based on the bar security tape only, and not on any added editorial content, consider the following scenario.

Suppose your law firm has agreed to represent the bartender and has assigned you to interview the client, the victim/bartender later today. You know that the person who attacked the bartender was an off-duty police officer. You have only the bar's video surveillance tape. Assume that the only defendant will be the off-duty police officer. During the client interview, you plan to ask broad, open-ended questions to elicit the client's story. You then plan to ask narrower questions. You know you will be likely to revisit the narrower topic of whether the off-duty police officer was acting under color of law.

In revisiting that particular topic—whether the officer acted under color of law—consider what narrow questions you will want to ask your client at the meeting. Draft those narrow questions.

For further discussion

1. The beginning of this Chapter noted that the Supreme Court has not yet determined when violent acts by police for personal reasons are private action or are instead state action, action "under color of law" under 42 U.S.C. § 1983. Despite the frequency of disputes arising from off-duty police conduct, the Supreme Court has so far declined to announce a national rule. Should it? Review the considerations the Supreme Court weighs in deciding whether to grant certiorari, set out in Rule 10 of the Rules of the Supreme Court (and included in the Guide to Law Practice Simulation 2 in Chapter 4). Under Rule 10(a), are there reasons the Supreme Court should grant certiorari? Under Rule 10(c) are there reasons the Supreme Court should grant certiorari? What are some of the practical reasons favoring a national rule on color of law in the context of off-duty police violence?

2. Can a private actor engage in state action? A private party can be held to have acted under color of state law under § 1983 where the private party has engaged in state action under the (1) public-function test, (2) the state-compulsion test, or (3) the nexus test. *See Manhattan Cmty. Access Corp. v. Halleck*, ___ U.S. ___, 139 S. Ct. 1921, 1928 (2019) (5–4 decision holding that public access cable company was not a state actor); *id.* at 1940 (Sotomayor, J., dissenting) (reasoning "*West* resolves this case. Although the settings are different, the legal features are the same: When a government (1) makes a choice that triggers constitutional obligations, and then (2) contracts out those constitutional responsibilities to a private entity, that entity—in agreeing to take on the job—becomes a state actor for purposes of § 1983").

The Sixth Circuit briefly summarized these three state-action tests in a First Amendment case. The case concerned whether a private contractor who trained public park rangers to cull wild deer on behalf of a local government had acted under color of law when the trainer erased video recorded by cameras hidden by an animal rights group at the site of the deer-culling:

> Because [the sharpshooter trainer] is not a government employee and [the organization contracted to cull wild deer] is not a government entity, we must determine whether they can be held liable under 42 U.S.C. § 1983. "First and Fourteenth Amendment protections, codified in 42 U.S.C. § 1983, are triggered only in the presence of state action and [] a private entity acting on its own cannot deprive a citizen of First Amendment rights." *Lansing v. City of Memphis*, 202 F.3d 821, 828 (6th Cir. 2000). On the other hand, "a private entity can be held to constitutional standards when its actions so approximate state action that they may be fairly attributed to the state." *Id.*
>
> Although the state-action analysis is a normative and fact-bound endeavor, *see Brentwood Acad. v. Tenn. Secondary Sch. Athletic Ass'n*, 531 U.S. 288, 295–96 (2001), we utilize three tests to assist us in our inquiry. *Lansing*, 202 F.3d at 828–30. These tests are the public-function test, the state-compulsion test, and the nexus test. *Id.* The plaintiffs argue that, even though [the sharpshooting trainer] is not a government employee and [the organization] is not a government entity, their actions so approximated state action that they are subject to liability under § 1983. We conclude that neither [the sharpshooting trainer] or [the organization] qualify as state actors under any of the state-action formulations.
>
> "The public function test requires that 'the private entity exercise powers which are traditionally exclusively reserved to the state, such as holding elections or eminent domain.'" *Id.* at 828 ... Having neglected to present an argument that deer-culling satisfies the requirements of the public-function test, plaintiffs have forfeited this argument [because a party forfeits an argument on appeal when it is mentioned in only a cursory manner].
>
> "The state compulsion test requires that a state exercise such coercive power or provide such significant encouragement, either overt or covert, that in law the choice of the private actor is deemed to be that of the state." *Lansing*, 202 F.3d at 829.... Here the plaintiffs point to the "encouragement" [two park rangers] gave to [the sharpshooting trainer] to delete the images on the tapes. Although there is a fact dispute as to how [the sharpshooting trainer] arrived at the ranger station, the version most favorable to the plaintiffs was that [two park rangers] asked him to come. At most, [two park rangers] asked if [the sharpshooting trainer] knew how to erase the tapes, and they did not stop him when he began to do so. Metro Parks [the government employer] had no knowledge of this activity at the time that it was occurring. On this record, there is no coercion; [the sharpshooting trainer] made a free-will choice to erase the images. Likewise, to the extent that [two

> park rangers] "encouraged" him, this is not the type of significant encouragement which would turn [the sharpshooting trainer]'s choice to delete the tapes into that of government action.
>
> "Under the nexus test, 'the action of a private party constitutes state action when there is a sufficiently close nexus between the state and the challenged action of the regulated entity so that the action of the latter may be fairly treated as that of the state itself.'" *Id.* at 830.... In *Brentwood*, the Supreme Court found state action based on the "pervasive entwinement," between the private actor and the state such that there was "no offsetting reason to see the association's acts in any other way." *Brentwood*, 531 U.S. at 291. Here the relationship between Metro Parks and [the organization] was a one-time contractual relationship whereby [the organization] provided deer-culling training to Metro Parks rangers. There was no on-going relationship. Despite the plaintiffs' argument to the contrary, this is far from "a complete [e]ntwinement of a private entity with a public entity." ... The relationship between [the organization] and Metro Parks is easily understood as two separate entities entering into a contractual arrangement to provide and receive a one-time service. Accordingly, [the sharpshooting trainer] and [the organization] are not state actors pursuant to the nexus test.

S.H.A.R.K. v. Metro Parks Serving Summit County, 499 F.3d 553, 564–65 (6th Cir. 2007). The Eighth Circuit summarized the three tests somewhat differently in holding that speech restrictions imposed by a private actor at an entertainment event staged at the city-owned airport and open to the public involved state action by the private party because the private party was "consistently entangled with the city in effectuating" the speech restrictions:

> ...
>
> In certain circumstances the government may become so entangled in private conduct that "the deed of an ostensibly private organization or individual is to be treated ... as if a State had caused it to be performed." *Brentwood Acad. v. Tenn. Secondary Sch. Ath. Ass'n*, 531 U.S. 288, 295 (2001).
>
> To ascertain whether there is state action in a case, we examine the record to determine "whether the conduct at issue is 'fairly attributable' to the state." *Montano v. Hedgepeth*, 120 F.3d 844, 848–849 (8th Cir. 1997) (quoting *Lugar v. Edmondson Oil Co.*, 457 U.S. 922, 937 (1982)).... The key issue is whether [the private party] may appropriately be considered a state actor in the circumstances presented. If a party's conduct meets the requirements for state action, the same acts also qualify as actions taken "under color of state law" for purposes of § 1983. *Lugar*, 457 U.S. at 935.
>
> The Supreme Court has recognized a number of circumstances in which a private party may be characterized as a state actor, such as where the state has delegated to a private party a power "traditionally exclusively reserved to the State," *see Jackson v. Metro. Edison Co.*, 419 U.S. 345, 352 (1974), where

a private actor is a "willful participant in joint activity with the State or its agents," *see Adickes v. S. H. Kress & Co.*, 398 U.S. 144, 151 (1970), and where there is "pervasive entwinement" between the private entity and the state, *see Brentwood*, 531 U.S. at 291. These particular circumstances are merely examples and not intended to be exclusive. *See id.* at 295.

Our ultimate conclusion must turn on the particular facts of the case, since "only by sifting facts and weighing circumstances can the nonobvious involvement of the State in private conduct be attributed its true significance." *Burton v. Wilmington Parking Auth.*, 365 U.S. 715, 722 (1961). The one unyielding requirement is that there be a "close nexus" not merely between the state and the private party, but between the state and the alleged deprivation itself. *See Brentwood*, 531 U.S. at 295. No such nexus exists where a private party acts with the mere approval or acquiescence of the state, *see Blum v. Yaretsky*, 457 U.S. 991, 1004–05 (1982), but a private entity may be considered a state actor if it "has acted together with or has obtained significant aid from state officials" in furtherance of the challenged action. *Lugar*, 457 U.S. at 937.

...

When a private entity has acted jointly and intentionally with the police pursuant to a "customary plan," it is proper to hold that entity accountable for the actions which it helped bring about. *See Murray v. Wal-Mart, Inc.*, 874 F.2d 555, 558–559 (8th Cir. 1989); *see also Dossett v. First State Bank*, 399 F.3d 940, 950 (8th Cir. 2005) (applying joint action test for state action to § 1983 action alleging First Amendment violation).

...

Since [the private actor] and the city were knowingly and pervasively entangled in the enforcement of the challenged speech restrictions, we conclude that [the private actor] was a state actor when it interfered with [protestors'] expressive activities.... [And its] curtailment of [the protestors'] freedom of expression constituted state action and was actionable under § 1983.

Wickersham v. City of Columbia, 481 F.3d 591, 597–600 (8th Cir.), *cert. denied*, 552 U.S. 950 (2007).

Guide to Law Practice Simulation 3

Description

This is an appellate oral argument before the fictional Twelfth Circuit based on the facts of *Martinez v. Colon*, 54 F.3d 980 (1st Cir. 1995). The Twelfth Circuit has never addressed the issue of what constitutes action under color of law in the context of personally-motivated police violence. This is a question of first impression. Two students represent the plaintiff. Two students represent the defendant officers other than the officer who shot plaintiff, Officer Valentin. Note that Valentin is *not* a defendant; rather, the defendants are the officers who did not intervene to stop Valentin. Two students are judges on the Twelfth Circuit.

To prepare, consider issues such as:

- What rule should the Twelfth Circuit adopt to distinguish between personally motivated violence that is, and is not, action under color of law?
- Is there any single fact that a rational jury could rely on to find action under color of law in this situation?
- Is what Martinez thought or believed relevant to whether Valentin acted under color of law?
- What additional fact would have made this an easy case of action under color of law by Valentin?
- Is this case like *Delacambre v. Delacambre*, 635 F.2d 407 (5th Cir. 1981) (as cited in *Barna*)?

Purpose

- Better understand general rules of 42 U.S.C. § 1983 "under color of" law doctrine by discussing legal tests and comparing variations in how it is applied, including *West, Martinez, Barna, Anderson,* and the jury instructions
- Explore the attorney's role in shaping color of law doctrine by simulating roles of attorneys applying doctrine to real facts (the *Martinez* facts)
- Prepare for law practice by either persuasively advocating a legal position and responding to questions, or by identifying ambiguities in doctrine or in its application to facts and posing questions to advocates
- Note there is no need to do any research—the relevant cases are in the casebook. You may use the First Circuit's *Martinez* majority or dissent as non-binding, persuasive authority.

Structure

- Attorneys for Plaintiff Martinez—Question and Answer with judges (8 minutes)
- Attorneys for Defendant Officers—Question and Answer with judges (8 minutes)
- After about 15 minutes, questioning will be opened up to the entire class
- Both sides—Question and Answer with judges and rest of class (15 minutes)
- Please prepare a question for every simulation, even if you are not one of the students playing a role
- To ensure full class participation, and as a courtesy to your fellow students, please close your laptops during the law practice simulation.

Chapter Six

Fourth Amendment Standards and Police Misconduct

The Fourth Amendment guarantees that "[t]he right of the people to be secure in their persons ... against unreasonable ... seizures, shall not be violated...."

A. Chapter Overview

In 1985, the Supreme Court used a Fourth Amendment analysis to hold that police have "seized" a person whenever they restrain the person's freedom to leave. Applying a balancing of competing interests test, the Court held that deadly force "may not be used unless it is necessary to prevent the escape and the officer has probable cause to believe that the suspect poses a significant threat of death or serious physical injury to the officer or others." *Tennessee v. Garner*, 471 U.S. 1, 3 (1985). In two cases decided a few years later, the Supreme Court clarified two aspects of *Garner*: first, that a "seizure" requires "governmental termination of freedom of movement through means intentionally applied," *Brower v. County of Inyo*, 489 U.S. 593, 596–97 (1989), and second, that all claims that police have used excessive force in effectuating a seizure are governed by the Fourth Amendment, not by the substantive due process clause of the 14th Amendment. *Graham v. Connor*, 490 U.S. 386, 395 (1989). *Graham* held that claims that police have used excessive force in the course of an arrest, investigatory stop or other seizure of a person are analyzed by asking "whether the officers' actions are 'objectively reasonable' in light of the facts and circumstances confronting them, without regard to their underlying intent or motivation." *Graham*, 490 U.S. at 397. The "objective reasonableness" standard contrasts with the Eighth Amendment standards in excessive force cases, where the prison guards' subjective motivations are an element of the cause of action. Because a "seizure" requires "governmental termination of freedom of movement through means intentionally applied," the Supreme Court subsequently held that an accidental termination of movement—*e.g.*, a car crash—would fall outside the Fourth Amendment. *County of Sacramento v. Lewis*, 523 U.S. 833, 844 (1998).

This Chapter includes examples of how the lower courts have applied *Graham* and *Garner* in jury instructions, in jury verdict questionnaires, and in narrowing the issues for trial of an excessive force claim involving a police dog bite.

In 2007, the Supreme Court held that *Garner* did not establish a magic "on/off" switch for when deadly force was permitted, but instead *Garner* was a specific application of the general "objective reasonableness" inquiry required by *Graham*. *Scott v. Harris*, 550 U.S. 372, 382 (2007). For that reason, courts analyzing claims of excessive force, including deadly force, must "slosh [their] way through the factbound morass of 'reasonableness.'" *Id.* at 383. In applying *Scott*, courts must grapple with whether *Scott* should be read narrowly—as confined to its facts—or broadly, for the proposition that a police officer's attempt to terminate a dangerous high-speed car chase that threatens the lives of innocent bystanders does not violate the Fourth Amendment, even when it places the fleeing driver at risk of serious injury or death.

Before reading the materials on Fourth Amendment standards and police misconduct, consider the job of a police officer.

B. Factual Context

> **Tennessee:** Around 6:30 a.m. on May 30, [2018], a 32-year-old sergeant with the Dickson County Sheriff's Office (DCSO) was shot and killed while answering a call for service in Dickson. The sergeant responded to a call for a welfare check on a vehicle parked on the wrong side of the road with two occupants inside who appeared to be sleeping or passed out. The veteran sergeant, who had 10 years of law enforcement experience, parked his marked patrol vehicle in front and to the side of the parked vehicle. He was wearing a body camera that recorded the incident. A female exited the passenger's side of the vehicle; the sergeant told her to return to the car. The sergeant approached the driver's side of the vehicle and asked the occupants for identification. Instead, the male suspect provided a Social Security number that was later found to be false. The sergeant radioed his location to a DCSO deputy then walked to the back of the vehicle and radioed the vehicle's tag number to dispatchers. The sergeant learned the vehicle had been reported as stolen, so he returned to the driver's side door and ordered the suspect to exit the vehicle. The suspect claimed the driver's side door wouldn't open, so the sergeant ordered the suspect to exit through the passenger's side door while keeping his hands visible. As the sergeant began to walk around the back of the vehicle toward the passenger's side, the suspect fired multiple rounds from a .45-caliber semiautomatic handgun, striking the sergeant. The sergeant ran toward the back of the vehicle to find cover and attempted to radio that shots had been fired; however, after running a short distance, the sergeant collapsed. The suspect exited the vehicle, walked over to the sergeant, stood over him, and shot him several more times. The sergeant received a total of six gunshot wounds to the side of the head, the front upper torso/chest, and the arms/hands. The suspect loaded the deceased sergeant into the back seat of the patrol vehicle. The suspect, posing as the sergeant, radioed dispatchers and reported everything was fine, and a suspect was in

> custody. Then he drove the patrol vehicle away from the scene. A DCSO deputy used the GPS in the sergeant's patrol vehicle to locate the vehicle in a field. Other units responded to the field and discovered the patrol vehicle was locked and filled with smoke; the suspect had started a fire inside before fleeing. Deputies broke the patrol vehicle's window and found the victim sergeant's body inside. The suspect had stolen the sergeant's service weapon (a 9 mm semiautomatic handgun), backup weapon (a .357-caliber semiautomatic handgun), and pocket knife. At some point during the attack, the female passenger had fled the scene on foot. Law enforcement located her a short time later in a neighboring county and took her into custody. On June 1, after a massive search, law enforcement located the suspect sitting on the side of a road and took him into custody. The suspect's backpack contained the victim sergeant's backup weapon and pocket knife, as well as the .45-caliber handgun. The 31-year-old suspect was charged with First-Degree Murder, Theft, Tampering with Evidence, and Criminal Impersonation. He was known to use and possess controlled substances and was on probation at the time of the incident. The suspect had a prior criminal record that included assault on a law enforcement officer, resisting arrest, a weapons violation, violent crime, and a drug law violation.[1]

In 2018, there were approximately 808,700 police and detectives. Local governments employed about 77%.[2] The United States Department of Labor summarized the work environment conditions of American police:

> Police and detective work can be very dangerous and stressful. Police officers and detectives have one of the highest rates of on-the-job injury and illness. In addition to the obvious dangers of confrontations with criminals, police officers and detectives need to be constantly alert and ready to deal appropriately with a number of other threatening situations. Many law enforcement officers witness death and suffering resulting from accidents and criminal behavior. A career in law enforcement may take a toll on their private lives.
>
> Uniformed officers, detectives, agents, and inspectors are usually scheduled to work 40-hour weeks, but paid overtime is common. Shift work is necessary because protection must be provided around the clock. Junior officers frequently work weekends, holidays, and nights. Police officers and detectives are required to work at any time their services are needed and may work long hours during investigations. In most jurisdictions, whether on or off

---

1. Federal Bureau of Investigation, U.S. Dept. of Justice, Criminal Justice Information Services, *Law Enforcement Officers Killed and Assaulted (2018), Summaries of Officers Feloniously Killed* at 32–33 (Released Spring 2019).

2. Bureau of Labor Statistics, U.S. Dept. of Labor, Occupational Outlook Handbook, 2018 Edition, Police and Detectives: Work Environment, https://www.bls.gov/ooh/protective-service/police-and-detectives.htm#tab-3.

> duty, officers are expected to be armed and to exercise their authority whenever necessary.[3]

Similarly, the President's Task Force on 21st Century Policing found that law enforcement officers "are subject to more stress than the general population owing to the nature of their jobs," which involve working "with difficult—even hostile—individuals responding to tragic events and sometimes coming under fire themselves."[4] Final Report (May 2015) at 63.

According to the Federal Bureau of Investigation, between 2009 and 2018, 510 law enforcement officers in the United States were feloniously killed[5] and 511 were accidentally killed.[6] According to the F.B.I., of the 60,211 officers assaulted in 2017, the largest percentage (30.4) "were responding to disturbance calls (family quarrels, bar fights, etc.)," "15.8 percent were attempting other arrests" and "12.4 percent were handling, transporting, or maintaining custody of prisoners."[7]

Police department education requirements "range from a high school diploma to a college degree. Most police and detectives must graduate from their agency's training academy before completing a period of on-the-job training. Candidates must be U.S. citizens, usually at least 21 years old, and able to meet rigorous physical and personal qualification standards."[8] "Knowledge of a foreign language is an asset in many ... geographical regions."[9]

Hiring criteria and salaries vary. According to the U.S. Department of Labor, in 2018, the "median annual wage for police and detectives was $63,380," the "lowest 10 percent earned less than $36,550, and the highest 10 percent earned more than $106,090."[10] Some departments pay more for bilingual police officers or those with

---

3. *Id.*; Bureau of Labor Statistics, U.S. Dept. of Labor, Occupational Outlook Handbook, 2018 Edition, Police and Detectives, http://www.bls.gov/ooh/protective-service/police-and-detectives.htm (police "may face physical injury when conflicts with criminals occur, during motor-vehicle pursuits, when exposure to communicable diseases occurs, or through many other high-risk situations").

4. Final Report of the President's Task Force on 21st Century Policing at 63 (2015), https://cops.usdoj.gov/pdf/taskforce/taskforce_finalreport.pdf.

5. Bureau of Investigation, U.S. Dept. of Justice, Criminal Justice Information Services, Law Enforcement Officers Killed and Assaulted, 2018, Law Enforcement Officers Feloniously Killed 2009–2018, Table 1 (Summer 2019).

6. Federal Bureau of Investigation, U.S. Dept. of Justice, Criminal Justice Information Services, Law Enforcement Officers Accidentally Killed, 2009–2018, Table 48 (Summer 2019), https://ucr.fbi.gov/leoka/2018/tables/table-48.xls.

7. Federal Bureau of Investigation, U.S. Dept. of Justice, Criminal Justice Information Services, Officers Assaulted Overview, Circumstances (Summer 2018), https://ucr.fbi.gov/leoka/2017/topic-pages/assaults_topic_page_-2017.

8. Bureau of Labor Statistics, U.S. Department of Labor, Occupational Outlook Handbook, 2018 Edition, Police and Detectives: How to Become a Police Officer or Detective, https://www.bls.gov/ooh/protective-service/police-and-detectives.htm#tab-4.

9. *Id.*

10. Bureau of Labor Statistics, U.S. Department of Labor, Occupational Outlook Handbook, 2018 Edition, Police and Detectives: Pay, https://www.bls.gov/ooh/protective-service/police-and-detectives.htm#tab-5.

college degrees.[11] For example, the Houston Police Department offers bonuses of several thousand dollars for higher education degrees.[12]

Once hired, police officers usually are trained in the wide variety of skills they will need on-the-job. "In State and large local departments, recruits get training in their agency's police academy, often for 12 to 14 weeks. In small agencies, recruits often attend a regional or State academy."[13] "Training includes classroom instruction in state and local laws and constitutional law, civil rights, and police ethics. Recruits also receive training and supervised experience in areas such as patrol, traffic control, firearm use, self-defense, first aid, and emergency response."[14] Some police specialize. For example, an officer in Houston, Texas, has the opportunity to specialize after the initial training in areas such as:

Alternative Dispute Resolution	Auto Theft	Bike Patrol
Burglary and Theft	Bomb Squad	Crime Scene Unit
Criminal Intelligence	Community Outreach	Dive Team
Helicopters	Homicide	Human Resources
Hostage Negotiations	Juvenile	K-9
Major Offenders	Missing Persons	Mounted Patrol
Narcotics	Robbery	Solo Motorcycles
SWAT	Traffic and Accident	Training Academy
Truck Enforcement	Vice	

Police are trained in a wide variety of skills. The Justice Department chart that follows summarizes training topics in the surveyed police academies in 2002, including the median number of hours per topic. As you review the chart, consider the 2015 recommendation of the President's Task Force on 21st Century Policing that law enforcement agency policies for training on use of force "should emphasize de-escalation and alternatives to arrest or summons, where appropriate" and include annual training "that includes shoot/don't shoot scenarios and the use of less than lethal technologies."[15] The chart shows the highest median hours were spent on firearms skills, fitness, investigations, criminal law, and patrol techniques:

---

11. *Id.*

12. Houston Police Department Careers, Benefits, https://www.hpdcareer.com/benefits.html.

13. Bureau of Labor Statistics, U.S. Department of Labor, Occupational Outlook Handbook, 2010–11 Edition, Police and Detectives: Training, Other Qualifications, and Advancement, https://www.credentialwatch.org/occ/2010-11OOH.pdf.

14. Bureau of Labor Statistics, U.S. Department of Labor, Occupational Outlook Handbook, 2018 Edition, Police and Detectives. How to Become a Police Officer or Detective: Training," https://www.bls.gov/ooh/protective-service/police-and-detectives.htm#tab-4.

15. Final Report of the President's Task Force on 21st Century Policing at 20–21 (2015), https://cops.usdoj.gov/pdf/taskforce/taskforce_finalreport.pdf.

Academies providing basic instruction on various topics, and number of hours of instruction required, 2002[16]

Training topic	Percent of academies providing training in topic area	Median hours of instruction required
Firearms skills	99%	60 hrs
Basic first-aid/CPR	99	24
Emergency vehicle operations	99	36
Self-defense	99	44
Criminal law	98	40
Domestic violence	98%	12 hrs
Ethics and integrity	98	8
Investigations	98	45
Patrol procedures/techniques	98	40
Juvenile law and procedures	98	8
Constitutional law	96%	11 hrs
Cultural diversity	95	8
Health and fitness	95	50
Officer civil/criminal liability	93	6
Human relations	92	11
Use of non-lethal weapons	91%	12 hrs
Community policing	90	8
Stress prevention/management	86	6
Hate crimes/bias crimes	85	4
Mediation skills/conflict management	83	8
Domestic preparedness	78%	8 hrs
Problem solving (…)	64	6
Computers/information systems	59	8
Basic foreign language (such as, survival Spanish)	35	16

16. Matthew J. Hickman, U.S. Dept. of Justice, Office of Justice Programs, Bureau of Justice Statistics, State and Local Law Enforcement Training Academies, 2002 at Table 16, p. 9 (Jan. 2005, NCJ 204030). A 2013 survey reflects some changes in training numbers. For example, while the median number of hours devoted to criminal and constitutional law had been 51 hours combined, the average in 2013 was 53; hours devoted to non-lethal weapons changed from a median of 12 to an average of 16; and to firearms, from a median of 60 to an average of 71. Brian Reaves, U.S. Dept. of Justice, Office of Justice Programs, Bureau of Justice Statistics, State and Local Law Enforcement Training Academies, 2013, at Table 6, p. 5 (July 2016, NCJ 249784), https://www.bjs.gov/content/pub/pdf/slleta13.pdf.

In addition to screening law enforcement applicants and training them after hiring, law enforcement agencies also "police the police" by enforcing standards of conduct. Apart from self-policing by law enforcement agencies, many cities have established civilian agencies to review citizen complaints of misconduct by police.[17] In a study titled "Mission Failure: Civilian Review of Policing in New York City 1994–2006," the New York Civil Liberties Union documented the kinds of complaints filed: "Half of all complaints filed with the [Civilian Complaint Review Board] charge that a police officer used excessive force.... In 2005 alone, civilians filed 6,264 complaint allegations of excessive force.... Other than allegations of excessive physical force, the allegations most frequently involve serious 'abuse of authority'—such as improper stop, frisk or search; unauthorized entry or search of premises; threat of arrest; threat of force...."[18]

A study published in 2019 found that "[f]or young men of color, police use of force is among the leading causes of death."[19] "Over the life course, about 1 in every 1,000 black men can expect to be killed by police. Risk of being killed by police peaks between the ages of 20 y[ears] and 35 y[ears] for men and women and for all racial and ethnic groups.";[20] *see also* Human Rights Watch, *"Get on the Ground": Policing, Poverty, and Racial Inequality in Tulsa, Oklahoma* (analysis of 2012–17 data showed that "black people in Tulsa are 2.7 times more likely to be subjected to physical force by police officers than white people on a per capita basis").[21] Even earlier, in 2010–12, nationwide "[y]oung black males [ages 15–19] ... were at a far greater risk of being shot dead by police than their white counterparts—21 times greater, according to a ProPublica analysis of federally collected data on fatal police shootings."[22] To equalize the risk, the report found, "[185] more whites over those three years would have had to have been killed ... more than one per week."[23]

In addition to other concerns, police misconduct costs taxpayers money. For example, in 2018, resolving claims for excessive force, civil rights violations, and other injuries allegedly caused by New York City police cost their taxpayers $229.8 million.[24] According to the New York Civil Liberties Union: "Between 2000 and 2004 New York City taxpayers have paid more than a quarter of a billion dollars in damages to compensate the victims

---

17. *See, e.g.*, Christopher Stone & Merrick Bobb, *Civilian Oversight of the Police in Democratic Societies*, Vera Institute for Justice Publications (2002).

18. Robert Perry, New York Civil Liberties Union, *Mission Failure: Civilian Review of Policing in New York City 1994–2006* at 1 (2007).

19. Frank Edwards, Hedwig Lee, and Michael Esposito, Risk of Being Killed by Police Use of Force in the United States by Age, Race, Ethnicity, and Sex at 1 (PNAS 2019).

20. *Id.*

21. Human Rights Watch, *"Get on the Ground": Policing, Poverty, and Racial Inequality in Tulsa, Oklahoma* at 6 (2019), https://www.hrw.org/sites/default/files/report_pdf/us0919_tulsa_web.pdf.

22. Ryan Gabrielson, Ryann Grochowski Jones and Eric Sagara, *Deadly Force in Black and White*, (Oct. 10, 2014), http://www.propublica.org/article/deadly-force-in-black-and-white?utm_source=et&utm_medium=email&utm_campaign=dailynewsletter.

23. *Id.*

24. New York City Comptroller Annual Report (April 2019) at 18–19, https://comptroller.nyc.gov/wp-content/uploads/documents/Claims-Report-FY-2018.pdf.

of police misconduct, and to pay the legal costs incurred by the city in defending law suits brought against police officers charged with acts of brutality."[25]

C. Supreme Court Application of the Fourth Amendment: Excessive Force

---

Questions to guide reading of *Garner*

1. According to *Garner*, what is a "seizure"?
2. What balancing test did *Garner* hold governs whether a seizure is constitutional?
3. Under what circumstances did *Garner* hold the use of deadly force would be reasonable?
4. Do you read *Garner* to establish a general test for when a police officer may use deadly force? Do you instead read *Garner* to be limited to its facts?

Tennessee v. Garner

471 U.S. 1 (1985)

Justice WHITE delivered the opinion of the Court.

This case requires us to determine the constitutionality of the use of deadly force to prevent the escape of an apparently unarmed suspected felon. We conclude that such force may not be used unless it is necessary to prevent the escape and the officer has probable cause to believe that the suspect poses a significant threat of death or serious physical injury to the officer or others.

I

At about 10:45 p.m. on October 3, 1974, Memphis Police Officers Elton Hymon and Leslie Wright were dispatched to answer a "prowler inside call." Upon arriving at the scene they saw a woman standing on her porch and gesturing toward the adjacent house. She told them she had heard glass breaking and that "they" or "someone" was breaking in next door. While Wright radioed the dispatcher to say that they were on the scene, Hymon went behind the house. He heard a door slam and saw someone run across the backyard. The fleeing suspect, who was appellee-respondent's decedent, Edward Garner, stopped at a 6-feet-high chain link fence at the edge of the yard. With the aid of a flashlight, Hymon was able to see Garner's face and hands. He saw no sign of a weapon, and, though not certain, was "reasonably sure" and "figured" that Garner was unarmed.... He thought Garner was 17 or 18 years old and about

---

25. Robert Perry, New York Civil Liberties Union, *Mission Failure: Civilian Review of Policing in New York City 1994–2006* (2007), at 3, *available at* https://www.nyclu.org/sites/default/files/publications/nyclu_pub_mission_failure.pdf.

5'5" or 5'7" tall.[2] While Garner was crouched at the base of the fence, Hymon called out "police, halt" and took a few steps toward him. Garner then began to climb over the fence. Convinced that if Garner made it over the fence he would elude capture, Hymon shot him. The bullet hit Garner in the back of the head. Garner was taken by ambulance to a hospital, where he died on the operating table. Ten dollars and a purse taken from the house were found on his body.

In using deadly force to prevent the escape, Hymon was acting under the authority of a Tennessee statute and pursuant to Police Department policy. The statute provides that "[i]f, after notice of the intention to arrest the defendant, he either flee or forcibly resist, the officer may use all the necessary means to effect the arrest." Tenn. Code Ann. § 40-7-108 (1982). The Department policy was slightly more restrictive than the statute, but still allowed the use of deadly force in cases of burglary.... The incident was reviewed by the Memphis Police Firearm's Review Board and presented to a grand jury. Neither took any action....

Garner's father then brought this action in the Federal District Court for the Western District of Tennessee, seeking damages under 42 U.S.C. § 1983 for asserted violations of Garner's constitutional rights.

...

II

Whenever an officer restrains the freedom of a person to walk away, he has seized that person.... [T]here can be no question that apprehension by the use of deadly force is a seizure subject to the reasonableness requirement of the Fourth Amendment.

A

A police officer may arrest a person if he has probable cause to believe that person committed a crime.... To determine the constitutionality of a seizure "[w]e must balance the nature and quality of the intrusion on the individual's Fourth Amendment interests against the importance of the governmental interests alleged to justify the intrusion." ... We have described "the balancing of competing interests" as "the key principle of the Fourth Amendment." ... Because one of the factors is the extent of the intrusion, it is plain that reasonableness depends on not only when a seizure is made, but also how it is carried out.... In each of these [above-discussed] cases, the question was whether the totality of the circumstances justified a particular sort of search or seizure.

B

The same balancing process applied in the cases cited above demonstrates that, notwithstanding probable cause to seize a suspect, an officer may not always do so by killing him. The intrusiveness of a seizure by means of deadly force is unmatched. The suspect's fundamental interest in his own life need not be elaborated upon. The

---

2. In fact, Garner, an eighth-grader, was 15. He was 5' 4" tall and weighed somewhere around 100 or 110 pounds....

use of deadly force also frustrates the interest of the individual, and of society, in judicial determination of guilt and punishment. Against these interests are ranged governmental interests in effective law enforcement.[8] It is argued that overall violence will be reduced by encouraging the peaceful submission of suspects who know that they may be shot if they flee. Effectiveness in making arrests requires the resort to deadly force, or at least the meaningful threat thereof....

Without in any way disparaging the importance of these goals, we are not convinced that the use of deadly force is a sufficiently productive means of accomplishing them to justify the killing of nonviolent suspects.... Petitioners and appellant have not persuaded us that shooting nondangerous fleeing suspects is so vital as to outweigh the suspect's interest in his own life.

The use of deadly force to prevent the escape of all felony suspects, whatever the circumstances, is constitutionally unreasonable. It is not better that all felony suspects die than that they escape. Where the suspect poses no immediate threat to the officer and no threat to others, the harm resulting from failing to apprehend him does not justify the use of deadly force to do so. It is no doubt unfortunate when a suspect who is in sight escapes, but the fact that the police arrive a little late or are a little slower afoot does not always justify killing the suspect. A police officer may not seize an unarmed, nondangerous suspect by shooting him dead. The Tennessee statute is unconstitutional insofar as it authorizes the use of deadly force against such fleeing suspects.

It is not, however, unconstitutional on its face. Where the officer has probable cause to believe that the suspect poses a threat of serious physical harm, either to the officer or to others, it is not constitutionally unreasonable to prevent escape by using deadly force. Thus, if the suspect threatens the officer with a weapon or there is probable cause to believe that he has committed a crime involving the infliction or threatened infliction of serious physical harm, deadly force may be used if necessary to prevent escape, and if, where feasible, some warning has been given. As applied in such circumstances, the Tennessee statute would pass constitutional muster.

III

A

It is insisted that the Fourth Amendment must be construed in light of the common-law rule, which allowed the use of whatever force was necessary to effect the arrest of a fleeing felon, though not a misdemeanant.

...

The State and city argue that because this was the prevailing rule at the time of the adoption of the Fourth Amendment and for some time thereafter, and is still in force in some States, use of deadly force against a fleeing felon must be "reasonable."

8. The dissent emphasizes that subsequent investigation cannot replace immediate apprehension. We recognize that this is so, *see* n. 13, *infra*; indeed, that is the reason why there is any dispute. If subsequent arrest were assured, no one would argue that use of deadly force was justified. Thus, we proceed on the assumption that subsequent arrest is not likely. Nonetheless, it should be remembered that failure to apprehend at the scene does not necessarily mean that the suspect will never be caught....

It is true that this Court has often looked to the common law in evaluating the reasonableness, for Fourth Amendment purposes, of police activity.... On the other hand, it "has not simply frozen into constitutional law those law enforcement practices that existed at the time of the Fourth Amendment's passage." [citation omitted]. Because of sweeping change in the legal and technological context, reliance on the common-law rule in this case would be a mistaken literalism that ignores the purposes of a historical inquiry.

B

It has been pointed out many times that the common-law rule is best understood in light of the fact that it arose at a time when virtually all felonies were punishable by death.

...

Almost all crimes formerly punishable by death no longer are or can be.... These changes have undermined the concept, which was questionable to begin with, that use of deadly force against a fleeing felon is merely a speedier execution of someone who has already forfeited his life....

There is an additional reason why the common-law rule cannot be directly translated to the present day. The common-law rule developed at a time when weapons were rudimentary. Deadly force could be inflicted almost solely in a hand-to-hand struggle during which, necessarily, the safety of the arresting officer was at risk.

...

In short, though the common-law pedigree of Tennessee's rule is pure on its face, changes in the legal and technological context mean the rule is distorted almost beyond recognition when literally applied.

C

...

It cannot be said that there is a constant or overwhelming trend away from the common-law rule. In recent years, some States have reviewed their laws and expressly rejected abandonment of the common-law rule. Nonetheless, the long-term movement has been away from the rule that deadly force may be used against any fleeing felon, and that remains the rule in less than half the States.

This trend is more evident and impressive when viewed in light of the policies adopted by the police departments themselves. Overwhelmingly, these are more restrictive than the common-law rule.... In light of the rules adopted by those who must actually administer them, the older and fading common-law view is a dubious indicium of the constitutionality of the Tennessee statute now before us.

D

...

Nor do we agree with petitioners and appellant that the rule we have adopted requires the police to make impossible, split-second evaluations of unknowable facts....

We do not deny the practical difficulties of attempting to assess the suspect's dangerousness. However, similarly difficult judgments must be made by the police in equally uncertain circumstances. *See, e.g., Terry v. Ohio*, 392 U.S., at 20, 27 (1968).... Moreover, the highly technical felony/misdemeanor distinction is equally, if not more, difficult to apply in the field. An officer is in no position to know, for example, the precise value of property stolen, or whether the crime was a first or second offense. Finally, as noted above, this claim must be viewed with suspicion in light of the similar self-imposed limitations of so many police departments.

IV

...

Officer Hymon could not reasonably have believed that Garner—young, slight, and unarmed—posed any threat. Indeed, Hymon never attempted to justify his actions on any basis other than the need to prevent an escape.

...

Justice O'CONNOR, with whom THE CHIEF JUSTICE and Justice REHNQUIST join, dissenting.

The Court today holds that the Fourth Amendment prohibits a police officer from using deadly force as a last resort to apprehend a criminal suspect who refuses to halt when fleeing the scene of a nighttime burglary. This conclusion rests on the majority's balancing of the interests of the suspect and the public interest in effective law enforcement.... Notwithstanding the venerable common-law rule authorizing the use of deadly force if necessary to apprehend a fleeing felon, and continued acceptance of this rule by nearly half the States ... the majority concludes that Tennessee's statute is unconstitutional inasmuch as it allows the use of such force to apprehend a burglary suspect who is not obviously armed or otherwise dangerous. Although the circumstances of this case are unquestionably tragic and unfortunate, our constitutional holdings must be sensitive both to the history of the Fourth Amendment and to the general implications of the Court's reasoning. By disregarding the serious and dangerous nature of residential burglaries and the longstanding practice of many States, the Court effectively creates a Fourth Amendment right allowing a burglary suspect to flee unimpeded from a police officer who has probable cause to arrest, who has ordered the suspect to halt, and who has no means short of firing his weapon to prevent escape. I do not believe that the Fourth Amendment supports such a right, and I accordingly dissent.

...

For further discussion

1. A court's decision can be read narrowly—as tailored to the particular facts before the court. Or a court's decision can be read broadly to stand for a more general proposition. For many years, *Garner* was read broadly to stand for the proposition that "where the suspect poses no immediate threat to the officer or to others, the

harm resulting from the failure to apprehend him does not justify the use of deadly force" and that "where the officer has probable cause to believe that the suspect does pose a threat of serious bodily injury to the officer or to others, then it is not constitutionally unreasonable to prevent escape with deadly force." *Ham v. Brice*, 203 F. App'x 631, 634 (5th Cir. 2006); *see Waller v. City of Danville*, 212 F. App'x 162, 169 (4th Cir. 2006) ("'[I]f the suspect threatens the officer with a weapon or there is probable cause to believe that he has committed a crime involving the infliction or threatened infliction of serious physical harm, deadly force may be used if necessary to prevent escape, and if, where feasible, some warning has been given.'") (quoting *Garner*, 471 U.S. at 11–12). Consider the circuits' broad reading of *Garner* as you read the Supreme Court's more recent decision in *Scott.*

2. What constitutes "deadly force"? The Supreme Court in *Garner* did not define the term. In the context of 4th Amendment excessive force claims, most circuits have adapted the Model Penal Code definition to hold that "deadly force" is force that creates a substantial risk of death or serious bodily injury. *Smith v. City of Hemet*, 394 F.3d 689, 705–707 (9th Cir. 2005) (*en banc*), *cert. denied*, 545 U.S. 1128 (2005) (citing, *e.g.*, *Gutierrez v. City of San Antonio*, 139 F.3d 441, 446 (5th Cir. 1998) (deadly force "creates a substantial risk of death or serious bodily injury").

3. Could the release of a police dog to apprehend a suspect constitute deadly force? To visualize how police use trained dogs, visit the companion website for this book, http://constitutionallitigation.rutgers.edu, click on the Resources link, and scroll down to the K9 video of dogs being trained in the "bite and hold" method.[26] While the circuits have not foreclosed the possibility that under certain circumstances the use of a police dog, particularly an improperly trained dog, could constitute deadly force, the Tenth Circuit concluded that it was "unaware of any circuit that has found that the use of a properly trained police dog constitutes deadly force." *Thomson v. Salt Lake County*, 584 F.3d 1304, 1316 n.4 (10th Cir. 2009) (citing, *e.g.*, *Jarrett v. Town of Yarmouth*, 331 F.3d 140, 148–51 (1st Cir. 2003), *cert. denied*, 540 U.S. 1017 (2003) (concluding that the "release of a dog trained to bite and hold" was nondeadly force that did not violate a constitutional right); *Robinette v. Barnes*, 854 F.2d 909, 912 (6th Cir. 1988) (finding that the use of a properly trained police dog to seize a felony suspect was not deadly force although the suspect in that case died as a result of being apprehended by the dog)).

26. Or search YouTube for a K9 police dog training video of the bite and hold method.

Questions to guide reading of *Graham*

1. What constitutional standard governs claims that a police officer used excessive force in making an arrest, investigatory stop, or other seizure?
2. What are factors that *Graham* identifies as relevant in deciding whether the use of force to bring about a seizure is reasonable? Assessed from whose perspective?
3. What constitutional question is left open in footnote 10? That issue is the subject of the jury charge conference simulation in Chapter 7.

Graham v. Connor

490 U.S. 386 (1989)

Chief Justice REHNQUIST delivered the opinion of the Court.

This case requires us to decide what constitutional standard governs a free citizen's claim that law enforcement officials used excessive force in the course of making an arrest, investigatory stop, or other "seizure" of his person. We hold that such claims are properly analyzed under the Fourth Amendment's "objective reasonableness" standard, rather than under a substantive due process standard.

In this action under 42 U.S.C. § 1983, petitioner Dethorne Graham seeks to recover damages for injuries allegedly sustained when law enforcement officers used physical force against him during the course of an investigatory stop. Because the case comes to us from a decision of the Court of Appeals affirming the entry of a directed verdict for respondents, we take the evidence hereafter noted in the light most favorable to petitioner. On November 12, 1984, Graham, a diabetic, felt the onset of an insulin reaction. He asked a friend, William Berry, to drive him to a nearby convenience store so he could purchase some orange juice to counteract the reaction. Berry agreed, but when Graham entered the store, he saw a number of people ahead of him in the checkout line. Concerned about the delay, he hurried out of the store and asked Berry to drive him to a friend's house instead.

Respondent Connor, an officer of the Charlotte, North Carolina, Police Department, saw Graham hastily enter and leave the store. The officer became suspicious that something was amiss and followed Berry's car. About one-half mile from the store, he made an investigative stop. Although Berry told Connor that Graham was simply suffering from a "sugar reaction," the officer ordered Berry and Graham to wait while he found out what, if anything, had happened at the convenience store. When Officer Connor returned to his patrol car to call for backup assistance, Graham got out of the car, ran around it twice, and finally sat down on the curb, where he passed out briefly.

In the ensuing confusion, a number of other Charlotte police officers arrived on the scene in response to Officer Connor's request for backup. One of the officers rolled Graham over on the sidewalk and cuffed his hands tightly behind his back, ignoring Berry's pleas to get him some sugar. Another officer said: "I've seen a lot of people with sugar diabetes that never acted like this. Ain't nothing wrong with the M.F. but drunk. Lock the S.B. up." ... Several officers then lifted Graham up from behind, carried him over to Berry's car, and placed him face down on its hood. Regaining consciousness, Graham asked the officers to check in his wallet for a diabetic decal that he carried. In response, one of the officers told him to "shut up" and shoved his face down against the hood of the car. Four officers grabbed Graham and threw him headfirst into the police car. A friend of Graham's brought some orange juice to the car, but the officers refused to let him have it. Finally, Officer Connor received a report that Graham had done nothing wrong at the convenience store, and the officers drove him home and released him.

At some point during his encounter with the police, Graham sustained a broken foot, cuts on his wrists, a bruised forehead, and an injured shoulder; he also claims to have developed a loud ringing in his right ear that continues to this day. He commenced this action under 42 U.S.C. § 1983 against the individual officers involved in the incident ... alleging that they had used excessive force in making the investigatory stop, in violation of "rights secured to him under the Fourteenth Amendment to the United States Constitution and 42 U.S.C. § 1983."

...

Fifteen years ago, in *Johnson v. Glick*, 481 F.2d 1028, *cert. denied*, 414 U.S. 1033 (1973), the Court of Appeals for the Second Circuit addressed a § 1983 damages claim filed by a pretrial detainee who claimed that a guard had assaulted him without justification. In evaluating the detainee's claim, Judge Friendly applied neither the Fourth Amendment nor the Eighth, the two most textually obvious sources of constitutional protection against physically abusive governmental conduct.[6] Instead, he looked to "substantive due process," holding that "quite apart from any 'specific' of the Bill of Rights, application of undue force by law enforcement officers deprives a suspect of liberty without due process of law." 481 F.2d, at 1032....

In the years following *Johnson v. Glick*, the vast majority of lower federal courts have applied its four-part "substantive due process" test indiscriminately to all excessive force claims lodged against law enforcement and prison officials under § 1983, without considering whether the particular application of force might implicate a more specific constitutional right governed by a different standard....

We reject this notion that all excessive force claims brought under § 1983 are governed by a single generic standard. As we have said many times, § 1983 "is not itself a source of substantive rights," but merely provides "a method for vindicating federal rights elsewhere conferred." ... In addressing an excessive force claim brought under

---

6. Judge Friendly did not apply the Eighth Amendment's Cruel and Unusual Punishments Clause to the detainee's claim for two reasons. First, he thought that the Eighth Amendment's protections did not attach until after conviction and sentence. 481 F.2d, at 1032. This view was confirmed by *Ingraham v. Wright*, 430 U.S. 651, 671, n. 40 (1977) ("Eighth Amendment scrutiny is appropriate only after the State has complied with the constitutional guarantees traditionally associated with criminal prosecutions")....

§ 1983, analysis begins by identifying the specific constitutional right allegedly infringed by the challenged application of force.... In most instances, that will be either the Fourth Amendment's prohibition against unreasonable seizures of the person, or the Eighth Amendment's ban on cruel and unusual punishments, which are the two primary sources of constitutional protection against physically abusive governmental conduct. The validity of the claim must then be judged by reference to the specific constitutional standard which governs that right, rather than to some generalized "excessive force" standard. *See Tennessee v. Garner*, 471 U.S., at 7–22 (claim of excessive force to effect arrest analyzed under a Fourth Amendment standard); *Whitley v. Albers*, 475 U.S. 312, 318–326 (1986) (claim of excessive force to subdue convicted prisoner analyzed under an Eighth Amendment standard).

Where, as here, the excessive force claim arises in the context of an arrest or investigatory stop of a free citizen, it is most properly characterized as one invoking the protections of the Fourth Amendment, which guarantees citizens the right "to be secure in their persons ... against unreasonable ... seizures" of the person. This much is clear from our decision in *Tennessee v. Garner*. In *Garner*, we addressed a claim that the use of deadly force to apprehend a fleeing suspect who did not appear to be armed or otherwise dangerous violated the suspect's constitutional rights, notwithstanding the existence of probable cause to arrest. Though the complaint alleged violations of both the Fourth Amendment and the Due Process Clause, *see* 471 U.S., at 5, ... we analyzed the constitutionality of the challenged application of force solely by reference to the Fourth Amendment's prohibition against unreasonable seizures of the person, holding that the "reasonableness" of a particular seizure depends not only on *when* it is made, but also on *how* it is carried out. *Id.*, at 7–8.... Today we make explicit what was implicit in *Garner's* analysis, and hold that *all* claims that law enforcement officers have used excessive force—deadly or not—in the course of an arrest, investigatory stop, or other "seizure" of a free citizen should be analyzed under the Fourth Amendment and its "reasonableness" standard, rather than under a "substantive due process" approach. Because the Fourth Amendment provides an explicit textual source of constitutional protection against this sort of physically intrusive governmental conduct, that Amendment, not the more generalized notion of "substantive due process," must be the guide for analyzing these claims.[10]

---

10. A "seizure" triggering the Fourth Amendment's protections occurs only when government actors have, "by means of physical force or show of authority, ... in some way restrained the liberty of a citizen," *Terry v. Ohio*, 392 U.S. 1, 19, n.16 (1968) ... Our cases have not resolved the question whether the Fourth Amendment continues to provide individuals with protection against the deliberate use of excessive physical force beyond the point at which arrest ends and pretrial detention begins, and we do not attempt to answer that question today. It is clear, however, that the Due Process Clause protects a pretrial detainee from the use of excessive force that amounts to punishment. *See Bell v. Wolfish*, 441 U.S. 520, 535–539 (1979). After conviction, the Eighth Amendment "serves as the primary source of substantive protection ... in cases ... where the deliberate use of force is challenged as excessive and unjustified." *Whitley v. Albers*, 475 U.S., at 327.... Any protection that "substantive due process" affords convicted prisoners against excessive force is, we have held, at best redundant of that provided by the Eighth Amendment. *Ibid.*

Determining whether the force used to effect a particular seizure is "reasonable" under the Fourth Amendment requires a careful balancing of " 'the nature and quality of the intrusion on the individual's Fourth Amendment interests' " against the countervailing governmental interests at stake. *Id.* at 8.... Our Fourth Amendment jurisprudence has long recognized that the right to make an arrest or investigatory stop necessarily carries with it the right to use some degree of physical coercion or threat thereof to effect it. *See Terry v. Ohio*, 392 U.S., at 22–27.... Because "[t]he test of reasonableness under the Fourth Amendment is not capable of precise definition or mechanical application," *Bell v. Wolfish*, 441 U.S. 520, 559 (1979), however, its proper application requires careful attention to the facts and circumstances of each particular case, including the severity of the crime at issue, whether the suspect poses an immediate threat to the safety of the officers or others, and whether he is actively resisting arrest or attempting to evade arrest by flight. *See Tennessee v. Garner*, 471 U.S., at 8–9 (the question is "whether the totality of the circumstances justifie[s] a particular sort of ... seizure").

The "reasonableness" of a particular use of force must be judged from the perspective of a reasonable officer on the scene, rather than with the 20/20 vision of hindsight. *See Terry v. Ohio*, 392 U.S., at 20–22.... With respect to a claim of excessive force, the same standard of reasonableness at the moment applies: "Not every push or shove, even if it may later seem unnecessary in the peace of a judge's chambers," *Johnson v. Glick*, 481 F.2d, at 1033, violates the Fourth Amendment. The calculus of reasonableness must embody allowance for the fact that police officers are often forced to make split-second judgments—in circumstances that are tense, uncertain, and rapidly evolving—about the amount of force that is necessary in a particular situation.

As in other Fourth Amendment contexts, however, the "reasonableness" inquiry in an excessive force case is an objective one: the question is whether the officers' actions are "objectively reasonable" in light of the facts and circumstances confronting them, without regard to their underlying intent or motivation.... [*S*]*ee also Terry v. Ohio*, 392 U.S., at 21 (in analyzing the reasonableness of a particular search or seizure, "it is imperative that the facts be judged against an objective standard"). An officer's evil intentions will not make a Fourth Amendment violation out of an objectively reasonable use of force; nor will an officer's good intentions make an objectively unreasonable use of force constitutional....

Because petitioner's excessive force claim is one arising under the Fourth Amendment, the Court of Appeals erred in analyzing it under the four-part *Johnson v. Glick* test. That test, which requires consideration of whether the individual officers acted in "good faith" or "maliciously and sadistically for the very purpose of causing harm," is incompatible with a proper Fourth Amendment analysis.... Whatever the empirical correlations between "malicious and sadistic" behavior and objective unreasonableness may be, the fact remains that the "malicious and sadistic" factor puts in issue the subjective motivations of the individual officers, which our prior cases make clear has no bearing on whether a particular seizure is "unreasonable" under the Fourth Amendment. Nor do we agree with the Court of Appeals' conclusion ... that because the subjective motivations of the individual officers are of central importance in deciding whether force used against a convicted prisoner violates the Eighth Amendment, *see Whitley v. Albers*, 475 U.S., at 320–321,[11] it cannot be reversible error to inquire into them in deciding whether force used against a suspect or arrestee violates the Fourth Amendment. Differing standards under the Fourth and Eighth Amendments are hardly surprising: the terms "cruel" and "punishments" clearly suggest some inquiry into subjective state of mind, whereas the term "unreasonable" does not. Moreover, the less protective Eighth Amendment standard applies "only after the State has complied with the constitutional guarantees traditionally associated with criminal prosecutions." *Ingraham v. Wright*, 430 U.S. 651, 671, n. 40 (1977). The Fourth Amendment inquiry is one of "objective reasonableness" under the circumstances, and subjective concepts like "malice" and "sadism" have no proper place in that inquiry.[12]

Because the Court of Appeals reviewed the District Court's ruling on the motion for directed verdict under an erroneous view of the governing substantive law, its judgment must be vacated and the case remanded to that court for reconsideration of that issue under the proper Fourth Amendment standard.

D. Development of Doctrine in the Lower Courts: Applying *Garner* & *Graham*

1. Fourth Amendment doctrine can be fact-specific. Moreover, federal circuits vary in their applications of Supreme Court precedent. For example, in the Tenth Circuit, "[t]he reasonableness of the use of force depends not only on whether the officers were in danger at the precise moment they used force but also on whether

11. In *Whitley*, we addressed a § 1983 claim brought by a convicted prisoner, who claimed that prison officials had violated his Eighth Amendment rights by shooting him in the knee during a prison riot. We began our Eighth Amendment analysis by reiterating the long-established maxim that an Eighth Amendment violation requires proof of the " '"unnecessary and wanton infliction of pain."' " 475 U.S., at 319, quoting *Ingraham v. Wright*, 430 U.S., at 670, in turn quoting *Estelle v. Gamble*, 429 U.S. 97, 103 (1976). We went on to say that when prison officials use physical force against an inmate "to restore order in the face of a prison disturbance, ... the question whether the measure taken inflicted unnecessary and wanton pain ... *ultimately turns* on 'whether the force was applied in a good faith effort to maintain or restore discipline or maliciously and sadistically for the very purpose of causing harm.'" 475 U.S., at 320–321 (emphasis added), quoting *Johnson v. Glick*, 481 F.2d, at 1033. We also suggested that the other prongs of the *Johnson v. Glick* test might be useful in analyzing excessive force claims brought under the Eighth Amendment. 475 U.S., at 321.... But we made clear that this was so *not* because Judge Friendly's four-part test is some talismanic formula generally applicable to all excessive force claims, but because its four factors help to focus the central inquiry in the Eighth Amendment context, which is whether the particular use of force amounts to the "unnecessary and wanton infliction of pain." *See id.*, at 320–321.... Our endorsement of the *Johnson v. Glick* test in *Whitley* thus had no implications beyond the Eighth Amendment context.

12. Of course, in assessing the credibility of an officer's account of the circumstances that prompted the use of force, a factfinder may consider, along with other factors, evidence that the officer may have harbored ill-will toward the citizen....

the officers' own conduct during the seizure unreasonably created the need to use such force ... However, only reckless and deliberate conduct that is 'immediately connected to the seizure will be considered.' ... Mere negligence or conduct attenuated by time or intervening events is not to be considered ... The mentally ill or disturbed condition of the suspect is a relevant factor in determining reasonableness of an officer's responses to a situation ... [citing precedent from 10th Circuit dating back to 1995]." *Estate of Ceballos v. Husk*, 919 F.3d 1204, 1214 (10th Cir. 2019) (further citation omitted). The Tenth Circuit has acknowledged that other circuits reject "the concept that pre-seizure conduct should be used in evaluating the reasonableness of an officer's actions." *Pauly v. White*, 874 F.3d 1197, 1219 n. 7 (10th Cir. 2017) (citing precedent from 4th, 7th, and 8th Circuits), *cert. denied*, ___ U.S. ___, 138 S.Ct. 2650 (2018). The Tenth Circuit has recognized further that "[t]he Supreme Court very recently had an opportunity to resolve this issue but declined to do so[.]" *Id.* (citing *County of Los Angeles v. Mendez*, ___ U.S. ___, 137 S.Ct. 1539, 1547 n. 8 (2017)).

2. The Supreme Court crafted the *Graham* standard for uses of force against adults. Should the *Graham* factors be modified when assessing uses of force in schools? Yes, argues Professor Alexis Karteron. In assessing whether a use of force against a student in school violates the Fourth Amendment, she argues courts should consider "the seriousness of the alleged infraction or crime; the likelihood that the student has committed an infraction or crime; the age of the student; the size and stature of the student; the likelihood of inflicting harm or trauma, especially in light of known disabilities or vulnerabilities; and the necessity of the enforcement action. A reasonableness test requiring consideration of these factors recognizes both the sensitivity of the school context and the unique vulnerabilities of juveniles." *Arrested Development: Rethinking the Fourth Amendment Standard for Seizures and Uses of Force in Schools*, 18 NEV. L. J. 863, 911 (2018).

For example, consider whether and how *Graham* should apply to a 7-year old second-grader, just over 4 feet tall and 60 lbs., who gets upset at being teased in class, leaves his seat, and yells at his second-grade classmate to "leave me alone. I'm not paying attention to you." Does this situation require police intervention? If the child leaves the classroom with a police officer but is crying and tries to wriggle out the officer's grasp, does the Fourth Amendment allow the officer to handcuff the 7-year old? Does the Fourth Amendment allow the officer and the principal to leave the child handcuffed for more than 15 minutes? *See K.W.P. v. Kansas City Public Schools*, 931 F.3d 813, 826 (8th Cir. 2019) (holding police officer and principal did not violate 7-year old's Fourth Amendment rights); *see* Brief of Plaintiff/Appellee in *K.W.P. v. Kansas City Public Schools*, 2018 WL 1763730 (April 2, 2018) at ii.

Jury Instructions

Recall from Chapter 2 that, before a jury retires to consider the evidence, the trial court judge instructs the jury on the law governing the plaintiff's claim. Recall that jury instructions are tailored by the judge (and law clerks) to the individual case but generally are based on published instructions, updated to reflect current law in the jurisdiction where the jury is seated. Below is an example of how district courts within the Eighth Circuit explain to juries how to evaluate a claim that a police officer used excessive force in seizing the plaintiff and thereby violated the plaintiff's 4th Amendment rights. The brackets indicate text that would only be shown to the jury if the district court judge who tailors the instructions considers it relevant to the plaintiff's claim. The footnotes to the instructions suggest how to use the instructions and identify the sources of each instruction for the district court judge to evaluate.

Excerpt from Eighth Circuit's Pattern Jury Instructions[27]

4.40 ELEMENTS OF CLAIM: EXCESSIVE USE OF FORCE—ARREST OR OTHER SEIZURE OF PERSON BEFORE CONFINEMENT FOURTH AMENDMENT

Your verdict must be for plaintiff [here insert name] and against defendant [here insert name] [here generally describe the claim][1] if all the following elements have been proved:[2]

First, the defendant [here describe an act such as "struck, hit, kicked, or shot"][4, 3] the plaintiff when [arresting or stopping][4] [him] [her]; and

Second, the force used was excessive because it was not reasonably necessary to [here describe the purpose for which force was used such as "arrest the plaintiff," or "take the plaintiff into custody," or "stop the plaintiff for investigation"]; and

Third, as a direct result, the plaintiff was injured;[5] and

[*Fourth*, the defendant was acting under color of state law.][6]

In determining whether the force, [if any][7] was "excessive," you must consider: the need for the application of force; the relationship between the need and the amount of force that was used; the extent of the injury inflicted; and whether a reasonable officer on the scene, without the benefit of hindsight, would have used that much force under similar circumstances. [You should keep in mind that the decision about how much force to use often must be made in circumstances that are tense, uncertain and rapidly changing.][8] [Deadly force[9] may be used only if it is reasonably believed necessary to [(apprehend a dangerous, fleeing felon) (prevent a significant threat of death or serious physical harm to the officer or others)].[10] A warning must be given, if [feasible] [possible], before deadly force may be used.] You must [decide] [determine] whether the officer's actions were reasonable in the light of the facts and cir-

---

27. Committee on Model Jury Instructions for the District Courts of the Eighth Circuit, 8th Cir. Civil Jury Instr. §4.40 (2019), http://www.juryinstructions.ca8.uscourts.gov.

cumstances confronting the officer [without regard to the officer's own state of mind, intention or motivation].[11]

If any of the above elements has not been proved, then your verdict must be for the defendant.

["Deadly force" is force intended or reasonably likely to cause death or serious physical injury.] [12]

Notes on Use

... 6. Use this language if there is an issue as to whether the defendant was acting under color of state law, a prerequisite to a claim under 42 U.S.C. § 1983. Typically, this element will be conceded by the defendant. If so, it need not be included in this instruction. Include this phrase if the defendant denies the use of any force.

...

9. Add the definition of deadly force if the phrase is used in the instruction.

10. Add this phrase or other appropriate language if deadly force is used. *See Rahn v. Hawkins*, 464 F.3d 813 (8th Cir. 2006); *Tennessee v. Garner*, 471 U.S. 1 (1985).

11. Add this phrase if there is evidence of the defendant officer's ill will toward the plaintiff. *See Graham v. Connor*, 490 U.S. 386 (1989).

12. Use this or another definition if deadly force was used, or may have been used. *See Kuha v. City of Minnetonka*, 365 F.3d 590, 597–98 (8th Cir. 2004) (use of police dog not deadly force); RESTATEMENT 2d OF TORTS § 131 (1965); *Black's Law Dictionary*, 718 (9th ed. 2009) ("violent action known to create a substantial risk of causing death or serious bodily harm"). There are a variety of formulations, all of which are similar.

Jury Verdict Sheet

When the jury retires to consider the evidence, the trial court judge often will provide the jury with a series of questions to answer. The jury verdict sheet, or special interrogatories, elicit the jury's answers to each of the key questions on the defendant's liability and the jury's award of damages. These questions function like a flowchart summarizing the legal analysis of plaintiff's case.

Below is the Eleventh Circuit's jury verdict form for a Fourth Amendment claim. Only the relevant portions of the bracketed material would be provided to the jury.

Eleventh Circuit Jury Verdict Form[28]

Do you find from a preponderance of the evidence:

1. That [name of defendant] intentionally committed acts that violated [name of plaintiff]'s right to [describe protected right]?

Answer Yes or No ____________

28. COMMITTEE ON PATTERN JURY INSTRUCTIONS, PATTERN CIV. JURY INSTR. 11th Cir. Ch. 5 Appendix B, 42 U.S.C. § 1983 CLAIMS FOR CASES BROUGHT BY NON-PRISONERS (PRISON-LITIGATION

If your answer is "No," this ends your deliberations, and your foreperson should sign and date the last page of this verdict form. If your answer is "Yes," go to the next question.

[2. That [name of defendant]'s actions were "under color" of state law?

Answer Yes or No ____________

If your answer is "No," this ends your deliberations, and your foreperson should sign and date the last page of this verdict form. If your answer is "Yes," go to the next question.]

3. That [name of defendant]'s conduct caused [name of plaintiff]'s injuries?

Answer Yes or No ____________

If your answer is "No," this ends your deliberations, and your foreperson should sign and date the last page of this verdict form. If your answer is "Yes," go to the next question.

4.a. That [name of plaintiff] should be awarded compensatory damages against [name of defendant]?

Answer Yes or No ____________

If your answer is "Yes," in what amount? $____________

—OR—

4.b. That [name of plaintiff] should be awarded nominal damages against [name of defendant]?

Answer Yes or No ____________

If your answer is "Yes," in what amount? $____________

[5. That punitive damages should be assessed against [name of individual defendant]?

Answer Yes or No ____________

If your answer is "Yes," in what amount? $____________]

SO SAY WE ALL.

DATE: ________________

___________________________ Foreperson's Signature

Exercise 6-A

1. You work for a law firm that frequently represents cities and towns. The Chief of Police for a city your firm represents has just learned that an on-duty police officer fatally shot a criminal suspect. The Chief texts you to

---

Reform Does Not Apply), Special Interrogatories To The Jury (2018), http://www.ca11.uscourts.gov/sites/default/files/courtdocs/clk/FormCivilPatternJuryInstruction.pdf.

call her in five minutes to discuss whether the officer's use of deadly force was constitutional. To prepare for the phone meeting, jot down a short list of questions to ask the Chief about the shooting.

2. Practice Pointer: If you had to quickly research the legal standards that govern a police officer's use of deadly force, what are some sources you could consult?

For further discussion

Since the early 1990's, law enforcement agencies have adopted various technologies intended to permit police to effect seizures using force less lethal than deadly force. Conducted energy devices (CEDs), sometimes known as "tasers" or "stun guns," use an electrical charge "to induce involuntary muscle contractions" that temporarily incapacitate the targeted person and "have become the less-lethal weapon of choice for a growing number of law enforcement agencies." *Study of Deaths Following Electro Muscular Disruption: Interim Report, U.S. Department of Justice*, Office of Justice Programs, National Institute of Justice, at 1 (June 2008). As of 2019, more than 15,000 law enforcement agencies in the U.S. have such electrical devices. Paul A. Haskins, National Institute of Justice, *Conducted Energy Devices: Policies on Use Evolve to Reflect Research and Field Deployment Experience* (May 2019).

Some people subjected to a charge from a CED have died. In a 2017 news story, Reuters news "documented 1,005 people who have died in the United States following encounters with police in which Tasers were used either on their own or, more often, as part of a larger mosaic of force. In at least 153 of those cases, Reuters found, coroners or medical examiners cited the Taser as a cause or contributing factor in the death." Peter Eisler, Grant Smith, and Jason Szep, *How Reuters Tracked Fatalities and Taser Incidents* (Aug. 22, 2017).

In addition, the devices may cause puncture wounds or burns and "head injuries or skeletal fractures may result from falls due to muscle incapacitation or intense muscle contraction." OFFICE OF JUSTICE PROGRAMS, NATIONAL INSTITUTE OF JUSTICE, STUDY OF DEATHS FOLLOWING ELECTRO MUSCULAR DISRUPTION, U.S. DEPARTMENT OF JUSTICE at 6 (May 2011). "There are groups who may be at risk for sudden death and those who are more vulnerable" to injury, such as "small children, those with diseased hearts, the elderly and pregnant women." *Id.* at 23. The Justice Department Report states: "use of a CED on these individuals when recognized during attempted subdual should be minimized or avoided unless the situation excludes other reasonable options." *Id.* at 24. The Justice Department further warns that "multiple or prolonged activations of CED as a means to accomplish subdual should be minimized or avoided" because those practices carry "unknown risks" and are involved with "most deaths associated with CED use." *Id.* at 27. The case below applies *Graham* in the context of a police officer's use of a Taser.

Bryan v. MacPherson

608 F.3d 614 (9th Cir. 2010)

WARDLAW, Circuit Judge.

[In 2005, Officer Brian MacPherson shot Carl Bryan with a taser during a morning traffic stop for a seatbelt violation. When Officer MacPherson stopped Mr. Bryan's car at an intersection, Bryan became angry at himself for failing to buckle his seatbelt. At the Officer's direction, Bryan parked his car on the curb. He hit his steering wheel and yelled expletives to himself, then stepped out of his car. "Bryan was agitated, standing outside his car, yelling gibberish and hitting his thighs, clad only in his boxer shorts and tennis shoes ... Bryan did not verbally threaten Officer MacPherson and ... was standing twenty to twenty-five feet away and not attempting to flee ... Officer MacPherson testified that Bryan took "one step" toward him, but Bryan says he did not take any step, and the physical evidence indicates that Bryan was actually facing away from Officer MacPherson. Without giving any warning, Officer MacPherson shot Bryan with his taser gun. One of the taser probes embedded in the side of Bryan's upper left arm. The electrical current immobilized him whereupon he fell face first into the ground, fracturing four teeth and suffering facial contusions." The Ninth Circuit held Officer MacPherson violated Mr. Bryan's 4th Amendment rights by using non-lethal but excessive force.]

We, along with our sister circuits, have held that tasers and stun guns fall into the category of non-lethal force. *See, e.g., Lewis* [*v. Downey*,] 581 F.3d [467,] 476 (7th Cir. 2009); *United States v. Fore*, 507 F.3d 412, 413 (6th Cir. 2007).... [H]owever ... all force—lethal and non-lethal—must be justified by the need for the specific level of force employed. *Graham* [*v. Connor*], 490 U.S. [386,] 395 (1989).... Nor is "non-lethal" a monolithic category of force. A blast of pepper spray and blows from a baton are not necessarily constitutionally equivalent levels of force simply because both are classified as non-lethal. Rather than relying on broad characterizations, we must evaluate the nature of the specific force employed in a specific factual situation ...

The physiological effects, the high levels of pain, and foreseeable risk of physical injury lead us to conclude that the X26 [taser] and similar devices are a greater intrusion than other non-lethal methods of force we have confronted. [We have] held that a jury could conclude that pepper spray was more than a "minimal intrusion" as it caused "intense pain..., an involuntary closing of the eyes, a gagging reflex, and temporary paralysis of the larynx." ... We similarly reject any contention that, because the taser results only in the "temporary" infliction of pain, it constitutes a nonintrusive level of force. The pain is intense, is felt throughout the body, and is administered by effectively commandeering the victim's muscles and nerves. Beyond the experience of pain, tasers result in "immobilization, disorientation, loss of balance, and weakness," even after the electrical current has ended ... Moreover, tasering a person may result in serious injuries when intense pain and loss of muscle control cause a sudden and uncontrolled fall.

The X26 thus intrudes upon the victim's physiological functions and physical integrity in a way that other non-lethal uses of force do not. While pepper spray causes an intense pain and acts upon the target's physiology, the effects of the X26 are not limited to the target's eyes or respiratory system. Unlike the police "nonchakus"..., the pain delivered by the X26 is far more intense and is not localized, external, [or] gradual.... We recognize the important role controlled electric devices like the Taser X26 can play in law enforcement. The ability to defuse a dangerous situation from a distance can obviate the need for more severe, or even deadly, force and thus can help protect police officers, bystanders, and suspects alike. We hold only that the X26 and similar devices constitute an intermediate, significant level of force that must be justified by "'a strong government interest [that] compels the employment of such force.'" [citation omitted].

...

Viewing the facts in the light most favorable to Bryan, the totality of the circumstances here did not justify the deployment of the Taser X26. The "most important" factor under *Graham* is whether the suspect posed an "immediate threat to the safety of the officers or others." *Smith v. City of Hemet*, 394 F.3d 689, 702 (9th Cir. 2005) (en banc).... While Bryan's behavior created something of an unusual situation, this does not, by itself, justify the use of significant force ... Rather, the objective facts must indicate that the suspect poses an immediate threat to the officer or a member of the public ... Bryan did not pose an immediate threat to Officer MacPherson or bystanders despite his unusual behavior. It is undisputed that Bryan was unarmed, and, as Bryan was only dressed in tennis shoes and boxer shorts, it should have been apparent that he was unarmed ... Although Bryan had shouted expletives to himself while pulling his car over and had taken to shouting gibberish, and more expletives, outside his car, at no point did he level a physical or verbal threat against Officer MacPherson. *See Smith*, 394 F.3d at 702–03 (recognizing that although the victim was shouting expletives, there was no threat leveled against the officer). Bryan was standing, without advancing, fifteen to twenty-five feet away from Officer MacPherson between the door and body of the car ... Not only was Bryan standing, unarmed, at a distance of fifteen to twenty-five feet, but the physical evidence demonstrates that Bryan was not even facing Officer MacPherson when he was shot: One of the taser probes lodged in the side of Bryan's arm, rather than in his chest, and the location of the blood on the pavement indicates that he fell away from the officer, rather than towards him. An unarmed, stationary individual, facing away from an officer at a distance of fifteen to twenty-five feet is far from an "immediate threat" to that officer. Nor was Bryan's erratic, but nonviolent, behavior a potential threat to anyone else, as there is no indication that there were pedestrians nearby or traffic on the street at the time of the incident. Finally, while confronting Bryan, Officer MacPherson had unholstered and charged his X26, placing him in a position to respond immediately to any change in the circumstances. The circumstances here show that Officer MacPherson was confronted by, at most, a disturbed and upset young man, not an immediately threatening one.

Officer MacPherson relies heavily on the Eleventh Circuit opinion in *Draper v. Reynolds*, 369 F.3d 1270 (11th Cir. 2004), which addressed the use of a taser during the arrest of an aggressive, argumentative individual. Although we do not adopt *Draper* as the law of this circuit, the present case is clearly distinguishable from the one before the Eleventh Circuit. Unlike Bryan, who was yelling gibberish and gave no sign of hearing or understanding Officer MacPherson's orders, it was undisputed in *Draper* that Draper heard and understood the officer's commands, and not only failed to comply, but engaged the officer in an increasingly heated argument. *Id.* at 1273. Four times the officer asked Draper to retrieve paperwork from the cab of his truck and four times Draper heard the officer, turned toward the truck to comply, but then turned around, walked back toward the officer and loudly accused the officer of "harassing" and "disrespecting" him, displaying a growing belligerence. *Id.* It was not until the fifth time that the officer requested the paperwork and Draper refused to comply, yelled at the officer, and paced toward him in agitation that the officer resorted to the taser. *Id.* The Eleventh Circuit determined that a verbal arrest command (when Draper had refused to comply with the first five commands) accompanied by an attempt to physically handcuff Draper "in these particular circumstances, may well have or would likely have escalated a tense and difficult situation into a serious physical struggle, in which either Draper or [the officer] would be seriously hurt." *Id.* at 1278.

Bryan never addressed, let alone argued with, Officer MacPherson once he left his car ... [T]he officer in *Draper* was confronting a belligerent, argumentative individual who was angrily pacing within feet of his position. Officer MacPherson, by contrast, was confronted with a half naked, unarmed, stationary, apparently disturbed individual shouting gibberish at a distance of approximately twenty feet. The only similarity to the factual circumstances in *Draper* is that both Draper and Bryan were stopped for a traffic violation, were loud, and were tasered by the police.

... It is undisputed that Bryan's initial "crime" was a mere traffic infraction — failing to wear a seatbelt — punishable by a fine. Traffic violations generally will not support the use of a significant level of force. *See Deville v. Marcantel*, 567 F.3d 156, 167 (5th Cir. 2009) ("Deville was stopped for a minor traffic violation ... making the need for force substantially lower than if she had been suspected of a serious crime.") ... Officer MacPherson now argues that use of the taser was justified because he believed Bryan may have been mentally ill and thus subject to detention. To the contrary: if Officer MacPherson believed Bryan was mentally disturbed he should have made greater effort to take control of the situation through less intrusive means ... Although we have refused to create two tracks of excessive force analysis, one for the mentally ill and one for serious criminals, we have found that even "when an emotionally disturbed individual is 'acting out' and inviting officers to use deadly force to subdue him, the governmental interest in using such force is diminished by the fact that the officers are confronted ... with a mentally ill individual." [Ninth Circuit citation omitted]. The same reasoning applies to intermediate levels of force. A mentally ill individual is in need of a doctor, not a jail cell, and in the usual case — where such an individual is neither a threat to himself nor to anyone else — the government's interest in deploying force to detain him is not as substantial as its interest in deploying that force to apprehend a dangerous criminal. Moreover, the purpose of detaining a mentally ill individual is not to punish him, but to help him. The government has an important interest in providing assistance to a person in need of psychiatric care; thus, the use of force that may be justified by that interest necessarily differs both in degree and in kind from the use of force that would be justified against a person who has committed a crime or who poses a threat to the community.

… The only resistance Officer MacPherson testified to was a failure to comply with his order that Bryan remain in his car. Shouting gibberish and hitting one's quadriceps is certainly bizarre behavior, but such behavior is a far cry from actively struggling with an officer attempting to restrain and arrest an individual. *Compare Abdullahi v. City of Madison*, 423 F.3d 763, 776 (7th Cir. 2005) (involving an arrestee swinging a belt at an officer and "strenuously resist[ing]" as the police attempted to handcuff him); *McCormick v. City of Fort Lauderdale*, 333 F.3d 1234, 1241–42 (11th Cir. 2003) (involving an arrestee engaging and advancing on officers with a stick)…. Two additional considerations militate against finding Officer MacPherson's use of force reasonable. First, it is undisputed that Officer MacPherson failed to warn Bryan that he would be shot with the X26 if he did not comply with the order to remain in his car … [P]olice officers normally provide such warnings where feasible, even when the force is less than deadly, and … the failure to give such a warning is a factor to consider … Here, it was feasible to give a warning that the use of force was imminent if Bryan did not comply. While a warning to Bryan may or may not have caused him to comply, there was "ample time to give that order or warning and no reason whatsoever not to do so." … Second, we have held that police are "required to consider '[w]hat other tactics if any were available' to effect the arrest." [We do not challenge the settled principle that police officers need not employ the "least intrusive" degree of force possible … We merely recognize the equally settled principle that officers must consider less intrusive methods of effecting the arrest and that the presence of feasible alternatives is a factor to include in our analysis.] … Objectively … there were clear, reasonable, and less intrusive alternatives. Officer MacPherson knew additional officers were en route to the scene … Officer MacPherson did not provide a warning before deploying the X26 and apparently did not consider less intrusive means of effecting Bryan's arrest factor significantly into our *Graham* analysis …

Our review of the *Graham* factors reveals that the government had, at best, a minimal interest in the use of force against Bryan … We thus conclude that the intermediate level of force employed by Officer MacPherson against Bryan was excessive in light of the governmental interests at stake. Bryan never attempted to flee. He was clearly unarmed and was standing, without advancing in any direction, next to his vehicle. Officer MacPherson was standing approximately twenty feet away observing Bryan's stationary, bizarre tantrum with his X26 drawn and charged. Consequently, the objective facts reveal a tense, but static, situation with Officer MacPherson ready to respond to any developments while awaiting backup. Bryan was neither a flight risk, a dangerous felon, nor an immediate threat … Officer MacPherson's desire to quickly and decisively end an unusual and tense situation is understandable. His chosen method for doing so violated Bryan's constitutional right to be free from excessive force.

For further discussion

1. In addition to *Bryan*, this book contains other examples of police encounters with emotionally agitated people, such as the police officers confronted by the armed father who had just murdered his children (*Castle Rock* in Chapter 8), the police officers attempting to arrest a suspect making verbal threats (*Espinosa* in Chapter 11), and the police officers who did not obtain medical treatment for an arrestee (*Canton* in Chapter 12). For factual background on police encounters with the mentally ill, *see* Chapter 11.

2. In 2017, Reuters news studied 442 Taser-related wrongful death lawsuits and found "34 percent involved allegations the person being shocked ... suffered from mental illness." Jason Szep, Peter Eisler, and Tim Reid, *'Breathe, Ronald, Breathe': The Court Case Curbing Taser Use,* Special Report, *Reuters* (August 23, 2017).

3. Chapter 11 revisits *Bryan* in the context of qualified immunity. Despite the court's ruling that Officer MacPherson violated Mr. Bryan's 4th Amendment rights, the Ninth Circuit held that the officer could not be held liable because of the powerful doctrine of qualified immunity.

Exercise 6-B

1. Consider whether the following situation is similar to *Bryan*. Did a police officer violate the Fourth Amendment by administering three five-second electrical shocks, over a two minute period, to a handcuffed, nonviolent traffic arrestee who was on the ground sobbing and who was not attempting to flee, where the purpose of the electrical shocks was to prompt the arrestee to stand up and enter the police car?

   - Is it relevant that the arrestee was refusing to stand up and complete the arrest?
   - Is it relevant that the officer repeatedly warned the arrestee that he would use the stun gun if the arrestee did not stand up and enter the police car?
   - Or that the officer was alone, at night, on a dark highway?

Assume the above scene was captured on police video. If you worked in a plaintiffs' law firm, would you represent the arrestee? What advice would you give a partner in your firm who was considering whether to represent the arrestee as a plaintiff in a suit alleging that the police officer used excessive force in the arrest? Is this situation similar to the facts of *Bryan*? In what ways is this situation different from *Bryan*?

2. This scenario is based on *Buckley v. Rackard*, 292 Fed. Appx. 791 (11th Cir. 2008), *cert. denied*, 556 U.S. 1235 (2009). Note that the Eleventh Cir-

cuit chose to decide the appeal in a non-precedential opinion. Yet the American Civil Liberties Union considered the case sufficiently important that it participated in filing a petition for certiorari on Mr. Buckley's behalf. Does it surprise you that a non-precedential opinion would concern an issue that a lawyer would consider not only important—but worthy of Supreme Court attention?

Exercise 6-C

Reflect on the issue of institutional competence in the context of tasers. Suppose the Mayor of the City asks the City Law Department which branch of government is best situated to define how police and correctional officers should use tasers: executive, legislative, or judicial. Further, suppose Mayor Valdez, who is a lawyer, asks whether the City should rely on federal courts to define the constitutionally permissible use of tasers through litigation or whether the City executive branch could provide better guidance to police and corrections officials on how to use tasers without violating constitutional rights. How would you respond?

Suppose further that the Mayor Valdez wants to hear different views on a possible Police Department policy to govern taser use by police. The Mayor invites three groups to propose a City policy: the Police Union, a non-profit advocacy group called Citizens Against Police Brutality, and the City Law Department (which represents both the Mayor and the Police Department). The Mayor's goal is to set a policy that enables police to carry out their dangerous duties while also preventing and deterring police violation of the constitutional rights of the citizens—and voters—of the City. What suggestions do you have for a City policy? Would your suggestions differ if you represented a different one of the three groups?

Preparing to negotiate to resolve a dispute

Exercise 6-D is a negotiation of an excessive force claim involving police use of a taser. The purpose of a negotiation is to get the other party to agree on terms as favorable as possible to your client. Everything about how and what you communicate should reflect that purpose.

Negotiating an end to litigation can be an opportunity to creatively deal with obstacles and craft a tailored solution. It can be collegial and cooperative. Negotiation can also be anxiety-producing if the lawyer is worried he or she will not have good enough information to avoid being misled, is mistrustful of negotiators on other side, is concerned about a disparity in power between the two sides, or is concerned about posturing by negotiators on the other side—yelling, abusive language, pounding the table, walking out.

A party's interests are the needs, desires, concerns, and fears that underlie the position of each side. Before the negotiation, try to identify both your own client's interests and the interests of the opposing party. Try to decide which interests take priority for each side. Examples of possible interests:

- resolving litigation promptly
- maintaining a beneficial long-term relationship
- maintaining reputation
- receiving money—how much and when
- psychological/emotional need for apology or admission of wrongdoing

Rights are independent legal rules or social standards that demonstrate the legitimacy or fairness of a party's position. The legal rules provide the context for a negotiation to resolve a dispute and help to predict what would happen if the litigation is not settled.

Most negotiations involve both an adversarial approach and a problem-solving approach. The adversarial approach focuses on the power and rights of the parties. Each party takes the position that s/he is entitled to something and the parties make concessions based on their perceptions of the strengths of their cases until an agreement is reached—or not reached.

The problem-solving approach focuses on the underlying interests of the parties and on how each can be better off by agreement, aiming for a win/win. A problem-solving approach requires each side to recognize its own interests and the interests of the other side. This approach can avoid parties getting locked into positions because they have invested energy in justifying those positions to opponents.

Before the negotiation, develop a Best Alternative to a Negotiated Agreement, BATNA, to measure the negotiation result. If the negotiation does not result in terms that are better than the BATNA, the negotiation will be abandoned and the litigation will proceed. Negotiators try to anticipate the other side's alternatives to settling, which is one way of measuring the strength or weakness of your own client's negotiating position. Good planning for the negotiator therefore involves imagining the other party's BATNA as well as your own.[29]

Exercise 6-D

In this exercise, you will strategize for a negotiation to settle a 4th Amendment excessive force claim against police that Ms. Brooks just filed. You represent either Ms. Brooks or the two police officers.

---

29. This brief introduction to negotiation is based on Stefan H. Krieger and Richard Neumann, Essential Lawyering Skills: Interviewing, Counseling, Negotiation, and Persuasive Fact Analysis (Aspen 2007).

Police tasered Ms. Brooks under the following circumstances. Consider why police used force on Ms. Brooks, the seriousness of the crime, whether Ms. Brooks was an immediate threat to the safety of the police or other people, whether she was actively resisting arrest, and whether she was trying to escape from police.

Ms. Brooks was driving her son to school. Two police officers stopped her for driving 32 miles per hour when the speed limit was 20. Brooks disagreed. From her seat in the car, she asked the Officer to let her accept the ticket without signing it. Officer Jones became angry and asked "*Can't you read?*" Brooks answered, "*Are you implying that I can't read because I'm black?*"

Officer Jones told Brooks that if she did not sign the speeding ticket she would be arrested. Brooks asked him "*For what?*" After Brooks refused to sign the ticket, the two police officers told Brooks she was under arrest. Police ordered Brooks out of the car.

Ms. Brooks refused to get out of the car. She explained to the police that she was seven months pregnant. She had already given the police officers her driver's license and asked the officers to allow her to take the ticket and leave. Officer Jones reached into the car, removed her keys, and dropped the keys on the floor of the car.

The two police officers tried to pull Brooks out of the car. She resisted by holding the steering wheel. The officers recognized that trying to pull Brooks from the car might risk injury to her or themselves. Instead, the officers decided to use a taser. The officers knew from training and experience that the taser causes pain but not injury and would not injure a pregnant woman. Officer Jones took out his taser. He warned Brooks that if she did not obey their order to get out of the car she would be tasered. She continued to resist arrest. Officer Jones applied the taser to her neck. Brooks shouted and honked the car horn. The 2 police were able to pull her from the car and handcuff her. Brooks admits she suffered no lasting physical injury from the taser, but does have a scar on her neck.

How do rules from *Graham*, *Bryan*, and the model jury instructions apply to your client's facts? In addition to that 4th Amendment excessive force authority, you may want to rely on *Bryan*'s summary of *Draper*, which held that police use of the taser did not violate the 4th Amendment. In planning your strategy for the negotiation, consider all of the following:

1. What are your client's interests?
2. What are the other party's interests?
3. What steps can your client take to change the power relationship? What steps can the other party take?
4. What is your client's Best Alternative to a Negotiated Agreement? Can you predict the other party's Best Alternative to a Negotiated Agreement?

5. What possible solutions can you suggest?
6. What information will you disclose? What will you try to conceal?
7. What negotiating style(s) will you use?

For further discussion

1. Each Fourth Amendment decision concerning tasers is a potential vehicle for the court to better define the constitutional law governing police use of tasers. Do you think Fourth Amendment doctrine in the context of tasers is sufficiently settled to be a routinely applied? Under what circumstances do you think a federal appellate court should designate an opinion concerning tasers to be non-precedential, binding only on the parties, rather than a precedent that will govern future use of tasers? What are the benefits of clarifying constitutional law governing tasers?

The Eleventh Circuit chose to label each of the below taser opinions as non-precedential decisions. That means the decisions do not have to be consistent with one another and can be ignored by future appellate panels, by district courts, and by administrators and police otherwise bound by Eleventh Circuit precedent.

- The Constitution could be violated when police tased a father who advised his son not to speak to the officers who were arresting the son, told the arresting officer not to be disrespectful, suggested the officer's microphone had recorded the officer's threat, and was on the ground and not resisting arrest himself when the officer tased the father in the back. *Thompson v. Mostert*, 489 Fed. Appx. 396 (11th Cir. 2012).
- The Constitution could be violated when police tased an unarmed man who "(1) was at least four feet up in a tree with his hands raised, (2) posed no threat to their safety or the safety of others, (3) had no chance, and did not attempt, to flee, and (4) merely put his hands in the air in compliance with the instructions of at least one officer," rendering the man paraplegic. *Harper v. Perkins*, 459 Fed. Appx. 822, 827 (11th Cir. 2012).
- The Constitution did not clearly prohibit police from tasing a noncompliant suspect three times, even "where the underlying crime was minor and where no violence had occurred." *Floyd v. Corder*, 426 Fed Appx. 790, 792 (11th Cir. 2011).
- The Constitution could be violated when police tased a woman twice, where she was non-threatening, the alleged crime was minor, and she was on the ground and unable to resist when police tased her a second time. *Powell v. Haddock*, 366 Fed. Appx. 29, 30 (11th Cir. 2010).

Over vigorous dissent, the Eleventh Circuit found no violation of the Fourth Amendment where a man was arrested for refusing to sign a speeding ticket and police tased him three times for refusing to stand and enter the police car, even though the man was handcuffed, on the ground, and sobbing. *Buckley v. Haddock*, 292 Fed. Appx. 791 (11th Cir. 2008), *cert. denied*, 556 U.S. 1235 (2009); *id.* at 799 (concurrence would have held third use of taser violated Constitution but that officer nevertheless had qualified immunity because the right was not "clearly established"). This book revisits the significance of clarity in constitutional rights in Chapter 11, Qualified Immunity.

2. In 2016, the Fourth Circuit adopted a "bright-line rule that only a need to protect police or others from a present threat—and not mere desire to control the subject—can justify CED use." Paul A. Haskins, National Institute of Justice, *Conducted Energy Devices: Policies on Use Evolve to Reflect Research and Field Deployment Experience* (May 2019)[30] (summarizing *Armstrong v. Pinehurst*, 810 F.3d 892 (4th Cir.), *cert. denied*, ___ U.S. ___, 137 S.Ct. 61 (2016)). In *Armstrong*, the Fourth Circuit "made it clear that the court saw CEDs as closer to the lethal-force end of the [use-of-force] spectrum." Haskins, *Conducted Energy Devices*.[31] Even if the suspect was not complying with police orders or engaged in nonviolent physical resistance, 810 F.3d at 904, the Fourth Circuit held "taser use is unreasonable force in response to resistance that does not raise a risk of immediate danger." *Id.* at 905. Rather, even if the suspect is not restrained, use of a CED should be as a response to danger: "A rule limiting Taser use to situations involving a proportional safety threat does not countenance use in situations where an unrestrained arrestee, though resistant, presents no serious safety threat." *Id.* at 904. The Fourth Circuit also "proscribed CED use on a fleeing subject, again absent an immediate danger posed to others. In contrast, [a National Institute of Justice-supported] pre-2010 survey of more than 500 law enforcement agencies found that almost three-fourths of the agencies using CEDs allowed their use against fleeing subjects." Haskins, *Conducted Energy Devices*.[32]

In the wake of *Armstrong*, Reuters news reported that, within the geographical region constrained by Fourth Circuit rulings:

> police are scaling back use [of Tasers]. At least eight major cities [within the Fourth Circuit] have adopted more restrictive Taser policies, Reuters found. In Baltimore, police used Tasers 47 percent fewer times [in 2016] than in 2015, according to records reviewed by Reuters. Deployments fell 65 percent in Virginia Beach; 60 percent in Greensboro, North Carolina; 55 percent in Charleston, South Carolina; and 52 percent in Huntington, West Virginia. Norfolk, Virginia, saw deployments plunge 95 percent.

Jason Szep, Peter Eisler, and Tim Reid, *Special Report, 'Breathe, Ronald, Breathe': The Court Case Curbing Taser Use*, Reuters (Aug. 23, 2017).

3. In 2019, the Camden County Police Department in New Jersey announced a new use of force policy it intends to be a national model. While the Constitution "provides a 'floor' for government action," Camden County "aspires to go beyond *Graham* and its minimum requirements ... [T]his directive is intended to ensure that de-escalation techniques are used whenever feasible, that force is only used when

---

30. The report is available at https://nij.ojp.gov/topics/articles/conducted-energy-devices-policies-use-evolve-reflect-research-and-field-deployment.

31. *Id.*

32. *Id.*

necessary, and that the amount of force used is proportionate to the situation that an officer encounters." Page 2. Drafted with help from the New York University Law School Police Project, the 18-page use of force policy is based on six core principles:

> CORE PRINCIPLE #1: Officers may use force only to accomplish specific law enforcement objectives.
>
> CORE PRINCIPLE #2: Whenever feasible, officers should attempt to de-escalate confrontations with the goal of resolving encounters without force. Officers may only use force that is objectively reasonable, necessary, and as a last resort.
>
> CORE PRINCIPLE #3: Officers must use only the amount of force that is proportionate to the circumstances.
>
> CORE PRINCIPLE #4: Deadly force is only authorized as a last resort and only in strict accordance with this directive.
>
> CORE PRINCIPLE #5: Officers must promptly provide or request medical aid.
>
> CORE PRINCIPLE #6: Employees have a duty to stop and report uses of force that violate any applicable law and/or this directive.

E. Application of Doctrine in the Trial Court: Evolution of a 4th Amendment Excessive Force Claim from Complaint to Verdict

At the time an attorney files a Complaint, the attorney does not have complete information about the underlying facts. This section illustrates how a legal claim can evolve over the course of the litigation, after the Complaint is filed. It illustrates how lawyers make educated guesses about litigation strategy based on incomplete information. For example, as plaintiff's counsel learns more about the facts of the case during the course of the litigation, the plaintiff's claims may change. The same is true for the defendant's choice of legal defenses. Plaintiff and defendant may also change legal theories in response to evidentiary rulings by the trial court. Often, government defendants will have exclusive knowledge of certain facts that the plaintiff will not learn about until obtaining discovery.

This section summarizes key steps in the litigation from the Complaint alleging a police dog bite to the jury's verdict. It demonstrate how Plaintiff changed the legal theory of a 4th Amendment excessive force claim after learning more through discovery about the city's canine policies. Further, it shows how the parties changed strategy in response to a pretrial court ruling. As you read, contrast the scope of the initial claims with the single claim ultimately heard by the jury.

The suit began with the allegations in Plaintiff's Complaint.

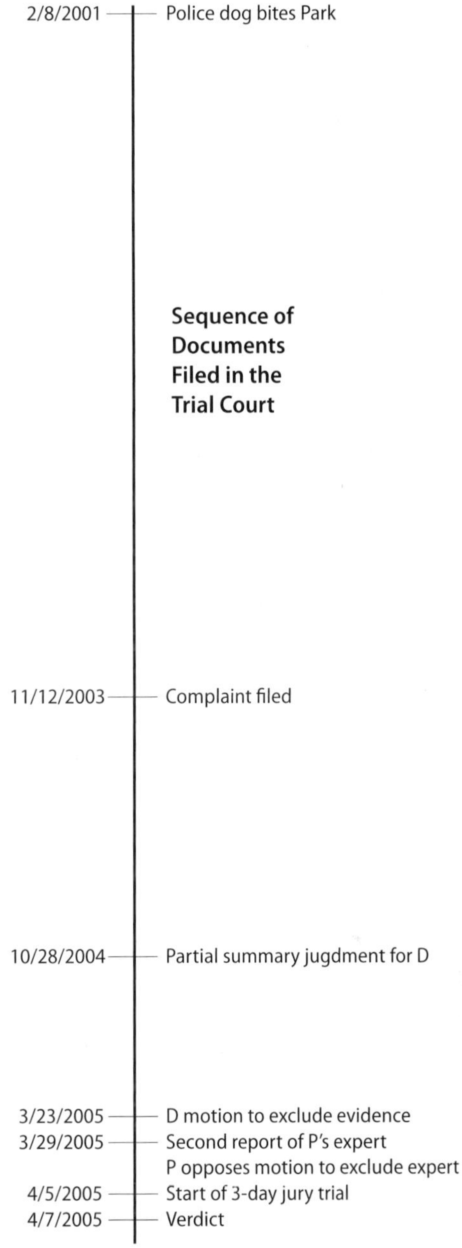

One night in 2001, Plaintiff was asleep in the restaurant where he worked. Plaintiff alleged his constitutional rights were violated when a barking dog awakened him and he was bitten by a police dog. When he filed his Complaint in November 2003, the gist of his federal claim against the two arresting officers was that they violated his 4th Amendment rights by searching and arresting him using "excessive force by releasing their canine dog, Ben, intentionally, into the premises of the Plaintiff, without probable cause," so that the dog could "inflict injury upon anyone lawfully upon the premises, including but not limited to the Plaintiff...." Complaint at ¶¶ 7, 9, 10 in *Park v. Miller*, 2003 WL 23843495 (D. Md. Nov. 12, 2003). Plaintiff alleged that the County was responsible for the police officers' actions, *id.* at ¶ 13, and for the 42 U.S.C. § 1983 violation, he sought $3,000,000 in compensatory damages, $3,000,000 in punitive damages, plus costs and attorneys' fees, *id.* at 4, Wherefore Clause, plus damages for violations of Maryland state law. *Id.*

A year later, the district court entered partial summary judgment for defendants on all claims except the excessive force claim against the dog-handler, Officer Eckley. The district court's opinion clarifies that, during the course of discovery and pre-trial briefing, Plaintiff had refined his excessive force claim to focus on injuries sustained "from a canine 'bite and hold' procedure," a procedure more likely to cause injury than a different method of using police dogs, the "bark and hold" procedure. *Park v. Miller*, 2004 WL 2415062 (D. Md. Oct. 28, 2004). The district court summarized the facts developed during discovery:

> On February 8, 2001 at 4:24 a.m., Sergeant Miller discovered an unsecured rear door to the Times Café ... while conducting a routine foot patrol of area businesses.... At the Times Café, Sergeant Miller opened the unlocked rear door and saw wet footprints leading into the kitchen which led him to suspect possible criminal activity, *i.e.*, suspected breaking and entering....

He then requested a canine team to respond to the location for a building search. Within a few minutes, PFC Eckley, a canine handler, arrived at the scene with his trained police canine, Ben. Beyond making a request for a canine team, Sergeant Miller is not trained to handle or command a police canine. Police radio records show that the building search was initiated by PFC Eckley at 4:36 a.m., and he made a radio request for an ambulance three minutes later.

Unknown to the officers at the time, Plaintiff Park, a part-time employee at the café, and Su Jin Lee, the manager and daughter of a co-owner of the business, were inside the Times Café on separate sofas ... In their depositions, both Park and Lee allege that they were asleep shortly before the canine entered the building, but awoke to sounds of a barking dog outside prior to the actual biting incident.... Neither person could determine where the barking sounds were coming from, and they prepared to leave the establishment after realizing the lateness of the hour. The officers testified that Lee's statements at the scene indicated that both she and Park may have been asleep immediately prior to Ben's seizure of Plaintiff Park....

Both Park and Lee testified at their depositions that they were awake and no oral warning from the police officer was given before the canine began to search the building. In direct contrast, Sergeant Miller and PFC Eckley testified that Eckley "yelled" his customary announcement and waited five to ten seconds before he commanded Ben to search the building. PFC Eckley described his customary announcement as: "County police canine, come out now or I'll release the dog." ...

Inside the café at PFC Eckley's command, the canine began a search for human scent and proceeded from the rear kitchen area into the seating area off-lead, *i.e.*, unrestrained by a leash. Sergeant Miller remained outside the building near the rear door, another officer stood in a surveillance position outside the front entrance, and PFC Eckley "took cover" behind the canine as he continued the building search. The canine tracked a human scent to Park's location behind a partition and bit him on the lower right ankle in order to hold him for PFC Eckley. At the same moment, PFC Eckley alleges that he saw a suspect's head look over the top of the booth. PFC Eckley moved closer to the booth where he discovered Park, who was held in a bite-grip by the canine, and Lee, who had suffered no injury. He ordered Park and Lee to show their hands and commanded the canine to release his bite-grip from Park's leg. PFC Eckley estimated that the bite lasted ten to fifteen seconds, and he observed two mouth bites on Park's lower right leg, which included an initial bite and then a readjust to get a firm hold when Park fell to the floor.

Sergeant Miller heard screams and entered the building upon PFC Eckley's radio request to his unit. Sergeant Miller proceeded into the seating area and arrived at the booth where PFC Eckley was questioning Park and Lee to as-

> certain their identities. Sergeant Miller participated in the dialogue and confirmed PFC Eckley's assertion to Lee and Park that PFC Eckley shouted a warning before Ben began to search the area. (Lee Dep., at 134.) Park alleges that during this questioning, PFC Eckley laughed at him and told him "not to worry" about the dog bite because the dog was "clean." (Lee Dep., at 138–39.) Lee alleges that the officers acted "like they were having a party. They were just talking to each other, you know, the joking." (*Id.*) In the course of this questioning collateral issues arose regarding some empty alcohol containers on the tabletops, whether the suspects had been drinking, and the location of the establishment's liquor license. In response to PFC Eckley's radio request made five minutes earlier, a paramedic unit arrived at the scene at 4:44 a.m. and transported Park to the hospital.... Park claims to have nerve damage to the affected area with symptoms of periodic numbness and burning in the sole of his right foot.

Park v. Miller, 2004 WL 2415062 at *1–*3 (D. Md. Oct. 28, 2004).

The district court entered judgment for Sergeant Miller because he did not actively participate in directing the dog's actions and entered judgment for the County because there was "no evidence demonstrating that the 'bite and hold' method is per se unconstitutional, that Howard County's use of force policy is unconstitutional, or that the county systematically fails to adequately train and supervise its officers in the proper use of police canines." *Id.* at *3–*4. The district court narrowed the issue for a jury trial to the excessive force claim against Officer Eckley, specifically holding that police officers generally must warn a suspect before releasing a dog and that, assuming Plaintiff's version of the facts to be true, Officer Eckley did not warn Mr. Park before releasing the dog. *Id.* at *3.

The parties changed litigation strategy in response to the district court's pretrial ruling. Several months after partial summary judgment was entered, and about two weeks before trial of the excessive force claim against Officer Eckley, Defendant moved to exclude testimony of Plaintiff's expert on police canine practices. Defendant argued that since the "bite and hold" police dog technique was not unconstitutional per se, and Officer Eckley was obligated to use the "bite and hold" technique because at the time the dog bit Mr. Park in 2001 "bite and hold" was the County's required method of using police dogs, the jury should not be permitted to hear the expert's testimony "attacking the legitimacy of the 'bite and hold' deployment method and opining that Eckley's dog should have been trained and deployed using the 'bark and hold' method instead." Memorandum of Law in Support of Motion in Limine of Defendants to Exclude Certain Evidence at Trial in *Park v. Miller*, 2005 WL 3776493 (D. Md. Mar. 23, 2005). Even though the County had since transitioned to using the "bark and hold" police dog technique, officers did not begin to routinely use that method until months after the dog bit Mr. Park. *Id.* Because Plaintiff's counsel had stated at the pretrial conference that he would argue that Officer Eckley had a choice between using the "bite and hold" and "bark and hold" methods, *id.* at n. 2, Defendant moved to exclude *all* evidence of "bark and hold" and *all* testimony by Plaintiff's police canine expert.

Six days later, Plaintiff's canine expert filed a second expert report:

> I am a retired Los Angeles County Deputy Sheriff having honorably served about 17 years as a Deputy. I have qualified in the past in a number of courts throughout the United States as an expert in the fields of use of police canines, as well as use of force.... One of the opinions that I have expressed in this case ... was,
>
> > "Regardless of whether adequate warnings were given and even assuming Officer Eckley kept the dog in sight and under his control at all times the dog attack on Mr. Park was still unnecessary and violated generally accepted law enforcement standards for the use of physical force."
>
> It is my opinion to a reasonable degree of probability within my field of expertise that Officer Eckley's release of the dog, knowing that it was going to bite Mr. Park when it found him, constituted excessive force under the circumstances and a violation of Howard County's own use of force policy.

Expert Report of VanNess H. Bogardus, III in *Park v. Miller*, 2005 WL 4012612 (D. Md. Mar. 29, 2005). In addition to filing the second expert report, Plaintiff opposed the motion to exclude evidence because he argued there was a factual dispute over what police dog technique Officer Eckley was required to use at the time the dog bit Mr. Park. Plaintiff's Opposition to Defendant's Motion in Limine, *Park v. Miller*, 2001 WL 34883252 (D. Md. Feb. 8, 2001).[33]

Defendant's trial counsel, Louis Ruzzi, recalls that no evidence of the "bark and hold" technique was presented at trial, that Plaintiff's expert did not testify, and that ultimately the trial turned on whether Officer Eckley properly followed the county's "bite and hold" canine policy by giving a verbal warning before releasing the dog.[34] After a 3-day jury trial, on April 7, 2005, the district court entered judgment in favor of defendant and against Plaintiff's claim.

Reflect on the changes in the litigation over time.

Recall that the Complaint alleged 4th Amendment claims against two police officers plus the County. Compare the scope of the Complaint's allegations (filed in 2003) to the single claim that went to trial two years later. That single claim was whether Officer Eckley used excessive force against Mr. Park by failing to properly apply the County's "bite and hold" policy by not warning Mr. Park before releasing the dog.

33. Despite the date of the citation, this document likely was filed in 2005, shortly before the trial.

34. Telephone interview with Louis Ruzzi, Philadelphia, PA (Feb. 4, 2010).

Consider the expenses incurred by Plaintiff's firm during those two years. Those expenses would include at least:

1. attorney time spent interviewing the client;
2. attorney time spent researching and drafting the Complaint, the briefs opposing summary judgment and evidentiary motions, and the jury instructions;
3. attorney time spent taking and defending depositions, appearing in court for pretrial conferences and the trial itself; and
4. money spent on the expert.

If Plaintiff's lawyer had realized at the outset of the litigation that when the dog bit Mr. Park the County had not yet implemented the "*bark* and hold" canine policy but instead was still following a "*bite* and hold" policy, and therefore the trial would focus on whether the dog-handler had properly followed the "*bite* and hold" policy, do you think Plaintiff's counsel would have agreed to represent Mr. Park? Consider also a plaintiff's disincentive to accept a settlement offer on the eve of trial if the offer does not cover the investment plaintiff's counsel has made in the claim. In *Park v. Miller*, for example, defense trial counsel Louis Ruzzi recalls that Plaintiff turned down a settlement offer of approximately $20,000 shortly before the trial.[35] While settlement of 42 U.S.C. § 1983 claims can entitle a plaintiff to an award of attorneys' fees, to do so settlements must meet certain criteria, a subject explored in Chapter 10.

F. Supreme Court Application of the Fourth Amendment: Excessive Force in the Context of Police Chases

Chapter 3 included materials concerning the prevalence of police car chases to apprehend crime suspects. The Supreme Court's decision in *Lewis* appeared in Chapter 3 and the facts of the case appear there. The following text was omitted from the earlier *Lewis* excerpt, which concerned the scope of substantive due process; the below text concerns the scope of a 4th Amendment seizure.

Questions to guide reading of *Lewis*

1. According to *Lewis*, what is a "seizure"?
2. Why was the passenger's claim in *Lewis* not properly analyzed as a 4th Amendment seizure?

---

35. *Id.*

County of Sacramento v. Lewis

523 U.S. 833 (1998)

Justice SOUTER delivered the opinion of the Court

...

Because we have "always been reluctant to expand the concept of substantive due process," ... we held in *Graham v. Connor*, 490 U.S. 386 (1989), that "[w]here a particular Amendment provides an explicit textual source of constitutional protection against a particular sort of government behavior, that Amendment, not the more generalized notion of substantive due process, must be the guide for analyzing these claims." *Albright v. Oliver*, 510 U.S. 266, 273 (1994) [further citation omitted]. Given the rule in *Graham*, we were presented at oral argument with the threshold issue raised in several amicus briefs, whether facts involving a police chase aimed at apprehending suspects can ever support a due process claim. The argument runs that in chasing the motorcycle, Smith was attempting to make a seizure within the meaning of the Fourth Amendment, and, perhaps, even that he succeeded when Lewis was stopped by the fatal collision. Hence, any liability must turn on an application of the reasonableness standard governing searches and seizures, not the due process standard of liability for constitutionally arbitrary executive action. *See Graham v. Connor*, *supra*, at 395 ... ("*All* claims that law enforcement officers have used excessive force—deadly or not—in the course of an arrest, investigatory stop, or other 'seizure' of a free citizen should be analyzed under the Fourth Amendment and its 'reasonableness' standard, rather than under a 'substantive due process' approach" (emphases in original)). *Albright v. Oliver*, 510 U.S., at 276 (GINSBURG, J., concurring); *id.*, at 288, n. 2 (SOUTER, J., concurring in judgment).

...

The argument is unsound. Just last Term, we explained that *Graham* "does not hold that all constitutional claims relating to physically abusive government conduct must arise under either the Fourth or Eighth Amendments; rather, *Graham* simply requires that if a constitutional claim is covered by a specific constitutional provision, such as the Fourth or Eighth Amendment, the claim must be analyzed under the standard appropriate to that specific provision, not under the rubric of substantive due process." *United States v. Lanier*, 520 U.S. 259, 272, n. 7 (1997). Substantive due process analysis is therefore inappropriate in this case only if respondents' claim is "covered by" the Fourth Amendment. It is not.

The Fourth Amendment covers only "searches and seizures," neither of which took place here. No one suggests that there was a search, and our cases foreclose finding a seizure. We held in *California v. Hodari D.*, 499 U.S. 621, 626 (1991), that a police pursuit in attempting to seize a person does not amount to a "seizure" within the meaning of the Fourth Amendment. And in *Brower v. County of Inyo*, 489 U.S. 593, 596–597 (1989), we explained that "a Fourth Amendment seizure does not occur whenever there is a governmentally caused termination of an individual's freedom of movement (the innocent passerby), nor even whenever there is a governmentally caused and governmentally *desired* termination of an individual's freedom of movement (the fleeing felon), but only when there is a governmental termination of freedom of movement through means intentionally applied." We illustrated the point by saying that no Fourth Amendment seizure would take place where a "pursuing police car sought to stop the suspect only by the show of authority represented by flashing lights and continuing pursuit," but accidentally stopped the suspect by crashing into him. *Id.*, at 597. That is exactly this case.... *Graham*'s more-specific-provision rule is therefore no bar to respondents' suit. *See, e.g., Frye v. Akron*, 759 F. Supp. 1320, 1324 (N.D. Ind. 1991) (parents of a motorcyclist who was struck and killed by a police car during a high-speed pursuit could sue under substantive due process because no Fourth Amendment seizure took place); *Evans v. Avery*, 100 F.3d, at 1036 (noting that "outside the context of a seizure, ... a person injured as a result of police misconduct may prosecute a substantive due process claim under section 1983"); *Pleasant v. Zamieski*, 895 F.2d 272, 276, n. 2 (CA6) (noting that *Graham* "preserve[s] fourteenth amendment substantive due process analysis for those instances in which a free citizen is denied his or her constitutional right to life through means other than a law enforcement official's arrest, investigatory stop or other seizure"), *cert. denied*, 498 U.S. 851 (1990).[7]

Questions to guide reading of Amicus Brief in *Scott*

Before reading the below amicus brief filed in *Scott* and the Supreme Court oral argument in *Scott*, you may want to read the facts of *Scott*, the next case in this Chapter.

1. Why does the brief argue that police department policies on ramming are relevant to the Court's consideration of Officer Scott's use of force?
2. According to the amicus brief, what is the significance of *Garner*?

Amicus Curiae Brief in *Scott v. Harris*

2007 WL 128585 (Jan. 16, 2007)

Brief of the National Police Accountability Project in Support of Respondent by Howard Friedman, Myong J. Joun, National Police Accountability Project; Karen Blum, Suffolk University Law School, with assistance of law students Zachary Hillman, Michael Lane, and Gregory Tumolo.

---

7. Several *amici* suggest that, for the purposes of *Graham*, the Fourth Amendment should cover not only seizures, but also failed attempts to make a seizure. *See, e.g.*, Brief for National Association of Counties et al. as *Amici Curiae* 10–11. This argument is foreclosed by *California v. Hodari D.*, 499 U.S. 621 (1991), in which we explained that "neither usage nor common-law tradition makes an *attempted* seizure a seizure. The common law may have made an attempted seizure unlawful in certain circumstances; but it made many things unlawful, very few of which were elevated to constitutional proscriptions." *Id.*, at 626, n.2.... Attempted seizures of a person are beyond the scope of the Fourth Amendment. *See id.*, at 646 ... (STEVENS, J., dissenting) (disagreeing with the Court's position that "an attempt to make [a] ... seizure is beyond the coverage of the Fourth Amendment").

IDENTITY AND INTEREST OF AMICUS CURIAE

The National Police Accountability Project ... was founded ... to end police abuse of authority and to provide support for grassroots and victims' organizations combating police misconduct.... The project provides training and support for attorneys and legal workers; public education and information on issues relating to police misconduct.... Police pursuits endanger the lives of the officers involved, as well as the lives of the suspects being pursued, and the public at large. [The project] has a strong interest in assuring that law enforcement agencies authorize high-speed pursuits only when necessary and under constraints that weigh heavily the dangers of such pursuits to all involved against the law enforcement interest that is furthered.... *Amicus Curiae* submits this brief to assist the Court in understanding that the conduct of Officer Scott was inconsistent with, and in violation of, the majority of pursuit policies of law enforcement agencies throughout the country. A determination by this Court that Officer Scott's conduct, when viewed at the summary judgment stage in the light most favorable to the respondent, was unreasonable and unconstitutional, will not interfere with, nor be contrary to, the stated policies of most federal, state, and local government law enforcement agencies. Indeed, responsible police officials recognize the dangers inherent in high-speed pursuits and many, like Chief James V. Murray of the Peachtree City Police Department, have called for the adoption of restrictive pursuit policies to put an end to "this high-speed police chase carnage...."

STATEMENT OF THE CASE

Viewed in the light most favorable to the respondent, a jury could find that petitioner used "deadly force" when he made contact with respondent's vehicle to terminate a high-speed pursuit; that respondent was a non-violent misdemeanant whose underlying offense was speeding (respondent's vehicle was clocked at 73 mph in a 55 mph zone); that there was no probable cause to believe "that respondent had committed a crime involving the infliction or threatened infliction of serious physical harm[;]" and that respondent, "prior to the chase, pose[d] [no] imminent threat of serious physical harm to [petitioner] or others[;]" that there were other means of tracking respondent down (pursuing officers had a description of his vehicle and the license plate number); and that absolutely no warning was given to respondent that petitioner intended to use deadly force to terminate the pursuit.

...

SUMMARY OF ARGUMENT

In *Tennessee v. Garner*, 471 U.S. 1 (1985), this Court held that

> [t]he use of deadly force to prevent the escape of all felony suspects, whatever the circumstances, is constitutionally unreasonable. It is not better that all felony suspects die than that they escape. Where the suspect poses no immediate threat to the officer and no threat to others, the harm resulting from failing to apprehend him does not justify the use of deadly force to do so.

Id. at 11. In reaching this conclusion, the Court took into consideration the fact "that a majority of police departments in this country [had] forbidden the use of deadly force against nonviolent suspects[,]" observing that "[i]f those charged with the enforcement of the criminal law have abjured the use of deadly force in arresting nondangerous felons, there is a substantial basis for doubting that the use of such force is an essential attribute of the arrest power in all felony cases." *Id.*

Amicus Curiae argues that Scott's conduct in using deadly force to terminate the pursuit of a traffic violator is conduct that is prohibited by the majority of police departments in this country. While the policies surveyed by *Amicus* vary as to when and under what circumstances they authorize the initiation of a high-speed pursuit ... and to the extent and pursuant to what guidelines they authorize the execution of a "PIT" maneuver[36] ... an overwhelming majority of the policies equate "ramming" with the use of deadly force, and prohibit "ramming," "bumping," or contact of any sort to terminate a pursuit at high speeds unless deadly force would be justified.

...

Amicus is not arguing that law enforcement agencies should never engage in high-speed pursuits or that well-trained officers, given appropriate conditions, should never use a PIT maneuver. Nor is *Amicus* equating conduct that violates police policies with conduct that violates the Constitution. However, to the extent that a determination of excessive force under the Fourth Amendment turns on the objective reasonableness of an officer's conduct, a review of a significant number of pursuit policies of law enforcement agencies should assist the Court in assessing what practices those in the profession deem reasonable....

Questions to guide reading of oral argument in *Scott*

1. How does Justice Souter characterize the question before the Court? Under Justice Souter's approach, why is Officer Scott's knowledge of the suspected underlying crime legally irrelevant?
2. Why did Justice Breyer suggest that *Garner* does not supply the correct analytic framework?
3. Why did Justice Scalia suggest that Mr. Harris was analogous to a burglar shooting as he leaves the burglarized residence?
4. According to Mr. Harris's lawyer, what is *Garner*'s bright line rule and why did it apply?
5. Note that, while the underlying offense was driving 73 in a 55 mph zone, once the chase was initiated, Mr. Harris drove at speeds in excess of 85 mph.

---

36. The PIT maneuver is used by police to terminate car pursuits by "intentionally nudging the pursued vehicle sideways" causing the pursued driver to lose control of the vehicle. Jing Zhou et al., *Vehicle Dynamics in Response to the Maneuver of Precision Immobilization Technique*, 2008 ASME Dynamic Systems and Control Conference (Oct. 20–22, 2008), *available at* http://jianbolu.tripod.com/paper/DSCC2008-2183.pdf.

Supreme Court Oral Argument in *Scott*

2007 WL 601927 (Feb. 26, 2007)

Craig T. Jones, Edmond & Jones, Atlanta, Ga., on behalf of respondent Mr. Harris.

...

JUSTICE SOUTER: ... Your answer up to this point is that well, [plaintiff Mr. Harris] used signal lights and his reflexes were good, and they sure were. But the question is whether [plaintiff Mr. Harris] was creating a substantial risk of death or serious bodily harm to others. And my question is ... how could the jury fail to find that he was creating such a risk?

MR. JONES: Well, the jury could certainly find he's creating a risk. But with regard to the other *Garner* factors that must be shown before deadly force can be used, he had not committed a violent felony, a crime involving the infliction or threat of infliction—

JUSTICE SOUTER: *Garner* was not talking about someone who at the time the deadly force was used was himself creating a substantial risk of death or serious bodily harm to others. That's what we are dealing with here. And the reasonableness of the officer's action depends on whether, at the summary judgment stage, a jury can reasonably find that, in fact, he was not creating at that moment, a substantial risk of serious bodily harm or death to others. And my question is, how could a jury find anything else?

MR. JONES: Well, a jury could find that the pursuit by the officer escalated the risk rather than diminishing the risk to others. And that given a choice between using deadly force to terminate a pursuit where the officer himself had escalated the risk versus backing off, letting the offender escape and then perhaps arresting him an hour later at the house.

...

JUSTICE BREYER: All right. If [police officer] Scott didn't know [that the underlying offense was speeding], I mean, my goodness, then I don't see the relevance of whether it was speeding or not.... I was on the other side.... Then I look at that tape, and ... my reaction was somewhat similar to Justice Alito's [that Plaintiff posed a tremendous risk to drivers on the road]. And so if it's doubtful and then you can't even show that the person who did it knew that this was for speeding rather than for murder, how can you get to the jury?

MR. JONES: Well, there is certainly a credibility issue as to whether Scott says he knew or didn't know. I mean, certainly the call on the radio he could have acquired. The thing is that—

JUSTICE KENNEDY: Well, as the Chief Justice indicated through a question earlier, isn't it reasonable for an officer to assume that it is—he is trying to escape because there is something more serious than speeding at stake? I mean, that's the assumption I would draw.

...

JUSTICE SOUTER: ... Let's assume Scott knew that this entire situation had eventuated out of an 18 mile in excess of speed act by the individual. Assume that. What Scott also knew at the point at which he joined the chase was that this individual was driving a car at 90 miles an hour. He was crossing yellow lines, going through red lights, et cetera. At that point, wasn't the only legally relevant data whether or not Harris was creating the risk of death or bodily harm to others?

MR. JONES: That's the issue. Was there an immediate risk of death or serious bodily harm—

...

JUSTICE BREYER: ... I'm uncertain about the standard for this. Because as you and the others have been arguing, if the question is one about rules surrounding the use of deadly force. But then ... it seemed to me that *Graham*, which comes after *Garner*, says that's not the standard. *Graham* is a standard of simple reasonableness and *Garner* is simply an illustration of that as applied to guns and a backyard chase, not as applied to cars which threaten other people much more.

...

MR. JONES: Well, whether you apply *Garner* or *Graham*, the result is the same in this case. And let me explain why. What *Graham* did is it expanded the *Garner* rule, which you can't use deadly force to stop a fleeing suspect who is merely fleeing, expanded that to include the entire range of use of force, deadly or nondeadly. And with regard to the factors that are to be considered in determining whether the use of force is reasonable under *Graham*, the balance with respect to a fleeing suspect who is subjected to deadly force was already drawn by *Garner*. *Garner* created a bright light rule. *Graham* extended that to an *ad hoc* balancing test with all use of force applications. But with respect to deadly force and a fleeing suspect, *Garner* still provides a bright line rule.

JUSTICE BREYER: So you're saying I cannot do the following under the law, which would seem to be contrary to common sense, to say there is a big difference between a policeman shooting a person who is running away and threatens no harm to others, and a policeman using a gun—using a car on a highway to try to get a person to stop who is threatening others. I have to treat those exactly as if they were the same thing.

MR. JONES: Yes....

...

CH. JUSTICE ROBERTS: ... You think what the officer should have done in this case was to let Mr. Harris go.

MR. JONES: That was one option. He could have continued the pursuit and simply decided not to mow him off the road at 90 miles an hour, or he could have stopped a pursuit and let him go which often happens in many pursuits.

CH. JUSTICE ROBERTS: Even though he doesn't know at that point that he will ever be able to arrest him later. He doesn't know if it's a stolen car or not.

MR. JONES: That's correct.

CH. JUSTICE ROBERTS: And he doesn't know why he is being pursued, whether it's for mass murder or terrorism or anything else.

MR. JONES: Well, that's correct. But in the majority of cases—and this is the only testimony in this record, Your Honors. Our experts testified on a study—based on a study which was commissioned for him by the Department of Justice, a study which has been cited by some of the amicus briefs on both sides in this case, Dr. Albert testified that 70 percent of the time, when police back off pursuit, the perpetrator stops running and they resume safe driving....

CH. JUSTICE ROBERTS: Once they have gotten away, I assume.

MR. JONES: Well, sometimes you have to let them get away. In *Garner*, it says, even if the guy has just broken into somebody's house in the middle of the night and committed a felony, if the choice is letting them go or using deadly force when the factors authorizing deadly force are not present, you have to let him go.

JUSTICE SCALIA: Not if he is shooting his way out of the house and endangering other people.

MR. JONES: That's correct.

JUSTICE SCALIA: I mean, that's a factor here, of course. If he has taken the jewelry and he's gone off into the night, if shooting at him might endanger somebody else, or even kill him, you have to let him go. I'm talking about a burglar who is, you know, who is shooting as he leaves.

MR. JONES:	You can shoot him. I'd be there shooting him, too.
JUSTICE SCALIA:	Of course you can shoot him.
MR. JONES:	Let me take that distinction and apply it to the vehicle, Justice Scalia. What we have to have to authorize deadly force in this context is something more than just unsafe flight. You've got to have someone who is behaving violently, who is menacing people, trying to ram people.
	...
JUSTICE GINSBURG:	The key point is that he is endangering the lives and safety of others. Anyone who has watched that tape has got to come to that conclusion, looking at the road and the way that this car was swerving, and the cars coming in the opposite direction. This was a situation fraught with danger.
MR. JONES:	Well, Justice Ginsburg, I hope I don't have you on my jury if that's—but what the trial court found was that construing the facts in a light most favorable to the Plaintiff as a nonmoving party, that reasonable jurors can find that this was simply a person who was driving fast. This was not a person who was driving assaultively. He wasn't driving violently. He wasn't a threat to anyone that would authorize the use of deadly force against him.
JUSTICE SCALIA:	Is that a factual finding of the, of the trial court here?
MR. JONES:	That is a factual finding.
JUSTICE SCALIA:	Are we bound by that fact?
MR. JONES:	We are bound by that. This is an interlocutory appeal....
JUSTICE SCALIA:	Even if having watched the tape, there is no way that, that factual finding can be accurate?
MR. JONES:	[Yes.] ...
	...
MR. JONES:	... This is the issue. If what this person is doing is driving, say driving unsafely, but they are not driving violently, they are not driving aggressively, they are not menacing anyone on the road. They are simply driving fast trying to get away, that in and of itself, is that going to be justification for the use of deadly force or is something more going to be required?
JUSTICE ALITO:	When someone is fleeing and ... creating a very grave danger for other drivers on the road, when in your view is it reasonable for the police to use deadly force to stop that, as opposed to breaking off the chase? What, what is the test.

MR. JONES: Well, under *Garner* the test is they have to be threatening violence or inflicting violence against someone. There have to be no other alternatives other than deadly force available to effect the apprehension. And assuming there is justification for deadly force, then there is a duty to give a warning where feasible before using deadly force. And the court below felt none of those three factors—

JUSTICE ALITO: How could you possibly give a warning in this situation?

MR. JONES: It's academic in this case, because the first two factors were not met. I mean, it's our position that you don't worry about giving a warning unless you have the right to use deadly force, and if you don't get to that point then it's—it's a moot question.

JUSTICE GINSBURG: Why wasn't there warning? There were lights, there were sirens. Surely the defendant knew that the police were trying to stop him.

MR. JONES: There was certainly warning that he needed—that he was expected to pull over. There was no warning of any intent to use deadly force.

JUSTICE BREYER: ... What am I supposed to assume? ... I looked at the tape and that tape shows he is weaving on both sides of the lane, swerving around automobiles that are coming in the opposite direction with their lights on, goes through a red light where there are several cars that are right there, weaves around them, and there are cars coming the other way, weaves back, goes down the road.... [A]m I supposed to pretend I haven't seen that? ...

MR. JONES: Well, I didn't see that.

...

MR. JONES: ... [M]y point is that if, if the drive—if the hazard caused by driving in and of itself is the only threat here, does that rise to a level of imminency and immediacy that justifies the use of deadly force? If it does, then any officer who perceives that someone is driving unsafely and that they may cause an accident to someone who may or may not be down the road if not stopped, would be justified in using deadly force, to literally take out anyone who is speeding.

JUSTICE SCALIA: It depends on how fast—if depends on how fast the car is going, whether it's a two-lane road or four-lane divided highway. All those factors come into, into account. And it doesn't seem to me that we have to adopt a rule that will, that will discourage police officers. There's, there's enough disincentive to engage in this kind of activity in the fact that the police officer may hurt himself. It's pretty risky to conduct this kind of a maneuver, don't you think? I wouldn't have done it if I was Scott.

...

JUSTICE SCALIA: Driving 90 miles an hour and comes up, approaches that car, that car swerved. Scott could have been killed, couldn't he?

...

JUSTICE SCALIA: So I don't think we need a whole lot of disincentive to stop police officers in engaging in frolicsome conduct.

MR. JONES: Well, not only that, Justice Scalia. The officer had no control over what was going to happen once he used deadly force.... [W]hen you hit the vehicle and knock a vehicle that has been in control and make it out of control, then it's now an unguided missile that could just as easily cross the center line and hit an innocent person.

...

CH. JUSTICE ROBERTS: And aren't you concerned that that creates an incentive in every case for anyone who, that sees the blue lights behind them to know that all they have to do is keep fleeing and the police are going to have to give up eventually?

MR. JONES: Well, let me respond by reading a portion of *Garner* that deals with that point, Mr. Chief Justice. These, these same important policy reasons were raised in *Garner*, that we don't want to encourage disobedience of issues. We want to discourage people from fleeing. And this is what the *Garner* Court said—

CH. JUSTICE ROBERTS: Well, *Garner*—*Garner* was the case involving shooting the guy in the back, right?

MR. JONES: Yes. He might easily break into someone else's house and perhaps end up killing them. This was a vigorous dissent in *Garner*. But this is what the majority said: "Without in any way disparaging the importance of these goals we are not convinced that the use of deadly force is a sufficiently productive means of accomplishing them to justify the killing of nonviolent suspects." And if unsafe driving—

...

JUSTICE SCALIA: ... I would have guessed that, if the police stopped chasing, you don't go 90 miles an hour anymore. But did this study show what the effect of a rule that says stop chasing when he hits 85, what the effect of that rule would be on, on fleeing speeders or fleeing felons, or fleeing anybody?

MR. JONES: Well, the rule simply says you don't kill him just because he is driving unsafely. And if, it simply says that if the choice is between killing him and letting him go, you have to let him go if the *Garner* factors aren't present. And we find nothing in the law and no reason to create a new exception in the law that says that *Garner* doesn't apply if you're fleeing by vehicle.

Questions to guide reading of *Scott*

1. Does the question presented by the majority make any assumptions? What crime was the driver suspected of?
2. Why does the majority characterize the video as showing a Hollywood car chase? Why does the majority reject Justice Stevens' suggestion that cars might have been on the shoulder because they reacted to the lights and sirens?
3. Why did the Supreme Court refuse to accept plaintiff's/respondent's view of the facts?
4. How did plaintiff/respondent urge the Court to use *Garner* to analyze the case? Why does the majority say that the plaintiff/respondent mischaracterized *Garner*?
5. Why does the majority hold that culpability is relevant to the reasonableness of the seizure? What consequence is likely if the culpability of the fleeing suspect is considered?
6. Does *Scott* stand for a general proposition? If so, what is it?
7. What facts does Justice Stevens say the majority omitted? Why does Justice Stevens state that the majority has usurped the jury's factfinding function?
8. If you represented a local government, how would you explain *Scott* to your police and city government clients?

Scott v. Harris

550 U.S. 372 (2007)

Justice SCALIA delivered the opinion of the Court.

We consider whether a law enforcement official can, consistent with the Fourth Amendment, attempt to stop a fleeing motorist from continuing his public-endangering flight by ramming the motorist's car from behind. Put another way: Can an officer take actions that place a fleeing motorist at risk of serious injury or death in order to stop the motorist's flight from endangering the lives of innocent bystanders?

I

In March 2001, a Georgia county deputy clocked respondent's vehicle traveling at 73 miles per hour on a road with a 55-mile-per-hour speed limit. The deputy activated his blue flashing lights indicating that respondent should pull over. Instead, respondent sped away, initiating a chase down what is in most portions a two-lane road, at speeds exceeding 85 miles per hour. The deputy radioed his dispatch to report that he was pursuing a fleeing vehicle, and broadcast its license plate number. Petitioner, Deputy Timothy Scott, heard the radio communication and joined the pursuit along with other officers. In the midst of the chase, respondent pulled into the parking lot of a shopping center and was nearly boxed in by the various police vehicles. Respondent evaded the trap by making a sharp turn, colliding with Scott's police car, exiting the parking lot, and speeding off once again down a two-lane highway.

Following respondent's shopping center maneuvering, which resulted in slight damage to Scott's police car, Scott took over as the lead pursuit vehicle. Six minutes and nearly 10 miles after the chase had begun, Scott decided to attempt to terminate the episode by employing a "Precision Intervention Technique ('PIT') maneuver, which causes the fleeing vehicle to spin to a stop." ... Having radioed his supervisor for permission, Scott was told to "'[g]o ahead and take him out.'" ... Instead, Scott applied his push bumper to the rear of respondent's vehicle.[1] As a result, respondent lost control of his vehicle, which left the roadway, ran down an embankment, overturned, and crashed. Respondent was badly injured and was rendered a quadriplegic.

Respondent filed suit against Deputy Scott and others under 42 U.S.C. § 1983, alleging ... use of excessive force resulting in an unreasonable seizure under the Fourth Amendment.

...

III A

The first step in assessing the constitutionality of Scott's actions is to determine the relevant facts.... [C]ourts are required to view the facts and draw reasonable inferences "in the light most favorable to the party opposing the [summary judgment] motion." ... In qualified immunity cases, this usually means adopting (as the Court of Appeals did here) the plaintiff's version of the facts.

There is, however, an added wrinkle in this case: existence in the record of a videotape capturing the events in question.... The videotape quite clearly contradicts the version of the story told by respondent and adopted by the Court of Appeals.[5] ... In-

1. ... It is irrelevant to our analysis whether Scott had permission to take the precise actions he took.

5. Justice STEVENS suggests that our reaction to the videotape is somehow idiosyncratic, and seems to believe we are misrepresenting its contents.... We are happy to allow the videotape to speak for itself. See Record 36, Exh. A, available at http://www.supremecourtus.gov/opinions/video/scott_v_harris.rmvb.

deed, reading the lower court's opinion, one gets the impression that respondent, rather than fleeing from police, was attempting to pass his driving test:

> "[T]aking the facts from the non-movant's viewpoint, [respondent] remained in control of his vehicle, slowed for turns and intersections, and typically used his indicators for turns. He did not run any motorists off the road. Nor was he a threat to pedestrians in the shopping center parking lot, which was free from pedestrian and vehicular traffic as the center was closed. Significantly, by the time the parties were back on the highway and Scott rammed [respondent], the motorway had been cleared of motorists and pedestrians allegedly because of police blockades of the nearby intersections." ...

The videotape tells quite a different story. There we see respondent's vehicle racing down narrow, two-lane roads in the dead of night at speeds that are shockingly fast. We see it swerve around more than a dozen other cars, cross the double-yellow line, and force cars traveling in both directions to their respective shoulders to avoid being hit.[6] We see it run multiple red lights and travel for considerable periods of time in the occasional center left-turn-only lane, chased by numerous police cars forced to engage in the same hazardous maneuvers just to keep up. Far from being the cautious and controlled driver the lower court depicts, what we see on the video more closely resembles a Hollywood-style car chase of the most frightening sort, placing police officers and innocent bystanders alike at great risk of serious injury.[7]

...

When opposing parties tell two different stories, one of which is blatantly contradicted by the record, so that no reasonable jury could believe it, a court should not adopt that version of the facts for purposes of ruling on a motion for summary judgment.

That was the case here with regard to the factual issue whether respondent was driving in such fashion as to endanger human life. Respondent's version of events is so utterly discredited by the record that no reasonable jury could have believed him.

---

6. Justice STEVENS hypothesizes that these cars "had already pulled to the side of the road or were driving along the shoulder because they heard the police sirens or saw the flashing lights," so that "[a] jury could certainly conclude that those motorists were exposed to no greater risk than persons who take the same action in response to a speeding ambulance." ... It is not our experience that ambulances and fire engines careen down two-lane roads at 85-plus miles per hour, with an unmarked scout car out in front of them. The risk they pose to the public is vastly less than what respondent created here. But even if that were not so, it would in no way lead to the conclusion that it was unreasonable to eliminate the threat to life that respondent posed. Society accepts the risk of speeding ambulances and fire engines in order to save life and property; it need not (and assuredly does not) accept a similar risk posed by a reckless motorist fleeing the police.

7. ... [T]he videotape validates the court's statement that when Scott rammed respondent's vehicle it was not threatening any other vehicles or pedestrians. (Undoubtedly Scott *waited* for the road to be clear before executing his maneuver.)

The Court of Appeals ... should have viewed the facts in the light depicted by the videotape.

B

... [I]t is quite clear that Deputy Scott did not violate the Fourth Amendment. Scott does not contest that his decision to terminate the car chase by ramming his bumper into respondent's vehicle constituted a "seizure." "[A] Fourth Amendment seizure [occurs] ... when there is a governmental termination of freedom of movement through means intentionally applied." *Brower v. County of Inyo*, 489 U.S. 593, 596–597 (1989) (emphasis deleted). *See also id.*, at 597 ("If ... the police cruiser had pulled alongside the fleeing car and sideswiped it, producing the crash, then the termination of the suspect's freedom of movement would have been a seizure"). It is also conceded, by both sides, that a claim of "excessive force in the course of making [a] ... 'seizure' of [the] person ... [is] properly analyzed under the Fourth Amendment's 'objective reasonableness' standard." *Graham v. Connor*, 490 U.S. 386, 388 (1989). The question we need to answer is whether Scott's actions were objectively reasonable.[8]

1

Respondent urges us to analyze this case as we analyzed *Garner*, 471 U.S. 1.... We must first decide, he says, whether the actions Scott took constituted "deadly force." ... If so, respondent claims that *Garner* prescribes certain preconditions that must be met before Scott's actions can survive Fourth Amendment scrutiny: (1) The suspect must have posed an immediate threat of serious physical harm to the officer or others; (2) deadly force must have been necessary to prevent escape;[9] and (3) where feasible, the officer must have given the suspect some warning ... Since these *Garner* preconditions for using deadly force were not met in this case, Scott's actions were *per se* unreasonable.

Respondent's argument falters at its first step; *Garner* did not establish a magical on/off switch that triggers rigid preconditions whenever an officer's actions constitute "deadly force." *Garner* was simply an application of the Fourth Amendment's "reasonableness" test, *Graham, supra*, at 388, to the use of a particular type of force in a particular situation. *Garner* held that it was unreasonable to kill a "young, slight, and

---

8. Justice STEVENS incorrectly declares this to be "a question of fact best reserved for a jury".... At the summary judgment stage, however, once we have determined the relevant set of facts and drawn all inferences in favor of the nonmoving party *to the extent supportable by the record*, ... the reasonableness of Scott's actions—or, in Justice STEVENS' parlance, "[w]hether [respondent's] actions have risen to a level warranting deadly force," ... —is a pure question of law.

9. ... [T]hat quote from *Garner* is taken out of context. The necessity described in *Garner* was, in fact, the need to prevent "serious physical harm, either to the officer or to others." By way of example only, *Garner* hypothesized that deadly force may be used "if necessary to prevent escape" when the suspect is known to have "committed a crime involving the infliction or threatened infliction of serious physical harm," so that his mere being at large poses an inherent danger to society. Respondent did not pose that type of inherent threat to society, since (prior to the car chase) he had committed only a minor traffic offense and, as far as the police were aware, had no prior criminal record. But in this case, unlike in *Garner*, it was respondent's flight itself (by means of a speeding automobile) that posed the threat of "serious physical harm ... to others." *Ibid.*

unarmed" burglary suspect, 471 U.S., at 21, by shooting him "in the back of the head" while he was running away on foot, *id.*, at 4, and when the officer "could not reasonably have believed that [the suspect] ... posed any threat," and "never attempted to justify his actions on any basis other than the need to prevent an escape," *id.*, at 21. Whatever *Garner* said about the factors that *might have* justified shooting the suspect in that case, such "preconditions" have scant applicability to this case, which has vastly different facts.... Nor is the threat posed by the flight on foot of an unarmed suspect even remotely comparable to the extreme danger to human life posed by respondent in this case. Although respondent's attempt to craft an easy-to-apply legal test in the Fourth Amendment context is admirable, in the end we must still slosh our way through the factbound morass of "reasonableness." Whether or not Scott's actions constituted application of "deadly force," all that matters is whether Scott's actions were reasonable.

2

In determining the reasonableness of the manner in which a seizure is effected, "[w]e must balance the nature and quality of the intrusion on the individual's Fourth Amendment interests against the importance of the governmental interests alleged to justify the intrusion." ... Scott defends his actions by pointing to the paramount governmental interest in ensuring public safety, and respondent nowhere suggests this was not the purpose motivating Scott's behavior. Thus, in judging whether Scott's actions were reasonable, we must consider the risk of bodily harm that Scott's actions posed to respondent in light of the threat to the public that Scott was trying to eliminate. Although there is no obvious way to quantify the risks on either side, it is clear from the videotape that respondent posed an actual and imminent threat to the lives of any pedestrians who might have been present, to other civilian motorists, and to the officers involved in the chase.... It is equally clear that Scott's actions posed a high likelihood of serious injury or death to respondent—though not the near certainty of death posed by, say, shooting a fleeing felon in the back of the head, *see Garner*, *supra*, at 4.... So how does a court go about weighing the perhaps lesser probability of injuring or killing numerous bystanders against the perhaps larger probability of injuring or killing a single person? We think it appropriate in this process to take into account not only the number of lives at risk, but also their relative culpability. It was respondent, after all, who intentionally placed himself and the public in danger by unlawfully engaging in the reckless, high-speed flight that ultimately produced the choice between two evils that Scott confronted. Multiple police cars, with blue lights flashing and sirens blaring, had been chasing respondent for nearly 10 miles, but he ignored their warning to stop. By contrast, those who might have been harmed had Scott not taken the action he did were entirely innocent. We have little difficulty in concluding it was reasonable for Scott to take the action that he did.[10]

---

10. ... Culpability *is* relevant, however, to the *reasonableness* of the seizure—to whether preventing possible harm to the innocent justifies exposing to possible harm the person threatening them.

But wait, says respondent: Couldn't the innocent public equally have been protected, and the tragic accident entirely avoided, if the police had simply ceased their pursuit? We think the police need not have taken that chance and hoped for the best. Whereas Scott's action—ramming respondent off the road—was certain to eliminate the risk that respondent posed to the public, ceasing pursuit was not. First of all, there would have been no way to convey convincingly to respondent that the chase was off, and that he was free to go. Had respondent looked in his rear-view mirror and seen the police cars deactivate their flashing lights and turn around, he would have had no idea whether they were truly letting him get away, or simply devising a new strategy for capture. Perhaps the police knew a shortcut he didn't know, and would reappear down the road to intercept him; or perhaps they were setting up a roadblock in his path.... Given such uncertainty, respondent might have been just as likely to respond by continuing to drive recklessly as by slowing down and wiping his brow.

Second, we are loath to lay down a rule requiring the police to allow fleeing suspects to get away whenever they drive *so recklessly* that they put other people's lives in danger. It is obvious the perverse incentives such a rule would create: Every fleeing motorist would know that escape is within his grasp, if only he accelerates to 90 miles per hour, crosses the double-yellow line a few times, and runs a few red lights. The Constitution assuredly does not impose this invitation to impunity-earned-by-recklessness. Instead, we lay down a more sensible rule: A police officer's attempt to terminate a dangerous high-speed car chase that threatens the lives of innocent bystanders does not violate the Fourth Amendment, even when it places the fleeing motorist at risk of serious injury or death.

* * *

The car chase that respondent initiated in this case posed a substantial and immediate risk of serious physical injury to others; no reasonable jury could conclude otherwise. Scott's attempt to terminate the chase by forcing respondent off the road was reasonable, and Scott is entitled to summary judgment....

Justice STEVENS, dissenting.

...

Relying on a *de novo* review of a videotape of a portion of a nighttime chase on a lightly traveled road in Georgia where no pedestrians or other "bystanders" were present, buttressed by uninformed speculation about the possible consequences of discontinuing the chase, eight of the jurors on this Court reach a verdict that differs from the views of the judges on both the District Court and the Court of Appeals who are surely more familiar with the hazards of driving on Georgia roads than we are. The Court's justification for this unprecedented departure from our well-settled standard of review of factual determinations made by a district court and affirmed by a court of appeals is based on its mistaken view that the [version of facts argued by respondent and adopted by the] Court of Appeals ... was "so utterly discredited by the record that no reasonable jury could have believed [it]." ...

Rather than supporting the conclusion that what we see on the video "resembles a Hollywood-style car chase of the most frightening sort," ... the tape actually confirms, rather than contradicts, the lower courts' appraisal of the factual questions at issue. More important, it surely does not provide a principled basis for depriving the respondent of his right to have a jury evaluate the question whether the police officers' decision to use deadly force to bring the chase to an end was reasonable.

Omitted from the Court's description of the initial speeding violation is the fact that respondent was on a four-lane portion of Highway 34 when the officer clocked his speed at 73 miles per hour and initiated the chase. More significant—and contrary to the Court's assumption that respondent's vehicle "force[d] cars traveling in both directions to their respective shoulders to avoid being hit" ... —a fact unmentioned in the text of the opinion explains why those cars pulled over prior to being passed by respondent. The sirens and flashing lights on the police cars following respondent gave the same warning that a speeding ambulance or fire engine would have provided. The 13 cars that respondent passed on his side of the road before entering the shopping center, and both of the cars that he passed on the right after leaving the center, no doubt had already pulled to the side of the road or were driving along the shoulder because they heard the police sirens or saw the flashing lights before respondent or the police cruisers approached. A jury could certainly conclude that those motorists were exposed to no greater risk than persons who take the same action in response to a speeding ambulance, and that their reactions were fully consistent with the evidence that respondent, though speeding, retained full control of his vehicle.

The police sirens also minimized any risk that may have arisen from running "multiple red lights," *ibid.* In fact, respondent and his pursuers went through only two intersections with stop lights and in both cases all other vehicles in sight were stationary, presumably because they had been warned of the approaching speeders. Incidentally, the videos do show that the lights were red when the police cars passed through them but, because the cameras were farther away when respondent did so and it is difficult to discern the color of the signal at that point, it is not entirely clear that he ran either or both of the red lights....

My colleagues on the jury saw respondent "swerve around more than a dozen other cars," and "force cars traveling in both directions to their respective shoulders," ... but they apparently discounted the possibility that those cars were already out of the pursuit's path as a result of hearing the sirens. Even if that were not so, passing a slower vehicle on a two-lane road always involves some degree of swerving and is not especially dangerous if there are no cars coming from the opposite direction. At no point during the chase did respondent pull into the opposite lane other than to pass a car in front of him; he did the latter no more than five times and, on most of those occasions, used his turn signal. On none of these occasions was there a car traveling in the opposite direction. In fact, at one point, when respondent found himself behind a car in his own lane and there were cars traveling in the other direction, he slowed and waited for the cars traveling in the other direction to pass before overtaking the car in front of him while using his turn signal to do so. This is hardly the stuff of Hollywood....

In sum ... the Court of Appeals ... correctly conclude[d] that there is no evidence that he ever lost control of his vehicle ... [and] correctly pointed out that the incident in the shopping center parking lot did not create any risk to pedestrians or other vehicles because the chase occurred just before 11 p.m. on a weekday night and the center was closed.... The only "innocent bystanders" who were placed "at great risk of serious injury," ... were the drivers who either pulled off the road in response to the sirens or passed respondent in the opposite direction when he was driving on his side of the road.

I recognize, of course, that even though respondent's original speeding violation on a four-lane highway was rather ordinary, his refusal to stop and subsequent flight was a serious offense that merited severe punishment. It was not, however, a capital offense, or even an offense that justified the use of deadly force rather than an abandonment of the chase. The Court's concern about the "imminent threat to the lives of any pedestrians who might have been present," ... should be discounted in a case involving a nighttime chase in an area where no pedestrians were present.

What would have happened if the police had decided to abandon the chase? We now know that they could have apprehended respondent later because they had his license plate number. Even if that were not true, and even if he would have escaped any punishment at all, the use of deadly force in this case was no more appropriate than the use of a deadly weapon against a fleeing felon in *Tennessee v. Garner*, 471 U.S. 1 (1985)....[5] The Court attempts to avoid the conclusion that deadly force was unnecessary by speculating that if the officers had let him go, respondent might have been "just as likely" to continue to drive recklessly as to slow down and wipe his brow.... Our duty to view the evidence in the light most favorable to the nonmoving party would foreclose such speculation if the Court had not used its observation of the video as an excuse for replacing the rule of law with its ad hoc judgment. There is no evidentiary basis for an assumption that dangers caused by flight from a police pursuit will continue after the pursuit ends. Indeed, rules adopted by countless police departments throughout the country are based on a judgment that differs from the Court's. *See, e.g.*, App. to Brief for Georgia Association of Chiefs of Police, Inc., as *Amicus Curiae* ("During a pursuit, the need to apprehend the suspect should always outweigh the level of danger created by the pursuit. When the immediate danger to the public created by the pursuit is greater than the immediate or potential danger to the public should the suspect remain at large, then the pursuit should be discontinued or terminated.... [P]ursuits should usually be discontinued when the violator's

5. In noting that Scott's action "was *certain* to eliminate the risk that respondent posed to the public" while "ceasing pursuit was not," the Court prioritizes total elimination of the risk of harm to the public over the risk that respondent may be seriously injured or even killed.... (emphasis in original). The Court is only able to make such a statement by assuming, based on its interpretation of events on the videotape, that the risk of harm posed in this case, and the type of harm involved, rose to a level warranting deadly force. These are the same types of questions that, when disputed, are typically resolved by a jury....

identity has been established to the point that later apprehension can be accomplished without danger to the public").

Although *Garner* may not, as the Court suggests, "establish a magical on/off switch that triggers rigid preconditions" for the use of deadly force, ... it did set a threshold under which the use of deadly force would be considered constitutionally unreasonable:

> "Where the officer has probable cause to believe that the suspect poses a threat of serious physical harm, either to the officer or to others, it is not constitutionally unreasonable to prevent escape by using deadly force. Thus, if the suspect threatens the officer with a weapon or there is probable cause to believe that he has committed a crime involving the infliction or threatened infliction of serious physical harm, deadly force may be used if necessary to prevent escape, and if, where feasible, some warning has been given." 471 U.S., at 11–12.

Whether a person's actions have risen to a level warranting deadly force is a question of fact best reserved for a jury. Here, the Court has usurped the jury's factfinding function and, in doing so, implicitly labeled the four other judges to review the case unreasonable ... [by] impl[ying] that no reasonable person could view the videotape and come to the conclusion that deadly force was unjustified. However, the three judges on the Court of Appeals panel apparently did view the videotapes ... and described a very different version of events:

> "At the time of the ramming, apart from speeding and running two red lights, Harris was driving in a non-aggressive fashion (*i.e.*, without trying to ram or run into the officers). Moreover, ... Scott's path on the open highway was largely clear. The videos introduced into evidence show little to no vehicular (or pedestrian) traffic, allegedly because of the late hour and the police blockade of the nearby intersections. Finally, Scott issued absolutely no warning (*e.g.*, over the loudspeaker or otherwise) prior to using deadly force." ...

If two groups of judges can disagree so vehemently about the nature of the pursuit and the circumstances surrounding that pursuit, it seems eminently likely that a reasonable juror could disagree with this Court's characterization of events. Moreover, under the standard set forth in *Garner*, it is certainly possible that "a jury could conclude that Scott unreasonably used deadly force to seize Harris by ramming him off the road under the instant circumstances." [citing Eleventh Circuit opinion].

The Court today sets forth a *per se* rule that presumes its own version of the facts: "A police officer's attempt to terminate a dangerous high-speed car chase *that threatens the lives of innocent bystanders* does not violate the Fourth Amendment, even when it places the fleeing motorist at risk of serious injury or death." (emphasis added). Not only does that rule fly in the face of the flexible and case-by-case "reasonableness" approach applied in *Garner* and *Graham v. Connor*, 490 U.S. 386 (1989), but it is also arguably inapplicable to the case at hand, given that it is not clear that this chase threatened the life of any "innocent bystande[r]." In my view, the risks inherent in justifying unwarranted police conduct on the basis of unfounded assumptions are unacceptable, particularly when less drastic measures—in this case, the use of stop sticks[9] or a simple warning issued from a loudspeaker—could have avoided such a tragic result. In my judgment, jurors in Georgia should be allowed to evaluate the reasonableness of the decision to ram respondent's speeding vehicle in a manner that created an obvious risk of death and has in fact made him a quadriplegic at the age of 19. I respectfully dissent.

For further discussion

1. The majority and the dissent both reference the video from the first officer's car (Car 1) and from Officer Scott's car (Car 2), which you can view on the website companion to this book, http://constitutionallitigation.rutgers.edu (select "Resources," then scroll down to 3rd and 4th videos), or by searching YouTube for Scott v. Harris. Whose characterization of the videos do you find more persuasive?

2. In concurrence, Justice Ginsburg stated that *Scott* did not "articulat[e] a mechanical, *per se* rule," but rather was a fact-specific ruling: "[t]he inquiry described by the Court is situation specific." *Scott*, 550 U.S. at 386 (Ginsburg, J., concurring). Do you agree?

3. Is the holding of *Scott* consistent with the statement in *Garner* that deadly force is different from other kinds of force and should be subject to a different legal analysis? Professor Karen Blum, co-author of the amicus brief excerpted earlier in this Chapter, argues that *Garner* "established a constitutional baseline for the use of deadly force, prohibiting its use unless an 'officer has probable cause to believe that the suspect poses a threat of serious physical harm, either to the officer or to others,'" and therefore "did establish a 'magical on/off switch' for uses of deadly force." Karen Blum, *Scott v. Harris: Death Knell for Deadly Force Policies and Garner Jury Instructions*?, 58 Syracuse L. Rev. 45, 56 (2007). Is this aspect of *Garner* limited or overruled by the instruction in *Scott* to wade through the factbound morass of reasonableness? Professor Blum argues that it is. "Justice Scalia's treatment of *Garner* is troubling. First, it reflects his own inability or unwillingness to recognize that death is different and that the employment of deadly force should be constrained by more stringent and more specific standards than the use of non-deadly force. Removing 'deadly force' from a special category of force that triggers certain preconditions will encourage police agencies to rewrite policies that currently treat deadly force as different, placing clear restraints on its use.... To the extent [*Scott*] establishes a per se rule, it is a dangerous one; in effect authorizing summary execution of anyone who flees from the police in a motor vehicle." *Id.* at 54–55. Review the note earlier in this Chapter on the circuits' definitions of deadly force. Given the holding in *Scott*, does determining whether a police officer used "deadly" force remain significant in analyzing whether the officer used excessive force?

---

9. "Stop sticks" are a device which can be placed across the roadway and used to flatten a vehicle's tires slowly to safely terminate a pursuit.

4. What are the practical consequences of the Supreme Court's addition of "culpability" to the considerations an officer should weigh before using deadly force? Should a passenger in a fleeing vehicle be considered culpable? In a high-speed pursuit, will the subject of the pursuit always be more culpable since the suspect could stop the chase by submitting to police authority? If so, is culpability a consideration to be weighed or a thumb on the scale that will help justify an officer's use of deadly force?

Professor George Dery argues that the addition of relative culpability "enabled the Court to apply the following unpalatable math: It was reasonable to take a greater risk (the 'larger probability') with Harris' life because he was more culpable in order to avoid the lesser risk (the 'lesser probability') to the lives of bystanders because they were less culpable ... How would the math change if the bystanders endangered were not so 'innocent?' Would the scales tip if the potential victims were motorists who themselves were exceeding the speed limit, failing to use signal indicators when turning, or double-parking? Would pedestrians be less deserving of police protection if they came out to watch the chase, to jaywalk in front of it, or even to cheer on the fleeing motorist?" *See* George M. Dery, *The Needless "Slosh" Through the "Morass of Reasonableness": The Supreme Court's Usurpation of Fact Finding Powers in Assessing Reasonable Force in* Scott v. Harris, 18 Geo. Mason U. Civ. Rts. L.J. 417, 449 (2008).

5. In *Scott*, the majority challenged readers to view the videotape of the police pursuit for themselves to assess the reasonableness of the officers' use of force. Professors Dan Kahan, David Hoffman, and Donald Braman took up the challenge and showed the video to a diverse sample of 1,350 people: "Overall, a majority agreed with the Court's resolution of the key issues, but within the sample there were sharp differences of opinion along cultural, ideological, and other lines." *See* Dan M. Kahan, David A. Hoffman, and Donald Braman, *Whose Eyes Are You Going To Believe?* Scott v. Harris *and the Perils of Cognitive Illiberalism*, 122 Harv. L. Rev. 837, 838 (2009). The study concluded that individuals who believe society should be "[hierarchical and individualistic] formed views emphatically in line with those of the Court majority. Those [who believe society should be egalitarian and communitarian] were more likely to see the police, not Harris, as the source of the risk to the public and to conclude that use of deadly force was not a justifiable response given the risk that Harris posed." *Id.* at 903.

6. Consider both Justice Stevens' dissent in *Scott* and the results of the above-quoted empirical study. Are images in a video susceptible to more than one interpretation? Professor Howard Wasserman criticizes the view apparently held by the *Scott* majority that video evidence is objective and subject to only a single interpretation:

> Like much else in the law, video is neither an unadorned good nor an unadorned bad; the reality is far more complex. As evidence, it has high probative value in advancing the search for truth, but not so high that it should dominate a jury and its deliberations. It is important evidence, but not an unassailable source of proof, not the objective, true, singular, unambiguous evidence it so often is thought to be. And it should not be an excuse for courts to disregard ordinary procedure and rely on their own interpretations of video to take cases away from juries on summary judgment.

Howard M. Wasserman, *Orwell's Vision: Video & the Future of Civil Rights Enforcement*, 68 Md. L. R. 600, 660–61 (2009).

Exercise 6-E

Your law firm frequently provides legal advice to local governments in your state. One of those local governments adopted the deadly force policy published by the Legal & Liability Risk Management Institute, which provides:

The use of deadly force is objectively reasonable when:

1. The officer is faced with an imminent threat of serious bodily harm or death to him/herself, or some other person who is present, or;
2. To prevent the escape of an individual in cases where the officer has probable cause to believe that the subject has committed a violent felony involving the infliction or threatened infliction of serious bodily harm or death AND by the subject's escape [he or she poses] an imminent threat of serious bodily harm or death to another.
3. Officers should warn the subject prior to using deadly force where feasible.

The local government seeks your advice as to whether it should amend the deadly force policy in light of *Scott* and, if so, how? Are there policy reasons for the local government to retain specific guidance for police officers' use of force, whether or not constitutionally required? *See* Karen Blum, Scott v. Harris*: Death Knell for Deadly Force Policies and Garner Jury Instructions?*, 58 Syracuse L. Rev. 45, 58 n.71 (2007) (quoting Legal & Liability Risk Management Institute, Model Policy: Response to Resistance 3 (2006) and noting that the policy is being adopted by nearly one thousand law enforcement departments).

Exercise 6-F

Recall that the jury instructions reproduced earlier in this Chapter specifically provided instructions for how juries should evaluate a police officer's use of deadly force. For example, relying in part on *Garner*, district courts within the Eighth Circuit instruct juries that "[Deadly force may be used only if it is reasonably believed necessary to [(apprehend a dangerous, fleeing felon) (prevent a significant threat of death or serious physical harm to the officer or others)]. A warning must be given, if [feasible] [possible], before deadly force may be used.]" Committee on Model Jury Instructions for the District Courts of the Eighth Circuit, 8th Cir. Civil Jury Instr. § 4.40 (2019), http://www.juryinstructions.ca8.uscourts.gov.

In light of *Scott*, should pattern jury instructions on deadly force be omitted in favor of general instructions on reasonable use of force? *See* Karen M. Blum, *Scott v. Harris: Death Knell for Deadly Force Policies and Garner Jury Instructions?*, 58 Syracuse L. Rev. 45, 76 (2007) (arguing that it is no longer necessary to instruct juries on the *Garner* preconditions; instead a jury charge must only help a jury to understand whether the force used was reasonable under all the circumstances); *Acosta v. Hill*, 504 F.3d 1323, 1323 (9th Cir. 2007) (district court did not err in only giving jury an excessive force instruction because, pursuant to *Scott*, "there is no special Fourth Amendment standard for unconstitutional deadly force" and district court need not give a separate deadly force instruction).

G. Development of Doctrine in the Circuits: Applying *Scott*

Questions to guide reading of *Lytle*

1. Did the majority read *Scott* as setting out a *per se* rule that deadly force is reasonable under the 4th Amendment when a suspect fleeing in a vehicle threatens the lives of innocent bystanders?
2. Did the dissent read *Scott* as setting out such a *per se* rule?
3. Is the majority's opinion more faithful to Justice Ginsburg's concurrence in *Scott* than to the majority opinion in *Scott*?
4. If the dissent's view had prevailed, under what circumstances would deadly force *not* be a reasonable way to terminate a police car chase?

Lytle v. Bexar County, Tex.

560 F.3d 404 (5th Cir. 2009), *cert. denied*, 559 U.S. 1007 (2010)

PRADO, Circuit Judge.

[Sheriff's Deputy Robert O'Donnell shot at the rear of a vehicle, striking and killing fifteen-year-old passenger Heather Lytle. Heather's father, Ernest Lytle, brought suit individually and on behalf of his daughter's estate against O'Donnell.]

A. Factual Background

On February 28, 2006, O'Donnell responded to a report that a complainant's ex-boyfriend had made threats of violence against her. The complainant stated that her ex-boyfriend was driving a stolen, primer-grey Ford Taurus. O'Donnell ... learned that the ex-boyfriend was a known car thief ... [and] was on bond for charges of felony theft and unlawfully carrying a weapon. O'Donnell later spotted a primer-black Ford Taurus—a possible match to the ex-boyfriend's vehicle—at a known drug location. After the Taurus left the location, O'Donnell began to follow it.

Shortly after O'Donnell began following the Taurus, it changed lanes without signaling. O'Donnell activated his emergency lights in an effort to initiate a traffic stop.

Instead of stopping, the Taurus turned right and began to accelerate. O'Donnell activated his siren and pursued the Taurus for a quarter-to-half mile. O'Donnell characterizes the chase as exceeding sixty-five miles per hour, while Lytle asserts that the speed was "well over" the thirty mile per hour speed limit. After this brief chase, the Taurus attempted to make a right turn, but it took the turn too widely and collided with a vehicle in the oncoming lane. The Taurus came to a stop and O'Donnell pulled his police cruiser twelve-to-fifteen feet behind the Taurus. The Taurus then began backing up toward O'Donnell's police cruiser.

The parties dispute what exactly happened next.... [S]ometime after O'Donnell stopped his police cruiser, he twice fired at the rear of the Taurus. Heather Lytle was sitting in the center of the back seat of the vehicle, and one of the shots struck and killed her. After firing, O'Donnell returned to his police cruiser and continued the pursuit. Upon later crashing the Taurus into a car port and fleeing on foot, the driver of the Taurus was apprehended.

...

[III.] A. The Constitutional Violation

Lytle asserts that O'Donnell used excessive force when he fired at the Taurus, implicating his daughter's Fourth Amendment right to be free from an unreasonable seizure ...

Assessing the reasonableness of a police officer's use of force involves "a careful balancing of 'the nature and quality of the intrusion on the individual's Fourth Amendment interests' against the countervailing governmental interests at stake." *Graham* [*v. Connor*], 490 U.S. [386,] 396 (1989) (quoting *Tennessee v. Garner*, 471 U.S. 1, 8 (1985)). This balancing "requires careful attention to the facts and circumstances of each particular case, including the severity of the crime at issue, whether the suspect poses an immediate threat to the safety of the officers or others, and whether he is actively resisting arrest or attempting to evade arrest by flight." *Id.* We judge the reasonableness of an officer's conduct "objectively," that is, without reference to the subjective intent or motivation that underlies the officer's conduct. *Id.* at 397. We must also look at the facts and circumstances "from the perspective of a reasonable officer on the scene, rather than with the 20/20 vision of hindsight." *Id.* at 396. And we must account for the difficult and often split-second decisions that police officers must make in carrying out their duties. *Id.* at 396–97.

There are few, if any, bright lines for judging a police officer's use of force; when determining whether an officer's conduct violated the Fourth Amendment, "we must ... slosh our way through the factbound morass of 'reasonableness.'" *Scott* [*v. Harris*, 550 U.S. 372,] 127 S.Ct. at 1777–78; *see also id.* (rejecting "an easy-to-apply legal test in the Fourth Amendment context").

...

O'Donnell asserts that his use of force was a reasonable response to the threat of harm that the Taurus posed to himself and the public. He further contends that this threat was ever-present, and thus suggests any dispute over the distance or direction that the Taurus had traveled was necessarily immaterial. In other words, according to O'Donnell, the threat that the Taurus posed was sufficiently grave whether the Taurus was immediately in front of him or four houses down the block.... O'Donnell misunderstands the issue, however, to be merely one of distance and direction.... [I]f the facts were as O'Donnell alleges—that is, he fired as or immediately after the Taurus was backing up toward him—he would likely be entitled to qualified immunity. This is due to the threat of immediate and severe physical harm that the reversing Taurus likely posed to O'Donnell himself. As discussed below, however, the threat of harm was potentially much different under Lytle's version of the facts. O'Donnell is thus mistaken in asserting that the distance and direction the Taurus traveled are irrelevant *because* the Taurus always posed a threat. They are instead relevant to *whether* the Taurus posed a threat.

Further, because we must look at all of the facts and circumstances relevant to the reasonableness of O'Donnell's conduct, he is mistaken to focus entirely on the threat of harm. Even were we to agree with O'Donnell as to the threat the Taurus posed, we would be remiss not to consider O'Donnell's conduct in response to that threat. It is unclear how firing at the back of a fleeing vehicle some distance away was a reasonable method of addressing the threat.... Were a jury to accept Lytle's version of the facts, it might very well be troubled by O'Donnell's act of firing his sidearm at the back of a vehicle three or four houses down the block of a residential area when he was unlikely to have a shot at—and apparently was not aiming for—the driver. A jury might also find that O'Donnell's act of firing at a vehicle driving away from him in a residential area posed a risk that the shots might strike an unintended target. Thus, even if we assumed that the Taurus posed a significant threat of harm, a jury could conclude that O'Donnell's conduct in response to that threat was unreasonable....

Moreover ... the distance and direction that the Taurus had traveled is essential to determining the extent of the threat that the Taurus actually posed—to both O'Donnell and the public in general—at the time O'Donnell fired. O'Donnell points to several factors that he argues indicate the severity of the threat posed by the vehicle. There was, first, the threat of harm that the Taurus posed to O'Donnell himself as it was backing up toward him. Further, O'Donnell reasonably believed (1) that the driver of the Taurus was the same individual that was on bond for charges of felony theft and unlawfully carrying a weapon, and (2) that the driver was driving a stolen vehicle. O'Donnell also knew that the driver of the Taurus (1) had committed the felony of fleeing from a police officer, (2) had left a known drug location, (3) had led O'Donnell on a high-speed chase through a residential area with children playing somewhere nearby, (4) had collided with an occupied car while attempting to make a right turn, (5) had refused orders to stop, (6) had reversed the Taurus toward O'Donnell, and (7) was fleeing into the neighborhood.

... To be sure, the Taurus might have posed an immediate and significant threat of harm to O'Donnell when it was backing up toward him. But an exercise of force that is reasonable at one moment can become unreasonable in the next if the justification for the use of force has ceased. *See* … *Ellis v. Wynalda*, 999 F.2d 243, 247 (7th Cir. 1993) ("When an officer faces a situation in which he could justifiably shoot, he does not retain the right to shoot at any time thereafter with impunity."); *see also Waterman v. Batton*, 393 F.3d 471, 481 (4th Cir. 2005) ("We therefore hold that force justified at the beginning of an encounter is not justified even seconds later if the justification for the initial force has been eliminated."). Thus, even were we to assume that shooting at the Taurus was reasonable at the moment it was backing up toward O'Donnell, that does not necessarily make his firing at the vehicle when it was driving away from him equally reasonable.

O'Donnell retorts that the events unfolded so quickly that, even if the vehicle was driving away when he fired, he should not be faulted for failing to recognize that the threat to him had passed.… [However] it was at least enough time for the Taurus to go from a full stop to a distance three or four houses down the block … anywhere from three to ten seconds, perhaps even more.… [D]rawing all reasonable inferences in the plaintiff's favor, we must assume that the Taurus backing up toward O'Donnell and the shooting were not [simultaneous and] … must therefore infer that sufficient time might have passed for O'Donnell to perceive that the threat to him had ceased … [and that] a jury could find that … this lack of a threat weighs against a conclusion of reasonableness.

… Invoking the Supreme Court's statement in *Scott* that "[a] police officer's attempt to terminate a dangerous high-speed car chase that threatens the lives of innocent bystanders does not violate the Fourth Amendment, even when it places the fleeing motorist at risk of serious injury or death," 127 S.Ct. at 1779, O'Donnell argues that the threat that the fleeing Taurus posed to the public renders his use of force objectively reasonable.

In *Scott*, the Court held that an officer's use of force to stop a fleeing motorist was reasonable in part because the suspect posed "an actual and imminent threat to the lives of any pedestrians who might have been present, to other civilian motorists, and to the officers involved in the chase." *Id.* at 1778 … [T]he Court's decision in *Scott* did not declare open season on suspects fleeing in motor vehicles. As Justice Ginsburg pointed out in her concurrence, *Scott* did not "articulat[e] a mechanical, *per se* rule." *Id.* at 1779 (Ginsburg, J., concurring).

> The inquiry described by the Court is situation specific. Among relevant considerations: Were the lives and well-being of others (motorists, pedestrians, police officers) at risk? Was there a safer way, given the time, place, and circumstances, to stop the fleeing vehicle?

Id. (citation omitted). Indeed, the reasoning of *Scott* itself—requiring courts to "slosh [their] way through the factbound morass of 'reasonableness,'" *id.* at 1778 (majority opinion)—belies such a per se approach. Consequently, the Taurus's flight does not *necessarily* render O'Donnell's conduct objectively reasonable. Nearly any suspect fleeing in a motor vehicle poses some threat of harm to the public. As the cases addressing this all-too-common scenario evince, the real inquiry is whether the fleeing suspect posed such a threat that the use of deadly force was justifiable.

For example, in *Cole v. Bone*, 993 F.2d 1328, 1330–31 (8th Cir. 1993), a police officer shot the driver of an eighteen-wheeler after the suspect led police on a fifty-mile chase exceeding speeds of ninety miles per hour, passed traffic on both shoulders, attempted to ram several police cruisers, ran a road block, and forced over one hundred vehicles out of its way. The Eighth Circuit held that the officer's conduct was reasonable because the officer was justified in believing that "the truck posed an imminent threat of serious physical harm to innocent motorists as well as to the officers themselves." *Id.* at 1333. Similarly, in *Williams v. City of Grosse Pointe Park*, 496 F.3d 482, 487 (6th Cir. 2007), the Sixth Circuit found the shooting of a fleeing motorist to be objectively reasonable. After the suspect's vehicle collided with a police cruiser, one officer approached the driver's window and stuck his gun into the vehicle, pointing it at the suspect's head. *Id.* at 484. The suspect began to drive away, knocking the officer to the ground. *Id.* The court in *Williams* found a second officer's shooting of the driver to be objectively reasonable based upon the threat that the driver posed to both the downed officer and the public. *Id.* at 487. And in *Abney v. Coe*, 493 F.3d 412, 418 (4th Cir. 2007), the Fourth Circuit held that an officer's conduct was reasonable where the officer stopped a suspect fleeing on a motorcycle by ramming the suspect with his police cruiser. The court found "abundant and uncontradicted evidence" that the suspect posed a substantial threat of harm to the public, including the fact that the suspect led police on an eight mile chase during "which he committed numerous dangerous traffic violations" and ran another motorist off the road. *Id.* at 416–17. This threat of harm rendered the officer's conduct objectively reasonable. *Id.* at 418....

In contrast, a number of courts have found police officers' shooting of fleeing motorists to be unreasonable—or at least potentially so, for the purposes of qualified immunity appeals—where the driver posed a lesser risk of harm to others. For example, in *Adams v. Speers*, 473 F.3d 989, 991 (9th Cir. 2007), a suspect had led police on a chase, "largely within the speed limit," for over an hour. An officer twice rammed the suspect's vehicle and later, without warning, shot and killed the suspect as the suspect's vehicle rolled away. *Id.* at 991–92. The Ninth Circuit found it "obvious" that "[n]o officer acting reasonably in these circumstances could have believed that he could use deadly force to apprehend" the suspect. *Id.* at 993–94. Similarly, in *Smith v. Cupp*, 430 F.3d 766, 770 (6th Cir. 2005), a police officer shot a suspect after the suspect had stolen the officer's police cruiser and began to drive away. The Sixth Circuit recognized that a suspect fleeing in a stolen police cruiser posed some danger to the public but held that the danger "was not so grave as to justify the use of deadly force." *Id.* at 773. As the plaintiff's version of the facts did not mention any bystanders "whose physical safety could have been endangered by [the suspect's] actions," *id.* at 774, the court held that a jury would "be entitled to determine that [the police officer's] use of force was unreasonable and accordingly unconstitutional," *id.* at 775....

As these decisions indicate, a suspect that is fleeing in a motor vehicle is not so inherently dangerous that an officer's use of deadly force is *per se* reasonable....

Taking the facts of the present case in the light most favorable to Lytle, a jury could conclude that the Taurus posed some threat of harm; the chase took place at high speeds within a residential area, there were children playing somewhere nearby, and the Taurus had collided with another vehicle. But we do not agree with O'Donnell that the Taurus was so menacing under Lytle's version of the facts that any use of force in an attempt to stop it would be objectively reasonable as a matter of law. A jury accepting Lytle's version of the facts could conclude that the Taurus did not pose a sufficient threat of harm such that the use of deadly force was reasonable. O'Donnell had pursued the Taurus for only a quarter-to-half mile before the shooting occurred, raising a question of whether O'Donnell had sufficient indicia to conclude that the Taurus posed such a threat of harm. Also, there were no children or bystanders in the path of the vehicle, indicating that no one was in immediate danger. The Taurus's collision with the oncoming vehicle while making a wide right turn does give us some pause, but we think the jury should assess the depravity that this collision evidenced. Thus, while any threat of harm to the public would weigh in favor of finding O'Donnell's conduct reasonable, the threat was not so great under Lytle's version of the facts that O'Donnell's conduct is beyond question.

When we consider the totality of the circumstances, we conclude that O'Donnell's conduct may not have been objectively reasonable. A rational jury could conclude that the Taurus did not pose an especially significant threat of harm such that the use of deadly force was justified. Further, when weighing the threat of harm posed by the Taurus against O'Donnell's chosen course of conduct—firing at the back of the vehicle from some distance—the jury could conclude that O'Donnell's conduct was not a reasonable response to any threat.

...

JERRY E. SMITH, Circuit Judge, dissenting.

... The majority errs, primarily in light of *Scott v. Harris*, 550 U.S. 372 (2007). The situation faced by the officers in *Scott* and the instant case are not different in any way that should make a difference ... In *Scott*, the Court, quite properly, focused on that threat—on what it termed "the extreme danger to human life posed by [the suspect]." *Scott*, 550 U.S. at 383. Addressing the statement in *Tennessee v. Garner*, 471 U.S. 1, 11 (1985), that, under the Fourth Amendment, "the fleeing suspect must have posed an immediate threat of serious physical harm to the officer or others," the *Scott* Court relied on the fact that "it was [the suspect's] flight itself (by means of a speeding automobile) that posed the threat of 'serious physical harm ... to others.'" *Scott*, 550 U.S. at 382 n. 9 (quoting *Garner*, 471 U.S. at 11).

We return, therefore, to the question whether, accepting Lytle's version of the facts, the threat to life and safety was sufficient to justify use of deadly force. The majority accurately sets forth several factors that [O'Donnell] argues indicate the severity of the threat posed by [the suspect's] vehicle....

For purposes of summary judgment, we cannot credit O'Donnell's disputed claim that the Taurus was backing toward him. The other facts, however, are not contested, and they closely mirror the considerations addressed in *Scott*, in which the Court asked whether,

> consistent with the *Fourth Amendment*, [an officer can] attempt to stop a fleeing motorist from continuing his public-endangering flight.... Put another way: Can an officer take actions that place a fleeing motorist at risk of serious injury or death on order to stop the motorist's flight from endangering the lives of innocent bystanders?

Scott, 550 U.S. at 374. The Court answered that question in the affirmative[.] ... The same result is called for here. It makes no difference if the dangerous suspect was three or four houses away instead of backing toward the officer. The obvious risk to the public was the same, as was the need for the officer to take action. The blame for the passenger's death falls squarely on the suspect, not the officer, who had no intention of hitting an innocent occupant of the Taurus with his shot. Officer O'Donnell did not violate the Fourth Amendment.... His actions, despite their unfortunate and unintended consequences, were not unreasonable. "[N]o reasonable jury could conclude otherwise." *Scott*, 550 U.S. at 386. I respectfully dissent.

For further discussion

A seizure may be permissible even though the police officer makes a reasonable factual mistake about the justification for the seizure. But what if the officer makes a reasonable *legal* mistake?

> In this case, an officer stopped a vehicle because one of its two brake lights was out, but a court later determined that a single working brake light was all the law required. The question presented is whether such a mistake of law can nonetheless give rise to the reasonable suspicion necessary to uphold the seizure under the Fourth Amendment. We hold that it can. Because the officer's mistake about the brake-light law was reasonable, the stop in this case was lawful under the Fourth Amendment.

Heien v. North Carolina, 574 U.S. 54, 135 S.Ct. 530, 534 (2014). In Chapter 11, this book returns to the significance of mistakes of fact and law in the context of qualified immunity from Section 1983 liability.

Practice Pointer

In practice, lawyers must research as efficiently as possible. To efficiently determine the current status of 4th Amendment law in your client's jurisdiction, secondary sources that summarize the topic can be a useful starting point. Before searching online for specific decisions, consider reviewing some of the following published resources to learn the vocabulary of the topic, to identify current issues, and to collect current citations. The focused treatise by Michael Avery, David Rudovsky & Karen Blum, POLICE MISCONDUCT:

LAW AND LITIGATION (3d Ed. Clark Boardman 2018), and the more comprehensive treatises by Sheldon Nahmod, CIVIL RIGHTS AND CIVIL LIBERTIES LITIGATION: THE LAW OF SECTION 1983 (4th ed., West 2019) and by Martin A. Schwartz, SECTION 1983 LITIGATION: CLAIMS AND DEFENSES (4th ed., Aspen 2009 & Supp. 2018), are all excellent sources for explanation of 4th Amendment concepts and identification of current citations, and are all available on WestlawEdge. Other very helpful treatises include Ivan E. Bodensteiner & Rosalie Berger Levinson, STATE AND LOCAL GOVERNMENT CIVIL RIGHTS LIABILITY (Thomson Reuters/West 2000 & Supp. 2011–19) and Martin A. Schwartz & Kathryn R. Urbonya, SECTION 1983 LITIGATION (3d ed., Federal Judicial Center 2014), both available on WestlawEdge, and Isidore Silver, POLICE CIVIL LIABILITY (Matthew Bender 1986 & Supp. 2019) and Joseph G. Cook & John L. Sobieski, Jr., CIVIL RIGHTS ACTIONS (Matthew Bender 1983 & Supp. 2019), both available on Lexis and Lexis Advance.

Other sources that can help you efficiently identify current 4th Amendment issues and locate recent citations to binding law are continuing legal education materials and practice guides. *See, e.g.*, Kathleen L. Daerr-Bannon, *Cause of Action Under 42 USC § 1983 for Use of Excessive Force by Police in Making Arrest*, 59 Causes of Action 2d 173 (2013, updated Oct. 2014). Model jury instructions—some of which are included in this Chapter—are useful for the same reasons and often are available on the federal circuit court websites.

American Law Reports articles provide useful summaries of particular 4th Amendment topics and citations to relevant cases, organized by jurisdiction with new cases added weekly. *See, e.g.*, Richard P. Shafer, *When does police officer's use of force during arrest become so excessive as to constitute violation of constitutional rights, imposing liability under Federal Civil Rights Act of 1871 (42 U.S.C.A. § 1983)*, 60 A.L.R. Fed. 204 (1982, updated weekly); Jay M. Zitter, *When Does Use of Taser Constitute Violation of Constitutional Rights*, 45 A.L.R.6th (2009, updated weekly). Legal encyclopedias can be helpful for the same reasons, although their treatment is less in-depth. *See, e.g.*, Ann Fagan Ginger & Louis H. Bell, *Police Misconduct Litigation—Plaintiff's Remedies*, 15 Am. Jur. Trials 555 (1968, updated Aug. 2019); Jim T. Priest & Reggie N. Whitten, *Defense of a Police Misconduct Suit*, 38 Am. Jur. Trials 493 (1989, updated Aug. 2019); William E. Ringel, Justin D. Franklin and Steven C. Bell, *Coverage of Fourth Amendment*, Searches and Seizures Arrests and Confessions § 2:2 (2d ed., updated July 2014).

All of the above sources may be available through electronic databases, depending on your employer's subscriptions. In addition, you can identify current issues and citations by searching the briefs filed recently in the relevant jurisdiction that are available in the WestlawEdge, Lexis Advance, or Lexis brief banks. Once you have located relevant, binding authority, be sure to update those sources via Shepard's on Lexis/Lexis Advance or KeyCite on WestlawEdge to confirm their accuracy and to locate additional, more recent authority.

Chapter Seven

Distinguishing 4th, 14th, and 8th Amendment Claims: Development of Doctrine in the Circuits

A. Chapter Overview

A claim that government officials used excessive force could be litigated under the 4th Amendment, the 14th Amendment, or the 8th Amendment. Which constitutional protection governs depends on the factual circumstances. Briefly, the 4th Amendment governs excessive force claims arising during arrest, the 14th Amendment governs claims arising during pretrial detention, and the 8th Amendment governs claims arising after conviction.

Before 2015, the Supreme Court had not decided how to analyze a claim concerning the use of excessive force by law enforcement "beyond the point at which arrest ends and pretrial detention begins," *Graham v. Connor*, 490 U.S. 386, 395 n.10 (1989), and the circuits were not uniform. In fact, for the more than two decades between 1989 and 2015, the federal circuits split on how to analyze a post-arrest excessive force claim. There was ambiguity about: (1) when a person under arrest becomes a pretrial detainee; (2) what legal standard governs a person in the "twilight zone" of post-arrest, pre-arraignment; and (3) what the substance of the 14th Amendment's standard governing pretrial detainees should be.

In 2015, the Supreme Court resolved the longstanding circuit split over whether custodial officials need to *subjectively* intend to inflict excessive force for a 14th Amendment claim of excessive force to succeed (*Kingsley*). This Chapter requires you to navigate the difficult legal landscape that lawyers, litigants, and courts inhabited in the decades before *Kingsley*, as a vehicle for grasping how doctrine evolves. This Chapter also considers what issues *Kingsley* left open.

Further, since 2015, several circuits have extended the logic of *Kingsley* to other 14th Amendment substantive due process claims by pretrial detainees. While *Kingsley* concerned an excessive force claim, some circuits have applied *Kingsley* outside the excessive force context, thereby changing how they analyze 14th Amendment prison condition claims. This Chapter discusses the resulting circuit split.

Claims arising from suicides by detainees also may require practicing lawyers and courts to determine whether the analysis is governed by the 14th or 8th Amendment. This Chapter includes factual background about suicide by detainees and an example of a circuit court application of the *Farmer* standard to the suicide of a pretrial detainee.

B. Excessive Force Claims Post-Arrest

Questions to guide reading of *Lopez*

Lopez is the basis of Simulation 4.

1. Why did the Seventh Circuit hold that the district court should have used the 4th Amendment instead of the 14th Amendment to analyze the plaintiff's claim?
2. In the Seventh Circuit, what event is necessary for a person arrested without a warrant to become a pretrial detainee? How does the Seventh Circuit differentiate protection under the 4th Amendment from protection under the 14th Amendment or 8th Amendment in the context of an excessive force claim? According to *Lopez*, why is a 14th Amendment standard more difficult for a plaintiff to satisfy?
3. What was the gist of the testimony by the plaintiff's police practices expert?
4. If you represented the detectives, what recommendations would you make to your clients after obtaining this court ruling?

Lopez v. City of Chicago

464 F.3d 711 (7th Cir. 2006)

SYKES, Circuit Judge.

Joseph Lopez was arrested by Chicago police for a murder he did not commit. The murder victim was a twelve-year-old boy, an innocent bystander hit by gunfire in a drive-by shooting. Lopez was arrested without a warrant, although with probable cause—an eyewitness identified him as the shooter.

Following his arrest, the individual defendants—all detectives with the Chicago Police Department—kept Lopez shackled to the wall of a windowless, nine-by-seven-foot interrogation room for four days and nights while they investigated the case. Lopez had nowhere to sleep but a four-foot-by-ten-inch metal bench or the dirty brick floor. The interrogation room had no toilet or sink; he had to "scream" for the detectives to let him out to use a bathroom. He was given only one bologna sandwich and one serving of juice as food and drink during the entire four days and nights he was kept in the interrogation room. The detectives questioned him from time to time and made him stand in two lineups.

After two-and-a-half days in these conditions, Lopez started to become disoriented and began hearing voices telling him to confess. He ultimately gave a statement containing a false confession that did not match the details of the crime. On the fifth day of his detention, Lopez was moved to the city lockup, charged, and finally taken to court. The following day, the police investigation led detectives to another individual who confessed to the murder. Lopez was released the next day.

Those were the facts the jury was entitled to believe based on evidence Lopez presented during a seven-day trial on his claim under 42 U.S.C. § 1983 for violation of his constitutional rights.... The detectives testified differently about their treatment of Lopez while he was in their custody, but there was no dispute that they detained him for five days after his warrantless arrest without taking him before a judge for a probable cause hearing. Remarkably, after hearing this evidence, the district court refused to submit the claims to the jury and instead granted the defendants' motion for judgment as a matter of law. We reverse.

...

There was conflicting evidence at trial on Lopez's treatment while in the detectives' custody, raising a jury issue on his constitutional claim relating to the conditions of his warrantless detention.... The district judge should not have taken these claims from the jury and resolved the factual conflict himself; they are remanded for retrial.

I. Background

[W]e recount the facts based on the evidence presented at trial in the light most favorable to Lopez, the party against whom the district court entered judgment as a matter of law....

On July 19, 2000, a twelve-year-old boy was shot and killed in a drive-by shooting in Lopez's Chicago neighborhood. Based on one eyewitness's identification, Chicago police officers arrested Lopez without a warrant at approximately 2 p.m. on July 20. Lopez stipulated at trial that the officers had probable cause to arrest him. The arresting officers took him to the Chicago Police Department's Area 5 detective headquarters where they left him in the custody of the defendant detectives: Jennifer Delucia, James Delafont, Daniel Jacobs, and Hector Vergara.

Lopez was placed in a nine-by-seven-foot interrogation room, and one of his arms was handcuffed to a metal ring fastened to the wall about three feet off the floor. When he asked if he could be unshackled from the wall, one of the detectives—Lopez does not remember who—told him "no" because he "was a murderer." The room's brick floor was dirtied with gum, cigarette butts, used matches, wrappers, and dust. Next to the wall and below the ring to which Lopez was shackled was a metal bench that was four feet long and ten inches wide. There was no sink, toilet, or running water in the room. There was a small window in the door, but it was covered over with paper so it was impossible to see through it. The room had no clock and Lopez did not have a watch or other timekeeping device with him, so he could not tell how long he was in the room or whether it was night or day. The detectives kept Lopez shackled to the wall of this room for four days and four nights.

Lopez's expert on police practices testified that a suspect should be held in such an interrogation room only for "short durations" not to exceed "eight hours." He testified that "generally you want to—you don't want to do it longer than what would normally be a business day or would normally be something somebody could tolerate for a period of time." He also said it would "[a]bsolutely not" be appropriate to hold a suspect in an interrogation room for even twenty-four hours, let alone the four days and nights Lopez endured.

The detectives let Lopez out of the interrogation room for only a few brief moments. They removed him twice to appear in police lineups, first on the evening of July 20 and then on the evening of July 21. At some point during his detention, the detectives transferred Lopez to a second interrogation room that was essentially the same as the first. To leave the interrogation room to use the bathroom, Lopez said he had to "scream[] from the top of [his] lungs" to get the detectives' attention in order to be let out. It is not clear how many times Lopez asked to use the bathroom. He implied on direct examination that it was multiple times: "Sometimes I'd be yelling for a while. I don't know how long. I couldn't time myself." But on cross-examination he said he thought he only asked once to use the bathroom. At any rate, because the interrogation room lacked a sink or running water, Lopez was unable to attend to his personal hygiene in any way for the four days. He realized he began to smell badly and Detective Jacobs told him he stunk.

Lopez had great difficulty sleeping during the four days and nights he was shackled to the wall of the interrogation room. He tried once to lie down on the brick floor to get some sleep, but he woke up with shooting pains down his shackled arm, which had begun to turn purplish blue, and pain in his shoulder, hip, and knees. Lopez then sat up on the bench and kept his shackled arm level with the ring on the wall in order to restore proper circulation. He gave up trying to sleep lying down and just sat on the bench and leaned back against the wall. It seemed to Lopez that whenever he fell asleep in that seated position, he would bump his head on the wall and wake up. The little sleep he got was not restful.

For his first two-and-a-half days in the interrogation room, no one brought Lopez anything to eat or drink. He testified that he was able to grab a drink of water during his trips to the bathroom. He said, "[T]he only way I could use the bathroom or drink some water [was] if the detectives that were working on my case were there. If not, I had to wait." Lopez testified that he became disoriented and began to hear voices in his head at some point after he was brought back from the second police lineup, about a day and a half into his detention. He told the jury:

> I couldn't even put my ideas in place. I couldn't even think straight. And every time I would, like, say something, I would tell myself man, you know, I didn't shoot that little boy and then a voice will click in and say yeah, you did shoot him.... It was just some voice that was coming from the back of

> my head just kept telling me yeah, you did shoot him. So after awhile me fighting against that voice, it just came true. I was like you know what, I started to believe that I did shoot [him].... I was sitting there for a while and after me crying so much and trying to put thoughts all together, which wasn't even going together, I was sitting looking at the wall and I would feel like the wall was like coming in closer. And as I would feel it, it looked like it was coming in closer to me.

Lopez told the jury that by this point in his detention he could no longer think rationally and that "[his] mind was nowhere near [his] head." About 60 hours into his detention, Lopez gave a statement to Detectives Jacobs and Delafont in which he falsely confessed to having shot the twelve-year-old boy.

The details of Lopez's confession did not match the forensic evidence from the crime scene, and shortly thereafter Detective Jacobs returned to the interrogation room and angrily called Lopez a liar. The detective told Lopez he did not deserve to be a father—Lopez's girlfriend was pregnant—and suggested that his girlfriend should get an abortion. Lopez retracted his confession and told Jacobs that he had not shot anyone. One of the detectives then brought Lopez a bologna sandwich and some juice; according to Lopez, it was the only food he received during his four-day stay. The detectives testified that they fed Lopez regularly by purchasing fast food with their own money, but they produced no receipts or other record of these purchases and there are no police documents indicating Lopez was fed in this manner.

On July 24, four days into Lopez's detention, an assistant state's attorney approved murder charges against him and he was transferred to the city lockup. There, Lopez was placed in a cell with a padded bunk for sleeping, a toilet, and a sink. He also received a meal that he recalls as a hot bologna sandwich, french fries, and a soda. All indications are that Lopez was fed regularly once he moved to the lockup.

Lopez appeared before a judge for arraignment and a probable cause hearing on July 25, five days after his warrantless arrest. The police continued to investigate the killing, and leads pointed to another individual, Miguel Figueroa, as the shooter. On July 26 Figueroa confessed to the murder. The state's attorney's office dropped the charges against Lopez and he was released on July 27.

Lopez sued ... the four detectives pursuant to 42 U.S.C. § 1983 alleging they had subjected him to an unconstitutional detention—because of the conditions he was subjected to and the extended duration of the detention in light of the warrantless arrest—in violation of the Fourth and Fourteenth Amendments.... The case was tried to a jury, which heard seven days of evidence. At the close of the evidence ... defendants moved for judgment as a matter of law ... [and] the court entered judgment for the defendants on [the conditions of detention] claim.

...

A. Unconstitutional Conditions of Confinement

[D]uring trial the parties agreed that the Fourth Amendment governed Lopez's claim that the detectives subjected him to unconstitutional conditions and treatment during his warrantless detention. The district judge thought otherwise and evaluated Lopez's unconstitutional conditions claim using the more demanding "deliberate indifference" standard applicable to convicted prisoners' claims of cruel and unusual punishment under the Eighth Amendment and similar claims of pretrial detainees under the Fourteenth Amendment. *See, e.g., Johnson v. Snyder*, 444 F.3d 579, 585 (7th Cir. 2006) (deliberate indifference requires a culpable state of mind such as ignoring a known risk of harm; it "is more than negligence and approaches intentional wrongdoing") (quotation marks and citation omitted).... The district court's application of the deliberate indifference standard made things more difficult for Lopez; the Fourth Amendment requires only proof that the defendants' conduct was objectively unreasonable under the circumstances....

The district court should have analyzed the detectives' conduct under the Fourth Amendment and its "objectively unreasonable" standard. The Fourth Amendment protects against unreasonable seizures; an arrest is a seizure, and the Fourth Amendment affords persons who are arrested the further, distinct right to a judicial determination of probable cause "as a prerequisite to extended restraint of liberty following arrest." *Gerstein* [*v. Pugh*], 420 U.S. [103,] 114 [(1975)]. The judicial determination of probable cause may be made before the arrest (in the form of an arrest warrant) or promptly after the arrest, at a probable cause hearing (sometimes called a *Gerstein* hearing). But whether the arresting officer opts to obtain a warrant in advance or present a person arrested without a warrant for a prompt after-the-fact *Gerstein* hearing, the Fourth Amendment requires a *judicial* determination of probable cause....

[P]ersons arrested without a warrant must receive a judicial determination of probable cause within 48 hours.... Because Lopez was arrested without a warrant and had not yet been presented for a probable cause hearing, the Fourth Amendment should have been applied to his claim relating to the treatment and conditions he endured during his four days and nights in warrantless detention. Although his claim does not challenge the existence of probable cause, our cases hold that the *Gerstein* probable cause hearing is the event that terminates the Fourth Amendment's applicability following a warrantless arrest.

Accordingly, we have held that "the Fourth Amendment governs the period of confinement between arrest without a warrant and the preliminary hearing at which a determination of probable cause is made, while due process regulates the period of confinement after the initial determination of probable cause." *Villanova v. Abrams*, 972 F.2d 792, 797 (7th Cir. 1992).... Our cases thus establish that the protections of the Fourth Amendment apply at arrest and through the *Gerstein* probable cause hearing, due process principles govern a pretrial detainee's conditions of confinement after the judicial determination of probable cause, and the Eighth Amendment applies following conviction.

[Defendants] argue that the claim is governed by the due process analysis applicable to claims of pretrial detainees, which borrows from the Eighth Amendment's "deliberate indifference" standard, applicable to conditions-of-confinement claims by convicted prisoners....

The defendants cite *Bell v. Wolfish*, 441 U.S. 520, 535 (1979), for the proposition that the Fourth Amendment does not apply to pretrial detainees. But *Bell* concerned "persons who have been charged with a crime but who have not yet been tried on the charge"—that is, pretrial detainees for whom a judicial determination of probable cause has already been made. *Id.* at 523. That the Fourth Amendment does not apply to postarraignment detention does not make its protections inapplicable to the period between Lopez's arrest and his probable cause hearing. *Bell* is inapposite.

Lopez's trial evidence, if credited by the jury, was more than adequate to support a finding that the detectives' conduct was objectively unreasonable under the circumstances. Indeed, this case should not have been taken from the jury even if the more burdensome standard of deliberate indifference applied. The defendants concede on appeal that the district court should have permitted the jury to consider Lopez's claim insofar as it alleged that shackling him to the wall of the interrogation room for four days and nights violated his constitutional rights. The jury should have been permitted to consider the *totality* of Lopez's evidence, not just the evidence of shackling. Lopez presented evidence that he was deprived of food, drink, and sleep during the four days and nights he spent shackled to the wall of the interrogation room, and was forced to yell for an extended period of time before being let out to use the bathroom. The defendants argue there is no evidence Lopez ever asked for food or drink or soiled himself. This is an argument for a jury, not a reviewing court.

If Lopez's version of events is believed, common sense alone would justify a conclusion that the detectives' conduct was objectively unreasonable; when the fact finder's task is to decide whether an act or omission is objectively unreasonable, reliance upon common sense is particularly appropriate.... But the jury need not have relied on common sense alone. Lopez's police practices expert testified that it would "[a]bsolutely not" be appropriate to confine an arrested person in an interrogation room for twenty-four hours, much less for four days. On this record, the district court's refusal to submit this claim to the jury was unjustified; the court impermissibly weighed the evidence and drew inferences in favor of the defendants rather than Lopez, contrary to Rule 50's governing standards. Lopez's unconstitutional conditions of confinement claim must be retried.

...

For further discussion

1. The *Lopez* facts do not present a typical physical beating scenario but a use of force—*e.g.*, chaining a man's arm midair to a wall for prolonged periods—that is akin to torture, in part because it caused sleep deprivation. Because of the American public debate about the use of "stress positions" in the conflicts in Iraq and Afghanistan, you may be aware of ways force can be used to coerce and injure, even if it does not leave marks.

2. Compare the treatment of Mr. Lopez with the treatment of some detainees held by the Central Intelligence Agency (CIA), as described in a 2014 Senate report. Ac-

cording to the report, multiple detainees at CIA detention sites were "forced to stand with their arms shackled above their heads for extended periods of time.... In one example, a U.S. military legal advisor observed the technique known as 'hanging,' involving handcuffing one or both wrists to an overhead horizontal bar. The legal advisor noted that one detainee was apparently left hanging 22 hours each day for two consecutive days to 'break' his resistance.... According to CIA cables, Abu Zubaydah was handcuffed 'high on the bars.'"[1] "Draft [CIA Office of Medical Services] guidelines on interrogations, noted that detainees could be shackled with their arms above their heads for 'roughly two hours without great concern,' and that the arms could be elevated for between two and four hours if the detainee was monitored for 'excessive distress.'"[2] In her forward to the Report, Senator Dianne Feinstein wrote:

> While the Office of Legal Counsel found otherwise between 2002 and 2007, it is my personal conclusion that, under any common meaning of the term, CIA detainees were tortured. I also believe that the conditions of confinement and the use of authorized and unauthorized interrogation and conditioning techniques were cruel, inhuman, and degrading.[3]

3. If you were Mr. Lopez's lawyer, would you have litigated this claim solely on behalf of Mr. Lopez, or would you have attempted to litigate this claim on behalf of other arrestees subjected to similar treatment by Chicago police? Strategically, what are the advantages of litigating on behalf of a single plaintiff as opposed to a class of similarly situated plaintiffs? What are some barriers to litigating on behalf of a class? The *Lopez* litigation is related to a suit against the City of Chicago itself, discussed in Chapter 12.

4. In *Lopez*, the Seventh Circuit recognized a neutral judicial determination of probable cause as dividing 4th Amendment from 14th Amendment protection. But since then, the Supreme Court has held that a defendant seized without probable cause can challenge his pretrial detention under the Fourth Amendment. *Manuel v. City of Joliet*, ___ U.S. ___, 137 S. Ct. 911, 917 (2017). In *Manuel*, the Supreme Court held that the Fourth Amendment protects a person from being seized without probable cause both at the time of arrest and "when legal process itself goes wrong—when, for example, a judge's probable-cause determination is predicated solely on a police officer's false statements.... Legal process has gone forward, but it has done nothing to satisfy the Fourth Amendment's probable-cause requirement. And for that reason, it cannot extinguish the detainee's Fourth Amendment claim—or somehow, as the Seventh Circuit has held, convert that claim into one founded on the Due Process Clause." *Id.* at 918–19; *id.* at 920, n.8 ("By contrast ... once a trial has occurred the Fourth Amendment drops out....").

5. Probable cause for the arrest was not contested in *Lopez*. The Supreme Court more recently has cautioned against assessing probable cause for an arrest by viewing

1. Senate Select Committee on Intelligence, Committee Study of the Central Intelligence Agency's Detention and Interrogation Program (Declassified Revisions Dec. 3, 2014), Section IX, Appendix 2: CIA Detainees from 2002–2008, at 497–98.

2. *Id.* at 498.

3. *Id.* at 4.

"each fact 'in isolation, rather than as a factor in the totality of the circumstances.'" *District of Columbia v. Wesby*, ___ U.S. ___, 138 S. Ct. 577, 588 (2018) (further citation omitted). "The totality-of-the-circumstances test 'precludes this sort of divide-and-conquer analysis.'" *Id.* Finding probable cause for the arrest of partygoers in a vacant house, the Supreme Court reasoned:

> [T]he officers found a group of people who claimed to be having a bachelor party with no bachelor, in a near-empty house, with strippers in the living room and sexual activity in the bedroom, and who fled at the first sign of police. The panel majority identified innocent explanations for most of these circumstances in isolation, but again, this kind of divide-and-conquer approach is improper.... [H]ere, the totality of the circumstances gave the officers plenty of reasons to doubt the partygoers' protestations of innocence.

Id. at 589.

Questions to guide reading of *Wilson*

1. According to *Wilson*, when is an excessive force claim governed by the 8th Amendment?
2. How does *Wilson* describe the split in the circuits about whether excessive force claims arising after arrest should be analyzed under the 4th or 14th Amendments? When does 4th Amendment protection end?
3. What standard did the Eighth Circuit apply in *Wilson*? If the 14th Amendment deliberate indifference standard had applied instead, what additional evidence would the jury have considered?
4. Based on your reading of *Lopez*, did the Eighth Circuit properly categorize the Seventh Circuit in footnote 2? How should a practicing lawyer approach such categorization in court decisions?

Wilson v. Spain

209 F.3d 713 (8th Cir. 2000)

BOWMAN, Circuit Judge.

...

I.

The undisputed facts are as follows. Officer [David] Spain, responding to a disturbance, arrested [Robert] Wilson for public intoxication. Another officer, Stanley Cain, took Wilson to the local jail. Both officers were involved in booking Wilson, who was uncooperative and hostile throughout much of the process. Spain allowed Wilson to call his brother to request a ride home. After the brother arrived, however, the officers decided to keep Wilson in custody. Officer Spain placed Wilson against a wall and frisked him. Wilson resisted, attempting to elbow Spain, and Spain wrestled

Wilson to the floor. Spain and Cain handcuffed Wilson, picked him up, and Spain then led Wilson into a holding cell.

Spain placed Wilson in the cell, shut the door, and placed a key into the latch to lock the door. Wilson was yelling and pounding on the door. Spain withdrew the key, paused for a moment, and then put the key back in the latch to unlock the door. Spain then pushed the door open, and the door hit Wilson, knocking him unconscious. Wilson was taken to the hospital shortly thereafter. A police department video camera captured most of these events on tape.

...

II.

Section 1983 does not confer substantive rights but merely provides a means to vindicate rights conferred by the Constitution or laws of the United States. "In addressing an excessive force claim brought under § 1983, analysis begins by identifying the specific constitutional right allegedly infringed by the challenged application of force." *Graham v. Connor*, 490 U.S. 386, 394 (1989). "[T]he two primary sources of constitutional protection against physically abusive governmental conduct" are the Fourth and Eighth Amendments. *Id.* The Fourth Amendment's prohibition against unreasonable seizures of the person applies to excessive-force claims that "arise[ ] in the context of an arrest or investigatory stop of a free citizen," *id.*, while the Eighth Amendment's ban on cruel and unusual punishment applies to excessive-force claims brought by convicted criminals serving their sentences. *See Whitley v. Albers*, 475 U.S. 312, 318–322 (1986).

Between arrest and sentencing lies something of a legal twilight zone. The Supreme Court has left open the question of how to analyze a claim concerning the use of excessive force by law enforcement "beyond the point at which arrest ends and pretrial detention begins," *Graham*, 490 U.S. at 395 n. 10, and the circuits are split.[2] This Court previously has applied the Fourth Amendment to situations very similar to this case. In *Moore v. Novak*, 146 F.3d 531 (8th Cir. 1998), law enforcement officers at a jail used force against an arrestee who was being violent and disruptive during the booking process. *See id.* at 532–33. We held that the district court appropriately applied Fourth Amendment standards to Moore's excessive-force claims. *See id.* at 535. Similarly, in *Mayard v. Hopwood*, 105 F.3d 1226 (8th Cir. 1997), we applied

2. Some circuits hold that after the act of arrest, substantive due process is the proper constitutional provision because the Fourth Amendment is no longer relevant. *See Riley v. Dorton*, 115 F.3d 1159, 1161–64 (4th Cir. 1997) (en banc), *cert. denied*, 522 U.S. 1030 (1997); *Cottrell v. Caldwell*, 85 F.3d 1480, 1490 (11th Cir. 1996); *Wilkins v. May*, 872 F.2d 190, 192–95 (7th Cir. 1989), *cert. denied*, 493 U.S. 1026 (1990). Other circuits hold that the Fourth Amendment applies until an individual arrested without a warrant appears before a neutral magistrate for arraignment or for a probable cause hearing, or until the arrestee leaves the joint or sole custody of the arresting officer or officers. *See Barrie v. Grand County*, 119 F.3d 862, 866 (10th Cir. 1997); *Pierce v. Multnomah County*, 76 F.3d 1032, 1042–43 (9th Cir. 1996), *cert. denied*, 519 U.S. 1006 (1996); *Powell v. Gardner*, 891 F.2d 1039, 1044 (2d Cir. 1989); *McDowell v. Rogers*, 863 F.2d 1302, 1306–07 (6th Cir. 1988).

Fourth Amendment standards not only to the act of arrest, but also to use of force against an arrestee who was restrained in the back of a police car. *See id.* at 1228. We therefore shall use the Fourth Amendment to analyze Wilson's federal claims. In doing so, we observe that if Wilson cannot win his case under Fourth Amendment standards, it is a certainty he cannot win it under the seemingly more burdensome, and clearly no less burdensome, standards that must be met to establish a Fourteenth Amendment substantive due process claim. *See County of Sacramento v. Lewis*, 523 U.S. 833, 845–54 (1998) (describing substantive due process inquiry as whether governmental conduct "shocks the conscience" in the circumstances)....

...

"The 'reasonableness' of a particular use of force must be judged from the perspective of a reasonable officer on the scene, rather than with the 20/20 vision of hindsight." *Graham*, 490 U.S. at 396. "The calculus of reasonableness must embody allowance for the fact that police officers are often forced to make split-second judgments—in circumstances that are tense, uncertain, and rapidly evolving—about the amount of force that is necessary in a particular situation." *Id.* at 396–97. Moreover, the officer's subjective intentions are irrelevant; a pure heart will not make unreasonable acts constitutional, nor will malice turn a reasonable use of force into a violation of the Fourth Amendment. *See id.* at 397.

The only evidence that bears on the objective reasonableness of Officer Spain's actions is the police videotape of the incident. As the District Court accurately described it, the videotape, which also has been viewed by this Court, shows Officer Spain "attempting to make a rapid re-entry into a cell containing a prisoner who had been very difficult to manage."... Wilson was banging on the door, and Officer Spain testified that he needed to re-enter the cell to quiet Wilson and to ensure that Wilson was not injuring himself. The videotape shows that Spain pushed the door open quickly, with both hands. While Spain might have known that the door could make contact with Wilson, a reasonable jury could not conclude from the videotape that the manner in which Spain opened the door was so forceful as to be objectively unreasonable in the circumstances. Once the door met resistance, Spain gave a stronger push and opened the door completely. The videotape shows that the door was of a solid construction, with only a narrow slit for an opening. Spain therefore could not see through the door and had no way of knowing what Wilson was doing or precisely how he was positioned. We hold that a jury could not reasonably find that Spain's split-second decision to push harder against the door was unreasonable.

The other evidence does not help Wilson make his case. Testimony from Wilson's brother, William Wilson, describing the events is not probative because he only saw the events on closed-circuit television, the same view that was captured on videotape. Evidence of statements allegedly made by Officer Spain might show that Spain was angry with Wilson, or even that Spain threatened Wilson, but Spain's mental state is not relevant to the objective reasonableness of his actions. We therefore conclude that Officer Spain was entitled to summary judgment ... on the merits of Wilson's claim against him in his individual capacity.

Questions to guide reading of Eleventh Circuit Pattern Jury Instructions

1. How would attorneys and the district court use pattern jury instructions to create jury instructions tailored to the evidence presented at an individual trial?
2. How does the Eleventh Circuit pattern instruction differ from the standard applied by the Eighth Circuit in *Wilson*?

Eleventh Circuit Jury Instructions

5.3 Civil Rights—42 U.S.C. § 1983 Claims—
Eighth or Fourteenth Amendment Claim—Convicted Prisoner or
Pretrial Detainee Alleging Excessive Force[4]

In this case, [name of plaintiff] claims that [name of defendant], while acting under color of law, intentionally deprived [him/her] of [his/her] rights under the United States Constitution. Specifically, [name of plaintiff] claims that [name of defendant], while working as a [correctional officer] at [name of corrections facility], intentionally violated [name of plaintiff]'s [Eighth Amendment right as a prisoner to be free from cruel and unusual punishment/Fourteenth Amendment right to be free from the use of excessive force against [him/her] while being detained as a pretrial detainee].

The Constitution guarantees that every person who is [convicted of a crime or a criminal offense has the right not to be subjected to cruel and unusual punishment] [arrested and detained} must not be subjected to excessive force while detained. This includes, of course, the right not to be assaulted or beaten without legal justification while incarcerated.

A person may sue in this court for an award of money damages against anyone who, under color of law, intentionally violates the person's rights under the United States Constitution. To succeed on this claim, [name of plaintiff] must prove each of the following facts by a preponderance of the evidence:

First: That [name of defendant] intentionally [describe the alleged conduct];

Second: That the force used against [name of plaintiff] by [name of defendant] was excessive;

Third: That [name of defendant] acted under color of law; and

Fourth: That [name of defendant]'s conduct caused [name of plaintiff]'s injuries. The United States Constitution guarantees the right not to be subjected

4. Committee on Pattern Jury Instructions of the Judicial Council of the Eleventh Circuit, 5.3 Civil Rights—42 U.S.C. § 1983 Claims, Eighth or Fourteenth Amendment Claim, Convicted Prisoner or Pretrial Detainee Alleging Excessive Force at 361–68 (2013), *superseded by 2018 Pattern Jury Instructions,* http://www.ca11.uscourts.gov/sites/default/files/courtdocs/clk/FormCivilPatternJuryInstruction.pdf.

> to excessive force by a law enforcement or corrections officer while being detained in custody. But not every push or shove—even if it later seems unnecessary—is a constitutional violation. Also, an officer always has the right to use the reasonable force that is necessary under the circumstances to maintain order and ensure compliance with jail or prison regulations.

You must decide whether any force used in this case was excessive based on whether the force, if any, was applied in a good-faith effort to maintain or restore discipline, or instead whether it was applied maliciously to cause harm. In making that decision you should consider the amount of force used in relationship to the need presented; the motive of [name of defendant]; the extent of the injury inflicted; and any effort made to temper the severity of the force used. Of course, officers may not maliciously or sadistically use force to cause harm regardless of the significance of the injury to the prisoner.

ANNOTATIONS AND COMMENTS

I. Eighth and Fourteenth Amendment Claims

. . .

"Each of these claims requires a two-prong showing: an objective showing of a deprivation or injury that is 'sufficiently serious' to constitute a denial of the 'minimal civilized measure of life's necessities' and a subjective showing that the official had a 'sufficiently culpable state of mind.'" [*Thomas v. Bryant*, 614 F.3d 1288, 1304 (11th Cir. 2010)] (quoting *Farmer v. Brennan*, 511 U.S. 825, 834 (1994))....

Claims by pretrial detainees challenging specific conditions of confinement [and] the excessive use of force ... are governed by the Fourteenth Amendment, which guarantees the same rights afforded to convicted prisoners under the Eighth Amendment. *Goebert v. Lee Cnty.*, 510 F.3d 1312, 1326 (11th Cir. 2007) (citation omitted); *Cottrell v. Caldwell*, 85 F.3d 1480, 1490 (11th Cir. 1996) ("[D]ecisional law involving prison inmates applies equally to cases involving arrestees or pretrial detainees."). Accordingly, this model instruction may be used for an excessive force claim brought by a pretrial detainee or a convicted prisoner.

II. Elements of Eighth Amendment Excessive Force Claim

As discussed above, an Eighth Amendment excessive force claim consists of an objective and a subjective component. With respect to the objective component, "not ... every malevolent touch by a prison guard gives rise to a federal cause of action." *Hudson v. McMillian*, 503 U.S. 1, 9 (1992). "The Eighth Amendment's prohibition of cruel and unusual punishments necessarily excludes from constitutional recognition *de minimis* uses of physical force, provided that the use of force is not of a sort repugnant to the conscience of mankind." *Id.* at 9–10 (internal quotations omitted)....

With respect to the subjective element of an Eighth Amendment excessive force claim, prison officials must not act maliciously and sadistically for the purpose of causing harm. *Id.* at 9; accord *Thomas*, 614 F.3d at 1304; *see also Whitley v. Albers*,

475 U.S. 312, 319 (1986) (holding that "unnecessary and wanton infliction of pain" constitutes cruel and unusual punishment forbidden by Eighth Amendment).

Questions to guide reading of Seventh Circuit Pattern Jury Instructions

1. Do you see any tension between the Seventh Circuit pattern jury instruction and the standard applied by the Seventh Circuit in *Lopez*?
2. How does the Seventh Circuit pattern instruction differ from the Eleventh Circuit pattern instruction?

Seventh Circuit Pattern Jury Instructions

7.08 FOURTH AMENDMENT/FOURTEENTH AMENDMENT: EXCESSIVE FORCE AGAINST ARRESTEE OR PRETRIAL DETAINEE—ELEMENTS[5]

In this case, Plaintiff claims that Defendant used excessive force against him. To succeed on this claim, Plaintiff must prove each of the following things by a preponderance of the evidence:

1. Defendant used unreasonable force against Plaintiff;

[2. Because of Defendant's unreasonable force, Plaintiff was harmed;]

[3. Defendant acted under color of law.]

If you find that Plaintiff has proved each of these things by a preponderance of the evidence, then you should find for Plaintiff, and go on to consider the question of damages.

If, on the other hand, you find that Plaintiff did not prove any one of these things by a preponderance of the evidence, then you should find for Defendant, and you will not consider the question of damages.

Committee Comments

a. **Unreasonable Force**: For authority regarding the "unreasonable force" element of the claim, see *Graham v. Connor*, 490 U.S. 386 (1989); *Tennessee v. Garner*, 471 U.S. 1 (1985); *Deering v. Reich*, 183 F.3d 645 (7th Cir. 1999). Although *Graham* and *Garner* are Fourth Amendment cases involving arrestees, *Wilson v. Williams*, 83 F.3d 870, 876 (7th Cir. 1996), states that the same standard applies to pretrial detainees. A separate instruction applies to cases involving convicted prisoners.

5. Andrew R. Klein & Paul E. Beam, Federal Civil Jury Instructions of the Seventh Circuit, 7.08 Fourth Amendment/Fourteenth Amendment: Excessive Force Against Arrestee or Pretrial Detainee—Elements at 146–47 (2009), *superseded by 2017 Pattern Jury Instruction 7.09*, http://www.ca7.uscourts.gov/pattern-jury-instructions/7th_cir_civil_instructions.pdf.

. . .

[b. **Harm:**] Though "harm" in the commonly-understood sense is likely to exist in most excessive force cases, some cases will arise in which it does not, *e.g.*, a situation in which an officer strikes the plaintiff with his hand but leaves no mark and causes no lingering injury or pain. In such cases, the court will need to determine whether the jury should be instructed on this point.

. . .

In *Lanigan v. Village of East Hazel Crest, Illinois*, 110 F.3d 467 (7th Cir. 1997), the court upheld a claim based on force consisting of "one violent push and poke," noting that the plaintiff "need not have been injured to have an excessive force claim." *Id.* at 470 n.3. In *McNair v. Coffey*, 279 F.3d 463 (7th Cir. 2002), the court addressed a claim arising from an incident in which no physical force was used, but officers pointed their weapons at the plaintiffs. Though it determined that the officers were entitled to qualified immunity, and indicated that the Fourth Amendment appeared to require *some* use of force, *id.* at 467, the majority ended its opinion with the statement "we do not foreclose the possibility that the circumstances of an arrest could become 'unreasonable' without the application of physical force." *Id.* at 468. *See also Herzog v. Village of Winnetka, Ill.*, 309 F.3d 1041, 1043 (7th Cir. 2002) (refusal to loosen chafing handcuffs or shoving an arrestee would constitute actionable excessive force)....

Practice Pointer

Before *Kingsley*, circuits split on the legal standard governing a post-arrest, pre-arraignment excessive force claim. Suppose the standard was unclear in plaintiff's circuit. In that situation, what standard should plaintiff use in drafting the Complaint? Further, consider the practical consequences of ambiguity in the governing legal standard for plaintiff's discovery strategy. Should plaintiff attempt to develop evidence of the police officer's subjective motivations? From defendant's perspective, what are some advantages of a 4th Amendment standard? Of a 14th Amendment standard? Revisit this issue after considering the materials on qualified immunity in Chapter 11.

Guide to Law Practice Simulation 4

Description

- Recall that trial court judges use jury instructions to explain the relevant law to the jury before they retire to consider the evidence. Often, the trial court judge will meet with counsel before the charge is finalized to hear arguments in favor and against including particular language in the jury charge. This Simulation is a jury charge conference before a district court judge in the fictional Twelfth Circuit, where the parties will discuss the instructions for a jury trial of the facts in *Lopez*.

- Assume the Supreme Court has not yet decided *Kingsley*. Assume the legal standard governing claims for physically abusive government conduct taking place post-arrest and pre-arraignment is a question of first impression in the Twelfth Circuit and is not addressed in the circuit pattern jury instructions.
- Two students represent the plaintiff arrestee. Two students represent the defendant police officers. One student is the trial court judge within the Twelfth Circuit.
- At the conclusion of the jury charge conference, the trial court judge should rule on how the judge will instruct the jury. If either the plaintiff or the defendant objects to the jury instruction chosen by the judge, the party will specify the objection on the record, and why, to preserve the issue for possible appeal.

To prepare, consider issues such as:

- Should the excessive force claim be measured by objective reasonableness (4th Amendment)?
- Should the jury not be permitted to consider any evidence of the detectives' state of mind, as in *Wilson*?
- Should the jury be told to apply the malicious and sadistic standard? Or deliberate indifference?
- Should the claim be governed by the 4th or 14th Amendment? If the judge decides that the claim is governed by the 14th Amendment, that does not necessarily answer what standard the district court should use to instruct the jury. Would plaintiff and defendant advocate for different standards to give content to the 14th Amendment?
- Should claims alleging physically abusive conduct by government actors, such as the "soft torture" facts in *Lopez*, be analyzed as excessive use of force or as conditions of confinement? Or does that only matter if the analysis will rely on 8th Amendment standards?

Purpose

- Better understand how to distinguish 4th, 14th, and 8th Amendment claims
- Better understand post-arrest excessive force doctrine by comparing variations in how it is applied, including *Lopez*, *Wilson*, Eleventh Circuit jury instructions, and Seventh Circuit jury instructions
- Explore attorney roles in shaping doctrine by simulating roles of attorneys, judge, and law clerk applying doctrine to real facts (the *Lopez* facts)

- Better understand the practical ramifications of ambiguity in legal standards on litigation decisions, such as how to draft a Complaint
- Prepare for law practice by simulating a jury charge conference, either by persuasively advocating a legal position and responding to questions or by identifying ambiguities in doctrine or in its application to facts and posing questions to advocates
- Prepare for law practice by preserving an issue before the trial court for potential appeal
- There is no need to do any research—the relevant authority is in the casebook. You may rely on the Seventh Circuit decision in *Lopez* as non-binding, foreign authority.
- Note that this Simulation takes place before the Supreme Court decided *Kingsley*.

Structure

- Attorneys for Plaintiff—Question and Answer with judge (8 minutes)
- Attorneys for Defendants—Question and Answer with judge (8 minutes)
- After 15 minutes, questioning will be opened up to the entire class
- Both Plaintiff and Defendants—Question and Answer with judge and rest of class (15 minutes)
- Please prepare a question for every simulation, even if you are not playing a role
- To ensure full class participation, and as a courtesy to your fellow students, please close your laptops during law practice simulations

---

Questions to guide reading of *Kingsley*

1. For a 14th Amendment excessive force claim, the Supreme Court holds that the officer must intentionally use physical force against the pretrial detainee. Why are accidental uses of force outside the 14th Amendment?
2. What two questions did the Supreme Court leave open in *Kingsley*?
3. How does the Court define "objective reasonableness" and what factors does the Court identify as relevant to the reasonableness of the use of force against pretrial detainees? Why does the Court predict this will be a "workable" standard?
4. Prison officials argued that excessive force claims by pretrial detainees should be judged under a subjective standard, that force was applied "maliciously and sadistically to cause harm." Why did the Supreme Court reject that argument?

5. Does the Supreme Court's reasoning in *Kingsley* suggest that the 8th Amendment standard for excessive force claims also should be objective? Why or why not?

Kingsley v. Hendrickson

576 U.S. ___, 135 S. Ct. 2466 (2015)

Justice BREYER delivered the opinion of the Court.

...

The question before us is whether, to prove an excessive force claim, a pretrial detainee must show that the officers were subjectively aware that their use of force was unreasonable, or only that the officers' use of that force was objectively unreasonable. We conclude that the latter standard is the correct one.

...

II. A.

We consider a legally requisite state of mind. In a case like this one, there are, in a sense, two separate state-of-mind questions. The first concerns the defendant's state of mind with respect to his physical acts—*i.e.*, his state of mind with respect to the bringing about of certain physical consequences in the world. The second question concerns the defendant's state of mind with respect to whether his use of force was "excessive." Here, as to the first question, there is no dispute. As to the second, whether to interpret the defendant's physical acts in the world as involving force that was "excessive," there is a dispute. We conclude with respect to that question that the relevant standard is objective not subjective. Thus, the defendant's state of mind is not a matter that a plaintiff is required to prove.

Consider the series of physical events that take place in the world—a series of events that might consist, for example, of the swing of a fist that hits a face, a push that leads to a fall, or the shot of a Taser that leads to the stunning of its recipient. No one here denies, and we must assume, that, as to the series of events that have taken place in the world, the defendant must possess a purposeful, a knowing, or possibly a reckless state of mind. That is because, as we have stated, "liability for *negligently* inflicted harm is categorically beneath the threshold of constitutional due process." *County of Sacramento v. Lewis*, 523 U.S. 833, 849 (1998) (emphasis added). *See also Daniels v. Williams*, 474 U.S. 327, 331 (1986) ("Historically, this guarantee of due process has been applied to *deliberate* decisions of government officials to deprive a person of life, liberty, or property"). Thus, if an officer's Taser goes off by accident or if an officer unintentionally trips and falls on a detainee, causing him harm, the pretrial detainee cannot prevail on an excessive force claim. But if the use of force is deliberate—*i.e.*, purposeful or knowing—the pretrial detainee's claim may proceed. In the context of a police pursuit of a suspect the Court noted, though without so holding, that recklessness in some cases might suffice as a standard for imposing liability. *See Lewis, supra*, at 849. Whether that standard might suffice for liability in the case of an alleged mistreatment of a pretrial detainee need not be decided here; for the officers do not dispute that they acted purposefully or knowingly with respect to the force they used against Kingsley.

We now consider the question before us here—the defendant's state of mind with respect to the proper interpretation of the force (a series of events in the world) that the defendant deliberately (not accidentally or negligently) used. In deciding whether the force deliberately used is, constitutionally speaking, "excessive," should courts use an objective standard only, or instead a subjective standard that takes into account a defendant's state of mind? It is with respect to this question that we hold that courts must use an objective standard. In short, we agree with ... the Seventh Circuit's jury instruction committee ... that a pretrial detainee must show only that the force purposely or knowingly used against him was objectively unreasonable.

[O]bjective reasonableness turns on the "facts and circumstances of each particular case." *Graham v. Connor*, 490 U.S. 386, 396 (1989). A court must make this determination from the perspective of a reasonable officer on the scene, including what the officer knew at the time, not with the 20/20 vision of hindsight. See *ibid.* A court must also account for the "legitimate interests that stem from [the government's] need to manage the facility in which the individual is detained," appropriately deferring to "policies and practices that in th[e] judgment" of jail officials "are needed to preserve internal order and discipline and to maintain institutional security." *Bell v. Wolfish*, 441 U.S. 520, 540, 547 (1979).

Considerations such as the following may bear on the reasonableness or unreasonableness of the force used: the relationship between the need for the use of force and the amount of force used; the extent of the plaintiff's injury; any effort made by the officer to temper or to limit the amount of force; the severity of the security problem at issue; the threat reasonably perceived by the officer; and whether the plaintiff was actively resisting. See, *e.g.*, *Graham*, *supra*, at 396. We do not consider this list to be exclusive. We mention these factors only to illustrate the types of objective circumstances potentially relevant to a determination of excessive force.

B

... [T]he appropriate standard for a pretrial detainee's excessive force claim is solely an objective one ... [I]t is consistent with our precedent. We have said that "the Due Process Clause protects a pretrial detainee from the use of excessive force that amounts to punishment." *Graham*, *supra*, at 395, n. 10 ... [T]he *Bell* Court ... explain[ed] that, in the absence of an expressed intent to punish, a pretrial detainee can nevertheless prevail by showing that the actions are not "rationally related to a legitimate nonpunitive governmental purpose" or that the actions "appear excessive in relation to that purpose." *Id.*, at 561. The *Bell* Court applied this latter objective standard to evaluate a variety of prison conditions, including a prison's practice of double-bunking. In doing so, it did not consider the prison officials' subjective beliefs about the policy. *Id.*, at 541–543. Rather, the Court examined objective evidence, such as the size of the rooms and available amenities, before concluding that the conditions were reasonably related to the legitimate purpose of holding detainees for trial and did not appear excessive in relation to that purpose. *Ibid.*

...

[E]xperience suggests that an objective standard is workable. It is consistent with the pattern jury instructions used in several Circuits ... Finally, the use of an objective standard adequately protects an officer who acts in good faith. We recognize that "[r]unning a prison is an inordinately difficult undertaking," ... and that "safety and order at these institutions requires the expertise of correctional officials, who must have substantial discretion to devise reasonable solutions to the problems they face," *Florence v. Board of Chosen Freeholders of County of Burlington*, 566 U.S. ___, ___ (2012). Officers facing disturbances "are often forced to make split-second judgments—in circumstances that are tense, uncertain, and rapidly evolving." *Graham*, 490 U.S., at 397. For these reasons, we have stressed that a court must judge the reasonableness of the force used from the perspective and with the knowledge of the defendant officer. We have also explained that a court must take account of the legitimate interests in managing a jail, acknowledging as part of the objective reasonableness analysis that deference to policies and practices needed to maintain order and institutional security is appropriate.... And we have limited liability for excessive force to situations in which the use of force was the result of an intentional and knowing act (though we leave open the possibility of including a "reckless" act as well). *Ibid.* Additionally, an officer enjoys qualified immunity and is not liable for excessive force unless he has violated a "clearly established" right, such that "it would [have been] clear to a reasonable officer that his conduct was unlawful in the situation he confronted." *Saucier v. Katz*, 533 U.S. 194, 202....

C

Respondents believe that the relevant legal standard should be subjective, *i.e.*, that the plaintiff must prove that the use of force was not "applied in a good-faith effort to maintain or restore discipline" but, rather, was applied "maliciously and sadistically to cause harm." ... [citing, *e.g.*, *Whitley v. Albers*, 475 U.S. 312 (1986) and *Hudson v. McMillian*, 503 U.S. 1 (1992)].

[*Whitley* and *Hudson*], however, concern excessive force claims brought by convicted prisoners under the Eighth Amendment's Cruel and Unusual Punishment Clause, not claims brought by pretrial detainees under the Fourteenth Amendment's Due Process Clause ... The language of the two Clauses differs, and ... most importantly, pretrial detainees (unlike convicted prisoners) cannot be punished at all, much less "maliciously and sadistically." *Ingraham v. Wright*, 430 U.S. 651, 671–672, n. 40 (1977); *Graham, supra*, at 395, n. 10 (1989).... Thus, there is no need here, as there might be in an Eighth Amendment case, to determine when punishment is unconstitutional. *Whitley* and *Hudson* are relevant here only insofar as they address the practical importance of taking into account the legitimate safety-related concerns of those who run jails. And, as explained above, we believe we have done so.

Lewis does not prove respondents' point, either. There, the Court considered a claim that a police officer had violated due process by causing a death during a high-speed automobile chase aimed at apprehending a suspect. We wrote that "[j]ust as a purpose to cause harm is needed for Eighth Amendment liability in a [prison] riot case, so it ought to be needed for due process liability in a pursuit case." 523 U.S., at 854.... [T]his statement referred to the defendant's intent to commit the acts in question, not to whether the force intentionally used was "excessive." 523 U.S., at 854, and n. 13.

...

We acknowledge that our view that an objective standard is appropriate in the context of excessive force claims brought by pretrial detainees pursuant to the Fourteenth Amendment may raise questions about the use of a subjective standard in the context of excessive force claims brought by convicted prisoners. We are not confronted with such a claim, however, so we need not address that issue today....

Justice SCALIA, with whom THE CHIEF JUSTICE and Justice THOMAS join, dissenting.

The Constitution contains no freestanding prohibition of excessive force. There are, however, four constitutional provisions that we have said forbid the use of excessive force in certain circumstances. The Fourth Amendment prohibits it when it makes a search or seizure "unreasonable." The Eighth Amendment prohibits it when it constitutes "cruel and unusual" punishment. The Fifth and Fourteenth Amendments prohibit it (or, for that matter, any use of force) when it is used to "deprive" someone of "life, liberty, or property, without due process of law."

This is a Fourteenth Amendment case ... Our cases hold that the intentional infliction of punishment upon a pretrial detainee may violate the Fourteenth Amendment; but the infliction of "objectively unreasonable" force, without more, is not the intentional infliction of punishment.

...

I disagree ... that any intentional application of force that is objectively unreasonable in degree is a use of excessive force that "amount[s] to punishment." *Bell*, 441 U.S., at 535 ... It is illogical, however, automatically to infer punitive intent from the fact that a prison guard used more force against a pretrial detainee than was necessary. That could easily have been the result of a misjudgment about the degree of force required to maintain order or protect other inmates, rather than the product of an intent to punish the detainee for his charged crime (or for any other behavior). An officer's decision regarding how much force to use is made "in haste, under pressure, and frequently without the luxury of a second chance," *Hudson v. McMillian*, 503 U.S. 1, 6 (1992) (internal quotation marks omitted), not after the considered thought that precedes detention-policy determinations like those at issue in *Bell*.... That an officer used more force than necessary might be evidence that he acted with intent to punish, but it is no more than that.

...

[O]ur Constitution is not the only source of American law. There is an immense body of state statutory and common law under which individuals abused by state officials can seek relief.

Exercise 7-A

The Supreme Court in *Kingsley* resolved a longstanding circuit split over whether custodial officials needed to *subjectively* intend to inflict excessive force in order for a 14th Amendment claim of excessive force to succeed. For decades, while a claim that could show *objectively* excessive force could prevail in some circuits, that same claim would have failed in other circuits because plaintiff could not prove the defendant *subjectively* intended force to be excessive.

- Is there any recourse for plaintiffs whose claims failed because, while they could demonstrate objective excessive force, they failed to prove a higher standard of subjective excessive force, or malicious and sadistic use of force?
- Suppose you represented a plaintiff in a pre-trial excessive force claim that was evaluated and rejected by a jury applying the Eleventh Circuit Jury Instructions in this Chapter. The jury reached its verdict in 2014. The deadline to appeal the verdict passed years ago. Your former client is now on the phone. She heard a news report about the new Supreme Court case and asks you how it can help her. Explain your answer in plain language to your former client.

Exercise 7-B

Review the Pattern Jury Instructions for the Eleventh Circuit reproduced earlier in this Chapter. Suppose you have been appointed to a distinguished panel of attorneys in the Eleventh Circuit. Your committee charge is to revise the pattern jury instructions to be consistent with the Supreme Court's decisions in *Kingsley* and *Wilkins*.

- What language will you propose for district court judges to instruct juries on claims of excessive force against pre-trial detainees?
- Consider how a district court should instruct a jury to evaluate evidence of the correctional officer's state of mind, the injury to plaintiff, and the institutional need to preserve order, among other factors.

For further discussion

1. Can 4th Amendment protections extend into pretrial detention? Yes, said the Supreme Court in a ruling after *Kingsley*. The Supreme Court held that the 4th

Amendment "governs a claim for unlawful pretrial detention even beyond the start of legal process." *Manuel v. City of Joliet*, ___ U.S. ___, 137 S. Ct. 911, 920 (2017). Police arrested Manuel without probable cause, based on his possession of pills that tested negative for an illegal substance. At the court proceeding initiating legal process, "[a]ll that the judge had before him were police fabrications about the pills' content." *Id.* at 919. The judge's order holding Manuel for trial therefore did not "expunge Manuel's Fourth Amendment claim because the process he received failed to establish what [the 4th] Amendment makes essential for pretrial detention—probable cause to believe he committed a crime." *Id.* at 919–20. Therefore, both Manuel's pretrial detention and his original arrest could violate his 4th Amendment rights. *Id.* at 920.

2. *Manuel* is consistent with *Kingsley*. While *Manuel* held that a defendant seized without probable cause can challenge pretrial detention under the 4th Amendment, "*Manuel* does not address the availability of due process challenges after a legal seizure ... [and] when the detention is legal, a pre-trial detainee subjected to excessive force properly invokes the Fourteenth Amendment." *Jauch v. Choctaw Cty.*, 874 F.3d 425, 429 (5th Cir. 2017).

While *Manuel* concerned a pretrial detainee's challenge to probable cause to detain him, *Kingsley* concerned a lawful pretrial detention. *Kingsley*, 576 U.S. ___, 135 S. Ct. at 2470. In *Kingsley*, a lawfully arrested pretrial detainee was awaiting trial when he claimed officers used excessive force in his cell. *Id.* (correctional officers applied a Taser to Kingsley's back while he was handcuffed in a jail cell). As the pretrial detainee in *Kingsley* did not challenge probable cause for his detention, but instead challenged the use of force during a lawful detention, the claim was properly analyzed under 14th Amendment due process.

3. *Kingsley* concerned an excessive force claim. Several federal circuits, however, have extended the logic of *Kingsley* to other 14th Amendment substantive due process claims by pretrial detainees. The Seventh Circuit recognized a circuit split in announcing that it would apply the *Kingsley* objective reasonableness standard to a 14th Amendment medical treatment claim by a pretrial detainee:

> The Ninth Circuit first extended *Kingsley*'s objective inquiry to detainees' Fourteenth-Amendment failure-to-protect claims. *Castro v. Cnty. of L.A.*, 833 F.3d 1060, 1070–71 (9th Cir. 2016) (*en banc*), *cert. denied*, ___ U.S. ___, 137 S.Ct. 831 (2017). Since then, that court has applied the *Kingsley* holding more broadly to a medical-need claim brought by a pretrial detainee. *Gordon v. Cnty. of Orange*, 888 F.3d 1118, 1120, 1122–25 (9th Cir. 2018). The Second Circuit followed suit, applying the objective standard to detainees' Fourteenth-Amendment complaints about their conditions of confinement; in the process it overruled a decision applying a subjective test to a medical-care claim. *Darnell v. Pineiro*, 849 F.3d 17, 34–35 (2d Cir. 2017) ... Later, the Second Circuit expressly applied an objective standard to a claim of deliberate indifference to a serious medical condition. *Bruno v. City of Schenectady*, 727 Fed. Appx. 717, 720 (2d Cir. 2018) (unpublished)....

> The Eighth, Eleventh, and Fifth Circuits have chosen to confine *Kingsley* to its facts—that is, to Fourteenth-Amendment claims based on excessive-force allegations in a pretrial setting. *E.g., Whitney v. City of St. Louis*, 887 F.3d 857, 860 n.4 (8th Cir. 2018); *Dang by & through Dang v. Sheriff, Seminole Cnty.*, 871 F.3d 1272, 1279 n.2 (11th Cir. 2017); *Alderson v. Concordia Parish Corr. Facility*, 848 F.3d 415, 419 n.4 (5th Cir. 2017) (following circuit precedent and concluding that the issue was not directly raised)....
>
> We ... conclude, along with the Ninth and Second Circuits, that medical-care claims brought by pretrial detainees under the Fourteenth Amendment are subject only to the objective unreasonableness inquiry identified in *Kingsley*.... The defendants here worry that an objective-reasonableness standard will impermissibly constitutionalize medical malpractice claims, because it would allow mere negligence to suffice for liability. A careful look at *Kingsley*, however, shows that this is not the case; the state-of-mind requirement for constitutional cases remains higher.... [Here, the first inquiry] asks whether the medical defendants acted purposefully, knowingly, or perhaps even recklessly when they considered the consequences of their handling of Gomes's case. *See* [*Kingsley*, 135 S. Ct.] at 2472, 2474 (discussing purposeful or knowing conduct and leaving open the possibility that recklessness would also suffice). The courts of appeals that have applied *Kingsley* to detainees' claims in contexts other than excessive force have taken that step, while continuing to recognize that it will not be enough to show negligence or gross negligence.... As *Kingsley* instructs, the second step is the objective one.

Miranda v. Cty. of Lake, 900 F.3d 335, 351–54 (7th Cir. 2018). As the circuits have split, you may be one of the lawyers who helps to craft a national rule for how to assess 14th Amendment claims by pretrial detainees outside of the context of excessive force.

C. Jail Suicide by Pretrial Detainees

Before reading about legal doctrine governing jail suicide by pretrial detainees, consider the following factual background:

> [U]ntil recently [suicide] was the leading cause of death in county jails and municipal police lockups (World Health Organization, 2007). Most jail suicides are perpetrated by hanging (self-asphyxiation) (Rosazza, 1994). The creation of a definitive profile of the pretrial detainee at greatest risk for suicide is problematic, because a large percentage of detainees have characteristics that heighten the risk for suicide and the base rates for suicide in this population are low (Rosazza, 1994). In such circumstances, accurate prediction is difficult and fraught with a high rate of false positives (Lurigio, 1986)....
>
> [J]ail detainees have disproportionately high rates of psychiatric, substance use, and personality disorders as well as unemployment, weak social ties, and homelessness—all of which increase the risk for suicide. In addition,

the majority of detainees are men, who are significantly more likely to commit suicide than women. These dispositional risk factors are difficult to modify in the short-term but must be addressed in any efforts to identity and monitor at-risk detainees (World Health Organization, 2007)....

[T]he jail environment and the experience of being in custody can be extremely stressful. Detainees are uncertain about their futures, lose their freedom, and could face substantial changes in their personal and professional lives. They are separated from their families, support networks, and jobs and forced to fend for themselves in a chaotic, loud, threatening and disorienting setting. Jails provide few immediate resources to assist detainees in coping with the overwhelming psychological stressors of pretrial status (World Health Organization, 2007).

Since 1983, the suicide rate in jails has dropped from 129 to 47 per 100,000 detainees. Nevertheless, suicide is the second leading cause of death in jails and responsible for 33 percent of detainees' deaths in custody.... In 2005, detainees with the highest risk of suicide were male, white, and members of the youngest (younger than 18) and oldest (55 or older) age groups of detainees and were charged with violent crimes (Mumola, 2005).[6]

Questions to guide reading of *Short*

1. How did the county jail policy and procedures manual require that potentially suicidal inmates be treated?
2. In what ways did the deputies fail to comply with the manual's suicide prevention procedures? How long was Mr. Short's body hanging before it was discovered?
3. The Fourth Circuit defines the constitutional right at stake as "the right of a detainee, whose jailers know that he is suicidal, to have his jailers take precautions against his suicide beyond merely placing him in a cell under video surveillance." Could the constitutional right have been defined more broadly, *e.g.*, a detainee's right to be free from a jailer's deliberate indifference to a substantial risk that he would commit suicide?
4. Why did the Fourth Circuit hold that the first-shift officers' conduct was objectively reasonable? Why did the Constitution not require additional precautions?
5. Should the various violations of the county jail's procedures have carried more legal significance—or would that "constitutionalize" a jail's procedures?
6. What is the gist of the dissent to the ruling on the first-shift officers?

---

6. James M. Byrne, Arthur J. Lurigio & Roger Pimentel, New Defendants, New Responsibilities: Preventing Suicide among Alleged Sex Offenders in the Federal Pretrial System, 73 Fed. Probation No. 2 (Sept. 2009), https://www.uscourts.gov/sites/default/files/73_2_5_0.pdf.

Short v. Smoot

436 F.3d 422 (4th Cir. 2006)

WILKINS, Chief Judge.

...

In reviewing an order denying summary judgment based on qualified immunity, we accept as true the facts that the district court concluded may be reasonably inferred from the record when viewed in the light most favorable to the plaintiff.... Thus, for purposes of resolving this appeal, we assume the following facts:

'[O]n January 8, 2004, ... Thomas Lee Short was arrested and jailed for assault and battery of his wife, in violation of a September 2003 protective order that prohibited Mr. Short from having any contact with her, from committing acts of family abuse, and from drinking alcoholic beverages. After his release on January 11, 2004, Short went to the Blue Ridge Motel in Front Royal, Virginia, and began drinking heavily. Around 9:30 p.m., Short called his wife, Mary Short, and told her that he was planning to kill himself. Mrs. Short, concerned that her husband would carry out his threat, called the Warren County Sheriff's office to request that they check the local bridges. That office advised her to call the Front Royal Town Police, which she did.

Soon after calling his wife, Mr. Short also called his daughter, Linda Good, to tell her that he "wanted to die," and to ask if she could come pick him up. When she arrived at the motel, Good found her father so drunk that she decided it would be better to let him sleep and return the next morning. Mr. Short called his wife again at 4:30 a.m. and repeated his threat to kill himself. He also called his daughter, who told him she would pick him up at noon the next day.

Before she returned to the hotel, Good spoke with Mrs. Short, and they decided to have Mr. Short arrested again for violating the September 2003 protective order, believing that this course of action would keep him from harming himself. Mrs. Short went to the Magistrate's Office to file a criminal complaint and the Magistrate issued a warrant for Mr. Short's arrest. The Magistrate then contacted the Front Royal Town Police and told the officer that Mr. Short was "basically a drunk," that he was intoxicated, and that he had called his wife threatening to kill himself. The officer, Sergeant Clint Keller, went to the Short residence, arrested Mr. Short, and transported him to the Warren County Jail.

Sergeant Keller took Mr. Short before the Magistrate, who issued an order remanding Mr. Short to custody until he could appear in Warren County General District Court the next day. Sergeant Keller then turned Mr. Short over to the deputies on duty at the jail. Defendants Smoot, Beatty, Oakes, and Lewis were in the jail's monitor room, where Sergeant Keller advised them that Mr. Short had been arrested for violation of a protective order, that he was drunk, and that he had been calling his wife threatening to kill himself.

The Warren County Jail Policy and Procedures manual, in effect on January 12, 2004, addressed proper treatment of potentially suicidal inmates. The manual required custodial officers to remove all potential tools such as sheets, blankets, and shoelaces, to conduct inmate checks at random intervals, at least twice per hour, and to make reports of any unusual occurrences. The defendant deputies also received training in treatment of potentially suicidal inmates. If the deputies were aware that the inmate was suicidal, they were instructed to remove his clothing, place him in a suicide "smock," call mental health services, and conduct checks at fifteen-minute intervals.

When an intoxicated inmate was brought to the jail, deputies would attempt to process him. If the inmate was unable to give a medical history, then the typical practice was to place the intoxicated inmate in the jail's sick cell, separate from the general population, to sober up, and also to remove all items that could be used for "self-destructive purposes."

Despite Sergeant Keller's statement that Short had threatened to kill himself, the deputies never removed Short's clothing and shoelaces or called for a mental health evaluation. Sergeant Smoot took him from the booking area to the bathroom and then to the sick cell, where he removed Short's belt. Several hours later, Smoot heard banging coming from the sick room. He asked Short if he was all right, and Short responded that he was fine. He did not apprise the other deputies of the disturbance, nor did he make a report of an unusual occurrence. Deputy Lewis checked on Short twice, at approximately 5:30 and 6:30 p.m.; both times Short was lying in bed with a sheet over him and appeared to be asleep. Deputy Oakes also checked on Short around 5:00 p.m., and observed that he was asleep.

Sergeant Smoot and Deputies Lewis, Oakes, and Beatty's shifts ended at 7:00 p.m. and defendants Deputies Ferguson, Kensy, and Seal arrived. No one in the departing shift informed the incoming deputies that Short had threatened to kill himself; the incoming deputies were only aware that an intoxicated detainee had been brought in and placed in the sick room.

The Warren County Jail used surveillance cameras to monitor inmate activity. There were a number of twelve-inch television screens that displayed images from these cameras in the jail's monitor room. During the evening shift, Deputy Ferguson, the officer-in-charge, was in the monitor room from approximately 7:00 to 8:30 p.m., and was responsible for observing monitors as well as answering the telephone and admitting any visitors. He acknowledged that he was aware that an inmate was in the sick cell on the evening of January 12, 2004, and that he observed the monitor showing activity in the sick cell. He left the monitor room for a short time at approximately 8:24 p.m. to respond to an inmate waving a towel at the camera. Deputy Seal was not working in the monitor room. He made rounds of the cells at approximately 7:15 p.m., and again between 8:00 and 8:30 p.m. Seal did not check on the sick cell where Short was housed, believing that it was unoccupied. Deputy Kensy was in the jail records room filing from 7:00 to 8:30 p.m. He passed through the monitor room for a few minutes, but was not present at the jail between 8:35 and 9:00.

The court has reviewed the videotape taken from the surveillance camera that recorded Short's activity in the sick room on January 12, 2004. Between approximately

7:00 and 7:30 p.m., Short removed the laces from his shoes, tied them together, and climbed from his bed to the bars of his cell. He tied the shoelaces to the bars and tested their strength. He then tied the laces around his neck. Short repeated this process a number of times, alternating between climbing on the bars and sitting on his bed for several minutes at a time. At approximately 7:36 p.m., Short again climbed from his bed to the bars of his cell, placed the noose around his neck, and hung himself. It was not until approximately 9:00 p.m., when Deputy Seal escorted a new detainee to the sick room, that the deputies discovered Short's body.

...

The district court denied [qualified immunity for] Deputies Smoot, Beatty, Oakes, and Lewis (the first-shift officers), concluding that the forecasted evidence permitted the reasonable inference that the conduct of the first-shift officers constituted deliberate indifference because the officers all were aware of the risk that Short would commit suicide yet failed to follow jail procedure or even "take the simple precaution of warning the next shift that Short was at risk." ... The court also denied the motion as to Deputy Ferguson, concluding that the forecasted evidence supported the inference that he exhibited deliberate indifference because he actually witnessed Ferguson's suicide in progress, understood what was happening, and yet made no attempt to intervene.

II.

[T]he district court erred in denying summary judgment to the first-shift officers ... The right in question here, defined at the appropriate level of specificity, is the right of a detainee, whose jailers know that he is suicidal, to have his jailers take precautions against his suicide beyond merely placing him in a cell under video surveillance. We hold that *Brown v. Harris*, 240 F.3d 383 (4th Cir. 2001), demonstrates that no such right derives from the Eighth Amendment.

The appropriate framework for evaluating constitutional claims arising from a prison official's "deliberate indifference" to "a substantial risk of serious harm to an inmate" is set out in *Farmer v. Brennan*, 511 U.S. 825, 828 (1994).... A substantial risk of suicide is sufficient to satisfy [the requirement that the alleged deprivation be objectively serious].... The subjective component of an Eighth Amendment claim challenging the conditions of confinement ... requires that a prison official actually know of and disregard an objectively serious condition, medical need, or risk of harm. *See id.* at 837....

Importantly, a prison official "who actually [knows] of a substantial risk to inmate health or safety may be found free from liability if [he] responded reasonably to the risk, even if the harm ultimately was not averted." *Farmer*, 511 U.S. at 844.... Although it is unclear whether the reasonableness of the response is part of the state of mind requirement or rather derives from the duty to "ensure reasonable safety," *Farmer* holds that "prison officials who act reasonably cannot be found liable under the Cruel and Unusual Punishments Clause." *Farmer*, 511 U.S. at 844–45....

Brown demonstrates that the first-shift officers' response to Short's risk of suicide was objectively reasonable and therefore sufficient to prevent liability under the Eighth Amendment. As is relevant here, *Brown*, like the case at bar, was an action alleging deliberate indifference by the defendants to a suicide risk of their detainee. There, Robert Brown was arrested by a probation officer (Svec), who had learned that Brown was taking 8–10 pills a day and had attempted suicide the prior week by overdosing on pills. *See Brown*, 240 F.3d at 385. Pursuant to subsequent searches, Svec found pills in Brown's bedroom and car, as well as on his person. *See id.* Svec then delivered Brown to the Virginia Beach General Jail for processing on a probation violation. *See id.*

At trial, the evidence was conflicting regarding what information Svec shared with the jail supervisor (Ogden). Svec testified that she told Ogden that Brown was suicidal, psychotic, and volatile. *See id.* On the other hand, Ogden testified that Svec informed him only that Brown had violent episodes and did not tell him that Brown was suicidal. *See id.* Ogden placed Brown on "medical watch," which established continuous video surveillance of Brown's cell. *Id.*... Nevertheless, Brown hanged himself three days after his arrival at the jail and eventually died as a result. *See id.* at 385–86.

We affirmed a district court order granting judgment as a matter of law to both Svec and Ogden.... [W]e assumed that Ogden had been informed of Brown's suicidal tendencies. *See id.* at 390. We nevertheless held that, as a matter of law, placement of a detainee in a cell under video surveillance constituted an objectively reasonable response by Ogden to the risk that Brown would kill himself. *See id.* We further concluded that the reasonableness of the response was not affected by the fact that there were additional precautions, such as placing Brown in a paper gown or having him examined by a medical professional, that Ogden also could have taken. *See id.* (explaining that even if Ogden "took less action than he ... should have ... [t]hat does not ... negate the reasonableness of his response")....

Here, the first-shift officers' response to the risk that Short would kill himself was the same as Ogden's response in *Brown*: they placed the detainee in a cell under video surveillance. Thus, under *Brown*, this response was sufficient under the Cruel and Unusual Punishments Clause regardless of whether additional precautions might also have been advisable.

Our dissenting colleague concludes that the officers' response was different from Ogden's in that the officers here "never observed Mr. Short on the video monitor." ... Initially, it is important to point out that it hardly seems unusual that none of the first-shift officers would have remembered observing Short on one of the many video monitors in their video monitor bank when the videotape of his time in the cell reveals that he was not doing anything out of the ordinary during their shift except for a couple of times when he banged his shoe against the cell bars or the sink. In fact, he spent most of the time in his bed covered with a sheet. In any event, it is unclear why our colleague considers the fact that the first-shift officers did not actually observe Short on the video monitors to be a difference between the two cases because there is no indication in our opinion in *Brown* that any officer, including Ogden, ever observed Brown on the video monitor until he had already hanged himself. *See Brown*, 240 F.3d at 385. The critical point is that despite the actual failure of the officers' measures to prevent the detainees' suicides, and despite possible inattentiveness of the officers whose duty it was at the time of the suicides to watch the monitors, in both *Brown* and the present case the officers placed their detainees in video-monitored cells, knowing that someone would be responsible for watching the monitors. *See id.* (stating that there was an officer responsible for viewing the video monitors); ... (Smoot's deposition testimony that during his shift, after a brief power outage, "[t]here was always someone" with the responsibility of watching the video monitors); ... (Ferguson's deposition testimony that he was responsible for watching the video monitors from 7:00 p.m. until after the time Short hanged himself).

...

Ogden's response [in *Brown*] was essentially identical to that of the first-shift officers here. Although the district court observed that the first-shift officers did not even so much as notify any second-shift officers of the risk that Short would commit suicide, a similar criticism could be leveled against Ogden, who apparently also did not share information about Brown's suicide risk with anyone (and indeed denied he ever received such information). In any event, the availability of additional precautions was immaterial to our decision in *Brown*, as we have explained.

III.

... [T]he district court correctly denied summary judgment [to Deputy Ferguson]. The district court concluded that the forecasted evidence supported the reasonable inference that Ferguson observed Short "removing the laces from his shoes and, over a period of twenty to thirty minutes, climbing on the bars of his cell, tying his shoelaces to the bar, placing a noose around his neck, and testing the weight of the rope." *Id.* at 1940. On this basis, the district court concluded that the record permitted a reasonable inference that Ferguson knew Short was attempting to commit suicide. *See id.* & n. 10. The court ruled that failure to make any effort to stop the ongoing suicide attempt, under such circumstances, would constitute deliberate indifference. *See id.* at 1940–41.

...

GREGORY, Circuit Judge, concurring in part and dissenting in part.

I fully agree with the majority's holding that the district court properly denied qualified immunity to Deputy Ferguson.

...

The majority concludes today that because the first-shift officers placed Short in a sick cell with a video camera, their actions were constitutionally sufficient under *Brown*. I disagree with this conclusion, because it is based on a dubious assumption—specifically, that an officer establishes constant video surveillance of an inmate by placing him in a cell with a video camera.... Sergeant Smoot, Deputy Beatty, Deputy Lewis, and Deputy Oakes each testified that he *never observed* Mr. Short on the video monitor.... Thus, even though the first shift officers placed Mr. Short in a cell with a video camera, they never established or maintained video surveillance. I, therefore, agree with the district court's conclusion that the first shift officers "did not take less action than they could have, rather, they did virtually nothing." ... Accordingly, I would also affirm the district court's denial of qualified immunity as to the first shift officers.

For further discussion

1. On remand, a jury rejected the plaintiff's only remaining claim, the claim against Deputy Ferguson.

2. Below is an expert report and affidavit filed in the *Short v. Smoot* case excerpted above.

> Report or Affidavit of Lindsay M. Hayes (August 13, 2004)[7]
>
> ...
>
> A nationally recognized expert in the field of suicide prevention in correctional facilities, this writer has served as project director for the *only* four national U.S. Justice Department-funded studies conducted of jail, prison, and juvenile suicide.... This writer has authored over 50 other publications in the area of suicide prevention in jail, prison, and juvenile facilities.... In addition, since 1983, this writer has served as a consultant in providing staff training and program assessment/development services in the area of suicide prevention in correctional facilities to numerous local and state jurisdictions throughout the country. This writer also serves as the suicide prevention consultant to the Special Litigation Section of the U.S. Justice Department's Civil Rights Division in its investigation of conditions of confinement in various correctional facilities.... Further, this writer has served as an expert witness/consultant in over 230 litigation cases involving suicide in correctional facilities, and has been qualified as an expert in both federal and state courts throughout the country....
>
> Documents Reviewed
>
> [include pleadings, briefs, report by Warren County Sheriff, autopsy, and videotape of the "sick room" cell that housed Mr. Short and the Warren County Jail's *Policies and Procedures Manual*] Finally, this writer has relied upon the Virginia Board of Corrections' *Minimum Standards for Jails and Lockups* (1995) and Virginia Board of Corrections' *Compliance Documentation for Local Jails and Lockups* (2002), as well as the American Correctional Association (ACA)'s *Standards for Adult Local Detention Facilities*, Third Edition (1991) and pertinent Supplements, and the National Commission on Correctional Health Care (NCCHC)'s *Standards for Health Services in Jails* (2003).
>
> Case Analysis
>
> ...

---

7. Expert Report and Affidavit of Lindsay M. Hayes, Project Director of the National Center on Institutions and Alternatives, No. 7:04-cv00531, 2004 WL 3712606 (Aug. 13, 2004).

This writer was asked by plaintiff counsel to ... give an opinion as to whether, through policy and practice, the actions and/or inactions by the Defendants were either contrary or inconsistent with both national correctional standards and standard correctional practice, constituted deliberate indifference, and were the proximate causes of Mr. Short's death.

...

Opinions

...

First, there appears to be a disputed fact as to whether officers at the Warren County Jail were informed that Thomas Short was possibly suicidal. According to Sergeant Clint Keller of the Front Royal Police Department, he informed several day shift correctional officers at the Warren County Jail on January 12, 2004 that Thomas Short was extremely intoxicated and had threatened suicide to his wife the previous evening. These officers have denied being informed of this information. If Sergeant Keller's statement and recorded interview with the sheriff's office investigator was truthful, then it would be this writer's opinion that the actions and inactions displayed by Warren County Jail staff were outrageous and reflected deliberate indifference to Mr. Short.

According to the Virginia Board of Corrections' *Minimum Standards for Jails and Lockups* (1995) and Virginia Board of Corrections' *Compliance Documentation for Local Jails and Lockups* (2002), the Warren County Jail was required to have a "suicide prevention and intervention plan" because:

"Statistics show that most suicides happen within the first 72 hours of arrest. The mental status of an inmate may vary greatly from day to day; therefore staff must employ good observational skills and be knowledgeable of signs and symptoms. Procedures should be in place for staff to notify the appropriate medical authority if concerns should arise (6 VAC15-40-450).

The Warren County Jail did have a suicide prevention and intervention plan which required that suicidal inmates not be placed in isolation, if possible, but housed with another inmate in a cell which does not contain various instruments utilized for hanging, *e.g.*, "sheets, blankets, shoestrings, etc." ... observed by correctional staff at least every 15 minutes, and referred to mental health personnel at Northwestern Community Services for assessment. Presuming that Warren County Jail staff had knowledge of Mr. Short's suicide risk, they displayed deliberate indifference by violating each of the conditions in the Jail's suicide prevention policy.

Second, according to the Virginia Board of Corrections' *Minimum Standards for Jails and Lockups* (1995) and Virginia Board of Corrections' *Compliance Documentation for Local Jails and Lockups* (2002), the Warren County Jail was required to have "a special housing area to provide for the temporary detention and care of persons under the influence of alcohol or narcotics;

who are uncontrollably violent, or self-destructive and those requiring medical supervision" ... Through his placement in the facility's "sick room" isolation cell, it would be this writer's opinion that Mr. Short was being housed in a "special purpose area" for safe-keeping and close observation.

In addition, according to the Warren County Jail's own Policies and Procedures Manual, "special management inmates are inmates segregated from the general jail population" because they are suicidal, mentally ill, alcoholic, and/or mentally retarded (at pages V-46 and V-47). At a minimum, Mr. Short met the criteria for a special management inmate based upon his intoxication. According to the policy pertaining to special management inmates, "jail personnel will ensure that items which could be used for self-destructive purposes are removed from the segregation cell of inmates who are mentally ill or intoxicated" (at page V-49). Warren County Jail personnel violated this policy by not removing Mr. Short's shoelaces prior to his placement in the sick room cell. These shoelaces formed the ligature that resulted in Mr. Short's suicide. Finally, Warren County Jail requires that correctional staff observe special management inmates "at least every 15 minutes" (at page V-51) and that these observations be documented in a special segregation log (at page V-52). Based upon the fact that correctional staff left Mr. Short unobserved in his cell for more than six hours, this policy was obviously violated in the case.

Third, according to the statements of several officers, they were aware that Mr. Short was being housed in the sick room isolation cell and needed to be processed. Despite the knowledge that he was housed in this cell as a special management inmate, these staff not only failed to provide any supervision of Mr. Short for more than six hours, but failed to conduct any intake medical screening. The Warren County Jail's own *Policies and Procedures Manual* provided very clear instructions regarding intake medical screening: "In order to protect the health and well being of the inmates and staff, each new inmate shall receive medical screening upon admission" (at page IV-34). Ironically, the policy manual also warned its correctional staff of the importance of completing the intake process by stating: "Correct intake procedures are VITAL for jail security and as a protection against lawsuits" (at page III-19).

Fourth, at least one correctional officer (Harry Ferguson) violated Warren County Jail policy, as well as state jail standards and national correctional standards and standard correctional practice, pertaining to emergency medical intervention. When Officer Ferguson went to the sick room cell and cut the noose from around Mr. Short's neck, he chose *not* to initiate CPR. During an interview with the sheriff's office investigator, Officer Ferguson gave several explanations for his failure to initiate CPR, including the comment that "I'm not much good at (it) and the man was pretty much dead already." Yet, although Officer Ferguson was presumably a certified jailer and trained in CPR, he was not qualified to determine that a victim was dead. According to Warren County Jail policy, "when a Correctional Officer or jail personnel discovers an inmate who is in need of emergency medical attention, he will apply first aid immediately" (at page IV-32). The application of first aid included CPR and use of an automated external defibrillator (at page IV-30). Officer Ferguson also told the investigator that he believed Mr. Short had only been hanging a short time (which was obviously false), yet still chose not to initiate any life-saving measures as directed by jail policy.

Fifth, based upon the videotape that recorded more than six hours of Mr. Short's confinement in the sick room isolation cell, it would appear that at least one correctional officer (and trustee) gave false and/or misleading testimony to the sheriff's office investigator, as well as falsified a document, regarding the observation of Mr. Short. For example, the Warren County Jail Check Register for January 12, 2004, which was completed by the officer-in-charge of each shift and documented various significant activities in the facility, suggested that security checks were made of all inmates at the following intervals:

15:48 (3:00pm)	19:25
16:15	19:59
16:45	20:24
17:15	20:58
17:45	21:25
18:13	21:59 (9:59pm)
18:47	

As required by both the Warren County Jail policy and state jail standards, correctional officers were to make "checks on inmates twice per hour" (at page V-38). The above notations were indeed within the required time frames. However, as indicated by the videotape that recorded more than six hours of Mr. Short's confinement in the sick room isolation cell, as well as statements of several correctional officers, *these cell checks never occurred.* Officer Ferguson told the investigator that as the officer-in-charge during the night shift, he was responsible for recording the cell checks on the Jail Check Register, as well as placing the initials of the officer physically performing the checks next to the time of the cell check round. During the night shift of January 12, 2004, three officers were on duty—Harry Ferguson, Kurt Kensy, and Jeremy Seal. Officer Ferguson stated that he stayed in the monitor room and did *not* conduct any cell check rounds. Officer Kensy stated he did *not* go to cell block area until Mr. Short was found hanging after 9:15 pm. Officer Seal stated that he was back in the cell block area during the shift, but did *not* make complete rounds (by checking each inmate), nor did he check Mr. Short's cell because "I didn't know Mr. Short was in there, the door was shut, and I didn't check the board." In addition, despite statements from the trustees that they brought Mr. Short a drink and/or ice at approximately 8:00 pm, this testimony was obviously false because Mr. Short was observed through the CCTV monitor to be hanging at 7:36 pm, and a trustee last interacted with him at 5:29 pm.

Therefore, not only did Officers Kensy and Seal fail to make cell block checks as required, Officer Ferguson falsely documented their initials in the Jail Check Register. In his interview with the sheriff's office investigator, Officer Ferguson acknowledged that Officer Kensy never told him he performed any cell block checks and justified the practice of falsifying cell check documents by stating that "you really don't know who's going back there[.]" Such conduct was outrageous and seriously compromised the safety and security of inmates within the Warren County Jail, including Thomas Short.

The practice of falsely documenting the Jail Check Register was apparently terminated immediately following Mr. Short's death.

Conclusion

In conclusion, the suicide of Thomas Short in the Warren County Jail was clearly preventable and his death was caused by correctional officers failing to comply with standard operating procedures, as well as simply ignoring Mr. Short's presence, health, and safety in the facility.

Specifically, it would be this writer's opinion that: 1) despite the fact that he was housed as a special management inmate requiring close observation (at a minimum of 15-minute intervals), correctional officers at the Warren County Jail ignored Mr. Short by failing to conduct physical checks of his cell for more than six hours, including the ignoring of Mr. Short for more than two hours as his suicide attempt and death were fully visible on the CCTV monitor; 2) the violation of numerous Warren County Jail policies, state jail standards, and national correctional standards and standard correctional practice, by several correctional officers was completely unreasonable, lacked any justification, and was a contributing factor to Mr. Short's suicide; 3) at least one correctional officer (and trustee) gave false and/or misleading testimony to the sheriff's office investigator, as well as falsified a document, regarding the observation of Mr. Short; and 4) presuming Sergeant Clint Keller of the Front Royal Police Department informed several correctional officers that Mr. Short was a possible risk for suicide, the failure of these officers to take appropriate steps to ensure his safety was unconscionable, reflected deliberate indifference, and was the proximate cause of his death.

3. Given what you have learned about jail suicide from both the factual background provided and the Expert Report and Affidavit above, do you agree with the Fourth Circuit's decision in *Short*? Why or why not?

4. Since Mr. Short was a pretrial detainee, why do you think the Fourth Circuit analyzed his claim under the 8th Amendment, which is supposed to apply only after conviction?

5. In the wake of the Supreme Court's 2015 decision in *Kingsley*, recall that some circuits have extended the *Kingsley* objective reasonableness standard to 14th Amendment substantive due process claims outside of the context of excessive force. Should the *Kingsley* objective reasonableness standard govern a substantive due process claim arising from the suicide of a pretrial detainee, such as the claim in *Short v. Smoot*? *See, e.g.*, *Estate of Vallina v. Cty. of Teller Sheriff's Office*, 757 F. App'x 643, 646 (10th Cir. 2018) (recognizing circuit split "on whether *Kingsley* alters the standard for conditions of confinement and inadequate medical care claims brought by pretrial detainees" and declining to reach the issue in evaluating a claim by the estate of a pretrial detainee who died by suicide).

6. What are the pros and cons of a correctional facility adopting department policies on prevention of jail suicide? Is there any risk in adopting a strict policy rather than a broad policy that leaves more discretion to the individual officers?

Chapter Eight

Procedural Due Process: Protection of Property Interests

The Due Process Clause of the 14th Amendment provides that no state shall "deprive any person of life, liberty, or property, without due process of law."

A. Procedural Due Process versus Substantive Due Process

Recall the distinction between procedural and substantive due process drawn by the Supreme Court in *Daniels v. Williams*, 474 U.S. 327 (1986):

Procedural Due Process: "By requiring the government to follow appropriate procedures when its agents decide to 'deprive any person of life, liberty, or property,' the Due Process Clause promotes fairness in such decisions."[1]

Substantive Due Process: "[B]y barring certain government actions regardless of the fairness of the procedures used to implement them, [due process] serves to prevent governmental power from being 'used for purposes of oppression.'"[2]

The focus of the procedural due process inquiry is on the fairness of the procedural steps, not on the fairness of the outcome. In practice, fair procedures are more likely to lead to a fair result. As stated in one of the briefs excerpted in this Chapter,

> The difference between substantive and procedural claims is not in whether the plaintiff alleges that she was deprived of a substantive benefit (to have an injury, she always must). Rather, it is in whether the plaintiff alleges that the denial is caused by the failure of the state to employ adequate procedures to guard against erroneous deprivation (procedural due process), or the

1. *Daniels*, 474 U.S. at 331.
2. *Id.*

failure of the state to provide an adequate justification for its action (substantive due process).[3]

B. Chapter Overview

Property protected by procedural due process means that the owner cannot be deprived of that interest by the government unless the government complies with certain procedural steps. What kinds of rights constitute "property" protected by procedural due process? Does procedural due process protect property interests other than land? What is necessary to show that an interest is sufficient to constitute "property" protected by procedural due process? Are property interests protected by procedural due process also protected by substantive due process?

This Chapter illustrates how the "property" protected by the 14th Amendment's Due Process Clause has evolved from the most obvious meaning of property, land, to the more abstract concept of government entitlements. The materials apply procedural due process doctrine in three different factual contexts:

(1) claims based on real property;

(2) claims based on public employment; and

(3) claims based on enforcement of protection from abuse orders.

These materials illustrate how lawyers can help shape legal doctrine by advocating novel legal theories. Novel legal theories sometimes prevail—such as the legal theory that property protected by procedural due process should include a government employee's entitlement to employment, the theory explored in *Roth* and *Loudermill*. Novel legal theories sometimes fail—such as the legal theory that a property interest in government employment should be protected by substantive due process, the theory rejected in *Nicholas*. Some claims in the context of employment involve both property and liberty interests protected by procedural due process (cases summarized in notes) or liberty interests alone (*Olivieri*).

This Chapter explores one novel legal theory in more depth, the theory rejected by the Supreme Court in *Castle Rock*, an unsuccessful attempt to expand the "property" protected by procedural due process to include a domestic violence victim's entitlement to enforcement of a restraining order.

Further, in the context of remedies for domestic violence, this Chapter invites you to consider how advocates seek to use the courts as an instrument of social change and the limits of federal constitutional law as an instrument of social change. This Chapter invites you to consider alternatives to constitutional litigation as paths to legal reform, such as legislation.

---

3. Brief of National Black Police Ass'n, *et al.* as Amici Curiae Supporting Respondent at 3, *Castle Rock v. Gonzales*, 545 U.S. 748 (2005), (No. 04-278), 2005 WL 328203, at *4. (Feb. 10, 2005).

C. Protection of Real Property Interests

Questions to guide reading of *Freeman*

1. Why did plaintiffs claim that they were deprived of their property without due process?
2. Why did the Fifth Circuit hold that plaintiffs received all the process that was due before the buildings were demolished?
3. Are you more persuaded by the majority or the dissent? Why?

Freeman v. City of Dallas

186 F.3d 601 (5th Cir. 1999), *cert. denied*, 534 U.S. 817 (2001)

DENNIS, Circuit Judge.

This case presents the questions of whether the seizure and destruction of the Plaintiffs' vacant apartment buildings by the City of Dallas, as "urban nuisances," based only on the findings and order of a panel of the City's Urban Rehabilitation Standards Board: (1) violated the Due Process Clause[] of the ... Fourteenth Amendment[] because the owners were not given an opportunity for an adversary hearing before a neutral magistrate and a judicial determination prior to the seizure and destruction of their real property....

A majority of this panel holds that the notice and hearings provided by the City satisfied the ... Fourteenth Amendment's guarantee[] against deprivation of property without due process of law.

...

I. FACTS AND PROCEDURAL HISTORY

Charles Freeman and Rosalyn Brown owned two apartment buildings in Dallas, Texas.... The buildings were vacant when Ms. Brown bought them and remained unoccupied until they were demolished.

The City of Dallas established the Urban Rehabilitation Standards Board ["Board"] to determine whether property condition reports by city inspectors constitute violations of the City's building code.... The [Board] may determine, after a hearing, whether a given structure is an "urban nuisance" and take various remedial measures. The [Board] is authorized by city ordinance to order repairs, receivership, the closing and vacating of buildings, demolition, and civil penalties up to $2,000 a day against property owners who fail to repair or demolish a structure after a valid determination and order has been issued by the [Board].

...

[In April and July of 1993, City code inspectors reported to the Board that the Plaintiffs' two apartment buildings needed repairs estimated at $84,290.00 and

$108,680.00.] The [Board] scheduled hearings to determine whether the buildings were in violation of the city building code and whether remedial steps should be taken.... The decision of a hearing panel is final except that rehearings may be granted in certain instances. Also, the code authorizes an affected property owner to appeal from the panel decision to the state district court for a "limited hearing under the substantial evidence rule." ...

Notice of the [Board] panel hearings with respect to the Plaintiffs' two buildings were mailed to the persons listed as owners on the title records. With regard to the building at 2621 Meyers Street, the City sent notices to Rosalyn Brown ... of the panel hearing "To Consider an Order of Repair or Correction of a Potential Urban Nuisance." Ms. Brown signed the return receipt on February 28, 1994. This notice listed all of the possible actions that the [Board] could take, including demolition: "If the board orders demolition, closure, vacation or removal, and if it is done by city forces, you will be required to pay for the expenses or a lien will be placed against the property." This notice concluded by stating, "It is important that you attend this hearing or send a representative." With regard to the structure at 2611 Meyers Street, an identical notice was sent to the person listed as the owner on the title, Robert Burkhead. Ms. Brown had purchased the property but had not yet filed her warranty deed. It appears that neither Burkhead nor the Plaintiffs received advance notice of the hearing with respect to the 2611 Meyers Street building, but Mr. Freeman learned that it was also involved when he attended the hearing in response to the notice sent to Ms. Brown concerning the 2621 Meyers Street property.

At the hearing concerning the two apartment buildings on February 28, 1994, Mr. Freeman testified and was questioned by the panel members. The panel looked at pictures of the structures, questioned Mr. Freeman about what plans he had to repair them, and asked whether he had the money or the time to accomplish the tasks. Mr. Freeman testified that he intended to repair the buildings himself and requested the panel to allow him sufficient time to do so. The panel members voiced their concerns about Mr. Freeman's ability to obtain the repair materials and his ability to renovate them by himself. The panel voted unanimously to demolish both structures.

Following this hearing, Freeman signed two notices of demolition for both apartment buildings. The City then sent out a "Notice of Demolition Order" for each building. As to the 2611 Meyers Street structure, the City sent notices to Freeman and Robert Burkhead. Freeman signed the return receipt on March 11, 1994, but Burkhead's notices were returned "Attempted—Not Known." Notices of a demolition order were sent to Rosalyn Brown and Charles Freeman as to the [Board]'s action concerning the 2621 Meyers Street building. Freeman signed return receipts of the notices on March 11, 1994. Each notice stated that the owners "may exercise your right to an administrative rehearing and review of this demolition order."

Mr. Freeman asked for and received a rehearing from the [Board] on May 23, 1994. At the rehearing, the [Board] members questioned Mr. Freeman about the two buildings, whether he had the materials to repair them, and whether any repairs had been made to the buildings since the last hearing. Mr. Freeman stated that had received some donated materials and he submitted pictures of one unit in the 2621 Meyers Street building that he had repaired. Several members of the [Board] panel expressed disbelief that Mr. Freeman could renovate the units for $2000 each as he claimed. The [Board] panel again voted to demolish both structures—the vote was unanimous as to the 2611 Meyers Street building, and it was five to two as to the 2621 Meyers Street building.

On the day of the hearing, Mr. Freeman signed the "Notice of Demolition" of both the 2611 and 2621 Meyers Street buildings. Neither Freeman nor Brown appealed the [Board] panel decision to the state district court. A notice entitled "Appeal Denied/Demolition" was sent to the owners of each building. Notice of the proposed demolition of 2611 Meyers Street was mailed to Freeman and Burkhead; notice of the proposed demolition for the other building was mailed to Freeman and Brown. Even though the notices for Freeman and Brown were sent to the same addresses at which they had received mail about earlier hearings, all of these were returned as "Unclaimed." No further notice was given to the Plaintiffs before the buildings were demolished in late December 1994. The costs of demolition by the City were assessed against Freeman and Brown in the amounts of $7954.72 for the building at 2611 Meyers Street and $7655.55 for the 2621 Meyers Street property.

...

III. DUE PROCESS

...

The Fourteenth Amendment prohibits the government from depriving "any person of life, liberty, or property, without due process of law." U.S. CONST. amend. XIV. This guarantee affords procedural protections. The government must give reasonable notice to an individual of its intention to deprive him of life, liberty, or property. It also must provide him with a meaningful opportunity to be heard. *Mathews v. Eldridge*, 424 U.S. 319, 333 (1976). Following *Mathews*, we assess what process is due by considering and balancing three distinct factors:

> First, the private interest that will be affected by the official action; second, the risk of an erroneous deprivation of such interest through the procedures used, and the probable value, if any, of additional or substitute procedural safeguards; and finally, the Government's interest, including the function involved and the fiscal and administrative burdens that the additional or substitute procedural requirement would entail.

Id., 424 U.S. at 335. This approach reflects the fact that "due process is flexible and calls for such procedural protections as the particular situation demands." ...

The Plaintiffs contend that they were denied a meaningful opportunity to be heard on the future of the apartment buildings because they were not told that the Department of Housing and Neighborhood Services had briefed panel members on their properties, they were not provided with the Department's information on their properties, they were not given notice of the tours of their properties by [Board] panel members, and the Department officials who reported the code violations were not present at either the hearings or the rehearings. We generally find a procedure to violate due process when the government fails to reveal its evidence. Non-disclosure by the government poses the risk of an erroneous deprivation because it forecloses the individual from testing the accuracy of the government's evidence. *See* [*Greene v. McElroy*, 360 U.S. 474,] 496–97 (1959). This threat is so great that it generally outweighs considerations favoring non-disclosure.

We conclude that the [Board] panel related to the Plaintiffs the evidence supporting the Department's recommendation to level the apartment buildings. During the rehearings, as well as the tour of 2621 Meyers Street preceding them, [Board] panel members conveyed to Freeman their concerns over the condition of the apartment buildings. Other members alerted him to the repair cost estimates. Freeman chose not to call the Department officials who had cited the apartment buildings for code violations or any other persons as witnesses. Nor did Freeman seek to learn more about the repair cost estimates after the panel informed him of them.... Because the [Board] panel made Freeman aware of the circumstances favoring demolition, Plaintiffs' assertion that the way in which the Board reached the decision to destroy the apartment buildings failed to accord with due process is without merit.

...

DENNIS, Circuit Judge, dissenting in part.

...

The City does not, and could not, dispute that the seizure and destruction of the plaintiffs' real property deprived them of property interests protected by the ... Fourteenth Amendment['s] Due Process Clause[]. The City argues, however, that a hearing before a panel of the City's own Urban Rehabilitation Standards Board afforded the plaintiffs all the process they were due before their property was seized and destroyed. Although the majority agrees, I believe that in the absence of an extraordinary situation, which did not exist in the present case, the Due Process Clauses require that, before a person is deprived of his real property by the government, he must be given notice and an opportunity for a meaningful hearing before a neutral magistrate, and that there must be a judicial determination that the seizure is justified.

Where the government seizes property not to preserve evidence of criminal wrongdoing but to assert ownership and control over the property, its action must also comply with the procedural protections of the Due Process Clause[] of the ... Fourteenth Amendment[]. The Supreme Court's precedents establish the general rule that Due Process requires that, absent an extraordinary situation, a party cannot invoke the power of the state to seize a person's property without a prior judicial determination that the seizure is justified.

...

Accordingly, the Due Process requirements of notice, a meaningful adversary hearing before a neutral magistrate, and a judicial determination of justification must be afforded to a person before his real property is seized and destroyed in order to abate or rehabilitate an "urban nuisance." In a case such as the present one, there is need for equally rigorous adherence to the principles of Due Process as in civil forfeitures of real property. The City of Dallas has pecuniary interests in the outcome of such proceedings, *e.g.*, justification for federal and state urban renewal grants; enhancement of the municipal tax base by promoting the replacement of old buildings with new ones. The need for safeguards against arbitrary, capricious or unreasonable seizures based on subjective standards may be even greater in "urban nuisance" or "urban rehabilitation" cases. Moreover, a post-seizure hearing cannot provide any remedy in such cases because the destroyed property cannot be restored and the best evidence of whether the seizure was justified will have been demolished also. It is not necessary to accomplish the City's legitimate goals of urban rehabilitation that an owner whose real property the City proposes to destroy be deprived of an opportunity for a meaningful pre-seizure adversary hearing before a neutral and impartial judge or magistrate. Requiring the city to postpone seizure and destruction until after such a hearing and judicial determination that the seizure is justified creates no significant administrative burden. And any harm that results from delay is minimal in comparison to the injury occasioned by the erroneous seizure and destruction of real property.[4]

For further discussion

What is necessary to show that an interest in land is sufficient to constitute "property" protected by procedural due process? In an opinion by now-Justice Sonia Sotomayor, the Second Circuit held that, for a real estate developer to establish a property interest protected by due process, the landowner must establish that state or local law "unambiguously limits" the government's discretion to deny the landowner's request for a government benefit:

> This Circuit applies a "clear entitlement" analysis to determine whether a landowner has a constitutionally cognizable property interest in the benefit sought.... This approach derives from the analysis set forth in *Board of Regents v. Roth*, 408 U.S. 564 (1972). In *Roth*, the Supreme Court held that, "[t]o have a property interest in a benefit, a person clearly must have more than an abstract need or desire for it. He must have more than a unilateral expectation of it. He must, instead, have a legitimate claim of entitlement to it." *Id.* at 577 ... In *RRI Realty Corp. v. Incorporated Village of Southampton*, 870 F.2d 911 (2d Cir. 1989), we ... enunciated a more stringent analysis: "Application of the test must focus primarily on the degree of discretion en-

4. Upon rehearing *en banc*, the Fifth Circuit wrote on a separate issue also decided by the *Freeman* panel and, without further discussion, affirmed that portion of the panel's ruling that the process afforded the building owner complied with due process. *Freeman v. City of Dallas*, 242 F.3d 642, 647 n.4 (5th Cir. 2001) (*en banc*).

> joyed by the issuing authority, not the estimated probability that the authority will act favorably in a particular case." *Id.* at 918. We noted that "[e]ven if in a particular case, objective observers would estimate that the probability of issuance was extremely high, the opportunity of the local agency to deny issuance suffices to defeat the existence of a federally protected property interest." *Id.*... Because we concluded that the proper focus for entitlement analysis is "on the degree of official discretion and not on the probability of its favorable exercise, the question of whether an applicant has a property interest will normally be a matter of law for the court." *Id.*... As we explained [in an earlier decision], "this standard appropriately balances the need for local autonomy, with recognition of constitutional protection at the very outer margins of municipal behavior ... It also recognizes that the Due Process Clause does not function as a general overseer of arbitrariness in state and local land-use decisions; in our federal system, that is the province of the state courts." [citation omitted].

Clubside, Inc. v. Valentin, 468 F.3d 144, 152–53 (2d Cir. 2006). The Second Circuit relied on *Roth*, the next case in this Chapter.

D. Protection of Non-Traditional Property Interests

1. Public Employment

In the 1970s, the Supreme Court expanded the concept of property protected by procedural due process to include:

> rights to some governmental benefits conferred by statute, *see, e.g., Goldberg v. Kelly*, 397 U.S. 254 (1970) (welfare payments), or by contract, *see, e.g., Perry v. Sindermann*, 408 U.S. 593 (1972) (tenured teaching position). The Court ... suggested that a rationale for constitutionalizing some of these so-called 'new property' rights is the functional importance of governmental benefits like welfare to citizens in contemporary society.

S & D Maint. Co., Inc. v. Goldin, 844 F.2d 962, 965 (2d Cir. 1988). The Supreme Court decisions below, *Roth* and *Loudermill*, explain the entitlement basis of this understanding of property.

Questions to guide reading of *Roth*

1. What procedural protections did Wisconsin state law provide for tenured faculty members? For new teachers without tenure?
2. What does a person have to show to prove a property interest in a governmental benefit—so that the benefit is protected by procedural due process?

3. Why were the Wisconsin Assistant Professor's due process rights not violated by the University's decision not to renew his contract, with no reason, review, or appeal? Can a state choose to provide a hearing or reasons for non-retention?

4. Suppose a fired public employee asked you to represent her in a suit alleging that the firing violated her right to procedural due process. Based on *Roth*, what information would help you determine whether the employee had a property interest in her job?

Bd. of Regents of State Colls. v. Roth

408 U.S. 564 (1972)

Mr. Justice STEWART delivered the opinion of the Court.

In 1968 the respondent, David Roth, was hired for his first teaching job as assistant professor of political science at Wisconsin State University-Oshkosh. He was hired for a fixed term of one academic year. The notice of his faculty appointment specified that his employment would begin on September 1, 1968, and would end on June 30, 1969. The respondent completed that term. But he was informed that he would not be rehired for the next academic year.

The respondent had no tenure rights to continued employment. Under Wisconsin statutory law a state university teacher can acquire tenure as a "permanent" employee only after four years of year-to-year employment. Having acquired tenure, a teacher is entitled to continued employment "during efficiency and good behavior." A relatively new teacher without tenure, however, is under Wisconsin law entitled to nothing beyond his one-year appointment. There are no statutory or administrative standards defining eligibility for re-employment. State law thus clearly leaves the decision whether to rehire a nontenured teacher for another year to the unfettered discretion of university officials.

The procedural protection afforded a Wisconsin State University teacher before he is separated from the University corresponds to his job security. As a matter of statutory law, a tenured teacher cannot be "discharged except for cause upon written charges" and pursuant to certain procedures. A nontenured teacher, similarly, is protected to some extent *during* his one-year term. Rules promulgated by the Board of Regents provide that a nontenured teacher "dismissed" before the end of the year may have some opportunity for review of the "dismissal." But the Rules provide no real protection for a nontenured teacher who simply is not re-employed for the next year. He must be informed by February 1 "concerning retention or non-retention for the ensuing year." But "no reason for non-retention need be given. No review or appeal is provided in such case."

In conformance with these Rules, the President of Wisconsin State University-Oshkosh informed the respondent before February 1, 1969, that he would not be rehired for the 1969–1970 academic year. He gave the respondent no reason for the decision and no opportunity to challenge it at any sort of hearing.

...

I.

The requirements of procedural due process apply only to the deprivation of interests encompassed by the Fourteenth Amendment's protection of liberty and property. When protected interests are implicated, the right to some kind of prior hearing is paramount.[7] But the range of interests protected by procedural due process is not infinite.

...

The Court has also made clear that the property interests protected by procedural due process extend well beyond actual ownership of real estate, chattels, or money. By the same token, the Court has required due process protection for deprivations of liberty beyond the sort of formal constraints imposed by the criminal process.

...

III.

The Fourteenth Amendment's procedural protection of property is a safeguard of the security of interests that a person has already acquired in specific benefits. These interests—property interests—may take many forms.

Thus, the Court has held that a person receiving welfare benefits under statutory and administrative standards defining eligibility for them has an interest in continued receipt of those benefits that is safeguarded by procedural due process. *Goldberg v. Kelly*, 397 U.S. 254. Similarly, in the area of public employment, the Court has held that a public college professor dismissed from an office held under tenure provisions, and college professors and staff members dismissed during the terms of their contracts, have interests in continued employment that are safeguarded by due process. Only last year, the Court held that this principle "proscribing summary dismissal from public employment without hearing or inquiry required by due process" also applied to a teacher recently hired without tenure or a formal contract, but nonetheless with a clearly implied promise of continued employment.

Certain attributes of "property" interests protected by procedural due process emerge from these decisions. To have a property interest in a benefit, a person clearly must have more than an abstract need or desire for it. He must have more than a unilateral expectation of it. He must, instead, have a legitimate claim of entitlement to it. It is a purpose of the ancient institution of property to protect those claims upon which people rely in their daily lives, reliance that must not be arbitrarily undermined. It is a purpose of the constitutional right to a hearing to provide an opportunity for a person to vindicate those claims.

---

7. Before a person is deprived of a protected interest, he must be afforded opportunity for some kind of a hearing, "except for extraordinary situations where some valid governmental interest is at stake that justifies postponing the hearing until after the event." ...

Property interests, of course, are not created by the Constitution. Rather they are created and their dimensions are defined by existing rules or understandings that stem from an independent source such as state law—rules or understandings that secure certain benefits and that support claims of entitlement to those benefits. Thus, the welfare recipients in *Goldberg v. Kelly* had a claim of entitlement to welfare payments that was grounded in the statute defining eligibility for them. The recipients had not yet shown that they were, in fact, within the statutory terms of eligibility. But we held that they had a right to a hearing at which they might attempt to do so.

Just as the welfare recipients' "property" interest in welfare payments was created and defined by statutory terms, so the respondent's "property" interest in employment at Wisconsin State University-Oshkosh was created and defined by the terms of his appointment. Those terms secured his interest in employment up to June 30, 1969. But the important fact in this case is that they specifically provided that the respondent's employment was to terminate on June 30. They did not provide for contract renewal absent "sufficient cause." Indeed, they made no provision for renewal whatsoever.

Thus, the terms of the respondent's appointment secured absolutely no interest in re-employment for the next year. They supported absolutely no possible claim of entitlement to re-employment. Nor, significantly, was there any state statute or University rule or policy that secured his interest in re-employment or that created any legitimate claim to it. In these circumstances, the respondent surely had an abstract concern in being rehired, but he did not have a *property* interest sufficient to require the University authorities to give him a hearing when they declined to renew his contract of employment.

IV.

Our analysis of the respondent's constitutional rights in this case in no way indicates a view that an opportunity for a hearing or a statement of reasons for nonretention would, or would not, be appropriate or wise in public colleges and universities. For it is a written Constitution that we apply. Our role is confined to interpretation of that Constitution.... [S]ummary judgment for the respondent should not have been granted, since the respondent has not shown that he was deprived of ... property protected by the Fourteenth Amendment.

Questions to guide reading of *Loudermill*

1. One of the public employers argued that state law defined not only the property right but also what procedures were required before deprivation of the property right. Why did the Supreme Court reject that view?
2. Why did the Supreme Court hold that the fired public employees were entitled to a pretermination opportunity to respond in addition to the post-termination procedures provided by state statute?
3. What are the essential requirements of a pretermination hearing?

Cleveland Bd. of Educ. v. Loudermill

470 U.S. 532 (1985)

Justice WHITE delivered the opinion of the Court.

In these cases we consider what pretermination process must be accorded a public employee who can be discharged only for cause.

I.

In 1979 the Cleveland Board of Education ... hired respondent James Loudermill as a security guard. On his job application, Loudermill stated that he had never been convicted of a felony. Eleven months later, as part of a routine examination of his employment records, the Board discovered that in fact Loudermill had been convicted of grand larceny in 1968. By letter dated November 3, 1980, the Board's Business Manager informed Loudermill that he had been dismissed because of his dishonesty in filling out the employment application. Loudermill was not afforded an opportunity to respond to the charge of dishonesty or to challenge his dismissal. On November 13, the Board adopted a resolution officially approving the discharge.

Under Ohio law, Loudermill was a "classified civil servant." Ohio Rev. Code Ann. § 124.11 (1984). Such employees can be terminated only for cause, and may obtain administrative review if discharged. § 124.34. Pursuant to this provision, Loudermill filed an appeal with the Cleveland Civil Service Commission on November 12. The Commission appointed a referee, who held a hearing on January 29, 1981. Loudermill argued that he had thought that his 1968 larceny conviction was for a misdemeanor rather than a felony. The referee recommended reinstatement. On July 20, 1981, the full Commission heard argument and orally announced that it would uphold the dismissal. Proposed findings of fact and conclusions of law followed on August 10, and Loudermill's attorneys were advised of the result by mail on August 21. [The other case concerned a school bus mechanic who was fired for failing an eye exam.]

...

II.

Respondents' federal constitutional claim depends on their having had a property right in continued employment. *Board of Regents v. Roth*, 408 U.S. 564, 576–78 (1972)....

Property interests are not created by the Constitution, "they are created and their dimensions are defined by existing rules or understandings that stem from an independent source such as state law...." [*Roth*], 408 U.S. at 577. The Ohio statute plainly creates such an interest. Respondents were "classified civil service employees," Ohio Rev. Code Ann. § 124.11 (1984), entitled to retain their positions "during good behavior and efficient service," who could not be dismissed "except ... for ... misfeasance, malfeasance, or nonfeasance in office," § 124.34.[4] The statute plainly supports the conclusion ... that respondents possessed property rights in continued employment....

---

4. The relevant portion of § 124.34 provides that no classified civil servant may be removed except

The Parma Board argues, however, that the property right is defined by, and conditioned on, the legislature's choice of procedures for its deprivation. The Board stresses that in addition to specifying the grounds for termination, the statute sets out procedures by which termination may take place. The procedures were adhered to in these cases.

...

[T]he Court has clearly rejected [this view]. In *Vitek v. Jones*, 445 U.S. 480, 491 (1980), we pointed out that "minimum [procedural] requirements [are] a matter of federal law, they are not diminished by the fact that the State may have specified its own procedures that it may deem adequate for determining the preconditions to adverse official action." ...

If a clearer holding is needed, we provide it today. The point is straightforward: the Due Process Clause provides that certain substantive rights—life, liberty, and property—cannot be deprived except pursuant to constitutionally adequate procedures. The categories of substance and procedure are distinct. Were the rule otherwise, the Clause would be reduced to a mere tautology. "Property" cannot be defined by the procedures provided for its deprivation any more than can life or liberty. The right to due process "is conferred, not by legislative grace, but by constitutional guarantee. While the legislature may elect not to confer a property interest in [public] employment, it may not constitutionally authorize the deprivation of such an interest, once conferred, without appropriate procedural safeguards." *Arnett v. Kennedy*, 416 U.S. 134, 167 (1974) (Powell, J., concurring in part and concurring in result in part)....

In short, once it is determined that the Due Process Clause applies, "the question remains what process is due." ... The answer to that question is not to be found in the Ohio statute.

III.

An essential principle of due process is that a deprivation of life, liberty, or property "be preceded by notice and opportunity for hearing appropriate to the nature of the case." ... We have described "the root requirement" of the Due Process Clause as being "that an individual be given an opportunity for a hearing *before* he is deprived of any significant property interest." ... This principle requires "some kind of a hearing" prior to the discharge of an employee who has a constitutionally protected property interest in his employment. [*Roth*], 408 U.S., at 569–70. Even decisions finding no constitutional violation in termination procedures have relied on the existence of some pretermination opportunity to respond....

The need for some form of pretermination hearing, recognized in these cases, is evident from a balancing of the competing interests at stake. These are the private interests in retaining employment, the governmental interest in the expeditious removal of unsatisfactory employees and the avoidance of administrative burdens, and

---

"for incompetency, inefficiency, dishonesty, drunkenness, immoral conduct, insubordination, discourteous treatment of the public, neglect of duty, violation of such sections or the rules of the director of administrative services or the commission, or any other failure of good behavior, or any other acts of misfeasance, malfeasance, or nonfeasance in office."

the risk of an erroneous termination. *See Mathews v. Eldridge*, 424 U.S. 319, 335 (1976).

First, the significance of the private interest in retaining employment cannot be gainsaid. We have frequently recognized the severity of depriving a person of the means of livelihood....

Second, some opportunity for the employee to present his side of the case is recurringly of obvious value in reaching an accurate decision. Dismissals for cause will often involve factual disputes. Even where the facts are clear, the appropriateness or necessity of the discharge may not be; in such cases, the only meaningful opportunity to invoke the discretion of the decisionmaker is likely to be before the termination takes effect.[8] ...

The cases before us illustrate these considerations. Both respondents had plausible arguments to make that might have prevented their discharge....

The governmental interest in immediate termination does not outweigh these interests. As we shall explain, affording the employee an opportunity to respond prior to termination would impose neither a significant administrative burden nor intolerable delays. Furthermore, the employer shares the employee's interest in avoiding disruption and erroneous decisions; and until the matter is settled, the employer would continue to receive the benefit of the employee's labors. It is preferable to keep a qualified employee on than to train a new one. A governmental employer also has an interest in keeping citizens usefully employed rather than taking the possibly erroneous and counterproductive step of forcing its employees onto the welfare rolls. Finally, in those situations where the employer perceives a significant hazard in keeping the employee on the job, it can avoid the problem by suspending with pay.

IV.

The foregoing considerations indicate that the pretermination "hearing," though necessary, need not be elaborate. We have pointed out that "[t]he formality and procedural requisites for the hearing can vary, depending upon the importance of the interests involved and the nature of the subsequent proceedings." In general, "something less" than a full evidentiary hearing is sufficient prior to adverse administrative action. *Mathews v. Eldridge*, 424 U.S., at 343. Under state law, respondents were later entitled to a full administrative hearing and judicial review. The only question is what steps were required before the termination took effect.

...

Here, the pretermination hearing need not definitively resolve the propriety of the discharge. It should be an initial check against mistaken decisions—essentially, a de-

8. This is not to say that where state conduct is entirely discretionary the Due Process Clause is brought into play.... The point is that where there is an entitlement, a prior hearing facilitates the consideration of whether a permissible course of action is also an appropriate one. This is one way in which providing "effective notice and informal hearing permitting the [employee] to give his version of the events will provide a meaningful hedge against erroneous action. At least the [employer] will be alerted to the existence of disputes about facts and arguments about cause and effect.... [H]is discretion will be more informed and we think the risk of error substantially reduced."

termination of whether there are reasonable grounds to believe that the charges against the employee are true and support the proposed action.

The essential requirements of due process, and all that respondents seek or the Court of Appeals required, are notice and an opportunity to respond. The opportunity to present reasons, either in person or in writing, why proposed action should not be taken is a fundamental due process requirement. The tenured public employee is entitled to oral or written notice of the charges against him, an explanation of the employer's evidence, and an opportunity to present his side of the story. To require more than this prior to termination would intrude to an unwarranted extent on the government's interest in quickly removing an unsatisfactory employee.

...

VI.

We conclude that all the process that is due is provided by a pretermination opportunity to respond, coupled with post-termination administrative procedures as provided by the Ohio statute. Because respondents allege in their complaints that they had no chance to respond, the District Court erred in dismissing for failure to state a claim....

For further discussion

1. What process is due is flexible depending on the circumstances. Once a plaintiff demonstrates a liberty or property interest protected by procedural due process, "'the question remains what process is due.'" *Cleveland Bd. of Educ. v. Loudermill*, 470 U.S. 532, 541 (1985) (further citation omitted). The Supreme Court outlined the analytical framework for assessing what process is due in *Mathews v. Eldridge*, 424 U.S. 319, 335 (1976), identifying three distinct factors to be weighed:

> First, the private interest that will be affected by the official action; second, the risk of an erroneous deprivation of such interest through the procedures used, and the probable value, if any, of additional or substitute procedural safeguards; and finally, the Government's interest, including the function involved and the fiscal and administrative burdens that the additional or substitute procedural requirement would entail.

Id.

A pre-deprivation hearing generally is required to reduce the risk of an erroneous deprivation of a constitutionally protected liberty or property interest. "An essential principle of due process is that a deprivation of life, liberty, or property 'be preceded by notice and opportunity for hearing appropriate to the nature of the case.'" *Loudermill*, 470 U.S. at 542 (quoting *Mullane v. Central Hanover Bank & Trust Co.*, 339 U.S. 306, 313 (1950)); *Board of Regents v. Roth*, 408 U.S. 564, 570 n.7 (1972) ("'it is fundamental that except in emergency situations ... due process requires that when a State seeks to terminate [a protected] interest ... it must afford "notice and opportunity for hearing appropriate to the nature of the case"'"); *see also Loudermill*, 470

U.S. at 546 ("The opportunity to present reasons, either in person or in writing, why proposed action should not be taken is a fundamental due process requirement.").

However, in " 'extraordinary situations where some valid government interest is at stake,' " it is permissible to postpone the hearing until after the deprivation. *Roth*, 408 U.S. at 570 n.7 (further citation omitted). For example, where a state employee holds a position of public trust, such as police officer, the state has a significant interest in "immediately suspending" that employee, without pay and prior to a hearing "when felony charges are filed against [the employee]." *Homar v. Gilbert*, 520 U.S. 924, 932 (1997). In such an emergency situation, the arrest and filing of charges relieves the state of the obligation to provide a pre-suspension hearing because the purpose that would have been served by a pre-suspension hearing—"to determine 'whether there are reasonable grounds to believe that the charges against the employee are true and support the proposed action,' " *id.* at 933 (quoting *Loudermill*, 470 U.S. at 545–46)—instead is served by the arrest and charge, since an independent third party found probable cause to believe the employee committed a serious crime. *Homar*, 520 U.S. at 933–34.

2. In the employment context, there is some distinction between the treatment of termination and suspension. "Unlike in the case of a termination, where we have recognized that 'the only meaningful opportunity to invoke the discretion of the decisionmaker is likely to be before the termination takes effect,' *Loudermill*, 470 U.S. at 543, in the case of a suspension there will be ample opportunity to invoke discretion later—and a short delay actually benefits the employee by allowing state officials to obtain more accurate information about the arrest and charges." *Homar*, 520 U.S. at 934–35. In *Homar*, for example, the Supreme Court ruled that a school campus police officer's due process rights were not violated when he was demoted following a hearing that took place after the officer had been suspended without a hearing when his employer learned of his arrest for possession of marijuana. *Homar*, 520 U.S. at 926–28, 931–35.

3. The formality of the process required by the Constitution depends on the circumstances. In the employment context, the pre-termination process to protect a tenured public employee's property interest in the job need not be elaborate but simply " 'an initial check against mistaken decisions' " by providing the employee "oral or written notice of the charges, an explanation of the employer's evidence, and an opportunity for the employee to tell his side of the story." *Homar*, 520 U.S. at 929 (quoting *Loudermill*, 470 U.S at 545–46). That is in part because the risk of mistaken deprivation of the property interest is also protected by post-termination process, such as grievance procedures under collective bargaining agreements.

By contrast, because of the nature of the harm, more extensive pre-deprivation process is due to protect a prisoner's liberty interest in avoiding transfer to a mental hospital and mistaken subjection to involuntary mental treatment. *See Vitek v. Jones*, 445 U.S. 480, 494, 495–96 (1980) (the risk of mistaken transfer, and "the stigmatizing consequences of a transfer to a mental hospital for involuntary psychiatric treatment, coupled with the subjection of the prisoner to mandatory behavior modification as a treatment for mental illness" requires a pre-deprivation adversarial hearing before a neutral decisionmaker). *But see Pierce v. Blaine*, 467 F.3d 362, 371 (3d Cir. 2006), *cert. denied*, 551 U.S. 1110 (2007) (at his own lawyer's request and over objections of district attorney, psychiatric evaluation of prisoner without predeprivation hearing permissible because "*Vitek* involved an open-ended civil commitment and involuntary treatment unrelated to any ongoing court proceedings rather than an inpatient evaluation for the limited purpose of determining competence to assist counsel").

Exercise 8-A

Suppose a fired public employee asked you to represent him in a suit alleging that the firing violated his right to procedural due process. Assume the employee had a property interest in his job. Based on *Loudermill* and *Homar* (summarized above), what information would help you determine whether the firing adequately protected the employee's property interest by complying with procedural due process?

For further discussion

1. In addition to alleging the deprivation of a *property* interest, a public employee may also bring a Section 1983 procedural due process claim for deprivation of a *liberty* interest arising from statements made at the time an employee suffers adverse employment action, such as firing or demotion. Because reputation alone is not a liberty interest protected by the Due Process Clause, *Paul v. Davis*, 424 U.S. 693, 701–12 (1976), defamation alone does not give rise to a due process claim. *Siegert v. Gilley*, 500 U.S. 226, 233–34 (1991). "Rather, to make out a due process claim for deprivation of a liberty interest in reputation, a plaintiff must show a stigma to his reputation plus deprivation of some additional right or interest," *Hill v. Borough of Kutztown*, 455 F.3d 225, 236 (3d Cir. 2006), known as the "stigma plus" standard. "For a defamation to give rise to a right to procedural due process, it is necessary ... that the defamation be accompanied by a discharge from government employment" or other adverse personnel action. *Mosrie v. Barry*, 718 F.2d 1151, 1161 (D.C. Cir. 1983).

"[T]he 'stigma-plus' standard [ ] requires a plaintiff to show that the government official's conduct deprived the plaintiff of a previously recognized property or liberty interest in addition to damaging the plaintiff's reputation." *Cypress Ins. Co. v. Clark*, 144 F.3d 1435, 1436–37 (11th Cir. 1998) (cited in *Dee v. Borough of Dunmore*, 549 F.3d 225, 234 n.11 (3d Cir. 2008)). A constitutionally protected property interest qualifies as a sufficient "plus." *See, e.g.*, *Greenwood v. New York*, 163 F.3d 119, 124 (2d Cir. 1998) ("Several circuits have held that the deprivation of a property interest satisfies the 'plus' prong of stigma plus. We agree with this position. And ... we hold that government defamation combined with the deprivation of a property interest ... g[i]ve[s] rise to a due process liberty interest." (internal citations omitted)) (cited in *Dee*, 549 F.3d at 234 n.11); *San Jacinto Sav. & Loan v. Kacal*, 928 F.2d 697, 701–02 (5th Cir. 1991) ("To establish the [plus] portion of the stigma plus infringement test, a claimant must establish that the state sought to remove or significantly alter a life, liberty, or property interest recognized and protected by state law or guaranteed by one of the provisions of the Bill of Rights that has been incorporated." (internal quotation marks omitted)) (cited in *Dee*, 549 F.3d at 234 n.11)); *Cooper v. Dupnik*, 924 F.2d 1520, 1532 n.22 (9th Cir. 1991), *vacated on other grounds*, 963 F.2d 1220 (9th Cir. 1992) (en banc), *cert. denied*, 506 U.S. 953 (1992) ("The 'plus' part of th[e stigma-plus] test can be met by either the denial of a right specifically secured by the Bill of Rights (such as the right to free speech or counsel), or the denial of a state-created property or liberty interest such that the Fourteenth Amendment's Due Process Clause is violated.")) (cited in *Dee*, 549 F.3d at 234 n.11). "Although the conceptual basis for reputation-plus claims is not fully clear, it presumably rests on the fact that official criticism will carry much more weight if the person criticized is at the same time demoted or fired." *O'Donnell v. Barry*, 148 F.3d 1126, 1140 (D.C. Cir. 1998).

2. The procedural due process remedy for a public employee who suffers stigma at the time he or she is deprived of a property interest in public employment is an opportunity to clear the employee's name. "[W]here a public-sector employer creates and disseminates a false and defamatory impression about an employee in connection with the employee's discharge," the Due Process Clause "require[s] the employer to provide the employee with an opportunity to dispute the defamatory allegations," and the employer's failure to do so is actionable under § 1983. *Wojcik v. Mass. State Lottery Comm'n.*, 300 F.3d 92, 103 (1st Cir. 2002); *Doe v. Dep't of Justice*, 753 F.2d 1092, 1113 n.25 (D.C. Cir. 1985) ("a government employee must be given a name-clearing hearing when the government disseminates allegedly false and reputation-destroying charges against her in the course of her discharge").

3. While the circuits are split about whether the stigmatizing allegations must be publicized, *see* the Seventh Circuit opinion below, the First Circuit has explained the "stigma" aspect of what a plaintiff must prove in that circuit to show an entitlement to a name-clearing hearing:

> First, the alleged statements must level a "charge against [the employee] that might seriously damage his standing and associations in his community" and place his "good name, reputation, honor, or integrity ... at stake." ... Second, the employee must dispute the charges made against him as false. Third, the stigmatizing statements or charges must have been intentionally publicized by the government. That is, the defamatory charges must have been aired "in a formal setting (and not merely the result of unauthorized 'leaks')." Fourth, the stigmatizing statements must have been made in conjunction with an alteration of the employee's legal status, such as the termination of his employment. Finally, the government must have failed to comply with the employee's request for an adequate name-clearing opportunity.

Wojcik, 300 F.3d at 103 (alteration and first omission in original) (citations omitted).

To guide reading of *Olivieri*

A public employee who does *not* have a property interest in the position may have a liberty interest protected by procedural due process and may be entitled to a name-clearing hearing when, in connection with the firing or demotion of the employee, the employer makes charges against the employee that significantly impair the employee's liberty to seek other employment. In *Olivieri v. Rodriguez*, 122 F.3d 406 (7th Cir. 1997), Judge Richard Posner analyzed such a claim and summarized the circuit split about the necessity of publicizing the defamatory charges.

Olivieri v. Rodriguez

122 F.3d 406 (7th Cir. 1997), *cert. denied*, 522 U.S. 1110 (1998)

POSNER, Chief Judge.

A probationary Chicago police officer fired on grounds of having sexually harassed female probationers at the police training academy sued the police superintendent under 42 U.S.C. § 1983. The basis of the suit was the ex-officer's claim that firing him on such a ground has prevented him from obtaining other employment as a police officer and by doing this has curtailed his liberty of employment without due process because, being merely a probationer, he was not granted a hearing before (or for that matter after) he was fired. The district court granted summary judgment for the superintendent.

A line of cases that reaches back to *Joint Anti-Fascist Refugee Comm. v. McGrath*, 341 U.S. 123 (1951), establishes that although defamation by a public officer is not a constitutional tort, because the interest that it invades, the interest in reputation, is not deemed liberty or property within the meaning of the due process clauses of the Constitution, *Paul v. Davis*, 424 U.S. 693, 701 (1976) ... when the character and circumstances of the defamation are such as to have "foreclose[d] his freedom to take advantage of other employment opportunities" he can bring a suit based on the deprivation of his liberty of employment or occupation. *Paul*, 424 U.S. at 710 (quoting *Board of Regents v. Roth*, 408 U.S. 564, 573 (1972)).... The classic case of this type, illustrated by *McGrath* itself, is a government blacklist, which when circulated or otherwise publicized to prospective employers effectively excludes the blacklisted individual from his occupation, much as if the government had yanked the license of an individual in an occupation that requires licensure. *See Roth*, 408 U.S. at 573–74.... The distinction between mere defamation and an infringement of liberty of occupation is merely one of degree, especially when the defamation relates to a person's fitness for a particular type of employment, but it is a distinction to which the courts are committed.

This case is unusual because there is no evidence that the defendant disclosed to anyone the grounds of the plaintiff's discharge. The plaintiff argues that this makes no difference to his employability because no police department will hire him without asking him why he was fired by the Chicago Police Department. If he answers truthfully, he will reveal the ground of the termination as effectively as (actually more effectively than) if the Department had taken out a full-page ad in every newspaper in the nation announcing the termination of Felix A. Olivieri for sexually harassing female probationary officers at the Chicago police training academy. This type of argument has persuaded three circuits that dissemination by the defendant in a case such as this is not required after all. [citing 2d, 4th, 11th Circuits]. Our court, however, insists on dissemination [citing 7th Circuit], as do the First and Third Circuits [citations omitted]. The Fifth and Eighth have hedged [citations omitted], and the others haven't addressed the issue.

We are not disposed to depart from our position in this intercircuit conflict, and not only because *stare decisis* has its claims. The contrary position resembles the largely discredited doctrine of "compelled republication" or (more vividly) "self-defamation," which allows the victim of a defamation to satisfy the requirement of publication by publishing it himself, for example to prospective employers as in the present case.... The doctrine is inconsistent with the fundamental principle of mitigation of damages. It is no doubt highly likely that the ground of Olivieri's discharge would become known to prospective employers, but it is not certain. A prospective employer might not ask him—might ask only the Chicago Police Department, which for all we know might refuse to disclose the grounds of Olivieri's discharge; many former employers refuse to answer such inquiries, because of fear of being sued for defamation. The principle of self-defamation, applied in a case such as this, would encourage Olivieri to apply for a job to every police force in the nation, in order to magnify his damages; and to blurt out to each of them the ground of his discharge in the most lurid terms, to the same end. Most states, as noted in the decisions cited above, reject self-defamation as a basis for a tort claim, and it would be odd for federal constitutional law to embrace this questionable doctrine.

A further consideration in favor of the majority position is brought to light by asking what the Chicago Police Department should have done when it decided to discharge Olivieri. His answer is that it should have granted him a hearing. This comes close to arguing that there is no such thing as probationary public employment—that no public employee can be fired without a hearing because if he is, and the ground of the discharge impugns his fitness for employment in a similar job, as it very often will, his employer will have violated his constitutional rights, no matter how secretive the employer is about the ground.

Finally, there is a qualitative difference, bearing on culpability, between publicizing a stigmatizing ground of dismissal and refusing to do so, that the plaintiff's position would erase. The public employer who goes out of his way to publicize the ground of the dismissal is deliberately taking measures to make it difficult or impossible for the employee to obtain comparable employment, and is thus acting with intent to infringe a constitutionally protected liberty. There is no similar intent in the case in which the employer does not disclose, let alone publicize, the ground of its action.

The effect on the employee's future employability is in that case the unavoidable by-product of action taken for a wholly different purpose, that of improving the employer's own work force. The employer in such a case would be unconcerned if the employee found comparable employment elsewhere. The case is thus at the farthest extreme from the blacklist cases out of which the constitutional doctrine arises.

For further discussion

The circuit split summarized by Judge Posner persists. *See, e.g., McGinnis v. D.C.*, 65 F. Supp. 3d 203, 221 n.3 (D.D.C. 2014) (summarizing decisions by the 1st, 3rd, 7th, and 8th Circuits that require proof that reputation-damaging statement in personnel file already has been disseminated to the public and contrasting with decisions by the 9th, 10th, and 11th Circuits requiring only that the personnel file could be viewed by the public); *Sciolino v. City of Newport News*, 480 F.3d 642, 655 (4th Cir.), *cert. denied*, 552 U.S. 1076 (2007) (Wilkinson, J., dissenting), ("[T]o say there is a circuit split is at once true and not indicative of the full extent of the problem. Whether a liberty interest is infringed by a letter in a file drawer has generated answers with shades and permutations that mock the clarity law must provide for human conduct.").

Exercise 8-B

You represent the City of Morgan. The Mayor of Morgan is on the phone. She tells you she has just fired employee Charlie Dolgenos. The Mayor is busy and you may not get a chance to speak with her again soon. While she is still on the phone, based on your understanding of *Roth*, *Loudermill*, *Homar*, *Olivieri*, and the accompanying notes, what questions do you want to ask the Mayor to determine whether the firing of Mr. Dolgenos complied with procedural due process? Depending on what you learn from the Mayor, are there any issues you might want your associate to research?

For further discussion

1. Students enrolled in public universities also may have property or liberty interests protected by procedural due process. While the Supreme Court has not squarely held that college or graduate students have a property interest in continued enrollment in a university (an interest that would be created by state law, such as a statute or contract guaranteeing an education) or a liberty interest in pursuing a chosen profession, the Court has assumed without deciding the existence of a protected interest and has reached the issue of whether the procedures used by the public university to dismiss a student accorded with procedural due process. *Board of Curators of Univ. of Mo. v. Horowitz*, 435 U.S. 78, 85 (1978); *see Tigrett v. Univ. of Va.*, 290 F.3d 620, 627 (4th Cir. 2002) ("[t]he Supreme Court has assumed, without actually deciding, that university students possess a 'constitutionally protectible right' in their continued enrollment in

a university"); *see also Univ. of Mich. v. Ewing*, 474 U.S. 214, 223 (1985) (assuming without deciding that a medical student had a property interest that gave rise to a substantive due process right to continued enrollment free from arbitrary state action).

The circuits are not uniform in ruling whether such a liberty or property interest exists. In *Hennessy v. City of Melrose*, 194 F.3d 237, 249–50 (1st Cir. 1999), the First Circuit reasoned that the "theoretical underpinnings" of a student's property interest "are shaky":

> The Supreme Court has not yet decided whether a student at a state university has a constitutionally protected property interest in continued enrollment ... [T]he claim to such a property interest is dubious ... and in this case it seems especially tenuous because Salem State did not expel the appellant, but merely precluded him from continuing in a particular program. In an abundance of caution, however, we assume for argument's sake that the appellant possessed a constitutionally protected property interest in completing the teacher certification program.

Compare Gorman v. Univ. of R.I., 837 F.2d 7, 12 (1st Cir. 1988) (public university student's "interest in pursuing an education is included within the fourteenth amendment's protection of liberty and property") and *Flaim v. Medical College of Ohio*, 418 F.3d 629, 633 (6th Cir. 2005) ("the Due Process Clause is implicated by higher education disciplinary decisions") with *Monroe v. Ark. State Univ.*, 495 F.3d 591, 594 (8th Cir. 2007) (assuming without deciding that nursing graduate student's "interest in pursuing his education constitutes a constitutionally protected interest"); *McGee v. Schoolcraft Cmty. Coll.*, 167 Fed. Appx. 429, 437 (6th Cir. 2006) ("whether a student's interest in continued enrollment at a post-secondary institution is protected by procedural due process has not been resolved"); *Fenje v. Feld*, 398 F.3d 620, 624, 627 (7th Cir. 2005) (where unchallenged, assuming existence of property interest in medical student's continued participation in residency program and liberty interest in pursuit of occupation and being free from stigmatizing dismissal); *Pugel v. Bd. of Trustees of the Univ. of Ill.*, 378 F.3d 659, 662 n.2 (7th Cir. 2004) ("open question" in Seventh Circuit "whether a college or university student has a property interest in enrollment" but assuming that physics graduate student dismissed as a student and teaching assistant for academic dishonesty had a liberty interest protected by due process); *Williams v. Wendler*, 530 F.3d 584, 589–90 (7th Cir. 2008) (affirming dismissal of due process claim by college sorority students suspended for injuring pledge in hazing ritual because students did not prove a property interest, such as a contractual "entitlement not to be suspended without good cause").

2. As noted above in the context of employment, damage to a graduate student's reputation, without more, is not a legally cognizable deprivation of a liberty interest. *See Tigrett v. Univ. of Va.*, 290 F.3d 620, 628 (4th Cir. 2002) ("an injury to reputation alone does not deprive an individual of a constitutionally protected liberty interest"); *Parker v. Duffey*, 251 Fed. Appx. 879, 883 (5th Cir. 2007) (same); *cf. Pugel*, 378 F.3d at 662 n.2 (assuming existence of liberty interest where graduate student was dismissed from her position as student and teaching assistant on charges of academic misconduct).

3. However, a student may have a liberty interest in pursuing a chosen occupation and damage to a student's reputation, if coupled with other evidence, may be a deprivation of that liberty interest. Relying in part on *Olivieri*, the stigma-plus case excerpted above, the Seventh Circuit recently held that a public university student adequately alleged that the university had deprived him of a protected liberty interest—his freedom to pursue a Navy career. *Doe v. Purdue Univ.*, 928 F.3d 652, 659–661 (7th Cir. 2019).

John Doe adequately alleged he had suffered "stigma-plus"; that is, the public university inflicted harm to his reputation by wrongfully labeling him a sex offender and changing his legal status by suspending him, thereby causing him to lose his Navy ROTC scholarship and precluding him from pursuing his chosen occupation. The Court rejected the university's argument that John did not allege "stigma" because John had authorized the university to disclose John's disciplinary record to the Navy.

The Seventh Circuit reasoned that Purdue, the public university:

> [is] trying to draw an analogy between John and a plaintiff who publishes damaging information about himself—because it is true that a plaintiff can't himself spill the beans and then blame the defendant for ruining his reputation. [In *Olivieri*, we held] that a plaintiff who publicizes negative information about himself cannot establish that the *defendant* deprived him of a liberty interest.... John's case is different. He does not claim simply that he might someday have to self-publish the guilty finding to future employers. Instead, John says that he had an obligation to authorize Purdue to disclose the proceedings to the Navy ... In contrast to *Olivieri*, where disclosure was voluntary and speculative, [here] it was compelled and certain.... [U]nlike in *Olivieri*, the disclosure was not self-published—it came from the defendant, even if the plaintiff had been obligated to authorize it ... [H]ere[,] Purdue, not John, revealed to the Navy that it had found him guilty of sexual violence, and John had a legal obligation to authorize the disclosure.
>
> Thus, if what John says is true, the university has stigmatized him by telling the Navy about the guilty finding ... John [also has alleged] that the stigma was accompanied by a change in legal status ... After conducting an adjudicatory proceeding, Purdue formally determined that John was guilty of a sexual offense. That determination changed John's status: he went from a full-time student in good standing to one suspended for an academic year.... And it was this official determination of guilt, not the preceding charges or any accompanying rumors, that allegedly deprived John of occupational liberty. It caused his expulsion from the Navy ROTC program (with the accompanying loss of scholarship) and foreclosed the possibility of his re-enrollment in it.

Purdue Univ., 928 F.3d at 662–63.

4. While graduate students in public schools who are sanctioned for academic reasons are entitled to less procedural protection than students sanctioned for disciplinary reasons, sometimes it is difficult to categorize the sanction. For example, in *Monroe v.*

Arkansas State University, a medical student took a leave of absence because of a drug abuse problem. 495 F.3d 591, 593 (8th Cir. 2007). The student received a grade of "incomplete," which ultimately led to his failure and dismissal from the program. *Id.* The court held that because the "incomplete" and subsequent failure was the basis of the plaintiff's claims, the dismissal was academic. *Id.* at 595. "[C]ourts have considered dismissals 'academic' in similar scenarios when the student's deficiencies, while arguably warranting disciplinary action, also bear on academic performance." *Id.* Similarly, in *Fenje v. Feld*, a medical student was terminated for "lack of candor" after the school discovered that he had lied on his medical school application and in his admission interview. 398 F.3d 620, 622 (7th Cir. 2005). The dismissal was held to be academic because the school stated the student's dishonesty would undermine his ability to be a credible source of information to patients and "[t]he nexus between Dr. Fenje's lack of candor in the application process and his capacity to be trusted with patient care clearly pushes this decision into the realm of an academic dismissal." *Id.* at 625–26.

When a student challenges an academic sanction, courts generally defer to the judgment of educators, and only informal procedures are required. Assuming there is a protected property or liberty interest, for an academic sanction to satisfy due process: (1) the student must have notice of the school's dissatisfaction with his or her academic progress, and (2) the decision to impose sanctions must be "careful and deliberate." *Univ. of Mo. v. Horowitz*, 435 U.S. 78, 85 (1978). Informal notice is sufficient. In *Monroe v. Arkansas State University*, 495 F.3d 591, 595 (8th Cir. 2007), the court held that the student's ability to log onto the school's web page and view his grade of "incomplete" constituted sufficient notice that he was in danger of failing and being dismissed. *Id.* at 595; *see Rogers v. Tenn. Bd. of Regents*, 273 Fed. Appx. 458, 462 (6th Cir. 2008) (notice was sufficient where instructor's evaluations conveyed dissatisfaction with student's work).

Similarly, informal fact-finding procedures satisfy the requirement of careful and deliberate decision-making, and a formal hearing is not required. *See, e.g., Trotter v. Univ. of N.M.*, 219 F.3d 1179, 1185 (10th Cir. 2000) ("the due process clause does not require that a student dismissed ... for academic reasons be given a hearing.") (citing *Horowitz*, 435 U.S. at 86–90). In *Fenje v. Feld*, where a medical student was dismissed for dishonesty in the application process, an academic dismissal, no pre- or post-termination hearing was required, and the student received more process than required because he was told of the medical school's concerns, he explained his position orally and in writing, the school was "careful and deliberate" in reaching its decision, and the student received both a post-termination hearing and an administrative appeal. 398 F.3d at 626. Similarly, in *Monroe*, where the dismissed student sent and received emails from school officials and had an informal meeting with them, the court held that even though an academic dismissal did not entitle the student to a hearing, the student in fact had received a hearing via the "conversations and interviews," including the emails. 495 F.3d at 596; *see Senu-Oke v. Jackson State Univ.*, 283 Fed. Appx. 236, 240 (5th Cir. 2008) (student dismissed from graduate program was not entitled to a face-to-face meeting and, whether dismissal was academic or disciplinary, opportunity to explain his position in emails and letters satisfied due process).

Practice Pointer

To research the current status of procedural due process protections for liberty or property interests in the relevant jurisdiction, generally it is more efficient to begin by reviewing sources that have done some of the research for your client. Before searching online for specific decisions, consider consulting some of the following published resources to learn the vocabulary of the field, to identify current debates, and to collect current citations. Review the Practice Pointers that conclude Chapters 2 and 6 for several helpful treatises that focus on constitutional litigation.

Articles in American Law Reports often contain summaries of a particular aspect of a legal claim, accompanied by practical suggestions and citations to relevant cases organized by jurisdiction. *See, e.g.*, James L. Buchwalter, *Application of Stigma-Plus Due Process Claims to Education Context*, 41 A.L.R. 6th 391 (2009 and updated weekly). Continuing legal education materials also identify current issues and supply recent citations to binding law. Westlaw's *Practical Law* series includes short overviews of frequently litigated claims. *See, e.g., Section 1983: Procedural Due Process Land Use Claims*, Government Practice: State & Local/Liability & Litigation/Practice Note (Maintained).

All of the above may be available on electronic databases, depending on your employer's subscriptions. Federal model jury instructions often include citations to current authority from the relevant jurisdiction and are another source that can help you research more efficiently. Jury instructions often are available directly from the website of the relevant federal circuit. Once you have located relevant, binding authority, be sure to update those sources via Shepard's on Lexis Advance or Lexis or Keycite on Westlaw Edge to confirm their accuracy and to locate additional, more recent authority.

Questions to guide reading of *Nicholas*

1. *Nicholas* is not a procedural due process decision but is included here to illustrate how procedural and substantive due process differ. What was plaintiff's substantive due process claim?
2. Why did the Third Circuit hold that plaintiff's property interest in public employment was not entitled to substantive due process protection; that is, that government action depriving a person of a property interest in public employment would be upheld as long as the state satisfies procedural due process?
3. If you represented Dr. Nicholas, how would you explain the ruling to your client?
4. *Nicholas* is an example of a failed attempt to expand an employee's due process protections. What factors do you think influenced plaintiff's counsel

in choosing to pursue this litigation strategy? If you had represented Dr. Nicholas, would you have made the same strategic decision?

Nicholas v. Pa. State Univ.

227 F.3d 133 (3d Cir. 2000)

ALITO, Circuit Judge:

Appellant, Dr. W. Channing Nicholas, was fired from his tenured professorship at Pennsylvania State University following a series of run-ins with his new supervisor.... [H]e claims that his tenured professorship was a property interest entitled to protection under the substantive component of the Due Process Clause....

...

I. A.

Nicholas claims that defendants violated the substantive component of the Fourteenth Amendment's Due Process Clause by firing him for an arbitrary, irrational, or improper reason. The chief issue in the appeal concerns whether Nicholas's property interest in his tenured professorship was entitled to substantive due process protection. We hold that it was not, and accordingly affirm the District Court's dismissal of his substantive due process claim.

...

As this Court has previously observed, substantive due process "is an area of law 'famous for controversy, and not known for its simplicity.'" ... Part of this conceptual confusion may arise from the fact that the fabric of substantive due process, as woven by our courts, encompasses at least two very different threads. Before ruling on Nicholas's claim, then, we will attempt to untwist this tangled skein.

The first thread of substantive due process applies when a plaintiff challenges the validity of a *legislative* act.[1] Typically, a legislative act will withstand substantive due process challenge if the government "identifies a legitimate state interest that the legislature could rationally conclude was served by the statute," although legislative acts that burden certain "fundamental" rights may be subject to stricter scrutiny....

The second thread of substantive due process, as identified by this Court, protects against certain types of *non-legislative* state action. Of course, the Due Process Clause's

---

1. It is crucial to keep in mind the distinction between legislative acts and non-legislative or executive acts. As we have previously explained, "[e]xecutive acts, such as employment decisions, typically apply to one person or to a limited number of persons, while legislative acts, generally laws and broad executive regulations, apply to large segments of society." *Homar v. Gilbert*, 89 F.3d 1009, 1027 (3d Cir. 1996) (Alito, J., concurring in part and dissenting in part); *see also McKinney v. Pate*, 20 F.3d 1550, 1557 n.9 (11th Cir. 1994).

primary protection against the arbitrary exercise of power by government officials is its requirement of fair procedures—that is, of procedural due process. This Court has nevertheless held that a non-legislative government deprivation "that comports with procedural due process may still give rise to a substantive due process claim 'upon allegations that the government deliberately and arbitrarily abused its power.'" *Indep. Enters. Inc. v. Pittsburgh Water & Sewer Auth.*, 103 F.3d 1165, 1179 (3d Cir. 1997) ... *see also Boyanowski v. Capital Area Intermediate Unit*, 215 F.3d 396, 399 (3d Cir. 2000) ("The substantive component of the Due Process Clause limits what governments may do regardless of the fairness of procedures that it employs, and covers government conduct in both legislative and executive capacities."). Accordingly, we have held that a property interest that falls within the ambit of substantive due process may not be taken away by the state for reasons that are "arbitrary, irrational, or tainted by improper motive," or by means of government conduct so egregious that it "shocks the conscience," *Boyanowski*, 215 F.3d 396, 401 (quoting *County of Sacramento v. Lewis*, 523 U.S. 833, 846 (1998)).

To prevail on a non-legislative substantive due process claim, "a plaintiff must establish as a threshold matter that he has a protected property interest to which the Fourteenth Amendment's due process protection applies." ... The text of the Fourteenth Amendment speaks of "property" without qualification, and it is well-settled that state-created property interests, including some contract rights, are entitled to protection under the procedural component of the Due Process Clause.... However, "not all property interests worthy of procedural due process protection are protected by the concept of substantive due process." Rather, to state a substantive due process claim, "a plaintiff must have been deprived of a *particular quality* of property interest." ...

On past occasion, we have lamented that "the case law of this circuit and the Supreme Court provides very little guidance as to what constitutes this 'certain quality' of property interest worthy of protection under the substantive due process clause." ... Nevertheless, we believe that a careful review of the case law does reveal one guiding principle: whether a certain property interest embodies this "particular quality" is not determined by reference to state law, but rather depends on whether that interest is "fundamental" under the United States Constitution. *See Regents of Univ. of Michigan v. Ewing*, 474 U.S. 214, 229 (1985) (Powell, J., concurring).... Justice Powell explained this distinction in his *Ewing* concurrence:

> Even if one assumes the existence of a property right ... not every such right is entitled to the protection of substantive due process. While property interests are protected by procedural due process even though the interest is derived from state law rather than the Constitution, substantive due process rights are created only by the Constitution.
>
> The history of substantive due process "counsels caution and restraint." The determination that a substantive due process right exists is a judgment that "'certain interests require particularly careful scrutiny of the state needs asserted to justify their abridgment.'" In the context of liberty interests, this Court has been careful to examine each asserted interest to determine whether

> it "merits" the protection of substantive due process. "Each new claim to [substantive due process] protection must be considered against a background of Constitutional purposes, as they have been rationally perceived and historically developed."
>
> The interest asserted by respondent [in continued university enrollment] is essentially a state-law contract right. It bears little resemblance to the fundamental interests that previously have been viewed as implicitly protected by the Constitution. It certainly is not closely tied to "respect for the teachings of history, solid recognition of the basic values that underlie our society, and wise appreciation of the great roles that the doctrines of federalism and separation of powers have played in establishing and preserving American freedoms." For these reasons, briefly summarized, I do not think the fact that Michigan may have labeled this interest "property" entitles it to join those other, far more important interests that have heretofore been accorded the protection of substantive due process.

Ewing, 474 U.S. at 229–30 (Powell, J., concurring) (citations omitted).

Following Justice Powell, this Circuit has adopted an approach to substantive due process that focuses on the nature of the property interest at stake. By way of illustration, we have so far limited non-legislative substantive due process review to cases involving real property ownership ("[land] ownership is a property interest worthy of substantive due process protection").

...

Heedful of the Supreme Court's admonition that we should exercise "utmost care whenever we are asked to break new ground in this field," *Collins v. City of Harker Heights*, 503 U.S. 115, 124 (1992), we have been reluctant to extend substantive due process protection to other, less fundamental property interests.... [W]e held that a service contract with the state failed to merit substantive due process protection ... [and] that a state-law entitlement to water and sewer services was not protected by the Due Process Clause's substantive component:

> Substantive due process refers to and protects federal rights. The provision of water and sewer services, whether by a municipality or by a private utility company, is not, however, a federally protected right. The legal fact that, once a municipality (or, for that matter, a private utility company) establishes a utility for its citizens, a citizen's expectation of receiving that service rises to the level of a property interest cognizable under the Due Process Clause, merely brings that expectation within the compass of the Fourteenth Amendment's procedural protection.... It does not transform that expectation into a substantive guarantee against the state in any circumstance.

[citation omitted].

...

Other cases have made explicit the requirement that a property interest must be constitutionally "fundamental" in order to implicate substantive due process.... [T]his

Court, citing Justice Powell's concurrence in *Ewing*, opined that a graduate student's interest in continued academic enrollment "bore 'little resemblance to the fundamental interests that previously had been viewed as implicitly protected by the Constitution.'" ... (quoting *Ewing*, 474 U.S. at 229 (Powell, J., concurring)). And, in *Independent Enterprises Inc. v. Pittsburgh Water & Sewer Authority*, we held that a low bidder's entitlement to state contract "is not the sort of 'fundamental' interest entitled to the protection of substantive due process." 103 F.3d [1165,] 1179 [(3d Cir. 1997)]. Distinguishing earlier cases containing "language indicating that substantive due process is violated whenever a governmental entity deliberately or arbitrarily abuses government power," the *Independent Enterprises* court explained that

> all of the cases involved zoning decisions, building permits, or other governmental permission required for some intended use of land owned by the plaintiffs, matters which were recognized in [an earlier 3d Circuit decision] as implicating the "fundamental" property interest in the ownership of land. Thus, in light of the court's explicit statement ... that some "particular quality of property interest" must be infringed before substantive due process protection may be invoked, these cases cannot be understood as affording substantive due process protection from every arbitrary and irrational governmental act, but *only for those that deprive the plaintiff of a fundamental property right "implicitly protected by the Constitution."*

103 F.3d at 1179 n.12 (citations omitted) (emphasis added).

To summarize: when a plaintiff challenges the validity of a legislative act, substantive due process typically demands that the act be rationally related to some legitimate government purpose. In contrast, when a plaintiff challenges a non-legislative state action (such as an adverse employment decision), we must look, as a threshold matter, to whether the property interest being deprived is "fundamental" under the Constitution. If it is, then substantive due process protects the plaintiff from arbitrary or irrational deprivation, regardless of the adequacy of procedures used. If the interest is not "fundamental," however, the governmental action is entirely outside the ambit of substantive process and will be upheld so long as the state satisfies the requirements of procedural due process.

With this framework in mind, we turn to whether Nicholas's tenured public employment is a fundamental property interest entitled to substantive due process protection. We hold that it is not, and thereby join the great majority of courts of appeals that have addressed this issue. [citing cases from the Eighth, Eleventh, Sixth, Fourth, Second, Seventh, and Ninth Circuits]. *But see Newman v. Massachusetts*, 884 F.2d 19, 25 (1st Cir. 1989) ("school authorities who make an arbitrary and capricious decision significantly affecting a tenured teacher's employment status are liable for a substantive due process violation").

Nicholas's tenured public employment is a wholly state-created contract right; it bears little resemblance to other rights and property interests that have been deemed fundamental under the Constitution. We agree ... that "it cannot be reasonably maintained that public employment is a property interest that is deeply rooted in the Nation's history and traditions." Nor does public employment approach the interests "'implicit in the concept of ordered liberty like personal choice in matters of marriage and family.'" *See also Collins*, 503 U.S. at 128 ("state law, rather than the Federal Constitution, governs the substance of the employment relationship"). Accordingly, we view public employment as more closely analogous to those state-created property interests that this Court has previous deemed unworthy of substantive due process[2] than to the venerable common-law rights of real property ownership....

Our decision also comports with the Supreme Court's admonition that the federal judiciary should not become a general court of review for state employment decisions:

> The federal court is not the appropriate forum in which to review the multitude of personnel decisions that are made daily by public agencies. We must accept the harsh fact that numerous individual mistakes are inevitable in the day-to-day administration of our affairs. The United States Constitution cannot feasibly be construed to require federal judicial review for every such error.... The Due Process Clause of the Fourteenth Amendment is not a guarantee against incorrect or ill-advised personnel decisions.

Bishop v. Wood, 426 U.S. 341, 359–60 (1976).

...

2. Enforcement of Restraining Orders

In *DeShaney v. Winnebago County*, 489 U.S. 189 (1989), the Supreme Court held that the substantive component of the Due Process Clause does not "requir[e] the State to protect the life, liberty, and property of its citizens against invasion by private actors." However, the Court declined to decide whether the child might have a property interest in child protective services; that is, whether state "child protection statutes gave [the child] an 'entitlement' to receive protective services in accordance with the terms of the statute, an entitlement which would enjoy due process protection...." *Id.* at 195, n.2. The Court decided a related issue in *Castle Rock v. Gonzales*, 545 U.S. 748 (2005), which can be read as a creative effort to circumvent *DeShaney*'s holding. Professor Laura Oren explains the connection to *DeShaney*:

> In *Castle Rock*, "the Court overruled an effort made by the state legislature to avoid the strictures of [substantive due process ruling in] *DeShaney* and the difficulties of proving the [substantive due process] state-created danger doctrine by taking another tack ... The *Castle Rock* district court dismissed claims based on substantive due process (state-created danger) and procedural due process, but the Tenth Circuit, in a panel decision, and then on rehearing en banc, was willing to let the procedural claim go forward ... Although only

2. [Citing cases concerning low bidder's entitlement to a state construction contract, contractor's right to payment for services rendered to the state, tenant's state law entitlement to sewer and water services, and graduate student's interest in continued studies at a state university.]

> the procedural part of the case was taken to rehearing and to the high Court, explicitly or implicitly a lot of the conversation was about *DeShaney* and the no affirmative duty paradigm."

Laura Oren, *Some Thoughts on the State-Created Danger Doctrine:* DeShaney *is Still Wrong and* Castle Rock *is More of Same*, 6 TEMP. POL. & CIV. RTS. L. REV. 47, 58–59 (2006).

In reading the *Castle Rock* materials below, keep in mind the Justice Department report from Chapter 6, which stated that in 2002 police academies required a median of 12 hours of domestic violence training (compared with, for example, 11 hours of constitutional law).[5]

Question to guide reading of *Castle Rock* facts

The facts of *Castle Rock* are taken from the Supreme Court majority opinion. According to the Complaint, how many times did Jessica Gonzales telephone or speak in person to police between 7:30 p.m. and 1:50 a.m. on the night her children were murdered?

Castle Rock v. Gonzales

545 U.S. 748 (2005)

SCALIA, J., delivered the opinion of the Court.

The horrible facts of this case are contained in the complaint.... Because the case comes to us on appeal from a dismissal of the complaint, we assume its allegations are true. Respondent alleges that petitioner, the town of Castle Rock, Colorado, violated the Due Process Clause of the Fourteenth Amendment to the United States Constitution when its police officers, acting pursuant to official policy or custom, failed to respond properly to her repeated reports that her estranged husband was violating the terms of a restraining order.

The restraining order ... issued by a state trial court several weeks earlier in conjunction with respondent's divorce proceedings ... commanded [Jessica Gonzalez's husband] not to "molest or disturb the peace of [respondent] or of any child," and to remain at least 100 yards from the family home at all times. The bottom of the pre-printed form noted that the reverse side contained "IMPORTANT NOTICES FOR RESTRAINED PARTIES AND LAW ENFORCEMENT OFFICIALS." ... The preprinted text on the back of the form included the following "**WARNING:**"

> "**A KNOWING VIOLATION OF A RESTRAINING ORDER IS A CRIME....** A VIOLATION WILL ALSO CONSTITUTE CONTEMPT OF COURT. **YOU MAY BE ARRESTED** WITHOUT NOTICE IF A LAW ENFORCEMENT OF-

---

5. MATTHEW J. HICKMAN, U.S. DEP'T JUST., OFFICE OF. JUSTICE PROGRAMS, BUREAU OF JUST. STAT., STATE AND LOCAL LAW ENFORCEMENT TRAINING ACADEMIES, 2002 at Table 16, p. 9 (Jan. 2005, NCJ 204030), http://bjs.ojp.usdoj.gov/content/pub/pdf/slleta02.pdf.

FICER HAS PROBABLE CAUSE TO BELIEVE THAT YOU HAVE KNOWINGLY VIOLATED THIS ORDER."

The preprinted text on the back of the form also included a "**NOTICE TO LAW ENFORCEMENT OFFICIALS**," which read in part:

"YOU SHALL USE EVERY REASONABLE MEANS TO ENFORCE THIS RESTRAINING ORDER. YOU SHALL ARREST, OR, IF AN ARREST WOULD BE IMPRACTICAL UNDER THE CIRCUMSTANCES, SEEK A WARRANT FOR THE ARREST OF THE RESTRAINED PERSON WHEN YOU HAVE INFORMATION AMOUNTING TO PROBABLE CAUSE THAT THE RESTRAINED PERSON HAS VIOLATED OR ATTEMPTED TO VIOLATE ANY PROVISION OF THIS ORDER AND THE RESTRAINED PERSON HAS BEEN PROPERLY SERVED WITH A COPY OF THIS ORDER OR HAS RECEIVED ACTUAL NOTICE OF THE EXISTENCE OF THIS ORDER."

On June 4, 1999, the state trial court modified the terms of the restraining order and made it permanent. The modified order gave respondent's husband the right to spend time with his three daughters (ages 10, 9, and 7) on alternate weekends, for two weeks during the summer, and, "'upon reasonable notice,'" for a mid-week dinner visit "'arranged by the parties'" [and] to visit the home to collect the children....

According to the complaint, at about 5 or 5:30 p.m. on ... June 22, 1999, respondent's husband took the three daughters while they were playing outside the family home. No advance arrangements had been made for him to see the daughters.... When respondent noticed the children were missing, she suspected her husband had taken them. At about 7:30 p.m., she called the Castle Rock Police Department, which dispatched two officers. The complaint continues: "When [the officers] arrived..., she showed them a copy of the TRO and requested that it be enforced and the three children be returned to her immediately. [The officers] stated that there was nothing they could do about the TRO and suggested that [respondent] call the Police Department again if the three children did not return home by 10:00 p.m."

At approximately 8:30 p.m., respondent talked to her husband on his cellular telephone. He told her "he had the three children [at an] amusement park in Denver." She called the police again and asked them to "have someone check for" her husband or his vehicle at the amusement park and "put out an [all points bulletin]" for her husband, but the officer with whom she spoke "refused to do so," again telling her to "wait until 10:00 p.m. and see if" her husband returned the girls.

At approximately 10:10 p.m., respondent called the police and said her children were still missing, but she was now told to wait until midnight. She called at midnight and told the dispatcher her children were still missing. She went to her husband's apartment and, finding nobody there, called the police at 12:10 a.m.; she was told to wait for an officer to arrive. When none came, she went to the police station at 12:50 a.m. and submitted an incident report. The officer who took the report "made no reasonable effort to enforce the TRO or locate the three children. Instead, he went to dinner."

At approximately 3:20 a.m., respondent's husband arrived at the police station and opened fire with a semiautomatic handgun he had purchased earlier that evening. Police shot back, killing him. Inside the cab of his pickup truck, they found the bodies of all three daughters, whom he already had murdered.

Questions to guide reading of *Amici Brief*

1. According to the Amici brief, both the statute and the order leave too much discretion to police for Ms. Gonzales to have a property interest. What examples of police discretion does the brief provide?
2. Even if there were a property interest, why do Amici argue that the police action here—answering the phone and listening to Ms. Gonzales—was all the process that was due? Do you agree?

Brief of Denver Police Protective Ass'n, et al. as Amici Curiae in *Castle Rock v. Gonzales*

2004 WL 3007307 (Dec. 13, 2004)

The Denver Police Protective Association, the Peace Officers Research Association of California Legal Defense Fund, and the Colorado Association of Chiefs of Police in Support of Petitioner by Julie C. Tolleson, David J. Bruno, Jeffrey J. Clayton & Michael T. Lowe.

. . .

SUMMARY OF ARGUMENT

In 1964, Charles Reich wrote: "We must create a new property." Charles A. Reich, *The New Property*, 73 YALE L.J. 733, 787 (1964). Reich's call to the Courts focused on the rising need to protect "privileges," created by a state statute, which were replacing traditional forms of property. He wrote:

> Society today is built around entitlements.... Many of the most important of these entitlements now flow from government.... Such sources of security, whether private or public, are no longer regarded as luxuries or gratuities; to the recipients they are essentials, fully deserved, and in no sense a form of charity.

Charles A. Reich, *Individual Rights and Social Welfare: The Emerging Legal Issues*, 74 YALE L.J. 1245, 1255 (1965).

Five years after its publication, Reich's article was cited with approval by a majority of this Court.... [T]his Court held that a determination of whether a right was sufficient to give rise to constitutionally adequate procedures did not depend on the distinction of whether such benefit was a right or a privilege. *Goldberg v. Kelly*, 397 U.S.

254, 262–63 (1970). Rather, the Court held that John Kelly had a property interest in continued welfare payments, the denial of which required pre-deprivation process consistent with the Fourteenth Amendment. Two years thereafter, in … *Board of Regents v. Roth*, 408 U.S. 564 (1972) … this Court held that a right to continued employment is, under certain circumstances, a property right which cannot be denied absent constitutionally sufficient procedures.…

This Court continued to recognize these "new" property rights over the course of the 1970s. As noted by the *en banc* panel of the Tenth Circuit, this Court has recognized that a person may have a property interest in professional licenses, driver's licenses, receipt of utility services, and disability benefits, *Gonzales v. City of Castle Rock*, 366 F.3d 1093 (10th Cir. 2004) (*en banc*) (citation omitted).… These interests, once thought merely privileges, have been recognized as property rights that cannot be denied absent constitutionally adequate procedures.

Today, the Court is asked to decide whether the Tenth Circuit *en banc* majority was correct in expanding this "new property" to the "reasonable" police enforcement of a domestic restraining order.… Once the emotion generated by the [undeniably tragic] facts is set aside, the inescapable conclusion is that the Plaintiff in this case has no constitutional right to any pre-deprivation procedure.… [T]he statute and restraining order at issue cannot create a reasonable expectation of a property right because too much is left to official discretion … [and] the legislative history does not suggest that the General Assembly intended to create a property right.

Finally … [i]f allowed to stand, the Tenth Circuit's analysis would dictate that certain tasks performed by public employees are not discretionary, but rather are mandatory, thus requiring a "street-level" pre-deprivation hearing. Such a requirement would bring government operations to a halt at the most basic level. The confusion created by this decision, if affirmed, will wreak its greatest havoc on the streets, where emergencies constantly force reallocation of scarce public safety resources.

ARGUMENT

…

I. Police Officers Have Discretion Under C.R.S. § 18-6-803.5 and the Court Order to Decide Whether to Arrest and When to Seek a Warrant, Thus Negating Any Reasonable Expectation of Enforcement of the Order Sufficient to be Termed Property Under *Roth*

The Tenth Circuit's analysis … would require District Courts to hold that many of the discretionary, executive functions engaged in by public employees actually create an expectation in members of the public that those duties are absolute.…

The Tenth Circuit in this case held that a determination of probable cause does not involve discretion. In passing, the Court says, "the officer is required to arrest or to seek a warrant to arrest the offending party." … While making a determination of probable cause could be said to be governed by objective predicates … [t]he determination of probable cause is not, in short, the *only* decision an officer has discretion to make under the statute and court order. The remaining discretion available to officers with no particularized predicates voids any notion that the statute and order confer a property interest.

First, the order and statute at issue leave to the officer's discretion the determination of whether the suspect "knowingly" violated the order, *Gonzales*, 366 F.3d at 1103. Certainly, making such a finding is discretionary, and no objective standards for rendering this decision are found.

Secondly, the restraining order is not clear as to what an official is required to do when the suspect is not in a location known to the police at the time the allegations against the suspect are made. Obviously, if officers do not know the location of the suspect, they cannot arrest him. The officers in the instant case had no information on the whereabouts of the suspect until 8:30 pm. At that time they discovered that the suspect was not in their jurisdiction.... Their decisions, at that point, were entirely discretionary under the language of the statute and order.

Even when the officers became aware of the suspect's location, their only defined duty was to "seek" a warrant for his arrest.... (citing C.R.S. § 18-6-803.5). The *en banc* panel noted that the officers were only under a duty to "use every reasonable means of enforcing the order." ... Under the language of the statute, officers have ultimate discretion to determine what is "reasonable" in any given instance. This discretion is broadened when the suspect's whereabouts are unknown or the suspect is known to be in another jurisdiction.

...

Further, the court order and statute at issue leave it up to officer discretion as to *when* such officer will "seek" an arrest warrant. C.R.S. § 18-6-803.5. Presumably, the officers in this case would have sought such an arrest warrant from a court had the suspect not violently ended his own life. The statute or order does not require the officer to *immediately* or *forthwith* obtain an arrest warrant if an arrest cannot be made. As such, a person can have no expectation as to *when* such an order will be sought, and thus can have no property interest of which she may be deprived.

In addition, the order and statute clearly contemplate that an officer will exercise his or her discretion as to whether to arrest since the statute permits officers to decide not to arrest if making an arrest would be "impracticable." C.R.S. § 18-6-803.5(3)(b).... An officer can thus refuse to arrest under the statute if he or she determines that it would be impracticable, inconvenient or difficult to arrest under the circumstances. There are no objective predicates set forth by the statute. The absence of such predicates defeats any expectation that the order or statute could confer a property right.

Ultimately, there is no way to assess what the officers were required to do in this instance. Officers were allegedly required to arrest. How could they arrest when the whereabouts of the suspect were unknown both to the officers and to Ms. Gonzales? The Officers were required to use every reasonable means to bring the suspect to justice, but were barred by State law from pursuing the suspect outside of their jurisdiction. Officers can, under the terms of the order and statute, simply refuse to arrest if doing so would be impracticable, inconvenient, or difficult. If Officers cannot arrest, they must seek a warrant. The statute or court order, however, does not require them to do so immediately. In short, the statute leaves far too much discretion to police officials to be considered a property right under ... *Roth*.

...

II. Assuming, *arguendo*, Plaintiffs Established That a Property Right Was Denied by Town of Castle Rock Officers, Plaintiffs Received All of the Process They Were Due Under the Constitution

In this case, the procedures employed were sufficient such that the constitution did not require more procedure than that which was supplied, *i.e.*, the opportunity to be heard in person and by phone, the opportunity to relate the facts as you know them, and the opportunity to make specific demands for action.

...

[T]he officers, as alleged in the complaint, took a restraining order call from Ms. Gonzales and went to her home. This seems a procedure suited for the circumstance. The Town offered Ms. Gonzales the opportunity to present her evidence in person to Town officials.

[O]n the facts plead, it is clear that Ms. Gonzales was heard: she expressed her complaint to officers in person at her home. She presented all of the evidence she had at that time, to which the officers listened. The suspect was not at the home, no one knew where he and the children were, and so the Officers went back to their duty. Then, as Ms. Gonzales learned more information, she shared that information with the police, who again heard it. This new information revealed that the suspect was in another jurisdiction. The process provided was ongoing.

Questions to guide reading of *Amici Brief*

1. Note that a law school clinic co-authored the brief below. What does the identity of the clients suggest about the diversity of views among law enforcement on the best practices in enforcing domestic violence restraining orders?
2. Why do Amici argue that the Court need not decide whether Ms. Gonzales had a protected property interest in the arrest of her estranged husband?
3. According to Amici, how does the legislative history of the Colorado statute demonstrate intent to confer an expectation of safety on recipients of protective orders?
4. How do Amici argue that the protection order created a property interest in enforcement of its terms? Why do Amici argue that police retention of discretion to choose means of enforcement and assess probable cause is consistent with creation of a property interest?
5. Would it be easy to distinguish between "lip service" and a police reaction that Amici would consider constitutional, such as the process outlined by the Tenth Circuit?

6. If assessment of probable cause and communication of an adverse decision is the process required, was the police response here all the process that was due?

Brief of National Black Police Ass'n, et al. as Amici Curiae in *Castle Rock v. Gonzales*

2005 WL 328203 (Feb. 10, 2005)

National Black Police Association, National Association of Black Law Enforcement Officers, Women in Federal Law Enforcement, the National Center for Women & Policing, and Americans for Effective Law Enforcement, Inc., ... Supporting Respondent by Joan S. Meier ... Domestic Violence, Legal Empowerment and Appeals Project, George Washington University Law School, Richard W. Smith, Francine A. Hochberg and Richard L. Sloane.

...

INTEREST OF THE AMICI CURIAE

Amici are law enforcement membership and educational organizations. They ... believe that, if the allegations in this case are correct, the conduct of the Castle Rock Police Department fell far beneath acceptable police standards. Amici seek to inform this Court about the widely recognized and adopted standard practices utilized by police around the country in responding to domestic violence, and to emphasize that the constitutional procedures adopted here would establish only a minimal floor that is far less burdensome than the "best practices" already typically employed by law enforcement in domestic violence cases.

...

ARGUMENT

...

II. COLORADO VESTED RESPONDENT WITH A PROPERTY INTEREST IN ENFORCEMENT OF HER PROTECTION ORDER.

The state of Colorado conferred upon Respondent a protected property interest in police enforcement of her protection order. The interest originated in Colorado law—which requires that police enforce domestic violence protection orders—and was bestowed upon Respondent individually when a Colorado court determined that her estranged husband posed a threat to her and her children and issued to her a protection order with explicit instructions to police and notice to her that it must be enforced.

A person obtains a property interest in a state benefit when she has "a legitimate claim of entitlement to it." [*Board of Regents v.*] *Roth*, 408 U.S. [564,] 577 [1972]. The touchstone of entitlement is mutual expectation.... *Vitek* [*v. Jones*], 445 U.S. [480,] 489 [(1980)]("justifiable expectations"); *see also Roth*, 408 U.S. at 577 ("more than a unilateral expectation"). States may create entitlements for a particular class of individuals if they define benefits and purposefully guide their officials to distribute those benefits to the class. *See Roth*, 408 U.S. at 577.... States do not create entitlements if they merely allow officials to award or deny benefits "for whatever reason or for no reason at all." *Olim v. Wakinekoba*, 461 U.S. 238 (1983) (quotation marks and citation omitted); *see also Cleveland Bd. of Educ. v. Loudermill*, 470 U.S. 532, 543–44 & n.9 (1985) (recognizing property interest despite discretion).

A. Colorado Law Explicitly Mandates Enforcement of Protection Orders.

Colorado law authorizes courts to issue protection orders in family cases and unambiguously requires state police to enforce them.... Once the state court awarded the protection order to Respondent and the order was served on Mr. Gonzales, its enforcement was made mandatory by Section 18-6-803.5.... That section requires that "[a] peace officer *shall* use *every* reasonable means to enforce a restraining order." *See id.* § 18-6-803.5(a) (emphasis added).

Petitioner and the United States contend that, despite the express terms of the statute, it does not create any mandatory benefit. This contention is unavailing....

[]Petitioner and its supporting amici wrongly frame this case as concerning an entitlement to "arrest." ... In fact, Respondent's claim is for "every reasonable means to enforce" the protection order.... "Enforcement," as used in the Colorado statute, may include arrest, and often must. But it may alternatively or additionally include obtaining a warrant or securing children. While amici believe an arrest was in fact mandated here, this Court need not decide whether Respondent had a protected property interest in an arrest *per se*. If, as the *en banc* court of appeals found, the state created an entitlement to "enforcement," regardless of the means chosen to effect it, she stated a claim.

...

[T]he legislative history of the statute confirms that the enforcement provisions are mandatory. The Colorado legislature adopted the mandatory enforcement statute specifically to protect women and children (such as Respondent) against abusive spouses and to remedy the police's long history of refusing to intervene on behalf of victims of domestic violence.... In 1994, when the mandatory enforcement provisions were enacted, it was understood that domestic violence was "the single largest cause of injury to women in the United States, more common than auto accidents, muggings, and rapes combined." *See* ... Colo. Rev. Stat. § 18-6-801.5 (finding that "domestic violence is frequently cyclical in nature, involves patterns of abuse, and can consist of harm with escalating levels of seriousness"). Colorado's criminal justice system was seen by the statutes' primary sponsors in the legislature as inconsistent and flawed. *See* Hearings, supra ... (statement of Rep. Kerns, sponsor) ("[T]he entire criminal justice system must act in a consistent manner, which does not now occur."). The legislature "wanted to put together a bill that would really attack the domestic violence problems ... and that is that the perpetrator has to be held accountable for his actions, and that the victim needs to be made to feel safe." *Id.* The legislature's solution, among other things, was to mandate enforcement of protection orders, thereby purposefully and intentionally empowering protected parties with the expectation of safety and statutorily reversing the history of police indifference. *See id.* ("The police must make probable cause arrests. The prosecutors must prosecute every case.")[.]

...

In short, if the Colorado domestic violence statute, with its plain meaning and clear legislative purpose, does not mandate enforcement, it is difficult to imagine how a state legislature could ever do so.

B. The Protection Order Personally Defined Respondent's Enforcement Right.

Respondent had a property right in enforcement because the Colorado protection order personally defined for her an otherwise general right of police enforcement. *See* ... *Coffman v. Wilson Police Dep't*, 739 F. Supp. 257, 264–65 (E.D. Pa. 1990) (finding that ordinarily "the duty to protect is owed by a municipality to the citizenry as a whole, rather to any individual," but "the orders of court create a property interest in police enforcement that is cognizable under *Roth*").

...

Respondent was entitled to rely on the order, the essence of which was enforcement. *See Roth*, 408 U.S. at 577 ("[I]t is a purpose of the ancient institution of property to protect those claims upon which people rely in their daily lives, reliance that must not be arbitrarily undermined."). Indeed, both the police and the courts regularly instruct victims of domestic violence that protection orders will entitle them to increased police protection, and victims typically rely on this expectation....

The Respondent's protection order evinced a judicial determination that she was within the class of persons entitled to receive the statutory benefit of enforcement. Once that individualized determination was made, it could not be withdrawn without adequate procedures.

...

C. Respondent's Property Interest Is Not Defeated by the Police's Limited Discretion.

Petitioner ... and the United States ... argue that police retain significant discretion under the statute for three reasons: 1) police discretion cannot be eliminated even by statutory mandates; 2) the statute itself contemplates substantial police discretion; and 3) a probable cause determination requires some discretion. These arguments vastly overstate whatever discretion remains in this purposefully mandatory statute, and underestimate the amount of discretion needed to defeat an entitlement.

First, the idea that police always retain discretion derives largely from treatises discussing only traditional criminal statutes using "shall." ... [Those are unlike] domestic violence enforcement statutes such as Colorado's, which were enacted for the specific purpose of eliminating the police's infamous history of abusing their discretion by failing to enforce protection orders.

...

Second, Petitioner conflates the Colorado statute's various *means* (which include arrest, warrant, etc.) with its singular *end* (which in accordance with the plain language and legislative intent, is unambiguously to enforce protection orders by "every reasonable means"). Petitioner argues that the phrase "every reasonable means" contemplates discretion and that the police must use discretion to decline arrests when violations are *de minimis*. *See* Pet. Br. 28 ("step back" order in response to restrained person stepping one yard inside restricted zone). In objectively *de minimis* situations, arrest may or may not be required. But that does not dilute the absolute requirement of "*enforcement*," and the word "every" which precedes it makes clear that "enforcement" is absolutely required. In short, whatever discretion the police possess with respect to the statute is constrained to selecting the means but not the end of enforcement. This is directly analogous to cases involving property rights (*e.g.* public education), where discretion to choose precise means (curricula) are left to decisionmakers (individual teachers), but the entitlement (education) is required. *See, e.g.*, *Goss v. Lopez*, 419 U.S. 565, 573–74 (1975).

...

Third, contrary to Petitioner's claim, the probable cause determination, while sometimes requiring the exercise of limited discretion, does not undermine the entitlement. This Court routinely finds protected interests arising out of state statutes and policies that allow much more discretion than whatever discretion is implicit in a probable cause determination. In *Loudermill*, for example, the Court noted that an Ohio statute "plainly" created a property interest in continued public employment, despite the fact that it allowed removal for subjective "incompetency, inefficiency, dishonesty, ... immoral conduct, insubordination, discourteous treatment ... or any other failure of good behavior." *Cleveland Bd. of Educ. v. Loudermill*, 470 U.S. at 538–39 & n.4 (1985). The Court expressly acknowledged that the decisionmaker retained "discretion" under the statute, and that the issues raised by *Loudermill* were "subjective." *Id.* at 543–44 & n.9.

...

III. RESPONDENT WAS DENIED CONSTITUTIONAL DUE PROCESS, EVEN THOUGH IT COULD EASILY HAVE BEEN PROVIDED.

A. Respondent's Pleas For Enforcement Were Arbitrarily Ignored Without Meaningful Process.

The essence of Respondent's complaint is that Petitioner arbitrarily ignored Respondent without employing *any valid process at all*.... Petitioner did not truly engage in an "informal consultation" with Respondent (who was "the principal or only witness available to police at the time"), nor did Petitioner make "an initial enforcement decision" after meaningfully considering her request.... Despite Respondent's five calls in five hours and midnight visit to the police station, Petitioner merely turned her away, telling Respondent that "there was nothing they could do" and to "call back later."

...

While it is true that Petitioner repeatedly took Respondent's calls, ... and that Petitioner allowed Respondent to file an incident report, ... those reflexive responses do not equate with genuine "process." They were mere lip service.... This historic police practice of ignoring and putting off victims of domestic violence is well-recognized, and is precisely why enforcement statutes like Colorado's are mandatory.

B. The *Mathews* Factors Weigh Heavily In Favor Of Requiring Minimal Procedural Safeguards.

...

The Court below held that due process in these circumstances requires the following: an objective, reasoned consideration of the complaint; an assessment of probable cause; a decision; and if adverse, notice to the complainant of the decision and the reasons.... These minimal steps appropriately balance the factors that this Court outlined in *Mathews* [*v. Eldridge*, 424 U.S. 319, 333 (1976)]: (i) the private interest at stake; (ii) the risk of an erroneous deprivation and probable value of additional safeguards; and (iii) the government's interest.

The Private Interest At Stake: ... Protective orders can quite literally save lives, if enforced. Once enforcement is denied, the damage caused to the victim may be permanent—no amount of retroactive relief will remedy her loss. *See Mathews*, 424 U.S. at 341 (weighing risk that denial "may deprive the eligible recipient of the very means by which to live while he waits").

The Risk of Erroneous Deprivation: This factor requires the Court to assess the extent to which the procedures actually employed by the state risk an erroneous decision. *Id.* Insofar as the Complaint alleges that Petitioner ignored Respondent's repeated pleas for assistance and gave no serious consideration to enforcement of her order ... the risk of error implicit in these non-"procedures" is unquestionably substantial.

...

Probable Value of Additional Safeguards: The procedures adopted by the *en banc* court of appeals are minimal, requiring no more than that which police are ordinarily expected to do in virtually any case: listen, give objective and unbiased consideration to the facts, make a decision about probable cause, and inform the complainant.... By requiring a decision to be made and expressly communicated to the complainant, it would require the police to treat her complaint as a potential crime and to assess probable cause. And by requiring the explanation for a decision against enforcement, it would allow the complainant to correct any misapprehensions and potentially seek supervisory review.

...

The Government's Interest: ... The state of Colorado has already ... adopt[ed] the mandatory enforcement statute.... A proactive police response is in states' interests because it deters future violence and reduces repeat domestic violence calls, thereby reducing the massive costs that future domestic violence incidents would impose.

...

Police practices adopted all over the country and championed by leading national law enforcement organizations ... recommend or mandate arrest where there is probable cause to believe a crime has been committed;[23] require police to locate the suspect when he is absent; and require police to file a detailed investigation report, regardless of whether an arrest is made. Notably, because violators of protection orders present a heightened danger to their victims, and because it is critical to enforce protection orders, those models that address violations of protection orders agree that when non-contact provisions of a protective order are violated, *arrest is required.*

...

Thus, while common police protocols require arrest, thorough probable cause assessments, detailed reporting, and follow-up when a suspect is absent, the Tenth Circuit's view of the Due Process Clause requires only reasoned consideration of the complaint, assessment of probable cause, and notice of the decision. The constitutionally sufficient procedures adopted by the *en banc* court are minimal—virtually trivial—in comparison to standard domestic violence police practices....

Questions to guide reading of *Castle Rock*

1. According to the majority, what is the significance of traditionally permitting law enforcement to exercise discretion?
2. Even if the statute could be construed as making enforcement of the restraining order mandatory, why does the majority suggest that such a construction would not mean that state law gave Ms. Gonzales an entitlement to enforcement of the mandate?
3. Does Section C of the majority opinion suggest that a state legislature could never enact a statute creating a property interest in enforcement of a restraining order?
4. What does it mean for the benefit of the government's enforcement action to be indirect and incidental?
5. Does the majority's view concede that the statute requires some enforcement? If the majority had characterized the property interest as a right to "some enforcement" as opposed to a "right to arrest," would the result have been different?
6. Under the concurrence's view, could a state legislature ever enact a statute creating a property interest in enforcing a restraining order?
7. According to the dissent, what is the significance of the legislative history of the Colorado statute, especially with regard to the traditional presumption of police discretion?
8. How does the dissent characterize the asserted property interest?

---

23. [Citing domestic violence guidelines from at least 12 states or cities.]

Town of Castle Rock v. Gonzales

545 U.S. 748 (2005)

SCALIA, J., delivered the opinion of the Court.

We decide in this case whether an individual who has obtained a state-law restraining order has a constitutionally protected property interest in having the police enforce the restraining order when they have probable cause to believe it has been violated. [The facts appear above.]

...

On rehearing *en banc*, a divided court ... conclud[ed] that respondent had a "protected property interest in the enforcement of the terms of her restraining order" and that the town had deprived her of due process because "the police never 'heard' nor seriously entertained her request to enforce and protect her interests in the restraining order." We granted certiorari.

II

Respondent [Gonzalez] claims ... she had a property interest in police enforcement of the restraining order against her husband; and that the town deprived her of this property without due process by having a policy that tolerated nonenforcement of restraining orders.

...

The procedural component of the Due Process Clause does not protect everything that might be described as a "benefit": "To have a property interest in a benefit, a person clearly must have more than ... a unilateral expectation of it. He must, instead, have a legitimate claim of entitlement to it." *Board of Regents of State Colleges v. Roth*, 408 U.S. 564, 577 (1972). Such entitlements are " 'of course, ... not created by the Constitution. Rather, they are created and their dimensions are defined by existing rules or understandings that stem from an independent source such as state law.' " ... (quoting *Roth*, *supra*, at 577).

A

Our cases recognize that a benefit is not a protected entitlement if government officials may grant or deny it in their discretion ... The Court of Appeals in this case determined that Colorado law created an entitlement to enforcement of the restraining order because the "court-issued restraining order ... specifically dictated that its terms must be enforced" and a "state statute command[ed]" enforcement of the order when certain objective conditions were met (probable cause to believe that the order had been violated and that the object of the order had received notice of its existence)....

We will not, of course, defer to the Tenth Circuit on the ultimate issue: whether what Colorado law has given respondent constitutes a property interest for purposes of the Fourteenth Amendment. That determination, despite its state-law underpinnings, is ultimately one of federal constitutional law.

...

B

The critical language in the restraining order came not from any part of the order itself ... but from the preprinted notice to law-enforcement personnel that appeared on the back of the order. That notice effectively restated the statutory provision describing "peace officers' duties" ... as follows:

> "(a) Whenever a restraining order is issued, the protected person shall be provided with a copy of such order. *A peace officer shall use every reasonable means to enforce a restraining order.*
>
> "(b) *A peace officer shall arrest, or, if an arrest would be impractical under the circumstances, seek a warrant for the arrest of a restrained person* when the peace officer has information amounting to probable cause that:
>
> > "(I) The restrained person has violated or attempted to violate any provision of a restraining order; and
> >
> > "(II) The restrained person has been properly served with a copy of the restraining order or the restrained person has received actual notice of the existence and substance of such order.
>
> "(c) ... *A peace officer shall enforce a valid restraining order whether or not there is a record of the restraining order in the registry.*" Colo. Rev. Stat. § 18-6-803.5(3) (Lexis 1999) (emphases added).

The Court of Appeals concluded that this statutory provision-especially taken in conjunction with a statement from its legislative history,[6] ... established the Colorado Legislature's clear intent "to alter the fact that the police were not enforcing domestic abuse retraining orders," and thus its intent "that the recipient of a domestic abuse restraining order have an entitlement to its enforcement." Any other result, it said, "would render domestic abuse restraining orders utterly valueless."

This last statement is sheer hyperbole. Whether or not respondent had a right to enforce the restraining order, it rendered certain otherwise lawful conduct by her husband both criminal and in contempt of court. *See* §§ 18-6-803.5(2)(a), (7). The creation of grounds on which he could be arrested, criminally prosecuted, and held in contempt was hardly "valueless"—even if the prospect of those sanctions ultimately failed to prevent him from committing three murders and a suicide.

We do not believe that these provisions of Colorado law truly made enforcement of restraining orders *mandatory*. A well established tradition of police discretion has long coexisted with apparently mandatory arrest statutes.

...

---

6. The Court of Appeals quoted one lawmaker's description of how the bill "'would really attack the domestic violence problems'":

> "'[T]he entire criminal justice system must act in a consistent manner, which does not now occur. The police must make probable cause arrests. The prosecutors must prosecute every case....'" "'[T]he entire system must send the same message ... [that] violence is criminal. And so we hope that House Bill 1253 starts us down this road.'"

[A] true mandate of police action would require some stronger indication from the Colorado Legislature than "shall use every reasonable means to enforce a restraining order" (or even "shall arrest ... or ... seek a warrant"), §§ 18-6-803.5(3)(a), (b).... It is hard to imagine that a Colorado peace officer would not have some discretion to determine that—despite probable cause to believe a restraining order has been violated—the circumstances of the violation or the competing duties of that officer or his agency counsel decisively against enforcement in a particular instance. The practical necessity for discretion is particularly apparent in a case such as this one, where the suspected violator is not actually present and his whereabouts are unknown....

The dissent correctly points out that, in the specific context of domestic violence, mandatory-arrest statutes have been found in some States to be more mandatory than traditional mandatory-arrest statutes. The Colorado statute mandating arrest for a domestic-violence offense is different from but related to the one at issue here, and it includes similar though not identical phrasing. Even in the domestic-violence context, however, it is unclear how the mandatory-arrest paradigm applies to cases in which the offender is not present to be arrested. As the dissent explains, much of the impetus for mandatory-arrest statutes and policies derived from the idea that it is better for police officers to arrest the aggressor in a domestic-violence incident than to attempt to mediate the dispute or merely to ask the offender to leave the scene. Those other options are only available, of course, when the offender is present at the scene.

...

Respondent does not specify the precise means of enforcement that the Colorado restraining-order statute assertedly mandated—whether her interest lay in having police arrest her husband, having them seek a warrant for his arrest, or having them "use every reasonable means, up to and including arrest, to enforce the order's terms," Brief for Respondent 29–30.[9] Such indeterminacy is not the hallmark of a duty that is mandatory. Nor can someone be safely deemed "entitled" to something when the identity of the alleged entitlement is vague. *See Roth*, 408 U.S., at 577 (considering whether "certain benefits" were "secure[d]" by rule or understandings). The dissent, after suggesting various formulations of the entitlement in question,[10] ultimately contends that the obligations under the statute were quite precise: either make an arrest

---

9. Respondent characterizes her entitlement in various ways. *See* Brief for Respondent 12 ("'entitlement' to receive protective services"); ("interest in police enforcement action"); ("specific government benefit" consisting of "the government service of enforcing the objective terms of the court order protecting her and her children against her abusive husband"); ("[T]he restraining order here mandated the arrest of Mr. Gonzales under specified circumstances, or at a minimum required the use of reasonable means to enforce the order").

10. *See* [*supra* at 2813–24] ("entitlement to police protection"); ("entitlement to mandatory individual protection by the local police force"); ("a right to police assistance"); ("a citizen's interest in the government's commitment to provide police enforcement in certain defined circumstances"); ("respondent's property interest in the enforcement of her restraining order"); (the "service" of "protection from her husband"); ("interest in the enforcement of the restraining order").

or (if that is impractical) seek an arrest warrant.... The problem with this is that the seeking of an arrest warrant would be an entitlement to nothing but procedure—which we have held inadequate even to support standing ...; much less can it be the basis for a property interest.... After the warrant is sought, it remains within the discretion of a judge whether to grant it, and after it is granted, it remains within the discretion of the police whether and when to execute it.[11] Respondent would have been assured nothing but the seeking of a warrant. This is not the sort of "entitlement" out of which a property interest is created.

Even if the statute could be said to have made enforcement of restraining orders "mandatory" because of the domestic-violence context of the underlying statute, that would not necessarily mean that state law gave *respondent* an entitlement to *enforcement* of the mandate. Making the actions of government employees obligatory can serve various legitimate ends other than the conferral of a benefit on a specific class of people. *See, e.g.*, *Sandin v. Conner*, 515 U.S. 472, 482 (1995) (finding no constitutionally protected liberty interest in prison regulations phrased in mandatory terms, in part because "[s]uch guidelines are not set forth solely to benefit the prisoner"). The serving of public rather than private ends is the normal course of the criminal law because criminal acts, "besides the injury [they do] to individuals, ... strike at the very being of society...." 4 W. Blackstone, Commentaries on the Laws of England 5 (1769)....

Respondent's alleged interest stems only from a State's *statutory* scheme—from a restraining order that was authorized by and tracked precisely the statute on which the Court of Appeals relied. She does not assert that she has any common-law or contractual entitlement to enforcement. If she was given a statutory entitlement, we would expect to see some indication of that in the statute itself. Although Colorado's statute spoke of "protected person[s]" such as respondent, it did so in connection with matters other than a right to enforcement. It said that a "protected person shall be provided with a copy of [a restraining] order" ...; that a law enforcement agency "shall make all reasonable efforts to contact the protected party upon the arrest of the restrained person," ... [and] most importantly, the statute spoke directly to the protected person's power to "initiate contempt proceedings against the restrained person if the order [was] issued in a civil action or request the prosecuting attorney to initiate contempt proceedings if the order [was] issued in a criminal action." § 18-6-803.5(7). The protected person's express power to "initiate" civil contempt proceedings contrasts tellingly with the mere ability to "request" initiation of criminal contempt proceedings—and even more dramatically with the complete silence about any power to "request" (much less demand) that an arrest be made.

The creation of a personal entitlement to something as vague and novel as enforcement of restraining orders cannot "simply g[o] without saying." *Post*, at 2821,

---

11. The dissent asserts that the police would lack discretion in the execution of this warrant, *post*, at 2820, n.12, but cites no statute mandating immediate execution. The general Colorado statute governing arrest provides that police "may arrest" when they possess a warrant "commanding" arrest. Colo. Rev. Stat. § 16-3-102(1) (Lexis 1999).

n.16 (STEVENS, J., dissenting). We conclude that Colorado has not created such an entitlement.

C

Even if we were to think otherwise concerning the creation of an entitlement by Colorado, it is by no means clear that an individual entitlement to enforcement of a restraining order could constitute a "property" interest for purposes of the Due Process Clause. Such a right would not, of course, resemble any traditional conception of property. Although that alone does not disqualify it from due process protection, as *Roth* and its progeny show, the right to have a restraining order enforced does not "have some ascertainable monetary value," as even our "*Roth*-type property-as-entitlement" cases have implicitly required.…[12] Perhaps most radically, the alleged property interest here arises *incidentally*, not out of some new species of government benefit or service, but out of a function that government actors have always performed—to wit, arresting people who they have probable cause to believe have committed a criminal offense.

The indirect nature of a benefit was fatal to the due process claim of the nursing-home residents in *O'Bannon v. Town Court Nursing Center*, 447 U.S. 773 (1980). We held that, while the withdrawal of "direct benefits" (financial payments under Medicaid for certain medical services) triggered due process protections, *id.*, at 786–787, the same was not true for the "indirect benefit[s]" conferred on Medicaid patients when the Government enforced "minimum standards of care" for nursing-home facilities, *id.*, at 787. "[A]n indirect and incidental result of the Government's enforcement action … does not amount to a deprivation of any interest in life, liberty, or property." *Ibid.* In this case, as in *O'Bannon*, "[t]he simple distinction between government action that directly affects a citizen's legal rights … and action that is directed against a third party and affects the citizen only indirectly or incidentally, provides a sufficient answer to" respondent's reliance on cases that found government-provided services to be entitlements. *Id.*, at 788.

III

We conclude, therefore, that respondent did not, for purposes of the Due Process Clause, have a property interest in police enforcement of the restraining order against her husband. It is accordingly unnecessary to address … [whether] the town's custom

12. The dissent suggests that the interest in having a restraining order enforced does have an ascertainable monetary value, because one may "contract with a private security firm … to provide protection" for one's family.… Respondent probably could have hired a private firm to guard her house, to prevent her husband from coming onto the property, and perhaps even to search for her husband after she discovered that her children were missing. Her alleged entitlement here, however, does not consist in an abstract right to "protection," but (according to the dissent) in enforcement of her restraining order through the arrest of her husband, or the seeking of a warrant for his arrest, after she gave the police probable cause to believe the restraining order had been violated. A private person would not have the power to arrest under those circumstances because the crime would not have occurred in his presence. Colo. Rev. Stat. § 16-3-201 (Lexis 1999). And, needless to say, a private person would not have the power to obtain an arrest warrant.

or policy prevented the police from giving her due process when they deprived her of that alleged interest....

In light of today's decision and that in *DeShaney*, the benefit that a third party may receive from having someone else arrested for a crime generally does not trigger protections under the Due Process Clause, neither in its procedural nor in its "substantive" manifestations. This result reflects our continuing reluctance to treat the Fourteenth Amendment as " 'a font of tort law,' " *Parratt v. Taylor*, 451 U.S. 527, 544 (1981) ... but it does not mean States are powerless to provide victims with personally enforceable remedies. Although the framers of the Fourteenth Amendment and the Civil Rights Act of 1871, 17 Stat. 13 (the original source of § 1983), did not create a system by which police departments are generally held financially accountable for crimes that better policing might have prevented, the people of Colorado are free to craft such a system under state law. *Cf. DeShaney*, 489 U.S., at 203.

...

Justice SOUTER, with whom Justice BREYER joins, concurring.

I agree with the Court that Jessica Gonzales has shown no violation of an interest protected by the Fourteenth Amendment's Due Process Clause, and I join the Court's opinion.... Gonzales's claim of a property right ... runs up against police discretion in the face of an individual demand to enforce, and discretion to ignore an individual instruction not to enforce (because, say, of a domestic reconciliation); no one would argue that the beneficiary of a Colorado order like the one here would be authorized to control a court's contempt power or order the police to refrain from arresting. These considerations argue against inferring any guarantee of a level of protection or safety that could be understood as the object of a "legitimate claim of entitlement," *Roth*, 408 U.S. 564, 577, in the nature of property arising under Colorado law. Consequently, the classic predicate for federal due process protection of interests under state law is missing....

[Gonzales's] argument is unconventional because the state-law benefit for which it claims federal procedural protection is itself a variety of procedural regulation, a set of rules to be followed by officers exercising the State's executive power: use all reasonable means to enforce, arrest upon demonstrable probable cause, get a warrant, and so on.

When her argument is understood as unconventional in this sense, a further reason appears for rejecting its call to apply *Roth*, a reason that would apply even if the statutory mandates to the police were absolute, leaving the police with no discretion when the beneficiary of a protective order insists upon its enforcement. The Due Process Clause extends procedural protection to guard against unfair deprivation by state officials of substantive state-law property rights or entitlements; the federal process protects the property created by state law. But Gonzales claims a property interest in a state-mandated process in and of itself. This argument is at odds with the rule that "[p]rocess is not an end in itself. Its constitutional purpose is to protect a substantive interest to which the individual has a legitimate claim of entitlement." *Olim v.*

Wakinekona, 461 U.S. 238, 250 (1983).... In putting to rest the notion that the scope of an otherwise discernible property interest could be limited by related state-law procedures, this Court observed that "[t]he categories of substance and procedure are distinct.... 'Property' cannot be defined by the procedures provided for its deprivation." *Cleveland Bd. of Ed. v. Loudermill*, 470 U.S. 532, 541 (1985). Just as a State cannot diminish a property right, once conferred, by attaching less than generous procedure to its deprivation, *ibid.*, neither does a State create a property right merely by ordaining beneficial procedure unconnected to some articulable substantive guarantee. This is not to say that state rules of executive procedure may not provide significant reasons to infer an articulable property right meant to be protected; but it is to say that we have not identified property with procedure as such. State rules of executive procedure, however important, may be nothing more than rules of executive procedure.

Thus, in every instance of property recognized by this Court as calling for federal procedural protection, the property has been distinguishable from the procedural obligations imposed on state officials to protect it. Whether welfare benefits, *Goldberg v. Kelly*, 397 U.S. 254 (1970), attendance at public schools, *Goss v. Lopez*, 419 U.S. 565 (1975), utility services, *Memphis Light, Gas & Water Div. v. Craft*, 436 U.S. 1 (1978), public employment, *Perry v. Sindermann*, 408 U.S. 593 (1972), professional licenses, *Barry v. Barchi*, 443 U.S. 55 (1979), and so on, the property interest recognized in our cases has always existed apart from state procedural protection before the Court has recognized a constitutional claim to protection by federal process. To accede to Gonzales's argument would therefore work a sea change in the scope of federal due process, for she seeks federal process as a substitute simply for state process. (And she seeks damages under ... 42 U.S.C. § 1983, for denial of process to which she claimed a federal right.) There is no articulable distinction between the object of Gonzales's asserted entitlement and the process she desires in order to protect her entitlement; both amount to certain steps to be taken by the police to protect her family and herself. Gonzales's claim would thus take us beyond *Roth* or any other recognized theory of Fourteenth Amendment due process, by collapsing the distinction between property protected and the process that protects it, and would federalize every mandatory state-law direction to executive officers whose performance on the job can be vitally significant to individuals affected.

The procedural directions involved here are just that. They presuppose no enforceable substantive entitlement, and *Roth* does not raise them to federally enforceable status in the name of due process.

Justice STEVENS, with whom Justice GINSBURG joins, dissenting.

The issue presented to us is ... whether the restraining order entered by the Colorado trial court on June 4, 1999, created a "property" interest that is protected from arbitrary deprivation by the Due Process Clause of the Fourteenth Amendment.

It is perfectly clear, on the one hand, that neither the Federal Constitution itself, nor any federal statute, granted respondent or her children any individual entitlement to police protection. *See DeShaney v. Winnebago County Dept. of Social Servs.*, 489

U.S. 189 (1989). Nor, I assume, does any Colorado statute create any such entitlement for the ordinary citizen. On the other hand, it is equally clear that federal law imposes no impediment to the creation of such an entitlement by Colorado law. Respondent certainly could have entered into a contract with a private security firm, obligating the firm to provide protection to respondent's family; respondent's interest in such a contract would unquestionably constitute "property" within the meaning of the Due Process Clause. If a Colorado statute enacted for her benefit, or a valid order entered by a Colorado judge, created the functional equivalent of such a private contract by granting respondent an entitlement to mandatory individual protection by the local police force, that state-created right would also qualify as "property" entitled to constitutional protection.

I do not understand the majority to rule out the foregoing propositions, although it does express doubts....

III

Three flaws in the Court's rather superficial analysis of the merits highlight the unwisdom of its decision to answer the state-law question *de novo*. First, the Court places undue weight on the various statutes throughout the country that seemingly mandate police enforcement but are generally understood to preserve police discretion. As a result, the Court gives short shrift to the unique case of "mandatory arrest" statutes in the domestic violence context; States passed a wave of these statutes in the 1980's and 1990's with the unmistakable goal of eliminating police discretion in this area. Second, the Court's formalistic analysis fails to take seriously the fact that the Colorado statute at issue in this case was enacted for the benefit of the narrow class of persons who are beneficiaries of domestic restraining orders, and that the order at issue in this case was specifically intended to provide protection to respondent and her children. Finally, the Court is simply wrong to assert that a citizen's interest in the government's commitment to provide police enforcement in certain defined circumstances does not resemble any "traditional conception of property"; in fact, a citizen's property interest in such a commitment is just as concrete and worthy of protection as her interest in any other important service the government or a private firm has undertaken to provide.

In 1994, the Colorado General Assembly passed omnibus legislation targeting domestic violence. The part of the legislation at issue in this case mandates enforcement of a domestic restraining order upon probable cause of a violation, § 18-6-803.5(3), while another part directs that police officers "shall, without undue delay, arrest" a suspect upon "probable cause to believe that a crime or offense of domestic violence has been committed," § 18-6-803.6(1). In adopting this legislation, the Colorado General Assembly joined a nationwide movement of States that took aim at the crisis of police underenforcement in the domestic violence sphere by implementing "mandatory arrest" statutes. The crisis of underenforcement had various causes, not least of which was the perception by police departments and police officers that domestic violence was a private, "family" matter and that arrest was to be used as a last resort.... In response ..."many states enacted mandatory arrest statutes under which a police officer must arrest an abuser when the officer has probable cause to believe that a domestic assault has occurred or that a protection order has been violated." ... [The purpose was] to "counter police resistance to arrests in domestic violence cases by removing or restricting police officer discretion; mandatory arrest policies would increase police response and reduce batterer recidivism."

Thus, when Colorado passed its statute in 1994, it joined the ranks of 15 States that mandated arrest for domestic violence offenses and 19 States that mandated arrest for domestic restraining order violations....

Given the specific purpose of these statutes, there can be no doubt that the Colorado Legislature used the term "shall" advisedly in its domestic restraining order statute. While "shall" is probably best read to mean "may" in other Colorado statutes that seemingly mandate enforcement, *cf.* Colo. Rev. Stat. § 31-4-112 (Lexis 2004) (police "*shall suppress* all riots, disturbances and breaches of the peace, *shall apprehend* all disorderly persons in the city ..." it is clear that the elimination of police discretion was integral to Colorado and its fellow States' solution to the problem of underenforcement in domestic violence cases. Since the text of Colorado's statute perfectly captures this legislative purpose, it is hard to imagine what the Court has in mind when it insists on "some stronger indication from the Colorado Legislature."

While Colorado case law does not speak to the question, it is instructive that other state courts interpreting their analogous statutes have not only held that they eliminate the police's traditional discretion to refuse enforcement, but have also recognized that they create rights enforceable against the police under state law. For example, in *Nearing v. Weaver*, 295 Or. 702, 670 P.2d 137 (1983) (*en banc*), the court held that although the common law of negligence did not support a suit against the police for failing to enforce a domestic restraining order, the statute's mandatory directive formed the basis for the suit because it was "a specific duty imposed by statute for the benefit of individuals previously identified by judicial order." *Id.*, at 707. [citing similar holdings from Tennessee, New Jersey, and Washington courts].... To what extent the Colorado Supreme Court would agree with the views of these courts is, of course, an open question, but it does seem rather brazen for the majority to assume that the Colorado Supreme Court would repudiate this consistent line of persuasive authority from other States.

Indeed, the Court fails to come to terms with the wave of domestic violence statutes that provides the crucial context for understanding Colorado's law. The Court concedes that, "in the specific context of domestic violence, mandatory-arrest statutes have been found in some States to be more mandatory than traditional mandatory-arrest statutes," ... but that is a serious understatement. The difference is not a matter of degree, but of kind. Before this wave of statutes, the legal rule was one of discretion; as the Court shows, the "traditional," general mandatory arrest statutes have always been understood to be "mandatory" in name only.... The innovation of the domestic violence statutes was to make police enforcement, not "more mandatory," but simply *mandatory*. If, as the Court says, the existence of a protected "entitlement" turns on whether "government officials may grant or deny it in their discretion," ... the new mandatory statutes undeniably create an entitlement to police enforcement of restraining orders.

Perhaps recognizing this point, the Court glosses over the dispositive question—whether the police enjoyed discretion to deny enforcement—and focuses on a different question—which "precise means of enforcement," were called for in this case. But that question is a red herring. The statute directs that, upon probable cause of a violation, "a peace officer shall arrest, or, if an arrest would be impractical under the circumstances, seek a warrant for the arrest of a restrained person." Colo. Rev. Stat. § 18-6-803.5(3)(b) (Lexis 1999). Regardless of whether the enforcement called for in this case was arrest or the seeking of an arrest warrant (the answer to that question probably changed over the course of the night as the respondent gave the police more information about the husband's whereabouts), the crucial point is that, under the statute, the police were *required* to provide enforcement; *they lacked the discretion to do nothing.*[12] The court suggests that the fact that "enforcement" may encompass different acts infects any entitlement to enforcement with "indeterminacy." But this objection is also unfounded. Our cases have never required the object of an entitlement to be some mechanistic, unitary thing. Suppose a State entitled every citizen whose income was under a certain level to receive health care at a state clinic. The provision of health care is not a unitary thing—doctors and administrators must decide what tests are called for and what procedures are required, and these decisions often involve difficult applications of judgment. But it could not credibly be said that a citizen lacks an entitlement to health care simply because the content of that entitlement is not the same in every given situation. Similarly, the enforcement of a restraining order is not some amorphous, indeterminate thing. Under the statute, if the police have probable cause that a violation has occurred, enforcement consists of either making an immediate arrest or seeking a warrant and then executing an arrest—traditional, well-defined tasks that law enforcement officers perform every day.[13]

---

12. Under the Court's reading of the statute, a police officer with probable cause is mandated to seek an arrest warrant if arrest is "impractical under the circumstances," but then enjoys unfettered discretion in deciding whether to *execute* that warrant. This is an unlikely reading given that the statute was motivated by a profound distrust of police discretion in the domestic violence context and motivated by a desire to improve the protection given to holders of domestic restraining orders. We do not have the benefit of an authoritative construction of Colorado law, but I would think that if an estranged husband harassed his wife in violation of a restraining order, and then absconded after she called the police, the statute would not only obligate the police to seek an arrest warrant, but also obligate them to execute it by making an arrest. In any event, under respondent's allegations, by the time the police were informed of the husband's whereabouts, an arrest was practical and, under the statute's terms, mandatory.

13. The Court wonders "how the mandatory-arrest paradigm applies to cases in which the offender is not present to be arrested." Again, questions as to the *scope* of the obligation to provide enforcement are far afield from the key issue—whether there exists an entitlement to enforcement.... Because the "scene" of the violation was wherever the husband was currently holding the daughters, this case does not implicate the question of an officer's duties to arrest a person who has left the scene and is no longer in violation of the restraining order. Second, to the extent that arresting the husband was initially "impractical under the circumstances" because his whereabouts were unknown, the Colorado

The Court similarly errs in speculating that the Colorado Legislature may have mandated police enforcement of restraining orders for "various legitimate ends other than the conferral of a benefit on a specific class of people." ... While the Court's concern would have some bite were we faced with a broadly drawn statute directing, for example, that the police "*shall suppress* all riots," there is little doubt that the statute at issue in this case conferred a benefit "on a specific class of people"—namely, recipients of domestic restraining orders. Here, respondent applied for and was granted a restraining order from a Colorado trial judge, who found a risk of "irreparable injury" and found that "physical or emotional harm" would result if the husband were not excluded from the family home. As noted earlier, the restraining order required that the husband not "molest or disturb" the peace of respondent and the daughters, and it ordered (with limited exceptions) that the husband stay at least 100 yards away from the family home. *Ibid.* It also directed the police to "use every reasonable means to enforce this ... order," and to arrest or seek a warrant upon probable cause of a violation. Under the terms of the statute, when the order issued, respondent and her daughters became "'protected person[s].'" § 18-6-803.5(1.5)(a) ("'Protected person' means the person or persons identified in the restraining order as the person or persons for whose benefit the restraining order was issued")....[16]

Because the statute's guarantee of police enforcement is triggered by, and operates only in reference to, a judge's granting of a restraining order in favor of an identified "'protected person,'" there is simply no room to suggest that such a person has received merely an "'incidental'" or "'indirect'" benefit. As one state court put it, domestic restraining order statutes "identify with precision when, to whom, and under what circumstances police protection must be afforded. The legislative purpose in requiring the police to enforce individual restraining orders clearly is to protect the named persons for whose protection the order is issued, not to protect the community at large by general law enforcement activity." *Nearing*, 295 Or. at 712....

IV

Given that Colorado law has quite clearly eliminated the police's discretion to deny enforcement, respondent is correct that she had much more than a "unilateral expectation" that the restraining order would be enforced; rather, she had a "legitimate claim of entitlement" to enforcement. *Roth*, 408 U.S., at 577. Recognizing respondent's

---

statute (unlike some other States' statutes) expressly addressed that situation—it *required* the police to seek an arrest warrant....

16. I find it neither surprising nor telling ... that the statute requires the restraining order to contain, "in capital letters and bold print," a "notice" informing protected persons that they can demand or request, respectively, civil and criminal contempt proceedings. § 18-6-803.5(7). While the legislature may have thought that these legal remedies were not popularly understood, a person's right to "demand" or "request" police enforcement of a restraining order simply goes without saying given the nature of the order and its language. Indeed, for a holder of a restraining order who has read the order's emphatic language, it would likely come as quite a shock to learn that she has no right to demand enforcement in the event of a violation....

property interest in the enforcement of her restraining order is fully consistent with our precedent. This Court has "made clear that the property interests protected by procedural due process extend well beyond actual ownership of real estate, chattels, or money." *Id.*, at 571–72. The "types of interests protected as 'property' are varied and, as often as not, intangible, 'relating to the whole domain of social and economic fact.'" *Logan v. Zimmerman Brush Co.*, 455 U.S. 422, 430 (1982). Thus, our cases have found "property" interests in a number of state-conferred benefits and services, including welfare benefits[,] disability benefits[,] public education[,] utility services[,] government employment[,] as well as in other entitlements that defy easy categorization, *see, e.g.*, *Bell v. Burson*, 402 U.S. 535 (1971) (due process requires fair procedures before a driver's license may be revoked pending the adjudication of an accident claim); *Logan*, 455 U.S. at 431 (due process prohibits the arbitrary denial of a person's interest in adjudicating a claim before a state commission).

Police enforcement of a restraining order is a government service that is no less concrete and no less valuable than other government services, such as education. The relative novelty of recognizing this type of property interest is explained by the relative novelty of the domestic violence statutes creating a mandatory arrest duty; before this innovation, the unfettered discretion that characterized police enforcement defeated any citizen's "legitimate claim of entitlement" to this service. Novel or not, respondent's claim finds strong support in the principles that underlie our due process jurisprudence. In this case, Colorado law *guaranteed* the provision of a certain service, in certain defined circumstances, to a certain class of beneficiaries, and respondent reasonably relied on that guarantee. As we observed in *Roth*, "[i]t is a purpose of the ancient institution of property to protect those claims upon which people rely in their daily lives, reliance that must not be arbitrarily undermined." 408 U.S. at 577. Surely, if respondent had contracted with a private security firm to provide her and her daughters with protection from her husband, it would be apparent that she possessed a property interest in such a contract. Here, Colorado undertook a comparable obligation, and respondent—with restraining order in hand—justifiably relied on that undertaking. Respondent's claim of entitlement to this promised service is no less legitimate than the other claims our cases have upheld, and no less concrete than a hypothetical agreement with a private firm. The fact that it is based on a statutory enactment and a judicial order entered for her special protection, rather than on a formal contract, does not provide a principled basis for refusing to consider it "property" worthy of constitutional protection.[20]

---

20. According to Justice SOUTER, respondent has asserted a property interest in merely a "state-mandated process," rather than in a state-mandated "substantive guarantee." This misunderstands respondent's claim.... [I]t is clear that respondent is in fact asserting a substantive interest in the "enforcement of the restraining order." Enforcement of a restraining order is a tangible, substantive act. If an estranged husband violates a restraining order by abducting children, and the police succeed in enforcing the order, the person holding the restraining order has undeniably just received a substantive benefit. As in other procedural due process cases, respondent is arguing that the police officers failed to follow fair procedures in ascertaining whether the statutory criteria that trigger their obligation to provide enforcement—*i.e.*, an outstanding order plus probable cause that it is being violated—

V

Because respondent had a property interest in the enforcement of the restraining order, state officials could not deprive her of that interest without observing fair procedures. Her description of the police behavior in this case and the department's callous policy of failing to respond properly to reports of restraining order violations clearly alleges a due process violation. At the very least, due process requires that the relevant state decisionmaker *listen* to the claimant and then *apply the relevant criteria* in reaching his decision. The failure to observe these minimal procedural safeguards creates an unacceptable risk of arbitrary and "erroneous deprivation[s]," *Mathews*, 424 U.S., at 335. According to respondent's complaint ... the process she was afforded by the police constituted nothing more than a "'sham or a pretense.'" ... Accordingly, I respectfully dissent.

For further discussion

1. After the murders of her children, Jessica Lenahan (formerly Gonzales) created a website in memory of her three daughters that included this photo of the girls.

2. After the *Castle Rock* decision, Jessica Lenahan filed a petition with the Inter-American Commission on Human Rights, represented by the ACLU Women's Rights

---

were satisfied in her case.... It is Justice SOUTER, not respondent, who makes the mistake of "collapsing the distinction between property protected and the process that protects it."

Justice SOUTER also errs in suggesting that respondent cannot have a property interest in enforcement because she would not be authorized to instruct the police to refrain from enforcement in the event of a violation. The right to insist on the provision of a service is separate from the right to refuse the service. For example, compulsory attendance laws deny minors the right to refuse to attend school. Nevertheless, we have recognized that minors have a property interest in public education and that school officials must therefore follow fair procedures when they seek to deprive minors of this valuable benefit through suspension.... In the end, Justice SOUTER overlooks the core purpose of procedural due process—ensuring that a citizen's reasonable reliance is not frustrated by arbitrary government action.

Program, the ACLU Human Rights Program, and Columbia Law School's Human Rights Clinic. The following is an excerpt from her 2007 statement in that proceeding:[6]

> I am a Latina and Native American woman from Pueblo, Colorado.... I married Simon [Gonzales] in 1990 and we moved to Castle Rock, Colorado in 1998. We lived together with our three children—Rebecca, Katheryn, and Leslie—and my son Jessie, from a previous relationship.
>
> Throughout our relationship, Simon was erratic and abusive toward me and our children.... He would break the children's toys and other belongings, harshly discipline the children, threaten to kidnap them, drive recklessly, exhibit suicidal behavior, and verbally, physically, and sexually abuse me. He was heavily involved with drugs. Simon's frightening and destructive behavior got worse and worse as the years went by.... Simon and I separated in 1999....
>
> On May 21, 1999, a Colorado court granted me a temporary restraining order that required Simon to stay at least 100 yards away from me, my home, and the children. The judge told me to keep the order with me at all times, and that the order and Colorado law required the police to arrest Simon if he violated the order. Having this court order relieved some of my anxiety.
>
> But Simon continued to terrorize me and the children even after I got the restraining order. He broke into my house, stole my jewelry, changed the locks on my doors, and loosened my house's water valves, flooding the entire street. I called the Castle Rock Police Department to report these and other violations of the restraining order. The police ignored most of my calls. And when they did respond, they were dismissive of me, and even scolded me for calling them.
>
> ...
>
> On June 4, Simon and I appeared in court, and the judge made the restraining order permanent.... Less than 3 weeks later, Simon violated the restraining order by kidnapping my three daughters from our yard on a day that he wasn't supposed to see the girls. When I discovered they were missing, I immediately called the police, told them that the girls were missing and that I thought Simon had abducted them in violation of a restraining order,

6. Jessica Lenahan, Statement of Jessica Lenahan for Inter-American Commission on Human Rights (Mar. 2, 2007), https://www.law.columbia.edu/sites/default/files/microsites/human-rights-institute/files/Gonzalesdocs/jess%20statement%20to%20iahcr%202008.pdf; *see also* Hearing Before Inter-American Commission on Human Rights (October 2008), https://www.law.columbia.edu/sites/default/files/microsites/human-rights-institute/files/Gonzalesdocs/merits%20hearing%20summary.pdf.

and asked them to find my daughters. The dispatcher told me she would send an officer to my house, but no one came.

I waited almost two hours for the police, and then called the station again. Finally two officers came to my house. I showed them the restraining order and explained that it was not Simon's night to see the girls, but that I suspected he had taken them. The officers said, "Well he's their father, it's okay for them to be with him." And I said, "No, it's not okay. There was no prearranged visit for him to have the children tonight." The officers said there was nothing they could do, and told me to call back at 10 p.m. if the children were still not home. I was flustered and scared. Unsure of what else I could say or do to make the officers take me seriously, I agreed to do what they suggested.

Soon afterwards, Simon's girlfriend called me and told me that Simon called her [and] was threatening to drive off a cliff. She asked him if he had a gun and whether or not he would hurt the children. I began to panic.

I finally reached Simon on his cell phone around 8:30 p.m. He told me he was with the girls at an amusement park in Denver, 40 minutes from Castle Rock. I immediately communicated this information to the police. I was shocked when they responded that there was nothing they could do, because Denver was outside of their jurisdiction. I called back and begged them to put out a missing child alert or contact the Denver police, but they refused. The officer told me I needed to take this matter to divorce court, and told me to call back if the children were not home in a few hours. The officer said to me, "At least you know the children are with their father." I felt totally confused and humiliated.

I called the police again and again that night. When I called at 10 p.m., the dispatcher said to me that I was being "a little ridiculous making us freak out and thinking the kids are gone." ... By midnight ... I called the police again. I could hardly believe it when, *seven hours after my first call to the police*, the dispatcher asked me how many girls were missing and what their ages were. The dispatcher promised to send out an officer, but no one ever arrived. Fighting panic and frustration, I drove to the police station and told yet another officer about the restraining order and that the girls had been gone for seven hours. After I left, that Officer went to a two-hour dinner and never contacted me again.

I asked the police for help nine separate times that night—two times in person and seven times on the phone. The police continued to ignore my cries for help. At 3:25 a.m., Simon's girlfriend called me to tell me that she had been on the phone with Simon when she heard shooting, and that she believed he and the girls were dead. I couldn't believe what she was telling me. I later learned that Simon had killed [my three little girls] earlier that evening.

After hearing about the [police shooting Simon], I drove to the police station. As I attempted to approach Simon's truck, I was taken away by the police and then to the local sheriff's office. Officials refused to give me any information about whether the girls were alive. They ignored my pleas to see my girls.... They detained me in a room for 12 hours and interrogated me throughout the early morning hours, as if I had a role in the children's deaths. They refused to let me see or call my family.... The media knew my girls were dead before my family or I did. I was finally told by state officials around 8 a.m. that Simon had murdered the girls before he arrived at the police station. However, I never learned any other details about how, when, and where the girls died. I continue to seek this information to this day.... My daughters' death certificates and the coroners' reports state no place, date, or time of death.

...

Today, nearly eight years after my tragedy, I continue to seek a thorough investigation into my babies' deaths. I see nothing being done in Castle Rock or nationwide to make police accountable to domestic violence victims. It's like rubbing salt in my wounds.

So why did the police ignore my calls for help? Was it because I was a woman? A victim of domestic violence? A Latina? Because the police were just plain lazy? I continue to seek answers to these questions.

We rely on the courts and the police for protection against violence. But I learned from my tragedy that the police have no accountability. The safety of my children was of such little consequence that the police took no action to protect my babies. If our government won't protect us, we should know that ... we are on our own when our lives are at risk.

Had I known that the police would do nothing to locate Rebecca, Katheryn, and Leslie or enforce my restraining order, I would have taken the situation into my own hands by looking for my children with my family and friends. I might have even bought a gun to protect us from Simon's terror.... But then I might be imprisoned right now. That is the dilemma for abused women in the United States.

After the girls' deaths, I was treated like a leper in my community. My co-workers told me that I did something to deserve what happened to me, that I filed the lawsuit because I was money-hungry, and that I would hurt them as taxpayers.... I have moved away from Colorado to try to escape the painful memories.... I've lost all faith in my government, in the law, and in humanity.

...

I brought this petition to the Inter-American Commission on Human Rights because I have been denied justice in the United States. It's too late for Rebecca, Katheryn, and Leslie but it's not too late to create good law and policies for others. Police have to be required to enforce restraining orders or else these orders are meaningless and give a false sense of security....

3. In 2011, the international court issued its opinion in favor of Jessica Lenahan. The remedy included the Recommendation "[t]o adopt multifaceted legislation at the federal and state levels, or to reform existing legislation, making mandatory the enforcement of protection orders and other precautionary measures to protect women from imminent acts of violence, and to create effective implementation mechanisms. These measures should be accompanied by adequate resources destined to foster their implementation; regulations to ensure their enforcement; training programs for the law enforcement and justice system officials who will participate in their execution; and the design of model protocols and directives that can be followed by police departments throughout the country." The full text of the opinion is on the companion website for this book, *available at* http://www.constitutionallitigation.rutgers.edu; select "Links," and scroll down. The opinion is also available from Columbia Law School's Human Rights Institute. Her lawyers included law school clinics at Columbia University and University of Miami law schools.

4. Video of Jessica Lenahan and her lawyers discussing the case is available at https://www.youtube.com/watch?v=sw58d7xLnus.

5. Consider the legal landscape for domestic violence victims seeking police enforcement of restraining orders before and after *Castle Rock*. Does the comparison suggest that there are risks to seeking court intervention to remedy perceived wrongs?

6. Do police officers commit acts of violence against their intimate partners at a rate higher than the general public? "Two studies have found that at least 40% of police officer families experience domestic violence, in contrast to 10% of families in the general population. A third study of older and more experienced officers found a rate of 24%, indicating that domestic violence is 2–4 times more common among police families than American families in general."[7] The International Association of Chiefs of Police states that "[t]he rate of domestic violence is estimated to be at least as common as that of the general population and limited research to date indicates the possibility of higher incidence of domestic violence among law enforcement professionals."[8] Since "the problem exists at some serious level and deserves careful attention," the Association has drafted a model policy for how individual law enforcement agencies should handle domestic violence committed by police officers.[9] When the batterer is a police officer, the victim may face special problems posed by the officer's access to weapons and surveillance tools, and training in techniques of physical intimidation.[10] The case below, *Burella*, involves a police officer with a history of domestic violence.

---

7. *Police Family Violence Fact Sheet*, Nat'l Ctr. for Women and Policing, http://womenandpolicing.com/violencefs.asp.

8. *Discussion Paper on IACP's Policy on Domestic Violence by Police Officers, Concept and Issues Paper*, Int'l Assoc. Chiefs of Police (July 2003), https://www.theiacp.org/resources/domestic-violence-by-law-enforcement-policy.

9. *Id.*

10. *See, e.g., When the Batterer Is a Cop: Domestic Violence in Police Families*, Purple Berets http://www.purpleberets.org/violence_police_families.html.

3. *Development of Doctrine in the Circuits: Applying* Castle Rock

---

Questions to guide reading of *Burella*

1. Why was the Pennsylvania statutory language "shall arrest" insufficient to strip police of discretion?
2. Why does the availability of a private criminal complaint not create a property interest in the enforcement of a restraining order?
3. Is the court's reasoning that police retain discretion not to arrest (even if the abuser is present) consistent with your understanding of the holding of *Loudermill*?
4. Do you read the concurrence to suggest that, even if a statute mandates arrest and confers on a victim the right to initiate a criminal prosecution, under *Castle Rock*, the District Attorney's retention of discretion not to pursue the suit defeats the victim's claim to a property interest?
5. Does the concurrence suggest that a state legislature could never draft a statute mandating arrest or creating a property interest in enforcement? What legal changes does the concurrence suggest instead?

Burella v. City of Philadelphia

501 F.3d 134 (3d Cir. 2007)

FUENTES, Circuit Judge.

In January 1999, George Burella, a ten-year veteran of the Philadelphia Police Department, shot and seriously injured his wife, Jill Burella, and then shot and killed himself. George Burella had emotionally and physically abused Jill Burella for years prior to the shooting. Although she reported numerous incidents of abuse to the police over the years, obtained several restraining orders just days before the shooting, and told police that her husband continued threatening her despite the orders, police failed to arrest him. This appeal concerns whether the police officers had a constitutional obligation to protect Jill Burella from her husband's abuse. Despite our grave concerns about the Philadelphia Police Department's alleged conduct in this case, we hold that the officers did not have such an obligation....

I. Background

The abuse began around February 1996, when George Burella was convicted of disorderly conduct for stalking his wife at her workplace and assaulting her male co-worker who he suspected was having an affair with her. [Detailing Mr. Burella's long history of physical and emotional abuse of Ms. Burella, Mr. Burella's mental health treatment and consequent restricted police duties, police programs internal investigations, employee assistance, and involvement of police supervisor.] ...

On December 24, 1998, George Burella again assaulted his wife, this time while she was visiting a friend. When Philadelphia police officers arrived, they allowed him to leave with the couple's youngest daughter, and then took Jill Burella and her two other children home, where her husband resumed beating her.

Over the course of the next few weeks, Jill Burella obtained the three protection from abuse orders relevant to this lawsuit. On January 2, 1999, she obtained an emergency *ex parte* protection from abuse order ... that prohibited her husband from "abusing, harassing, stalking and/or threatening" her, and from "living at, entering, attempting to enter or visiting" the couple's home. The order further provided that officers "shall ... arrest the defendant if he/she fails to comply with this Order." The next day, Officer Reamer served the order on George Burella, who, according to Jill Burella, immediately violated it by shouting at and threatening her. Despite witnessing the alleged violation, Officer Reamer permitted George Burella to enter the house.

The next day, Jill Burella obtained another temporary protection from abuse order, which essentially repeated the terms set forth in the January 2 order. In addition, the court awarded her temporary custody of the couple's three children, prohibited George Burella from having "any contact" with her, and ordered him to relinquish all guns other than his service weapon, which he was required to turn over to his commanding officer at the end of every shift. The order also stated that "[t]his Order shall be enforced by any law enforcement agency in a county where a violation of this Order occurs."

Later that day, Jill Burella called 911 after she received threatening phone calls from her husband. After officers arrived, and while in their presence, she received several more calls from her husband. The officers told her they could not do anything unless her husband was physically present. When Jill Burella called the police the next day, again they told her that nothing could be done unless her husband was physically present at her house.

On January 8, 1999, Jill Burella obtained a final order of protection. Four days later, following an appointment with a psychiatrist at the City Medical Department, George Burella went to the house he formerly shared with his wife and shot her in the chest. He then immediately shot and killed himself. Although she suffered serious injuries, Jill Burella survived the shooting.

...

2. *Procedural Due Process*

The District Court held that Jill Burella had a procedural due process claim under *Board of Regents v. Roth*, 408 U.S. 564 (1972)....

[The district court followed another district court in reasoning that, although property interests generally arise from sources other than judicial orders, it was "in no way remarkable that an order could create such an entitlement."] ... Therefore, the District Court reasoned, the orders of protection, coupled with the Pennsylvania statute, left officers without discretion not to arrest George Burella for a violation and, thereby, conferred on Jill Burella an entitlement to police enforcement of the orders.

...

Jill Burella argues that the Supreme Court's decision in *Castle Rock* does not prevent her from succeeding on her procedural due process claim because the Pennsylvania Protection from Abuse Act states that police "*shall arrest* a defendant for violating an order." *See* 23 Pa. Cons. Stat. Ann. §6113(a) (emphasis added)....

[H]owever, the Court in *Castle Rock* unambiguously stated that absent a "clear indication" of legislative intent, a statute's mandatory arrest language should not be read to strip law enforcement of the discretion they have traditionally had in deciding whether to make an arrest. 545 U.S. at 761. Although the Supreme Court did not specify what language would suffice to strip the police of such discretion, it is clear after *Castle Rock* that the phrase "shall arrest" is insufficient. As previously noted, the Supreme Court explicitly stated that "a true mandate of police action would require some stronger indication from the Colorado Legislature than ... 'shall arrest.'" *Id.*

In addition, we note that Jill Burella's argument fails to address the Supreme Court's observation in *Castle Rock* that even if the Colorado domestic violence statute mandated an arrest, it would not necessarily mean the victim would have an "entitlement" to an arrest. That is, although the Pennsylvania statute allows a victim of domestic violence to "file a private criminal complaint against a defendant, alleging indirect criminal contempt" for violation of a protective order, 23 Pa. Cons. Stat. §6113.1(a), or "petition for civil contempt" against the violator, 23 Pa. Cons. Stat. §6114.1(a), like the Colorado statute, it is silent as to whether a victim can request, much less demand, an arrest. *See* 23 Pa. Cons. Stat. Ann. §6113.1(a). In fact, "[w]hen an individual files a private criminal complaint [under §6113.1], the district attorney has the discretion to refrain from proceeding for policy reasons."

Moreover, Jill Burella's attempt to limit the Supreme Court's holding in *Castle Rock* to situations in which the abuser is not present at the time of the alleged violation is unconvincing. She is correct that the Supreme Court stated that "[t]he practical necessity for [police] discretion is particularly apparent in a case such as this one, where the suspected violator is not actually present and his whereabouts are unknown." *Id.* at 762. But, in our view, the Court's holding in *Castle Rock* did not depend on the absence of the perpetrator. Indeed, we agree with the officers that the perpetrator's absence "was only additional fodder for discretion, not a necessary ingredient."

Finally, we cannot ignore that despite framing the issue as one of procedural due process, what Jill Burella appears to seek is a substantive due process remedy: that is, the right to an arrest itself, and not the pre-deprivation notice and hearing that are the hallmarks of a procedural due process claim.

In short ... Jill Burella does not have a cognizable claim that the officers' failure to enforce the orders of protection violated her due process rights.

...

AMBRO, Circuit Judge, concurring in part.

...

Ms. Burella contends that Pennsylvania's Protection from Abuse Act of 1994 provided sufficiently clear indication of mandatory police action. While Pennsylvania's

General Assembly has made a valiant effort to do so[,] ... for any claim to afford constitutional relief in preventing domestic violence and protecting future victims of abuse, Pennsylvania's legislators would need to go back to the drawing board.

...

In essence, *Castle Rock* recognized that a state statute *could* create a mandatory arrest scheme when the statutory language strongly signals an intent to curtail police discretion to enforce a protection order (1) with clearly commanding language, (2) by excluding the indeterminacies accompanying the option either to arrest or to seek a warrant, and (3) by creating a direct entitlement permitting the victim herself to pursue enforcement. The Pennsylvania Protection Act no doubt comes closer than Colorado in meeting these tests. Alas, it too fails.

The language of the Pennsylvania Protection Act differs markedly from Colorado's discretionary language. Unlike Colorado's law, Pennsylvania's statute did not simply state that "[a] peace officer *shall use every reasonable means to enforce* a protection order" and "*shall arrest, or,* if an arrest would be impractical under the circumstances, *seek a warrant,*" Colo. Rev. Stat. § 18-6-803.5(3) (emphases added). Rather, the Pennsylvania Protection Act, when enacted in 1976, required no warrant where there was probable cause to believe that a suspect had violated a protection-from-abuse (PFA) order. Following amendments in 1994, the statute now provides that officers "shall arrest a defendant for violating an order." 23 Pa. Con. Stat. § 6113(a). This amended language restricts the window of discretion by omitting language granting officers the option to seek a warrant rather than to arrest. The 1994 amendments also permitted victims to pursue directly (although, as noted below, with limits) criminal prosecution of protection-order violators.... In addition, violation of the PFA order itself became a crime—that of criminal contempt. In effecting these three principal changes and some others, Pennsylvania provided deliberate and strong indication that it intended arrest to be mandatory under the statute. No longer did it give police the option to arrest; it now commanded it.

The issue is whether this intent to mandate arrest can get around the "deep-rooted nature of law-enforcement discretion, even in the presence of seemingly mandatory legislative commands," *Castle Rock*, 545 U.S. at 761, and particularly in light of the presumption that "*all* police officers must use some discretion in deciding when and where to enforce [statutes]." ... (emphasis added)....

To be sure, state and federal criminal statutes typically specify crimes and penalties without dictating the way law enforcement will arrest and prosecute suspected criminals, leaving that to the executive's discretion. But if courts recognize that it is ever possible for legislatures to mandate the police to arrest, as *Castle Rock* seemed to do, 545 U.S. at 761, I do not see why police officers' decisions in how to carry out their duty to arrest, or even their inability to arrest in certain situations should the perpetrator be absent, compromise the extent to which a statute mandates arrest (as the Pennsylvania Protection Act purports to do). After all, the absence of the perpetrator in Pennsylvania would not lessen the statutory requirement to arrest him for violation of a PFA order; it would simply mean the impossibility of carrying out the mandate at some particular time.

If the Protection Act is read to mandate arrest, a byproduct of that mandate is of course the specification of a definite entitlement: arrest for a violation. *Castle Rock* noted that even if Colorado's statutory language required truly mandatory arrest, it did not create an entitlement because it did not grant the victim the right to bring a criminal action against the violator to enforce the order. 545 U.S. at 765–66. It instead permitted the victim to initiate *civil* contempt proceedings directly or *to request* initiation of *criminal* contempt proceedings. *Id.* at 766. This rendered any government's enforcement action "indirect and incidental" to the victim. *Id.* at 767.

...

The Pennsylvania General Assembly attempted to avoid this infirmity by granting the victim the right to initiate a criminal prosecution herself. While this gives hope to victims of abuse, my colleagues correctly point out that proceeding with any such suit is within the discretion of the local district attorney. Without commenting on the practical wisdom of stripping the district attorney of this discretion, it would need to be eliminated were the Protection Act amended further.

...

I reluctantly concede my colleagues are correct to suggest that a legislature would be hard-pressed to draft around *Castle Rock* in light of the "well-established tradition of police discretion [that] has long coexisted with apparently mandatory arrest statutes." Maj. Op. at 144 (citing *Castle Rock*, 545 U.S. at 760). Although the Supreme Court has not held explicitly that a state legislature can never mandate arrest or that abuse-protection statutes can never create a constitutionally protected interest, the perception persists that few (if any) paths to those results are available.

The next version of the Protection Act to be written (if at all) by the Pennsylvania General Assembly requires resolving conflicts of policy—the protection of citizens and the discretion accorded police officers and district attorneys in carrying out that function....[24]

Questions to guide reading of *Hudson*

1. Is the Sixth Circuit's reasoning consistent with the suggestion in *Castle Rock* that a state could create a property interest but that "a true mandate of police action would require some stronger indication" than statutory

24. What then can be done? The answer may simply be to take this case out of a constitutional context and into one of state tort law. This, of course, would require a waiver of immunity under the Commonwealth's Political Subdivision Tort Claims Act. Currently under that Act, the Pennsylvania government [has a blanket grant of immunity with only eight exceptions.] These exceptions currently do not provide for governmental liability for police officers' failure to protect victims of domestic abuse. ...

language such as "shall use every reasonable means to enforce" or "shall arrest"?

2. Does the Sixth Circuit's reasoning essentially track Justice Souter's concurrence in *Castle Rock*, and thus suggest that a state could never confer such a property interest?

Hudson v. Hudson

475 F.3d 741 (6th Cir. 2007)

COOK, Circuit Judge.

...

Jennifer Braddock was issued three protective orders against James Hudson, the father of her son, because Hudson repeatedly abused Braddock. In August 2001, while the third protective order was in effect, Hudson broke into Braddock's home and threatened her. She called the Memphis Police Department, but it made no attempt to find him. Hudson eventually was convicted of aggravated criminal trespass, vandalism, and violating the protective order, and sentenced to one week in jail. Over the next two years, Braddock called the police several times to complain about various violations of the protective order, including acts of physical violence, but the Memphis Police took no action. Braddock's struggle against Hudson's violence ended when Hudson broke into her home, killed her and two of her friends, then turned the gun on himself and committed suicide.

Justin Hudson, Braddock's son with Hudson, and Pamela Davis, Braddock's mother and Justin's guardian, sued James's sister Susan Hudson, who drove James Hudson to Braddock's house on the day of the shooting, the Memphis Police Department, and a number of Memphis Police Officers for violating the Fourteenth Amendment and various state-law rights.

...

To establish a procedural due process claim, a plaintiff must show that she had a property interest of which she was deprived without due process of law. U.S. Const. amend. XIV. We must determine "whether what [Tennessee] law has given [Braddock] constitutes a property interest for purposes of the Fourteenth Amendment." *Castle Rock*, 545 U.S. at 757. We first determine whether Tennessee has created a property interest under its law, *see Bd. of Regents v. Roth*, 408 U.S. 564, 577 (1972), and then decide whether that interest is protected by the Fourteenth Amendment, an issue that "is ultimately one of federal constitutional law." *Castle Rock*, 545 U.S. at 757. Mandatory enforcement of a protective order does not necessarily give a petitioner an entitlement to its enforcement, nor does it "resemble any traditional conception of property." *Id.* at 766.

...

Even if Tennessee law might be read to create some type of property interest, that interest must still rise to the level of a constitutionally protected interest under the

Due Process Clause of the Fourteenth Amendment. Braddock's interest in the enforcement of the protection order, specifically the arrest of Hudson, would arise incidentally "out of a function that government actors have always performed—to wit, arresting people who they have probable cause to believe have committed a criminal offense." *Castle Rock*, 545 U.S. at 767. We share the Supreme Court's skepticism in *Castle Rock* that this type of entitlement could ever "constitute a 'property' interest for purposes of the Due Process Clause." *Id.* Imbuing these restraining orders with constitutional property value, protected by the Due Process Clause, would needlessly interfere with Tennessee's choice of how to allocate the resources necessary to enforce its domestic violence laws. We thus hold that the enforcement of Tennessee protective orders does not create a property interest protected by the Due Process Clause of the Fourteenth Amendment.

...

While this loss of life was undeniably tragic, these officers simply did not violate the United States Constitution by failing to prevent James Hudson from murdering Jennifer Braddock.

...

Guide to Law Practice Simulation 5

Description

This simulation involves testimony before a state legislative committee considering the domestic violence Bill below, *The Domestic Violence Victim Protection Act*. Testifying before the legislative committee are Counsel for a non-profit, the Coalition for Domestic Violence Victims (1 student); Counsel for an executive agency, the State Domestic Violence Agency (1 student); Counsel for a statewide organization of municipalities, the Local Government Alliance (1 student); and Counsel for the statewide Chiefs of Police Association (1 student). Hearing testimony and asking questions are State legislators who did not author the Bill. Both legislators and those testifying are free to offer amendments to the Bill or to offer a different Bill.

To prepare, consider issues such as:

If you were an attorney for a domestic violence advocacy organization, in light of *Castle Rock*, what statutory language would you advocate to create a property interest in enforcement of restraining orders?

- Should the statute combine "shall enforce" with an express statement that, while police have discretion to choose the method of enforcement, enforcement of restraining orders is not discretionary but mandatory?
- Or add language clarifying that recipients of restraining orders are intended, not incidental, beneficiaries of police protection against known perpetrators?

- Should the legislative findings specify that the amendments to the statute are intended to overcome deficiencies identified in the Colorado statute by *Castle Rock*?
- Should an executive signing statement reinforce that the traditional discretion afforded law enforcement is intended to be overridden by the mandatory enforcement language?

Suppose you represented an organization of municipalities or law enforcement personnel that sought to ensure that whatever the legislature enacts does *not* create a property interest in enforcement of restraining orders. What language would you advocate in testimony before the legislature?

If you were a legislator on the committee hearing testimony, what questions would you ask? What amendments would you advocate? Or would you advocate for a Bill other than the one proposed in this Simulation?

Purposes

- Better understand procedural due process protection of property interests by comparing variations in how it is applied, including by amici briefs, *Castle Rock*, *Burella*, and *Hudson*
- Explore attorney roles in shaping doctrine by understanding *Castle Rock*, *Burella* and *Hudson* as creative attempts to circumvent the substantive due process rule of *DeShaney*
- Explore attorney role in shaping legislative remedies to adverse court decisions and non-enforcement of domestic violence restraining orders
- Prepare for law practice by simulating legislative hearing involving attorneys both testifying and questioning witnesses
- There is no need to do any research. The relevant authority is in the casebook.

Structure

- Domestic violence agency, Coalition for victims—Question and Answer with legislators (8 minutes)
- Local government alliance, Chiefs of Police—Question and Answer with legislators (8 minutes)
- After 15 minutes, questioning will open to the entire class
- All witnesses—Question and Answer with legislators and rest of class (15 minutes)
- Please prepare a question for every simulation, even if you are not playing a role
- To ensure full class participation, and as a courtesy to your fellow students, please close your laptops during law practice simulations.

Committee on Families and Youth

Chair: Sen. Amy Pearl

The State Senate

Eighty-Ninth Legislature

Tuesday, March 8 — 10:00 AM
Room 300N State Office Building

AGENDA

Public Hearing: SB 2135 Domestic Violence Victim Protection Act

Scheduled testimony: State Domestic Violence Agency, Coalition for Domestic Violence Victims, Local Government Alliance, Chiefs of Police Association

Domestic Violence Victim Protection Act

A BILL

Legislative findings. The State Legislature hereby finds that:

(a) Domestic violence is the single largest cause of injury to women in the United States, more common than auto accidents, muggings, and rapes combined;

(b) Underenforcement of protection from abuse orders is caused in part by police treating domestic violence as a private family matter;

(c) Police discretion to not enforce the terms of protection from abuse orders is inconsistent with the State's goal of protecting victims of domestic violence from further abuse;

(d) Curtailment of police discretion to refuse to enforce the terms of protection from abuse orders is necessary to remedy the long history of police refusing to intervene on behalf of victims of domestic violence;

(e) The Supreme Court's decision in *Castle Rock* allows state legislatures to create a property interest in enforcement of protection from abuse orders that will be protected by procedural due process.

Section (1) This Act is intended to directly benefit the narrow class of persons who are recipients of judicial protection from abuse orders by conferring an entitlement to police enforcement of such orders on the protected class.

Section (2) An arrest for violation of a protection from abuse order may be without warrant upon probable cause to believe the defendant has violated a provision of the order, whether or not the violation is committed in the presence of the police officer. The police officer may verify the existence of a protection order by telephone, radio or other electronic communication with the appropriate police department, State Police registry, protection order file or issuing authority.

Section (3) Upon probable cause to believe that a defendant has violated a protection from abuse order, a police officer shall enforce the terms of the protection from abuse order.

(a) Police enforcement of the order is a mandatory duty. Police shall not retain discretion to not enforce the terms of the order.

(b) Police shall retain discretion to choose the method of enforcement, including arrest.

(c) If the police officer does not arrest the defendant, the officer shall provide the recipient of the protection from abuse order with reasons for the decision.

(d) The police officer who responds to the complaint shall provide a written report to the State Domestic Violence Agency following response to or investigation of an allegation of a violation of a protection from abuse order, whether or not an arrest is made. If an arrest is not made, the officer shall provide a written explanation of the reasons.

Guide to Law Practice Simulation 6

Description

This is a meeting of in-house counsel with the Mayor of Metropolis to decide how to maximize the deterrent effect of adverse 42 U.S.C. § 1983 rulings and settlements on future conduct by city social workers and police.

Two teams of Metropolis Law Department lawyers (two lawyers on each) will propose and advocate for policy changes based on the facts below. Each team should prepare to discuss both legal and practical reasons for and against adopting their proposals. The proposals may or may not include any of the following:

- suggestions to improve accountability, training, hiring, investigations of misconduct, investigations of citizen complaints, or supervision of employees;
- proposal that individual city agencies responsible for the adverse rulings or settlements should have to pay the verdict and settlement amounts out of their own agency budgets, thus reducing money for other agency priorities;
- proposal that employees whose conduct contributes to an adverse ruling or settlement should be disciplined;
- proposal that individual city agencies responsible for the adverse rulings or settlement should study any patterns of social worker or police mis-

conduct (such as whether there are certain officers or certain precincts that account for more complaints; or whether there are certain kinds of conduct that account for many complaints);

- proposal that individual city agencies responsible for adverse rulings or settlements should work with the Metropolis Law Department lawyers to better educate the social workers and police to prevent future claims. To date, the Law Department has not had a role in attempting to prevent claims by educating clients about their legal obligations;
- any other proposal likely to reduce future 42 U.S.C. § 1983 claims against Metropolis police or social workers.

To prepare, consider:

For this simulation, the following facts should be considered. The Metropolis budget is $864 million. There is no possibility of increasing the City's budget as the Mayor and City Council both are trying to reduce the tax burden on citizens. The Department of Human Services budget is $75 million. During the last two years, the verdicts and settlements in social work cases totaled $2 million for 50 cases (with 2 highly-publicized cases accounting for $500,000) two years ago and $2.5 million for 75 cases last year. The factual settings varied but included foster care and services provided to abused children in their homes.

The Police Department budget is $300 million. During the last two years, the verdicts and settlements in police cases totaled $3.2 million for 110 cases two years ago; and $3 million for 100 cases last year. The factual settings varied but included off-duty police violence and excessive use of force, including dog bite cases and misuse of Tasers. While not all of them result in lawsuits, a recent report by the ACLU found that half of all complaints filed with the Civilian Complaint Review Board allege that an officer used excessive force.

Purpose

- Think creatively about the real-world local government policy implications of the 4th and 14th Amendment police and social worker decisions you have read
- Explore attorney roles in counseling and advising clients
- Think creatively about how city lawyers can proactively counsel city clients to reduce the expense of civil rights violations by avoiding violations or by reducing the costs of violations
- Prepare for law practice by simulating a client meeting, either by persuasively advocating a policy position and responding to questions or by identifying concerns about policy proposals posing questions to advocates
- There is no need to do any legal research—the relevant cases are in the casebook.

- You are free to research possible policy proposals. If your proposal to the client will include any facts in addition to the information in this Guide, be sure to allow time for other students to consider the information by providing the entire class with the additional material at least one course meeting in advance of Simulation 6.

Structure

- Advocates Team 1—Question and Answer with Mayor (8 minutes)
- Advocates Team 2—Question and Answer with Mayor (8 minutes)
- After about 15 minutes, questioning will be opened up to the entire class.
- All advocates—Question and Answer with Mayor and rest of class (15 minutes)
- Please prepare a question for every Simulation, even if you are not one of the students playing a role.
- To ensure full class participation, and as a courtesy to your fellow students, please close your laptops during law practice simulations.

Chapter Nine

Absolute Immunity

A. Chapter Overview

This book opened by examining the statute that is the vehicle for bringing most constitutional claims, 42 U.S.C. § 1983. It then turned to the constitutional grounds for litigation under the 8th, 14th, and 4th Amendments. Chapter 5 and this Chapter return to the § 1983 statute.

Individual defendants may be entitled to either qualified immunity, the subject of Chapter 11, or to absolute immunity, the subject of this Chapter. The Supreme Court has summarized the rationale for absolute immunity: "[i]n cases involving prosecutors, legislators, and judges we have repeatedly explained that the immunity serves the public interest in enabling such officials to perform their designated functions effectively without fear that a particular decision may give rise to personal liability." *Clinton v. Jones*, 520 U.S. 681, 693 (1997).[1]

The materials in this Chapter explain that, beginning in medieval times, judges were held absolutely immune from suits by disgruntled litigants as a way to establish appeals as the vehicle for correcting judicial errors and thereby protecting judicial independence (*Forrester*). Because of the public interest in a judiciary free to act on disputes within their jurisdiction without fear of later suits by dissatisfied litigants, judicial immunity extends even to judges allegedly motivated by malice or corruption (*Pierson*).

The materials in this Chapter explain that generally, to decide whether an individual defendant is entitled to absolute immunity, a court will examine the function of the individual defendant (*Forrester*). Whether the individual is entitled to absolute immunity under 42 U.S.C. § 1983 depends on whether that function was entitled to immunity under the common law in 1871, when the predecessor to § 1983 was enacted (*Pierson*, *Forrester*).

The functional inquiry to determine the availability of absolute immunity is relatively straightforward for judges acting in their judicial roles (*Pierson*), as long as the judge has not acted in the complete absence of jurisdiction (*Stump*, *Mirales*). Similarly, the functional inquiry is relatively straightforward for prosecutors acting in their advocacy roles because then the prosecutors' actions are closely associated

1. *See, e.g.*, *Tenney v. Brandhove*, 341 U.S. 367, 376–77 (1951) (legislative immunity); *Pierson v. Ray*, 386 U.S. 547, 554–55 (1967) (judicial immunity); *Imbler v. Pachtman*, 424 U.S. 409, 422–23 (1976) (prosecutorial immunity).

with the judicial phase of criminal process (*Imbler, Kalina*). "'[A] prosecutor's absolute immunity reflects "a balance" of "evils" [and it] has been thought in the end better ... to leave unredressed the wrongs done by dishonest officers than to subject those who try to do their duty to the constant dread of retaliation.'" *Van de Kamp v. Goldstein*, 555 U.S. 335, 340 (2009) (quoting *Gregoire v. Biddle*, 177 F.2d 579, 581 (2d Cir. 1949) (Hand, C.J.)).

The functional inquiry to determine the availability of absolute immunity is more complicated if it is not clear whether the conduct was a judicial act or simply an act by a person who is a judge. While judges do perform roles other than judicial decision-making, such as administrative roles, the availability of absolute immunity turns on whether the acts complained of were judicial acts (*Forrester*). Similarly, while prosecutors do perform roles that are not intimately associated with preparing for and/or presenting the state's case to a court, prosecutors do not have absolutely immunity for actions taken in their administrative or other roles (*Kalina, Van de Kamp*). The functional inquiry becomes more complex when government employees whose professions did not exist in 1871—such as child protective service workers or social workers—are sued for performing functions that might or might not be analogous to prosecutorial functions and therefore closely involved in the judicial process (*Ernst, Holloway*).

B. Judicial Function

Questions to guide reading of *Pierson*

1. What public policy purpose is served by immunizing judges from civil liability for acts within their jurisdiction?
2. Would the same public policy considerations require that absolute immunity be extended to judges for non-judicial acts?
3. According to the majority, why is absolute immunity for judges consistent with the plain language of § 1983? In the dissent, how did Justice Douglas invoke the legislative history of the Ku Klux Klan Act of 1871?

Pierson v. Ray

386 U.S. 547 (1967)

Mr. Chief Justice WARREN delivered the opinion of the Court.

These cases present issues involving the liability of local police officers and judges under ... 42 U.S.C. § 1983. Petitioners ... were members of a group of 15 white and Negro Episcopal clergymen who attempted to use segregated facilities at an interstate bus terminal in Jackson, Mississippi, in 1961. They were arrested by respondents Ray, Griffith, and Nichols, policemen of the City of Jackson, and charged with violating ... the Mississippi Code, which makes guilty of a misdemeanor anyone who congregates with others in a public place under circumstances such that a breach of the peace may be occasioned thereby, and refuses to move on when ordered to do so by a police officer. Petitioners waived a jury trial and were convicted of the offense by respondent Spencer, a municipal police justice. They were each given the maximum sentence of four months in jail and a fine of $200. On appeal petitioner Jones was accorded a trial de novo in the County Court, and after the city produced its evidence the court granted his motion for a directed verdict. The cases against the other petitioners were then dropped.

Having been vindicated in the County Court, petitioners brought this action for damages ... alleging that respondents had violated § 1983.... We granted certiorari ... to consider whether a local judge is liable for damages under § 1983 for an unconstitutional conviction....

...

The evidence at the federal trial showed that petitioners and other Negro and white Episcopal clergymen undertook a 'prayer pilgrimage' in 1961 from New Orleans to Detroit. The purpose of the pilgrimage was to visit church institutions and other places in the North and South to promote racial equality and integration, and, finally, to report to a church convention in Detroit. Letters from the leader of the group to its members indicate that the clergymen intended from the beginning to go to Jackson and attempt to use segregated facilities at the bus terminal there, and that they fully expected to be arrested for doing so. The group made plans based on the assumption that they would be arrested if they attempted peacefully to exercise their right as interstate travelers to use the waiting rooms and other facilities at the bus terminal, and the letters discussed arrangements for bail and other matters relevant to arrests.

The ministers stayed one night in Jackson, and went to the bus terminal the next morning to depart for Chattanooga, Tennessee. They entered the waiting room, disobeying a sign at the entrance that announced 'White Waiting Room Only—By Order of the Police Department.' They then turned to enter the small terminal restaurant but were stopped by two Jackson police officers, respondents Griffith and Nichols, who had been awaiting their arrival and who ordered them to 'move on.' The ministers replied that they wanted to eat and refused to move on. Respondent Ray, then a police captain and now the deputy chief of police, arrived a few minutes later. The ministers were placed under arrest and taken to the jail.

All witnesses including the police officers agreed that the ministers entered the waiting room peacefully and engaged in no boisterous or objectionable conduct while in the 'White Only' area. There was conflicting testimony on the number of bystanders present and their behavior. Petitioners testified that there was no crowd at the station, that no one followed them into the waiting room, and that no one uttered threatening words or made threatening gestures. The police testified that some 25 to 30 persons followed the ministers into the terminal, that persons in the crowd were in a very dissatisfied and ugly mood, and that they were mumbling and making unspecified threatening gestures. The police did not describe any specific threatening incidents, and testified that they took no action against any persons in the crowd who were threatening violence because they 'had determined that the ministers was the cause of the violence if any might occur,' although the ministers were concededly orderly and polite and the police did not claim that it was beyond their power to control the allegedly disorderly crowd. The arrests and convictions were followed by this lawsuit.

We find no difficulty in agreeing with the Court of Appeals that Judge Spencer is immune from liability for damages for his role in these convictions. The record is barren of any proof or specific allegation that Judge Spencer played any role in these arrests and convictions other than to adjudge petitioners guilty when their cases came before his court. Few doctrines were more solidly established at common law than the immunity of judges from liability for damages for acts committed within their judicial jurisdiction, as this Court recognized when it adopted the doctrine, in *Bradley v. Fisher*, 13 Wall. 335 (1872). This immunity applies even when the judge is accused of acting maliciously and corruptly, and it 'is not for the protection or benefit of a malicious or corrupt judge, but for the benefit of the public, whose interest it is that the judges should be at liberty to exercise their functions with independence and without fear of consequences.' ... It is a judge's duty to decide all cases within his jurisdiction that are brought before him, including controversial cases that arouse the most intense feelings in the litigants. His errors may be corrected on appeal, but he should not have to fear that unsatisfied litigants may hound him with litigation charging malice or corruption. Imposing such a burden on judges would contribute not to principled and fearless decisionmaking but to intimidation.

We do not believe that this settled principle of law was abolished by § 1983, which makes liable 'every person' who under color of law deprives another person of his civil rights. The legislative record gives no clear indication that Congress meant to abolish wholesale all common-law immunities. Accordingly, this Court held in *Tenney v. Brandhove*, 341 U.S. 367 (1951), that the immunity of legislators for acts within the legislative role was not abolished. The immunity of judges for acts within the judicial role is equally well established, and we presume that Congress would have specifically so provided had it wished to abolish the doctrine.

...

Mr. Justice DOUGLAS, dissenting.

I do not think that all judges, under all circumstances, no matter how outrageous their conduct are immune from suit under ... 42 U.S.C. § 1983. The Court's ruling is not justified by the admitted need for a vigorous and independent judiciary, is not commanded by the common-law doctrine of judicial immunity, and does not follow inexorably from our prior decisions.

... To most, 'every person' [in § 1983] would mean every person, not every person except judges.

...

The congressional purpose [in enacting § 1983 in 1871] seems to me to be clear. A condition of lawlessness existed in certain of the States, under which people were being denied their civil rights. Congress intended to provide a remedy for the wrongs being perpetrated. And its members were not unaware that certain members of the judiciary were implicated in the state of affairs which the statute was intended to rectify. It was often noted that '(i)mmunity is given to crime, and the records of the public tribunals are searched in vain for any evidence of effective redress.' Cong. Globe, 42d Cong., 1st Sess., 374. Mr. Rainey of South Carolina noted that '(T)he courts are in many instances under the control of those who are wholly inimical to the impartial administration of law and equity.' Id., at 394. Congressman Beatty of Ohio claimed that it was the duty of Congress to listen to the appeals of those who 'by reason of popular sentiment or secret organizations or prejudiced juries or bribed judges, (cannot) obtain the rights and privileges due an American citizen * * *.' Id., at 429. The members supporting the proposed measure were apprehensive that there had been a complete breakdown in the administration of justice in certain States and that laws nondiscriminatory on their face were being applied in a discriminatory manner, that the newly won civil rights of the Negro were being ignored, and that the Constitution was being defied. It was against this background that the section was passed, and it is against this background that it should be interpreted.

It is said that, at the time of the statute's enactment, the doctrine of judicial immunity was well settled and that Congress cannot be presumed to have intended to abrogate the doctrine since it did not clearly evince such a purpose. This view is beset by many difficulties. It assumes that Congress could and should specify in advance all the possible circumstances to which a remedial statute might apply and state which cases are within the scope of a statute.

...

The position that Congress did not intend to change the common-law rule of judicial immunity ignores the fact that every member of Congress who spoke to the issue assumed that the words of the statute meant what they said and that judges would be liable. Many members of Congress objected to the statute because it imposed liability on members of the judiciary. Mr. Arthur of Kentucky opposed the measure because:

> 'Hitherto * * * no judge or court has been held liable, civilly or criminally, for judicial acts * * *. Under the provisions of (section 1) every judge in the State court * * * will enter upon and pursue the call of official duty with the sward of Damocles suspended over him * * *.' Cong. Globe, 42d Cong., 1st Sess., 365–366.

...

Yet despite the repeated fears of its opponents, and the explicit recognition that the section would subject judges to suit, the section remained as it was proposed: it applied to 'any person.' There was no exception for members of the judiciary. In light of the sharply contested nature of the issue of judicial immunity it would be reasonable to assume that the judiciary would have been expressly exempted from the wide sweep of the section, if Congress had intended such a result.

For further discussion

1. Recall that the legislative history of the Ku Klux Klan Act of 1871 was invoked by the majority in both *Monroe* and *Monell*, excerpted in Chapter 1. For what purpose was it invoked in each case?

2. Justice Douglas quotes Mr. Rainey of South Carolina on the legislative history of the statute that became § 1983. Mr. Rainey was among the sixteen blacks to serve in Congress during Reconstruction. Eric Foner, Reconstruction: America's Unfinished Revolution 1863–1877 (Harper & Row, New York 1988) 352 and n. 12; *see* Philip Dray, Capitol Men: The Epic Story of Reconstruction Through the Lives of the First Black Congressmen (Houghton Mifflin Co. 2008).

3. What is a "judicial act"? In *Stump v. Sparkman*, 435 U.S. 349 (1978), an Indiana judge granted a mother's petition to sterilize her fifteen-year-old daughter, *ex parte*, without a hearing, and without notice to the daughter or appointment of a guardian. *Id.* The daughter believed she was having her appendix removed and only later discovered the sterilization, whereupon she sued the judge and others. *Id.* The Court held judicial immunity applied when the judge "had jurisdiction over the subject matter before him," which must be "construed broadly." *Id.* at 356. The Court held: "A judge will not be deprived of immunity because the action he took was in error, was done maliciously, or was in excess of his authority; rather, he will be subject to liability only when he has acted in the 'clear absence of all jurisdiction.'" *Id.* at 356–57 (further citation omitted). Further, an action can be judicial even if the judge commits "grave procedural errors." Whether an act by a judge is "judicial" depends on "the nature of the act itself, *i.e.*, whether it is a function normally performed by a judge," and on "the expectations of the parties, *i.e.*, whether they dealt with the judge in his judicial capacity." *Id.* at 362. The Court held the judge entitled to absolute immunity. *Id.* at 364. Construing jurisdiction broadly, the Court reasoned that granting a petition was within the general jurisdiction of the state court, *id.* at 350, and rejected the daughter's argument that the judge's act was "so unfair and so totally devoid of judicial concern for the interests and wellbeing of the young-girl involved as to disqualify it as a judicial act." *Id.* at 363; *see, e.g., Archie v. Lanier*, 95 F.3d 438, 441 (6th Cir. 1996) (rejecting invocation of judicial immunity because stalking and sexually assaulting a person are not "judicial acts" even though the assailant was a judge).

4. In deriving its test for a "judicial act," the Supreme Court in *Stump* relied in part on the Fifth Circuit's test for determining whether a judge's actions were judicial. The Fifth Circuit more recently articulated the four factors it weighs: "(1) whether the precise act complained of is a normal judicial function; (2) whether the acts occurred in the courtroom or appropriate adjunct spaces such as the judge's chambers; (3) whether the controversy centered around a case pending before the court; and (4) whether the acts arose directly out of a visit to the judge in his official capacity." *Davis v. Tarrant County Tex.*, 565 F.3d 214, 222 (5th Cir.), *cert. denied*, 558 U.S. 1024 (2009).

5. Can a judge be entitled to absolute immunity from Section 1983 damages even for non-judicial acts? A federal district court in Pennsylvania answered no. In *Wallace*

v. Powell, the district court held that a state-court judge could be held liable for damages for conduct that was not judicial. 2014 WL 70092 (M.D. Pa. Jan. 9, 2014). *Wallace* concerned a Pennsylvania judge who accepted bribes from the operator of private prisons, encouraged construction of a private juvenile-detention facility, and took actions to fill the private cells with juveniles. Colloquially known as "Kids for Cash," the scandal is the subject of a documentary by the same name.

The non-judicial acts for which the state-court judge could be held liable for damages included:

- initiating the plan to bring together people with the financial ability to construct a new juvenile-detention facility;
- assisting in closing the public jail by "appearing on television urging a shutdown of a county-run detention facility" and helping to hire staff "for a private detention facility [neither of which are] functions 'normally performed by a judge.'" *Wallace*, 2014 WL 70092 at *9;
- expanding a "no tolerance" probation policy for curfew, appointment, drug-and-alcohol, and other probation violations that increased the number of juveniles who appeared before the judge, an administrative and not a judicial act; and
- failing to disclose the more than $2.7 million he and another judge received from the private juvenile-jail operator "while sending juveniles to his detention facility."

Wallace, 2014 WL 70092 at *9–*10.

By contrast, the Sixth Circuit recently held differently: Yes, a judge can be absolutely immune from Section 1983 damages for non-judicial acts. In *King v. McCree*, during a child-support hearing, the judge flirted with the child's mother when the judge first saw her. 573 F. App'x 430, 440 (6th Cir. 2014). The judge soon began a months-long sexual relationship with the child's mother, gave her thousands of dollars, and instructed her to keep the relationship secret. *Id.* The judge continued to preside over the child-support case for several months, until transferring it to another judge. *Id.* at 433–35. Upon learning of the sexual relationship between the judge and the child's mother, the child's father sued the judge for denial of due process. *Id.* at 436.

In a non-precedential opinion, the Sixth Circuit held the judge immune from Section 1983 liability, not only for the judge's courtroom conduct but for his acts outside the courtroom. The Sixth Circuit agreed that the judge's personal relationship with the child's mother "consisted of non-judicial acts." *King*, 573 F. App'x at 443, n.7. Nevertheless, the Sixth Circuit held that the judge's acts "though often reprehensible, did not directly involve [the child's father, the plaintiff]." *Id.* at 440. "We hold that a [plaintiff] cannot avoid the bar of judicial immunity by relying on non-judicial, out-of-court acts that may have affected in-court judicial acts. Personal bias alone of a judge—when not serving in a judicial function—does not create a due-process violation." *Id.* at 441. The Sixth Circuit distinguished *Wallace*, the Kids for Cash bribery case. The Sixth Circuit reasoned that in *Wallace*, the corrupt state-court judge's non-judicial acts—of advocating closure of the public jail and the construction of a private facility, helping to staff the private facility, enacting the zero-tolerance probation policy, and actively concealing the bribes—"*directly* deprived the [juveniles] of their rights." *King*, 573 F. App'x at 442; *id* (judge in *Wallace* was "liable for non-judicial acts that directly harmed the plaintiffs"). Without expressly stating so, the Sixth Circuit held the judge's non-judicial acts in *King*—essentially, conducting a sexual relationship with one of the two litigants while presiding over the litigation—did not directly harm the plaintiff. More importantly, the Sixth Circuit's reasoning differed from *Wallace*, where the classification of the conduct as either judicial acts or non-judicial acts was key to the threshold inquiry of judicial immunity.

Curiously, while the Sixth Circuit in *King* cited its own precedent, *Archie v. Lanier*, in holding that the judge's personal relationship was not a judicial act, the Sixth Circuit did not distinguish the holding of *Archie v. Lanier*, 95 F.3d 438, 441 (6th Cir. 1996) (rejecting invocation of judicial immunity because stalking and sexually assaulting a person are not "judicial acts" even though the assailant was a judge). The plaintiff in *King* petitioned for certiorari and, in 2015, the Supreme Court declined review.

6. What is the difference between a judge acting "in the clear absence of all jurisdiction" and "in excess" of jurisdiction? The Supreme Court used this example to illustrate the distinction between lack of jurisdiction and excess of jurisdiction: "if a probate judge, with jurisdiction over only wills and estates, should try a criminal case, he would be acting in the clear absence of jurisdiction and would not be immune from liability for his action; on the other hand, if a judge of a criminal court should convict a defendant of a nonexistent crime, he would merely be acting in excess of his jurisdiction and would be immune." *Stump*, 435 U.S. at 357 n.7 (citing *Bradley*, 13 Wall at 352). The Court explained further: "'Where there is clearly no jurisdiction over the subject-matter any authority exercised is a usurped authority, and for the exercise of such authority, when the want of jurisdiction is known to the judge, no excuse is permissible. But where jurisdiction over the subject-matter is invested by law in the judge, or in the court which he holds, the manner and extent in which the jurisdiction shall be exercised are generally as much questions for his determination as any other questions involved in the case....'" *Stump*, 435 U.S. at 356 n.6 (quoting *Bradley*, 13 Wall at 351–352).

Questions to guide reading of *Forrester*

1. Generally, why do government officials have some immunity from damages?
2. According to *Forrester*, what purposes are served by permitting judges to be immune from § 1983 actions?
3. What does the Supreme Court mean by a "functional" approach to immunity?
4. What are some examples of judicial acts? Non-judicial acts?
5. Why was the judge in *Forrester* not entitled to absolute immunity?

Forrester v. White

484 U.S. 219 (1988)

Justice O'CONNOR delivered the opinion of the Court.

This case requires us to decide whether a state-court judge has absolute immunity from a suit for damages under 42 U.S.C. § 1983 for his decision to dismiss a subordinate court employee. The employee, who had been a probation officer, alleged that she was demoted and discharged on account of her sex, in violation of the Equal Protection Clause of the Fourteenth Amendment. We conclude that the judge's decisions were not judicial acts for which he should be held absolutely immune.

[State of Illinois Judge Howard Lee White] had the authority to hire adult probation officers, who were removable in his discretion.... [and] the authority to appoint juvenile probation officers to serve at his pleasure....

In April 1977, Judge White hired petitioner Cynthia A. Forrester as an adult and juvenile probation officer. Forrester prepared presentence reports for Judge White in adult offender cases, and recommendations for disposition and placement in juvenile cases. She also supervised persons on probation and recommended revocation when necessary. In July 1979, Judge White appointed Forrester as Project Supervisor of the Jersey County Juvenile Court Intake and Referral Services Project, a position that carried increased supervisory responsibilities. Judge White demoted Forrester to a nonsupervisory position in the summer of 1980. He discharged her on October 1, 1980.

Forrester filed this lawsuit ... alleg[ing] violations of ... 42 U.S.C. § 1983. A jury found that Judge White had discriminated against Forrester on account of her sex, in violation of the Equal Protection Clause of the Fourteenth Amendment. The jury awarded her $81,818.80 in compensatory damages under § 1983.

...

II

Suits for monetary damages are meant to compensate the victims of wrongful actions and to discourage conduct that may result in liability. Special problems arise, however, when government officials are exposed to liability for damages.... Because government officials are engaged by definition in governing, their decisions will often have adverse effects on other persons. When officials are threatened with personal liability for acts taken pursuant to their official duties, they may well be induced to act with an excess of caution or otherwise to skew their decisions in ways that result in less than full fidelity to the objective and independent criteria that ought to guide their conduct. In this way, exposing government officials to the same legal hazards faced by other citizens may detract from the rule of law instead of contributing to it.

Such considerations have led to the creation of various forms of immunity from suit for certain government officials. Aware of the salutary effects that the threat of liability can have, however, as well as the undeniable tension between official immunities and the ideal of the rule of law, this Court has been cautious in recognizing claims that government officials should be free of the obligation to answer for their acts in court. Running through our cases, with fair consistency, is a "functional" approach to immunity questions other than those that have been decided by express constitutional or statutory enactment. Under that approach, we examine the nature of the functions with which a particular official or class of officials has been lawfully entrusted, and we seek to evaluate the effect that exposure to particular forms of liability would likely have on the appropriate exercise of those functions. Officials who seek exemption from personal liability have the burden of showing that such an exemption is justified by overriding considerations of public policy, and the Court has recognized a category of "qualified" immunity that avoids unnecessarily extending the scope of the traditional concept of absolute immunity.

...

This Court has generally been quite sparing in its recognition of claims to absolute official immunity. One species of such legal protection is beyond challenge: the legislative immunity created by the Speech or Debate Clause, U.S. Const., Art. I, §6, cl. 1. Even here, however, the Court has been careful not to extend the scope of the protection further than its purposes require.... Furthermore, on facts analogous to those in the case before us, the Court indicated that a United States Congressman would not be entitled to absolute immunity, in a sex-discrimination suit filed by a personal aide whom he had fired, unless such immunity was afforded by the Speech or Debate Clause.

...

Among executive officials, the President of the United States is absolutely immune from damages liability arising from official acts. *Nixon v. Fitzgerald*, 457 U.S. 731 (1982). This immunity, however, is based on the President's "unique position in the constitutional scheme," *id.*, at 749, and it does not extend indiscriminately to the President's personal aides, *see Harlow* [*v. Fitzgerald*, 457 U.S. 800, (1982)], or to Cabinet level officers, *Mitchell v. Forsyth*, 472 U.S. 511 (1985)....

III.

As a class, judges have long enjoyed a comparatively sweeping form of immunity, though one not perfectly well-defined. Judicial immunity apparently originated, in medieval times, as a device for discouraging collateral attacks and thereby helping to establish appellate procedures as the standard system for correcting judicial error.... Besides protecting the finality of judgments or discouraging inappropriate collateral attacks, the *Bradley* Court [*Bradley v. Fisher*, 13 Wall. 335, 347 (1872)] concluded, judicial immunity also protected judicial independence by insulating judges from vexatious actions prosecuted by disgruntled litigants. *Id.*, at 348.

In the years since *Bradley* was decided, this Court has not been quick to find that federal legislation was meant to diminish the traditional common-law protections extended to the judicial process. *See, e.g.*, *Pierson v. Ray*, 386 U.S. 547 (1967). On the contrary, these protections have been held to extend to Executive Branch officials who perform quasi-judicial functions, *see Butz v. Economou*, supra, 438 U.S., at 512 ... or who perform prosecutorial functions that are "intimately associated with the judicial phase of the criminal process," *Imbler v. Pachtman*, 424 U.S. 409, 430 (1976).... The common law's rationale for these decisions—freeing the judicial process of harassment or intimidation—has been thought to require absolute immunity even for advocates and witnesses. See *Briscoe v. LaHue*, 460 U.S. 325 (1983); *Butz v. Economou*, 438 U.S., at 512.

...

The purposes served by judicial immunity from liability in damages have been variously described. In *Bradley v. Fisher*, *supra*, at 348, and again in *Pierson v. Ray*, *supra*, at 554, the Court emphasized that the nature of the adjudicative function requires a judge frequently to disappoint some of the most intense and ungovernable desires that people can have. As Judge Posner pointed out in his dissenting opinion below, this is the principal characteristic that adjudication has in common with legislation and with criminal prosecution, which are the two other areas in which absolute immunity has most generously been provided. [*Forrester v. White*,] 792 F.2d [647,] 660 [(7th Cir. 1986) (Posner, J., dissenting)]. If judges were personally liable for erroneous decisions, the resulting avalanche of suits, most of them frivolous but vexatious, would provide powerful incentives for judges to avoid rendering decisions likely to provoke such suits. *Id.*, at 660–661. The resulting timidity would be hard to detect or control, and it would manifestly detract from independent and impartial adjudication. Nor are suits against judges the only available means through which litigants can protect themselves from the consequences of judicial error. Most judicial mistakes or wrongs are open to correction through ordinary mechanisms of review, which are largely free of the harmful side-effects inevitably associated with exposing judges to personal liability.

When applied to the paradigmatic judicial acts involved in resolving disputes between parties who have invoked the jurisdiction of a court, the doctrine of absolute judicial immunity has not been particularly controversial. Difficulties have arisen primarily in attempting to draw the line between truly judicial acts, for which immunity is appropriate, and acts that simply happen to have been done by judges. Here, as in other contexts, immunity is justified and defined by the *functions* it protects and serves, not by the person to whom it attaches.

This Court has never undertaken to articulate a precise and general definition of the class of acts entitled to immunity. The decided cases, however, suggest an intelligible distinction between judicial acts and the administrative, legislative, or executive functions that judges may on occasion be assigned by law to perform. Thus, for example, the informal and *ex parte* nature of a proceeding has not been thought to imply that an act otherwise within a judge's lawful jurisdiction was deprived of its judicial character. *See Stump v. Sparkman*, 435 U.S. 349, 363, n. 12 (1978). Similarly, acting to disbar an attorney as a sanction for contempt of court, by invoking a power "possessed by all courts which have authority to admit attorneys to practice," does not become less judicial by virtue of an allegation of malice or corruption of motive. *Bradley v. Fisher*, 13 Wall., at 354. As the *Bradley* Court noted: "Against the consequences of [judges'] erroneous or irregular action, from whatever motives proceeding, the law has provided for private parties numerous remedies, and to those remedies they must, in such cases, resort." *Ibid.*

Administrative decisions, even though they may be essential to the very functioning of the courts, have not similarly been regarded as judicial acts. In *Ex parte Virginia*, 100 U.S. (10 Otto) 339 (1880), for example, this Court declined to extend immunity to a county judge who had been charged in a criminal indictment with discriminating on the basis of race in selecting trial jurors for the county's courts. The Court reasoned:

> Whether the act done by him was judicial or not is to be determined by its character, and not by the character of the agent. Whether he was a county judge or not is of no importance. The duty of selecting jurors might as well have been committed to a private person as to one holding the office of a judge.... That the jurors are selected for a court makes no difference. So are court-criers, tipstaves, sheriffs, &c. Is their election or their appointment a judicial act? *Id.*, at 348.

Although this case involved a criminal charge against a judge, the reach of the Court's analysis was not in any obvious way confined by that circumstance.

Likewise, judicial immunity has not been extended to judges acting to promulgate a code of conduct for attorneys.... In explaining why legislative, rather than judicial, immunity furnished the appropriate standard, we said: "Although it is clear that under Virginia law the issuance of the Bar Code was a proper function of the Virginia Court, propounding the Code was not an act of adjudication but one of rulemaking." Similarly, in the same case, we held that judges acting to enforce the Bar Code would be treated like prosecutors, and thus would be amenable to suit for injunctive and declaratory relief.... Once again, it was the nature of the function performed, not the identity of the actor who performed it, that informed our immunity analysis.

IV.

In the case before us, we think it clear that Judge White was acting in an administrative capacity when he demoted and discharged Forrester. Those acts—like many others involved in supervising court employees and overseeing the efficient operation of a court—may have been quite important in providing the necessary conditions of a sound adjudicative system. The decisions at issue, however, were not themselves judicial or adjudicative. As Judge Posner pointed out below, a judge who hires or fires a probation officer cannot meaningfully be distinguished from a district attorney who hires and fires assistant district attorneys, or indeed from any other Executive Branch official who is responsible for making such employment decisions. Such decisions, like personnel decisions made by judges, are often crucial to the efficient operation of public institutions (some of which are at least as important as the courts), yet no one suggests that they give rise to absolute immunity from liability in damages under § 1983.

The majority below thought that the threat of vexatious lawsuits by disgruntled ex-employees could interfere with the quality of a judge's decisions....

There is considerable force in this analysis, but it in no way serves to distinguish judges from other public officials who hire and fire subordinates.... This does not imply that qualified immunity, like that available to Executive Branch officials who make similar discretionary decisions, is unavailable to judges for their employment decisions.... Absolute immunity, however, is "strong medicine, justified only when the danger of [officials' being] deflect[ed from the effective performance of their duties] is very great." 792 F.2d, at 660 (Posner, J., dissenting). The danger here is not great enough. Nor do we think it significant that, under Illinois law, only a judge can hire or fire probation officers. To conclude that, because a judge acts within the scope of his authority, such employment decisions are brought within the court's "jurisdiction," or converted into "judicial acts," would lift form above substance....

We conclude that Judge White was not entitled to absolute immunity for his decisions to demote and discharge Forrester.

...

For further discussion

1. In *Mireles v. Waco*, 502 U.S. 9 (1991) (*per curiam*), a public defender scheduled to appear before a judge alleged that, when he failed to appear, the judge ordered police officers to bring the public defender from another courtroom where he was waiting to appear. *Id.* at 10. The attorney alleged that the judge instructed the police to use force, that the officers violently dragged him backwards from the other courtroom, cursing him and calling him names, and that all of this conduct was approved by the judge. *Id.* The Supreme Court clarified that judicial immunity "is overcome in only two sets of circumstances. First, a judge is not immune from liability for nonjudicial actions, *i.e.*, actions not taken in the judge's judicial capacity.... Second, a judge is not immune for actions, though judicial in nature, [that were] taken in the complete absence of all jurisdiction." *Id.* at 11–12. Focusing on the nature of the alleged act—that the judge issued an order to the officers, *id.* at 13—the Court held this was a judicial act to which judicial immunity applied, regardless of any malicious motivation. *Id.* at 12. Justice Stevens dissented, reasoning that "[o]rdering a battery has no relation to a function normally performed by a judge." *Id.* at 14 (Stevens, J., dissenting).

2. In 1996, Congress amended 42 U.S.C. § 1983 to broaden judicial immunity to include not only immunity from damages but also immunity from injunctive relief in most circumstances. Section 1983 is quoted in full in Chapter 1. While the statute generally provides for liability "to the party injured in an action at law, suit in equity, or other proper proceeding for redress," this Chapter has explained how that language has been construed to exempt judges from liability for damages for their judicial acts. In 1996, to supersede *Pulliam v. Allen*, 466 U.S. 522 (1984), Congress amended Section 1983 to insulate judges from prospective injunctive relief; the statute now provides for liability "except that in any action brought against a judicial officer for an act or omission taken in such officer's judicial capacity, injunctive relief shall not be granted unless a declaratory decree was violated or declaratory relief was unavailable." *See, e.g.*, *Conway v. Garvey*, 117 F. App'x 792, 793 (2d Cir. 2004) (since state court judge

had not violated declaratory decree and plaintiff parent in a child custody suit had not shown declaratory relief was unavailable, § 1983 barred injunctive relief against state court judge).

3. Apart from civil liability under § 1983, what legal remedies might exist for corrupt acts by judges? Part of the public policy justification for absolute immunity from § 1983 damages actions is the availability of the appeals process for correcting judicial error. In addition, a judge can be criminally prosecuted for corrupt acts.

Further, a party can move that a judge recuse him or herself from considering a particular case. *See, e.g.*, 28 U.S.C. § 144 (1949) (personal bias or prejudice of district court judge); 28 U.S.C. § 455 (1948) (appearance of impartiality). The normal process is for a federal judge whose disqualification is sought to decide the motion to recuse. In 2009, Congress held hearings on whether to amend the federal court recusal process. Professor Charles Geyh testified in support of a proposal to amend 28 U.S.C. § 455 to require that contested disqualification motions be decided by a different judge rather than asking the judge to "grade his own paper." Charles G. Geyh, Assoc. Dean of Research, John F. Kimberly Chair in Law, Indiana Univ. Maurer School of Law at Bloomington, Testimony Before the House Subcommittee on Courts and Competition (Dec. 10, 2009).

4. Since *Forrester*, the Supreme Court has revisited absolute immunity for the President. In *Clinton v. Jones*, the Supreme Court reasoned that "[t]he principal rationale for affording certain public servants immunity from suits for money damages arising out of their official acts is inapplicable to unofficial conduct," 520 U.S. 681, 693 (1997), and therefore the President could be sued while in office for conduct that allegedly took place outside of his official duties and before his election as President. *Id.* at 694.

5. Absolute immunity from § 1983 damages actions has been extended to Executive Branch officials who perform quasi-judicial functions. *E.g.*, *Butz v. Economou*, 438 U.S. 478 (1978) (holding that officials who perform quasi-judicial and quasi-prosecutorial functions in administrative agency adjudications are entitled to the same immunities afforded to judges and prosecutors at common law); *Swift v. California*, 384 F.3d 1184, 1189 (9th Cir. 2004) (holding that parole board officials are entitled to absolute quasi-judicial immunity from suits arising from decisions to grant, deny, or revoke parole). In *Butz*, the Court identified factors to be weighed in determining whether a non-judicial officer performs quasi-judicial functions and therefore is entitled to judicial immunity:

> (a) the need to assure that the individual can perform his functions without harassment or intimidation; (b) the presence of safeguards that reduce the need for private damages actions as a means of controlling unconstitutional conduct; (c) insulation from political influence; (d) the importance of precedent; (e) the adversary nature of the process; and (f) the correctability of error on appeal.

Butz, 438 U.S. at 512–13. Considering these factors, in *Cleavinger v. Saxner*, 474 U.S. 193, 203 (1985), the Supreme Court rejected absolute immunity for prison disciplinary hearing panels, even though members of such panels do adjudicate whether the accused inmate is guilty of a prison rule violation based on testimony, credibility determinations, documents, and weighing the evidence, and even though disappointed inmates might harass or intimidate members of the hearing panel. Nevertheless, the Supreme Court reasoned:

> We do not perceive the discipline committee's function as a "classic" adjudicatory one.... Surely, the members of the [prison hearing panels], unlike a federal or state judge, are not 'independent'; to say that they are is to ignore reality. They are not professional hearing officers, as are administrative law judges. They are, instead, prison officials, albeit no longer of the rank and file, temporarily diverted from their usual duties. They are employees of the [prison] and they are the direct subordinates of the warden who reviews their decision. They work with the fellow employee who lodges the charge against the inmate upon whom they sit in judgment. The credibility determination they make often is one between a co-worker and an inmate. They thus are under obvious pressure to resolve a disciplinary dispute in favor of the institution and their fellow employee.

Id. at 203–04.

6. Absolute immunity from § 1983 damages actions has been extended to witnesses testifying at trial. *Briscoe v. LaHue*, 460 U.S. 325, 334 (1983). Invocation of absolute immunity by clerks employed by the judiciary, however, has met with mixed results. *See, e.g.*, *Antoine v. Byers & Anderson*, 508 U.S. 429, 435 (1993) (holding that court reporter was not absolutely immune from damages action for failing to produce trial transcript because verbatim transcription is not discretionary and judicial immunity is intended to protect the "independent and impartial exercise of judgment vital to the judiciary" which otherwise "might be impaired by exposure to potential damages liability"); *compare Stein v. Disciplinary Board of Sup. Ct. of New Mexico*, 520 F.3d 1183, 1192 (10th Cir. 2008) (declining to determine "the precise boundaries of absolute quasijudicial immunity for clerks"); *but see Rodriguez v. Weprin*, 116 F.3d 62, 66–67 (2d Cir. 1997) (holding that court clerks alleged to have improperly managed the court calendar were entitled to absolute immunity because a "court's inherent power to control its docket is part of its function of resolving disputes between parties").

In *Rehberg v. Paulk*, 566 U.S. 356 (2012), the Yale Law School Supreme Court Clinic was on the litigation team for petitioner Charles Rehberg. Rehberg was a certified public accountant who criticized management of a hospital. Allegedly as a favor to the hospital's leadership, Rehberg was criminally investigated by James Paulk, the district attorney's chief investigator and the "complaining witness" who testified before the grand jury.

In *Rehberg*, the Supreme Court held that a complaining witness in a grand jury proceeding is entitled to absolute immunity because a witness's fear of liability could impair the truth-seeking process and the threat of perjury provides sufficient deterrent to false testimony. *Id.* at 367. The Court reasoned:

> The factors that justify absolute immunity for trial witnesses apply with equal force to grand jury witnesses. In both contexts, a witness' fear of retaliatory litigation may deprive the tribunal of critical evidence. And in neither context is the deterrent of potential civil liability needed to prevent perjurious testimony. In *Briscoe*, the Court concluded that the possibility of civil liability was not needed to deter false testimony at trial because other sanctions—chiefly prosecution for perjury—provided a sufficient deterrent. *Id.*, at 342. Since perjury before a grand jury, like perjury at trial, is a serious criminal offense ... there is no reason to think that this deterrent is any less effective in preventing false grand jury testimony.

Id.

> [W]e conclude that grand jury witnesses should enjoy the same immunity as witnesses at trial. This means that a grand jury witness has absolute immunity from any § 1983 claim based on the witness' testimony. In addition, as the Court of Appeals held, this rule may not be circumvented by claiming that a grand jury witness conspired to present false testimony or by using evidence of the witness' testimony to support any other § 1983 claim concerning the initiation or maintenance of a prosecution. Were it otherwise, 'a criminal defendant turned civil plaintiff could simply reframe a claim to attack the preparation instead of the absolutely immune actions themselves." *Buckley v. Fitzsimmons*, 509 U.S. 259, 283 (1993) (KENNEDY, J., concurring in part and dissenting in part)....

Id. at 369.

7. The next section addresses the extension of absolute immunity to prosecutors when they perform functions intimately associated with the judicial process and to social workers when they perform functions analogous to prosecutors.

C. Prosecutorial Function

Questions to guide reading of *Kalina*

1. According to *Kalina*, what considerations supported absolute immunity for prosecutors in *Imbler*?
2. According to *Kalina*, why was absolute immunity unavailable for certain of the prosecutors' functions in *Burns*, *Buckley*, and *Kalina* itself?

Kalina v. Fletcher

522 U.S. 118 (1997)

Justice STEVENS delivered the opinion of the Court.

The question presented is whether 42 U.S.C. § 1983 creates a damages remedy against a prosecutor for making false statements of fact in an affidavit supporting an application for an arrest warrant, or whether, as she contends, such conduct is protected by "the doctrine of absolute prosecutorial immunity."

I.

Petitioner is a Deputy Prosecuting Attorney for King County, Washington. Following customary practice, on December 14, 1992, she commenced a criminal proceeding against respondent by filing three documents in the King County Superior Court. Two of those documents—an information charging respondent with burglary and a motion for an arrest warrant—were unsworn pleadings. The burglary charge was based on an alleged theft of computer equipment from a school.

Washington Criminal Rules require that an arrest warrant be supported by an affidavit or "sworn testimony establishing the grounds for issuing the warrant." To satisfy that requirement, petitioner supported her motion with a third document—a "Certification for Determination of Probable Cause"—that summarized the evidence supporting the charge. She personally vouched for the truth of the facts set forth in the certification under penalty of perjury. Based on petitioner's certification, the trial court found probable cause and ordered that an arrest warrant be issued.

Petitioner's certification contained two inaccurate factual statements. After noting that respondent's fingerprints had been found on a glass partition in the school, petitioner stated that respondent had "never been associated with the school in any manner and did not have permission to enter the school or to take any property." In fact, he had installed partitions on the premises and was authorized to enter the school. She also stated that an employee of an electronics store had identified respondent "from a photo montage" as the person who had asked for an appraisal of a computer stolen from the school. In fact, the employee did not identify respondent.

Respondent was arrested and spent a day in jail. About a month later, the charges against him were dismissed on the prosecutor's motion.

II.

Respondent brought this action under ... 42 U.S.C. § 1983, seeking damages from petitioner based on her alleged violation of his constitutional right to be free from unreasonable seizures.... Respondent's complaint focuses on the false statements made by petitioner in the certification.

...

III.

Section 1983 is a codification of § 1 of the Civil Rights Act of 1871. The text of the statute purports to create a damages remedy against every state official for the violation of any person's federal constitutional or statutory rights.... We have nevertheless recognized that Congress intended the statute to be construed in the light of common-law principles that were well settled at the time of its enactment.

...

In *Imbler v. Pachtman*, 424 U.S. 409 (1976), we held that a former prisoner whose conviction had been set aside in collateral proceedings could not maintain a § 1983 action against the prosecutor who had litigated the charges against him. Relying in part on common-law precedent, and perhaps even more importantly on the policy considerations underlying that precedent, we concluded that "a state prosecuting attorney who acted within the scope of his duties in initiating and pursuing a criminal prosecution" was not amenable to suit under § 1983. *Id.*, at 410.

...

The policy considerations that justified the common-law decisions affording absolute immunity to prosecutors when performing traditional functions ... included both the interest in protecting the prosecutor from harassing litigation that would divert his time and attention from his official duties and the interest in enabling him to exercise independent judgment when "deciding which suits to bring and in conducting them in court." *Id.*, at 424. The former interest would lend support to an immunity from all litigation against the occupant of the office whereas the latter is applicable only when the official is performing functions that require the exercise of prosecutorial discretion. Our later cases have made it clear that it is the interest in protecting the proper functioning of the office, rather than the interest in protecting its occupant, that is of primary importance.

In *Imbler*, we did not attempt to define the outer limits of the prosecutor's absolute immunity, but we did recognize that our rationale would not encompass some of his official activities. Thus, while we concluded that Pachtman's "activities were intimately associated with the judicial phase of the criminal process, and thus were functions to which the reasons for absolute immunity apply with full force," *id.*, at 430, we put to one side "those aspects of the prosecutor's responsibility that cast him in the role of an administrator or investigative officer rather than that of advocate," *id.*, at 430–431.

Subsequent cases have confirmed the importance to the judicial process of protecting the prosecutor when serving as an advocate in judicial proceedings. Thus, in *Burns v. Reed*, 500 U.S. 478 (1991), after noting the consensus among the Courts of Appeals concerning prosecutorial conduct before grand juries, *id.*, at 490, n. 6, we held that the prosecutor's appearance in court in support of an application for a search warrant and the presentation of evidence at that hearing were protected by absolute immunity, *id.*, at 492. And in *Buckley* [*v. Fitzsimmons*], we categorically stated that "acts undertaken by a prosecutor in preparing for the initiation of judicial proceedings or for trial, and which occur in the course of his role as an advocate for the State, are entitled to the protections of absolute immunity." 509 U.S., 259, 273 (1993).

In both of those cases, however, we found the defense unavailable when the prosecutor was performing a different function. In *Burns*, the provision of legal advice to the police during their pretrial investigation of the facts was protected only by qualified, rather than absolute, immunity. 500 U.S., at 492–496. Similarly, in *Buckley*, the prosecutor was not acting as an advocate either when he held a press conference, 509 U.S., at 276–278, or when he allegedly fabricated evidence concerning an unsolved crime. With reference to the latter holding, we explained:

> There is a difference between the advocate's role in evaluating evidence and interviewing witnesses as he prepares for trial, on the one hand, and the detective's role in searching for the clues and corroboration that might give him probable cause to recommend that a suspect be arrested, on the other hand. When a prosecutor performs the investigative functions normally performed by a detective or police officer, it is "neither appropriate nor justifiable that, for the same act, immunity should protect the one and not the other." *Id.* at 273–74.

These cases make it clear that the absolute immunity that protects the prosecutor's role as an advocate is not grounded in any special "esteem for those who perform these functions, and certainly not from a desire to shield abuses of office, but because any lesser degree of immunity could impair the judicial process itself." *Malley* [*v. Briggs*], 475 U.S., [335,] 342 [1986]. Thus, in determining immunity, we examine "the nature of the function performed, not the identity of the actor who performed it." *Forrester v. White*, 484 U.S. 219, 229 (1988).

...

In *Malley* we considered, and rejected ... immunity [for] a police officer who had caused an unconstitutional arrest by presenting a judge with a complaint and supporting affidavit that failed to establish probable cause.... [The Supreme Court rejected the police officer's proffered analogy] between his conduct and the functions often performed by prosecutors. As we explained:

> ... [C]laiming absolute immunity, [the police officer] draws an analogy between an officer requesting a warrant and a prosecutor who asks a grand jury to indict a suspect. Like the prosecutor, [the police officer] argues, the officer must exercise a discretionary judgment based on the evidence before him, and like the prosecutor, the officer may not exercise his best judgment if the threat of retaliatory lawsuits hangs over him. Thus, [he] urges us to read § 1983 as giving the officer the same absolute immunity enjoyed by the prosecutor. *Cf. Imbler v. Pachtman*, 424 U.S. 409 (1976).
>
> ....
>
> We intend no disrespect to the officer applying for a warrant by observing that his action, while a vital part of the administration of criminal justice, is further removed from the judicial phase of criminal proceedings than the act of a prosecutor in seeking an indictment. Furthermore, [the officer's] analogy, while it has some force, does not take account of the fact that the prosecutor's act in seeking an indictment is but the first step in the process of seeking a conviction. Exposing the prosecutor to liability for the initial phase of his prosecutorial work could interfere with his exercise of independent judgment at every phase of his work, since the prosecutor might come to see later decisions in terms of their effect on his potential liability. Thus, we shield the prosecutor seeking an indictment because any lesser immunity could impair the performance of a central actor in the judicial process. 475 U.S., at 341–343.

These cases make it quite clear that [the prosecutor's] activities in connection with the preparation and filing of two of the three charging documents—the information and the motion for an arrest warrant—are protected by absolute immunity. Indeed, except for her act in personally attesting to the truth of the averments in the certification, it seems equally clear that the preparation and filing of the third document in the package was part of the advocate's function as well. The critical question, however, is whether she was acting as a complaining witness rather than a lawyer when she executed the certification "[u]nder penalty of perjury." We now turn to that question.

IV.

The Fourth Amendment requires that arrest warrants be based "upon probable cause, supported by Oath or affirmation"—a requirement that may be satisfied by an indictment returned by a grand jury, but not by the mere filing of criminal charges in an unsworn information signed by the prosecutor....

Although the law required that document to be sworn or certified under penalty of perjury, neither federal nor state law made it necessary for the prosecutor to make that certification. In doing so, petitioner performed an act that any competent witness might have performed.... Indeed, tradition, as well as the ethics of our profession, generally instruct counsel to avoid the risks associated with participating as both advocate and witness in the same proceeding.

...

Nevertheless, petitioner argues that the execution of the certificate was just one incident in a presentation that, viewed as a whole, was the work of an advocate and was integral to the initiation of the prosecution. That characterization is appropriate for her drafting of the certification, her determination that the evidence was sufficiently strong to justify a probable-cause finding, her decision to file charges, and her presentation of the information and the motion to the court. Each of those matters involved the exercise of professional judgment; indeed, even the selection of the particular facts to include in the certification to provide the evidentiary support for the finding of probable cause required the exercise of the judgment of the advocate. But that judgment could not affect the truth or falsity of the factual statements themselves. Testifying about facts is the function of the witness, not of the lawyer.... Even when the person who makes the constitutionally required "Oath or affirmation" is a lawyer, the only function that she performs in giving sworn testimony is that of a witness.

Finally, petitioner argues that denying her absolute immunity will have a "chilling effect" on prosecutors in the administration of justice. We are not persuaded.

...

[W]e merely hold that § 1983 may provide a remedy for respondent insofar as petitioner performed the function of a complaining witness. We do not depart from our prior cases that have recognized that the prosecutor is fully protected by absolute immunity when performing the traditional functions of an advocate. See *Imbler*, 424 U.S., at 431; *Buckley*, 509 U.S., at 273.

For further discussion

1. While the individual prosecutor is protected by absolute immunity, should former criminal defendants be permitted to sue for damages under 42 U.S.C. § 1983 if they claim that constitutional errors at trial were caused by the *supervisors* of the individual prosecutor? The Supreme Court unanimously answered "no." In *Van de Kamp v. Goldstein*, 555 U.S. 335 (2009), the Court held that a prosecutor's absolute immunity extends to claims of constitutional errors in the prosecution "due to: (1) a failure to properly train prosecutors, (2) a failure to properly supervise prosecutors, or (3) a failure to establish an information system containing potential impeachment material about informants." *Id.* at 338–39.

Thomas Goldstein was convicted of murder. Over two decades later, federal courts granted Mr. Goldstein habeas corpus relief because prosecutors had failed to provide his trial attorney with information that could have been used to impeach the testimony of a jailhouse informant, allegedly resulting in Goldstein's erroneous conviction. Rather than retry Mr. Goldstein, the Los Angeles District Attorney's Office released him. Mr. Goldstein filed a 42 U.S.C. § 1983 damages action against the chief supervisory attorneys, alleging that their failure to train and supervise prosecutors who worked for them, and failure to establish an information system about informants, had resulted in the prosecution's failure to tell his defense attorney that the jailhouse informant had received reduced sentences for providing prosecutors with favorable testimony in other cases, a violation of their constitutional duty. *Id.* at 339–40.

The Supreme Court held the supervisors absolutely immune, despite agreeing with Mr. Goldstein that he was attacking the prosecutors' "administrative procedures." *Id.* at 344. The Court explained:

> [W]e conclude that prosecutors involved in such supervision or training or information-system management enjoy absolute immunity from the kind of legal claims at issue here. Those claims focus upon a certain kind of administrative obligation—a kind that itself is directly connected with the conduct of a trial. Here, unlike with other claims related to administrative decisions, an individual prosecutor's error in the plaintiff's specific criminal trial constitutes an essential element of the plaintiff's claim. The administrative obligations at issue here are thus unlike administrative duties concerning, for example, workplace hiring, payroll administration, the maintenance of physical facilities, and the like. Moreover, the types of activities on which Goldstein's claims focus necessarily require legal knowledge and the exercise of related discretion, *e.g.*, in determining what information should be included in the training or the supervision or the information-system management. And in that sense also Goldstein's claims are unlike claims of, say, unlawful discrimination in hiring employees.

Id. at 344. Since "supervisory prosecutors [would be] immune in a suit directly attacking their actions related to an *individual trial*, we must find they are similarly immune in the case before us." *Id.* at 346. Under *Imbler*'s functional analysis, both "a suit charging that a supervisor made a mistake directly related to a particular trial, on the one hand, and a suit charging that a supervisor trained and supervised inadequately, on the other" would result in absolute immunity, *id.*, because the prosecutors' behavior in both situations "would involve '[p]reparation ... for ... trial,' [*Imbler*,] 424 U.S., at 431, n. 33, and would be 'intimately associated with the judicial phase of the criminal process' because [both] concern[] the evidence presented at trial. *Id.*, at 430." *Van de Kamp*, 555 U.S. at 345. Practically, "it will often prove difficult to draw a line between general office supervision or office training ... and specific supervision or training related to a particular case." *Id.* at 346. "Most important, the ease with which a plaintiff could restyle a complaint charging a trial failure so that it becomes a complaint charging a failure of training or supervision would eviscerate *Imbler*." *Id.* at 347.

While the absolute immunity inquiry can be more complex when prosecutors are sued for actions taken in their administrative roles, *Van de Kamp* clarifies that a plaintiff cannot circumvent absolute immunity for individual prosecutors by suing their supervisors for failure to adequately train or supervise the individual prosecutors.

2. Recall that the Supreme Court denied absolute immunity for hiring and firing decisions by judges because such employment claims "cannot meaningfully be distinguished from a district attorney who hires and fires assistant district attorneys ... [and] no one suggests that [such employment decisions] give rise to absolute immunity from liability in damages under § 1983." *Forrester*, 484 U.S. at 229. Can you reconcile the reasoning of *Forrester* and of *Van de Kamp*?

3. Absolute immunity is limited to individuals. Absolute immunity is not available as a defense to governments. "[C]ounties and other local governments—while 'persons' for the purposes of § 1983 liability in the sense that they can be sued—do not enjoy the defenses of absolute and qualified immunity that are available to human defendants sued in their individual capacities. *See Owen v. City of Independence*, 445 U.S. 622, 650 (1980); *Monell v. Dep't of Social Serv.*, 436 U.S. 658, 694 (1978)." *Holloway v. Brush*, 220 F.3d 767, 772 (6th Cir. 2000).

4. The Supreme Court was to consider the scope of absolute immunity for prosecutors in *Pottawattamie County v. McGhee*, 556 U.S. 1181 (2009) (granting certiorari). There, two men who had served more than two decades in prison alleged that prosecutors had obtained murder convictions by coercing false testimony from third-party witnesses, introducing that testimony at trial, and withholding exculpatory evidence of a different murder suspect. In an amicus brief in support of the prosecutors, the United States summarized the current understanding of and justification for absolute immunity:

> ... If the allegations here are true, [prosecutors] engaged in prosecutorial misconduct of an execrable sort, involving a complete breach of the public trust. But absolute immunity reflects a policy judgment that such conduct is properly addressed not through civil liability, but through a host of other deterrents and punishments, including judicial oversight of criminal trials, and criminal and professional disciplinary proceedings against prosecutors. *Imbler* [*v. Pachtman*], 424 U.S. [409,] 429 [(1976)]. The Court has long held

that, given these alternative tools, allowing criminal defendants to bring civil suits against prosecutors will produce few additional benefits and could cause serious harm.

What respondents seek here is, in every effect, a subversion of absolute prosecutorial immunity. To be sure, this Court has recognized that a prosecutor "neither is, nor should consider himself to be, an advocate"—and thus not absolutely immune—"before he has probable cause to have anyone arrested." *Buckley v. Fitzsimmons*, 509 U.S. 259, 274 (1993). But the Court has never said that a prosecutor can be liable for actions at trial, simply because they relate back to earlier conduct at the investigatory stage (*i.e.*, before probable cause is established). To do so would transform the absolute immunity of *Imbler* into little more than a pleading rule; plaintiffs barred under *Imbler* would simply draft their complaint to refer to the prosecutor's investigation and preparation of the case instead of his activity at trial.

...

Imbler's promise of absolute immunity becomes meaningless if any acquitted individual could pierce the prosecutor's protection by pleading that he was somehow involved in a pre-trial investigation. The common law has never recognized such a theory of liability, and because that theory would undermine the purposes of absolute prosecutorial immunity, the Court should not do so now.

Brief for the United States as Amicus Curiae Supporting Petitioners, *Pottawattamie Cty. v. McGhee*, No. 08-1065, 2009 WL 2159654 (July 20, 2009).

Yet the Supreme Court did not decide the case. After the oral argument the government defendants settled with the two former criminal defendants. *See* Lee Rood, *$12 million wrongful conviction settlement is hailed*, Des Moines Register (Jan. 5, 2010), and the Supreme Court dismissed certiorari. *See Pottawattamie Cty. v. McGhee*, 558 U.S. 1103 (2010). Given the cost and effort of petitioning for certiorari, briefing the merits, preparing for argument, and delivering oral argument, why do you think the government defendants settled the case after the oral argument? Given the Supreme Court's apparent interest in the issue, do you think it is likely that the Supreme Court will consider the scope of absolute prosecutorial immunity in the near future?

D. Development of Doctrine in the Circuits: Absolute Immunity for Social Workers

The following cases illustrate differing approaches to immunity for social workers and child protective service workers. Before reading these cases, consider the factual information in Chapter 4 about the working conditions of social workers and others charged with protecting children on behalf of the state.

Questions to guide reading of *Ernst*

1. Under what circumstances did the Third Circuit hold that a social worker is entitled to absolute immunity? How does *Ernst* summarize the steps in the historical and functional analysis?
2. What public policy considerations supported absolute immunity for social workers? Other than § 1983 actions, what safeguards exist to protect parents from unconstitutional actions by social workers?
3. Why did the Third Circuit hold the individual social worker defendants had absolute immunity in *Ernst*?

Ernst v. Child and Youth Services of Chester County

108 F.3d 486 (3d Cir.), *cert. denied*,
522 U.S. 850 (1997)

STAPLETON, Circuit Judge.

A grandmother alleges in this civil rights action that she was deprived of the custody of her granddaughter for five years in violation of rights secured by the Constitution. The defendants are Chester County Children & Youth Services ("CYS") ... caseworkers.... We are called upon to decide whether and to what extent child welfare workers ... who represent child welfare agencies are entitled to absolute immunity for actions taken in connection with dependency proceedings in state court. This is an issue of first impression in this circuit. Like the other courts of appeals that have addressed the issue, we hold that child welfare workers ... who prosecute dependency proceedings on behalf of the state are entitled to absolute immunity from suit for all of their actions in preparing for and prosecuting such dependency proceedings.

I. Facts

Sylvia Ernst ("Ernst") was the sole guardian of her minor granddaughter Susanne from infancy until the child was nine years old. At about that time, during the 1987–88 school year, a number of people in the Downingtown, Pennsylvania area where Ernst and Susanne lived became concerned about Susanne's well-being....

The Downingtown police conducted an investigation and learned that the Family Court of Nassau County, New York, had issued warrants for the arrest of Ernst and her daughter for child neglect and that a petition for custody of Susanne had been filed in 1981 but never served on Ernst. Nassau County officials informed the Downingtown police that the warrants had been vacated and the petition for custody of Susanne had been withdrawn. The police informed a CYS employee of its investigation and of the status of the warrants, but the CYS personnel responsible for the decision to seek custody of Susanne were apparently unaware at the time of their decision that the Nassau County warrants had been withdrawn.

School officials at several schools Susanne attended became concerned about Susanne's frequent tardiness, poor attendance, and inability to separate from Ernst at the start of the school day. The days would often begin with a scene outside Susanne's classroom during which Susanne would cry and scream and refuse to let go of her grandmother. On May 3, 1988, after another morning tantrum, [school] officials ... requested immediate [CYS] intervention. CYS believed Susanne's attachment to Ernst was sufficiently extreme to be unhealthy and filed a petition that same day seeking an adjudication of dependency[3] and emergency custody of Susanne. After an immediate detention hearing, [the state court] found that a *prima facie* case of dependency had been presented, and ordered Susanne placed in a psychiatric institution for a complete evaluation.

At a subsequent hearing on May 18, 1988, the parties stipulated to an adjudication of dependency, which resulted in temporary legal custody remaining with CYS. The stipulation provided that CYS's goal was the reunification of the family and that Ernst could receive counseling and treatment at the institution at which Susanne was being treated.

CYS retained custody of Susanne for the next five years. During that time, Ernst and CYS waged an intense legal battle over Susanne's dependency status and custody. They also developed an extremely contentious relationship. CYS caseworkers found Ernst to be uncooperative, antagonizing, and unwilling to acknowledge her parenting problems. They also complained that she frequently made negative comments about CYS and Susanne's foster families during visits with Susanne. As CYS caseworkers became increasingly frustrated with Ernst, they sought and obtained restrictions on her visits with Susanne. Ultimately, with the approval of the [state courts], they changed CYS's goal for Susanne from family reunification to long-term foster placement. Meanwhile, Susanne occupied eight different placements at various foster homes and institutions. Ultimately, her emotional and intellectual development deteriorated significantly.

Finally, in April 1993, a new judge assigned to review Susanne's placement recognized that "[t]he adversarial air of the proceeding [concerning Susanne's dependency] ... at times ... captured the focus of many of those involved in this case instead of focusing on Susanne." ... Concluding that "[w]e have come to the point where state intervention in Susanne's life is now doing more harm than good," the court ordered that physical custody of Susanne be returned to Ernst, with legal custody remaining with CYS. Ernst was granted legal custody on November 17, 1993.

During the pendency of the state court proceedings, Ernst filed this action in federal court under 42 U.S.C. § 1983 against ... various CYS caseworkers who were involved in Susanne's case (the "CYS defendants").... Ernst's complaint alleged (1) violation of procedural and substantive due process by all defendants for their improper "seizure" of Susanne; (2) violation of substantive due process by ... the CYS defendants ... for the imposition of restrictions on visitation and for the recommendation of long-term placement instead of reunification....

3. A child is "dependent" under Pennsylvania law if he or she is "without proper parental care or control, subsistence, education as required by law, or other care or control necessary for his physical, mental, or emotional health, or morals."....

. . .

A. CYS Defendants' Absolute Immunity

Ernst challenges the district court's grant of partial summary judgment to the CYS defendants based on absolute immunity "insofar as they acted in their prosecutorial capacity of filing petitions and making recommendations to the court." She contends that the CYS defendants cannot claim entitlement to immunity from suit under § 1983 because child welfare workers employed by the state did not exist, and thus enjoyed no immunity from suit at common law, in 1871 when § 1983 was enacted. Although we recognize that state-employed social workers enjoyed no common law immunity from suit in 1871, we nonetheless hold that the CYS defendants are entitled to absolute immunity for their actions in petitioning and in formulating and making recommendations to the state court because those actions are analogous to functions performed by state prosecutors, who were immune from suit at common law.

... Despite its broad language, the Supreme Court has consistently held that [42 U.S.C. § 1983] did not abolish long-standing common law immunities from civil suits. *See Burns v. Reed*, 500 U.S. 478, 484 (1991) (citing *Pierson v. Ray*, 386 U.S. 547, 554 (1967)); *Imbler v. Pachtman*, 424 U.S. 409, 418 (1976). Instead, courts must determine whether a particular governmental official is entitled to immunity according to the following analysis:

> [The] initial inquiry is whether [the] official claiming immunity under § 1983 can point to a common-law counterpart to the privilege he asserts. If "an official was accorded immunity from tort actions at common law when the Civil Rights Act was enacted in 1871, the Court next considers whether § 1983's history or purposes nonetheless counsel against recognizing the same immunity in § 1983 actions."

Malley v. Briggs, 475 U.S. 335, 340 (1986) [further citation omitted]. Courts "look to the common law and other history for guidance because [their] role is 'not to make a freewheeling policy choice,' but rather to discern Congress' likely intent in enacting § 1983." *Burns*, 500 U.S. at 493 (quoting *Malley*, 475 U.S. at 342).

The fact that a particular public official did not enjoy absolute immunity at common law is not, however, determinative of the absolute immunity issue. Where the official claiming immunity occupies a governmental position that did not exist at common law, he may still be entitled to immunity if he performs official functions that are analogous to functions performed by those who were immune at common law. *See Butz v. Economou*, 438 U.S. 478 (1978) (holding that officials who perform quasi-judicial and quasi-prosecutorial functions in administrative agency adjudications are entitled to the same immunities afforded to judges and prosecutors at common law); *see also Forrester v. White*, 484 U.S. 219, 224 (1988) ("Running through our cases, with fair consistency, is a 'functional' approach to immunity questions other than those that have been decided by express constitutional or statutory enactment. Under that approach, we examine the nature of the functions with which a particular official or class of officials has been lawfully entrusted, and we seek to evaluate the effect that exposure to particular forms of liability would likely have on the appropriate exercise of those functions."). It is therefore necessary for us to review the functions performed by officials to whom absolute immunity has been accorded in order to determine if child welfare workers perform analogous functions.

Under its historical and functional approach, the Supreme Court has held that certain officials "functioning as integral parts of the judicial process" are absolutely immune from civil suits under § 1983.... For example, the Court has declared that judges, *Pierson v. Ray*, 386 U.S. 547 (1967), prosecutors, *Imbler v. Pachtman*, 424 U.S. 409 (1976), and witnesses, *Briscoe v. LaHue*, 460 U.S. 325 (1983), are entitled to absolute immunity when they perform judicial or quasi-judicial acts that are integral parts of the judicial process.

In *Imbler v. Pachtman*, the Court held that prosecutors were absolutely immune at common law from civil liability for malicious prosecution and that public policy considerations countenanced a similar absolute immunity from suits under § 1983. 424 U.S. at 424. The relevant public policy considerations were numerous. First, a prosecutor's exercise of his independent judgment would likely be compromised if he were threatened with suits for damages for his actions in initiating and prosecuting criminal cases in court. *Id.* at 424–25. Such suits "could be expected with some frequency, for a defendant often will transform his resentment at being prosecuted into the ascription of improper and malicious actions to the State's advocate." *Id.* at 425. Second, the prosecutor's energy would be diverted from his official duties if he were forced to defend himself against § 1983 actions. *Id.* Third, defending against § 1983 actions likely would be particularly difficult for a prosecutor:

> [T]he honest prosecutor would face greater difficulty in meeting the standards of qualified immunity than other executive or administrative officials. Frequently acting under serious constraints of time and even information, a prosecutor inevitably makes many decisions that could engender colorable claims of constitutional deprivation. Defending these decisions, often years after they were made, could impose unique and intolerable burdens upon a prosecutor responsible annually for hundreds of indictments and trials.

Id. at 425–26. Fourth, failure to afford absolute immunity to prosecutors might undermine the functioning of the criminal justice system because it might lead prosecutors concerned about personal liability not to tender evidence that, while relevant, might conceivably turn out to be fabricated by the witness. *Id.* at 426. Fifth, failure to afford absolute immunity might weaken the fairness of the criminal justice system by clouding postconviction review with "the subconscious knowledge that a post-trial decision in favor of the accused might result in the prosecutor's being called upon to respond in damages for his error or mistaken judgment." *Id.* at 427. Finally, the court noted that absolute immunity for prosecutors would not leave the public without any means to punish or deter unconstitutional conduct because the availability of both judicial review and professional disciplinary procedures would protect the public and punish the errant prosecutor. *Id.* at 429. Thus, the Court concluded that "in initiating a prosecution and in presenting the State's case, the prosecutor is immune from a civil suit for damages under § 1983." *Id.* at 431.

In *Burns v. Reed*, 500 U.S. 478 (1991), and *Buckley v. Fitzsimmons*, 509 U.S. 259 (1993), the Court clarified the scope of a prosecutor's absolute immunity from suit under § 1983. In *Burns*, the Court held that a prosecutor was absolutely immune from liability for his presentation of evidence in a probable cause hearing but was not absolutely immune for the provision of legal advice to police officers investigating a case. Emphasizing its "functional approach" to immunity under § 1983, the Court reiterated that absolute immunity extends only to prosecutorial activities that are "intimately associated with the judicial phase of the criminal process." *Burns*, 500 U.S. at 493 (quoting *Imbler*, 424 U.S. at 430). Such activities include both the initiation and prosecution of the State's case and certain "actions preliminary to the initiation of a prosecution" but nonetheless integral to the judicial prosecution of the case. *Id.* at 491 (quoting *Imbler*, 424 U.S. at 431 n. 33).

In *Buckley v. Fitzsimmons*, the Court again declared that "the *Imbler* approach focuses on the conduct for which immunity is claimed," 509 U.S. at 271–72 (emphasis added), and the "functional tie" between that conduct and the judicial process in a criminal case. *Id.* at 277–78. It distinguished between a prosecutor's functioning as an "advocate" in judicial proceedings on behalf of the State, which is entitled to immunity, and as an investigator searching for clues that might lead to an arrest, which is not entitled to absolute immunity.

Applying the principles set forth in *Butz*, *Imbler*, and their progeny to the instant case, we hold that the CYS defendants are entitled to absolute immunity for their actions on behalf of the state in preparing for, initiating, and prosecuting dependency proceedings. Their immunity is broad enough to include the formulation and presentation of recommendations to the court in the course of such proceedings. We reach this conclusion because (1) the functions performed by the CYS defendants in dependency proceedings are closely analogous to the functions performed by prosecutors in criminal proceedings; (2) the public policy considerations that countenance immunity for prosecutors are applicable to child welfare workers performing these functions; and (3) dependency proceedings incorporate important safeguards that protect citizens from unconstitutional actions by child welfare workers. With this holding, we join the courts of appeals of the Fourth, Sixth, Seventh, Eighth, and Ninth Circuits....[6]

---

6. Justices Thomas and Scalia recently criticized the appellate court cases that have held that social workers are entitled to absolute immunity for quasi-prosecutorial acts on the ground that

> [a]n official seeking ... immunity ... must at the outset show that a "counterpart to the privilege he asserts" was recognized at common law in 1871.... The courts that have accorded absolute immunity to social workers appear to have overlooked the necessary historical inquiry; none has seriously considered whether social workers enjoyed absolute immunity for their official duties in 1871. If they did not, absolute immunity is unavailable to social workers under § 1983. This all assumes, of course, that "social workers" (at least as we now understand the term) even existed in 1871. If that assumption is false, the argument for granting absolute immunity becomes (at least) more difficult to maintain.

The functions performed by child welfare workers like the CYS defendants in dependency proceedings are closely analogous to those performed by prosecutors. As the Ninth Circuit has explained,

> [a]lthough child services workers do not initiate criminal proceedings, their responsibility for bringing dependency proceedings, and their responsibility to exercise independent judgment in determining when to bring such proceedings, is not very different from the responsibility of a criminal prosecutor. The social worker must make a quick decision based on perhaps incomplete information as to whether to commence investigations and initiate proceedings against parents who may have abused their children.

Meyers v. Contra Costa County Dep't of Soc. Servs., 812 F.2d 1154, 1157 (9th Cir. 1987).

In addition, child welfare workers involved in the prosecution of dependency proceedings clearly serve "as advocate for the State," *Imbler*, 424 U.S. at 430–31 n. 33, in a capacity that is "intimately associated with the judicial phase of the [child protection] process." *Id.* at 430. A CYS court liaison officer and a case work supervisor testified that CYS caseworkers, after consultation with their supervisors and other professionals such as psychologists and school officials, determine what recommendations are made to the court in dependency proceedings. Even when they work with an attorney who represents CYS in the dependency proceeding, the attorney plays no role in formulating the recommendations made to the court; she merely "expresses [CYS's] recommendations on [its] behalf." ... Because CYS caseworkers are directly responsible for the recommendations made to the court in dependency proceedings, their actions in determining those recommendations and communicating them to the court are "intimately associated" with the judicial process in much the same way as are a prosecutor's actions in representing the state in criminal prosecutions.

Moreover, we conclude that the public policy considerations supporting absolute immunity for prosecutors are equally applicable to child welfare workers acting in a quasi-prosecutorial capacity in dependency proceedings. Like a prosecutor, a child welfare worker must exercise independent judgment in deciding whether or not to bring a child dependency proceeding, and such judgment would likely be compromised if the worker faced the threat of personal liability for every mistake in judgment. Certainly, we want our child welfare workers to exercise care in deciding to interfere in parent-child relationships. But we do not want them to be so overly cautious, out of fear of personal liability, that they fail to intervene in situations in which children are in danger.... *cf. DeShaney v. Winnebago County Dep't of Soc. Servs.*, 489 U.S. 189, 191–93 (1989).

In the absence of absolute immunity, we would expect suits in retaliation for the initiation of dependency proceedings to occur with even greater frequency than suits

---

Hoffman v. Harris, 511 U.S. 1060 (1994) (Thomas, J., dissenting from denial of certiorari) (citations omitted). However, there has been no indication that the other justices on the Court perceive the appropriate historical inquiry in the same way as do Justices Thomas and Scalia. Indeed, it seems to us inconsistent with the Court's holding in *Butz* to do so.

against prosecutors. Parents involved in seemingly unjustified dependency proceedings are likely to be even more resentful of state interference in the usually sacrosanct parent-child relationship than are defendants of criminal prosecution.... In turn, the likely frequency of such suits would result in a significant diversion of the energies of child welfare workers away from their official duties to the defense of § 1983 litigation. Further, defending against § 1983 actions would likely be as difficult for child welfare workers as it would be for prosecutors because child welfare workers, like prosecutors, must make quick decisions on the basis of limited information. "Defending these decisions, often years after they are made, could impose unique and intolerable burdens on [child welfare workers] responsible annually for hundreds of [dependency and child abuse cases]." *Imbler*, 424 U.S. at 425–26.

Finally, as with prosecutors, there are alternative mechanisms other than the threat of § 1983 liability that protect the public against unconstitutional conduct by child welfare workers. First, the judicial process itself provides significant protection.... Child welfare workers must seek an adjudication of dependency from a neutral judge whose decisions are guided by the "best interests of the child" and subject to appellate review. Second, although child welfare workers are not subject to the comprehensive system of professional responsibility applicable to prosecutors, they are under the supervision of the agency that employs them. The agency has an incentive to ensure that its employees do not violate constitutional rights because it is not immune from suit for abuses committed by employees with policy-making authority or acting pursuant to agency policy or custom.

Reviewing Ernst's Third Amended Complaint, it is clear that all of the claims against the CYS defendants concern actions taken by the defendants in connection with the formulation and presentation of recommendations to the state court regarding Susanne's dependency status and disposition. Because all of these actions are analogous to a prosecutor's preparation for and initiation and presentation of a criminal prosecution, we hold that the CYS defendants are entitled to absolute immunity for the conduct that Ernst challenges here.[7]

We cannot agree with the district court's conclusion that the CYS defendants' actions in preparing and formulating recommendations to the state court were not within the

---

7. We emphasize that our holding concerns only actions taken by child welfare workers in the context of dependency proceedings. Like our sister courts in the Fifth, Sixth, Seventh, and Tenth Circuits, we would be unwilling to accord absolute immunity to "investigative or administrative" actions taken by child welfare workers outside the context of a judicial proceeding. *See Snell v. Tunnell*, 920 F.2d 673 (10th Cir. 1990) (holding that pre-adjudicatory investigative activities by child welfare workers are entitled only to qualified immunity); *Achterhof v. Selvaggio*, 886 F.2d 826 (6th Cir. 1989) (holding that opening and investigating child abuse case and placing parent's name on central registry of abusers are investigative and administrative activities entitled only to qualified immunity); *Austin v. Borel*, 830 F.2d 1356 (5th Cir. 1987) (holding that filing of complaint that allowed child services to obtain custody but did not initiate adjudicative proceeding was analogous to police officer's complaint filed to obtain arrest warrant and was therefore entitled only to qualified immunity) (citing *Malley v. Briggs*, 475 U.S. 335 (1986)); *Millspaugh v. County Dep't of Pub. Welfare of Wabash County*, 937 F.2d 1172 (7th Cir. 1991) (same).

scope of their absolute immunity. The Supreme Court has explicitly rejected the idea that absolute prosecutorial immunity "extends only to the act of initiation itself and to conduct occurring in the courtroom." *Buckley*, 509 U.S. at 272. Moreover, the Court has expressly embraced the idea that immunity must be afforded to the evaluation of available data to determine whether and in what manner to seek judicial action:

> We expressly stated [in *Imbler*] that "the duties of the prosecutor in his role as advocate for the State involve actions preliminary to the initiation of a prosecution and actions apart from the courtroom," and are nonetheless entitled to absolute immunity.... We have not retreated ... from the principle that acts undertaken by a prosecutor in preparing for the initiation of judicial proceedings or for trial, and which occur in the course of his role as an advocate for the State, are entitled to the protections of absolute immunity. Those acts must include the professional evaluation of the evidence assembled by the police and appropriate preparation for its presentation at trial or before a grand jury after a decision to seek an indictment has been made.

Id. at 272–73.

Ernst here challenges the CYS defendants' formulation of professional judgments that served as the basis for a series of recommendations they made to the [state court]. To grant them absolute immunity for the recommendations they made to the court but deny them such immunity for the observations and judgments that were the necessary predicate for those recommendations would eviscerate the immunity they did receive and undermine the purposes sought to be advanced by the grant of absolute immunity. We therefore conclude that, like a prosecutor's evaluation of evidence in preparation for indictment or trial, the CYS defendants' gathering and evaluation of information and professional opinions regarding the relationship between Ernst and Susanne in preparation for the dependency proceedings must be protected. Accordingly, we will affirm the grant of judgment for the CYS defendants' for their actions in formulating recommendations concerning Susanne's dependency proceedings on the ground of absolute immunity....

...

Questions to guide reading of *Holloway*

Holloway is the basis for Law Practice Simulation 7.

1. How does the court describe prosecutorial immunity?
2. Under what circumstances did the court hold social workers analogous to prosecutors?
3. Why did the majority hold social worker Brush was not entitled to absolute immunity?
4. Why would the dissent have held Brush entitled to absolute immunity?

Holloway v. Brush

220 F.3d 767 (6th Cir. 2000)

BOGGS, Circuit Judge.

... Sammye Holloway's § 1983 suit for damages [concerns] terminat[ion of] her parental rights and [a] grant [of] permanent custody of her children to the Clermont County Department of Human Services ("CCDHS").... [The full court] *en banc* [today] decide[s] the question of the extent to which a public child services agency caseworker, in this case Sally Brush, may be entitled to immunity for her acts in connection with a child custody proceeding....

I

Sammye Holloway, a mother who despite a high-school diploma reads and writes at a third-grade level due to dyslexia, lost track of her two children, then six months and two years old, when, as alleged in her complaint, her husband threw her out of their Oklahoma home in November 1988 and absconded with the children to another state. Over several years, she made numerous attempts to locate them through the relevant agencies of many states. She had no success until, in 1992, her letter to authorities in the State of Washington led them to notify Ohio, resulting ultimately in contact between Holloway and the CCDHS in the person of Sally Brush, a caseworker there. The sequence of events appears to be as follows.

In 1990, after an odyssey through several states, a sequence of failed jobs and the three of them living out of vehicles, the father and the children were stranded in Clermont County, Ohio after his car broke down there. In November, Ohio authorities became aware that the children were living in a car, in extremely unsanitary conditions. Proceedings were instituted to deprive the father of custody on grounds of abuse and to award custody to CCDHS, preparatory to having the children adopted. CCDHS was granted temporary custody of the Holloway children on November 29, 1990. Efforts to notify Holloway by mail were fruitless, so Clermont County attempted to notify her of the proceedings by publication in the spring of 1991. CCDHS also attempted to place the children with a paternal relative in Spokane, Washington, but this was unsuccessful and the children were returned to Ohio in May or June of 1992. Brush began administering the children's case plan on March 1, 1992. In November 1992, Brush provided an affidavit that Sammye Holloway's whereabouts were unknown, permitting her to be served with notice by publication in The Clermont Sun. On December 15, 1992, Brush testified before a referee appointed by the Clermont County Juvenile Court that the children's father should not regain custody and recommended that permanent custody be awarded to CCDHS. The referee agreed, embodying his recommendations in a report filed on January 26, 1993. Ohio law provides that such a referee's recommendations are to be reviewed, and may be adopted, modified, or set aside by the juvenile court, which also "may hear additional testimony...." Ohio Rev. Code Ann. § 2151.16 (Baldwin 1994). Brush continued to follow the process throughout 1993, in coordination with Clermont County Assistant Prosecutor Thomas Flessa.

On May 12, 1993, the Washington Department of Social and Health Services wrote to CCDHS, addressing the letter to both [a] Supervisor, and Sally Brush, Social Worker, attaching the letter Washington had received from Holloway requesting information about her children. A copy of the letter was sent to Holloway. Brush received that letter on May 18th, and called Flessa about it that day. Her notes on this call read: "5-18-93 Telephone call to Tom Flessa, told him about letter. Legally we have custody." On May 20, 1993, Brush received a letter from Holloway requesting that she put the children on a plane to Kansas City, where Holloway proposed to pick them up. The following day Brush and Holloway spoke by telephone.

At that time, CCDHS had temporary custody of the children, while the juvenile court was considering the referee's recommendation regarding permanent custody for CCDHS. But that is not what Brush told Holloway. For reasons that have not been satisfactorily explained, in their telephone conversation on May 21, 1993 Brush falsely informed Holloway that CCDHS had already been awarded permanent custody of her children. Brush concedes this, but characterizes it as a "misstatement." Brush's own notes of that conversation, however, indicate she did not merely mis-speak: "I told Mrs. Holloway her best bet is to talk to a lawyer about her rights. At this point, our agency has permanent custody." Moreover, Holloway claims that Brush told her "they had taken away her parental rights whether she likes it or not," and refused to discuss the matter further, advising Holloway to get a lawyer. Brush repeated the latter advice in a letter to Holloway dated June 2, 1993. Although the matter of awarding permanent custody to CCDHS was still pending before the juvenile court, the long-sought appearance of the children's mother, who had not been heard at the December proceeding, was not brought to the court's attention by Brush, nor by assistant prosecutor Flessa, who knew as early as May 18th that Holloway had surfaced. Indeed, Holloway alleges that when, on May 24, 1993 Brush failed to keep an appointment to speak with Holloway by phone, due (as Brush's June 2nd letter states) to the fact that Brush was out of her office that afternoon, Brush was actually in court to file a document related to the Holloway custody case ... The record indicates that a Case Plan Document Amendment was in fact filed on that date.

Brush's telephone log of this period continues with entries relating to the children's medical coverage, placement in school as foster children, and other details. On June 15th, the day before the court acted on permanent custody, there is the following entry: "6-15-93 Telephone call to [assistant prosecutor] Tom Flessa. He is writing the letter to Sammye Holloway. I should not worry needlessly at this point about her *disrupting the whole process*. We did everything legally as to publication/notice" (emphasis added)....

On June 16, 1993, the court accepted the referee's report by written order, awarding permanent custody of the children to CCDHS.... On June 18, 1993, two days after the juvenile court acted, Flessa wrote Sammye Holloway to inform her that CCDHS had permanent custody of her sons, and continued "I suggest that you contact an attorney in regard to your legal rights, as our plan is to seek adoptive homes for the children."

Sammye Holloway moved to have the order of permanent custody set aside by the juvenile court; the motion was denied and Holloway appealed. The Ohio Court of

Appeals ruled that Clermont County had not followed proper procedures to give her notice, and remanded the case for a new hearing.... Nevertheless, to this day, seven years after CCDHS secured permanent custody of the Holloway children without their mother being heard, no rehearing has taken place and Holloway's sons remain in the care of the foster parents who adopted them.

...

III

Judges and other court officers are absolutely immune from suit on claims arising out of their performance of judicial or quasi-judicial functions, *Pierson v. Ray*, 386 U.S. 547, 553–54 (1967) ... but not from suits that arise out of other conduct, *Forrester v. White*, 484 U.S. 219, 228 (1988); *Clinton v. Jones*, 520 U.S. 681, 694–95 (1997). Absolute immunity is determined by a functional analysis that looks to "'the nature of the function performed, not the identity of the actor who performed it.'" *Buckley v. Fitzsimmons*, 509 U.S. 259, 269 (1993) (quoting *Burns v. Reed*, 500 U.S. 478, 486 (1991)). The official seeking absolute immunity bears the burden of showing that immunity is justified in light of the function she was performing. *See Burns*, 500 U.S. at 486.

This court has held that under certain circumstances, social workers are entitled to absolute immunity. [citing 6th Circuit decisions holding social workers entitled to absolute immunity when prosecuting child delinquency petitions and when filing child abuse petitions but not when deciding whether to open or continue an investigation or when deciding to enter a parent's name in a central register of abusers, which are administrative or investigative, not prosecutorial]. [In all of these cases] this court has explicitly analogized the social workers to prosecutors for purposes of the functional analysis. Thus, to determine the scope of the immunity extended to social workers, we look to the scope of prosecutorial immunity.

Absolute prosecutorial immunity is justified "only for actions that are connected with the prosecutor's role in judicial proceedings, not for every litigation-inducing conduct." *Burns*, 500 U.S. at 494. "Prosecutors are entitled to absolute immunity for conduct 'intimately associated with the judicial phase of the criminal process.'" *Imbler v. Pachtman*, 424 U.S. 409, 430 (1976). Prosecutors are not absolutely immune when they perform administrative, investigative, or other functions; for example, when they give legal advice to the police, hold a press conference, or fabricate evidence. *Ibid.* "[T]he actions of a prosecutor are not absolutely immune merely because they are performed by a prosecutor. Qualified immunity represents the norm.... *The question, then, is whether the prosecutors have carried their burden of establishing that they were functioning as 'advocates'*" when they performed the actions complained of. *Buckley*, 509 U.S. at 273–74 (emphasis added). The Supreme Court has extended absolute immunity to prosecutors only where their challenged acts were performed while serving as an advocate in legal proceedings. *Kalina v. Fletcher*, 522 U.S. 118, 125 (1997).

This Circuit has followed the Supreme Court closely. Prosecutorial immunity extends to "'a prosecutor's decision to file a criminal complaint and seek an arrest warrant and the presentation of these materials to a judicial officer.' ..." Prosecutors are not absolutely immune, however, when they perform administrative, investigative, or other functions. [citation omitted] (denying absolute immunity to a prosecutor for investigating a couple and holding them on extortion charges without probable cause). "Sixth Circuit precedent has established that 'the critical inquiry is how closely related is the prosecutor's challenged activity to his *role as an advocate* intimately associated with the judicial phase of the criminal process.'" ...

The analytical key to prosecutorial immunity, therefore, is advocacy—whether the actions in question are those of an advocate. *See Buckley*, 509 U.S. at 273–74; *Kalina*, 522 U.S. at 125.... By analogy, social workers are absolutely immune only when they are acting in their capacity as legal advocates—initiating court actions or testifying under oath—not when they are performing administrative, investigative, or other functions. The case before us turns on whether the actions of which Holloway complains were taken by Brush in her capacity as a legal advocate.

IV

As a caseworker, Brush's official position and responsibilities were defined by Ohio statutes. These provide that a "public children services agency ... shall prepare and maintain a case plan for any child to whom the agency is providing services;" this applies, for example, when, as in this case, that agency has temporary custody of the child. Ohio Rev. Code Ann. § 2151.412(A) and (A)(2) (Baldwin 1994). Day-to-day responsibility for that case plan's management is in the hands of the caseworker. *Id.* at § 2151.416(B)(1). In such a situation, the agency preparing the case plan "shall attempt to obtain an agreement among all parties, including, but not limited to, the parents, guardian, or custodian of the child and the guardian ad litem of the child regarding the content of the case plan." *Id.* at § 2151.412(D).

Two aspects of this statutory scheme are of considerable relevance to this case. First, the agency, CCDHS, as temporary custodian of the children, was one of the parties. Second, it was a party with a statutorily created duty to attempt to obtain the agreement of the other parties, including the parents. As the agency caseworker, this was plainly Brush's responsibility, but Brush chose to construe her role otherwise. In violation of the clear mandate of the statute, she described herself to Holloway as her "adversary." Rather than first seeking to forge an agreement with Holloway, as the law required her to do, she refused to discuss the case with that parent. Instead, she advised Holloway to obtain an attorney. Had Brush attempted to obtain Holloway's participation in the proceedings and agreement with the case plan, and failed to obtain such agreement, then perhaps Brush and Holloway would have become adverse parties in a court hearing. In that event, however, the advocate for the child services agency would be, not Brush, but the county prosecutor and assistant prosecutors. To be sure, in such a case, Brush would have absolute immunity for her testimony or recommendations given in court concerning the children's best interests as she saw the matter. But in claiming absolute immunity for her out-of-court actions as a caseworker, Brush arrogates to herself an adversarial and quasi-prosecutorial role which Ohio law did not intend her to have.

Once again, absolute immunity extends to social workers only when they are acting in the capacity of legal advocates. It is apparent that Ohio law does not envision a caseworker's principal function as that of an advocate, although at a certain stage in custody proceedings a caseworker might be called by the prosecutor to present reports or make recommendations that, functionally, constitute advocacy. But the acts for which Brush is being sued—failing to notify the trial court that Plaintiff had made contact and wished to assert her parental rights, telling Plaintiff that her rights had been severed when they had not yet been, and withholding information that would have enabled Plaintiff to raise her rights in court before her rights were severed—do not come within that description.

The information withheld by Brush in the case before us was not analogous to the evidence that may be analyzed, and presented or withheld, by a prosecutor in a criminal proceeding. Rather, it was the fact that a party long sought by the court had appeared and wished to address the court to assert her legal rights; it was the fact that the juvenile court's decision on the recommendations of the referee, who had held the December 15, 1992 hearing and filed the January 26, 1993 report, was still pending, and the fact that in April 1993 a hearing had been held to afford the children's father an opportunity to assert his rights; it was the fact that Holloway, had she not been misinformed by Brush, would have been able to ask the court for a similar hearing on her rights before a decision were made. This is not evidence in the case, but rather administrative information about the case and its posture.

Nor are Brush's actions analogous to a prosecutor's decision about whether a given witness shall or shall not testify, which is entitled to absolute immunity. *See Buckley*, 509 U.S. at 272–73 (citing *Imbler*, 424 U.S. at 430 n. 32). Whatever latitude a prosecutor has to control the testimony of his witness is irrelevant here. Witnesses other than the defendant generally have no right to testify in criminal proceedings. But Holloway did have a right to be heard by the juvenile court. Moreover, Holloway was in no sense Brush's witness, and this is not a situation of a prosecutor's controlling Brush's actions. Holloway was a party, analogous to a defendant in a criminal proceeding, whose right to be heard in court may have been denied by Brush's actions under color of law.

Once such potential analogies to prosecutorial functions are seen as spurious, it is difficult to see in what sense Brush's actions were, in the words of the [district court], "an integral part of the judicial process...." It is true that Brush was involved "in initiating the court proceedings involving the Holloway children and in testifying on behalf of the interests of the children in court." But those are not the actions complained of. It is her out-of-court actions, misinforming Holloway and failing to inform the court of the latter's appearance, that are the basis of this suit. Brush may have been an integral part of the judicial process at other stages. But such an involvement is not, by itself, sufficient for absolute immunity. The Supreme Court has explicated the appropriate standard on several occasions. "The question ... is whether the prosecutors have carried their burden of establishing that they were functioning as 'advocates'" (as opposed, for example, to auxiliary police) when they performed the actions complained of. *Buckley*, 509 U.S. at 274; *see also Kalina*, 522 U.S. at 125 (extending absolute immunity to prosecutors only where their challenged acts were performed while serving as an advocate in legal proceedings).... Even if Brush could successfully explain how failing to tell the court that Holloway had appeared and wished to assert her parental rights, lying to Holloway about her rights, and failing to inform Holloway that the matter was still pending were intimately connected with the judicial process, she has not explained how they were the functions of an advocate or consistent with her statutory role.

Nor are the actions of which Holloway complains analogous to recommendations made by caseworkers to the court, or the "formulation of professional judgments that served as the basis for" such recommendations, which the Third Circuit has held are entitled to immunity. *See Ernst v. Child & Youth Servs.*, 108 F.3d 486 (3d Cir. 1997). In *Ernst*, the court had the opportunity to evaluate the caseworkers' actions and to accept or reject their suggestions. In the case before us, Brush's actions denied the court the opportunity to accept or reject the results of her judgment. A jury could reasonably find that Brush appropriated the entire judicial process to herself by hiding Holloway and the court from each other and feeding them inaccurate information by act (in Holloway's case) and omission (in both cases). Even granting arguendo that Brush's actions were motivated by her "formulations of professional judgment," the actions themselves bear no resemblance to recommendations made to the court. They were, rather, usurpations of the court's authority. Even if such motivations could legitimate Brush's actions, it would be through qualified immunity, not absolute immunity, and she has not claimed qualified immunity.

...

What Brush did was not the evaluation and presentation of evidence. It was not controlling the testimony of her witness. It was not intimately associated with the judicial process, nor was it the function of an advocate. Finally, it was not a recommendation to the county court. It was a usurpation of the judicial process that denied Holloway her right to be heard in court. The proper test is whether Brush has carried her burden of establishing that she was functioning as an advocate when she performed the actions complained of. *See Buckley*, 509 U.S. at 274. She was not. The judgment of the district court granting summary judgment on grounds of absolute immunity to Defendant Brush is REVERSED.

...

CLAY, Circuit Judge, dissenting.

... This case is nothing more than an improper attempt by Plaintiff to use the heavy hand of the federal court to usurp the state court's authority in a child custody case. In its judicial activism, the majority has ignored the truth of this matter in order to set an unwarranted precedent in this circuit regarding the level of immunity to be afforded social workers.... I believe with even greater conviction that Sally Brush is entitled to absolute immunity for her actions at issue in this case which were prosecutorial in nature.

...

Specifically, Plaintiff claims that Ms. Brush denied Plaintiff her right to procedural due process of law when Ms. Brush 1) failed to notify the trial court that Plaintiff had made contact and wished to assert her parental rights, 2) told Plaintiff that her rights had been severed when they had not yet been, and 3) withheld information that would have enabled Plaintiff to raise her rights in court before they had been terminated....

The relevant inquiry into the level of immunity afforded to Ms. Brush for the three alleged actions is whether those actions can be considered "prosecutorial, judicial, or otherwise intimately related to the judicial process." [citing 6th Circuit]. If they can be so considered, then Ms. Brush is entitled to absolute immunity. *Id.* If the actions are considered "investigatory or administrative" in nature, then Ms. Brush would only be entitled to qualified immunity. *See id.* In deciding whether the acts were prosecutorial or administrative/investigatory in nature so as to impose the proper level of immunity, a reviewing court employs the "functional approach" announced by the Supreme Court; which is to say, a court looks to "[']the nature of the function performed, not the identity of the actor who performed it.'" *Buckley v. Fitzsimmons*, 509 U.S. 259, 269 (1993) (quoting *Forrester v. White*, 484 U.S. 219, 229 (1988)).

Because social workers are analogized to prosecutors for immunity purposes, and because I acknowledge that in determining whether a prosecutor is entitled to absolute immunity we look to how closely related the challenged activity is to the prosecutor's role as an advocate ... I agree that for purposes of determining whether a social worker is entitled to absolute immunity for an alleged action, we look to whether she was functioning as an advocate for the state at the time. However, I disagree with the majority's myopic view of those instances when a social worker is functioning as an advocate. In other words, I disagree with the majority's attempt to strictly limit the actions for which a social worker is absolutely immune to instances where she is "initiating court actions or testifying under oath," such that the majority characterizes these actions as being confined to filing a complaint or testifying in court. Indeed, the majority's extreme position was advanced by the petitioner in *Buckley* regarding absolute immunity afforded to prosecutors, and was expressly rejected by the Supreme Court:

> Petitioner argues that *Imbler*'s protection for a prosecutor's conduct in initiating a prosecution and in presenting the State's case, extends only to the act of initiation itself and to conduct occurring in the courtroom. This extreme position is plainly foreclosed by our opinion in *Imbler* [*v. Pachtman*, 424 U.S. 409 (1996)] itself. We expressly stated that the duties of the prosecutor in his role as advocate for the State involve actions preliminary to the initiation of a prosecution and actions apart from the courtroom, and are nonetheless entitled to absolute immunity. We noted in particular that an out-of-court effort to control the presentation of [a] witness' testimony was entitled to absolute immunity because it was fairly within [the prosecutor's] function as an advocate. To be sure, *Burns* made explicit the point we had reserved in *Imbler*: A prosecutor's administrative duties and those investigatory

> functions that do not relate to an advocate's preparation for the initiation of a prosecution or for judicial proceedings are not entitled to absolute immunity. *We have not retreated, however, from the principle that acts undertaken by a prosecutor in preparing for the initiation of judicial proceedings or for trial, and which occur in the course of his role as an advocate for the State are entitled to the protections of absolute immunity. Those acts must include the professional evaluation of the evidence assembled by the police and appropriate preparation for its presentation at trial or before a grand jury after a decision to seek an indictment has been made.*

Buckley, 509 U.S. at 272–73 (internal quotation marks and citations omitted; emphasis added).

Furthermore, in her role as social worker with the Clermont County Department of Social Services, Ms. Brush was an advocate for the state regarding child custody issues, especially for purposes of determining immunity.... The analogy goes as follows: a prosecutor functions as an advocate for the state in bringing a defendant to trial for his alleged acts against a crime victim; a social worker functions as an advocate for the state in bringing parents or legal custodians of children to "trial" for their alleged actions, or perhaps inactions, against children who are victims or abuse or neglect....

Turning to the matter at hand, the majority bases its holding that Ms. Brush is not entitled to absolute immunity for her actions of which Plaintiff complains on the ground that the CCDHS had a statutory duty to attempt to incorporate Plaintiff into the case plan pursuant to § 2151.412.... In other words, the majority claims that Ms. Brush was not functioning as an advocate for the state regarding the actions for which Plaintiff complains, because the actions somehow come down to a violation of Ms. Brush's duty under § 2151.412 and § 2151.416 to make Plaintiff part of the case plan, where Ms. Brush was standing in the shoes of the CCDHS which was a party to the case. Simply put, the majority contends that because Ms. Brush was standing in the shoes of a party in failing to incorporate Plaintiff into the plan, she could not be considered an advocate for the state; rather, Ms. Brush should have been some sort of advocate for Plaintiff. I disagree with what I believe to be the majority's flawed logic.

...

Whether Ms. Brush had such a statutory duty to Plaintiff, and whether Ms. Brush violated that duty if she in fact had one, is not relevant to the matter at hand. Instead, we look to Ms. Brush's actions for which Plaintiff complains, and whether those actions can be considered prosecutorial, judicial, or otherwise intimately related to the judicial process, whether inside or outside of the courtroom, such that Plaintiff was acting as an advocate for the state at the time. We do not look to the actor involved, nor the statute under which she may have been acting in determining the level of immunity to be afforded. *See Buckley*, 509 U.S. at 269. Rather, we look to the nature of the function performed. *Id.*

However, even when considering the statute cited by the majority and Ms. Brush's duty to include Plaintiff in the case plan, I disagree with the majority's contention that Ms. Brush was not acting in an adversarial role toward Plaintiff or as an advocate for the state. As a child social worker for the State of Ohio, Ms. Brush is not an advocate for parents or legal custodians. Rather, her advocacy efforts lie in assisting the state to secure whatever is in the best interests of the children, which the state expressly says supersedes the interests of the parent. Indeed, the theory behind affording social workers immunity is to allow them to proceed on behalf of the children's best interests without fear of reprisal from disgruntled parents. Therefore, by the very nature of the work they perform, child social workers are not seen by parents as individuals acting on their behalf; rather, they are viewed as parental adversaries, whether in the course of developing a case plan or performing some other task, where their efforts may ultimately lead to a termination of parental rights.

Focusing on the relevant acts for which Plaintiff complains, failing to notify the trial court that Plaintiff had made contact and wished to assert her parental rights; telling Plaintiff that her rights had been severed when they had not yet been; and withholding information that would have enabled Plaintiff to raise her rights in court before they had been terminated, I believe that all of these acts were intimately associated with the judicial process such that Ms. Brush was functioning as an advocate at the time and should therefore be entitled to absolute immunity. [This] case is unique because Plaintiff is seeking to hold Ms. Brush liable for acts that she did not perform, as opposed to affirmative acts performed, as is usually the case. However, by analogy and negative implication, Ms. Brush's actions would be protected by absolute immunity.

For example, Ms. Brush's actions may be analogized to a prosecutor who would be protected by absolute immunity for initiation of a case against a defendant. Indeed, the majority claims that Ms. Brush should have done exactly that—initiated proceedings when Plaintiff surfaced. It follows that since Ms. Brush would have been entitled to absolute immunity had she initiated proceedings against Plaintiff and incorporated her into a case plan, Ms. Brush should be entitled to absolute immunity for her failure to do so. *See Buckley*, 509 U.S. at 272–73; *Ernst v. Child and Youth Servs.*, 108 F.3d 486, 495 (3d Cir. 1997) (holding that child social workers "are entitled to absolute immunity for their actions on behalf of the state in preparing for, initiating, and prosecuting dependency hearings" as well as "the formulation and presentation of recommendations to the court in the course of such proceedings").

Likewise, any actions taken by Ms. Brush in the preparation, evaluation, and formulation of recommendations which may or may not have eventually been made to the court, are entitled to absolute immunity. *See Ernst*, 108 F.3d at 497–98. As the Court of Appeals for the Third Circuit held in *Ernst*, "[t]o grant [child social workers] absolute immunity for the recommendations that they made to the court but deny them such immunity for the observations and judgments that were the necessary predicate for those recommendations would eviscerate the immunity they did receive and undermine the purposes sought to be advanced by the grant of absolute immunity." *Id.* at 498. Therefore, it follows that Ms. Brush is absolutely immune for her actions in evaluating information concerning Plaintiff making contact, even if that evaluation and judgment did not lead to a recommendation to the court. *Id.* at 498 (noting that "the [Supreme] Court has expressly embraced the idea that immunity must be afforded to the evaluation of available data to determine *whether* and in what manner to seek judicial action") (emphasis added) (citing *Buckley*, 509 U.S. at 272–73). In a similar vein, any professional judgment that Ms. Brush may have exercised, correctly or incorrectly, regarding the status of the ongoing judicial proceeding which may have prevented Plaintiff from immediately presenting herself to the court is entitled to absolute immunity. *See id.* at 497–98....

Characterizing Ms. Brush's actions as usurpations of the court's authority, the majority contends that *Ernst* does not apply because all of Ms. Brush's actions denied the court the opportunity to evaluate any recommendations. In other words, the majority claims that *Ernst* extends only to recommendations that a social worker makes to the court, and not to the judgment exercised by the social worker leading up to deciding what to recommend and whether to recommend anything at all. However, as stated above, *Ernst* expressly held that a social worker is entitled to absolute immunity for the formulation of judgments "to determine whether and in what manner to seek judicial action," and that denying absolute immunity for the actions which led to recommendations—whether or not the result of the exercise of professional judgment led to a recommendation to the court at all—would "eviscerate" the absolute immunity afforded to them. *See Ernst*, 108 F.3d at 497 (citing *Buckley*, 509 U.S. at 272–73).

Finding that Ms. Brush is entitled to absolute immunity for her actions—or perhaps more accurately stated, for her inactions—of which Plaintiff complains, comports with strong policy reasons based upon the welfare of our children and the body of those individuals who have made it their chosen profession to act in best interests of children. In stating these policy reasons and in finding Ms. Brush absolutely immune, in no way do I wish to suggest that a parent's custody right to his or her children is not strong. However, what we must keep in mind is that parental rights are not absolute and that they bow to what is in the children's best interests. The policy reasons for affording Ms. Brush immunity are two-fold.

First, parents have available to them other means than suits filed under § 1983 in order to protect against alleged unconstitutional behavior by child social workers, in the same way that alternative means are available to the public from such conduct by prosecutors and judges. *See Imbler v. Pachtman*, 424 U.S. 409, 428–29 (1976). For example, appellate review is available. *See id.*; *see also Butz v. Economou*, 438 U.S. 478, 512 (1985); *Ernst*, 108 F.3d at 497.... In addition, the agency which employs social workers ha[s] an incentive to insure that its employees do not violate the Constitution, because the agencies are not immune from liability for abuses committed by employees with policy-making authority. *See Ernst*, 108 F.3d at 497. And, of course, social workers, like prosecutors and judges, are subject to criminal prosecution under 18 U.S.C. § 242 for willful deprivations of constitutional rights, even if absolutely immune from civil liability. *See Briscoe v. LaHue*, 460 U.S. 325, 345 (1983).

Second, child social workers are better able to perform their jobs—and therefore ostensibly protect our children—if their judgment is not compromised by the threat of personal liability under § 1983 from a disgruntled parent. As recognized by the Supreme Court, "if litigation expenses mount, social workers ... may well become less willing to seek placements for children over their parents' objections, whether rational or irrational, even though in their honest judgment the child's best interests demand it." *Lehman v. Lycoming County Children's Servs. Agency*, 458 U.S. 502, 514 n. 18 (1982). Indeed, "[s]ocial workers often act on limited information; those who tarry, or resolve all doubts in favor of the parents, chance enduring damage to the children." [7th Circuit decision citing *DeShaney v. Winnebago County Dep't of Soc. Servs.*, 489 U.S. 189 (1989)]. Likewise, defending against such suits would divert the social worker's time and attention away from her official duties, in which case innocent children are the parties who suffer the consequences. *See Imbler*, 424 U.S. at 424–25. Imposing liability and requiring social workers to defend such suits would impose "intolerable burdens" upon the caseworker who is likely working under serious time constraints and carrying a heavy case load. *See id.*

In short, "immunity helps social workers put their private interests aside and concentrate on the welfare of children. Unfortunately, immunity also may embolden social workers to pursue their private agendas.... One effect is inseparable from the other.".... However, it is for the greater good that child social workers proceed in their quasi-judicial capacities without fear of redress from parents who, perhaps sometimes through no fault of their own, simply cannot properly care for their children.... Allowing the case against Ms. Brush to proceed, thereby subjecting her to potential liability, may provide Plaintiff with money damages to cover expenses for a short period of time; however, it will also send a message to child social workers causing them to second-guess their actions in a way which could forever affect the lives of children who are victims of neglect and abuse....

For further discussion

The Sixth Circuit summarized its approach to absolute immunity for social workers:

> '[S]ocial workers are absolutely immune only when they are acting in their capacity as *legal advocates*—initiating court actions or testifying under oath—not when they are performing administrative, investigative, or other functions.' [citation omitted]. When applied, '[t]he defense of absolute immunity provides a shield from liability for acts performed erroneously, even if alleged to have been done maliciously or corruptly.' *Dean v. Byerley*, 354 F.3d 540, 554 (6th Cir. 2004). Social workers often engage in prosecutorial functions when carrying out their duties. As we explained in *Pittman* [*v. Cuyahoga Cnty. Dep't of Children & Fam. Servs.*, 640 F.3d 716, 724 (6th Cir. 2011], absolute immunity based on a prosecutorial function covers interactions with a court, such as "testimony or recommendations given in court concerning the child's best interests as she saw the matter." [*Id.*] at 725 (internal quotation

> marks omitted). However, this immunity does not extend to "participating in agency decisions." *Id.* at 726 (internal quotation marks omitted); *see also Holloway v. Brush,* 220 F.3d 767, 776 (6th Cir. 2000) (en banc) ("It is her *out-of-court* actions, misinforming Holloway and failing to inform the court of the latter's appearance, that are the basis of this suit."). "Social workers who initiate judicial proceedings against those suspected of child abuse or neglect perform a prosecutorial duty, and so are entitled to absolute immunity." *Rippy v. Hattaway,* 270 F.3d 416, 421 (6th Cir. 2001) (internal quotation marks omitted).

Kovacic v. Cuyahoga Cnty. Dep't of Children & Family Servs., 724 F.3d 687, 694 (6th Cir. 2013), *cert. denied sub nom. Campbell-Ponstingle v. Kovacic,* 572 U.S. 1149 (2014).

Orally Briefing a Non-Lawyer Client

In preparing to orally brief the client, try to anticipate what information a client may need to make an informed decision about the next steps in the litigation. Anticipate the questions a client might ask. Try to anticipate questions a client might not think to ask and prepare to address those also. In outlining what the lawyer plans to say, consider how much detail the client likely will need to make an informed decision.

While the client will want the lawyer's prediction for how a court is likely to apply law to the client's facts, the client also will need to consider the practical context for the decision. Consider available alternative steps and the legal and practical consequences of each alternative.

Before orally briefing a client, consider whether the client is likely to understand legal terms. If not, consider how the lawyer can explain legal concepts without using vocabulary more likely to confuse than clarify the client's understanding of the options. Consider whether the lawyer will call the client by the client's title, name, or nickname.

Try to communicate in a professional, yet conversational, tone that conveys seriousness of purpose and confidence in the thoroughness of your work. "Avoid complex sentences and unusual vocabulary words.... By choosing commonly used words and simple sentence phrasing (subject before action verb, for example)" your oral briefing will be more easily understood by the client.[2]

---

2. Christine Coughlin, Joan Malmud Rocklin & Sandy Patrick, A LAWYER WRITES: A PRACTICAL GUIDE TO LEGAL ANALYSIS (2d ed. 2013) 287; *see also* Sarah Morath, *From Awkward Law Student to Articulate Attorney: Teaching the Oral Research Report*, 27 THE SECOND DRAFT: THE OFFICIAL MAGAZINE OF THE LEGAL WRITING INST. 6 (2013).

Guide to Law Practice Simulation 7

Description

This Simulation involves briefing the client, who is trying to decide whether to settle or appeal a federal district court decision. The district court decision is the *Holloway v. Brush*, 220 F.3d 767 (6th Cir. 2000) majority's discussion of absolute immunity for social worker Brush. The appeal would be to the fictional Twelfth Circuit where the issue of whether social workers are entitled to absolute immunity is a question of first impression.

Four students are attorneys for the social worker. Two think the client should settle. Two think the client should appeal. One student is the client—the local government agency that employs the social worker. The social worker would seek absolute immunity only; she would not seek qualified immunity.

The client is not a lawyer but is a high-level city manager. The client will need to understand the risks and benefits of the choice to appeal or to settle.

To prepare, consider issues such as:

- Be sure to communicate with your client without jargon, in language your client can understand.
- What are the practical consequences of the decision facing the client? Are there any risks to appealing? How will the resolution of this case affect the city social workers' ability to invoke absolute immunity in future cases?
- Is it relevant to a settlement decision that this would be a question of first impression? Or that the mother is sympathetic?
- Why isn't this situation just like *Ernst*?
- By withholding relevant information from the court, did Brush undermine the judicial process?
- Isn't any preparation, evaluation, and formulation of recommendations which may or may not be made to the court entitled to absolute immunity—like *Ernst*?
- Does the city have an institutional interest in establishing absolute immunity for social workers?

Purpose

- Better understand absolute immunity for government employees by comparing variations in how absolute immunity is applied, including *Kalina, Ernst,* and *Holloway*
- Explore attorney roles in shaping doctrine by understanding *Ernst* and *Holloway* as attempts to analogize the functions of social workers/child protective service workers to prosecutors

- Prepare for law practice by simulating interoffice settlement discussion among attorneys with different views of the case and advocating different strategies
- Prepare for law practice by explaining strategic litigation choices to a client who may have different views and may be sophisticated but may not fully grasp legal terms
- There is no need to do any research—the relevant cases are in the casebook. You may rely on the Sixth Circuit decision in *Holloway* as non-binding authority.

Structure

- Attorneys advocating appeal of adverse trial court decision—Question & Answer with client (8 minutes)
- Attorneys advocating settlement—Question & Answer with client (8 minutes)
- After about 15 minutes, questioning will be opened up to the entire class
- All attorneys—Question & Answer with client and rest of class (15 minutes)
- Please prepare a question for every simulation, even if you are not one of the students playing a role.
- To ensure full class participation, and as a courtesy to your fellow students, please close your laptops during law practice simulations.

Chapter Ten

Other Statutes: Attorney's Fees, the Prison Litigation Reform Act, and Selected Recurring Procedural Issues in 42 U.S.C. § 1983 Actions

A. Chapter Overview

The "American Rule" in litigation is that each side pays its own attorney's fees. In 42 U.S.C. § 1988(b), Congress created an exception to the usual rule by requiring an unsuccessful party, usually the defendant, to bear the cost of the prevailing party's counsel. *See Sole v. Wyner*, 551 U.S. 74, 77 (2007); *Buckhannon Bd. & Care Home, Inc. v. W. Va. Dep't of Health & Human Res.*, 532 U.S. 598, 602–03 (2001). The statute provides that "the court, in its discretion, may allow the prevailing party, other than the United States, a reasonable attorney's fee as part of the costs." 42 U.S.C. § 1988(b) (2000). The fee-shifting provision provides an incentive for plaintiffs to file claims under 42 U.S.C. § 1983. The purpose is "to make it possible for those who cannot pay a lawyer for his time and effort to obtain competent counsel." *Pennsylvania v. Delaware Valley Citizens' Council For Clean Air*, 483 U.S. 711, 725 (1987).

What do the statutory terms "prevailing party" and "reasonable attorney's fees" mean in practice? The Supreme Court has held that a prevailing party requires "the material alteration of the legal relationship of the parties" and "judicial imprimatur." *Buckhannon*, 532 U.S. at 604–05. In *Buckhannon*, the Supreme Court did not expressly define "judicial imprimatur" but stated that enforceable judgments on the merits and consent decrees are sufficient for prevailing party status. *Id.* at 604. By contrast, a defendant's voluntary change in conduct in response to the plaintiff's lawsuit but not in response to a court order lacks the necessary judicial imprimatur to establish prevailing party status. *Id.* at 601, 605. As a result, in the absence of a judgment on the merits or a consent decree, it is not easy to determine whether a plaintiff should be considered a "prevailing party" under § 1988. Further, even if a plaintiff should be considered a prevailing party under § 1988, determining what amount constitutes a "reasonable" attorney's fee is an additional subject of litigation. Both of these questions of statutory interpretation are explored in the excerpts below.

As explained in Chapter 1, the availability of statutory attorney's fees since 1976 is one reason for the increase in federal civil rights litigation. In 1995, Congress reacted to that increase in litigation by enacting the Prison Litigation Reform Act. This Chapter introduces that statute, which placed new hurdles in the path of a prisoner seeking to file a civil rights claim and substituted a new attorney's fee provision for prisoner litigation.

This Chapter also flags several recurring procedural issues in § 1983 actions, such as pleading requirements, statute of limitations concerns, the *Heck v. Humphrey* bar confronted by former criminal defendants, and removal to federal court of cases originally filed in state court.

Questions to guide reading of Attorney's Fees statute

1. Does the statute require any particular method of calculating attorney's fees?
2. Are expert fees part of the attorney's fee in § 1983 litigation? Why do you agree or disagree with that Congressional choice?

---

42 U.S.C. § 1988 Civil Rights Attorney's Fees

(b) Attorney's fees

In any action or proceeding to enforce a provision of section[] ... 1983 ... the court, in its discretion, may allow the prevailing party, other than the United States, a reasonable attorney's fee as part of the costs, except that in any action brought against a judicial officer for an act or omission taken in such officer's judicial capacity such officer shall not be held liable for any costs, including attorney's fees, unless such action was clearly in excess of such officer's jurisdiction.

(c) Expert fees

In awarding an attorney's fee under subsection (b) [of this section] in any action or proceeding to enforce a provision of section 1981 or 1981a of this title, the court, in its discretion, may include expert fees as part of the attorney's fee.

...

HISTORICAL AND STATUTORY NOTES

Revision Notes and Legislative Reports[.]1976 Acts. Senate Report No. 94-1011, see 1976 U.S. Code Cong. and Adm. News, p. 5908.

...

Questions to guide reading of Senate Judiciary Committee Report

1. What is the concept of the "private attorney general" and why is it relevant to the attorney's fees statute?
2. What guidance does the legislative history provide on the meaning of a "prevailing party"?
3. Is there any hint in the Senate Report on the bill that the attorney's fees statute might encourage more civil rights litigation?

The Civil Rights Attorney's Fees Awards Act of 1976

SENATE REPORT NO. 94-1011 June 29, 1976

PURPOSE

This amendment to the Civil Rights Act of 1866..., Revised Statutes Section 722, gives the Federal courts discretion to award attorneys' fees to prevailing parties in suits brought to enforce the civil rights acts which Congress has passed since 1866. The purpose of this amendment is to remedy anomalous gaps in our civil rights laws created by the United States Supreme Court's recent decision in *Alyeska Pipeline Service Co. v. Wilderness Society*, 421 U.S. 240 (1975), and to achieve consistency in our civil rights laws.

HISTORY OF THE LEGISLATION

The bill grows out of six days of hearings on legal fees held before the Subcommittee on the Representation of Citizen Interests of this Committee in 1973. There were more than thirty witnesses, including Federal and State public officials, scholars, practicing attorneys from many areas of expertise, and private citizens.

...

STATEMENT

The purpose and effect of S. 2278 are simple—it is designed to allow courts to provide the familiar remedy of reasonable counsel fees to prevailing parties in suits to enforce the civil rights acts which Congress has passed since 1866. S. 2278 follows the language of [other civil rights statutes.] All of these civil rights laws depend heavily upon private enforcement, and fee awards have proved an essential remedy if private citizens are to have a meaningful opportunity to vindicate the important Congressional policies which these laws contain.

In many cases arising under our civil rights laws, the citizen who must sue to enforce the law has little or no money with which to hire a lawyer. If private citizens are to be able to assert their civil rights, and if those who violate the Nation's fundamental laws are not to proceed with impunity, then citizens must have the opportunity to recover what it costs them to vindicate these rights in court.

Congress recognized this need when it made specific provision for such fee shifting in Titles II and VII of the Civil Rights Act of 1964:

> When a plaintiff brings an action under (Title II) he cannot recover damages. If he obtains an injunction, he does so not for himself alone but also as a 'private attorney general,' vindicating a policy that Congress considered of the highest priority. If successful plaintiffs were routinely forced to bear their own attorneys' fees, few aggrieved parties would be in a position to advance the public interest by invoking the injunctive powers of the Federal courts. Congress therefore enacted the provision for counsel fees—* * * to encourage individuals injured by racial discrimination to seek judicial relief under Title II.'

Newman v. Piggie Park Enterprises, Inc., 390 U.S. 400, 402 (1968).

The idea of the 'private attorney general' is not a new one, nor are attorneys' fees a new remedy. Congress has commonly authorized attorneys' fees in laws under which 'private attorneys general' play a significant role in enforcing our policies. We have, since 1870, authorized fee shifting under more than 50 laws....

...

Modern civil rights legislation reflects a heavy reliance on attorneys' fees as well. In 1964, seeking to assure full compliance with the Civil Rights Act of that year, we authorized fee shifting for private suits establishing violations of the public accommodations and equal employment provisions.... Since 1964, every major civil rights law passed by the Congress has included, or has been amended to include, one or more fee provisions....

These fee shifting provisions have been successful in enabling vigorous enforcement of modern civil rights legislation, while at the same time limiting the growth of the enforcement bureaucracy. Before May 12, 1975, when the Supreme Court handed down its decision in *Alyeska Pipeline Service Co. v. Wilderness Society*, 421 U.S. 240 (1975), many lower Federal courts throughout the Nation had drawn the obvious analogy between the Reconstruction Civil Rights Acts and these modern civil rights acts, and, following Congressional recognition in the newer statutes of the 'private attorney general' concept, were exercising their traditional equity powers to award attorneys' fees under early civil rights laws as well.

...

This bill, S. 2278, is an appropriate response to the *Alyeska* decision. It is limited to cases arising under our civil rights laws, a category of cases in which attorneys' fees have been traditionally regarded as appropriate.

...

A party seeking to enforce the rights protected by the statutes covered by S. 2278, if successful, 'should ordinarily recover an attorney's fee unless special circumstances would render such an award unjust.' *Newman v. Piggie Park Enterprises, Inc.*, 390 U.S. 400, 402 (1968).... Such a party, if unsuccessful, could be assessed his opponent's fee only where it is shown that his suit was clearly frivolous, vexatious, or brought for harassment purposes. *United States Steel Corp. v. United States*, 385 F. Supp. 346 (W.D. Pa. 1974), *aff'd*, 9 E.P.D. 10,225 (3d Cir. 1975).

...

Moreover for purposes of the award of counsel fees, parties may be considered to have prevailed when they vindicate rights through a consent judgment or without formally obtaining relief. *Kopet v. Esquire Realty Co.*, 523 F.2d 1005 (2d Cir. 1975), and cases cited therein [citing cases from the Third and Eighth Circuits and from federal district courts].

...

This bill creates no startling new remedy—it only meets the technical requirements that the Supreme Court has laid down if the Federal courts are to continue the practice of awarding attorneys' fees which had been going on for years prior to the Court's May decision. It does not change the statutory provisions regarding the protection of civil rights except as it provides the fee awards which are necessary if citizens are to be able to effectively secure compliance with these existing statutes. There are very few provisions in our Federal laws which are self-executing. Enforcement of the laws depends on governmental action and, in some cases, on private action through the courts. If the cost of private enforcement actions becomes too great, there will be no private enforcement. If our civil rights laws are not to become mere hollow pronouncements which the average citizen cannot enforce, we must maintain the traditionally effective remedy of fee shifting in these cases.

...

For further discussion

1. In *Buckhannon Bd. & Care Home, Inc. v. W. Va. Dep't of Health & Human Res.*, 532 U.S. 598 (2001), the Supreme Court struck down the "catalyst theory" under which a party was a "prevailing party" where the defendant took voluntary action in response to the litigation. In so holding, the Court rejected the view that the legislative history of 42 U.S.C. § 1988(b) demonstrated Congressional intent to permit the award of attorney's fees in the absence of a judgment on the merits or a consent decree:

> The House Report to § 1988 states that "[t]he phrase 'prevailing party' is not intended to be limited to the victor only after entry of a final judgment following a full trial on the merits," H.R. Rep. No. 94-1558, p. 7 (1976), while the Senate Report explains that "parties may be considered to have prevailed when they vindicate rights through a consent judgment or without formally obtaining relief," S. Rep. No. 94-1011, p. 5 (1976), U.S. Code Cong. & Admin. News 1976, pp. 5908, 5912. Petitioners argue that these Reports ... indicate Congress' intent to adopt the "catalyst theory." We think the legislative history cited by petitioners is at best ambiguous as to the availability of the "catalyst theory" for awarding attorney's fees. Particularly in view of the

> "American Rule" that attorney's fees will not be awarded absent "explicit statutory authority," such legislative history is clearly insufficient to alter the accepted meaning of the statutory term.... [S]ee also *Hanrahan* [*v. Hampton*, 446 U.S. 754, 758 (1980)] ("[O]nly when a party has prevailed on the merits of at least some of his claims ... has there been a determination of the 'substantial rights of the parties,' which Congress determined was a necessary foundation for departing from the usual rule in this country that each party is to bear the expense of his own attorney" (quoting H.R. Rep. No. 94-1558, at 8)).

Buckhannon, 532 U.S. at 607–08. Do you agree with that reading of the Senate Judiciary Committee Report? This Chapter discusses *Buckhannon* further in the context of later Supreme Court and circuit court decisions.

2. Should Congress repudiate the *Buckhannon* holding by amending § 1988 to allow a plaintiff to recover attorney's fees when the government defendant voluntarily complies with plaintiff's demands? That is, should Congress allow plaintiffs to qualify as a prevailing party under the catalyst theory? What arguments support redefining "prevailing party" to include "a voluntary or unilateral change in position by the agency"? What are arguments against Congress so amending the statute?

3. Either plaintiff or defendant may qualify as a prevailing party under § 1988, but for a defendant to qualify, the litigation must have been frivolous or vexatious. *See, e.g., Gen. Camera Corp. v. Urban Dev. Corp.*, 734 F.2d 468, 468–69 (2d Cir. 1984) (defendant entitled to attorney's fees under 42 U.S.C. § 1988 as prevailing parties in a § 1983 action because plaintiff's action was frivolous). The Supreme Court held in *Fox v. Vice*, 563 U.S. 826, 836–38 (2011) that, under Section 1988, a defendant can obtain "only the portion of his fees that he would not have paid but for the frivolous claim," which includes (1) fees for defending a non-frivolous claim that was only performed because of the potential damage liability on a frivolous claim; (2) fees incurred because the frivolous claim drove up litigation expenses by enabling removal to federal court; and (3) fees incurred because the frivolous claim reasonably caused defendant to hire specialized and more expensive counsel). Counsel for the defendants included the University of Virginia School of Law Supreme Court Clinic.

4. The Supreme Court reversed a state court interpretation of 42 U.S.C. § 1988 because it "is a federal statute" and the "Idaho Supreme Court, like any other state or federal court, is bound by this Court's interpretation of federal law." *James v. City of Boise*, 577 U.S. ___, 136 S.Ct. 685 (2016) (*per curiam*).

5. *Abeyta v. City of New York* is notable both for an award of legal fees to a prevailing municipal defendant in a Section 1983 excessive force case and for the defendants' creative use of discovery to discredit the plaintiff's allegations.[1] In a rare move, the

---

1. This summary of *Abeyta* is by Cecilia A. Silver, formerly Senior Counsel in the New York City Law Department's Special Federal Litigation Division, and currently on the Brooklyn Law School faculty. *See* Michael Schwirtz, *Plaintiff in Police Lawsuit Is Ordered to Pay New York City's Legal Fees*, N.Y. Times, Mar. 9, 2014, at A27

district court judge invited the defendants to pursue attorneys' fees under 42 U.S.C. § 1988 because the plaintiff's case was revealed at trial to be "frivolous, unreasonable, and without foundation." *Abeyta v. City of N.Y.*, 2014 WL 929838, at *1–*2 (S.D.N.Y. Mar. 7, 2014). In *Abeyta*, the plaintiff, a Columbia University graduate, celebrated his 24th birthday at a bar. *Id.* at *1. After consuming several drinks, the plaintiff got on his bicycle, approached two police officers, and insulted them. *Id.* Mr. Abeyta asserted that because he offended the officers, they slammed his head into the hood of their squad car, resulting in head pain, nausea, and dizziness; he later claimed that he suffered life-altering brain injuries. *Id.* at *2. Plaintiff alleged that post-concussion syndrome prevented him from returning to work and forced him to move in with his mother to seek treatment.[2]

But Mr. Abeyta's spending records painted a different picture. According to a receipt produced in discovery, just seven hours after his purportedly life-changing concussion, Mr. Abeyta went to a bar and ordered three of the bar's signature cocktail, a frozen margarita mixed with beer.[3] Plaintiff's debit card records revealed that after the incident, he continued playing video games and frequenting strip clubs, undermining his claim that he could not look at a computer screen or tolerate crowds and loud noises because of his injury.[4]

The district court granted the City of New York $211,747.50 in legal fees. 2014 WL 929838 at *6. While the court acknowledged that the fee award was "significant," it chastised "plaintiff [for bringing] it upon himself" by taking a case to trial based on "fictitious facts" and requiring defendants to "spend a great deal of time, energy, and money." *Id.* at *6 n. 10. Plaintiff's spending records proved to be a key to the case, illustrating how thinking resourcefully about document discovery can influence the outcome of litigation.

Question to guide reading of *Sole*

After *Sole*, if a plaintiff succeeds in obtaining a preliminary injunction, is that party likely to qualify as a "prevailing party" entitled to attorney's fees? What additional information would you need to make a prediction?

Sole v. Wyner

551 U.S. 74 (2007)

Justice GINSBURG delivered the opinion of the Court.

For private actions brought under 42 U.S.C. § 1983 ... Congress established an exception to the "American Rule" that "the prevailing litigant is ordinarily not entitled

---

2. Schwirtz, *supra* note 1, at A27.

3. Receipt from the bar, Diablo Royale (Apr. 15, 2012) (on file with Cecilia A. Silver).

4. Schwirtz, *supra* note 1, at A27; *see also* Andrew Abeyta Citibank Debit Card Records (Apr. 9, 2012–June 9, 2013) (on file with Cecilia A. Silver) (showing multiple visits to video game retailer and regular ATM withdrawals at Xposed Gentlemen's Club).

to collect [counsel fees] from the loser." ... That exception, codified in 42 U.S.C. § 1988(b), authorizes federal district courts, in their discretion, to "allow the prevailing party ... a reasonable attorney's fee as part of the costs." This case presents a sole question: Does a plaintiff who gains a preliminary injunction after an abbreviated hearing, but is denied a permanent injunction after a dispositive adjudication on the merits, qualify as a "prevailing party" within the compass of § 1988(b)?

Viewing the two stages of the litigation as discrete episodes, plaintiffs ... maintain that they prevailed at the preliminary injunction stage, and therefore qualify for a fee award for their counsels' efforts to obtain that interim relief. Defendants ... regard the case as a unit; they urge that a preliminary injunction holds no sway once fuller consideration yields rejection of the provisional order's legal or factual underpinnings. We agree with the latter position and hold that a final decision on the merits denying permanent injunctive relief ordinarily determines who prevails in the action for purposes of § 1988(b). A plaintiff who achieves a transient victory at the threshold of an action can gain no award under that fee-shifting provision if, at the end of the litigation, her initial success is undone and she leaves the courthouse emptyhanded.

> [Plaintiffs who wished to stage a nude antiwar display on a public Florida beach obtained a preliminary injunction prohibiting police enforcement of the ban on nudity during the Valentine's Day 2003 peace display because, at the preliminary injunction hearing, the district court understood that beach-goers who did not wish to see the nudity would be shielded from the display by a screen. However, the nude participants did not set up the display behind the screen. Upon seeking a permanent injunction to permit a repeat performance for Valentine's Day 2004, the district court granted summary judgment for defendants.]

...

II.

"The touchstone of the prevailing party inquiry," this Court has stated, is "the material alteration of the legal relationship of the parties in a manner which Congress sought to promote in the fee statute." ... *cf. Buckhannon Board & Care Home, Inc. v. West Virginia Dept. of Health and Human Resources*, 532 U.S. 598, 605(2001) (precedent "counsel[s] against holding that the term 'prevailing party' authorizes an award of attorney's fees without a corresponding alteration in the legal relationship of the parties").[3]

---

3. *Buckhannon Board & Care Home, Inc. v. West Virginia Dept. of Health and Human Resources*, 532 U.S. 598, 600 (2001), held that the term "prevailing party" in the fee-shifting provisions of the Fair Housing Amendments Act of 1988 and the Americans with Disabilities Act of 1990 does not "includ[e] a party that has failed to secure a judgment on the merits or a court-ordered consent decree, but has nonetheless achieved the desired result because the lawsuit brought about a voluntary change in the defendant's conduct." The dissent in *Buckhannon* would have deemed such a plaintiff "prevailing," not because of any temporary relief gained (in that case, a consent stay pending litigation), but because the lawsuit caused the State to amend its laws, terminating the controversy between the parties, and permanently giving plaintiff the real-world outcome it sought. *See id.*, at 622, 624–625 (opinion of

...

Prevailing party status, we hold, does not attend achievement of a preliminary injunction that is reversed, dissolved, or otherwise undone by the final decision in the same case.

At the preliminary injunction stage, the court is called upon to assess the probability of the plaintiff's ultimate success on the merits.... Of controlling importance to our decision, the eventual ruling on the merits for defendants, after both sides considered the case fit for final adjudication, superseded the preliminary ruling. [Plaintiff's] temporary success rested on a premise the District Court ultimately rejected. That court granted preliminary relief on the understanding that a curtain or screen [on the beach between the public and the nude participants in the antiwar display] would adequately serve Florida's interest in shielding the public from nudity that recreational beach users did not wish to see.... At the summary judgment stage, with the benefit of a fuller record, the District Court recognized that its initial assessment was incorrect. Participants in the peace symbol display were in fact unwilling to stay behind a screen that separated them from other park visitors.... In light of the demonstrated inadequacy of the screen to contain the nude display, the District Court determined that enforcement of the Bathing Suit Rule was necessary to "preserv[e] park aesthetics" and "protect the experiences of the visiting public."

...

III.

[Plaintiff] is not a prevailing party, we conclude, for her initial victory was ephemeral.... We are presented with, and therefore decide, no broader issue in this case.

We express no view on whether, in the absence of a final decision on the merits of a claim for permanent injunctive relief, success in gaining a preliminary injunction may sometimes warrant an award of counsel fees. We decide only that a plaintiff who gains a preliminary injunction does not qualify for an award of counsel fees under § 1988(b) if the merits of the case are ultimately decided against her.

...

B. Development of Doctrine in the Circuits

The excerpts below further explain why the Supreme Court in *Buckhannon* rejected the "catalyst" theory for defining a "prevailing party" under federal fee-shifting statutes and explore how, since *Buckhannon*, the federal courts have continued to refine what it means for a party to prevail in federal civil rights litigation under § 1988.

GINSBURG, J.). Our decision today is consistent with the views of both the majority and the dissenters in *Buckhannon*.

Questions to guide reading of *Roberson*

1. How did the Second Circuit in *Roberson* explain the "catalyst" theory rejected by the Supreme Court in *Buckhannon*?
2. After *Buckhannon*, what is necessary to be a "prevailing party" entitled to attorney's fees? What two examples did *Buckhannon* identify?
3. Why did the Second Circuit in *Roberson* hold that the district court's retention of jurisdiction to enforce the settlement agreement provided sufficient judicial sanction to confer "prevailing party" status on the plaintiffs? Would a private settlement agreement standing alone likely entitle plaintiff to "prevailing party" status?
4. Post-*Buckhannon* and *Roberson*, what are some steps a careful Plaintiff's attorney might take when settling litigation to protect the right to collect attorney's fees? Note that the Brennan Center for Justice at New York University Law School was involved in the *Roberson* litigation.

Roberson v. Giuliani

346 F.3d 75 (2d Cir. 2003)

FEINBERG, Circuit Judge.

Plaintiffs-appellants appeal from a [district court order] denying their motion for attorney's fees in this action brought under 42 U.S.C. § 1983. The sole issue on appeal is whether plaintiffs may be considered a "prevailing party" under the applicable fee-shifting statute where they resolved their dispute with defendants through a private settlement agreement over which the district court retained enforcement jurisdiction.... [W]e hold that on the record before us the court's retention of jurisdiction carried sufficient judicial approval of the settlement agreement to support an award of attorney's fees....

I. Background

In October 1999, plaintiffs filed this § 1983 class action against (1) the Mayor of the City of New York and the Commissioner of the New York City Department of Social Services (collectively, "City defendants").... [P]laintiffs challenged defendants' policies regarding the disposition of applications for food stamps, Medicaid and public assistance benefits.... [P]laintiffs and City defendants entered into a settlement agreement [under which] City defendants denied any liability ... but agreed to various changes in the way future benefits claims would be handled.

...

In consideration for [promises relating to administration of public benefits], plaintiffs agreed to dismiss all outstanding claims against City defendants and release them from all liability arising out of the allegations in the complaint. The Agreement also provided that it "shall not become effective if the Order of Discontinuance in the above-captioned action does not include a provision retaining jurisdiction over enforcement." In addition, the Agreement provided, "The issue of plaintiffs' entitlement to an award of attorneys' fees and costs and disbursements is reserved for later determination upon application to the Court...."

In June 2001, plaintiffs submitted to the district court an order dismissing their claims against City defendants and requested the court to sign it. A copy of the Agreement was provided to the court.... A week later, the plaintiffs and City defendants executed a Stipulation and Order of Discontinuance (the "dismissal Order"), which acknowledged that the parties had entered into a settlement agreement and dismissed plaintiffs' claims with prejudice as to City defendants. The dismissal Order also provided, "This Court shall retain jurisdiction over the settlement agreement for enforcement purposes." The Agreement, however, was not otherwise incorporated into the dismissal Order.

In September 2001, plaintiffs moved for $140,060.25 in attorney's fees and costs pursuant to 42 U.S.C. § 1988, which provides, "In any action or proceeding to enforce a provision of section[ ] ... 1983 [of this title] ... the court, in its discretion, may allow the prevailing party, other than the United States, a reasonable attorney's fee as part of the costs." City defendants opposed the motion on the grounds that (1) plaintiffs were not prevailing parties in the underlying action....

II. Discussion

...

Generally, the Supreme Court has given a "generous formulation" to the term prevailing party, stating that plaintiffs may be entitled to attorney's fees "if they succeed on any significant issue in litigation which achieves some of the benefit the parties sought in bringing suit." *Hensley v. Eckerhart*, 461 U.S. 424, 433 (1983) (internal quotation marks omitted). However, the Court recently took a somewhat more restrictive approach in its 2001 *Buckhannon* decision.[3]

A. The *Buckhannon* Opinion

In October 1997, the plaintiffs in *Buckhannon* brought suit against the State of West Virginia and twenty other defendants seeking declaratory and injunctive relief. The lawsuit claimed that a provision of the West Virginia code requiring all residents of residential board and care homes to be capable of "self-preservation" violated federal law. After the parties began discovery, the West Virginia Legislature eliminated the self-preservation provision and the district court dismissed the case as moot. Thereafter, plaintiffs sought attorney's fees as a prevailing party on the ground that their lawsuit was the "catalyst" in forcing the defendants to change the law....

In *Buckhannon* the Supreme Court considered whether a plaintiff could be a prevailing party under what was termed the "catalyst theory." As described by the Court,

---

3. *Buckhannon* concerned different fee-shifting provisions from [§ 1988. H]owever, "the standards used to interpret the term prevailing party under any given fee-shifting statute are generally applicable in all cases in which Congress has authorized an award of fees to a prevailing party." [citing Second Circuit application of *Buckhannon* to § 1988].

the catalyst theory posits that "a plaintiff is a 'prevailing party' if it achieves the desired result because the lawsuit brought about a voluntary change in the defendant's conduct." 532 U.S. at 601. Prior to *Buckhannon,* most Courts of Appeals to have considered the issue had held that the catalyst theory was an appropriate basis for an award of attorney's fees. The Supreme Court disagreed.

[T]he Supreme Court held that "a 'prevailing party' is one who has been awarded some relief by the court." *Id.* at 603. It rejected the catalyst theory as a basis for an award of fees because it "allows an award where there is no judicially sanctioned change in the legal relationship of the parties" and "lacks the necessary judicial imprimatur." *Id.* at 605. Essentially, in order to be considered a "prevailing party" after *Buckhannon,* a plaintiff must not only achieve some "material alteration of the legal relationship of the parties," but that change must also be judicially sanctioned....

The *Buckhannon* Court gave two examples of the types of relief that carry sufficient judicial imprimatur to form the basis for awarding attorney's fees to a plaintiff: judgments on the merits and settlement agreements that are enforced through court-ordered consent decrees. The Court noted that a consent decree is sufficient even without an admission of liability by the defendant because it constitutes a "court ordered change in the legal relationship between the plaintiff and the defendant." 532 U.S. at 604 (internal marks omitted). The Court also stated in a footnote, "Private settlements do not entail the judicial approval and oversight involved in consent decrees. And federal jurisdiction to enforce a private contractual settlement will often be lacking unless the terms of the agreement are incorporated into the order of dismissal." 532 U.S. at 604 n.7.

...

[I]t seems clear from even the majority opinion in *Buckhannon* that the Court intended its statements about judgments on the merits and court-ordered consent decrees as merely "examples" of the type of judicial action that could convey prevailing party status.[6] 532 U.S. at 605 ("We think, however, the 'catalyst theory' falls on the other side of the line *from these examples.*" (emphasis added)). We therefore join the majority of courts to have considered the issue since *Buckhannon* in concluding that judicial action other than a judgment on the merits or a consent decree can support an award of attorney's fees, so long as such action carries with it sufficient judicial imprimatur. *See Am. Disability Ass'n, Inc. v. Chmielarz,* 289 F.3d 1315, 1319 (11th Cir. 2002) ("[T]he district court interpreted *Buckhannon* to stand for the proposition that a plaintiff could be a 'prevailing party' only if it achieved one of those two results. That reading of *Buckhannon,* however, is overly narrow."); *Barrios v. Cal. Interscholastic Fed'n,* 277 F.3d 1128, 1134–35 n.5 (9th Cir. 2002) ("While dictum in *Buckhannon* suggests that a plaintiff 'prevails' only when he or she receives a favorable judgment

6. The Supreme Court split five to four in the *Buckhannon* decision. The four dissenters would have accepted even the catalyst theory as a basis for an award of attorney's fees.

on the merits or enters into a court-supervised consent decree, we are not bound by that dictum...."); *Oil, Chem. & Atomic Workers Int'l Union v. Dep't of Energy*, 288 F.3d 452, 458–59 (D.C. Cir. 2002) (holding that parties' stipulation and order of dismissal did not "meaningfully alter the legal relationship of the parties," but implying that had there been such a change, *Buckhannon* would not preclude an award of fees); *Smyth v. Rivero*, 282 F.3d 268, 281 (4th Cir. 2002) ("We doubt that the Supreme Court's guidance in *Buckhannon* was intended to be interpreted so restrictively as to require that the words 'consent decree' be used explicitly."); *Truesdell v. Philadelphia Hous. Auth.*, 290 F.3d 159, 165 (3d Cir. 2002) ("We do not agree with the District Court's conclusion that the parties' settlement was an inappropriate basis for an award of attorney's fees."); *but see Christina A. v. Bloomberg*, 315 F.3d 990, 993 (8th Cir. 2003) ("*Buckhannon*, as indicated, makes it clear that a party prevails only if it receives either an enforceable judgment on the merits or a consent decree.").

Although the district court here took the correct general approach, its analysis did not fully appreciate the implications of its retention of jurisdiction over enforcement of the Agreement. [Because the district court in this case explicitly retained jurisdiction over enforcement of the Agreement, we need not decide whether a settlement agreement standing alone would justify an award of attorney's fees.] The Supreme Court's decision in *Kokkonen v. Guardian Life Insurance of America*, 511 U.S. 375 (1994), cited with approval in *Buckhannon*, 532 U.S. at 604 n.7, is instructive in this regard. In *Kokkonen*, the Supreme Court considered whether a federal district court had the "inherent power" to enforce a settlement agreement that resulted in the dismissal of a case pending before it. The Court stressed the limited jurisdiction of the federal courts stating, "They possess only that power authorized by Constitution and statute, which is not to be expanded by judicial decree." *Id.* at 377 (citations omitted). It held that the district court lacked ancillary jurisdiction to issue an order enforcing the private settlement agreement, but also noted,

> The situation would be quite different if the parties' obligation to comply with the terms of the settlement agreement *had been made part of the order of dismissal*—either by separate provision (*such as a provision "retaining jurisdiction" over the settlement agreement)* or by incorporating the terms of the settlement agreement in the order. In that event, a breach of the agreement would be a violation of the order, and ancillary jurisdiction to enforce the agreement would therefore exist.

Id. at 381 (emphasis added).

Viewed in the light of *Kokkonen*, the district court's retention of jurisdiction in this case is not significantly different from a consent decree and entails a level of judicial sanction sufficient to support an award of attorney's fees. First, despite the district court's statements that it had not specifically reviewed or approved the terms of the settlement agreement, the district court retained jurisdiction to enforce the Agreement. Under *Kokkonen*, when the district court retained jurisdiction, it necessarily made compliance with the terms of the agreement a part of its order so that "a breach of the agreement would be a violation of the order." 511 U.S. at 381. Further, because the court has the general responsibility to ensure that its orders are fair and lawful, it retains some responsibility over the terms of a settlement agreement as the parties' obligation to comply with the agreement was made a part of its order.

. . .

Thus, when the district court retained jurisdiction according to the procedures approved in *Kokkonen* it gave judicial sanction to a change in the legal relationship of the parties, regardless of the actual scrutiny applied.

Second, while the district court was correct that courts have inherent jurisdiction to enforce consent decrees, that jurisdiction is no different from the jurisdictional basis in this case. Consent decrees are enforceable in federal court because they are orders of the court; the Agreement is enforceable in federal court because a violation of the Agreement is a violation of the court's dismissal Order. Both are, in the terms used by the *Buckhannon* Court, "court-ordered change[s] in the legal relationship between the plaintiff and the defendant." 532 U.S. at 604. Third, even if the district court was correct that our holding in [a 2d Circuit decision] precludes a court from using its contempt power in the first instance to enforce a private settlement agreement over which it has retained jurisdiction, we do not think this is significant enough to deprive plaintiffs of prevailing party status. In the case of both consent decrees and private settlement agreements over which a district court retains enforcement jurisdiction, the district court has the authority to force compliance with the terms agreed upon by the parties. In the latter instance, the court at most would need to take an extra step by first ordering specific performance and then, if a party does not comply, finding that party in contempt. We doubt that the definition of "prevailing party" should turn on such a difference.

Our decision that the Agreement received sufficient judicial sanction to justify considering plaintiffs prevailing parties is strengthened by the clause it contains conditioning its effectiveness on the district court's retention of jurisdiction. The district court's dismissal Order in this case did not, as City defendants assert, simply preserve a federal forum in which the parties could adjudicate disputes. It effectuated the obligations of the parties under the Agreement because until the district court signed the dismissal Order retaining jurisdiction, the Agreement was not yet in effect. In a very literal sense, it was the court's order that created the change in the legal relationship between plaintiffs and City defendants.

. . .

Questions to guide reading of *Walker*

1. In addition to the two examples listed in *Buckhannon*, according to *Walker*, how else can a party qualify for attorney's fees in the Seventh Circuit?
2. In comparison with the Second Circuit in *Roberson*, does the Seventh Circuit in *Walker* require more evidence of judicial involvement for a settlement agreement to be analogous to a consent decree?

3. If there are circuit variations in what level of judicial involvement is sufficient for a settlement agreement to be analogous to a consent decree, what steps might a careful plaintiff's attorney take when settling litigation to ensure the right to collect attorney's fees?

Walker v. Calumet City

565 F.3d 1031 (7th Cir. 2009)

MANION, Circuit Judge.

Ayanna Walker wanted to sell a dwelling she owned in Calumet City ("the City"), but she found that a local ordinance imposed obstacles that interfered with her ability to dispose of her property. She sued the City, alleging that the ordinance violated her right to procedural due process and unreasonably restrained the alienability of her property. After the City stated that it would not enforce the ordinance against Walker, the district court dismissed the case as moot. Subsequently, the district court held that Walker was a prevailing party and awarded her attorney fees [of $189,000 under § 1988]. The City appeals, and we reverse.

...

II.

On appeal, the City argues that the district court erred in awarding attorney fees to Walker under 42 U.S.C. § 1988(b), which states that in a § 1983 suit, "the court, in its discretion, may allow the prevailing party ... a reasonable attorney's fee as part of the costs." Prior to 2001, this court commonly evaluated the awarding of attorney fees using the "catalyst rule," which stated that "a plaintiff may be a prevailing party for purposes of section 1988 even if the defendant voluntarily provides the relief sought rather than litigating the suit to judgment." [Seventh Circuit citation omitted]. However, the United States Supreme Court rejected the catalyst rule in *Buckhannon Board & Care Home, Inc. v. West Virginia Department of Health & Human Resources*, 532 U.S. 598 (2001). *Buckhannon* "emphasized that in order to be deemed a prevailing party, there must be a 'material alteration in the legal relationship of the parties.'" [citation omitted] (quoting *Buckhannon*, 532 U.S. at 606). This alteration must arise from a court order.... In other words, "there must be a judicial imprimatur on the change." [Seventh Circuit cites omitted].

In *Buckhannon*, the Supreme Court gave two examples of when a party should be considered prevailing: first, when "the plaintiff has received a judgment on the merits"; second, when the plaintiff has "obtained a court-ordered consent decree." *Buckhannon*, 532 U.S. at 605. In general, we have stated that "[i]t could not be clearer that a voluntary settlement by the defendant ... does not entitle a plaintiff to attorneys' fees." [Seventh Circuit citation omitted]....

Here, the dismissal order stated:

> 3. The Court bases its decision that Walker's claim are [*sic*] moot on the following representations made by City: (a) because Walker has already sub-

> mitted the property ... to an annual inspection ... and has corrected all identified Code violations in accordance with the terms thereof, Walker does not need to pass a redundant point-of-sale inspection in order for her to sell the Subject Property; (b) City will not otherwise enforce its Point of Sale Inspection [POS] Ordinance ... as to the Subject Property ... and (d) City has certified that the Subject Property is a legal nonconforming use under City's Zoning Ordinance, a status which runs with the land....

...

This case does not fit within the first category enunciated in *Buckhannon*, namely where "the plaintiff has received a judgment on the merits." 532 U.S. at 605. We have permitted attorney fees when a case has been declared moot if, prior to the change in circumstances, the court made a decision on the merits in favor of the plaintiff. *See, e.g., Palmetto Props., Inc. v. County of DuPage*, 375 F.3d 542 (7th Cir. 2004). Here, the district court never reached the merits of Walker's claim.... The court never decided whether the POS ordinance unreasonably restrained the alienability of Walker's property or violated her procedural due process rights, or whether a due process violation arose from the potential deeming of her property as "illegally nonconforming." Accordingly, because no judgment was rendered by the district court on the merits of her claims, Walker is not a prevailing party under the first example given in *Buckhannon*.

Second, *Buckhannon* stated that a plaintiff may be deemed prevailing if he "obtained a court-ordered consent decree." 532 U.S. at 605. Walker did not obtain a consent decree in this case; hence, the second *Buckhannon* example does not apply.

Although *Buckhannon* only refers to two types of outcomes that will give rise to prevailing party status, we have also hypothesized that "some settlement agreements, even though not explicitly labeled as a 'consent decree' may confer 'prevailing party' status, if they are sufficiently analogous to a consent decree." *T.D. v. La Grange Sch. Dist. No. 102*, 349 F.3d 469, 478 (7th Cir. 2003). *T.D.* suggested that such a settlement agreement might arise if the settlement "(1) contained mandatory language, (2) was entitled 'Order,' (3) bore the signature of the District Court judge, not the parties' counsel, and (4) provided for judicial enforcement." *Id.* at 478–79.[1] However, this case

1. Citing *T.D.*, later cases of this circuit have opined that "a settlement short of a consent decree may qualify if, for instance, the terms of the settlement were incorporated into the dismissal order and the order was signed by the court rather than the parties, or the order provided that the court would retain jurisdiction to enforce the terms of the settlement." *Petersen v. Gibson*, 372 F.3d 862, 866–67 (7th Cir. 2004). *See also Gautreaux v. Chicago Hous. Auth.*, 491 F.3d 649, 655 (7th Cir. 2007) (citing *Petersen*). Because *T.D.* required all four criteria to be met before a party would be considered prevailing, *Petersen* and *Gautreaux* appear to be in some tension with *T.D.* However, the statements in both *Petersen* and *Gautreaux* were dicta. In *Petersen*, there was no court order at all; moreover, *Petersen* specifically eschewed establishing a new test, saying that "[w]e need not concern ourselves here with the precise boundaries between a settlement that meets the prevailing party definition and one that falls short." 372 F.3d at 867. In *Gautreaux*, the parties had entered a consent decree and attorney fees had been awarded after the court enforced and modified the decree. 491 F.3d at 652–54. Hence, the legal effect of settlements that functioned similarly to consent decrees was not at issue.

does not involve a settlement at all. Instead, the suit was deemed moot based on voluntary actions by the City. Accordingly, the exception noted in *T.D.* does not apply.

In an attempt to make the possible *T.D.* exception relevant, Walker likens this case to a settlement.... Walker's argument fails because the dismissal order does not meet all four criteria delineated in *T.D.* Although the order was entitled a "final dismissal order" and was signed by the district court judge, it did not provide for judicial enforcement. Rather, the order noted that Walker could bring a motion for attorney fees but gave no option for Walker to seek enforcement of its provisions and did not vest the court with continuing jurisdiction. Moreover, the order did not contain mandatory language that would convert the dismissal order into an effective consent decree. Instead, the order listed and accepted the representations made by the City.... [T]he case [was] moot because the City did not intend to enforce the POS ordinance against Walker. She wanted to sell and the City agreed not to apply the POS because the requirements had already been met.

To show that she obtained permanent relief by the district court's order, and thereby obtained a judgment on the merits, Walker asserts that, under the dismissal order, the City "is forever barred from requiring a point-of-sale inspection of the property before its sale and is thus forever barred from requiring [Walker], or any subsequent owner, to make repairs to the property as a condition of the right to sell it." However, Walker mischaracterizes the dismissal order. The order merely states that Walker's property has already been inspected and thus the POS ordinance will not be enforced and transfer stamps will be issued when Walker pays the pertinent fees. Nowhere does the order state that later owners will not be subject to the ordinance.... Although the dismissal order states that the "legal nonconforming status" will "run with the land," viewed in context this statement indicates solely that, under the present City ordinances, the property is being used lawfully. Should the property no longer conform to the specified ordinances, that status may be revoked. Accordingly, contrary to Walker's position the order does not grant Walker and her assigns permanent relief from the application of the POS ordinance.

...

The dismissal of the case for mootness did not impose a judicial imprimatur that would permit awarding attorney fees under Buckhannon. There was no final judgment on the merits in Walker's favor and no consent decree was entered.

Questions to guide reading of *Dearmore*

1. In *Sole*, the Supreme Court left open "whether, in the absence of a final decision on the merits of a claim for permanent injunctive relief, success in gaining a preliminary injunction may sometimes warrant an award of counsel fees." 551 U.S. at 86. According to *Dearmore*, what are some of the ways that the federal circuits have decided the open question of whether a plaintiff can qualify as a prevailing party if the plaintiff obtains a preliminary injunction that is not ultimately decided for defendant on the merits?

2. Why would the result in *Dearmore* be different if the City had voluntarily changed its position before judicial action had been taken? Why might a government defendant want to moot an action and label its change in conduct voluntary, as opposed to involuntary, *i.e.*, a change prompted by the entry of a preliminary injunction?

Dearmore v. City of Garland

519 F.3d 517 (5th Cir.), *cert. denied*, 555 U.S. 938 (2008)

CLEMENT, Circuit Judge.

...

This appeal presents an issue of first impression in this Circuit: Whether a plaintiff qualifies as a "prevailing party" under § 1988(b) when he obtains a preliminary injunction after the district court makes an unambiguous indication of probable success on the merits of his claim and the defendant subsequently moots the case before trial in direct response to the court's preliminary injunction order.

...

Although an enforceable judgment on the merits and a court-ordered consent decree have sufficient judicial imprimatur [to establish prevailing party status under § 1988(b)], these examples are not exclusive. *See Buckhannon Board & Care Home, Inc. v. West Virginia Dept. of Health and Human Resources*, 532 U.S. 598, 605 (2001) (referencing the judgment on the merits and consent decree as mere "examples") ... *Watson v. County of Riverside*, 300 F.3d 1092, 1096 (9th Cir. 2002). As a result, lower courts have had difficulties in ascertaining what other forms of judicial action have the "necessary judicial imprimatur" to create prevailing party status, particularly in the context of preliminary injunctions. The Supreme Court has never expressed a view "on whether, in the absence of a final decision on the merits of a claim for permanent injunctive relief, success in gaining a preliminary injunction may ... warrant an award of counsel fees." *Sole* [*v. Wyner*, 551 U.S. 74, 86 (2007)].... As this Court has noted,

> several circuits have determined that a preliminary injunction that merely preserves the status quo temporarily will not confer "prevailing party" status on a party; instead, the preliminary injunction must (i) reflect a merits-based decision on an issue involved in the case, *see, e.g.*, *John T. v. Del. County Intermediate Unit*, 318 F.3d 545, 558–59 (3d Cir. 2003); *Dubuc v. Green Oak Twp.*, 312 F.3d 736, 753 (6th Cir. 2002); *Taylor v. City of Fort Lauderdale*, 810 F.2d 1551, 1558 (11th Cir. 1987); (ii) constitute substantive, indefeasible relief akin to final relief on the merits because, for example, "the party's claim [for a] permanent injunction is rendered moot by the impact of the preliminary injunction," *N. Cheyenne Tribe v. Jackson*, 433 F.3d 1083, 1086 (8th Cir. 2006); *see also, e.g.*, *Dupuy v. Samuels*, 423 F.3d 714, 719, 723 (7th Cir. 2005); (iii) grant the party concrete and irreversible relief in a merits-based decision that vindicates the party's claim and is not

> appealed by the opposing party, *see, e.g.*, *Select Milk Producers, Inc. v. Johanns*, 400 F.3d 939, 947–48 (D.C. Cir. 2005); or (iv) incorporate some combination of these factors.

Yousuf v. Motiva Enters. LLC, 246 Fed. Appx. 891, 894 (5th Cir. 2007) (per curiam) (citation omitted). "The Ninth Circuit has … taken a relatively generous approach, at least in principle, stating that a 'preliminary injunction issued by a judge carries all the "judicial imprimatur" necessary to satisfy *Buckhannon*.'" [citing Fifth Circuit] (quoting *Watson*, 300 F.3d at 1096) … "By contrast, the Fourth Circuit has expressed strong skepticism that a preliminary injunction could ever serve as the basis for prevailing party status," because "'the merits inquiry in the preliminary injunction context is necessarily abbreviated.'" [citation omitted] (quoting *Smyth v. Rivero*, 282 F.3d 268, 276 (4th Cir. 2002)).

…

[T]he Sixth Circuit provides that a plaintiff is a prevailing party if the preliminary injunction represents an "unambiguous indication of probable success on the merits, and not merely a maintenance of the status quo ordered because the balance of equities greatly favors the plaintiff." *Dubuc*, 312 F.3d at 753 (internal quotations omitted). Likewise, the Seventh Circuit states that a plaintiff may obtain attorney's fees when the district court engaged in a discussion on the merits of the claim when considering a preliminary injunction motion, and the case was mooted after the plaintiffs were granted a preliminary injunction but before they requested attorney's fees. *See Dupuy*, 423 F.3d at 722–23. Further, the Ninth Circuit holds that a plaintiff is entitled to attorney's fees if he obtained a preliminary injunction and the case was subsequently mooted. *See Watson*, 300 F.3d at 1096. Here, the district court considered the merits of [Plaintiff] Dearmore's claim and clearly concluded that a provision of the Ordinance violated the Fourth Amendment. In response to the district court's grant of this preliminary injunction, the City [of Garland] amended the offending provision of the Ordinance, thereby mooting the case. Under these facts, at a minimum, it appears that Dearmore qualifies as a prevailing party under the Sixth, Seventh, and Ninth Circuits' tests.

…

Contrary to the City's argument, *Buckhannon* does not stand for the proposition that a defendant should be allowed to moot an action to avoid the payment of the plaintiff's attorney's fees when a district court grants a preliminary injunction based upon an unambiguous indication of probable success on the merits. Instead, we agree with Dearmore that this preliminary injunction, coupled with the City's subsequent mooting of the case, is sufficient to establish prevailing party status.

Under these facts, to qualify as a prevailing party under § 1988(b), we hold that the plaintiff (1) must win a preliminary injunction, (2) based upon an unambiguous indication of probable success on the merits of the plaintiff's claims as opposed to a mere balancing of the equities in favor of the plaintiff, (3) that causes the defendant to moot the action, which prevents the plaintiff from obtaining final relief on the merits. Such a test satisfies *Buckhannon,* because it requires that a party obtain a judicial ruling which results in a material change in the legal relationship between the parties. It also does not implicate the "catalyst theory," which the Supreme Court struck down in *Buckhannon,* because this test grants prevailing party status only when the defendant moots the plaintiff's action in response to a court order, not just in response to the filing of a lawsuit.

...

Dearmore clearly satisfies the three-prong test for prevailing party status announced herein. First, it is undisputed that the district court granted Dearmore a preliminary injunction—an enforceable judgment—by court order on November 3, 2005. Thus, Dearmore has satisfied the first prong of the test.

Second, the district court granted the preliminary injunction based upon its assessment that Dearmore would likely succeed on the merits of his Fourth Amendment claim, not because of any balancing of the equities in his favor.... Third, the district court's grant of the preliminary injunction directly caused the City to amend the offending portion of the Ordinance, thereby mooting the case and preventing Dearmore from obtaining final relief on the merits.... [I]f the City had mooted the case through amending the Ordinance before the court granted the preliminary injunction, then Dearmore could not qualify as a prevailing party under *Buckhannon* because it would have improperly invoked the "catalyst theory." The City, however, mooted the case after and in direct response to the district court's preliminary injunction order. There is an obvious direct causal link between the district court' s issuance of the preliminary injunction and the City's subsequent amendment of the Ordinance to moot the case. Almost immediately following the district court's issuance of the preliminary injunction, counsel for the City informed counsel for Dearmore that ... the City planned to amend the Ordinance to address the district court's concerns. Twelve days after the district court issued the injunction, the Garland City Council amended the provision of the Ordinance that the district court held to be violative of the Fourth Amendment. Dearmore has satisfied the third prong of the test, and thus he is entitled to attorney's fees and costs under § 1988(b).[4]

[T]he merits-based preliminary injunction here, coupled with the City's mooting of the action in direct response to the injunction, caused a material alteration in the legal relationship between the parties. The fact that Dearmore never obtained a final judgment on the merits does not affect our ruling, as a final judgment is not required. We, like the District of Columbia Circuit, conclude that "*Buckhannon* embraces the possibility that, under certain circumstances, a preliminary injunction, like a consent decree [which does not always include an admission of liability], may result in a court-ordered change in the legal relationship between the parties that is sufficient

4. [T]his test does not signal any disagreement with the approaches adopted by the other circuits, with the exception of the Fourth Circuit.

to make the plaintiff a 'prevailing party' under a fee-shifting statute." *Select Milk Producers*, 400 F.3d at 945. This is such a case. When the district court granted the preliminary injunction, it provided Dearmore with the interim judicial relief that he requested—it blocked the City from enforcing the portion of the Ordinance that violated the Fourth Amendment.... When the City modified its behavior in direct response to the injunction and mooted the case, it ultimately provided Dearmore with his desired result....

For further discussion

1. Under Section 1988, a demonstrator who successfully obtained an injunction against police officials' standing threat to prohibit him from carrying anti-abortion signs was a "prevailing party" normally entitled to attorney's fees. *Lefemine v. Wideman*, 568 U.S. 1, 5 (2012) (*per curiam*). The district court's injunction "worked the requisite material alteration in the parties' relationship" because "[b]efore the ruling, the police intended to stop [the demonstrator] from protesting with his signs; after the ruling, the police could not prevent him from demonstrating in that manner." *Id.*

2. A plaintiff who recovers only nominal damages is a prevailing party eligible to recover attorneys' fees under § 1988(b), but a reasonable fee in those circumstances usually is either no fee or a very low fee. *Farrar v. Hobby*, 506 U.S. 103, 114–15 (1992).

3. How should a court decide what fee is "reasonable" under § 1988(b)? While the statute does not define "reasonable," to calculate the attorney fee, generally a district court multiplies the reasonable number of hours worked by attorneys on the case by hourly rates that reflect the skill of the individual timekeepers to calculate the "lodestar" amount. "Because considerations concerning the quality of a prevailing party's counsel's representation normally are reflected in the reasonable hourly rate, the overall quality of performance ordinarily should not be used to adjust the lodestar, thus removing any danger of 'double counting.'" *Pennsylvania v. Delaware Valley Citizens' Council for Clean Air*, 478 U.S. 546, 566 (1986). Upon objection by defendant, a trial court may reduce the attorney hours to be counted in the lodestar. In *McKenna v. City of Philadelphia*, for example, the Third Circuit affirmed the reduction of attorney hours where defendants objected to the hours "in light of the [confusing] quality of the work produced, noting that '[counsel's] written work, including the complaint, motions, jury instructions, and the instant petition for attorneys' fees, is careless, vague, ambiguous, unintelligible, verbose, and repetitive.'" 582 F.3d 447, 459 (3d Cir. 2009).

4. Should the fee be increased based on high quality representation? In *Perdue v. Kenny* A., the Supreme Court granted certiorari to consider the following question: "Can a reasonable attorney's fee award under a federal fee-shifting statute ever be enhanced based solely on quality of performance and results obtained when these factors already are included in the lodestar calculation?" Petition for Writ of Certiorari,

Perdue v. Kenny A., No. 08-970, 2009 WL 245095, at *i (Jan. 29, 2009). Advocating for the answer "yes," an amici brief on behalf of law professors specializing in economics argued as follows:

> [T]he fees awarded under Section 1988 must provide lawyers the opportunity to earn remuneration comparable to what they could earn in other matters, and should provide them with the incentive to accept meritorious cases and resolve those cases in the most efficient manner.... [P]rohibiting courts from taking into account the actual quality of performance and result achieved, would severely undermine the statutory objective. First, it would discourage lawyers from taking civil rights cases because they would not have the opportunity to earn, on average, remuneration comparable to what they could earn in other matters. Second, when compensation is based in part on the quality of performance and result, lawyers who are best suited to handle meritorious cases will have an increased economic incentive to accept those cases.... Third, rewarding actual performance and result encourages lawyers to pursue the most efficient means to resolve a matter successfully, rather than ... the means that is likely to result in the highest lodestar fee. To provide the appropriate incentives for lawyers to accept and efficiently resolve meritorious civil rights cases, courts must have the flexibility to enhance (or diminish) the lodestar fee, in appropriate cases, to account for the quality of performance and result. That conclusion is consistent with the statutory text and purpose, this Court's cases, and sound economic principles.

Brief for Law and Economics Scholars Lucian A. Bebchuk, *et al.* as Amici Curiae Supporting Respondents, *Perdue v. Kenny A.*, No. 08-970, 2009 WL 2777659, at *4–*5 (Aug. 28, 2009).

In *Perdue v. Kenny A.*, 559 U.S. 542 (2010), the Supreme Court decided that "the calculation of an attorney's fee, under federal fee-shifting statutes, based on the 'lodestar,' *i.e.*, the number of hours worked multiplied by the prevailing hourly rates, may be increased due to superior performance and results." *Id.* at 546. While the Court reaffirmed that "such an increase is permitted in extraordinary circumstances," *id.*, it also reaffirmed that "there is a strong presumption that the lodestar is sufficient; factors subsumed in the lodestar calculation cannot be used as a ground for increasing an award above the lodestar; and a party seeking fees has the burden of identifying a factor that the lodestar does not adequately take into account and proving with specificity that an enhanced fee is justified." *Id.*

The Supreme Court further explained that "Section 1988 serves an important public purpose by making it possible for persons without means to bring suit to vindicate their rights. But unjustified enhancements that serve only to enrich attorneys are not consistent with the statute's aim. In many cases, attorney's fees awarded under § 1988 are not paid by the individuals responsible for the constitutional or statutory violations on which the judgment is based. Instead, the fees are paid in effect by state and local taxpayers, and because state and local governments have limited budgets, money that is used to pay attorney's fees is money that cannot be used for programs that provide vital public services." *Id.* at 559.

Exercise 10-A

You are counsel to a non-profit organization that frequently litigates § 1983 suits against local governments. Because of your organization's expertise, you represent clients throughout the country. The Board emails you that the non-profit would like to increase the amounts it receives as attorney's fees when it prevails in litigation. The Board asks: "Since the purpose of § 1988 is 'to make it possible for those who cannot pay a lawyer for his time and effort to obtain competent counsel,' *Delaware Valley*, 483 U.S. at 725, should we seek to amend 42 U.S.C. § 1988? If so, what amendments should we seek?" Draft a response to the Board's question. Consider the definition of "prevailing party," the catalyst theory, your non-profit's expertise, and any other factors that may influence your non profit's view of the statutory language of § 1988.

C. Prison Litigation Reform Act of 1995

Questions to guide reading of *Jones*

1. The Prison Litigation Reform Act (PLRA) requires prisoners to exhaust administrative remedies before filing a 42 U.S.C. § 1983 suit. What are some of the purposes served by this procedural hurdle imposed on prisoners?
2. Contrast the explanation of the PLRA exhaustion requirements in *Jones* with the Supreme Court's decision in *Monroe* (Chapter 1). How does the exhaustion requirement imposed on prisoners differ from the "no exhaustion" rule for other 42 U.S.C. § 1983 claims?
3. Note that the circuit court decisions challenged in *Jones* were non-precedential. Does that surprise you, given that between them these decisions implicated three different circuit splits?
4. What are the three circuit splits identified by the Supreme Court in *Jones*?

Jones v. Bock

549 U.S. 199 (2007)

Chief Justice ROBERTS delivered the opinion of the Court.

In an effort to address the large number of prisoner complaints filed in federal court, Congress enacted the Prison Litigation Reform Act of 1995 (PLRA) ... 42 U.S.C. § 1997e *et seq.* Among other reforms, the PLRA mandates early judicial screening of prisoner complaints and requires prisoners to exhaust prison grievance procedures before filing suit. 28 U.S.C. § 1915A; 42 U.S.C. § 1997e(a). The Sixth Circuit, along with some other lower courts, adopted several procedural rules designed to implement this exhaustion requirement and facilitate early judicial screening. These rules require a prisoner to allege and demonstrate exhaustion in his complaint, permit suit only against defendants who were identified by the prisoner in his grievance, and require courts to dismiss the entire action if the prisoner fails to satisfy the exhaustion requirement as to any single claim in his complaint. Other lower courts declined to adopt such rules. We granted *certiorari* to resolve the conflict and now conclude that these rules are not required by the PLRA, and that crafting and imposing them exceeds the proper limits on the judicial role.

I

Prisoner litigation continues to "account for an outsized share of filings" in federal district courts. *Woodford v. Ngo*, 548 U.S. 81, 94, n.4 (2006). In 2005, nearly 10 percent of all civil cases filed in federal courts nationwide were prisoner complaints challenging prison conditions or claiming civil rights violations.[1] Most of these cases have no merit; many are frivolous. Our legal system, however, remains committed to guaranteeing that prisoner claims of illegal conduct by their custodians are fairly handled according to law. The challenge lies in ensuring that the flood of nonmeritorious claims does not submerge and effectively preclude consideration of the allegations with merit....

Congress addressed that challenge in the PLRA. What this country needs, Congress decided, is fewer and better prisoner suits.... To that end, Congress enacted a variety of reforms designed to filter out the bad claims and facilitate consideration of the good. Key among these was the requirement that inmates complaining about prison conditions exhaust prison grievance remedies before initiating a lawsuit.

The exhaustion provision of the PLRA states:

> "No action shall be brought with respect to prison conditions under [42 U.S.C. § 1983], or any other Federal law, by a prisoner confined in any jail, prison, or other correctional facility until such administrative remedies as are available are exhausted." 42 U.S.C. § 1997e(a).

Requiring exhaustion allows prison officials an opportunity to resolve disputes concerning the exercise of their responsibilities before being haled into court. This has the potential to reduce the number of inmate suits, and also to improve the quality of suits that are filed by producing a useful administrative record. *Woodford*, 548 U.S. at 94–95. In an attempt to implement the exhaustion requirement, some

1. *See* Administrative Office of the United States Courts, Judicial Facts and Figures, Tables 4.4, 4.6, http://www.uscourts.gov/ judicialfactsfigures/contents.html (as visited Jan. 17, 2007, and available in Clerk of Court's case file). That number excludes habeas corpus petitions and motions to vacate a sentence. If these filing are included, prisoner complaints constituted 24 percent of all civil filings in 2005.

lower courts have imposed procedural rules that have become the subject of varying levels of disagreement among the federal courts of appeals.

The first question presented centers on a conflict over whether exhaustion under the PLRA is a pleading requirement the prisoner must satisfy in his complaint or an affirmative defense the defendant must plead and prove. The Sixth Circuit, adopting the former view, requires prisoners to attach proof of exhaustion—typically copies of the grievances—to their complaints to avoid dismissal. If no written record of the grievance is available, the inmate must plead with specificity how and when he exhausted the grievance procedures....

The next issue concerns how courts determine whether a prisoner has properly exhausted administrative remedies—specifically, the level of detail required in a grievance to put the prison and individual officials on notice of the claim. The Sixth Circuit requires that a prisoner have identified, in the first step of the grievance process, each individual later named in the lawsuit to properly exhaust administrative remedies.... Other circuits have taken varying approaches to this question, *see, e.g.*, [Ninth Cir.](proper exhaustion requires use of the administrative process provided by the State; if that process does not require identification of specific persons, neither does the PLRA); [Fifth Cir.] ("[T]he grievance must provide administrators with a fair opportunity under the circumstances to address the problem that will later form the basis of the suit"); [Seventh Cir.] (exhaustion satisfied if grievance "served its function of alerting the state and inviting corrective action"), none going as far as the Sixth Circuit in requiring in every case that the defendants have been named from the beginning of the grievance process.

Finally, the circuits are divided over what the PLRA requires when both exhausted and unexhausted claims are included in a complaint. Some circuits, including the Sixth Circuit, apply a "total exhaustion" rule, under which no part of the suit may proceed if any single claim in the action is not properly exhausted.... Among circuits requiring total exhaustion there is further disagreement over what to do if the requirement is not met. Most courts allow the prisoner to amend his complaint to include only exhausted claims, e.g., [Eighth Cir.], but the Sixth Circuit denies leave to amend, dismisses the action, and requires that it be filed anew with only unexhausted claims.... Other circuits reject total exhaustion altogether, instead dismissing only unexhausted claims and considering the rest on the merits. *See, e.g.*, [Second Cir.]

A

Petitioners are inmates in the custody of the Michigan Department of Corrections (MDOC). [The Michigan prison policy] set forth the applicable grievance procedures....

Inmates must first attempt to resolve a problem orally within two business days of becoming aware of the grievable issue. If oral resolution is unsuccessful, the inmate may proceed to Step I of the grievance process, and submit a completed grievance form within five business days of the attempted oral resolution. The Step I grievance form provided by MDOC (a one-page form on which the inmate fills out identifying information and is given space to describe the complaint) advises inmates to be "brief and concise in describing your grievance issue." The inmate submits the grievance to a designated grievance coordinator, who assigns it to a respondent—generally the supervisor of the person being grieved.

If the inmate is dissatisfied with the Step I response, he may appeal to Step II by obtaining an appeal form within five business days of the response, and submitting the appeal within five business days of obtaining the form. The respondent at Step II is designated by the policy, (*e.g.*, the regional health administrator for medical care grievances). If still dissatisfied after Step II, the inmate may further appeal to Step III using the same appeal form; the MDOC director is designated as respondent for all Step III appeals.

Lorenzo Jones

Petitioner Lorenzo Jones is incarcerated at the MDOC's Saginaw Correctional Facility. In November 2000, while in MDOC's custody, Jones was involved in a vehicle accident and suffered significant injuries to his neck and back. Several months later Jones was given a work assignment he allegedly could not perform in light of his injuries. According to Jones, respondent Paul Morrison—in charge of work assignments at the prison—made the inappropriate assignment, even though he knew of Jones's injuries. When Jones reported to the assignment, he informed the staff member in charge—respondent Michael Opanasenko—that he could not perform the work; Opanasenko allegedly told him to do the work or " 'suffer the consequences.' " Jones performed the required tasks and allegedly aggravated his injuries. After unsuccessfully seeking redress through the MDOC's grievance process, Jones filed a complaint in the Eastern District of Michigan under 42 U.S.C. § 1983 for deliberate indifference to medical needs, retaliation, and harassment.

...

In his complaint, Jones provided the dates on which his claims were filed at various steps of the MDOC grievance procedures. He did not, however, attach copies of the grievance forms or describe the proceedings with specificity. Respondents attached copies of all of Jones's grievances to their own motion to dismiss, but the District Judge ruled that Jones's failure to meet his burden to plead exhaustion in his complaint could not be cured by respondents. The Sixth Circuit agreed ... and [held] that, even if Jones had shown that he exhausted the claims against [certain defendants], dismissal was still required under the total exhaustion rule, [135 F. App'x 837, 839 (2005)].

Timothy Williams

Petitioner Timothy Williams is incarcerated at the MDOC's Adrian Correctional Facility. [He also filed a complaint alleging denial of medical care when prison officials rejected a prison doctor's recommendation for surgery and denied Williams housing in a handicapped cell.]

...

The District Judge found that Williams had failed to exhaust his administrative remedies with regard to his medical care claim because he had not identified any of the respondents named in his lawsuit during the grievance process. Although Williams's claim concerning the handicapped cell had been properly exhausted, the District Judge—applying the total exhaustion rule—dismissed the entire suit. The Sixth Circuit affirmed. 136 F. App'x 859, 861–863 (2005).

...

B

Jones ... argu[es] that the Sixth Circuit's heightened pleading requirement and total exhaustion rule contravene the clear language of the Federal Rules of Civil Procedure and the PLRA. Williams ... contend[s] that the rule requiring every defendant to be named during the grievance process is not required by the PLRA, and also challeng[es] the total exhaustion rule....

II

There is no question that exhaustion is mandatory under the PLRA and that unexhausted claims cannot be brought in court.... What is less clear is whether it falls to the prisoner to plead and demonstrate exhaustion in the complaint, or to the defendant to raise lack of exhaustion as an affirmative defense. The minority rule, adopted by the Sixth Circuit, places the burden of pleading exhaustion in a case covered by the PLRA on the prisoner; most courts view failure to exhaust as an affirmative defense.

We think petitioners, and the majority of courts to consider the question, have the better of the argument. Federal Rule of Civil Procedure 8(a) requires simply a "short and plain statement of the claim" in a complaint, while Rule 8(c) identifies a nonexhaustive list of affirmative defenses that must be pleaded in response. The PLRA itself is not a source of a prisoner's claim; claims covered by the PLRA are typically brought under 42 U.S.C. § 1983, which does not require exhaustion at all, see *Patsy v. Board of Regents of Fla.*, 457 U.S. 496, 516 (1982). Petitioners assert that courts typically regard exhaustion as an affirmative defense in other contexts.... The PLRA dealt extensively with the subject of exhaustion, see 42 U.S.C. §§ 1997e(a), (c)(2), but is silent on the issue whether exhaustion must be pleaded by the plaintiff or is an affirmative defense. This is strong evidence that the usual practice should be followed, and the usual practice under the Federal Rules is to regard exhaustion as an affirmative defense.

In a series of recent cases, we have explained that courts should generally not depart from the usual practice under the Federal Rules on the basis of perceived policy concerns. Thus, in *Leatherman v. Tarrant County Narcotics Intelligence and Coordination Unit*, 507 U.S. 163 (1993), we unanimously reversed the court of appeals for imposing a heightened pleading standard in § 1983 suits against municipalities.

...

The Sixth Circuit and other courts requiring prisoners to plead and demonstrate exhaustion in their complaints contend that if the "new regime" mandated by the PLRA for prisoner complaints is to function effectively, prisoner complaints must be treated outside of this typical framework.... These courts explain that the PLRA not only imposed a new mandatory exhaustion requirement, but also departed in a fundamental way from the usual procedural ground rules by requiring judicial screening to filter out nonmeritorious claims: Courts are to screen inmate complaints "before docketing, if feasible, or ... as soon as practicable after docketing," and dismiss the complaint if it is "frivolous, malicious, ... fails to state a claim upon which relief may be granted[,] or ... seeks monetary relief from a defendant who is immune from such relief." 28 U.S.C. §§ 1915A(a), (b). All this may take place before any responsive pleading is filed—unlike in the typical civil case, defendants do not have to respond to a complaint covered by the PLRA until required to do so by the court, and waiving the right to reply does not constitute an admission of the allegations in the complaint. *See* 42 U.S.C. § 1997e(g)(1), (2). According to respondents, these departures from the normal litigation framework of complaint and response mandate a different pleading requirement for prisoner complaints, if the screening is to serve its intended purpose....

We think that the PLRA's screening requirement does not—explicitly or implicitly—justify deviating from the usual procedural practice beyond the departures specified by the PLRA itself. Before the PLRA, the *in forma pauperis* provision of § 1915, applicable to most prisoner litigation, permitted *sua sponte* dismissal only if an action was frivolous or malicious. 28 U.S.C. § 1915(d) (1994 ed.).... In the PLRA, Congress added failure to state a claim and seeking monetary relief from a defendant immune from such relief as grounds for *sua sponte* dismissal of *in forma pauperis* cases, § 1915(e)(2)(B) (2000 ed.), and provided for judicial screening and *sua sponte* dismissal of prisoner suits on the same four grounds, § 1915A(b); 42 U.S.C. § 1997e(c)(1). Although exhaustion was a "centerpiece" of the PLRA, *Woodford*, 548 U.S. at 84, failure to exhaust was notably not added in terms to this enumeration. There is thus no reason to suppose that the normal pleading rules have to be altered to facilitate judicial screening of complaints specifically for failure to exhaust.

...

The argument that screening would be more effective if exhaustion had to be shown in the complaint proves too much; the same could be said with respect to any affirmative defense. The rejoinder that the PLRA focused on exhaustion rather than other defenses simply highlights the failure of Congress to include exhaustion in terms among the enumerated grounds justifying dismissal upon early screening. As noted, that is not to say that failure to exhaust cannot be a basis for dismissal for failure to state a claim. It is to say that there is no basis for concluding that Congress implicitly meant to transform exhaustion from an affirmative defense to a pleading requirement by the curiously indirect route of specifying that courts should screen PLRA complaints and dismiss those that fail to state a claim.

Respondents point to 42 U.S.C. § 1997e(g) as confirming that the usual pleading rules should not apply to PLRA suits, but we think that provision supports petitioners. It specifies that defendants can waive their right to reply to a prisoner complaint without the usual consequence of being deemed to have admitted the allegations in the complaint. *See* § 1997e(g)(1) (allowing defendants to waive their response without admitting the allegations "[n]otwithstanding any other law or rule of procedure"). This shows that when Congress meant to depart from the usual procedural requirements, it did so expressly.

We conclude that failure to exhaust is an affirmative defense under the PLRA, and that inmates are not required to specially plead or demonstrate exhaustion in their complaints...." Whatever temptations the statesmanship of policy-making might wisely suggest," the judge's job is to construe the statute—not to make it better. Frankfurter, *Some Reflections on the Reading of Statutes*, 47 Colum. L. Rev. 527, 533 (1947).... Given that the PLRA does not itself require plaintiffs to plead exhaustion, such a result "must be obtained by the process of amending the Federal Rules, and not by judicial interpretation." *Leatherman*, 507 U.S., at 168[.]

III

The Sixth Circuit threw out the Williams ... suit[] because [he] had not identified in [his] initial grievances each defendant ... later sued. 136 F. App'x, at 862–863; *id.*, at 848–849.[7] Here again the lower court's procedural rule lacks a textual basis in the PLRA. The PLRA requires exhaustion of "such administrative remedies as are available," 42 U.S.C. § 1997e(a), but nothing in the statute imposes a "name all defendants" requirement along the lines of the Sixth Circuit's judicially created rule....

Woodford held that "proper exhaustion" was required under the PLRA, and that this requirement was not satisfied when grievances were dismissed because prisoners had missed deadlines set by the grievance policy. *Id.*, at 93–95[.] At the time each of the grievances at issue here was filed, in contrast, the MDOC policy did not contain any provision specifying who must be named in a grievance.... Nothing in the MDOC policy itself supports the conclusion that the grievance process was improperly invoked simply because an individual later named as a defendant was not named at the first step of the grievance process.

Nor does the PLRA impose such a requirement. In *Woodford*, we held that to properly exhaust administrative remedies prisoners must "complete the administrative review process in accordance with the applicable procedural rules," 548 U.S., at 88—rules that are defined not by the PLRA, but by the prison grievance process itself. Compliance with prison grievance procedures, therefore, is all that is required by the PLRA to "properly exhaust." The level of detail necessary in a grievance to comply with the grievance procedures will vary from system to system and claim to claim, but it is the prison's requirements, and not the PLRA, that define the boundaries of proper exhaustion. As the MDOC's procedures make no mention of naming particular officials, the Sixth Circuit's rule imposing such a prerequisite to proper exhaustion is unwarranted.

---

7. This "name all defendants" rule apparently applies even when a prisoner does not learn the identity of the responsible party until a later step of the grievance process. Upon learning the identity of the responsible party, the prisoner is required to bring an entirely new grievance to properly exhaust....

We have identified the benefits of exhaustion to include allowing a prison to address complaints about the program it administers before being subjected to suit, reducing litigation to the extent complaints are satisfactorily resolved, and improving litigation that does occur by leading to the preparation of a useful record.... [E]xhaustion is not per se inadequate simply because an individual later sued was not named in the grievances. We leave it to the court below in the first instance to determine the sufficiency of the exhaustion in these cases.

IV

The final issue concerns how courts should address complaints in which the prisoner has failed to exhaust some, but not all, of the claims asserted in the complaint. All agree that no unexhausted claim may be considered. The issue is whether the court should proceed with the exhausted claims, or instead—as the Sixth Circuit has held—dismiss the entire action if any one claim is not properly exhausted.

Here the Sixth Circuit can point to language in the PLRA in support of its rule. Section 1997e(a) provides that "[n]o action shall be brought" unless administrative procedures are exhausted. Respondents argue that if Congress intended courts to dismiss only unexhausted claims while retaining the balance of the lawsuit, the word "claim" rather than "action" would have been used in this provision.... There are many instances in the Federal Code where similar language is used, but such language has not been thought to lead to the dismissal of an entire action if a single claim fails to meet the pertinent standards. [citing, e.g., statutes of limitations].

...

As a general matter, if a complaint contains both good and bad claims, the court proceeds with the good and leaves the bad.

...

In pressing the total exhaustion argument, respondents also marshal the policy and purpose underlying the PLRA.... [I]f the exhaustion requirement of § 1997e(a) is not effectuated by a total exhaustion rule, they argue, inmates will have little incentive to ensure that they have exhausted all available administrative remedies before proceeding to court. The PLRA mandated early judicial screening to reduce the burden of prisoner litigation on the courts; a total exhaustion rule allows courts promptly to dismiss an action upon identifying an unexhausted claim. The alternative approach turns judges into editors of prisoner complaints, rather than creating an incentive for prisoners to exhaust properly....

We are not persuaded by these policy arguments. In fact, the effect of a total exhaustion rule could be that inmates will file various claims in separate suits, to avoid the possibility of an unexhausted claim tainting the others. That would certainly not comport with the purpose of the PLRA to reduce the quantity of inmate suits. Additionally, district judges who delve into a prisoner complaint only to realize it contains an unexhausted claim, requiring dismissal of the entire complaint under the total exhaustion rule, will often have to begin the process all over again when the prisoner refiles. In light of typically short prison grievance time limits, prisoners' refiled complaints will often be identical to what the district court would have considered had it simply dismissed unexhausted claims as it encountered them and proceeded with the exhausted ones. Perhaps filing fees and concerns about the applicability of the "three strikes" rule, 28 U.S.C. § 1915(g), would mitigate these effects, but the debate about consequences is close enough that there is no clear reason to depart from the more typical claim-by-claim approach.

* * *

We are not insensitive to the challenges faced by the lower federal courts in managing their dockets and attempting to separate, when it comes to prisoner suits, not so much wheat from chaff as needles from haystacks. We once again reiterate, however—as we did unanimously in Leatherman ... that adopting different and more onerous pleading rules to deal with particular categories of cases should be done through established rulemaking procedures, and not on a case-by-case basis by the courts.

...

To guide reading of Attorney's Fees provision of Prison Litigation Reform Act

Compare the method of calculating attorney's fees under the Prison Litigation Reform Act with the attorney's fees provision in § 1988 discussed earlier in this Chapter. Do you think the Prison Litigation Reform Act provision encourages or discourages attorneys from representing prisoners?

Attorney's Fees Provision of Prison Litigation Reform Act

42 U.S.C.A. § 1997e(d) (West 1996)

(d) Attorney's fees

(1) In any action brought by a prisoner who is confined to any jail, prison, or other correctional facility, in which attorney's fees are authorized under section 1988 of this title, such fees shall not be awarded, except to the extent that—

(A) the fee was directly and reasonably incurred in proving an actual violation of the plaintiff's rights protected by a statute pursuant to which a fee may be awarded under section 1988 of this title; and

(B)(i) the amount of the fee is proportionately related to the court ordered relief for the violation; or

(ii) the fee was directly and reasonably incurred in enforcing the relief ordered for the violation.

(2) Whenever a monetary judgment is awarded in an action described in paragraph (1), a portion of the judgment (not to exceed 25 percent) shall be applied to satisfy the amount of attorney's fees awarded against the defendant. If the award of at-

torney's fees is not greater than 150 percent of the judgment, the excess shall be paid by the defendant.

(3) No award of attorney's fees in an action described in paragraph (1) shall be based on an hourly rate greater than 150 percent of the hourly rate established under section 3006A of Title 18 for payment of court-appointed counsel.

(4) Nothing in this subsection shall prohibit a prisoner from entering into an agreement to pay an attorney's fee in an amount greater than the amount authorized under this subsection, if the fee is paid by the individual rather than by the defendant pursuant to section 1988 of this title.

...

For further discussion

The Supreme Court reaffirmed that the Prison Litigation Reform Act requires an inmate to exhaust available administrative remedies before bringing suit to challenge prison conditions, but clarified that the inmate "need not exhaust remedies if they are not 'available.'" *Ross v. Blake*, 578 U.S. ___, 136 S. Ct. 1850, 1855 (2016). "[A]n administrative procedure is unavailable when (despite what regulations or guidance materials may promise) it operates as a simple dead end ... [*e.g.*] a prison handbook directs inmates to submit their grievances to a particular administrative office—but in practice that office disclaims the capacity to consider those petitions.... [Or, an administrative scheme might be unavailable if] some mechanism exists to provide relief, but no ordinary prisoner can discern or navigate it ... [or] when prison administrators thwart inmates from taking advantage of a grievance process through machination, misrepresentation, or intimidation." *Ross*, 136 S. Ct. at 1859–60.

No Equal Justice: The Prison Litigation Reform Act in the United States

David Fathi, Human Rights Watch (June 15, 2009)
© Human Rights Watch

Trap for the Unwary

... Many cases are dismissed because the prisoner used the wrong form, or wrote to the wrong entity within the prison system. Cases have been dismissed, in whole or in part, because the prisoner:

- Submitted a form to the "inmate appeals branch" rather than to the "appeals coordinator."[53]
- Filed an "administrative appeal" rather than a "disciplinary appeal."[54] ...

53. *Chatman v. Johnson*, 2007 WL 2023544 at *6 (E.D. Cal. 2007) (report and recommendation adopted 2007 WL 2796575 (E.D. Cal. 2007)).

54. *Richardson v. Spurlock*, 260 F.3d 495, 499 (5th Cir. 2001).

- Sent appeal documents to the secretary of the Department of Corrections rather than to the secretary's Office of Inmate Grievances and Appeals.[56]
- Filed a new grievance rather than seeking reinstatement of a previous grievance (the court characterized its dismissal of the case as "hyper-technical" but required by the PLRA).[57]

No Exceptions, No Excuses

[The Supreme Court stated "we will not read futility or other exceptions into [PLRA] statutory exhaustion requirements. *Booth v. Chorner*, 532 U.S. 731, 741 n.6 (2001).] Courts have not been receptive to the argument that the exhaustion requirement should be excused, even when there is good cause for the prisoner's failure to pursue remedies within the prison grievance system. Among the justifications for non-exhaustion courts have rejected are:

Dyslexia[58]

Illiteracy[59]

Inability to read English[60]

Cerebral palsy[61]

Mental illness[62] ...

Being in a coma[65]

... In a case involving the exhaustion requirement, the US Supreme Court said that "[b]eyond doubt, Congress enacted [the PLRA] to reduce the quantity and improve the quality of prisoner suits."[67] A central argument of the PLRA's supporters was that the law would filter out only frivolous or plainly meritless prisoner suits, but would not affect those that raised serious issues. As Senator Orrin Hatch put it, "I do not want to prevent inmates from raising legitimate claims. This legislation will not prevent those claims from being raised. The legislation will, however, go far in preventing inmates from abusing the Federal judicial system."[68] Representative Charles Canady sounded a similar note: "These reasonable requirements will not impede meritorious claims by inmates but will greatly discourage claims that are without merit."[69]

---

56. *Keys v. Craig*, 160 F. App'x 125, 126 (3d Cir. 2005).

57. *Whitney v. Simonson*, 2007 WL 3274373 at *2 (E.D. Cal. 2007) (report and recommendation adopted 2007 WL 4591593 (E.D. Cal. 2007), *aff'd.* 2009 WL 604912 (9th Cir. 2009)).

58. *Williams v. Pettiford*, 2007 WL 3119548 at *3 (D.S.C. 2007).

59. *Ramos v. Smith*, 187 F. App'x 152, 154 (3d Cir. 2006).

60. *Benavidez v. Stansberry*, 2008 WL 4279559 at *4 (N.D. Ohio 2008).

61. *Elliott v. Monroe Correctional Complex*, 2007 WL 208422 at *3 (W.D. Wash. 2007).

62. *Yorkey v. Pettiford*, 2007 WL 2750068 at *4 (D.S.C. 2007).

65. *Parker v. Adjetey*, 89 F. App'x 886, 887–88 (5th Cir. 2004).

67. *Porter v. Nussle*, 534 U.S. 516, 524 (2002).

68. Statement of Senator Orrin Hatch (R-UT), September 29, 1995, Congressional Record, vol. 141, 1995, p. S14,62[6].

69. Statement of Representative Charles Canady (R-FL), February 9, 1995, Congressional Record, vol. 141, 1995, p. H1480.

But the exhaustion requirement has nothing to do with the merit of the prisoner's underlying claim. It requires dismissal of the case—regardless of its merit—if the prisoner has failed to comply with the procedural requirements, however petty, of the prison grievance regime. The legality or illegality of the conduct the prisoner is complaining of, or the magnitude of the harm she has suffered, simply do not matter....

The Physical Injury Requirement

... The PLRA ... provides that a prisoner may not sue "for mental or emotional injury suffered while in custody without a prior showing of physical injury [or the commission of a sexual act]."[85] [This provision does not preclude nominal or punitive damages or declaratory or injunctive relief.] The physical injury requirement simply declares a certain category of injury to be noncompensable, without regard to the merit of the prisoner's claim or the culpability of the defendant. Thus, even a prisoner who is the victim of intentionally abusive staff conduct, resulting in extreme emotional distress, cannot recover compensation. As one federal judge put it,

> [I]magine a sadistic prison guard who tortures inmates by carrying out fake executions—holding an unloaded gun to a prisoner's head and pulling the trigger, or staging a mock execution in a nearby cell, with shots and screams, and a body bag being taken out (within earshot and sight of the target prisoner). The emotional harm could be catastrophic but would be non-compensable [under the PRLA].[86]

One witness testifying before the Commission on Safety and Abuse in America's Prisons suggested that this provision of the PLRA "seems to make it national policy ... that mental torture is not actionable."[87] ... Indeed, some courts have ruled that the PLRA bars compensation for even the most extreme mistreatment of prisoners. Stephen Jarriett filed a lawsuit alleging that prison officials forced him to stand in a two-and-a-half foot square cage for about 13 hours, naked for the first eight to ten hours, and unable to sit for more than 30 or 40 minutes of this time. He was in acute pain from a clearly visible swelling in his leg from a previous injury and repeatedly asked to see a doctor, but his requests were ignored. The court ruled that the PLRA barred compensation for this treatment because any physical injury was "de minimis," a legal term meaning too trivial to deserve the court's attention.[90]

Although the plain language of the PLRA suggests that any "physical injury" is enough to support compensation, many courts have ruled that injuries they deem

---

85. 42 U.S.C. 1997e(e).

86. *Siggers-El v. Barlow*, 433 F. Supp. 2d 811, 816 (E.D. Mich. 2006) (quoting with approval a hypothetical set forth in plaintiff's brief) [Plaintiff was represented by University of Michigan Clinical Law Programs].

87. Commission on Safety and Abuse in America's Prisons, *Confronting Confinement*, p. 86. This provision of the PLRA does not affect the availability of injunctive relief....

90. *Jarriett v. Wilson*, 162 F. App'x 394, 403 (6th Cir. 2005) (Karen Nelson Moore, J., dissenting).

minor do not qualify. Conditions courts have found insufficient to satisfy the PLRA's physical injury requirement include: ...

- An "open wound" to the head causing "severe pain"[92]
- Being forced to defecate in one's clothing and sleep in feces[93]
- An asthma attack requiring hospitalization in the critical care unit[94]
- Extreme pain resulting from broken teeth with exposed nerve[95]

For further discussion

1. Should the attorney's fee provision of the Prison Litigation Reform Act be stricken, so that prisoner's claims are again subject to the § 1988 attorney's fee provision? Why or why not?

2. Is relief available in the absence of physical injury or commission of a sexual act? The circuits are split over whether Section 1997e(e) precludes compensatory damages in the absence of an allegation of physical injury. *See* Petition for Writ of Certiorari, *Zamiara v. King*, 136 S. Ct. 794 (No. 15-259), 2015 WL 5158773, at *3 (Aug. 31, 2015) (arguing seven circuits apply this limitation to all federal civil actions but three circuits, including the Sixth Circuit, hold that "deprivations of First Amendment rights are themselves injuries, apart from any mental, emotional, or physical injury"), *cert. denied*, ___ U.S. ___, 136 S. Ct. 794 (2016); *Siggers-El v. Barlow*, 433 F. Supp. 2d 811, 816 (E.D. Mich. 2006) ("physical injury" requirement of PLRA does not apply to First Amendment claim; litigated by University of Michigan Clinical Law Programs). Even in the absence of physical injury, several circuits have held that § 1997e(e) does not preclude other forms of relief. In *Royal v. Kautzky*, 375 F.3d 720, 723 (8th Cir. 2004), *cert. denied*, 544 U.S. 1061 (2005), for example, the Eighth Circuit held:

> To the extent Royal argues nominal damages, punitive damages, and injunctive and declaratory relief are available to him, we agree. Congress did not intend section 1997e(e) to bar recovery for all forms of relief. *See, e.g.*, *Memphis Cmty. Sch. Dist. v. Stachura*, 477 U.S. 299, 308 (1986) (holding nominal damages should be granted for section 1983 claims when actual injury cannot be shown); *Smith v. Wade*, 461 U.S. 30, 56 (1983) (holding punitive damages are authorized for violations of constitutional rights); *Hughes v. Lott*, 350 F.3d 1157, 1162 (11th Cir. 2003) (holding section 1997e(e) does not preclude nominal damages); *Thompson [v. Carter]*, 284 F.3d [411,] 418 [(2d Cir. 2002] (holding section 1997e(e) does not preclude injunctive relief or nominal damages); *Searles [v. Van Bebber]*, 251 F.3d [869,] 878–79 [10th Cir.

---

92. *Diggs v. Emfinger*, 2008 WL 544293 at *4 (report and recommendation rejected on other grounds, 2008 WL 516378 (W.D. La. 2008)).

93. *Brooks v. Delta Correctional Facility*, 2007 WL 2219303 at *1 (N.D. Miss. 2007).

94. *Williams v. Smith*, 2006 WL 938980 at *2 (W.D. Ky. 2006).

95. *Olivas v. Corrections Corp. of America*, 408 F. Supp. 2d 251, 254, 259 n.4 (N.D. Tex. 2006).

2001](holding section 1997e(e) does not preclude nominal damages); *Davis v. Dist. of Columbia*, 158 F.3d 1342, 1346 (D.C. Cir. 1998) (stating section 1997e(e) does not preclude injunctive relief); *Zehner v. Trigg*, 133 F.3d 459, 462 (7th Cir. 1997) (same).

3. The "vast majority of circuits" agree Section 1997e(e) does not limit the availability of punitive damages to plaintiffs who plead only mental or emotional injury, without a showing of physical harm. *See Aref v. Lynch*, 833 F.3d 242, 266 (D.C. Cir. 2016) (noting that the D.C. Circuit has held punitive damages are precluded for plaintiffs who plead mental or emotional injury in the absence of physical harm).

4. Unlike § 1988 attorney's fees, the Prison Litigation Reform Act requires a prevailing prisoner to pay a defined portion of the recovery to satisfy attorney's fees. In *Murphy v. Smith*, ___ U.S. ___, 138 S. Ct. 784, 787 (2018), the Court held that "the [district] court (1) *must* apply judgment funds toward the fee award (2) with the *purpose* of (3) *fully discharging* the fee award. And to meet *that* duty, a district court must apply as much of the judgment as necessary to satisfy the fee award, without of course exceeding the 25% cap." *Id.* at 787. The statutory phrase "shall be applied," *id.*, required the district court to "apply as much of the judgment as necessary, up to 25%, to satisfy an award of attorney's fees." *Id.* at 790. In so holding, the Supreme Court abrogated rulings from several circuits. While those circuits had recognized 25% as the maximum portion of the award to be applied towards attorney's fees, they had allowed plaintiffs to pay less than 25%. Brief for Petitioner in *Murphy v. Smith*, No. 16-1067, 2017 WL 4404062, at *12 (Sept. 29, 2017).

D. Selected Recurring Procedural Issues in § 1983 Litigation

The below sampling of recurring procedural issues is included to "red flag" these as potential issues you may encounter in practice. For each, there is a developed body of case law that a careful litigator must research within the relevant jurisdiction.

1. Statute of Limitations

Claims brought pursuant to 42 U.S.C. § 1983 are characterized as claims for personal injury and the appropriate statute of limitations for § 1983 claims is borrowed from the forum state's statute of limitations for personal injury suits. *See Wilson v. Garcia*, 471 U.S. 261, 275–79 (1985), *superseded by statute on other grounds, as stated in Jones v. R.R. Donnelley & Sons Co.*, 541 U.S. 369, 377–378 (2004); *Owens v. Okure*, 488 U.S. 235, 236 (1989) (where a state has one or more statutes of limitations for certain intentional torts, and a residual statute for all other personal injury actions, the latter applies to § 1983 actions). Accordingly, while the statute of limitations for § 1983 is uniform within a particular state, the statute of limitations may vary among different states.

2. Heck v. Humphrey *Bar on 42 U.S.C. § 1983 Actions*

When a § 1983 claim accrues depends on the nature of the claim. Usually, a claim accrues at the time of the injury. For example, an excessive force claim accrues at the time the force is used, whether the claim arises under the 4th, 8th, or 14th Amendments to the Constitution. *See* Chapter 6.

However, a § 1983 claim for unlawful conviction or confinement does not accrue until the underlying conviction has been invalidated. *See Heck v. Humphrey*, 512 U.S. 477, 486–87 (1994) (limiting damages actions that would imply the invalidity of a conviction or sentence to those where plaintiff can "prove that the conviction or sentence has been reversed on direct appeal, expunged by executive order, declared invalid by a state tribunal authorized to make such determination, or called into question by a federal court's issuance of a writ of habeas corpus"). Similarly, a "fabricated-evidence challenge to criminal proceedings" does not accrue as a § 1983 cause of action until "the criminal proceeding has ended in the defendant's favor, or a resulting conviction has been invalidated within the meaning of *Heck*." *McDonough v. Smith*, ___ U.S. ___, 139 S. Ct. 2149, 2156–58 (2019); *compare Skinner v. Switzer*, 562 U.S. 521, 534 (2011) (Section 1983 action seeking post-conviction access to DNA evidence was not barred by *Heck* because it did not necessarily imply the conviction was invalid).

What event triggers the start of the statute of limitations for a claim that pretrial detention violates probable cause? *Manuel* held a pretrial detainee's challenge to the validity of the probable cause resulting in the detention is governed by the 4th Amendment. *Manuel v. City of Joliet*, ___ U.S. ___, 137 S. Ct. 911, 920 (2017). But in *Manuel*, the Supreme Court declined to reach what accrual rule should govern a § 1983 challenge to post-legal-process pretrial detention. *Id.* at 921–22.

Plaintiff argued that the Fourth Amendment claim should accrue upon termination of the criminal prosecution in favor of the accused, analogizing the constitutional claim to the tort of malicious prosecution. That accrual date would avoid "conflicting resolutions" in § 1983 litigation and criminal proceedings by "preclud[ing] the possibility of the claimant succeeding in the tort action after having been convicted in the underlying criminal prosecution." *Id.* at 921. In support of that accrual date, the Supreme Court in *Manuel* explicitly noted "all but two of the ten Courts of Appeals that have recognized a Fourth Amendment claim like his have incorporated a 'favorable termination' element and so pegged the statute of limitations to the dismissal of the criminal case." *Id.*

By contrast, defendants argued that the Fourth Amendment claim should accrue on the date of the initiation of legal process, analogizing the constitutional claim to the tort of false arrest. Further, defendants argued, "even if malicious prosecution were the better comparison," a court should reject "that tort's favorable-termination element" because "'the Fourth Amendment is concerned not with the outcome of a prosecution, but with the legality of searches and seizures." *Id.* (summarizing defendants' argument). Finally, defendants argued plaintiff had "forfeited an alternative theory" that "his pretrial detention 'constitute[d] a continuing Fourth Amendment violation,' each day of which triggered the statute of limitations anew." *Id.* (further summarizing defendants' argument).

3. *Accrual of a False Arrest Claim and the* Heck v. Humphrey *Bar*

Unlike a "fabricated-evidence challenge to criminal proceedings," which is analogous to a malicious prosecution claim, *McDonough*, 139 S.Ct. at 2156–58, a false arrest claim under the 4th Amendment is instead analogous to a false imprisonment claim. A claim based upon a warrantless arrest therefore accrues at the time the alleged false imprisonment ends, *i.e.*, at the time the claimant appears before a magistrate and is bound over for trial; it does not accrue later, upon the claimant's release from custody after criminal charges are dropped. *Wallace v. Kato*, 549 U.S. 384, 389–90 (2007).

Because the false arrest claim accrues before the outcome of the criminal trial, plaintiffs confront a procedural challenge for plaintiff since, under *Heck*, a § 1983 claim challenging the validity of a criminal conviction may not be brought unless and until the conviction is vacated or set aside. *Heck*, 512 U.S. at 486–87. The plaintiff in *Wallace*, following *Heck's* dictate that no § 1983 claim for abuse of process accrues until the underlying conviction is invalidated, waited to bring a false imprisonment claim under § 1983 until all charges in the underlying criminal suit against him had been dropped. 549 U.S. at 392. The Court held that petitioner's claim was barred by the statute of limitations since the statute of limitations had begun to run when plaintiff was bound over for trial. *Id.* at 391–92.

Since a false arrest claim accrues at the time the alleged false imprisonment ends, the statute of limitations begins to run at that time, even though a claim of false arrest may not be ripe for consideration by a trial court unless and until a resulting criminal conviction is set aside. *Id.* at 393–94. Plaintiffs must file within the limitations period to protect the right to assert the false arrest claim if and when the criminal conviction is set aside. *Id. Wallace* therefore has complicated the litigation tactics of plaintiffs' counsel, who, depending on the forum state's statute of limitations, may be forced to file a § 1983 suit while the underlying criminal proceeding is pending. In anticipation of this procedural challenge, the Court noted that district court judges have discretion to stay the civil proceeding until the resolution of the underlying criminal matter. *Id.*

4. *42 U.S.C. § 1983 Pleading Requirements*

The federal rules require general notice pleading for most causes of action. Under Fed. R. Civ. P. Rule 8, a complaint must contain "a short and plain statement of the grounds for the court's jurisdiction ... a short and plain statement of the claim showing that the pleader is entitled to relief; and a demand for the relief sought." Fed. R. Civ. P. 8(a)(1)–(3).

The Supreme Court reemphasized the applicability of general pleading standards for § 1983 claims in *Gomez v. Toledo*, 446 U.S. 635 (1980). The Court held that § 1983 required "two—and only two—allegations," *id.* at 640, that (1) someone acting under color of state law (2) deprived plaintiff of a federal statutory or constitutional right. *Id.* During the 1970s and 80s, however, some courts imposed heightened pleading standards for § 1983 claims. *See, e.g., Elliott v. Perez*, 751 F.2d 1472 (5th Cir. 1985); *Strauss v. City of Chicago*, 760 F.2d 765 (7th Cir. 1985); *Batista v. Rodriguez*, 702 F.2d 393 (2d Cir. 1983).

Since then, the Supreme Court has further clarified its rejection of heightened pleading requirements to § 1983 complaints. In *Leatherman v. Tarrant Cty.*, the Court rejected heightened pleading for municipal liability claims, reasoning that Rule 8 should apply to § 1983 complaints. 507 U.S. 163, 168 (1993). In *Swierkiewicz v. Sorema*, the Court rejected heightened pleading for employment discrimination claims. 534 U.S. 506 (2002). Citing *Leatherman*, the Court reasoned:

> Rule 8(a)'s simplified pleading standard applies to all civil actions, with limited exceptions. Rule 9(b), for example, provides for greater particularity in all averments of fraud or mistake. This Court, however, has declined to extend such exceptions to other contexts.... Just as Rule 9(b) makes no mention of municipal liability under ... [§ 1983], neither does it refer to employment discrimination.

Id. at 513. The Court again relied on the interplay between Rule 8 and Rule 9 to reject a heightened pleading standard to a § 1983 claim brought after Congress enacted the Prison Litigation Reform Act. The Court in *Jones v. Bock* relied on *Leatherman* and *Swierkiewicz* in reasoning that "adopting different and more onerous pleading rules to deal with particular categories of cases should be done through established rulemaking procedures, and not on a case-by-case basis by the courts." 549 U.S. 199, 224 (2007).

More recently, however, the Supreme Court may have changed the meaning of Rule 8 notice pleading. Beginning in *Bell Atlantic Corp. v. Twombly*, 550 U.S. 544 (2007) and again in *Ashcroft v. Iqbal*, 556 U.S. 662 (2009), the Court construed Rule 8(a) and Rule 12(b)(6) to require the factual allegations in a civil complaint to meet a plausibility standard to survive a motion to dismiss. In *Iqbal*, the Supreme Court clarified that, in evaluating a Rule12(b)(6) motion, the trial court should not assume the truth of legal conclusions if they are not supported by allegations of fact and should subject all factual allegations assumed to be true to a 'plausibility' standard:

> [A] court considering a motion to dismiss can choose to begin by identifying pleadings that, because they are no more than conclusions, are not entitled to the assumption of truth. While legal conclusions can provide the framework of a complaint, they must be supported by factual allegations. When there are well-pleaded factual allegations, a court should assume their veracity and then determine whether they plausibly give rise to an entitlement to relief.

556 U.S. at 679.

Determining whether the factual allegations state a plausible claim for relief requires the trial court judge to draw on his or her "judicial experience and common sense." *Id.* Though the plaintiff need not establish a probability of misconduct at the pleading stage, a 12(b)(6) motion to dismiss may be granted "[w]here a complaint pleads facts that are 'merely consistent with' a defendant's liability, [because such a complaint] 'stops short of the line between possibility and plausibility of "entitlement to relief."'" *Id.* at 678 (further citation omitted).

The full consequences of the current 12(b)(6) standard are not yet clear. Does the Supreme Court's application of the "plausibility" standard suggest that it is now harder for § 1983 plaintiffs to survive a motion to dismiss? Or harder for § 1983 plaintiffs to survive a motion to dismiss a constitutional claim that requires proof of the defendant's state of mind, since the claim in *Iqbal* was that defendants intentionally discriminated against plaintiff? Does it surprise you that the current standard under Rule 8(a) means that a complaint could be dismissed for failure to state a claim where it pleads facts that are "merely consistent with" a defendant's liability because that "stops short of the line between possibility and plausibility of entitlement to relief"? Are civil rights plaintiffs subject to a heightened pleading standard? *See, e.g., E.E.O.C. v. Port Auth. of New York & New Jersey*, 768 F.3d 247, 254 (2d Cir. 2014) ("[A]long with several of our sister circuits, we recognize that *Swierkiewicz* has continuing viability, as modified by *Twombly* and *Iqbal*"); *compare Johnson v. City of Shelby, Miss.*, 574 U.S. 10, 135 S. Ct. 346, 347 (2014) (*per curiam*) (*Iqbal* and *Twombly* concern factual allegations only and "no heightened pleading rule requires plaintiffs seeking damages for violations of constitutional rights to invoke § 1983 expressly in order to state a claim").

Recall that this Chapter began by noting the "private attorney general" justification for enacting the Civil Rights Attorney's Fees Awards Act of 1976. Consider that concept in reading the late Pennsylvania Senator Arlen Specter's reasons for introducing a bill to overrule *Twombly/Iqbal.* Senator Specter stated that the effect of the Supreme Court's decisions in *Twombly* and *Iqbal* will be "to deny many plaintiffs with meritorious claims access to the federal courts.... [T]hat is an especially unwelcome development at a time when, with the litigating resources of our executive-branch and administrative agencies stretched thin, the enforcement of federal antitrust, consumer protection, civil rights and other laws that benefit the public will fall increasingly to private litigants." 155 Cong. Rec. S7871-01 (2009).

Senator Specter's bill would have returned federal courts to the pre-*Twombly* standard for dismissing a complaint for failure to state a claim set forth in *Conley v. Gibson*, 355 U.S. 41 (1957). Notice Pleading Restoration Act of 2009, S. 1504, 111th Cong. § (2009). More recently, Professor Benjamin Spencer has argued that "plausibility pleading is indefensible, 'assuming one cares about enabling private litigants to vindicate substantive law violations through the courts.' Ultimately, it may be that some defenders of *Twombly* and *Iqbal* simply do not fully embrace that goal. My hope is that this goal can at least be kept in mind as the Supreme Court and others who influence federal civil procedure interpret and apply plausibility pleading going forward."[5]

5. Federal Rule of Civil Procedure 68 Offers of Judgment

The purpose of Fed. R. Civ. P. 68 is to encourage settlement of litigation before either side has spent a lot. Under Rule 68, a defendant may make a written offer to allow the entry of judgment against the defendant along with costs then accrued and, if the plaintiff rejects the offer and later prevails at trial but for less than the amount of the offer, then "the offeree must pay the costs incurred after the making of the offer." Fed. R. Civ. P. 68(d). In *Delta Air Lines, Inc. v. August*, the Supreme Court held that the plain language, purpose, and history of Rule 68 meant that the Rule applies only when a defendant makes an offer of judgment and then later plaintiff prevails. 450 U.S. 346, 348–49, 352 (1981).

In *Marek v. Chesny*, the Supreme Court held that because 42 U.S.C. § 1988 states that a prevailing plaintiff in a § 1983 action may be awarded attorney's fees "as part of the costs," attorney's fees are "costs" under Rule 68. 473 U.S. 1, 9 (1985). In *Marek*, the defendants in a § 1983 action successfully argued that because the plaintiff had rejected their Rule 68 offer and then failed to obtain a more favorable judgment, the defendants were not liable for the plaintiff's post-offer attorney's fees. *Id.* at 4, 12. By rejecting the offer, the prevailing civil rights plaintiff forfeited the post-offer attorney's fees that he would otherwise have been entitled to pursuant to § 1988. *Id.*

A Rule 68 offer of judgment is a useful tool for a defendant where the plaintiff is likely to prevail, the amount of recovery is uncertain, and the defendant wants to keep costs low. Before rejecting a Rule 68 offer, a plaintiff will want to analyze how likely it is that s/he will both prevail at trial and obtain a damage award higher than the defendant's offer.

6. Summary Judgment

Local government defendants often move for summary judgment based on absolute immunity, qualified immunity, or municipal liability. "This is true not only where qualified immunity is raised at the district court level but also where the district court denies a defense motion for summary judgment based on qualified immunity, and the defendant files an interlocutory appeal."1 Sheldon Nahmod, Civil Rights & Civil Liberties Litigation: The Law of Section 1983 § 1:45. Absolute immunity is the subject of Chapter 9 and qualified immunity is the subject of Chapter 11.

Note there is tension between the substantive constitutional law and summary judgment principles. For example, Federal Rule of Civil Procedure 56 requires the

5. A. Benjamin Spencer, *Pleading and Access to Civil Justice: A Response to Twiqbal Apologists*, 60 U.C.L.A L. Rev. 1710, 1737–38 (2013).

court to view facts in the light most favorable to the non-moving party, typically the plaintiff. But in an excessive force case, the Fourth Amendment requires the court to ascertain what facts the officer knew at the time, meaning the facts as seen and heard by the officer. Based on those facts, and other evidence, the court then assesses whether the officer's conduct was reasonable.

In the excerpt below, Justice Sotomayor, joined by Justice Ginsburg, dissented from the Supreme Court's refusal to grant certiorari because, she argued, the lower courts incorrectly applied summary judgment standards. Justice Sotomayor's succinct reasoning illustrates the complex decision-making process of a federal court evaluating whether a case should be resolved by summary judgment:

> Just after midnight on October 29, 2010, a Houston police officer shot petitioner Ricardo Salazar-Limon in the back. Salazar-Limon claims the officer shot him as he tried to walk away from a confrontation with the officer on an overpass. The officer, by contrast, claims that Salazar-Limon turned toward him and reached for his waistband—as if for a gun—before the officer fired a shot. The question whether the officer used excessive force in shooting Salazar-Limon thus turns in large part on which man is telling the truth. Our legal system entrusts this decision to a jury sitting as finder of fact, not a judge reviewing a paper record.
>
> The courts below thought otherwise. The District Court credited the officer's version of events and granted summary judgment to respondents—the officer and the city. [citation omitted]. The Fifth Circuit affirmed. [citation omitted]. But summary judgment is appropriate only where "there is no genuine dispute as to any material fact." Fed. Rule Civ. Proc. 56(a). The courts below failed to heed that mandate. Three Terms ago, we summarily reversed the Fifth Circuit in a case "reflect[ing] a clear misapprehension of summary judgment standards." *Tolan v. Cotton,* 572 U.S. ___, ___, 134 S.Ct. 1861, 1868 (2014) (*per curiam*). This case reflects the same fundamental error. I respectfully dissent from the Court's failure to grant certiorari and reverse.
>
> . . .
>
> II
>
> This is not a case that should have been resolved on summary judgment. Summary judgment is appropriate only where "there is no genuine dispute as to any material fact and the movant is entitled to judgment as a matter of law." Fed. Rule Civ. Proc. 56(a). A "judge's function" in evaluating a motion for summary judgment is not "to weigh the evidence and determine the truth of the matter but to determine whether there is a genuine issue for trial." *Anderson v. Liberty Lobby, Inc.,* 477 U.S. 242, 249 (1986); see also *First Nat. Bank of Ariz. v. Cities Service Co.,* 391 U.S. 253, 289 (1968) (the question at summary judgment is whether a jury should "resolve the parties' differing versions of the truth at trial"). In doing so, the court must "view the facts and draw rea-

sonable inferences 'in the light most favorable to the party opposing the ... motion.'" *Scott v. Harris,* 550 U.S. 372, 378 (2007) [further citation omitted].

Applying that rule to this case is easy work. The question before the lower courts was whether the facts, taken in the light most favorable to Salazar-Limon, entitled Thompson to judgment on Salazar-Limon's excessive-force claim. *Saucier v. Katz,* 533 U.S. 194, 201 (2001); *Graham v. Connor,* 490 U.S. 386, 394 (1989). Although such cases generally require courts to wade through the "factbound morass of 'reasonableness,'" *Scott,* 550 U.S., at 383, here the question whether Thompson's use of force was reasonable turns in large part on exactly what Salazar-Limon did in the moments before Thompson shot him. Indeed, the courts below needed to ask only one question: Did Salazar-Limon turn and reach for his waistband, or not? If he did, Thompson's use of force was reasonable. If he did not, a jury could justifiably decide that the use of force was excessive.

Given that this case turns in large part on what Salazar-Limon did just before he was shot, it should be obvious that the parties' competing accounts of the event preclude the entry of summary judgment for Thompson. Thompson attested in a deposition that he fired his gun only *after* he saw Salazar-Limon turn and "ma[k]e [a] motion towards his waistband area." [citation omitted]. Salazar-Limon, by contrast, attested that Thompson fired either "immediately" or "seconds" after telling Salazar-Limon to stop—and in any case *before* Salazar-Limon turned toward him. [citation omitted]. These accounts flatly contradict each other. On the one, Salazar-Limon provoked the use of force by turning and raising his hands toward his waistband. On the other, Thompson shot without being provoked. It is not for a judge to resolve these "differing versions of the truth" on summary judgment, [citation omitted]; that question is for a jury to decide at trial.

The courts below reached the opposite conclusion only by disregarding basic principles of summary judgment. The District Court reasoned that Salazar-Limon "offered no controverting evidence" against Thompson's testimony that he turned and reached for his waistband before he was shot, [citation omitted], and the Fifth Circuit similarly reasoned that Salazar-Limon had not "submitted any other controverting evidence" regarding that fact, [citation omitted]. This is plainly wrong. Salazar-Limon's own testimony "controverted" Thompson's claim that Salazar-Limon had turned and reached for his waistband. The sworn testimony of an eyewitness is competent summary judgment evidence. And Salazar-Limon's testimony "controverted" Thompson's; indeed, the two contradict one another in every material way. Salazar-Limon needed no other evidence to defeat summary judgment.

Respondents defend the judgment below on the ground that Salazar-Limon "had the opportunity to directly contradict Officer Thompson's testimony," but did not do so. [citation omitted]. Justice ALITO advances the same argument. *Ante,* at 1277 (concurring opinion). They argue that Salazar-

> Limon never explicitly stated, "I did not reach for my waistband," and that his failure to do so permitted the courts below to grant summary judgment to Thompson. But this inference is questionable at best: Salazar-Limon had no need to introduce such an explicit statement, given respondents' concession that the events immediately preceding the gunshot (including the alleged waistband reach) were subject to dispute. [citation omitted]. And even if the inference respondents suggest was a reasonable one, it would be improper at the summary judgment stage. At that stage, all "reasonable inferences should be drawn in favor of the nonmoving party"—here, Salazar-Limon. *Tolan,* 572 U.S., at ___, 134 S.Ct., at 1868. The most natural inference to be drawn from Salazar-Limon's testimony was that he neither turned nor reached for his waistband before he was shot—especially as no gun was ever recovered. See *Cruz v. Anaheim,* 765 F.3d 1076, 1079 (C.A.9 2014) ("In this case, there's circumstantial evidence that could give a reasonable jury pause. Most obvious is the fact that [the victim] didn't have a gun on him, so why would he have reached for his waistband?"). Respondents' argument to the contrary "reflects a clear misapprehension of summary judgment standards." *Tolan,* 572 U.S., at ___, 134 S.Ct., at 1868.
>
> This is not a difficult case. When a police officer claims that the victim of the use of force took some act that would have justified that force, and the victim claims he did not, summary judgment is improper ... Only Thompson and Salazar-Limon know what happened on that overpass on October 29, 2010. It is possible that Salazar-Limon did something that Thompson reasonably found threatening; it is also possible that Thompson shot an unarmed man in the back without justification. What is clear is that our legal system does not entrust the resolution of this dispute to a judge faced with competing affidavits. The evenhanded administration of justice does not permit such a shortcut. Our failure to correct the error made by the courts below leaves in place a judgment that accepts the word of one party over the word of another.

Salazar-Limon v. City of Houston, Tex., ___ U.S. ___, 137 S. Ct. 1277, 1278–83 (2017) (Sotomayor, J. and Ginsburg, J., dissenting from denial of certiorari).

7. Removal of 42 U.S.C. § 1983 Cases from State to Federal Court[6]

Defendants sued under § 1983 in state court must decide whether to remove to federal court. Pursuant to 28 U.S.C. § 1441, a defendant may remove from state to federal court only where the "district courts of the United States have original jurisdiction," such as diversity and/or federal question jurisdiction. 28 U.S.C. § 1441(a).

6. Based on research and interviews by Patrick A. Castañeda, Camden, New Jersey (Spring 2009).

Of the 230,637 civil cases filed in the United States District Courts during the 2018 fiscal year, 32, 779 were removals from state court.[7]

What influences defense counsel decisions to remove § 1983 cases? In 2008, a law student interviewed four attorneys who defended § 1983 claims against cities in California, Michigan, Illinois and Texas. All four attorneys stated that they routinely removed § 1983 claims from state to federal court. But they did so for different reasons. Among the factors identified by the defense counsel interviewed were:

- Quality of judges and law clerks
- Substantive law and court rules
- Formality
- Technological savvy
- Jury unanimity
- Potential bias of judges
- Jury composition
- Attorney comfort
- Speed of litigation
- Settlement prospects

Each interview began with a two-part question: "Do you, as a matter of routine practice, remove § 1983 claims from state to federal court? Why?" Below are synopses of their responses.

a. Cory Brente — Assistant City Attorney for Los Angeles

Mr. Brente defends Los Angeles police and the city from § 1983 claims. He removes "just about all" § 1983 cases from state to federal court. There is no formal or informal policy regarding removal in the Police Litigation Division. Rather, the office provides attorneys flexibility in handling cases. He mentioned that federal judges do not like removal and they will try to find any flaw to remand the case back to state court.

First, Mr. Brente prefers federal courts because they require a unanimous verdict, while California state courts do not, and it is therefore harder for the plaintiffs to prevail in federal court. Second, he believes that federal judges have more familiarity with § 1983 law. Specifically, the judges are more knowledgeable about the *defenses* to such claims, such as absolute and qualified immunity. Third, he has extensive federal court experience and is more comfortable there. The federal judges are more strict and formal and the buildings and courtrooms are nicer and more technologically advanced. Fourth, he is wary of possible bias in the state courts. Many of his cases

7. Table 4.3, *U.S. District Courts. Civil Cases Filed, by Origin, available at* https://www.uscourts.gov/sites/default/files/data_tables/jff_4.3_0930.2018.pdf.

are controversial and, unlike federal judges who are appointed for life, state judges must face re-election.

While plaintiffs in federal court have more access to police personnel records than they would in state court because state rules of discovery are more liberal, Mr. Brente was clear that the advantages of federal court outweigh the disadvantages.

b. Robert Davis — Attorney Defending City of Plano, Texas in § 1983 Suits

Mr. Davis is a partner in Matthews, Stein, Shiels, Pearce, Knott, Eden, & Davis, L.L.P., located in Dallas, Texas. As is true for many cities, in-house counsel for Plano rarely handle § 1983 claims. Instead, § 1983 claims are referred to outside counsel. About 60% of Mr. Davis' caseload involves federal courts and he "absolutely" removes § 1983 claims from state to federal court.

First, Mr. Davis has more confidence in the federal judges and their staff. It is hard for a state court to grasp the idea that force resulting in death can be used without the city incurring liability. Second, Mr. Davis handles some controversial cases and he prefers not to litigate before state judges who must face re-election: "they are more subject to the whims of public opinion." Third, the technological resources are better in federal court. He can file electronically and receives emails when something is filed. By contrast, in state court he sometimes is not notified when the plaintiff files a document. Fourth, there are fewer surprises in federal court because federal judges are less likely than state judges to permit last minute actions before trial. Mr. Davis believes the federal law on procedure, summary judgment, attorney's fees, and immunities is better for defendants than the corresponding state law. While Mr. Davis noted his preference for the unanimity requirement for jury verdicts in federal court, which is not required for Texas state juries, a higher priority for him is the larger jury pool in federal court. In state court, Mr. Davis' jury would be drawn from one county, whereas in federal court the jury is drawn from four counties.

c. Jacob Schwarzberg — Senior Trial Attorney for Detroit Law Department

While working full-time for the Detroit Police Department, ultimately as a Sergeant, Mr. Schwarzberg earned a law degree from the Detroit College of Law, and has almost twenty years of trial experience in both private practice and with the City of Detroit Law Department, largely defending municipalities and police personnel.

Mr. Schwarzberg "automatically" and "regularly" removes § 1983 cases from state to federal court, even though it is his experience that about one-third of federal judges remand the claims. First, Mr. Schwarzberg prefers the atmosphere and civility of the federal courts. Second, federal judges have more expertise with § 1983 claims, including complex doctrines such as qualified immunity and municipal liability. Third, federal judges, appointed for life, are less likely to be influenced by local politics or public opinion. Fourth, rules regarding the sequence, duration and scope of discovery

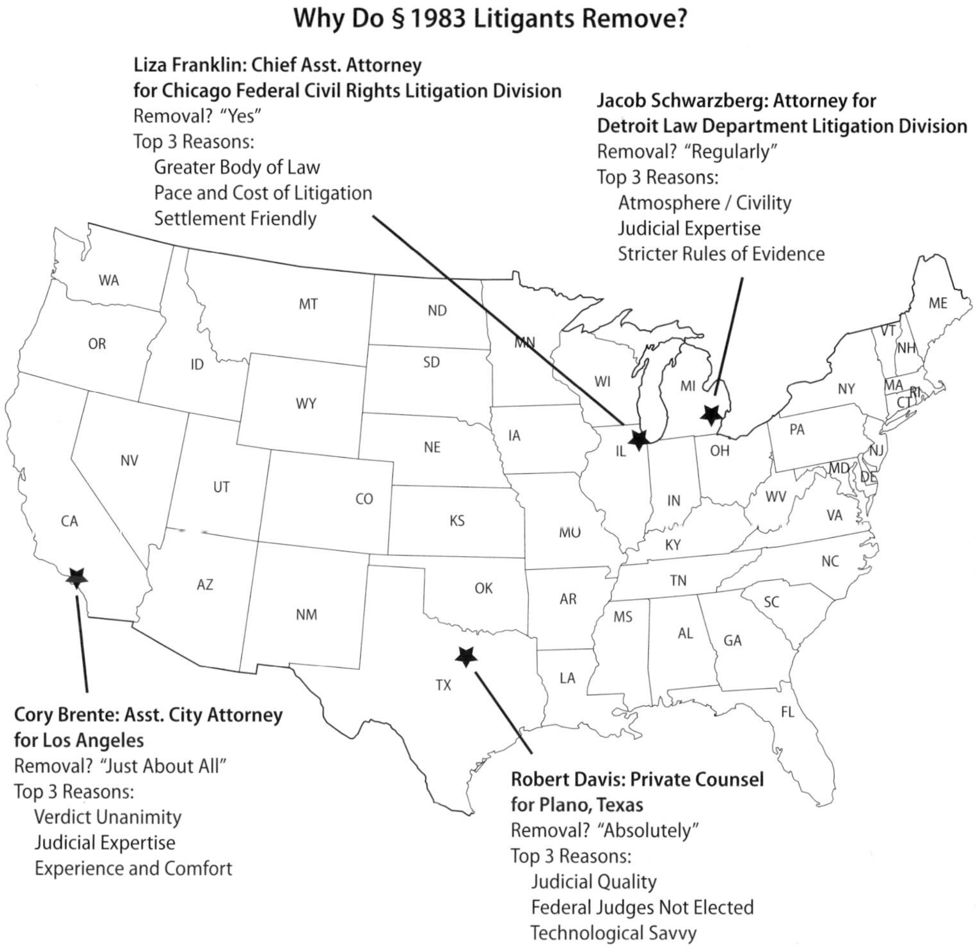

and pre-trial practice, as well as the use of experts and reporting requirements, are specifically delineated and, in his experience, strictly enforced in federal court. Fifth, a federal district court draws prospective jurors from a large geographic area, with a broader cross-section of citizens, including some socio-economic groups that tend to be conservative and pro-law enforcement. Thus, jury verdicts are more likely to be in favor of the officer.

d. Liza Franklin—Chief Assistant Attorney for Chicago

Ms. Franklin, an attorney in the City of Chicago's Federal Civil Rights Litigation Division, routinely removes § 1983 claims from state to federal court. First, Ms. Franklin believes federal judges are "more familiar with the [constitutional] issues than state court judges." Second, the pace and cost of litigation in federal court favors removal because "[d]eadlines are stricter in federal court, which helps with moving the cases along and making decisions to settle." Finally, "[f]ederal judges have more of an idea of what cases are worth" and "have the time [or] make the time to have settlement conferences."

8. New York's Alternative Dispute Resolution for § 1983 Police Misconduct Cases

New York Legal Aid recently released a searchable database culled from approximately 2,350 federal civil rights lawsuits filed from 2015–2018 against more than 3,900 New York Police officers.[8] To help courts and litigants manage the crowded civil rights caseload against New York City police, the federal court for the Southern District of New York designed an alternative dispute resolution system tailored to police misconduct litigation.[9]

For the last several years, the Southern District has automatically referred certain § 1983 cases against the New York City Police Department for streamlined discovery and mediation.[10] Briefly, the New York program applies to counseled plaintiffs alleging Section 1983 claims for excessive force, false arrest, or malicious prosecution against the New York Police Department or the City itself.[11] Instead of the normal discovery process, litigants must automatically make available certain factual information, such as medical and sealed arrest records, reports from the Civilian Complaint Review Board and Internal Affairs Board, and other key documents. On a quick timeline, the program requires a settlement demand, defendant's settlement offer, and mediation. While from 2012–2014 "approximately 70%" of the Section 1983 mediated cases settled, both the number of filings and settlement rates declined in 2015–16.[12]

---

8. Andrew Denney, *Legal Aid Posts Database of Federal Civil Rights Suits Against NYPD Officers* (March 6, 2019), *available at* https://www.legalaidnyc.org/news/2019/3/6/legal-aid-launches-capstat-a-public-database-of-federal-civil-rights-lawsuits-nypd-disciplinary-summaries-and-nypd-payroll-data.

9. Local Civil Rule 83.10, Plan for Certain § 1983 Cases Against the City of New York (Southern District Only) (Sept. 23, 2014), *available at* http://www.nysd.uscourts.gov/docs/mediation/Local%20Civil%20Rule%2083.10.Final.pdf.

10. Rebecca Price, *Mediation Program Annual Report January 1, 2016–December 31, 2016* at 2 (Dec. 5, 2017), *available at* http://nysd.uscourts.gov/docs/mediation/Annual_Reports/2016/Annual%20Report.2016.Final%20Draft.pdf.

11. Local Civil Rule 83.10, *supra* n. 9.

12. 2016 *Mediation Program Annual Report* at 2, *supra* n. 10.

Chapter Eleven

Qualified Immunity

A. Introduction

Amadou Diallo, an unarmed 22-year-old West African immigrant standing in the vestibule of his own home, was shot and killed by four New York City undercover police officers. The officers shot 41 times. The officers said they mistakenly believed that Mr. Diallo was reaching for a gun, when he was reaching for his wallet. All four officers were criminally prosecuted[1] and acquitted.[2] Mr. Diallo's family settled a state civil claim against New York City for $3 million.[3] After the settlement, Diallo's mother established the Amadou Diallo Foundation, built a school in her son's name in Guinea, and advocated for policy changes in prosecuting police use of excessive force.[4]

The tragic circumstances of Mr. Diallo's death prompted street protests.[5] A different gauge of the political and emotional reaction to Mr. Diallo's death are the many songs written about the shooting by artists such as Wyclef Jean, Akon, and others.[6] While Mr. Diallo's case did not concern qualified immunity, consider the mistake of fact made by the police officers in the Diallo case, and how that mistake compares to the facts of two qualified immunity cases included in this Chapter, *Carr* and *Espinosa.* Below is an excerpt from Bruce Springsteen's song about Mr. Diallo's death:

41 shots, and we'll take that ride
'Cross this bloody river to the other side

---

1. The shooting was widely publicized and the trial was moved outside New York City because the pretrial publicity had tainted the jury pool. The trial court reasoned in granting the change of venue: "The prospective jurors of Bronx County, and the rest of New York City, have been subjected to an endless repetition of the notion that the two undisputed facts, namely that 41 shots were fired and that Mr. Diallo was unarmed, conclusively establish defendants' guilt and are dispositive of all possible factual and legal issues." *People v. Boss*, 701 N.Y.S.2d 342, 344 (N.Y. App. Div. 1999).

2. *See* Alan Feuer, *$3 Million Deal in Police Killing of Diallo in '99*, N.Y. Times, Jan. 7, 2004, at 1.

3. *Id.*

4. Christian Red, *20 years after police killed Amadou Diallo, his mother still fights 'this good fight,'* Philadelphia Tribune, July 19, 2019.

5. *See* Andy Newman, *Prayer in New York, Protest in Washington*, N.Y. Times (Feb. 16, 1999) (reporting 1,500 gathered in New York; 400 in Washington), http://www.nytimes.com/1999/02/16/nyregion/prayer-in-new-york-protest-in-washington.html; Kevin Flynn, *8 Arrested Near City Hall in Protest on Police Shooting*, New York Times (Feb. 23, 1999), http://www.nytimes.com/1999/02/23/nyregion/8-arrested-near-city-hall-in-protest-on-police-shooting.html.

6. *See* Shooting of Amadou Diallo, Wikipedia, http://en.wikipedia.org/wiki/Amadou_Diallo.

41 shots, cut through the night
You're kneeling over his body in the vestibule
Praying for his life

Well, is it a gun, is it a knife
Is it a wallet, this is your life
It ain't no secret (it ain't no secret)
It ain't no secret (it ain't no secret)
No secret my friend
You can get killed just for living in your American skin

(41 shots)
(41 shots)
(41 shots)
(41 shots)

41 shots, Lena gets her son ready for school
She says "On these streets, Charles
You've got to understand the rules
If an officer stops you, promise me you'll always be polite
And that you'll never ever run away
Promise Mama you'll keep your hands in sight"

Well, is it a gun, is it a knife
Is it a wallet, this is your life
It ain't no secret (it ain't no secret)
It ain't no secret (it ain't no secret)
No secret my friend
You can get killed just for living in your American skin[7]

B. Chapter Overview

Under 42 U.S.C. § 1983, individual defendants may be entitled to either absolute immunity, the subject of Chapter 9, or qualified immunity, the subject of this Chapter. Qualified immunity protects government officials performing discretionary functions from personal liability for damages as long as their conduct does not violate clearly established statutory[8] or constitutional rights (*Harlow*, *Hope*, *Brousseau*, *Pearson*, *Plumhoff*, *Mullenix*). The defense "provides ample protection to all but the plainly incompetent or those who knowingly violate the law." *Malley v. Briggs*, 475 U.S. 335, 341 (1986).

7. Bruce Springsteen, American Skin (41 Shots) (Columbia Records 2001), Thousands of New York police and their supporters gathered in a New York park in part to protest this Springsteen song. *Police Protest Song at Rally*, N.Y. Times (June 14, 2000), http://www.nytimes.com/2000/06/14/nyregion/police-protest-song-at-rally.html.

8. This book focuses on the protection of certain constitutional, but not statutory, rights.

Qualified immunity is not just a defense to liability but rather provides the defendant with immunity from suit. A court should decide qualified immunity at the earliest opportunity, either on a motion to dismiss or on summary judgment. *See, e.g., Mitchell v. Forsyth*, 472 U.S. 511, 526 (1985). Because qualified immunity is "immunity from suit," it is "effectively lost if a case is erroneously permitted to go to trial." *Id.* For that reason, pretrial denial of qualified immunity is immediately appealable. *Id.* (*Plumhoff*).

Until the Supreme Court decided *Pearson* in 2009, the constitutional inquiry required that the following two questions be answered in sequence: did the official violate a constitutional right and, if so, was the constitutional right "clearly established" at the time of the conduct (not at the time of the court's decision) (*Lewis, Saucier*). After *Pearson*, that sequence is no longer mandatory: without first deciding whether the official violated a constitutional right, a court may hold that an official is entitled to qualified immunity because the constitutional right was not "clearly established" at the time of the official's conduct.

Difficult questions under qualified immunity include how specifically the constitutional right must be defined (*e.g., Anderson, Hope, Brousseau, Plumhoff, Wesby*), what sources of law a court should consult in deciding whether a constitutional right was "clearly established" at the time of the official's conduct (*e.g., Hope, Brousseau, Plumhoff, Mullenix*), how similar the allegedly unconstitutional conduct must be to conduct held unconstitutional in earlier cases (*e.g., Brousseau, Plumhoff, Mullenix*), and whether the inquiry should begin by deciding whether the official violated a constitutional right or skip to the question of whether the right was "clearly established" (*Saucier, Pearson, Plumhoff*).

More fundamentally, some question the doctrine of qualified immunity itself. For example, Justice Thomas critiqued the current doctrine as unmoored from the historical inquiry of whether the common law in 1871 would have accorded immunity to government officials facing similar claims. *Ziglar v. Abbasi*, ___ U.S. ___, 137 S. Ct. 1843, 1872 (2017). Further, a recent amicus brief to the Supreme Court argued that qualified immunity "enables public officials who violate federal law to sidestep their legal obligations to the victims of their misconduct," thereby "corrod[ing] the public's trust in those officials—law enforcement in particular...."[9]

Questions to guide reading of *Harlow*

1. What did *Harlow* identify as the basic reasons high level executive branch officials are entitled to qualified immunity?
2. In balancing the need for a damages remedy against the costs to society of claims against innocent government officials, what specific social costs did *Harlow* identify?

---

9. Brief of Cross-Ideological Groups Dedicated to Ensuring Official Accountability, Restoring the Public's Trust in Law Enforcement, and Promoting the Rule of Law as *Amici Curiae* in Support of Petitioner, *Baxter v. Bracey*, 2019 WL 2370285, at *6 (May 31, 2019). Cert was denied in 2020.

3. Before *Harlow*, qualified immunity had both a subjective and an objective aspect. What reasons did *Harlow* identify for eliminating the subjective aspect of qualified immunity? What "special costs" of the subjective inquiry into the good faith of government officials did *Harlow* identify? What reasons did *Harlow* give for limiting the qualified immunity test to the objective aspect?
4. How did the Court in *Harlow* envision the summary judgment process disposing of claims on qualified immunity grounds?
5. What is the relevant time period for the "clearly established" law inquiry—clearly established *at what time*?
6. What guidance did *Harlow* give (or not give) in footnote 32 about the sources of law relevant to the "clearly established" inquiry? If *Harlow* had been decided this morning, how would you explain its holding to a non-lawyer client?

Harlow v. Fitzgerald

457 U.S. 800 (1982)

Justice POWELL delivered the opinion of the Court.

The issue in this case is the scope of the immunity available to the senior aides and advisers of the President of the United States in a suit for damages based upon their official acts.

I

In this suit for civil damages petitioners Bryce Harlow and Alexander Butterfield are alleged to have participated in a conspiracy to violate the constitutional and statutory rights of the respondent A. Ernest Fitzgerald. Respondent avers that petitioners entered the conspiracy in their capacities as senior White House aides to former President Richard M. Nixon.

...

Petitioner Butterfield also is alleged to have entered the conspiracy not later than May 1969. Employed as Deputy Assistant to the President and Deputy Chief of Staff to H. R. Haldeman, Butterfield circulated a White House memorandum in that month in which he claimed to have learned that Fitzgerald planned to "blow the whistle" on some "shoddy purchasing practices" by exposing these practices to public view. Fitzgerald characterizes this memorandum as evidence that Butterfield had commenced efforts to secure Fitzgerald's retaliatory dismissal.

...

II

As we reiterated today in *Nixon v. Fitzgerald*, 457 U.S. 731, our decisions consistently have held that government officials are entitled to some form of immunity from suits for damages. As recognized at common law, public officers require this protection to shield them from undue interference with their duties and from potentially disabling threats of liability.

Our decisions have recognized immunity defenses of two kinds. For officials whose special functions or constitutional status requires complete protection from suit, we have recognized the defense of "absolute immunity." The absolute immunity of legislators, in their legislative functions ... and of judges, in their judicial functions ... now is well settled. Our decisions also have extended absolute immunity to certain officials of the Executive Branch. These include prosecutors and similar officials ... executive officers engaged in adjudicative functions ... and the President of the United States....

For executive officials in general, however, our cases make plain that qualified immunity represents the norm.

...

III

A

Petitioners argue that they are entitled to a blanket protection of absolute immunity as an incident of their offices as Presidential aides.

...

Having decided in *Butz* [*v. Economou*, 438 U.S. 478 (1978)], that Members of the Cabinet ordinarily enjoy only qualified immunity from suit, we conclude today that it would be equally untenable to hold absolute immunity an incident of the office of every Presidential subordinate based in the White House.... It is no disparagement of the offices held by petitioners to hold that Presidential aides, like Members of the Cabinet, generally are entitled only to a qualified immunity.

B

...

[I]n general our cases have followed a "functional" approach to immunity law. We have recognized that the judicial, prosecutorial, and legislative functions require absolute immunity.... In *Gravel*, for example, we emphasized that Senators and their aides were absolutely immune only when performing "acts legislative in nature," and not when taking other acts even "in their official capacity." [*Gravel v. United States*,] 408 U.S. 606, 625 (1972).... Our cases involving judges and prosecutors have followed a similar line. The undifferentiated extension of absolute "derivative" immunity to the President's aides therefore could not be reconciled with the "functional" approach that has characterized the immunity decisions of this Court....

...

IV

Even if they cannot establish that their official functions require absolute immunity, petitioners assert that public policy at least mandates an application of the qualified immunity standard that would permit the defeat of insubstantial claims without resort to trial. We agree.

A

The resolution of immunity questions inherently requires a balance between the evils inevitable in any available alternative. In situations of abuse of office, an action for damages may offer the only realistic avenue for vindication of constitutional guarantees.... It is this recognition that has required the denial of absolute immunity to most public officers. At the same time, however, it cannot be disputed seriously that claims frequently run against the innocent as well as the guilty—at a cost not only to the defendant officials, but to society as a whole. These social costs include the expenses of litigation, the diversion of official energy from pressing public issues, and the deterrence of able citizens from acceptance of public office. Finally, there is the danger that fear of being sued will "dampen the ardor of all but the most resolute, or the most irresponsible [public officials], in the unflinching discharge of their duties." [citation omitted].

In identifying qualified immunity as the best attainable accommodation of competing values, ... we relied on the assumption that this standard would permit "[i]nsubstantial lawsuits [to] be quickly terminated." [*Butz,*] 438 U.S., at 507–508.... Yet petitioners advance persuasive arguments that the dismissal of insubstantial lawsuits without trial—a factor presupposed in the balance of competing interests struck by our prior cases—requires an adjustment of the "good faith" standard established by our decisions.

B

Qualified or "good faith" immunity is an affirmative defense that must be pleaded by a defendant official.... Decisions of this Court have established that the "good faith" defense has both an "objective" and a "subjective" aspect. The objective element involves a presumptive knowledge of and respect for "basic, unquestioned constitutional rights." ... The subjective component refers to "permissible intentions." [*Wood v. Strickland*, 420 U.S. 308, 322 (1975)]. Characteristically the Court has defined these elements by identifying the circumstances in which qualified immunity would not be available. Referring both to the objective and subjective elements, we have held that qualified immunity would be defeated if an official "*knew or reasonably should have known* that the action he took within his sphere of official responsibility would violate the constitutional rights of the [plaintiff], *or* if he took the action *with the malicious intention* to cause a deprivation of constitutional rights or other injury...." *Ibid.* (emphasis added).

The subjective element of the good-faith defense frequently has proved incompatible with our admonition in *Butz* that insubstantial claims should not proceed to trial. Rule 56 of the Federal Rules of Civil Procedure provides that disputed questions of fact ordinarily may not be decided on motions for summary judgment. And an official's subjective good faith has been considered to be a question of fact that some courts have regarded as inherently requiring resolution by a jury.

...

[I]t now is clear that substantial costs attend the litigation of the subjective good faith of government officials. Not only are there the general costs of subjecting officials to the risks of trial—distraction of officials from their governmental duties, inhibition of discretionary action, and deterrence of able people from public service. There are special costs to "subjective" inquiries of this kind. Immunity generally is available only to officials performing discretionary functions. In contrast with the thought processes accompanying "ministerial" tasks, the judgments surrounding discretionary action almost inevitably are influenced by the decisionmaker's experiences, values, and emotions. These variables explain in part why questions of subjective intent so rarely can be decided by summary judgment. Yet they also frame a background in which there often is no clear end to the relevant evidence. Judicial inquiry into subjective motivation therefore may entail broad-ranging discovery and the deposing of numerous persons, including an official's professional colleagues. Inquiries of this kind can be peculiarly disruptive of effective government.[29]

...

[W]e conclude today that bare allegations of malice should not suffice to subject government officials either to the costs of trial or to the burdens of broad-reaching discovery. We therefore hold that government officials performing discretionary functions generally are shielded from liability for civil damages insofar as their conduct does not violate clearly established statutory or constitutional rights of which a reasonable person would have known[30]....

Reliance on the objective reasonableness of an official's conduct, as measured by reference to clearly established law, should avoid excessive disruption of government

29. As Judge Gesell observed in his concurring opinion in *Halperin v. Kissinger*, 606 F.2d 1192, 1214 (1979), *aff'd in pertinent part by an equally divided Court*, 452 U.S. 713 (1981):

> "We should not close our eyes to the fact that with increasing frequency in this jurisdiction and throughout the country plaintiffs are filing suits seeking damage awards against high government officials in their personal capacities based on alleged constitutional torts. Each such suit almost invariably results in these officials and their colleagues being subjected to extensive discovery into traditionally protected areas, such as their deliberations preparatory to the formulation of government policy and their intimate thought processes and communications at the presidential and cabinet levels. Such discover [sic] is wide-ranging, time-consuming, and not without considerable cost to the officials involved. It is not difficult for ingenious plaintiff's counsel to create a material issue of fact on some element of the immunity defense where subtle questions of constitutional law and a decisionmaker's mental processes are involved. A sentence from a casual document or a difference in recollection with regard to a particular policy conversation held long ago would usually, under the normal summary judgment standards, be sufficient [to force a trial].... The effect of this development upon the willingness of individuals to serve their country is obvious."

30. This case involves no issue concerning the elements of the immunity available to state officials sued for constitutional violations under 42 U.S.C. § 1983. We have found previously, however, that it would be "untenable to draw a distinction for purposes of immunity law between suits brought against state officials under § 1983 and suits brought directly under the Constitution against federal officials." *Butz v. Economou*, 438 U.S., at 504.... Our decision in no way diminishes the absolute immunity currently available to officials whose functions have been held to require a protection of this scope.

and permit the resolution of many insubstantial claims on summary judgment. On summary judgment, the judge appropriately may determine, not only the currently applicable law, but whether that law was clearly established at the time an action occurred.[32] If the law at that time was not clearly established, an official could not reasonably be expected to anticipate subsequent legal developments, nor could he fairly be said to "know" that the law forbade conduct not previously identified as unlawful. Until this threshold immunity question is resolved, discovery should not be allowed. If the law was clearly established, the immunity defense ordinarily should fail, since a reasonably competent public official should know the law governing his conduct. Nevertheless, if the official pleading the defense claims extraordinary circumstances and can prove that he neither knew nor should have known of the relevant legal standard, the defense should be sustained. But again, the defense would turn primarily on objective factors.

By defining the limits of qualified immunity essentially in objective terms, we provide no license to lawless conduct. The public interest in deterrence of unlawful conduct and in compensation of victims remains protected by a test that focuses on the objective legal reasonableness of an official's acts. Where an official could be expected to know that certain conduct would violate statutory or constitutional rights, he should be made to hesitate; and a person who suffers injury caused by such conduct may have a cause of action. But where an official's duties legitimately require action in which clearly established rights are not implicated, the public interest may be better served by action taken "with independence and without fear of consequences." *Pierson v. Ray*, 386 U.S. 547, 554 (1967).[34]

Exercise 11-A

The "clearly established" inquiry is an exception to the normal rule that a court applies the law as of the date of the court's decision. While the law as of the date of the decision determines the constitutional question, for the qualified immunity "clearly established" inquiry, the relevant time is the date of the defendant's action. A qualified immunity judicial decision, then, may analyze law at two separate times.

Suppose you found a Twelfth Circuit court decision issued on January 1, 2020 that held that there was a constitutional violation. Suppose further that the court held the defendant was qualifiedly immune because the act took place on August 14, 2018 and the law was not clearly established on August 14, 2018. How are you likely to be able to use the 2020 decision?

---

32. … [W]e need not define here the circumstances under which "the state of the law" should be "evaluated by reference to the opinions of this Court, of the Courts of Appeals, or of the local District Court."

34. We emphasize that our decision applies only to suits for civil damages arising from actions within the scope of an official's duties and in "objective" good faith. We express no view as to the conditions in which injunctive or declaratory relief might be available.

1. to argue that conduct that occurred *after* January 1, 2020 violated the constitution?
2. to argue that conduct that *pre-dated* 2018 violated the constitution?
3. to argue that conduct that occurred *between* August 15, 2018 and January 1, 2020 violated the constitution?

For further discussion

1. The Supreme Court later clarified that to be "clearly established" for purposes of qualified immunity, "[t]he contours of the right must be sufficiently clear that a reasonable official would understand that what he is doing violates that right." *Anderson v. Creighton*, 483 U.S. 635, 640 (1987). The Court explained that "clearly established":

> depends substantially upon the level of generality at which the relevant 'legal rule' is to be identified. For example, the right to due process of law is quite clearly established by the Due Process Clause, and thus there is a sense in which any action that violates that Clause (no matter how unclear it may be that the particular action is a violation) violates a clearly established right. Much the same could be said of any other constitutional or statutory violation. But if the test of 'clearly established law' were to be applied at this level of generality, it would bear no relationship to the 'objective legal reasonableness' that is the touchstone of *Harlow*. Plaintiffs would be able to convert the rule of qualified immunity that our cases plainly establish into a rule of virtually unqualified liability simply by alleging violation of extremely abstract rights. *Harlow* would be transformed from a guarantee of immunity into a rule of pleading ... It should not be surprising, therefore, that our cases establish that the right the official is alleged to have violated must have been 'clearly established' in a more particularized, and hence more relevant, sense: The contours of the right must be sufficiently clear that a reasonable official would understand that what he is doing violates that right. This is not to say that an official action is protected by qualified immunity unless the very action in question has previously been held unlawful, *see Mitchell* [*v. Forsyth*,] 472 U.S. [511,] 535, n. 12; but it is to say that in the light of pre-existing law the unlawfulness must be apparent.

Anderson, 483 U.S. at 639–640. *See Reichle v. Howards*, 566 U.S. 658, 665 (2012) ("[T]he right allegedly violated must be established, '"not as a broad general proposition,"' *Brosseau v. Haugen*, 543 U.S. 194, 198 (2004) (*per curiam*), but in a 'particularized' sense so that the 'contours' of the right are clear to a reasonable official") (further citation omitted); *Ashcroft v. al-Kidd*, 563 U.S. 731, 742 (2011) ("We have repeatedly told courts—and the Ninth Circuit in particular ... not to define clearly established law at a high level of generality ... The general proposition, for example, that an unreasonable search or seizure violates the Fourth Amendment is of little help in determining whether the violative nature of particular conduct is clearly established").

The Supreme Court more recently further defined its "clearly established" principle:

> The rule must be "settled law," ... which means it is dictated by "controlling authority" or "a robust 'consensus of cases of persuasive authority,'" ... It is not enough that the rule is suggested by then-existing precedent. The precedent must be clear enough that every reasonable official would interpret it to establish the particular rule the plaintiff seeks to apply. *See Reichle* [*v. Howards*], 566 U.S. [658,] 666 [(2012)]. Otherwise, the rule is not one that "every reasonable official" would know. *Id.*, at 664 (internal quotation marks omitted).
>
> The "clearly established" standard also requires that the legal principle clearly prohibit the officer's conduct in the particular circumstances before him. This requires a high "degree of specificity." *Mullenix v. Luna*, 577 U.S. ___, ___, 136 S.Ct. 305, 309 (2015) (*per curiam*).... We have stressed that the "specificity" of the rule is "especially important in the Fourth Amendment context." *Mullenix, supra*, at 308.... Thus, we have stressed the need to "identify a case where an officer acting under similar circumstances ... was held to have violated the Fourth Amendment." *White v. Pauly*, 580 U.S. ___, ___, 137 S.Ct. 548, 552 (2017) (*per curiam*); *e.g., Plumhoff* [*v. Rickard*, 572 U.S. 765, 779 (2014)]. While there does not have to be "a case directly on point," existing precedent must place the lawfulness of the particular arrest "beyond debate." [*Ashcroft v.*] *al-Kidd*, 563 U.S. [731,] 741 [(2011)]. Of course, there can be the rare "obvious case," where the unlawfulness of the officer's conduct is sufficiently clear even though existing precedent does not address similar circumstances. *Brosseau v. Haugen*, 543 U.S. 194, 199 (2004) (*per curiam*). But "a body of relevant case law" is usually necessary to "'clearly establish' the answer" with respect to probable cause. *Ibid.*

District of Columbia v. Wesby, 538 U.S. ___, 138 S. Ct. 577, 589–90 (2018); *see City of Escondido v. Emmons*, ___ U.S. ___, 139 S. Ct. 500, 504 (2019) (*per curiam* and without briefing on the merits) ("'[W]e have stressed the need to identify a case where an officer acting under similar circumstances was held to have violated the Fourth Amendment'") (quoting *Wesby*); *White v. Pauly*, 580 U.S. ___, ___, 137 S. Ct. 548, 552 (2017) (*per curiam*) ("[c]learly established federal law does not prohibit a reasonable officer who arrives late to an ongoing police action in circumstances like this from assuming that proper procedures, such as officer identification, have already been followed"). *Brousseau*, *Plumhoff*, and *Mullenix* are excerpted in this Chapter.

2. Whether the law is "clearly established" can depend on how generally or specifically the right is defined. Usually, will plaintiff or defendant want to define the right more generally? As you read each case in this Chapter, consider what constitutional right was asserted, whether that right was "clearly established" in a particularized sense, and why.

3. A core concept of qualified immunity is fairness to the defendant. It would not be fair to hold a defendant liable for violating a right that a reasonable official would not realize existed. Similarly, the doctrine of qualified immunity promotes fairness to defendants by allowing defendants to make mistakes. For example, the Supreme

Court clarified in *Saucier v. Katz*, 533 U.S. 194, 205–06 (2001), *overruled on other grounds*, *Pearson v. Callahan*, 555 U.S. 223 (2009), that the 4th Amendment permits a police officer to make a reasonable mistake of fact and that the qualified immunity doctrine permits the officer to make a reasonable mistake of law. The Court explained:

> Because "police officers are often forced to make split-second judgments—in circumstances that are tense, uncertain, and rapidly evolving—about the amount of force that is necessary in a particular situation," [*Graham*,] 490 U.S. 386 (1989), at 397, the reasonableness of the officer's belief as to the appropriate level of force should be judged from that on-scene perspective, *id.*, at 396. We set out a test that cautioned against the "20/20 vision of hindsight" in favor of deference to the judgment of reasonable officers on the scene. *Id.*, at 393, 396. *Graham* sets forth a list of factors relevant to the merits of the constitutional excessive force claim, "requir[ing] careful attention to the facts and circumstances of each particular case, including the severity of the crime at issue, whether the suspect poses an immediate threat to the safety of the officers or others, and whether he is actively resisting arrest or attempting to evade arrest by flight." *Id.*, at 396. If an officer reasonably, but mistakenly, believed that a suspect was likely to fight back, for instance, the officer would be justified in using more force than in fact was needed.
>
> The qualified immunity inquiry, on the other hand, has a further dimension. The concern of the immunity inquiry is to acknowledge that reasonable mistakes can be made as to the legal constraints on particular police conduct. It is sometimes difficult for an officer to determine how the relevant legal doctrine, here excessive force, will apply to the factual situation the officer confronts. An officer might correctly perceive all of the relevant facts but have a mistaken understanding as to whether a particular amount of force is legal in those circumstances. If the officer's mistake as to what the law requires is reasonable, however, the officer is entitled to the immunity defense.
>
> *Graham* does not always give a clear answer as to whether a particular application of force will be deemed excessive by the courts ... Qualified immunity operates in this case, then, just as it does in others, to protect officers from the sometimes "hazy border between excessive and acceptable force," *Priester v. Riviera Beach*, 208 F.3d 919, 926–927 (C.A.11 2000), and to ensure that before they are subjected to suit, officers are on notice their conduct is unlawful.

Saucier, 533 U.S. at 205–06. *See District of Columbia v. Wesby*, 538 U.S. ___, 138 S. Ct. 577, 591 (2018) ("Even assuming the officers lacked actual probable cause to arrest the partygoers, the officers are entitled to qualified immunity because they 'reasonably but mistakenly conclude[d] that probable cause [wa]s present'") (further citation omitted); *Ashcroft v. al-Kidd*, 563 U.S. 731, 743 (2011) ("Qualified immunity gives government officials breathing room to make reasonable but mistaken judgments about open legal questions"). Recall from Chapter 6 that neither a police officer's reasonable mistake of fact nor reasonable mistake of law will violate the 4th Amendment.

4. *Harlow* reserved the question of whether qualified immunity was a defense to a suit seeking injunctive or declaratory relief. *Harlow v. Fitzgerald*, 457 U.S. 800, 819 n.34 (1982). The Supreme Court later clarified that qualified immunity is unavailable "in a suit to enjoin future conduct [and] in an action against a municipality...." *Sacramento v. Lewis*, 523 U.S. 833, 841 n.5 (1998); *see, e.g., Adler v. Pataki*, 185 F.3d 35, 48 (2d Cir. 1999) ("[q]ualified immunity shields the defendants only from claims for monetary damages and does not bar actions for declaratory or injunctive relief") (further citation omitted).

5. Qualified immunity of state officials sued under 42 U.S.C. § 1983 is equated with the immunity of federal officers sued directly under the Constitution. *Harlow*, 457 U.S. at 818 n.30 ("We have found previously ... that it would be 'untenable to draw a distinction for purposes of immunity law between suits brought against state officials under § 1983 and suits brought directly under the Constitution against federal officials'") (further citation omitted). As a practical matter, that means that, in general, § 1983 defendants can rely on qualified immunity decisions involving federal defendants—such as the defendants in *Harlow*.

6. Employees of private prisons under contract with state or local governments may be sued under 42 U.S.C. § 1983 but are not entitled to invoke qualified immunity. *Richardson v. McNight*, 521 U.S 399, 401 (1997). For example, in *Harrison v. Ash*, 539 F.3d 510, 524–25 (6th Cir. 2008), the Sixth Circuit refused to extend qualified immunity to nurses employed by a for-profit prison health care company:

> Applying the wisdom of *Richardson* to the instant case, we find that the purposes of qualified immunity do not support the extension of the doctrine to nurses employed by a private medical provider. With respect to unwarranted timidity, the most important rationale underlying qualified immunity, it is clear that market forces will operate to insure that CMS [the private for-profit medical provider] and its employees will effectively execute their contractual duties.... To the extent that CMS performs its contractual duties [to provide medical care in prisons and jails] in a manner that is overly cautious or unduly concerned with its bottom line at the expense of inmate care, its performance will be subject to review at the end of the contractual term and it will likely face "pressure from potentially competing firms who can try to take its place." *Richardson*, 521 U.S. at 410. Thus, CMS and its employees have an incentive to perform in a manner that comports with constitutional standards and with the expectations of the contracting governmental entity.
>
> Additionally, a finding that CMS nurses are ineligible for qualified immunity will not deter talented candidates from serving in such a capacity. Even in the absence of qualified immunity, CMS may attract candidates for nursing and other positions by increasing pay, benefits packages and obtaining adequate insurance coverage. Although such measures will not entirely eliminate the distraction caused by the threat of damages from a § 1983 suit, any distraction caused by the threat of suit is certainly no greater than the threat of malpractice suits faced by other medical professionals.

> In short, we find that, like *Richardson*, public policy considerations do not militate in favor of qualified immunity for Defendant nurses. Here, as in *Richardson*, there are no special concerns to distinguish CMS from other private firms and thus, there is no need to extend qualified immunity to Defendant nurses. Importantly, like the company in *Richardson*, CMS is a for-profit entity that has undertaken the major administrative task of providing health care to Macomb County inmates, operates with little supervision from Jail authorities, and is subject to the pressures of the marketplace.

7. But qualified immunity *does* extend to some who are not full-time government employees. In *Filarsky v. Delia*, the Supreme Court held that an individual hired to do government work is permitted to invoke qualified immunity even though "he works for the government on something other than a permanent or full-time basis." 566 U.S. 377, 380 (2012). Justice Roberts wrote for the unanimous Court:

> Affording immunity not only to public employees but also to others acting on behalf of the government similarly serves to '"ensure that talented candidates [are] not deterred by the threat of damages suits from entering public service."' *Richardson* [*v. McKnight*, 521 U.S. 399, 408 (1997) (further citation omitted)]. The government's need to attract talented individuals is not limited to full-time public employees. Indeed, it is often when there is a particular need for specialized knowledge or expertise that the government must look outside its permanent work force to secure the services of private individuals. This case is a good example: Filarsky had 29 years of specialized experience as an attorney in labor, employment, and personnel matters, with particular expertise in conducting internal affairs investigations.

Id. at 390.

> *Richardson v. McKnight*, 521 U.S. 399 (1997) [is] not to the contrary.
>
> . . .
>
> In *Richardson*, we considered whether guards employed by a privately run prison facility could seek the protection of qualified immunity. Although the Court had previously determined that public-employee prison guards were entitled to qualified immunity, *see Procunier v. Navarette*, 434 U.S. 555 (1978), it determined that prison guards employed by a private company and working in a privately run prison facility did not enjoy the same protection. We explained that the various incentives characteristic of the private market in that case ensured that the guards would not perform their public duties with unwarranted timidity or be deterred from entering that line of work. 521 U.S., at 410–411.
>
> *Richardson* was a self-consciously 'narrow[]' decision. *Id.*, at 413 ('[W]e have answered the immunity question narrowly, in the context in which it arose'). The Court made clear that its holding was not meant to foreclose all claims of immunity by private individuals. *Ibid.* Instead, the Court emphasized that the particular circumstances of that case—'a private firm, systematically organized to assume a major lengthy administrative task (managing an institution) with

> limited direct supervision by the government, undertak[ing] that task for profit and potentially in competition with other firms'—combined sufficiently to mitigate the concerns underlying recognition of governmental immunity under § 1983. *Ibid.* Nothing of the sort is involved here, or in the typical case of an individual hired by the government to assist in carrying out its work.

Id. at 392–93.

Justice Sotomayor concurred, emphasizing that "it does not follow that *every* private individual who works for the government in some capacity necessarily may claim qualified immunity when sued under 42 U.S.C. § 1983." *Filarsky*, 566 U.S. at 397 (Sotomayor, J., concurring). She reasoned that, in *Richardson v. McKnight*, 521 U.S. 399 (1997),

> we left open … the question whether immunity would be appropriate for 'a private individual briefly associated with a government body, serving as an adjunct to government in an essential governmental activity, or acting under close official supervision.' *Id.*, at 413 … [T]here is no doubt that Filarsky worked alongside the employees in investigating [the firefighter suspected of abusing sick leave]. In such circumstances, I agree that Filarsky should be allowed to claim qualified immunity from a § 1983 suit.
>
> This does not mean that a private individual may assert qualified immunity only when working in close coordination with government employees. For example, *Richardson*'s suggestion that immunity is also appropriate for individuals 'serving as an adjunct to government in an essential governmental activity,' 521 U.S., at 413, would seem to encompass modern-day special prosecutors and comparable individuals hired for their independence.

Filarsky, 566 U.S. at 397–98 (Sotomayor, J., concurring). *See Currie v. Chhabra*, 728 F.3d 626, 631–32 (7th Cir. 2013) (finding persuasive that, while "tracking the Court's analysis in *Filarsky*, the Sixth Circuit recently held that a doctor providing psychiatric services to inmates at a state prison is not entitled to assert qualified immunity") (further citation omitted).

9. The Supreme Court clarified the pleading standard that applies in the qualified immunity context in *Wood v. Moss*, 572 U.S. 744, 757 (2014) (qualified immunity protects from civil damages "unless a plaintiff pleads facts showing (1) that the official violated a statutory or constitutional right, and (2) that the right was 'clearly established' at the time of the challenged conduct") (further citation omitted).

Questions to guide reading of *Lewis*

1. The facts and text of *Lewis* are excerpted in Chapter 3. In *Lewis*, the Supreme Court directed that the qualified immunity analysis proceed in what sequence?
2. Why could constitutional standards remain "uncertain" if courts avoided constitutional decisions by disposing of cases on qualified immunity grounds alone when the constitutional right is not clearly established?

County of Sacramento v. Lewis

523 U.S. 833 (1998)—Footnote 5

Footnote 5. As in any action under § 1983, the first step is to identify the exact contours of the underlying right said to have been violated. *See Graham v. Connor*, 490 U.S. 386, 394 (1989). The District Court granted summary judgment to [the pursuing police officer] on the basis of qualified immunity, assuming without deciding that a substantive due process violation took place but holding that the law was not clearly established in 1990 so as to justify imposition of § 1983 liability. We do not analyze this case in a similar fashion because, as we have held, the better approach to resolving cases in which the defense of qualified immunity is raised is to determine first whether the plaintiff has alleged a deprivation of a constitutional right at all. Normally, it is only then that a court should ask whether the right allegedly implicated was clearly established at the time of the events in question. *See Siegert v. Gilley*, 500 U.S. 226, 232 (1991) ("A necessary concomitant to the determination of whether the constitutional right asserted by a plaintiff is 'clearly established' at the time the defendant acted is the determination of whether the plaintiff has asserted a violation of a constitutional right at all," and courts should not "assum[e], without deciding, this preliminary issue").

... [T]he generally sound rule of avoiding determination of constitutional issues does not readily fit the situation presented here; when liability is claimed on the basis of a constitutional violation, even a finding of qualified immunity requires some determination about the state of constitutional law at the time the officer acted. What is more significant is that if the policy of avoidance were always followed in favor of ruling on qualified immunity whenever there was no clearly settled constitutional rule of primary conduct, standards of official conduct would tend to remain uncertain, to the detriment both of officials and individuals. An immunity determination, with nothing more, provides no clear standard, constitutional or nonconstitutional.... [T]herefore the better approach is to determine the right before determining whether it was previously established with clarity.

Questions to guide reading of *Hope*

1. What sequence did the Supreme Court follow in deciding the qualified immunity question?
2. What sources of law and other authority did the Supreme Court rely on in considering whether the guards had "fair warning" that their conduct violated a clearly established constitutional right? Was it fair to the individual defendants to hold them responsible for information in the Department of Justice report? Why or why not?
3. Why did the Supreme Court hold the Eleventh Circuit's approach to qualified immunity was wrong?

4. Did *Hope* hold that the "clearly established" inquiry does not require a factually similar case and, separately, that the 8th Amendment violation was obvious? Or did *Hope* hold that *because* there was an obvious constitutional violation, the "clearly established" inquiry did not require a factually similar case? Consider this question in reading *Brousseau*, the case that follows *Hope*.

Hope v. Pelzer

536 U.S. 730 (2002)

Justice STEVENS delivered the opinion of the Court.

...

In 1995, Alabama was the only State that followed the practice of chaining inmates to one another in work squads. It was also the only State that handcuffed prisoners to "hitching posts" if they either refused to work or otherwise disrupted work squads.[1] Hope was handcuffed to a hitching post on two occasions. On May 11, 1995, while Hope was working in a chain gang near an interstate highway, he got into an argument with another inmate. Both men were taken back to the Limestone prison and handcuffed to a hitching post. Hope was released two hours later, after the guard captain determined that the altercation had been caused by the other inmate. During his two hours on the post, Hope was offered drinking water and a bathroom break every 15 minutes, and his responses to these offers were recorded on an activity log. Because he was only slightly taller than the hitching post, his arms were above shoulder height and grew tired from being handcuffed so high. Whenever he tried moving his arms to improve his circulation, the handcuffs cut into his wrists, causing pain and discomfort.

On June 7, 1995, Hope was punished more severely. He took a nap during the morning bus ride to the chain gang's worksite, and when it arrived he was less than prompt in responding to an order to get off the bus. An exchange of vulgar remarks led to a wrestling match with a guard. Four other guards intervened, subdued Hope, handcuffed him, placed him in leg irons and transported him back to the prison where he was put on the hitching post. The guards made him take off his shirt, and he remained shirtless all day while the sun burned his skin.[2] He remained attached to the post for approximately seven hours. During this 7-hour period, he was given water only once or twice and was given no bathroom breaks. At one point, a guard

---

1. [T]he hitching post is a horizontal bar "'made of sturdy, nonflexible material,'" placed between 45 and 57 inches from the ground. Inmates are handcuffed to the hitching post in a standing position and remain standing the entire time they are placed on the post. Most inmates are shackled to the hitching post with their two hands relatively close together and at face level. [citation omitted].

2. "The most repeated complaint of the hitching post, however, was the strain it produced on inmates' muscles by forcing them to remain in a standing position with their arms raised in a stationary position for a long period of time[, i]n addition to their exposure to sunburn [and] dehydration...."

taunted Hope about his thirst. According to Hope's affidavit: "[The guard] first gave water to some dogs, then brought the water cooler closer to me, removed its lid, and kicked the cooler over, spilling the water onto the ground."

...

II

The threshold inquiry a court must undertake in a qualified immunity analysis is whether plaintiff's allegations, if true, establish a constitutional violation. *Saucier v. Katz*, 533 U.S. 194, 201 (2001).

...

"'[T]he unnecessary and wanton infliction of pain ... constitutes cruel and unusual punishment forbidden by the Eighth Amendment.'" *Whitley v. Albers*, 475 U.S. 312, 319 (1986) (some internal quotation marks omitted). We have said that "[a]mong 'unnecessary and wanton' inflictions of pain are those that are 'totally without penological justification.'" *Rhodes v. Chapman*, 452 U.S. 337, 346 (1981). In making this determination in the context of prison conditions, we must ascertain whether the officials involved acted with "deliberate indifference" to the inmates' health or safety. *Hudson v. McMillian*, 503 U.S. 1, 8 (1992). We may infer the existence of this subjective state of mind from the fact that the risk of harm is obvious. *Farmer v. Brennan*, 511 U.S. 825, 842 (1994).

As the facts are alleged by Hope, the Eighth Amendment violation is obvious. Any safety concerns had long since abated by the time petitioner was handcuffed to the hitching post because Hope had already been subdued, handcuffed, placed in leg irons, and transported back to the prison. He was separated from his work squad and not given the opportunity to return to work.

Despite the clear lack of an emergency situation, the respondents knowingly subjected him to a substantial risk of physical harm, to unnecessary pain caused by the handcuffs and the restricted position of confinement for a 7-hour period, to unnecessary exposure to the heat of the sun, to prolonged thirst and taunting, and to a deprivation of bathroom breaks that created a risk of particular discomfort and humiliation.[8] The use of the hitching post under these circumstances [is] punitive treatment [which] amounts to gratuitous infliction of "wanton and unnecessary" pain that our precedent clearly prohibits.

---

8. The awareness of the risk of harm attributable to any individual respondent may be evaluated in part by considering the pattern of treatment that inmates generally received when attached to the hitching post. In *Austin v. Hopper*, the District Court cited examples of humiliating incidents resulting from the denial of bathroom breaks. One inmate "was not permitted to use the restroom or to change his clothing for four and one-half hours after he had defecated on himself." 15 F. Supp. 2d, at 1246. "Moreover, certain corrections officers not only ignored or denied inmates' requests for water or access to toilet facilities, but taunted them while they were clearly suffering from dehydration...." *Id.*, at 1247.

III

Despite their participation in this constitutionally impermissible conduct, respondents may nevertheless be shielded from liability for civil damages if their actions did not violate "clearly established statutory or constitutional rights of which a reasonable person would have known." *Harlow v. Fitzgerald*, 457 U.S. 800, 818 (1982). In assessing whether the Eighth Amendment violation here met the *Harlow* test, the Court of Appeals required that the facts of previous cases be " 'materially similar' to Hope's situation." ... This rigid gloss on the qualified immunity standard, though supported by Circuit precedent, is not consistent with our cases.

As we have explained, qualified immunity operates "to ensure that before they are subjected to suit, officers are on notice their conduct is unlawful." *Saucier v. Katz*, 533 U.S., at 206. For a constitutional right to be clearly established, its contours "must be sufficiently clear that a reasonable official would understand that what he is doing violates that right. This is not to say that an official action is protected by qualified immunity unless the very action in question has previously been held unlawful, *see Mitchell* [*v. Forsyth*, 472 U.S. 511,] 535, n. 12; but it is to say that in the light of pre-existing law the unlawfulness must be apparent." *Anderson v. Creighton*, 483 U.S. 635, 640 (1987).

...

Our opinion in [*United States v.*] *Lanier* [, 520 U.S. 259 (1997)] makes clear that officials can still be on notice that their conduct violates established law even in novel factual circumstances. Indeed, in *Lanier*, we expressly rejected a requirement that previous cases be "fundamentally similar." Although earlier cases involving "fundamentally similar" facts can provide especially strong support for a conclusion that the law is clearly established, they are not necessary to such a finding. The same is true of cases with "materially similar" facts. Accordingly, pursuant to *Lanier*, the salient question that the Court of Appeals ought to have asked is whether the state of the law in 1995 gave respondents fair warning that their alleged treatment of Hope was unconstitutional....

IV

The use of the hitching post as alleged by Hope "unnecessar[ily] and wanton[ly] inflicted pain," *Whitley*, 475 U.S., at 319 (internal quotation marks omitted), and thus was a clear violation of the Eighth Amendment.... Arguably, the violation was so obvious that our own Eighth Amendment cases gave respondents fair warning that their conduct violated the Constitution. Regardless, in light of binding Eleventh Circuit precedent, an Alabama Department of Corrections (ADOC) regulation, and a [Department of Justice] report informing the ADOC of the constitutional infirmity in its use of the hitching post, we readily conclude that the respondents' conduct violated "clearly established statutory or constitutional rights of which a reasonable person would have known." *Harlow*, 457 U.S., at 818.

...

[A Fifth Circuit decision binding on the Eleventh Circuit] squarely held that several ... "forms of corporal punishment run afoul of the Eighth Amendment [and] offend contemporary concepts of decency, human dignity, and precepts of civilization which we profess to possess" [including] "handcuffing inmates to the fence and to cells for long periods of time ... and forcing inmates to stand, sit or lie on crates, stumps, or otherwise maintain awkward positions for prolonged periods." *Ibid*.... [F]or the purpose of providing fair notice to reasonable officers administering punishment for past misconduct ... there [is no] reason to draw a constitutional distinction between a practice of handcuffing an inmate to a fence for prolonged periods and handcuffing him to a hitching post for seven hours. The Court of Appeals' conclusion to the contrary exposes the danger of a rigid, overreliance on factual similarity.

...

The reasoning, though not the holding, in a case decided by the Eleventh Circuit in 1987 sent the same message to reasonable officers in that Circuit. In *Ort v. White*, 813 F.2d 318, the Court of Appeals held that an officer's temporary denials of drinking water to an inmate who repeatedly refused to do his share of the work assigned to a farm squad "should not be viewed as punishment in the strict sense, but instead as necessary coercive measures undertaken to obtain compliance with a reasonable prison rule, *i.e.*, the requirement that all inmates perform their assigned farm squad duties." *Id*., at 325.... The court cautioned, however, that a constitutional violation might have been present "if later, once back at the prison, officials had decided to deny [Ort] water as punishment for his refusal to work." *Id*., at 326. So too would a violation have occurred if the method of coercion reached a point of severity such that the recalcitrant prisoner's health was at risk. *Ibid*. Although the facts of the case are not identical, *Ort's* premise is that "physical abuse directed at [a] prisoner after he terminate[s] his resistance to authority would constitute an actionable Eighth amendment violation." *Id*., at 324. This premise has clear applicability in this case. Hope was not restrained at the worksite until he was willing to return to work. Rather, he was removed back to the prison and placed under conditions that threatened his health. *Ort* therefore gave fair warning to respondents that their conduct crossed the line of what is constitutionally permissible.

Relevant to the question whether *Ort* provided fair warning to respondents that their conduct violated the Constitution is a regulation ... authoriz[ing] the use of the hitching post when an inmate refuses to work or is otherwise disruptive to a work squad. It provides that an activity log should be completed for each such inmate, detailing his responses to offers of water and bathroom breaks every 15 minutes.... [T]he record indicates that the periodic offers contemplated by the regulation were not made.... The regulation also states that an inmate "will be allowed to join his assigned squad" whenever he tells an officer "that he is ready to go to work." ... [T]his important provision of the regulation was frequently ignored by corrections officers. If regularly observed, a requirement that would effectively give the inmate the keys to the handcuffs that attached him to the hitching post would have made this case more analogous to the practice upheld in *Ort*, rather than the kind of punishment *Ort* described as impermissible. A course of conduct that tends to prove that the requirement was merely a sham, or that respondents could ignore it with impunity, provides equally strong support for the conclusion that they were fully aware of the wrongful character of their conduct.

Respondents violated clearly established law. Our conclusion that "a reasonable person would have known," *Harlow*, 457 U.S., at 818, of the violation is buttressed by the fact that the DOJ specifically advised the ADOC of the unconstitutionality of its practices before the incidents in this case took place.... [A] DOJ report noted that ADOC's officers consistently failed to comply with the policy of immediately releasing any inmate from the hitching post who agrees to return to work.... [T]he DOJ advised the ADOC to cease use of the hitching post in order to meet constitutional standards.... [and] informed the ADOC that, "'[a]lthough an emergency situation may warrant drastic action by corrections staff, our experts found that the "rail" is being used systematically as an improper punishment for relatively trivial offenses. Therefore, we have concluded that the use of the "rail" is without penological justification.'" *Ibid.* Although there is nothing in the record indicating that the DOJ's views were communicated to respondents, this exchange lends support to the view that reasonable officials in the ADOC should have realized that the use of the hitching post under the circumstances alleged by Hope violated the Eighth Amendment prohibition against cruel and unusual punishment.

The obvious cruelty inherent in this practice should have provided respondents with some notice that their alleged conduct violated Hope's constitutional protection against cruel and unusual punishment. Hope was treated in a way antithetical to human dignity—he was hitched to a post for an extended period of time in a position that was painful, and under circumstances that were both degrading and dangerous. This wanton treatment was not done of necessity, but as punishment for prior conduct. Even if there might once have been a question regarding the constitutionality of this practice, the Eleventh Circuit precedent of *Gates* and *Ort*, as well as the DOJ report condemning the practice, put a reasonable officer on notice that the use of the hitching post under the circumstances alleged by Hope was unlawful. The "fair and clear warning," *Lanier*, 520 U.S., at 271, that these cases provided was sufficient to preclude the defense of qualified immunity at the summary judgment stage.... The judgment of the Court of Appeals is reversed....

Justice THOMAS, with whom THE CHIEF JUSTICE and Justice SCALIA join, dissenting.

The Court today subjects three prison guards to suit based on facts not alleged, law not clearly established, and its own subjective views on appropriate methods of prison discipline. Qualified immunity jurisprudence has been turned on its head.

...

II

Once petitioner's allegations regarding respondents' conduct are separated from his other grievances and the mistreatment invented by the Court, this case presents one simple question: Was it clearly established in 1995 that the mere act of cuffing petitioner to the restraining bar (or, in the case of Officer McClaran, ordering petitioner's attachment to the restraining bar) violated the Eighth Amendment? The answer to this question is also simple: Obviously not.

...

Finally, the "binding Eleventh Circuit precedent" relied upon by the Court ... was plainly insufficient to give respondents fair warning that their alleged conduct ran afoul of petitioner's Eighth Amendment rights. The Court of Appeals held in *Ort v. White*, 813 F.2d 318 (C.A.11 1987), that a prison guard did not violate an inmate's Eighth Amendment rights by denying him water when he refused to work.... [T]he Court ... claims that the "reasoning" in *Ort* "gave fair warning to respondents that their conduct crossed the line of what is constitutionally permissible."

...

To be sure, the Court correctly notes that the Court of Appeals in *Ort* suggested that it "might have reached a different decision" had the prison officer denied the inmate water after he had returned to the prison instead of while he was out with the work squad. *Id.*, at 326. But the suggestion in *dicta* that a guard might have violated a prisoner's Eighth Amendment rights by denying him water once he returned from work duty does not come close to clearly establishing the unconstitutionality of attaching a disruptive inmate to a restraining bar after he is removed from his work squad and back within prison walls.

Admittedly, the other case upon which the Court relies, *Gates v. Collier*, 501 F.2d 1291 (C.A.5 1974), is more on point. Nevertheless, *Gates* is also inadequate to establish clearly the unlawfulness of respondents' alleged conduct. In *Gates*, the Court of Appeals listed "handcuffing inmates to [a] fence and to cells for long periods of time" as one of many unacceptable forms of "physical brutality and abuse" present at a Mississippi prison. *Id.*, at 1306. Others included administering milk of magnesia as a form of punishment, depriving inmates of mattresses, hygienic materials, and adequate food, and shooting at and around inmates to keep them standing or moving. *See ibid.* The Court of Appeals had "no difficulty in reaching the conclusion that these forms of corporal punishment run afoul of the Eighth Amendment." *Ibid.*

It is not reasonable, however, to read *Gates* as establishing a bright-line rule forbidding the attachment of prisoners to a restraining bar. For example, in referring to the fact that prisoners were handcuffed to a fence and cells "for long periods of time," the Court of Appeals did not indicate whether it considered a "long period of time" to be 1 hour, 5 hours, or 25 hours. The Court of Appeals also provided no explanation of the circumstances surrounding these incidents. The opinion does not indicate whether the handcuffed prisoners were given water and suitable restroom breaks or whether they were handcuffed in a bid to induce them to comply with prison rules. In the intervening 21 years between *Gates* and the time respondents affixed petitioner to the restraining bar, there were no further decisions clarifying the contours of the law in this area. Therefore, as another court interpreting *Gates* has noted: "There is no blanket prohibition against the use of punishment such as the hitching post in *Gates* which would signal to the Commissioner of Corrections [let alone ordinary corrections officers] that the mere use of the hitching post would be a constitutional violation." *Fountain v. Talley*, 104 F. Supp. 2d 1345, 1354 (M.D. Ala. 2000).

Moreover, Eighth Amendment law has not stood still since *Gates* was decided. In *Farmer v. Brennan*, 511 U.S. 825 (1994), this Court elucidated the proper test for measuring whether a prison official's state of mind is one of "deliberate indifference," holding that "a prison official cannot be found liable under the Eighth Amendment for denying an inmate humane conditions of confinement unless the official knows of and disregards an excessive risk to inmate health or safety; the official must both be aware of facts from which the inference could be drawn that a substantial risk of serious harm exists, and he must also draw the inference." *Id.*, at 837. Because the Court of Appeals in *Gates* did not consider this subjective element, *Gates* alone could not have clearly established that affixing prisoners to a restraining bar was clearly unconstitutional in 1995. Also, in the face of recent Federal District Court decisions specifically rejecting prisoners' claims that Alabama prison guards violated their Eighth Amendment rights by attaching them to a restraining bar as well as a state regulation authorizing such conduct, it seems contrary to the purpose of qualified immunity to hold that one vague sentence plucked out of a 21-year-old Court of Appeals opinion provided clear notice to respondents in 1995 that their conduct was unlawful.

....

For further discussion

In 2010, in a non-precedential decision, the Eleventh Circuit reversed a district court's denial of qualified immunity to police officers who fatally shot a man with a weapon called a beanbag gun. The Eleventh Circuit held the law was not clearly established so as to give the officers fair warning that shooting a beanbag gun under the circumstances would have been illegal:

> [There is no] roughly analogous case law that would suffice to put the officers on notice of the illegality of their conduct in these "tense, uncertain" circumstances. On April 4, 2005, there were no cases in the relevant jurisdictions on the use of less than deadly force (here a beanbag munition) to subdue a suspect who had threatened to shoot at officers who were in front of his house, spoke about killing children, and threatened suicide. There were reported cases involving handguns, *see, e.g.*, *Carr v. Tatangelo*, 338 F.3d 1259 (11th Cir. 2003), and a case involving the use of a Taser gun, *see Draper v. Reynolds*, 369 F.3d 1270 (11th Cir. 2004), but this weapon (a beanbag gun) lies in the unwashed middle somewhere between deadly force and the use of a Taser gun.

Glenn v. City of Columbus, 375 F. App'x 928, 933 (11th Cir.) (*per curiam*), *cert. denied*, 562 U.S. 895 (2010). On remand, the district court reluctantly entered summary judgment in favor of the officers, "[a]lthough this Court finds the holding and rationale of the Court of Appeals to be remarkably charitable to law enforcement officers who used deadly force against an unarmed man under dubious circumstances...."

Glenn v. City of Columbus, No. 4:07-CV-52 (CDL), 2010 WL 2600718, at *2 (M.D. Ga. June 23, 2010). (Note that *Carr* is excerpted in this Chapter and *Draper* is referenced in Chapter 6.)

Questions to guide reading of *Brosseau*

1. In *Saucier* (as summarized in *Brosseau*), the Supreme Court directed that the qualified immunity analysis proceed in what sequence?
2. Why does qualified immunity shield a police officer from suit even when the officer makes a constitutionally deficient decision that "reasonably misapprehends the law governing the circumstances she confronted"?
3. According to the *per curiam* decision, why did *Graham* and *Garner* not provide "fair warning" to a reasonable police officer that the conduct in *Brosseau* would be unlawful? Did *Brousseau* limit *Hope*?
4. In determining that the 4th Amendment right asserted by plaintiff was not "clearly established," what sources of law did the Supreme Court consider? Does the Court expect careful defense lawyers to keep their clients current on law from other jurisdictions?
5. Why did the Supreme Court reverse the Ninth Circuit's qualified immunity ruling without even asking the parties for briefs on the merits?
6. Why did three Justices question the sequence of the qualified immunity analysis required by *Saucier*?
7. Why did Justice Stevens dissent?
8. Note that the majority and dissent differently characterize the circuit court decisions in *Cole* and *Smith*. As a matter of litigation strategy, how is the rhetorical technique of reading a precedent broadly (to stand for a general proposition) or reading a precedent narrowly (to be tied to specific facts) likely to be invoked in the qualified immunity context?

Brosseau v. Haugen

543 U.S. 194 (2004)

PER CURIAM.

Officer Rochelle Brosseau, a member of the Puyallup, Washington, Police Department, shot Kenneth Haugen in the back as he attempted to flee from law enforcement authorities in his vehicle ... Following the two-step process set out in *Saucier v. Katz*, 533 U.S. 194 (2001), the Court of Appeals found, first, that Brosseau had violated Haugen's Fourth Amendment right to be free from excessive force and, second, that the right violated was clearly established and thus Brosseau was not entitled to qualified immunity. Brosseau ... request[ed] that we review both of the Court of Appeals' determinations. We grant the petition on the second, qualified immunity question and reverse.

The material facts, construed in a light most favorable to Haugen, are as follows. On the day before the fracas, Glen Tamburello went to the police station and reported to Brosseau that Haugen, a former crime partner of his, had stolen tools from his shop. Brosseau later learned that there was a felony no-bail warrant out for Haugen's arrest on drug and other offenses. The next morning, Haugen was spray-painting his Jeep Cherokee in his mother's driveway. Tamburello learned of Haugen's whereabouts, and he and cohort Matt Atwood drove a pickup truck to Haugen's mother's house to pay Haugen a visit. A fight ensued, which was witnessed by a neighbor who called 911.

Brosseau heard a report that the men were fighting in Haugen's mother's yard and responded. When she arrived, Tamburello and Atwood were attempting to get Haugen into Tamburello's pickup. Brosseau's arrival created a distraction, which provided Haugen the opportunity to get away. Haugen ran through his mother's yard and hid in the neighborhood. Brosseau requested assistance, and, shortly thereafter, two officers arrived with a K-9 to help track Haugen down. During the search, which lasted about 30 to 45 minutes, officers instructed Tamburello and Atwood to remain in Tamburello's pickup. They instructed Deanna Nocera, Haugen's girlfriend who was also present with her 3-year-old daughter, to remain in her small car with her daughter. Tamburello's pickup was parked in the street in front of the driveway; Nocera's small car was parked in the driveway in front of and facing the Jeep; and the Jeep was in the driveway facing Nocera's car and angled somewhat to the left. The Jeep was parked about 4 feet away from Nocera's car and 20 to 30 feet away from Tamburello's pickup.

An officer radioed from down the street that a neighbor had seen a man in her backyard. Brosseau ran in that direction, and Haugen appeared. He ran past the front of his mother's house and then turned and ran into the driveway. With Brosseau still in pursuit, he jumped into the driver's side of the Jeep and closed and locked the door. Brosseau believed that he was running to the Jeep to retrieve a weapon.

Brosseau arrived at the Jeep, pointed her gun at Haugen, and ordered him to get out of the vehicle. Haugen ignored her command and continued to look for the keys so he could get the Jeep started. Brosseau repeated her commands and hit the driver's side window several times with her handgun, which failed to deter Haugen. On the third or fourth try, the window shattered. Brosseau unsuccessfully attempted to grab the keys and struck Haugen on the head with the barrel and butt of her gun. Haugen, still undeterred, succeeded in starting the Jeep. As the Jeep started or shortly after it began to move, Brosseau jumped back and to the left. She fired one shot through the rear driver's side window at a forward angle, hitting Haugen in the back. She later explained that she shot Haugen because she was "'fearful for the other officers on foot who [she] believed were in the immediate area, [and] for the occupied vehicles in [Haugen's] path and for any other citizens who might be in the area.'" [*Haugen v. Brosseau*,] 339 F.3d [857,] 865 [(9th Cir. 2003)].

Despite being hit, Haugen, in his words, "'st[ood] on the gas'"; navigated the "'small, tight space'" to avoid the other vehicles; swerved across the neighbor's lawn; and continued down the street. *Id.*, at 882. After about a half block, Haugen realized that he had been shot and brought the Jeep to a halt. He suffered a collapsed lung and was airlifted to a hospital. He survived the shooting and subsequently pleaded guilty to the felony of "eluding." ... By so pleading, he admitted that he drove his Jeep in a manner indicating "a wanton or wilful [sic] disregard for the lives ... of others." *Ibid.*

...

When confronted with a claim of qualified immunity, a court must ask first the following question: "Taken in the light most favorable to the party asserting the injury, do the facts alleged show the officer's conduct violated a constitutional right?" *Saucier v. Katz*, 533 U.S., at 201. As the Court of Appeals recognized, the constitutional question in this case is governed by the principles enunciated in *Tennessee v. Garner*, 471 U.S. 1 (1985), and *Graham v. Connor*, 490 U.S. 386 (1989). These cases establish that claims of excessive force are to be judged under the Fourth Amendment's "'objective reasonableness'" standard. *Id.*, at 388. Specifically with regard to deadly force, we explained in *Garner* that it is unreasonable for an officer to "seize an unarmed, nondangerous suspect by shooting him dead." 471 U.S., at 11. But "[w]here the officer has probable cause to believe that the suspect poses a threat of serious physical harm, either to the officer or to others, it is not constitutionally unreasonable to prevent escape by using deadly force." *Ibid.*

We express no view as to the correctness of the Court of Appeals' decision on the constitutional question itself. We believe that, however that question is decided, the Court of Appeals was wrong on the issue of qualified immunity.[3]

Qualified immunity shields an officer from suit when she makes a decision that, even if constitutionally deficient, reasonably misapprehends the law governing the circumstances she confronted. *Saucier v. Katz*, 533 U.S., at 206 (qualified immunity operates "to protect officers from the sometimes 'hazy border between excessive and acceptable force'"). Because the focus is on whether the officer had fair notice that her conduct was unlawful, reasonableness is judged against the backdrop of the law at the time of the conduct. If the law at that time did not clearly establish that the officer's conduct would violate the Constitution, the officer should not be subject to liability or, indeed, even the burdens of litigation.

It is important to emphasize that this inquiry "must be undertaken in light of the specific context of the case, not as a broad general proposition." *Id.*, at 201. As we previously said in this very context:

> "[T]here is no doubt that *Graham v. Connor* ... clearly establishes the general proposition that use of force is contrary to the Fourth Amendment if it is

3. We have no occasion in this case to reconsider our instruction in *Saucier v. Katz*, *supra*, that lower courts decide the constitutional question prior to deciding the qualified immunity question. We exercise our summary reversal procedure here simply to correct a clear misapprehension of the qualified immunity standard.

> excessive under objective standards of reasonableness. Yet that is not enough. Rather, we emphasized in *Anderson* [*v. Creighton,*] 'that the right the official is alleged to have violated must have been "clearly established" in a more particularized, and hence more relevant, sense: The contours of the right must be sufficiently clear that a reasonable official would understand that what he is doing violates that right.' 483 U.S. [635,] 640 [(1987)]. The relevant, dispositive inquiry in determining whether a right is clearly established is whether it would be clear to a reasonable officer that his conduct was unlawful in the situation he confronted." *Id.*, at 201–202.

The Court of Appeals acknowledged this statement of law, but then proceeded to find fair warning in the general tests set out in *Graham* and *Garner*. In so doing, it was mistaken. *Graham* and *Garner*, following the lead of the Fourth Amendment's text, are cast at a high level of generality. *See Graham v. Connor*, *supra*, at 396 ("'[T]he test of reasonableness under the Fourth Amendment is not capable of precise definition or mechanical application'"). Of course, in an obvious case, these standards can "clearly establish" the answer, even without a body of relevant case law. *See Hope v. Pelzer*, 536 U.S. 730, 738, (2002) (noting in a case where the Eighth Amendment violation was "obvious" that there need not be a materially similar case for the right to be clearly established).... The present case is far from the obvious one where *Graham* and *Garner* alone offer a basis for decision.

We therefore turn to ask whether, at the time of Brosseau's actions, it was "'"clearly established"'" in this more "'particularized'" sense that she was violating Haugen's Fourth Amendment right. *Saucier v. Katz*, 533 U.S., at 202. The parties point us to only a handful of cases relevant to the "situation [Brosseau] confronted": whether to shoot a disturbed felon, set on avoiding capture through vehicular flight, when persons in the immediate area are at risk from that flight.[4] *Ibid.* Specifically, Brosseau points us to *Cole v. Bone*, 993 F.2d 1328 (C.A.8 1993), and *Smith v. Freland*, 954 F.2d 343 (C.A.6 1992).

In these cases, the courts found no Fourth Amendment violation when an officer shot a fleeing suspect who presented a risk to others. *Cole v. Bone*, *supra*, at 1333 (holding the officer "had probable cause to believe that the truck posed an imminent threat of serious physical harm to innocent motorists as well as to the officers themselves"); *Smith v. Freland*, 954 F.2d, at 347 (noting "a car can be a deadly weapon" and holding the officer's decision to stop the car from possibly injuring others was reasonable). *Smith* is closer to this case. There, the officer and suspect engaged in a car chase, which appeared to be at an end when the officer cornered the suspect at the back of a dead-end residential street. The suspect, however, freed his car and

---

4. The parties point us to a number of other cases in this vein that postdate the conduct in question, *i.e.*, Brosseau's February 21, 1999, shooting of Haugen. *See Cowan ex rel. Estate of Cooper v. Breen*, 352 F.3d 756, 763 (C.A.2 2003); *Pace v. Capobianco*, 283 F.3d 1275, 1281–1282 (C.A.11 2002); *Scott v. Clay County*, 205 F.3d 867, 877 (C.A.6 2000); *McCaslin v. Wilkins*, 183 F.3d 775, 778–779 (C.A.8 1999); *Abraham v. Raso*, 183 F.3d 279, 288–296 (C.A.3 1999). These decisions, of course, could not have given fair notice to Brosseau and are of no use in the clearly established inquiry.

began speeding down the street. At this point, the officer fired a shot, which killed the suspect. The court held the officer's decision was reasonable and thus did not violate the Fourth Amendment. It noted that the suspect, like Haugen here, "had proven he would do almost anything to avoid capture" and that he posed a major threat to, among others, the officers at the end of the street. *Ibid.*

Haugen points us to *Estate of Starks v. Enyart*, 5 F.3d 230 (C.A.7 1993), where the court found summary judgment inappropriate on a Fourth Amendment claim involving a fleeing suspect. There, the court concluded that the threat created by the fleeing suspect's failure to brake when an officer suddenly stepped in front of his just-started car was not a sufficiently grave threat to justify the use of deadly force. *Id.*, at 234.

These three cases taken together undoubtedly show that this area is one in which the result depends very much on the facts of each case. None of them squarely governs the case here; they do suggest that Brosseau's actions fell in the " 'hazy border between excessive and acceptable force.' " *Saucier v. Katz, supra*, at 206. The cases by no means "clearly establish" that Brosseau's conduct violated the Fourth Amendment.

The judgment of the United States Court of Appeals for the Ninth Circuit is therefore reversed, and the case is remanded for further proceedings consistent with this opinion.

Justice BREYER, with whom Justice SCALIA and Justice GINSBURG join, concurring.

I join the Court's opinion but write separately to express my concern about the matter to which the Court refers in footnote 3, namely, the way in which lower courts are required to evaluate claims of qualified immunity under the Court's decision in *Saucier v. Katz*, 533 U.S. 194, 201 (2001). As the Court notes ... *Saucier* requires lower courts to decide (1) the constitutional question prior to deciding (2) the qualified immunity question. I am concerned that the current rule rigidly requires courts unnecessarily to decide difficult constitutional questions when there is available an easier basis for the decision (*e.g.*, qualified immunity) that will satisfactorily resolve the case before the court. Indeed when courts' dockets are crowded, a rigid "order of battle" makes little administrative sense and can sometimes lead to a constitutional decision that is effectively insulated from review, *see Bunting v. Mellen*, 541 U.S. 1019, 1025 (2004) (SCALIA, J., dissenting from denial of certiorari). For these reasons, I think we should reconsider this issue.

Justice STEVENS, dissenting.

In my judgment, the answer to the constitutional question presented by this case is clear: Under the Fourth Amendment, it was objectively unreasonable for Officer Brosseau to use deadly force against Kenneth Haugen in an attempt to prevent his escape. What is not clear is whether Brosseau is nonetheless entitled to qualified immunity because it might not have been apparent to a reasonably well trained officer in Brosseau's shoes that killing Haugen to prevent his escape was unconstitutional. In my opinion that question should be answered by a jury.

...

The most common justifications for the use of deadly force are plainly inapplicable to this case. Respondent Haugen had not threatened anyone with a weapon, and petitioner Brosseau did not shoot in order to defend herself. Haugen was not a person who had committed a violent crime; nor was there any reason to believe he would do so if permitted to escape. Indeed, there is nothing in the record to suggest he intended to harm anyone. The "threat of serious physical harm, either to the officer or to others," *id.*, at 11, that provides the sole justification for Brosseau's use of deadly force was the risk that while fleeing in his vehicle Haugen would accidentally collide with a pedestrian or another vehicle. Whether Brosseau's shot enhanced or minimized that risk is debatable, but the risk of such an accident surely did not justify an attempt to kill the fugitive. Thus, I have no difficulty in endorsing the Court's assumption that Brosseau's conduct violated the Constitution.

II

...

[W]e have recognized that "general statements of the law are not inherently incapable of giving fair and clear warning," *United States v. Lanier*, 520 U.S. 259, 271 (1997), and have firmly rejected the notion that "an official action is protected by qualified immunity unless the very action in question has previously been held unlawful," *Anderson v. Creighton*, 483 U.S. 635, 640 (1987).

Thus, the Court's search for relevant case law applying the *Garner* standard to materially similar facts is both unnecessary and ill-advised. *See Hope*, 536 U.S., at 741 ("Although earlier cases involving 'fundamentally similar' facts can provide especially strong support for a conclusion that the law is clearly established, they are not necessary to such a finding").... Indeed, the cases the majority relies on are inapposite and, in fact, only serve to illuminate the patent unreasonableness of Brosseau's actions.[4]

Rather than uncertainty about the law, it is uncertainty about the likely consequences of Haugen's flight—or, more precisely, uncertainty about how a reasonable officer making the split-second decision to use deadly force would have assessed the

4. In *Cole v. Bone*, 993 F.2d 1328 (C.A.8 1993), an 18-wheel tractor-trailer sped through a tollbooth and engaged the police in a high-speed pursuit in excess of 90 miles per hour on a high-traffic interstate during the holiday season. During the course of the pursuit, the driver passed traffic on both shoulders of the interstate, repeatedly attempted to ram several police cars, drove more than 100 passenger vehicles off the road, ran through several roadblocks, and continued driving after the officer shot out the wheels of the fugitive's truck. *Id.*, at 1330–1331. Only then did the officer finally resort to deadly force to disable the driver. Similarly, in *Smith v. Freland*, 954 F.2d 343 (C.A.6 1992), the suspect led a police officer on a high-speed chase, reaching speeds in excess of 90 miles per hour. When the officer initially cornered the suspect in a field, the driver repeatedly swerved directly toward the police car, forcing the officer to move out of the way and allowing the suspect to continue the chase. *Id.*, at 344. Only after additional officers cornered the suspect for a second time, and after the suspect smashed directly into an unoccupied police car and began to flee again, did the officer finally shoot the driver. *Ibid.*

In stark contrast, at the time Brosseau shot Haugen, the Jeep was immobile, or at best, had just started moving. Haugen had not driven at excess speeds; nor had he rammed, or attempted to ram, nearby police cars or passenger vehicles. In sum, there was no ongoing or prior high-speed car chase to inform the probable cause analysis.

foreseeability of a serious accident—that prevents me from answering the question of qualified immunity that this case presents. This is a quintessentially "fact-specific" question, not a question that judges should try to answer "as a matter of law."

...

For further discussion

Several years after *Brosseau*, the Supreme Court granted certiorari in a Tenth Circuit decision and, in its Order, directed the parties to argue an additional question. Based on the below Order granting certiorari, what can you surmise about the attitude of at least some Supreme Court Justices toward the analytical sequence required by *Saucier*?

> Petition ... granted. In addition to the questions presented by the petition, the parties are directed to brief and argue the following question: 'Whether the Court's decision in *Saucier v. Katz*, 533 U.S. 194 (2001) should be overruled?'

Pearson v. Callahan, 552 U.S. 1279 (2008).

Questions to guide reading of Amicus Brief

1. The ACLU argued that the *Saucier* sequence resolved a "troubling pattern" that had developed in qualified immunity claims. What problem did the ACLU argue was created by permitting courts to skip the constitutional violation inquiry? Why did it argue that, pre-*Saucier*, defendants had more than "one free constitutional violation"?
2. How does the ACLU summarize the critique of the *Saucier* sequence and how does the brief refute those critiques?

Brief Amicus Curiae of the ACLU in *Pearson*

2008 WL 3851627 (August 11, 2008)

By Allen M. Hopper and Adam B. Wolf, American Civil Liberties Union Foundation, Santa Cruz, California and Steven R. Shapiro; and Catherine Crump, American Civil Liberties Union Foundation, New York, New York

I. *Saucier*'s Two-Step Rule For Resolving Qualified Immunity Claims Is Critical For Clarifying Constitutional Rights and Should Be Retained

The two-step rule announced in *Saucier* was not developed in a vacuum. Rather, it responded to a troubling pattern that had developed in addressing qualified immunity claims. With disturbing frequency, such claims were upheld on the basis that the defendant's conduct did not violate a clearly established right without determining whether any rights had actually been violated.

This unresolved ambiguity produced two unfortunate results. First, it failed to provide government officials with the legal guidance they need, and ideally should want, to perform their duties in a constitutional manner. Second, by perpetuating a state of legal ambiguity, it diminished the chance that victims of unconstitutional state action could recover damages for their injury in subsequent actions.

Saucier remedied both problems by insisting that courts presented with a qualified immunity claim initially determine if there has been a constitutional violation on the facts alleged before deciding whether that right was clearly established.... Although *Saucier* has been criticized as inflexible, it has largely accomplished its intended purpose ... [and] any exceptions to its rule should be carefully defined and narrowly circumscribed.

A. *Saucier* Serves Important Goals That Should Not Be Abandoned

By having courts decide what the law requires before deciding whether that requirement was clearly established at the time defendants acted, *Saucier* "promotes clarity in the legal standards for official conduct, to the benefit of both the officers and the general public." *Wilson v. Layne*, 526 U.S. 603, 609 (1999). Public officials who can reasonably claim that they were uncertain of their legal obligations remain entitled to qualified immunity. But *Saucier* simultaneously ensures that the grant of immunity does not short circuit a salutary "process for the law's elaboration from case to case." *Saucier*, 533 U.S. at 201.

Saucier thus shields public officials from liability from damages when they act in a context where the rules are unclear, while placing them on notice that they will be held accountable for future violations of rights that have been clearly announced. *Saucier* thereby helps to ensure that the qualified immunity inquiry promotes rather than frustrates the deterrent function of § 1983. *See Owen v. City of Independence*, 445 U.S. 622, 651 (1980) (stating that "§ 1983 was intended not only to provide compensation to the victims of past abuses, but to serve as a deterrent against future constitutional deprivations, as well.").

Returning to a pre-*Saucier* regime would once again transform qualified immunity from a rule that gives officers "one liability-free violation of the Constitution" to a rule that allows for "multiple bites of a constitutionally forbidden fruit." ... This is because "[a]n immunity determination, with nothing more, provides no clear standard, constitutional or nonconstitutional," *County of Sacramento v. Lewis*, 523 U.S. 833, 841 n.5 (1998). As a result, unconstitutional conduct could proliferate yet escape review as defendants rely on the absence of clearly established rights to avoid liability.... This ongoing uncertainty will inevitably deter future victims from seeking redress for similar constitutional injuries. *See Owen*, 445 U.S. at 651 n.33 (noting "the deleterious effect of freezing constitutional law in its current state of development" if individuals were to lose incentive to seek vindication of constitutional rights).

To be sure, some constitutional rights can be clarified and become clearly established in contexts where qualified immunity does not apply, such as ... suits against municipalities.... [W]hile municipalities are not protected by qualified immunity, *see Owen v. City of Independence*, 445 U.S. 622 (1980), they can only be sued for damages where plaintiffs can prove the existence of an unconstitutional policy or custom. *Monell v. Dep't of Social Services*, 436 U.S. 658, 694 (1978).

...

Likewise, the doctrine of constitutional avoidance does not dictate a departure from the *Saucier* rule.... "If the policy of avoidance were always followed in favor of ruling on qualified immunity whenever there was no clearly settled constitutional rule of primary conduct, standards of official conduct would tend to remain uncertain, to the detriment both of officials and individuals." *County of Sacramento*, 523 U.S. at 841 n.5.

Finally, critics of *Saucier* argue that the rule is unfair because government defendants who lose on step one but prevail on step two will be left with a constitutional ruling that they are unable to appeal.... [That] concern disappears entirely if the plaintiff appeals the qualified immunity decision in defendant's favor since both stages of the *Saucier* inquiry will then be before the reviewing court. *See Hope v. Pelzer*, 536 U.S. 730, 736 (2002) (reviewing the constitutional issue that the plaintiff had won in the lower court).... More traditionally, if the underlying constitutional ruling is a close or controversial one, it is likely to provoke a circuit conflict that is grounds for review under this Court's normal rules. In short, the unappealability problem arises infrequently and is resolvable by this Court when it arises.

Questions to guide reading of *Pearson*

1. *Pearson* overruled the sequence of the qualified immunity inquiry required by *Saucier*. How was this change foreshadowed by the *Brousseau* concurrences and the Supreme Court's order granting certiorari in *Pearson*?
2. *Pearson* held that a court may choose either to follow the *Saucier* sequence or may skip the question of whether the conduct violated the constitution and move directly to whether the right was clearly established. Can you tell what standard courts should use in choosing whether to move directly to the "clearly established" inquiry?
3. Do you think either plaintiffs or defendants might have a preference for the *Saucier* sequence? Would a plaintiff litigating a novel theory of constitutional liability be more likely to prevail under the *Saucier* sequence or under the *Pearson* rule permitting the court to skip to the "clearly established" inquiry?
4. Why will it conserve judicial resources to give courts the option of either deciding the constitutional issue or instead jumping to the "clearly established" inquiry? If courts frequently exercise that option, is there a risk that an area of constitutional law could indefinitely be "not clearly established"?
5. *Pearson* reasons that its rule will conserve the resources of the parties because they will avoid unnecessary litigation of constitutional issues. Is that likely? Since the decision of whether to follow the *Saucier* sequence or jump to the clearly established inquiry is the court's choice, will the parties proceed differently during pleading, discovery, and summary judgment?
6. Is the Supreme Court reluctant for courts to follow the *Saucier* sequence when the constitutional question is fact-bound? If so, is there tension be-

tween that reluctance and the requirement that, to hold a government official liable, the constitutional right must be defined sufficiently for a reasonable official to know that what he is doing violates that right?

Pearson v. Callahan

555 U.S. 223 (2009)

Justice ALITO delivered the opinion of the Court.

This is an action brought by respondent under 42 U.S.C. § 1983, against state law enforcement officers who conducted a warrantless search of his house incident to his arrest for the sale of methamphetamine to an undercover informant whom he had voluntarily admitted to the premises.... Following the procedure we mandated in *Saucier v. Katz*, 533 U.S. 194 (2001), the Court of Appeals held, first, that respondent adduced facts sufficient to make out a violation of the Fourth Amendment and, second, that the unconstitutionality of the officers' conduct was clearly established.... We now hold that the *Saucier* procedure should not be regarded as an inflexible requirement and that petitioners are entitled to qualified immunity on the ground that it was not clearly established at the time of the search that their conduct was unconstitutional. We therefore reverse.

...

The doctrine of qualified immunity protects government officials "from liability for civil damages insofar as their conduct does not violate clearly established statutory or constitutional rights of which a reasonable person would have known." *Harlow v. Fitzgerald*, 457 U.S. 800, 818 (1982). Qualified immunity balances two important interests—the need to hold public officials accountable when they exercise power irresponsibly and the need to shield officials from harassment, distraction, and liability when they perform their duties reasonably. The protection of qualified immunity applies regardless of whether the government official's error is "a mistake of law, a mistake of fact, or a mistake based on mixed questions of law and fact." *Groh v. Ramirez*, 540 U.S. 551, 567 (2004) (Kennedy, J., dissenting) [further citation omitted].

Because qualified immunity is "an immunity from suit rather than a mere defense to liability ... it is effectively lost if a case is erroneously permitted to go to trial." *Mitchell v. Forsyth*, 472 U.S. 511, 526 (1985).... Indeed, we have made clear that the "driving force" behind creation of the qualified immunity doctrine was a desire to ensure that " 'insubstantial claims' against government officials [will] be resolved prior to discovery." *Anderson v. Creighton*, 483 U.S. 635, 640, n. 2 (1987). Accordingly, "we repeatedly have stressed the importance of resolving immunity questions at the earliest possible stage in litigation." *Hunter v. Bryant*, 502 U.S. 224, 227 (1991) (*per curiam*).

In *Saucier*, 533 U.S. 194, this Court mandated a two-step sequence for resolving government officials' qualified immunity claims. First, a court must decide whether the facts that a plaintiff has alleged (*see* Fed. Rules Civ. Proc. 12(b)(6), (c)) or shown (*see* Rules 50, 56) make out a violation of a constitutional right. 533 U.S., at 201. Second, if the plaintiff has satisfied this first step, the court must decide whether the right at issue was "clearly established" at the time of defendant's alleged misconduct. *Ibid.* Qualified immunity is applicable unless the official's conduct violated a clearly established constitutional right. *Anderson, supra,* at 640.

Our decisions prior to *Saucier* had held that "the better approach to resolving cases in which the defense of qualified immunity is raised is to determine first whether the plaintiff has alleged a deprivation of a constitutional right at all." *County of Sacramento v. Lewis,* 523 U.S. 833, 841, n. 5 (1998). *Saucier* made that suggestion a mandate. For the first time, we held that whether "the facts alleged show the officer's conduct violated a constitutional right ... *must* be the initial inquiry" in every qualified immunity case. 533 U.S., at 201 (emphasis added). Only after completing this first step, we said, may a court turn to "the next, sequential step," namely, "whether the right was clearly established." *Ibid.*

This two-step procedure, the *Saucier* Court reasoned, is necessary to support the Constitution's "elaboration from case to case" and to prevent constitutional stagnation. *Ibid.* "The law might be deprived of this explanation were a court simply to skip ahead to the question whether the law clearly established that the officer's conduct was unlawful in the circumstances of the case." *Ibid.*

B

In considering whether the *Saucier* procedure should be modified or abandoned, we must begin with the doctrine of *stare decisis. Stare decisis* "promotes the evenhanded, predictable, and consistent development of legal principles, fosters reliance on judicial decisions, and contributes to the actual and perceived integrity of the judicial process." ... Revisiting precedent is particularly appropriate where, as here, a departure would not upset expectations, the precedent consists of a judge-made rule that was recently adopted to improve the operation of the courts, and experience has pointed up the precedent's shortcomings.

"Considerations in favor of *stare decisis* are at their acme in cases involving property and contract rights, where reliance interests are involved; the opposite is true in cases ... involving procedural and evidentiary rules" that do not produce such reliance. [citations omitted]. Like rules governing procedures and the admission of evidence in the trial courts, *Saucier*'s two-step protocol does not affect the way in which parties order their affairs....

Nor does this matter implicate "the general presumption that legislative changes should be left to Congress." ... [T]he *Saucier* rule is judge made and implicates an important matter involving internal Judicial Branch operations. Any change should come from this Court, not Congress....

Lower court judges, who have had the task of applying the *Saucier* rule on a regular basis for the past eight years, have not been reticent in their criticism of *Saucier*'s "rigid order of battle." ... Members of this Court have also voiced criticism of the *Saucier* rule. *See* ... *Brosseau v. Haugen,* 543 U.S. 194, 201–202 (2004) (Breyer, J., joined by Scalia and Ginsburg, JJ., concurring) (urging Court to reconsider *Saucier*'s "rigid 'order of battle,'" which "requires courts unnecessarily to decide difficult constitutional questions when there is available an easier basis for the decision (*e.g.*, qualified immunity) that will satisfactorily resolve the case before the court"); *Saucier*, 533 U.S., at 210 (Ginsburg, J., concurring in judgment) ("The two-part test today's decision imposes holds large potential to confuse").

III

On reconsidering the procedure required in *Saucier*, we conclude that, while the sequence set forth there is often appropriate, it should no longer be regarded as mandatory. The judges of the district courts and the courts of appeals should be permitted to exercise their sound discretion in deciding which of the two prongs of the qualified immunity analysis should be addressed first in light of the circumstances in the particular case at hand.

A

Although we now hold that the *Saucier* protocol should not be regarded as mandatory in all cases, we continue to recognize that it is often beneficial. For one thing, there are cases in which there would be little if any conservation of judicial resources to be had by beginning and ending with a discussion of the "clearly established" prong. "[I]t often may be difficult to decide whether a right is clearly established without deciding precisely what the constitutional right happens to be." [citation omitted]. In some cases, a discussion of why the relevant facts do not violate clearly established law may make it apparent that in fact the relevant facts do not make out a constitutional violation at all. In addition, the *Saucier* Court was certainly correct in noting that the two-step procedure promotes the development of constitutional precedent and is especially valuable with respect to questions that do not frequently arise in cases in which a qualified immunity defense is unavailable.

B

At the same time, however, the rigid *Saucier* procedure comes with a price. The procedure sometimes results in a substantial expenditure of scarce judicial resources on difficult questions that have no effect on the outcome of the case. There are cases in which it is plain that a constitutional right is not clearly established but far from obvious whether in fact there is such a right. District courts and courts of appeals with heavy caseloads are often understandably unenthusiastic about what may seem to be an essentially academic exercise.

Unnecessary litigation of constitutional issues also wastes the parties' resources. Qualified immunity is "an immunity from suit rather than a mere defense to liability." *Mitchell*, 472 U.S., at 526 (emphasis deleted). *Saucier*'s two-step protocol "disserve[s] the purpose of qualified immunity" when it "forces the parties to endure additional burdens of suit—such as the costs of litigating constitutional questions and delays attributable to resolving them—when the suit otherwise could be disposed of more readily." ...

Although the first prong of the *Saucier* procedure is intended to further the development of constitutional precedent, opinions following that procedure often fail to make a meaningful contribution to such development. For one thing, there are cases in which the constitutional question is so fact-bound that the decision provides little guidance for future cases. *See Scott v. Harris*, 550 U.S. 372, 388 (2007) (Breyer, J., concurring) (counseling against the *Saucier* two-step protocol where the question is "so fact dependent that the result will be confusion rather than clarity")....

...

Rigid adherence to the *Saucier* rule may make it hard for affected parties to obtain appellate review of constitutional decisions that may have a serious prospective effect on their operations. Where a court holds that a defendant committed a constitutional violation but that the violation was not clearly established, the defendant may face a difficult situation. As the winning party, the defendant's right to appeal the adverse holding on the constitutional question may be contested. *See* [*Mellen v.*]*Bunting*, 541 U.S., [1019,] 1025 [(2004)] (Scalia, J., dissenting from denial of certiorari) ("The perception of unreviewability undermines adherence to the sequencing rule we ... created" in *Saucier*)[.][2] ... In cases like *Bunting*, the "prevailing" defendant faces an unenviable choice: "compl[y] with the lower court's advisory dictum without opportunity to seek appellate [or certiorari] review," or "def[y] the views of the lower court, adher[e] to practices that have been declared illegal, and thus invit[e] new suits" and potential "punitive damages." ...

Adherence to *Saucier*'s two-step protocol departs from the general rule of constitutional avoidance and runs counter to the "older, wiser judicial counsel 'not to pass on questions of constitutionality ... unless such adjudication is unavoidable.'" *Scott*, 550 U.S., at 388 (Breyer, J., concurring)....

...

This flexibility properly reflects our respect for the lower federal courts that bear the brunt of adjudicating these cases. Because the two-step *Saucier* procedure is often, but not always, advantageous, the judges of the district courts and the courts of appeals are in the best position to determine the order of decisionmaking [that] will best facilitate the fair and efficient disposition of each case.

C

...

Our decision does not prevent the lower courts from following the *Saucier* procedure; it simply recognizes that those courts should have the discretion to decide

---

2. In *Bunting*, the Court of Appeals followed the *Saucier* two-step protocol and first held that the Virginia Military Institute's use of the word "God" in a "supper roll call" ceremony violated the Establishment Clause, but then granted the defendants qualified immunity because the law was not clearly established at the relevant time. *Mellen v. Bunting*, 327 F.3d 355, 365–376 (C.A.4 2003), *cert. denied*, 541 U.S. 1019 (2004). Although they had a judgment in their favor below, the defendants asked this Court to review the adverse constitutional ruling. Dissenting from the denial of certiorari, Justice Scalia, joined by Chief Justice Rehnquist, criticized "a perceived procedural tangle of the Court's own making." 541 U.S., at 1022. The "tangle" arose from the Court's "'settled refusal' to entertain an appeal by a party on an issue as to which he prevailed" below, a practice that insulates from review adverse merits decisions that are "locked inside" favorable qualified immunity rulings. *Id.*, at 1023, 1024.

whether that procedure is worthwhile in particular cases. Moreover, the development of constitutional law is by no means entirely dependent on cases in which the defendant may seek qualified immunity. Most of the constitutional issues that are presented in § 1983 damages actions and *Bivens* cases also arise in cases in which that defense is not available, such as criminal cases and § 1983 cases against a municipality, as well as § 1983 cases against individuals where injunctive relief is sought instead of or in addition to damages. *See Lewis*, 523 U.S., at 841, n. 5 (noting that qualified immunity is unavailable "in a suit to enjoin future conduct, in an action against a municipality, or in litigating a suppression motion").

We also do not think that relaxation of *Saucier*'s mandate is likely to result in a proliferation of damages claims against local governments. *Compare* Brief for Nat. Assn. of Counties *et al.*, as Amici Curiae 29, 30 ("[T]o the extent that a rule permitting courts to bypass the merits makes it more difficult for civil rights plaintiffs to pursue novel claims, they will have greater reason to press custom, policy, or practice [damages] claims against local governments"). It is hard to see how the *Saucier* procedure could have a significant effect on a civil rights plaintiff's decision whether to seek damages only from a municipal employee or also from the municipality. Whether the *Saucier* procedure is mandatory or discretionary, the plaintiff will presumably take into account the possibility that the individual defendant will be held to have qualified immunity, and presumably the plaintiff will seek damages from the municipality as well as the individual employee if the benefits of doing so (any increase in the likelihood of recovery or collection of damages) outweigh the litigation costs.

For further discussion

1. The Supreme Court's decision in *Pearson* has been criticized for failing to provide a standard for federal courts to use in deciding whether to reach the constitutional violation in a particular case, and instead leaving that decision to the complete discretion of the federal judges. *See* Jack M. Beermann, *Qualified Immunity and Constitutional Avoidance*, 2009 SUP. CT. REV. 139 (2009). *Plumhoff*, the next case in this Chapter, is a post-*Pearson* decision that followed the *Saucier* sequence.

2. *Harlow* reserved the question of whether the "state of the law" should be "evaluated by reference to the opinions of this Court, of the Courts of Appeals, or of the local District Court." *Harlow v. Fitzgerald*, 457 U.S. 800, 819 n.32 (1982). *Hope* later clarified that "[a]lthough earlier cases involving 'fundamentally similar' facts can provide especially strong support for a conclusion that the law is clearly established, they are not necessary to such a finding." *Hope v. Pelzer*, 536 U.S. 730, 741 (2002).

As of 2018, the Supreme Court still had not resolved what sources of authority can sufficiently define a constitutional right in the context of qualified immunity. For example, the Court found a circuit court's reliance on a single binding precedent—even though it was from the relevant circuit—to be insufficient to "clearly establish" a constitutional right "because it was not 'settled law.'" *District of Columbia v. Wesby*, 538 U.S. ___, 138 S. Ct. 577, 591 (2018) (further citation omitted). The

Court acknowledged that it had not yet resolved what sources of law render a constitutional right "clearly established":

> We have not yet decided what precedents—other than our own—qualify as controlling authority for purposes of qualified immunity.... We express no view on that question here. Relatedly, our citation to and discussion of various lower court precedents should not be construed as agreeing or disagreeing them, or endorsing a particular reading of them.

Id. at 591 n.8 (internal citations omitted). For similar reasons, the Supreme Court held in 2015 that prison officials were entitled to qualified immunity from the claim that they had violated plaintiff's "right to the proper implementation of adequate suicide prevention protocols" because such a right was not clearly established in 2004. *Taylor v. Barkes*, 575 U.S. ___, 135 S. Ct. 2042 (2015) (per curiam). The Court reasoned:

> No decision of this Court establishes a right to the proper implementation of adequate suicide prevention protocols. No decision of this Court even discusses suicide screening or prevention protocols. And "to the extent that a 'robust consensus of cases of persuasive authority'" in the Courts of Appeals "could itself clearly establish the federal right respondent alleges," *City and County of San Francisco v. Sheehan*, 575 U.S. ___, ___ (2015) (slip op., at 16), the weight of that authority at the time of Barkes's death suggested that such a right did not exist. [citing decisions of Sixth, Eleventh, Fifth, and Fourth Circuits].
>
> The Third Circuit nonetheless found this right clearly established by two of its own decisions, both stemming from the same case. Assuming for the sake of argument that a right can be "clearly established" by circuit precedent despite disagreement in the courts of appeals, neither of the Third Circuit decisions relied upon clearly established the right at issue.

Taylor, 135 S. Ct. at 2044–45. *See Lane v. Franks*, 573 U.S. 228, 243–46 (2014) (holding no "clearly established" constitutional right existed where there was "a discrepancy" in the relevant circuit's precedent, "no decision of this Court was sufficiently clear to cast doubt on the controlling [c]ircuit['s] precedent," and the controlling circuit's precedent conflicted with precedent from other circuits); *compare Carroll v. Carman*, 574 U.S. 13, 135 S. Ct. 348, 350 (2014) (per curiam) ("assuming for the sake of argument that a controlling circuit precedent could constitute clearly established federal law"); *Reichle v. Howards*, 566 U.S. 658, 665–66 (2012) (no clearly established right "[a]ssuming arguendo that controlling Court of Appeals' authority could be a dispositive source of clearly established law").

In *Reichle*, a post-*Pearson* decision, the Supreme Court declined to decide the constitutional question, and held that Secret Service agents were entitled to qualified immunity because the constitutional right allegedly violated by their arrest of plaintiff was not "clearly established" at the time of the arrest. In holding that the constitutional right had not been "clearly established" at the time of the arrest, the Court considered (1) its own precedent; (2) controlling precedent from the relevant circuit; and (3) one precedential decision from a different circuit that predated the arrest. In addition, to support its reasoning that the constitutional right remained unclear after the date of plaintiff's arrest in *Reichle*, the Supreme Court relied on (4) one precedential and one non-precedential decision from different circuits that *post*-dated the arrest. *Id.* at 665–71.

3. To determine whether a constitutional right is "clearly established," what sources of law do circuit courts rely on and direct trial courts and litigants to consult? *See, e.g.*, *Leiser v. Kloth*, 933 F.3d 696, 702 (7th Cir. 2019) ("We first look to whether the Supreme Court or this circuit has previously held that conduct analogous to the present case violates the right at issue ... The lack of specific precedent is not necessarily fatal to a qualified immunity defense because the Supreme Court has recognized that 'officials can still be on notice that their conduct violates established law ... in novel factual circumstances.' *Safford Unified Sch. Dist. No. 1 v. Redding*, 557 U.S. 364, 377–78 (2009).... If no existing precedent puts the conduct beyond debate, we next consider if this is one of the rare cases, like *Hope*, where the state official's alleged conduct is so egregious that it is an obvious violation of a constitutional right.") (further citation omitted); *Barna v. Bd. of Sch. Dirs. of the Panther Valley Sch. Dist.*, 877 F.3d 136, 142 (3d Cir. 2017) ("In conducting the inquiry into whether a right is clearly established, we look first for applicable Supreme Court precedent.... If none exists, we consider whether there is a case of controlling authority in our jurisdiction or a robust consensus of cases of persuasive authority in the Courts of Appeals [that] could clearly establish a right for purposes of qualified immunity.") (citations omitted); *McKenney v. Mangino*, 873 F.3d 75, 81 (1st Cir. 2017) ("[P]laintiff must point to 'controlling authority' or a 'consensus of cases of persuasive authority' that broadcasts 'a clear signal to a reasonable official that certain conduct falls short of the constitutional norm.'") (citation omitted); *Carollo v. Boria*, 833 F.3d 1322, 1333 (11th Cir. 2016) ("'Our Circuit uses two methods to determine whether a reasonable official would understand that his conduct violates a constitutional right.' 'The first asks whether binding opinions from the United States Supreme Court, the Eleventh Circuit Court of Appeals, and the highest court in the state where the action is filed ... gave [the defendant] fair warning that his treatment of [the plaintiff] was unconstitutional.' The second asks whether a public official's 'conduct lies so obviously at the very core of what [federal law] prohibits that the unlawfulness of the conduct was readily apparent to [the public official], notwithstanding the lack of fact-specific case law on point.'") (citations omitted); *Brown v. Chapman*, 814 F.3d 447, 461–62 (6th Cir. 2016) (relying on three non-precedential opinions to determine "that an individual's right to be free from a taser is clearly established when the individual is not actively resisting arrest or is already detained"); *Story v. Foote*, 782 F.3d 968, 970–71 (8th Cir. 2015) ("The Supreme Court recently has reserved judgment twice on the question whether decisions of a federal court of appeals are a source of clearly established law for purposes of qualified immunity analysis ... Following the approach of the Court in [*Reichle* and *Carroll*,] we assume for the sake of analysis that our decisions clearly establish that a convicted inmate has rights under the Fourth Amendment against unreasonable searches of his body"); *Irving v. Dormire*, 519 F.3d 441, 451 (8th Cir.

2008) ("[N]otwithstanding the lack of a decision squarely on point within our circuit, we conclude that given the clear weight of the circuits that have ruled on the question, [defendant] was on fair notice that to falsely label an inmate a snitch is to unreasonably subject that inmate to the threat of a substantial risk of harm at the hands of his fellow inmates."); *Burgess v. Lowery*, 201 F.3d 942, 944–45 (7th Cir.), *cert. denied*, 531 U.S. 817 (2000) ("[T]he absence of a decision by the Supreme Court or this court cannot be conclusive on the issue whether a right is clearly established in this circuit. There might be no decision in either court simply because the existence of the right was so clear, as a matter of the wording of a constitutional or statutory provision or decision in other circuits or in the state courts, that no one thought it worthwhile to litigate the issue ... To rule that until the Supreme Court has spoken, no right of litigants in this circuit can be deemed established before we have decided the issue would discourage anyone from being the first to bring a damages suit in this court; he would be *certain* to be unable to obtain any damages") (Posner, J.).

4. Will the *Pearson* option of disposing of cases on "clearly established" grounds without reaching the constitutional question result in perpetually unenforceable rights? A Sixth Circuit judge raised that "troubling potential" in the context of 14th Amendment police pursuit cases:

> ... As the Court notes, neither party has cited a single example of a case, from any circuit or district court, in which an officer's actions in a police chase have ultimately been found to shock the conscience, and I am aware of no such case. Thus, it appears that the set of examples of constitutionally impermissible police-pursuit behavior is currently an empty one. Although surprising, this was not especially troubling under the mandatory analytical regime set forth in *Saucier v. Katz*, 533 U.S. 194 (2001).
>
> ...
>
> But [*Saucier*] is no longer the law of the land; *Pearson* ... is. Under *Pearson*, ... a court may avoid deciding whether a constitutional violation occurred if the court is of the belief that, even assuming a violation, it was not clearly established at the time of the incident that the officer's actions crossed whatever constitutional line is at play in a given case ... However, ... the set of examples of impermissible police-pursuit behavior remains empty. I am therefore concerned about applying *Pearson* in future police-pursuit cases. Except in the most overwhelmingly egregious case, an officer that crosses the Fourteenth Amendment's threshold likely still would be entitled to qualified immunity because it was not clearly established that his specific actions were of the kind that crossed the line. Under *Pearson*, the court confronted with this officer's actions could avoid the constitutional question entirely and resolve the case on the clearly established prong. And so too could all subsequent courts.
>
> This, of course, results in a self-perpetuating cycle in Fourteenth Amendment police-pursuit cases: district courts will skip the constitutional inquiry in favor of disposing of cases on the "clearly established" prong, so there

> will never be an actual finding that an officer's conduct shocks the conscience, so courts will continue to be able to dispose of cases on the "clearly established" prong, and so on ... The set of conscience-shocking fact patterns could remain empty, and no body of case law will develop to define the parameters of what police conduct in a pursuit case could shock the conscience.
>
> This is a troubling potential because reflexive exercise of *Pearson* discretion in police-pursuit cases could result in essentially writing that cause of action off the books ... [Because I] read *Pearson* to encourage and support continued development of the constitutional law using a more targeted approach in small subsets of qualified immunity cases, such as police-pursuit cases, where the body of law still needs fattening ... I further encourage the district courts and future panels of this Court to follow suit in these kinds of cases by continuing to employ [*Saucier*'s] analytical sequence.

Jones v. Byrnes, 585 F.3d 971, 978–80 (6th Cir. 2009) (Martin, J., concurring). An amicus brief to the Supreme Court argued that *Pearson* has in fact created the "troubling" "self-perpetuating cycle" anticipated by the Sixth Circuit judge:

> The *Pearson* escape hatch creates a vicious cycle. Violations must be clearly established to survive qualified immunity; but qualified immunity itself stunts the development of the law and prevents it from becoming clearly established.... [*S*]*ee generally* Aaron L. Nielson & Christopher J. Walker, *The New Qualified Immunity*, 89 S. Cal. L. Rev. 1, 6 (2015) (federal courts "find constitutional violations yet grant qualified immunity less frequently now (less than one-tenth of the time) than they did before *Pearson*"). That some untold number of federal violations now passes through the federal courts without ever being acknowledged undercuts Section 1983's central accountability function.

Brief of Cross-Ideological Groups Dedicated to Ensuring Official Accountability, Restoring the Public's Trust in Law Enforcement, and Promoting the Rule of Law as Amici Curiae in Support of Petitioner, *Baxter v. Bracey*, No. 18-1287, 2019 WL 2370285, at *16–17 (May 31, 2019) (petition for certiorari denied while this book was in press). Likewise, a Fifth Circuit judge critiqued *Pearson* for allowing courts to grant immunity despite avoiding the constitutional issue by "skipping to the simpler second prong: no factually analogous precedent":

> Forgoing a knotty constitutional inquiry makes for easier sledding, no doubt. But the inexorable result is 'constitutional stagnation'—fewer courts establishing law at all, much less *clearly* doing so. Section 1983 meets Catch-22. Plaintiffs must produce precedent even as fewer courts are producing precedent. Important constitutional questions go unanswered precisely because no one's answered them before ... No precedent = no clearly established law = no liability ... Heads government wins, tails plaintiff loses.

Zadeh v. Robinson, 928 F.3d 457, 479–80 (5th Cir. 2019) (Willett, J., concurring in part)(petition for certiorari denied while this book was in press).

5. Recall Justice Breyer's concern in his concurrence in *Brosseau* that *Saucier*'s "rigid" sequence "can sometimes lead to a constitutional decision that is effectively insulated from review," a critique also referenced by the ACLU in its amicus brief in *Pearson*. Since *Brosseau* was decided, not only has *Pearson* allowed courts to reach the "clearly established" inquiry before deciding the constitutional question—one solution to Justice Breyer's concern—but the Supreme Court also has created an alternate path to review the constitutional question. In *Camreta v. Greene*, 563 U.S. 692 (2011), the Court held that it "may review a lower court's constitutional ruling at the behest of a government official granted immunity." *Id.* at 698. Article III's case-or-controversy requirement may be met when officials who prevailed on qualified immunity grounds before the appellate court seek to challenge a ruling that their conduct violated the Constitution:

> That is ... because the judgment may have prospective effect on the parties. The court in such a case says: 'Although this official is immune from damages today, what he did violates the Constitution and he or anyone else who does that thing again will be personally liable.' If the official regularly engages in that conduct as part of his job (as [the child protective service worker here] does), he suffers injury caused by the adverse constitutional ruling. So long as it continues in effect, he must either change the way he performs his duties or risk a meritorious damages action.... Only by overturning the ruling on appeal can the official gain clearance to engage in the conduct in the future. He thus can demonstrate, as we demand, injury, causation, and redressability. And conversely, if the person who initially brought the suit may again be subject to the challenged conduct, she has a stake in preserving the court's holding.

Id. at 702–03. The Court held that the adverse constitutional rulings challenged by government officials who prevailed on qualified immunity grounds before the circuit court "are rulings that have a significant future effect on the conduct of public officials—both the prevailing parties and their co-workers—and the policies of the government units to which they belong." *Id.* at 704. The Court explained that constitutional rulings adverse to the government and imbedded in opinions holding the government actors qualifiedly immune nevertheless are intended to shape future conduct by better defining constitutional rights. The Court further explained:

> [T]hey are rulings self-consciously designed to [effect future conduct of public officials] by establishing controlling law and preventing invocations of immunity in later cases. And still more: they are rulings designed this way with this Court's permission, to promote clarity—and observance—of constitutional rules.
>
> ...
>
> Consider a plausible but unsettled constitutional claim asserted against a government official in a suit for money damages. The court does not resolve the claim because the official has immunity. He thus persists in the challenged practice; he knows that he can avoid liability in any future damages action, because the law has still not been clearly established. Another plaintiff brings

> suit, and another court both awards immunity and bypasses the claim. And again, and again, and again. So the moment of decision does not arrive. Courts fail to clarify uncertain questions, fail to address novel claims, fail to give guidance to officials about how to comply with legal requirements.... Qualified immunity thus may frustrate 'the development of constitutional precedent' and the promotion of law-abiding behavior. *Pearson v. Callahan*, 555 U.S. 223, 237 (2009).

Id. at 704–06. The Court limited its holding in two ways. It clarified that there was no change in how it would decide whether to grant certiorari. *Id.* at 708–09. Further, the Court did not decide whether a court of appeals—as opposed to the Supreme Court—could hear an appeal from a government official who prevailed on immunity grounds. Because district court decisions are not binding "[m]any Courts of Appeals ... decline to consider district court precedent when determining if constitutional rights are clearly established for purposes of qualified immunity ... Otherwise said, district court decisions—unlike those from the courts of appeals—do not necessarily settle constitutional standards or prevent repeated claims of qualified immunity." *Id.* at 709 n.7.

6. For more on the practical consequences of *Pearson*, *see* Pamela S. Karlan, *Shoe-Horning, Shell Games, and Enforcing Constitutional Rights in the Twenty-first Century*, 78 U.M.K.C. L. Rev. 875 (2010) (arguing that the Supreme Court may be using the presence of the exclusionary rule in criminal cases as a rationale for weakening § 1983 damages remedies, and vice versa).

Questions to guide reading of *Plumhoff*

1. Why do you think that the Sixth Circuit decided *Plumhoff* in a non-precedential opinion?
2. *Plumhoff* was decided after *Pearson*. Yet the Court reached the constitutional question before deciding whether the constitutional right was clearly established. Why?
3. Why was there no Fourth Amendment violation in *Plumhoff*?
4. Litigants often argue in the alternative. That means the litigant makes two arguments that are inconsistent with one another and the second argument assumes the failure of the first argument. Should the Supreme Court decide qualified immunity cases in the alternative, as it did in *Plumhoff*? Why?

Plumhoff v. Rickard

572 U.S. 765 (2014)

Justice ALITO delivered the opinion of the Court.

The courts below denied qualified immunity for police officers who shot the driver of a fleeing vehicle to put an end to a dangerous car chase. We reverse and hold that the officers did not violate the Fourth Amendment. In the alternative, we conclude that the officers were entitled to qualified immunity because they violated no clearly established law.

...

III. A

Petitioners contend that ... they did not violate [decedent Donald] Rickard's Fourth Amendment rights and that, in any event, their conduct did not violate any Fourth Amendment rule that was clearly established at the time of the events in question. When confronted with such arguments, we held in *Saucier v. Katz*, 533 U.S. 194, 200 (2001), that "the first inquiry must be whether a constitutional right would have been violated on the facts alleged." Only after deciding that question, we concluded, may an appellate court turn to the question whether the right at issue was clearly established at the relevant time. *Ibid.*

We subsequently altered this rigid framework in *Pearson*, declaring that "*Saucier*'s procedure should not be regarded as an inflexible requirement." 555 U.S., at 227. At the same time, however, we noted that the *Saucier* procedure "is often beneficial" because it "promotes the development of constitutional precedent and is especially valuable with respect to questions that do not frequently arise in cases in which a qualified immunity defense is unavailable." 555 U.S., at 236....

Heeding our guidance in *Pearson*, we begin in this case with the question whether the officers' conduct violated the Fourth Amendment. This approach, we believe, will be "beneficial" in "develop[ing] constitutional precedent" in an area that courts typically consider in cases in which the defendant asserts a qualified immunity defense. *See Pearson*, *supra*, at 236.

B

A claim that law-enforcement officers used excessive force to effect a seizure is governed by the Fourth Amendment's "reasonableness" standard. *See Graham v. Connor*, 490 U.S. 386 (1989); *Tennessee v. Garner*, 471 U.S. 1 (1985).... [In *Scott*, w]e held that a "police officer's attempt to terminate a dangerous high-speed car chase that threatens the lives of innocent bystanders does not violate the Fourth Amendment, even when it places the fleeing motorist at risk of serious injury or death." [550 U.S. 372,] 386 [2007].

...

We see no basis for reaching a different conclusion here. As we have explained [in this opinion], the chase in this case exceeded 100 miles per hour and lasted over five minutes. During that chase, Rickard passed more than two dozen other vehicles, several of which were forced to alter course. Rickard's outrageously reckless driving posed a grave public safety risk. And while it is true that Rickard's car eventually collided with a police car and came temporarily to a near standstill, that did not end the chase. Less than three seconds later, Rickard resumed maneuvering his car. Just before the shots were fired, when the front bumper of his car was flush with that of one of the police cruisers, Rickard was obviously pushing down on the accelerator because the car's wheels were spinning, and then Rickard threw the car into reverse "in an attempt to escape." Thus, the record conclusively disproves respondent's claim that the chase in the present case was already over when petitioners began shooting. Under the circumstances at the moment when the shots were fired, all that a reasonable police officer could have concluded was that Rickard was intent on resuming his flight and that, if he was allowed to do so, he would once again pose a deadly threat for others on the road. Rickard's conduct even after the shots were fired—as noted, he managed to drive away despite the efforts of the police to block his path—underscores the point.

In light of the circumstances we have discussed, it is beyond serious dispute that Rickard's flight posed a grave public safety risk, and here, as in *Scott*, the police acted reasonably in using deadly force to end that risk.

2

We now consider respondent's contention that, even if the use of deadly force was permissible, petitioners acted unreasonably in firing a total of 15 shots. We reject that argument. It stands to reason that, if police officers are justified in firing at a suspect in order to end a severe threat to public safety, the officers need not stop shooting until the threat has ended.... Here, during the 10-second span when all the shots were fired, Rickard never abandoned his attempt to flee. Indeed, even after all the shots had been fired, he managed to drive away and to continue driving until he crashed. This would be a different case if petitioners had initiated a second round of shots after an initial round had clearly incapacitated Rickard and had ended any threat of continued flight, or if Rickard had clearly given himself up. But that is not what happened.

In arguing that too many shots were fired, respondent relies in part on the presence of [passenger] Kelly Allen in the front seat of the car, but we do not think that this factor changes the calculus. Our cases make it clear that "Fourth Amendment rights are personal rights which ... may not be vicariously asserted." [citations omitted]. Thus, the question before us is whether petitioners violated Rickard's Fourth Amendment rights, not Allen's.... But Allen's presence in the car cannot enhance Rickard's Fourth Amendment rights. After all, it was Rickard who put Allen in danger by fleeing and refusing to end the chase, and it would be perverse if his disregard for Allen's safety worked to his benefit.

C

We have held that petitioners' conduct did not violate the Fourth Amendment, but even if that were not the case, petitioners would still be entitled to summary judgment based on qualified immunity.

An official sued under § 1983 is entitled to qualified immunity unless it is shown that the official violated a statutory or constitutional right that was "'clearly established'" at the time of the challenged conduct. *Ashcroft v. al-Kidd*, 563 U.S. ___, ___, 131 S.Ct. 2074, 2080 (2011). And a defendant cannot be said to have violated a clearly established right unless the right's contours were sufficiently definite that any reasonable official in the defendant's shoes would have understood that he was violating it. *Id.*, at 2083–2084. In other words, "existing precedent must have placed the statutory or constitutional question" confronted by the official "beyond debate." *Ibid.* In addition, "[w]e have repeatedly told courts ... not to define clearly established law at a high level of generality," id., at 2074, since doing so avoids the crucial question whether the official acted reasonably in the particular circumstances that he or she faced. We think our decision in *Brosseau v. Haugen*, 543 U.S. 194 (2004) (*per curiam*) squarely demonstrates that no clearly established law precluded petitioners' conduct at the time in question. In *Brosseau*, we held that a police officer did not violate clearly established law when she fired at a fleeing vehicle to prevent possible harm to "other officers on foot who [she] believed were in the immediate area, ... occupied vehicles in [the driver's] path[,] and ... any other citizens who might be in the area." Id., at 197 [further citation omitted]. After surveying lower court decisions regarding the reasonableness of lethal force as a response to vehicular flight, we observed that this is an area "in which the result depends very much on the facts of each case" and that the cases "by no means 'clearly establish[ed]' that [the officer's] conduct violated the Fourth Amendment." 543 U.S., at 201. In reaching that conclusion, we held that *Garner* and *Graham*, which are "cast at a high level of generality," did not clearly establish that the officer's decision was unreasonable. 543 U.S., at 199.

Brosseau makes plain that as of February 21, 1999—the date of the events at issue in that case—it was not clearly established that it was unconstitutional to shoot a fleeing driver to protect those whom his flight might endanger. We did not consider later decided cases because they "could not have given fair notice to [the officer]." Id., at 200, n. 4. To defeat immunity here, then, respondent must show at a minimum either (1) that the officers' conduct in this case was materially different from the conduct in *Brosseau* or (2) that between February 21, 1999, and July 18, 2004, there emerged either "'controlling authority'" or a "robust 'consensus of cases of persuasive authority,'" *al-Kidd*, *supra*, at 2084 (quoting *Wilson v. Layne*, 526 U.S. 603, 617); some internal quotation marks omitted), that would alter our analysis of the qualified immunity question. Respondent has made neither showing.

To begin, certain facts here are more favorable to the officers. In *Brosseau*, an officer on foot fired at a driver who had just begun to flee and who had not yet driven his car in a dangerous manner. In contrast, the officers here shot at Rickard to put an end to what had already been a lengthy, high-speed pursuit that indisputably posed a danger both to the officers involved and to any civilians who happened to be nearby.... Attempting to distinguish *Brosseau*, respondent focuses on the fact that the officer there fired only 1 shot, whereas here three officers collectively fired 15 shots. But it was certainly not clearly established at the time of the shooting in this case that the number of shots fired, under the circumstances present here, rendered the use of force excessive.

Since respondent cannot meaningfully distinguish *Brosseau*, her only option is to show that its analysis was out of date by 2004. Yet respondent has not pointed us to any case—let alone a controlling case or a robust consensus of cases—decided between 1999 and 2004 that could be said to have clearly established the unconstitutionality of using lethal force to end a high-speed car chase.

. . .

For further discussion

1. *Plumhoff* concerned the claim of the driver of the car, who was killed. *Plumhoff* did not concern a claim by the passenger in the car, who also was killed. Footnote 4 of *Plumhoff* identifies "some disagreement" about a potential passenger claim:

> There seems to be some disagreement among lower courts as to whether a passenger in Allen's situation can recover under a Fourth Amendment theory. *Compare Vaughan v. Cox*, 343 F.3d 1323 (C.A.11 2003) (suggesting yes), and *Fisher v. Memphis*, 234 F.3d 312 (C.A.6 2000) (same), with *Milstead v. Kibler*, 243 F.3d 157 (C.A.4 2001) (suggesting no), and *Landol-Rivera v. Cruz Cosme*, 906 F.2d 791 (C.A.1 1990) (same). We express no view on this question. We also note that in *County of Sacramento v. Lewis*, 523 U.S. 833, 836 (1998), the Court held that a passenger killed as a result of a police chase could recover under a substantive due process theory only if the officer had "a purpose to cause harm unrelated to the legitimate object of arrest."

Plumhoff v. Rickard, 572 U.S. 765, 778 n.4 (2014). Review the excerpt from *Lewis* in Chapter 6, Section F, discussing the distinction between claims under the 4th and 14th Amendments. Given your reading of the *Lewis* excerpt, why do you think the Supreme Court in *Plumhoff* "express[ed] no view" on the issue of whether the passenger could assert a Fourth Amendment claim?

2. In *Tolan v. Cotton*, 572 U.S. 650 (2014) (*per curiam*), the Supreme Court took the unusual step of granting certiorari to correct a circuit court's application of a well-settled legal rule, the summary judgment standard. The Supreme Court vacated the judgment "so that the court can determine whether, when [the injured party's] evidence is properly credited and factual inferences are reasonably drawn in his favor, [the police officer's] actions violated clearly established law." *Id.* at 660.

> During the early morning hours of New Year's Eve, 2008, police sergeant Jeffrey Cotton fired three bullets at Robert Tolan; one of those bullets hit its target and punctured Tolan's right lung. At the time of the shooting, Tolan was unarmed on his parents' front porch about 15 to 20 feet away from Cotton.
>
> . . .
>
> [U]nder either prong [of the qualified immunity analysis], courts may not resolve genuine disputes of fact in favor of the party seeking summary judgment. *See Brosseau v. Haugen*, 543 U.S. 194, 195, n. 2 (2004) (*per curiam*); *Saucier*, *supra*, at 201; *Hope*, *supra*, at 733, n. 1.... Our qualified-immunity cases illustrate the importance of drawing inferences in favor of the nonmovant, even when, as here, a court decides only the clearly-established

> prong of the standard. In cases alleging unreasonable searches or seizures, we have instructed that courts should define the 'clearly established' right at issue on the basis of the 'specific context of the case.' *Saucier*, *supra*, at 201; *see also Anderson v. Creighton*, 483 U.S. 635, 640–641 (1987). Accordingly, courts must take care not to define a case's 'context' in a manner that imports genuinely disputed factual propositions. *See Brosseau*, *supra*, at 195, 198 (inquiring as to whether conduct violated clearly established law '"in light of the specific context of the case"' and construing "facts ... in a light most favorable to" the nonmovant).... In holding that Cotton's actions did not violate clearly established law, the Fifth Circuit failed to ... credit evidence that contradicted some of its key factual conclusions[,] improperly "weigh[ed] the evidence" and resolved disputed issues in favor of the moving party, *Anderson*, 477 U.S., at 249.
>
> First, the court relied on its view that at the time of the shooting, the Tolans' front porch was 'dimly-lit.' ... Second, the Fifth Circuit stated that Tolan's mother 'refus[ed] orders to remain quiet and calm,' thereby 'compound[ing]' Cotton's belief that Tolan 'presented an immediate threat to the safety of the officers.'.... But here, too, the court did not credit directly contradictory evidence.... Third, the Court concluded that Tolan was 'shouting,' ... and 'verbally threatening' the officer, ... in the moments before the shooting.... [T]he parties agree, that while Cotton was grabbing the arm of his mother, Tolan told Cotton, '[G]et your fucking hands off my mom.'... But Tolan testified that he 'was not screaming.'.... A jury could well have concluded that a reasonable officer would have heard Tolan's words not as a threat, but as a son's plea not to continue any assault of his mother. Fourth, the Fifth Circuit inferred that at the time of the shooting, Tolan was 'moving to intervene in Sergeant Cotton's' interaction with his mother....
>
> The witnesses on both sides come to this case with their own perceptions, recollections, and even potential biases. It is in part for that reason that genuine disputes are generally resolved by juries in our adversarial system.... [T]he court should have acknowledged and credited Tolan's evidence with regard to the lighting, his mother's demeanor, whether he shouted words that were an overt threat, and his positioning during the shooting....

Tolan, 572 U.S. at 651–60. Consider *Tolan* in preparing for Simulation 9.

3. In a dissent joined by Justice Ginsburg, Justice Sotomayor sounded an alarm about the trajectory of Supreme Court qualified immunity jurisprudence. Justice Sotomayor wrote:

> [T]his Court routinely displays an unflinching willingness 'to summarily reverse courts for wrongly denying officers the protection of qualified immunity' but 'rarely intervene[s] where courts wrongly afford officers the benefit of qualified immunity in these same cases.' [quoting her own earlier dissent] ... Such a one-sided approach to qualified immunity transforms the doctrine

> into an absolute shield for law enforcement officers, gutting the deterrent effect of the Fourth Amendment.
>
> The majority today exacerbates that troubling asymmetry. Its decision is not just wrong on the law; it also sends an alarming signal to law enforcement officers and the public. It tells officers that they can shoot first and think later, and it tells the public that palpably unreasonable conduct will go unpunished.

Kisela v. Hughes, ___ U.S. ___, 138 S. Ct. 1148, 1162 (2018) (Sotomayor, J., dissenting). The next Supreme Court case excerpted, *Mullenix*, is an example of a summary reversal of a circuit court's denial of qualified immunity.

Questions to guide reading of *Mullenix*

1. In a single decision in *Mullenix*, the Supreme Court both granted certiorari and ruled on the merits. Why do you think the Court did not require briefing or argument on the merits?
2. In *Mullenix*, the Supreme Court applies several decisions excerpted in this book, such as *Scott* (Chapter 6), *Lytle* (Chapter 6), and *Brousseau* (this Chapter). Do you agree with its reading of those cases?
3. Do you see tension between the 2002 holding of *Hope* and the holdings of more recent qualified immunity decisions, such as *Mullenix*, *Brousseau*, and *Ashcroft v. al-Kidd*?

Mullenix v. Luna

___ U.S. ___, 136 S. Ct. 305 (2015)

PER CURIAM.

[This § 1983 action alleges Trooper Chadrin Mullenix violated the Fourth Amendment by using excessive force against Israel Leija, Jr. Leija led police on an 18-minute chase at speeds between 85 and 110 miles per hour. Leija called police, claiming to have a gun and threatening to shoot at police officers if they did not abandon their pursuit. Police set up tire spikes. Trooper Mullenix drove to an overpass, intending to set up a spike strip, but considered shooting at Leija's car to disable it. Mullenix had not received training in this tactic and had not attempted it before. Mullenix took a shooting position on the overpass, 20 feet above the highway. Respondents allege that Mullenix still could hear his supervisor's response to "stand by" and "see if the spikes work first." From the overpass, Mullenix fired six shots in the dark at a car traveling 85 miles per hour, killing Leija. A second later, the car hit spike strips deployed to stop it.]

We address only the qualified immunity question, not whether there was a Fourth Amendment violation in the first place.... In this case, the Fifth Circuit held that Mullenix violated the clearly established rule that a police officer may not " 'use deadly force against a fleeing felon who does not pose a sufficient threat of harm to the officer or others.'" 773 F.3d, at 725.... The relevant inquiry is whether existing precedent placed the conclusion that Mullenix acted unreasonably in these circumstances "beyond debate." [*Ashcroft v. al-Kidd*, 563 U.S. 731, 741 (2011)]. The general principle that deadly force requires a sufficient threat hardly settles this matter. *See* [Fifth Circuit precedent from 2009] ("[I]t would be unreasonable to expect a police officer to make the numerous legal conclusions necessary to apply *Garner* to a high-speed car chase ...").

Far from clarifying the issue, excessive force cases involving car chases reveal the hazy legal backdrop against which Mullenix acted. In *Brosseau* itself, the Court held that an officer did not violate clearly established law when she shot a fleeing suspect out of fear that he endangered "other officers on foot who [she] *believed* were in the immediate area," "the occupied vehicles in [his] path," and "any other citizens who *might* be in the area." 543 U.S., at 197.... The threat Leija posed was at least as immediate as that presented by a suspect who had just begun to drive off and was headed only in the general direction of officers and bystanders. *Id.*, at 196–197. By the time Mullenix fired, Leija had led police on a 25-mile chase at extremely high speeds, was reportedly intoxicated, had twice threatened to shoot officers, and was racing towards an officer's location.

...

The Court has thus never found the use of deadly force in connection with a dangerous car chase to violate the Fourth Amendment, let alone to be a basis for denying qualified immunity. Leija in his flight did not pass as many cars as the drivers in *Scott* [Chapter 6] or *Plumhoff* [Chapter 11]; traffic was light on [the highway]. At the same time, the fleeing fugitives in *Scott* and *Plumhoff* had not verbally threatened to kill any officers in their path, nor were they about to come upon such officers. In any event, none of our precedents "squarely governs" the facts here. Given Leija's conduct, we cannot say that only someone "plainly incompetent" or who "knowingly violate[s] the law" would have perceived a sufficient threat and acted as Mullenix did. *Malley*, 475 U.S., at 341.

The dissent [argues Mullenix violated] clearly established law because he did not wait to see if the spike strips would work before taking action.... The dissent can cite no case from this Court denying qualified immunity because officers entitled to terminate a high-speed chase selected one dangerous alternative over another.

Even so, the dissent argues, there was no governmental interest that justified acting before Leija's car hit the spikes. [Mullenix feared Leija might shoot at or run over officers manning the spike strips and that, if Leija hit the spike strips, he might continue driving toward officers.] Ultimately, whatever can be said of the wisdom of Mullenix's choice, this Court's precedents do not place the conclusion that he acted unreasonably in these circumstances "beyond debate." *al-Kidd*, 563 U.S., at 741.

...

Cases decided by the lower courts since *Brosseau* likewise have not clearly established that deadly force is inappropriate in response to conduct like Leija's. The Fifth Circuit here principally relied on its own decision in *Lytle v. Bexar County,* 560 F.3d 404 (2009) [Chapter 6] denying qualified immunity to a police officer who had fired at a fleeing car and killed one of its passengers. That holding turned on the court's assumption, for purposes of summary judgment, that the car was moving away from the officer and had already traveled some distance at the moment the officer fired. See *id.,* at 409.... Without implying that *Lytle* was either correct or incorrect, it suffices to say that *Lytle* does not clearly dictate the conclusion that Mullenix was unjustified in perceiving grave danger and responding accordingly, given that Leija was speeding towards a confrontation with officers he had threatened to kill.

Cases that the Fifth Circuit ignored also suggest that Mullenix's assessment of the threat Leija posed was reasonable. [citing decisions from Eleventh and Sixth Circuits]. Other cases are simply too factually distinct to speak clearly to the specific circumstances here. [*e.g.,* suspects who may have done little more than flee at relatively low speeds]. These cases shed little light on whether the far greater danger of a speeding fugitive threatening to kill police officers waiting in his path could warrant deadly force.... [Q]ualified immunity protects actions in the "'hazy border between excessive and acceptable force.'" *Brosseau, supra,* at 201 (citation omitted). Because the constitutional rule applied by the Fifth Circuit was not "'beyond debate,'" *Stanton v. Sims,* 571 U.S. ___, ___, 134 S. Ct. 3, 7 (2013) (*per curiam*), we grant Mullenix's petition for certiorari and reverse the Fifth Circuit's determination that Mullenix is not entitled to qualified immunity.

For further discussion

Should the doctrine of qualified immunity doctrine be substantially curtailed? Some say yes. For example, Justice Thomas criticized the qualified immunity doctrine as a free-wheeling policy choice unmoored from both its statutory origin and the proper historical inquiry of whether the government officials would have been immune from analogous claims under 1871 common law. *Ziglar v. Abbasi,* ___ U.S. ___, 137 S. Ct. 1843, 1872 (2017) (Thomas, J., concurring). Justice Thomas warned: "Until we shift the focus of our inquiry to whether immunity existed at common law, we will continue to substitute our own policy preferences for the mandates of Congress. In an appropriate case, we should reconsider our qualified immunity jurisprudence." *Id.* at 1872 (Thomas, J., concurring). *See* Joanna C. Schwartz, *The Case Against Qualified Immunity*, 93 Notre Dame L. Rev. 1797, 1799 n.10 (2018) (summarizing Justice Sotomayor's dissents in 2015 (*Mullenix*) and again in 2018 (*Kisela*) as "express[ing] concern that the Court's qualified immunity decisions contribute to a culture of police violence"); *For further discussion*, Note 3, before *Mullenix* (excerpting Justice Sotomayor's dissent in *Kisela*).

Similarly, a recent amicus brief to the Supreme Court argued that:

> qualified immunity often bars even those plaintiffs who can prove their case from remedying a wrong: harm, but no foul. Qualified immunity thus enables public officials who violate federal law to sidestep their legal obligations to

> the victims of their misconduct. In so doing, the doctrine corrodes the public's trust in those officials—law enforcement in particular—making on-the-ground policing more difficult and dangerous for all officers, including that vast majority who endeavor to uphold their constitutional obligations. And the doctrine's primary justification, to prevent public officials from paying their own judgments, has proven empirically unfounded as the widespread availability of indemnification already provides that protection. Neither the text nor the history of Section 1983 compels this perverse outcome. *See, e.g.*, William Baude, *Is Qualified Immunity Unlawful?*, 106 Cal. L. Rev. 45 (2018).

Amici Brief of Cross-Ideological Groups in *Baxter v. Bracey*, No. 18-1287 2019 WL 2370285, at *6–7 (May 30, 2019). Likewise, the Cato Institute's amicus brief in the same case argued that *stare decisis* did not preclude revisiting qualified immunity doctrine:

> [C]ontemporary qualified-immunity doctrine is not just legally unfounded—it is also proving practically unworkable in the lower courts, and it is severely undermining official accountability across the nation. If the Court is inclined to reconsider qualified immunity, it should not hesitate to do so based on *stare decisis*. The amorphous nature of the "clearly established law" test has precluded the doctrine from effecting the stability and predictability that normally justify respect for precedent. Moreover, the Court has already treated qualified immunity as a judge-made, common-law doctrine, and thus appropriate for revision. *See Pearson v. Callahan*, 555 U.S. 223, 233–34 (2009).

Brief of Cato Institute as Amicus Curiae Supporting Petitioner, *Baxter v. Bracey*, No. 18-1287, 2019 WL 2354727, at *2–3 (May 30, 2019). While this book was in press, the petition for certiorari was denied.

Also recently, Fifth Circuit Judge Don R. Willett opined that, to some, "qualified immunity smacks of unqualified impunity, letting public officials duck consequences for bad behavior ... as long as they were the *first* to behave badly." *Zadeh v. Robinson*, 928 F.3d 457, 479 (5th Cir. 2019) (Willett, J., concurring in part). Judge Willett broadly critiqued the doctrinal muddle of the "clearly established" prong, and expressed particular concern about its consequences for defining constitutional rights in the face of changing technology:

> Merely proving a constitutional deprivation doesn't cut it; plaintiffs must cite functionally identical precedent that places the legal question 'beyond debate' to 'every' reasonable officer ... This current 'yes harm, no foul' imbalance leaves victims violated but not vindicated ... But courts of appeals are divided—intractably—over precisely what degree of factual similarity must exist. How indistinguishable must existing precedent be? On the one hand, the Supreme Court reassures plaintiffs that its caselaw 'does not require a case directly on point for a right to be clearly established.' On the other hand, the Court admonishes that 'clearly established law must be "particularized" to the facts of the case.' How to square these abstract instructions?
>
> ...

> Second, constitutional litigation increasingly involves cutting-edge technologies. If courts leapfrog the underlying constitutional merits in cases raising novel issues like digital privacy, then constitutional clarity—matter-of-fact guidance about what the Constitution requires—remains exasperatingly elusive.... Indeed, it's curious how this entrenched, judge-created doctrine excuses constitutional violations by limiting the statute Congress passed to redress constitutional violations.

Id. at 479–81 (Willett, J., concurring in part) (further citation omitted). Cert was denied in 2020.

In 2019, the Supreme Court declined to consider a challenge to the broad scope of qualified immunity doctrine. One brief in support of certiorari had argued:

> Courts now rarely provide substantive analysis of constitutional claims against state officials and such officials are increasingly insulated from § 1983 liability as new fact patterns, technologies, and applications of the Constitution arise. *See* [Karen] Blum, [*Qualified Immunity: Time to Change the Message,*] 93 Notre Dame L. Rev. [1885], 1902–1903 (2018).... Current doctrine thus forces § 1983 plaintiffs to find 'existing precedent' that puts 'the statutory or constitutional question *beyond debate,*' *Mullenix,* 136 S. Ct. at 308 (emphasis added) (quoting *al-Kidd,* 563 U.S. at 741), even as the Court has all but halted the development of new precedents to rely on in the future.
>
> The effect of the current jurisprudence is to shield unconstitutional conduct by state actors rather than protecting people from such conduct. Courts' frequent rejection of § 1983 claims without analysis of the claimed violation, even where the conduct at issue appears plainly unconstitutional, sends an "alarming signal" to other potential offenders: that "palpably unreasonable conduct will go unpunished." *Kisela,* 138 S. Ct. at 1162 (Sotomayor, J., dissenting); *see also Mullenix,* 136 S. Ct. at 316 (Sotomayor, J., dissenting); *Young v. Borders,* 850 F.3d 1274, 1299–1300 (11th Cir. 2017) (Martin, J., dissenting from denial of rehearing en banc)....

Brief for Scholars of the Law of Qualified Immunity as Amici Curiae Supporting Petitioners in *I.B. v. Woodard,* No. 18-1173, 2019 WL 1596321, at *3–4 (April 10, 2019).

C. Development of Doctrine in the Circuits

This book occasionally uses a single case to illustrate multiple legal doctrines. It does so in part to help you appreciate the intellectual challenge of sophisticated law practice, where a single case may involve more than one legal doctrine. It also does so to facilitate learning of multiple legal concepts without requiring you to learn new facts.

For example, note that *Butera* was included in Chapter 4 to illustrate the state-created danger doctrine; *Butera* is included later in Chapter 13 to illustrate the evolution of the parental liberty interest doctrine; and *Butera* is excerpted below to illustrate the development of qualified immunity in the circuit courts. *Butera* is also the basis for Law Practice Simulation 8.

Judicial opinions excerpted in casebooks are significantly edited to focus on one or two concepts. In law practice, by contrast, lawyers read and use unedited cases that may illustrate multiple legal principles. Practicing lawyers draft pleadings and briefs that address multiple legal principles and discuss multiple legal principles involved in a client's case in oral interactions with opposing counsel, neutral decision makers, and other lawyers representing the same client. In civil rights litigation, it is not uncommon for a single Complaint to allege multiple theories of recovery under federal and state law and for lawyers to have to develop facts to support (or refute) all of those theories. It is not uncommon for a single summary judgment brief or appellate brief to address several complex constitutional and statutory issues. Often, litigants will brief arguments in the alternative, such as the absence of a constitutional violation and, in the alternative, the applicability of qualified immunity. Reading unedited judicial decisions is a good reminder of how complex—and challenging—law practice can be. In lieu of assigning any case by citation, this book instead uses certain cases to illustrate multiple doctrines.

In reading the circuit court applications of the qualified immunity doctrine, put yourself in the shoes of a practitioner and consider whether more recent Supreme Court decisions affect the analysis, *e.g.*, the Supreme Court's decisions in *Mullenix* (2015), *Plumhoff* (2014), *Tolan* (2014), and *Pearson* (2009).

Exercise 11-B

When is a constitutional right "clearly established"? The below facts, concerning Officer MacPherson's traffic stop of Mr. Bryan, may be familiar to you from Chapter 6. Consider two opposing views of whether a 4th Amendment right was clearly established. Both views analyze the same facts. As you read, consider these questions: (1) How is the constitutional right defined in the 2009 opinion? Contrast how the constitutional right is defined in the 2010 opinion. (2) Contrast how the two opinions read *Hope*. (3) Is one "clearly established" analysis more persuasive to you than the other? Why?

The 2009 opinion:

[Mr. Bryan already had lived through an emotionally trying morning when Officer MacPherson approached Bryan's car at an intersection because he was not wearing a seatbelt. Bryan realized that he had mistakenly failed to buckle his seatbelt and, becoming angry at himself, simply stared straight ahead. Although Bryan complied with Officer MacPherson's request to pull over to the curb, because he was angry with himself, he hit his steering wheel and was yelling expletives to himself when he stepped out of his car.]

"There is no dispute that Bryan was agitated, standing outside his car, yelling gibberish and hitting his thighs, clad only in his boxer shorts

> and tennis shoes. It is also undisputed that Bryan did not verbally threaten Officer MacPherson and, according to Officer MacPherson, was standing twenty to twenty-five feet away and not attempting to flee. The one material dispute concerns whether Bryan made any movement toward the officer. Officer MacPherson testified that Bryan took 'one step' toward him, but Bryan says he did not take any step, and the physical evidence indicates that Bryan was actually facing away from Officer MacPherson. Without giving any warning, Officer MacPherson shot Bryan with his taser gun. One of the taser probes embedded in the side of Bryan's upper left arm. The electrical current immobilized him whereupon he fell face first into the ground, fracturing four teeth and suffering facial contusions."

The Ninth Circuit concluded that Bryan's 4th Amendment rights were violated; below is its initial analysis of whether that 4th Amendment right was "clearly established":

> [W]here an officer's conduct so clearly offends an individual's constitutional rights, we do not need to find closely analogous case law to show that a right is clearly established.... *Hope v. Pelzer*, 536 U.S. 730, 741 (2002) ("[O]fficials can still be on notice that their conduct violates established law even in novel factual circumstances.") ... In the excessive force context, it is clearly established that "force is least justified against nonviolent misdemeanants who do not flee or actively resist and pose little or no threat to the security of the officers or the public." *Brown v. City of Golden Valley*, 574 F.3d 491, 499 (8th Cir. 2009); *see also Casey v. City of Federal Heights*, 509 F.3d 1278, 1285 (10th Cir. 2007). No reasonable officer confronting a situation where the need for force is at its lowest—where the target is a nonviolent, stationary misdemeanant twenty feet away—would have concluded that deploying intermediate force without warning was justified. We thus hold that Officer MacPherson's use of significant force in these circumstances does not constitute a "reasonable mistake" of either fact or law.... Officer MacPherson is therefore not entitled to qualified immunity for his use of the Taser X26 against Bryan.[10]

Six months later, the same Ninth Circuit panel issued a superseding opinion. While adhering to the finding that Officer MacPherson had violated Mr. Bryan's 4th Amendment rights, the Ninth Circuit reached the opposite conclusion on whether that right was "clearly established."

---

10. *Bryan v. McPherson*, 590 F.3d 767, 781–82 (9th Cir. 2009), *superseded by* 608 F.3d 614, 629 (9th Cir. 2010). The June 2010 opinion was superseded by an opinion in November 2010 that reached the same result and also denied rehearing *en banc*. 630 F.3d 805 (9th Cir. 2010).

The 2010 opinion:

> We do not need to find closely analogous case law to show that a right is clearly established ... *Hope v. Pelzer*, 536 U.S. 730, 741 (2002) ("[O]fficials can still be on notice that their conduct violates established law even in novel factual circumstances."); *Oliver* [*v. Fiorino*], 586 F.3d [898,] 907 [(11th Cir. 2009)] (finding that a right can be clearly established where the officer's conduct "lies so obviously at the very core of what the Fourth Amendment prohibits that the unlawfulness of the conduct was readily apparent to [the officer], notwithstanding the lack of fact-specific case law"). However, as of July 24, 2005, there was no Supreme Court decision or decision of our court addressing whether the use of a taser, such as the Taser X26, in dart mode constituted an intermediate level of force. Indeed, before that date, the only statement we had made regarding tasers in a published opinion was that they were among the "variety of non-lethal 'pain compliance' weapons used by police forces." *San Jose Charter of Hells Angels Motorcycle Club* [*v. City of San Jose*], 402 F.3d [962,] 969 n.8 [(9th Cir. 2005)]. And, as the Eighth Circuit has noted, "[t]he Taser is a relatively new implement of force, and case law related to the Taser is developing." *Brown v. City of Golden Valley*, 574 F.3d 491, 498 n.5 (8th Cir. 2009). Two other panels have recently, in cases involving different circumstances, concluded that the law regarding tasers is not sufficiently clearly established to warrant denying officers qualified immunity. [citing two Ninth Circuit decisions issued in 2010 but concerning events in 2004 and 2006]. Based on these recent statements regarding the use of tasers, and the dearth of prior authority, we must conclude that a reasonable officer in Officer MacPherson's position could have made a reasonable mistake of law regarding the constitutionality of the taser use in the circumstances Officer MacPherson confronted in July 2005. Accordingly, Officer MacPherson is entitled to qualified immunity.[11]

- The first opinion was issued on December 28, 2009. The superseding opinion was issued on June 18, 2010. If you were advising a city government in the Ninth Circuit, from which date would you consider the 4th Amendment law governing the use of Tasers to have been altered by *Bryan*?

  1) after the June 2010 decision?
  2) after the December 2009 decision?
  3) before July 2005, the date of Officer MacPherson's traffic stop?
  4) between July 2005–June 18, 2010?

11. *Bryan v. MacPherson*, 608 F.3d 614, 629 (9th Cir. 2010).

- The 4th Amendment law governing the use of tasers is still developing. But developing that law is not free. Plaintiff's counsel in *Bryan* likely paid for research, drafting the complaint, taking or defending at least two depositions, and briefing summary judgment; in addition, Plaintiff's counsel may have spent resources on court appearances, discovery, reviewing documents, and oral argument. Should Plaintiff's counsel be entitled to attorney's fees under § 1988? Was the attorney's role in developing the constitutional standards for use of tasers consistent with the "private attorney general" concept that motivated Congress to enact the attorney's fees statute?
- Consider the interplay between qualified immunity and the attorney's fees statute. If an individual defendant violated a person's constitutional rights but was entitled to qualified immunity because the right was not clearly established, the plaintiff may have successfully demonstrated the violation of a constitutional right and thereby helped define a new right—but plaintiff's attorney would not be entitled to attorney's fees. *See Hewitt v. Helms*, 482 U.S. 755 (1987) ("[w]e conclude that a favorable judicial statement of law in the course of litigation that results in judgment against the plaintiff does not suffice to render him a 'prevailing party'"). One blog devoted to Section 1983 litigation summarized one view of the "doctrines and disincentives" facing plaintiff's counsel:

  Let's look at the tangles:

  - A state actor is entitled to qualified immunity.
  - Qualified immunity applies when the law has not been clearly established.
  - Courts are more willing than ever to find in favor of defendants based on qualified immunity.
  - A lawyer who creates clearly-established law will not get paid.[12]
- Is there tension between the purpose of § 1988 and the § 1983 doctrine of qualified immunity? In light of the above, revisit Exercise 10-A and consider whether you would draft an additional amendment to § 1988 to address qualified immunity. Or should a defendant who is held immune from liability not be liable for any attorney's fees, because to do otherwise would frustrate the very purpose of qualified immunity?

---

12. *See* Mike Tuesday, *Time To Amend 42 U.S.C. Section 1988 (As Qualified Immunity Has Gutted It)*, Section 1983 Blog (May 25, 2010), http://www.section1983blog.com/2010/05/time-to-amend-42-usc-section-1988-as.html.

Questions to guide re-reading of *Butera*

Butera is the basis for Law Practice Simulation 8. Note that *Butera* was included in Chapter 4 (state-created danger) and is in Chapter 13 (evolution of the parental liberty interest).

1. How did *Butera* identify the two prongs of the qualified immunity analysis?
2. Why did the D.C. Circuit hold in *Butera* that the district court erred in defining Eric Butera's constitutional right as a right to "life, bodily integrity, personal security and personal privacy"? What policy reasons support defining constitutional rights more specifically in the context of qualified immunity? How did the D.C. Circuit instead define the constitutional right at stake?
3. In *Butera*, the D.C. Circuit adopted the state-created danger/state endangerment theory. How did *Butera* define the substantive due process right that it is adopting?
4. In *Butera*, the D.C. Circuit recognized that, per *Lewis*, conduct that is "conscience-shocking" in one context may not be in another. Why does *Butera* hold that, to "shock the conscience" under the circumstances of this case, the police officers only had to have been "deliberately indifferent" to Eric Butera's safety? Could the court have instead required the higher fault standard of "intent to harm"? Why or why not?
5. In deciding whether the constitutional right was "clearly established" as of December 1997, what sources of law did the D.C. Circuit consult? How is footnote 11 relevant to the potential significance of *DeShaney*'s relationship to state-created danger doctrine? How is footnote 11 potentially relevant to the "clearly established" inquiry?
6. *Butera* held that, in December 1997, Eric Butera's constitutional right to protection by the District of Columbia from third-party violence was not clearly established. What two reasons did *Butera* give for that holding?
7. How did *Butera* suggest that the voluntariness of Eric Butera's conduct might be relevant to the "clearly established" inquiry?

Butera v. District of Columbia

235 F.3d 637 (D.C. Cir. 2001)

ROGERS, Circuit Judge.

This appeal arises from the tragic death of 31-year-old Eric Butera while he served as an undercover operative for the ... Police Department of the District of Columbia. [Please review the facts set out in Chapter Four.]

...

Qualified immunity ... generally shields State officials from liability for their discretionary functions "insofar as their conduct does not violate clearly established statutory or constitutional rights of which a reasonable person would have known." *Harlow v. Fitzgerald*, 457 U.S. 800, 818 (1982). To evaluate a substantive due process claim in which State officials have raised the defense of qualified immunity, and particularly where defendants can be spared the burdens of long trials and where the court can provide clarity in standards for official conduct, the Supreme Court has instructed that courts ordinarily follow a two-prong analysis. *See Wilson v. Layne*, 526 U.S. 603, 609 (1999); *County of Sacramento v. Lewis*, 523 U.S. 833, 841 n. 5 (1998).... First, courts must address the threshold issue in any action brought under § 1983: "whether the plaintiff has alleged the deprivation of an actual constitutional right at all." *Wilson*, 526 U.S. at 609 ... *see also Sacramento*, 523 U.S. at 841 n. 5.... In this stage, courts must not define the relevant constitutional right in overly general terms, lest they strip the qualified immunity defense of all meaning:

> For example, the right to due process of law is quite clearly established by the Due Process Clause, and thus there is a sense in which any action that violates that Clause (no matter how unclear it may be that the particular action is a violation) violates a clearly established right. Much the same could be said of any other constitutional or statutory violation. But if the test of "clearly established law" were to be applied at this level of generality, it would bear no relationship to the "objective legal reasonableness" that is the touchstone of *Harlow*. Plaintiffs would be able to convert the rule of qualified immunity that our cases plainly establish into a rule of virtually unqualified liability simply by alleging violation of extremely abstract rights.

Anderson v. Creighton, 483 U.S. 635, 639 (1987). Consequently, the court must define the right to a degree that would allow officials "reasonably [to] anticipate when their conduct may give rise to liability for damages," thus preserving "the balance that [Supreme Court] cases strike between the interests in vindication of citizens' constitutional rights and in public officials' effective performance of their duties." *Id.* [further citation omitted]. Put otherwise, the constitutional right must be identified "at the appropriate level of specificity" for a court to determine the second prong of the inquiry: whether the right was "clearly established." *Wilson*, 526 U.S. at 615. A constitutional right was "clearly established" at the time of the events in question only if "[t]he contours of the right [were] sufficiently clear that a reasonable officer would understand that what he [was] doing violate[d] that right." *Anderson*, 483 U.S. at 640....

The district court ruled in denying summary judgment to the District of Columbia that Eric Butera had a constitutional right to "life," and that Terry Butera had a "constitutionally protected liberty interest" in the companionship of her son.... At trial, the district court instructed the jury that Eric Butera's right to "life," "personal security," "bodily integrity," and "personal privacy," and Terry Butera's right to her son's companionship, were "clearly-established constitutional rights as of the date of the incident, December 4, 1997." On appeal, the court reviews *de novo* the district court's legal conclusion that the constitutional rights allegedly violated existed and that they were clearly established as a matter of law in December 1997....

Under the first stage of the *Wilson* inquiry—whether the plaintiff has asserted the relevant constitutional rights at the appropriate level of specificity—we conclude, consistent with the Supreme Court's instructions in *Anderson* and *Wilson*, that the district court erred by defining the constitutional rights as Eric Butera's right to life, bodily integrity, personal security, and personal privacy, and as Terry Butera's "liberty interest" in the companionship of her son. Although courts have acknowledged the existence of these general rights in certain circumstances, *see, e.g.*, ... *Stanley v. Illinois*, 405 U.S. 645, 651 (1972); *Kneipp v. Tedder*, 95 F.3d 1199, 1201 (3d Cir. 1996); *Wood v. Ostrander*, 879 F.2d 583, 589 (9th Cir. 1989), they are overly broad where a qualified immunity defense is asserted. Applying the standards of *Wilson* and *Anderson*, we conclude that the relevant inquiries are (1) whether Eric Butera has a constitutional right to protection by the District of Columbia from danger that it created or enhanced that resulted in harm by third parties....[13] This narrower definition of the rights allows a reasonable police officer to anticipate whether his actions amount to a constitutional violation.

A. State Endangerment.

As a general matter, a State's failure to protect an individual from private violence, even in the face of a known danger, "does not constitute a violation of the Due Process Clause." *DeShaney v. Winnebago County Dep't of Soc. Servs.*, 489 U.S. 189, 197 (1989).... The Due Process Clause, the Supreme Court has emphasized, is "phrased as a limitation on the State's power to act, not as a guarantee of certain minimal levels of safety and security." *DeShaney*, 489 U.S. at 195.... It followed in *DeShaney* that the State was not constitutionally liable for the permanent brain damage to a child who was beaten severely by his father, notwithstanding evidence that the State was aware of the child's physical abuse yet failed to remove the child from his father's custody. *See id.* at 202.

Despite this general rule, the *DeShaney* Court acknowledged that, in "certain limited circumstances[,] the Constitution imposes upon the State affirmative duties of care and protection with respect to particular individuals." *Id.* at 198. One such circumstance, the Court stated, arises when the State "takes a person into its custody and holds him there against his will," hence depriving him of liberty. *Id.* at 199–200; *see also Youngberg v. Romeo*, 457 U.S. 307, 317 (1982); *Estelle v. Gamble*, 429 U.S. 97, 103–04 (1976)....[9]

In addition to custody, the *DeShaney* Court left open the possibility that, under a second set of circumstances, the State could be liable for harm inflicted to an individual by third parties. In explaining the absence of constitutional liability for the child's physical abuse by his father, the Court stated:

---

13. Editor: The second constitutional right asserted "(2) whether Terry Butera has a liberty interest in the society and companionship of her independent adult child," is the subject of Chapter 13.

9. In *Estelle*, the Supreme Court held that the cruel and unusual punishment clause of the Eighth Amendment obliges the State to provide medical care to prisoners. *See* 429 U.S. at 103–04. *Youngberg* extended this obligation as a matter of substantive due process to mental patients who were involuntarily committed. *See* 457 U.S. at 315–16....

> While the State may have been aware of the dangers that Joshua faced in the free world, it played no part in their creation, nor did it do anything to render him more vulnerable to them.

DeShaney, 489 U.S. at 201. All circuit courts of appeals, except this circuit, have by now relied on this passage in *DeShaney* to acknowledge that there may be possible constitutional liability under § 1983 "where the state creates a dangerous situation or renders citizens more vulnerable to danger."[10] *Reed v. Gardner*, 986 F.2d 1122, 1125 (7th Cir. 1993), *cert. denied*, 510 U.S. 947 (1993).[11] In *Reed*, police officers arrested a presumably sober driver and left behind an obviously intoxicated passenger, who subsequently drove the car and was involved in a collision with the victims. The Seventh Circuit held that the victims of the collision stated a substantive due process claim because "[p]olice officers who remove sober drivers and leave behind drunk passengers with keys may be said to create a danger." *Id.* at 1125. Similarly, in *Wood* [*v. Ostrander*, 879 F.2d 583, 589–90 (9th Cir. 1989), *cert. denied*, 498 U.S. 938 (1990)], a police officer arrested a drunk driver at 2:30 a.m. and impounded his vehicle, leaving the driver's female passenger by the side of the road in a high-crime area. The passenger, who was five miles from her home, accepted a ride from a stranger, who raped her. *See* 879 F.2d at 586. The Ninth Circuit held that the passenger had "raised a triable issue of fact as to whether [the police officer] affirmatively placed [her] in a position of danger." *Id.* at 589–90 (citation omitted). Additionally, in *Kallstrom v. City of Columbus*, 136 F.3d 1055 (6th Cir. 1998), city officials released personal information from the files of undercover police officers (including names, addresses, and telephone numbers of the officers and their families) to defense counsel for the alleged drug conspirators whom the officers had investigated. The Sixth Circuit held that "the City's actions placed the officers and their family members in 'special danger' by substantially increasing the likelihood that a private actor would deprive them of their liberty interest in personal security." *Id.* at 1067.

The circuit courts have adopted the State endangerment concept in a range of fact patterns concerning alleged misconduct by State officials. Regardless of the conduct at issue, however, the circuits have held that a key requirement for constitutional liability is affirmative conduct by the State to increase or create the danger that results in harm to the individual. No constitutional liability exists where the State actors "had no hand in creating a danger but [simply] 'stood by and did nothing when suspicious circumstances dictated a more active role for them.'" *Reed*, 986 F.2d at 1125 (quoting *DeShaney*, 489 U.S. at 203); *see also Kallstrom*, 136 F.3d at 1066; *Armijo v. Wagon Mound Public Schools*, 159 F.3d 1253, 1262–63 (10th Cir. 1998); *Frances-Colon v. Ramirez*, 107 F.3d 62, 64 (1st Cir. 1997); *Estate of Stevens v. City of Green Bay*, 105 F.3d 1169, 1176–77 (7th Cir. 1997); *Johnson v. Dallas Indep. Sch. Distr.*, 38 F.3d 198, 201 (5th Cir. 1994); *Dwares v. City of New York*, 985 F.2d 94, 99 (2d Cir.

10. [Citing cases from First–Eleventh Circuits.]

11. Even before *DeShaney*, several courts of appeals had recognized a State's constitutional duty to protect an individual whom the State placed in a situation of heightened danger. [citing cases from 1988, 1986, 1985 and 1982, from the Eighth, Ninth, First, Eleventh, and Seventh Circuits].

1993); *Gregory v. City of Rogers*, 974 F.2d 1006, 1010 (8th Cir. 1992) (*en banc*); *L.W. v. Grubbs*, 974 F.2d 119, 121 (9th Cir. 1992). Absent such affirmative conduct by the State to endanger an individual, courts have rejected liability under a State endangerment concept. *See, e.g., S.S. v. McMullen*, 225 F.3d 960, 962 (8th Cir. 2000) (*en banc*); *Stevens v. Umsted*, 131 F.3d 697, 705 (7th Cir. 1997).

...

The development of the State endangerment concept by the circuit court of appeals is consistent with the notion, implied in *DeShaney*, that something less than physical custody may suffice to present a substantive due process claim. We join the other circuits in holding that, under the State endangerment concept, an individual can assert a substantive due process right to protection by the District of Columbia from third-party violence when District of Columbia officials affirmatively act to increase or create the danger that ultimately results in the individual's harm. In so doing, we are "mindful of the caution we must exercise in expanding the liberty interests protected by substantive due process," ... (citing and quoting *Collins v. City of Harker Heights*, 503 U.S. 115, 125 (1992)), but conclude that the circuits' exposition of the concept has mitigated some of the general concerns about the lack of guideposts; to that extent, the court is hardly "break[ing] new ground in this field." *Collins*, 503 U.S. at 125.

To assert a substantive due process violation, however, the plaintiff must also show that the District of Columbia's conduct was "so egregious, so outrageous, that it may fairly be said to shock the contemporary conscience." [*Lewis v.*] *Sacramento*, 523 U.S. at 847 n. 8. This stringent requirement exists to differentiate substantive due process, which is intended only to protect against arbitrary government action, from local tort law. *See id.* at 845–46, 848–49; *Daniels v. Williams*, 474 U.S. 327, 331 (1986).... Hence, while it may be possible under District of Columbia tort law for a plaintiff to obtain a remedy by proving mere negligence or failure to exercise due care, this "lowest common denominator of customary tort liability" is "categorically beneath the threshold of constitutional due process." [*Lewis v.*] *Sacramento*, 523 U.S. at 848–49.

> It is, on the contrary, behavior at the other end of the culpability spectrum that would most probably support a substantive due process claim; conduct intended to injure in some way unjustifiable by any government interest is the sort of official action most likely to rise to the conscience-shocking level.

Id. at 849 ...

The Supreme Court in [*Lewis v.*] *Sacramento* acknowledged, however, that in some circumstances the "point of the conscience shocking" can be reached by proving "something more than negligence but 'less than intentional conduct, such as recklessness or gross negligence.'" *Id.* (citation omitted). While such proof "is a matter for closer calls," *id.*, this lower threshold, the Supreme Court has instructed, is appropriate in circumstances where the State has a heightened obligation toward the individual. For example, where the State has taken a person into custody, it "so restrains [his] liberty that it renders him unable to care for himself"; therefore, the "Constitution imposes upon [the State] a corresponding duty to assume some responsibility for his safety and general well-being." *Id.* at 851 (quoting *DeShaney*, 489 U.S. at 199–200). Further, where an individual is in State custody, prison officials have "the luxury ... of ... time to make unhurried judgments, upon the chance for repeated reflection, largely uncomplicated by the pulls of competing obligations." *Id.* at 853. Because of these special circumstances, a State official's deliberate indifference in the context of state custody can be "truly shocking." *Id.*

As in the context of State custody, the State also owes a duty of protection when its agents create or increase the danger to an individual. Like prison officials who are charged with overseeing an inmate's welfare, State officials who create or enhance danger to citizens may also be in a position where "actual deliberation is practical." *Id.* at 851. In the instant case, the officers had the opportunity to plan the undercover operation with care. In view of the officers' duty to protect Eric Butera, he may prove that the officers' treatment of him in connection with the attempted undercover drug buy "shocked the conscience" by meeting the lower threshold of "deliberate indifference." ...

The remaining question, under the second prong of the *Wilson* test, is whether, in December 1997, the law surrounding the violation of Eric Butera's asserted due process right to be protected from third-party violence in the context of State endangerment was "sufficiently clear that a reasonable officer would understand that what he [was] doing violate[d] that right." *Anderson*, 483 U.S. at 640; *see also Wilson*, 526 U.S. at 615. Qualified immunity is intended to "provide government officials with the ability 'reasonably to anticipate when their conduct may give rise to liability for damages,'" *Anderson*, 483 U.S. at 646 (citation omitted). In light of this purpose, an official "[cannot] reasonably be expected to anticipate subsequent legal developments, nor ... fairly be said to 'know' that the law forb[ids] conduct not previously identified as unlawful." *Harlow*, 457 U.S. at 818. Consequently, the court must determine whether the Supreme Court, the District of Columbia Circuit, and, to the extent that there is a consensus, other circuits have spoken clearly on the lawfulness of the conduct at issue.[17]

Upon examining relevant case law on the "State endangerment" exception to *DeShaney*, we conclude that, in December 1997, Eric Butera's constitutional right to protection by the District of Columbia from third-party violence was not clearly established within the meaning of *Anderson*. First, as discussed, this circuit has never recognized constitutional liability in the context of a State endangerment claim, and the court in [an earlier D.C. Circuit decision] intimated that it would construe narrowly the express custody exception set forth in *DeShaney* ... Moreover, the only Supreme Court authority to support a State endangerment concept consisted of the often-quoted dictum in *DeShaney*, which simply "leaves the door open for liability" in this context. *Reed*, 986 F.2d at 1125.

---

17. In *Anderson*, the Supreme Court made clear that, in evaluating whether the right at issue was clearly established, a court need not have found the very action in question unlawful in the past. *See id.* at 640. Rather, a court must consider whether "in the light of pre-existing law the unlawfulness [was] apparent." *Id.* To make this determination, however, the parties have pointed us to no source other than case law from the Supreme Court and the circuits.

Second, as of 1997, the "contours" of the rights created by the State endangerment concept were not settled among the circuits. *See Anderson*, 483 U.S. at 640. While courts of appeals had adopted the State endangerment concept without prompting Supreme Court review, [citing denial of *certiorari* in six circuit court decisions,] there was little consistency in courts' explanations of the types of actions that would amount to constitutional liability. The Eighth Circuit, for example, first acknowledged that "[i]t is not clear, under *DeShaney*, how large a role the state must play in the creation of danger and in the creation of vulnerability before it assumes a corresponding constitutional duty to protect." *Freeman v. Ferguson*, 911 F.2d 52, 55 (8th Cir. 1990). The court later stated that, to establish constitutional liability, the plaintiff must demonstrate that he "would not have been in harm's way but for the government's affirmative actions." *Carlton v. Cleburne County*, 93 F.3d 505, 508 (8th Cir. 1996). The Seventh Circuit, in turn, provided a slightly different standard, finding State endangerment where the State "*greatly* increased the danger to [the plaintiff] while constricting access to self-help." *Estate of Stevens v. City of Green Bay*, 105 F.3d 1169, 1177 (7th Cir. 1997) (emphasis added). Other circuits, however, adopted more elaborate tests to determine whether the actions of State officials amounted to State endangerment and therefore triggered constitutional liability.[20]

While all of these tests share the key element of State endangerment, namely, affirmative conduct by State actors, *see, e.g.*, *Reed*, 986 F.2d at 1126, they are inconsistent in their elaborations of the concept. For example, the circuits have adopted

---

20. For example, while stating in 1995 that it had "yet to decide definitively whether the State endangerment theory is a viable mechanism for finding a constitutional injury," the Third Circuit identified four elements that State endangerment cases from other circuits had "in common":

> (1) the harm ultimately caused was foreseeable and fairly direct; (2) the state actor acted in willful disregard for the safety of the plaintiff; (3) there existed some relationship between the state and the plaintiff; [and] (4) the state actors used their authority to create an opportunity that otherwise would not have existed for the third party's crime to occur.

Mark v. Borough of Hatboro, 51 F.3d 1137, 1152 (3d Cir. 1995). In 1996, the Third Circuit applied the four elements outlined in *Mark* to hold that an individual could assert a constitutional claim based on the State endangerment theory. *See Kneipp*, 95 F.3d at 1208–11. The Fifth Circuit, in turn, stated the following common elements, while also acknowledging in 1994 that it had never predicated relief based on a State endangerment claim:

> [T]he environment created by the state actors must be dangerous; they must know it is dangerous; and ... they must have used their authority to create an opportunity that would not otherwise have existed for the third party's crime to occur.

Johnson, 38 F.3d at 201. Finally, the Tenth Circuit expounded a multi-part test to determine whether the defendant created a "special danger" sufficient to trigger the State's constitutional liability:

> Plaintiff must demonstrate that (1) [plaintiff] was a member of a limited and specifically definable group; (2) Defendants' conduct put [the plaintiff] ... at substantial risk of serious, immediate and proximate harm; (3) the risk was obvious or known; (4) Defendants acted recklessly in conscious disregard of that risk; and (5) such conduct, when viewed in total, is conscience shocking.

Uhlrig [v. Harder, 64 F.3d 567, 574 (10th Cir. 1995), *cert. denied*, 516 U.S. 1118 (1996)]. In 1998, the Tenth Circuit added another criterion to the *Uhlrig* test: Plaintiff must show "that the charged state entity and the charged individual defendant actors created the danger or increased the plaintiff's vulnerability to the danger in some way." *Armijo*, 159 F.3d at 1263.

different nexus requirements, *compare Mark v. Borough of Hatboro*, 51 F.3d 1137, 1152 (3d Cir. 1995), and *Carlton*, 93 F.3d at 508, with *Uhlrig v. Harder*, 64 F.3d 567, 574 (10th Cir. 1995), and employed differing degrees of specificity in defining actionable conduct, *compare Estate of Stevens*, 105 F.3d at 1177, and *Carlton*, 93 F.3d at 508, with *Johnson*, 38 F.3d at 201, *Mark*, 51 F.3d at 1152, and *Uhlrig*, 64 F.3d at 574. Moreover, although we do not suggest that State liability would necessarily be eliminated or mitigated, to date no circuit has applied the State endangerment concept where an arguably voluntary informant, much less a police operative like Eric Butera, was involved. This lack of clarity in the law of the circuits leads us to conclude that no reasonable police officer would have known that his or her actions were subject to a State endangerment limitation. *See Anderson*, 483 U.S. at 640 …

Given the criteria imposed by the qualified immunity defense, as well as the absence of Supreme Court and District of Columbia Circuit precedent, we hold that the law in this circuit was insufficiently clear in December 1997 to alert the District of Columbia and its police officers to possible constitutional liability (as distinct from tort liability) for their conduct in using Eric Butera as a police operative in an undercover operation. While the law was evolving in the circuits to cover situations where either (1) there was State control or custody, or (2) the State knowingly created or increased the risk that an individual would be exposed to danger, we do not know whether, had a State endangerment concept been recognized in this circuit in 1997, Eric Butera's claim would have survived. In any event, the officers were entitled to qualified immunity.

…

Questions to guide reading of *Carr*

Carr is the basis for Law Practice Simulation 9.

1. As to the 4th Amendment claim by Carr against Officer Fortson, what are the relevant facts? Does drawing a picture help to visualize them?
2. What does *Carr* identify as the two basic steps of qualified immunity analysis? What constitutional right did Carr claim Officer Fortson violated by shooting Carr?
3. Why did the Eleventh Circuit in *Carr* hold that Officer Fortson was entitled to qualified immunity from Carr's 4th Amendment claim of excessive force, even though Carr claimed he did not have a gun and no gun was found?
4. Does the court's analysis assume that neither Carr nor Wymbs had a gun and that Officer Fortson made a mistake of fact? If so, why does the court quote the exchange in footnote 25? In other ways, is the court's analysis entirely consistent with the court's obligation to view the facts in the light most favorable to the non-moving party and to refrain from making credibility determinations?
5. Is what Carr thought relevant to the police officers' decision to shoot?

6. Instead of reaching qualified immunity, could the court have held that there was no constitutional violation? Is the court's analysis consistent with that view?

Carr v. Tatangelo

338 F.3d 1259 (11th Cir. 2003)

BIRCH, Circuit Judge.

I. BACKGROUND

In the early morning hours of Sunday, October 24, 1999, in Monroe, Georgia, defendants-appellees, Officers Joseph Tatangelo, Anthony Fortson, and Damien Mercer, were pursuing an individual who had fled during an investigatory stop that involved plaintiffs-appellants Romeo Carr and Cedrick Wymbs.[1] The officers decided to patrol ... a high-crime area known for drug trafficking, to look for the individual who had fled as well as to watch for drug activity.[2] While the officers were observing a pay telephone and the street for evidence of drug activity, visibly intoxicated Harold Henderson appeared, and Officer Mercer asked him what he was doing in the area at that time. Henderson, who said that he was going to get drugs for others at Carr's house, gave his name as Harold Wade and consented to a pat-down search. In Henderson's wallet, Officer Mercer found Henderson's parole identification card, which revealed that Henderson had given the officers an incorrect name and birth date. The officers also called into dispatch to see if Henderson had any outstanding warrants.

To avoid going to jail, Henderson proposed a "deal" to the officers: in exchange for letting him go, Henderson volunteered to go to Carr's house and have somebody come out with drugs for the officers to arrest.... The officers agreed and let Henderson walk to Carr's house, although Officer Mercer kept his wallet. After Henderson had departed from the presence of the officers, they learned that there were three outstanding warrants for his arrest, including theft by taking and parole violation by escape.... At that point, the objective of the officers' surveillance changed, and they went to Carr's house to watch for Henderson to emerge so that they could apprehend and arrest him. The officers never saw Henderson again.

The officers positioned themselves behind trees and bushes near Carr's house to give them a view of the house without being seen. Officer Tatangelo was across the street from Carr's house in an area where there were bushes and shrubs; Officer Fortson was on the same side of the street as Officer Tatangelo, but farther away from

---

1. This investigatory stop at approximately 1:30 A.M.... was the subject of a prior 42 U.S.C. § 1983 case in which the district court accorded the officers qualified immunity for handcuffing Carr, Wymbs, and others to secure them while Officer Mercer chased the individual who had run from the scene. ...

2. Officer Tatangelo testified that, in addition to drug trafficking, this area had "shootings, aggravated assaults," and other crimes.... While the officers were on duty in those early morning hours, seventeen-year-old Chris Peters was riding with Officer Fortson in his patrol car as part of the police ride-along program. Peters accompanied the officers in their surveillance, which is the subject of this case, and was left to fend for himself when the shooting occurred.

the house; and Officer Mercer was on the side of Carr's house lying on the ground in some bushes. As the officers watched, a car with three or four women drove up in front of Carr's house, and the horn sounded. Carr went out to the car and conversed with the women from the passenger's side.

As Carr walked out to the vehicle and Wymbs walked outside and down the street to use the pay telephone, Henderson entered the house. As he returned from the pay telephone and walked toward Carr's house, Wymbs noticed movement in the bushes across the street, which he believed to be a person. When he reached the car where Carr was talking to the women, Wymbs asked Carr to come to the rear of the vehicle, told Carr of his concern, asked him to come and look with him, and threw a rock into the bushes where he had detected movement "[t]o see whether it was a real person." ... After throwing his rock, Wymbs asked: "[W]ho is that over there?" ... He then called: "Reggie, Reggie."[5] ... Noticing no movement after Wymbs had thrown his rock and also thinking that the hidden individual might be Williams, Carr threw a rock hard and had his hand raised to throw another rock when he was shot.[6]

Wymbs testified that, when he walked back from the pay telephone and threw rocks into the bushes, his sunglasses were on top of his head.... After throwing rocks, Wymbs "was folding [his sunglasses] up and putting them in [his] pocket," and Carr "was about to throw his [rock], [when the police officers] started shooting." ... Carr has suggested that Wymbs's folding his sunglasses was the "click-clack noise" that the officers heard that caused them to start shooting.... Carr testified that the noise of Wymbs's removing his glasses and placing them in his pocket had caused him to think that Wymbs "had shot [Carr] at first." ...

The police officers related the incident as they perceived it from their hidden locations. Officer Fortson testified that Officer Mercer communicated over the police radio that Carr and Wymbs knew that the officers were in the bushes ... Carr and Wymbs walked across the street and were pointing and looking into the bushes. Officer Fortson testified that one asked: "[I]s that the 'po-po'?" ... The other responded: "[T]hat's not the 'po-po.'" ... Immediately thereafter, Officer Fortson "heard someone racking a round,"[7] ... which caused him to draw his weapon, although he did not fire because there was no target; he waited until he "actually perceived a threat," ... Officer Tatangelo then screamed "'[P]olice,'" ... whereupon Officer Fortson could see Carr and Wymbs pointing a weapon at Officer Tatangelo ... Officer Fortson

5. Reggie Williams was the individual who had stabbed Carr's brother in an altercation the previous night. The brother was in a hospital ... and Carr had visited him there earlier that evening.

6. Carr testified that he believed that Williams might harm "somebody," either Carr "or anybody who would come out of our house." ... He further testified: "If the police would have never said they shot me, I wouldn't even know today who it was."

7. In addition to his professional experience as a police officer, Officer Fortson had military experience that had taught him the distinctive sound of the chambering of a bullet in a gun: "[e]ight years in the military, three years in the infantry, two years as a unit armorer taking care of the weapons, and a total of five years' law enforcement experience." ... Although he did not see a gun at the time ... he heard the unique sound of someone racking a gun: "It's kind of a combination between a click and a sliding sound...."

verified: "I'm certain that one of them pointed a weapon at Officer Tatangelo." ... Officer Tatangelo testified that, when the gun was pointed at him, it "scared the hell out of me." ... Then Officer Tatangelo "heard the rack of the gun [Carr or Wymbs] was holding," ... and he saw "what [he] believed to be a small portion of the barrel" of a semi-automatic weapon ...[9]

Officer Fortson testified that he was the first to fire his weapon because Carr and Wymbs "pointed a weapon at Officer Tatangelo," ... and he "was protecting a third party," ... Officer Fortson fired only once because he saw the muzzle of Officer Tatangelo's gun, knew that he was moving toward Officer Fortson, and he did not want him to be in his line of fire. Officer Tatangelo testified that, following Officer Fortson's one shot, he fired his gun "eight" times and that he was shooting to kill. He believed that Carr had shot at him, and he shot so many times "[t]o eliminate the threat."[10]

Like Officer Tatangelo, Officer Fortson testified that he believed that his life was in danger when he heard the chambering of a bullet, that he "thought [Carr and Wymbs] were going to shoot Officer Tatangelo," ... and believed that, if they would "shoot him," then they would shoot Officer Fortson also.... When Officer Fortson shot his gun, he aimed at center mass consistent with his training. Although Officer Fortson testified that "I'm the one who hit Romeo Carr," ... he also stated that, at the time, "I d[id]n't know whether I hit him or not,".... Moreover, Carr and Wymbs "took off running towards the house roughly almost instantaneously after the first shot." ...

After Officers Tatangelo and Fortson had ascertained that they were not wounded, and Officer Mercer had run across the street to join them, all the officers ran back to their cars following the shooting to await backup that they had summoned. Officer Fortson testified that they did not know "how far away backup was" and that they "didn't want to be in a hostile area," which did not "make good common sense." ... Consequently, the officers ran back to their cars in a more secure area rather than pursuing Carr and Wymbs.[11] Frightened by his first experience of being close to gunfire in

---

9. Similarly, Officer Mercer, who had "been around guns and hunting all [his] life" was "[a]bsolutely 100 percent positive" that he heard the racking of a gun ... He further testified that he "was almost 100 percent sure that [Officers Tatangelo and Fortson] were working with their guns cocked and ready to fire" because most officers "carry a loaded weapon at work"; otherwise, "you might as well not have one." ... He emphasized that "[p]olice officers don't rack guns before they shoot them." ...

10. Officer Tatangelo explained the threat that he was trying to eliminate: "The threat was that he had a gun, he was pointing it at me, and I pulled my weapon to defend myself, my fellow officers, and the citizens of the city of Monroe. That's what I was doing.... It just happened so fast." ...

11. Officer Fortson explained the reason for not pursuing Carr and Wymbs: "I wasn't going to chase somebody with a gun, not when they go into their own house." ... He also explained the officers' reasoning for leaving an unsecured area and running to their cars in a secure area to wait for backup:

> [W]e were in basically a very unsecured area, we needed to get back to an area where we were secured, we were safe, and we could get backup to come in there without them being compromised.
>
> ...
>
> An unsecured area is an area that we don't have control over. I had no control over that street whatsoever. By me standing there doesn't mean I had control over it. I could not control if

the line of duty, Officer Mercer radioed that shots had been fired, and, in addition to regular police backup, he "called for the National Guard," Mercer Dep. at 90, and a helicopter to search the woods with light, *id.* at 96. No gun that Carr or Wymbs may have had was located outside or inside Carr's house, and they denied having a gun.[12]

When the shooting began, Carr "took off running" and did not realize that he had been shot until he was inside his house.... Moreover, Carr outran Wymbs, who had not been shot, was the first back at his house, and dove in the front door.... He lay on the floor in the front hallway until the paramedics arrived.

After the shooting stopped, approximately twenty people came out into the street, and they were angry about the shooting. Wymbs and Carr's brother ran outside, stopped a county police car that was driving by, and informed that Carr had been shot. The county police called for backup and an ambulance. Wymbs testified that, from the end of the shooting until the county police were notified, was "less than five minutes." ... The Monroe City Police arrived in "less than two minutes" and secured the scene.... Then, the ambulance arrived and took Carr to the hospital for medical assistance.

...

II. DISCUSSION

...

Under qualified immunity, "government officials performing discretionary functions generally are shielded from liability for civil damages insofar as their conduct does not violate clearly established statutory or constitutional rights of which a reasonable person would have known." *Harlow v. Fitzgerald*, 457 U.S. 800, 818 (1982). This defense "provides ample protection to all but the plainly incompetent or those who knowingly violate the law." *Malley v. Briggs*, 475 U.S. 335, 341 (1986). "[Q]ualified immunity operates 'to ensure that before they are subjected to suit, officers are on notice their conduct is unlawful.'" *Hope v. Pelzer*, 536 U.S. 730, 739 (2002) (quoting *Saucier v. Katz*, 533 U.S. 194, 206 (2001)).

"The threshold inquiry a court must undertake in a qualified immunity analysis is whether plaintiff's allegations, if true, establish a constitutional violation." *Id.* at 736. Even "constitutionally impermissible conduct" might not render government officials liable for civil damages if those actions had not been clearly established as violative of the Constitution when they occurred. *Id.* at 739.

> For a constitutional right to be clearly established, its contours "must be sufficiently clear that a reasonable official would understand that what he is

---

> somebody were to come out with an AK-47 and waste all of us. I couldn't control that. Back at our cars, back at our patrol cars, we had a little bit more control of the area as far as we knew that no one was going to walk out the door with a weapon, or we had a safe assumption that nobody was going to walk out their door with a weapon.

...

12. Wymbs testified that neither he nor Carr had a gun when they were throwing rocks at the figure in the bushes....

> doing violates that right. This is not to say that an official action is protected by qualified immunity unless the very action in question has previously been held unlawful, but it is to say that in the light of pre-existing law the unlawfulness must be apparent."

Id. (quoting *Anderson v. Creighton*, 483 U.S. 635, 640 (1987)) (internal citation omitted). Accordingly, if the issues that Carr ... ha[s] raised on appeal establish a constitutional violation, then we must determine if Officers Tatangelo, Fortson, and Mercer violated the constitutional rights of appellant[] and, if so, whether they had "fair warning" under clearly established law that their conduct was unconstitutional. *Id.*

A. Excessive Force

Carr ... contend[s] that Officers Tatangelo and Fortson's shooting ... constituted excessive force.... "Violation of the Fourth Amendment requires an *intentional* acquisition of physical control." *Brower v. County of Inyo*, 489 U.S. 593, 596 (1989) (emphasis added). Fourth Amendment analysis of intentional physical control by police officers in § 1983 cases alleging excessive force, "[a]s in other Fourth Amendment contexts," is subject to an objective reasonableness inquiry: "the question is whether the officers' actions are 'objectively reasonable' in light of the facts and circumstances confronting them, without regard to their underlying intent or motivation."[16] *Graham v. Connor*, 490 U.S. 386, 397 (1989); *see Tennessee v. Garner*, 471 U.S. 1, 9 (1985) (noting that the constitutional justification of a particular seizure is determined by "the totality of circumstances").

> The "reasonableness" of a particular use of force must be judged from the perspective of a reasonable officer on the scene, rather than with the 20/20 vision of hindsight.... The calculus of reasonableness must embody allowance for the fact that police officers are often forced to make split-second judgments—in circumstances that are tense, uncertain, and rapidly evolving—about the amount of force that is necessary in a particular situation.

Graham, 490 U.S. at 396–97.[17]

An intentional seizure of a person "readily bears the meaning of a laying on of hands or application of physical force to restrain movement, even when it is ultimately unsuccessful." *California v. Hodari D.*, 499 U.S. 621, 626 (1991). "While it is not always clear just when minimal police interference becomes a seizure, there can be no question that apprehension by the use of deadly force is a seizure subject to the reasonableness requirement of the Fourth Amendment." *Garner*, 471 U.S. at 7 (internal citation omitted). The Supreme Court has instructed that determination of the con-

---

16. To the extent that Carr has suggested that the officers bore ill will toward Carr and Wymbs from their encounter with them earlier that night, not only is there no evidence that was the case, but also subjective intent is inappropriate in qualified immunity, objective reasonableness analysis.

17. Carr ... ha[s] taken issue with the district court for considering the officers' responses and reactions to their respective perceptions that Carr or Wymbs was pointing a gun and chambering a bullet at Officer Tatangelo. Yet, *Graham* requires an evaluation of the officers' reasonable apprehension to assess their responses to the circumstances confronting them, particularly in a rapidly evolving situation.

stitutionality of a seizure requires "'balanc[ing] the nature and quality of the intrusion on the individual's Fourth Amendment interests against the importance of the governmental interests alleged to justify the intrusion.'" *Id.* at 8 (citation omitted) ... [I]t is constitutionally permissible for an officer to use deadly force when "the officer has probable cause to believe that the suspect poses a threat of serious physical harm, either to the officer or to others." *Id.* at 11....

Carr has argued that a seizure did not occur under the Fourth Amendment because he was not stopped but ran back to his house. The seizure occurred when Carr was struck by the bullet from Officer Fortson's gun; in running away he submitted by retreating, although he was not stopped until he reached his house ... Officer Fortson had shot to kill to save the life of Officer Tatangelo, and it is his intent and the physical contact of the bullet from his gun that governs our Fourth Amendment, seizure analysis. Although Carr was not immediately stopped by the bullet from Officer Fortson's gun, he nevertheless was seized within the meaning of the Fourth Amendment when the bullet struck or contacted him.

...

Having determined that Carr has stated a cognizable Fourth Amendment seizure claim, we must decide if the officers violated clearly established law in shooting him. "An officer is entitled to qualified immunity if a reasonable officer, under the circumstances, might have thought that the use of force did not violate the federal law at the time of the incident." [citing 11th Circuit precedent.] Although he had drawn his weapon, Officer Fortson did not fire his gun until he saw Carr point what he believed to be a gun into the bushes behind which Officer Tatangelo was hiding and heard the sound of the chambering of a bullet. Both he and Officer Tatangelo testified that they heard this distinctive sound.

Officer Fortson testified that he shot Carr with the intention of killing him, as he had been trained, in order to prevent Carr from shooting Officer Tatangelo. In a split-second, rapidly escalating situation involving perceived deadly force, coupled with his police response training, Officer Fortson acted in an objectively reasonable manner to the apparent imminent threat to his fellow officer to save his life. Officer Tatangelo's subsequent shooting of bullets that did not strike Carr ... was reaction to the same perceived threat of a gun and the chambering of bullets to protect himself. A reasonable but mistaken belief that probable cause exists for using deadly force is not actionable under § 1983.[19]

---

19. Acknowledging *Garner* as "[t]he clearly established standard" in a similar case that occurred in 1992, the Fourth Circuit explained "that a police officer's use of deadly force is not excessive where he has probable cause to believe a suspect poses a threat of serious physical harm to the officer or others." *McLenagan v. Karnes*, 27 F.3d 1002, 1006–07 (4th Cir. 1994). "Regardless of whether probable cause actually existed, if a reasonable officer possessing the same particularized information as [the subject officer] could have, in light of *Garner*, believed that his conduct was lawful, then [the officer] is entitled to qualified immunity." *Id.* at 1007.

In *McLenagan*, the defendant police officer heard another police officer yell: "The man has got a gun!" *Id.* at 1005. The officer immediately drew his gun, turned around, and saw the suspect almost

When Carr was shot in 1999, *Garner*, permitting an officer to use deadly force to protect himself or others, had been Supreme Court law for fourteen years.[20] ... [W]hen a seizure by shooting occurred in a rapidly escalating situation that resulted in death: "'Reconsideration will nearly always reveal that something different could have been done if the officer knew the future before it occurred. This is what we mean when we say we refuse to second-guess the officer.'" [citing 11th Circuit precedent.] In determining whether the officers in this case are entitled to qualified immunity, we analyze the precise circumstances immediately preceding Carr's being shot and not the earlier surveillance decisions or the events following the shooting. Under the Fourth Amendment objective reasonableness standard applied to the officers' defense of themselves and a fellow officer, Officers Fortson, Tatangelo, and Mercer are entitled to qualified immunity on Carr's Fourth Amendment, seizure argument.[22]

...

We first examine the need for force and the amount of force used. In those dark, early Sunday morning hours, Officers Tatangelo, Fortson, and Mercer were conducting surveillance in a high-crime neighborhood. They were hidden and watching for Hen-

---

upon him. *Id.* Although the officer could not see whether the suspect had a gun, he shot him anyway. *Id.* As the suspect fell to the ground with "serious injuries to his hands and abdomen," the officer saw that he had no weapon. *Id.*

The Fourth Circuit determined that this use of force was reasonable under the circumstances and that a warning was unnecessary in the particular situation. *Id.* at 1007–08.

> For all [the officer] knew, the hesitation involved in giving a warning could readily cause such a warning to be his last. *We decline, therefore, to fashion an inflexible rule that, in order to avoid civil liability, an officer must always warn his suspect before firing—particularly where, as here, such a warning might easily have cost the officer his life.*
>
> ... It is true that [the officer] did not see a gun in [the suspect's] hands, but it is also true that he could not confirm that [the suspect] was unarmed. *We will not second-guess the split-second judgment of a trained police officer merely because that judgment turns out to be mistaken, particularly where inaction could have resulted in death or serious injury to the officer and others.* Although it is extremely unfortunate that [the suspect] was seriously injured, *§ 1983 does not purport to redress injuries resulting from reasonable mistakes.*
>
> ... [I]n this case, [the officer] had no time to consider anything at all-except his and the public's immediate safety. At the moment of truth, [the officer] acted well within the range of behavior expected of a police officer. What happened after the critical time had passed is simply irrelevant.

Id. (first, second, and third emphases added). We agree with the reasoning of the Fourth Circuit in *McLenagan*, which is analogous to the shooting incident in this case. This reasoning is particularly relevant to Carr['s] contention[] that the officers should have warned or identified themselves, a fact that is in contention.

20. Carr's arguments that the officers were not chasing him as a fleeing felon or attempting to arrest him and take him into custody are inapposite. At the time when the shooting occurred, the appropriate analysis under *Garner* was defense of self and others.

...

22. Although the parties have not provided, and we have not located, a case with precisely these circumstances, the pre-existing Supreme Court decisions in *Garner* as well as *Graham* and *Brower* clearly established that Officers Tatangelo, Fortson, and Mercer acted in an objectively reasonable manner in this situation. *Hope* [*v. Pelzer*, 536 U.S. 730, 739 (2002)].

derson, with outstanding warrants, to emerge from Carr's house so that they could arrest him, which was characteristic police work. While Officers Tatangelo and Fortson were hidden by bushes across the street from Carr's house, Carr and Wymbs began to throw rocks into the bushes behind which they were hidden. They then walked in front of the bushes behind which Officer Tatangelo was hidden, and both officers believed that they saw either Carr or Wymbs point a gun at Officer Tatangelo. Whatever doubt as to their perception of a gun was eliminated when both officers heard a click-clack sound, a noise each officer independently identified from his training and experience with weapons as the distinctive sound of the chambering of a bullet in a gun. Although Carr now claims that the click-clack sound was Wymbs folding his sunglasses, significantly, he testified that he thought Wymbs had shot him, which indicates that Carr believed that Wymbs had a gun.[25] Thus, three people at the scene of the shooting believed that Carr or Wymbs had a gun, including Officers Tatangelo and Fortson, who testified that they saw the gun from behind the bushes. When both Officers Tatangelo and Fortson reasonably believed that deadly force had been drawn on Officer Tatangelo, their surveillance ended, and they were entitled to respond in kind with deadly force to protect themselves. The amount of force with which they responded was directly proportional to that with which they were confronted.

III. CONCLUSION

Carr ... ha[s] appealed the district court's granting qualified immunity to the police officers involved in the challenged shooting incident based on claims of excessive force.... While the officers may not have exhibited paradigmatic police work in the course of the night and early morning hours in question, Carr ... ha[s] failed to state

---

25. We note, as did defense counsel at the summary judgment hearing, that it is unusual for someone to be wearing sunglasses in such early morning hours when it is dark.... Regarding whether Carr and Wymbs had a gun when they thought that Williams, who had stabbed Carr's brother, was in the bushes, the district judge had an insightful exchange with defense counsel at the summary judgment hearing:

> THE COURT: But, I mean, it doesn't really add up. You're afraid that Reggie Williams is out there, he has already stabbed your brother, you're a little afraid-you are afraid of him. Are you going to make him even madder by throwing rocks at him?
>
> [DEFENSE COUNSEL]: Your honor, I completely agree with the preposterousness of that position, which is exactly why I kind of label this you-don't-bring-a-rock-to-a-gun fight, and which also makes it ... a lot less likely that these plaintiffs, who believe that this guy has stabbed one of their brothers is in the bushes, that they're lobbing rocks rather than pointing a gun and make[s] their story a lot less plausible.

Id. at 19. Additionally, the fact that a gun was not located outside or inside Carr's house is not determinative. Defense counsel gave a reasonable explanation of how the gun could have disappeared:

> [I]t is important to note that there were numerous people inside the Carr residence. Cedric[k] Wymbs and Romeo Carr both fled directly into the residence after the shooting.
>
> There were numerous people in there at that time, and those people, one of those persons could have easily taken the gun and gone out the back of the house before any other officers came up because our officers went ... back to their car to get help.

In fact, Harold Henderson, who had gone into the Carr residence, was not there when the other officers came to assist Mr. Carr with his injury. So at least one person who had been in the house was not there afterwards....

[a] constitutional violation[] or show that the officers' conduct was unreasonable under clearly established law on the objective facts of this case that would render the officers liable for damages. Accordingly, … summary judgment based on qualified immunity to Officers Tatangelo, Fortson, and Mercer is AFFIRMED.

Questions to guide reading of *Espinosa*

1. What mistake of fact did Officers Avis and Keesor make? Was their mistake similar to the mistake of fact by the officers in *Carr*?
2. Note that the majority states that the officers would be entitled to qualified immunity if they did not violate a constitutional right. Does a court *need* to reach the issue of immunity if there is no constitutional violation?
3. Why did the majority hold the reasonableness of the mistake of fact was a jury question?
4. Why did the dissent instead argue that the judgment should be reversed and remanded for the district court to consider whether the undisputed facts show that the shooting was objectively reasonable?

Espinosa v. City and County of San Francisco

598 F.3d 528 (9th Cir. 2010), *cert. denied sub. nom Alvis v. Espinosa*, 565 U.S. 1156 (2012)

HUG, Senior Circuit Judge.

[This is an interlocutory appeal by San Francisco police officers from the district court's denial of their summary judgment motion in this 42 U.S.C. § 1983 action brought by survivors of Asa Sullivan. Plaintiffs allege that Officers Paulo Morgado, Michelle Alvis, and John Keesor violated Asa Sullivan's Fourth Amendment rights by using unreasonable force.] The three officers entered an apartment in which Asa Sullivan was staying, searched it, and Officers Alvis and Keesor fatally shot Sullivan.

…

The district court properly denied defendants' summary judgment motion regarding whether Officers Morgado, Alvis, and Keesor are entitled to qualified immunity for the alleged Fourth Amendment violations … For qualified immunity, we determine whether the facts show that (1) the officer's conduct violated a constitutional right; and (2) the right which was violated was clearly established at the time of the violation. *Saucier v. Katz*, 533 U.S. 194, 201 (2001).… If the officers did not violate a constitutional right, then they are entitled to immunity … If the officers violated such a right, but it was not clearly established, then they are entitled to immunity.…

In this case, the district court properly denied the summary judgment motion because there are genuine issues of fact regarding whether the officers violated Asa Sullivan's Fourth Amendment rights. Those unresolved issues of fact are also material to a proper determination of the reasonableness of the officers' belief in the legality of their actions. *See Santos v. Gates*, 287 F.3d 846, 855 n. 12 (9th Cir. 2002) (finding it premature to decide the qualified immunity issue "because whether the officers may be said to have made a 'reasonable mistake' of fact or law may depend on the jury's resolution of disputed facts and the inferences it draws therefrom") (internal cite omitted).

On June 6, 2006, Officers Morgado, Alvis, and Keesor entered an apartment in which Sullivan, the victim, was staying, and shot and killed him. Evidence indicated that Sullivan was staying at the apartment with the permission of [a] resident, Jason Martin. That evening, the police received a call in which a neighbor stated that the front door of the apartment was swinging open and that the location could be a drug house. Officer Morgado arrived and saw that the apartment door was closed.... Officer Morgado then pushed open the apartment door and ... saw a bloody shirt hanging over the top of an interior door. In a post-incident interview with investigators, he stated that he could not tell if the blood was fresh or dry, but later stated it appeared fresh.

Officers Alvis and Keesor arrived and entered the apartment. All three officers searched the first floor and found nothing except paint cans and painting sheets. Officer Keesor ... stated that they found nothing to indicate an emergency, except for the bloody shirt. [O]n the second floor, they found a locked bedroom. They announced that they were the police and kicked down the bedroom door. Inside the room, they found resident, Jason Martin. They ordered him to the ground and handcuffed him. He was cooperative and complied with their requests. They searched him and found a knife. Then, they heard noises coming from the attic indicating that someone was in the attic.

Officer Alvis climbed into the attic with her gun drawn. Officers Morgado and Keesor entered the attic after Officer Alvis with their guns drawn as well. It was dark, but Officers Alvis and Morgado had flashlights. Officer Alvis shouted that she saw Sullivan. An officer responded over the radio "Hey, why don't we just pull back really quick, set up a perimeter and just try to get him later." Officer Alvis then shouted, "Cover both closets. I have him at gunpoint. He's not going anywhere...." The officers told Sullivan to put up his hands, but he failed to follow the instruction. Officers Keesor and Alvis fired their guns at Sullivan, fatally wounding him. Officer Keesor stated that he shot because he believed that he saw something black in Sullivan's hand that looked like a gun. Officer Alvis stated that she shot because she thought she saw something in Sullivan's hand and that she saw him move his right arm. Sullivan was unarmed.

...

II. Unreasonable Force

The district court properly denied defendants' summary judgment motion regarding whether the officers are entitled to qualified immunity for allegedly violating Sullivan's Fourth Amendment rights by using excessive force. Fourth Amendment claims of excessive or deadly force are analyzed under an objective reasonableness standard.

Scott v. Harris, 550 U.S. 372, 381 (2007). To determine if a Fourth Amendment violation has occurred, we must balance the extent of the intrusion on the individual's Fourth Amendment rights against the government's interests to determine whether the officer's conduct was objectively reasonable based on the totality of the circumstances. *Graham v. Connor*, 490 U.S. 386, 396–97 (1989).... Our analysis involves three steps. First, we must assess the severity of the intrusion on the individual's Fourth Amendment rights by evaluating "the type and amount of force inflicted." [citing 9th Circuit precedent]. Next, we must evaluate the government's interests by assessing (1) the severity of the crime; (2) whether the suspect posed an immediate threat to the officers' or public's safety; and (3) whether the suspect was resisting arrest or attempting to escape ... *Graham*, 490 U.S. at 396. Third, "we balance the gravity of the intrusion on the individual against the government's need for that intrusion." [citing 9th Circuit precedent]. Ultimately, we must balance the force that was used by the officers against the need for such force to determine whether the force used was "greater than is reasonable under the circumstances." *Santos v. Gates*, 287 F.3d 846, 854 (9th Cir. 2002). In deadly force cases, "[w]here the suspect poses no immediate threat to the officer and no threat to others, the harm resulting from failing to apprehend him does not justify the use of deadly force to do so." *Tennessee v. Garner*, 471 U.S. 1, 11–12 (1985). The parties "relative culpability" *i.e.*, which party created the dangerous situation and which party is more innocent, may also be considered. *Scott*, 550 U.S. at 384. Finally, this court has often held that in police misconduct cases, summary judgment should only be granted "sparingly" because such cases often turn on credibility determinations by a jury.

Here, defendants failed to show that there are no questions of fact regarding whether Officers Morgado, Keesor and Alvis used unreasonable force when they entered the attic and pointed loaded guns at Sullivan. The three officers climbed into the attic and each pointed a gun at Sullivan. With regard to the force used, pointing a loaded gun at a suspect, employing the threat of deadly force, is use of a high level of force. The officers pointed guns at Sullivan knowing that he had not been accused of any crime. Sullivan had not caused the officers to forcibly enter the home; he ran from them. Sullivan did not present a danger to the public. Sullivan could not escape from the attic because it had only one exit. The bloody shirt and finding a knife on resident Jason Martin may have suggested some risk of harm. However, the officers offered inconsistent testimony regarding whether the blood appeared fresh or old. Viewing the evidence most favorably for plaintiffs, the officers did not know if the blood was new or old. With regard to the knife, according to Officer Keesor, the officers kicked down Martin's bedroom door, Martin put his hands up, allowed the officers to handcuff him even though he had not been accused of any crime, and complied with their demands. After he was arrested, they found a knife. However, his behavior did not make future danger more likely. Viewing the evidence in the light most favorable to plaintiffs, even considering the shirt and knife, defendants fail to show that there are not questions of fact regarding whether the level of force used was reasonable at the point when they entered the attic given the low level of threat.

. . .

In addition, there are questions of fact regarding whether Officer Keesor's and Alvis's use of deadly force was reasonable. Both officers fired their entire magazines at Sullivan. Officer Keesor fired 12 shots at Sullivan. Officer Alvis fired 13 shots at Sullivan. All shots were fired at close range. The officers stated that Sullivan refused to show his hands and made disturbing statements, such as "Kill me or I'll kill you" and "Are you ready to shoot me?" Officer Alvis stated that she thought she saw something in Sullivan's hands and when he moved his right arm that she thought he was going to shoot her. Officer Keesor stated that he saw something that looked like a gun in Sullivan's hand, heard a pop, and began shooting at Sullivan. According to the officers, Sullivan was resisting arrest and posed a high risk to their safety. Still, Sullivan had not been accused of any crime. He was not a threat to the public and could not escape. He had not initially caused this situation. He had not brandished a weapon, spoken of a weapon, or threatened to use a weapon. Sullivan, in fact, did not have a weapon. Viewing the evidence in the light most favorable to the plaintiffs, defendants have failed to show that there are no questions of fact regarding whether the use of deadly force was reasonable.

. . .

WU, District Judge, concurring in part and dissenting in part.

. . .

[I disagree with the majority's resolution of the qualified immunity question in the contexts of the unreasonable force.]

B. Analysis

1. The Officers' Pointing their Guns at Sullivan

There were two instances of force applied as to Sullivan which must be addressed and analyzed. First is the officers' act of training their firearms on Sullivan … Second is the actual shooting of the firearms by Officers Alvis and Keesor.

Turning to the facts and circumstances confronting the officers, while encountering the bloody T-shirt would not by itself constitute probable cause to believe that a crime had been committed, it would certainly give rise to a reasonable belief that caution (because of possible danger to the officers) was appropriate. Another factor was the officers' being denied immediate access to the first bedroom following their identifying themselves as police officers and requests for the door to be opened. Thereafter, the officers found Martin in the bedroom who cooperated with their commands. From the sounds of movement coming from the attic at that point, it was rational to conclude that there was another individual who was attempting to flee from the officers and who was in the attic or on the roof. Before climbing into the attic, a knife was found on Martin's person. Upon entering the attic, the officers found it to be extremely dark, illuminated only by the flashlights which they carried in one hand, and filled with rafters and other obstructions which hampered both movement and vision. When the person in the attic did not respond to their presence or announcements and remained hidden, in light of all of the referenced factors, it was objectively reasonable for the officers to have drawn their guns because of the possibility of danger to the officers in that situation.

Thereafter, the officers located Sullivan who was in a position in between sitting and lying down on his back between two wooden beams on the floor, and partly covered by the insulation material. Despite the officers' repeated demands for him to show them his hands, he never raised his right hand which was underneath the insulation and, periodically, he would move his left hand in and out of the insulation material. Consequently, at no time during the entire incident could the officers have determined whether or not Sullivan was armed with a gun, knife or other weapon. Sullivan was a 25-year-old able-bodied, five foot nine inch, 208 pound man. Thus, pointing their weapons at him cannot be found to have been objectively unreasonable ... Here, Sullivan was not cooperative, was indicating that he would not be taken into custody, and was possibly armed with a weapon, plus all of the participants were in a dark, confined and obstructed location. In light of the above facts, the defendant officers are entitled to qualified immunity as to this portion of plaintiffs' unreasonable force claim. [No firearm or other weapon was found on or near Sullivan's body. A dark eyeglass case was located underneath his right forearm.]

...

2. Officers Alvis and Keesor's Shooting of Sullivan

...

On the issue of the shooting, all of the previously discussed facts/evidence would come into play. Furthermore, the officers continually made requests throughout the incident for Sullivan to show both his hands, but he never did so. Additionally, he made statements which: 1) indicated his intent not to be taken into custody; 2) were of a threatening nature in regards to the officers' safety; and 3) led the officers to believe that he was contemplating "suicide by cop." [One officer stated that before the shooting, Sullivan said: "hey, tell my mom that I love her, and tell my girl that I love her. You guys, I'm gonna make my move and you'll be sorry."] In addition, once the officers encountered Sullivan in the attic, they did not act precipitously. They did not rush and attempt to subdue him. [Sullivan kicked a hole in the attic floor that opened to the bathroom below.] As the time elapsed, [police] considered options such as using less than lethal weapons and trying to force a larger hole through the bathroom ceiling/attic flooring to gain access to Sullivan's person. Also, they had made a request for a canine unit and were waiting for it to arrive.

Finally, and most importantly, one must consider what was happening just before the officers' use of the force. Here, there was testimony that immediately preceding the shooting, there were: 1) Sullivan's sudden movement of his right hand behind his back, 2) Sullivan's sudden lifting of his right arm, 3) Sullivan's raising something in one or both of his hands, 4) the sound of a "pop" that, to certain of the officers, was like a gunshot, and 5) a muzzle flash as if from a gun. Officer Alvis stated that she believed that Sullivan was shooting a gun at her so she returned fire. Officer

Keesor testified that he thought that Sullivan had shot Alvis after he heard the pop and she fell from his peripheral view. He then opened fire. Although it is not disputed that Sullivan had no firearm to shoot, the question not addressed by the district court is whether Alvis and Keesor had objectively reasonable beliefs that Sullivan had a gun and was using it at the time they fired their weapons.[14]

For further discussion

1. In *Espinosa*, the police officers at one point believed that Mr. Sullivan was attempting to commit "suicide-by-cop." Suicide-by-cop is a colloquial reference to "incidents in which individuals intend to end their own lives by engaging in criminal behavior to prompt a lethal response by law enforcement officers...." Melissa Reuland *et al.*, COUNCIL OF STATE GOV'TS JUSTICE CTR., LAW ENFORCEMENT RESPONSES TO PEOPLE WITH MENTAL ILLNESSES 5 (2009). The Ninth Circuit found that experts in the relevant fields recognized the suicide-by-cop theory and that two other circuits also had referenced the theory. *Boyd v. City & Cty. of San Francisco*, 576 F.3d 938, 945–46 n.5 (9th Cir. 2009) (citing cases from 5th and 7th Circuits). Earlier, this book included a likely "suicide-by-cop" scenario. In *Castle Rock*, in Chapter 8, a father murdered his three children, then drove to a police station and opened fire on police, who killed him.

While some suicide-by-cop situations "arise spontaneously out of the anger and panic" of the moment, others "appear to be planned, as evidenced by the presence of a suicide note...."[14] It is emotionally difficult for police officers to become the instrument of a suicide attempt. Officers "often feel a sense of powerlessness and manipulation." *Id.* On a website intended to "offer support to officers who have been inexplicably drawn into the emotional upheaval of those who choose to end their lives," one police officer described his emotional response to killing a person who provoked the shooting: "The man I killed that night pointed an unloaded 30.06 at

---

14. The majority Opinion seems to imply that there are factual questions in regards to the use of deadly force because Officers Keesor and Alvis emptied their entire magazines when firing at Sullivan and because, in the majority's view, Sullivan "had not initially caused this situation." A question arises as to why the majority feels that, under the facts herein, it makes any difference whether the officers fired one bullet or "12 shots." If there was a reasonable basis to believe that deadly force was appropriate in the situation, given the darkness of the location, the rafters and other obstructions, and additional factors which impeded the officers' determination as to the accuracy of their shots, there is no basis to believe that it would have been rational for the officers to count the number of bullets fired and to stop at some arbitrary figure.

Additionally, to claim that Sullivan "had not initially caused this situation" is highly questionable. Had Sullivan remained in the first bedroom when the officers announced their presence, had he shown both of his hands when repeatedly requested to do so by the officers, and had he not made the statements to the officers which were of a threatening and uncooperative nature, then the "situation" would have been entirely different.

14. Laurence Miller, *Suicide by Cop: Prevention, Response and Recovery*, POLICEONE (Mar. 18, 2007), http://www.policeone.com/police-products/communications/crisis-communications/articles/1228463-Suicide-by-cop-Prevention-response-and-recovery/.

my partner and I. Why? Who knows! I do know that there is hell on earth and I have been there."[15]

2. Police often encounter mentally ill people. For example,

- In a six-year period (1998–2004), the Akron (Ohio) Police Department responded to 10,004 calls related to a "mental disturbance." This represents 6.55 percent of the total call load (1,527,281 calls) during that period.
- Approximately 12,000 emergency calls for service to the Los Angeles (Calif.) Police Department (2.3 percent) annually are coded as "mental disturbance calls."
- In 174 U.S. police departments serving more than 100,000 people examined in 1998, approximately seven percent of all police contacts—including both investigations and complaints—involved a person believed to have a mental illness.[16]

Most police encounters with mentally ill people involve low level crimes or the person's threat to hurt him or herself:

> What may begin as a call from a business owner to "do something" about the unkempt young man pacing in front of his store, or community demands to keep individuals from sleeping on park benches—to the more extreme 9-1-1 report from a frightened caller that his or her loved one is threatening to hurt someone, or him-or-herself—will prompt a police response that can result in myriad outcomes. Officers on patrol will themselves encounter those who seem to be in crisis or are in violation of some "quality-of-life" law, such as urinating in public or sleeping in doorways. How police respond to such individuals can have a tremendous impact on how encounters will be resolved and on what future these individuals can expect.[17]

Some law enforcement agencies now collaborate with mental health professionals "to design specialized responses to people with mental illnesses."[18] For example, in April 2014, the Civil Rights Division of the Justice Department found that the "policies, training, and supervision" of the Albuquerque Police Department were "insufficient to ensure that officers encountering people with mental illness or in distress do so in a manner that respects their rights and is safe for all involved." The reforms ordered by the Justice Department are explained in Chapter 12 (Local Government Liability). *See* Letter from Civil Rights Div. of the Dep't of Justice to The Honorable Richard J. Berry (Apr. 10, 2014).

---

15. *See* Louise C. Pyers, *Suicide by Cop—The Ultimate "Trap,"* 3 FBI Nat'l Acad. Assocs. Mag. (July/Aug. 2001), http://www.theppsc.org/Staff_Views/Pyers/suicide_by_cop.htm.

16. Melissa Reuland *et al.*, Council of State Gov'ts Justice Ctr., Law Enforcement Responses to People with Mental Illnesses 5–7 (2009) (citations omitted), http://csgjusticecenter.org/wp-content/uploads/2012/12/le-research.pdf.

17. Council of State Gov'ts, Criminal Justice/Mental Health Consensus Project 34 (2002), https://csgjusticecenter.org/wp-content/uploads/2013/03/consensus-project-full-report.pdf.

18. Reuland *et al.*, *supra* note 16 at 9.

Exercise 11-C

If Congress were to codify qualified immunity, what standards and provisions would you advocate? Would you support a broad qualified immunity defense, where only the Supreme Court could define "clearly established" rights? Or only the Supreme Court and the binding circuit court? Alternatively, would you support a narrower qualified immunity doctrine by allowing the "clearly established" inquiry to be answered by referencing any circuit court decision, whether or not there was a consensus or majority view? Would you include any circuit court decision, whether precedential or non-precedential? Or would you include any federal court decision?

Guide to Law Practice Simulation 8

Description

This is an interoffice debate among the attorneys representing the plaintiff/estate of Eric Butera, based on the facts of *Butera v. District of Columbia*, 235 F.3d 637 (D.C. Cir. 2001). The attorneys must decide whether to seek certiorari to the U.S. Supreme Court on the issue of qualified immunity for the police officers on the estate's state-created danger claim only. Assume only the individual officers are defendants. All five students represent the plaintiff estate. Two students are junior counsel who do not want to seek certiorari. Two students are junior counsel who do want to seek certiorari. One student is senior counsel who will make the decision whether or not to recommend seeking certiorari to the client/representative of the estate.

Please review Rule 10 of the Rules of the Supreme Court of the United States, Considerations Governing Review on Certiorari:

> Review on a writ of certiorari is not a matter of right, but of judicial discretion. A petition for a writ of certiorari will be granted only for compelling reasons. The following, although neither controlling nor fully measuring the Court's discretion, indicate the character of the reasons the Court considers:
>
> (a) a United States court of appeals has entered a decision in conflict with the decision of another United States court of appeals on the same important matter; has decided an important federal question in a way that conflicts with a decision by a state court of last resort; or has so far departed from the accepted and usual course of judicial proceedings, or sanctioned such a departure by a lower court, as to call for an exercise of this Court's supervisory power; …
>
> (c) … a United States court of appeals has decided an important question of federal law that has not been, but should be, settled by this

Court, or has decided an important federal question in a way that conflicts with relevant decisions of this Court.

A petition for a writ of certiorari is rarely granted when the asserted error consists of erroneous factual findings or the misapplication of a properly stated rule of law.

To prepare, consider issues such as:

- Is it relevant that nearly every circuit has recognized the state-created danger doctrine? Are the variations in state-created danger tests surveyed by *Butera* legally significant?
- Is *Butera*'s "clearly established" analysis inconsistent with Supreme Court precedent because federal circuit courts had recognized the state-created danger theory before *DeShaney* and those pre-existing decisions were not abrogated by *DeShaney*?
- Is it time for the Supreme Court to directly decide the contours of the state-created danger doctrine? Are there any risks for Mr. Butera's estate? For future plaintiffs?
- Was there a constitutional violation at all? Was there any evidence that the officers were not deliberately indifferent to Mr. Butera's safety since Mr. Butera safely had visited the location before and did not want to wear a wire? Was there no constitutional violation because the court should have applied a higher standard of fault—intent to harm? Was there no constitutional violation because the officers did not create a unique opportunity for this harm to occur?
- What is the purpose of permitting a defendant to be immune even when the defendant violated a person's constitutional rights?

Purpose

- Better understand qualified immunity for government employees by comparing variations in how qualified immunity is applied, including *Harlow, Lewis, Hope, Brosseau, Tolan, Plumhoff, Mullenix, Butera, Carr,* and *Espinosa*
- Better understand 14th Amendment state-created danger doctrine and its interplay with *DeShaney* (addressed in Chapter 4) and *Lewis* (addressed in Chapter 3) by talking through qualified immunity analysis in the context of state-created danger
- Explore attorney role in shaping both qualified immunity and 14th Amendment doctrine by simulating role of attorneys applying doctrine to real facts (the *Butera* facts) and by understanding how law develops by application to analogous or new facts
- Prepare for law practice by simulating interoffice discussion among attorneys advocating different strategies

- Learn distinction between grounds for petition for certiorari and normal brief on the merits
- Prepare for law practice by discussing practical considerations underlying litigation decisions (*e.g.*, cost, time, risks) and by either persuasively advocating legal positions and responding to questions or by identifying ambiguities in doctrine or in its application to facts and posing questions to advocates
- There is no need to do any research—the relevant cases are in the casebook

Structure

- Advocates for seeking certiorari—Question & Answer with senior attorney (8 minutes)
- Advocates for not seeking certiorari—Question & Answer with senior attorney (8 minutes)
- After about 15 minutes, questioning will be opened up to the entire class
- All attorneys—Question & Answer with senior attorney and rest of class (15 minutes)
- Please prepare a question for every simulation, even if you are not one of the students playing a role.
- To ensure full class participation, and as a courtesy to your fellow students, please close your laptops during law practice simulations.

Guide to Law Practice Simulation 9

Description

This is a settlement conference before federal appellate mediators. The parties must decide whether to settle the litigation or to pursue the appeal of a federal district court decision on qualified immunity. The district court decision is *Carr v. Tatangelo*, 338 F.3d 1259 (11th Cir. 2003). Plaintiff's appeal of the qualified immunity ruling would be to the fictional Twelfth Circuit and would concern only the 4th Amendment claim by Mr. Carr against Officer Fortson. The mediation takes place after the trial court has decided the case and after the notice of appeal has been filed. The parties have not yet briefed the appeal and no briefing schedule will issue if the parties can agree to settle. At the settlement conference, be prepared to discuss both the likelihood of success on appeal (legal issues) and a specific dollar amount. Two students are attorneys for the defendant police officer Fortson. Two students are attorneys for the plaintiff Carr. One student is the federal appellate mediator. For a brief description of a federal appellate mediation program, please visit the website for the Sixth Circuit's program: https://www.ca6.uscourts.gov/about-mediation-conferences.

To prepare, consider issues such as:

- Plaintiff's main incentive to settle is the adverse district court ruling. Plaintiff's and defendant's incentives to settle may include the costs of litigation, *e.g.*, the time and effort of briefing and arguing an appeal. In addition, defendant risks reversal of the favorable qualified immunity ruling on appeal, if there are good reasons the Twelfth Circuit might not affirm.
- The Supreme Court in *Garner* recommended police issue a warning before using deadly force, if feasible. Is that relevant here?
- Did Officer Fortson make a mistake of fact when he thought he saw and heard a gun? Is that a reasonable mistake of fact permitted under *Saucier*?
- Did the district court make a credibility determination about Carr's and Wymb's statements denying either had a gun?
- Before the settlement conference, review the guidance on negotiation in Chapter 6, Exercise 6-D.
- In addition to the legal issues, prepare to discuss settlement value. Each side should arrive at the mediation with authority from the client to settle for a particular dollar amount or range. In evaluating a settlement amount acceptable to your "client," consider the chance each side has of prevailing in the appeal, the monetary value of the damages, each side's incentives to settle, and each side's obstacles to settlement.

Purpose

- Better understand qualified immunity for government employees by comparing variations in how qualified immunity is applied, including *Harlow, Lewis, Saucier, Hope, Brosseau, Tolan, Plumhoff, Mullenix, Butera, Carr,* and *Espinosa*
- Better understand 4th Amendment doctrine (addressed in Chapter 6) by talking through qualified immunity analysis in context of 4th Amendment claim
- Explore attorney role in shaping both qualified immunity and 4th Amendment doctrine by simulating role of attorneys applying doctrine to real facts (the *Carr* facts) and by understanding how law develops by application to analogous or new facts
- Prepare for law practice by simulating settlement discussion with supervision of appellate mediator and by discussing practical considerations underlying litigation decisions (*e.g.*, cost)
- Prepare for law practice by persuasively advocating legal position, posing or responding to questions, and by understanding how ambiguities in doctrine or in its application to facts may influence settlement decisions
- There is no need to do any research on the legal issues—the relevant cases are in the casebook.

- To research a realistic settlement amount, consider the amount of verdicts and settlements of similar claims. Consult a Tool such as "Case Evaluator" on WestlawEdge. Under "Civil Rights and Constitutional Law," select "Excessive force," and choose from categories such as "Jurisdictions" or "Injury," then select "Generate Report."

Structure

- Counsel for defendant Fortson—Question & Answer with mediator (8 minutes)
- Counsel for plaintiff Carr—Question & Answer with mediator (8 minutes)
- After about 15 minutes, questioning will be opened up to the entire class
- All counsel—Question & Answer with mediator and rest of class (15 minutes)
- Please prepare a question for every simulation, even if you are not one of the students playing a role.
- To ensure full class participation, and as a courtesy to your fellow students, please close your laptops during law practice simulations.

Chapter Twelve

Local Government Liability

A. Chapter Overview

Claims under 42 U.S.C. § 1983 can be brought against both individual defendants and against local governments, the two paths to liability introduced in Chapter 1. Suits against state governments are subject to the 11th Amendment, the subject of Chapter 15.

This Chapter addresses what plaintiffs must prove to prevail in § 1983 claims against local governments. In *Collins*, the Supreme Court held that municipal liability under § 1983 requires answering two questions: "(1) whether plaintiff's harm was caused by a constitutional violation, and (2) if so, whether the city is responsible for that violation." *Collins v. City of Harker Heights*, 503 U.S. 115, 120 (1992).

A local government can be liable for causing its employees to violate the constitution or for condoning such violations. But a local government cannot be liable simply because it employs a constitutional wrongdoer. The Supreme Court in *Monell* rejected *respondeat superior* liability under § 1983 and instead held that only "when execution of a government's policy or custom" causes the constitutional violation is the government defendant liable. *Monell v. Dep't of Soc. Serv.*, 436 U.S. 658, 694 (1978). Identifying a policy or custom can be difficult. The easy case is when the local government's lawmakers, *e.g.* City Council members, formally enact a rule or ordinance (*Monell*). It is more difficult to identify a policy or custom made informally by policymakers, "those whose edicts or acts may fairly be said to represent official policy," *id.*, meaning "those officials or governmental bodies who speak with final policymaking authority for the local governmental actor" concerning the specific subject of the alleged constitutional violation. *Jett v. Dallas Indep. Sch. Dist.*, 491 U.S. 701, 737 (1989).

A governmental custom or policy that is not authorized by written law is a practice "so permanent and well settled" as to have "the force of law." *Monell*, 436 U.S. at 691. A custom or policy can be demonstrated by acquiescence in a longstanding practice (*Jett*, *Bordanaro*). A custom or policy can also be demonstrated by the local government's failure to train its employees when, in light of the employees' duties, the failure to train constitutes deliberate indifference to constitutional rights (*Canton*, *Bordanaro*). "Where ... a claim of municipal liability is predicated upon a failure to act, the requisite degree of fault must be shown by proof of a background of events and circumstances which establish that the 'policy of inaction' is the functional equivalent of a decision by the city itself to violate the Constitution." *City of Canton v. Harris*, 489 U.S. 378, 395 (1989) (O'Connor, J., concurring in part and dissenting in part). The Supreme Court narrowed but did not foreclose the possibility that a plaintiff could demonstrate deliberate indifference to the need for training in the absence of prior, similar violations if the need for training is "obvious" (*Connick*).

To illustrate different theories of municipal liability, this Chapter includes (1) a Complaint alleging municipal customs or policies that caused police to violate constitutional rights of detainees (*Dunn*); (2) a court decision setting out in detail why a jury correctly held a local government was itself liable for the constitutional violations inflicted by its police officers (*Bordanaro*); and (3) a settlement agreement between a local government and a class of inmates who alleged a wide range of prison practices violated their constitutional rights (*McLendon*).

If the individual government employee has not inflicted constitutional harm, the Supreme Court has held that the municipal employer cannot be liable (*Heller*). Yet the circuits are not uniform in how they apply *Heller*. For example, the Third Circuit held in a precedential decision that a local government could be liable under § 1983 for a substantive due process violation even if no individual violated the Constitution (*Fagan*), but diverged from that position in non-precedential decisions. This Chapter invites reflection on the practical challenges faced by litigants and district courts confronted by a lack of doctrinal uniformity in municipal liability precedents and, more generally, lack of doctrinal uniformity between precedential and non-precedential decisions of the same circuit court.

Does the frequently-invoked doctrine of "supervisory liability" still exist? In conjunction with claims that local governments are liable, plaintiffs often bring claims against supervisors of the individuals alleged to have violated plaintiffs' constitutional rights. While formulated differently by the circuits, under supervisory liability, the supervisor of an employee who violated a person's rights may be individually liable if the supervisor played a role in the violation or knew of the violation and condoned or acquiesced in the conduct.

Despite seemingly settled doctrine, the Supreme Court in 2009 called into question the continuing existence of supervisory liability (*Iqbal*). As federal courts vary in how they apply *Iqbal*, even within a single circuit, the doctrine of supervisory liability remains in flux.

B. Theories of Local Government Liability: The Supreme Court

Questions to guide reading of *Monell*

(excerpted in Chapter 1)

1. Under what circumstances did *Monell* hold that a local government can be liable under § 1983? Is *Monell* a constitutional or a statutory decision?
2. Do you agree that vicarious liability is inconsistent with the statutory language "shall subject or cause to be subjected"?
3. Who were the policymakers in *Monell*?

Questions to guide reading of law review article

1. What kinds of documentary evidence would a plaintiff need to present to prove each of the theories of municipal liability summarized by Professor Achtenberg?
2. Why might there be the strategic advantages for a plaintiff to allege municipal liability?
3. Why might there be strategic disadvantages for a plaintiff to allege municipal liability?

Law Review Article

David Jacks Achtenberg, *Taking History Seriously: Municipal Liability Under 42 U.S.C. § 1983 and the Debate Over Respondeat Superior*, 73 Fordham L. Rev. 2183, 2187–90 (2005)[1]

In its current incarnation, the *Monell* doctrine has replaced *respondeat superior* with four distinct theories under which cities can be held liable: liability based on formal policy, liability based on governmental custom, liability based on inadequate training or supervision, and liability based on improper hiring. The four theories, while sometimes overlapping, provide quite different standards for determining whether a municipality will be liable for its employee's wrongful act. A separate requirement cuts across and modifies these four theories: the policy, custom, training, or hiring must somehow be tied to actions by certain high-ranking, policymaking officials.

1. Professor Achtenberg attributed the municipal liability doctrine to *Monell* for ease of reference but noted that various aspects of the doctrine properly are attributed to several cases: *Bd. of the Cty. Comm'rs v. Brown*, 520 U.S. 397 (1997) (standard for hiring-based liability); *City of Canton v. Harris*, 489 U.S. 378 (1989) (standard for training/supervision-based liability); *City of St. Louis v. Praprotnik*, 485 U.S. 112 (1988); *Pembaur v. City of Cincinnati*, 475 U.S. 469 (1986); *Owen v. City of Independence*, 445 U.S. 622 (1980). *See* Achtenberg, *Taking History Seriously*, 73 Fordham L. Rev. at 2187 n.19–20.

1. Formal Policy-Based Liability

Under the first theory, a municipality will be liable for an employee's constitutional wrong if the employee's conduct executed or implemented an official policy adopted by the city's lawmakers. *Monell* itself was such a case. The Board of Education and the Department of Social Services had each officially adopted an unconstitutional maternity leave policy, and the plaintiffs' supervisors simply carried out that policy when they directed the plaintiffs to take medically unnecessary maternity leaves.

2. Custom-Based Liability

Under the second theory, a municipality will be liable if the employees acted pursuant to the city's governmental custom, even if that custom had never been formally adopted by the city's lawmakers. Custom-based municipal liability recognizes the existence of practices that might be considered the city's administrative common law—a set of practices so well-settled that they have the force of law. For example, a municipal police department may have a longstanding, consistent practice of treating domestic violence cases less seriously than other violent crimes, and a person injured as a result of such a custom may sue the city even without showing that the municipal policymakers had formally approved the practice.

3. Training/Supervision-Based Liability

Under the inadequate training or supervision theory, cities are liable for the constitutional wrongs of their employees if two requirements are met: First, the failure to train or supervise must be so deficient that it shows "deliberate indifference to the rights" of those with whom the employees will interact. [citing *City of Canton v. Harris*, 489 U.S. 378, 388 (1989).] Second, the failure must have actually caused the wrongdoing to occur. [*Id.* at 390.] Deliberate indifference will be found where the nature of the employees' duties or a previous pattern of violations makes it obvious that, without further training, the employees are highly likely to violate citizens' federally protected rights. [*Id.* at 390 n.10.] Thus, for example, failure to train police officers not to commit perjury does not, by itself, show deliberate indifference since the officers should not need training to know that perjury is unacceptable. However, if the officers demonstrate a pattern of lying under oath, the need for further training or supervision becomes obvious, and the continued failure to provide it will constitute deliberate indifference. Even if the need is obvious, the city will not be liable unless adequate training or supervision would have prevented the violation. [*Id.* at 391.] Thus, the municipality will not be liable if the officer would have committed the same violation even if properly trained and supervised. [*Id.*]

4. Hiring-Based Liability

In quite limited circumstances a municipality will be held liable for its employees' constitutional wrongs on the basis that the city failed to adequately screen the employees before hiring them. For the city to be liable under this theory, a plaintiff must show that "adequate scrutiny of an applicant's background would [have led] a reasonable policymaker to conclude that the plainly obvious consequence of the decision to hire ... would be the deprivation of a third party's federally protected right," [*Bd.*

of County Comm'rs v. Brown, 520 U.S. 397, 411 (1997)] and that adequate screening would have shown that "this officer was highly likely to inflict the particular injury suffered by the plaintiff." [*Id.* at 412.] *A fortiori*, plaintiffs could also prevail if they show that the city hired the employee despite having actual knowledge of facts demonstrating this high likelihood of employee misconduct.

5. The Overarching Requirement: Actions of City Policymakers

Each of these methods of establishing municipal liability is limited by an overarching requirement that, for a municipality to be liable, the constitutional wrongdoing must result from action or inaction by a person who can be categorized as an official municipal policymaker. Thus, formal policy can be seen as action formally taken by employees who qualify as policymakers. Custom can be defined as a practice that is so widespread that the municipal policymakers must have been aware of it and may be deemed to have adopted it as their policy.[35] Liability based on inadequate training or supervision requires a finding that it should have been "plainly obvious" to the city's policymakers that further training or supervision was necessary and the conclusion that failure to provide it showed that those policymakers were "deliberately indifferent" to the high likelihood of constitutional wrongs. [*City of Canton*, 489 U.S. at 390 n.10.] Finally, hiring-based liability can only be maintained when proper screening would have revealed the damning background information to a municipal policymaker. Thus, every form of municipal liability under *Monell* requires some form of action or culpable inaction by an identifiable individual who can properly be characterized as a municipal policymaker.

For further discussion

1. Should *Monell* be overruled? Professor Achtenberg argues that "*Monell* relies on an historical analysis that is simply wrong," that the Reconstruction-era Congress "would have expected courts to treat the common law not as a set of ironclad rules, but instead as a flexible decision-making process," and that "application of that process to current municipal employment relations would lead to reinstating *respondeat superior*." David Jacks Achtenberg, *Taking History Seriously: Municipal Liability Under 42 U.S.C. § 1983 and the Debate Over Respondeat Superior*, 73 Fordham L. Rev. 2183, 2185–86 (2005). More recently, Professor Karen Blum argued that both qualified immunity and municipal liability doctrine have become too complex and that the fix lies in overruling *Monell*'s rejection of *respondeat superior* to instead hold local governments liable for the constitutional violations of their employees. Karen M.

---

35. *See Jett v. Dallas Indep. Sch. Dist.*, 491 U.S. 701, 737 (1989) (holding that municipal liability for custom exists if the policymakers have acquiesced in the custom); *City of St. Louis v. Praprotnik*, 485 U.S. 112, 130 (1988) (same); *Bielevicz v. Dubinon*, 915 F.2d 845, 851 (3d Cir. 1990) (suggesting that the policymakers must have been aware of the custom). *But see Sorlucco v. N.Y.C. Police Dep't*, 971 F.2d 864, 871 (2d Cir. 1992) (noting that constructive notice is enough without evidence of actual knowledge or acquiescence to senior policymakers).

Blum, *Qualified Immunity: Time to Change the Message*, 93 Notre Dame L. Rev. 1887, 1932–33 (2018). Professor Blum argued:

> The *Monell* Court's misreading of the legislative history and common law surrounding the rejection of the Sherman Amendment and its implications for *respondeat superior* liability under Section 1983 have long been criticized.... [R]ejection of the Sherman Amendment, which would have imposed strict liability on municipalities for acts of private violence committed within their borders by members of the Ku Klux Klan, was *not* a rejection of *respondeat superior* liability for constitutional torts committed by employees of the local government entity. The Court was just flat out wrong about this.
>
> ...
>
> [Because] government indemnification of officials found liable under Section 1983 is the norm, not the exception, so making *respondeat superior* the rule would not impose a change in standard operating procedure for those cases in which officers are found to have violated the Constitution and do not prevail on qualified immunity; nor, obviously, would it affect those cases where defendants prevail because there has been no constitutional violation. And officers who would prevail under qualified immunity under the current doctrine would still be protected from exposure to individual liability. What *respondeat superior* would accomplish is what Congress originally intended: the provision of a remedy for those whose constitutional rights have been violated by those acting pursuant to authority vested in them by the state. Establishing the underlying constitutional violation by a government employee would still be no walk in the park.
>
> ...
>
> By adopting the doctrine of *respondeat superior* in Section 1983 litigation, the Court would not only rectify the mistake it made in *Monell* forty years ago, but it would "fix" the doctrine of qualified immunity by making it largely irrelevant ... It is time to take another look at the message Congress intended in the Civil Rights Act of 1871. Correcting the Court's error in *Monell* and recognizing that *respondeat superior* was part of the original scheme would be a good first step towards cleaning up the mess of qualified immunity and clarifying the message that Section 1983 was intended to restore, rather than restrict, civil rights.

Blum, 93 Notre Dame L. Rev. at 1933–35 (further citation and footnotes omitted). If *Monell* were overruled, and plaintiffs could obtain damages from government employers based on *respondeat superior*, what are some possible responses by local governments?

2. The Supreme Court recently reaffirmed the core holding of *Monell*. *See Lozman v. City of Riviera Beach*, ___ U.S. ___, 138 S. Ct. 1945, 1951 (2018) ("It is well established that in a § 1983 case a city or other local governmental entity cannot be

subject to liability at all unless the harm was caused in the implementation of 'official municipal policy.' ").

3. The majority of lower courts have extended *Monell*'s *respondeat superior* exemption to private parties subject to § 1983 but the Supreme Court has not yet addressed the issue. Richard Frankel, *Regulating Privatized Government Through § 1983*, 76 U. Chic. L. Rev. 1449, 1457 (2009). Professor Frankel argues that, unlike local governments, private entities subject to § 1983 should be subject to *respondeat superior* because the justifications for exempting local governments from *respondeat superior* do not apply to private entities and, as a matter of policy, damages awards will better deter private companies than governmental entities from constitutional violations. *Id.*

4. Local government liability is subject to stringent causation standards. "[I]n enacting § 1983, Congress did not intend to impose liability on a municipality unless *deliberate* action attributable to the municipality itself is the 'moving force' behind the plaintiff's deprivation of federal rights." *Bd. of the Cty Com'rs of Bryan County, Okl. v. Brown*, 520 U.S. 397, 400 (1997) (quoting *Monell*, 436 U.S. at 694). "Where a plaintiff claims that the municipality has not directly inflicted an injury, but nonetheless has caused an employee to do so, rigorous standards of culpability and causation must be applied to ensure that the municipality is not held liable solely for the actions of its employee." *Brown*, 520 U.S. at 405 (further citation omitted).

5. Government officials can be sued in their individual capacities or in their official capacities or both. Naming the defendant in the official capacity is the equivalent of suing the governmental entity itself and requires proof of governmental, not individual, liability. *See, e.g.*, *Martinez v. Beggs*, 563 F.3d 1082, 1091 (10th Cir.), *cert. denied*, 558 U.S. 877 (2009).

6. Qualified immunity is not available to government defendants. That defense is limited to individual defendants. *Owen v. City of Independence*, 445 U.S. 622, 657 (1980); *but see* Karen Blum, *Qualified Immunity: Time to Change the Message*, 93 Notre Dame L. Rev. 1887, 1932 n.276 (2018) ("One rather perverse intersection of qualified immunity with municipal liability doctrine is exemplified by cases holding that, although municipalities are not entitled to qualified immunity, if an individual officer prevails on the clearly established law prong of the immunity analysis, a government entity cannot be held liable on a 'failure to train' claim because it could not have been deliberately indifferent under [*Canton*], in not training as to the violation of a right that was not clearly established. For examples of such cases, *see Arrington-Bey v. City of Bedford Heights*, 858 F.3d 988, 995 (6th Cir. 2017) ('The absence of a clearly established right spells the end of this *Monell* claim.'); *Hollingsworth v. City of St. Ann*, 800 F.3d 985, 992 (8th Cir. 2015) ('As it was not clearly established in July 2009 that force resulting in only *de minimis* injury could violate the Fourth Amendment, the City did not act with deliberate indifference by failing to train its officers that use of a Taser in these circumstances was impermissible.')...."). Local governments, however, are immune from punitive damages. *City of Newport v. Fact Concerts*, 453 U.S. 247, 267, 271 (1981).

7. The *Monell* requirement that plaintiffs establish a municipal policy or custom applies whether plaintiff seeks monetary, declaratory, or injunctive relief. *Los Angeles County v. Humphries*, 562 U.S. 29, 30 (2010). In 2010, the Supreme Court granted certiorari to decide whether "claims for declaratory relief against a local public entity [are] subject to the requirement of *Monell* that the plaintiff demonstrate that the constitutional violation was the result of a policy, custom or practice attributable to the local public entity as determined by the First, Second, Fourth and Eleventh Circuits, or are such claims exempt from *Monell*'s requirement as determined by the Ninth Circuit?" *Los Angeles County v. Humphries*, 559 U.S. 935 (2010). The Supreme Court resolved the circuit split by rejecting the Ninth Circuit's position.

8. A local government can be liable for a single decision by a policymaker. In *Pembaur v. City of Cincinnati*, 475 U.S. 469, 480 (1986), the county prosecutor directed police to break down the door of a physician's office in order to locate witnesses to alleged welfare fraud. The Supreme Court held that the local government could be liable for this 4th Amendment violation inflicted by police at the direction of the county prosecutor, acting as a final decisionmaker, because a single decision by a policymaker is sufficient to establish a government's policy. *Id.* at 481.

9. *Monell* held that "it is when execution of a government's policy or custom, whether made by its lawmakers or by those whose edicts or acts may fairly be said to represent official policy, inflicts the injury that the government as an entity is responsible under § 1983." *Monell v. Dep't of Soc. Serv.*, 436 U.S. 658, 694 (1978). How is it decided whether a government employee is a "policymaker"? The Supreme Court later clarified that the district court, not the jury, decides as a matter of state law whether a local government official has final policymaking authority in the area that is the subject of the suit:

> '[W]hether a particular official has "final policymaking authority" is a question of state law.' [*St. Louis v. Praprotnik*, 485 U.S. 112,] 123, quoting *Pembaur* [*v. Cincinnati*], 475 U.S. [469,] 483 (plurality opinion).... [T]he identification of those officials whose decisions represent the official policy of the local governmental unit is itself a legal question to be resolved by the trial judge *before* the case is submitted to the jury. Reviewing the relevant legal materials, including state and positive law, as well as " 'custom or usage' having the force of law," *Praprotnik*, *supra*, at 124 n.1, the trial judge must identify those officials or governmental bodies who speak with final policymaking authority for the local governmental actor concerning the action alleged to have caused the particular constitutional ... violation at issue. Once those officials who have the power to make official policy on a particular issue have been identified, it is for the jury to determine whether their decisions have caused the deprivation of rights at issue by policies which affirmatively command that it occur, *see Monell*, 436 U.S. at 661, n. 2, or by acquiescence in a longstanding practice or custom which constitutes the 'standard operating procedure' of the local governmental entity. *See Pembaur*, *supra*, at 485–87 (White, J., concurring).

Jett v. Dallas Indep. Sch. Dist., 491 U.S. 701, 737 (1989).

10. Who can be a policymaker according to the circuits? As noted, that is a question of state law. For example, whether a police chief is a final policymaker in a particular case depends on the subject matter of the complaint and whether, under the particular state's law, the police chief has final authority over that subject matter. A police chief may be the final decision maker for personnel decisions in one city but not in another. The table below illustrates that the answer to the question "is a police chief a final policymaker" can vary within a federal circuit because the answer depends on state law.

Is a Police Chief a Final Policymaker?
A Sampling of the Circuits

Lytle v. Doyle 326 F.3d 463, 472 (4th Cir. 2003)	"[c]hief of [p]olice could be considered a final policymaker for the police department[]"
Fairley v. Luman 281 F.3d 913, 918 (9th Cir.), *cert. denied*, 537 U.S. 1044 (2002)	police chief was policymaker for law enforcement issues within the city
Dill v. City of Edmond 155 F.3d 1193, 1211 (10th Cir. 1998)	police chief was policymaker for discipline and transfer of police officers, even though city charter and policies did not speak to that issue
Flanagan v. Munger 890 F.2d 1557, 1568 (10th Cir. 1989)	police chief was final policymaker regarding police personnel policy
***But see*:**	
Young v. City of Providence 404 F.3d 4, 30 n.21 (1st Cir. 2005)	Commissioner of Public Safety was policymaker on police training; declining to decide whether police chief was policymaker
Dempsey v. City of Baldwin 143 Fed. Appx. 976, 987 (10th Cir. 2005)	City Council, not police chief, was final policymaker for the City's personnel actions
Hunter v. Town of Mocksville 897 F.3d 538, 561 (4th Cir. 2018)	Town Manager, not police chief, was final municipal policymaker with respect to personnel policy because the police chief's personnel decisions were always subject to Town Manager's review

---

Questions to guide reading of *Canton*

In *Monell*, it was easy to determine how the local government itself caused the constitutional violation because the violation (medically unnecessary maternity leaves) was inflicted pursuant to a formally-enacted city rule. But a local government also can be liable for an unwritten governmental custom or policy. *Canton* established that a municipality can be liable for failing to train employees where the failure to train amounts to deliberate indifference to the constitutional rights of persons the employees are likely to encounter in their work. *Canton* itself concerned police encounters with people who require medical treatment.

1. Is this a constitutional or a statutory decision? What arguments did the city make to contest municipal liability?
2. According to *Canton*, under what circumstances can a local government be liable under § 1983 for inadequate training of police? *Canton* lists several examples of allegations that would not be sufficient to prove that a municipality has a "policy" of failing to train employees. What are they?
3. How can a plaintiff satisfy the rigorous causation standard imposed by *Canton*? Is the proof different if the need for training is "obvious," as explained in footnote 10?
4. How does Justice O'Connor's concurrence flesh out the two paths to liability for failure to train employees?
5. How is the concept of "notice" to defendants relevant in the context of *Canton* local government liability? In Chapter 11, notice to defendants was relevant to the doctrine of qualified immunity and in Chapter 2, notice to defendants also was relevant to the 8th Amendment standard of deliberate indifference. Why is notice to defendants important in each of these contexts?
6. If you were the plaintiff's attorney, what documentary evidence would you seek to prove municipal liability for the constitutional violation assumed to exist in *Canton*?

City of Canton v. Harris

489 U.S. 378 (1989)

Justice WHITE delivered the opinion of the Court.

In this case, we are asked to determine if a municipality can ever be liable under 42 U.S.C. § 1983 for constitutional violations resulting from its failure to train municipal employees. We hold that, under certain circumstances, such liability is permitted by the statute.

I

In April 1978, respondent Geraldine Harris was arrested by officers of the Canton Police Department. Mrs. Harris was brought to the police station in a patrol wagon.

When she arrived at the station, Mrs. Harris was found sitting on the floor of the wagon. She was asked if she needed medical attention, and responded with an incoherent remark. After she was brought inside the station for processing, Mrs. Harris slumped to the floor on two occasions. Eventually, the police officers left Mrs. Harris lying on the floor to prevent her from falling again. No medical attention was ever summoned for Mrs. Harris. After about an hour, Mrs. Harris was released from custody, and taken by an ambulance (provided by her family) to a nearby hospital. There, Mrs. Harris was diagnosed as suffering from several emotional ailments; she was hospitalized for one week and received subsequent outpatient treatment for an additional year.

Some time later, Mrs. Harris commenced this action ... seeking [*inter alia*] to hold the city liable under 42 U.S.C. § 1983 for its violation of Mrs. Harris' right, under the Due Process Clause of the Fourteenth Amendment, to receive necessary medical attention while in police custody.

A jury trial was held on Mrs. Harris' claims. Evidence was presented that indicated that, pursuant to a municipal regulation, shift commanders were authorized to determine, in their sole discretion, whether a detainee required medical care. In addition, testimony also suggested that Canton shift commanders were not provided with any special training (beyond first-aid training) to make a determination as to when to summon medical care for an injured detainee....

III

In *Monell v. New York City Dept. of Social Services*, 436 U.S. 658 (1978), we decided that a municipality can be found liable under § 1983 only where the municipality itself causes the constitutional violation at issue. *Respondeat superior* or vicarious liability will not attach under § 1983. *Id.* at 694–695. "It is only when the 'execution of the government's policy or custom ... inflicts the injury' that the municipality may be held liable under § 1983." ... (quoting *Monell*, *supra*, 436 U.S. at 694).

Thus, our first inquiry in any case alleging municipal liability under § 1983 is the question whether there is a direct causal link between a municipal policy or custom and the alleged constitutional deprivation. The inquiry is a difficult one; one that has left this Court deeply divided in a series of cases that have followed *Monell*;[4] one that is the principal focus of our decision again today.

A

... [P]etitioner urges us to adopt the rule that a municipality can be found liable under § 1983 only where "the policy in question [is] itself unconstitutional." ... Whether such a rule is a valid construction of § 1983 is a question the Court has left unresolved. *See, e.g.*, ... *Oklahoma City v. Tuttle*, 471 U.S. [808,] 824, n.7 (1985). Under such an approach, the outcome here would be rather clear: we would have to reverse and remand the case with instructions that judgment be entered for petitioner. There can be little doubt that on its face the city's policy regarding medical treatment for detainees is constitutional. The policy states that the city jailer "shall ... have [a person needing medical care] taken to a hospital for medical treatment, with permission of his supervisor...."

...

4. *See, e.g.*, ... *Los Angeles v. Heller*, 475 U.S. 796 (1986)....

Nor, without more, would a city automatically be liable under § 1983 if one of its employees happened to apply the policy in an unconstitutional manner, for liability would then rest on *respondeat superior*. The claim in this case, however, is that if a concededly valid policy is unconstitutionally applied by a municipal employee, the city is liable if the employee has not been adequately trained and the constitutional wrong has been caused by that failure to train. For reasons explained below, we conclude ... that there are limited circumstances in which an allegation of a "failure to train" can be the basis for liability under § 1983. Thus, we reject petitioner's contention that only unconstitutional policies are actionable under the statute.

B

... We hold today that the inadequacy of police training may serve as the basis for § 1983 liability only where the failure to train amounts to deliberate indifference to the rights of persons with whom the police come into contact.[8] This rule is most consistent with our admonition in *Monell*, 436 U.S. at 694 ... that a municipality can be liable under § 1983 only where its policies are the "moving force [behind] the constitutional violation." Only where a municipality's failure to train its employees in a relevant respect evidences a "deliberate indifference" to the rights of its inhabitants can such a shortcoming be properly thought of as a city "policy or custom" that is actionable under § 1983. As Justice Brennan's opinion in *Pembaur v. Cincinnati*, 475 U.S. 469, 483–484 (1986) (plurality) put it: "[M]unicipal liability under § 1983 attaches where—and only where—a deliberate choice to follow a course of action is made from among various alternatives" by city policymakers. *See also Oklahoma City v. Tuttle*, 471 U.S., at 823 (opinion of Rehnquist, J.). Only where a failure to train reflects a "deliberate" or "conscious" choice by a municipality—a "policy" as defined by our prior cases—can a city be liable for such a failure under § 1983.

Monell's rule that a city is not liable under § 1983 unless a municipal policy causes a constitutional deprivation will not be satisfied by merely alleging that the existing

8. The "deliberate indifference" standard we adopt for § 1983 "failure to train" claims does not turn upon the degree of fault (if any) that a plaintiff must show to make out an underlying claim of a constitutional violation. For example, this Court has never determined what degree of culpability must be shown before the particular constitutional deprivation asserted in this case—a denial of the due process right to medical care while in detention—is established. Indeed, in *Revere v. Massachusetts General Hospital*, 463 U.S. 239, 243–245 (1983), we reserved decision on the question whether something less than the Eighth Amendment's "deliberate indifference" test may be applicable in claims by detainees asserting violations of their due process right to medical care while in custody. We need not resolve here the question left open in *Revere* for two reasons. First, petitioner has conceded that, as the case comes to us, we must assume that respondent's constitutional right to receive medical care was denied by city employees—whatever the nature of that right might be ... Second, the proper standard for determining when a municipality will be liable under § 1983 for constitutional wrongs does not turn on any underlying culpability test that determines when such wrongs have occurred....

training program for a class of employees, such as police officers, represents a policy for which the city is responsible. That much may be true. The issue in a case like this one, however, is whether that training program is adequate; and if it is not, the question becomes whether such inadequate training can justifiably be said to represent "city policy." It may seem contrary to common sense to assert that a municipality will actually have a policy of not taking reasonable steps to train its employees. But it may happen that in light of the duties assigned to specific officers or employees the need for more or different training is so obvious, and the inadequacy so likely to result in the violation of constitutional rights, that the policymakers of the city can reasonably be said to have been deliberately indifferent to the need.[10] In that event, the failure to provide proper training may fairly be said to represent a policy for which the city is responsible, and for which the city may be held liable if it actually causes injury.[11]

In resolving the issue of a city's liability, the focus must be on adequacy of the training program in relation to the tasks the particular officers must perform. That a particular officer may be unsatisfactorily trained will not alone suffice to fasten liability on the city, for the officer's shortcomings may have resulted from factors other than a faulty training program. *See ... Oklahoma City v. Tuttle, supra*, 471 U.S. at 821 (opinion of Rehnquist, J.). It may be, for example, that an otherwise sound program has occasionally been negligently administered. Neither will it suffice to prove that an injury or accident could have been avoided if an officer had had better or more training, sufficient to equip him to avoid the particular injury-causing conduct. Such a claim could be made about almost any encounter resulting in injury, yet not condemn the adequacy of the program to enable officers to respond properly to the usual and recurring situations with which they must deal. And plainly, adequately trained officers occasionally make mistakes; the fact that they do says little about the training program or the legal basis for holding the city liable.

Moreover, for liability to attach in this circumstance the identified deficiency in a city's training program must be closely related to the ultimate injury. Thus in the case at hand, respondent must still prove that the deficiency in training actually

---

10. For example, city policymakers know to a moral certainty that their police officers will be required to arrest fleeing felons. The city has armed its officers with firearms, in part to allow them to accomplish this task. Thus, the need to train officers in the constitutional limitations on the use of deadly force, *see Tennessee v. Garner*, 471 U.S. 1 (1985), can be said to be "so obvious," that failure to do so could properly be characterized as "deliberate indifference" to constitutional rights. It could also be that the police, in exercising their discretion, so often violate constitutional rights that the need for further training must have been plainly obvious to the city policymakers, who, nevertheless, are "deliberately indifferent" to the need.

11. The record indicates that the city did train its officers and that its training included first-aid instruction.... Petitioner argues that it could not have been obvious to the city that such training was insufficient to administer the written policy, which was itself constitutional. This is a question to be resolved on remand....

caused the police officers' indifference to her medical needs. Would the injury have been avoided had the employee been trained under a program that was not deficient in the identified respect? Predicting how a hypothetically well-trained officer would have acted under the circumstances may not be an easy task for the factfinder, particularly since matters of judgment may be involved, and since officers who are well trained are not free from error and perhaps might react very much like the untrained officer in similar circumstances. But judge and jury, doing their respective jobs, will be adequate to the task.

To adopt lesser standards of fault and causation would open municipalities to unprecedented liability under § 1983. In virtually every instance where a person has had his or her constitutional rights violated by a city employee, a § 1983 plaintiff will be able to point to something the city "could have done" to prevent the unfortunate incident. *See Oklahoma City v. Tuttle*, 471 U.S. at 823 (opinion of Rehnquist, J.). Thus, permitting cases against cities for their "failure to train" employees to go forward under § 1983 on a lesser standard of fault would result in *de facto respondeat superior* liability on municipalities—a result we rejected in *Monell*, 436 U.S., at 693–694. It would also engage the federal courts in an endless exercise of second-guessing municipal employee-training programs. This is an exercise we believe the federal courts are ill suited to undertake, as well as one that would implicate serious questions of federalism....

Consequently, while claims such as respondent's—alleging that the city's failure to provide training to municipal employees resulted in the constitutional deprivation she suffered—are cognizable under § 1983, they can only yield liability against a municipality where that city's failure to train reflects deliberate indifference to the constitutional rights of its inhabitants.

...

Justice O'CONNOR, with whom Justice SCALIA and Justice KENNEDY join, concurring in part and dissenting in part.

...

[T]he Court's opinion correctly requires a high degree of fault on the part of city officials before an omission that is not in itself unconstitutional can support liability as a municipal policy under *Monell*. As the Court indicates, "it may happen that ... the need for more or different training is so obvious, and the inadequacy so likely to result in the violation of constitutional rights, that the policymakers of the city can reasonably be said to have been deliberately indifferent to the need." ... Where a § 1983 plaintiff can establish that the facts available to city policymakers put them on actual or constructive notice that the particular omission is substantially certain to result in the violation of the constitutional rights of their citizens, the dictates of *Monell* are satisfied. Only then can it be said that the municipality has made " 'a deliberate choice to follow a course of action ... from among various alternatives.' " [quoting majority] quoting *Pembaur v. Cincinnati*, 475 U.S. 469, 483–484 (1986).

In my view, it could be shown that the need for training was obvious in one of two ways. First, a municipality could fail to train its employees concerning a clear constitutional duty implicated in recurrent situations that a particular employee is certain to face. As the majority notes ... the constitutional limitations established by this Court on the use of deadly force by police officers present one such situation. The constitutional duty of the individual officer is clear, and it is equally clear that failure to inform city personnel of that duty will create an extremely high risk that constitutional violations will ensue.

...

Second, I think municipal liability for failure to train may be proper where it can be shown that policymakers were aware of, and acquiesced in, a pattern of constitutional violations involving the exercise of police discretion. In such cases, the need for training may not be obvious from the outset, but a pattern of constitutional violations could put the municipality on notice that its officers confront the particular situation on a regular basis, and that they often react in a manner contrary to constitutional requirements. The lower courts that have applied the "deliberate indifference" standard we adopt today have required a showing of a pattern of violations from which a kind of "tacit authorization" by city policymakers can be inferred.

...

Exercise 12-A

To prove that a local government has a policy or custom of failing to train or discipline its employees, plaintiff must request relevant documents from the defendant local government. Below are several examples of document requests by a plaintiff seeking to prove that a local government had a custom of tolerating police use of excessive force in making arrests:

- Any and all documents, materials and writings that concern or are at all relevant to any allegations of misconduct or complaints made against Defendant Police Officer Jason Fortenberry in connection with his employment for Arthur Township for the entire period of his employment.
- All documents, materials and writings which relate to incidents in the Arthur Township for the past five years in which it was alleged that Arthur police officers used unreasonable force or excessive force on citizens.
- All Arthur Township documents, memoranda, materials and writings which relate to the procedures for handling incidents involving reports and allegations that Arthur police used unreasonable force or excessive force on citizens in effect on February 21, 2019.
- Provide copies of all documents, writings, directives and materials which relate to the means by which Arthur Township monitors the per-

> formance of its police officers, investigates allegations of misconduct by its police officers, and imposes discipline and other remedial measures to police officers who are alleged to have engaged in misconduct or to have violated established practices and procedures of Arthur Township[5]

With the above examples in mind, if you represented the plaintiff in *Canton*, what document requests would you draft to obtain evidence to prove the failure to train alleged in the *Canton* litigation?

TO PROVE X	→	REQUEST Y DOCUMENT

For further discussion

1. The *Canton* deliberate indifference standard applies to claims that a local government has exposed its citizens to the likelihood of constitutional violations by failing to train its employees and also to claims that the local government has failed to take such actions as supervising or disciplining employees. "Although *City of Canton* addressed a claim of a failure to train, the stringent causation and culpability requirements set out in that case have been applied to a broad range of supervisory liability claims. *See, e.g., Amnesty* [*America v. Town of West Hartford*], 361 F.3d [113,] 127 [(2d Cir. 2004)] (failure to supervise); *Berry v. City of Detroit*, 25 F.3d 1342, 1354 (6th Cir. 1994) (failure to discipline)." *Reynolds v. Giuliani*, 506 F.3d 183, 192 (2d Cir. 2007). *See, e.g., Brammer-Hoelter v. Twin Peaks Charter Acad.*, 602 F.3d 1175, 1189 (10th Cir. 2010) ("municipal liability may be based on injuries caused by a failure to adequately train or supervise employees, so long as that failure results from 'deliberate indifference' to the injuries that may be caused"); *Lewis v. City of West Palm Beach*, 561 F.3d 1288, 1293 (11th Cir. 2009), *cert. denied*, 559 U.S. 936 (2010) ("To establish a city's deliberate indifference, 'a plaintiff must present some evidence that the municipality knew of a need to train and/or supervise in a particular area and the municipality made a deliberate choice not to take any action'") (further citation omitted).

2. Recall that, under the Supreme Court's decision in *Collins*, municipal liability requires answering a constitutional inquiry and a statutory inquiry: "(1) whether plaintiff's harm was caused by a constitutional violation, and (2) if so, whether the city is responsible for that violation." *Collins*, 503 U.S. at 120. *Canton* is not a constitutional decision. Rather, in *Canton* the Supreme Court assumed an underlying constitutional violation and addressed the question of whether, under 42 U.S.C.

5. Only the names and date have been changed from real discovery requests included in Paul M. Messing, *Framing the Causes of Action: Actionable Police Misconduct*, Civil Rights: How Lawyers Protect the Constitution through Section 1983 Civil Litigation (Pa. Bar Institute 2010) at 155–56.

§ 1983, the local government should be held liable for that constitutional violation. 489 U.S. at 389 n.8. The "deliberate indifference" standard in *Canton*, therefore, is a statutory standard.

3. The meaning of "deliberate indifference" in *Canton* differs from the meaning of that term in the 8th Amendment constitutional context. In *Farmer v. Brennan*, 511 U.S. 825, 837 (1994), the Supreme Court held that "deliberate indifference" in the Eighth Amendment context means that a government defendant subjectively appreciated the risk of harm to an inmate and recklessly disregarded the risk—a subjective, not an objective standard. The Supreme Court explained in *Farmer* how that standard differed from the objective statutory standard in *Canton*:

> Because 'deliberate indifference' is a judicial gloss, appearing neither in the Constitution nor in a statute, we could not accept petitioner's argument that the test for 'deliberate indifference' described in *Canton v. Harris*, 489 U.S. 378 (1989), must necessarily govern here. In *Canton*, interpreting 42 U.S.C. § 1983, we held that a municipality can be liable for failure to train its employees when the municipality's failure shows 'a deliberate indifference to the rights of its inhabitants.' 489 U.S., at 389.... Justice O'Connor's separate opinion for three Justices agreed with the Court's 'obvious[ness]' test and observed that liability is appropriate when policymakers are 'on actual or constructive notice' of the need to train, *id.*, at 396 (opinion concurring in part and dissenting in part). It would be hard to describe the *Canton* understanding of deliberate indifference, permitting liability to be premised on obviousness or constructive notice, as anything but objective.
>
> *Canton*'s objective standard, however, is not an appropriate test for determining the liability of prison officials under the Eighth Amendment as interpreted in our cases. Section 1983, which merely provides a cause of action, 'contains no state-of-mind requirement independent of that necessary to state a violation of the underlying constitutional right.' *Daniels v. Williams*, 474 U.S. 327, 330 (1986). And while deliberate indifference serves under the Eighth Amendment to ensure that only inflictions of punishment carry liability ... the 'term was used in the *Canton* case for the quite different purpose of identifying the threshold for holding a city responsible for the constitutional torts committed by its inadequately trained agents,' *Collins v. Harker Heights*, 503 U.S. 115, 124 (1992), a purpose the *Canton* Court found satisfied by a test permitting liability when a municipality disregards 'obvious' needs. Needless to say, moreover, considerable conceptual difficulty would attend any search for the subjective state of mind of a governmental entity, as distinct from that of a governmental official. For these reasons, we cannot accept petitioner's argument that *Canton* compels the conclusion here that a prison official who was unaware of a substantial risk of harm to an inmate may nevertheless be held liable under the Eighth Amendment if the risk was obvious and a reasonable prison official would have noticed it.

511 U.S. at 840–42; *see, e.g.*, *Layton v. Bd. of Cty. Comm'rs*, 512 F. App'x 861, 868 n. 5 (10th Cir. 2013) ("'In the prison conditions context, deliberate indifference is a subjective standard requiring actual knowledge of a risk by the official." ... In contrast, "[i]n the municipal liability context, deliberate indifference is an objective standard which is satisfied if the risk is so obvious that the official should have known of it"') (citations omitted).

4. Justice O'Connor explained that a local government could be liable for failure to train "where it can be shown that policymakers were aware of, and acquiesced in, a pattern of constitutional violations...." *Canton*, 489 U.S. at 1209 (O'Connor, J., concurring in part and dissenting in part); *see also Forrest v. Parry*, 930 F.3d 93, 117–18 (3d Cir. 2019) ("[A] claim predicated on a municipality's failure or inadequacy in training, supervision, or otherwise ... must make the deliberate indifference showing ... [that] '(1) municipal policymakers know that *employees* will confront a particular situation; (2) the situation involves a difficult choice or a history of employees mishandling; and (3) the wrong choice by an employee will frequently cause deprivation of constitutional rights'") (citation omitted).

What constitutes a "pattern"? What evidence is enough to preclude summary judgment on a claim that there has been a "pattern" of constitutional violations? Circuits differ on how many earlier incidents and how similar those earlier incidents must be to the alleged conduct to constitute a pattern of constitutional violations sufficient to put the city's policymakers on notice. In *Okin v. Village of Cornwall-On-Hudson Police Dept.*, 577 F.3d 415, 439–40 (2d Cir. 2009), for example, the Second Circuit held that a domestic violence victim's "more than a dozen" complaints to different officers showed a triable issue about whether a local government had a custom of acquiescing in unconstitutional police conduct. "These incidents suggest a consistent pattern of failing to adequately respond to [the victim's] complaints, to implement the [state] mandatory arrest statute, to interview the alleged abuser, or to file domestic incident reports, a pattern which may have encouraged further violence. We therefore find sufficient evidence in the record to create a genuine issue of fact as to whether the officers' conduct indicates a practice, tacitly endorsed by the [local government]." *See, e.g.*, *Young v. City of Providence ex rel. Napolitano*, 404 F.3d 4, 28 (1st Cir. 2005) (where estate of off-duty minority officer shot by on-duty officers presented "some evidence from which a jury could find that it was common knowledge within the [city police department] that misidentifications of off-duty officers responding to an incident often occurred in [the city], particularly misidentification of minority officers ... [i]t is clear that a jury could find a pattern of knowledge of prior misidentifications"); *Beck v. City of Pittsburgh*, 89 F.3d 966, 972 (3d Cir. 1996), *cert. denied*, 519 U.S. 1151 (1997) (five complaints of excessive force in less than five years was sufficient to establish a pattern of excessive force that should have put the City on notice of the risk of the current excessive force incident); *Sanchez v. Gomez*, 283 F. Supp. 3d 524, 536–37 (W.D. Tex. 2017), *appeal dismissed sub nom. Sanchez v. City of El Paso*, 2018 WL 1989633 (5th Cir. 2018) ("statistics combined with the numerous past cases of excessive force in similar circumstances ... followed by the repeated denial of wrongdoing" plausibly allege "a pattern" of El Paso police "unreasonable use of force" on individuals "exhibiting signs of mental illness").

By contrast, in *Peterson v. City of Fort Worth*, 588 F.3d 838, 851 n.4 (5th Cir. 2009), *cert. denied*, 562 U.S. 827 (2010), the Fifth Circuit held that no reasonable jury could find a municipal policy of using or condoning excessive force by police in making arrests because "[t]wenty-seven incidents in four years, with no context as to the overall number of arrests or any comparisons to other cities, is not sufficient evidence of a pattern rising to the level of a policy. The burden of providing a context that would show such a pattern falls on the plaintiff, not on the City, and [plaintiff] has failed to meet that burden." *See, e.g., Jenkins v. Bartlett*, 487 F.3d 482, 493 (7th Cir.), *cert. denied*, 552 U.S. 1039 (2007) (four incidents of an officer firing at a suspect in a vehicle over five years was not enough to put the municipality on notice of the alleged pattern of the municipality's failure to train and supervise officers with respect to the use of deadly force on suspects in vehicles); *Estate of Davis ex rel. McCully v. City of North Richland Hills*, 406 F.3d 375, 382 (5th Cir. 2005) (testimony by former member of SWAT team that offending officer improperly fired his weapon on three occasions during training exercises and that the offending officer's superiors knew or should have known that the officer was likely to fire his weapon, a background investigation report indicating that the offending officer had a tendency to act too aggressively, and evidence that the offender's superior failed to discipline him when a citizen warned offender's superiors that he was "going to kill somebody" after a traffic stop encounter was not similar enough to the alleged improper shooting to put the city on notice of the risk); *Deborah O By & Through Thomas O v. Lake Cent. Sch. Corp.*, 61 F.3d 905 (Table) (7th Cir. 1995) (student allegedly stalked and raped by teacher; one prior incident of inappropriate teacher touching of student and one prior incident of student-on-student assault did not establish a pattern because they were "unrelated to the situation in this case" and did not establish "the kind of 'recurrent situations' required to give school officials proper notice of a constitutional problem").

5. Does local government liability for failing to fulfill an "obvious" need for training survive the Supreme Court's decision in *Connick*, the next case excerpted in this book? That is not yet clear. Under *Canton*, even in the absence of a prior pattern of constitutional violations, a local government could be liable for failure to train its employees where the need for training was "obvious." *Canton*, 489 U.S. at 390 n.10. The example *Canton* provided was equipping police with guns; the need to train officers on the constitutional limitations on using deadly force is obvious and therefore failure to do so constitutes deliberate indifference to constitutional rights. However, stringent causation requires that inadequate training *cause* the constitutional violation; employees do not require training to avoid blatant violations of constitutional rights. For example, prison guards and police do not need training to realize it is wrong to sexually assault those in their custody. *Barney v. Pulsipher*, 143 F.3d 1299, 1308 (10th Cir. 1998) ("[e]ven if the courses concerning gender issues and inmates' rights were less than adequate, we are not persuaded that a plainly obvious consequence of a deficient training program would be the sexual assault of inmates. Specific or extensive

training hardly seems necessary for a jailer to know that sexually assaulting inmates is inappropriate behavior"); *Andrews v. Fowler*, 98 F.3d 1069, 1077 (8th Cir. 1996) ("In light of the regular law enforcement duties of a police officer, we cannot conclude that there was a patently obvious need for the city to specifically train officers not to rape young women"). But in 2011, the Supreme Court decided *Connick*, the case below, which may have altered the meaning of an "obvious" need for training.

Questions to guide reading of *Connick*

1. Plaintiff did not argue that he had proved a pattern of constitutional violations. Even so, the majority stated that plaintiff's evidence was insufficient to have put Connick on notice that the office's *Brady* training was inadequate. Why was the evidence insufficient to show a pattern?
2. Is *Connick* limited to lawyer-employees? Does the reasoning of *Connick* apply to government employees who do *not* undergo years of professional training before accepting a government job, such as correctional officers or child protection caseworkers?
3. After *Connick*, is a government policymaker entitled to rely on the professional training of government employees (such as social workers) as sufficient to prevent constitutional violations? Unless the policymaker has a reason not to rely on that professional training, such as a pattern of violations?
4. Contrast how the majority and dissent describe the preparedness of recent law graduates to decide what *Brady* evidence to produce. Which description do you think is more accurate?

Connick v. Thompson

563 U.S. 51 (2011)

Justice THOMAS delivered the opinion of the Court.

The Orleans Parish District Attorney's Office now concedes that, in prosecuting respondent John Thompson for attempted armed robbery, prosecutors failed to disclose evidence that should have been turned over to the defense under *Brady v. Maryland*, 373 U.S. 83 (1963). Thompson was convicted. Because of that conviction Thompson elected not to testify in his own defense in his later trial for murder, and he was again convicted. Thompson spent 18 years in prison, including 14 years on death row. One month before Thompson's scheduled execution, his investigator discovered the undisclosed evidence from his armed robbery trial. The reviewing court determined that the evidence was exculpatory, and both of Thompson's convictions were vacated.

After his release from prison, Thompson sued petitioner Harry Connick, in his official capacity as the Orleans Parish District Attorney, for damages under ... 42 U.S.C. § 1983. Thompson alleged that Connick had failed to train his prosecutors adequately about their duty to produce exculpatory evidence and that the lack of training had caused the nondisclosure in Thompson's robbery case. The jury awarded Thompson $14 million.... We granted certiorari to decide whether a district attorney's office may be held liable under § 1983 for failure to train based on a single *Brady* violation. We hold that it cannot.

...

The *Brady* violation conceded in this case occurred when one or more of the four prosecutors involved with Thompson's armed robbery prosecution failed to disclose the crime lab report to Thompson's counsel. Under Thompson's failure-to-train theory, he bore the burden of proving both (1) that Connick, the policymaker for the district attorney's office, was deliberately indifferent to the need to train the prosecutors about their *Brady* disclosure obligation with respect to evidence of this type and (2) that the lack of training actually caused the *Brady* violation in this case. Connick argues that he was entitled to judgment as a matter of law because Thompson did not prove that he was on actual or constructive notice of, and therefore deliberately indifferent to, a need for more or different *Brady* training. We agree.

...

In limited circumstances, a local government's decision not to train certain employees about their legal duty to avoid violating citizens' rights may rise to the level of an official government policy for purposes of § 1983. A municipality's culpability for a deprivation of rights is at its most tenuous where a claim turns on a failure to train. *See Oklahoma City v. Tuttle*, 471 U.S. 808, 822–823 (1985) (plurality opinion) ("[A] 'policy' of 'inadequate training'" is "far more nebulous, and a good deal further removed from the constitutional violation, than was the policy in *Monell*"). To satisfy the statute, a municipality's failure to train its employees in a relevant respect must amount to "deliberate indifference to the rights of persons with whom the [untrained employees] come into contact." *Canton*, 489 U.S., at 388. Only then "can such a shortcoming be properly thought of as a city 'policy or custom' that is actionable under § 1983." *Id.*, at 389.

"'[D]eliberate indifference' is a stringent standard of fault, requiring proof that a municipal actor disregarded a known or obvious consequence of his action." *Bryan Cty.*, 520 U.S., at 410. Thus, when city policymakers are on actual or constructive notice that a particular omission in their training program causes city employees to violate citizens' constitutional rights, the city may be deemed deliberately indifferent if the policymakers choose to retain that program. *Id.*, at 407. The city's "policy of inaction" in light of notice that its program will cause constitutional violations "is the functional equivalent of a decision by the city itself to violate the Constitution." *Canton*, 489 U.S., at 395 (O'Connor, J., concurring in part and dissenting in part). A less stringent standard of fault for a failure-to-train claim "would result in de facto *respondeat superior* liability on municipalities...." *Id.*, at 392 ...

A pattern of similar constitutional violations by untrained employees is "ordinarily necessary" to demonstrate deliberate indifference for purposes of failure to train. *Bryan Cty.*, 520 U.S., at 409. Policymakers' "continued adherence to an approach that they know or should know has failed to prevent tortious conduct by employees may establish the conscious disregard for the consequences of their action—the 'deliberate indifference'—necessary to trigger municipal liability." *Id.*, at 407. Without notice that a course of training is deficient in a particular respect, decisionmakers can hardly be said to have deliberately chosen a training program that will cause violations of constitutional rights.

Although Thompson does not contend that he proved a pattern of similar *Brady* violations ... he points out that, during the ten years preceding his armed robbery trial, Louisiana courts had overturned four convictions because of *Brady* violations by prosecutors in Connick's office. Those four reversals could not have put Connick on notice that the office's *Brady* training was inadequate with respect to the sort of *Brady* violation at issue here. None of those cases involved failure to disclose blood evidence, a crime lab report, or physical or scientific evidence of any kind. Because those incidents are not similar to the violation at issue here, they could not have put Connick on notice that specific training was necessary to avoid this constitutional violation.

...

Instead of relying on a pattern of similar *Brady* violations, Thompson relies on the "single-incident" liability that this Court hypothesized in *Canton*. He contends that the *Brady* violation in his case was the "obvious" consequence of failing to provide specific *Brady* training, and that this showing of "obviousness" can substitute for the pattern of violations ordinarily necessary to establish municipal culpability.

In *Canton*, the Court left open the possibility that, "in a narrow range of circumstances," a pattern of similar violations might not be necessary to show deliberate indifference. *Bryan Cty.*, *supra*, at 409. The Court posed the hypothetical example of a city that arms its police force with firearms and deploys the armed officers into the public to capture fleeing felons without training the officers in the constitutional limitation on the use of deadly force. *Canton*, *supra*, at 390, n. 10. Given the known frequency with which police attempt to arrest fleeing felons and the "predictability that an officer lacking specific tools to handle that situation will violate citizens' rights," the Court theorized that a city's decision not to train the officers about constitutional limits on the use of deadly force could reflect the city's deliberate indifference to the "highly predictable consequence," namely, violations of constitutional rights. *Bryan Cty.*, *supra*, at 409. The Court sought not to foreclose the possibility, however rare, that the unconstitutional consequences of failing to train could be so patently obvious that a city could be liable under § 1983 without proof of a pre-existing pattern of violations.

Failure to train prosecutors in their *Brady* obligations does not fall within the narrow range of *Canton*'s hypothesized single-incident liability. The obvious need for specific legal training that was present in the *Canton* scenario is absent here. Armed police must sometimes make split-second decisions with life-or-death consequences. There is no reason to assume that police academy applicants are familiar with the constitutional constraints on the use of deadly force. And, in the absence of training, there is no way for novice officers to obtain the legal knowledge they require. Under those circumstances there is an obvious need for some form of training.

In stark contrast ... [a]ttorneys are trained in the law and equipped with the tools to interpret and apply legal principles, understand constitutional limits, and exercise legal judgment. Before they may enter the profession and receive a law license, all attorneys must graduate from law school or pass a substantive examination; attorneys in the vast majority of jurisdictions must do both.... These threshold requirements are designed to ensure that all new attorneys have learned how to find, understand, and apply legal rules....

Nor does professional training end at graduation. Most jurisdictions require attorneys to satisfy continuing-education requirements.... Attorneys who practice with other attorneys, such as in district attorney's offices, also train on the job as they learn from more experienced attorneys....

In addition, attorneys in all jurisdictions must satisfy character and fitness standards to receive a law license and are personally subject to an ethical regime designed to reinforce the profession's standards ... Among prosecutors' unique ethical obligations is the duty to produce *Brady* evidence to the defense.... An attorney who violates his or her ethical obligations is subject to professional discipline, including sanctions, suspension, and disbarment.

...

In light of this regime of legal training and professional responsibility, recurring constitutional violations are not the "obvious consequence" of failing to provide prosecutors with formal in-house training about how to obey the law. *Bryan Cty.*, 520 U.S., at 409. Prosecutors are not only equipped but are also ethically bound to know what *Brady* entails and to perform legal research when they are uncertain. A district attorney is entitled to rely on prosecutors' professional training and ethical obligations in the absence of specific reason, such as a pattern of violations, to believe that those tools are insufficient to prevent future constitutional violations in "the usual and recurring situations with which [the prosecutors] must deal." *Canton*, 489 U.S., at 391. A licensed attorney making legal judgments, in his capacity as a prosecutor, about *Brady* material simply does not present the same "highly predictable" constitutional danger as *Canton*'s untrained officer.

A second significant difference between this case and the example in *Canton* is the nuance of the allegedly necessary training. The *Canton* hypothetical assumes that the armed police officers have no knowledge at all of the constitutional limits on the use of deadly force. But it is undisputed here that the prosecutors in Connick's office were familiar with the general *Brady* rule. Thompson's complaint therefore cannot rely on the utter lack of an ability to cope with constitutional situations that underlies the *Canton* hypothetical, but rather must assert that prosecutors were not trained about particular *Brady* evidence or the specific scenario related to the violation in his case. That sort of nuance simply cannot support an inference of deliberate indifference here. As the Court said in *Canton*, "[i]n virtually every instance where a person has had his or her constitutional rights violated by a city employee, a § 1983 plaintiff will be able to point to something the city 'could have done' to prevent the unfortunate incident." 489 U.S., at 392 (citing *Tuttle*, 471 U.S., at 823 (plurality opinion)).

Thompson suggests that the absence of any formal training sessions about *Brady* is equivalent to the complete absence of legal training that the Court imagined in *Canton*. But failure-to-train liability is concerned with the substance of the training, not the particular instructional format. The statute does not provide plaintiffs or courts carte blanche to micromanage local governments throughout the United States.

We do not assume that prosecutors will always make correct *Brady* decisions or that guidance regarding specific *Brady* questions would not assist prosecutors. But showing merely that additional training would have been helpful in making difficult decisions does not establish municipal liability. "[P]rov[ing] that an injury or accident could have been avoided if an [employee] had had better or more training, sufficient to equip him to avoid the particular injury-causing conduct" will not suffice. *Canton*, supra, at 391. The possibility of single-incident liability that the Court left open in *Canton* is not this case.

The dissent rejects our holding that *Canton*'s hypothesized single-incident liability does not, as a legal matter, encompass failure to train prosecutors in their *Brady* obligation. It would instead apply the *Canton* hypothetical to this case, and thus devotes almost all of its opinion to explaining why the evidence supports liability under that theory. But ... [t]he reason why the *Canton* hypothetical is inapplicable is that attorneys, unlike police officers, are equipped with the tools to find, interpret, and apply legal principles.

...

The District Court and the Court of Appeals panel erroneously believed that Thompson had proved deliberate indifference by showing the "obviousness" of a need for additional training. They based this conclusion on Connick's awareness that (1) prosecutors would confront *Brady* issues while at the district attorney's office; (2) inexperienced prosecutors were expected to understand *Brady*'s requirements; (3) *Brady* has gray areas that make for difficult choices; and (4) erroneous decisions regarding *Brady* evidence would result in constitutional violations ... This is insufficient.

It does not follow that, because *Brady* has gray areas and some *Brady* decisions are difficult, prosecutors will so obviously make wrong decisions that failing to train them amounts to "a decision by the city itself to violate the Constitution." *Canton*, 489 U.S., at 395 (O'Connor, J., concurring in part and dissenting in part). To prove deliberate indifference, Thompson needed to show that Connick was on notice that, absent additional specified training, it was "highly predictable" that the prosecutors in his office would be confounded by those gray areas and make incorrect *Brady* decisions as a result. In fact, Thompson had to show that it was so predictable that failing to train the prosecutors amounted to conscious disregard for defendants' *Brady* rights. *See Bryan Cty.*, 520 U.S., at 409; *Canton*, *supra*, at 389. He did not do so.

...

We conclude that this case does not fall within the narrow range of "single-incident" liability hypothesized in *Canton* as a possible exception to the pattern of violations necessary to prove deliberate indifference in § 1983 actions alleging failure to train. The District Court should have granted Connick judgment as a matter of law on the failure-to-train claim because Thompson did not prove a pattern of similar violations that would "establish that the 'policy of inaction' [was] the functional equivalent of a decision by the city itself to violate the Constitution." *Canton, supra*, at 395 (opinion of O'Connor, J.).

Justice GINSBURG, with whom Justice BREYER, Justice SOTOMAYOR, and Justice KAGAN join, dissenting.

...

Connick should have comprehended that Orleans Parish prosecutors lacked essential guidance on *Brady* and its application. In fact, Connick has effectively conceded that *Brady* training in his Office was inadequate....

In 1985, Connick acknowledged, many of his prosecutors "were coming fresh out of law school," and the Office's "[h]uge turnover" allowed attorneys with little experience to advance quickly to supervisory positions.... [I]t was possible for "inexperienced lawyers, just a few weeks out of law school with no training," to bear responsibility for "decisions on ... whether material was *Brady* material and had to be produced." [citation omitted].

Thompson's expert characterized Connick's supervision regarding *Brady* as "the blind leading the blind." ... For example, in 1985 trial attorneys "sometimes ... went to Mr. Connick" with *Brady* questions, "and he would tell them" how to proceed. But Connick acknowledged that he had "stopped reading law books ... and looking at opinions" when he was first elected District Attorney in 1974....

Prosecutors confirmed that training in the District Attorney's Office, overall, was deficient. Soon after Connick retired, a survey of assistant district attorneys in the Office revealed that more than half felt that they had not received the training they needed to do their jobs.

Thompson, it bears emphasis, is not complaining about the absence of formal training sessions ... His complaint does not demand that *Brady* compliance be enforced in any particular way. He asks only that *Brady* obligations be communicated accurately and genuinely enforced. Because that did not happen in the District Attorney's Office, it was inevitable that prosecutors would misapprehend *Brady*.

...

For further discussion

1. Note that *Connick* reaffirmed that, under § 1983, a local government's deliberate indifference to constitutional rights is measured objectively: "when city policymakers

are on actual or constructive notice that a particular omission in their training program causes city employees to violate citizens' constitutional rights, the city may be deemed deliberately indifferent if the policymakers choose to retain that program." *Contrast* the meaning of "deliberate indifference" in the Eighth Amendment context. *See Farmer v. Brennan*, Chapter 2 (rejecting an objective measure of deliberate indifference and holding a prison official liable only where the official was "aware of facts from which the inference could be drawn that a substantial risk of serious harm exist[ed], and he [drew] the inference").

2. Recall from Chapter 9 that, in the context of deciding whether individual social workers were entitled to absolute immunity, the Third Circuit reasoned that mechanisms other than the threat of § 1983 liability would protect the public against constitutional violations by child protective service workers. Those protections include the government employer's incentive to ensure that its employees did not violate constitutional rights because the local government itself is not immune from suit. *See Ernst v. Child & Youth Servs. of Chester County*, Chapter 9. Is there tension between the reasoning in *Ernst* and the holding of *Connick*?

3. Did *Connick* foreclose the possibility of a plaintiff demonstrating deliberate indifference to the need for training even in the absence of prior, similar violations by showing an "obvious" need for training? No, that path is narrow but remains open, says the Sixth Circuit. For example, in lieu of a pattern of 8th Amendment violations, a plaintiff instead can establish a prison health care corporation was deliberately indifferent to an obvious need for training nurses:

> "a single violation of federal rights, accompanied by a showing that [the for-profit health corporation] has failed to train its employees to handle recurring situations presenting an obvious potential" for a constitutional violation. *Bryan Cnty.*, 520 U.S. at 409. This second mode of proof is available "in a narrow range of circumstances" where a federal rights violation "may be a highly predictable consequence of a failure to equip [employees] with specific tools to handle recurring situations." *Id.* [also relying on *Canton*]. This method of proof does not require [plaintiff] to show that [the for-profit health provider] had actual or constructive notice that its nurses were deficiently trained ... ; proof of actual or constructive notice is necessary only when a plaintiff pursues § 1983 liability on the pattern theory of constitutional violations. *See Connick*, 131 S. Ct. at 1360–61.
>
> The likelihood that a particular situation will recur and the probability that an employee who lacks proper tools to respond to the situation will violate a citizen's federal rights could lead to a finding that the policymaker's decision not to train reflects deliberate indifference "to the obvious consequence of the policymakers' choice—namely, a violation of a specific constitutional or statutory right." *Bryan Cnty.*, 520 U.S. at 409. "The high degree of predictability may also support an inference of causation—that the municipality's indifference led directly to the very consequence that was so predictable." *Id.* at 409–10.

...

> [Here, the for-profit health corporation] chose by contract to assume the county's constitutional medical obligations to its prisoners. [Its] administrators knew that the ... nurses interacted with dozens of inmates presenting a wide and recurring range of medical conditions that required timely and accurate diagnosis and treatment.... [A] reasonable jury could find that the potential risk of the commission of constitutional torts by ... nurses who lack the essential knowledge, tools, preparation, and authority to respond to the recurring medical needs of prisoners in the jail setting is so obvious that [the corporation's] failure to provide adequate training and supervision to those nurses constitutes deliberate indifference to the risk.

Shadrick v. Hopkins County, 805 F.3d 724, 739–40 (6th Cir. 2015). *But compare Pollard v. District of Columbia*, 698 F. App'x 616, 623 (D.C. Cir. 2017) (concurrence applying *Connick* to reason that it is not clear "that 'city policymakers know to a moral certainty' recurring constitutional violations will result from not further training police officers in how to identify and engage with individuals with intellectual disabilities" because even if " 'additional training would have been helpful in making difficult decisions [that] does not establish municipal liability' ") (further citations omitted). The consequences of *Connick* will become clearer as federal courts, local governments, and litigants apply the Supreme Court's ruling to new factual situations.

Exercise 12-B

Review the chart in Chapter 4 of typical police academy topics and median hours spent on each subject. With that in mind, if you represented 4 different plaintiffs allegedly injured by different kinds of conduct by different Bryce City police officers this year, and you did not have the resources to prove a prior pattern of similar constitutional violations by the police department in any of the three different cases, could you credibly argue that the need for police training was "obvious" in any of the below situations:

- the Bryce City police department purchased tasers in 2015, required officers to take a one-day course in their use in 2015, has used tasers ever since, and Plaintiff 1 was injured by a taser;[2]
- the Bryce City police department does not train officers how to transport a handcuffed person from a prone to a standing position, and Plaintiff 2 was injured when the officer lifted her from behind, by the handcuffs;[3]

2. *Estate of Gilliam v. City of Prattville*, 667 F. Supp. 2d 1276, 1292–93 (M.D. Ala. 2009), *rev'd in part*, 639 F.3d 1041 (11th Cir.), *cert. denied sub. nom. Waldroup v. Emmanuel*, 565 U.S. 1079 (2011).
3. *Klemash v. Monroe Tp.*, 2010 WL 455263 at *11 (D.N.J. Feb. 4, 2010).

- the Bryce City police department does not train officers to arrest people without sexually assaulting arrestees and Plaintiff 3 was sexually assaulted while in police custody;[4]

Could the police department credibly argue that the need for police training was *not* obvious in any of these situations?

For further discussion

1. Should the existence of a constitutional written policy insulate the local government from liability? A plurality of the Supreme Court suggested "yes" in *City of St. Louis v. Praprotnik* by stating "[w]hen an official's discretionary decisions are constrained by policies not of that official's making, those policies, rather than the subordinate's departures from them, are the act of the municipality." 485 U.S. 112, 127 (1988). However, the plurality in *Praprotnik* also suggested that a written policy might not be conclusive if the evidence showed that the policy was regularly disregarded. *Id.* at 131. Currently, because actual practice can differ from a city's written policies, in at least some jurisdictions a plaintiff can pursue a custom of failure to train, supervise, or discipline claim even if the local government has a constitutional written policy. *See, e.g.*, *Price v. Sery*, 513 F.3d 962, 973–74 (9th Cir. 2008) (finding Portland's deadly force policy complied with Fourth Amendment and nevertheless reaching plaintiff's argument "that the City's alleged failure to train its police officers appropriately as to the use of deadly force amounts to a constitutional violation by itself").

2. According to a petition for certiorari, the circuits are split on whether a constitutional written policy protects the local government from liability:

> In the Ninth and Eleventh Circuits the existence of such a written standard is of limited or no relevance to whether a city is liable for a constitutional violation. On the other hand, in the Fifth and Seventh Circuits such a written standard generally precludes the imposition of liability on a city. The Eighth and Tenth Circuits have taken an intermediate position.
>
> In *Lytle v. Carl*, 382 F.3d 978 (9th Cir. 2004), the Ninth Circuit concluded that *Praprotnik* does not permit a government body to insulate itself from liability simply by adopting a standard prohibiting constitutional violations. In that case a school district had authorized the school superintendent to discipline employees "in accordance with the applicable ... laws." 382 F.3d at 984.... [The Ninth Circuit held a] general statement by a school board or board of trustees that a superintendent is not authorized to violate the law, without more, cannot be enough to insulate the school district from liability.
>
> ...
>
> In the Seventh Circuit, on the other hand, the existence of a written standard precluding a particular type of constitutional violation does insulate a city

4. *Campbell v. Anderson County*, 695 F. Supp. 2d 764, 774–75 (E.D. Tenn. 2010).

from liability for such a violation. In *Auriemma v. Rice*, 957 F.2d 397 (7th Cir. 1992), several Chicago city employees had been demoted shortly after the election of a new mayor; they asserted that the demotions had been ordered by the Chief of Police, with the concurrence of the mayor, because of the political views of the plaintiffs. The court of appeals acknowledged that such patronage practices were widespread and longstanding in the city of Chicago. 957 F.2d at 399. It held, nonetheless, that the city was not liable for those actions.

> Ordinances applicable to the police department unequivocally ban ... political discrimination.... If ... [the Chief] discriminated on account of ... politics, he violated rather than implemented the policy of Chicago.

957 F.2d at 399–401.

Petition for Writ of Certiorari, *Bolton v. The City of Dallas*, 2008 WL 5083094 at *34–39 (Nov. 26, 2008). The Supreme Court denied certiorari in 2009.

Interview with David Rudovsky, Plaintiff's Counsel in *Canton*[3]

LISA HERNANDEZ: Did you enjoy [being a student at New York University Law School]?

DAVID RUDOVSKY: Yes.... [My first] summer, I got an internship to work with a lawyer named C.B. King in Albany, Georgia. So it was the summer of '65, really the height of the civil rights movement, and he was, he's probably the most extraordinary lawyer that I've ever met. The only black lawyer in all of southwest Georgia at that time.... [E]very day hundreds of people were being arrested in demonstrations and protests over segregation.... [I]t was really an extraordinary experience. Not only from what I learned from the legal issues that were involved, and a lot of them in terms of representing persons involved in social protest, both the criminal and civil side, but also seeing how an individual who was constantly under fire, literally under fire.... [W]hat first struck [me] when I first saw his office was that the entire front of the office had been bricked over, where there had been windows and there were no longer windows.... Sure enough, three months before, somebody had fired at him with a rifle outside the office, missing him by just a couple of feet, so they decided to brick off the office....

HERNANDEZ: As a professor [at University of Pennsylvania Law School] ... is there anything in particular that you think makes you different from other professors? ...

---

3. David Rudovsky, Founding Partner, Kairys, Rudovsky, Messing & Feinberg, and Senior Fellow at the University of Pennsylvania Law School. Lisa Hernandez, *Oral Legal History Project Interview with David Rudovsky* (Nov. 16, 1999), *available at* https://www.law.upenn.edu/library/archives/other/oralhistory/interviews/transcripts/rudovsky.php.

RUDOVSKY: … I've practiced for over 30 years.… I think I have a sense of what happens in the real world in terms of how doctrines are applied or misapplied, how courts operate, how lawyers handle problems, how trials emerge and issues get joined, so I think I bring some practical experience to the classroom.… I don't think I could teach these classes, quite frankly, unless I had, I had been immersed professionally in those issues, as a lawyer. Some people can, I think you have to really be smart to teach stuff that you haven't practiced in.

…

[My law partners and I] were extremely lucky.… [F]or the entire time we've been in operation … we've been able to pick our cases, and do probably 98% … civil rights, civil liberties, or criminal defense. Which isn't often easy to do in terms of sustaining a practice, but we've been fortunate enough to get some interesting cases, to get paid enough to make the operation go over the years, enough to support families and so on and really to do the kind of work we wanted to do.…

HERNANDEZ: [Y]ou've argued in front of the Supreme Court, is that correct?

…

RUDOVSKY: I've been there twice, two civil rights cases in the Supreme Court. [*Canton*, included in this Chapter, and *Mitchell*, included in Chapter 11] … What they say is final, and there are issues of major importance that are going to impact a lot of cases, and so there's usually much more at stake than in an individual case you may argue in a trial court. In terms of nine justices and questions and so on … [b]y the time you've written a brief, and thought about the argument, and gone through some test arguments, mock arguments, you're pretty well prepared. And … it's the rare situation when the judges know a lot more about the case than you do. Occasionally, you'll get a question that you haven't thought about, but, the questions were fairly predictable in terms of who they came from and what they were in terms of substance, and it was a challenging and interesting experience. I couldn't say, there's the usual thing of being very nervous right beforehand, but as soon as you stand up and start talking, it feels like you've been there before. Kind of mixed results in both cases, I think the results were fairly predictable going in, you can kind of usually count heads pretty well as to where the Court was, and we were pretty close in both cases. But an experience I certainly enjoyed.

…

HERNANDEZ: [You earned a] MacArthur Foundation Award … what [is that]?

RUDOVSKY: The MacArthur Foundation gives away these awards each year, which they call "Genius Awards", kind of an embarrassing title, but that was really out of the blue.... [Y]ou don't know you're under consideration.... And it's a very generous award. It's five years, several hundred thousand dollars. And it really is no strings attached. I mean, they tell you, you can do whatever you want with this money.... I continued to do what I was doing, but it was actually a nice opportunity because it kind of took the pressure off, financially, my practice. I could be more selective in the cases I took, could do a little bit more work outside my practice in terms of writing and research. I think it helped, not so much personally, but in the area I was working in. Kind of helped legitimize some of the work we were doing.

HERNANDEZ: Finally, what advice do you have, drawing from all of your expertise, for law students and young lawyers ...?

RUDOVSKY: ... [P]ick an area that you're going to be happy with the work you're doing. I mean, the money is important, and you've got loans to pay off and families to support, and I understand that, but I've seen a lot of law students and a lot of lawyers over the years involved in a lot work they don't like doing and are basically unhappy.... [T]he challenge is to find something that really grabs you, with some intensity that you feel strongly about. Do that, the rest will follow. And leave some time for other stuff ... you know, your personal life and your family life.

C. Development of Doctrine in the Circuits: Applying *Monell* and *Canton*

Questions to guide reading of *Bordanaro*

1. To prove a custom, did the court require involvement of a policymaking official?
2. What evidence did the court rely on in upholding the jury finding that the police department had a longstanding practice of breaking down doors without a warrant when arresting a felon?
3. What evidence did the court rely on in upholding the jury finding that the policymaking officials had constructive knowledge of the unconstitutional custom?
4. Why was the unconstitutional custom of arresting felons without a warrant by breaking down doors the "moving force" behind the plaintiff's injury?

5. What evidence did the court rely on in upholding the jury finding that the police department had a policy of inadequate training, supervising, or disciplining its officers?
6. What evidence did the court rely on in upholding the jury finding that the policymaking officials of the city were deliberately indifferent to the inadequate training, supervision, or discipline of the police?
7. Why was the municipal policy of inadequate training, supervision, or discipline the moving force behind the constitutional violations?
8. Why do you think the government decided to go forward with the trial on evidence this egregious?

Bordanaro v. Mcleod

871 F.2d 1151 (1st Cir. 1989), *cert. denied*, 493 U.S. 820 (1989)

BOWNES, Circuit Judge.

This appeal arises out of brutal beatings that plaintiffs-appellees received at the hands of Everett, Massachusetts police officers. Those injured and the estate of a person killed in the attack were awarded substantial verdicts[1] in their actions based upon 42 U.S.C. § 1983....

We affirm the verdicts....

3. THE FACTS

... In the early morning hours of July 23, 1982, Everett policeman, John McLeod, who was off duty, escorted Beverly Ferrairo to a bar located inside the King Arthur Motel in Chelsea, Massachusetts. An altercation soon began between McLeod and plaintiff Alfred "Da" Mattuchio. As McLeod was about to land the first punch against Mattuchio, Charles Dimino intervened and fisticuffs ensued between Dimino and McLeod. Dimino proved the better pugilist and McLeod, beaten and bloody, was thrown out of the bar.

McLeod then went to a nearby security hut and had the attendant call the Everett Police Department for reinforcements. At the Everett station house, Lieutenant Baker and Sergeant Ferullo listened on the radio as the entire night watch of the Everett Police Department—five officers—reported that they were en route to aid McLeod. The Chelsea Police Department also responded and sent officers to the scene.

When these officers arrived, McLeod took a set of nunchaku from the trunk of one of the cruisers and joined the other officers as they moved toward the King Arthur Motel in force. As the police approached the locked glass doors of the motel, the plaintiffs, all patrons of the bar, viewed them with apprehension. The officers shouted threats to the plaintiffs and demanded entry. Before the manager could open the

---

1. The total award was approximately $3,488,356 in compensatory damages and $819,983 in punitive damages.

doors, the police shattered the glass with their nightsticks. Fearing for the safety of the plaintiffs, the manager sent them upstairs to Room 209, while he went to unlock the doors. Once the doors had been opened, the police rushed into the motel and mounted the stairs in pursuit of the plaintiffs.

The owner of the King Arthur Motel, Arthur Guttardaro, and the manager followed the police up to Room 209. The police began banging on the door with their nightsticks, threatening to kill the occupants of the room. Guttardaro and the manager offered to open the door with a pass key. Instead of accepting their offer, Officers McLeod, Macauda and Aiello assaulted and beat Guttardaro and the manager. Both men managed to drag themselves to safety despite suffering injuries.

The police officers were armed with nightsticks, clubs, bats, tire-irons, and a fire axe, in addition to their service revolvers. They banged repeatedly on the door, demanding entry and continuing to threaten the plaintiffs. A hole was hastily drilled in the door through which mace was injected into the room. Soon thereafter, Officer McClusky fired two shots from his pistol through the door.

When the door gave way, the armed force of officers entered the room. They then savagely beat the heads and bodies of the unarmed plaintiffs until most were reduced to an unconscious or semi-conscious state. McLeod repeatedly slammed Vincent Bordanaro's head against the wall and clubbed the other plaintiffs with a bat, all the while stating again and again, "Remember my name, John McLeod, don't forget it."

At some point before the door caved in, Sergeant Ferullo arrived at the entrance to Room 209. He stayed near the doorway a few moments after the door had been forced open, then left saying, "Frig this. I'm going downstairs." Most of the persons in Room 209 sustained severe injuries. Vincent Bordanaro died as a result of the repeated blows to his head.

...

The jury returned a verdict against Everett, its Mayor (Edward Connolly) and its Chief of Police (Donald Bontempo) [hereinafter defendants, appellants, or Everett].

...

III. MUNICIPAL ... LIABILITY UNDER 42 U.S.C. § 1983

...

A. Municipal Liability Based on an Unconstitutional Custom

...

[C]ourts have established two requirements for plaintiffs to meet in maintaining a § 1983 action grounded upon an unconstitutional municipal custom. First, the custom or practice must be attributable to the municipality. In other words, it must be so well settled and widespread that the policymaking officials of the municipality can be said to have either actual or constructive knowledge of it yet did nothing to end the practice.... Second, the custom must have been the cause of and the moving force behind the deprivation of constitutional rights....

4. Existence of the Custom.

Testimonial evidence from Sergeant Ferullo showed that the Everett Police Department had a longstanding, wide-spread, and facially unconstitutional practice of breaking down doors without a warrant when arresting a felon. Based upon his uncontroverted testimony and inferences reasonably drawn therefrom, the jury could have found that:

- The sergeant had been present at either "about 20 or 30" or "50, 60" situations involving door breakdowns over his 24-year tenure as a police officer.
- A 12-pound sledge hammer was provided by the City of Everett for use in breaking down doors.
- Numerous occasions in which doors were broken down by Everett officers involved the unconstitutional practice of breaking down doors without a warrant when attempting to arrest a felon. When asked whether this type of force was used by the Everett Police in effecting arrests the sergeant stated: "[Y]es, that's the way we've always applied it."

...

- In breaking down the door at the King Arthur Motel, the officers were following what had been accepted departmental practice in the past.

This uncontradicted version of the arrest practice that was employed by the Everett Police Department proved that such an unconstitutional custom was "'the way things [were] done and [had] been done'" in the City of Everett.

...

Additional support for the existence of such a practice can be inferred from the event itself. This incident involved the joint actions of the entire night watch of the Everett Police Department. A reasonable inference to draw from this is that all of the officers involved were operating under a shared set of rules and customs. The fact that all of these officers acted in concert is further evidence that there was a pre-existing practice of breaking down doors when apprehending felons.... While it is true that evidence of a single event alone cannot establish a municipal custom or policy, *see, e.g.*,[*Oklahoma City v.*] *Tuttle*, 471 U.S. [808,] 823–24 [(1985)] (opinion of Rehnquist, J.), where other evidence of the policy has been presented and the "single incident" in question involves the concerted action of a large contingent of individual municipal employees, the event itself provides some proof of the existence of the underlying policy or custom.[5] ...

5. Attribution to the Municipality.

Although there was no direct evidence that the Chief of Police had actual knowledge of this policy of breaking down doors without a warrant, the evidence does support a finding of his constructive knowledge of it. Constructive knowledge "may be evi-

---

5. We are mindful of the difficulty plaintiffs encounter in proving the existence of such police department policies and customs. Plaintiffs are likely to encounter hostile witnesses and incomplete documentation of past abuses....

denced by the fact that the practices have been so widespread or flagrant that in the proper exercise of [their] official responsibilities the [municipal policymakers] should have known of them." ... The evidence is sufficient to prove that the Chief should have known of the unconstitutional arrest practice. The Chief's own testimony and that of others was that he oversaw the operations of the department and set much of its policy. The evidence showed that the Chief utilized an extensive report review process to monitor the conduct of his officers and to ensure their compliance with the rules of the department. Such a review process would alert the Chief to practices that transgressed department policy. Knowledge of the practice may thus be imputed to the Chief. And allowing this custom to continue amounted to a deliberate indifference to the rights of the citizens of Everett, making a constitutional violation "'almost bound to happen, sooner or later.'" ... In this case, the jury could conclude that there was "supervisory encouragement, condonation and even acquiescence" in the unconstitutional practice.... Chief Bontempo's failure to eradicate this facially unconstitutional practice from the police department attributes that custom to the municipality.

Everett's contention that the Chief of Police cannot be considered a policymaker for the police department is unavailing. Testimony from the Chief and Mayor Connolly established that, in regard to law enforcement decisions, the Chief was one "whose acts or edicts may fairly be said to represent official policy." *Monell* [*v. Dep't of Soc. Serv.*], 436 U.S. [658,] 694 [(1978)]

....

6. The Causal Link.

The Supreme Court has declared that to support liability under § 1983, a municipal custom must have been the "moving force" behind the plaintiff's injury. *See Tuttle*, 471 U.S. at 819; *Monell*, 436 U.S. at 694–95.... There must be some "affirmative link" between the municipal custom and the constitutional deprivation. *See Tuttle*, 471 U.S. at 824–25 & n.8 (opinion of Rehnquist, J.) ... *see also City of Canton* [*v. Harris*], 489 U.S. [378,] 390–92 [(1989)]. Everett argues that there is no evidence that the officers were following the alleged custom on the night of July 22–23, 1982. It contends that the police were not apprehending felons but, rather, were seeking revenge. We disagree.

Testimony from a number of sources indicated that the officers were in the process of arresting one or more felons. Most importantly, Sergeant Ferullo testified that the officers on the scene had told him they were in the process of apprehending and arresting certain individuals and, later, that he was told arrests were made. Moreover, as Sergeant Ferullo noted, the breaking down of the door at the King Arthur Motel was no different from previous cases, in that all involved situations where doors had been broken down to apprehend felons. The officers were, therefore, following regular police practice.

The jury could reasonably have concluded that the plaintiffs' injuries occurred as a direct and immediate consequence of this unconstitutional municipal custom. Everett's arrest practice was both affirmatively linked to and the moving force behind the plaintiffs' constitutional deprivations. If a *constitutional* practice of arrest had been the accepted norm in the Everett Police Department, the officers would have been forced to obtain a warrant before entering Room 209. The additional cooling-off time that this would have afforded and the imposition of an impartial judicial officer's assessment of the situation would have greatly reduced, if not totally removed, the likelihood of any police overzealousness in this case.... Under the existing practice, however, the officers knew they could knock down the door to Room 209 and reach the persons inside without violating department policy. The jury's conclusion that this custom caused the plaintiffs' injuries is thus amply supported by the record.

In sum, a well-settled, unconstitutional practice of breaking down doors without warrants existed in Everett as of July 22–23, 1982. The Chief of Police had constructive knowledge of this custom yet did nothing to stop the practice. This made it almost inevitable that a constitutional injury would be suffered by some future party. The custom was the moving force behind and the cause of the violation in this case. Therefore, the jury's imposition of § 1983 liability on Everett based upon this unconstitutional custom is affirmed.

B. Municipal Liability Based on a Deficient Custom or Policy in the ... Training, Supervision or Discipline of Everett Police Officers

The City was also found liable under § 1983 for having a policy of inadequate ... training, supervision or discipline of its police officers. The jury found that this policy evidenced gross negligence amounting to deliberate indifference to the constitutional rights of those with whom the police would come into contact. Everett now argues that the evidence was insufficient as a matter of law to support this finding. We disagree.

...

With these teachings [from *Canton*] in mind, we address the question of whether the evidence presented at trial was sufficient to prove that Everett officials were deliberately indifferent to the need for better ... training, supervision and discipline of the city's police force.

7. The Existence of the Policy.

The evidence adduced at trial supports the finding that the City of Everett failed to provide minimally acceptable standards of ... training, supervision or discipline of its police force. In the instant action, ... "[t]here was direct evidence presented to the jury of the City of [Everett's] failure to train and supervise its officers in a number of key areas of law enforcement and of its indifference to the circumstances of [the plaintiffs' beatings]." ... The evidence on this issue and reasonable inferences to be drawn from it was as follows:

- The City of Everett was operating under a set of rules and regulations promulgated in 1951 and last distributed to the officers in the mid-sixties. The Rules and Regulations of the Everett Police Department, which comprised the day-to-day guidelines for the department, failed to address contemporary law enforcement issues and lacked sufficient detail to serve as the operating directives of a modern police force. Specifically, they failed to address up-to-date standards governing search and seizure, hot pursuit and the use of deadly force. Reiter, the plaintiffs' expert on police procedures, testified that these regulations were deficient in almost every way.

- Aside from emergency medical instruction, Everett officers received little or no formal training after completing their initial police academy courses. The officers thus lacked up-to-date direction in many police procedures, including the proper use of force.
- The City of Everett discouraged officers from seeking out supplementary training courses.

...

- There was no supervisory or command training required upon promotion to a higher rank. Supervisory officers, therefore, lacked the basic training due all officers and the command training necessary to effectively supervise and operate a police force.

...

- In the past, discipline had been meted out haphazardly, inconsistently, and infrequently to Everett officers.
- No disciplinary actions were instituted against the officers involved in this incident until over one month after the episode. A number of the officers were then suspended, because they had been indicted by the Suffolk County District Attorney.
- A full, internal investigation by the Everett Police Department did not occur until over one year after the King Arthur incident.
- Sergeant Ferullo received a short suspension as a result of this investigation. His suspension was subsequently overturned on appeal based, in part, on the fact that he had received inadequate supervisory training to be a police sergeant.
- Reiter testified that the Chief's review of civil grievances filed against Everett officers for their misconduct fell well below accepted levels. Indeed, many complaints were placed in a dead letter drawer never to be seen again.

...

- The Chief and the Mayor had received oral and written requests for better training and organizational improvements prior to the incident at King Arthur. They were aware of the issue, discussed it, and decided to institute no additional training programs. Later requests for better training by Everett police officers were ignored.
- Prior to the incident at the King Arthur Motel, Lieutenant Stewart, the main advocate for better training and guidance among the Everett officers, told both the Mayor and the Chief that something bad would happen if more instruction were not provided to the police force.

In addition to the evidence outlined above, we believe that the jury could have considered the incident itself in determining what type of ... training, supervision and discipline were given to Everett police officers. As with the unconstitutional custom of breaking down doors discussed, *supra*, there is independent evidence concerning the police department policy. The incident involved a series of interrelated acts of assault carried out by individual police officers. This, combined with the fact that there was other, independent evidence regarding police department policy, makes the police conduct at the motel evidence directly bearing on the officers'... training, supervision and discipline. It is reasonable to infer from what happened that these police officers received the same training and supervision and had similar understandings about whether they would be subject to discipline for their actions.

...

Based upon all the foregoing, the jury was well within its discretion in finding that the ... training, supervision or discipline of Everett police officers was grossly and flagrantly deficient.

8. Attribution to the Municipality.

In addition to proving the great inadequacies in the ... training, supervision or discipline of Everett police officers, plaintiffs must also establish that municipal officials charged with the responsibility of making policy for the police department were "deliberately indifferent" to these failings. *See City of Canton*, 489 U.S. at 388–89.... [T]he Chief of Police, and ultimately the Mayor of Everett, were responsible for the ... training, supervision and discipline of the Everett police force ... [and] both of these men were ones "whose acts or edicts may fairly be said to represent official policy." *Monell*, 436 U.S. at 694.... They were the policymakers for the city regarding law enforcement matters.

Based on the following evidence the jury could have found that both the Chief and the Mayor had express knowledge of the lack of any effective policy for the ... training, supervision or discipline of Everett police officers:

- Each had received complaints from Everett officers concerning inadequate police training and the dangers that this presented to civilians. The issue and its consequences were discussed by the Mayor and the Chief. They determined that no more training would be provided.
- Everett officers who sought out further training were affirmatively discouraged from doing so.
- The testimony of the Mayor and the Chief indicate clearly that they knew that there was no mandatory training required of Everett patrolmen or supervisory officers, aside from emergency medical instruction and police academy training.
- The Mayor had been sued by Everett police officers to force him to pay the monetary benefits due them under a state law that compelled municipalities to give

economic incentives to police officers who voluntarily take college-level law enforcement courses.

- Both men had the responsibility for overseeing the department and the discipline of its officers. The Mayor and the Chief were aware of the acts perpetrated at the King Arthur Motel yet chose to take no disciplinary actions against the officers until they had been indicted.

The jury had solid evidentiary grounds for finding that the failure of the Mayor and the Chief of Police to institute a minimally acceptable program of ... training, supervision or discipline amounted to a deliberate indifference to the constitutional rights of the city's inhabitants. *See City of Canton*, 489 U.S. at 391. The consequence of this policy was that the Everett police force was ill-prepared and ill-equipped to perform the obvious and recurring duties of police officers. *See id.*, at 389–91; *id.* at 395–96 (O'Connor, J., concurring in part and dissenting in part). The "do nothing policy" of the Mayor and the Chief exposed the citizens of Everett to imminent police misconduct, and was attributable to the municipality. *See id.* at 389–91.

9. The Causal Link.

In order to hold the city liable for their injuries under § 1983, the plaintiffs must also establish that there was a direct causal connection between the policy of inadequate ... training, supervision or discipline and the deprivations of their constitutional rights.... To form the basis for liability under § 1983, a municipal policy must be affirmatively linked to and the moving force behind the constitutional violation. *See Monell*, 436 U.S. at 694....

The jury could have found that the failure of the entire night watch of the Everett Police Department to act at even minimally acceptable levels of police conduct was directly linked to the city's policy of deficient ... training, supervision and discipline of its police force. The Rules and Regulations contained no information, and the Everett officers were given no up-to-date training on, the use of force—deadly or otherwise—hot pursuit, or search and seizure. The lack of proper training on these essential elements of law enforcement led directly to the constitutional violations at the King Arthur Motel. Due to the inadequacy of his supervisory training, Sergeant Ferullo abdicated his responsibility to the plaintiffs and left a volatile scene that demanded control by a supervisory officer. The absence of a strictly enforced disciplinary system led the officers at the King Arthur Motel to believe they were above the law and would not be sanctioned for their misconduct. A sufficiently supervised, properly ... trained and disciplined group of officers would not have acted so far below the level of accepted police behavior.

Based on all the foregoing, we affirm both the jury's finding that the plaintiffs' injuries were caused by a policy of the City of Everett and its imposition of § 1983 liability on the city. We point out that liability is levied here not because the city hired "one 'bad apple,'" *see Tuttle*, 471 U.S. at 821, but because the city's police policy produced an entire barrel of bad apples.

Exercise 12-C

Consider the evidence the court relied on in *Bordanaro* and the sample discovery requests included in Exercise 12-A in thinking about what discovery would be necessary for a plaintiff to prove that a constitutional violation had been caused by a municipal custom. For example, visit YouTube and search for the bar security camera tape of an off-duty Chicago police officer assaulting a bartender (Chicago Police Officer Attacks Female Bartender or Drunk Cop Beats Female Bartender and Gets Probation). Consider the security tape only, not any added editorial content. Suppose that your client, the bartender, plans to file a complaint alleging that the City of Chicago should be held liable for the off-duty police officer's assault. What theories of municipal liability do you think the bartender might pursue? What document requests would you draft to help establish municipal liability?

TO PROVE X	→	REQUEST Y DOCUMENT

Questions to guide reading of jury instructions

1. At several points, this book includes model jury instructions, the written instructions trial court judges read to the jurors before they retire to consider the evidence. A judge tailors model jury instructions to the evidence presented at trial by filling in the blanks. The judge (and law clerks) make sure the jury instructions reflect current law for the particular jurisdiction in which the jury is sitting.
2. While the jury instructions do not explicitly state that a policymaker is required for a claim based on a custom, do the instructions implicitly require that a policymaker be linked to the alleged custom?
3. In what ways do the federal model jury instructions emphasize causation?

Federal Jury Practice and Instructions

C. Essential Elements of Plaintiff's Claim

§ 165.25. Custom, policy, ordinance, regulation or decision

Plaintiff ________ claims defendant *[city]*, a municipality, is liable to plaintiff ________ for the denial of constitutional rights the plaintiff ________ alleges. Defendant *[city]* may be liable where you find that plaintiff ________ has been deprived of his constitutional rights and such deprivation was done pursuant to a governmental custom, policy, ordinance, regulation or decision.

When a person is injured as the *[proximate] [direct]* result of a government's policy, custom, regulation or decision, whether made by its lawmakers or by those officials whose statements or acts may fairly be said to represent official policy, defendant *[city]* itself is responsible for the injury that it caused.

Defendant *[city]* may be liable to plaintiff ________ if you find that the deprivation was done pursuant to a custom, policy, ordinance, regulation, or decision of defendant *[city]* that was the *[proximate] [direct]* cause of the deprivation of plaintiff's constitutional rights. Whether a custom or policy exists is a question of fact for you to determine.

[*The [Mayor, City Council] [was an official] [were officials] whose acts constitute final official policy of defendant [city]. Therefore, if you find that the acts of the [Mayor, City Council] deprived plaintiff ________ of plaintiff's constitutional rights, defendant [city] may be liable for such deprivations.*]

[*It has been shown that there was a [statute] [ordinance] [regulation] authorizing the actions that is the basis of plaintiff's claim. That is a sufficient basis for finding that defendant [city] caused the action at issue.*]

NOTES [to jury instructions]

...

In *City of St. Louis v. Praprotnik*, 485 U.S. 112 (1988), the plurality opinion stated that identification of policymaking officials is not a question of fact in the usual sense, but a determination to be based upon the law. The plurality opinion stated:

> In any event, however, a federal court would not be justified in assuming that municipal policymaking authority lies somewhere other than where the applicable law purports to put it. And certainly there can be no justification for giving a jury the discretion to determine which officials are high enough in the government that their actions can be said to represent a decision of the government itself.

485 U.S. at 126 ...

Proof of a single incident of unconstitutional activity is insufficient to impose liability under *Monell* unless proof of the incident includes proof that it was caused by an existing municipal policy which policy can be attributed to a municipal policymaker. *City of Oklahoma City v. Tuttle*, 471 U.S. 808, 823 (1985). In this case, a police officer shot plaintiff's deceased out of fear that the deceased was preparing to fire upon him. An instruction that allowed the jury "to infer a thoroughly nebulous 'policy' of 'inadequate training' on the part of the municipal corporation from the single incident described earlier in this opinion, and at the same time sanctioned the inference that the policy was the cause of the incident" was held to be improper. 471 U.S. at 823–824. The Court rejected plaintiff's argument that Oklahoma City had a policy of "inadequate training."

...

Proof of the mere existence of an unlawful policy or custom is not enough to establish municipal liability under Section 1983. The plaintiff bears the burden of proving that the municipal practice was the proximate cause of the injuries suffered. *Bielevicz v. Dubinon*, 915 F.2d 845, 850 (3d Cir. 1990) (plaintiff must demonstrate a plausible nexus or affirmative link between municipality's custom and specific deprivation of constitutional rights at issue). *See also Sivard v. Pulaski County*, 17 F.3d 185, 188 (7th Cir. 1994) (there must be an affirmative link between municipal policy and alleged constitutional violation for municipality to be held liable under Section 1983); *Hinton v. City of Elwood*, 997 F.2d 774, 782 (10th Cir. 1993) (municipality may not be held liable under Section 1983 solely because its employees inflicted injury on plaintiff, but plaintiff must show existence of municipal policy or custom and direct causal link between policy or custom and injury alleged).

...

See Los Angeles County, Cal. v. Humphries, 131 S. Ct. 447 (2010) (requirement that, in order for civil rights plaintiffs to successfully sue a municipal entity under § 1983, they must show their injury was caused by municipal policy or custom is equally applicable, irrespective of whether the remedy sought is money damages or prospective relief).[6]

To guide reading of Complaint

Lopez v. City of Chicago in Chapter 7 illustrated the difficulty of analyzing post-arrest, pre-conviction excessive force claims before *Kingsley*. Like *Lopez*, the below class action Complaint also was filed before the Supreme Court decided *Kingsley*.

Like the plaintiff in *Lopez*, Plaintiffs in the class action challenged Chicago police practices for detaining arrestees. In fact, Plaintiffs' Complaint relied in part on evidence discovered in the *Lopez* litigation. The Complaint further alleged that *Lopez* put Chicago on notice that people were being subjected to unconstitutional conditions while detained in police departments.

In reading the Complaint, focus on the municipal liability allegations by one class of arrestees. Notice the many ways Plaintiffs plead that the city itself is the moving force behind the alleged constitutional violations: by maintaining unconstitutional policies and customs, by failing to train and discipline police, and by being deliberately indifferent to the need for different policies, training, or discipline.

---

6. Kevin F. O'Malley, Jay E. Grenig, & Hon. William C. Lee, 3B Fed. Jury Prac. & Instr. § 165.26 (6th ed.) (updated Aug. 2019).

Dunn v. City of Chicago

2004 WL 2815185 (N.D. Ill. Oct. 21, 2004)

...

1. This is a class action pursuant to 42 U.S.C Section 1983 challenging the Chicago Police Department's ("CPD" or "Department") inhumane and unlawful system for detaining persons under the Department's control.

...

Interrogation Room Detentions: *The Use of "Soft" Torture In Chicago's Detective Divisions*

11. Many persons who are detained by the CPD for extended periods are held in Detective Division interrogation rooms—small, bare rooms, approximately ten feet in length and eight feet in width.

12. The rooms contain only a four foot by ten inch metal bench. There is no place to sleep or to relieve oneself and no access to running water. Because the rooms are wholly inadequate to meet the detainee's basic needs, it is inhumane and cruel to hold a detainee in these rooms for extended periods of time....

13. The CPD, however, maintains no policies regarding the length of time a detainee may be held in these rooms. It is not uncommon for a detainee to be kept in such rooms for several days while CPD detectives interrogate them and attempt to extract a confession.

14. Exacerbating the torturous conditions, CPD policies and procedures require that all suspects held in an interrogation room be shackled—arm to a ring on the wall or to a bar on the bench, for the entire time they are detained in the room.

16. If a suspect needs food or water, he/she can only get it if the detectives bring some. There is no scheduled food service for persons detained in these rooms. If a person needs to use the bathroom, they are at the whim of the detectives to unshackle them, let them out of the room and escort them to a restroom. It is not uncommon for persons detained in the interrogations rooms for extended periods to urinate or defecate on themselves or on the floor.

17. These interrogation room detentions are not only physically torturous, they are psychologically disorienting in a manner that can lead to increased suggestibility for the suspect being interrogated and, ultimately, to false confessions. These very conditions are recognized world-wide as a means of psychological torture to overcome a human being's reason and will.

...

Other Inhumane Conditions Inflicted By The CPD's System

...

24. The Department has an obligation to ensure, at a minimum, that detainees' basic needs for sustenance, hygiene and sleep are met while they are in the Department's charge. However ... [a]s a general and widespread practice and policy:

a. The CPD holds detainees in oppressive conditions;

b. The CPD furnishes no mattress or other bedding for overnight detentions....;

c. The CPD provides wholly inadequate access to restrooms and means of personal hygiene; and

d. The CPD furnishes detainees little if any food or drink during extended detentions. Even when the CPD does furnish food to those in its custody, it is always limited to a pork bologna sandwich, which, as the final policymakers of the CPD well know, violates the religious beliefs of many of its detainees, and is inedible to them.

...

Class Allegations

...

49. Named Plaintiffs Kimble and Robinson seek to represent Class I. Class I consists of: All persons detained in a CPD interrogation room for more than eight hours in a 24 hour period at any time form March 15, 1999 to the date of the order granting certification in this case....

a. On information and belief, at least 200,000 persons have been arrested by the CPD each year since 1999;

b. The CPD maintains no policy, directive or procedure limiting the amount of time that an arrestee may be kept in an interrogation room....

51. There are questions of law and fact common to the claims of Class I. Among these common questions are:

a. Whether it is unconstitutional to hold detainees in an interrogation for extended periods of time;

b. Whether it is unconstitutional to shackle persons to a wall in an interrogation room for extended periods of time;

c. Whether the conditions of confinement in the interrogation rooms deprive detainees of acceptable means of sleep in an unconstitutional manner;

d. Whether CPD policy allows the misuse of interrogations rooms for extended detentions in the manner alleged herein;

e. Whether there is a custom or practice within the CPD of misusing interrogation rooms in the manner alleged herein;

f. Whether CPD final policymakers have condoned or been deliberately indifferent to the misuse of interrogations rooms for extended detentions in the manner alleged herein; and

g. Whether extended detentions in the interrogation rooms violate detainees' rights under state law.

...

72. In direct response to the challenge in *Lopez,* the CPD modified its directive for processing arrestees to forbid detentions in excess of 48 hours in the absence of judicial approval or extraordinary circumstances.

73. The modification was enacted by the CPD's final policymaker or makers. The modification became effective in August of 2003.

74. The final policymakers of the CPD remain deliberately indifferent despite their having adopted the modification. Ignoring the allegations in *Lopez* of torturous conditions of confinement during CPD detentions, the final policymakers enacted no directive or modification to limit the amount of time a detainee may be held in an interrogation room other than the 48 hour general limitation on all detentions. Neither was a directive modified or adopted to require adequate accommodations for sleeping or adequate provision of nutrition or sanitation.

...

76. The modification was not implemented in a genuine manner that would actually change the CPD's widespread practice of unlawful detentions. The modification has not been subject of adequate dissemination, training and/or enforcement, and violations of the 48 hour requirement have not been adequately investigated and disciplined.

77. Rather, the final policymakers of the City of Chicago have been and remain deliberately indifferent to the widespread practice of detaining arrestees in excess of 48 hours without judicial approval. As a result, such detentions remain widespread practice in the CPD.

...

COUNT I—42 U.S.C. § 1983 Claim for Unlawful Interrogation Room Detentions

...

87. As described more fully above, Named Plaintiffs Kimble and Robinson and the members of the Class I have been detained in CPD interrogation rooms for unconstitutional lengths of time and have been damaged as a direct and proximate result.

88. The City of Chicago caused this deprivation of rights and is liable for Plaintiffs' and the Class Members' damages, *inter alia,* because the City of Chicago maintains unconstitutional policies, customs and widespread practices that caused these violations. Moreover, the City of Chicago fails to adequately train and discipline its officers in a manner that causes such violations. Further, the City of Chicago has been deliberately indifferent to the need for different policies, training and discipline. Also, the City of Chicago has failed to act to remedy the patterns of misconduct described in the preceding paragraphs, despite actual knowledge of the same, thereby causing the types of injuries alleged here.

COUNT II—42 U.S.C. § 1983 Claim For Deprivation of Adequate Accommodations For Sleep

...

COUNT III—42 U.S.C. § 1983 Claim For Excessive Detention

...

WHEREFORE, PLAINTIFFS DUNN, ROBINSON and KIMBLE, on behalf of themselves and a class of others similarly situated, demand judgment against the CITY OF CHICAGO awarding their actual damages, costs and a reasonable attorneys fee, together with any other relief that may be just; and further demand that a common fund be established to compensate them and their attorneys and to reimburse all expenses in connection with obtaining this relief.

For further discussion

1. The City of Chicago settled *Dunn* in 2010 for $16.5 million. Over 500,000 people may have been entitled to damages, including the thousands of arrestees over a nine-year period who did not receive probable cause hearings within 48 hours (up to $3,000 each); those held in interrogation rooms for more than 16 hours without regular bathroom breaks, meals, or a place to sleep (up to $2,000 each); and those held overnight without bedding (up to $90 each).[7]

2. When plaintiffs attempt to prove liability via use of expert witnesses, circuits require the expert to prove a clear training deficiency and direct link between that deficiency and the defendant's actions. For example, the Fifth Circuit concurred with the Seventh in finding a fatal flaw when "the plaintiff relied upon expert testimony that did not include any reference to the relevant training that the offending officers had actually received." *Pineda v. City of Houston*, 291 F.3d 325, 334 (5th Cir. 2002), *cert. denied*, 537 U.S. 1110 (2003); *see also Carr v. Castle*, 337 F.3d 1221, 1230 (10th Cir. 2003) ("that someone with the opportunity to prepare an expert report at leisure opines that well-trained officers would have performed differently under pressure does not rise to the legal standard of deliberate indifference on the part of the City, for [the expert] fails to point to any evidence placing the City on actual or constructive notice that the asserted failures to train were substantially certain to result in a constitutional violation").

Questions to guide reading of Settlement Agreement of Prison Litigation

1. Why do you think the settlement agreement twice references compliance with the Prison Litigation Reform Act?
2. Why do you think the parties included the American Correctional Association standards if those standards are not binding on defendants?

---

7. *See* Sandra Quinlan, *Chicago IL Civil Rights: City recommends $16.5 settlement in police custody suit*, JUSTICE NEW FLASH (May, 12, 2010), http://www.justicenewsflash.com/2010/05/13/city-recommends-165-settlement-in-police-custody-suit_201005134308.html.

3. Why do you think the prison population provision merited further explanation?
4. Is this settlement agreement analogous to a consent decree that would entitle plaintiff to "prevailing party" status under 42 U.S.C. § 1988? If so, why do you think the agreement provides for attorneys' fees?

McLendon v. City of Albuquerque

2005 WL 6003617 (D.N.M. June 30, 2005)

Stipulated Settlement Agreement Between Plaintiffs and Defendants

The Plaintiffs and Defendants agree that it is in their respective best interest to enter into this Stipulated Settlement Agreement.[5] The Plaintiffs and Defendants agree that this Stipulated Settlement Agreement complies with all of the requirements of the Prison Litigation Reform Act, 18 U.S.C. § 3626, *et seq.*

Nothing contained in this Stipulated Settlement Agreement constitutes an admission by the Defendants that they have ever violated the constitutional rights of any inmates, or that the Defendants have ever violated any Order of Court and nothing in this Stipulated Settlement Agreement should be construed as an admission by the Defendants that any prior or present policy, procedure, practice, event, circumstance, act or failure to act by the Defendants, their elected officials, contractors, agents or employees violated the civil rights laws of the United States, failed to meet applicable federal or constitutional standards, failed to comply with any Order of Court, or otherwise fell short of any standard of care imposed by law.

The Plaintiffs and Defendants enter into this Stipulated Settlement Agreement for the purpose of avoiding the risks and burdens of litigation and in order to describe conditions both parties wish to see maintained or improved at the Bernalillo County Metropolitan Detention Center.... The Plaintiffs and Defendants intend that this Stipulated Settlement Agreement will maintain and improve the conditions at the Metropolitan Detention Center for the benefit of the Defendants, their employees, agents and staff and for the benefit of the Plaintiff class.

... If necessary, the Defendants will revise and/or develop as necessary the policies, procedures, protocols, training materials and practices to ensure that the Defendants continue to comply with the policies and procedures of the Metropolitan Detention Center and that these policies and procedures are consistent with the requirements of the United States Constitution, the advisory standards of the American Correctional Association's Standards for Adult Detention Centers (which do not establish any minimum constitutional standard but which reflect prevailing professional practices) and the terms set forth in this Stipulated Settlement Agreement.

---

5. Counsel for Defendants was Jeffrey L. Baker, Esq., The Baker Law Firm. Counsel for Plaintiffs were Brian Pori, Esq., Inocente P.C. and Marc Lowry, Esq., Rothstein, Donatelli, Hughes Dahlstrom & Schoenburg LLP.

Plaintiffs and Defendants will jointly select two Auditor(s) (one Auditor for items 1–14 below, and one Auditor for medical issues) who will, over a nine month period (or sooner), evaluate the Defendants' compliance with the policies and procedures of the Metropolitan Detention Center, the United States Constitution, the advisory standards set forth in the American Correctional Association's Standards for Adult Detention Centers, and the terms set forth in this Stipulated Settlement Agreement and report in writing to the Plaintiffs and Defendants concerning the following aspects of the Bernalillo County Metropolitan Detention Center:

1. Population Management Initiatives (as more fully described *infra*)

2. Facility maintenance and sanitation (including the provision of adequate linen, bedding, and hygiene supplies)

3. Inmate safety (including, but not limited to, use of excessive force by officers and protection against a known risk of assault by other inmates)

4. Inmate access to law library

5. Food services

6. Inmate disciplinary process (including the provision of an inmate handbook in each housing unit which describes the disciplinary process)

7. Inmate grievance process (including the provision of an inmate handbook in each housing unit which describes the grievance process and other inmate rights and responsibilities)

8. Inmate programming (excluding mental health programming)

9. Inmate classification (consistent with the advisory standards of the American Correctional Association's Standards for Adult Detention Centers)

10. Inmate case management

11. Inmate access to mail

12. Inmate access to telephones

13. Inmate access to commissary

14. Inmate visitations (including the provision of an inmate handbook in each housing unit which describes the visitation process)

15. Medical services (including good faith efforts to comply with the advisory Guidelines of the National Commission on Correctional Health Care)

...

In evaluating the Defendants' compliance with Item Number One, Population Management Initiatives, the Auditor will recognize that many factors affect the population at the Metropolitan Detention Center which are beyond the control of the Defendants. Therefore, in evaluating the Defendants' compliance with Item Number One, Population Management Initiatives, the Auditor will ensure only that the Defendants will employ their best efforts to manage the population of the Metropolitan Detention Center.... The purpose of all of these population management initiatives is to assist the Defendants in using their best efforts to manage the population of the Metropolitan Detention Center because the parties realize that the unabated rise in the population of the Metropolitan Detention Center places unnecessary burdens on all aspects of the jail, its staff, and the provision of basic resident services.

The Auditor(s) shall have free access to all areas of the Metropolitan Detention Center, at such times and for such duration as the Auditor(s) desire. The Auditor(s) shall have unlimited access to all Metropolitan Detention Center personnel and records, and to all inmates of the Metropolitan Detention Center. The Defendants will provide the Auditor(s) with unlimited access to all personnel who work for the Metropolitan Detention Center, their private vendors, their independent contractors, or their agents who provide services to the Metropolitan Detention Center.

The Auditor(s) will notify the Director or his designee of the Auditor's visits to the Metropolitan Detention Center, so that the Auditor's personal security can be assured....

The Defendants will ensure that the Auditor(s) shall have the opportunity to conduct confidential interviews with inmates, as well as the opportunity to conduct interviews with Metropolitan Detention Center staff, their private vendor staff, their independent contractors, or their agents, outside the presence of other staff supervisors. The only exception would be when an active criminal investigation is ongoing, so as not to compromise the integrity of the criminal investigation.

...

If any items in the above list (1–15) are determined by the Auditor(s) not to be in compliance with United States constitutional requirements, the policies and procedures of the Metropolitan Detention Center, the advisory standards of the American Correctional Association's Standards for Local Detention Facilities, and the terms of this Stipulated Settlement Order, the Auditor(s) shall continue to evaluate and report on any such items until such time as all fifteen listed items are in compliance with the United States constitutional requirements, the policies and procedures of the Metropolitan Detention Center, the advisory standards of the American Correctional Association, and this Stipulated Settlement Agreement.

Once the Auditor(s) reports that an item complies with United Slates constitutional requirements, the policies and procedures of the Metropolitan Detention Center, the advisory standards of the American Correctional Association's Standards for Local Detention Facilities, and the terms of this Stipulated Settlement Agreement, the Auditor will cease reviewing this area.

Plaintiffs' class will move to dismiss this case, with prejudice, when the Defendants obtain compliance in all areas.

...

The Auditor(s) will be compensated by the Defendants, at rates to be negotiated between the Auditor(s) and the Defendants.

During the initial nine month period (or shorter), Plaintiffs agree their counsel will be compensated at the rate of $ 135.00 per hour ... for the monitoring activities of [two named counsel], not to exceed a combined twenty (20) hours per month, and $65.00 per hour ... for the monitoring activities of paralegals, not to exceed a combined twenty-five (25) hours per month. At the end of the nine month period (or sooner), if any items listed above have not met the requirements of this Stipulated Settlement Agreement, Plaintiffs' lawyers and paralegals will continue to be limited to the hourly rates and number of hours described above for monitoring activities, unless modified in writing between Plaintiffs and Defendants. However, any such hours which Plaintiffs' counsel and paralegals bill the Defendants will still be subject to the requirements of reasonableness.

...

The Defendants will not file any motion in the future asserting that this Stipulated Settlement should be terminated under the Prison Litigation Reform Act ... Any claimed breach of this Stipulated Settlement Agreement will be mediated by the United States Magistrate Judge before it is submitted to the District Court.

IT IS SO ORDERED.

D. The Relationship of Municipal Liability and Individual Liability for Constitutional Violations: The Supreme Court

---

Questions to guide reading *of Heller*

1. Under *Heller*, when the individual police officer has not inflicted constitutional harm, can the municipal employer still be held liable?
2. Based on *Heller*, do you think defendants would have an incentive to seek bifurcation of the trial against individuals from trial against the municipality? Would plaintiffs have the opposite incentive? Why?
3. Why does the dissent argue that a verdict for the officer would not necessarily be inconsistent with a possible verdict against the city?
4. Given your understanding of qualified immunity, why would a plaintiff be permitted to pursue local government liability even if the individual defendant was entitled to qualified immunity?
5. Do you think *Heller* should be accorded any more or less weight because it was decided *per curiam*, without briefs on the merits or oral arguments?

City of Los Angeles v. Heller

475 U.S. 796 (1986)

PER CURIAM.

Respondent Ronald Heller sued petitioners, city of Los Angeles, and individual members of the Los Angeles Police Commission, and two Los Angeles police officers in the United States District Court for the Central District of California under the provisions of 42 U.S.C. § 1983. He claimed damages by reason of having been arrested without probable cause and having been the victim of excessive force in the making of the arrest. The incident arose as a result of the two Los Angeles police officers stopping him because of a suspicion that he was driving while intoxicated. In the words of the Court of Appeals for the Ninth Circuit:

"The officers administered a series of field sobriety tests. Apparently dissatisfied with the results, the officers decided to take Heller to the station to undergo a breath test. When notified that he was under arrest, however, Heller became belligerent. One of the defendants, Officer Bushey, attempted to handcuff him. An altercation ensued. In the course of the struggle, Heller fell through a plate glass window." *Heller v. Bushey*, 759 F.2d 1371, 1372–1373 (9th Cir. 1985).

The District Court held a bifurcated trial, and first heard respondent's claims against one of the individual police officers.* The jury was instructed that Heller would make out his constitutional claim if he were arrested without reasonable cause, or if he were arrested with "unreasonable force" that exceeded the force necessary under the circumstances to effect arrest. *Id.* at 1374. The jury was not instructed on any affirmative defenses that might have been asserted by the individual police officer.... The jury returned a verdict for the defendant police officer and against respondent. The District Court then dismissed the action against petitioners, concluding that if the police officer had been exonerated by the jury there could be no basis for assertion of liability against the city or the persons constituting its Police Commission.

Respondent appealed to the Court of Appeals for the Ninth Circuit, and that court reversed the judgment of the District Court dismissing respondent's case against petitioners even though it did not disturb the verdict for the defendant police officer. Respondent urged, and the Court of Appeals apparently agreed, that "the jury could have believed that Bushey, having followed Police Department regulations, was entitled in substance to a defense of good faith. Such a belief would not negate the existence of a constitutional injury". *Id.* at 1373–74.

The difficulty with this position is that the jury was not charged on any affirmative defense such as good faith which might have been availed of by the individual police officer. Respondent contends in his brief in opposition to certiorari that even though no issue of qualified immunity was presented to the jury, the jury might nonetheless have considered evidence which would have supported a finding of such immunity.

---

* The second of the two police officers named as defendants was granted summary judgment by the District Court.

But the theory under which jury instructions are given by trial courts and reviewed on appeal is that juries act in accordance with the instructions given them ... and that they do not consider and base their decisions on legal questions with respect to which they are not charged. We think that the Court of Appeals' search for ambiguity in the verdict was unavailing; as that court itself noted later in its opinion, "[b]ecause the instructions required a verdict for [respondent] if *either* the due process *or* the excessive force claim was found, the jury's verdict for the defendant required a negative finding on both claims." *Id.* at 1374, n.3. This negative, it seems to us, was conclusive not only as to Officer Bushey, but also as to the city and its Police Commission. They were sued only because they were thought legally responsible for Bushey's actions; if the latter inflicted no constitutional injury on respondent, it is inconceivable that petitioners could be liable to respondent.

The Court of Appeals also stated:

> "We must conclude that the general verdict does not foreclose a finding that Heller suffered a constitutional deprivation. Heller's *Monell* claim survived the general verdict.... The jury verdict, of course, conclusively determined that there was probable cause to arrest Heller. On the other hand, it is equally clear that whether the application of force in accordance with Police Department regulations in this case exceeded constitutional limits has not been determined." *Id.* at 1374–75.

But this was an action for damages, and neither *Monell v. New York City Dept. of Social Services*, 436 U.S. 658 (1978), nor any other of our cases authorizes the award of damages against a municipal corporation based on the actions of one of its officers when in fact the jury has concluded that the officer inflicted no constitutional harm. If a person has suffered no constitutional injury at the hands of the individual police officer, the fact that the departmental regulations might have *authorized* the use of constitutionally excessive force is quite beside the point.

The petition for certiorari is granted, the judgment of the Court of Appeals is reversed, and the case is remanded for further proceedings consistent with this opinion. It is so ordered.

...

Justice STEVENS, with whom Justice MARSHALL joins, dissenting.

...

The District Court's decision to dismiss the action against the city, the Police Department, and the Police Commissioners necessarily rested on two assumptions: (1) there was an inherent inconsistency between the jury verdict in favor of Officer Bushey and a possible verdict against the municipal defendants and (2) that inconsistency required the dismissal of the action against the municipal defendants.... In my view, neither of the necessary assumptions for the District Court's action—and for this Court's reinstatement of its decision—is remotely present in this case.

I

The first necessary assumption is that there would be an inevitable inconsistency between the jury verdict of no liability for Officer Bushey and a possible verdict of liability against the municipal entities; in the absence of such an inconsistency, the District Court's decision, and this Court's reinstatement of it, are simply inexplicable.

It is undisputed that Ronald Heller crashed through a plate-glass window after some kind of an altercation with Officer Bushey. He had been stopped on suspicion of driving while intoxicated and given sobriety tests. In his claim against the municipal entities, Heller contended that the city and the Police Department had adopted a policy of condoning excessive force in making arrests, that the policy was unlawful, and that he had been injured by the application of that policy at the time of his arrest. In his claim against Officer Bushey, Heller contended that his constitutional rights were violated because Officer Bushey had employed "unreasonable force" in arresting him.

...

In the proceeding against Officer Bushey, considerable evidence of the Los Angeles Police Department's policy and custom on the use of force was introduced. An expert witness testified regarding Los Angeles' officially sanctioned use of "escalating force," culminating in the use of the notorious "chokehold." Officer Bushey himself testified that Heller's flight through the window resulted from his attempt to impose a chokehold, and that he was carefully following official Police Department policy. Officer Bushey's superior, Sergeant Shrader, also testified that Officer Bushey's actions were in complete compliance with official Police Department policy. Finally, Officer Bushey's attorney repeatedly emphasized that his client's actions were entirely consistent with established Department policy.

In submitting the claim against Officer Bushey to the jury, the trial judge gave an instruction that simply stated that whether or not the force used in making an arrest is unreasonable "is an issue to be determined in the light of all the surrounding circumstances." After deliberating several hours, the jury returned a general verdict in favor of the officer.

Thus, despite the majority's summary assertion to the contrary, it is perfectly obvious that the general verdict rejecting the excessive force claim against Officer Bushey did not necessarily determine the constitutionality of the city's "escalating force" policy—a subject on which the jury had received no instructions at all. The verdict merely determined that the officer's action was not unreasonable "in the light of all the surrounding circumstances"—which, of course, included the evidence that Officer Bushey was merely obeying orders and following established Police Department policy.

As a result, there was no necessary inconsistency between the verdict for Officer Bushey and a possible verdict of liability against the municipal defendants.

II

In view of the fact that the Court of Appeals correctly concluded that there was no necessary inconsistency between a verdict exonerating Officer Bushey and a verdict holding the city and Police Department liable for the "escalating force" policy, it did not have to consider the appropriate response to a possible inconsistency in the context of a bifurcated trial.

. . .

If the Court's unprecedented, ill-considered, and far-reaching decision happens to be correct, defendants as a class have been presented with a tactical weapon of great value. By persuading trial judges to bifurcate trials in which both the principal and its agents are named as defendants, and to require the jury to bring in its verdict on the individual claim first, they may obtain the benefit of whatever intangible factors have prompted juries to bring in a multitude of inconsistent verdicts in past years; defendants will no longer have to abide the mechanisms that courts have used to mitigate and resolve apparent inconsistencies. Perhaps that is an appropriate response to the current widespread concern about the potential liabilities of our municipalities, but I doubt it.

. . .

III

The Court today reverses an interlocutory decision in a constitutional rights case on the basis of assumptions that dramatically conflict with the record and with settled legal principles. The Court mistakenly assumes that there was a necessary inconsistency between the verdict of no liability against the individual officer and a possible verdict against the municipal defendants; it then mistakenly assumes that dismissal was an appropriate response to the perceived inconsistency. Perhaps not coincidentally, the Court achieves these results without the aid of briefs or argument, and relies on an anonymous author to explain what it has done. I respectfully dissent.

For further discussion

Defendants may move to bifurcate the claim against the individual defendants from the claim against the municipality as "a strategy that may eliminate the need to proceed against the municipality, either because the plaintiff fails to establish a constitutional wrong or because the city agrees initially to indemnify and pay any judgment should the plaintiff prevail against the individual officer." Karen M. Blum, *Making Out the Monell Claim Under Section 1983*, 25 Touro L. Rev. 829, 852 (2009). Plaintiffs might oppose bifurcation if testimony on injuries and damages to plaintiff is relevant to the issue of liability, *e.g.*, how severe the injuries are is relevant to whether a police officer's use of force was excessive, and if the same witnesses will testify as to liability and damages. Paul M. Messing, *Framing the Causes of Action: Actionable Police Misconduct*, Civil Rights: How Lawyers Protect the Constitution through Section 1983 Civil Litigation (Pa. Bar Institute 2010) at 83.

E. Development of Doctrine in the Circuits: Applying *Heller*

Most circuits have read *Heller* to preclude municipal liability in the absence of a constitutional violation by the individual local government actors whose conduct inflicted plaintiff's injuries. *See, e.g.*, *Trigalet v. City of Tulsa*, 239 F.3d 1150, 1154–56 (10th Cir.), *cert. denied*, 534 U.S. 814 (2001). For a time, the Third Circuit did not. The law review article excerpted below is included to illustrate the following:

1) in practice, lawyers and courts may confront circuit precedent that is arguably inconsistent with Supreme Court precedent;
2) in practice, lawyers and courts may confront non-precedential federal appellate opinions that are inconsistent with circuit precedent; and
3) inconsistency in the decisions of the hierarchically superior courts has practical consequences for litigation strategy.

The article is also included as an example of how lawyers may slowly chip away at precedent without overtly seeking its reversal, and how judges may do the same, without overtly announcing its reversal.

Questions to guide reading of law review article

1. What is the *Fagan* theory of municipal liability? Why is it potentially inconsistent with *Heller*?
2. How did non-precedential opinions on municipal liability diverge from *Fagan*?
3. Based on the excerpt from the summary judgment oral argument, what was the district court judge's attitude toward non-precedential opinions?
4. What are some of the practical ramifications of the doctrinal divergence between precedential and non-precedential applications of municipal liability for litigants and district courts bound by the *Fagan* precedent?

Law Review Article

The following is an excerpt from Sarah E. Ricks, *The Perils of Unpublished Non-precedential Federal Appellate Opinions: A Case Study of the State-Created Danger Doctrine in One Circuit*, 81 Wash. L. Rev. 217 (2006) (documenting four doctrinal divergences between the precedential and non-precedential Third Circuit opinions applying one constitutional doctrine).

D. Example Four: 42 U.S.C. § 1983 Municipal Liability

A final doctrinal divergence between precedential and non-precedential opinions concerns municipal liability for state-created danger. In 1994, Third Circuit precedent held that municipalities could be liable under 42 U.S.C. § 1983 for constitutional wrongdoing even in the absence of liability by an individual state actor. This precedent was widely criticized. Perhaps in response to such criticism, in two non-precedential opinions in 2000, the Third Circuit purported to modify its precedential theory. Even after the 2003 issuance of a precedential opinion on municipal liability for state-created danger in the absence of individual liability, the contours of the theory remain too unclear for non-precedential application, which should be limited to applications of settled doctrine.

1. Third Circuit Precedent Required Examination of Municipal Liability Even in the Absence of Constitutional Wrongdoing by Individual Actors

The Supreme Court held in *Collins v. City of Harker Heights, Texas*, that a municipal liability claim under 42 U.S.C. § 1983 should be analyzed in two steps: "(1) whether plaintiff's harm was caused by a constitutional violation, and (2) if so, whether the city is responsible for that violation." Over a decade ago, the Third Circuit apparently read the Supreme Court's statutory standard for holding a government liable for the constitutional wrongdoing of its employee to instead create a direct constitutional theory of municipal liability. In *Fagan v. City of Vineland*, [22 F.3d 1283 (3d Cir. 1994)] a high speed police chase case, the Third Circuit held that municipal liability under § 1983 for a substantive due process violation does not depend on the individual employee's liability and that a constitutional violation can exist even if no individual police officer violated the Constitution.

A year after *Fagan*, in a precedential state-created danger decision, the Third Circuit acknowledged "some inconsistency in our circuit as to the standard governing the underlying constitutional violation in policy, custom or practice cases" because the *Fagan* panel may have misread the statutory standard for holding a municipality liable for an employee's constitutional wrongdoing to instead describe a separate constitutional standard. The court suggested that the *Fagan* panel had skipped the first prong of the municipal liability analysis required by the Supreme Court in *Collins*:

> [T]he *Fagan* panel opinion appeared to hold that a plaintiff can establish a constitutional violation predicate to a claim of municipal liability simply by demonstrating that the policymakers, acting with deliberate indifference, enacted an inadequate policy that caused an injury. It appears that, by focusing almost exclusively on the 'deliberate indifference' prong of the *Collins* test, the panel opinion did not apply the first prong—establishing an underlying constitutional violation.

Federal and state courts have widely rejected the *Fagan* panel decision and both courts and commentators have criticized it as inconsistent with Supreme Court doctrine. The validity of that criticism is beyond the scope of this Article. What is significant here is that Third Circuit precedent has adhered to *Fagan*. In its precedent adopting the state-created danger doctrine, the Third Circuit chastised the district court for failing to evaluate the claim against the city because "[t]he precedent in our circuit requires the district court to review the plaintiffs' municipal liability claims independently of the § 1983 claims against the individual police officers." Yet the Third Circuit continued to send conflicting signals to litigants and district courts by acknowledging Supreme Court authority for the proposition that a municipal liability claim will fail in the absence of an underlying constitutional violation.

2. Non-Precedential Municipal Liability Opinions Permitted Rejection of Claims Against Individuals to Be Dispositive of the Municipal Liability Claim

Following criticism of *Fagan*, the Third Circuit issued two non-precedential opinions in 2000 that permitted rejection of claims against individuals to be dispositive of municipal liability claims by distinguishing *Fagan* on analytically unsound grounds. In both non-precedential opinions, the Third Circuit held that plaintiffs failed to show substantive due process violations by the individual police officers and that this conclusion was dispositive of the § 1983 claims against the municipalities. The Third Circuit's non-precedential distinction of *Fagan* was accomplished with semantic sleight of hand: the panels inquired only into constitutional wrongdoing by the individual defendants and, without inquiring into direct constitutional wrongdoing by the municipality as *Fagan* requires, concluded there had been no constitutional wrongdoing, and therefore no municipal liability. The non-precedential decisions reasoned identically, using nearly identical language, suggesting one followed the other:

> Whether there is an underlying constitutional violation also will help clarify municipal liability for if there is no violation, there can be no municipal liability. *Cf. City of Los Angeles v. Heller*, 475 U.S. 796, 799 (1986) (per curiam) ("If a person has suffered no constitutional injury at the hands of the individual police officers, the fact that the departmental regulations might have authorized the use of constitutionally excessive force is quite beside the point.").

. . .

> The absence of a constitutional violation also resolves the question of municipal liability. Although it is undoubtedly true that a municipality's "liability under section 1983 for a substantive due process violation does not depend upon an individual officer's liability," *Fagan*, 22 F.3d at 1293, it is equally true that a Section 1983 claim requires a constitutional violation. *See Heller*, 475 U.S. at 799. As there is no constitutional violation, there is no municipal liability.

Whether consistent with Supreme Court teaching, the non-precedential distinction of *Fagan* is not consistent with how the Third Circuit had instructed district courts to apply *Fagan*'s theory of direct municipal liability for substantive due process claims. Neither opinion explained the failure to undertake *Fagan*'s theory of direct municipal liability once the individual defendants had been absolved of inflicting "a constitutional injury." The appellate court function of ensuring doctrinal uniformity was undermined by the Third Circuit's broad reading of the Supreme Court's *Heller* decision in two non-precedential decisions because the Third Circuit's precedential decisions required district courts and litigants to analyze its direct theory of constitutional wrongdoing by the municipality itself.

The two non-precedential opinions were not, however, the circuit's only state-created danger municipal liability decisions. The court issued non-precedential opinions on at least seven other state-created danger claims concerning municipal liability between its precedential decisions in 1997 and 2003. Two did not differentiate claims against individuals from those against the municipality. But five appear consistent with *Fagan* as each analyzed constitutional wrongdoing by the municipality despite the absence of constitutional wrongdoing by an individual.

3. Practical Consequences of Doctrinal Inconsistency for District Courts and Litigants

The lack of doctrinal uniformity left litigants and district courts confused about how to apply the Third Circuit's criticized theory that municipal liability in substantive due process cases can be independent of claims against individual state actors, rather than derivative of claims against individuals. Some government litigants relied on the non-precedential distinction of *Fagan*. Meanwhile, district courts were struggling to reconcile the independent theory of municipal liability articulated in *Fagan* both with Supreme Court decisions that preexisted *Fagan* (*Heller*, *Collins*, and *City of Canton, Ohio v. Harris* [489 U.S. 378 (1989)]) and with Supreme Court decisions that postdated *Fagan* (*Lewis*).

Doctrinal inconsistency may have caused federal courts to expend more resources in resolving state-created danger litigation and discouraged settlement of municipal liability claims, thus undercutting the efficiency rationale for issuing non-precedential opinions. For example, one district court required a trial of state-created danger claims against the municipality even after granting judgment to all individual defendants. Other district courts instead ignored the Third Circuit's independent theory of municipal liability and treated substantive due process claims against cities as derivative of claims against individual defendants. At least one district court suggested that the Third Circuit revisit its theory of municipal liability independent of individual substantive due process violations while acknowledging it was meanwhile bound by *Fagan*.

Because they are unavailable on Westlaw or Lexis and are not published in a print reporter, many district courts likely were unaware of the non-precedential opinions issued before 2002. However, one district court flatly rejected a municipal litigant's attempted reliance on one of the non-precedential decisions discussed above, which the litigant had cited in distinguishing *Fagan*. Further, the district court criticized another district court for having followed the non-precedential opinions:

THE COURT:	... Do you rely on [a non-precedential Third Circuit opinion]?
MR. WINEBRAKE:	We rely on [the] District Court decision in [that case], and we apprised the Court of the unpublished opinion because we think it's good to know that the Third Circuit in a seemingly well thought out opinion written by Judge Scirica upheld [the district court].
THE COURT:	Well, that's very interesting. It was not for publication and has no precedential value. At a conference of the Third Circuit, the Court of Appeals defended their un-

published opinions on the ground that they're not well reasoned, they don't give them much thought. So it's hard to say that that's a well-reasoned opinion that has any precedential value.

MR. WINEBRAKE: Well, we concede—

THE COURT: It's instructive on what they'll do without much thought.

MR. WINEBRAKE: True. But it's instructive, Your Honor, and it's also—it's also interesting to see how they handled some of the issues—how they handled the *Fagan* issue, for example.

THE COURT: I don't intend to rely on the affirmance by the Court of Appeals in [the non-precedential opinion]. I think it was incorrect of [another district court judge] to cite [Third Circuit non-precedential state-created danger opinions] as he did. What I mean—

MR. WINEBRAKE: Your Honor—

THE COURT: [The other district court] may be correct in his ultimate decision [citing non-precedential opinions], but I think that the Court of Appeals has instructed us not to rely on unpublished opinions, and we're obliged to comply with that instruction.

Had the non-precedential distinction of *Fagan* instead been precedential, and therefore binding on the district court, the district court would not have been free to ignore the Third Circuit's retreat from its criticized municipal liability theory.

4. The Doctrine of Independent Municipal Liability for State-Created Danger Is Insufficiently Settled for Non-Precedential Application

Recent Third Circuit state-created danger precedent suggests that, even now, the contours of *Fagan*'s theory of independent substantive due process violations by a municipality remain insufficiently settled for routine, non-precedential application. A precedential opinion issued by the Third Circuit in 2003 acknowledged the widespread criticism of *Fagan*. That 2003 precedent could be read broadly to link the existence of constitutional harm to the conduct of the individuals, eviscerating the Third Circuit's theory of independent municipal liability for state-created danger claims, and thereby making precedential the distinction of *Fagan* first articulated in non-precedential opinions years earlier. But the 2003 precedent simultaneously adhered to *Fagan*, holding that "[i]t is possible for a municipality to be held independently liable for a substantive due process violation even in situations where none of its employees are liable." [*Brown v. Commonwealth of Pa. Dep't of Health Emergency Med. Servs. Training Inst.*, 318 F.3d 473, 482 (3d Cir. 2003) (citing *Fagan* at 1292).] Direct municipal liability for state-created danger, therefore, remains insufficiently clear for non-precedential application, which should be restricted to application of settled law.

For further discussion

1. Based on the doctrinal evolution outlined in the article above, what litigation strategy would you recommend to plaintiffs and defendants bound by the Seventh Circuit's decision in *Thomas v. Cook County Sheriff's Dept.*, 604 F.3d 293 (7th Cir. 2010)? *Thomas* read *Heller* narrowly, to preclude municipal liability in the absence of underlying constitutional wrongdoing by an individual *only if* such a finding would produce an inconsistent verdict. *Id.* at 305. The Seventh Circuit reasoned:

> The plaintiff presented evidence of County customs and practices that caused [a pretrial detainee's] death.... The testimony at trial leads us to conclude that the jury had a sufficient basis to find a widespread practice of [medical technicians] failing to collect medical request forms, and that this failure caused [the detainee's] death.
>
> Furthermore, we find unpersuasive the County's argument that it cannot be held liable under *Monell* because none of its employees were found to have violated [the detainee's] constitutional rights.... The County, in this case, appears to push for a rule that requires individual officer liability before a municipality can ever be held liable for damages under *Monell.* This is an unreasonable extension of *Heller.* What if the plaintiff here had only sued the County, or didn't know, because of some breakdown in recording shifts, who the [medical technicians] on duty were? The actual rule, as we interpret it, is much narrower: a municipality can be held liable under *Monell*, even when its officers are not, unless such a finding would create an inconsistent verdict. *See Heller*, 475 U.S. at 798–99; *see also id.* at 801 (Stevens, J., dissenting). So, to determine whether the County's liability is dependent on its officers, we look to the nature of the constitutional violation, the theory of municipal liability, and the defenses set forth.

Id. at 303–05. If you represented Cook County, would you seek certiorari? Why?

2. In 2018, the Supreme Court denied a petition for certiorari asserting a circuit split about local government liability in the absence of a constitutional violation by the individual employee. The certiorari petition argued that the federal circuits had been divided "for decades" over the scope of the Supreme Court's ruling in *Heller.* Petition for Writ of Certiorari in *Medrano-Arzate v. May*, 2016 WL 9997910, No. 17-601, at *2 (Oct. 18, 2016). Petitioner summarized the argument:

> II. The Circuits Are Deeply Divided Over Whether Municipal Liability Under Section 1983 Can Inhere Absent a Constitutionally Culpable Act by the Individual Employee
>
> A. Five Circuits Read *Heller* Narrowly, Resulting in Ampler Municipal Liability
>
> B. Six Circuits Read *Heller* Too Broadly, Prematurely Foreclosing Section 1983 Claims Against Municipal Defendants

Id. at ii. In categorizing the Third Circuit as reading *Heller* narrowly, the Petition relied heavily on the Third Circuit's opinion in *Fagan* to illustrate the point. Based on your reading of the law review excerpt, and the doctrinal divergence between the Third Circuit's precedential and non-precedential opinions, would you categorize the Third Circuit in the same way? *See also* Petition for Writ of Certiorari, *Barnwell v. Douglas County*, 2010 WL 4314347, No. 10-574 at *8–10 (Oct. 28, 2010), *cert. denied*, 562 U.S. 1137 (2011) (relying in part on *Fagan* and *Thomas v. Cook County Sheriff's Department*, 604 F.3d 293, 305 (7th Cir. 2010) to argue that, "[i]n the wake of *Heller*, the Second, Third, Seventh, and Eighth Circuits have adopted the view that *Heller* does not impose upon *Monell* an absolute requirement that the plaintiff prove liability on the part of an individual officer as a prerequisite to the local government's liability" while the First, Fourth, Sixth, Tenth, and Eleventh Circuits "have adopted a restrictive view, holding that *Heller* creates an absolute legal bar to municipal liability absent proof of an individual officer's liability... The restrictive view is inconsistent with *Monell*'s holding that local governments are "persons" that are liable under § 1983 when their policies or customs result in constitutional injuries. *Monell* made clear that municipal liability under § 1983 is not derivative of an individual employee's liability, and does not sound in *respondeat superior*.").

F. The Murky Landscape of Post-*Iqbal* Supervisory Liability: Is it Statutory or Constitutional? Is Intent Required?

The current status of § 1983 supervisory liability is uncertain. Below is a brief overview of the doctrine before and after the Supreme Court's surprising decision in *Iqbal*. A close-up of the varying ways one circuit, the Seventh, has applied the supervisory liability doctrine gives a snapshot of the doctrinal uncertainty in the wake of *Iqbal*.

*1. Pre-*Iqbal *Supervisory Liability*

It is well settled that there is no *respondeat superior* liability under § 1983. *See* Chapter 1. But for many years, federal appellate courts have recognized supervisory liability as a kind of individual liability under § 1983. While formulated differently by the circuits, supervisory liability permits the supervisor of an employee who violated a person's rights to be liable for the supervisor's own conduct, such as when the supervisor played a role in the violation or knew of the violation and condoned or acquiesced in the conduct. For example, the Fourth Circuit required a plaintiff to prove all of the following to prevail on a § 1983 supervisory liability claim:

> (1) that the supervisor had actual or constructive knowledge that his subordinate was engaged in conduct that posed 'a pervasive and unreasonable risk' of constitutional injury to citizens like the plaintiff;
>
> (2) that the supervisor's response to that knowledge was so inadequate as to show 'deliberate indifference to or tacit authorization of the alleged offensive practices'; and

> (3) that there was an 'affirmative causal link' between the supervisor's inaction and the particular constitutional injury suffered by the plaintiff.

Shaw v. Stroud, 13 F.3d 791, 799 (4th Cir.), *cert. denied*, 513 U.S. 813 (1994). Similarly, in the context of alleged sexual abuse of a minor public school child by a school employee, the Fifth Circuit held a supervisory school official could be liable under § 1983 when:

> (1) the defendant learned of facts or a pattern of inappropriate sexual behavior by a subordinate pointing plainly toward the conclusion that the subordinate was sexually abusing the student; and
>
> (2) the defendant demonstrated deliberate indifference toward the constitutional rights of the student by failing to take action that was obviously necessary to prevent or stop the abuse; and
>
> (3) such failure caused a constitutional injury to the student.

Doe v. Taylor Indep. Sch. Dist., 15 F.3d 443, 454 (5th Cir.) (en banc), *cert. denied*, 513 U.S. 815 (1994).

2. Iqbal *on Supervisory Liability*

In a surprising 2009 decision discussed in Chapter 10, the Supreme Court called into question the continuing existence of supervisory liability. In *Ashcroft v. Iqbal*, 556 U.S. 662 (2009), a Pakistani Muslim filed suit against federal officials based on his arrest and detention following the September 11, 2001, attacks. The Supreme Court's decision could be read to eliminate supervisory liability in the federal analog to a § 1983 case, a *Bivens* action, for reasons equally applicable to § 1983 claims.[8]

The Court rejected plaintiff's claim that '"knowledge and acquiescence [by supervisors] in their subordinates' use of discriminatory criteria to make classification decisions among detainees'" was sufficient to find that the supervisors had committed a constitutional violation and concluded that "the term 'supervisory liability' is a misnomer" in a section 1983 suit or a *Bivens* suit. *Iqbal*, 556 U.S. at 677

In dissent, Justice Souter, joined by three other Justices, canvassed the circuits' various supervisory liability tests, argued that the Court failed to recognize the distinction between *respondeat superior* and supervisory liability, and argued further that the Court should not have reached the issue of supervisory liability because it had neither been briefed nor argued:

> [T]here is quite a spectrum of possible tests for supervisory liability: it could be imposed where a supervisor has actual knowledge of a subordinate's constitutional violation and acquiesces [citing 3d and 10th Circuit]; or where supervisors "'know about the conduct and facilitate it, approve it, condone it, or turn a blind eye for fear of what they might see,'" [quoting D.C. Circuit]

8. The federal analog to 42 U.S.C. § 1983 action was created in *Bivens v. Six Unknown Named Agents of Fed. Bureau of Narcotics*, 403 U.S. 388, 389 (1971), where the Supreme Court held that an implied cause of action exists against officials acting under color of federal law who violate an individual's constitutional rights.

> (quoting *Jones v. Chicago*, 856 F.2d 985, 992 (7th Cir. 1988) (Posner, J.)); or where the supervisor has no actual knowledge of the violation but was reckless in his supervision of the subordinate [citing 8th Circuit]; or where the supervisor was grossly negligent [citing 1st Circuit].

Iqbal, 556 U.S. at 693–94 (Souter, J., dissenting). Justice Souter predicted that *Iqbal* eliminated supervisory liability: "Lest there be any mistake ... the majority ... is eliminating *Bivens* supervisory liability entirely. The nature of a supervisory liability theory is that the supervisor may be liable, under certain conditions, for the wrongdoing of his subordinates, and it is this very principle that the majority rejects." *Iqbal*, 556 U.S. at 693 (Souter, J., dissenting).

At least one commentator considered Justice Souter's dissent alarmist and counseled courts to read *Iqbal* to have narrowed but not eliminated supervisory liability. Professor Stein argued *Iqbal* denied the existence of supervisory liability "only in regard to claims of intentional discrimination; insofar as [the federal supervisory officials] were only charged with intentional discrimination, that intentionality must be their own, not that of their subordinates. That intentionality presumably could be established either through their own discriminatory policy, or through knowledge of and indifference to their subordinate's discriminatory conduct." Allan R. Stein, *Confining Iqbal*, 45 Tulsa L. Rev. 277, 290 & n.87 (2010).

3. Doctrinal Uncertainty: The Seventh Circuit's Applications of Supervisory Liability

The uncertain status of supervisory liability since *Iqbal* is illustrated by the Seventh Circuit's various approaches. Existing Seventh Circuit precedent analyzes claims against supervisors (1) as a question of causation under § 1983 by asking if the supervisor knew about the conduct and turned a blind eye (*Backes*); (2) as a constitutional question where the standard varies with the requirements of the constitutional claim (*T.E.*; *Arnett; Paine*); (3) as a constitutional question but reserving the question of whether a supervisor must intend to violate the constitution even if the constitutional standard does not require intent (*Arnett*); (4) as a constitutional question and holding a supervisor must intend to violate the constitution even if the constitutional standard does not require intent but holding subjective deliberate indifference is a form of intent (*Vance*).

a. Is Supervisory Liability a Statutory Claim about § 1983 Causation?

The Seventh Circuit in one precedent appeared to treat supervisory liability as unchanged by *Iqbal*, that is, as a question of statutory construction of the § 1983 causation language requiring that the underlying constitutional violation be *caused by* the supervisor. *Backes v. Village of Peoria Heights*, 662 F.3d 866 (7th Cir. 2011). Without even citing *Iqbal*, the Seventh Circuit reasoned:

> [A] defendant need not 'participate[] directly in the deprivation' for liability to follow under § 1983. [citing 7th Circuit precedent]. Indeed, a supervisor may

> still be personally liable for the acts of his subordinates if he 'approves of the conduct and the basis for it.' [citing 7th Circuit precedent] '[S]upervisors must know about the conduct and facilitate it, approve it, condone it, or turn a blind eye for fear of what they might see. They must in other words act either knowingly or with deliberate, reckless indifference.' *Id.* [quoting 7th Circuit precedent].

Backes, 662 F.3d at 869–70.

b. Is Supervisory Liability a Constitutional Question Where the Standard Varies Depending on the Constitutional Claim?

By contrast, citing *Iqbal,* the Seventh Circuit has analyzed claims against supervisors as independent constitutional claims. The Seventh Circuit held that a public school principal could be liable for concealing reports of sexual abuse by a teacher and "creating an atmosphere that allowed abuse to flourish" because such conduct was "not mere failure of supervisory officials to act" but a claim that a defendant's "own misconduct" and "deliberate indifference" deprived students of their liberty interests in violation of substantive due process, "regardless whether a supervisor or a subordinate." *T.E. v. Grindle*, 599 F.3d 583, 590–91 (7th Cir. 2010); *see Arnett v. Webster*, 658 F.3d 742, 758 (7th Cir. 2011) (similarly, suggesting that a supervisor's failure to act can be culpable where plaintiff can show the supervisor knew of a substantial risk of serious harm to plaintiff, the same 8th Amendment standard that applies to non-supervisors).

Consistently with analyzing claims against supervisors as constitutional claims (rather than statutory claims based on the causation language of Section 1983), the Seventh Circuit, again citing *Iqbal*, has plainly stated that a police supervisor "can only be liable for what he did; there is no doctrine of supervisory liability for the errors of subordinates such as [police]." *Paine v. Cason*, 678 F.3d 500, 512 (7th Cir. 2012) (supervisor could be liable for denying a clearly established constitutional right to medical care based on supervisor's own observation of a mentally disturbed arrestee and own treatment of call from arrestee's father as a prank).

c. Is Intent to Harm Required for All Claims, Not Just for Invidious Discrimination Claims?

But even if the claim against the supervisor is constitutional and not based on the causation language of the § 1983 statute, it is not clear what standard governs. The Seventh Circuit explicitly has recognized that, after *Iqbal*, if plaintiff's constitutional claim requires not intent to harm but the lesser standard of deliberate indifference, it is not clear whether a supervisor nevertheless must *intend* to violate the constitution. While *Iqbal* "was a discrimination case involving discriminatory purpose," *Arnett*, 658 F.3d at 757, the Supreme Court "stated that 'purpose rather than knowledge is required to impose *Bivens* liability,'" *id.* (citing *Iqbal*, 556 U.S. at 677, and therefore the reasoning of *Iqbal* "has raised questions about whether a stricter standard of personal liability for supervisors applies in deliberate indifference suits." *Arnett*, 658 F.3d at 757. The Seventh Circuit concluded that "[t]he *landscape of such claims after Iqbal remains murky*...." *Id.* (emphasis added).

d. If Intent to Harm Is Required, Is It Satisfied by Subjective Deliberate Indifference?

The Seventh Circuit addressed the implications of *Iqbal* on a claim against a supervisor for a constitutional violation that does not itself require intent. *Vance v. Rumsfeld*, 701 F.3d 193 (7th Cir. 2012) (en banc), *cert. denied*, 569 U.S. 1038 (2013). Unlike *Iqbal*, the constitutional right was not invidious discrimination but a constitutional claim governed by a standard less than intent. Yet the Seventh Circuit held that the supervisor's intent was required: "[k]nowledge of a subordinate's misconduct is not enough for liability. The supervisor can be liable only if he *wants* the unconstitutional or illegal conduct to occur." *Vance*, 701 F.3d at 203 (emphasis added). While the Seventh Circuit held that "[t]he supervisor must want the forbidden outcome to occur," since subjective deliberate indifference "is a form of intent," inaction also could be culpable if "the public official knew of risks with sufficient specificity to allow an inference that inaction is designed to produce or allow harm." *Id* at 204.

Vance does not fully answer the question of what standard governs a constitutional claim against supervisors. Plaintiffs in *Vance* were security contractors in Iraq who were detained by the military and subjected to violence, sleep deprivation, and other "harsh interrogation methods" authorized by Defense Secretary Donald Rumsfeld for enemy combatants, but not authorized for civilian contractors. *Vance*, 701 F.3d at 196; *id.* at 203. Plaintiffs sued very high level officials of a very large bureaucracy, the U.S. military. Perhaps *Vance* will be limited to *Bivens* claims, or to high-ranking officials in huge agencies with a long chain of subordinates between them and the actors who inflicted harm. But dicta suggests that *Vance* also applies to lower ranking officials subject to Section 1983 liability. *Id.* at 205 ("Every police chief knows that some officers shoot unnecessarily ... [b]ut heads of organizations have never been held liable on the theory that they did not do enough to combat subordinates' misconduct, and the Supreme Court made it clear in *Iqbal* that such theories of liability are unavailing"). The Supreme Court could have clarified the standard but denied certiorari in 2013.

e. Continuing Uncertainty

The various approaches taken by just one circuit, the Seventh, highlight the continuing uncertainty about *Iqbal*'s effect on supervisory liability. *Iqbal*'s holding on supervisory liability "has bedeviled the Courts of Appeals to have considered it, producing varied interpretations of its effect on supervisory liability." *Barkes v. First Corr. Med., Inc.*, 766 F.3d 307, 318 (3d Cir. 2014), *rev'd. on other grounds*, ___U.S. ___, 135 S.Ct. 2042 (2015). According to the Third Circuit, "[m]ost courts have ... recognize[ed] that because the state of mind necessary to establish a § 1983 or *Bivens* claim varies with the constitutional provision at issue, so too does the state of mind necessary to trigger liability in a supervisory capacity." *Id.*; *see, e.g.*, Avery, Rudovsky, Blum & Laurin, Police Misconduct: Law and Litigation § 4:4 (Oct. 2018 update) (*Iqbal* does "[not] undermine in *all* cases those authorities permitting supervisory liability to attach upon a showing of deliberate indifference or recklessness" and may mean simply that when the "constitutional right at issue requires a showing of discriminatory purpose, plaintiffs will be required to allege and prove that the supervisor had the discriminatory purpose, and will not be permitted to assert liability based on mere knowledge and acquiescence").

Until the doctrinal significance of *Iqbal* has been resolved, courts confronted with claims of 42 U.S.C. § 1983 supervisory liability may opt to apply the circuit's pre-existing doctrine as an alternate ground for the decision. *See, e.g., Maldonado v. Fontanes*, 568 F.3d 263, 274 n.7 (1st Cir. 2009) (while *Iqbal* "may call into question our prior circuit law" on the § 1983 standard for supervisory liability, "[w]e need not resolve this issue" because "plaintiffs have not pled facts sufficient to make out a plausible entitlement to relief under our previous formulation of the standards for supervisory liability"). What are some practical consequences for litigation strategy if courts decide supervisory claims under both pre-and post-*Iqbal* standards?

While *Iqbal* did not address local government liability, Professor Karen Blum predicts that "*Iqbal* and *City of Canton* may be on a collision course." Karen Blum, *Section 1983 Litigation: Post-Pearson and Post-Iqbal*, 26 Touro L. Rev. 433, 462 (2010).

> [In *City of Canton*,] the city did not commit a constitutional violation, but rather was deliberately indifferent in that it knew, or should have known that its failure to train, supervise, discipline, *etc.*, would cause the underlying constitutional violation. The Court adopted a causation approach to § 1983, and stated that an entity can be liable for causing a constitutional violation. There is no requirement under *City of Canton* that the governmental entity or any policymaker must be shown to have the particular state of mind required by the underlying constitutional offense.
>
> *Iqbal*, on the other hand, insists that the supervisor not merely cause a constitutional violation, but must himself or herself demonstrate the level of culpability needed to make out the underlying constitutional wrong. It is difficult to reconcile *Iqbal* with *City of Canton* unless one accepts that the Court is drawing a distinction between the types of "persons" who may be sued under § 1983 and establishing different standards for entity and individual liability.

Id. at 462–63.

Practice Pointer

Absolute immunity, qualified immunity, and local government liability are all based on the statute, 42 U.S.C. § 1983. Usually, an efficient way to begin statutory research is to consult the annotated statute and skim the relevant annotations. That is not the most efficient way to do § 1983 research, however, because of the great volume of litigation. Rather, to research the current status of § 1983 immunity defenses or local government liability, the most efficient methods are those explained in the Practice Pointers earlier in this book. That is, begin by reviewing secondary sources that can identify relevant vocabulary and current debates and have done some of the research for your client, such as treatises, American Law Reports, encyclopedias, continuing legal education materials, online brief banks, and the other sources mentioned earlier.

Chapter Thirteen

Case Study of a Legal Doctrine: The Evolving Scope of the Parental Liberty Interest

A. Introduction

This section documents the evolution of a legal doctrine over about thirty years. The doctrine is substantive due process protection for a parental liberty interest in *adult* children. That is the substantive due process claim asserted by the mother in *Butera*, whose son was murdered while serving as an undercover drug informant, and for which the jury awarded $34 million.

The parental liberty interest in raising minor children is well established. The Supreme Court has held that the "interest of parents in the care, custody and control of their children ... is perhaps the oldest of the fundamental liberty interests recognized by this Court." *Troxel v. Granville*, 530 U.S. 57, 65 (2000) (plurality); *accord*, *M.L.B. v. S.L.J.*, 519 U.S. 102, 116 (1996) ("[c]hoices about marriage, family life, and the upbringing of children are among associational rights this Court has ranked as 'of basic importance in our society'") (further citation omitted); *Prince v. Massachusetts*, 321 U.S. 158, 166 (1944) ("the custody, care and nurture of the child reside first in the parents, whose primary function and freedom include preparation for obligations the state can neither supply nor hinder").

As noted in Chapter 4, Section 1983 claims alleging violations of the parental liberty interest are frequently litigated when state actors such as social workers investigate allegations of child abuse or neglect, remove children from their parents' custody, refuse to return children to their parents' custody, or seek to terminate parental rights to a child. A parental liberty interest in minor children may be protected by both procedural and substantive due process. Litigation of the scope of the parental liberty interest in the substantive due process context takes place against the backdrop of the Supreme Court's reluctance to expand substantive due process protections, a concept introduced in the earlier Substantive Due Process Chapters (Chapters 3 and 4) and explored in this Chapter.

While a parental liberty interest in raising a minor child is well settled, in recent decades, parents of *adults* have asserted a parental liberty interest, with varying success. Parents of adults have litigated these claims particularly where a son or daughter's death was caused by government conduct, such as a police shooting. This Chapter examines the evolving scope of the parental liberty interest, an issue that has split the federal circuits, with one circuit reversing its precedent to switch sides in the circuit split (*Bell*, *Russ*). As explained in this Chapter, while the Supreme Court twice has granted certiorari to consider a parental liberty interest in an adult child, the Court both times dismissed certiorari without reaching the merits, and has not agreed to hear the issue since.

Sketching the evolution of this doctrine serves several purposes. One is to underscore a theme of this book, that constitutional law is not static. Another is to provide an example of the role of lawyers in shaping legal doctrine. Even when district courts within a circuit have treated an issue as settled, the doctrine can be successfully challenged at the trial and appellate level. The same principle applies to Supreme Court litigation: even if an issue has been treated as settled within a circuit, the doctrine can be successfully challenged before the Supreme Court.

As you read the below materials about the evolving scope of the parental liberty interest, keep in mind that the Supreme Court has not yet ruled on the issue. You may be the lawyer who litigates this issue before the Supreme Court.

B. Recognizing a Parental Liberty Interest in Companionship of Children

---

Questions to guide reading of *Bell*

1. In *Bell*, the Seventh Circuit found that the legislative history of § 1983 included a remedy "to the woman whose husband has been murdered; to the children whose father has been killed." Cong. Globe, 42d Cong., 1st Sess. 807. Why did *Bell* find that language relevant to the father's constitutional claim?
2. What is the liberty interest protected by substantive due process in *Bell*?
3. Why does *Bell* hold that the fact that Daniel was 23 when he was killed is not significant to the constitutional question of whether there is a parental liberty interest?
4. Would the reasoning in *Bell* logically extend to protect a child's claim for the governmentally-caused death of a parent? A spouse's claim for the governmentally-caused death of a husband or wife?

Bell v. City of Milwaukee

746 F.2d 1205 (7th Cir. 1984)

CUMMINGS, Chief Judge.

[Daniel Bell was shot and killed by police. The police officers conspired to cover up the shooting by falsely claiming that Mr. Bell was armed at the time of the shooting. Years later, one of the officers confessed. The Seventh Circuit summarized the facts:[1]

"On February 2, 1958, Milwaukee police officers Thomas Grady, Jr. and Louis Krause observed Daniel Bell, a 23-year-old black man, driving a vehicle that was missing a tail-light. Grady pulled over Bell's car, and Bell jumped out of the car and ran away. [746 F.2d 1205, 1215 (7th Cir. 1984)]. Grady and Krause pursued Bell—first by car, and then on foot. *Id.* Grady was carrying a loaded revolver. As he caught up with Bell, Grady extended his hand to grab Bell. The gun discharged, shooting Bell in the upper back. *Id.* The defendants claimed that the shot was accidental; Bell's family members, who later sued, believed that Grady intentionally pulled the trigger. *Id.* at 1215 n.2.

After determining that Bell was dead, Grady planted a knife in Bell's right hand. He and Krause then agreed on the story they would tell about what had happened: that Bell had jumped out of the car armed with a knife and yelled: "You won't catch me, I'm a holdup man!" *Id.* at 1216. Other witnesses at the scene testified that they saw nothing in Bell's hands nor did they observe Bell swing or lunge at Grady, as the officers claimed. *Id.* at 1221–22.

After an internal investigation, the district attorney and medical examiner held an inquest into Bell's death, which returned a verdict that the killing was justifiable. *Id.* at 1222. Daniel Bell's father, Dolphus Bell, died in 1962 without recovering for the death of his son. *Id.* at 1223.

Twenty years later, in 1978, Krause revealed that he and Grady had lied about what had occurred during the Bell shooting. *Id.* On August 29, 1979, Grady pleaded guilty to homicide by reckless conduct and perjury. He was sentenced to seven years of imprisonment and was paroled after three years. *Id.*

In October 1979, Daniel Bell's sister and eleven brothers filed suit in federal court on behalf of themselves, the estate of Daniel Bell, and the estate of Dolphus Bell. *Id.* at 1224. Their complaint ... alleged various constitutional violations arising out of the killing of Daniel Bell. After a ten-week trial, the jury found, among other things, that Grady violated Daniel Bell's constitutional rights by shooting and killing him, and awarded Daniel Bell's estate $100,000 in compensatory damages and $25,000 in punitive damages. *Id.* at 1225. The jury awarded the estate of Dolphus Bell $75,000 for the loss of society and companionship of Daniel Bell, plus funeral expenses, and

---

1. This summary of the facts is quoted from a later Seventh Circuit decision, *Russ v. Watts*, 414 F.3d 783, 785–86 (7th Cir. 2005), *cert. denied*, 546 U.S. 1094 (2006). *Russ* overruled *Bell* on the scope of the parental liberty interest. This summary of the facts is quoted because it is concise and focused on the facts relevant to the parental liberty interest.

awarded a total of $100,000 to Daniel's twelve siblings for the loss of society and companionship. The jury also found that the defendants had conspired to cover up the facts of the shooting of Daniel Bell, depriving his family of due process of law and racial equality, and awarded compensatory and punitive damages. *Id.*"]

...

A. Whether the Father or Siblings Possessed a Constitutional Liberty Interest in Their Association With Daniel Bell

The Supreme Court has yet to address whether a parent or sibling has a liberty interest in the continued association of a sibling or child, protected from unlawful state interference by the due process clause of the Fourteenth Amendment, in the context of a Section 1983 death action....

Supreme Court decisions examining the parameters of the constitutional protection afforded the parent-child relationship more forcefully indicate that Daniel Bell's father possessed a constitutional liberty interest in his relationship with his son. The Court has frequently emphasized the primacy of the parent-child relationship. The rights to conceive and to raise one's children have been deemed "essential," *Meyer v. Nebraska*, 262 U.S. 390, 399 [1923], "[r]ights far more precious ... than property rights." *May v. Anderson*, 345 U.S. 528, 533 [1953]. "Marriage and procreation are fundamental to the very existence and survival of the race." *Skinner v. Oklahoma*, 316 U.S. 535, 541 [1942]. "It is cardinal with us that the custody, care and nurture of the child reside first in the parents, whose primary function and freedom include preparation for obligations the state can neither supply nor hinder." *Prince v. Massachusetts*, 321 U.S. 158, 166 [1944].

The due process clause requires that severances in the parent-child relationship caused by the state occur only with rigorous protections for the individual liberty interests at stake. [citations to Supreme Court cases omitted]. The state may not separate the parent from the child, even temporarily, without according them due process of law to protect their liberty interests....

Additionally, the legislative history of the Ku Klux Klan Act of 1871, though not expressive on the specific issues, indicates that the Act was meant to create a remedy where the parent-child relationship was interfered with by lawless, racially-motivated violence. Representative Butler described the Act:

> This then is what we offer to the people of the United States as a remedy for wrongs, arsons and murders done. This is what we offer to a man whose house has been burned, as a remedy; to the woman whose husband has been murdered, as a remedy;[48] to the children whose father has been killed, as a remedy.

Cong. Globe, 42d Cong., 1st Sess. 807.

---

48. Because this case does not present the issue, any pronouncement would be unnecessary regarding whether one possesses a constitutional right under Section 1983 to recover for the loss of society and companionship resulting from the death of a spouse.

Although the above-quoted legislative history makes a clearer case for recovery to the child due to loss of support or loss of society and companionship of a parent, recognition of the child's rights vis-à-vis parental loss logically implies the reciprocal recognition of the parent's rights vis-à-vis the loss of a child. In contrast to the mentioning of the parent-child relationship, however, a discussion of intra-sibling interests is lacking in the legislative history of the Ku Klux Klan Act.

...

Defendants point out that Daniel was 23 years old and thus no longer a minor when he was killed. They contend that a parent's interest in the society and companionship of a child is less substantial when the child is an adult and not living with the parent. However, we are unpersuaded that a constitutional line based solely on the age of the child should be drawn. The Supreme Court's decisions protect more than the custody dimension of the parent-child relationship. The protected relationship includes the parent's "interest in the companionship, care, custody, and management" of the child. *Stanley v. Illinois*, 405 U.S. 645, 651 [1972]. The continued interest in the care and companionship of a child is afforded due process protection where the parent raised and nurtured the child, even where the parent has never had legal custody. [citations to Supreme Court cases omitted].

Moreover, Daniel was single and had no children. He had not become a part of another family unit; his father's family was his immediate family.... Also, there was substantial testimony regarding the warm and close relationship between Daniel Bell and his father. Further, this deprivation was far more substantial than the unlawful removal of a child from the parent's custody; it was the annihilation of the parent-child relationship. The jury was fully aware that Daniel was no longer a minor, and it was appropriate for them to consider that fact (as they were instructed to do) in assessing the damages awarded to Dolphus Bell's estate for loss of Daniel's society and companionship. Daniel's age and separate residence were matters for the jury to consider when determining damages. These were not a bar to any recovery at all.

Questions to guide reading of *Kelson*

1. What is the liberty interest protected by substantive due process in *Kelson*?
2. How do the Supreme Court cases on which *Kelson* relied articulate the liberty interest protected by substantive due process?

Kelson v. City of Springfield

767 F.2d 651 (9th Cir. 1985)

ALARCON, Circuit Judge.

Duane and Eleanor Kelson (the Kelsons) appeal from the district court's dismissal of their complaint alleging a violation of 42 U.S.C. § 1983 ... arising out of the suicide of their fourteen-year-old son, Brian Kelson. This appeal requires us to resolve the narrow question whether parents possess a constitutionally protected liberty interest in the companionship and society of their child, deprivation of which is actionable under section 1983. Because we conclude that a cognizable liberty interest does exist in the circumstances of this case, we reverse.

I. PERTINENT FACTS AND PROCEDURAL HISTORY

On the morning of March 15, 1982, Brian confronted a teacher in his classroom, brandishing a .38 caliber revolver and demanding that the teacher place the coins in his desk drawer on the desk top. The teacher complied, and then persuaded Brian to accompany him to an empty room where the vice principal, Ronald Schiessel (Schiessel), was waiting. Brian showed Schiessel a suicide note....

Meanwhile, school officials called the Springfield Police Department. The police in turn called the Kelsons to notify them of the situation. As Brian and Schiessel left the empty room on their way to the vice principal's office, they were confronted by Officer Jerry Smith (Smith). Smith informed Brian that he was "in trouble with the law." Five minutes later Brian left Schiessel, entered the boys' restroom and shot himself. Brian died later that morning.

The Kelsons filed a complaint under 42 U.S.C. § 1983 alleging violations of their ... right to association with their son....

II. EXISTENCE OF A FUNDAMENTAL PARENTAL RIGHT TO THE COMPANIONSHIP AND SOCIETY OF A CHILD

...

The district court's conclusion that parents do not possess a constitutionally protected interest in the companionship and society of their children is erroneous.[2] This court has previously held that such a liberty interest exists and is cognizable under section 1983. In *Morrison v. Jones*, 607 F.2d 1269 (9th Cir. 1979), *cert. denied*, 445 U.S. 962 (1980) ... [we held] that the parent-child relationship is constitutionally protected and that governmental interference with it gives rise to a section 1983 action for damages. *Id.* at 1275....

The Supreme Court has repeatedly reaffirmed the existence of a constitutional right to the maintenance of a parent-child relationship. In *Little v. Streater*, 452 U.S. 1 (1981), the Court held that an indigent defendant in a paternity proceeding brought by the State has a Fourteenth Amendment due process right to receive blood grouping tests. *Id.* at 17. The Court stressed the importance of familial bonds and reasoned that their imposition by the state (via a paternity suit) demands procedural fairness.

2. Appellees construe the complaint as alleging a violation of Brian Kelson's civil rights—a loss of life without due process of law—and argue that the Kelsons lack standing to assert the rights of their son. On the contrary, the complaint alleges only a deprivation of a liberty right—the right to associate with one's child. The Kelsons do not sue in their representative capacity on behalf of Brian's estate, nor do they argue that their familial relationship affords them the right to sue on his behalf. Instead, they assert a violation of their parental rights and seek damages to compensate them for loss of their son's companionship and for their own mental distress....

Id. at 13. In *Lassiter v. Department of Social Services*, 452 U.S. 18 (1981), the Court held that due process must be afforded to a parent prior to state termination of her parental status on grounds of unfitness. *Id.* at 27. The Court stated:

> This Court's decisions have by now made plain beyond the need for multiple citation that a parent's desire for and right to 'the companionship, care, custody, and management of his or her children' is an important interest that 'undeniably warrants deference and, absent a powerful countervailing interest, protection'....

Id. (footnote omitted) (citations omitted).

Finally, in *Santosky v. Kramer*, 455 U.S. 745 (1982), the Court held that natural parents have a constitutionally protected liberty interest in the care, custody and management of their child which entitles them to due process at a state-initiated parental rights termination proceeding. *Id.* at 752–57. The Court noted that its decisions in *Lassiter* and *Streater*, among others, rendered beyond dispute the proposition that parents have a fundamental liberty interest in maintaining a relationship with their children which is protected by the Fourteenth Amendment. *Id.* at 753.

Several federal appellate courts have recognized this right in the context of a killing of a child by a state agent. *See, e.g., Bell v. City of Milwaukee*, 746 F.2d 1205, 1242–45 (7th Cir. 1984) (parents have constitutionally protected liberty interest in continued association with their children and may recover under section 1983 for killing of their son by police officer); *Mattis v. Schnarr*, 502 F.2d 588, 593–95 (8th Cir. 1976) (father whose son was shot and killed while attempting to escape arrest had a constitutionally protected liberty interest under the due process clause of Fourteenth Amendment which was cognizable under section 1983) ...[4]

In short, existing Supreme Court and Ninth Circuit precedent establish that a parent has a constitutionally protected liberty interest in the companionship and society of his or her child. The state's interference with that liberty interest without due process of law is remediable under section 1983. The district court erred in deter-

---

4. Moreover, a more recent case from the District of Colorado ... observed:

> It would be ironic indeed to recognize, on the one hand, the constitutional rights to marry, *Loving v. Virginia*, [388 U.S. 1 (1967)], to procreate, *Skinner v. Oklahoma*, [316 U.S. 535 (1942)], to supervise the upbringing of children, *Pierce v. Society of Sisters*, [268 U.S. 510 (1925)], *Prince v. Massachusetts*, [321 U.S. 158 (1944)], to retain custody of one's illegitimate children, *Stanley v. Illinois*, [405 U.S. 645 (1972)], and to live in the same residence with one's 'family,' *Moore v. East Cleveland*, [431 U.S. 494 (1977)], but on the other hand, to deny parents constitutional protection for the continued life of their child. State action that wrongfully kills one's child certainly interferes with fruition and fulfillment of the fundamental right to procreate. A parent cannot benefit from his constitutionally protected rights to supervise the upbringing, retain custody, or live in the same residence with a child if state action unlawfully takes the child's life. To constitutionally protect families from lesser intrusions into family life, yet allow the state to destroy the family relationship altogether, would drastically distort the concept of ordered liberty protected by the Due Process Clause.

[citation omitted].

mining that the Kelsons did not allege a deprivation of a constitutionally protected liberty interest....

C. Refusing to Recognize a Parental Liberty Interest in Companionship Alone

Questions to guide reading of *Butera*

1. What was the liberty interest asserted by the mother in *Butera*?
2. The D.C. Circuit rejected the mother's claimed parental liberty interest. What were some of its reasons?
3. What parental liberty interest do you think the D.C. Circuit would recognize?
4. In its survey of the circuits, how does the D.C. Circuit categorize the Third Circuit's *Bailey* precedent?

Butera v. District of Columbia

235 F.3d 637 (D.C. Cir. 2001)

ROGERS, Circuit Judge.

[*Butera* concerns a private citizen who volunteered for an undercover police operation and was beaten to death during the police sting. This book has included *Butera* twice before.]

B. Right to the Companionship of an Adult Child.

Terry Butera's claim of a constitutional right to the companionship of her 31-year-old son ... fails.... The Supreme Court has not spoken to the precise issue, and the precedent in this and nearly all of the other circuits suggests that no such right exists.

Terry Butera testified that her son was an adult, living on his own, and that he was not providing her with any financial assistance at the time of his death. The evidence further showed that Eric Butera had moved out of his mother's house when he was eighteen years old, married, moved to Pennsylvania, and had a child. In allowing Terry Butera to claim a due process interest in the society and companionship of her adult son, the district court relied solely on our opinion in [a D.C. Circuit decision]....

On appeal, Terry Butera relies on [the D.C. Circuit decision], as well [as] on cases from other circuits that recognize parents' constitutionally protected liberty interest in the companionship and custody of their children and in the "maintenance and integrity of the family." *Estate of Bailey v. County of York*, 768 F.2d 503, 509 n.7 (3d Cir. 1985), *overruled in part by DeShaney*, 489 U.S. at 202; *see also Kelson v. City of Springfield*, 767 F.2d 651, 653–54 (9th Cir. 1985); *Bell v. City of Milwaukee*, 746 F.2d 1205, 1243–44 (7th Cir. 1984). In *Bell*, the Seventh Circuit recognized this constitutional interest in the context of a plaintiff's twenty-three-year-old son.[21] *See* 746 F.2d at 1242–45.

The general statements in [the D.C Circuit decision], as well as in the Supreme Court cases on which [that decision] relies, focus on securing the rights of parents to have custody of and to raise their minor children in a manner that develops "parental and filial bonds free from government interference." ... This emphasis is clear in cases such as *Prince v. Massachusetts*, 321 U.S. 158 (1944), where, in the context of the prosecution of a child's guardian for furnishing her with religious literature to sell on the public streets in violation of child labor laws, the Court stated that "the custody, care, and nurture of the child reside first in the parents," *id.* at 166, and *Ginsberg v. New York*, 390 U.S. 629 (1968), where the Court recognized parents' right "to direct the rearing of their children [as] basic in the structure of our society." *Id.* at 639. Moreover, while the Court in *Stanley v. Illinois*, 405 U.S. 645 (1972), recognized a parent's constitutional interest in the "companionship" of his children, it did so in the context of a parent's right to the custody and care of a minor child. *See id.* at 651. We find nothing in Supreme Court case law to indicate an intention to extend these concerns in support of a constitutional liberty interest in a parent's relationship with her adult son. Indeed, two of the three cases on which Terry Butera relies were also decided in the context of minor (not adult) children. *See Kelson*, 767 F.2d at 652–54; *Estate of Bailey*, 768 F.2d at 505, 509 n.7. In the third case, *see Bell*, 746 F.2d at 1245, the Seventh Circuit relied largely on the same Supreme Court cases that this court cited in [the D.C. Circuit decision], as well as on others that focus on parents' relationships with their minor children, to reject the notion that "a constitutional line based solely on the age of the child should be drawn." *Id.*

This circuit has indicated that it is not prepared to adopt the interpretation that the Seventh Circuit espoused in *Bell.* [This Court has] acknowledged different constitutional treatment when the parent-child relationship involves two adults:

> When children grow up, their dependence on their parents for guidance, socialization, and support gradually diminishes. At the same time, the strength and importance of the emotional bonds between them and their parents usually decrease. Concededly, the bond between a parent and child when the child is an adult usually bears some resemblance to the same bond when the child was a minor. But, as a long line of Supreme Court cases attests, the differences between the two stages of the relationship are sufficiently marked to warrant sharply different constitutional treatment.

Franz v. United States, 712 F.2d 1428, 1432 (D.C. Cir. 1983) (citation omitted). While the court acknowledges the importance of the parent-child relationship regardless

21. In recognizing a constitutional right for Bell's father (the plaintiff), the Seventh Circuit noted that the decedent was single, had no children, and had not become part of another family unit other than his father's, although the two lived apart. *See Bell*, 746 F.2d at 1245. The court concluded that the victim's age and separate residence were relevant only to the amount of damages to be awarded to the father for the loss of his son's society and companionship. *See id.*

of the child's age, and the court does not minimize the devastating loss that a parent can experience from the death of an adult child, this consideration, in view of circuit precedent, is insufficient to establish a constitutional liberty interest under § 1983. We do not think ... the Supreme Court cases and other authorities on which *Bell* relied can be read to support Terry Butera's constitutional claim. Therefore, we hold that a parent does not have a constitutionally-protected liberty interest in the companionship of a child who is past minority and independent....[23]

For further discussion

This book has included *Butera* twice before, in the Chapters concerning state-created danger and qualified immunity. Including a single case to illustrate multiple concepts is intended both (1) to help you keep in mind that civil rights pleadings, discovery, briefs, and oral arguments often address multiple complex constitutional and statutory issues, and (2) to facilitate learning new doctrine by not asking you to learn new facts for each concept.

D. Doctrinal Shift: Evolution of the Parental Liberty Interest in Companionship of Children

Beginning in 1988, district courts within the Third Circuit began to recognize a parental liberty interest in adult children. Some did so because they believed that by referencing *Bell* in a footnote in *Estate of Bailey v. County of York*, 768 F.2d 503 (3d Cir. 1985), the Third Circuit had endorsed the Seventh Circuit's reasoning in *Bell*. Other district courts recognized a parental liberty interest in adult children because they predicted that the Third Circuit would follow *Bell*—a prediction also based on the footnote in *Bailey*.

Questions to guide reading of *Amici Brief*

1. What was the liberty interest asserted by the father in *McCurdy?*
2. Why did the Amici Cities argue that recognizing the father's asserted liberty interest would require the expansion of substantive due process doctrine?
3. Given the existence of more than a decade of district court decisions recognizing a parental liberty interest in adult children, why was it strategically

---

23. Because we hold that a parent-child relationship between two independent adults does not invoke constitutional "companionship" interests, we do not reach the District of Columbia's contention that Terry Butera's claim fails because the District of Columbia's actions were not intentionally directed or aimed at her relationship with her son....

important to get the Third Circuit to recognize the narrowness of the parental liberty interest in *Bailey*?

4. Why did Amici argue that the Third Circuit precedent in *Bailey* is consistent with Supreme Court definitions of the scope of the parental liberty interest?
5. The facts of *McCurdy* are barely alluded to by Amici. After reading the summary of the facts in the *Trial Magazine* article that follows the Amici Brief, can you explain why the lawyer chose not to focus on the facts in the brief?

Amici Curiae Brief in *McCurdy v. Dodd*

Brief of Cities of Harrisburg and Pittsburgh, PA and Newark and Camden, NJ by Sarah E. Ricks, Rutgers Law School—Camden, with Marie Saraceni, 2002 WL 32819435 (Dec. 9, 2002)

STATEMENT OF IDENTITY, INTEREST AND AUTHORITY

...

This Section 1983 appeal concerns an open issue in this Circuit, about which the federal Circuits have split: Should a biological father have a substantive due process right to companionship with his independent adult son when the father had no custody or control of his adult son and the governmental conduct at issue, a police shooting of the adult son, was not focused on the parent/child relationship.

Recognition of the overly expansive parental liberty interest asserted in this appeal would be inconsistent with Supreme Court substantive due process principles, would likely result in a proliferation of claims by relatives of plaintiffs injured by government conduct, and would have a potentially catastrophic economic effect on municipalities bound by this Court's rulings on federal constitutional claims, such as Camden, Newark, Harrisburg and Pittsburgh. In one recent case in which a parent made the same substantive due process claim asserted in this appeal, the jury awarded the parent $34,000,000 against the municipal defendants. *See Butera v. District of Columbia*, 235 F.3d 637, 644 (D.C. Cir. 2001) (rejecting parent's substantive due process claim on appeal)....

SUMMARY OF ARGUMENT

One person cannot sue for the deprivation of another person's civil rights. While the facts of this case are undeniably tragic, Mr. McCurdy must show that the government conduct violated his own constitutional rights, not those of his adult son Donta Dawson. Neither the Supreme Court nor this Court has ever recognized the constitutional right Mr. McCurdy urges this Court to declare today: that a father has a substantive due process right to companionship with his independent adult son where the government conduct at issue—a police shooting—was not directed at the parent/child relationship.

Mr. McCurdy urges this Court to expand substantive due process in three ways: to establish a liberty interest in "familial companionship" outside of the context of parental decisionmaking about a child's care, custody and control; to establish a parental liberty interest in a parent's relationship with an independent adult son; and to establish a parental liberty interest where the government action complained-of was not concerned with, nor even cognizant of, any parent/child relationship.

Mr. McCurdy's expansive view of substantive due process is inconsistent with Supreme Court precedent recognizing a parental liberty interest where the child is a minor and the government action at issue was an attempt to preempt parental decisionmaking in the rearing of young children or was otherwise focused on the parent/child relationship. Mr. McCurdy's expansive view of substantive due process is inconsistent with this Court's own precedent in *Estate of Bailey v. County of York*, 768 F.2d 503 (3d Cir. 1985), which recognized a parental liberty interest in the life and custody of a minor child under circumstances where the government action was focused on the parent/child relationship. This Court should not expand the parental liberty interest recognized in Bailey, which is consistent with precedent from courts within at least the 1st, 4th, 5th, 6th, 8th and D.C. Circuits.

Substantive due process only protects against deliberate state action. Even if this Court were to expand substantive due process to announce a parental liberty interest in companionship with an adult son, it should decline to expand substantive due process to protect that interest against government conduct which only incidentally affects the parental relationship. Otherwise, parents could bring independent substantive due process claims any time government conduct having nothing to do with the parental relationship—such as an arrest, prosecution, jail suicide—injured a person who happened to have a parent. Recognition of such a broad parental right would serve no Section 1983 deterrent function. On the contrary, this expansion would create a whole new category of unpredictable and financially significant tort claims under cover of the federal Constitution.

I. Judgment Should Be Affirmed Because There Is No Parental Liberty Interest in Companionship of an Adult Independent Son When the Government Conduct Was Not Focused on the Parent/Child Relationship

... To allege a constitutional claim here, Donta Dawson's biological father must claim the deprivation of his own constitutional rights. He cannot. While Mr. McCurdy casually asserts in an uninformative stringcite that this Court already has recognized a parental liberty interest in the relationship between a parent and his adult offspring, and should do so again today, he is wrong on both counts....

A. Recognition of Mr. McCurdy's Claim Would Require this Court to Significantly Expand Substantive Due Process in Three Ways

No binding authority recognizes a parental liberty interest as broad as Mr. McCurdy's claim here. Neither the Supreme Court nor this Court has ever held that the biological father of an adult son has a constitutionally-protected liberty interest in continued companionship with his son. To the contrary, this Court has twice explicitly declined to decide the issue of whether the liberty interest that a parent has in the care and custody of a minor child extends to the life of an independent adult son or daughter. *Freedman v. City of Allentown*, 853 F.2d 1111, 1117 n.5 (3d Cir. 1988) ("we do not reach the issue of whether parents of an adult decedent may maintain a Section 1983 claim"); *Solum v. Yerusalim*, No. 99-1607 (3d Cir. March 8, 2000) (unpublished and non-precedential) (declining to reach issue) ... The Supreme Court dismissed *certiorari* as improvidently granted in a case concerning a parental liberty interest where a child was killed by government actors. "The Supreme Court has not spoken to the precise issue [of whether a parent has a liberty interest in the companionship of an independent adult son] and the precedent in [the D.C. Circuit] and nearly all of the other circuits suggests that no such right exists." *Butera v. District of Columbia*, 235 F.3d 637, 654 (D.C. Cir. 2001).

Lacking binding precedent to support his claim to constitutional protection of companionship between a biological parent and his independent adult son where the police conduct at issue had nothing to do with the parent/child relationship, Mr. McCurdy resorts to the semantic dodge of pronouncing his constitutional claim to be "clear." ... What is clear is that recognition of the parental liberty interest urged by Mr. McCurdy would require this Court to expand substantive due process in each of three ways:

1. expand substantive due process to establish a right to "familial companionship," outside of the context of parental responsibility for care, custody and control (Complaint—Fourth Count); and
2. expand substantive due process to protect a biological father's interest in his relationship with an independent adult son, over whom the father had no custody or control; and
3. expand substantive due process to announce a parental liberty interest where the government action complained-of was focused on the adult son, and not concerned with, nor even cognizant of, any parent/child relationship.

In light of the limitations on the parental substantive due process right recognized by the Supreme Court, and this Court's own precedent, this Court should not break new ground to expand substantive due process to establish the parental liberty interest claimed by Mr. McCurdy, and should affirm judgment against Mr. McCurdy's § 1983 claim.

B. The "Established Guideposts" of the Parental Liberty Interest Require Government Action Focused on the Parent/Child Relationship and Parental Decisionmaking in Rearing of Minor Children

The Supreme Court and this Court have repeatedly warned against "expand[ing] the concept of substantive due process because guideposts for responsible decisionmaking in this uncharted area are scarce and open-ended [and] [t]he doctrine of judicial self-restraint requires us to exercise the utmost care whenever we are asked to break new ground in this field." [internal citations omitted] ... This Court therefore "requires scrupulous attention to the guideposts that have previously been established" when addressing a substantive due process claim....

The Supreme Court's most recent articulation of the parental liberty interest in children reaffirms that the substantive component of "the Due Process Clause of the

Fourteenth Amendment protects the fundamental right of parents to make decisions concerning *the care, custody and control of their children*." *Troxel v. Granville*, 530 U.S. 57, 66 (2000) (plurality) (emphasis added). Significantly omitting mention of "companionship," the Supreme Court plurality four times defined the parental liberty interest protected by due process as limited to the "*right to make decisions concerning the care, custody and control*" of children. *Id.* at 75 (emphasis added); *id.* at 66; *id.* at 72.

Recognition of that liberty interest makes sense only so long as a parent is in a position to make life's difficult decisions for his children, such as when the child is a minor in his parents' custody or otherwise dependent on his parents. Every single decision relied on by the Supreme Court in defining the parental liberty interest in *Troxel* recognized the existence of this parental liberty interest when the child was a minor and the government action at issue attempted to preempt parental decision-making in the rearing of young children or was otherwise focused on the parent/child relationship. *See Troxel*, 530 U.S. at 65–66 (citing cases). After carefully examining much the same precedent, the D.C. Court of Appeals held just last year: "We find nothing in Supreme Court case law to indicate an intention to extend these concerns in support of a constitutional liberty interest in a parent's relationship with her *adult* son." *Butera*, 235 F.3d at 655 (emphasis added).

Appellant Mr. McCurdy does not and cannot point to any binding authority holding "companionship" itself to be an independently protected parental liberty interest. The Supreme Court's repeated formulation in *Troxel* of a constitutionally-protected parental liberty interest in "*mak[ing] decisions concerning the care, custody and control of their children*," does not specify a parent's interest in "companionship" of children shorn of the context of the parent's decisionmaking responsibility for the care, custody and control of a minor child. *Troxel*, 530 U.S. at 66 (emphasis added). As the D.C. Court of Appeals recently stated, "[w]hile the Court in *Stanley v. Illinois*, [405 U.S. 645, 651 (1972)] recognized a parent's constitutional interest in the 'companionship' of his children, it did so *in the context of a parent's right to the custody and care of a minor child*." *Butera*, 235 F.3d at 655 (emphasis added).

Yet the substantive due process right Mr. McCurdy urges this Court to establish in this case is "familial companionship" outside the context of parental care, custody and control of the child.... "Companionship" isolated from a parental right to care, custody and control of a minor child—companionship between two adults—apparently has been recognized by some district courts within this Circuit in stretching a parental liberty interest to include ongoing relationships of parents with their adult, independent offspring....

Mr. McCurdy's expansive view of substantive due process would require this Court to venture beyond the [Supreme Court's] established guideposts of *Troxel* and the parental liberty cases it synthesized, to announce a parental liberty interest even where the son was an independent adult over whom the parent had no right to make decisions concerning care, custody or control, and even where the government action complained-of was focused on the adult son, and not concerned with nor even cognizant of any parent/child relationship....

C. This Court's *Bailey* Precedent is Consistent with the Supreme Court's Definition of the Parental Liberty Interest in *Troxel* and Does Not Support Mr. McCurdy's Claim

This Court has never recognized a parental liberty interest as broad as Mr. McCurdy's asserted right. To the contrary, this Court's existing definition of the parental liberty interest is consistent with the established guideposts set out in the Supreme Court plurality's decision in *Troxel.*

The Supreme Court's definition of the parental interest in *Troxel* is consistent with this Court's footnote holding in *Estate of Bailey v. County of York*, 768 F.2d 503 (3d Cir. 1985), *overruled on other grounds by DeShaney v. Winnebago County Dept. of Social Services*, 489 U.S. 189 (1989). *Bailey* concerned a 5-year-old girl who was removed by a government child welfare agency from her mother's custody because of suspected child abuse, and then returned to her mother's custody, whereupon the mother and her boyfriend murdered the child. The girl's father in his own right sued the child protection agency. *Bailey*, 768 F.2d at 505–06.

The actual holding of the *Bailey* footnote is narrow. This Court held that a parent of a minor child had a liberty interest in protecting the life and safety of that child—because of the parent's interest in custody and maintaining the family—under circumstances where government action was focused on the parent/child relationship. *Id.*at 509 n.7....[4] In the *Bailey* footnote, this Court did not hold that any parent—even a parent whose sole contribution to the parenting process was some DNA—had a liberty interest in any child—whether an adult son or a son who was himself a parent—which was implicated whenever the child died as a consequence of any government action—whether the government action was aimed directly at the parent/child relationship, as in *Bailey*, or entirely unrelated to the parent/child relationship, as when the police approach the driver of a car on the street....

In holding that the parent of a minor had a protected liberty under circumstances where the government action at issue was focused on the parent/child relationship, the footnote in *Bailey* cited *Bell v. City of Milwaukee*, 746 F.2d 1205, 1242–45 (7th Cir. 1984).... Mr. McCurdy's assertion that this Court thereby adopted the entirety of *Bell* is flat out wrong.... In a subsequent decision also written by the author of *Bailey*, Judge Sloviter, this Court cited *Bailey* and specifically held that whether parents of an adult decedent have a constitutionally protected liberty interest was an open issue in the Third Circuit. *See Freedman*, 853 F.2d at 1117 n.5 (citing *Bell*); *see Solum v. Yerusalim*, No. 99-1607 (3d Cir. March 8, 2000) (unpublished and non-precedential) (declining to reach issue)....[5]

---

4. This Circuit has elsewhere recognized that substantive due process protects a parent's liberty interest in the care and custody of a minor child when government action targets the parent/child relationship. *See e.g.*, *Miller v. City of Philadelphia*, 174 F.3d 368, 374 (3d Cir. 1999) (mother sued social worker for temporarily depriving her of custody of her child)....

5. Some district courts have misread *Bell* in the same way Appellant McCurdy does here. *See Cooper v. Leamer*, 705 F. Supp. 1081, 1087 (M.D. Pa. 1989) (erroneously reading *Bailey* to have adopted *Bell's* ruling on parental interest in companionship of adult children); *Agresta* [*v. Sambor*], 687 F. Supp. [162,] 164 [E.D. Pa. 1988] (same).

D. Expansion of the Parental Liberty Interest Beyond the Established Confines of *Bailey* Would Be Inconsistent With *Troxel* and Precedent from Other Circuits

This Court's narrow holding in the *Bailey* footnote—that the parent of a minor had a protected liberty interest under circumstances where the government action at issue was focused on the parent/child relationship—is consistent with *Troxel* and with precedent from courts within at least the 1st, 4th, 5th, 6th, 8th and D.C. Circuits.

Bailey is consistent with *Ortiz v. Burgos*, 807 F.2d 6 (1st Cir. 1986), where a panel including now-Justice Breyer concluded that the stepfather of an adult inmate allegedly beaten to death by guards had no constitutionally protected liberty interest in the companionship of his adult son and that its reasoning also would preclude the mother's claim. *Id.* at 7 n.1. Neither of the two categories of Supreme Court cases protecting parental care and custody of children supported expanding substantive due process to the parental claim asserted. Cases holding that the government may not interfere in particularly private family decisions (such as procreation or religious schooling) apply only to a parent's care for minor children and when the state attempts to preempt parental decisionmaking. "[T]his case differs because ... Decedent, who was over 21 at the time of his death, was not a minor child still within 'the care, custody, and management' of his parents. Nor did the state seek here to impose upon his family its own choice as to how or by whom he should be reared." *Ortiz*, 807 F.2d at 8.

Nor was the parental claim in *Ortiz* supported by Supreme Court cases recognizing a parental liberty interest "when the state seeks to change or affect the relationship of parent and child in furtherance of a legitimate state interest" (such as termination of parental rights or the custody rights of an unwed father), since the government action complained of—the alleged beating of the son to death—was targeted at the son, not at the parent/child relationship. *Ortiz*, 807 F.2d at 8. While the parent/child relationship was irreversibly affected by the prison beating death of the plaintiffs' child, the Supreme Court "has never held that governmental action that affects the parental relationship only incidentally—as in this case—is susceptible to challenge for a violation of due process." *Id.* The holding of *Ortiz* is entirely consistent with *Bailey*, which recognized a parental liberty interest when the government action concerned physical custody of a minor child: "*We decline to make the leap ... from the realm of governmental action directly aimed at the relationship between a parent and a young child to an incidental deprivation of the relationship between a parent and a young child to an incidental deprivation of the relationship between [the stepfather] and [his] adult relative.*" *Id.* (emphasis added)....[7]

---

7. There is contrary authority. *See, e.g., Strandberg v. City of Helena*, 791 F.2d 744, 748 and n.1 (9th Cir. 1986); *Bell v. City of Milwaukee*, 746 F.2d 1205, 1242–45 (7th Cir. 1984). The Seventh Circuit has declined to extend *Bell* to constitutionalize a wife's claim for loss of consortium, and has recognized that *Bell*'s permitting family members to bring substantive due process claims "even though the plaintiff was not the target of the wrongful conduct" has "evoked a measure of skepticism in other circuits," especially in light of Supreme Court precedent that negligent infliction of harm is not actionable under Section 1983. *Niehus v. Liberio*, 973 F.2d 526, 533 (7th Cir. 1992).

This Circuit's *Bailey* precedent, which concerned a parental liberty interest in a minor child, also is consistent with the D.C. Circuit's bright line rule limiting the liberty interest to parents of minors. The D.C. Circuit recently rejected a mother's claim that government conduct causing the death of her adult son thereby deprived her of a liberty interest: "[A] parent does not have a constitutionally protected liberty interest in the companionship of a child who is past minority and independent." *Butera*, 235 F.3d at 656.... That Donta Dawson was an independent adult would alone be sufficient to defeat Mr. McCurdy's claim under that bright line rule.

... In light of *Troxel*'s definition of the parental liberty interest in decisionmaking concerning the care, custody and control of children, which is consistent with *Bailey*, it would be a significant expansion of substantive due process protection for this Court to extend that parental liberty interest to include a father who did not have the right to make decisions concerning the care, custody and control of his adult son, such as Mr. McCurdy. It would be a further expansion of the Supreme Court's defined parental liberty interest for this Court to recognize a right of ongoing companionship with an independent adult son, such as Donta Dawson. It would be a further expansion of Supreme Court and this Court's precedent to recognize a parental interest in ongoing companionship with an independent adult son in the context of government action which was not directed at nor even cognizant of the parent/child relationship, such as a police stop of an adult man on the street.

Yet for Mr. McCurdy to pursue a substantive due process claim to vindicate his alleged parental liberty interest in the continued companionship of his independent adult son in the context of this case, this Court must make all three of the above expansions of substantive due process protection. To do so would be inconsistent with Supreme Court and this Court's precedent, and persuasive precedent from other circuits.

E. Even If This Court Were To Recognize a Liberty Interest in an Adult Son, it Should Not Expand Substantive Due Process to Protect Against Government Action Which Incidentally Affects the Parental Relationship Because Substantive Due Process Only Protects Against Deliberate State Action

Even if this Circuit were to expand substantive due process to recognize a parental liberty interest in companionship with an independent adult son, it should not expand substantive due process to recognize such a parental liberty interest when the government action at issue was neither an attempt to preempt parental choices in peculiarly private areas nor targeted at the parent/child relationship, but instead affected that relationship only incidentally.

"[T]he Due Process Clause of the Fourteenth Amendment was intended to prevent government 'from abusing [its] power, or employing it as an instrument of oppression.'" *Collins* [*v. City of Harker Heights*,] 503 U.S. [115,] 126 [1992] (citations omitted). "'Historically, this guarantee of due process has been applied to deliberate decisions of government officials to deprive a person of life, liberty or property.'" *Id.* at 127 n.10 (quoting *Daniels v. Williams*, 474 U.S. 327, 331 (1986)). This Court should hold that state action that affects the parent/child relationship only incidentally, even though the deprivation may be permanent—as in this case—does not implicate a constitutionally protected liberty interest, because only deliberate government actions depriving a person of liberty are actionable under substantive due process. *Daniels*, 474 U.S. at 331.... [H]ere, the responding police officers were not focused on whether Mr. Dawson had parents or children or was an orphan, and the state action—the shooting of Mr. Dawson—was an on-the-street reaction to suspected criminal activity, not a deliberate attempt to affect Mr. Dawson's relationship with his biological father.

In the "unchartered area" of substantive due process, judicial restraint requires that there be a principled limitation on the parental liberty interest. *Collins*, 503 U.S. at 125.... Not all wrongs are constitutional wrongs. "[A] conclusion that governmentally caused termination of ... the parental interest in the continued relationship with a child always is actionable would constitutionalize adjudication in a myriad of situations we think inappropriate for due process scrutiny, including the alleged wrongful prosecution and incarceration of a child or the alleged wrongful discharge of a child from a state job, forcing the child to seek employment in another part of the country." *Ortiz*, 807 F.2d at 9.

If the familial liberty interest were recognized outside of situations where the government conduct deliberately affected the parent/child relationship, parents could bring independent substantive due process claims any time government conduct having nothing to do with the parental relationship—such as an arrest, prosecution, excessive use of force, jail suicide—was alleged to have injured a person who happened to have a custodial parent, a non-custodial parent, a child or several step-children. *See, e.g.*, ... *Smith v. Fontana*, 818 F.2d 1411, 1419 (9th Cir. 1987), *cert. denied*, 484 U.S. 935 (1987), *overruled on other grounds*, *Hodgers v. de la Vina*, 199 F.3d 1037 (9th Cir. 1999) (adult and minor children of man shot by police have liberty interest in companionship with father); *Freedman*, 853 F.2d at 1113 and 1117 n.5 (parents of adult jail suicide [victim] claimed violation of their own liberty interests).

...

Recognition of a parental liberty interest when the government action is not focused on the parent/child relationship—such as a police stop of a man in a car—would not serve the deterrent function of Section 1983, because the responding officer does not know whether the person the officer is stopping is an orphan or has a single parent or has two step-parents, nor would or should that knowledge affect the police action, because the government action is concerned only with the child, and the child's parental relationship is affected only incidentally by the government action.

...

Questions to guide reading of Trial Magazine article

1. In *McCurdy*, the Third Circuit rejected the father's claim to a parental interest in companionship of his independent adult child as an unwarranted "broad

expansion of due process." What reasons did *McCurdy* give for rejecting the parental liberty interest proposed by the father?

2. Why do you think the City's lawyers chose *McCurdy* as a vehicle for litigating the scope of the parental liberty interest?

U.S. Courts Grapple with Constitutional Claims for Loss of Adult Children

Carmel Sileo, TRIAL MAGAZINE, March 1, 2004

Shortly after midnight on October 1, 1988, two Philadelphia police officers noticed a car parked in the middle of the road, its engine running. They found 19-year-old Donta Dawson in the driver's seat, apparently unconscious and unhurt, and he did not respond to their questions or get out of the car when asked. Finally, one officer reached into the car and saw the young man's arm move; the officer, convinced that he had seen a gun, killed Donta with a shot to the head. Later, the officers discovered that Donta was unarmed.

The courts found that the shooting officer had acted reasonably and dismissed three criminal charges against him. Donta's mother, Cynthia, filed a federal civil rights lawsuit against the city and several police officers. She sought damages for violations of Donta's civil rights, wrongful death, and for violations of her own civil rights by depriving her of her right to Donta's companionship. The city settled with Cynthia in what the Philadelphia City Paper called "one of the largest ever—and one of the fastest" city settlements. Since she released the defendants from all claims in the settlement agreement, Cynthia's claim that her civil rights had been violated was not considered.

But a few months later Donta's father, Bobby McCurdy, filed his own suit, claiming that the police officer's actions had denied him, too, a constitutionally protected right to his relationship with his son. McCurdy filed under § 1983 of the Civil Rights Act. (*McCurdy v. Dodd*, 352 F. 3d 820 (3d Cir. 2003).)

His suit brought to the forefront a question that has bedeviled courts across the country: Is a parent's right to a relationship with an adult child constitutionally protected? The Seventh and Tenth circuits, for instance, have adopted an expansive view of the parental liberty interest, allowing parents (and even siblings) to sue under § 1983, while the First and District of Columbia circuits have taken a much narrower view—and the Supreme Court has never had to decide the issue.

McCurdy's suit progressed to the Third Circuit, where it was dismissed in December 2003. Writing for the majority, Judge Julio Fuentes noted that while "we are mindful of the broad remedial purposes of § 1983 grounded on alleged parental liberty interests, we are venturing into the murky area of unenumerated constitutional rights."

The court found that McCurdy was proposing too broad an expansion of due process rights and that the state had not specifically intended to interfere with his relationship with Donta. (Intent is a crucial element in finding a due process violation.)

The judges also noted that there was no evidence to show a close relationship between McCurdy and Donta and that Cynthia had largely raised him on her own. Finally, Fuentes concluded that while the definition of a "child" is fluid, it would be a "serious mistake ... to extend the liberty interests of parents into the amorphous open-ended area of a child's adulthood."

Blame it on Bailey

The *McCurdy* ruling repudiates almost 20 years of district court decisions in the Third Circuit that go back to a landmark ruling, *Estate of Bailey v. County of York*. The *Bailey* judges recognized a "cognizable liberty interest in preserving the life and safety of a minor child"; yet the decision has been cited routinely to support claims that involve adult children. (768 F.2d 503 (3d Cir. 1985).)

"District courts misread a footnote in *Bailey*, thinking [the parental liberty question] was a decided issue," explained Sarah Ricks, a former attorney for the city and a Rutgers School of Law professor, who wrote an amicus brief in *McCurdy*.

"They never recognized that it was, in fact, undecided in the Third Circuit and split in the federal circuits. But since then, the courts have consistently misread that decision and ruled in favor of this expanded parental liberty interest. What *McCurdy* did was to recognize the split in the courts, and to finally decide it with a ruling firmly grounded in U.S. Supreme Court analysis." In fact, the trial court cited *Bailey* when it allowed Cynthia to press her § 1983 claim.

The *McCurdy* decision is one of two key Third Circuit cases that deal with this issue. The other was brought by the family of a 23-year-old murder victim, Shannon Schieber.

In May 1998, Philadelphia police officers responded to an early-hours emergency call from Schieber's neighbor, who reported that he and his wife heard a scream and "a choking sound." This was in a neighborhood where several recent rapes had been attributed to the so-called Center City rapist. When the police arrived, the neighbors expressed some doubt about the origin of the noises. The officers knocked on Schieber's door; when no one answered, they told the neighbors to call 911 again if they heard anything, and left.

The next day, Schieber's brother broke into her apartment; she had been raped and murdered. A few months later, the Schiebers sued the city and the police officers in federal court, under the same due process theory that McCurdy used. Senior District Judge Norma Shapiro, ruling that the case could go before a jury, agreed that the officers had violated Shannon Schieber's civil rights by placing her "in a worse situation than if they had not responded at all"—the so-called state-created-danger doctrine. Given that Schieber was probably still alive when the officers arrived, and that they knew the Center City rapist was still at large, Shapiro agreed they should have foreseen serious danger.

The judge also ruled unequivocally that the parents of an adult child have a liberty interest in their child's life "because of the parents' interest in custody and maintaining the family."

The Third Circuit granted summary judgment for the officers in February 2003, saying that there was no evidence that Shannon's civil rights had been violated, and remanded the case to the trial court. Significantly, the judges left open the parental liberty question. In the words of the chief judge: "I express no view on whether the Schiebers, as parents, had a liberty interest in the continued companionship of their adult, emancipated child." (*Schieber v. City of Philadelphia*, 320 F.3d 409 (3d Cir. 2003).)

With the question of parental liberty still undecided, resolving the debate was left to the judges in *McCurdy*. Ricks said *McCurdy* sets the precedent for any similar claims that the court will consider in the future: "This totally changes the framework. It puts an end to these parental claims, and does so by being grounded in Supreme Court holdings."

While the Supreme Court has never ruled specifically on the relationship between parents and their adult children, it has examined related issues. *Troxel v. Granville* first established that "the parent-child relationship is constitutionally protected" by the Due Process Clause of the Fourteenth Amendment and that parents have a constitutional right to the "care, custody, and control" of their children. But the justices made it clear that this applied only to minor children, on the assumption that parents do not "control" their adult children. (530 U.S. 57 (2000).)

... [F]or a government action to be unconstitutional, it had to be specifically aimed at harming the parent-child relationship. In *McCurdy*'s case, noted Ricks, "the relationship of Donta Dawson to his parents was not on the police officer's mind when he pulled the trigger."

...

An ongoing fight?

Constitutional arguments are also wending their way into typical wrongful death cases that involve parents' loss of adult children. One reason is that the states vary widely in the compensation they allow for losses related to an adult child's wrongful death (a few states don't allow any), and plaintiff attorneys are looking to federal remedies.

...

[A plaintiff's attorney in Iowa] called *McCurdy* "a bad decision," saying, "All of these arguments about the constitutional liberty interest focus on the age concept. The Supreme Court has ruled only on cases involving minors, and there is absolutely no dispute that the right to a relationship with your child is a constitutional right. So why does this right disappear when your child reaches majority?"

...

Change in the law can be slow. Ricks noted that the city of Philadelphia had waited "about 10 years," letting many similar cases go by unchallenged, before finding the one that could settle the parental liberty issue, at least in the Third Circuit. "It's been a conscious, long-term strategy of waiting for the right case, and finally, this was it."

E. Doctrinal Shift: Post-*Butera/McCurdy* Evolution of the Parental Liberty Interest in Adult Children

When the *McCurdy* brief was filed in the Third Circuit in 2002, the scope of the parental liberty interest protected by substantive due process had split the federal circuits, with the Seventh[2] and Ninth[3] agreeing that parents had a protected interest in companionship with their adult children.[4] At that time, more than a dozen years of district court decisions within the Third Circuit had recognized the same parental substantive due process right, either because they believed the Third Circuit already had endorsed that view, or because they predicted that the Third Circuit would do so when confronted with the issue.

The legal landscape has changed dramatically since the time the *McCurdy* brief was filed. In December 2003, the Third Circuit adopted much of the reasoning of the excerpted Amici Cities Brief and of the litigant they supported, the City of Philadelphia, holding that "the fundamental guarantees of the Due Process Clause do not extend to a parent's interest in the companionship of his independent adult child."[5] In *McCurdy*, the Third Circuit rejected the claims of the biological father of an independent, adult son that the father had a federal constitutional right to sue police for the deprivation of the son's companionship, where the son was killed in a police shooting. In rejecting the father's assertion of a parental liberty interest in the companionship of an adult son, the Third Circuit repudiated more than a dozen years of district court decisions within the Third Circuit recognizing such a constitutional right as having "misinterpreted" Third Circuit law.

The Third Circuit accepted both major grounds advocated by the cities for rejecting the father's constitutional claim. It held that "a broad expansion of due process protections to encompass [the parent's] proposed definition is unwarranted" because the Supreme Court's definition of the parental liberty interest "concerns the right of parents to make critical child-rearing decisions concerning the care, custody, and control of minors."[6] That right "must cease to exist" when the child begins to make decisions for him or herself, presumably at the state age of majority or when the child is emancipated.[7]

---

2. *Bell v. City of Milwaukee*, 746 F.2d 1205, 1242–45 (7th Cir. 1984), *overruled by Russ v. Watts*, 414 F.3d 783, 791 (7th Cir. 2005).

3. *Strandberg v. City of Helena*, 791 F.2d 744, 748 (9th Cir. 1986); *Smith v. City of Fontana*, 818 F.2d 1411, 1419 (9th Cir. 1987), *overruled on other grounds by Hodgers-Durgin v. de la Vina*, 199 F.3d 1037 (9th Cir. 1999).

4. Based on Sarah Ricks, *Evolution of a Doctrine: The Scope of the Parental Liberty Interest Protected by Substantive Due Process After McCurdy*, 3 Rutgers J. L. & Urb. Pol'y 138 (2005).

5. *McCurdy v. Dodd*, 352 F.3d 820, 830 (3d Cir. 2003).

6. *Id.* at 829 (citing *Troxel v. Granville*, 530 U.S. 57, 66 (2000)).

7. *Id.*

The Third Circuit also accepted the other ground advocated in the Amici Cities' brief. "It would ... stretch the concept of due process too far if we were to recognize a constitutional violation based on official actions that were not directed at the parent-child relationship."[8] When the police officer shot the plaintiff's son, "[h]is actions were directed solely at the person at the center of that volatile situation—[the son] himself. [The mother, the father] and the parent-child relationships between them and their son were not on [the officer's] mind when he pulled the trigger."[9]

The Third Circuit's resolution of the parental liberty interest in adult children was not the only change in the legal landscape. More dramatically, in 2005, the Seventh Circuit switched sides in the circuit split.[10] In light of other circuits' rejections of its view, the Seventh Circuit revisited its 21-year-old precedent and overruled it as "wrongly decided,"[11] "not well grounded in the Constitution or Supreme Court case law,"[12] and "not appropriately moored to Supreme Court precedents establishing the contours of the parental liberty interest."[13] Citing *McCurdy* and several precedents on which the Third Circuit had relied, the Seventh Circuit concluded in *Russ v. Watts*: "[w]e therefore overrule our decision [from 1984] insofar as it recognized a constitutional right to recover for the loss of the companionship of an adult child when that relationship is terminated as a result of state action."[14] The Seventh Circuit's decision in *Russ v. Watts* is the next case in this book.

Within weeks of the Seventh Circuit's defection to the opposite side in the circuit split, in 2005 the Eleventh Circuit weighed in on the existence of a parental liberty interest in a continued relationship with an adult child, a question of first impression for that court.[15] The Eleventh Circuit held that "the Fourteenth Amendment's substantive due process protections do not extend to the relationship between a mother and her adult son."[16]

Questions to guide reading of *Russ*

1. In 2005, the Seventh Circuit switched sides in the circuit split, overruling its earlier decision in *Bell*. Does the Seventh Circuit suggest that only state conduct that deliberately interferes with the parent-child relationship will implicate a parental liberty interest? Why?

---

8. *Id.* at 830.
9. *Id.*
10. *Russ v. Watts*, 414 F.3d 783 (7th Cir. 2005), *cert. denied*, 546 U.S. 1094 (2006) (reversing *Bell*).
11. *Id.* at 788.
12. *Id.*
13. *Id.* at 790.
14. *Id.* at 791.
15. *Robertson v. Hecksel*, 420 F.3d 1254 (11th Cir. 2005), *cert. denied*, 547 U.S. 1162 (2006).
16. *Id.* at 1255.

2. How does the Seventh Circuit's refusal to recognize a parental liberty interest in society and companionship of an adult child reflect a concern for differentiating federal constitutional law from state tort law?
3. Should a minor's need for parental guidance warrant different constitutional treatment than an adult's relationship with a parent? As a policy matter, what are the advantages of drawing lines such as the age of majority? What are the alternatives?

Russ v. Watts

414 F.3d 783 (7th Cir. 2005), *cert. denied*, 546 U.S. 1094 (2006)

FLAUM, Chief Judge.

This case arises out of the tragic and fatal shooting of Robert Russ, a 22-year-old student at Northwestern University, by Chicago police officer Van B. Watts. The issue before us is whether the United States Constitution, through the federal civil rights statute 42 U.S.C. § 1983, provides Russ's parents with a cause of action for the loss of the society and companionship of their son. That question leads us to revisit our decision in *Bell v. City of Milwaukee*, 746 F.2d 1205 (7th Cir. 1984), in which we held that a parent's constitutional liberty interest in his relationship with his adult son was violated when his son was killed by police. After careful consideration, we conclude that *Bell* was wrongly decided and must be overruled. We hold that the federal Constitution does not allow a parent to recover in such circumstances, and, on this basis, we affirm the district court's entry of summary judgment in favor of defendants.

I. Background

...

On June 5, 1999, just a few weeks before his graduation, Robert Russ was driving from the Northwestern campus in Evanston, Illinois to his mother's home in Calumet City, Illinois. At approximately 1:00 A.M., Chicago police officer Phillip Banazkiewicz attempted to pull over Russ's car. When Russ did not stop, a chase ensued, with three officers—Banazkiewicz, Watts, and Deputy Sheriff Robert Helson of the Cook County Sheriff's Department—pursuing Russ in three separate police vehicles.

... The chase finally ended after Russ's car collided with several of the police vehicles. Once stopped, the three police officers exited their vehicles and surrounded Russ's car with their weapons drawn. Officer Watts positioned himself on the driver's side of Russ's vehicle, and Officers Banazkiewicz and Helson stood on the passenger's side. Watts broke the rear window on the driver's side and fired a single shot, striking and killing Russ.

Several months before he was killed, Russ had conceived a child with Erin Lewis. Lewis gave birth to Russ's son on September 26, 1999, over four months after Russ's death ... On October 17, 2003, a jury found Watts liable for Russ's death and awarded $9.6 million in damages to Russ's estate.... Russ's parents and siblings filed separate actions in federal district court against [the] Officers....

...

II. Discussion

...

We held in *Bell* that a father whose son was killed by a Milwaukee police officer during a chase could recover under § 1983 for the violation of his substantive due process right to associate with his son. 746 F.2d at 1243–44.

...

We upheld the award to Dolphus Bell's estate for the loss of society and companionship, concluding that Daniel Bell's father "possessed a constitutional liberty interest in his relationship with his son." *Id.* at 1243. In reaching this conclusion, we relied on the Supreme Court decisions "examining the parameters of the constitutional protection afforded the parent-child relationship." *Id.* (citing *Meyer v. Nebraska*, 262 U.S. 390, 399 (1923) ... *Skinner v. Oklahoma*, 316 U.S. 535, 541 (1942); *Prince v. Massachusetts*, 321 U.S. 158, 166 (1944)). We also found support in the Supreme Court decisions protecting the parental relationship from state interference. We concluded:

> The due process clause requires that severances in the parent-child relationship caused by the state occur only with rigorous protections for the individual liberty interests at stake. The state may not separate the parent from the child, even temporarily, without according them due process of law to protect their liberty interests.

Id. at 1243–44 [further citation omitted].

We held that Daniel's status as an adult living on his own at the time he was killed did not preclude recovery, stating, "we are unpersuaded that a constitutional line based solely on the age of the child should be drawn." *Id.* at 1245. We explained that "[t]he Supreme Court's decisions protect more than the custody dimension of the parent-child relationship" and that the protected relationship "includes the parent's 'interest in the companionship, care, custody, and management' of the child." *Id.* (quoting *Stanley* [*v. Illinois*], 405 U.S. [645,] 651 [1972]). We also noted that Daniel Bell was single, had no children, and had not become part of another family unit. "[H]is father's family was his immediate family." *Id.* Moreover, we observed, the Wisconsin wrongful death statute permitted recovery for loss of society and companionship regardless of the age of the child at his death ... We therefore concluded that Daniel's age and separate residence were matters for the jury to consider when determining damages, but were not a bar to recovery. *Id.*

Our opinion declined to extend constitutional protection to the relationship between *Bell* and his siblings, remarking that were we to rule otherwise, "there could be no principled way of limiting such a holding to the immediate family or perhaps even to blood relationships." *Id.* at 1247. We noted that Supreme Court decisions examining the Fourteenth Amendment liberty interests were based primarily on the parents' constitutional right to raise, associate with, and make decisions affecting the family, even though they also alluded to the importance of the integrity of the family unit as a whole. *Id.* at 1245–46.

...

Since *Bell*, several of our sister circuits have considered whether the Constitution protects a parent's relationship with his adult children in the context of state action which has the incidental effect of severing that relationship. No other court of which we are aware has allowed a parent to recover for the loss of his relationship with his child in these circumstances. Most courts that have considered the issue have expressly declined to find a violation of the familial liberty interest where the state action at issue was not aimed specifically at interfering with the relationship. *See Trujillo v. Bd. of County Comm'rs*, 768 F.2d 1186, 1190 (10th Cir. 1985) (plaintiffs' § 1983 action for the wrongful death of their son and brother while he was in state custody was properly dismissed because plaintiffs did not allege that defendants intended to deprive them of their protected relationship with the decedent); *Valdivieso Ortiz v. Burgos*, 807 F.2d 6, 9 (1st Cir. 1986) (declining to find violation of substantive due process right based on government action causing only an "incidental deprivation" of the relationship between appellants and their adult relative when he was allegedly beaten to death by guards while in prison); *McCurdy v. Dodd*, 352 F.3d 820, 830 (3d Cir. 2003) (where officer shot and killed individual after he refused demands to hold up his hands, father could not recover for deprivation of his relationship with his son because the official action was not "directed at the parent-child relationship") ... *Shaw v. Stroud*, 13 F.3d 791, 804–05 (4th Cir. 1994) (declining to recognize wife and minor child's Fourteenth Amendment claim for loss of love and support of their husband and father after he was shot by police officer). *But see Kelson v. City of Springfield*, 767 F.2d 651, 655 (9th Cir. 1985) (parents had a constitutionally protected liberty interest in the companionship and society of their 14-year-old son and stated claim under § 1983 against school officials after their son committed suicide while at school).

Courts have also been reluctant to extend the constitutional protections afforded the parent-child relationship to cases involving adult children. *See Valdivieso Ortiz*, 807 F.2d at 8 (noting that decedent was over 21 at the time of his death and was "not a minor child still within 'the care, custody, and management' of his parents"); *Butera v. District of Columbia*, 235 F.3d 637, 656 (D.C. Cir. 2001) (holding that a "parent does not have a constitutionally protected liberty interest in the companionship of a child who is past minority and independent"); *McCurdy*, 352 F.3d at 829 (parental liberty interest as defined by the Supreme Court "must cease to exist at the point at which a child begins to assume that critical decisionmaking responsibility for himself or herself").

An analysis of the decisions of our sister circuits as well as a reexamination of our own rationale in *Bell* convinces us that *Bell* was wrongly decided. We do not make such a declaration lightly. Although we must give considerable weight to our prior decisions, we are not bound by them absolutely and may overturn Circuit precedent for compelling reasons.... Other circuits' rejection of our position provides one such compelling reason. As we have previously explained:

> When a number of other circuits reject a position that we have taken, and no other circuit accepts it, the interest in avoiding unnecessary intercircuit conflicts comes into play; and if we are asked to reexamine our position, we can hardly refuse. That is not to say that reexamination will cause us to relinquish the position.... But if upon conscientious reexamination we are persuaded that the other circuits have the better of the argument, we should abandon our position in order to spare the Supreme Court extra work.

United States v. Hill, 48 F.3d 228, 232 (7th Cir. 1995) (internal citations omitted).

That *Bell* stands alone causes us to reconsider its holding. We now see that our conclusion that Dolphus Bell's parental liberty interest was violated by the killing of his son was not well grounded in the Constitution or Supreme Court case law. The Supreme Court has recognized violations of the due process liberty interest in the parent-child relationship only where the state took action specifically aimed at interfering with that relationship. As the Supreme Court has explained, "[h]istorically, the guarantee of due process has been applied to deliberate decisions of government officials to deprive a person of life, liberty, or property." *Daniels v. Williams*, 474 U.S. 327, 331 (1986) (collecting cases).

The Supreme Court has "always been reluctant to expand the concept of substantive due process because guideposts for responsible decisionmaking in this unchartered area are scarce and open-ended." *Washington v. Glucksberg*, 521 U.S. 702, 720 (1997) (citations omitted). The Court has cautioned that we must "exercise the utmost care" in extending constitutional protection to an asserted right or liberty interest because, in doing so, we "place the matter outside the arena of public debate and legislative action." *Id.* With these principles in mind, we turn to the liberty interest asserted by plaintiffs.

Although it is well established that parents have a fundamental constitutional liberty interest in the "care, custody, and control of their children," *Troxel v. Granville*, 530 U.S. 57, 65 (2000), the appropriate framework for analyzing claims alleging a violation of this interest is less than clear....

Under any standard, finding a constitutional violation based on official actions that were not directed at the parent-child relationship would stretch the concept of due process far beyond the guiding principles set forth by the Supreme Court. *See McCurdy*, 352 F.3d at 830; *Valdivieso Ortiz*, 807 F.2d at 9.

Our finding of a constitutional violation in *Bell* was not appropriately moored to Supreme Court precedents establishing the contours of the parental liberty interest. The decisions on which we relied as "indicat[ing] that Daniel Bell's father possessed a constitutional liberty interest in his relationship with his son" all dealt with the right to procreate and make decisions about rearing one's minor children without state inference. *See Meyer*, 262 U.S. at 400 (right of parents to engage teacher to instruct child in foreign language); *Skinner*, 316 U.S. at 541 (state-imposed sterilization "forever deprives" individual of a "basic liberty"); *Prince*, 321 U.S. at 165–66 (parental right to give children religious training and encourage them in practice of religious beliefs).... These precedents certainly did not compel the result we reached in *Bell*.

Similarly, all the cases we cited in *Bell* for the proposition that the state may interfere with the parental relationship only after providing sufficient procedural protection involved state action that purposefully interfered with the family relationship. *See Lassiter*, 452 U.S. at 31 (addressing due process requirements in parental termination proceedings) ... *Smith*, 431 U.S. at 854–56 (examining constitutional adequacy of notice, pre-removal conference, and post-removal hearing in administrative action to remove child from custody of foster parents); *Stanley*, 405 U.S. at 649 (due process entitles unwed father to a hearing on his fitness as a parent before removing minor children from his custody) [further citation omitted].

Neither *Bell* nor the instant case involved intentional action by the state to interfere with a familial relationship; plaintiffs in this case have not alleged that Watts shot Russ for the specific purpose of terminating Russ's relationship with his family. Affording plaintiffs a constitutional due process right to recover against the state in these circumstances would create the risk of constitutionalizing all torts against individuals who happen to have families. Upon reconsideration, we now recognize that the finding of a violation of the parental liberty interest in *Bell* is no longer supportable. Furthermore, although we need not impose an absolute rule that parents of adult children lack any liberty interest in their relationship with their children, we agree with our sister circuits that minor children's need for the guidance and support of their parents warrants "sharply different constitutional treatment." *Butera*, 235 F.3d at 656; *McCurdy*, 352 F.3d at 829.

We therefore overrule our decision in *Bell* insofar as it recognized a constitutional right to recover for the loss of the companionship of an adult child when that relationship is terminated as an incidental result of state action. Having concluded that Russ's parents have no constitutional right to recover for the loss of society and companionship of Russ in these circumstances, we need not address the other issues raised by the parties.

For further discussion

Although *Russ* is a panel decision of the Seventh Circuit, it overruled *Bell*, an earlier Seventh Circuit panel decision. The Seventh Circuit is unusual in not abiding by the *en banc* requirement for a subsequent panel to overrule a prior panel. Why do you think that most circuits follow the practice of only permitting a panel decision to be overruled by the *en banc* court?

Questions to guide reading of *Smith*

1. What is the attitude of the district court toward the Ninth Circuit precedent it was bound to follow in *Smith*? Was the district court sending an implicit message to the Ninth Circuit? Or to the Supreme Court if it should decide to address the scope of the parental liberty interest in an adult son or daughter?
2. Could a defendant bound by Ninth Circuit precedent make a credible argument in support of the view that parents of an independent adult son or

daughter should not have a substantive due process right to companionship of their child? Can you craft such an argument?

Smith v. Pierce Cty.

218 F. Supp. 3d 1220 (W.D. Wash. 2016)

SETTLE, District Court Judge.

[Matthew Smith was arrested and held in a county jail. When Smith was booked into Jail, the County Jail's medical providers knew Smith suffered from Crohn's, a potentially dangerous disease. Smith began to suffer symptoms of Crohn's. Within six weeks, Smith died on the floor of the jail's medical clinic, while awaiting medical treatment. Smith was 47. Among other claims, the parents of the decedent, Ben Smith and Nona Smith, seek recovery of damages for violation of their own federal constitutional rights for loss of association with their son.]

C. Parents' Individual Standing for § 1983 Claims

...

Mr. and Mrs. Smith allege claims for the deprivation of their own Fourteenth Amendment right to the companionship and society of their son. The Ninth Circuit "has recognized that parents have a Fourteenth Amendment liberty interest in the companionship and society of their children." *Wilkinson v. Torres*, 610 F.3d 546, 554 (9th Cir. 2010). "Parents and children may assert Fourteenth Amendment substantive due process claims if they are deprived of their liberty interest in the companionship and society of their child or parent through official conduct." *Lemire v. California Dept. of Corrections and Rehabilitation*, 726 F.3d 1062, 1075 (9th Cir. 2013). *See also Curnow v. Ridgecrest Police*, 952 F.2d 321, 325 (9th Cir. 1991) (citing *Strandberg v. City of Helena*, 791 F.2d 744, 748 (9th Cir. 1986); *Kelson v. City of Springfield*, 767 F.2d 651, 653–55 (9th Cir. 1985))....

In its reply, the County argues, in essence, that the prevailing Ninth Circuit precedent is bad law ... The County indicates that the Supreme Court has remained silent on whether a parent may maintain an individual § 1983 substantive due process claim resulting from the death of an adult nondependent child ... Indeed, "the Supreme Court cases [addressing the parental liberty interest] focus on securing the rights of parents to have custody of and to raise their *minor* children in a manner that develops parental and filial bonds free from government interference." *Butera v. D.C.*, 235 F.3d 637, 655 (D.C. Cir. 2001) (internal quotation omitted). *See, e.g., Troxel v. Granville*, 530 U.S. 57, 66 (2000) ("[W]e have recognized the fundamental right of parents to make decisions concerning the care, custody, and control of their children."). Accordingly, "the Courts of Appeals are divided on the issue of whether the Due Process Clause protects a parent's right to the companionship of his or her adult son." *McCurdy v. Dodd*, 352 F.3d 820, 828 (3d Cir. 2003).

Examining the Ninth Circuit line of cases, it could be argued that a parent's right to sue under § 1983 based on the loss of society and companionship of an adult nondependent child is an improper exaggeration of the well-established right to direct the care, custody, and control of dependent children. In *Kelson*, the Ninth Circuit held that a fourteen-year-old boy's suicide while under the supervision of school officials implicated a § 1983 claim for interference with "a constitutional right to the maintenance of a parent-child relationship." 767 F.2d at 654. In reaching its conclusion, the Ninth Circuit relied on various authorities recognizing a parent's liberty interest in the care, custody, and control of *minor dependent* children. *Kelson*, 767 F.2d at 653–55 [citations omitted].

The *Kelson* decision also relied on *Bell v. City of Milwaukee*, 746 F.2d 1205 (7th Cir. 1984), which held that a father could claim a due process deprivation for the death of his nondependent 23-year-old son; but *Bell* was subsequently overruled. *See Russ v. Watts*, 414 F.3d 783, 790 (7th Cir. 2005) ("Our finding ... in *Bell* was not appropriately moored to Supreme Court precedents establishing the contours of the parental liberty interest. The decisions on which we relied as indicating that [a] father possessed a constitutional liberty interest in his relationship with his [adult] son all dealt with the right to procreate and make decisions about rearing one's minor children without state inference.") (quotation marks omitted).

Subsequently, in *Strandberg*, the Ninth Circuit relied on *Kelson* to bifurcate the parental liberty interest into separate rights to (1) raise minor children and (2) enjoy the companionship and society inherent to a parent-child relationship. 791 F.2d at 748 n.1. Under this approach, the Ninth Circuit found that parents could bring § 1983 claims for Fourteenth Amendment violations based on the death of their 22-year-old son while in jail. *Id.* at 748. Later, in *Curnow*, the Ninth Circuit cited *Kelson* and *Strandberg* and allowed parents to pursue § 1983 claims based on the Fourteenth Amendment after the fatal shooting of their adult son by police. 952 F.2d at 325. Since *Curnow*, the Ninth Circuit has consistently recognized that § 1983 claims may proceed under the theory that the Fourteenth Amendment protects the right to the companionship and society between parents and their adult children. [citations omitted].

This Court is not the first district court to consider the evolution of the parent-child right to society and companionship in the Ninth Circuit. In *Rentz v. Spokane Cty.*, 438 F. Supp. 2d 1252 (E.D. Wash. 2006), Judge McDonald (who also authored the *Curnow* opinion while sitting by designation) offered a careful examination of the Ninth Circuit's *Strandberg-Curnow* line of cases. There, Judge McDonald allowed the parents' § 1983 claims to proceed, stating: "the development of this precedent in the Ninth Circuit, even be it inadvertent and/or not particularly well thought out under Supreme Court precedent, is nonetheless binding authority upon this district court." 438 F. Supp. 2d at 1265.

Here, the Court reaches the same conclusion. This Court is bound to apply the prevailing law of the Ninth Circuit.... Although the Ninth Circuit's *Strandberg-Curnow* line of cases arguably overexpanded the parental interest recognized by the Supreme Court, the Supreme Court authority does not necessarily contradict the Ninth Circuit. Therefore, Mr. and Mrs. Smith may bring § 1983 substantive due process claims for the loss of society and companionship of their adult nondependent son.

For further discussion

1. The U.S. Supreme Court has not yet decided the scope of the parental liberty interest in adult children, an issue that it might have addressed in two cases in which the Court dismissed certiorari as improvidently granted.[17] While evidence of how Supreme Court Justice Stephen Breyer might rule on this issue can be gleaned from his participation on the First Circuit panel that rejected the parental claim,[18] less can be learned from Justice Samuel Alito's participation on the Third Circuit panel that decided *McCurdy*, as then-Judge Alito concurred in the judgment only, and for other reasons.[19]

2. In 2018, the parties in *Smith* settled. If you represented the defendants in *Smith*, would you recommend settling instead of pursuing the litigation? Even if the Ninth Circuit ultimately rejected defendants' arguments that the parental liberty interest asserted by plaintiffs did not exist, could the defendants later seek certiorari to the Supreme Court? If you were choosing a test case to litigate the scope of the parental liberty interest before the Supreme Court, would you choose *Smith*?

3. A federal trial court in 2016 summarized the continuing circuit split:

> There is a split among the circuit courts as to whether parents have [a] protected liberty interest in the companionship of their adult children under Fourteenth Amendment. *See Robertson v. Hecksel*, 420 F.3d 1254, 1255 (11th Cir. 2005) (holding mother did not have constitutionally protected liberty interest in her relationship with her adult son, who was fatally shot by police officer during traffic stop, because "the Fourteenth Amendment's substantive due process protections do not extend to the relationship between a mother and her adult son"). *Compare with Chaudhry v. City of Los Angeles*, 751 F.3d 1096, 1106 (9th Cir. 2014), *cert. denied sub nom. City of Los Angeles, Cal. v. Chaudhry*, 135 S. Ct. 295 (2014) ("Our decisions recognize that parents have a liberty interest in the companionship of their adult children and have a cause of action under the Fourteenth Amendment when the police kill an adult child without legal justification."). These cases discuss substantive due process protection of the parent-child relationship as it relates to the loss of companionship with a child.

Moreno v. Mcallen Indep. Sch. Dist., No. 7:15-CV-162, 2016 WL 1258410, at *6, n. 83 (S.D. Tex. Mar. 31, 2016); *see id.* ("'the Supreme Court has protected the parent only when the government directly acts to sever or otherwise affect his or her legal relationship with a child. The Court has never held that governmental action that

17. *McCurdy*, 352 F.3d at 828 n.5 (further citation omitted).

18. *Ortiz v. Burgos*, 807 F.2d 6 (1st Cir. 1986).

19. *McCurdy*, 352 F.3d at 831 n.9 (concurring in the judgment "for essentially the reasons given by the District Court").

affects the parental relationship only incidentally ... is susceptible to challenge for a violation of due process'") (quoting *Malagon de Fuentes v. Gonzales*, 462 F.3d 498, 505 (5th Cir. 2006) (quoting *McCurdy*); *see also Gorman v. Rensselaer Cty.*, 910 F.3d 40, 48 (2d Cir. 2018) (holding that, "[b]ased on the Supreme Court's directive that only deliberate conduct implicates due process, we join the consensus view of the circuit courts: a claim under the Due Process Clause for infringement of the right to familial associations requires the allegation that state action was specifically intended to interfere with the family relationship").

4. The Ninth Circuit rejected a police defendant's argument that a distant parent/child relationship could preclude a parent's claim as a matter of law, instead considering such information to be factual, not legal. *Johnson v. Bay Area Rapid Transit Dist.*, 724 F.3d 1159, 1170 (9th Cir. 2013) (declining "to find, as a matter of law, that [decedent] Grant and his father lacked a sufficiently strong father—son bond to support the father's Fourteenth Amendment claim").

5. The law review Notes excerpted below explore additional arguments in favor of recognizing a parental liberty interest in companionship of adult children.

Questions to guide reading of law review Note

1. How does the Note writer suggest a parental liberty interest in adult children should be defined?
2. What are some of the practical litigation consequences of not defining the parental liberty interest by what the Note writer calls the "arbitrary bright line" of age but instead by whether the parent shared a close and loving relationship with the adult son or daughter?

Towards the Recognition of a Parental Right of Companionship in Adult Children under the 14th Amendment Substantive Due Process Clause

By Romana Kaleem, 35 Seton Hall L. Rev. 1121 (2005)

Conclusion: A Framework for Recovery

Although the Supreme Court has urged restraint in implying fundamental rights, the recognition of a parental right of companionship in adult children does not stray from substantive due process guidelines. The crux of substantive due process analysis looks to the traditions and culture of the American people in determining whether or not there exists a fundamental right that deserves constitutional protection. Over the years, the Supreme Court has consistently explained that American tradition emphasizes familial relationships, especially those of parent and child. Additionally, the Court has, on numerous occasions, discouraged the imposition of bright line rules in fundamental rights analysis and favored a fact-intensive approach. For these reasons, it is anomalous to cut off a parental constitutional right of companionship at the age of majority. Even more so, it seems illogical to recognize a right to keep the family together and a right to the companionship, care, custody, and management of one's children, but to not allow a general parental right of companionship in children.

Courts should extend a constitutional fundamental right to parents in the companionship of their adult children. This right should extend to foster parents and unwed natural parents as well as married biological parents. A survey of substantive due process cases illustrates that the Court has refused to assume that the nature of a foster parent's or unwed parent's relationship with her child is automatically less worthy of constitutional protection than a married natural parent's relationship with her child. Thus, the right to companionship of an adult child should not be automatically defined to exist only for natural, married parents.

Because of the great weight the Supreme Court has accorded the parent-child relationship, the circuits that have refused to recognize a right of companionship between parents and adult children are wrong. The allowance of the right is in line with substantive due process analysis because the court has repeatedly shunned the use of arbitrary lines and markers. Refusing to extend the right of companionship between parents and children beyond the age of eighteen is exactly that—an arbitrary marker. Furthermore, the courts that refuse to recognize the right base much of their analysis on the fact that the parent-child relationship grows weaker with age. Significantly, however, current research indicates otherwise.

Using the state's age of majority as a marker for recovery creates the illogical situation where a deadbeat father is unjustly enriched from his child's death as long as the child is a minor, and an involved and attached father gets no recovery because his child happens to be an adult. Rather than cutting off a right of companionship at the age of majority, a court should determine whether a parent has a valid constitutional claim for loss of companionship in a child based on the relationship that he and his child shared.

For example, when due to unlawful state action, a father loses a minor child with whom he has not spoken in years, he should not be able to recover on a constitutional right of companionship, regardless of the fact that his child was a minor. On the other hand, when a father loses an adult child with whom he has a close and loving relationship, he should be able to recover for his loss, regardless of the fact that his child was nineteen years old or even thirty. Although no amount of damages can compensate for the death of a child, such a framework for recovery comes closer to compensating parents justly.

Along with being in line with general substantive due process guidelines, the recognition of a parental right of companionship in adult children is in line with the reality of parent-child relationships in America. "Researchers have exploded the myth that families abandon their elderly relatives." In fact, parents and adult children often share intimate relationships that can be more rewarding than the relationships they shared early in life. Though not a part of substantive due process analysis, social and economic trends also indicate that recognition of the right would be wise.

The Supreme Court has consistently recognized the importance of familial relationships without the imposition of arbitrary markers. The Fourteenth Amendment parental right of companionship in adult children is not the place to begin to impose such arbitrary bright line rules.

For further discussion

Other commentators advocating for a parental liberty interest in grown children have taken different paths to that result. One Note argued:

> [T]here is a constitutionally protected parental interest in the companionship of an adult child. Under the approach advanced in this Note, the parental liberty interest alters in scope during the two phases of a child's life. During a child's minor years, the parental liberty interest contains the full constellation of rights. The parent of such a minor child has a constitutionally protected interest in the companionship, care, custody, and management of his or her children. The scope of the parental liberty interest, however, fundamentally changes as the child matures in adulthood. Many liberties in the constellation would conflict with the adult child's own constitutional liberty and autonomy. Under the second tier, therefore, the parental liberty interest would extend only to the companionship and care of the adult child, provided that a companionship relationship had been developed before the occurrence of any state action that may have limited it.
>
> Though this Note arguably advances the expansion of substantive due process, and for that reason could be viewed as activist, it can also be viewed as conservative in that it furthers the profound value that American society has placed on the intimacy of family life. The two-tiered approach to the parental liberty interest continues in the tradition of Supreme Court precedent on the family and logically flows from the special rights and obligations imposed on individuals by virtue of the relationship of a parent and her adult child. This Note also goes further and attempts to honor the normative values of the family that the Court previously has previously been unwilling to acknowledge explicitly. Once one views the family unit not just in utilitarian terms of economic support or guardian, but as a source for emotional support and nurture, it makes perfect sense to afford constitutional protection to the companionship interest of a parent and her adult child.

Isaac J.K. Adams, *Growing Pains: The Scope of Substantive Due Process Rights of Parents of Adult Children*, 57 Vand. L. Rev. 1883, 1932–33 (2004) (footnotes omitted). Another Note argued:

> By finding that there is a constitutionally protected right for a parent to associate with an adult child based on the importance of family relationships, the Ninth Circuit complies with the Supreme Court's constant reminders of the value of the family. To abide by § 1983, this right should only be actionable in situations where the governmental action is deliberately aimed at disrupting the parent-adult child relationship, as agreed on by most of the courts of

appeal. Lastly, the original approach of the Seventh Circuit, holding that the right should be protected only when certain factors are met, is most practical and best avoids unnecessary litigation. This mixed approach is consistent with the large precedent expanding due process familial rights, and takes the accepted right to a parent's companionship with a minor child and logically extends it to an adult child.

Meir Weinberg, *The Fourteenth Amendment Due Process Right of Companionship Between A Parent and His or Her Adult Child: Examination of A Circuit Split*, 43 New Eng. L. Rev. 271, 299 (2009).

Guide to Law Practice Simulation 10

Description

The fictional Twelfth Circuit has scheduled oral argument in an appeal raising a question of first impression, specifically: "Does the father of an adult son have a protected liberty interest in companionship of his adult son?" The oral argument before the Twelfth Circuit is based on the facts of the hypothetical district court decision below, *Aryn v. Lily*. Two students represent the plaintiff/appellant. Two students represent the defendant/appellee police officer. One student is a Twelfth Circuit judge.

To prepare, consider issues such as:

- Is it relevant that the government conduct was not directed at the parent/child relationship, but only affected the parent/child relationship incidentally?
- Should the parental liberty interest terminate at the time a child reaches the age of majority? At the age of 18? At the age of 21? If so, why? What principle supports your view?
- If there is a protected interest in "companionship," why should this liberty interest be limited to parent/child relationships? Shouldn't it also apply to grandparents, siblings, uncles, *etc.*?
- In *Bell*, the Seventh Circuit found that the legislative history of § 1983 included a remedy "to the woman whose husband has been murdered; to the children whose father has been killed." Cong. Globe, 42d Cong., 1st Sess. 807 (noting the same language, then finding that the father of an adult child who was killed by police could recover under § 1983). Is that legislative history relevant here? Why, since the question here is constitutional, not statutory?
- Would a parent have a liberty interest in companionship with the child when the child is still dependent on the parent financially, or when the child still lives in the parent's house, or the parent has significant control over what the child does?

Purpose

- Better understand 14th Amendment substantive due process and the scope of the parental liberty interest by comparing varying discussions in *Bell*, *Kelson*, *Butera*, *McCurdy*, *Russ*, *Smith* and law reviews
- Explore attorney role in shaping 14th Amendment substantive due process doctrine by simulating role of attorneys and judge applying doctrine to realistic facts and by exploring a question of first impression that has split the federal circuits
- Prepare for law practice either by persuasively advocating client's legal position and responding to questions or by identifying ambiguities in doctrine or in its application to facts and posing questions to advocates
- There is no need to do any research—the relevant cases are in the casebook.

Structure

- Appellant/plaintiff Aryn—Question & Answer with judge (8 minutes)
- Appellee/defendant Lily—Question & Answer with mediator (8 minutes)
- After about 15 minutes, questioning will be opened up to the entire class
- All counsel—Question & Answer with judge and rest of class (15 minutes)
- Please prepare a question for every simulation, even if you are not one of the students playing a role.
- To ensure full class participation, and as a courtesy to your fellow students, please close your laptops during law practice simulations.

UNITED STATES DISTRICT COURT

FRED ARYN	:	
v.	:	
EISENREICH LILY	:	NO. 20-1776

OPINION OF THE COURT

KATHERINE DOLGENOS, **U.S. District Court Judge.**

Early in the morning of October 1, 2019, Murphy City Police Officer Eisenreich Lily shot and killed Alexander Hamilton, tragically ending an ill-fated confrontation that began when officers pulled aside Mr. Hamilton's stopped vehicle to render assistance, and which deteriorated into an armed stand-off precipitated by Police Officer Lily's mistaken belief that Mr. Hamilton was in possession of and attempting to hide a handgun. Mr. Hamilton was 22 years old. He lived separately from and was not financially supported by his parents. Plaintiff Fred Aryn, the biological father of the adult decedent, sought recovery for a violation of his own constitutional rights pursuant to 42 U.S.C. § 1983 and 42 U.S.C. § 1988. Plaintiff commenced the instant action in state court and defendant removed the action to the federal district court, citing the federal court's original jurisdiction under 28 U.S.C. § 1331.

Defendant Lily has moved for summary judgment pursuant to Rule 56 of the Federal Rules of Civil Procedure. Mr. Aryn's claim is for damages arising out of the allegedly unconstitutional deprivation of Plaintiff's liberty interest in familial companionship. Plaintiff alleged that he "was deprived of the care, comfort, aid, society, affection, companionship, services, assistance and other interpersonal relationships which he would have received from his son for the remainder of his life."

This case squarely presents an issue of first impression in this Circuit: whether Plaintiff Aryn may maintain a Section 1983 action for loss of companionship of his adult son. In Plaintiff Aryn's Complaint, he asserts a Section 1983 claim, in his own right, alleging that the defendant Lily's treatment of Mr. Hamilton deprived Mr. Aryn of his liberty interest in the companionship of his child. Here, Plaintiff does not seek to recover damages for injuries suffered by Alexander Hamilton; rather, he seeks recovery for his own constitutional injuries stemming from Mr. Hamilton's death. The question that arises in connection with the plaintiff's Complaint, therefore, is whether a parent may maintain a Section 1983 loss of companionship claim relating to the defendant's treatment of his adult child.

This is an open issue in this Circuit. The Twelfth Circuit's sole reference to the issue is the following footnote in a 2004 decision, Gottlieb v. Istvan: "While we recognize the death of the Youngs' son as tragic, we express no view on whether the Youngs, as parents, had a liberty interest in the continued companionship of their adult, emancipated child. *Compare* Bell v. City of Milwaukee, 746 F.2d 1205 (7th Cir. 1984), *with* Butera v. District of Columbia, 235 F.3d 637 (D.C. Cir. 2001); Ortiz v. Burgos, 807 F.2d 6 (1st Cir. 1986)." Since the Twelfth Circuit has left open whether the natural father of an adult decedent may bring an action for loss of companionship of his son, the claim Plaintiff pursues for "familial companionship" has not yet been recognized in this Circuit. Further, for the reasons set out in Ortiz and Butera, we do not believe the Twelfth Circuit will recognize the parental liberty interest advocated by Plaintiff. We note that the Seventh Circuit overruled Bell in 2005. We choose to follow the First and D.C. Circuits' reasoning in Ortiz and Butera.

For the foregoing reasons, we will grant the summary judgment motion of Murphy City Police Officer Eisenreich Lily and enter judgment in his favor.

Chapter Fourteen

Protecting Freedom of Religion in Prison: The Free Exercise Clause and RLUIPA

Exercise 1: Chapter Problem

There are approximately 50,000 inmates in New York State prisons.[1] Robert Sand is one of these inmates. He is incarcerated at Clinton Correctional Facility, a maximum-security prison.[2]

Mr. Sand claims that his right to freely exercise his religion was violated when prison officials refused to allow him to practice his religion in accordance with his sincere religious beliefs. When he entered prison, Sand declared that he was Jewish. He began attending Jewish services, but quickly came to the conclusion that the Rabbi employed by the facility—Rabbi Samuel Cohen—did not practice Judaism correctly.

Sand became disruptive and argumentative during Jewish services and refused to follow the Rabbi's instructions. For example, he wrote notes during services held on the Sabbath and insisted on writing out the full name of God, even though the Rabbi explained that these practices violated Jewish law. He openly told other members of the congregation that the Rabbi was not knowledgeable about Judaism, interrupted the Rabbi during services to argue his own views, and refused to call the Rabbi by his proper title. Based on this behavior, Rabbi Cohen determined that Sand was not a bona fide member of the Jewish religion, that he was disruptive during services, and that he could no longer attend Jewish services at Clinton Correctional Facility.

1. Data provided in the Under Custody Report, Profile of Inmate Population Under Custody on January 1, 2018, issued by the State of New York Department of Corrections and Community Supervision; see also, Jennifer Bronson, et al., Prisoners in 2017, Bureau of Justice Statistics, U.S. Dept. of Justice (2019).

2. This exercise is based on the facts in *Sebok v. Friedman*, No. 99-CV-86 (N.D.N.Y. filed July 12, 2000). Some of the facts have been changed for educational purposes. Because the facts do not precisely track those in the actual case, the names of the parties have been changed.

According to Sand, Rabbi Cohen's views made it impossible for him to properly practice his religion. Rabbi Cohen is the only Rabbi at Clinton, so Sand requested that prison administrators either provide another Rabbi who recognized his religious beliefs or allow him to conduct religious services himself. He has a following of six inmates who have already expressed an interest in attending his services.

Clinton Correctional Facility's administrators denied Sand's request to lead religious services and refused to provide another Rabbi. They also denied several of Sand's other requests for religious accommodations. They denied his request to light candles in his cell on Saturdays—the Jewish Sabbath—and on Chanukah. They also denied his requests to have a mezuzah[3] placed outside his cell door and to have three boxes of books delivered to his cell, so he can continue to study Jewish law. Sand is permitted to observe other aspects of his religion in his cell.

As you read this chapter, assume that you are the attorney for Sand. Will you advise your client that he is likely to succeed on his First Amendment claims? Would he succeed on these claims under the Religious Land Use and Institutionalized Persons Act (RLUIPA)? What additional facts would you want from Sand before making this determination? Use the case law and other materials provided in this chapter to determine what questions you will ask your client.

After acting as attorney for Sand, change sides and assume that you are the attorney for the New York State Department of Correctional Services. What additional facts do you want from your client to defend a possible action for violation of Sand's religious rights? Again, use the case law and materials provided in this chapter to determine the questions you will ask.

A. Balancing Religious Freedoms against Institutional Safety, Financial, and Administrative Concerns

Prisoners in federal and state institutions do not lose all of their religious freedoms due to their incarceration. They retain some religious rights under the First Amendment of the United States Constitution, which protects "the free exercise [of religion]," and under federal statutes including the Religious Freedom Restoration Act (RFRA) and RLUIPA. Prison administrators also have incentives to foster religion in prisons because religious programs are helpful in rehabilitating prisoners and maintaining

3. For a description of a mezuzah, *see infra*.

State Prison, at Sing Sing, New York, a wood engraving, originally published Nov. 1885 in Ballou's Pictoral Drawing-Room Companion, Boston, Massachusetts. This media file is in the public domain in the United States.

order and security.[4] The challenge for prison administrators is to balance the religious privileges granted to prisoners against the institution's legitimate concerns regarding safety, security, and budgetary restraints.[5]

The very nature of prison life—compared to life outside the prison—gives inmates enormous incentives to request religious accommodations. Outside of prison, citizens are responsible for paying for their religious needs and have much more control over their lives. They are required to pay for their churches and temples and for the clergy who provide their services. Private citizens control how they spend their free time, what they eat, what they wear, and how long they grow their hair. If, for example, the government tried to prevent an individual from wearing a crucifix, the courts would almost certainly find a first amendment violation.[6]

On the other hand, inside the prison, many of the inmates' religious needs are provided by the correctional facilities. The prison must provide the chaplains, special meals, holiday breaks, meeting rooms, and some items necessary for worship. Because

4. U.S. Comm'n on Civil Rights, Enforcing Religious Freedom in Prison 30 (2008), *available at* http://www.usccr.gov/pubs/STAT2008ERFIP.pdf (last visited July 2019).

5. *Id.* at xiii; *see also id.* at 31 (addressing Stiles Unit, Supplemental Response to U.S. Comm'n on Civil Rights Interrogatories, Response to Interrogatory Request 24 (2008); Ronald G. Turner, *The Religious Land Use and Institutionalized Persons Act of 2000: The Impact of People in Prison*, 45-JAN Tenn. B. J. 25, 25 (2009).

6. U.S. Comm'n on Civil Rights, *supra* note 4, at 135.

prisons are very restrictive and inmates have limited freedoms, inmates may have substantial incentives to request religious privileges[7] even those they may not have purchased for themselves outside the prison.[8] Indeed, while most inmates' religious requests are undoubtedly based on sincere religious beliefs, some inmates have feigned conversion to other religions and even invented religious beliefs in order to gain benefits and privileges that they would otherwise not be entitled to receive.[9] Some extreme examples include an inmate group, known as the Church of New Song (CONS), that claimed that their religion required that they have steak and wine[10] and an inmate who claimed that his religion—the Jack Daniels Faith—"required that he consume a fifth of whiskey each week."[11] While these claims were not successful, they provide an example of how religious requests can lead to attempts to obtain all sorts of privileges. If the inmate's beliefs are sincere, they must be accommodated unless the denial of privileges is based on compelling prison concerns. As discussed later in this chapter, determining sincerity is a very difficult task.

Even when inmates purchase their own religious items or want to perform their own religious services, they need prison administrators to sanction the services and the use of items they feel are necessary to meet their religious needs. Meeting inmate requests may be difficult for prison administrators due to the unique concerns in a prison setting. For example, maximum-security prisons must ban items that can be used as weapons.[12] Inmates are very ingenious in shaping weapons out of the objects they have available.[13] In the past, inmates have sharpened toothbrush handles, lids of food cans, and even plastic eyeglasses to use as weapons.[14] Given this history, should maximum security prisons allow inmates to have metal crucifixes?[15] How about wooden crucifixes that can be sharpened to gouge out an eye?[16] In considering these questions, remember that the crucifix may provide considerable comfort to a religious inmate. Should the prison evaluate the security threat posed by each individual inmate before making this determination or should the prison instead have a uniform policy? Should

---

7. Noha Moustafa, *The Right to Free Exercise of Religion in Prisons: How Courts Should Determine Sincerity of Religious Beliefs Under* RLUIPA, 20 Mich. J. Race and Law 213, 224 (2014); *see also* Morgan F. Johnson, *Heaven Help Us: The Religious Land Use and Institutionalized Persons Act's Prisoners Provisions in the Aftermath of the Supreme Court's Decision in Cutter v. Wilkinson*, 14 Am. U. J. Gender Soc. Pol'y & L. 585, 608 (2006).

8. U.S. Comm'n on Civil Rights, *supra* note 4, at 125.

9. Johnson, *supra* n. 7, at 610–11.

10. U.S. Comm'n on Civil Rights, *supra* note 4, at 124 n. 22 (citing Lindell v. McCallum, 352 F.3d 1107, 1108 (7th Cir. 2003), Wood v. Me. Dep't of Corr., No. 06-156-B-W, 2007 U.S. Dist. LEXIS 81146, at *3–*5 (D. Me. Oct. 25, 2007), and Theriault v. Silber, 453 F. Supp. 254, 260 (W.D. Tex. 1978)).

11. *See* Doty v. Lewis, 995 F. Supp. 1081, 1085 (D. Ariz. 1998).

12. U.S. Comm'n on Civil Rights, *supra* note 4, at 135.

13. N.Y.S. Dep't of Corr. Serv., Prison Safety in New York: Working Together for Public Protection, VII (2006).

14. *Id.*

15. *See* Sasnett v. Litchser, 197 F.3d 290, 291 (7th Cir. 1999).

16. U.S. Comm'n on Civil Rights, *supra* note 4, at 135.

prison administrators honor the requests of Wotanists and Asatru members,[17] who claim that their religion entitles them to white supremacist literature?

Examples of Approved Religious Items[18]

Rosary beads. Black only. Beads must be made of plastic resin or acrylic and cannot be altered; string may not be made of metal or dangerous material.	**Runes.** Runes are to be made of lightweight wood and measure no larger than a domino. Use in cell only.	**Tarot cards.** One set or deck may be possessed measuring no more than 3.5" x 5" in cell only.
		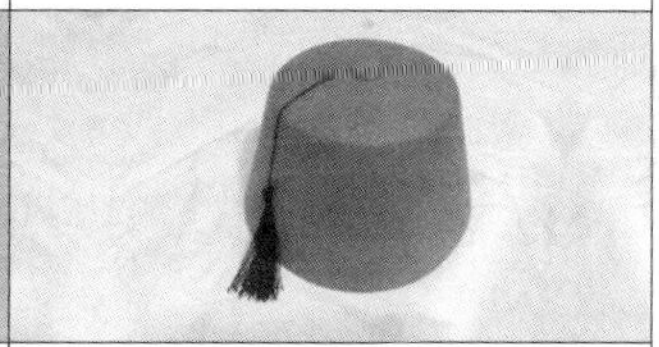
Mala Beads. Beads are only to be held or carried in-cell or to worship but should not be worn. May not exceed 108 beads plus 1 starter bead.	**Star of David pendant.** Maximum of two inches in diameter; no stones or protrusions or sharp edges. It must be covered completely underneath clothing.	**Fez.** A red brimless, cone-shaped, flat-crowned hat; with a tassel not to exceed 3", made of felt; worn by men. The tassel may be attached to a small string measuring up to 3". The tassel and the string may be a maximum of 6".

The large number of religions and the growing religious diversity of the inmate population compound the challenge of accommodating inmate beliefs.[19] For example, the New York State Department of Correctional Services has recorded more than 53 religions in its prisons.[20]

17. *Id.* at 124, 143 (noting that Wotanists worship Norse gods and tend to promote white supremacist teachings); *see also* Borzych v. Frank, 439 F.3d 388, 390 (7th Cir. 2006); Wood v. Me. Dep't of Corr., No. 06-156-BW, 2007 U.S. Dist. LEXIS 81146, at *6, *10 (D. Me. Oct. 25, 2007) (an inmate was denied access to reading materials that were found not to be religious in nature because the religion "*as practiced by Wood* [is] one that advocates white supremacy and encourages contempt and denigration of other races.") (emphasis in original).

18. Information provided by the New York State Department of Corrections and Community Supervision (NYS DOCS): Religious Holy Day Calendar (2019); Photographs by Stephanie Reighart.

19. Turner, *supra* note 5, at 26.

20. Data provided by the New York State Department of Corrections and Community Supervision (NYS DOCS): Subcategories (2019); data for chart provided in 2018; Under Custody Report, *supra* note 1.

Religious Populations in New York State Prisons

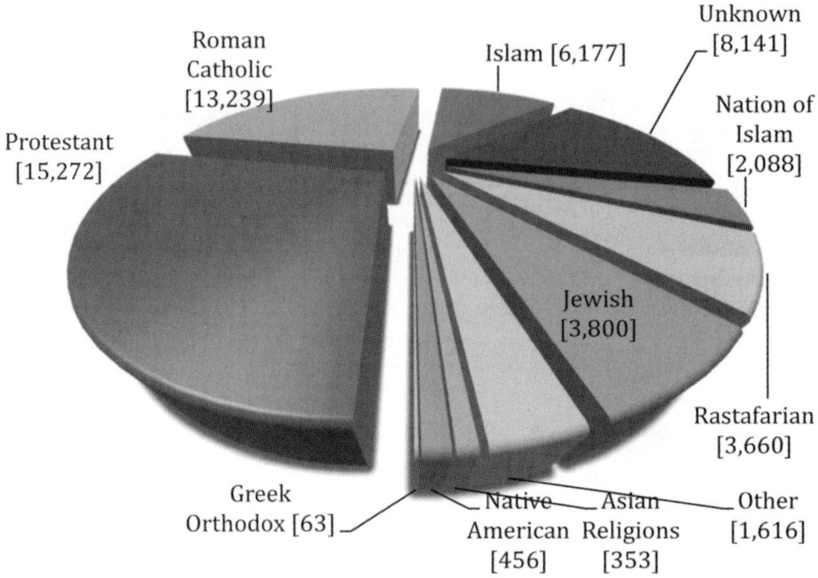

Subcategories:

- Within Protestant: Adventist; Assemblies of God; Baptist; Brethren; Christian Scientist; Church of Christ; Church of God; Episcopal; Evangelical Covenant; Friends/Quakers; Fundamentalist; Jehovah's Witnesses; Lutheran; Messianic Jewish; Methodist; Mormon; Nazarene; Pentecostal; Protestant; Presbyterian; Reformed; Salvation Army; Seventh Day Adventist; United Church of Christ; Unitarian/Universalist.
- Within Islam: American Muslim Mission; Islam; Mohammedan; Moslem; Shiite Muslim; Sunni.
- Within Jewish: Jewish; Orthodox Jewish.
- Within Other: Agnostic; Animism; Atheist; Buddhist; Five Percenter; Hindu; Moorish Science Temple; Odinist/Wodinist; Orisini; Santeria; Satanism; Sikh; Taoist; Vudu; Wiccan/Pagan; Yoruba.
- Within Unknown: Not Specified; Not Coded.

The numerous practices, holidays, religious leaders, dietary needs, clothing requirements, and personal property items needed for each religion make it difficult for prisons to meet all of the prisoners' religious requests. To accommodate the religious holidays alone, the New York State Department of Correctional Services must recognize 126 different religious holidays, each with its own requirements and practices.[21]

21. Data provided by NYS DOCS, Religious Holy Day Calendar (2019).

Religious Holidays Recognized by the New York State
Department of Correctional Services (2019)

January						
		1	2	3	4	5
6	7	8	9	10	11	12
13	14	15	16	17	18	19
20	21	22	23	24	25	26
27	28	29	30	31		

February						
					1	2
3	4	5	6	7	8	9
10	11	12	13	14	15	16
17	18	19	20	21	22	23
24	25	26	27	28		

March						
					1	2
3	4	5	6	7	8	9
10	11	12	13	14	15	16
17	18	19	20	21	22	23
24	25	26	27	28	29	30
31						

April						
	1	2	3	4	5	6
7	8	9	10	11	12	13
14	15	16	17	18	19	20
21	22	23	24	25	26	27
28	29	30				

May						
			1	2	3	4
5	6	7	8	9	10	11
12	13	14	15	16	17	18
19	20	21	22	23	24	25
26	27	28	29	30	31	

June						
						1
2	3	4	5	6	7	8
9	10	11	12	13	14	15
16	17	18	19	20	21	22
23	24	25	26	27	28	29
30						

July						
	1	2	3	4	5	6
7	8	9	10	11	12	13
14	15	16	17	18	19	20
21	22	23	24	25	26	27
28	29	30	31			

January
Mid-Winter (NA)
Moorish-American New Year (MSTA)
Solemnity of Mary (RC)
Epiphany (RC, PROT, RC)
Eve of Epiphany (RC)
Ethiopian Christmas (RAST)
Prophet Noble Drew Ali's Birthday (MSTA)
Skadi Blot/Thorr Blot (WOT)
Ho-On-Ko (BDH)
Three Kings (PROT)
Baptism of the Lord Jesus (PROT)
Week of Prayer for Christian Unity (PROT)
Solemnity of Mary (RC)
Maghi (SIK)
Jewish Arbor Day (JW)

February
Mid-Winter (NA)
Great Lent (GOC, RC) (40 days)
Nirvana (BOH)
Feast of Vail (WOT)
Saviour's Day (NOI)
Purim (JW) (2 days)
Meatfare Sunday (GOC)
Cheesefare Sunday (GOC)
Clean Monday (GOC)
Imbolc/Imbolg/Candlemas (WIC)
Allah's Physical Birthday (NGD)
Transfiguration Sunday (PROT)

March
Ash Wednesday (RC)
Moorish American Flag Day (MSTA)
Spring O-Higan (BDH)
Fast of Esither (JW)
First days Passover (JW) (3 days)
Ostara (WIC)
High Feast of Ostara (WOT)
Annunciation to the Virgin Mary (GOC)
Fast of Esther (JW)
Purim (JW)
Maple Tree Ceremony (NA)
Battle of Adwa Victory (RAST)
Baha'I Fast (BAH)
Naw-Ruz (BAH)
Mahashivarathri/Shiva Puja (HIN)
Holi (HIN)

April
Holy Thursday (PROT, RC)
Good Friday (PROT, RC)
Easter (PROT, RC, MOR, SDA)
Vaisakhi (SIK)
Last days of Passover (JW)
Ridvan (BAH)**April, cont.**
Sigr Blot (WOT)
Buddha's Birth Date (BDH)
Palm Sunday (GOC, RC)
Holy Friday (GOC)
Pascha (GOC)
Memorial of Christ's Death (JHW)
First Days of Passover (JW)
Intermediate Days of Passover (JW)
Family Observance of Passover (JW)
Thunder Ceremony (NA)
Holy Saturday (PROT, RC)
Holy Mother Empress Menen Day (RAST)
Grounation Day (RAST)

May
Pascha (GOC)
Ascension Thursday (RC)
Lailatul Qadr (ISL, SHI)
Pentecost Sunday (GOC)
Frigga Blot (WOT)
Planting Ceremony (NA)
National Day of Prayer (PROT)
Ascension of Jesus (PROT)
Victory Day (RAST)
Africa OAU/AU Day (RAST)
Beltane (WIC)
Declaration of the Ba'b (BAH)
Ascension of the Baha'u'llah (BAH)
Ramadan (ISL, NOI, SHI)
Night of Power (NOI)
Djehuti Brings Back Tefnut (SN)

June
Ascension Thursday (GOC)
Gempo Memorial (BDH)
Shavuot (JW) (3 days)
High Feast of Baldor/Midyear (WOT)
St. John the Baptist (RC)
Fast for the Holy Apostles (GOC)
Pentecost (PROT, RC)
Trinity Sunday (PROT)
Ramadan (ISL, NOI, SHI)
Eidul Fitr (ISL, NOI, SHI)
Six Days of Shawwal (ISL, SHI)
Allah's Show and Prove (NGE)
Remembrance of Guru Arjan (SIK)
Saga Dawa Duchen (BDH)
Strawberry Ceremony (NA)
Patriarch Leonard Percival Howell Day (RAST)
Saint Anthony/Eleggua (SAN)
Litha (WIC)

July
Founders Day (WOT)
O-Bon (BDH) (2 days)
Constitution Day (RAST)
Fast of the 17th Tammuz (JW)
Fast of 9th of Av (JW (2 days)
Nine Days Before Tisha B'Av (JW)
Chokhor Duchen (BDH)
Our Authority Day (MSTA)
Pioneer Day (MOR)
Green Bean Ceremony (NA)
Birthday of Goddess Nebthet (SN)
Birthday of God Asar (SN)
Birthday of God Heru the Elder (SN)
Birthday of God Set (SN)
Birthday of Goddess Aset (SN)
Beginning of the Rise of Sopdu (SN)
Beginning of the Neterian New Year (SN)
Martyrdom of the Ba'b (BAH)
Tafari (RAST)

August						
				1	2	3
4	5	6	7	8	9	10
11	12	13	14	15	16	17
18	19	20	21	22	23	24
25	26	27	28	29	30	31

September						
1	2	3	4	5	6	7
8	9	10	11	12	13	14
15	16	17	18	19	20	21
22	23	24	25	26	27	28
29	30					

October						
		1	2	3	4	5
6	7	8	9	10	11	12
13	14	15	16	17	18	19
20	21	22	23	24	25	26
27	28	29	30	31		

November						
					1	2
3	4	5	6	7	8	9
10	11	12	13	14	15	16
17	18	19	20	21	22	23
24	25	26	27	28	29	30

December						
1	2	3	4	5	6	7
8	9	10	11	12	13	14
15	16	17	18	19	20	21
22	23	24	25	26	27	28
29	30	31				

Key:
BAH: Bahai
BDH: Buddhist
GOC: Greek Orthodox Christian
HIN: Hindu
ISL: Islam
JHW: Jehovah's Witnesses
JW: Jewish
MSTA: Moorish Science Temple of America
MOR: Mormon
NGE: Nation of Gods and Earths
NOI: Nation of Islam
NA: Native American
PROT: Protestant
RAST: Rastafarian
RC: Roman Catholic
SAN: Santeria
SDA: Seventh Day Adventist
SN: Shetaut Neter
SHI: Shi'a
SIK: Sikh
WIC: Wicca
WOT: Wotanist

August
Fast for Assumption of Mary (GOC) (14 days)
Assumption of Mary (GOC, RC)
Transfiguration of our Lord (GOC)
Beheading of St. John the Forerunner (GOC)
Freyfaxi (WOT)
Green Corn Ceremony (NA)
Prophet Marcus Mosiah Garvey Day (RAST)
Lammas (WIC)
Eidul Adha (ISL, NOI, SHI)
Djehuti Heals the Eye of Heru (SN)
Sri Krishnas Janmashtani (HIN)
Allah Social (NGE)
Day of Battle Between Heru and Set (SN)

September
Isrs and Miraj (ISL)
Eid-Ul-Fitra
Rastafarian New Year (RAST)
Elevation of the Holy Cross (GOC)
Autumn O-Higan (BDH)
Winter Finding (WOT)
Nufus Shaban (ISL)
Rosh Hashanah (JW) (2 days)
End of Ramadan (ISL)
Harvest Ceremony (NA)
Ethiopian New Year (RAST)
Our Lady of Regla (SAN)
Our Lady of Charity (SAN)
Our Lady of Mercy (SAN)
Installation of the Adi Granth (SIK)
Mabon (WIC)
The Days of Ashura (ISL, SHI)
Sri Ganesha Chaturthi/Sri Ganesha Puja (HIN)

October
Negus Day (RAST)
Bodhidharma (BDH)
Savior's Day (NOI)
Holy Day of Atonement (NOI) (2 days)
Night of Power (ISL)
Yom Kippur (JW)
First Days of Sukkot (JW) (2 days)
Intermediate Days of Sukkot (JW)
Last Days of Sukkot (JW)
Fast of Gedaliah (JW)
Winter Nights (WOT)
Day of Ghadir (ISL, SHI)
Mubahilah (ISL, SHI)
Harvest Ceremony (NA)
Reformation Day (PROT)
Samhain (WIC)
Birth of the Ba'b (BAH)
Birth of Baba'u'llah (BAH)
Dussera (HIN)
Diwali (HIN)
Birth of Nation of Gods and Earths (NGE)
Thunder Ceremony (NA)
Bandi Chor Divas (SIK)

November
All Saints' (PROT, RC)
All Souls' Day (PROT, RC)
Transfiguration (RAST)
Christmas Advent (GOC, PROT, RC)
Feast of Ullr (WOT)
Harvest Ceremony (NA)
Thunder Ceremony (NA)
Birthday of Guru Nanak (SIK)
Coronation Day (RAST)

December
Chanukah (JW) (8 days)
Christmas Eve (PROT)
Christmas (GOC, PROT, RC, MOR, SDA)
Christmastime (PROT)
Watch Night (PROT)
High Feast of Yule (WOT)
Anniversary of Sister's Auxiliary (MSTA)
Anniversary of Young Moslem League (MSTA)
Immaculate Conception (RC)
Mid-Winter Ceremony (NA)
Buddha's Enlightenment Day (BDH)
New Year's Eve (BDH)
Saint Barbara (SAN)
Winter Solstice/Yule (WIC)
Thunder Ceremony (NA)
Our Lady of Guadalupe (RC)
Birth of Heru (SN)

One of the more burdensome religious requests made by inmates was a request by Native Americans for a sweat lodge.[22] Sweat lodges are dome-shaped structures designed to give privacy to those participating in the ceremonies that take place inside.[23] The ceremonies in the sweat lodge involve the use of burning hot coals, large rocks, and metal tools to create steam.[24] It is easy to understand why these lodges might create security concerns in a prison. Some religions have special meal requirements that can strain prison budgets. For example, kosher meals required by the Jewish faith can cost almost twice as much as a standard meal. In 2016, the certified religious meal, which includes kosher meals, in Florida cost $3.55, while a standard meal cost $1.89.[25] Even religious requirements regarding hair length can cause significant burdens in the prison setting.[26] Rastafarians and members of some Native American religions believe that their religion requires them to wear their hair long and Orthodox Jews believe they must grow long beards.[27] Many prisons forbid long hair because it can be used to hide contraband.[28] Officers at the prison can avoid this problem by requiring inmates to comb through their hair at various check points. However, this accommodation requires officers to carry combs with them, take the time to have inmates comb through their hair, and constantly wash the combs to ensure they are clean.[29]

Free exercise issues such as these, which can only be accommodated by exceptions to the prisons' general rules and practices, require prison officials to evaluate the extent to which the prison can accommodate religious freedoms given the realities of prison life, including security, safety, budgetary and staffing constraints. The court decisions in this area are often inconsistent due to the importance of inmates' religious rights and the difficulties involved in effectively and efficiently managing a population of inmates.[30]

To further complicate matters, not only do prison officials have to be concerned about religious rights, but they must also be careful not to violate the Establishment Clause of the First Amendment. The Establishment Clause mandates that "Congress

---

22. U.S. Comm'n on Civil Rights, *supra* note 4, at 135; Fowler v. Crawford, 534 F.3d 931, 939–42 (8th Cir. 2008).

23. *Id.* at 934.

24. *Id.* at 935.

25. United States v. Sec'y, Fla. Dep't of Corr., 828 F.3d 1341, 1345 (11th Cir. 2016).

26. Most of the examples in this section involve male inmates because the "overwhelming majority" of free exercise cases are brought by males. U.S. Comm'n on Civil Rights, *supra* note 4, at 81, 83.

27. Michael B. Mushlin, *Rights of Prisoners* 722 (3d ed., West 2002).

28. N.Y.S. Dep't of Corr. Serv., *supra* note 13, at 24; U.S. Comm'n on Civil Rights, *supra* note 4, at 137 (adding that contraband "may be hidden in long hair" and may also "help alter an inmate's appearance after escape").

29. N.Y.S. Dep't of Corr. Serv., *supra* note 13, at 44; *see also* Jean-Laurent v. Wilkerson, 438 F. Supp. 2d 318, 323–24 (S.D.N.Y. 2006) (discussing that plaintiff was a Muslim inmate who claimed that a strip search violated his religious belief that he not be naked in front of strangers).

30. *See* Turner, *supra* note 5, at 30.

shall make no law respecting an establishment of religion...."[31] The courts have interpreted this provision to mean that government cannot establish a national religion,[32] favor one religion over another, or spend taxpayer money to advance religion.[33] Given these general principles, does the government violate the Establishment Clause by, for example, building chapels in prison or providing chaplains to help meet the inmates' religious needs?[34] Do prison officials violate the Establishment Clause by providing religious inmates with special privileges, such as special diets or holiday breaks? The more prison officials deviate from general prison rules to accommodate inmates' free exercise rights, the greater their risk of running afoul of the Establishment Clause.[35]

In *Kaufman v. McCaughtry*,[36] the Seventh Circuit held that atheism qualified as a religion for first amendment purposes and that atheists were arguably entitled to study groups. Would study groups for atheists solve the Establishment Clause concerns? If prison officials provide some religious accommodations, must similar accommodations be provided to other religious groups? If the burdens and benefits are not spread equitably among religious groups, might there also be valid equal protection claims?

As this discussion demonstrates, accommodating inmates' religious needs, while also balancing the legitimate concerns of prison officials, is a daunting task. The following discussion addresses the standards the courts and Congress have developed to deal with the difficult legal issues related to religion in prison.

B. Development of the Law Relating to Inmates' Religious Rights

1. The Supreme Court Sets the Standard for Deciding First Amendment Free Exercise Cases in Prisons

In 1963 and 1972, in *Sherbert v. Verner*[37] and *Wisconsin v. Yoder*,[38] the Supreme Court set the standard for deciding religion cases—outside of prisons—under the First Amendment of the United States Constitution. In those cases, the Supreme

31. U.S. Const. amend. I., cl. 1. ("Congress shall make no law respecting an establishment of religion, or prohibiting the free exercise thereof; or abridging the freedom of speech, or of the press; or the right of the people peaceably to assemble, and to petition the Government for a redress of grievances.").

32. Everson v. Bd. of Educ. of Ewing Tp., 330 U.S. 1, 15 (1947).

33. Mushlin, *supra* note 27, at 699–700.

34. *Id.* at 700; *see also* Lynn S. Branham, *"The Devil is in the Details": A Continued Dissection of the Constitutionality of Faith-Based Prison Units*, 6 Ave Maria L. Rev 409, 416, 422 (2008).

35. Cutter v. Wilkinson, 544 U.S. 709, 719 (2005).

36. 419 F.3d 678, 682 (7th Cir. 2005).

37. 374 U.S. 398 (1963).

38. 406 U.S. 205 (1972).

Court determined that the Free Exercise Clause prevented the government from enforcing a law—even a neutral law of general applicability—in a manner that substantially burdened the exercise of religion unless the law was justified by a compelling state interest and was narrowly tailored to meet the government's purpose.[39]

It was unclear whether this strict scrutiny standard was to be applied in prisons, or even whether prisoners retained First Amendment free exercise rights, until these questions were partially answered by the Supreme Court in *Cruz v. Beto*.[40] In *Cruz*, decided in 1972, an inmate brought an equal protection claim alleging that Buddhist prisoners were not afforded the same rights as Christian inmates. The Supreme Court found that "reasonable opportunities must be afforded to all prisoners to exercise the religious freedom guaranteed by the First and Fourteenth Amendments...."[41] Although the Court explicitly held that inmates retain some religious rights, the Court did not discuss the scope of these rights or whether the *Sherbert* standard should be used by the courts in deciding whether an inmate's First Amendment rights are infringed.

The Supreme Court did not directly address the appropriate standard to be used in prisoner free exercise cases until 1987. In that year, the Court decided *O'Lone v. Shabazz*,[42] a case in which Muslim inmates claimed they had a right to attend Friday afternoon Jumu'ah services. In reaching its decision in *O'Lone*, the Supreme Court applied the test developed in *Turner v. Safley*,[43] a case decided earlier that year involving the constitutionality of prison regulations concerning inmate correspondence and marriage.

Questions to guide reading of *O'Lone v. Shabazz*

1. In *O'Lone*, did the Supreme Court apply the strict scrutiny test set out in *Sherbert* and *Yoder* or a lower level of scrutiny?
2. How did the Court choose to balance the religious privileges granted to prisoners and the concerns of prison administrators? In other words, according to *O'Lone*, how much deference should be given to the decisions of prison administrators? What language do you rely on in reaching your conclusion? What reasons does the Court give for applying this level of deference?
3. In *Turner v. Safley*, the Supreme Court developed a four-part test for determining whether an inmate's constitutional rights have been violated by the government. These four factors are applied in *O'Lone*. What are they?

---

39. Sarah Keeton Campbell, *Restoring RLUIPA's Equal Terms Provision*, 58 Duke L. J. 1071, 1076–77 (2009); Spencer T. Proffitt, *Gods Behind Bars: How Religious Liberty Has Been Sent Directly to Jail, and How to Get Out of Jail Free*, 40 Ariz. St. L.J. 1401, 1412–13 (2008).

40. 405 U.S. 319 (1972).

41. *Id.* at 322 n. 2.

42. 482 U.S. 342 (1987).

43. 482 U.S. 78 (1987).

4. Did the Court require the prison officials in *O'Lone* to show that the Muslim inmates were provided with Jumu'ah services at a time other than Friday afternoon? Were the prison officials required to show that the Muslim inmates received religious accommodations other than Jumu'ah services?
5. What facts did the Court consider most important in deciding that the inmates' free exercise rights were not violated? Make sure you know which facts were used to show that the prison policy met each one of the four *Turner* factors.
6. Does the dissent advocate applying the strict scrutiny standard set out in *Sherbert-Yoder* or a lower level of scrutiny?
7. In what ways does the dissenting opinion apply the *Turner* factors differently than the majority?

O'Lone, Administrator, Leesburg Prison Complex v. Estate of Shabazz

482 U.S. 342 (1987)

CHIEF JUSTICE REHNQUIST delivered the opinion of the Court.

Respondents, members of the Islamic faith, were prisoners in New Jersey's Leesburg State Prison. They challenged policies adopted by prison officials which resulted in their inability to attend Jumu'ah, a weekly Muslim congregational service regularly held in the main prison building and in a separate facility known as "the Farm." Jumu'ah is commanded by the Koran and must be held every Friday after the sun reaches its zenith and before the Asr, or afternoon prayer. There is no question that respondents' sincerely held religious beliefs compelled attendance at Jumu'ah. We hold that the prison regulations here challenged did not violate respondents' rights under the Free Exercise Clause of the First Amendment to the United States Constitution.

Inmates at Leesburg are placed in one of three custody classifications. Maximum security and "gang minimum" security inmates are housed in the main prison building, and those with the lowest classification—full minimum—live in "the Farm." Both respondents were classified as gang minimum security prisoners when this suit was filed, and respondent Mateen was later classified as full minimum.... [G]ang minimum inmates [are] ordinarily assigned jobs outside the main building. These inmates work in details of 8 to 15 persons, supervised by one guard. [F]ull minimum inmates work outside the main institution, whether on or off prison grounds, or in a satellite building such as the Farm....

Significant problems arose with those inmates assigned to outside work details. Some avoided reporting for their assignments, while others found reasons for returning to the main building during the course of the workday (including their desire to attend religious services). Evidence showed that the return of prisoners during the day resulted in security risks and administrative burdens that prison officials found unacceptable. Because details of inmates were supervised by only one guard, the whole detail was forced to return to the main gate when one prisoner desired to return to the facility. The gate was the site of all incoming foot and vehicle traffic during the day, and prison officials viewed it as a high security risk area. When an inmate returned, vehicle traffic was delayed while the inmate was logged in and searched.

In response to these burdens, Leesburg officials took steps to ensure that those assigned to outside details remained there for the whole day. Thus, arrangements were made to have lunch and required medications brought out to the prisoners, and appointments with doctors and social workers were scheduled for the late afternoon.... [I]nmates assigned to outside work details [were also prohibited]from returning to the prison during the day except in the case of emergency.

The prohibition of returns prevented Muslims assigned to outside work details from attending Jumu'ah. Respondents filed suit under 42 U.S.C. § 1983 alleging that the prison policies unconstitutionally denied them their free exercise rights under the First Amendment, as applied to the States through the Fourteenth Amendment.... Several general principles guide our consideration of the issues presented here. First, "convicted prisoners do not forfeit all constitutional protections by reason of their conviction and confinement in prison." *Bell* v. *Wolfish*, 441 U.S. 520, 545 (1979). See *Turner* v. *Safley, ante*, at 84; *Jones* v. *North Carolina Prisoners' Labor Union, Inc.*, 433 U.S. 119, 129 (1977). Inmates clearly retain protections afforded by the First Amendment, including its directive that no law shall prohibit the free exercise of religion. See *Cruz* v. *Beto*, 405 U.S. 319 (1972) *(per curiam)*. Second, "lawful incarceration brings about the necessary withdrawal or limitation of many privileges and rights, a retraction justified by the considerations underlying our penal system." *Price* v. *Johnston*, 334 U.S. 266, 285 (1948). The limitations on the exercise of constitutional rights arise both from the fact of incarceration and from valid penological objectives—including deterrence of crime, rehabilitation of prisoners, and institutional security. *Pell* v. *Procunier, supra*, at 822–823; *Procunier* v. *Martinez*, 416 U.S. 396, 412 (1974).

In considering the appropriate balance of these factors, we have often said that evaluation of penological objectives is committed to the considered judgment of prison administrators, "who are actually charged with and trained in the running of the particular institution under examination." *Bell* v. *Wolfish, supra*, at 562. See *Turner* v. *Safley, ante*, at 86–87. To ensure that courts afford appropriate deference to prison officials, we have determined that prison regulations alleged to infringe constitutional rights are judged under a "reasonableness" test less restrictive than that ordinarily applied to alleged infringements of fundamental constitutional rights. See, *e.g., Jones* v. *North Carolina Prisoners' Labor Union, Inc., supra*, at 128. We recently restated the proper standard: "When a prison regulation impinges on inmates' constitutional rights, the regulation is valid if it is reasonably related to legitimate penological interests." *Turner* v. *Safley, ante*, at 89.[2]

FN2. Our decision in *Turner* v. *Safley* rejected respondents' principal argument in this case—that more rigorous scrutiny is appropriate unless a court can conclude that the activity for which prisoners seek protection is "presumptively dangerous." *See* Brief of Respondents at 30, *Turner v. Safley*, No. 85-1384 (U.S. Sept. 11, 1986). *See also Abdul Wali v. Coughlin*, 754 F.2d 1015,

> 1033 (2d Cir. 1985). As we noted in *Turner*, "[t]he determination that an activity is 'presumptively dangerous' appears simply to be a conclusion about the reasonableness of the prison restriction in light of the articulated security concerns. It therefore provides a tenuous basis for creating a hierarchy of standards of review." *Id. at 89.*
>
> Nor are we convinced that heightened scrutiny is appropriate whenever regulations effectively prohibit, rather than simply limit, a particular exercise of constitutional rights. *See* Brief for the Respondents, *Turney v. Safley*, 482 U.S. 78, (1987) (No. 85-1384). As *Turner* makes clear, the presence or absence of alternative accommodations of prisoners' rights is properly considered a factor in the reasonableness analysis rather than a basis for heightened scrutiny. *See Turner*, 482 U.S. 78 at 88, 90–91.

This approach ensures the ability of corrections officials "to anticipate security problems and to adopt innovative solutions to the intractable problems of prison administration," *ibid.*, and avoids unnecessary intrusion of the judiciary into problems particularly ill suited to "resolution by decree." *Procunier* v. *Martinez, supra*, at 405. *See also Turner* v. *Safley, ante*, at 89; *Bell* v. *Wolfish, supra*, at 548.

We think the Court of Appeals decision in this case was wrong when it established a separate burden on prison officials to prove "that no reasonable method exists by which [prisoners'] religious rights can be accommodated without creating bona fide security problems." 782 F.2d, at 420. See also *id.*, at 419 (Prison officials should be required "to produce convincing evidence that they are unable to satisfy their institutional goals in any way that does not infringe inmates' free exercise rights"). Though the availability of accommodations is relevant to the reasonableness inquiry, we have rejected the notion that "prison officials ... have to set up and then shoot down every conceivable alternative method of accommodating the claimant's constitutional complaint." *Turner* v. *Safley, ante*, at 90–91. By placing the burden on prison officials to disprove the availability of alternatives, the approach articulated by the Court of Appeals fails to reflect the respect and deference that the United States Constitution allows for the judgment of prison administrators.

Turning to consideration of the policies challenged in this case, we think the findings of the District Court establish clearly that prison officials have acted in a reasonable manner. *Turner* v. *Safley* drew upon our previous decisions to identify several factors relevant to this reasonableness determination. First, a regulation must have a logical connection to legitimate governmental interests invoked to justify it. The policies at issue here clearly meet that standard. The requirement that full minimum and gang minimum prisoners work outside the main facility was justified by concerns of institutional order and security, for the District Court found that it was "at least in part a response to a critical overcrowding in the state's prisons, and ... at least in part designed to ease tension and drain on the facilities during that part of the day when the inmates were outside the confines of the main buildings." 595 F. Supp., at 929. We think it beyond doubt that the standard is related to this legitimate concern.

The subsequent policy prohibiting returns to the institution during the day also passes muster under this standard. Prison officials testified that the returns from outside work details generated congestion and delays at the main gate, a high risk area in any event. Return requests also placed pressure on guards supervising outside details, who previously were required to "evaluate each reason possibly justifying a return to the facilities and either accept or reject that reason." *Id.*, at 931. Rehabilitative concerns further supported the policy; corrections officials sought a simulation of working conditions and responsibilities in society. Chief Deputy Ucci testified: "One of the things that society demands or expects is that when you have a job, you show up on time, you put in your eight hours, or whatever hours you are supposed to put in, and you don't get off.... If we can show inmates that they're supposed to show up for work and work a full day, then when they get out at least we've done something." Tr. 89. These legitimate goals were advanced by the prohibition on returns; it cannot seriously be maintained that "the logical connection between the regulation and the asserted goal is so remote as to render the policy arbitrary or irrational." *Turner* v. *Safley, ante*, at 89–90.

Our decision in *Turner* also found it relevant that "alternative means of exercising the right ... remain open to prison inmates." *Ante*, at 90. There are, of course, no alternative means of attending Jumu'ah; respondents' religious beliefs insist that it occur at a particular time. But the very stringent requirements as to the time at which Jumu'ah may be held may make it extraordinarily difficult for prison officials to assure that every Muslim prisoner is able to attend that service. While we in no way minimize the central importance of Jumu'ah to respondents, we are unwilling to hold that prison officials are required by the Constitution to sacrifice legitimate penological objectives to that end.... [W]e think it appropriate to see whether under these regulations respondents retain the ability to participate in other Muslim religious ceremonies. The record establishes that respondents are not deprived of all forms of religious exercise, but instead freely observe a number of their religious obligations. The right to congregate for prayer or discussion is "virtually unlimited except during working hours," (testimony of O'Lone), and the state-provided imam has free access to the prison. Muslim prisoners are given different meals whenever pork is served in the prison cafeteria. Special arrangements are also made during the month-long observance of Ramadan, a period of fasting and prayer. During Ramadan, Muslim prisoners are awakened at 4 a.m. for an early breakfast, and receive dinner at 8:30 each evening. We think this ability on the part of respondents to participate in other religious observances of their faith supports the conclusion that the restrictions at issue here were reasonable.

Finally, the case for the validity of these regulations is strengthened by examination of the impact that accommodation of respondents' asserted right would have on other inmates, on prison personnel, and on allocation of prison resources generally. See *Turner* v. *Safley, ante*, at 90. Respondents suggest several accommodations of their practices, including placing all Muslim inmates in one or two inside work details or providing weekend labor for Muslim inmates.... [E]ach of respondents' suggested accommodations would, in the judgment of prison officials, have adverse effects on the institution ... [They would require] extra supervision ... [and] "would be a drain on scarce human resources" at the prison. 595 F. Supp., at 932. Prison officials determined that the alternatives would also threaten prison security by allowing "affinity groups" in the prison to flourish. Administrator O'Lone testified that "we have found out and think almost every prison administrator knows that any time you put a group of individuals together with one particular affinity interest ... you wind up with ... a leadership role and an organizational structure that will almost invariably challenge the institutional authority." Finally, the officials determined that special arrangements for one group would create problems as "other inmates [see] that a certain segment is escaping a rigorous work detail" and perceive favoritism. *Id.*, at 178–179. These concerns of prison administrators provide adequate support for the conclusion that accommodations of respondents' request to attend Jumu'ah would have undesirable results in the institution. These difficulties also make clear that there are no "obvious, easy alternatives to the policy adopted by petitioners." *Turner* v. *Safley*, *ante*, at 93.

We take this opportunity to reaffirm our refusal, even where claims are made under the First Amendment, to "substitute our judgment on ... difficult and sensitive matters of institutional administration," *Block* v. *Rutherford*, 468 U.S. 576, 588 (1984), for the determinations of those charged with the formidable task of running a prison. Here the District Court decided that the regulations alleged to infringe constitutional rights were reasonably related to legitimate penological objectives. We agree with the District Court, and it necessarily follows that the regulations in question do not offend the Free Exercise Clause of the First Amendment to the United States Constitution. The judgment of the Court of Appeals is therefore *Reversed.*

DISSENT BY: JUSTICE BRENNAN, with whom JUSTICE MARSHALL, JUSTICE BLACKMUN, and JUSTICE STEVENS join, dissenting.

The religious ceremony that these respondents seek to attend is not presumptively dangerous, and the prison has completely foreclosed respondents' participation in it. I therefore would require prison officials to demonstrate that the restrictions they have imposed are necessary to further an important government interest, and that these restrictions are no greater than necessary to achieve prison objectives. See *Turner* v. *Safley*, *ante*, at 101, n. 1 (STEVENS, J., concurring in part and dissenting in part) (citing *Abdul Wali* v. *Coughlin*, 754 F.2d 1015 (CA2 1985))....

Prisoners are persons whom most of us would rather not think about. Banished from everyday sight, they exist in a shadow world that only dimly enters our awareness. They are members of a "total institution" that controls their daily existence in a way that few of us can imagine[.] ...

The challenge for this Court is to determine how best to protect those prisoners' rights that remain. Our objective in selecting a standard of review is therefore *not*, as the Court declares, "to ensure that courts afford appropriate deference to prison officials." The Constitution was not adopted as a means of enhancing the efficiency with which government officials conduct their affairs, nor as a blueprint for ensuring sufficient reliance on administrative expertise. Rather, it was meant to provide a bulwark against infringements that might otherwise be justified as necessary expedients of governing....

In my view, adoption of "reasonableness" as a standard of review for *all* constitutional challenges by inmates is inadequate to this task. Such a standard is categorically deferential, and does not discriminate among degrees of deprivation. From this perspective, restricting use of the prison library to certain hours warrants the same level of scrutiny as preventing inmates from reading at all. Various "factors" may be weighed differently in each situation, but the message to prison officials is clear: merely act "reasonably" and your actions will be upheld. If a directive that officials act "reasonably" were deemed sufficient to check all exercises of power, the Constitution would hardly be necessary. Yet the Court deems this single standard adequate to restrain *any* type of conduct in which prison officials might engage....

Once we provide such an elastic and deferential principle of justification, "the principle ... lies about like a loaded weapon ready for the hand of any authority that can bring forth a plausible claim of an urgent need. "... Mere assertions of exigency have a way of providing a colorable defense for governmental deprivation, and we should be especially wary of expansive delegations of power to those who wield it on the margins of society. Prisons are too often shielded from public view; there is no need to make them virtually invisible.

An approach better suited to the sensitive task of protecting the constitutional rights of inmates is laid out by Judge Kaufman in *Abdul Wali* v. *Coughlin*, 754 F.2d 1015 (CA2 1985).... Where exercise of the asserted right is not presumptively dangerous [ ] and where the prison has completely deprived an inmate of that right, then prison officials must show that "a particular restriction is necessary to further an important governmental interest, and that the limitations on freedoms occasioned by the restrictions are no greater than necessary to effectuate the governmental objective involved." *Ibid.*...

The prison in this case has completely prevented respondent inmates from attending the central religious service of their Muslim faith. I would therefore hold prison officials to the standard articulated in *Abdul Wali*, and would find their proffered justifications wanting. The State has neither demonstrated that the restriction is necessary to further an important objective nor proved that less extreme measures may not serve its purpose. Even if I accepted the Court's standard of review, however, I could not conclude on this record that prison officials have proved that it is reasonable to preclude respondents from attending Jumu'ah. Petitioners have provided mere unsubstantiated assertions that the plausible alternatives proposed by respondents are infeasible.

II

In *Turner*, the Court set forth a framework for reviewing allegations that a constitutional right has been infringed by prison officials. The Court found relevant to that review "whether there are alternative means of exercising the right that remain open to prison inmates." The Court in this case acknowledges that "respondents' sincerely held religious beliefs compe[l] attendance at Jumu'ah," and concedes that there are "no alternative means of attending Jumu'ah." Nonetheless, the Court finds that prison policy does not work a complete deprivation of respondents' asserted religious right, because respondents have the opportunity to participate in other religious activities. This analysis ignores the fact that, as the District Court found, Jumu'ah is the central religious ceremony of Muslims, "comparable to the Saturday service of the Jewish faith and the Sunday service of the various Christian sects." *Shabazz* v. *O'Lone*, 595 F. Supp. 928, 930 (NJ 1984). As with other faiths, this ceremony provides a special time in which Muslims "assert their identity as a community covenanted to God." Brief for Imam Jamil Abdullah Al-Amin et al. as *Amici Curiae* 32. As a result:

> "unlike other Muslim prayers which are performed individually and can be made up if missed, the Jumu'ah is obligatory, cannot be made up, and must be performed in congregation. The Jumu'ah is therefore regarded as the central service of the Muslim religion, and the obligation to attend is commanded by the Qur'an, the central book of the Muslim religion." 595 F. Supp. at 930.

Jumu'ah therefore cannot be regarded as one of several essentially fungible religious practices. The ability to engage in other religious activities cannot obscure the fact that the denial at issue in this case is absolute: respondents are completely foreclosed from participating in the core ceremony that reflects their membership in a particular religious community. If a Catholic prisoner were prevented from attending Mass on Sunday, few would regard that deprivation as anything but absolute, even if the prisoner were afforded other opportunities to pray, to discuss the Catholic faith with others, and even to avoid eating meat on Friday if that were a preference. Prison officials in this case therefore cannot show that " 'other avenues' remain available for the exercise of the asserted right." *Turner, ante*, at 90 (quoting *Jones* v. *North Carolina Prisoners' Union*, 433 U.S. 119, 131 (1977)).

Under the Court's approach, as enunciated in *Turner*, the availability of other means of exercising the right in question counsels considerable deference to prison officials. By the same token, the infliction of an absolute deprivation should require more than mere assertion that such a deprivation is necessary. In particular, "the existence of obvious, easy alternatives may be evidence that the regulation is not reasonable, but is an 'exaggerated response' to prison concerns." *Ibid.*...

That Muslim inmates are able to participate in Jumu'ah throughout the entire federal prison system suggests that the practice is, under normal circumstances, compatible with the demands of prison administration. Indeed, the Leesburg State Prison permitted participation in this ceremony for five years, and experienced no threats to security or safety as a result. In light of both standard federal prison practice and Leesburg's own past practice, a reasonableness test in this case demands at least minimal substantiation by prison officials that alternatives that would permit participation in Jumu'ah are infeasible. Under the standard articulated by the Court in *Turner*, this does not mean that petitioners are responsible for identifying and discrediting these alternatives; "prison officials do not have to set up and then shoot down every conceivable alternative method of accommodating the claimant's constitutional complaint." When prisoners themselves present alternatives, however, and when they fairly call into question official claims that these alternatives are infeasible, we must demand at least some evidence beyond mere assertion that the religious practice at issue cannot be accommodated. Examination of the alternatives proposed in this case indicates that prison officials have not provided such substantiation.

III

Respondents' first proposal is that gang minimum prisoners be assigned to an alternative inside work detail on Friday, as they had been before the recent change in policy. Prison officials testified that the alternative work detail is now restricted to maximum security prisoners, and that they did not wish maximum and minimum security prisoners to mingle. Even the District Court had difficulty with this assertion, as it commented that "the defendants did not explain why inmates of different security levels are not mixed on work assignments when otherwise they are mixed." 595 F. Supp. at 932.... The record as it now stands thus does not establish that the Friday alternative work detail would create a problem for the institution.

Respondents' second proposal is that gang minimum inmates be assigned to work details inside the main building on a regular basis. While admitting that the prison used inside details in the kitchen, bakery, and tailor shop, officials stated that these jobs are reserved for the riskiest gang minimum inmates, for whom an outside job might be unwise. *Ibid.* Thus, concluded officials, it would be a bad idea to move these inmates outside to make room for Muslim gang minimum inmates. Respondents contend, however, that the prison's own records indicate that there are a significant number of jobs inside the institution that could be performed by inmates posing a lesser security risk. This suggests that it might not be necessary for the riskier gang minimum inmates to be moved outside to make room for the less risky inmates. Officials provided no data on the number of inside jobs available, the number of high-risk gang minimum inmates performing them, the number of Muslim inmates that might seek inside positions, or the number of staff that would be necessary to monitor such an arrangement. Given the plausibility of respondents' claim, prison officials should present at least this information in substantiating their contention that inside assignments are infeasible.

Third, respondents suggested that gang minimum inmates be assigned to Saturday or Sunday work details, which would allow them to make up any time lost by attending Jumu'ah on Friday. While prison officials admitted the existence of weekend work details, they stated that "since prison personnel are needed for other programs on weekends, the creation of additional weekend details would be a drain on scarce human resources." *Ibid.* The record provides no indication, however, of the number of Muslims that would seek such a work detail, the current number of weekend details, or why it would be infeasible simply to reassign current Saturday or Sunday workers to Friday, rather than create additional details. The prison is able to arrange work schedules so that Jewish inmates may attend services on Saturday and Christian inmates may attend services on Sunday. *Id.*, at 935. Despite the fact that virtually all inmates are housed in the main building over the weekend, so that the demand on the facility is greater than at any other time, the prison is able to provide sufficient staff coverage to permit Jewish and Christian inmates to participate in their central religious ceremonies. Given the prison's duty to provide Muslims a "reasonable opportunity of pursuing [their] faith comparable to the opportunity afforded fellow prisoners who adhere to conventional religious precepts," *Cruz* v. *Beto*, 405 U.S. 319, 322 (1972), prison officials should be required to provide more than mere assertions of the infeasibility of weekend details for Muslim inmates.

Finally, respondents proposed that minimum security inmates living at the Farm be assigned to jobs either in the Farm building or in its immediate vicinity. Since [prison rules] permit such assignments for full minimum inmates, and since such inmates need not return to prison facilities through the main entrance, this would [not] interfere ... with ... the no-return policy. Nonetheless, prison officials stated that such an arrangement might create an "affinity group" of Muslims representing a threat to prison authority. Officials pointed to no such problem in the five years in which Muslim inmates were permitted to assemble for Jumu'ah, and in which the alternative Friday work detail was in existence. Nor could they identify any threat resulting from the fact that during the month of Ramadan all Muslim prisoners participate in both breakfast and dinner at special times. Furthermore, there was no testimony that the concentration of Jewish or Christian inmates on work details or in religious services posed any type of "affinity group" threat. As the record now stands, prison officials have declared that a security risk is created by a grouping of Muslim inmates in the least dangerous security classification, but not by a grouping of maximum security inmates who are concentrated in a work detail inside the main building, and who are the only Muslims assured of participating in Jumu'ah. Surely, prison officials should be required to provide at least some substantiation for this facially implausible contention.

Petitioners also maintained that the assignment of full minimum Muslim inmates to the Farm or its near vicinity might provoke resentment because of other inmates' perception that Muslims were receiving special treatment. Officials pointed to no such perception during the period in which the alternative Friday detail was in existence, nor to any resentment of the fact that Muslims' dietary preferences are accommodated and that Muslims are permitted to operate on a special schedule during the month of Ramadan. Nor do they identify any such problems created by the accommodation of the religious preferences of inmates of other faiths. Once again, prison officials should be required at a minimum to identify the basis for their assertions.

Despite the plausibility of the alternatives proposed by respondents in light of federal practice and the prison's own past practice, officials have essentially provided mere pronouncements that such alternatives are not workable. If this Court is to take seriously its commitment to the principle that "prison walls do not form a barrier separating prison inmates from the protections of the Constitution," *Turner, ante*, at 84, it must demand more than this record provides to justify a Muslim inmate's complete foreclosure from participation in the central religious service of the Muslim faith.

IV ...

Incarceration by its nature denies a prisoner participation in the larger human community. To deny the opportunity to affirm membership in a spiritual community, however, may extinguish an inmate's last source of hope for dignity and redemption.... While I would prefer that this case be analyzed under the approach set out in Part I, *supra*, I would at a minimum remand to the District Court for an analysis of respondents' claims in accordance with the standard enunciated by the Court in *Turner* and in this case. I therefore dissent.

2. *Congress Passes the Religious Freedom Restoration Act (RFRA) in Response to* Smith *and* O'Lone

O'Lone was the start of a bigger retreat by the Supreme Court from the *Sherbert-Yoder* standard.[44] Three years later, in 1990, the Court decided *Employment Division, Dep't of Human Resources of Oregon v. Smith*,[45] a case challenging an Oregon law that prohibited possession of controlled substances unless they were prescribed by a physician. The Native American church claimed that this law interfered with its members' rights to use peyote for sacramental purposes in religious ceremonies. The Supreme Court upheld the Oregon law using rational basis review. In a departure from the compelling interest test developed in *Sherbert*, the Court found that valid and neutral laws of general applicability do not offend the First Amendment, even if they incidentally burden the free exercise of religion. According to the Court, the laws are only suspect if they target a particular religious group or if their intent is to interfere with the free exercise of religion.

Congress responded to the Supreme Court's decision in *Smith* by passing the Religious Freedom Restoration Act (RFRA) in 1993. In RFRA, Congress expressly stated that the purpose of the Act was to override *Smith*[46] and "restore the compelling interest test set forth in *Sherbert v. Verner* and *Wisconsin v. Yoder*."[47] The statute prohibited federal, state, and local governments from substantially burdening the free exercise of religion—even if the burden arose from a neutral law of general applicability—unless the burden was justified by a compelling state interest and was the least restrictive means of satisfying that interest.

The legislative history of RFRA made clear that the statute was to be applied in prisons. For example, the Senate Report issued by the Judiciary Committee stated that the "intent of the act is to restore the [ ] protection afforded to prisoners to observe their religions which was weakened by the decision in *O'Lone v. Estate of Shabazz*."[48] Thus, strict scrutiny was to be applied to rules substantially burdening the free exercise of religion, even in a prison context.

Despite Congress's direct support for a compelling interest standard, RFRA governed free exercise cases for less than four years. In 1997, the Supreme Court declared

44. Derek L. Gaubatz, *RLUIPA at Four: Evaluating the Success and Constitutionality of RLUIPA's Prisoner Provisions*, 28 Harv. J.L. & Pub. Pol'y 501, 508 (2005).

45. 494 U.S. 872 (1990).

46. Religious Freedom Restoration Act, 42 U.S.C. § 2000bb(a)(4) (1993).

47. *Id.* at § 2000bb(b).

48. S. Rep. No 103-111 (1993), reprinted in 1993 U.S.C.C.A.N. 1892, 1899.

in *City of Boerne v. Flores*[49] that RFRA was unconstitutional as applied to states and localities. The Court held that Congress exceeded its constitutional powers by invoking section 5 of the Fourteenth Amendment, also known as the Enforcement Clause, to enact RFRA and apply its provisions to the states. As the Court explained, section 5 gives Congress the power "to enact legislation designed to prevent, as well as remedy, constitutional violations" by the states.[50] But RFRA was not enacted to "counteract state laws likely to be unconstitutional because of their treatment of religion,"[51] rather its purpose was to change the standard for deciding First Amendment free exercise cases. The Court thus concluded that Congress did not design RFRA to remedy or prevent constitutional violations as authorized by section 5, but rather to impose a standard contrary to *Smith* and, in this way, to make a substantive change in the rights granted by the constitution. Free exercise rights would change under RFRA because some state laws that would be valid under *Smith* would fall under RFRA.[52] The Court wrote:

> Legislation which alters the meaning of the Free Exercise Clause cannot be said to be enforcing the Clause. Congress does not enforce a constitutional right by changing what the right is. It has been given the power 'to enforce,' not the power to determine what constitutes a constitutional violation.[53]

The Court also indicated that, by enacting RFRA under section 5, Congress violated the separation of powers doctrine set forth in the Constitution. Citing *Marbury v. Madison*, the Court found that the Judicial Branch has the exclusive power to interpret the Constitution, "which embraces the duty to say what the law is."[54] By enacting RFRA, Congress, in effect, usurped the judiciary's role as interpreter of the constitution.

Because the Supreme Court's analysis in *City of Boerne* focused on Congress's powers to legislate under section 5 of the Fourteenth Amendment, the decision invalidated RFRA as applied to states and localities, but not as applied to federal prisons.[55] However, *City of Boerne* did have the effect of depriving most prisoners of the protections in RFRA. Of the approximately 1.5 million prisoners in the United States, almost 88 percent are in state and local prisons and jails.[56] After *City of Boerne*, the courts returned to applying the *Turner* factors set forth in *O'Lone* to the free exercise claims of state and local prisoners.[57]

---

49. 521 U.S. 507 (1997).
50. *Id.* at 517.
51. *Id.* at 534–35.
52. *Id.* at 534.
53. *Id.* at 519.
54. *Id.* at 536.
55. Turner, *supra* note 5, at 27.
56. Jennifer Bronson, et al., Prisoners in 2017, Bureau of Justice Statistics, U.S. Dept. of Justice (2019).
57. Mushlin, *supra* note 27, at 689; *see also* U.S. Comm'n on Civil Rights, *supra* note 4, at 8 (some states responded to the Supreme Court's decision in *City of Boerne* by passing their own laws known as "state RFRAs").

Standards for Reviewing the Free Exercise Claims of Prisoners

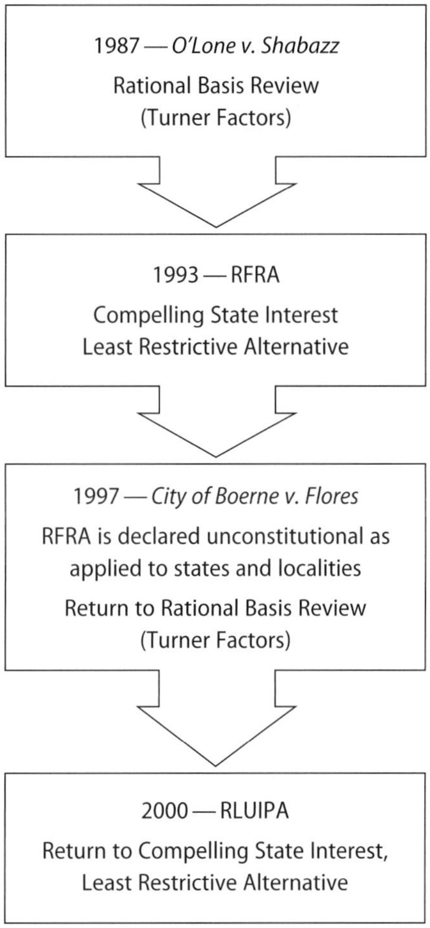

3. Congress Responds to City of Boerne *by Passing the Religious Land Use and Institutionalized Persons Act (RLUIPA)*

Congress responded to *City of Boerne* by overwhelmingly passing the Religious Land Use and Institutionalized Persons Act (RLUIPA) in 2000. The purpose of RLUIPA was to revive the strict scrutiny standard set out in RFRA for deciding some cases in which state laws substantially burden the free exercise of religion.

Congress took three major steps to address the concerns in *City of Boerne* and ensure that RLUIPA—unlike RFRA—stood up to constitutional attack.[58] First, Congress narrowed the scope of the religious protections contained in RLUIPA to land use regulations and institutionalized persons, the two areas that Congress de-

58. Patricia E. Salkin, *The Genesis of RLUIPA and Federalism: Evaluating the Creation of a Federal Statutory Right and Its Impact on Local Government*, 40 Urb. Law. 195, 210 (2008).

termined had the strongest problems related to free exercise of religion.[59] With respect to institutionalized persons, RLUIPA provides that state action that substantially burdens an institutionalized person's religious exercise is unlawful unless it is the least restrictive means of furthering a compelling state interest.[60] Institutionalized persons include those in prisons and psychiatric hospitals[61] but most of the cases invoking RLUIPA's protections for institutionalized persons involve prisoners.

Second, to show the need for RLUIPA, Congress held three years of hearings and made specific findings.[62] With respect to prisons, Congress found that inmates are often subject to arbitrary rules that deny them the freedom to practice their religion.[63]

Third, because *City of Boerne* precluded Congress from using section 5 of the Fourteenth Amendment to enact a stricter standard of review for free exercise cases, Congress used its powers under the Spending and Commerce Clauses to enact RLUIPA. RLUIPA only applies where the religious burden at issue "is imposed in a program or activity that receives Federal financial assistance"[64] or where "the substantial burden affects, or removal of that substantial burden would affect, commerce with foreign nations, among the several States, or with Indian tribes."[65] The Spending Clause is generally more important in prisoner cases and the Commerce Clause in land use cases.[66] "Every State ... accepts federal funding for its prisons."[67]

The Spending Clause gives Congress the power to attach conditions to the receipt of federal funds to further its policy objectives.[68] Although Congress cannot deprive citizens of their constitutional protections, Congress's powers under the Spending Clause allow it to require stronger civil rights protections than those set out in the constitution. Congress used the Spending Clause to require all prisons—as a condition for accepting federal funds—to comply with the provisions in RLUIPA.

The steps Congress took to ensure the constitutionality of RLUIPA have paid off. Since it became law, the constitutionality of RLUIPA has been repeatedly challenged and upheld. All of the Circuit courts that have considered the constitutionality of using the Spending Clause to enact RLUIPA have agreed that Congress acted properly.[69]

---

59. Gaubatz, *supra* note 44, at 510.

60. *See* 42 U.S.C. § 2000cc-1(a).

61. *See* Cutter v. Wilkinson, 544 U.S. 709, 710 (2005).

62. *Id.* at 716.

63. *Id.*

64. *See* 42 U.S.C. § 2000cc-1(b)(1).

65. *See* 42 U.S.C. § 2000cc-1(b)(2).

66. Salkin, *supra* note 58, at 212.

67. Cutter v. Wilkinson, 544 U.S. at 716 n. 4.

68. *See* South Dakota v. Dole, 483 U.S. 203, 206 (1987). *Dole* also sets forth limits on federal spending powers. *Id.* at 207–08. To validly exercise its spending powers, Congress must act within these limits. *Id.* at 207.

69. *See* Madison v. Virginia, 474 F.3d 118 (4th Cir. 2006) (rejecting Spending Clause challenge to RLUIPA § 3); Cutter v. Wilkinson, 423 F.3d 579, 590 (6th Cir. 2005) (rejecting Spending Clause and Tenth Amendment challenges to RLUIPA § 3); Charles v. Verhagen, 348 F.3d 601 (7th Cir. 2003) (rejecting Establishment Clause, Spending Clause, and Tenth Amendment challenges to RLUIPA § 3);

The Ninth Circuit also found that RLUIPA does not infringe on the separation of powers mandated by the constitution. As long as Congress is acting pursuant to the Spending Clause, it can provide greater protections than those found in the constitution without violating separation of powers principles. As the Ninth Circuit wrote, the separation of powers principle is not violated because "the statute does not overturn the Court's constitutional interpretation in *Smith*," but "[r]ather ... provides additional protection for religious worship, respecting that *Smith* set only a constitutional floor—not a ceiling—for the protection of personal liberty."[70]

The Sixth Circuit did hold, in *Cutter v. Wilkinson*, that RLUIPA violated the Establishment Clause.[71] But that decision was later overturned by the Supreme Court.

Questions to guide reading of the Supreme Court's decision in *Cutter v. Wilkinson*

1. What is the main reason the Court gives to support its holding that RLUIPA does not violate the Establishment Clause even though it requires prisons to accommodate religious practices?
2. Use the discussion in *Cutter* to explain how the Establishment Clause and the Free Exercise Clause "often exert conflicting pressures."
3. The Sixth Circuit found that RLUIPA unconstitutionally promotes religion in violation of the Establishment Clause by, *inter alia*, "encouraging prisoners to become religious in order to enjoy greater rights."[72] How does *Cutter* deal with this issue? Is the Court's response to the Sixth Circuit convincing?
4. How does *Cutter* deal with the Sixth Circuit's finding that RLUIPA "impermissibly advanc[es] religion by giving greater protection to religious rights than to other constitutionally protected rights"?[73]
5. Find and highlight all of the places in *Cutter* where the Court discusses deference to the judgment of prison officials. Does *Cutter* advocate a strict scrutiny standard of review for deciding RLUIPA cases or a new standard of review—one that is strict yet deferential?

Mayweathers v. Newland, 314 F.3d 1062 (9th Cir. 2002), *cert denied*, 540 U.S. 815 (2003) (rejecting Establishment Clause, Spending Clause, Tenth Amendment, Eleventh Amendment, and separation of powers challenges to RLUIPA § 3); Benning v. Georgia, 391 F.3d 1299 (11th Cir. 2004) (rejecting Spending Clause, Establishment Clause, and Tenth Amendment challenges to RLUIPA § 3). Section 2 of RLUIPA relates to land use and section 3 to institutionalized persons. For a list of district court cases addressing the constitutionality of RLUIPA, *see* Derek L. Gaubatz, *supra* note 44, at 572 n. 297.

70. Mayweathers v. Newland, 314 F.3d 1062, 1070 (9th Cir. 2002).

71. 349 F.3d 257 (6th Cir. 2003).

72. *Id.* at 266.

73. *Id.* at 264.

Cutter v. Wilkinson, Director, Ohio Department of Rehabilitation and Correction

544 U.S. 709 (2005)

JUSTICE GINSBURG delivered the opinion of the Court.

Section 3 of the Religious Land Use and Institutionalized Persons Act of 2000 (RLUIPA or Act), 114 Stat. 804, 42 U.S.C. § 2000cc-1(a)(1)–(2), provides in part: "No government shall impose a substantial burden on the religious exercise of a person residing in or confined to an institution," unless the burden furthers "a compelling governmental interest," and does so by "the least restrictive means." Plaintiffs below, petitioners here, are current and former inmates of institutions operated by the Ohio Department of Rehabilitation and Correction and assert that they are adherents of "nonmainstream" religions: the Satanist, Wicca, and Asatru religions, and the Church of Jesus Christ Christian. They complain that Ohio prison officials (respondents here), in violation of RLUIPA, have failed to accommodate their religious exercise "in a variety of different ways, including retaliating and discriminating against them for exercising their nontraditional faiths, denying them access to religious literature, denying them the same opportunities for group worship that are granted to adherents of mainstream religions, forbidding them to adhere to the dress and appearance mandates of their religions, withholding religious ceremonial items that are substantially identical to those that the adherents of mainstream religions are permitted, and failing to provide a chaplain trained in their faith." Brief for United States 5.

For purposes of this litigation at its current stage, respondents have stipulated that petitioners are members of bona fide religions and that they are sincere in their beliefs. *Gerhardt* v. *Lazaroff*, 221 F. Supp. 2d 827, 833 (SD Ohio 2002).

In response to petitioners' complaints, respondent prison officials have mounted a facial challenge to the institutionalized-persons provision of RLUIPA; respondents contend, *inter alia*, that the Act improperly advances religion in violation of the First Amendment's Establishment Clause. The District Court denied respondents' motion to dismiss petitioners' complaints, but the Court of Appeals reversed that determination. The appeals court held, as the prison officials urged, that the portion of RLUIPA applicable to institutionalized persons, 42 U.S.C. § 2000cc-1, violates the Establishment Clause. We reverse the Court of Appeals' judgment.

"This Court has long recognized that the government may ... accommodate religious practices ... without violating the Establishment Clause." *Hobbie* v. *Unemployment Appeals Comm'n of Fla.*, 480 U.S. 136, 144–145 ... (1987). Just last Term, in *Locke* v. *Davey*, 540 U.S. 712 ... (2004), the Court reaffirmed that "there is room for play in the joints between" the Free Exercise and Establishment Clauses, allowing the government to accommodate religion beyond free exercise requirements, without offense to the Establishment Clause. *Id.*, at 718 ... (quoting *Walz* v. *Tax Comm'n of City of New York*, 397 U.S. 664, 669 ... (1970)). "At some point, accommodation may devolve into 'an unlawful fostering of religion.'" *Corporation of Presiding Bishop of Church of Jesus Christ of Latter-day Saints* v. *Amos,* 483 U.S. 327, 334–335 ... (1987) (quoting *Hobbie,* 480 U.S. at 145 ...). But § 3 of RLUIPA, we hold, does not, on its face, exceed the limits of permissible government accommodation of religious practices.

I A ...

Before enacting § 3, Congress documented, in hearings spanning three years, that "frivolous or arbitrary" barriers impeded institutionalized persons' religious exercise. See 146 Cong. Rec. 16698, 16699 (2000) (joint statement of Sen. Hatch and Sen. Kennedy on RLUIPA) (hereinafter Joint Statement) ("Whether from indifference, ignorance, bigotry, or lack of resources, some institutions restrict religious liberty in egregious and unnecessary ways.").[5] To secure redress for inmates who encountered undue barriers to their religious observances, Congress carried over from RFRA the "compelling governmental interest"/"least restrictive means" standard. See *id.*, at 16698. Lawmakers anticipated, however, that courts entertaining complaints under § 3 would accord "due deference to the experience and expertise of prison and jail administrators." *Id.*, at 16699 (quoting S. Rep. No. 103-111, p. 10 (1993)).

FN 5. The hearings held by Congress revealed, for a typical example, that "[a] state prison in Ohio refused to provide Moslems with Hallal food, even though it provided Kosher food." Hearing on Protecting Religious Freedom After *Boerne* v. *Flores* before the Subcommittee on the Constitution of the House Committee on the Judiciary, 105th Cong., 2d Sess., pt. 3, p. 11, n. 1 (1998) (hereinafter Protecting Religious Freedom) (prepared statement of Marc D. Stern, Legal Director, American Jewish Congress). Across the country, Jewish inmates complained that prison officials refused to provide sack lunches, which would enable inmates to break their fasts after nightfall. *Id.*, at 39 (statement of Isaac M. Jaroslawicz, Director of Legal Affairs for the Aleph Institute). The "Michigan Department of Corrections ... prohibited the lighting of Chanukah candles at all state prisons" even though "smoking" and "votive candles" were permitted. *Id.*, at 41 (same). A priest responsible for communications between Roman Catholic dioceses and corrections facilities in Oklahoma stated that there "was [a] nearly yearly battle over the Catholic use of Sacramental Wine ... for the celebration of the Mass," and that prisoners' religious possessions, "such as the Bible, the Koran, the Talmud or items needed by Native Americans[,] ... were frequently treated with contempt and were confiscated, damaged or discarded" by prison officials. *Id.*, pt. 2, at 58–59 (prepared statement of Donald W. Brooks, Reverend, Diocese of Tulsa, Oklahoma).

B ...

We granted certiorari to resolve the conflict among Courts of Appeals on the question whether RLUIPA's institutionalized-persons provision, § 3 of the Act, is consistent with the Establishment Clause of the First Amendment. 543 U.S. 924 ... (2004). Compare 349 F.3d 257 with *Madison* v. *Riter*, 355 F.3d 310, 313 (CA4 2003) (§ 3 of RLUIPA does not violate the Establishment Clause); *Charles* v. *Verhagen*, 348 F.3d 601, 610–611

(CA7 2003) (same); *Mayweathers* v. *Newland*, 314 F.3d 1062, 1068–1069 (CA9 2002) (same). We now reverse the judgment of the Court of Appeals for the Sixth Circuit.

II A

The Religion Clauses of the First Amendment provide: "Congress shall make no law respecting an establishment of religion, or prohibiting the free exercise thereof." The first of the two Clauses, commonly called the Establishment Clause, commands a separation of church and state. The second, the Free Exercise Clause, requires government respect for, and noninterference with, the religious beliefs and practices of our Nation's people. While the two Clauses express complementary values, they often exert conflicting pressures. See *Locke,* 540 U.S., at 718 ... ("These two Clauses ... are frequently in tension."); *Walz,* 397 U.S., at 668–669 ... ("The Court has struggled to find a neutral course between the two Religion Clauses, both of which are cast in absolute terms, and either of which, if expanded to a logical extreme, would tend to clash with the other.").

Our decisions recognize that "there is room for play in the joints" between the Clauses, *id.*, at 669..., some space for legislative action neither compelled by the Free Exercise Clause nor prohibited by the Establishment Clause. See, *e.g.*... *Sherbert* v. *Verner*, 374 U.S. 398 ... (1963) (Harlan, J., dissenting) ("The constitutional obligation of 'neutrality' is not so narrow a channel that the slightest deviation from an absolutely straight course leads to condemnation." (citation omitted)). In accord with the majority of Courts of Appeals that have ruled on the question, ... we hold that § 3 of RLUIPA fits within the corridor between the Religion Clauses: On its face, the Act qualifies as a permissible legislative accommodation of religion that is not barred by the Establishment Clause.

Foremost, we find RLUIPA's institutionalized-persons provision compatible with the Establishment Clause because it alleviates exceptional government-created burdens on private religious exercise. See *Board of Ed. of Kiryas Joel Village School Dist.* v. *Grumet,* 512 U.S. 687 ... (1994) (government need not "be oblivious to impositions that legitimate exercises of state power may place on religious belief and practice"); *Amos,* 483 U.S., at 349 ... (O'CONNOR, J., concurring in judgment) (removal of government-imposed burdens on religious exercise is more likely to be perceived "as an accommodation of the exercise of religion rather than as a Government endorsement of religion"). Furthermore, the Act on its face does not founder on shoals our prior decisions have identified: Properly applying RLUIPA, courts must take adequate account of the burdens a requested accommodation may impose on nonbeneficiaries, see *Estate of Thornton* v. *Caldor, Inc.,* 472 U.S. 703 ... (1985); and they must be satisfied that the Act's prescriptions are and will be administered neutrally among different faiths, see *Bd. of Ed. of Kiryas Joel School Dist. v. Grumet,* 512 U.S. 687 ... (1994).[8]

FN 8. Directed at obstructions institutional arrangements place on religious observances, RLUIPA does not require a State to pay for an inmate's devotional accessories. See, *e.g.*, *Charles* v. *Verhagen*, 348 F.3d 601, 605 (CA7 2003) (overturning prohibition on possession of Islamic prayer oil but leaving inmate-plaintiff with responsibility for purchasing the oil).

"The 'exercise of religion' often involves not only belief and profession but the performance of ... physical acts [such as] assembling with others for a worship service [or] participating in sacramental use of bread and wine...." *Smith*, 494 U.S. at 877.... Section 3 covers state-run institutions—mental hospitals, prisons, and the like—in which the government exerts a degree of control unparalleled in civilian society and severely disabling to private religious exercise. 42 U.S.C. § 2000cc-1(a); § 1997; see Joint Statement 16699 ("Institutional residents' right to practice their faith is at the mercy of those running the institution.").[9] RLUIPA thus protects institutionalized persons who are unable freely to attend to their religious needs and are therefore dependent on the government's permission and accommodation for exercise of their religion.[10]

FN 9. See, *e.g.*, *ibid.* (prison's regulation prohibited Muslim prisoner from possessing ritual cleansing oil); *Young* v. *Lane*, 922 F.2d 370, 375–376 (CA7 1991) (prison's regulation restricted wearing of yarmulkes); *Hunafa* v. *Murphy*, 907 F.2d 46, 47–48 (CA7 1990) (noting instances in which Jewish and Muslim prisoners were served pork, with no substitute available).

FN 10. Respondents argue, in line with the Sixth Circuit, that RLUIPA goes beyond permissible reduction of impediments to free exercise. The Act, they project, advances religion by encouraging prisoners to "get religion," and thereby gain accommodations afforded under RLUIPA. Brief for Respondents 15–17; see 349 F.3d at 266 ("One effect of RLUIPA is to induce prisoners to adopt or feign religious belief in order to receive the statute's benefits."). While some accommodations of religious observance, notably the opportunity to assemble in worship services, might attract joiners seeking a break in their closely guarded day, we doubt that all accommodations would be perceived as "benefits." For example, congressional hearings on RLUIPA revealed that one state corrections system served as its kosher diet "a fruit, a vegetable, a granola bar, and a liquid nutritional supplement—each and every meal." Protecting Religious Freedom, pt. 3, at 38 (statement of Jaroslawicz).

The argument, in any event, founders on the fact that Ohio already facilitates religious services for mainstream faiths. The State provides chaplains, allows inmates to possess religious items, and permits assembly for worship. See App. 199 (affidavit of David Schwarz, Religious Services Administrator for the South Region of the Ohio Dept. of Rehabilitation and Correction (Oct. 19, 2000)) (job duties include "facilitating the delivery of religious services in 14 correctional institutions of various security levels throughout ... Ohio"); Ohio Dept. of Rehabilitation and Correction, Table of Organization (April 2005), available at http://www.drc.state.oh.us/web/DRCORG1.pdf (as visited May 27, 2005, and available in Clerk of Court's case file) (department includes "Religious Services" division); Brief for United States 20, and n. 8 (citing, *inter alia*, *Gawloski* v. *Dallman*, 803 F. Supp. 103, 113 (SD Ohio 1992) (inmate in protective custody allowed to attend a congregational religious service, possess a Bible and other religious materials, and receive chaplain visits);

> *Taylor* v. *Perini*, 413 F. Supp. 189, 238 (ND Ohio 1976) (institutional chaplains had free access to correctional area)).

We note in this regard the Federal Government's accommodation of religious practice by members of the military. See, *e.g.*, 10 U.S.C. § 3073 (referring to Army chaplains); *Katcoff* v. *Marsh*, 755 F.2d 223, 225–229 (CA2 1985) (describing the Army chaplaincy program). In *Goldman* v. *Weinberger*, 475 U.S. 503 ... (1986), we held that the Free Exercise Clause did not require the Air Force to exempt an Orthodox Jewish officer from uniform dress regulations so that he could wear a yarmulke indoors. In a military community, the Court observed, "there is simply not the same [individual] autonomy as there is in the larger civilian community." *Id.* at 507 ... (brackets in original; internal quotation marks omitted). Congress responded to *Goldman* by prescribing that "a member of the armed forces may wear an item of religious apparel while wearing the uniform," unless "the wearing of the item would interfere with the performance [of] military duties [or] the item of apparel is not neat and conservative." 10 U.S.C. § 774(a)–(b).

We do not read RLUIPA to elevate accommodation of religious observances over an institution's need to maintain order and safety. Our decisions indicate that an accommodation must be measured so that it does not override other significant interests. In *Caldor*, the Court struck down a Connecticut law that "armed Sabbath observers with an absolute and unqualified right not to work on whatever day they designated as their Sabbath." 472 U.S., at 709.... We held the law invalid under the Establishment Clause because it "unyieldingly weighted" the interests of Sabbatarians "over all other interests." *Id.* at 710....

We have no cause to believe that RLUIPA would not be applied in an appropriately balanced way, with particular sensitivity to security concerns. While the Act adopts a "compelling governmental interest" standard, see *supra*, at 715, "context matters" in the application of that standard. See *Grutter* v. *Bollinger*, 539 U.S. 306 ... (2003).[11] Lawmakers supporting RLUIPA were mindful of the urgency of discipline, order, safety, and security in penal institutions. See, *e.g.*, 139 Cong. Rec. 26190 (1993) (remarks of Sen. Hatch). They anticipated that courts would apply the Act's standard with "due deference to the experience and expertise of prison and jail administrators in establishing necessary regulations and procedures to maintain good order, security and discipline, consistent with consideration of costs and limited resources." Joint Statement 16699 (quoting S. Rep. No. 103-111, at 10).

> FN 11. The Sixth Circuit posited that an irreligious prisoner and member of the Aryan Nation who challenges prison officials' confiscation of his white supremacist literature as a violation of his free association and expression rights would have his claims evaluated under the deferential rational-relationship standard described in *Turner* v. *Safley*, 482 U.S. 78 ... (1987). A member of the Church of Jesus Christ Christian challenging a similar withholding, the Sixth Circuit assumed, would have a stronger prospect of success because a court would review his claim under RLUIPA's compelling-interest standard. 349 F.3d at 266 (*citing Madison* v. *Riter*, 240 F. Supp. 2d 566, 576

> (WD Va. 2003)). Courts, however, may be expected to recognize the government's countervailing compelling interest in not facilitating inflammatory racist activity that could imperil prison security and order. Cf. *Reimann* v. *Murphy*, 897 F. Supp. 398, 402–403 (ED Wis. 1995) (concluding, under RFRA, that excluding racist literature advocating violence was the least restrictive means of furthering the compelling state interest in preventing prison violence); *George* v. *Sullivan*, 896 F. Supp. 895, 898 (WD Wis. 1995) (same).

Finally, RLUIPA does not differentiate among bona fide faiths. In *Kiryas Joel*, we invalidated a state law that carved out a separate school district to serve exclusively a community of highly religious Jews, the Satmar Hasidim. We held that the law violated the Establishment Clause, 512 U.S. at 690..., in part because it "singled out a particular religious sect for special treatment," *id.* at 706 ... (footnote omitted). RLUIPA presents no such defect. It confers no privileged status on any particular religious sect, and singles out no bona fide faith for disadvantageous treatment.

B

The Sixth Circuit misread our precedents to require invalidation of RLUIPA as "impermissibly advancing religion by giving greater protection to religious rights than to other constitutionally protected rights." 349 F.3d at 264.

...

Were the Court of Appeals' view the correct reading of our decisions, all manner of religious accommodations would fall.... Ohio could not, as it now does, accommodate "traditionally recognized" religions, 221 F. Supp. 2d, at 832: The State provides inmates with chaplains "but not with publicists or political consultants," and allows "prisoners to assemble for worship, but not for political rallies," Reply Brief for United States 5.

In upholding RLUIPA's institutionalized-persons provision, we emphasize that respondents "have raised a facial challenge to [the Act's] constitutionality, and have not contended that under the facts of any of [petitioners'] specific cases ... [that] applying RLUIPA would produce unconstitutional results." 221 F. Supp. 2d, at 831. The District Court, noting the underdeveloped state of the record, concluded: A finding "that it is *factually impossible* to provide the kind of accommodations that RLUIPA will require without significantly compromising prison security or the levels of service provided to other inmates" cannot be made at this juncture. *Id.* at 848 (emphasis added).[13] We agree.

> FN 13. Respondents argue that prison gangs use religious activity to cloak their illicit and often violent conduct.... It bears repetition, however, that prison security is a compelling state interest, and that deference is due to institutional officials' expertise in this area. See *supra*, at 722–723. Further, prison officials may appropriately question whether a prisoner's religiosity, asserted as the basis for a requested accommodation, is authentic. Although RLUIPA bars inquiry into whether a particular belief or practice is "central"

> to a prisoner's religion, see 42 U.S.C. § 2000cc-5(7)(A), the Act does not preclude inquiry into the sincerity of a prisoner's professed religiosity. Cf. *Gillette* v. *United States,* 401 U.S. 437 ... (1971) ("'The "truth" of a belief is not open to question'; rather, the question is whether the objector's beliefs are 'truly held.'" (quoting *United States* v. *Seeger,* 380 U.S. 163 ... (1965)).

"For more than a decade, the federal Bureau of Prisons has managed the largest correctional system in the Nation under the same heightened scrutiny standard as RLUIPA without compromising prison security, public safety, or the constitutional rights of other prisoners." Brief for United States 24 (citation omitted). The Congress that enacted RLUIPA was aware of the Bureau's experience. See Joint Statement 16700 (letter from Dept. of Justice to Sen. Hatch) ("We do not believe [RLUIPA] would have an unreasonable impact on prison operations. RFRA has been in effect in the Federal prison system for six years and compliance with that statute has not been an unreasonable burden to the Federal prison system."). We see no reason to anticipate that abusive prisoner litigation will overburden the operations of state and local institutions....

Should inmate requests for religious accommodations become excessive, impose unjustified burdens on other institutionalized persons, or jeopardize the effective functioning of an institution, the facility would be free to resist the imposition. In that event, adjudication in as-applied challenges would be in order.

For the reasons stated, the judgment of the United States Court of Appeals for the Sixth Circuit is reversed, and the case is remanded for further proceedings consistent with this opinion.

It is so ordered.[74]

Law Practice Simulation # 1

RLUIPA requires courts to use strict scrutiny to review rules that substantially burden religious exercise. *Cutter* appears to uphold this strict scrutiny standard, but also requires deference to the expertise of prison officials. Is it possible to have a strict, but deferential, standard of review? Is the Court creating a new standard of review that operates between strict scrutiny and rational basis?

Assume that you work for a Congressman and that you have been asked to redraft RLUIPA to clarify the standard of review. Your job is to incorporate the deference to prison officials required in *Cutter* so RLUIPA can be applied by the lower courts without any confusion. The relevant provisions of RLUIPA are set forth below.

§ 2000cc-1. Protection of religious exercise of institutionalized persons

(a) General rule

> No government shall impose a substantial burden on the religious exercise of a person residing in or confined to an institution ... even if the burden

---

74. The concurring opinion of Justice Thomas has been omitted.

results from a rule of general applicability, unless the government demonstrates that imposition of the burden on that person—

(1) is in furtherance of a compelling governmental interest; and

(2) is the least restrictive means of furthering that compelling governmental interest.

...

§ 2000cc-3. Rules of construction ...

(g) Broad construction

This chapter shall be construed in favor of a broad protection of religious exercise, to the maximum extent permitted by the terms of this chapter and the Constitution.

...

4. The Law Regarding Inmates' Religious Rights since RLUIPA

Because the constitutionality of RLUIPA has been upheld, it remains good law and provides the standard for deciding free exercise cases brought by inmates in state prisons and local jails. Federal inmates can rely on RFRA and all inmates can also file their claims under the First Amendment of the U.S. Constitution. Indeed, many RLUIPA claims are filed in tandem with First Amendment claims[75]—even though the First Amendment standard is rational basis, rather than strict scrutiny—because plaintiffs cannot recover money damages under RLUIPA.[76]

75. Salkin, *supra* note 58, at 217.

76. *See* Sossamon v. Texas, 563 U.S. 277 (2011) ("States, in accepting federal funding, do not consent to waive their sovereign immunity to private suits for money damages under RLUIPA because no statute expressly and unequivocally includes such a waiver."). In order to circumvent the ruling in Sossamon, some inmates brought their claims for money damages against prison officials in their individual capacities rather than against the state correctional facilities. However, the Circuit Courts have uniformly held that RLUIPA does not support such a claim. See, e.g., Washington v. Gonyea, 731 F.3d 143, 145 (2d Cir. 2013) ("We adopt the reasoning of our sister circuits in concluding that RLUIPA does not provide a cause of action against state officials in their individual capacities because the legislation was enacted pursuant to Congress' spending power, ... which allows the imposition of conditions, such as individual liability, only on those parties actually receiving state funds."); Stewart v. Beach, 701 F.3d 1322, 1335 (10th Cir. 2012) ("There is no cause of action under RLUIPA for individual capacity claims."). For a discussion of the Eleventh Amendment and individual capacity lawsuits, see Chapter 15.

Although inmates can recover money damages under the First Amendment, they are unlikely to receive this relief. *See* Joseph Thomas Wilson, *The Big Man in the Big House: Prisoner Free Exercise in Light of Employment Division v. Smith*, 73 La. L. Rev. 219, 248 (2012) ("[J]udges rarely award monetary relief for prisoners' First Amendment free-exercise claims. In order to receive a monetary award under Turner, a prisoner must show that the alleged violation of his First Amendment rights resulted in a physical injury—a highly unlikely scenario.").

Standards for Deciding Free Exercise Claims

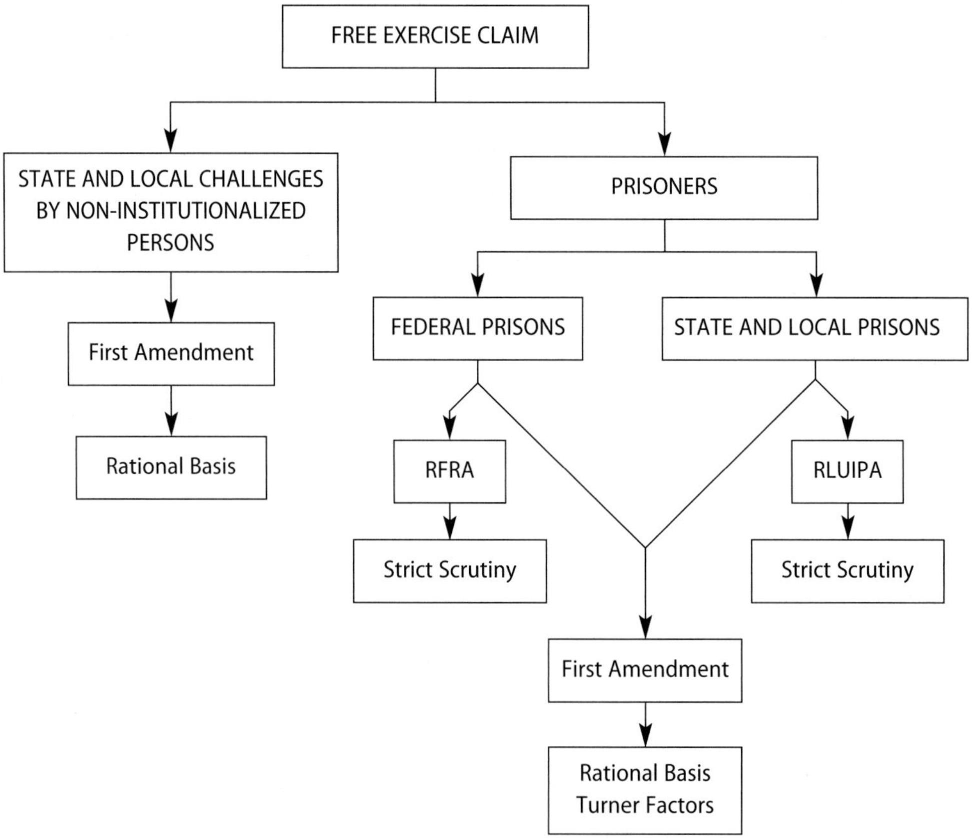

To succeed on a RLUIPA claim, a prisoner must first make a prima facie showing that prison officials "impose[d] a substantial burden on [his or her] religious exercise."[77] Congress did not define the term "substantial burden" in RLUIPA and the Circuit courts have differing interpretations of what the term means.[78] Basically, "substantial burden" means that a government action "puts substantial pressure on an adherent to modify his behavior and to violate his beliefs."[79] The pressure exerted by the gov-

77. 42 U.S.C. § 2000cc-1(a).

78. Washington v. Klem, 497 F.3d 272, 277–281 (3d Cir. 2007) (this case contains a lengthy discussion of "substantial burden" and includes the differing definitions in the Circuit courts); *see also* Mark Strasser, *Free Exercise & Substantial Burdens Under Federal Law,* 94 Neb. L. Rev. 633, 634 (2016) (noting that the U.S. Supreme Court has "sent mixed signals regarding how to define substantial" and the circuits have "adopted different and conflicting tests.").

79. Lovelace v. Lee, 472 F.3d 174, 187 (4th Cir. 2006); *see also* Hartmann v. Cal. Dep't of Corr. & Rehab., 707 F.3d 1114, 1125 (9th Cir. 2013) ("a substantial burden occurs 'where the state ... denies [an important benefit by] putting substantial pressure on an adherent to modify his behavior and violate his beliefs.'") (citation omitted); Adkins v. Kaspar, 393 F.3d 559, 570 (5th Cir. 2004) (defining "substantial burden" as government action which "truly pressures the adherent to significantly modify his religious behavior and significantly violate his religious beliefs."); Barrick Bollman, *Deference and Prisoner Accommodations Post-Holt: Moving RLUIPA Toward "Strict in Theory, Strict in Fact,"* 112 Nw U. L. Rev. 839, 847 (2018) ("[Holt v. Hobbs, 135 S. Ct. 853, 862 (2015)] clarified this [substantial

ernment need not be directed at religious activity. RLUIPA explicitly provides that the burden can "result[ ] from a rule of general applicability."[80] Prison officials can even exert substantial pressure by creating a neutral rule or policy that has the unintended effect of forcing an inmate to choose between receiving a benefit available to other inmates or violating his sincere religious beliefs.[81]

Inmates not only must show a substantial burden, but also that the burden is imposed on a "religious exercise." RLUIPA broadly defines "religious exercise" to include "any exercise of religion, whether or not compelled by, or central to, a system of religious belief."[82] Thus, the "religious exercise" being burdened can be merely a discretionary religious activity. For example, a Muslim may want to use prayer oils or a Catholic may prefer to pray using a rosary.[83] Although these practices may not be mandated or key to the religion, they are protected under RLUIPA.

The religious exercise must, however, be based on a sincere belief and be religious in nature. To qualify as religious in nature, the activity cannot be based solely on moral, secular, or political beliefs.[84] While it is clear that moral, religious, and secular beliefs are not "religious," the courts have had difficulty finding a precise definition of religion that selects out sham "religions" designed solely to obtain advantages in prison while also protecting unfamiliar faiths with unusual beliefs and traditions.[85] A religious belief can be subjective and can qualify for protection even if it does not include belief in a Supreme Being or is considered bizarre to most.[86]

The Supreme Court has defined religion to include a "belief occupy[ing] the same place in the life of the [adherent] as an orthodox belief in God...."[87] The Third Circuit found three factors helpful in determining whether an inmate's beliefs were religious:

> First, a religion addresses fundamental and ultimate questions having to do with deep and imponderable matters. Second, a religion is comprehensive

---

burden] test by requiring an individualized assessment of the plaintiff's subjective sincerity and a determination of whether the prisoner must actually choose between following religious belief or following prison policy.").

80. 42 U.S.C. § 2000cc-1(a).

81. *See* Washington v. Klem, 497 F.3d at 280.

82. 42 U.S.C. § 2000cc-5(7)(A).

83. Gaubatz, *supra* note 44, at 522.

84. Mushlin, *supra* note 27, at 714; *see also* Africa v. Commonwealth of Pa., 662 F.2d 1025, 1034 (3d Cir. 1981).

85. *See* Africa v. Commonwealth of Pa., 662 F.2d at 1031 ("Few tasks that confront a court require more circumspection than that of determining whether a particular set of ideas constitutes a religion....").

86. *See* Reed v. Faulkner, 842 F.2d 960, 962 (7th Cir. 1988) ("religious beliefs often strike the nonbeliever as bizarre."); *see also Recent Case: First Amendment—Free Exercise in Prisons—Fifth Circuit Holds that Prison's Prohibition on All Objects over Twenty-Five Dollars Did Not Violate Prisoner's First Amendment Rights or Substantially Burden His Religion Under RLUIPA—McFaul v. Valenzuela, 684 F.3d 564 (5th Cir. 2012)*, 126 Harv. L. Rev. 1154, 1159–60 (2013) ("Numerous scholars have pointed out that judicial determinations about the sincerity of a particular individual's beliefs are hazardous because judges are likely to be more sympathetic to mainstream religious practices than to those practices that are idiosyncratic.").

87. U.S. v. Seeger, 380 U.S. 163, 184 (1965).

> in nature; it consists of a belief-system as opposed to an isolated teaching. Third, a religion often can be recognized by the presence of certain formal and external signs.[88]

These factors have not been adopted by the Supreme Court, but have been used by five Circuit courts.[89] The Second Circuit has used a more subjective test and limited "the factfinder's inquiry to a determination of whether 'the beliefs professed ... are, in [the claimant's] own scheme of things, religious.'"[90] While the definition of a religion is not settled, the issue is an important one. Courts have already had to decide whether groups such as the Black Muslims, Rastafarians, Five Percenters and MOVE, qualify as religions and entitle prisoners to the accommodations granted other religious groups.[91]

To succeed on a RLUIPA claim, the inmate's beliefs must also be sincerely held. As the Supreme Court stated, "while the 'truth' of a belief is not open to question, there remains the significant question whether it is 'truly held.'"[92] Determining whether a belief is sincere is very difficult and has been described by the Second Circuit as "exceedingly amorphous, requiring the factfinder to delve into the claimant's most veiled motivations ..."[93] and "'an awesome problem,' capable of resolution only by reference to a panoply of subjective factors."[94] One way to avoid the problem of determining sincerity would be to simply accept the inmate's declarations that his beliefs are truly held. However, without some sincerity requirement, inmates would be able to avoid valid prison requirements simply by fabricating religious beliefs.[95]

A hearing is almost always necessary to determine questions of sincerity.[96] But even a hearing cannot solve the difficulties inherent in making this determination. A belief can be sincere even if an adherent does not belong to any organized religion[97] and even if he does not follow all of the dictates of his declared religion.[98] As one court wrote, "[it] would be bizarre for prisons to undertake in effect to promote strict orthodoxy, by forfeiting the religious rights of any inmate [who] ... does not adhere

88. Africa v. Commonwealth of Pa., 662 F.2d at 1032.

89. Ronald G. Turner, *supra* note 5, at 31.

90. Patrick v. LeFevre, 745 F.2d 153, 158–59 (2d Cir. 1984) (quoting U.S. v. Seeger, 380 U.S. 163, 185 (1965)).

91. *See* Mushlin, *supra* note 27, at 706–07; Holt v. Hutto, 363 F. Supp. 194, 202 (E.D. Ark. 1973) (Black Muslim group qualifies as a religion); Reed v. Faulkner, 653 F. Supp. 965, 971 (N.D. Ind. 1987) (Rastafarian qualifies as a religion); Patrick v. LeFevre, 745 F.2d at 157–58 (remanding the issue of whether the beliefs of an inmate identifying himself as a member of the Five Percenter Nation of Islam are sincerely held and religious in nature); Africa v. Commonwealth of Pa., 662 F.2d at 1032 (MOVE does not qualify as a religion afforded First Amendment protection).

92. U.S. v. Seeger, 380 U.S. at 185.

93. Patrick v. LeFevre, 745 F.2d at 157.

94. *Id.* at 159.

95. *See* Africa v. Commonwealth of Pa., 662 F.2d at 1031.

96. *See* Shaheed-Muhammad v. DiPaolo, 393 F. Supp. 2d 80, 90 (D. Mass. 2005).

97. Mosier v. Maynard, 937 F.2d 1521, 1523 (10th Cir. 1991).

98. Reed v. Faulkner, 653 F. Supp. 965, 971 (N.D. Ind. 1987).

steadfastly to every tenet of his faith."[99] Thus, the courts may find an inmate's religious beliefs to be sincere even if the prison authorities can show that the inmate has not declared himself a member of a religion and even if he fails to follow the requirements of the religion. Indeed, all the courts may agree upon is that the inmate should have some knowledge of his professed religious faith.[100]

Once the inmate makes a prima facie showing that the prison has substantially burdened a religious exercise, the burden shifts to the government to prove that imposing the burden is the least restrictive means of furthering a compelling government interest.[101] Before RLUIPA, the prisoner had the burden of proving that prison administrators had no legitimate reason for imposing a burden on the exercise of his religion.[102] Under RLUIPA, the government—not the prisoner—has the burden of proving that its reasons for imposing a substantial burden on the inmate's religious exercise are compelling.[103] Interests that are merely important or rational are not sufficient under RLUIPA.[104]

The government must also prove that there are no alternative means of meeting its interests without burdening the inmate's exercise of his religion.[105] This least restrictive alternative test is the more difficult part of the government's burden.[106]

Questions to guide reading of *Washington v. Klem*

1. According to *Washington*, is the Pennsylvania Department of Corrections' (DOC's) ten-book limit on the number of books an inmate can have in his cell supported by a compelling governmental interest? Why or why not?
2. What reasons did the court give for finding that the ten-book limit was not the Pennsylvania DOC's least restrictive alternative?
3. According to *Washington*, can prisoners use the fact that other prisons successfully used a less restrictive policy to prove that the Pennsylvania DOC's policy is not the least restrictive alternative? Can prisoners use the fact that a less restrictive policy was used in the same prison in relation to other prisoners to argue that the DOC's policy is not the least restrictive alternative?

---

99. Reed v. Faulkner, 842 F.2d at 963; *see also* Holt v. Hobbs, 574 U.S. ___, 135 S. Ct. 853 (2015) ("[T]he protection of RLUIPA, no less than the guarantee of the Free Exercise Clause, is 'not limited to beliefs which are shared by all of the members of a religious sect.'") (citation omitted).

100. *See* Mushlin, *supra* note 27, at 713.

101. Washington v. Klem, 497 F.3d at 283.

102. Gaubatz, *supra* note 44, at 543.

103. *Id.*

104. *Id.* at 540, 545, *see also* Mayfield v. Tex. Dep't of Criminal Justice, 529 F.3d 599, 612 (5th Cir. 2008) ("RLUIPA imposes a higher burden than does the First Amendment in that the statute requires prison regulators to put forth a stronger justification for regulations that impinge on the religious practices of prison inmates.").

105. *Id.* at 541.

106. Mushlin, *supra* note 27, at 695.

RLUIPA

The prisoner must initially show that the following two factors are met:

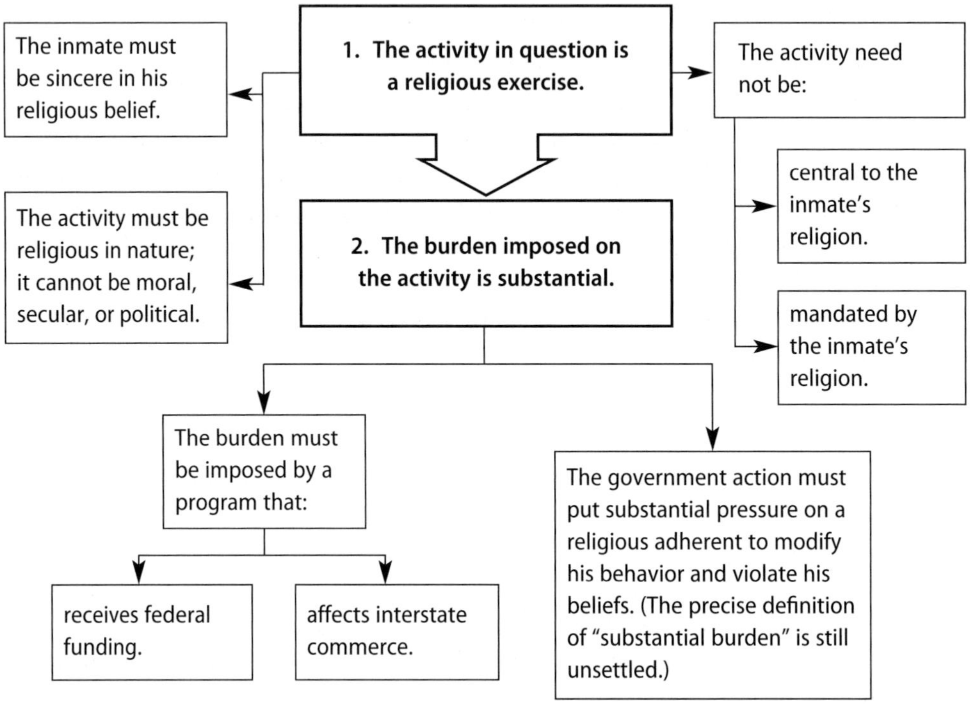

If the prisoner meets the above burden, the burden shifts to the correctional facility to show the following two factors are met:

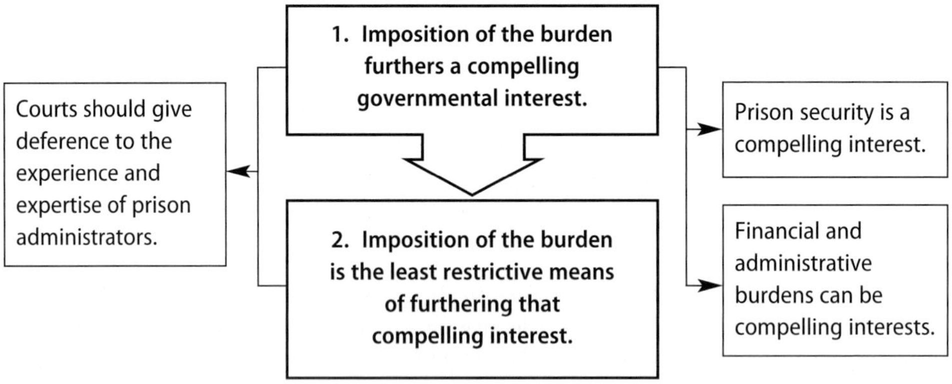

4. According to *Washington*, does the Pennsylvania DOC have to consider other specific alternative policies before it can conclude that the policy it has chosen is the least restrictive alternative?
5. Does the court suggest how the Pennsylvania DOC could create a rule that would withstand review under RLUIPA while still restricting the number of books allowed in a prison cell?

Washington v. Klem

497 F.3d 272 (3d Cir. 2007)

OPINION OF THE COURT—SMITH, *Circuit Judge.*

This case requires us to ... determine whether the Pennsylvania Department of Corrections' (DOC's) restriction on inmates that they possess in their cells only ten books at a time substantially burdens inmate Henry Unseld Washington's religious exercise. We hold that it does. Because the DOC is unable to show that its ten-book policy is the least restrictive means to further its compelling governmental interest in the safety and health of prisoners and prison employees, we will reverse the District Court's order dismissing Washington's RLUIPA claim and remand with instructions to consider whether any factual issues remain when that claim is evaluated under the proper legal standard.

I.

Henry Unseld Washington is an inmate in the custody of the Pennsylvania DOC who has attempted to practice his religion while incarcerated. Washington founded and has been a practitioner of the Children of the Sun Church for over two decades. According to Washington, the Children of the Sun Church supports the development of "Pan-Afrikanism" whereby adherents to the religion stress that "only through Pan-Afrikanism can Afrikan people worldwide, be able to change the conditions of Afrikan people in the diaspora and the motherland." To this end, Washington's Church states that "[f]or every Afrikan's eyes you open with his teachings you will gain rewards in the life everafter." One of the rituals requires a practitioner to read four different Afro-centric books per day.[1] This ritual is aimed at educating the adherent to doctrine, so that he is able to teach others more effectively. Washington views this ritual as necessary to his Church's proselytization requirement, so that the books "are in essence the religion itself."

FN 1. Washington quotes Church doctrine to require "a daily reading of Afro-kentrick books, newspaper, newsletters, magazines, etc., (at least four different sources on the same topic a must!!!) view Afrikan-centerd books, plays, dances, etc." While this statement seems to permit Washington to use non-books to fulfill the four source requirement, the Pennsylvania DOC stipulates that Washington is supposed to read four books per day as part of his religious practice.

The Pennsylvania DOC limits the amount of property any inmate may store in his cell. The DOC's policy states that "limitations on the amount and variety of inmate property may be imposed for security, hygiene and/or safety reasons." With respect to publications, each inmate is permitted to retain three newspapers, ten magazines, and ten books, "unless additional books are approved by the facility's education department." This provision applies to every prison in the Pennsylvania DOC. The DOC also permits "storage space equal to four records center boxes. This space may be made up of the four records center boxes or one footlocker and two records center boxes. In cells that have either a built-in or a free standing storage cabinet, the inmate is permitted to use that space and either two records center boxes or one footlocker."

The conflict in this case arises from the clash between Washington's interest in practicing what he claims is his religion and the prison's interest in limiting, for security, hygiene, and safety reasons, the amount of inmate property that may be held in a cell. In July 2000, Washington was transferred from the State Correctional Institution (SCI) at Mahanoy to SCI-Retreat. In February 2001, Washington's books, religious literature, and legal materials arrived at SCI-Retreat in thirteen boxes. In December 2001, authorities at SCI-Retreat informed Washington that he was in possession of property in his cell that exceeded the amount of property permitted. The excess property was removed from Washington's cell, although authorities permitted Washington to choose which ten books to keep in his cell. SCI-Retreat authorities gave Washington the option of mailing the books out of the prison or having the books destroyed by the DOC because of a lack of adequate storage space for excess inmate property. The Superintendent of SCI-Retreat wrote to Washington personally, stating that Washington could also donate the books to the prison library so he could still access them on an as-needed basis. The prison, though, had a policy limiting the number of trips an inmate could take to the library to one per week. Library policy allowed inmates to check out four books per visit. SCI-Retreat did not destroy the property, and shipped it to SCI-Albion when Washington was transferred there in December 2002.

Washington, proceeding pro se, sued several employees of Pennsylvania's DOC pursuant to 42 U.S.C. § 1983 and 42 U.S.C. §§ 2000cc–2000cc-5 (the Religious Land Use and Institutionalized Persons Act of 2000, or RLUIPA) in December 2001. His suit alleged that the ten-book policy violated his First Amendment rights and the terms of RLUIPA....

II. ...

In our view, the Pennsylvania DOC's ten-book limitation in a prisoner's cell constitutes a substantial burden which impedes Washington from exercising his professed religion.

Washington argues that the ten-book limitation places a substantial burden on his religious exercise because it prevents him from reading four books per day and teaching others about the African people.... Further, Washington argues that his ability to teach others about the African people exists only to the extent that he himself has learned about the African people.

The Pennsylvania DOC contends that limiting the number of books that Washington may keep in his cell at any one time does not significantly inhibit or constrain his conduct, or the expression, of his religious beliefs. This book limitation, it asserts, does not prohibit Washington from adhering to his faith or deny him the opportunity to engage in activity fundamental to his religion. The Pennsylvania DOC also argues that its regulations do not render Washington's religious exercise effectively impracticable....

The DOC has, for whatever reason, elected not to challenge the sincerity of Washington's religious beliefs. The brief for the DOC prison officials states that those officials "do not dispute that Washington's beliefs are sincerely held religious beliefs and that the books are necessary to enable him to fulfill his religious missionary work...." Washington's religion contains two interrelated components—reading four books per day about Africa and African people, and then proselytizing about what he has read. The record amply supports the proposition that Washington cannot practice his religion in the absence of reading these books. Washington is therefore correct in his assertion that "his books and his religion are one and the same; his religion is destroyed in the absence of his religious books."

The ten-book limitation substantially burdens ... Washington's religious exercise ... because it severely inhibits his ability to read four new books per day. Before the end of three days, Washington would run out of new books. In response, the Pennsylvania DOC makes two arguments. First, the DOC states that the prison library is available for Washington's use and that he would be permitted to read books that are housed in the library. The fatal flaw in this argument is that, as we have mentioned, Washington was permitted to visit the library only once a week and could take out just four books at a time. This policy precludes Washington from reading twenty-eight Afrocentric books per week. Thus, even if the Pennsylvania DOC is correct that Washington could house his own books in the prison library, this policy would still not permit him to read four books per day. Second, the Pennsylvania DOC argues that there is no prohibition on Washington's trading those ten books for another ten books at any time. We find nothing in the record to show that Washington could freely trade books that were located inside the prison. Similarly, forcing Washington, an indigent prisoner, to have outsiders continuously mail books to him severely inhibits his ability to read four new books per day. Coupling Washington's sincerity of religious belief with the inseparability of the four-book requirement from the exercise of his religion leads us to the conclusion that the Pennsylvania DOC's ten-book limitation substantially burdens the practice of Washington's religion.

2. Compelling Governmental Interest

Washington has satisfied his burden to show that the Pennsylvania DOC's ten-book limitation substantially burdens his exercise of religion. 42 U.S.C. § 2000cc-2(b). Accordingly, the burden shifts to the Pennsylvania DOC to show that the policy is in furtherance of a compelling governmental interest and is the least restrictive means of furthering this interest. 42 U.S.C. § 2000cc-1(a).

Interests of safety and health play a particularly important role in the institutional setting. *Williams v. Morton*, 343 F.3d 212, 218 (3d Cir. 2003) (stating that "when a challenged regulation implicates security ... judicial deference is especially appropriate") (internal quotation omitted); *Lovelace*, 472 F.3d at 210–11 (Wilkinson, J., dissenting) (chastising the majority for not properly accounting for the prison's compelling interest in safety and security). The Supreme Court in *Cutter v. Wilkinson*, 544 U.S. 709, 125 S. Ct. 2113, 161 L. Ed. 2d 1020 (2005), *repeatedly referenced* the importance of according deference to prison authorities' choices about how to run their institution. The Court plainly stated that "[w]e do not read RLUIPA to elevate accommodation of religious observances over an institution's need to maintain *order and safety*." *Cutter*, 544 U.S. at 722 (emphasis added); *Baranowski v. Hart*, 486 F.3d 112, 125 (5th Cir.

2007) (a policy that "is related to maintaining good order and controlling costs" serves a compelling governmental interest). The Court in *Cutter* noted the importance of order, security, and the granting of deference to prison administrators' expertise, and also displayed "particular sensitivity to security concerns." 544 U.S. at 722–23. Further, "context matters in the application of that standard." *Id.* at 723 (internal quotation omitted). *See Hoevenaar v. Lazaroff*, 422 F.3d 366, 370–72 (6th Cir. 2005); *see also Lovelace*, 472 F.3d at 212 (Wilkinson, J., dissenting) ("As the Supreme Court recognized in *Cutter*, it is simply impossible to divorce a prison's compelling interests in safety and security from internal administration and order."). Even in light of the substantial deference given to prison authorities, the mere assertion of security or health reasons is not, by itself, enough for the Government to satisfy the compelling governmental interest requirement. Rather, the particular policy must further this interest. *See, e.g.*, *Spratt*, 482 F.3d at 39; *Murphy*, 372 F.3d at 988–89; *Gonzales v. O Centro Espirita Beneficente Uniao do Vegetal*, 546 U.S. 418, 126 S. Ct. 1211, 1225, 163 L. Ed. 2d 1017 (2006) (rejecting the government's reliance on a general interest in health and safety in the related RFRA context). A conclusory statement is not enough.

In this case, Washington argues that general assertions of safety and security are not sufficient to establish a compelling governmental interest. He points to the Pennsylvania Administrative Code, which recommends that prisoners should be allowed "a reasonable quantity of reading materials," and that "[n]eatness and good order should be of primary concern rather than a specified number of publications." 37 PA. CODE § 95.245. As further support, Washington points out the arbitrary nature of the ten-book limitation. One DOC policy allows for an exception to the limitation when the books are for educational purposes. Also, an inmate may have ten magazines and three newspapers in addition to the ten books. Similarly, an inmate may have as many non-literature items as will fit in four storage boxes in his cell. If safety and security are the paramount concerns, these exceptions seem to undermine the *compelling* nature of the ten-book limitation.

The Pennsylvania DOC responds that its limitation on the number of books in a cell furthers a compelling governmental interest in protecting the safety and health of prisoners and DOC employees. The District Court agreed with the DOC that the policy furthers the state's compelling governmental interest. The DOC contends that an excess number of books can create a fire hazard, provide a place to conceal weapons or other contraband, and also create a sanitation problem in the relatively small confines of a prison cell.

Certainly, the Pennsylvania DOC has asserted a valid interest, but it fails to make clear how its ten-book limitation furthers this interest. It is unclear how the book limitation decreases the likelihood of a fire in a cell or provides hiding places for contraband when a prisoner in that same cell is permitted to have magazines and newspapers in addition to ten books. We suppose that books eleven through twenty, for example, provide more hiding places than books one through ten. It is also plausible that the physical space taken by these extra books might make a cell dirtier. In this sense, the ten-book limitation might further the Pennsylvania DOC's interest in safety and health. Yet even assuming that the DOC has shown that its ten-book limitation serves a compelling governmental interest, it falls short of satisfying its burden that this DOC policy is the least restrictive means for achieving this interest....

3. Least Restrictive Means

In other strict scrutiny contexts, the Supreme Court has suggested that the Government must consider and reject other means before it can conclude that the policy chosen is the least restrictive means. *See Warsoldier*, 418 F.3d at 999 (citing *United States v. Playboy Entm't Group, Inc.*, 529 U.S. 803, 824, 120 S. Ct. 1878, 146 L. Ed. 2d 865 (2000); *City of Richmond v. J.A. Croson*, 488 U.S. 469, 507, 109 S. Ct. 706, 102 L. Ed. 2d 854 (1989)). In light of the statute's text and legislative history, we agree with the Ninth Circuit in *Warsoldier* that this requirement applies with equal force to RLUIPA. Additionally, the phrase "least restrictive means" is, by definition, a relative term. It necessarily implies a comparison with other means. Because this burden is placed on the Government, it must be the party to make this comparison.

The Pennsylvania DOC argues that the manner in which its policies were applied to Washington were the least restrictive means of furthering the compelling governmental interest in health and safety. To support this point, the DOC emphasizes that the policies were applied to Washington in a flexible manner. The DOC notes that none of Washington's books was ever destroyed, Washington could have donated his books to the prison library so that they would be available to him, and Washington could have exchanged his books for new ones. Because of this flexibility, according to the Pennsylvania DOC, the policy was applied to him in the least restrictive manner possible. There are two interrelated problems with the Pennsylvania DOC's argument. First, this discussion occurred in the District Court against the backdrop of the incorrect assumption that Washington had the burden to prove that there were other less restrictive means available. The District Court noted that "[w]e cannot comprehend, and Washington has not suggested, any way in which the Defendants can better keep inmates' cells safe, other than limiting the amount of personal property inmates may store within their cells." RLUIPA, however, mandates that the Government has the burden to prove that its policy is the least restrictive means. 42 U.S.C. §2000cc-1(a).

Once we place this burden on the proper party, the second problem arises. This problem is that the ten-book limitation, either facially or as applied to Washington, arbitrarily limits the property an inmate may possess. The record indicates that Pennsylvania DOC policies permit prisoners to have personal property up to a limit of four storage boxes or their equivalent. However, an inmate is not permitted to fill these boxes with more than ten books, although the inmate may fill the boxes with other property. The least restrictive means would be to allow an inmate to choose what property he may keep in the storage units so long as the property does not violate prison policy for an independently legitimate reason. A prisoner could not, for example, keep a knife in the storage unit. Additionally, prison policy permits more than ten books when the books are approved for educational purposes. Finally, inmates are permitted to have ten books, ten magazines, and three newspapers, but not more books instead of fewer magazines and newspapers. Put simply, these two policies evince a flexibility in the prison regulations that belies the "compelling" nature of the policies with respect to safety and security.

There is also flexibility within the Pennsylvania DOC system. Prior to transferring to SCI-Retreat, Washington spent two decades incarcerated, apparently in the Pennsylvania DOC system. We can find nothing in the record to indicate that prison authorities at these other institutions objected to Washington possessing his books. *See Warsoldier*, 418 F.3d at 1000 ("[T]he failure of a defendant to explain why another institution with the same compelling interests was able to accommodate the same religious practices may constitute a failure to establish that the defendant was using the least restrictive means.")....

We are satisfied that a ruling in favor of the plaintiff will not lead to judicial micro-management of the Pennsylvania DOC. Here, we are doing no more than examining prison policies on their own terms to determine whether the ten-book limitation is the least restrictive means to achieving a compelling interest in health, safety, and security. The Pennsylvania DOC's own policies state that safety and security of a prison cell are satisfied when the prisoner possesses storage boxes that have the capacity to hold more than ten books. Given the existence of those policies, falling back on safety and security concerns, while possibly satisfying the compelling governmental interest prong of strict scrutiny, will not, independent of other reasoning, also satisfy the least restrictive means test.[10] *See Warsoldier*, 418 F.3d at 998–99 (rejecting the state's "conclusory statements that the [policy in question] is the least restrictive means to ensuring prison security"). We are not facially invalidating the ten-book limitation. We do hold that its application in this case has substantially burdened the exercise of Washington's religious beliefs—the sincerity of which the Pennsylvania DOC does not challenge—and that the DOC has not shown that this burden is the least restrictive means to further its interest in safety and security.

FN 10. If the books themselves preached violence that undermined safety and security within the prison, then this would be a different case. *See Borzych v. Frank*, 439 F.3d 388 (7th Cir. 2006) (purportedly religious texts advocated white-supremacist violence).

III.

For the above-stated reasons, we will *reverse* the District Court's Order dismissing Washington's RLUIPA claim and *remand* with instructions to consider whether any factual issues remain when that claim is evaluated under the proper legal standard. On the current record, the DOC has failed to demonstrate that its policy is the least restrictive means to further its interest in safety and security. However, we recognize that the Pennsylvania DOC has not had a full opportunity to rebut Washington's assertions because the District Court appeared to place the least restrictive means burden on Washington rather than the DOC. On remand, the DOC will have the opportunity to do so.

Law Practice Simulation # 2

In Exercise 1, Clinton Correctional Facility refused Sand's request to have three boxes of books delivered to his cell so he can continue to study Jewish law. Assume that you are an attorney for the New York State Department of Correctional Services (DOCS). Write a prison policy that would allow DOCS to limit the number of books Sand can have in his cell. The policy should be written so that it will withstand a RLUIPA challenge. In writing this policy, you should:

1. Include the reasons for the policy.
2. Consider whether the policy should be applied only at Clinton Correctional Facility or at all DOCS facilities.
3. Include alternatives that were considered if you think that is necessary.
4. Decide if there should be any exceptions to the policy.
5. Consider the reasoning in *Washington* in constructing your policy.

Law Practice Simulation # 3

In Exercise 1, Clinton Correctional Facility refused Sand's request to light candles in his cell on Saturdays—the Jewish Sabbath—and on Chanukah. Assume that you are the attorney for Sand. What facts would you want to know from Sand before commencing a lawsuit under RLUIPA challenging the denial of these requests? In constructing your fact questions, remember that Sand has the initial burden of showing that prison officials imposed a substantial burden on his religious exercise. (Assume for purposes of this simulation that Sand's beliefs are "religious").

You should also ask Sand questions that would prepare you to answer the government's arguments that the policy is based on compelling state interests and is the least restrictive means of furthering those interests. Determine what facts the *Washington* court found important and use these facts to help you draft your questions.

For further discussion

Assume that there were several fires in apartment buildings in the City of Berne. The City studied the cause of the fires and determined that some of them were caused by candles during a city-wide blackout. To help avoid a future disaster, the City passed a candle ordinance prohibiting tenants in apartment buildings from lighting candles in their apartments.

James Levin was Jewish and lit candles in his apartment on Friday night to celebrate the Sabbath. He was arrested and found guilty of violating the candle ordinance.

Levin was sentenced to two months in jail. While incarcerated in the local jail, he requested permission to light candles in his cell on Friday nights to celebrate the Sabbath. His request was denied based on a prison policy prohibiting the lighting of candles in jail cells.

Levin claims that the candle ordinance and the jail policy forbidding the lighting of candles violates his free exercise rights under the First Amendment of the U.S. Constitution and under RLUIPA.

1. Will his challenge to the candle ordinance be decided using strict scrutiny or a rational basis test? Explain.

2. Will his challenge to the jail policy be decided using strict scrutiny or a rational basis test? Explain.

3. Based on your answers to 1 and 2 above, is it possible that Levin might be successful in compelling the jail to allow him to light candles in his cell on the Sabbath and unsuccessful in his challenge to the candle ordinance? Do the religious rights of convicted inmates receive more protection than the religious rights of law-abiding citizens? Explain. Does this mean that Levin might be able to compel the jail to allow him to engage in exactly the activity that caused him to be incarcerated in the first place?[107]

Law Practice Simulation # 4

In Exercise 1, Clinton Correctional Facility refused Sand's request to have a mezuzah placed outside his cell door. A mezuzah—literally meaning "doorpost" in Hebrew—is a small case containing Judaism's holiest prayer—the Shema—written on a piece of parchment and is intended to be affixed to the doorposts of Jewish homes, businesses, and synagogues.[108] The case containing the Shema can be made of wood, metal, glass, or other materials and is often decorated.[109] The practice of using mezuzahs derives from the Jewish Torah's commandment to inscribe the words of the Shema on the doorposts of your house and on your gates.[110]

Assume that you are an attorney for DOCS. What compelling interests might justify prohibiting placement of a mezuzah outside an inmate's cell door?

---

107. For a further discussion of this conundrum, *see* Spencer T. Proffitt, *GODS Behind Bars: How Religious Liberty Has Been Sent Directly to Jail, and How to Get Out of Jail Free*, 40 Ariz. St. L.J. 1401, 1403 (2008).

108. *See* http://www.aish.com/jl/m/mm/48948731.html (last visited July 2019) (providing a definition and explanation of the mezuzah and the mezuzah case); *see also* CHABAD.ORG, *Mezuzah: What is a Mezuzah?* https://www.chabad.org/library/article_cdo/aid/256915/jewish/What-Is-a-Mezuzah.htm (last visited July 2019) (defining mezuzah and providing a religious overview of the practice).

109. Judaica Mall, *Glossary of Terms*, http://www.judaica-mall.com/glossary-terms.htm (last visited July 2019) (defining mezuzah case and listing materials commonly used in making a mezuzah case).

110. *See* http://www.religionfacts.com/mezuzah (last visited July 2019).

Write a prison policy for Clinton Correctional Facility prohibiting the placement of mezuzahs outside the inmates' cell doors. What additional facts would you want from DOCS to insure that your policy would withstand a RLUIPA challenge?

Now, assume that you are the attorney for Sand. What additional facts would you want from Sand to support a RLUIPA challenge to the mezuzah policy you have written? Do you think your policy will stand up to the challenge? If you are unsure, what facts do you think are pivotal in making this determination?

Above: Decorative Menorah.
Photograph by Max Damashek

Right: Mezuzah fastened to a door.
Photograph by Jonathan Gillerman.

5. Meetings and Inmate Religious Leaders

In most religions, congregate services are an important part of the religious experience.[111] Group religious meetings provide an opportunity for members of a particular faith to get together and learn the tenets of their religion with the assistance of a religious leader.[112]

Prison chaplains are generally charged with providing religious counseling to all of the facility's inmates regardless of their faith.[113] The chaplains also lead services in their own faith and assist inmates in finding religious leaders in other faiths.[114] In

111. Mushlin, *supra* note 27, at 741.

112. *Id.*

113. U.S. Comm'n on Civil Rights, *supra* note 4, at 16.

114. *Id.; see also* RELIGION IN PRISONS: A 50-STATE SURVEY OF PRISON CHAPLAINS, Pew Research Center, Religion and Public Life, https://www.pewresearch.org/wp-content/uploads/sites/7/2012/03/Religion-in-Prisons.pdf ("Nearly all the [state] chaplains (92 percent) say their work includes personally leading worship services, religious instruction and spiritual counseling sessions.").

2007, there were 251 chaplains employed by the Federal Bureau of Prisons.[115] There is at least one full-time chaplain employed at each federal and state prison.[116]

If the prison does not have a chaplain who can meet the religious needs of a particular religious group, the prison will attempt to either contract with outside clergy or use outside volunteers to meet these needs.[117] In 2007, the Federal Bureau of Prisons had between 27 and 150 volunteer religious leaders in each facility.[118]

If an outside religious leader or volunteer cannot be found to meet a religious group's needs, some prisons will allow inmate-led services. However, inmate-led services create substantial concerns for prison administrators.[119] Gang activity is one of the biggest security problems facing prison administrators and inmate-led religious services can be used as a disguise for gang meetings.[120] Religious meetings can also be used, *inter alia*, to plan escapes, to engage in illegal drug transactions, to recruit radical groups, to undermine security, and to plot assaults on staff and other inmates.[121] For these reasons, when inmate-led services are allowed, the prison authorities generally attend and monitor the services.[122]

Questions to guide reading of *Spratt v. Rhode Island* Department of Corrections

1. What was the reason given by the Rhode Island Department of Corrections (RIDOC) for prohibiting Spratt from preaching to his fellow inmates during religious services?

---

115. U.S. Comm'n on Civil Rights, *supra* note 4, at 16; *see also* RELIGION IN PRISONS: A 50-STATE SURVEY OF PRISON CHAPLAINS, Pew Research Center, Religion and Public Life, https://www.pewresearch.org/wp-content/uploads/sites/7/2012/03/Religion-in-Prisons.pdf (In 2011, there were 1,474 professional chaplains working in state prisons across the country.).

116. U.S. Comm'n on Civil Rights, *supra* note 4, at 16–17 ("[e]ach of the federal prisons surveyed had a minimum of two full-time chaplains and some had up to four.... All of the state prisons surveyed engage the services of at least one full-time chaplain.").

117. *Id.* at 16, 39 ("[f]ederal and state prisons have indicated a difficulty in recruiting chaplains of other faiths, specifically chaplains of non-Christian faiths such as Islam and Wicca. As a result, both federal and state correctional institutions rely heavily on religious contractors, volunteers and faith-based organizations to meet inmates' religious needs.").

118. *Id.* at 16.

119. Mushlin, *supra* note 27, at 742.

120. U.S. Comm'n on Civil Rights, *supra* note 4, at 30; Michael Keegan, *The Supreme Court's "Prisoner Dilemma:" How Johnson, RLUIPA, and Cutter Re-Defined Inmate Constitutional Claims*, 86 Neb. L. Rev. 279, 325 (2007) ("[c]ontrolling prison gangs is the foremost problem facing prison administrators and guards...."); *see* Aiello v. West, 207 F. Supp. 3d 886, 890 (W.D. Wisc. 2016); *see also* National Gang Crime Research Center, THE PROBLEM OF GANGS AND SECURITY THREAT GROUPS (STG'S) IN AMERICAN PRISONS AND JAILS TODAY: RECENT FINDINGS FROM THE 2012 NGCRC NATIONAL GANG/STC SURVEY (2012).

121. U.S. Comm'n on Civil Rights, *supra* note 4, at 30–31; *see* Mushlin, *supra* note 27, at 741.

122. *See* U.S. Comm'n on Civil Rights, *supra* note 4, at 31.

2. Was Spratt successful in his claim that he should be allowed to continue to preach during religious services? What relief was awarded by the court? Why did the court choose to grant this relief?
3. According to *Spratt*, does a court have to consider and reject other alternatives before deciding that Spratt cannot preach during religious services? If your answer is yes, does this mean that RIDOC must consider every possible option or just some alternatives? Is RIDOC responsible for explaining why it rejected the alternatives?
4. Does RIDOC have to consider Spratt as an individual in deciding that there are no less restrictive measures that would further its compelling interest in prohibiting inmate preaching or can RIDOC have a well-justified uniform policy concerning inmate preaching? Can the court both make a case-by-case individualized assessment and consider the success of alternative policies at other institutions?
5. The court found significant that Spratt had preached during religious services in the prison for seven years without incident. Does this mean that an inmate who has never had a chance to preach during services would have less chance of prevailing on a similar claim?

Spratt v. Rhode Island Department of Corrections

482 F.3d 33 (1st Cir. 2007)

JUDGES: Before Torruella, Lynch, and Lipez, Circuit Judges.

TORRUELLA, *Circuit Judge.* Wesley Spratt ("Spratt") is a prisoner in the Adult Correctional Institution ("ACI") in Rhode Island. After prison officials prohibited Spratt from preaching to his fellow inmates, he filed suit against the Rhode Island Department of Corrections and its director, A.T. Wall (collectively, "RIDOC") under the Religious Land Use and Institutionalized Persons Act, 42 U.S.C. § 2000cc *et seq.* ("RLUIPA"). The district court granted summary judgment to RIDOC. After careful consideration, we reverse and remand for further proceedings.

I. *Background*

Spratt is a prisoner in the maximum security unit and is serving a life sentence for murder. *See State* v. *Spratt*, 742 A.2d 1194 (R.I. 1999). In 1995, Spratt underwent a religious awakening, and began attending Christian services at the ACI. Impressed with his commitment and devotion, the prison chaplains began allowing Spratt to preach[1] to inmates during weekly services. In 2000, Spratt was ordained as a minister by the Universal Life Church. From 1995 until 2003, no prison official interfered with Spratt's religious activities. Spratt's preaching during this seven year period did not lead to any apparent disciplinary problems at the ACI.

FN1. To be clear, we use the word "preach" to refer to the activity of commenting or expounding upon some religious text. RIDOC continues to allow

Spratt to read scripture aloud during religious services so long as he does not add any commentary.

In 2003, then-Warden Whitman was replaced by Warden Weeden, who remains the warden of the ACI. On October 15, 2003, Spratt was told by a correctional officer that he was no longer allowed to preach in the chapel. When Spratt approached Warden Weeden about the matter, he was told that preaching by prisoners was not allowed under prison regulations. Spratt formalized his complaint in writing, and Warden Weeden responded that inmate preaching was prohibited by RIDOC Policy # 26.01-2DOC, which states that all religious services are scheduled, supervised, and directed by institutional chaplains. Weeden also informed Spratt that if he was found to be preaching, he would be subject to disciplinary action. Spratt then filed a complaint with A.T. Wall, director of RIDOC, stating the aforementioned facts, and asking that Wall allow him to preach. Wall responded in a letter dated December 15, 2003, which states:

Mr. Spratt, you do have the right to practice your religion under the constitution subject to reasonable restrictions. Because you are not an acknowledged member of the clergy, you do not have the right to proselytize or preach to the inmate population. Therefore, your request for my intervention is denied.

Spratt proceeded to file a pro se complaint against Wall and RIDOC in the United States District Court for the District of Rhode Island, asking for relief under the First Amendment, the Fourteenth Amendment, and the Religious Freedom Restoration Act, 42 U.S.C. § 2000bb-1(c) ("RFRA").[4] ...

FN4. Spratt initially filed suit under RFRA. However, RFRA was found to be unconstitutional as applied to purely state (as opposed to federal) action in *City of Boerne* v. *Flores*, 521 U.S. 507, 117 S. Ct. 2157, 138 L. Ed. 2d 624 (1997). In its response to Spratt's complaint, RIDOC noted that Spratt would likely refile his complaint under RLUIPA. Since then, the district court and the parties have treated Spratt's complaint as arising out of RLUIPA. We do not disturb this decision.

RIDOC submitted a [ ] memorandum acknowledging that it was subject to RLUIPA ... and attached an affidavit from Jake Gadsden, Assistant Director of Operations for the Rhode Island Department of Corrections. The affidavit briefly reviews Gadsden's professional experience, and states that inmates may not lead religious services in RIDOC facilities. Gadsden explains in the affidavit that inmate preaching could be dangerous because "placing an inmate in a position of actual or perceived leadership before an inmate group threatens security, as it provides the perceived inmate leader with influence within the administration." Gadsden further states in the affidavit that "there is no less restrictive manner to accommodate Spratt's desire to preach to an inmate congregation, other than an outright ban," because even an inmate preaching under RIDOC supervision would be perceived as having influence. Finally, the affidavit states that Gadsden was familiar with a program in the Texas Correctional System which he identified as the "trustee" program, in which inmates were given certain leadership roles. Gadsden states that Texas abolished the program because the inmate leaders abused their positions to garner favors from fellow inmates.

Spratt filed an affidavit in response, which states that he acknowledges Gadsden's "noteworthy" credentials, but that Gadsden's conclusions are "exaggerat[ion] and speculation." Spratt also stated in a memorandum of law that he would willingly submit to further RIDOC supervision of his preaching activities. He also suggested that RIDOC could retain their policy against inmate preaching but grant limited exemptions when enforcement of the policy would result in a violation of RLUIPA. Spratt noted that RIDOC allows inmates to congregate and talk freely about non-religious topics during recreational time, and that this had not been found to pose a threat to prison security....

II. *Analysis*

A. Standard of Review

We review a grant of summary judgment *de novo*, viewing the record in the light most favorable to the non-moving party. *Iverson* v. *City of Boston*, 452 F.3d 94, 98 (1st Cir. 2006). Summary judgment is appropriate only if there are no material disputes of fact, and if the moving party is entitled to judgment as a matter of law. *Id.*

B. RLUIPA ...

A claim under RLUIPA includes four elements. On the first two elements, (1) that an institutionalized person's religious exercise has been burdened and (2) that the burden is substantial, the plaintiff bears the burden of proof. *Id.* § 2000cc-2(b). Once a plaintiff has established that his religious exercise has been substantially burdened, the onus shifts to the government to show (3) that the burden furthers a compelling governmental interest and (4) that the burden is the least restrictive means of achieving that compelling interest. *Id.*

1. Spratt's Burden

For purposes of this appeal, the state does not seriously dispute that Spratt's evidence on his prima facie case is sufficient to survive summary judgment. As an inmate in a state correctional facility, Spratt is an institutionalized person within the definition of RLUIPA. *See id.* § 1997(1) ("The term 'institution' means any facility or institution—(A) which is owned, operated, or managed by, or provides services on behalf of any State or political subdivision of a State; and (B) which is—(ii) a jail, prison, or other correctional facility...."). Furthermore, it is clear that preaching is a form of religious exercise. *See McDaniel* v. *Paty*, 435 U.S. 618, 626, 98 S. Ct. 1322, 55 L. Ed. 2d 593 (1978) ("[T]he right to the free exercise of religion unquestionably encompasses the right to preach, proselyte, and perform other similar religious functions.").

As to the second prong, RIDOC devotes a footnote in its brief to suggesting that Spratt's "exercise of ... religion in general is not being substantially burdened." Appellees' Br. at 11 n.6. RIDOC points out that "Spratt may still attend and participate in religious services. He may pray, sing, or recite during such services just as every other inmate may." *Id.*... Spratt has stated that RIDOC will not allow him to preach anytime or anywhere, threatening that if he does so, he will be subject to disciplinary sanctions. As such, for the purposes of this appeal, Spratt has made a prima facie showing that his religious exercise has been substantially burdened.

2. RIDOC's Burden

The burden thus shifts to RIDOC to demonstrate that its ban on inmate preaching, as applied to Spratt, furthers a "compelling governmental interest" and is the least restrictive means of achieving that interest. 42 U.S.C. § 2000cc-1. We are mindful, however, that in passing RLUIPA, Congress stated that we should continue to give "due deference to the experience and expertise of prison and jail administrators" in determining prison policy. *Cutter*, 544 U.S. at 717 (internal quotation marks omitted) (quoting 146 Cong. Rec. S7774, S7775 (daily ed. July 27, 2000) (joint statement of Sens. Hatch and Kennedy on RLUIPA)). However, as the Congressional sponsors of RLUIPA stated, "inadequately formulated prison regulations and policies grounded on mere speculation, exaggerated fears, or post-hoc rationalizations will not suffice to meet the act's requirements." 146 Cong. Rec. at S7775 (internal quotation marks omitted).

RIDOC asserts that it has a compelling state interest in maintaining prison security. We agree. *See, e.g., Cutter*, 544 U.S. at 725 n.13 ("It bears repetition ... that prison security is a compelling state interest, and that deference is due to institutional officials' expertise in this area."). However, merely stating a compelling interest does not fully satisfy RIDOC's burden on this element of RLUIPA; RIDOC must also establish that prison security is furthered by barring Wesley Spratt from engaging in any preaching at any time.

RIDOC has offered just one piece of evidence to support this assertion: the Gadsden affidavit. This affidavit, which cites no studies and discusses no research in support of its position, simply describes the equation thus: if Spratt is a preacher, he is a leader; having leaders in prison (even those sanctioned by the administration) is detrimental to prison security; thus, Spratt's preaching activity is detrimental to prison security. But to prevail on summary judgment, RIDOC "must do more than merely assert a security concern." *Murphy* v. *Mo. Dep't of Corr.*, 372 F.3d 979, 988 (8th Cir. 2004). The Gadsden affidavit offers only one reference to another prison in support of its assertion that inmate preaching is a security concern: the affidavit mentions a situation in Texas which was described as a "trustee" system. We believe that Gadsden was referring to the "building tender" system present in Texas prisons in the 1970s. This situation, of course, is radically different: building tenders were inmates who were armed, served as official guards within the prison, and who were serving in supervisory capacities in the prison system. *See generally Ruiz* v. *Estelle*, 503 F. Supp. 1265, 1294–98 (S.D. Tex. 1980). Whereas it is quite easy to see how armed prisoners granted nearly indiscriminate authority to brutalize fellow prisoners are a threat to institutional security, the same cannot be said about a preacher who offers a weekly sermon under the direction of the prison chaplain.

Beyond the Texas "trustee system," Gadsden cites no past instances where having inmates in leadership positions endangered security, nor does he explain why a person who expounds on the scripture during a weekly religious service would be considered a leader. Self-serving affidavits that do not "contain adequate specific factual information based on personal knowledge" are insufficient to defeat a motion for summary judgment, let alone to sustain one. *Quinones* v. *Houser Buick*, 436 F.3d 284, 290 (1st Cir. 2006); *see also Hayes*, 8 F.3d at 92 ("Although an expert affidavit need not include details about all of the raw data used to produce a conclusion, or about scientific or other specialized input which might be confusing to a lay person, it must at least include the factual basis and the process of reasoning which makes the conclusion viable in order to defeat a motion for summary judgment.").

In addition, RIDOC's initial explanation for the preaching ban was that only ordained ministers were allowed to preach, and that Spratt was not ordained. However, according to materials submitted in connection with Spratt's motion for summary judgment, he had been an ordained minister since 2000. RIDOC now claims that its initial explanation was "incomplete," and that the real reason is that no inmates are allowed to preach at all. At the very least, the inconsistencies between RIDOC's various explanations for its policy require further explanation.[9]

> FN9. RIDOC offers a third explanation for its prohibition on inmate preaching. RIDOC suggests that inmate-led religious activities could foment terrorism-related activity. *See* Appellee's Br. at 18 n.8 (citing Frank Cilluffo et al., Geo. Wash. Univ. Homeland Sec. Policy Inst. and Univ. of Va. Critical Incident Analysis Group, *Out of the Shadows: Getting Ahead of Prisoner Radicalization* (2006), *available at* http://www.gwumc.edu/hspi/reports/rad/Out%20of%20the%20shadows.pdf). The report cited by RIDOC describes the formation of terror cells in prisons by radicalized Muslim inmates. This explanation for the blanket ban on inmate preaching further demonstrates that RIDOC has not engaged in any individualized consideration of Spratt's preaching whatsoever. *Cf. Gonzales* v. *O Centro Espirita Beneficente Uniao do Vegetal*, 546 U.S. 418, 126 S. Ct. 1211, 1221, 163 L. Ed. 2d 1017 (2006) (requiring that the government engage in individualized consideration of the necessity of a burden on religious exercise).

Finally, RIDOC claims that it was merely "lucky" that institutional security was not threatened during Spratt's seven year stint as a preacher, and that it need not wait for a dangerous situation to occur before it takes steps to remedy the threat. *See Casey* v. *Lewis*, 4 F.3d 1516, 1521 (9th Cir. 1993) (noting that "failure to specify a past event" that threatened institutional security "does not render irrational the adoption and implementation of a ... policy" to address future events that might pose a threat). RIDOC also claims that its policy is long-standing, and that prison officials who permitted Spratt to preach were in violation of it. However, Spratt's seven-year track record as a preacher, which is apparently unblemished by any hint of unsavory activity, at the very least casts doubt on the strength of the link between his activities and institutional security. While we recognize that prison officials are to be accorded substantial deference in the way they run their prisons, this does not mean that we will "rubber stamp or mechanically accept the judgments of prison administrators." *Lovelace*, 472 F.3d at 190.

Even if we assume that RIDOC has shown a link between Spratt's preaching and institutional security, RIDOC still has not shown that the blanket ban on all inmate preaching is the "least restrictive means" available to achieve its interest. A prison "cannot meet its burden to prove least restrictive means unless it demonstrates that it has actually considered and rejected the efficacy of less restrictive measures before adopting the challenged practice." *Warsoldier* v. *Woodford*, 418 F.3d 989, 999 (9th Cir. 2005); *Murphy*, 372 F.3d at 989 ("It is not clear that MDOC seriously considered any other alternatives, nor were any explored before the district court."); *cf. Casey* v. *City of Newport*, 308 F.3d 106, 114 (1st Cir. 2002) ("[T]he narrow-tailoring test requires the district court to consider whether the regulation challenged on First Amendment grounds sweeps more broadly than necessary to promote the government's interest. That consideration, in turn, cannot be done without some evaluation of the alternative measures put in issue by the parties.").[11] Rather than considering alternatives, RIDOC argues that inmate preaching is an "all or nothing" issue: any amount of inmate preaching, it contends, is dangerous to institutional security under any circumstances. As such, RIDOC argues, there are no "less restrictive alternatives." However, it is not clear how RIDOC has come to this conclusion. *See Warsoldier*, 418 F.3d at 999 (explaining that a California prison had done "nothing to ... discuss whether it has ever considered a less restrictive approach" to a blanket ban on long hair). RIDOC offers no explanation for why alternative policies would be unfeasible, or why they would be less effective in maintaining institutional security.

FN11. It is important to note that we do not construe RLUIPA to "require prison administrators to refute every conceivable option in order to satisfy the least restrictive means prong of RFRA." *Hamilton* v. *Schriro*, 74 F.3d 1545, 1556 (8th Cir. 1996). However, to meet the least restrictive means test, prison administrators generally ought to explore at least some alternatives, and their rejection should generally be accompanied by some measure of explanation. A blanket statement that all alternatives have been considered and rejected, such as the one here, will ordinarily be insufficient.

RIDOC responds by pointing to the Eighth Circuit's decision in *Hamilton* v. *Schriro*, 74 F.3d 1545 (8th Cir. 1996), in which that court accepted prison administrators' contention that a regulation requiring inmates to have short hair was the least restrictive means of achieving prison security. However, the court in *Hamilton* made this determination after considering lengthy testimony by the prison administrators in the district court, something which is notably absent here. *Id.* at 1555. In addition, the Eighth Circuit relied on several district court decisions upholding hair length regulations against RFRA challenges, at least one of which appears to have considered and rejected alternatives to the regulation. *Id.* at 1555 n.12. In contrast, RIDOC offers no case finding that blanket bans on inmate preaching satisfy the least restrictive means test, and none appear to exist.[12] Finally, the Eighth Circuit explicitly acknowledged that "prison authorities must do more than offer conclusory statements and post hoc rationalizations for their conduct." *Id.* at 1554 n.10. Thus, *Hamilton* lends little support to RIDOC's argument here.

FN12. Past decisions have found that restricting inmate preaching "reasonably" furthered institutional security. *See, e.g.*, *Anderson* v. *Angelone*, 123 F.3d 1197, 1199 (9th Cir. 1997) ("Requiring an outside minister to lead religious activity among inmates undoubtedly contributes to prison security."); *Hadi* v. *Horn*, 830 F.2d 779, 785 n.9 (7th Cir. 1987). However, these cases were decided under the pre-RLUIPA standard of *Turner* v. *Safley*, which states that a "[prison] regulation is valid if it is reasonably related to legitimate penological interests." 482 U.S. 78, 89, 107 S. Ct. 2254, 96 L. Ed. 2d 64 (1987). The RLUIPA standard, which requires that prison administrators achieve a "compelling interest" by the "least restrictive means," imposes a different burden on prison officials. *See Lovelace*, 472 F.3d at 199–200 ("[T]he First Amendment affords less protection to inmates' free exercise rights than does RLUIPA.").

In fact, RIDOC's "all or nothing" argument raises many questions. Why are inmates banned from preaching when they are free to become leaders under other circumstances? Likewise, why is Spratt still allowed to stand in front of his congregation and read scripture if it is his appearance in the pulpit that is problematic? If it is the "teaching" element of scripture that is so troubling, why are inmates permitted to assist instructors in educational programs at the prison? Why would allowing preaching only under strict prison supervision be a less effective solution to the purported "threat to institutional security"? These questions, all unanswered, suggest that RIDOC has not given consideration to possible alternatives.[13]

FN13. This list of questions is offered by way of example, and is not exhaustive. We leave it to the district court to determine whether RIDOC has adequately shown that its policy is the least restrictive means of achieving prison security.

Furthermore, "[e]qually problematic ... is that other prison systems, including the Federal Bureau of Prisons, do not have such ... policies or, if they do, [they] provide ... exemptions." *Warsoldier*, 418 F.3d at 999. As Spratt points out, the Federal Bureau of Prisons policy on religious practices appears to contemplate inmate-led religious services in certain circumstances. *See* Federal Bureau of Prisons, *Program Statement: Religious Beliefs and Practices*, Statement P5360.09 (2004) P 7(d) ("Inmate-led religious programs require constant staff supervision."); *id.* P 7(a) ("Inmates may recite formulaic prayers in the language required by their religion. Sermons, original oratory, teachings and admonitions must be delivered in English."). We recognize that "prison officials ... are infinitely more familiar with their own institutions than outside observers," *Hamilton*, 74 F.3d at 1556 n.15, and that as such, evidence of policies at one prison is not conclusive proof that the same policies would work at another institution. However, in the absence of any explanation by RIDOC of significant differences between the ACI and a federal prison that would render the federal policy unworkable, the Federal Bureau of Prisons policy suggests that some form of inmate preaching could be permissible without disturbing prison security.

Simply put, RIDOC must "demonstrate, and not just assert, that the rule at issue is the least restrictive means of achieving a compelling governmental interest." *O'Bryan*

v. *Bureau of Prisons*, 349 F.3d 399, 401 (7th Cir. 2003). This does not conflict with our policy of deferring to the judgment of prison administrators. Rather, before we can evaluate whether deference is due, we require that prison administrators explain in some detail what their judgment is.[14] Here, RIDOC "offer[s] conclusory statements that a limitation on religious freedom is required for security, health or safety." *Weaver* v. *Jago*, 675 F.2d 116, 119 (6th Cir. 1982). To prevail on summary judgment, RIDOC must do more.

FN14. The level of deference to be accorded to prison administrators under RLUIPA remains an open question. RLUIPA's statutory requirement that we apply strict scrutiny to prison policies that substantially burden religious exercise may be in tension with the legislative history which suggests that courts should continue to defer to the expertise of prison administrators. Obviously, courts will need to find some balance between scrutiny of and deference to prison regulations. We need not resolve that question now because RIDOC has yet to present any reasoned judgment to justify the policies at issue in this case.

C. Remedy

Spratt asks that we enter summary judgment in his favor.... Summary judgment is proper only when "there is no genuine issue as to any material fact." Fed. R. Civ. P. 56(c). Denial of summary judgment is also appropriate where factual records are "disturbingly thin," "contain gaps," and require judgment calls which depend on evidence not in the record but readily obtainable. *See Mandel* v. *The Boston Phoenix, Inc.*, 456 F.3d 198, 205–07 (1st Cir. 2006). Notwithstanding Spratt's protestations to the contrary, it is clear that there are factual disputes, including whether a ban on inmate preaching furthers prison security, and whether a blanket ban is the least restrictive means necessary. The factual record on these issues is quite thin. As such, it would also be improvident at this point to grant summary judgment in favor of Spratt. We have held that entry of summary judgment for defendant was not warranted. Each side, on remand, may present further evidence and argument.

III. *Conclusion*

For the foregoing reasons, we reverse the judgment of the district court and remand for further disposition in accordance herewith.

Reversed and Remanded.

Questions to guide reading of *Baranowski v. Hart*

1. What facts did the court find most significant in denying Baranowski's First Amendment free exercise claim that his rights were violated because the prison failed to provide weekly Sabbath and other holy day services even though these services could be provided if inmates were allowed to lead them?
2. Why did the court deny Baranowski's equal protection claim even though Christian and Muslim services were conducted more frequently than Jewish services and other religious groups had more access to the chapel?

3. What was the court's rationale for denying Baranowski's RLUIPA claim? How did the court deal with Baranowski's argument that inmates should be allowed to lead Jewish services when no Rabbi or outside volunteer is available?
4. Can the reasoning in *Baranowski* be reconciled with the reasoning in *Spratt*? How are these two cases different? Do the defendants in *Baranowski* provide more or less specific factual information to support their policy of denying inmates the right to conduct religious services than the defendants in *Spratt*?

Baranowski v. Hart

486 F.3d 112 (5th Cir. 2007)

JUDGES: Before HIGGINBOTHAM, WIENER, and PRADO, Circuit Judges.

PRADO, Circuit Judge:

In this appeal, a Texas prisoner contends that the defendants-appellees violated his rights under the First Amendment, the Fourteenth Amendment, and the Religious Land Use and Institutionalized Persons Act, 42 U.S.C. § 2000cc-1 et seq., by failing to provide weekly Sabbath and other holy day services [and] by failing to allow Jewish prisoners to use the chapel for their religious services.... For the reasons that follow, we AFFIRM the district court's order granting summary judgment in favor of the defendants-appellees.

I. FACTUAL AND PROCEDURAL BACKGROUND

Thomas H. Baranowski ("Baranowski"), an inmate incarcerated in the Huntsville Unit of the Texas Department of Criminal Justice ("TDCJ"), proceeding pro se and *in forma pauperis*, filed a civil rights complaint in federal district court, pursuant to 42 U.S.C. § 1983, against employees and officials of the TDCJ: Defendants-Appellees Larry Hart ("Hart"), Huntsville Unit Chaplain; Lawrence Hodges, Huntsville Unit Warden; ...; Bill Pierce ("Pierce"), Director of the TDCJ Chaplaincy Department; and Douglas Dretke, former Director of the TDCJ (collectively, "Defendants").... Baranowski, a member of the Jewish faith, alleged that Defendants ... deprived him and other Jewish inmates of access to Friday Sabbath services in September and October 2003 and High Holy Day services [and] deprived him and other Jewish inmates of access to the Huntsville Unit chapel for their religious observances.... Baranowski also claimed that prisoners of other religious faiths were treated more favorably than Jewish prisoners, citing limited religious services and chapel access for Jewish prisoners.

Defendants moved for summary judgment, filing copies of various prison policies and sworn affidavits in support. In his affidavit, Pierce, the Director of the TDCJ Chaplaincy Department, testified that "TDCJ allows all offenders to worship according to their faith preference in their cell[s] using allowed items such as sacred texts, devotional items, and materials." According to Pierce, TDCJ policy is to allow inmates as much freedom and opportunity as possible for pursuing their individual beliefs and practices, consistent with agency security, safety, order, and rehabilitation concerns. Pierce explained that religious services are provided based on demand, need, and resources. He further testified that "[c]haplaincy services are nondiscriminatory in the treatment of offenders' religious beliefs, but TDCJ policy attempts to take space, time, and staffing restraints into consideration."

Pierce stated that of the 145,000 offenders currently confined in TDCJ, only 900 are self described as Jewish. Of those, only 70 to 75 are "recognized" as actually practicing their faith, with 90 in the conversion process. According to Pierce, these numbers are very small when compared to the number of observant Protestants, Catholics, and Muslims.

Pierce also stated that although Jewish programs and activities are not available at every unit, they are available at the Huntsville Unit, which is one of seven Jewish "host" units within the TDCJ. He explained that "[r]abbis, not offenders, lead Jewish services to ensure that religious practices reflect Jewish doctrines. There is no other way for TDCJ to accommodate the demand for Jewish congregational services from practicing Jews." According to Pierce, "[b]ecause of the small number of inmates who actually practice Judaism and attend Jewish services, as well as the limited availability of rabbis in certain geographical areas of the state, TDCJ is unable to hold Jewish services at every Jewish host unit on a weekly basis." Pierce testified that services are held at least monthly at each of the Jewish host units. Pierce explained that in addition to monthly services, however, the TDCJ recognizes twenty-one Jewish holy days (compared with two for Christians), and that time off is permitted for eight of those days....

Defendants also introduced affidavit testimony of Hart, a chaplain at the Huntsville Unit, in support of their summary judgment motion. Hart testified that because rabbis or approved outside volunteers lead Jewish services, "[s]cheduled events may be delayed or canceled when qualified spiritual leaders are not available." The Huntsville Unit has a contract rabbi who works with Hart to schedule Jewish services, order religious items, and authorize time off for Jewish holy days. Hart explained that Jewish services in September and October 2003 were canceled, as complained of by Baranowski, because a rabbi or qualified volunteer was not available.

Hart also testified about the use of the Huntsville Unit chapel. He explained that Friday night Sabbath services for the twelve Jewish inmates who routinely attend are held in the Education Department and not the chapel because the chapel is made available to the New Birth Bible Program, a group consisting of approximately 175 participants. Hart pointed out that the chapel is open to all offenders from 10:30 a.m. until 11:30 a.m. on Monday through Thursday for religious study.

The district court granted summary judgment and entered a judgment dismissing the complaint with prejudice.... Baranowski now appeals....

III. DISCUSSION ...

A. Free Exercise Claim

Baranowski argues that Defendants have impeded his free exercise of religion under the First Amendment by denying him access to Jewish Sabbath and other holy day services ... and by denying him access to the Huntsville Unit chapel for religious observances. Defendants counter that valid penological objectives, including security, staff and space limitations ... justify TDCJ's policies, and that Baranowski has alternative means of practicing his religion.

This court reviews prison policies that impinge on fundamental constitutional rights under the deferential standard set forth in *Turner v. Safley*, 482 U.S. 78, 107 S. Ct. 2254, 96 L. Ed. 2d 64 (1987). Under *Turner*, a prison regulation that impinges on an inmate's constitutional rights is valid if it is reasonably related to legitimate penological interests. Id. at 89. *Turner* requires the court to consider four factors: (1) whether a valid and rational connection exists between the prison regulation and the legitimate governmental interest put forward to justify it; (2) whether there are alternative means of exercising the right that remain open to prison inmates; (3) the impact of the accommodation on prison guards, other inmates, and the allocation of prison resources generally; and (4) whether there are "ready alternatives" to the regulation in question. Id. at 89–90. "A court 'must determine whether the government objective underlying the regulation at issue is legitimate and neutral, and that the regulations are rationally related to that objective.'" *Freeman*, 369 F.3d at 860 (*quoting Thornburgh v. Abbott*, 490 U.S. 401, 414–15, 109 S. Ct. 1874, 104 L. Ed. 2d 459 (1989)); *see also Scott v. Miss. Dep't of Corr.*, 961 F.2d 77, 80–81 (5th Cir. 1992) (explaining that a court need not "weigh evenly, or even consider, each of these factors," as rationality is the controlling standard).

Turning to the *Turner* factors, we hold that the TDCJ policies on the availability of religious services and use of the chapel pass constitutional muster.... The record demonstrates that the prison policies at issue here are logically connected to legitimate penological concerns of security, staff and space limitations, and that there are no obvious or easy alternatives. Baranowski's main complaint is that the prison could accommodate the need for weekly Jewish services if inmates were permitted to lead the services without the assistance of a rabbi or approved outside volunteer.... The summary judgment evidence shows that despite being denied weekly Sabbath services and other holy day services when a rabbi or approved volunteer is not present, Baranowski retains the ability to participate in alternative means of exercising his religious beliefs, including the ability to worship in his cell using religious materials and the ability to access the chapel and lockers containing religious materials on certain days and times. *See O'Lone v. Estate of Shabazz*, 482 U.S. 342, 351–52, 107 S. Ct. 2400, 96 L. Ed. 2d 282 (1987) (upholding a regulation that prevented Muslim prisoners from attending Friday Jumu'ah services, and recognizing that although there were "no alternative means of attending Jumu'ah [since] respondents' religious beliefs insist that it occur at a particular time," inmates were "not deprived of all forms of religious exercise, but instead freely observe a number of their religious obligations"); *see also Turner*, 482 U.S. at 90 ("Where other avenues remain available for the exercise of asserted rights, courts should be particularly conscious of the measure of judicial deference owed to corrections officials in gauging the validity of the regulation.") (internal quotation marks, citations, and alterations omitted). Finally, the Jewish population at the TDCJ constitutes less than one percent of the total inmate population. If this court were to require the TDCJ to accommodate every religious holiday and requirement of the Jewish faith, regardless of the availability of qualified volunteers and adequate space and security, we "would spawn a cottage industry of litigation and could have a negative impact on prison staff, inmates, and prison resources." *Freeman*, 369 F.3d at 862. We decline to yield to Baranowski's demands....

B. Equal Protection Claim

Baranowski next alleges that Defendants violated his equal protection rights by favoring other religions over Judaism. Specifically, he contends Christian and Muslim services are conducted more frequently than Jewish services, and that other groups have greater access to the chapel. Defendants respond that Baranowski has provided no summary judgment evidence of purposeful discrimination regarding any of his allegations.

To succeed on his equal protection claim, Baranowski " 'must prove purposeful discrimination resulting in a discriminatory effect among persons similarly situated.' " *Adkins*, 393 F.3d at 566 (*quoting Muhammad v. Lynaugh*, 966 F.2d 901, 903 (5th Cir. 1992)). "However, the Fourteenth Amendment does not demand 'that every religious sect or group within a prison—however few in numbers—must have identical facilities or personnel.' " *Freeman*, 369 F.3d at 862–63 (*quoting Cruz v. Beto*, 405 U.S. 319, 322 n.2, 92 S. Ct. 1079, 31 L. Ed. 2d 263 (1972)). Rather, prison officials must afford prisoners "reasonable opportunities ... to exercise the religious freedom guaranteed by the First and Fourteenth Amendment[s]." *Cruz*, 405 U.S. at 322 n.2. "*Turner* applies with corresponding force to equal protection claims." *Freeman*, 369 F.3d at 863.

Baranowski's equal protection claim must fail. He has offered no competent summary judgment evidence that similarly situated faiths are afforded superior treatment, or that TDCJ's policies are the product of purposeful discrimination. Although Baranowski claims that other religious groups have greater access to the chapel, it is recognized that "[a] special chapel or place of worship need not be provided for every faith regardless of size; nor must a chaplain, priest, or minister be provided without regard to the extent of the demand." *Cruz*, 405 U.S. at 322 n.2. It is therefore not constitutionally impermissible for Defendants to consider the demand and need of the group requesting the chapel, along with space and staffing limitations, when deciding where religious groups will conduct their services. *See id.* (noting that the Constitution does not demand that every religious group, regardless of size, have identical facilities).

In sum, Baranowski has failed to provide anything more than bald and unsubstantiated allegations that Defendants purposefully discriminated against him. This is not enough to succeed on an equal protection claim. *See Adkins*, 393 F.3d at 566. We therefore affirm the district court's dismissal of this claim.

C. RLUIPA Claim

Baranowski next argues that his inability to observe Sabbath and other holy day services ... substantially burden his ability to practice Judaism, in violation of RLUIPA.

As a "Torah-observant Jew," Baranowski claims that he is compelled to observe the Sabbath and other holy days.... He contends that the substantial burdens imposed by Defendants pressure him to modify his behavior and to violate his sincerely held religious beliefs. Defendants counter that Baranowski has failed to establish that his religious practices are substantially burdened. In the alternative, Defendants argue that their policies are the least restrictive means of furthering their compelling interests of security [and] safety ... for the prison and its inmates and employees....

The threshold inquiry under RLUIPA is whether the challenged governmental action substantially burdens the exercise of religion. The burden of proving the existence of a substantial interference with a religious exercise rests on the religious adherent. 42 U.S.C. § 2000cc-2(b). If such a substantial burden is proven, it is then up to the government to demonstrate that the compelling interest test is satisfied. *See id.*

RLUIPA defines "religious exercise" to include "any exercise of religion, whether or not compelled by, or central to, a system of religious belief." *Id.* § 2000cc-5(7)(A). "'[T]he 'exercise of religion' often involves not only belief and profession but the performance of ... physical acts [such as] assembling with others for a worship service [or] participating in sacramental use of bread and wine....'" *Cutter*, 544 U.S. at 720 (*quoting Employment Div., Dep't of Human Res. of Ore. v. Smith*, 494 U.S. 872, 877, 110 S. Ct. 1595, 108 L. Ed. 2d 876 (1990)). There is no question that the activities alleged to be burdened in this case—Jewish Sabbath and holy day services ...—qualify as "religious exercises" for the practice of Judaism under RLUIPA's generous definition. *See Adkins*, 393 F.3d at 567–68 (stating that Sabbath and holy day gatherings "easily qualify as 'religious exercise'")....

In *Adkins*, we considered the meaning of "substantial burden," which is not defined by the statute. We held that "for purposes of applying the RLUIPA in this circuit, a government action or regulation creates a 'substantial burden' on a religious exercise if it truly pressures the adherent to significantly modify his religious behavior and significantly violate his religious beliefs." 393 F.3d at 569–70. The court cautioned, however, that "our test requires a case-by-case, fact-specific inquiry to determine whether the government action or regulation in question imposes a significant burden on an adherent's religious exercise ..." *Id.* at 571.

We first consider whether Baranowski's religious exercise was substantially burdened when he was prevented from congregating with other Jewish inmates on many Sabbath and Jewish holy days. The uncontroverted summary judgment evidence shows that on the days Baranowski claims that services were not provided, no rabbi or approved religious volunteer was available to lead the services. This court considered a similar claim under RLUIPA in *Adkins*; the plaintiff in that case was prevented from gathering with other YEA members for various religious observances. We explained that the plaintiff and other YEA members were not prevented from congregating by prison policy but by the dearth of clergy and authorized volunteers. Id. We held that the requirement of an outside volunteer did not place a substantial burden on the plaintiff's religious exercise under RLUIPA. Id. In light of this court's decision in *Adkins* and the summary judgment evidence before us, we are convinced that the acts of Defendants regarding religious services have not placed a substantial burden on Baranowski's free exercise of his Jewish faith, within the contemplation of RLUIPA. *See id.*...

IV. CONCLUSION

For the reasons stated above, we affirm the district court's grant of summary judgment.

For further discussion

The Texas Department of Criminal Justice (TDCJ) assumed that Baranowski had adequate alternative means of exercising his religion because he could "worship in his cell using religious materials [and] access the chapel and lockers containing religious materials on certain days and times."[123] However, Baranowski was a Torah-observant Jew and solitary prayer is not an appropriate alternative for this group.

> In order to hold many religious services, a Jewish prayer service requires the assembly of a minyan—a quorum of at least ten men. Denied the right to assemble even without a rabbi or volunteer, Baranowski was unable to read from the Torah. Baranowski was also unable to read certain prayers, including but not limited to the Kaddish. These aspects of the prayer service are of fundamental importance to Torah-observant Jews given that they are called for in the Torah and Talmud, the principal sources of Jewish law.
>
> ...
>
> [A] rabbi or approved outside volunteer is not preferable or necessarily more competent than a Torah-observant Jewish inmate at leading religious services. Orthodox rabbis often do not lead their congregations in religious services because of the perceived conflict between being a community leader who may make decisions that his congregants may oppose and a prayer leader who represents each congregant. Consequently, a non-rabbi leader is often preferred by Torah-observant Jews.[124]

Do you think that if this additional information was submitted to the court, the decision in *Baranowski* would have been the same with respect to the First Amendment claim? Why or why not? Would the decision have been the same with respect to the RLUIPA claim? Why or why not?

For a related case, see *Aiello v. West*, 207 F. Supp. 3d 886 (W.D. Wisc. 2016).

Law Practice Simulation # 5

In Exercise 1, Rabbi Cohen determined that Sand was not a bona fide member of the Jewish religion, that he was disruptive, and that he could

---

123. Baranowski v. Hart, 486 F.3d 112, 121 (5th Cir. 2007).

124. Ian J. Silverbrand, *Baranowski v. Hart: Limitations on Jailhouse Religion Despite the Free Exercise Clause and RLUIPA*, 85 U. Det. Mercy L. Rev. 587, 598–600 (2008).

no longer attend Jewish services at Clinton Correctional Facility. Sand requested that the Correctional Facility either provide another Rabbi or allow him to conduct the religious services himself. DOCS denied his request.

Assume that Sand commenced an action in federal court claiming that his rights under RLUIPA were violated because he could not attend Jewish services at the prison and was not allowed to conduct the religious services himself. To determine if DOCS violated RLUIPA, you would first want to review DOCS' policy with respect to inmate-led services. DOCS' policies are contained in DOCS' directives and DOCS Directive 4202 controls inmate-led services.[125]

STATE OF NEW YORK DEPARTMENT OF CORRECTIONS AND COMMUNITY SUPERVISION **DIRECTIVE**	TITLE **Religious Programs and Practices**		NO. 4202 DATE 10/19/2015
SUPERSEDES DIR# 4202 Dtd. 07/24/2014	DISTRIBUTION A B	PAGES PAGE 1 OF 13	DATE LAST REVISED
REFERENCES (Include but are not limited to) Annual Religious Calendar Directives #4022, #4200, #4572, #4911, #4913, #4914, #4750, #4752, #4930, #4933	APPROVING AUTHORITY Jeff McKoy		

I. SCOPE: This directive concerns religious programs and practices within facilities of the New York State Department of Corrections and Community Supervision (DOCCS), and covers the religious rights and obligations of inmates and Chaplains within these facilities.

II. BACKGROUND: The Division of Ministerial, Family and Volunteer Services (MFVS), which falls under the jurisdiction of the Deputy Commissioner for Program Services, is responsible for ensuring that all religious programs and practices are carried out in accordance with the established tenets and practices of the faiths, the United States Constitution, as well as the policies and procedures of DOCCS. For religions not represented by DOCCS Chaplains, the Director of MFVS will seek advice on matters of religious doctrine, practice, and tradition from recognized religious authorities in the outside community. Due to the large number of unfamiliar faith groups in the community, any in-

125. Some portions of Directive 4202 have been omitted for educational purposes. The provisions deleted include religious head coverings, religious medallions, beads and shrines, religious publications and texts, dietary considerations and Native American religious items. The full directive can be accessed at http://www.doccs.ny.gov/directives/4202.pdf (last visited July 2019).

mate who wishes to practice one of these religions/faiths will be required to make an official request by using Form #4202E, "Request for New Religion." The form must be completed in its entirety and submitted to the Coordinating Chaplain. The Chaplain will keep a copy on file and forward the original to the Director of MFVS. The Director's determination will be returned to the Coordinating Chaplain with a copy to the Deputy Superintendent for Program Services (DSP).

The Director reports to the Assistant Commissioner for Program Services and is responsible for its day-to-day activities and the involvement of facility Chaplains and their approved programs. The Coordinating Chaplain will be responsible for monitoring these activities for compliance. Facility Chaplains are responsible for carrying out all aspects of the religious programs of their respective faiths and for ensuring that the approved accommodations for each faith group are afforded to the adherents of other identified groups. This responsibility will include the supervision of religious volunteers. Directive #4200, "Functions of the Division of Ministerial, Family & Volunteer Services," sets forth the mission and internal organization of the Division. DOCCS' Religious Calendar, in conjunction with this directive, Directive #4911, "Packages & Articles Sent or Brought to Facilities," Directive #4913, "Inmate Property," and Directive #4914, "Inmate Grooming Standards," sets forth DOCCS standards that must be adhered to when making religious accommodations for all inmate faith groups.

III. **POLICY**: In recognition of the First Amendment right of "religious liberty" and in pursuit of the objective of assisting inmates to live as law abiding citizens, it is the intent of DOCCS to extend to inmates as much spiritual assistance as possible, as well as to provide as many opportunities as feasible for the practice of their chosen faiths, consistent with the safe and secure operations of the DOCCS correctional facilities. This includes provisions for religious volunteers who must be fully registered (see Directive #4750, "Volunteer Services Program") to participate in authorized facility religious programs.

In situations where an inmate's faith may not be represented by a Chaplain at his or her facility, the inmate may contact and refer an outside clergyperson to contact the Coordinating Chaplain for discussion. If appropriate, they may apply to become a religious volunteer. If a Chaplain or an outside religious volunteer is not available to serve the spiritual needs of a particular faith group, the facility Superintendent, in consultation with the Director of MFVS, may authorize a faith group member to facilitate a religious education class **or** congregate worship service with staff monitoring. (See "Protocol; Inmate Facilitators," Attachment A.) If an inmate wishes to follow an unfamiliar or new religion he or she must complete Form #4202E, "Request for New Religion."

It should be clearly understood that DOCCS takes no position "acknowledging" any particular religion within its inmate population. DOCCS merely attempts to identify particular faiths within the population in an effort to accommodate the legitimate spiritual needs of its inmates as reasonably as possible in a manner which is commensurate with its legitimate correctional interests and the safety and security of its respective facilities.

DOCCS employees, including Chaplains and volunteers, in addition to inmate facilitators, shall refrain from disparaging in any manner whatsoever either the doctrines, beliefs, practices, or teachings of any other religious faith or any inmate or group of inmates who are adherents of any other religious faith or sect. Under no circumstances will proselytizing be permitted on the part of staff, volunteers, or inmates.

In addition to the Religious Calendar, Ministerial Program Coordinators (MPCs) and facility Chaplains should be consulted with regard to the tenets, practices, holy day observances, etc. of their respective faiths. The MPC, in consultation with the Director of MFVS or designee, will provide all necessary information where a particular faith is not represented by an employee Chaplain.

IV. **RESPONSIBILITIES OF MINISTERIAL PROGRAM COORDINATOR** (MPC): Ministerial Program Coordinators report to the Assistant Director of Ministerial Services. The responsibilities include but are not limited to:

- Serve as a liaison between Central Office Ministerial Services and the field
- Serve as the contact person for facilities with regard to all faith group inquiries
- Assist with facilitation of HUB Chaplains trainings and meetings
- Assist facility Chaplains to increase volunteer recruitment for all faith groups, but particularly for the emerging faith groups

V. **RESPONSIBILITIES OF THE FACILITY COORDINATING CHAPLAIN**: Each facility should have a Coordinating Chaplain who will serve as the principal adviser to the Superintendent on religious programs and practices. In addition to the tasks performed by Facility Chaplains, in collaboration with all other Chaplains assigned to the facility, the Coordinating Chaplain will also oversee and monitor the religious programs that are offered at the facility. He or she will be responsible for informing the DSP of religious program progress as well as collecting Form #3304, "Chaplain's Monthly Report," from all Chaplains and submitting them along with Form MFVS-MCS, "Monthly Chaplain's Summary," on a monthly basis. The reports should be forwarded to the MPC via Outlook e-mail, as attachments, with a copy to the Division of Ministerial, Family and Volunteer Services (DOCCS.sm.MFVS), no later than the Monday of the last full week of each month.

The Coordinating Chaplain will coordinate the various religious functions and the use of designated religious space, in conjunction with the overall functions of the institution. He or she will act as the liaison between the facility administration and the Chaplains assigned to the facility to ensure that policy and policy changes are shared; Chaplain's meetings should be held at least every two months. Coordinating Chaplains are expected to attend Central Office trainings as required. In conjunction with the facility Chaplains, the Coordinating Chaplain will also be responsible for enhancing the facility religious activities through the presence of community volunteers.

The Coordinating Chaplain will not have direct supervision of other Chaplains assigned to the facility; however, he or she will be required to know other Chaplain's work schedules and religious schedules to coordinate the religious area more efficiently. This includes assisting with completing religious event packages for groups that are overseen by a Chaplain that is assigned to provide coverage to multiple facilities. The responsibilities of the Coordinating Chaplain can be divided among one or more Chaplains.

VI. RELIGIOUS WORSHIP SERVICES AND PROGRAMS

A. Chaplain's Leadership Role: Each facility Chaplain is responsible to personally lead the primary congregational worship and prayer services of his or her particular faith on a regular basis at his or her assigned facility(ies). Although the Chaplain is responsible for leading worship services for his or her faith group, a volunteer may conduct the religious educational class/group. In these instances, the material that is presented by the volunteer must be submitted to the Chaplain and approved in advance. In addition, each Chaplain shall share responsibility for assisting faith groups not represented by a facility Chaplain in the exercise of their faith's practices. Chaplains shall not defer their leadership role to any person from outside the facility except on rare or special occasions, and only with the expressed consent of the facility Superintendent. In accordance with policy, inmates may facilitate but shall not provide any leadership role for the worshipping inmate community since this is properly the function of the facility Chaplains. Inmates who are themselves legitimately ordained clergy are not permitted to practice their profession while incarcerated.

B. Attendance

1. Chaplain work schedules should be consistent with inmate program modules.

2. To the extent possible and consistent with the safety and security of the facility, registered adherents may submit a request to the Superintendent:

a. To observe their congregational worship services when led by employee Chaplains or outside religious volunteers, or

b. To attend religious classes facilitated by a Chaplain, an approved volunteer, or an approved facilitator.

(1) Facilitation by a facilitator will only be considered under the following conditions:

(a) There must be a request from the inmate population for congregate worship or religious education classes;

(b) The religious faith must have tenets that can be expressed, taught, or practiced in a group setting by a facilitator;

(c) No employee Chaplain or outside religious volunteer of this particular faith is available to serve in a leadership capacity; and

(d) **The inmate facilitator must be specifically approved by the Superintendent after consultation with the Coordinating Chaplain and the Director of MFVS.** "Protocol; Inmate Facilitators," Attachment A, must also be completed with a copy placed in the correspondence section of the inmate's Guidance folder and with the Coordinating Chaplain.

(e) Due to the unique role that inmate facilitators perform, they should be reviewed on an annual basis and, for security reasons, they should serve terms not to exceed 36 months.

(2) If the class/service is facilitated by a volunteer or inmate, an outline of the discussion/service must be submitted to the designated Chaplain advisor for pre-approval.

(3) The Superintendent shall make a determination on each request to form a study group or congregation within 14 days of the request. Factors to be considered include, but are not limited to, the total number of inmates making the request, availability of space, and staffing.

If approved, the number of congregate gatherings will be determined in the following manner:

- Requests from five (5) or less will be approved to meet once a month.
- Requests from six (6)—ten (10) will be approved to meet twice a month.
- Requests from eleven (11)—twenty (20) will be approved to meet three times per month.
- Requests from more than twenty (20) will be approved to meet weekly.
- If a group requests more than the allotted number of meetings, the Superintendent has the discretion to approve such requests if the accommodation can be made without incurring any additional costs/resources.

(4) Inmate facilitated meetings and inmate facilitated congregate worship will be conducted only with appropriate oversight by staff. This may include electronic recording (audio or videotaping) of the meeting or congregate worship for review by the Coordinating Chaplain or other person designated by the Superintendent. Questions regarding the appropriateness of inmate facilitated congregate worship should be addressed to the MPC or to the Director of MFVS or designee.

3. Ordinarily an inmate may attend only the religious programs of his or her designated religion as noted in facility records. However, it is acceptable for those who desire to learn more about the religious practices of another faith to request permission to attend up to three classes/services per year from the Chaplain of that faith group. In case there is no Chaplain of that

faith group, the request should be made to the Coordinating Chaplain. (This does not include those interested in the Native American faith unless the inmate has met all conditions of the verification process.) If attendance can be accommodated, the Chaplain will advise the DSP that the inmate will be placed on a call-out.

4. Participation by an inmate in any religious celebration, service, or study group is voluntary. Therefore, it is the responsibility of the inmate to request to participate in all religious activities of interest. Once they have been placed on the call-out, it is their responsibility to attend. Completed call-outs and sign in sheets should be kept on file by the Chaplain. If an inmate does not regularly attend the program the Chaplain should meet with him or her to determine his or her interest in continued participation. If there is no further interest then a notation should be made and the inmate's name should be removed from the call-out.

5. The Superintendent or designee, in consultation with the assigned Chaplain for the affected faith group and the Director of MFVS or designee, shall resolve any conflicts pertaining to the scheduling and conduct of worship services.

VII. **RELIGIOUS CELEBRATIONS OR OBSERVANCES OF RELIGIOUS HOLY DAYS:** The Division of Ministerial, Family and Volunteer Services will compile a list of the approved dates of observance/celebrations, protocols, and accommodations for each identified faith group in the form of the annual Religious Calendar. The Division will also provide guidance and direction regarding the sacramental or ritual needs of each group.

A. Calendar: The Deputy Commissioner for Program Services or designee will issue a Religious Holy Day Calendar on an annual basis. This Calendar will list by faith group, the **one** designated family event and the High Holy days or days of observance. It will also note if special accommodations, such as Off Work and Programs (OWP), Family Events (FE), and Menu Considerations (MC), are required. These may involve work prohibition or restrictions, special ceremonies, additional chapel time, etc. In addition to the yearly calendar of religious days of observance, specific faith group instructions may be issued preceding a specific holy day or day of observance when needed. These holidays should be noted on a facility events calendar so that all groups are afforded the designated accommodations. There should be no deviation from these instructions without Central Office approval.

B. Schedules and Arrangements: Chaplains shall notify each religious community of upcoming celebrations along with a deadline to sign up to participate. This should be documented in writing and be included in the packet. The event packet must be submitted to the DSP **no less than forty five (45) days prior to the event.** (See Directive #4022, "Special Events Program," for policy regarding special/family event program administration.) Inmates are required to provide a separate written request to participate in each religious celebration or observance that they are interested in. If an inmate transfers into a facility after the deadline has passed and requests to participate in the observance, the request should be approved. It is the responsibility of the designated Chaplain to schedule the above activities and to document requests for attendance. Where a particular faith is not represented by a facility Chaplain, these responsibilities rest with the Coordinating Chaplain or assigned Chaplain.

VIII. **CHANGE OF RELIGIOUS DESIGNATION:** After reception/classification, an inmate may request an initial change of his or her religious affiliation, as recorded in Departmental records, by completing Form #4202C, "Change of Religious Designation Form," and presenting it to the facility Coordinating Chaplain. The Coordinating Chaplain will maintain a log of such requests and will ensure that the affected Chaplains are made aware of the change. The Chaplain of the inmate's former religion, if any, and the Chaplain of the inmate's newly designated religion, if any, shall both sign Form #4202C. In the absence of a Chaplain of a particular faith group, this will become the responsibility of the Coordinating Chaplain. Native American designations can only be approved after appropriate verification of the inmate's ancestry by the Director of MFVS in consultation with the DOCCS Native American Chaplains. Upon approval, the Coordinating Chaplain will forward the completed form to the facility Inmate Records Coordinator (IRC) for entry into the Department's central computer system, and distribute a copy to the Offender Rehabilitation Coordinator (ORC) for placement in the guidance file and a copy to the inmate. It is expected that the change will be accomplished within fourteen (14) business days. Subsequent changes of religion will be permitted only at twelve (12)-month intervals. There may be occasions when it is believed that there is a need to update a designation prior to the twelve (12)-month rule. These cases should be referred to the Director who will decide whether to approve an override or not. Inmates may not change their religious designation while a Superintendent's hearing is pending, while they are initially confined to a cell, room, or Special Housing Unit. However, if the confinement is twelve (12) months or longer, the inmate may change his or her faith after the twelve (12) months. Form #4202C is not to be handed out at religious services or classes.

Departmental guidelines must be adhered to when approving a religious designation. Whenever policy requires additional information in order to complete the verification process, it will be the inmate's responsibility to acquire it from outside religious authorities.

IX. **AREAS DESIGNATED FOR WORSHIP AND RELIGIOUS PROGRAMS**

A. The Superintendent, after consultation with the assigned Chaplain or Coordinating Chaplain, shall provide suitable areas for scheduled worship services and scheduled religious programs by the approved religious groups.

Adequate time shall be allowed. All spaces in facilities that are designated as places for religious worship are to be reserved for religious uses only. Under some very extraordinary circumstances, the occasional use of such spaces for non-religious purposes may be permitted but only after consultation with the Coordinating Chaplain and Superintendent approval. Always, the spaces designated for religious purposes are to be dealt with in a respectful manner.

B. In some facilities, because of space limitations, religious activities are now scheduled to be held at specific times in multipurpose or all-purpose spaces such as classrooms, gymnasiums, or meeting halls. Where this practice is required, respect should always be given to the sometime sacred and religious use of the space. The area should be large enough to accommodate the group and should be provided with the necessary furnishings such as chairs, tables, lecterns, cushions, altars, and rugs.

C. Shared areas for worship and programs should not include fixed visible symbols, posters, wall hangings, mirrors, etc.

D. If a serious question arises regarding the appropriateness of a given activity for a religious space, the Superintendent or designee should consult the Director of MFVS in order to decide how to resolve the issue.

X. ATTENDANCE AT CONGREGATE RELIGIOUS SERVICES BY INMATES WHO ARE IN KEEPLOCK STATUS

A. Upon commencement of keeplock or confinement status, an inmate may submit a written request to attend regularly scheduled congregate religious services.

B. Such requests shall be made in writing to the Deputy Superintendent for Security (DSS) or designee using Form #2175, "Request to Attend Scheduled Religious Service by Keeplocked Inmate." A request must be submitted 48 hours before the time of the scheduled service unless the inmate has been placed in keeplock or confinement less than 48 hours before the service. In such a case, the request must be submitted within 24 hours after the inmate has been placed in keeplock or confinement. A separate request must be submitted for each religious service that an inmate desires to attend. The final decision to permit attendance rests with the DSS.

XI. PRAYER OR DEVOTIONS

A. Individual demonstrative prayer by inmates will only be allowed in the privacy of their own living quarters and in designated religious areas whenever feasible, as determined by the Superintendent.

B. Congregate or group prayer may only occur in a designated religious area during a religious service or at other times authorized by the Superintendent.

XII. **RELIGIOUS MATERIALS:** The Religious Land Use and Institutionalized Persons Act (RLUIPA), Pub. L. 106-274, **codified as 42 U.S.C § 2000 cc et seq.**, is a United States Federal Law that prohibits the imposition of burdens on the ability of prisoners to worship as they please. The general rule is that no government shall impose a substantial burden on the religious exercise of a person residing or confined to an institution unless the government demonstrates that imposition of the burden on that person is in furtherance of a compelling governmental interest and is the least restrictive means of furthering that compelling governmental interest. As a result, DOCCS will provide a list of approved religious items that inmates may possess regardless of their designated faith group. These items will only be allowed for individual worship and may only be possessed as outlined in policy. In order to maintain the integrity of specific religions, the Calendar notes the only items that are allowed for congregate worship.

A. In accordance with sound security practice and in the best interest of the safe, secure, and orderly operations of correctional facilities, **staff and volunteers may only bring religious items into a facility if they have been appropriately approved via a gate clearance by the facility administration. The gate clearance must include an accurate description of the item, what faith group it is associated with, and indicate the specific purpose of the item.**

Religious materials for a faith group can also be obtained via purchase request when deemed appropriate by the Chaplain, or the group's staff advisor, and upon approval by the DSP.

If religious materials are received via an outside donation, a facility Chaplain shall review the materials in consultation with the DSP and the MPC if necessary. Donated materials will be accepted in accordance with Directive #4752, "Receipt of Donated Material." In addition, approved items may be donated by family members as long as the facility Chaplain is notified in advance and the items are shipped to the facility directly from an approved vendor.

Whether via purchase requests, through a gate clearance, or from an outside donation, religious media, such as, but not limited to, books, DVDs, or magazines, must be submitted to the Media Review Committee for approval. If there are questions regarding the religious significance of the material a Chaplain should be consulted and if need be, the assigned MPC as well. If further clarification is required the MPC will consult with the Director of MFVS, or designee, to assist the facility with the review. The DSP has the final discretion as to whether the materials are approved for purchase or entrance into the facility.

NOTE: Please ensure that storage of media, such as DVDs, is in accordance with Directive #4930, "Tool Control."

B. During the conduct of religious services, Chaplains and outside clergy may wear their religious vestments and/or insignia. Ceremonial candles should be affixed to candelabras that are securely fastened to prevent overturning. Electric candles are approved for congregate gatherings only. Incense should only be used during religious worship when the ceremony calls for it as noted in the Calendar.

C. An inmate's use of or request for any particular religious article shall be limited to those items that have been approved by DOCCS. If the validity of a religious item is in question, a Chaplain must be consulted prior to confiscating the item. If a Chaplain is unavailable, then the MPC or Director of MFVS should be consulted.

If you represented DOCS and wanted a further explanation of Directive 4202 and how it would be applied in the Sand case, you might contact John Lomane, the Director of Ministerial and Family Services for DOCS. Assume that Mr. Lomane prepared the following affidavit, with your assistance, explaining the DOCS' Directive.

UNITED STATES DISTRICT COURT
NORTHERN DISTRICT OF NEW YORK

ROBERT SAND,

Plaintiff,

No.19-CV-0086

-against-

AFFIDAVIT

(TJM)(RWS)

SAMUEL COHEN, Jewish Chaplin,
Clinton Corr. Facility; JOHN LOMANE
Dir. Ministerial and Family Services,
N.Y. Dept. of Correctional Services;
DANIEL SMITH, Superintendent,
Clinton Corr. Facility

Defendants.

STATE OF NEW YORK)
) SS:
COUNTY OF CLINTON)

JOHN LOMANE,[126] being duly sworn, deposes and says:

1. I am the Director of Ministerial and Family Services for the New York State Department of Correctional Services (DOCS). I have held this position for approximately one year. Prior to this position, I was a Regional Coordinator at DOCS for five years and the Imam at Bare Hill Correctional Facility for approximately

126. This affidavit is from *Sebok v. Friedman*, No. 99-CV-86 (N.D.N.Y. filed July 12, 2000). For educational purposes, some of the facts have been omitted and there has been some minor editing of the language in the original affidavit. The names of the parties have also been changed.

eight years. My responsibilities include ensuring that all religious programs are carried out in accordance with the policies and procedures of DOCS and are supervised by a qualified religious leader. I make this affidavit in support of defendants' motion for summary judgment. The information in this affidavit is based on documents maintained by DOCS and my own personal knowledge.

A. DOCS Policy

2. DOCS has traditionally sanctioned several religions with a large inmate following for group activities. These religions include: Catholic, Protestant, Jewish, and Muslim.

3. DOCS also sanctions other religions for group activities that have fewer inmates participating. These religions include: Rastafarian, Native American, and Santeria.

4. DOCS will officially sanction any other religion for group activities that has a body of dogma, a religious leader outside of the prison, and some traditions indicating the religion was not formed in prison.

5. Officially sanctioning a religious group for group activities means that the religious practices of these groups are accommodated by DOCS to the fullest extent possible, taking into consideration the security, administrative, and monetary restrictions of the Department and its correctional facilities.

6. The religious practices that are accommodated include, but are not limited to, arranging regular services and holiday services conducted by an approved religious leader.

7. Every medium and maximum security facility has a full-time Chaplain who coordinates religious activities at that facility. Once a religious group or inmate shows the facility Chaplain that there is a written body of religious dogma concerning the religion, the facility Chaplain will assist the inmate in contacting a person outside the prison who has the appropriate credentials for that religion and who can verify the existence of the religion outside of the prison and its traditions. Where possible, DOCS will provide those inmates with access to that religious leader.

8. For example, DOCS has, in the past, officially sanctioned the religions of Odinism and Taino for group activities, because inmates could provide a written body of dogma and a religious leader outside of the prison was able to verify the existence and traditions of the religion.

9. Once a religion is officially sanctioned for group activities, DOCS will accommodate the religious practices of the religion as set forth in paragraph 5 above.

B. Determining Membership in Religious Groups

10. When an inmate enters the prison he/she voluntarily states his/her religion. If the inmate selects any group that has been officially sanctioned for group activities (hereafter a religious group), the inmate is then allowed to attend the group's religious services.

11. The determination of whether an inmate can continue to attend the group religious services is made by that group's leader.
12. All religious leaders at DOCS must be approved by the Department of Corrections. DOCS will only hire religious leaders who are endorsed by their religion. For example, a Rabbi must be endorsed by the New York Board of Rabbis, Catholic clergy must be endorsed by the Archdiocese, Protestants must be endorsed by the Community of Churches, and Muslim Imams must be endorsed by the World Community of Islam. This ensures that the religious leaders will act in accordance with the dictates of the religion and that the religious leader is not a front for illicit activities.
13. A religious leader can only refuse to allow the inmate to attend the services of the religion he/she has selected if the inmate is not a bona fide member of the religion or if the inmate is disruptive.
14. DOCS delegates the determination of whether an inmate is a bona fide member of a religious group and whether an inmate is disrupting services to the religious leader of the group. DOCS does not require the religious leader to use any particular method for making these determinations.
15. DOCS agents, such as corrections officers and other correctional facility personnel, are not qualified to assess whether an inmate is a bona fide member of the religion because they are not familiar with the accepted norms of practice, and they are not sufficiently knowledgeable concerning the importance of various beliefs and practices to the differing religious groups.
16. If DOCS officials made the decision concerning whether an inmate is a bona fide member of a religious group, a group may be forced to accept a member who does not meet their criteria and does not properly follow the religion's tenets. This may affect the group's ability to effectively practice the religion. For example, some religious groups, including Jewish groups, are more comfortable praying with others who share their religious beliefs.
17. There is also a danger that DOCS officials may misinterpret the dictates of a religion and decide that an inmate is not a member of a religion when the religious group believes the inmate is a member of the group.
18. DOCS officials are also not qualified to determine whether an inmate is disrupting services. An inmate who disrupts services affects the ability of other inmates to practice their religion and the ability of the religious leader to effectively conduct services.
19. It would be difficult for DOCS to determine if particular behavior is disruptive. For example, Jews forbid the name of God to be spoken in Temple. An official would have to be aware of this religious dictate before determining that the use of this word was disruptive.
20. If an inmate is determined to be a bona fide member of the religious group, he/she is entitled to all of the religious privileges afforded to that religious group.

If an inmate is disruptive, and thus removed from group religious services, that inmate is still entitled to the privileges of his/her religion, except for attending group religious services.

C. Safeguards

21. DOCS does not delegate unbridled authority to the religious leaders. DOCS has safeguards to ensure that religious leaders do not arbitrarily deprive inmates of religious privileges.

22. As stated previously, DOCS only hires religious leaders who are endorsed by their religion. This helps ensure that the religious leader will act in accordance with the dictates of the religion.

23. Also, if an inmate believes that a religious leader is arbitrarily denying the inmate access to religious privileges, the inmate may grieve the decision of the religious leader.

24. If it appears that an inmate's complaint about a religious leader is not frivolous, the facility administration will communicate with the religious leader and attempt to work out accommodations that suit both the religious leader and the inmate. If the facility receives many complaints about a particular religious leader, the religious leader may be dismissed.

25. The inmates can also complain directly to the head Chaplain at the facility, the Superintendent at the facility and/or myself (the Director of Ministerial and Family Services) if they feel the individual religious leader is treating them unfairly. The religious leader will then be investigated and, if necessary, removed from the position.

26. In addition, the endorsing religious bodies generally monitor the activities of their own religious leaders and will remove a religious leader who is not acting appropriately.

D. Individualized Belief Systems

27. Even if an inmate is disruptive, or found not to be a bona fide member of a religious group, he may still have sincere religious beliefs. An inmate can have individualized beliefs that do not have any supporting body of dogma and/or do not have any support by a religious leader outside of the prison. An inmate can also claim to be a member of a religious group, but insist that he practices the religion in his own unique way. He may claim that he needs special accommodations in addition to those of the religious group to which he belongs or that he needs different accommodations than the religious group.

28. For example, Mr. Sand claims that he practices Judaism differently than Rabbi Cohen and that Rabbi Cohen's manner of practicing Judaism is incorrect.

29. DOCS cannot realistically accommodate the religious practices of every inmate who claims his individualized requests for privileges are based on religious beliefs not common to any religious group, or claims his request for privileges is based on the unique way in which he practices a group religion.

E. DOCS' Accommodations of Individualized Beliefs

30. To deal with these individualized beliefs, DOCS has established general guidelines that enable inmates who have individualized beliefs to practice their religion while recognizing the necessary limitations in a prison setting. These general guidelines provide all inmates with many religious privileges.

31. For example, while inmates with individualized beliefs are not given individualized services, they are given accommodations that enable them to pray and receive religious guidance. All inmates, regardless of their religious status, are allowed to pray and study in their cells and receive religious publications. The only restriction on religious publications is that inmates are not allowed material that will incite violence.

32. Inmates can also meet individually with any facility religious leader. All facility Chaplains and religious leaders are encouraged to meet with inmates individually, regardless of their religious beliefs, to discuss religious issues and provide as much spiritual guidance as possible.

33. The restraints on DOCS' ability to fully accommodate all inmates' individualized beliefs is due to: 1) the difficulty in determining whether individualized beliefs are sincere, 2) the substantial administrative burdens, and 3) security concerns.

F. Sincerity

34. It would be difficult to determine if an inmate is sincere in his individualized religious beliefs because of the strong incentives in a prison setting to construct beliefs that will help inmates obtain certain special privileges.

35. While some religious observances require sacrifices on the part of the inmate, many religious practices provide inmates with privileges that they have no other way of obtaining. Religious accommodations can also enable inmates to alter their daily routines and to gather for holiday services.

G. Administrative Burden

36. Inmates with individualized religious beliefs could claim they needed their own religious services. According to DOCS Directive 4202 (I), religious services should generally be held in areas designated for religious purposes only. The Directive states: "All spaces in facilities that are designated as places for religious worship are to be reserved for religious uses only."

37. There is not enough room in the facilities to designate religious worship areas for all inmates with individualized religious beliefs.

38. For example, Mr. Sand claims he cannot practice his religion with Rabbi Cohen, the only Rabbi at Clinton Correctional Facility. Accommodating Mr. Sand's individualized beliefs would require that he have his own Rabbi and a separate place or time to worship.

39. Allowing each inmate to select holidays from many religions would create other major administrative concerns. Each religion can have many religious observances.

For example, there are eight major holidays for the American Indian Religion alone. Zen Buddhism has eleven religious holidays, one of which lasts a month. There is no limit to the number of potential religious holidays that inmates might claim need to be accommodated.

40. Allowing each individual inmate to practice his religion in his own unique way might require modification of work and school schedules. Also the limited prison personnel would have to be available to supervise the varying inmate schedules.

H. Security

41. Gangs are the most common cause of violence in correctional facilities. Gang members may act violently toward other gangs, toward correctional facility personnel, or toward other individual inmates. Making inmates choose one religion helps ensure that the group meetings associated with that religion are necessary for religious purposes and not to promote illicit activities.

42. For example, only Auburn Correctional Facility has the religious personnel and other accommodations necessary to practice the Long House religion. In the past, inmates claimed they were members of the Long House religion and requested to be transferred to Auburn Correctional Facility not because of their alleged religious beliefs, but because of gang membership.

43. Similarly, at Adirondack Correctional Facility, several inmates claimed they were members of a new religion called the Moorish Science Temple religion. The inmates then used the religious meetings for prohibited gang meetings.

44. Limiting religious groups to those with a body of dogma, some verifiable tradition outside the prison, and an outside religious leader helps prevent religious meetings from being used as gang meetings, thus reducing the risk of violence within the correctional facilities. If any inmate or group of inmates were allowed to gather as a group simply by claiming they had a religious need, inmates could easily hold gang meetings.

45. In sum, due to the foregoing concerns, DOCS assumes each inmate's individualized beliefs are sincere and then accommodates individuals who want to practice a group religion in their own unique way, or who claim to practice a religion that has no body of dogma and/or outside religious leader and tradition. DOCS does this through a uniform set of guidelines that enables all inmates to receive religious counseling and to satisfy many aspects of their religious needs.

WHEREFORE, your affiant requests that defendants' motion for summary judgment dismissing the complaint and action be granted in its entirety.

____

JOHN LOMANE

Sworn to before me

____

Notary Public

Is Sand likely to win on his claim that DOCS violated his religious rights under RLUIPA by not providing another Rabbi or allowing him to conduct religious services himself? In answering this question, assume that you are representing DOCS and consider the following:

1. Did DOCS violate Sand's rights under RLUIPA by allowing the Rabbi to determine that he was not a bona fide member of the Jewish religion and that he could no longer attend Jewish services at Clinton Correctional Facility?
2. Does DOCS Directive 4202 substantially burden Sand's religious exercise by preventing him from conducting his own services when "an employee chaplain or outside religious volunteer of his particular faith is available to serve in a leadership capacity."
3. Does DOCS have a compelling interest in having a uniform policy regarding an inmate's unique exercise of an established religion?
4. If your answer to 3 is yes, is DOCS' policy the least restrictive means of furthering that compelling interest?
5. What additional facts, if any, would you add to the Lomane affidavit to make DOCS' position stronger?

After answering the questions above, determine the best arguments for Sand by considering questions 1 through 4 above.

Law Practice Simulation # 6

In 2015, the United States Supreme Court decided *Holt v. Hobbs*, a case that addresses several of the major issues covered in this chapter. In that case, inmate Gregory Houston Holt, also known as Abdul Maalik Muhammad, challenged the Arkansas Department of Correction policy that prohibited him from growing a beard. Holt claimed that his fundamentalist Muslim religion required that he let his beard grow, but as a compromise, he proposed limiting the length of his beard to half an inch. The prison refused to allow him to grow a beard of any length.

Excerpts from the oral arguments in the U.S. Supreme Court are included below. When you read the oral arguments, determine whether you would answer the Justices' questions in the same way and if not, how your answers would differ. Then read the Supreme Court's decision and focus on how the Court responded to the parties' answers.

When reading the oral argument, consider specifically how the parties responded to questions on the following issues. Were their answers consistent with the reasoning used in other court decisions contained in this chapter?

1. In Law Practice Simulation # 1, you were asked to determine how to incorporate deference to prison officials into RLUIPA's strict scrutiny standard of review. What standard does each of the parties propose with respect to the level of deference that should be shown to prison officials under RLUIPA? Do the parties clearly state the standard to be applied?
2. Holt's attorney argues that other prisons successfully use a less restrictive policy regarding beard length and that the prison where Holt is incarcerated also has a less restrictive beard policy with respect to some other inmates at the same prison. What facts does Holt's attorney use to support his argument? How does the attorney for the Arkansas Department of Correction respond? Are Arkansas's arguments convincing?
3. Does Holt's attorney argue that other specific alternative policies must be considered by the Arkansas Department of Correction before it can conclude that its policy is the least restrictive alternative?
4. To what extent would a ruling in Holt's favor apply to other prison grooming policies that infringe on inmates' religious beliefs, such as how long prisoners can wear their hair?
5. Would the Arkansas Department of Correction's argument have been more convincing if the attorney abandoned his weaker justification for the prison policy and stuck to his stronger argument? Why or why not?

IN THE SUPREME COURT OF THE UNITED STATES

---x

GREGORY HOUSTON HOLT,

AKA ABDUL MAALIK MUHAMMAD,

Petitioner **No. 13-6827**

v.

RAY HOBBS, DIRECTOR, ARKANSAS

DEPARTMENT OF CORRECTION, ET AL.

Respondents.

---x

Washington, D.C.

Tuesday, October 7, 2014

The above-entitled matter came on for oral argument before the Supreme Court of the United States at 10:04 a.m.[127]

127. This is an excerpt of the official transcript of the oral argument in *Holt v. Hobbs* before the United States Supreme Court. For educational purposes, parts of the transcript have been clarified and parts have been omitted.

CHIEF JUSTICE ROBERTS: We'll hear argument first this morning in Case 13-6827, Holt verses Hobbs. Mr. Laycock.

ORAL ARGUMENT OF DOUGLAS LAYCOCK, ESQ. on behalf of Petitioner.

MR. LAYCOCK: Mr. Chief Justice, and may it please the Court:

40 other prison systems permit beards without a length limit, yet Arkansas prohibits even half an inch. And in their brief, they reject every means that courts have devised to evaluate their testimony.

So what they really seek is absolute deference to anything [prison officials] say just because they say it. And that would be to repeal [RLUIPA] de facto.

There may be deference to prison officials, but there must be concrete limits to that deference.

JUSTICE GINSBURG: If this prisoner wanted to have a full beard, would RLUIPA require that the prison administration allow him to do that?

MR. LAYCOCK: Well, some courts have said yes. There's very little in this record about full beards and whether they're safe or whether they're dangerous, but the 40 States that permit them suggest that the State would have a difficult burden of proof. But that question is not presented here.

JUSTICE SCALIA: Mr. Laycock, the problem I have with—with your client's claim of—religious requirement is the religious requirement is to grow a full beard, isn't it? Now, let's assume in the religion that requires polygamy.

I mean, could—could I say to the prison, well, you know, okay, I won't have three wives; just let me have two wives. I mean, you're still violating your religion, it seems to me, if he allows his beard to be clipped to one—one inch, isn't he?

MR. LAYCOCK: Well, the religious teaching is a full beard. He testified that religiously half an inch is better than nothing, and he explained that in terms of Hadith that he referenced.

He's in a very difficult situation. I don't think he should be penalized for being reasonable here. He offered an extremely conservative compromise to the prison—

JUSTICE SCALIA: Well, religious beliefs aren't reasonable. I mean, religious beliefs are categorical. You know, it's God tells you. It's not a matter of being reasonable. God be reasonable? He's supposed to have a full beard.

JUSTICE KENNEDY:	Do you—do you think RLUIPA displaces Turner as the right standard?
MR. LAYCOCK:	It was clearly intended to replace Turner. It textually replaces Turner.
JUSTICE KENNEDY:	And what is the test insofar as you're concerned?
MR. LAYCOCK:	The test is compelling interests and least restrictive means and deference must be administered in the context of that standard, not instead of that standard. So, if it's a close case on compelling interest, they may well get deference. If they give a reasoned and well-considered and informed explanation, they deserve more deference. More deference would be due. Cutter says some—Cutter says they get due deference, but Cutter had no occasion to decide how much deference is due or—or how that—how that should be administered. The textual standard is clearly compelling interest and least restrictive means.
JUSTICE GINSBURG:	... What about a ¼ inch rule? Because that's what they allowed for people who have dermatological problems.
MR. LAYCOCK:	They allow—they allow a quarter inch for medical beards. They don't allow even a quarter inch for religious beards. But the quarter inch, I think, for medical beards, I think, fatally undermines their claim that they can't administer a length limit. And it—and it somewhat undermines all their other claims about—about a ½-inch beard ... [t]he medical exception undermines all the alleged reasons for not allowing a religious exception.
JUSTICE GINSBURG:	There are—there are some religious practices—I think that the Sikh practice of not cutting hair ranks as a religious practice. So not cutting hair and wearing a turban, consistent with what you say is the standard, could a prison say, we won't allow that because it is too easy to hide contraband?
MR. LAYCOCK:	Yeah, that may be. I don't know what the evidence would show about Sikh hair wrapped in a—in a turban. But that's clearly a much more serious issue than—than what's presented in this case. You know, Sikh hair wrapped in a turban may well be different, but we don't

have any evidence about in this case. We don't really have a way to know on the record in this case.

ORAL ARGUMENT OF ANTHONY A. YANG, ESQ., Assistant to the Solicitor General, Department of Justice, Washington, D.C.; on behalf of United States, as amicus curiae, supporting Petitioner.

JUSTICE GINSBURG: So they would—all those [prison policies] that we approved, correspondence limitations, all those would have to be looked at anew under the RLUIPA standard.

MR. YANG: I think that's right, because if you were to go back to pre-RLUIPA case law, no one would doubt that a State could, in fact, prohibit a ½-inch beard under the prior constitutional standards. But Congress has set a higher bar and it imposes upon States the obligation to come forward to explain and justify it. Now—

CHIEF JUSTICE ROBERTS: Where—where are you on the full beard?

MR. YANG: On the full beard, I think there might well be a difference. But again, RLUIPA depends on a showing in litigation by the State that the means selected is the least restrictive means. A State may well be able to show that a full beard would run real risks that are just not present in the ½-inch beard that we have here.

CHIEF JUSTICE ROBERTS: Well, assuming that's the case, assuming they have some evidence of concealment or whatever in—in a full beard, what do we do? Just litigate a dozen cases till we settle on one and three quarters inches, or what?

MR. YANG: Well, I think—

CHIEF JUSTICE ROBERTS: What I'm doing, it's the same question I asked your friend—

MR. YANG: Yes. There's going to be a—

CHIEF JUSTICE ROBERTS: —which is what's the legal principle? And if there is no direct legal principle, then isn't it a situation in which you would employ deference to the administrative judgment?

MR. YANG: I think that's exactly right, that there is going to be a ... range of reasonableness that courts will find appropriate to defer to predictive judgments by expert officials in various contexts. Now—

JUSTICE SCALIA: Well, wait a minute.... We're talking here about a compelling State interest. Bear in mind I would not have enacted this statute, but there it is. It says there has to be a compelling State interest. And you're—you're asking, well, let's balance things; let's be reasonable. Compelling State interest is not a reasonableness test at all.

MR. YANG: It's not me, Your Honor. I think it's what the Court actually recognized in Cutter. The Court, and I'll quote, said that "The Act needs to be applied in an appropriately balanced way, with particular sensitivity to security concerns, and that accommodation must be measured so that it does not override other significant interests."

ORAL ARGUMENT OF DAVID A. CURRAN, ESQ. on behalf of the Respondents.

JUSTICE SCALIA: .... What prevents you from taking a photograph before he grows the ½-inch beard, which can then be distributed to police departments if he escapes?

MR. CURRAN: You know, I agree Your Honor. I mean, there—there are scenarios—

JUSTICE SCALIA: This is not an evidentiary matter at all.

MR. CURRAN: The—the point of identification within the prison, though, is an evidentiary matter on this record, and let me get to that, because it's very important to understand this in our prison's unique environment. Morton Lay[128] testified that shaving a beard can enable an inmate to get into an area where he's not supposed to be in—that's at Joint Appendix page 104—and that a beard can enable an inmate to deviate from an inmate's appearance on an ID badge. That's at Joint Appendix 100. And, of course, a beard is one of the quickest and easiest ways to change one's appearance. That's on page 97 of the Joint Appendix.

And, of course, the grooming policy itself speaks in terms of maintaining the standard appearance throughout the period of incarceration, minimizing opportunities for disguise. And let me explain a minute why this matters in our prison's unique environment and why we're different, because it's a very important point here.

The testimony on the record on page 101 of the Joint Appendix was that we have a very different situation with barracks housing and inmates going outside the

128. Gaylon Lay is a defendant and Warden of the Cummins Unit of the Arkansas Department of Correction, where Holt was incarcerated.

fence in large groups of 30 to 60 per barracks unit every day. It's a very high-traffic, maximum security facility where they come out of a large barracks holding 30 or 60 inmates, go out, and then come back.

And there's a lot of traffic there, and in that environment rapid and accurate identification of the inmate by his face, his—his ID badge and the like, but also general familiarity with the inmate and who the guards are dealing with is very important in that process. And if a mistake is made, an inmate could get into the barracks where he is not supposed to be in and an assault could occur. And [the inmates are assigned to barracks in order to separate] enemies and the like. And that is very serious in our environment. It was made on the record, and it differentiates Arkansas from every State mentioned by the Petitioner in the United States.

Chief Justice Roberts: But you have no example of that ever happening.

Mr. Curran: I have no example of a—well, let me say this. In our brief, on footnote 13 and on page 26 of the 18 States amicus brief, there are examples. There are no record—there are no record examples here.

Justice Ginsburg: What about the argument that it's—never mind the least restrictive means, you have no comparable rule about hair on one's head, where it seems more could be hidden than in the beard, where [ ] something [is hidden] in a beard and it might drop out.

Mr. Curran: Yes, Justice Ginsburg. The material difference there [in] our professional judgment is the disguise-related component of a beard and shaving that beard is more profound than one on the head. So your point speaks to one of contraband and I agree as a matter of common sense and logic there is a length and gravity component to a head that's different than a beard, for sure. But the risk is still there [all] the same. I mean, there is an interest in regulating the contraband element, but the head hair doesn't [present] the same disguise-related problem as a beard.

Justice Alito: Why is that? Why is that so? Are you saying that somebody with or without a ½-inch beard—that's a bigger difference than somebody who has longish hair versus the same person with a shaved head?

Mr. Curran:	In our professional judgment, it is, yes, that's correct. Because you're looking at the essential features of a person's face, their jawline, their chin and the like, and that's the means by which we identify each other. And so that is a significant difference in our view. And really the head-hair policy complements the facial identification policy because it's not allowed to get to a length that could obscure the [face] and that's the rationale for that.
Justice Kagan:	Mr. Laycock characterizes your position as being essentially all deference all the time. So I'll give you an opportunity to say when would deference be inappropriate?
Mr. Curran:	Deference would be inappropriate when the explanation offered on the witness stand in the record of compelling interest and the least restrictive means is—neither comports with logic or common sense.
Justice Scalia:	Mr. Curran, ... I—I thought earlier that you had pretty much abandoned the concealment justification for the policy. Do you—do you still—and were relying upon the identification justification?
Mr. Curran:	No. We think each justification stands on its own weight and we're—
Justice Scalia:	You think something can be concealed within a ½-inch beard?
Mr. Curran:	I think that on this record that something as small as a SIM card, which the Court found compelling, could. I do think that the identification within the prison is more weighty here.
Justice Alito:	As far as concealment is concerned, what—what is the difference between a ½-inch beard and hair on the head that's much longer?
Mr. Curran:	Well, the testimony on the record was that your common sense view that longer hair is a better way to conceal contraband, I think, is a right one. The question really is: Is a beard an unlikely place? Well, the testimony here is not only can something fit in—in a beard, but correctional officers very likely will be somewhat reluctant to do a full search of the beard like they would with, say, head hair.
Justice Breyer:	I take it there's no example, not a single example in any State, that allows beard policies where somebody did hide something in his beard.

MR. CURRAN:	I think that's mostly right, Your Honor. I think there's an affidavit—
JUSTICE BREYER:	So we have no example.
MR. CURRAN:	There is no example.
JUSTICE ALITO:	Well, as far as searching a beard is concerned, why can't the prison just give the inmate a comb, you could develop whatever kind of comb you want, and say comb your beard, and if there's anything in there, if there's a SIM card in there or a revolver or anything else you think—
(Laughter.)	
JUSTICE ALITO:	—can be hidden in a ½-inch beard, a tiny revolver, it'll fall out.
MR. CURRAN:	You know, I suppose that's a possible alternative. I think the concern there is there's no perfect way of searching and—and there's a lot of area there and you're going to have to really monitor to make sure they get all the spots. But—
JUSTICE ALITO:	Do you really think that would be difficult, to say here's a comb, comb your beard?
MR. CURRAN:	I don't think it would be that difficult. I mean, I'm not in the prison environment. It really wasn't raised on this record. My clients might think that it is, but based on the information I have, I would agree that sounds like that would be something that could be done....

REBUTTAL BY DOUGLAS LAYCOCK, ESQ. on behalf of Petitioner.

JUSTICE KAGAN:	You made a statement..., Mr. Laycock, about how to think about deference in the context of this statute and it's something that still troubles me, so I'm going to ask you to expand on that. To say—it just seems like a contradiction in terms, so I want to understand how it's not a contradiction in terms.
MR. LAYCOCK:	Well, it—there's obviously some tension here, but the legislative history says due deference. The Cutter opinion quotes that legislative history and says due deference to expertise. It doesn't say how much deference is due. That's the question to be decided here. You know, we think the more informed and considered and well-explained [the prison officials' decisions], the

> more deference [they] naturally deserve[ ], the more deference is due. But they have to take some account of the prisoner's religious needs. They have to take some account of solutions that have been found to work in other States.
>
> If it's something so dangerous no one would ever try it ... then of course you wouldn't expect examples. But here 43 States have tried [allowing prisoners to have beards], Arkansas tried it for years throughout—in a situation like that, where there ought to be plenty of examples if there's a problem, they ought to have to produce some of those examples.
>
> So the degree of deference [a decision] is due depends on the quality of their explanation, the quality of their consideration of the issue, and here there's no indication they ever considered the religious needs of the prisoners in the adoption of this rule, or if they ever took a second look at it after RLUIPA was adopted. And the testimony is very conclusory, devoid of examples, devoid of attention to other jurisdictions.
>
> The level of deference cannot be so great as to negate the statutory standard. You have to administer deference within that standard, not substitute deference for the standard, and the statutory standard is still compelling interest and least restrictive means.

Questions to guide reading of *Holt v. Hobbs*

1. What level of deference should be given to prison officials under RLUIPA? Did the Court use the parties' answers during oral argument to determine the level of deference? What rule for determining the level of deference is set out in Justice Sotomayor's concurring opinion? Does the rule clarify the majority's decision? Would the rule set out in the concurring opinion be easy to apply?
2. What weight does the Court give to the fact that Muslim inmates could practice some aspects of their religion at the prison? What is the Court's reasoning with respect to the alternate means of practicing religion argument?
3. Does the Court find the fact that other prisons have a less restrictive beard policy relevant in determining whether the Arkansas Department of Correction's policy is the least restrictive alternative? Does the Court find the fact that a less restrictive beard policy was applied to other prisoners in the same prison relevant in determining whether the Arkansas Department of

Correction's policy is the least restrictive alternative? Explain your answers using the language in the Court's decision.

4. Does a state prison system have to consider other specific alternative policies before it can conclude that the policy it has chosen is the least restrictive alternative? Does the prison system have to consider alternatives if the inmate plaintiff does not suggest any? What language in the Court's decision and in the concurring opinion did you rely on to reach your answer?
5. Does the Supreme Court find that a court must consider Holt as an individual in deciding that there are no less restrictive measures that would further its compelling interest in prohibiting inmates from growing beards or can the prison system have a well-justified uniform policy? Would considering each inmate's religious needs on a case-by-case basis lead to equal protection and security concerns?
6. Does the Supreme Court suggest how the Arkansas Department of Correction could create a rule that would withstand review under RLUIPA while still restricting the inmates' beard length?

Supreme Court of the United States Gregory Houston Holt, AKA Abdul Maalik Muhammad, Petitioner v. Ray Hobbs, Director, Arkansas Department of Correction, et al.

On Writ of Certiorari to the United States Court of Appeals for the Eighth Circuit
January 20, 2015

JUSTICE ALITO delivered the opinion of the Court.

Petitioner Gregory Holt, also known as Abdul Maalik Muhammad, is an Arkansas inmate and a devout Muslim who wishes to grow a ½-inch beard in accordance with his religious beliefs. Petitioner's objection to shaving his beard clashes with the Arkansas Department of Correction's grooming policy, which prohibits inmates from growing beards unless they have a particular dermatological condition. We hold that the Department's policy, as applied in this case, violates the Religious Land Use and Institutionalized Persons Act of 2000 (RLUIPA), 114 Stat.803, 42 U.S.C. § 2000cc *et seq.*, which prohibits a state or local government from taking any action that substantially burdens the religious exercise of an institutionalized person unless the government demonstrates that the action constitutes the least restrictive means of furthering a compelling governmental interest.

We conclude in this case that the Department's policy substantially burdens petitioner's religious exercise.

Although we do not question the importance of the Department's interests in stopping the flow of contraband and facilitating prisoner identification, we do doubt whether the prohibition against petitioner's beard furthers its compelling interest about contraband. And we conclude that the Department has failed to show that its policy is the least restrictive means of furthering its compelling interests. We thus reverse the decision of the United States Court of Appeals for the Eighth Circuit.

... B

Petitioner, as noted, is in the custody of the Arkansas Department of Correction and he objects on religious grounds to the Department's grooming policy, which provides that "[n]o inmates will be permitted to wear facial hair other than a neatly trimmed mustache that does not extend beyond the corner of the mouth or over the lip." App. to Brief for Petitioner 11a. The policy makes no exception for inmates who object on religious grounds, but it does contain an exemption for prisoners with medical needs: "Medical staff may prescribe that inmates with a diagnosed dermatological problem may wear facial hair no longer than one quarter of an inch." *Ibid.* The policy provides that "[f]ailure to abide by [the Department's] grooming standards is grounds for disciplinary action." *Id.*, at 12a. Petitioner sought permission to grow a beard and, although he believes that his faith requires him not to trim his beard at all, he proposed a "compromise" under which he would grow only a ½-inch beard. App. 164. Prison officials denied his request, and the warden told him: "[Y]ou will abide by [Arkansas Department of Correction] policies and if you choose to disobey, you can suffer the consequences." No. 5:11-cv-00164 (ED Ark., July 21,2011), Doc. 13, p. 6 (Letter from Gaylon Lay to Gregory Holt (July 19, 2011)).

Petitioner filed a *pro se* complaint in Federal District Court challenging the grooming policy under RLUIPA. We refer to the respondent prison officials collectively as the Department. In October 2011, the District Court granted petitioner a preliminary injunction and remanded to a Magistrate Judge for an evidentiary hearing. At the hearing, the Department called two witnesses. Both expressed the belief that inmates could hide contraband in even a ½-inch beard, but neither pointed to any instances in which this had been done in Arkansas or elsewhere. Both witnesses also acknowledged that inmates could hide items in many other places, such as in the hair on their heads or their clothing. In addition, one of the witnesses—Gaylon Lay, the warden of petitioner's prison—testified that a prisoner who escaped could change his appearance by shaving his beard, and that a prisoner could shave his beard to disguise himself and enter a restricted area of the prison. Neither witness, however, was able to explain why these problems could not be addressed by taking a photograph of an inmate without a beard, a practice followed in other prison systems. Lay voiced concern that the Department would be unable to monitor the length of a prisoner's beard to ensure that it did not exceed one-half inch, but he acknowledged that the Department kept track of the length of the beards of those inmates who are allowed to wear a ¼-inch beard for medical reasons.

As a result of the preliminary injunction, petitioner had a short beard at the time of the hearing, and the Magistrate Judge commented: "I look at your particular circumstance and I say, you know, it's almost preposterous to think that you could hide contraband in your beard." App. 155. Nevertheless, the Magistrate Judge recommended that the preliminary injunction be vacated and that petitioner's complaint be dismissed for failure to state a claim on which relief can be granted. The Magistrate Judge emphasized that "the prison officials are entitled to deference," *id.*, at 168, and that the grooming policy allowed petitioner to exercise his religion in other ways, such as by praying on a prayer rug, maintaining the diet required by his faith, and observing religious holidays.

The District Court adopted the Magistrate Judge's recommendation in full, and the Court of Appeals for the Eighth Circuit affirmed in a brief *per curiam* opinion, holding that the Department had satisfied its burden of showing that the grooming policy was the least restrictive means of furthering its compelling security interests. 509 Fed. Appx. 561 (2013)....

We entered an injunction pending resolution of petitioner's petition for writ of certiorari, 571 U.S. ___ (2013), and we then granted certiorari, 571 U.S. ___ (2014).

II

Under RLUIPA, petitioner bore the initial burden of proving that the Department's grooming policy implicates his religious exercise. RLUIPA protects "any exercise of religion, whether or not compelled by, or central to, a system of religious belief," § 2000cc-5(7)(A), but, of course, a prisoner's request for an accommodation must be sincerely based on a religious belief and not some other motivation, see *Hobby Lobby*, 573 U.S., at ___, n. 28 [134 S. Ct. 2751, 2773, n. 28]. Here, the religious exercise at issue is the growing of a beard, which petitioner believes is a dictate of his religious faith, and the Department does not dispute the sincerity of petitioner's belief.

In addition to showing that the relevant exercise of religion is grounded in a sincerely held religious belief, petitioner also bore the burden of proving that the Department's grooming policy substantially burdened that exercise of religion. Petitioner easily satisfied that obligation. The Department's grooming policy requires petitioner to shave his beard and thus to "engage in conduct that seriously violates [his] religious beliefs." *Id.*, at ___ [134 S. Ct. at 2775]. If petitioner contravenes that policy and grows his beard, he will face serious disciplinary action. Because the grooming policy puts petitioner to this choice, it substantially burdens his religious exercise. Indeed, the Department does not argue otherwise.

The District Court reached the opposite conclusion, but its reasoning (adopted from the recommendation of the Magistrate Judge) misunderstood the analysis that RLUIPA demands. First, the District Court erred by concluding that the grooming policy did not substantially burden petitioner's religious exercise because "he had been provided a prayer rug and a list of distributors of Islamic material, he was allowed to correspond with a religious advisor, and was allowed to maintain the required diet and observe religious holidays." App. 177. In taking this approach, the District Court improperly imported a strand of reasoning from cases involving prisoners' First Amendment rights. See, *e.g.*, *O'Lone* v. *Estate of Shabazz*, 482 U.S. 342, 351–352 (1987); see also *Turner* v. *Safley*, 482 U.S. 78, 90 (1987). Under those cases, the availability of alternative means of practicing religion is a relevant consideration, but RLUIPA provides greater protection. RLUIPA's "substantial burden" inquiry asks whether the government has substantially burdened religious exercise (here, the growing of a ½-inch beard), not whether the RLUIPA claimant is able to engage in other forms of religious exercise.

Second, the District Court committed a similar error in suggesting that the burden on petitioner's religious exercise was slight because, according to petitioner's testimony, his religion would "credit" him for attempting to follow his religious beliefs, even if that attempt proved to be unsuccessful. RLUIPA, however, applies to an exercise of religion regardless of whether it is "compelled." § 2000cc-5(7)(A).

Finally, the District Court went astray when it relied on petitioner's testimony that not all Muslims believe that men must grow beards. Petitioner's belief is by no means idiosyncratic. See Brief for Islamic Law Scholars as *Amici Curiae* 2 ("hadith requiring beards ... are widely followed by observant Muslims across the various schools of Islam"). But even if it were, the protection of RLUIPA, no less than the guarantee of the Free Exercise Clause, is "not limited to beliefs which are shared by all of the members of a religious sect." *Thomas* v. *Review Bd. of Indiana Employment Security Div.*, 450 U.S. 707, 715–716 (1981).

III

Since petitioner met his burden of showing that the Department's grooming policy substantially burdened his exercise of religion, the burden shifted to the Department to show that its refusal to allow petitioner to grow a ½-inch beard "(1) [was] in furtherance of a compelling governmental interest; and (2) [was] the least restrictive means of furthering that compelling governmental interest." § 2000cc-1(a).

The Department argues that its grooming policy represents the least restrictive means of furthering a " 'broadly formulated interes[t],' " see *Hobby Lobby*, *supra*, at ___ [134 S. Ct. at 2779] (quoting *O Centro*, 546 U.S., at 431), namely, the Department's compelling interest in prison safety and security. But RLUIPA, like RFRA, contemplates a " 'more focused' " inquiry and " 'requires the Government to demonstrate that the compelling interest test is satisfied through application of the challenged law "to the person"—the particular claimant whose sincere exercise of religion is being substantially burdened.' " *Hobby Lobby*, 573 U.S., at ___ [134 S. Ct. at 2779] (quoting *O Centro*, *supra*, at 430–431 (quoting § 2000bb-1(b))). RLUIPA requires us to " 'scrutiniz[e] the asserted harm of granting specific exemptions to particular religious claimants' " and "to look to the marginal interest in enforcing" the challenged government action in that particular context. *Hobby Lobby*, *supra*, at ___ [134 S. Ct. at 2779](quoting *O Centro*, *supra*, at 431; alteration in original). In this case, that means the enforcement of the Department's policy to prevent petitioner from growing a ½-inch beard.

The Department contends that enforcing this prohibition is the least restrictive means of furthering prison safety and security in two specific ways.

A

The Department first claims that the no-beard policy prevents prisoners from hiding contraband. The Department worries that prisoners may use their beards to conceal all manner of prohibited items, including razors, needles, drugs, and cellular phone subscriber identity module (SIM) cards.

We readily agree that the Department has a compelling interest in staunching the flow of contraband into and within its facilities, but the argument that this interest would be seriously compromised by allowing an inmate to grow a ½-inch beard is hard to take seriously. As noted, the Magistrate Judge observed that it was "almost preposterous to think that [petitioner] could hide contraband" in the short beard he had grown at the time of the evidentiary hearing. App. 155. An item of contraband would have to be very small indeed to be concealed by a ½-inch beard, and a prisoner seeking to hide an item in such a short beard would have to find a way to prevent the item from falling out. Since the Department does not demand that inmates have shaved heads or short crew cuts, it is hard to see why an inmate would seek to hide contraband in a ½-inch beard rather than in the longer hair on his head.

Although the Magistrate Judge dismissed the possibility that contraband could be hidden in a short beard, the Magistrate Judge, the District Court, and the Court of Appeals all thought that they were bound to defer to the Department's assertion that allowing petitioner to grow such a beard would undermine its interest in suppressing contraband. RLUIPA, however, does not permit such unquestioning deference. RLUIPA, like RFRA, "makes clear that it is the obligation of the courts to consider whether exceptions are required under the test set forth by Congress." *O Centro*, *supra*, at 434. That test requires the Department not merely to explain why it denied the exemption but to prove that denying the exemption is the least restrictive means of furthering a compelling governmental interest. Prison officials are experts in running prisons and evaluating the likely effects of altering prison rules, and courts should respect that expertise. But that respect does not justify the abdication of the responsibility, conferred by Congress, to apply RLUIPA's rigorous standard. And without a degree of deference that is tantamount to unquestioning acceptance, it is hard to swallow the argument that denying petitioner a ½-inch beard actually furthers the Department's interest in rooting out contraband.

Even if the Department could make that showing, its contraband argument would still fail because the Department cannot show that forbidding very short beards is the least restrictive means of preventing the concealment of contraband. "The least-restrictive-means standard is exceptionally demanding," and it requires the government to "sho[w] that it lacks other means of achieving its desired goal without imposing a substantial burden on the exercise of religion by the objecting part[y]." *Hobby Lobby*, *supra*, at ___ [134 S. Ct. at 2780]. "[I]f a less restrictive means is available for the Government to achieve its goals, the Government must use it." *United States* v. *Playboy Entertainment Group, Inc.*, 529 U.S. 803, 815 (2000).

The Department failed to establish that it could not satisfy its security concerns by simply searching petitioner's beard. The Department already searches prisoners' hair and clothing, and it presumably examines the ¼-inch beards of inmates with dermatological conditions. It has offered no sound reason why hair, clothing, and ¼-inch beards can be searched but ½-inch beards cannot. The Department suggests that requiring guards to search a prisoner's beard would pose a risk to the physical safety of a guard if a razor or needle was concealed in the beard. But that is no less true for searches of hair, clothing, and ¼-inch beards. And the Department has failed to prove that it could not adopt the less restrictive alternative of having the prisoner run a comb through his beard. For all these reasons, the Department's interest in eliminating contraband cannot sustain its refusal to allow petitioner to grow a ½-inch beard.

B

The Department contends that its grooming policy is necessary to further an additional compelling interest, *i.e.*, preventing prisoners from disguising their identities. The Department tells us that the no-beard policy allows security officers to identify prisoners quickly and accurately. It claims that bearded inmates could shave their beards and change their appearance in order to enter restricted areas within the prison, to escape, and to evade apprehension after escaping.

We agree that prisons have a compelling interest in the quick and reliable identification of prisoners, and we acknowledge that any alteration in a prisoner's appearance, such as by shaving a beard, might, in the absence of effective countermeasures, have at least some effect on the ability of guards or others to make a quick identification. But even if we assume for present purposes that the Department's grooming policy sufficiently furthers its interest in the identification of prisoners, that policy still violates RLUIPA as applied in the circumstances present here. The Department contends that a prisoner who has a beard when he is photographed for identification purposes might confuse guards by shaving his beard. But as petitioner has argued, the Department could largely solve this problem by requiring that all inmates be photographed without beards when first admitted to the facility and, if necessary, periodically thereafter. Once that is done, an inmate like petitioner could be allowed to grow a short beard and could be photographed again when the beard reached the ½-inch limit. Prison guards would then have a bearded and clean-shaven photo to use in making identifications. In fact, the Department (like many other States, see Brief for Petitioner 39) already has a policy of photographing a prisoner both when he enters an institution and when his "appearance changes at any time during [his] incarceration." Arkansas Department of Correction, Inmate Handbook 3–4 (rev. Jan. 2013).

The Department argues that the dual-photo method is inadequate because, even if it might help authorities apprehend a bearded prisoner who escapes and then shaves his beard once outside the prison, this method is unlikely to assist guards when an inmate quickly shaves his beard in order to alter his appearance within the prison. The Department contends that the identification concern is particularly acute at petitioner's prison, where inmates live in barracks and work in fields. Counsel for the Department suggested at oral argument that a prisoner could gain entry to a restricted area by shaving his beard and swapping identification cards with another inmate while out in the fields. Tr. of Oral Arg. 28–30, 39–43.

We are unpersuaded by these arguments for at least two reasons. First, the Department failed to show, in the face of petitioner's evidence, that its prison system is so different from the many institutions that allow facial hair that the dual-photo method cannot be employed at its institutions. Second, the Department failed to establish why the risk that a prisoner will shave a ½-inch beard to disguise himself is so great that ½-inch beards cannot be allowed, even though prisoners are allowed to grow mustaches, head hair, or ¼-inch beards for medical reasons. All of these could also be shaved off at a moment's notice, but the Department apparently does not think that this possibility raises a serious security concern.

C

In addition to its failure to prove that petitioner's proposed alternatives would not sufficiently serve its security interests, the Department has not provided an adequate response to two additional arguments that implicate the RLUIPA analysis.

First, the Department has not adequately demonstrated why its grooming policy is substantially underinclusive in at least two respects. Although the Department denied petitioner's request to grow a ½-inch beard, it permits prisoners with a dermatological condition to grow ¼-inch beards. The Department does this even though both beards pose similar risks. And the Department permits inmates to grow more than a ½-inch of hair on their heads. With respect to hair length, the grooming policy provides only that hair must be worn "above the ear" and "no longer in the back than the middle of the nape of the neck." App. to Brief for Petitioner 11a. Hair on the head is a more plausible place to hide contraband than a ½-inch beard—and the same is true of an inmate's clothing and shoes. Nevertheless, the Department does not require inmates to go about bald, barefoot, or naked. Although the Department's proclaimed objectives are to stop the flow of contraband and to facilitate prisoner identification, "[t]he proffered objectives are not pursued with respect to analogous nonreligious conduct," which suggests that "those interests could be achieved by narrower ordinances that burdened religion to a far lesser degree." *Church of Lukumi Babalu Aye, Inc.* v. *Hialeah*, 508 U.S. 520, 546 (1993).

In an attempt to demonstrate why its grooming policy is underinclusive in these respects, the Department emphasizes that petitioner's ½-inch beard is longer than the ¼-inch beard allowed for medical reasons. But the Department has failed to establish (and the District Court did not find) that a ¼-inch difference in beard length poses a meaningful increase in security risk. The Department also asserts that few inmates require beards for medical reasons while many may request beards for religious reasons. But the Department has not argued that denying petitioner an exemption is necessary to further a compelling interest in cost control or program administration. At bottom, this argument is but another formulation of the "classic rejoinder of bureaucrats throughout history: If I make an exception for you, I'll have to make one for everybody, so no exceptions." *O Centro*, 546 U.S., at 436. We have rejected a similar argument in analogous contexts, see *ibid.*; *Sherbert*, 374 U.S., at 407, and we reject it again today.

Second, the Department failed to show, in the face of petitioner's evidence, why the vast majority of States and the Federal Government permit inmates to grow ½-inch beards, either for any reason or for religious reasons, but it cannot. See Brief for Petitioner 24–25; Brief for United States as *Amicus Curiae* 28–29. "While not necessarily controlling, the policies followed at other well-run institutions would be relevant to a determination of the need for a particular type of restriction." *Procunier* v. *Martinez*, 416 U.S. 396, 414, n. 14 (1974). That so many other prisons allow inmates to grow beards while ensuring prison safety and security suggests that the Department could satisfy its security concerns through a means less restrictive than denying petitioner the exemption he seeks.

We do not suggest that RLUIPA requires a prison to grant a particular religious exemption as soon as a few other jurisdictions do so. But when so many prisons offer an accommodation, a prison must, at a minimum, offer persuasive reasons why it believes that it must take a different course, and the Department failed to make that showing here. Despite this, the courts below deferred to these prison officials' mere say-so that they could not accommodate petitioner's request. RLUIPA, however, demands much more. Courts must hold prisons to their statutory burden, and they must not "assume a plausible, less restrictive alternative would be ineffective." *Playboy Entertainment*, 529 U.S., at 824.

We emphasize that although RLUIPA provides substantial protection for the religious exercise of institutionalized persons, it also affords prison officials ample ability to maintain security. We highlight three ways in which this is so. First, in applying RLUIPA's statutory standard, courts should not blind themselves to the fact that the analysis is conducted in the prison setting. Second, if an institution suspects that an inmate is using religious activity to cloak illicit conduct, "prison officials may appropriately question whether a prisoner's religiosity, asserted as the basis for a requested accommodation, is authentic." *Cutter* v. *Wilkinson*, 544 U.S. 709, 725, n. 13 (2005). See also *Hobby Lobby*, 573 U.S., at ___, n. 28 [134 S. Ct. at 2773, n. 28]. Third, even if a claimant's religious belief is sincere, an institution might be entitled to withdraw an accommodation if the claimant abuses the exemption in a manner that undermines the prison's compelling interests.

IV

In sum, we hold that the Department's grooming policy violates RLUIPA insofar as it prevents petitioner from growing a ½-inch beard in accordance with his religious beliefs. The judgment of the United States Court of Appeals for the Eighth Circuit is reversed, and the case is remanded for further proceedings consistent with this opinion.

It is so ordered.

JUSTICE SOTOMAYOR, concurring.[129]

I concur in the Court's opinion, which holds that the Department failed to show why the less restrictive alternatives identified by petitioner in the course of this litigation were inadequate to achieve the Department's compelling security-related interests. I write separately to explain my understanding of the applicable legal standard.

---

129. Justice Ginsburg's concurring opinion has been omitted.

Nothing in the Court's opinion calls into question our prior holding in *Cutter* v. *Wilkinson* that "[c]ontext matters" in the application of the Religious Land Use and Institutionalized Persons Act of 2000 (RLUIPA), 114 Stat. 803, 42 U.S.C. § 2000cc *et seq.* 544 U.S. 709, 723 (2005) (internal quotation marks omitted). In the dangerous prison environment, "regulations and procedures" are needed to "maintain good order, security and discipline, consistent with consideration of costs and limited resources." *Ibid.* Of course, that is not to say that cost alone is an absolute defense to an otherwise meritorious RLUIPA claim. See § 2000cc-3(c). Thus, we recognized "that prison security is a compelling state interest, and that deference is due to institutional officials' expertise in this area." *Cutter,* 544 U.S., at 725, n. 13.

I do not understand the Court's opinion to preclude deferring to prison officials' reasoning when that deference is due—that is, when prison officials offer a plausible explanation for their chosen policy that is supported by whatever evidence is reasonably available to them. But the deference that must be "extend[ed to] the experience and expertise of prison administrators does not extend so far that prison officials may declare a compelling governmental interest by fiat." *Yellowbear* v. *Lampert,* 741 F. 3d 48, 59 (CA10 2014). Indeed, prison policies " 'grounded on mere speculation' " are exactly the ones that motivated Congress to enact RLUIPA. 106 Cong. Rec. 16699 (2000) (quoting S. Rep. No. 103-111, 10 (1993)).

Here, the Department's failure to demonstrate why the less restrictive policies petitioner identified in the course of the litigation were insufficient to achieve its compelling interests—not the Court's independent judgment concerning the merit of these alternative approaches—is ultimately fatal to the Department's position. The Court is appropriately skeptical of the relationship between the Department's no-beard policy and its alleged compelling interests because the Department offered little more than unsupported assertions in defense of its refusal of petitioner's requested religious accommodation. RLUIPA requires more.

One final point bears emphasis. RLUIPA requires institutions refusing an accommodation to demonstrate that the policy it defends "is the least restrictive means of furthering [the alleged] compelling ... interest[s]." § 2000cc-1(a)(2); see also *Washington* v. *Klem,* 497 F. 3d 272, 284 (CA3 2007) ("[T]he phrase 'least restrictive means' is, by definition, a relative term. It necessarily implies a comparison with other means"); *Couch* v. *Jabe,* 679 F. 3d 197, 203 (CA4 2012) (same). But nothing in the Court's opinion suggests that prison officials must refute every conceivable option to satisfy RLUIPA's least restrictive means requirement. Nor does it intimate that officials must prove that they considered less restrictive alternatives at a particular point in time. Instead, the Court correctly notes that the Department inadequately responded to the less restrictive policies that petitioner brought to the Department's attention during the course of the litigation, including the more permissive policies used by the prisons in New York and California. See, *e.g., United States* v. *Wilgus,* 638 F. 3d 1274, 1289 (CA10 2011) (observing in the analogous context of the Religious Freedom Restoration Act of 1993 that the government need not "do the impossible—refute each and every conceivable alternative regulation scheme" but need only "refute the alternative schemes offered by the challenger").

Because I understand the Court's opinion to be consistent with the foregoing, I join it.

Chapter Fifteen

The Eleventh Amendment

A. Introduction and Chapter Overview

This chapter addresses the Eleventh Amendment, the central limitation in the Constitution on the power of the federal courts to hear lawsuits against states and state officials for violating constitutional and federally created statutory rights. The Amendment, which is only 43 words, states:

> The Judicial power of the United States shall not be construed to extend to any suit in law or equity, commenced or prosecuted against one of the United States by Citizens of another State, or by Citizens or Subjects of any Foreign State.

Although the terms of the Amendment address suits against a state by persons outside of its borders, the Supreme Court has interpreted the Amendment to prevent the federal courts from intruding on state sovereignty and therefore to bar any lawsuits against a state or state agency in federal court, unless the state consents to be sued.

If the Eleventh Amendment deprives the federal courts of judicial authority over lawsuits against a state, how can the federal courts provide remedies for violations of federal civil rights laws by states and state officials? This chapter begins with a historical discussion of the Eleventh Amendment and why it was included in the Constitution. It will then discuss some of the seminal cases affecting the modern-day interpretation of the Eleventh Amendment and conclude with a discussion of some of the most important Eleventh Amendment issues that have arisen in the past two decades.

B. Historical Background

1. The Constitutional Debates

At the time of the Constitutional Convention in 1787, it was well-established that a sovereign, or self-governing state, was immune from suit without its express consent. *See Alden v. Maine*, 527 U.S. 706, 715–16 (1999) ("[T]he doctrine that a sovereign could not be sued without its consent was universal in the States when the Constitution was drafted and ratified.") (citations omitted); *Hans v. Louisiana*, 134 U.S. 1, 16 (1890) ("The suability of a state, without its consent, was a thing unknown to the law."). When the states entered the Union, it was generally understood that their sovereignty remained intact, except insofar as they gave up certain specified authority to the new national government.[1]

However, the principle of sovereign immunity was not included in the Constitution itself. Indeed, the Constitution, as drafted in 1787, provided that the states could be sued under certain circumstances. Article III, Section 2, Clause 1, which addresses the scope of federal judicial power, provides:

> The judicial power shall extend to all Cases, in Law and Equity, arising under this Constitution, the Laws of the United States, and Treaties made, or which shall be made, under their Authority; ... to all Cases affecting Ambassadors, other public Ministers and Consuls; ... to all Cases of admiralty and maritime Jurisdiction; ... to Controversies to which the United States shall be a Party; ... to Controversies between two or more States; ... between a State and Citizens of another State; ... between Citizens of different States; ... between Citizens of the same State claiming Lands under Grants of different States, and between a State, or the Citizens thereof, and foreign States, Citizens or Subjects.

Historical Debate Simulation

The class should be divided into two groups to discuss the merits and disadvantages of maintaining state sovereign immunity. Both groups consist of delegates at the ratification convention in Virginia. Ratification conventions were held by each individual state for the purpose of deciding whether the state should ratify the Constitution. Group 1 supports ratifying the Constitution without an express provision protecting Virginia's sovereign immunity. Group 2 opposes ratification unless such a provision is included in the Constitution.

Group 1: Prepare a list of arguments and proposals (possible provisions) that might persuade your opponents to support the Constitution without an express provision protecting Virginia from suit in federal court by a citizen of Virginia or another state. What if you knew that Virginia's decision to ratify the Constitution was critical to the success of the new nation? (Note that three-fourths [nine out of thirteen] of the states had to ratify the Constitution for it to take effect.)

Group 2: This group is concerned that Virginia's sovereignty will be compromised if a federal court could entertain a lawsuit by a private citizen against it. Discuss the potential disadvantages of allowing the federal courts

---

1. *See* Blatchford v. Native Vill. of Noatak, 501 U.S. 775, 779 (1991) ("we have understood the Eleventh Amendment to stand not so much for what it says, but for the presupposition of our constitutional structure which it confirms: that the States entered the federal system with their sovereignty intact; that the judicial authority in Article III is limited by this sovereignty") (citations omitted).

to have jurisdiction over these lawsuits. Prepare a list of arguments that might persuade your opponents to oppose ratification unless the Constitution is changed to provide explicitly that states are immune from suit. Is there a middle ground that would allow you to support the Constitution without this provision? What questions would you ask to make up your mind?

Questions for both sides to consider

1. Would the newly created federal courts protect Virginia's interests in the same way that the state courts of Virginia would protect her sovereignty? Is there any way to ensure that the federal courts would adequately protect Virginia's sovereignty?
2. Would the newly established federal courts acknowledge Virginia's sovereign immunity from suit given the express language in Article III of the Constitution?
3. Even if Virginia were protected from suit in federal court by a citizen of Virginia or another state, such as North Carolina, would it also be protected from suit by a sister state or by the new national government?
4. If Virginia could be sued in federal court by a citizen of another state, could the federal court enforce a potential money judgment against the State of Virginia? (Note: At the time of the ratification debates, the state governments were very concerned about their economic situations).

At the Virginia Convention, James Madison and John Marshall assured opponents of the Constitution, such as George Mason and Patrick Henry, that Virginia's sovereign immunity was secure despite the language in Article III. Madison stated:

> [The federal courts' jurisdiction] in controversies between a state and citizens of another state is much objected to, and perhaps without reason. It is not in the power of individuals to call any state into court. The only operation it can have, is that, if a state should wish to bring a suit against a citizen, it must be brought before the federal court. This will give satisfaction to individuals, as it will prevent citizens on whom a state may have a claim being dissatisfied with the state courts.

J. Elliot, *The Debates in the Several State Conventions on the Adoption of the Federal Constitution* vol. 3, 533 (2d Ed. 1863).

John Marshall similarly stated:

> With respect to disputes between *a state and the citizens of another state*, its jurisdiction has been decried with unusual vehemence. I hope that no gentleman will think that a state will be called at the bar of the federal court.... It is not rational to suppose that the sovereign power should be dragged

> before a court. The intent is to enable states to recover claims of individuals residing in other states.... But, say they, there will be partiality in it if a state cannot be a defendant—if an individual cannot proceed to obtain judgment against a state, though he may be sued by a State. It is necessary to be so, and cannot be avoided. I see a difficulty in making a state defendant, which does not prevent its being plaintiff.

Id. at 555–56 (emphasis in original).

Alexander Hamilton, one of the authors of the Federalist Papers, was also a firm supporter of sovereign immunity. He wrote:

> It is inherent in the nature of sovereignty not to be amenable to the suit of an individual *without its consent.* This is the general sense, and the general practice of mankind; and the exemption, as one of the attributes of sovereignty, is now enjoyed by the government of every State in the Union. Unless, therefore, there is a surrender of this immunity in the plan of the convention, it will remain with the States.

Federalist Papers, No. 81, at 487–88 (emphasis in original).

A similar debate took place at the ratification conventions in New York and Rhode Island. At both conventions, some delegates supported a constitutional amendment to clarify that the states retained their sovereign immunity from suit. The leaders of those conventions made clear that they understood the Constitution, as written, to preserve the states' immunity from private suits.

J. Elliot, *Debates on the Federal Constitution* vol. 1, 327, 329 (New York), 336 (Rhode Island).

Not everyone agreed with the Madison-Marshall-Hamilton point of view, including some who served on the Committee on Detail, the Committee that added the jurisdictional clause—which became Article III—to the Constitution. James Wilson[2] explained that "[w]hen a citizen has a controversy with another state, there ought to be a tribunal where both parties may stand on a just and equal footing." J. Elliot, *Debates on the Federal Constitution* vol. 2, 491 (1876 ed.).[3]

In the end, the supporters of the Madison-Marshall-Hamilton position carried the day. C. Warren, *The Supreme Court in United States History* vol. 1, 91 (rev. ed. 1973) ("the existence of any such right [of the Federal Judiciary to summon a State as defendant and to adjudicate its rights and liabilities] had been disclaimed by many of the most eminent advocates of the new Federal Government, and it was largely owing to their successful dissipation of the fear of the existence of such Federal power that the Constitution was finally adopted"). New York and Rhode Island expressly included in their statements in support of ratification that they understood that the

---

2. James Wilson is one of the Founding Fathers of the United States and contributed to the drafting of the United States Constitution. He later served as Associate Justice of the Supreme Court of the United States.

3. Quoted in Nevada v. Hall, 440 U.S. 410, 419 n. 17 (1979).

judicial power of the United States would not extend to any suit by a private person against a state.[4]

2. Chisholm v. Georgia, *the First Supreme Court Case to Address Federal Court Jurisdiction under Article III*

The law did not develop in the manner Madison, Marshall, and Hamilton had anticipated. Four years after the Constitution took effect—before the enactment of the Eleventh Amendment—the Supreme Court decided *Chisholm v. Georgia* and resolved that a citizen of one state could sue another state in federal court. *Chisholm* was an action in assumpsit, meaning a lawsuit seeking the recovery of damages by reason of the breach or nonperformance of a contract. The case was filed by a citizen of South Carolina—the executor of a South Carolina estate—to recover money owed to the estate by the State of Georgia.

There were five justices on the Court at the time and each justice wrote a separate opinion. When the votes were tallied, the Court held 4:1 that a state could be sued for damages by a private person. U.S. Attorney General Randolph represented the plaintiff Chisholm. The State of Georgia submitted a written response and declined to argue its case before the Court.

Oral Argument of U.S. Attorney General Randolph

[After quoting from Article III, Section 2 of the Constitution] The judicial power is extended to controversies between a State and citizens of another State. I pass over the word, 'between,' as in no respect indicating who is to be Plaintiff or who Defendant.... Is not a defendant a party as well as a plaintiff? ... What is to be done, if in consequence of a bill of attainder, or an ex post facto law, the estate of a citizen shall be confiscated, and deposited in the treasury of a State? What, if a State should adulterate or coin money below the Congressional standard, emit bills of credit, or enact unconstitutional tenders, for the purpose of extinguishing its own debts? What if a State should impair her own contracts? These evils, and others which might be enumerated like them, cannot be corrected without a suit against the State. It is not denied, that one State may be sued by another; and the reason would seem to be the same, why an individual, who is aggrieved, should sue the State aggrieving.... [The Constitution] derives its origin immediately from the people; and the people individually are, under certain limitations, subject to the legislative, executive, and judicial authorities thereby established. The States are in fact assemblages of these individuals who are liable to process.... The [Judiciary Act of 1789] recognizes the jurisdiction over States. Instead

4. J. Elliot, *Debates on the Federal Constitution* vol. 1, 327, 329 (New York), 336 (Rhode Island).

of using the first expression in the Constitution, to wit, 'controversies, between, etc.' it adopts the second, namely, 'where a State shall be a party.' Thus it makes no distinction between a State as Plaintiff, or as Defendant; but evidently comprehends in the word 'party' a State, as Defendant in one case at least, where a State is opposed to a State.

Note: The Judiciary Act of 1789 was enacted by the First Congress to implement Article III of the Constitution. The Act established the federal courts and prescribed the types of cases the federal courts could entertain.

Questions to guide reading of *Chisholm v. Georgia*

1. Did the *Chisholm* Court agree with Attorney General Randolph that a suit by an individual against a state should be treated the same for purposes of federal jurisdiction as a suit by one state against another? Why or why not?
2. Do you agree with Chief Justice Jay that suability and sovereignty are not incompatible because the Constitution derives from the people? Discuss your position.
3. Do you agree with Chief Justice Jay that the language in Article III contains an implicit exception barring suit against the United States, but not against an individual state? Do you agree with his reasoning in support of that conclusion? Explain your answer.
4. Do you think Justice Iredell's dissent was based solely on the fact that Congress had not yet enacted a law to implement Article III of the Constitution? If Congress had enacted a law allowing states to be sued, do you think Justice Iredell would have upheld this law as within Congress's authority? Why or why not?

Chisholm v. Georgia

2 Dall 419 (1793)

Opinion of Chief Justice John Jay

The question we are now to decide has been accurately stated, viz. Is a State suable by individual citizens of another State?.... In order to ascertain the merits..., let us enquire, 1st. In what sense Georgia is a sovereign State. 2nd. Whether suability is incompatible with such sovereignty. 3rd. Whether the Constitution (to which Georgia is a party) authorizes such an action against her.... [T]he people, in their collective and national capacity, established the present Constitution. It is remarkable that in establishing it, the people exercised their own rights, and their own proper sovereignty, and conscious of the plenitude of it, they declared with becoming dignity, 'We the people of the United States, do ordain and establish this Constitution.' Here we see the people acting as sovereigns of the whole country; and in the language of sovereignty, establishing a Constitution by which it was their will, that the State Governments should be bound, and to which the State Constitutions should be made to conform.... 2nd. The second object of enquiry now presents itself, viz. whether suability is compatible with State sovereignty. Suability, by whom? Not a subject, for in this country there are none; not an inferior, for all the citizens being as to civil rights perfectly equal, there is not, in that respect, one citizen inferior to another. It is agreed, that one free citizen may sue another; the obvious dictates of justice, and the purposes of society demanding it. It is agreed, that one free citizen may sue any number on whom process can be conveniently executed; nay, in certain cases one citizen may sue forty thousand; for where a corporation is sued, all the members of it are actually sued, though not personally, sued. In this city there are forty odd thousand free citizens, all of whom may be collectively sued by any individual citizen. In the State of Delaware, there are fifty odd thousand free citizens, and what reason can be assigned why a free citizen who has demands against them should not prosecute them? Can the difference between forty odd thousand, and fifty odd thousand make any distinction as to right?.... Grant that the Governor of Delaware holds an office of superior rank to the Mayor of Philadelphia, they are both nevertheless the officers of the people; and however more exalted the one may be than the other, yet in the opinion of those who dislike aristocracy, that circumstance cannot be a good reason for impeding the course of justice.... There is at least one strong undeniable fact against this incompatibility, and that is this, any one State in the Union may sue another State, in this Court, that is, all the people of one State may sue all the people of another State. It is plain then, that a State may be sued, and hence it plainly follows, that suability and state sovereignty are not incompatible. As one State may sue another State in this Court, it is plain that no degradation to a State is thought to accompany her appearance in this Court. It is not therefore to an appearance in this Court that the objection points. To what does it point? It points to an appearance at the suit of one or more citizens. But why it should be more incompatible, that all the people of a State should be sued by one citizen, than by one hundred thousand, I cannot perceive, the process in both cases being alike; and the consequences of a judgment alike. Nor can I observe any greater inconveniencies in the one case than in the other, except what may arise from the feelings of those who may regard a lesser number in an inferior light. But if any reliance be made on this inferiority as an objection, at least one half of its force is done away by this fact, viz. that it is conceded that a State may appear in this Court as Plaintiff against a single citizen as Defendant; and the truth is, that the State of Georgia is at this moment prosecuting an action in this Court against two citizens of South Carolina. (fn. omitted)

The only remnant of objection therefore that remains is, that the State is not bound to appear and answer as a Defendant at the suit of an individual: but why it is unreasonable that she should be so bound, is hard to conjecture: That rule is said to be a bad one, which does not work both ways; the citizens of Georgia are content with a right of suing citizens of other States; but are not content that citizens of other States should have a right to sue them.... The question now before us renders it necessary to pay particular attention to that part of the second section [Note: this is a reference to Article III, § 2], which extends the judicial power 'to controversies between a state and citizens of another state.' It is contended, that this ought to be construed to reach none of these controversies, excepting those in which a State may be Plaintiff. The ordinary rules for construction will easily decide whether those words are to be understood in that limited sense.... If the Constitution really meant to extend these powers only to those controversies in which a State might be Plaintiff, to the exclusion of those in which citizens had demands against a State, it is inconceivable that it should have attempted to convey that meaning in words, not only so incompetent, but also repugnant to it; if it meant to exclude a certain class of these controversies, why were they not expressly excepted; on the contrary, not even an intimation of such intention appears in any part of the Constitution.... The exception contended for, would contradict and do violence to the great and leading principles of a free and equal national government, one of the great objects of which is, to ensure justice to all: To the few against the many, as well as to the many against the few. It would be strange, indeed, that the joint and equal sovereigns of this country, should, in the very Constitution by which they professed to establish justice, so far deviate from the plain path of equality and impartiality, as to give to the collective citizens of one State, a right of suing individual citizens of another State, and yet deny to those citizens a right of suing them....

I perceive, and therefore candor urges me to mention, a circumstance, which seems to favor the opposite side of the question. It is this: the same section of the Constitution which extends the judicial power to controversies 'between a State and the citizens of another State,' does also extend that power to controversies to which the United States are a party. Now, it may be said, if the word party comprehends both Plaintiff and Defendant, it follows, that the United States may be sued by any citizen, between whom and them there may be a controversy. This appears to me to be fair reasoning; but the same principles of candor which urge me to mention this objection, also urge me to suggest an important difference between the two cases. It is this: in all cases of actions against States or individual citizens, the National Courts are supported in all their legal and Constitutional proceedings and judgments, by the arm of the Executive power of the United States; but in cases of actions against the United States, there is no power which the Courts can call to their aid. From this distinction important conclusions are deducible, and they place the case of a State, and the case of the United States, in very different points of view.

I wish the state of society was so far improved, and the science of government advanced to such a degree of perfection, as that the whole nation could, in the peaceable course of law, be compelled to do justice, and be sued by individual citizens. Whether that is or is not now the case ought not to be thus collaterally and incidentally decided. I leave it a question....

For my own part, I am convinced that the sense in which I understand and have explained the words "controversies between States and citizens of another State" is the true sense. The extension of the judiciary power of the United States to such controversies appears to me to be wise, because it is honest and because it is useful. It is honest because it provides for doing justice ... and, by securing individual citizens as well as States in their respective rights, performs the promise which every free government makes to every free citizen of equal justice and protection. It is useful because it is honest; because it leaves not even the most obscure and friendless citizen without means of obtaining justice from a neighbouring State; because it obviates occasions of quarrels between States on account of the claims of their respective citizens; because it recognizes and strongly rests on this great moral truth that justice is the same whether due from one man or a million, or from a million to one man; because it teaches and greatly appreciates the value of our free republican national government, which places all our citizens on an equal footing, and enables each and every of them to obtain justice without any danger of being overborne by the weight and number of their opponents; and because it brings into action and enforces this great and glorious principle—that the people are the sovereign of this country, and consequently that fellow citizens and joint sovereigns cannot be degraded by appearing with each other in their own courts to have their controversies determined. The people have reason to prize and rejoice in such valuable privileges, and they ought not to forget that nothing but the free course of constitutional law and government can ensure the continuance and enjoyment of them....

Dissenting Opinion of Justice Iredell

The particular question then before the Court, is, will an action of assumpsit lie against a State?.... If it will, it must be in virtue of the Constitution of the United States, and of some law of Congress conformable thereto.... This appears to me to be one of those cases, with many others, in which an article of the Constitution cannot be effectuated without the intervention of the Legislative authority.... I believe there is no doubt that neither in the State now in question nor in any other in the Union, any particular legislative mode, authorizing a compulsory suit for the recovery of money against a State, was in being either when the Constitution was adopted, or at the time the Judicial Act was passed. Since that time, an Act of Assembly for such a purpose has been passed in Georgia. But that surely could have no influence in the construction of an act of the Legislature of the United States passed before.... Every State in the Union, in every instance where its sovereignty has not been delegated to the United States, I consider to be as completely sovereign as the United States are in respect to the powers surrendered. The United States are sovereign as to all the powers of Government actually surrendered: each State in the Union is sovereign as to all the powers reserved. It must necessarily be so, because the United States have no claim to any authority but such as the States have surrendered to them. Of course, the part not surrendered must remain as it did before....

I have now, I think, established the following particulars. 1st. That the Constitution, so far as it respects the judicial authority, can only be carried into effect by acts of the legislature appointing courts and prescribing their methods of proceeding. 2nd. That Congress has provided no new law in regard to this case, but expressly referred us to the old. 3rd. That there are no principles of the old law, to which, we must have recourse that in any manner authorize the present suit, either by precedent or by analogy. The consequence of which, in my opinion, clearly is that the suit in question cannot be maintained, nor, of course, the motion made upon it be complied with.... If, upon a fair construction of the Constitution of the United States, the power contended for really exists, it undoubtedly may be exercised, though it be a power of the first impression.... But it is of extreme moment that no judge should rashly commit himself upon important questions which it is unnecessary for him to decide. My opinion being that, even if the Constitution would admit of the exercise of such a power, a new law is necessary for the purpose, since no part of the existing law applies, this alone is sufficient to justify my determination in the present case. So much, however, has been said on the Constitution that it may not be improper to intimate that my present opinion is strongly against any construction of it which will admit, under any circumstances, a compulsive suit against a State for the recovery of money. I think every word in the Constitution may have its full effect without involving this consequence, and that nothing but express words, or an insurmountable implication (neither of which I consider, can be found in this case) would authorize the deduction of so high a power.... With regard to the policy of maintaining such suits, that is not for this Court to consider, unless the point in all other respects was very doubtful. Policy might then be argued from with a view to preponderate the judgment. Upon the question before us, I have no doubt. I have therefore nothing to do with the policy. But I confess, if I was at liberty to speak on that subject, my opinion on the policy of the case would also differ from that of the Attorney General. It is, however, a delicate topic. I pray to God that, if the Attorney General's doctrine as to the law be established by the judgment of this Court, all the good he predicts from it may take place, and none of the evils with which, I have the concern to say, it appears to me to be pregnant.

3. Congress Enacts the Eleventh Amendment in Response to Chisholm

Chisholm "created such a shock of surprise throughout the country that, at the first meeting of congress thereafter [in 1794], the eleventh amendment to the constitution was almost unanimously proposed, and was in due course adopted by the legislatures of the states." *Hans v. Louisiana*. 134 U.S. at 11. The Amendment passed very quickly because there was considerable concern that state sovereignty had been threatened and that the door was now wide open to prospective raids on depleted state treasuries. *Pennhurst State Sch. and Hosp. v. Halderman*, 465 U.S. 89, 151 (1984) (Stevens, J., dissenting) ("There is general agreement that the Amendment was passed because the States were fearful that federal courts would force them to pay their Revolutionary War debts, leading to their financial ruin."). (fn. omitted)[5]

5. The decision in *Chisholm* "fell upon the country with a profound shock." C. Warren, *The Supreme Court in United States History* vol. 1, 96 (rev. ed. 1926). Newspapers throughout the country "representing a rainbow of opinion protested what they viewed as an unexpected blow to state sovereignty. Others spoke more concretely of prospective raids on state treasuries." D. Currie, *The Con-*

4. Developments through 1908

During the next 125 years, the Court addressed two fundamental questions related to the interpretation of the Eleventh Amendment. First, should the Amendment be interpreted literally based on its plain text? And second, should the interpretation of the Eleventh Amendment be affected by the subsequent ratification of the Fourteenth Amendment?

The language in the Eleventh Amendment did not fully protect individual states from lawsuits in federal courts. The Amendment only bars lawsuits brought against a state in federal court by citizens of another state or citizens of a foreign state. Therefore, the literal text would allow a state to be sued by its own citizens, by foreign states, by corporations, by other states, and by the federal government.

Likewise, if the corresponding language of Article III, Section 2, Clause 1 is read broadly, the Amendment would not bar a lawsuit against a state in admiralty or maritime court or when the underlying claim involves a federal question, i.e., a claim based upon the Federal Constitution, federal law, or a federal treaty. Furthermore, it would not apply where a suit was brought against a state instrumentality or a state official, as opposed to the state itself.

In *Hans v. Louisiana*, the Supreme Court addressed the issue of whether the Eleventh Amendment should be interpreted literally based on its plain text.

Questions to guide reading of *Hans v. Louisiana*

1. The *Hans* majority rejects a literal interpretation of the Eleventh Amendment in favor of a broader reading. Does the majority provide any criteria for determining how to interpret the Eleventh Amendment?
2. In Justice Harlan's concurring opinion, he stated that it was unnecessary for the Court to disavow the majority opinion in *Chisholm* and rely on Justice Iredell's dissenting opinion. What does Justice Harlan rely on in making this determination?

Hans v. Louisiana

134 U.S. 1 (1890)

MR. JUSTICE BRADLEY delivered the opinion of the Court.

The question is presented whether a State can be sued in a Circuit Court of the United States by one of its own citizens upon a suggestion that the case is one that arises under the Constitution or laws of the United States.

The ground taken is that under the Constitution, as well as under the act of Congress passed to carry it into effect, a case is within the jurisdiction of the federal

---

stitution in Congress: The Federalist Period 1789–1801 196 (1997). This combination of public opinion and media attention created the impetus for passage of the Eleventh Amendment.

courts, without regard to the character of the parties, if it arises under the Constitution or laws of the United States, or, which is the same thing, if it necessarily involves a question under said Constitution or laws. The language relied on is that clause of the 3rd article of the Constitution which declares that

> the judicial power of the United States shall extend to all cases in law and equity arising under this Constitution, the laws of the United States, and treaties made, or which shall be made, under their authority;

and the corresponding clause of the act conferring jurisdiction upon the Circuit Court which, as found in the act of March 3, 1875, is as follows, to-wit:

> That the Circuit Courts of the United States shall have original cognizance, concurrent with the courts of the several States, of all suits of a civil nature, at common law or in equity, ... arising under the Constitution or laws of the United States, or treaties made, or which shall be made, under their authority....

In the present case, the plaintiff in error contends that he, being a citizen of Louisiana, is not embarrassed by the obstacle of the Eleventh Amendment inasmuch as that Amendment only prohibits suits against a State which are brought by the citizens of another State, or by citizens or subjects of a foreign state. It is true the Amendment does so read, and, if there were no other reason or ground for abating his suit, it might be maintainable; and then we should have this anomalous result, that, in cases arising under the Constitution or laws of the United States, a State may be sued in the federal courts by its own citizens, though it cannot be sued for a like cause of action by the citizens of other States, or of a foreign state; and may be thus sued in the federal courts, although not allowing itself to be sued in its own courts. If this is the necessary consequence of the language of the Constitution and the law, the result is no less startling and unexpected than was the original decision of this Court, that, under the language of the Constitution and of the Judiciary Act of 1789, a State was liable to be sued by a citizen of another State or of a foreign country. That decision was made in the case of *Chisholm v. Georgia*, 2 Dall. 419, and created such a shock of surprise throughout the country that, at the first meeting of Congress thereafter, the Eleventh Amendment to the Constitution was almost unanimously proposed, and was in due course adopted by the legislatures of the States. This amendment, expressing the will of the ultimate sovereignty of the whole country, superior to all legislatures and all courts, actually reversed the decision of the Supreme Court. It did not, in terms, prohibit suits by individuals against the States, but declared that the Constitution should not be construed to import any power to authorize the bringing of such suits.... Looking back from our present standpoint at the decision in *Chisholm v. Georgia*, we do not greatly wonder at the effect which it had upon the country. Any such power as that of authorizing the federal judiciary to entertain suits by individuals against the States had been expressly disclaimed, and even resented, by the great defenders of the Constitution while it was on its trial before the American people....

It seems to us that these views of those great advocates and defenders of the Constitution were most sensible and just, and they apply equally to the present case as to that then under discussion. The letter is appealed to now, as it was then, as a ground for sustaining a suit brought by an individual against a State. The reason against it is as strong in this case as it was in that. It is an attempt to strain the Constitution and the law to a construction never imagined or dreamed of. Can we suppose that, when the Eleventh Amendment was adopted, it was understood to be left open for citizens of a State to sue their own State in the federal courts, while the idea of suits by citizens of other States, or of foreign states, was indignantly repelled? Suppose that Congress, when proposing the Eleventh Amendment, had appended to it a proviso that nothing therein contained should prevent a State from being sued by its own citizens in cases arising under the Constitution or laws of the United States, can we imagine that it would have been adopted by the States? The supposition that it would is almost an absurdity on its face....

The suability of a State without its consent was a thing unknown to the law. This has been so often laid down and acknowledged by courts and jurists that it is hardly necessary to be formally asserted. It was fully shown by an exhaustive examination of the old law by Mr. Justice Iredell in his opinion in *Chisholm v. Georgia*, and it has been conceded in every case since where the question has in any way been presented, even in the cases which have gone furthest in sustaining suits against the officers or agents of States.... In all these cases, the effort was to show, and the court held, that the suits were not against the State or the United States, but against the individuals; conceding that, if they had been against either the State or the United States, they could not be maintained....

Undoubtedly a State may be sued by its own consent, as was the case in ... *Clark v. Barnard*, 108 U.S. 436, 108 U.S. 447.... But this Court decided, in *Beers v. Arkansas*, 61 U.S. 527, that the State could repeal that law at any time; ... The judgment of the Circuit Court is Affirmed.

MR. JUSTICE HARLAN, concurring.

I concur with the Court in holding that a suit directly against a State by one of its own citizens is not one to which the judicial power of the United States extends, unless the State itself consents to be sued. Upon this ground alone, I assent to the judgment. But I cannot give my assent to many things said in the opinion. The comments made upon the decision in *Chisholm v. Georgia* do not meet my approval. They are not necessary to the determination of the present case. Besides, I am of opinion that the decision in that case was based upon a sound interpretation of the Constitution as that instrument then was.

For further discussion

For the next hundred years, the Supreme Court attempted to further elucidate the meaning of *Hans*. In doing so, it continually reaffirmed the basic principle in that case. The Court made clear that the most critical aspect of the Eleventh Amendment was that it restored the original interpretation of the Constitution as espoused by Madison-Marshall-Hamilton;[6] the Amendment was intended to reinforce that the foundational principle of sovereign immunity is part of the constitutional framework. Therefore, the precise language in the Amendment itself does not fully define the scope of the states' sovereign immunity from suit.

In later years, individual Justices expressed the view that *Hans* was wrongly decided.[7] Nevertheless, both the decision in *Hans* and its broad principles have retained the support of a majority of the Supreme Court.

Indeed, the Court's most recent pronouncement on the meaning and scope of the Eleventh Amendment also reaffirms that the principle of sovereign immunity is part of the Constitution as it was adopted by the framers and ratified by the states, even though sovereign immunity is not explicitly referred to in the Constitution.[8] "[T]he States retained their sovereign immunity except as" altered by the principles underlying the framework of the Constitution or constitutional amendment.[9] The Court has construed this alteration narrowly—by following the positions advanced by Hamilton, Madison and Marshall during the ratification debates—to include only two types of lawsuits, those brought against a state by one or more sister states and suits brought by the United States against a state.[10]

In light of the broad construction given to the Eleventh Amendment in *Hans* and the retention of the principle of sovereign immunity in the Constitution as discussed in *Franchise Tax Bd.*, which of the following federal lawsuits against a state would you find are barred by the Eleventh Amendment? To complete this exercise, you need only accept the main principle underlying *Hans*, i.e., that the Amendment is intended to reinforce the principle that sovereign immunity remains a component of our constitutional design and limits the jurisdiction of the federal courts under Article III. The principal exception to this rule is that the Amendment does not apply in those specific instances where the states forfeited their historic sovereign immunity as a condition of their agreement to join the Union. Note: none of these lawsuits is prohibited by the literal text of the Amendment.

i) a suit by a private corporation created by an act of Congress;

ii) a suit by a foreign state;

iii) a suit brought in admiralty;

iv) a suit by a Native American tribe;

---

6. *See* Principality of Monaco v. Mississippi, 292 U.S. 313, 329 (1934) ("Superseding the decision in *Chisholm*, ... the Amendment established in effective operation the principle asserted by Madison, Hamilton, and Marshall in expounding the Constitution and advocating its ratification.").

7. *See e.g.*, Hess v. Port Authority Trans-Hudson Corp., 513 U.S. 30, 53–54 (1994) (Stevens, J., dissenting); Employees v. Missouri Pub. Health & Welfare Dept., 411 U.S. 279, 313 (1973) (Brennan J., dissenting); Blatchford v. Native Vill. of Noatak, 510 U.S. at 789 (Blackmun, J., with whom Marshall, J. and Stevens, J., join, dissenting).

8. Franchise Tax Bd. of Cal. v. Hyatt, 587 U.S. ___, 139 S. Ct. 1485, 203 L. Ed. 2d 768 (2019).

9. Franchise Tax Bd., supra, 587 U.S. at ___, 139 S. Ct. 1485, 1493 (2019).

10. Franchise Tax Bd., supra, 587 U.S. at ___, 139 S. Ct. 1485, 1493 (2019).

v) a suit by a private party against a state or state agency in the state or local courts of a sister state; and

vi) an administrative adjudicatory proceeding brought before the federal maritime commission.[11]

C. What Constitutes "The State" for Purposes of the Eleventh Amendment?

This section addresses the question of who, other than a state itself, is eligible to receive the protections of the Eleventh Amendment and sovereign immunity. States operate through municipalities, agencies, departments, authorities, and many other governmental instrumentalities. In addition, states employ thousands of workers to set policies and to implement those policies. What factors would you use to determine if an instrumentality qualifies as a state entity or whether a state official should be entitled to invoke the state's Eleventh Amendment immunity from suit?

1. Should Municipal Entities That Perform a Governmental Function on Behalf of the State Be Entitled to Assert the State's Eleventh Amendment Immunity from Suit?

Municipal governments and local entities are often created by state law and empowered to perform governmental functions on behalf of the state. However, these political subdivisions are not entitled to Eleventh Amendment immunity. In *Mt. Healthy City Board of Educ. v. Doyle,* 429 U.S. 274, 280 (1977), the Supreme Court made clear that a governmental entity only qualifies for Eleventh Amendment immunity if it is considered an arm of the state. An entity that is functionally independent of the state or is considered to be similar to a municipal corporation or a county does not receive the benefit of the state's Eleventh Amendment immunity.

In *Northern Ins. Co. of New York v. Chatham County,* 547 U.S. 189 (2006), the Supreme Court similarly noted that state sovereign immunity does not extend to municipalities and other political subdivisions of the state even though these entities exercise a "slice of state power." In that case, Chatham County operated and maintained a bridge on behalf of the State of Georgia. When it was sued over a bridge accident, the County argued that it was entitled to rely on what it called a common law "residual" sovereign immunity that would extend to protect a political subdivision from

11. To find the cases determining whether each of these lawsuits is barred by the Eleventh Amendment, *see* (i) Smith v. Reeves, 178 U.S. 436, 449 (1900); (ii) Principality of Monaco v. Mississippi, 292 U.S. at 313; (iii) Ex parte New York (No. 1), 256 U.S. 490, 500 (1921); (iv) Blatchford v. Native Vill. of Noatak, 501 U.S. 775 (1991); (v) Franchise Tax Bd. of Cal. v. Hyatt, 587 U.S. ___, 139 S. Ct. 1485, 203 L. Ed. 2d 768 (2019), *overruling* Nevada v. Hall, 440 U.S. 410 (1979); (vi) Federal Maritime Comm'n v. South Carolina State Ports Auth., 535 U.S. 743 (2002).

suit. The Supreme Court rejected that argument, emphasizing that it has consistently held that state sovereign immunity does not extend to municipalities and other political subdivisions of the state.

2. Should the Eleventh Amendment Apply to Lawsuits against State Agencies and Instrumentalities?

The Supreme Court has long recognized that a state's sovereign immunity would be ineffectual if a lawsuit could proceed in federal court because it was brought against an agency of the state. Thus, "[i]t has long been settled that the [Eleventh Amendment applies] not only [to] actions in which a State is actually named as the defendant, but also [to] certain actions against state agents and state instrumentalities."[12]

A suit against a state agency or state instrumentality is deemed to have been brought against the state itself when the agency or instrumentality is determined to be an alter ego or arm of the state.[13] Federal law determines whether a particular governmental instrumentality is an arm or alter ego of the state for Eleventh Amendment purposes, but the federal question can be answered "only after considering the provisions of state law that define the agency's character."[14]

There is no uniform rule to help determine whether an instrumentality is an arm or alter-ego of the state. The Supreme Court has not written definitively on this issue and there is no single test used by the Circuits. As the Second Circuit noted, "[t]he jurisprudence over how to apply the arm-of-the-state doctrine is, at best confused." *Mancuso v. New York State Thruway Auth.*, 86 F.3d 289, 293 (2d Cir.), *cert. denied*, 519 U.S. 992 (1996). The First Circuit added that "the Eleventh Amendment demands a case-by-case inquiry into the specific structure and functions of the public entity in question." *Wojcik v. Massachusetts State Lottery Comm'n*, 300 F.3d 92, 101 (1st Cir. 2002).

Of course, there are some factors that the courts routinely consider in determining whether an instrumentality is an alter-ego of the state. For example, most Circuits

12. Regents of the Univ. of Cal. v. Doe, 519 U.S. 425, 429 (1997) (citations omitted); *see also* Scheuer v. Rhodes, 416 U.S. 232, 237 (1974) (the Amendment "bars suits not only against the State when it is the named party but also when it is the party in fact...."); Edelman v. Jordan, 415 U.S. 651, 663 (1974) (Eleventh Amendment bars certain lawsuits even where "a State is not named a party to the action").

13. *See* Regents of the Univ. of Cal. v. Doe, 519 U.S. at 429; *see also* Ex parte New York, 256 U.S. at 500 ("As to what is to be deemed a suit against a state, ... it is now established that the question is to be determined not by the mere names of the titular parties, but by the essential nature and effect of the proceeding, as it appears from the entire record."); Watson v. Univ. of Utah Med. Ctr., 75 F.3d 569, 574 (10th Cir. 1996) ("The arm-of-the-state doctrine bestows immunity on entities created by state governments that operate as alter egos or instrumentalities of the states") (citation omitted).

14. Regents of the Univ. of Cal. v. Doe, 519 U.S. at 429 n. 5; Woods v. Rondout Valley Cent. Sch. Dist. Bd. of Educ., 466 F.3d 232, 237 (2d Cir. 2006); Sturdevant v. Paulsen, 218 F.3d 1160, 1164 (10th Cir. 2000) ("Although ultimately a matter of federal law, arm-of-the-state status must be determined in each case by reference to the particular state laws characterizing the entity.").

have concluded that the effect of a judgment on state finances is the most important factor to be considered. Other factors include the state's control over the instrumentality and the degree of state funding.

Sturdevant v. Paulsen is a representative Circuit decision that addresses in depth some of the issues considered by the courts in determining whether a governmental entity is entitled to Eleventh Amendment immunity.

Questions to guide reading of *Sturdevant v. Paulsen*

1. What factors did the Court consider in determining whether the Colorado State Board for Community Colleges and Occupational Education was an arm of the state? Are certain factors more important than others?
2. The Court begins its analysis by looking at the extent to which the entity has autonomy under state law and whether the state is liable for judgments issued against the entity. Do you agree that both of these considerations should be relevant factors in determining whether the entity is an arm of the state? Explain.
3. The Court goes to great lengths to determine whether the state treasury is legally obligated to pay the State Board's judgments or whether it will, *as a practical matter*, pay those judgments. Why is that distinction relevant?
4. The Court decides that it cannot resolve the "arm of the state" issue based upon who has the legal responsibility to pay the State Board's judgments. Do you agree with the Circuit Court that it can, nevertheless, determine whether the State Board is an arm of the State of Colorado based solely on the other factors set forth in the decision?
5. Since the State Board is created by state law and provides an important state educational function, why are those two factors alone insufficient to conclude that the Board is an "arm of the state" of Colorado?

Sturdevant v. Paulsen

218 F.3d 1160 (10th Cir. 2000)

LUCERO, Circuit Judge.

This interlocutory appeal of the district court's denial of Eleventh Amendment immunity presents the legal issue of whether the Colorado State Board for Community Colleges and Occupational Education ("the Board") is an "arm of the state" for purposes of the Eleventh Amendment. Resolution of this issue requires an inquiry into the financial relationships between the state and the Board, as well as the Board's degree of autonomy, but fundamentally comes down to the following question: Is the Board more like a political subdivision such as a local school district, or is it an alter ego of the state such as the governing board of a state university system? We conclude it is more akin to the latter, and reverse.

[The court's discussion of the facts follows—plaintiff, a full-time history instructor at a Community College, asserts wrongful termination claims against the Board.]

Colo. Rev. Stat. 23-60-104 establishes and sets forth the powers and duties of the Board, which governs the State of Colorado's community college and occupational education system. *See id.* 23-60-102. The Board "is charged to develop and establish state policy for occupational education and to govern the state system of community colleges." Colo. Rev. Stat. 23-60-102(1). It is defined as a "body corporate" with the power to hold "money, lands, or other property" and to use such property in the interests of community and occupational education. Colo. Rev. Stat. 23-60-104(1)(b). Nine of its eleven members are appointed by the governor with the consent of the Senate, subject to certain political and geographical diversity requirements. *See* Colo. Rev. Stat. 23-60-104(2)(a)(I). A student and faculty member from among the state community colleges, elected according to Board-established procedures, fill the additional two positions. *See* Colo. Rev. Stat. 23-60-104(2)(a)(II).

The Board controls and administers a "state board for community colleges and occupational education fund." Colo. Rev. Stat. 23-60-107(1). This fund contains money obtained by legislative appropriation as well as grant, contract, gift, sale, or other means. *See id.* Fund balances do not revert to the general fund at the end of the year. *See id.*

Board powers and duties over the state system of community and technical colleges include, in part, constructing facilities and issuing "revenue bonds and other revenue obligations," Colo. Rev. Stat. 23-60-202(1)(b); fixing the "tuition and fees to be charged in the community and technical colleges" in accordance with the level of legislative appropriation therefore, Colo. Rev. Stat. 23-60-202(1)(c); and planning and implementing policies for the community and technical educational system generally, *see* Colo. Rev. Stat. 23-60-202. In many respects, however, the Board's powers are subordinate to the oversight of the Colorado Commission on Higher Education ("CCHE"). The CCHE may approve or modify the Board's proposed budget before making a funding recommendation to the governor and general assembly, *see* Colo. Rev. Stat. 23-1-105(2), establishes binding policies on tuition and fees, *see id.* 23-1-108(12), and must approve the service area of, and all educational programs at, Board-governed institutions, see id. 23-1-107, -109. Finally, with respect to its oversight of community and technical colleges, the Board enjoys and is subject to the same powers and duties as "the governing boards of institutions of higher education," Colo. Rev. Stat. 23-60-202(1).

In determining that the Board does not enjoy the State's Eleventh Amendment immunity, the district court concluded that it constitutes a political subdivision rather than an arm of the state. Specifically, the district court looked to the following factors: the Board's status as a "body corporate," its powers to raise and administer revenues, its "significant degree of autonomy," the fact that its funds do not annually revert to the state, and, most importantly, a conclusion that although the state risk management fund would pay any judgment against the Board, "the state of Colorado would not be legally liable to pay a judgment against the Board." (Appellant's App. at 88–89.) Considering these factors de novo and in light of the fundamental purpose of Eleventh Amendment arm-of-the-state doctrine, we disagree....

Eleventh Amendment immunity is a question of federal law reviewed de novo.... We give some deference to the rationale of state court decisions regarding the arm-of-the-state status of a particular entity, but do not regard them as dispositive....

Our inquiry under the arm-of-the-state doctrine is well defined.

> The issue here ... turns on whether the [entity] is to be treated as an arm of the State partaking of the State's Eleventh Amendment immunity, or is instead to be treated as a municipal corporation or other political subdivision to which the Eleventh Amendment does not extend. The answer depends, at least in part, on the nature of the entity created by state law....

In other words, the inquiry with regard to a particular entity is whether it is "more like a county or city than ... like an arm of the state?" ... Although ultimately a matter of federal law, arm-of-the-state status must be determined in each case by reference to the particular state laws characterizing the entity....

In [*Watson v. University of Utah Med. Ctr.*, 75 F.3d 569 (10th Cir. 1996)], we further elaborated on the *Mt. Healthy* test for arm-of-the-state status. To determine whether an entity is an arm of the state

> we engage in two general inquiries. [T]he court first examines the degree of autonomy given to the agency, as determined by the characterization of the agency by state law and the extent of guidance and control exercised by the state. Second, the court examines the extent of financing the agency receives independent of the state treasury and its ability to provide for its own financing. The governmental entity is immune from suit if the money judgment sought is to be satisfied out of the state treasury.

Watson, 75 F.3d at 574–75 (internal quotations and citations omitted). With respect to the last and particularly important factor of state treasury liability, "[w]e interpret [the Supreme Court's decision in *Regents of the Univ. of Cal. v.* Doe, 519 U.S. at 431], to require us to focus on legal liability for a judgment, rather than practical, or indirect, impact a judgment would have on a state's treasury." ... Although our consideration of the various enumerated factors requires consideration of certain aspects of a state entity in multiple contexts, we nevertheless pursue the factors in detail, because they lead us to a different conclusion than that of the district court.

A. Legal Liability for a Judgment

Because we held in [*Duke v. Grady Mun. Schs., 127 F.3d 972 (10th Cir. 1997),*] that state treasury liability strongly favors arm-of-the-state status, we address that issue first. The Board claims that damages against it would be paid out of the state risk management fund. This fund is authorized "[t]o pay liability claims and expenses related thereto, brought against the state, its officials, or its employees pursuant to the 'Colorado Governmental Immunity Act.'... and claims against the state, its officials, or its employees arising under federal law." Colo. Rev. Stat. 24-30-1510(3)(a). It appears that one colorable reading of the statute is that the Board is a covered state agency for purposes of the risk management fund by virtue of being a "state institution of higher education *or other instrumentality thereof*." Colo. Rev. Stat. 24-30-1502(5) (emphasis added). Sturdevant, however, argues that her claims are not federal claims and therefore not explicitly covered by Colo. Rev. Stat. 24-30-1510(3). According to Sturdevant, insofar as the risk management statute incorporates the Colorado Governmental Immunity Act, that statute covers only state law tort and not state law contract claims, and therefore a judgment in her favor would not implicate the risk management fund. *See* Colo. Rev. Stat. 24-30-1510(3)(a) (providing that the risk management fund will pay claims against the state, its officials, or its employees "arising under federal law" and pursuant to the Colorado Governmental Immunity Act); *id.* 24-10-105 (stating that it is the intent of governmental immunity act to cover tort actions); but *see id.* 24-30-1510(4)(b) (stating that the risk management fund will not be used to pay contract claims, "except for claims relating to employment contracts"). Although such a distinction appears to have some support in the Colorado statutory provisions at issue, Sturdevant's Eleventh Amendment argument necessarily relies on the proposition that the details of a risk management fund can render a particular state entity an arm of the state for purposes of certain claims and a political subdivision for purposes of other claims. We have found no cases supporting such an approach. Moreover, we do not consider such a distinction consistent with the fundamental goal of the *Mt. Healthy* analysis: distinguishing political subdivisions from governmental entities that are effectively arms of the state. *See Mt. Healthy*, 429 U.S. at 280. We therefore expressly decline to answer the state law question of the precise application of the risk management statute to particular claims....

More importantly for purposes of the Federal constitutional question, it is not at all clear that even if a risk management fund must pay a judgment, this obligation renders that judgment a judgment against the state for Eleventh Amendment purposes. "The key question is whether funds to satisfy a money judgment would come directly from the state, or indirectly through commingled state and local funds or state indemnification provisions." ...

Because its moneys are placed in a fund within the state treasury, see Colo. Rev. Stat. 23-60-107(1), the Board additionally argues that any judgment against it, whether reimbursed by the Risk Management Fund or not, will be assessed directly against the state's treasury. This argument is more directly relevant to Duke's emphasis on the legal incidence of any judgment, and finds some support in Graham's statement that a judgment against the University of Northern Colorado—whose moneys are likewise placed in a fund within the state treasury, see Colo. Rev. Stat. 23-40-103.5(1)—would "likely be enforceable against the state" as well as satisfied by risk management funds. *Graham*, 956 P.2d at 565. Unfortunately, the Colorado Supreme Court's statement that there is a likelihood of enforceability falls short of amounting to an explicit resolution of the question of the legal incidence of the judgment. Moreover, it appears that the Board's fund within the state treasury may well contain commingled funds from state and local sources....

We need not resolve conclusively the questions of operation of the risk management fund and the state's legal liability for a potential judgment. In *Sutton*, 173 F.3d at 1233, confronted with an analogous lack of clarity as to the legal liability for the judgment against a governmental defendant, we proceeded to resolve the question based on the remaining factors of the *Mt. Healthy* test, without definitively resolving the state law question of liability for the judgment: "It is not clear from Utah's statutory scheme and case law how the State School for the Deaf and Blind satisfies money judgments against it. Nevertheless, we are persuaded that the State School for the Deaf and Blind is an 'arm of the state' entitled to Eleventh Amendment immunity." *Id.* at 1233. (footnote omitted) "[E]ven after *Hess* and *Doe*, which emphasized the primacy of the impact on the state treasury as a factor in determining immunity, other factors remain relevant." *Duke*, 127 F.3d at 978. We therefore turn to the other factors delineated in our arm-of-the-state case law. Concluding that these other factors decisively resolve the question in favor of Eleventh Amendment immunity, we decline to address further the ambiguities attendant upon the question of legal liability for a judgment.

B. Factors of Autonomy and Financial Independence

Under the general rubrics of autonomy and financial independence, we have identified several other factors relevant to the arm-of-the-state determination:

> (1) the characterization of the governmental unit under state law; (2) the guidance and control exercised by the state over the governmental unit; (3) the degree of state funding received; and (4) the governmental unit's ability to issue bonds and levy taxes on its own behalf....

We note that other circuits have considered additional factors in applying the *Mt. Healthy* test, including "whether the entity is concerned primarily with local as opposed to statewide problems." ...

1. Characterization under State Law

The Board is not explicitly defined by state statute as either an arm of the state or a political subdivision. It is defined as a "body corporate." Colo. Rev. Stat. 23-60-104(1)(b). *Graham*, 956 P.2d at 556, provides some guidance as to that term's meaning under Colorado law and its import in the context of our Eleventh Amendment analysis. In determining whether the University of Northern Colorado ("UNC") is a "person" for purposes of 42 U.S.C. 1983, the Colorado Supreme Court concluded that UNC is an arm of the state under the *Mt. Healthy* test. *See id.* at 562, 565–66. In reaching that conclusion, the Court considered the status of UNC's board as a "body corporate," noting that such status is comparable to that of a municipality, but concluded that the general assembly's choice of corporate form did not evince an intent to waive sovereign immunity. *See id.* at 563. Rather, the Court held that "such characterization appears to be for the purpose of providing a convenient means for allowing UNC to pursue the ends of higher education." *Id.* at 565; ... More to the point, the Colorado Court of Appeals [in National Camera] has construed the relevant statutory provisions to conclude that the Board is an arm of the state traditionally immune from damages liability under the Eleventh Amendment and therefore not a "person" for purposes of liability under 42 U.S.C. 1983.... Although we are not bound by state court decisions regarding arm-of-the-state status, we defer to the rationale of National Camera insofar as it interprets state law....

The Board is indisputably a kind of state-wide entity and absent from those provisions of Colorado law that define political subdivisions. *See, e.g.*, Colo. Rev. Stat. 1-7.5-103(6). We therefore conclude that the state law classification of the Board as analogous to "the governing boards of institutions of higher education," Colo. Rev. Stat. 23-60-202(1), coupled with the holding of the Colorado Court of Appeals in National Camera, 832 P.2d at 963–64, weighs strongly in favor of the conclusion that the Board is an instrumentality of the State of Colorado.

2. State Control

The district court surveyed the governing statutory provisions and concluded that the Board "operates with a significant degree of autonomy." (Appellant's App. at 88). Appellant vigorously contests this characterization. Our review of the Colorado statutory provisions confirms that although the Board enjoys a significant degree of autonomy, the extent of state control over its operations is greater than the district court indicated. For example, while the Board has the authority to fix tuition and fees, see Colo. Rev. Stat. 23-60-202(c), it can do so only "in accordance with the level of cash fund appropriations set by the general assembly for such institutions," id., and subject to review and approval by the CCHE, see id. 23-1-105(2), -108(12).... The relative lack of local involvement or even involvement by the member institutions in determining the makeup of the Board's voting members further buttresses that conclusion. Cf. Sutton, 173 F.3d at 1232 (noting that, unlike local school districts, members of state school boards are members of the state board of education).

In addition, although both local districts and the Board are subject to some mixture of autonomy and oversight by state executive or legislative bodies, the Board is explicitly focused on state-wide rather than local concerns: The Board is "charged to develop and establish state policy for occupational education and to govern the state system of community colleges." Colo. Rev. Stat. 23-60-102(1) (emphasis added) ... Considering the genesis of the arm/subdivision distinction in *Mt. Healthy*, 429 U.S. at 280, we conclude that the district court gave insufficient weight to the Board's primary focus on state-wide issues, the governor's authority to appoint eleven of its thirteen members, and the degree to which its decisions are supervised by the CCHE and state legislature. Therefore, we conclude that considerations of autonomy and control weigh in favor of characterizing the Board as an arm of the state rather than as a political subdivision.

3. Degree of State Funding and the Ability to Issue Bonds and Levy Taxes

The third and fourth factors identified in *Sutton* concern "the degree of state funding received ... and ... the governmental unit's ability to issue bonds and levy taxes on its own behalf." 173 F.3d at 1232.... While these factors overlap somewhat with the question of "whether a judgment against the [defendant] would be paid out of the state treasury," *id.* at 1233..., as discussed above, uncertainty as to liability does not preclude consideration of other aspects of the financial relationship between state and entity, *see id.* at 1233 & n.6, to provide guidance in applying our arm-of-the-state analysis.

a. Sources of Funding

A discrete fund within the state treasury—one that does not revert to the legislature annually—falls under the control of the Board.... Our review of the Colorado statutes leads us to conclude, however, that a local school district's reliance in practice on state grants is qualitatively different, for purposes of the *Mt. Healthy* analysis, than the CCHE's direct supervision over the means by which the Board both raises and spends the moneys within its fund, whatever their source. Thus, factors relating to sources of funding weigh in on both sides of the arm-of-the-state/political subdivision scale.

b. Ability to Issue Bonds and Levy Taxes

Although the Board has the power, with certain limits, to issue bonds, unlike a county, city, or even school district, it most certainly lacks the power to levy taxes. The absence of this characteristic attribute of political subdivisions is a relevant distinction in the case law.... Because of the open-ended nature of the arm-of the-state analysis, it is easy to become caught up in the minutiae of state law, such as the extent of control over the Board by the executive and legislature, the details of the risk management fund's operation, and the proportional sources of the Board's funding. These details, however, must not eclipse a fundamental distinction that emerges from *Mt. Healthy* and the cases following it—between alter egos or instrumentalities of states on the one hand, and political subdivisions such as cities and counties on the other. Considering the various factors in context, the Board lacks a fundamental characteristic of a political subdivision—political control by some community other than the state as a whole....

Review of Tenth Circuit precedent in this area underscores the importance of this fundamental distinction. We have consistently held that state colleges and universities are arms of the state, whereas local school boards are political subdivisions, even if largely dependent on state funding and subject to state control.... *Sturdevant* has identified no significant respect in which the relationship of the community colleges to the State of Colorado differs from the relationships of the universities in the above cases to their respective states; it would be anomalous to find the very instrumentality and intermediary of state control and funding to be somehow less of an alter ego of the state than the local and regional institutions it supervises on the state's behalf. Upon examination of the statutory scheme for the Board, we hold it to be an "instrumentality of the state," far more akin to state universities and their governing bodies than to a municipalities and local school boards. Therefore, the Board enjoys Eleventh Amendment immunity as an instrumentality or "arm" of the State of Colorado.

3. Should the Eleventh Amendment Apply to Lawsuits against State Officials?

Allowing lawsuits to be brought against state officials in federal court could also result in an end-run around the Eleventh Amendment where the real party in interest is the state itself. On the other hand, prohibiting such lawsuits could insulate any misconduct of state officials from judicial scrutiny in federal court. For the past two centuries, the Court has struggled with how to ensure that the federal courts have authority, consistent with the constraints of the Eleventh Amendment, to compel state officials to conform their conduct to federal law.

a. Suing State Officials in their Official Capacity

In *Ex parte Young*, the Supreme Court constructed a legal fiction to balance the competing interests of state sovereignty and federal supremacy. The Court held that a state official sued in his official capacity in federal court is not entitled to rely on the state's Eleventh Amendment immunity when (1) the state official is about to act, or has already begun to act, in violation of the Federal Constitution or federal law; and (2) the lawsuit seeks to enjoin the official from undertaking or continuing such future action (i.e., the plaintiff seeks prospective equitable relief).

Questions to guide reading of *Ex parte Young*

1. Why was the Minnesota Attorney General, petitioner Young, held in contempt by a federal court? Do you think it was reasonable for the Attorney General, at that time, to believe that a state act of the legislature was superior to an order of the federal circuit court? How likely is it today that a state official would fail to obey an order of the federal court?
2. Was the shareholders' argument that they could not risk violating state law because of the severe penalties that would be imposed for a violation a valid point? Could they have sought the same or similar relief from a state court?
3. The Court first concludes that it has jurisdiction over the lawsuit because of the presence of several federal questions and then addresses whether it is deprived of jurisdiction by the Eleventh Amendment. Why do you think the Court approached the issue in the way it did?
4. Was the Court's ruling that it had jurisdiction over the lawsuit because of the presence of federal questions in conflict with the holding of *Hans v. Louisiana*? Explain.
5. The Court holds that a state law that conflicts with the Federal Constitution "is void because [it is] unconstitutional." Why was that conclusion necessary for the Court to get around the Eleventh Amendment?
6. Justice Harlan's dissent makes clear that Attorney General Young was sued only in his official capacity. According to Justice Harlan, what was the significance of that fact?
7. Do you agree with Justice Harlan's statement that "[t]h[e] principle [that emerges from the majority's decision], if firmly established, would work a radical change in our governmental system"? Why or why not?

Note that Justice Harlan concludes that the Eleventh Amendment was not modified by the Fourteenth Amendment. The majority avoided deciding that issue, but Justice Harlan's view did not prevail. The Fourteenth Amendment's impact on the Eleventh Amendment will be discussed later in this chapter.

Ex parte Young

209 U.S. 123 (1908)

Statement by Mr. Justice Peckham:

An original application was made to this court for leave to file a petition for writs of habeas corpus and certiorari in behalf of Edward T. Young, petitioner, as attorney general of the state of Minnesota....

The facts are these: The legislature of the state of Minnesota duly created a railroad and warehouse commission, and that commission, on the 6th of September, 1906, made an order fixing the rates for the various railroad companies for the carriage of merchandise between stations in that state of the kind and classes specified in what is known as the 'Western Classification.' These rates materially reduced those then existing, and were by the order to take effect November 15, 1906. In obedience to the order the railroads filed and published the schedules of rates, which have ever since that time been carried out by the companies....

On the 4th of April, 1907, the legislature of the state of Minnesota passed an act fixing 2 cents a mile as the maximum passenger rate to be charged by railroads in Minnesota. (The rate had been theretofore 3 cents per mile.) The act was to take effect on the 1st of May, 1907, and was put into effect on that day by the railroad companies, and the same has been observed by them up to the present time. It was provided in the act that 'any railroad company, or any officer, agent, or representative thereof, who shall violate any provision of this act, shall be guilty of a felony, and, upon conviction thereof, shall be punished by a fine not exceeding five thousand ($5,000) dollars, or by imprisonment in the state prison for a period not exceeding five (5) years, or both such fine and imprisonment.'

On the 18th of April, 1907, the legislature passed an act (chapter 232 of the laws of that year), which established rates for the transportation of certain commodities.... Section 6 directed that every railroad company in the state should adopt and publish and put into effect the rates specified in the statute, and that every officer, director, traffic manager, or agent, or employee of such railroad company should cause the adoption, publication, and use by such railroad company of rates not exceeding those specified in the act; 'and any officer, director, or such agent or employee of any such railroad company who violates any of the provisions of this section, or who causes or counsels, advises or assists, any such railroad company to violate any of the provisions of this section, shall be guilty of a misdemeanor, and may be prosecuted therefore....

The railroad companies did not obey the provisions of this act so far as concerned the adoption and publication of rates as specified therein. On the 31st of May, 1907, the day before the act was to take effect, nine suits in equity were commenced in the circuit court of the United States for the district of Minnesota, third division, each suit being brought by stockholders of the particular railroad mentioned in the bill, and in each case the defendants named were the railroad company of which the complainants were, respectively, stockholders, and the members of the railroad and warehouse commission, and the attorney general of the state, Edward T. Young, and individual defendants, representing the shippers of freight upon the railroad....

It was averred in the bill that the suit was not a collusive one to confer on the court jurisdiction of a case of which it could not otherwise have cognizance, but that the objects and purposes of the suit were to enjoin the railway company from publishing or adopting (or continuing to observe, if already adopted) the rates and tariffs prescribed and set forth in the two acts of the legislature above mentioned and in the orders of the railroad and warehouse commission, and also to enjoin the other defendants from attempting to enforce such provisions, or from instituting any action or proceeding against the defendant railway company, its officers, etc., on account of any violation thereof, for the reason that the said acts and orders were and each of them was violative of the Constitution of the United States....

The bill further alleged that the orders of the commission of September, 1906, and May, 1907, and the acts of April 4, 1907, and April 18, 1907, were, in the penalties prescribed for their violation, so drastic that no owner or operator of a railway property could invoke the jurisdiction of any court to test the validity thereof, except at the risk of confiscation of its property, and the imprisonment for long terms in jails and penitentiaries of its officers, agents, and employees. For this reason the complainants alleged that the above-mentioned orders and acts, and each of them, denied to the defendant railway company and its stockholders, including the complainants, the equal protection of the laws, and deprived it and them of their property without due process of law, and that each of them was, for that reason, unconstitutional and void.

The bill also contained an averment that if the railway company should fail to continue to observe and keep in force, or to observe and put in force, the orders of the commission and the acts of April 4, 1907, and April 18, 1907.... that if the company should fail to obey the order of the commission or the acts of April 4, 1907, and April 18, 1907, the said Edward T. Young, as attorney general of the state of Minnesota, would, as complainants were advised and believed, institute proceedings by mandamus or otherwise against the railway company, its officers, directors, agents, or employees, to enforce said orders and all the provisions thereof, ... Appropriate relief by injunction against the action of the defendant Young and the railroad commission was asked for.

A temporary restraining order was made by the circuit court, which only restrained the railway company from publishing the rates as provided for in the act of April 18, 1907, and from reducing its tariffs to the figures set forth in that act; ... but it restrained Edward T. Young, attorney general, from taking any steps against the railroads to enforce the remedies or penalties specified in the act of April 18, 1907.

Copies of the bill and the restraining order were served, among others, upon the defendant Mr. Edward T. Young, attorney general, who appeared specially and only for the purpose of moving to dismiss the bill as to him, on the ground that the court had no jurisdiction over him as attorney general; and he averred that the state of Minnesota had not consented, and did not consent, to the commencement of this suit against him as attorney general of the state, which suit was in truth and effect a suit against the said state of Minnesota, contrary to the 11th Amendment of the Constitution of the United States.

Thereupon, on the 23rd of September, 1907, the court, after a hearing of all parties and taking proofs in regard to the issues involved, ordered a temporary injunction to issue against the railway company, restraining it, pending the final hearing of the cause, from putting into effect the tariffs, rates, or charges set forth in the act approved April 18, 1907. The court also enjoined the defendant Young, as attorney general of the state of Minnesota, pending the final hearing of the cause, from taking or instituting any action or proceeding to enforce the penalties and remedies specified in the act above mentioned, or to compel obedience to that act, or compliance therewith, or any part thereof....

The day after the granting of this preliminary injunction the attorney general, in violation of such injunction, filed a petition for an alternative writ of mandamus in one of the courts of the state, and obtained an order from that court, September 24, 1907, directing the alternative writ to issue as prayed for in the petition. The writ was thereafter issued and served upon the Northern Pacific Railway Company, commanding the company, immediately after its receipt, 'to adopt and publish and keep for public inspection, as provided by law, as the rates and charges to be made, demanded, and maintained by you for the transportation of freight between stations in the state of Minnesota of the kind, character, and class named and specified in chapter 232 of the Session Laws of the state of Minnesota for the year 1907, rates and charges which do not exceed those declared to be just and reasonable in and by the terms and provisions of said chapter 232.'

Upon an affidavit showing these facts the United States circuit court ordered Mr. Young to show cause why he should not be punished as for a contempt for his misconduct in violating the temporary injunction issued by that court in the case therein pending.

Upon the return of this order the Attorney General filed his answer, in which he set up the same objections which he had made to the jurisdiction of the court in his motion to dismiss the bill, and in his demurrer; he disclaimed any intention to treat the court with disrespect in the commencement of the proceedings referred to, but believing that the decision of the court in the action, holding that it had jurisdiction to enjoin him, as attorney general, from performing his discretionary official duties, was in conflict with the 11th Amendment of the Constitution of the United States, as the same has been interpreted and applied by the United States Supreme Court, he believed it to be his duty, as such Attorney General, to commence the mandamus proceedings for and in behalf of the state, and it was in this belief that the proceedings were commenced solely for the purpose of enforcing the law of the state of Minnesota. The order adjudging him in contempt was then made....

We recognize and appreciate to the fullest extent the very great importance of this case, not only to the parties now before the court, but also to the great mass of the citizens of this country, all of whom are interested in the practical working of the courts of justice throughout the land, both Federal and state, and in the proper exercise of the jurisdiction of the Federal courts, as limited and controlled by the Federal Constitution and the laws of Congress....

The question of jurisdiction, whether of the circuit court or of this Court, is frequently a delicate matter to deal with, and it is especially so in this case, where the material and most important objection to the jurisdiction of the circuit court is the assertion that the suit is, in effect, against one of the states of the Union. It is a question, however, which we are called upon, and which it is our duty to decide.... [A]n examination of the record before us shows that there are Federal questions in this case....

[T]he question really to be determined under this objection is whether the acts of the legislature and the orders of the railroad commission, if enforced, would take property without due process of law; and although that question might incidentally involve a question of fact, its solution, nevertheless, is one which raises a Federal question....

Another Federal question is the alleged unconstitutionality of these acts because of the enormous penalties denounced for their violation, which prevent the railway company, as alleged, or any of its servants or employees, from resorting to the courts for the purpose of determining the validity of such acts.... Still another Federal question is urged, growing out of the assertion that the laws are, by their necessary effect, an interference with and a regulation of interstate commerce, the grounds for which assertion it is not now necessary to enlarge upon. The question is not, at any rate, frivolous. We conclude that the circuit court had jurisdiction in the case before it, because it involved the decision of Federal questions arising under the Constitution of the United States.... It may therefore be said that when the penalties for disobedience are by fines so enormous and imprisonment so severe as to intimidate the company and its officers from resorting to the courts to test the validity of the legislation, the result is the same as if the law in terms prohibited the company from seeking judicial construction of laws which deeply affect its rights....

We hold, therefore, that the provisions of the acts relating to the enforcement of the rates, either for freight or passengers, by imposing such enormous fines and possible imprisonment as a result of an unsuccessful effort to test the validity of the laws themselves, are unconstitutional on their face, without regard to the question of the insufficiency of those rates. We also hold that the circuit court had jurisdiction under the cases already cited (and it was therefore its duty) to inquire whether the rates permitted by these acts or orders were too low and therefore confiscatory, and, if so held, that the court then had jurisdiction to permanently enjoin the railroad company from putting them in force, and that it also had power, while the inquiry was pending, to grant a temporary injunction to the same effect....

We have, therefore, upon this record, the case of an unconstitutional act of the state legislature and an intention by the Attorney General of the state to endeavor to enforce its provisions, to the injury of the company, in compelling it, at great expense, to defend legal proceedings of a complicated and unusual character, and involving questions of vast importance to all employees and officers of the company, as well as to the company itself. The question that arises is whether there is a remedy that the parties interested may resort to, by going into a Federal court of equity, in a case involving a violation of the Federal Constitution, and obtaining a judicial investigation of the problem, and, pending its solution, obtain freedom from suits, civil or criminal, by a temporary injunction, and, if the question be finally decided favorably to the contention of the company, a permanent injunction restraining all such actions or proceedings.

This inquiry necessitates an examination of the most material and important objection made to the jurisdiction of the circuit court—the objection being that the suit is, in effect, one against the state of Minnesota, and that the injunction issued against the Attorney General illegally prohibits state action, either criminal or civil, to enforce obedience to the statutes of the state. This objection is to be considered with reference to the 11th and 14th Amendments to the Federal Constitution.... We think that whatever the rights of complainants may be, they are largely founded upon that [14th] Amendment, but a decision of this case does not require an examination or decision of the question whether its adoption in any way altered or limited the effect of the earlier Amendment. We may assume that each exists in full force, and that we must give to the 11th Amendment all the effect it naturally would have, without cutting it down or rendering its meaning any more narrow than the language, fairly interpreted, would warrant.... Since that time there have been many cases decided in this court involving the 11th Amendment, among them [what follows is a discussion of many of the Court's Eleventh Amendment cases, beginning with *Osborn v. Bank of United States* (1824) 9 Wheat. 738, 846, 857, 6 L. Ed. 204, 229, 232.]

The various authorities we have referred to furnish ample justification for the assertion that individuals who, as officers of the state, are clothed with some duty in regard to the enforcement of the laws of the state, and who threaten and are about to commence proceedings, either of a civil or criminal nature, to enforce against parties affected an unconstitutional act, violating the Federal Constitution, may be enjoined by a Federal court of equity from such action....

In making an officer of the state a party defendant in a suit to enjoin the enforcement of an act alleged to be unconstitutional, it is plain that such officer must have some connection with the enforcement of the act, or else it is merely making him a party as a representative of the state, and thereby attempting to make the state a party.

It is also argued that the only proceeding which the attorney general could take to enforce the statute, so far as his office is concerned, was one by mandamus, which would be commenced by the state, in its sovereign and governmental character, and that the right to bring such action is a necessary attribute of a sovereign government. It is contended that the complainants do not complain and they care nothing about any action which Mr. Young might take or bring as an ordinary individual, but that he was complained of as an officer, to whose discretion is confided the use of the name of the state of Minnesota so far as litigation is concerned, and that when or how he shall use it is a matter resting in his discretion and cannot be controlled by any court.

The answer to all this is the same as made in every case where an official claims to be acting under the authority of the state. The act to be enforced is alleged to be unconstitutional; and if it be so, the use of the name of the state to enforce an unconstitutional act to the injury of complainants is a proceeding without the authority of, and one which does not affect, the state in its sovereign or governmental capacity. It is simply an illegal act upon the part of a state official in attempting, by the use of the name of the state, to enforce a legislative enactment which is void because unconstitutional. If the act which the state attorney general seeks to enforce be a violation of the Federal Constitution, the officer, in proceeding under such enactment, comes into conflict with the superior authority of that Constitution, and he is in that case stripped of his official or representative character and is subjected in his person to the consequences of his individual conduct. The state has no power to impart to him any immunity from responsibility to the supreme authority of the United States. *See Re Ayers*, 123 U.S. 507, 31 L. ed. 230, 8 Sup. Ct. Rep. 164. It would be an injury to complainant to harass it with a multiplicity of suits or litigation generally in an endeavor to enforce penalties under an unconstitutional enactment, and to prevent it ought to be within the jurisdiction of a court of equity. If the question of unconstitutionality, with reference, at least, to the Federal Constitution, be first raised in a Federal court, that court, as we think is shown by the authorities cited hereafter, has the right to decide it, to the exclusion of all other courts.

The question remains whether the attorney general had, by the law of the state, so far as concerns these rate acts, any duty with regard to the enforcement of the same. By his official conduct it seems that he regarded it as a duty connected with his office to compel the company to obey the commodity act, for he commenced proceedings to enforce such obedience immediately after the injunction issued, at the risk of being found guilty of contempt by so doing....

It would seem to be clear that the attorney general, under his power existing at common law, and by virtue of these various statutes, had a general duty imposed upon him, which includes the right and the power to enforce the statutes of the state, including, of course, the act in question, if it were constitutional. His power by virtue of his office sufficiently connected him with the duty of enforcement to make him a proper party to a suit of the nature of the one now before the United States circuit court....

And, again, it must be remembered that jurisdiction of this general character has, in fact, been exercised by Federal courts from the time of *Osborn v. Bank of United States* up to the present; the only difference in regard to the case of *Osborn* and the case in hand being that in this case the injury complained of is the threatened commencement of suits, civil or criminal, to enforce the act, instead of, as in the *Osborn* Case, an actual and direct trespass upon or interference with tangible property. A bill filed to prevent the commencement of suits to enforce an unconstitutional act, under the circumstances already mentioned, is no new invention, as we have already seen. The difference between an actual and direct interference with tangible property and the enjoining of state officers from enforcing an unconstitutional act, is not of a radical nature, and does not extend, in truth, the jurisdiction of the courts over the subject-matter. In the case of the interference with property, the person enjoined is assuming to act in his capacity as an official of the state, and justification for his interference is claimed by reason of his position as a state official. Such official cannot so justify when acting under an unconstitutional enactment of the legislature. So, where the state official, instead of directly interfering with tangible property, is about to commence suits which have for their object the enforcement of an act which violates the Federal Constitution, to the great and irreparable injury of the complainants, he is seeking the same justification from the authority of the state as in other cases. The sovereignty of the state is, in reality, no more involved in one case than in the other. The state cannot, in either case, impart to the official immunity from responsibility to the supreme authority of the United States. See *Re Ayers*, 123 U.S. 507, 31 L. ed. 230, 8 Sup. Ct. Rep. 164.

Mr. Justice Harlan, dissenting:

Let it be observed that the suit instituted by Perkins and Shepard in the circuit court of the United States was, as to the defendant Young, one against him as, and only because he was, Attorney General of Minnesota. No relief was sought against him individually, but only in his capacity as Attorney General. And the manifest, indeed the avowed and admitted, object of seeking such relief, was to tie the hands of the state so that it could not in any manner or by any mode of proceeding, in its own courts, test the validity of the statutes and orders in question. It would therefore seem clear that within the true meaning of the 11th Amendment the suit brought in the Federal court was one, in legal effect, against the state—as much so as if the state had been formally named on the record as a party—and therefore it was a suit to which, under the Amendment, so far as the state or its attorney general was concerned, the judicial power of the United States did not and could not extend. If this proposition be sound it will follow—indeed, it is conceded that if, so far as relief is sought against the Attorney General of Minnesota, this be a suit against the state—then, the order of the Federal court enjoining that officer from taking any action, suit, step, or proceeding to compel the railway company to obey the Minnesota statute was beyond the jurisdiction of that court and wholly void; in which case, that officer was at liberty to proceed in the discharge of his official duties as defined by the laws of the state, and the order adjudging him to be in contempt for bringing the mandamus proceeding in the state court was a nullity....

When, therefore, the Federal court forbade the defendant Young, as Attorney General of Minnesota, from taking any action, suit, step, or proceeding whatever looking to the enforcement of the statutes in question, it said in effect to the state of Minnesota: 'It is true that the powers not delegated to the United States by the Constitution, nor prohibited by it to the states, are reserved to the states respectively or to its people, and it is true that, under the Constitution, the judicial power of the United States does not extend to any suit brought against a state by a citizen of another state or by a citizen or subject of a foreign state, yet the Federal court adjudges that you, the state, although a sovereign for many important governmental purposes, shall not appear in your own courts, by your law officer, with the view of enforcing, or even for determining the validity of, the state enactments which the Federal court has, upon a preliminary hearing, declared to be in violation of the Constitution of the United States.'

This principle, if firmly established, would work a radical change in our governmental system. It would inaugurate a new era in the American judicial system and in the relations of the national and state governments. It would enable the subordinate Federal courts to supervise and control the official action of the states as if they were 'dependencies' or provinces. It would place the states of the Union in a condition of inferiority never dreamed of when the Constitution was adopted or when the 11th Amendment was made a part of the supreme law of the land. I cannot suppose that the great men who framed the Constitution ever thought the time would come when a subordinate Federal court, having no power to compel a state, in its corporate capacity, to appear before it as a litigant, would yet assume to deprive a state of the right to be represented in its own courts by its regular law officer. That is what the court below did, as to Minnesota, when it adjudged that the appearance of the defendant Young in the state court, as the attorney general of Minnesota, representing his state as its chief law officer, was a contempt of the authority of the Federal court, punishable by fine and imprisonment....

The essential and only question now before us or that need be decided is whether an order by the Federal court which prevents the state from being represented in its own courts, by its chief law officer, upon an issue involving the constitutional validity of certain state enactments, does not make a suit against the state within the meaning of the 11th Amendment. If it be a suit of that kind, then, it is conceded, the circuit court was without jurisdiction to fine and imprison the petitioner, and he must be discharged, whatever our views may be as to the validity of those state enactments. This must necessarily be so unless the Amendment has less force and a more restricted meaning now than it had at the time of its adoption, and unless a suit against the attorney general of a state, in his official capacity, is not one against a state under the 11th Amendment when its determination depends upon a question of Constitutional power or right under the 14th Amendment. In that view I cannot concur. In my opinion the 11th Amendment has not been modified in the slightest degree as to its scope or meaning by the 14th Amendment, and a suit which, in its essence, is one against the state, remains one of that character and is forbidden even when brought to strike down a state statute alleged to be in violation of that clause of the 14th Amendment, forbidding the deprivation by a state of life, liberty, or property without due process of law.... Parties cannot, in any case, obtain redress by a suit against the state. Such has been the uniform ruling in this court, and it is most unfortunate that it is now declared to be competent for a Federal circuit court, by exerting its authority over the chief law officer of the state, without the consent of the state, to exclude the state, in its sovereign capacity, from its own courts when seeking to have the ruling of those courts as to its powers under its own statutes. Surely, the right of a state to invoke the jurisdiction of its own courts is not less than the right of individuals to invoke the jurisdiction of a Federal court. The preservation of the dignity and sovereignty of the states, within the limits of their Constitutional powers, is of the last importance, and vital to the preservation of our system of government. The courts should not permit themselves to be driven by the hardships, real or supposed, of particular cases, to accomplish results, even if they be just results, in a mode forbidden by the fundamental law. The country should never be allowed to think that the Constitution can, in any case, be evaded or amended by mere judicial interpretation, or that its behests may be nullified by an ingenious construction of its provisions....

In support of the contention that the present suit is not one against the state, reference was made by counsel to several cases, ... Upon examination it will be found that the defendants in each of those cases were officers of the state, especially charged with the execution of a state enactment alleged to be unconstitutional, but under the authority of which, it was averred, they were committing or were about to commit some specific wrong or trespass, to the injury of the plaintiff's rights. There is a wide difference between a suit against individuals, holding official positions under a state, to prevent them, under the sanction of an unconstitutional statute, from committing, by some positive act, a wrong or trespass, and a suit against officers of a state merely to test the constitutionality of a state statute, in the enforcement of which those officers will act only by formal judicial proceedings in the courts of the state. In the present case, as we have said, neither of the state officers named held any special relation to the particular statute alleged to be unconstitutional. They were not expressly directed to see to its enforcement. If, because they were law officers of the state, a case could be made for the purpose of testing the constitutionality of the statute, by an injunction suit brought against them, then the constitutionality of every act passed by the legislature could be tested by a suit against the governor and attorney general, based upon the theory that the former, as the executive of the state, was, in a general sense, charged with the execution of all its laws, and the latter, as attorney general, might represent the state in litigation involving the enforcement of its statutes. That would be a very convenient way for obtaining a speedy judicial determination of questions of constitutional law which may be raised by individuals, but it is a mode which cannot be applied to the states of the Union consistently with the fundamental principle that they cannot, without their assent, be brought into any court at the suit of private persons....

I am justified, by what this court has heretofore declared, in now saying that the men who framed the Constitution, and who caused the adoption of the 11th Amendment, would have been amazed by the suggestion that a state of the Union can be prevented, by an order of a subordinate Federal court, from being represented by its Attorney General in a suit brought by it in one of its own courts; and that such an order would be inconsistent with the dignity of the states as involved in their Constitutional immunity from the judicial process of the Federal courts (except in the limited cases in which they may Constitutionally be made parties in this court), and would be attended by most pernicious results.

I dissent from the opinion and judgment.

For further discussion

Young is so important because the Court ruled against the State Attorney General even though the injunctive remedy being sought was directed against him in his "official capacity," the Attorney General was acting under "color of state law," and the relief being sought would impose binding obligations on a high-level official of the State of Minnesota.[15] Significantly, the relief awarded in *Young* was prospective only, i.e., the Minnesota Attorney General was enjoined to conform his *future* conduct in his official position to the requirements of the Fourteenth Amendment.

In *Edelman v. Jordan*, 415 U.S. 651 (1974), the Court concluded that *Young* applies only when the equitable relief sought is prospective in nature, and that a request for retroactive relief is functionally the same as suing a state official in his official capacity for money damages. In that case, a class of public assistance recipients sued Illinois officials for failing to process public assistance grants within the time limits set forth in federal law. The state officials were instead processing the grants within the longer time periods contained in state regulations. With respect to plaintiffs' claim for retroactive relief, the Court concluded that a payment of welfare benefits from the state treasury for past wrongful conduct was tantamount to an award of damages against the state and was barred by the principle of sovereign immunity that underlies the Eleventh Amendment. On the other hand, the Court relied on *Young* to enjoin defendants' future conduct because the state officials were acting in violation of federal law and the Court was enjoining the officials from continuing this unlawful future action. In other words, *Edelman* held that the Eleventh Amendment barred suit against a state official to the extent the lawsuit sought to extract money for an accrued liability, but did not bar suit to compel a state official to expend funds in the future to comply with federal law.[16]

---

15. *See* Florida Dept. of State v. Treasure Salvors, Inc., 458 U.S. 670, 685 (1982) (opinion of Stevens, J.) (*Young* created the "well-recognized irony" that an official's unconstitutional conduct constitutes "state action" under the Fourteenth Amendment, "yet [is] not attributable to the State for purposes of" the Eleventh Amendment).

16. The lower federal courts continue to struggle with the issue of whether certain relief is permissible prospective relief under *Young* or impermissible retroactive relief under *Edelman*. *See e.g.*, Native Vill. of Noatak v. Blatchford, 38 F.3d 1505, 1512 (9th Cir. 1994) ("In discerning whether the relief sought is prospective or retroactive for purposes of the Eleventh Amendment bar, we must analyze the substance, not the form, of the relief."); Independent Living Center v. Maxwell-Jolly, 572 F.3d 644, 661 n.19 (9th Cir. 2009) (order providing for payment of Medicaid monies for services performed prior to date of order barred under *Edelman* as retroactive relief in the nature of damages. "In so deciding, we employ the approach used by the Second, Fourth, and Seventh Circuits, i.e., whether relief is prospective or retrospective in the Medicaid payment context turns on the date of service, not the date of payment.") (citations omitted): *accord* New York City Health & Hosp. Corp. v. Perales, 50 F.3d 129, 137 (2d Cir. 1995).

In 2011, the Court reaffirmed the vitality of *Young* in a lawsuit that was brought in federal court by a state entity—Virginia Office for Protection and Advocacy—against state officials at the Virginia Department of Behavioral Health and Developmental Services to compel them to produce certain records relating to its investigation into the death or serious injury of three people in facilities operated by that agency. In *Commonwealth of Virginia v. Reinhard*,[17] the Fourth Circuit had dismissed the case holding that *Young* could not be used to adjudicate "intramural state conflicts" because doing so would encroach on the dignity and sovereignty of the state and conflict directly with the principles of federalism that underlie the Eleventh Amendment.

The Supreme Court reversed[18] and held that a state agency could sue state officials under the doctrine of *Ex parte Young* to protect the rights of the developmentally disabled. In an opinion by Justice Scalia, the six-member majority explained that the interests that underlie *Ex parte Young*, specifically the vindication of federal rights, were not diminished because the plaintiff was a state entity. The Court wrote: "[W]e do not understand how a State's stature could be diminished to any greater degree when its own agency polices its officers' compliance with their federal obligations, than when a private person hales those officers into federal court for the same purpose—something everyone agrees is proper."[19] The Court also explained that not every indignity offends the doctrine of sovereign immunity. Rather, the type of indignity that the doctrine protects is suing a state without its consent when the object of the lawsuit is to infringe upon the state's sovereign interests, such as seeking funds from the state's treasury. This kind of indignity "does not occur just because the suit happens to be brought by another state agency"[20] for relief that could have properly been obtained by a private individual.

17. 568 F.3d 110, 119–21 (4th Cir. 2009).

18. Virginia Office for Protection and Advocacy v. Stewart, 563 U.S. 247 (2011).

19. *Id.* at 257–58 (emphasis in original; fn. omitted). The Court also noted that the state law itself had authorized the state agency to sue to protect the rights of the developmentally disabled.

20. *Id.* Note also that the United States, as amicus, urged the Court to reverse the Fourth Circuit's decision, arguing, *inter alia*, that "the suit here involves an independent entity that the Commonwealth voluntarily established to participate in federal programs that protect vulnerable individuals.... When petitioner sues state officials to enforce its rights under the [federal laws that protect the developmentally disabled], then, petitioner is implementing federal law and policy, not seeking relief that might be characterized as intramural in nature." U.S. Amicus Brief, p. 19, *available at* https://dlcv.org/wp-content/uploads/2016/08/US-Amicus-VOPA.pdf (last visited Nov. 2019).

Rules for Applying the Eleventh Amendment When a State Official Is Sued in Her Official Capacity

Lawsuit seeks money damages.	Eleventh Amendment is a complete defense.
Lawsuit seeks equitable relief and there is no claim that the official's conduct violates federal law or the Federal Constitution.	Eleventh Amendment is a complete defense.
Lawsuit seeks equitable relief and it is alleged that the official is acting ultra vires.*	Eleventh Amendment does not apply, but only where the allegation is that the official's actions lack any colorable legal authority.
Lawsuit seeks equitable relief and it is alleged that the official is acting in violation of the Federal Constitution or federal law.	Under *Ex parte Young*, Eleventh Amendment does not apply where the relief is prospective in nature, i.e., it applies to future conduct.

* The ultra vires doctrine applies only when the state official acts in the absence of any colorable legal authority. *See* Pennhurst State Sch. & Hosp. v. Halderman, 465 U.S. at 110–114, fns 20–23.

The Supreme Court has also recognized the importance of applying *Young* to "ensure that the doctrine of sovereign immunity remains meaningful, while also giving recognition to the need to prevent violations of federal law." *Idaho v. Coeur d'Alene Tribe of Idaho*, 521 U.S. 261, 269 (1997). To reach this balance, the Court has carved out three areas where *Young* does not apply even though the underlying claim is based upon a state official's alleged violation of federal law or a pendent state claim.

i. Cases in which *Young* would be inconsistent with a detailed statutory or regulatory scheme provided in the federal statute that forms the basis for the underlying claim. In these cases, the Supreme Court concluded that, where Congress has crafted a detailed remedial scheme in a federal law to deal with the violation of a federal right, federal supremacy is vindicated by using the remedies contained in that scheme rather than the more general prospective equitable relief available under *Young*.[21]

ii. Cases that implicate special state sovereignty interests, such as a quiet title action. In these cases, the Eleventh Amendment applies to actions that might otherwise be allowed under *Young* because of the enormous impact the lawsuit may have on the state's sovereign interests.[22]

---

21. *See* Seminole Tribe of Fla. v. Florida, 517 U.S. 44, 74–76 (1996) (holding that the existence of a detailed remedial scheme for enforcement of the Indian Gaming Regulatory Act shows congressional intent to prohibit recourse to a broader equitable action against state officials based on *Young*).

22. *See* Idaho v. Coeur d'Alene Tribe of Idaho, 521 U.S. 261, 270, 281–82 (1997) (federally recognized Indian Tribe and individual tribe members brought action in federal court for declaratory and injunctive relief against the State of Idaho and various state officials and agencies alleging that the Tribe owned submerged lands as well as the bed of a lake and its tributaries under treaties establishing the boundaries of the Tribe's reservation. The Court dismissed the lawsuit under the Eleventh Amendment, concluding that the Tribe's suit was the functional equivalent of a quiet title action which implicates special sovereignty interests especially where, if the Tribe succeeds, all benefits of ownership and regulatory control of the affected lands would shift from the State to the Tribe.

The suit would diminish, even extinguish, the State's control over a vast reach of lands and

iii. Cases brought in federal court against state officials raising separate, but related claims, called pendent claims, under state law. In these cases, the Supreme Court determined that the need to vindicate the supremacy of federal law is not at issue and, therefore, there is no need to use the *Young* exception.[23]

b. Understanding the Difference between an Official Capacity and a Personal Capacity Lawsuit

Individuals injured by the actions of state officials will often sue the official—as opposed to the agency that employs the person—in his or her official capacity in order to avoid having the case dismissed under the Eleventh Amendment. An official capacity federal lawsuit is in all respects, except for the name of the defendant, a suit against the entity that employs the individual.[24] For example, if the person works for the State Department of Widgets, the official capacity claim is, as a practical matter, considered to be brought against the Department that employs him or her. If the Department is an agency of the state, the suit is essentially brought against the state.

In an official capacity claim, if the official dies or leaves government service, his or her successor is automatically substituted as a party litigant in the case.[25] In other words, the official is being sued not for his individual actions, but as an alter ego of the governmental entity that employs him.[26] Because the suit is essentially against the state and any monetary relief would be paid from the state treasury, the Supreme Court has concluded that a suit for money damages against a state official in her official capacity is barred by the Eleventh Amendment.[27] Using this logic, it would

---

> waters long deemed by the State to be an integral part of its territory. To pass this off as a judgment causing little or no offense to Idaho's sovereign authority and its standing in the Union would be to ignore the realities of the relief the Tribe demands.

Id. at 282; *see also* W. Mohegan Tribe & Nation v. Orange County, 395 F.3d 18 (2d Cir. 2004) (applying *Coeur d' Alene* and holding that quiet title action against New York's Governor was barred by Eleventh Amendment immunity); Ysela del sur Pueblo v. Raney, 199 F.3d 281 (5th Cir. 2000) (lawsuit by Indian Tribe seeking to eject state officers from land they allegedly occupied in violation of federal law was barred by Eleventh Amendment immunity); MacDonald v. Vill. of Northport, Mich., 164 F.3d 964 (6th Cir. 1999) (Eleventh Amendment barred a federal lawsuit against the Michigan State Treasurer seeking a declaration that the plaintiffs owned a right-of-way which provided access to a navigable waterway).

23. *See* Pennhurst State Sch. & Hosp. v. Halderman, 465 U.S. at 105–06 (the Court concluded that pendent state law claims do not implicate the supremacy of federal law).

24. Brandon v. Holt, 469 U.S. 464, 471–72 (1985) ("[A] judgment against a public servant 'in his official capacity' imposes liability on the entity that he represents provided, of course, the public entity received notice and an opportunity to respond.") (fn. omitted).

25. For example, in Smith v. Reeves, 178 U.S. 436, 437 (1900), the Court noted that the original defendant was J.R. McDonald, as Treasurer of the State of California, and that he was succeeded in the office by Levi Rackliffe, W.S. Green, and Truman Reeves, in the order named, each of whom had been substituted for his predecessor as a defendant in the lawsuit. The substitution was allowed because the defendant was sued in his official capacity; *see also* Fed. R. Civ. Pro. 25(d).

26. Smith v. Reeves, 178 U.S. at 440 ("We are clearly of opinion that ... this suit, though in form against an officer of the state, is against the state itself.").

27. *See* Ford Motor Co. v. Dept. of the Treasury, 323 U.S. 459, 464 (1945) (Eleventh Amendment bars suit against state officials when "the action is in essence one for the recovery of money from the

appear that a suit for injunctive relief against a state official should also be barred by the Eleventh Amendment because it is also essentially a suit against the state and would intrude on the state's sovereign immunity. However, the Court created a legal fiction in *Young* to allow state officials to be sued for prospective injunctive relief if the official is violating federal law or the Federal Constitution.[28] The Court determined that allowing state officials to continue violating federal law and/or the Federal Constitution would so weaken federal supremacy that this exception was necessary.

Are the State and Widget Department responsible for every action taken by their employees? The courts have held that in order to hold the entity itself liable in an official capacity lawsuit, the entity must be the "'moving force' behind" the challenged action or deprivation.[29] Therefore, an official capacity lawsuit requires the plaintiff to show that a government statute, rule, policy, or custom played a part in the violation of federal law.[30]

A lawsuit may also be brought against a state official in her personal/individual capacity, rather than her official capacity, for unconstitutional or otherwise wrongful conduct.[31] In an individual capacity lawsuit, the wrongful conduct must be fairly attributable to the actions or inactions of the official herself and the relief must be sought directly from that person and not from the state treasury.

Based on these rules, when would you sue a state official in her official capacity and when would you sue her in her individual capacity? The simple answer is that if you are seeking equitable relief, such as an injunction or a declaration, you would usually sue the state official in her official capacity, and if you are seeking money damages, you would sue the official in her individual capacity. You would seek equitable relief if your lawsuit is based on a state rule or policy that has caused you injury. The person you are suing would, by virtue of her position, have responsibility for enforcing the challenged rule or policy. Thus, in an official capacity suit, your focus is not on the particular individual, but rather on the office or position that a particular individual holds.

On the other hand, when you sue a state official in her individual capacity for money damages, the claim must be based on the wrongful conduct of that particular

---

state [because] the state is the real, substantial party in interest and is entitled to invoke its sovereign immunity from suit even though individual officials are nominal defendants.").

28. The legal fiction is that the lawsuit can proceed, despite the Eleventh Amendment, because the lawsuit is not against the State itself, but rather is against the individual in order to vindicate federal supremacy rights.

29. *See* Kentucky v. Graham, 473 U.S. 159, 166 (1985) ("More is required in an official-capacity action, however, for a governmental entity is liable under section 1983 only when the entity itself is a 'moving force' behind the deprivation").

30. *Id.* ("[I]n an official-capacity suit the entity's 'policy or custom' must have played a part in the violation of federal law") (citations omitted).

31. *See* Scheuer v. Rhodes, 416 U.S. at 238 ("damages against individual defendants are a permissible remedy in some circumstances notwithstanding the fact that they hold public office") (citations omitted); Hafer v. Melo, 502 U.S. 21, 30–31 (1991) ("the Eleventh Amendment does not erect a barrier against suits to impose 'individual and personal liability' on state officials under section 1983") (quoting Scheuer v. Rhodes, 416 U.S. at 238).

employee towards you. You are not seeking money damages against the office or position the person holds. State officials can however, be sued in both their official and individual capacities in the same lawsuit for both injunctive relief and damages. These suits would involve both wrongful conduct on the part of the particular employee and conduct by the state official based on the agency's policy and custom.

Even though a state official is being sued in her individual or personal capacity, the underlying conduct at issue will usually be based upon conduct that arose in the course of her official duties. While the Eleventh Amendment does not apply to bar such lawsuits, officials sued for money damages in their personal capacities are eligible in many states, as a matter of state law, to indemnification by the state for any money judgment.

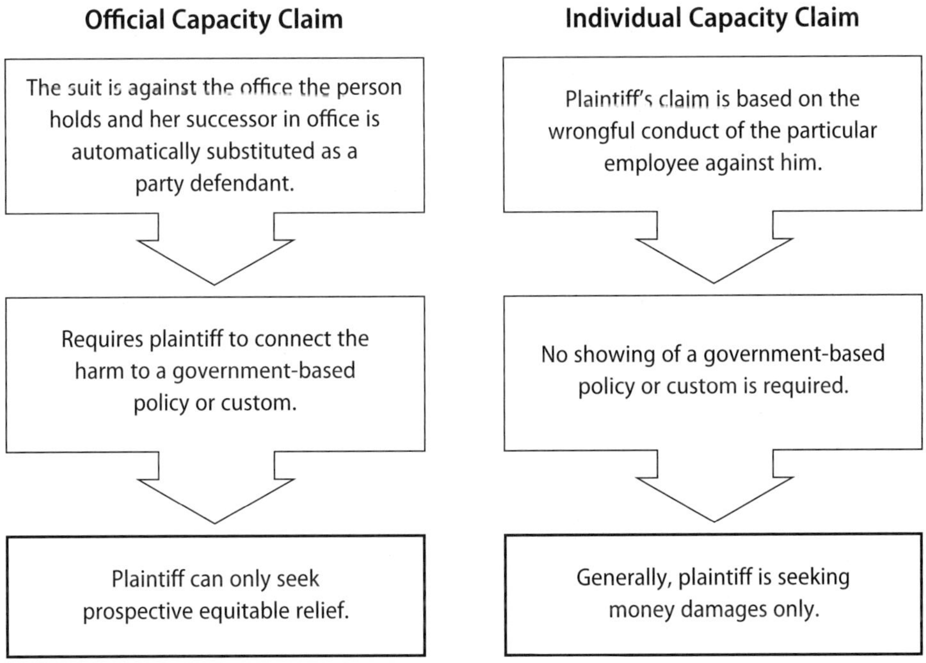

D. The Eleventh Amendment vs. the Fourteenth Amendment — Balancing State Sovereign Interests with Enforcement of Civil Rights Guaranteed by the Fourteenth Amendment

The Fourteenth Amendment was ratified in 1868, shortly after the Civil War ended. Section 1 of the Amendment protects all individuals from state action that would result in the loss of life, liberty, and property without due process of law or in the denial of equal protection of the laws. That section provides, in relevant part:

> No State shall make or enforce any law which shall abridge the privileges or immunities of citizens of the United States; nor shall any State deprive any person of life, liberty, or property, without due process of law; nor deny to any person within its jurisdiction the equal protection of the laws.

In addition, the Fourteenth Amendment contains a catchall provision, known as Section 5, which authorizes Congress to enact appropriate laws to enforce the guarantees of the Amendment. Section 5 provides that "The Congress shall have power to enforce, by appropriate legislation, the provisions of this article."

Three years after the Fourteenth Amendment was ratified, Congress enacted the Civil Rights Act of 1871, the predecessor to 42 U.S.C. § 1983 (section 1983), which allows any person to sue a state official for violating his or her rights under the Federal Constitution or federal law.

Beginning in the 1960s, section 1983 became one of the most important weapons for protecting the civil rights of minorities and others injured by state action. Relying on *Young*, individuals injured by governmental action sued state officials in their official capacities for injunctive relief to stop them from continuing to violate their federal constitutional and statutory rights.

Because section 1983 also makes any person who causes a deprivation of another person's civil and constitutional rights liable for damages, the lawsuits were also brought against state officials in their individual capacities for damages. But plaintiffs injured by the conduct of state and local officials sometimes needed to hold states and state instrumentalities themselves liable for damages under section 1983 in order to get full relief. For example, government officials might be protected by absolute or qualified immunity, but these defenses are not available to states and state agencies. To get around the Eleventh Amendment bar, these litigants argued that, since section 1983 was enacted to enforce the Fourteenth Amendment, the provisions of that Amendment trumped those in the Eleventh Amendment.

In the 1970s, the Supreme Court resolved two of the fundamental issues involving the interplay of the Fourteenth Amendment, section 1983, and the Eleventh Amendment.

1. The first issue was whether laws enacted under Section 5 of the Fourteenth Amendment could be enforced despite the Eleventh Amendment. This issue is described as whether a law enacted by Congress under section 5 and directed at the states can "abrogate" the states' Eleventh Amendment immunity. The most important case addressing this issue was *Fitzpatrick v. Bitzer*, 427 U.S. 445 (1976). That case involved an alleged violation of Title VII of the Civil Rights Act of 1964, as amended. In general, Title VII prohibits state and local officials from discriminating with respect to the terms and conditions of employment on the basis of race, gender, and ethnicity. In *Fitzpatrick*, the Court held that Title VII was validly enacted under Section 5, i.e., it was appropriate legislation to enforce the Fourteenth Amendment, and that the effect of that enactment was to abrogate the state's sovereign immunity from suit. The ra-

tionale behind *Fitzpatrick* was that the Fourteenth Amendment, by expanding federal power at the expense of state autonomy, had fundamentally altered the balance of power between the states and the federal government from what it was in the original Constitution.[32]

After establishing this general rule, the Court made clear that abrogation of Eleventh Amendment immunity is to be strictly limited because it "upsets 'the fundamental constitutional balance between the Federal Government and the states,' placing a considerable strain on '[t]he principles of federalism that inform Eleventh Amendment doctrine.'"[33]

2. *Fitzpatrick* set the stage for resolution of the second issue—what attributes must a law possess to be considered appropriate legislation under Section 5 of the Fourteenth Amendment?

   a. The Clear Statement Rule

   In *Edelman v. Jordan*, 415 U.S. 651 (1974) and *Quern v. Jordan*, 440 U.S. 332, 342 (1979), the Supreme Court established that a law enacted under Section 5 can only abrogate the state's Eleventh Amendment immunity if Congress clearly intended the law at issue to be used by individuals to sue states. This has become known as the "clear legislative statement rule." Under this rule, there can be no abrogation of Eleventh Amendment immunity unless Congress makes clear—in express terms in the language of the statute—that states themselves are both covered by the law and can be sued to enforce the law.

   After reviewing the language in section 1983 and its legislative history, the Supreme Court in *Quern* concluded that Congress did not clearly demonstrate the intent to allow suits to be brought directly against states in that statute, but only intended that suit be brought against state officials. One of the primary reasons for the difference in outcome between *Fitzpatrick* (Title VII) and *Quern* (section 1983) was that when Congress amended Title VII in 1972, it expressly authorized injured persons to sue states, but Congress failed to do the same when it enacted section 1983.

For further discussion

Below are several examples of language crafted by Congress in federal laws that were alleged to abrogate Eleventh Amendment immunity. Decide in each case whether the language is sufficient to satisfy the clear legislative statement rule. If you believe the language is not sufficiently clear, do you think the legislative history of the statute could be used to provide further guidance?

32. Fitzpatrick v. Bitzer, 427 U.S. at 455.
33. Dellmuth v. Muth, 491 U.S. 223, 227 (1989) (citations omitted).

1. [The law] applies to "any recipient of Federal assistance." Note that all states receive federal money.[34]
2. "Nothing in this [law] shall preclude a[n aggrieved party] from bringing a suit on behalf of individuals with developmental disabilities against a State, or an agency or instrumentality of a State."[35]
3. Under this law, employees may sue for back pay "against any employer (including a public agency) in any Federal or State court of competent jurisdiction." Public agency is defined to include "the government of a State or political subdivision thereof," and "any agency of ... a State."[36]
4. Under this law, "[a]ny state ... shall not be immune, under the Eleventh Amendment of the Constitution of the United States or under any other doctrine of sovereign immunity, from suit in Federal court ... for infringement of a patent."[37]

---

b. The law must secure the guarantees of the Fourteenth Amendment

Assuming that the clear legislative statement rule is met, the court must decide whether the law is appropriate to enforce the Fourteenth Amendment.[38] In order to be appropriate, the law must secure the guarantees of

---

34. This language was included in section 504 of the Rehabilitation Act of 1973. The Supreme Court concluded that it did not provide a clear statement of intent to cover states because it was too general to give states fair notice that they would be subject to the provisions of this federal law by receiving federal money. In explaining its reasoning the Court wrote: "A general authorization for suit in federal court is not the kind of unequivocal statutory language sufficient to abrogate the Eleventh Amendment. When Congress chooses to subject the States to federal jurisdiction, it must do so specifically." Atascadero State Hosp. v. Scanlon, 473 U.S. 234, 242 (1985).

35. This language is contained in 42 U.S.C. § 15044(b)(1), a section within the federal Developmental Disabilities Assistance and Bill of Rights Act of 2000, 42 U.S.C. §§ 15001–15115. The Fourth Circuit concluded that the language of the statute did not provide the clear expression of legislative intent necessary to abrogate the State's sovereign immunity because it did not explicitly state that the States' Eleventh Amendment immunity from suit is waived. Commonwealth of Virginia v. Reinhard, 568 F.3d 110, 116–17 (4th Cir. 2009), *rev'd on other grounds,* 563 U.S. 247 (2011). The Circuit Court wrote:

> We agree with the district court that the provision ... is not sufficiently explicit to waive Virginia's sovereign immunity. Indeed, the language in that provision is far from the emphatic, 'express' and 'unequivocal' statement that is necessary to constitute a waiver.

36. This language from the Fair Labor Standards Act, which was cross-referenced in the Age Discrimination in Employment Act (ADEA), was found sufficient to waive the states' sovereign immunity from suit under the ADEA. Kimel v. Florida Bd. of Regents, 528 U.S. 62, 67–68, 73–74 (2000) (quoting 29 U.S.C. § 216(b), as cross-referenced in 29 U.S.C. § 626(b); definition of public agency found at 29 U.S.C. § 203(x)).

37. This language was found sufficient to waive the state's sovereign immunity from suit under the Patent Remedy Act. Florida Prepaid Postsecondary Educ. Expense Bd. v. Coll. Sav. Bank, 527 U.S. 627, 635 (1999) (interpreting the Patent Remedy Act, 35 U.S.C. § 296(a)).

38. Katzenbach v. Morgan, 384 U.S. 641, 651 (1966).

the Fourteenth Amendment either by prohibiting conduct that on its face violates section 1 of the Fourteenth Amendment or by regulating conduct that is facially constitutional, but that can, over time, lead to a violation of section 1 of the Fourteenth Amendment. The latter is known as prophylactic legislation.

As the Supreme Court explained, Section 5 gives Congress "the power 'to enforce,' not the power to determine what constitutes a constitutional violation."[39] Therefore, Section 5 legislation must remedy or prevent constitutional violations, rather than create new standards or make substantive changes to rights contained in the Constitution.[40]

c. History and pattern of discrimination

To show that the law is appropriate to guarantee the rights in the Constitution, Congress must identify a history or pattern of unconstitutional discrimination by states that the law is targeted to remedy.[41] The evidentiary burden imposed on Congress depends on the nature of the classification that Congress is seeking to remedy. For example, states may not discriminate on the basis of race or gender without satisfying a stringent standard known as strict or intermediate scrutiny. Therefore, Congress has greater leeway in enacting laws under Section 5 that prohibit states from discriminating on the basis of these characteristics. On the other hand, Congress has a stricter burden in showing the need to enact age or disability laws because states are ordinarily given deference in these areas and need only meet a rational basis standard to overcome a constitutional challenge.

d. The congruence and proportionality standard

Not only must Congress show a need for the legislation, but the statute's remedial scheme must also be sufficiently targeted to prevent and/or remedy the unconstitutional discrimination that the law was designed to remedy. In other words, the court evaluates whether the rights and remedies contained in the statutory scheme are "congruent and proportional" to the documented harm. "There must be a congruence and proportionality between the injury to be prevented or remedied and the means adopted to that end."[42]

Between 1996 and 2006, the Court decided whether some of the most important civil rights laws were properly enacted under Section 5 of the Fourteenth Amendment. The stakes were high. Those laws found not to be "appropriate" legislation under

39. City of Boerne v. Flores, 521 U.S. 507, 519 (1997).

40. *See id.* at 534.

41. *See id.* at 508–09.

42. *Id.* at 520.

Section 5 could not trump the states' Eleventh Amendment immunity and, as a result, private parties subject to discrimination on the basis of age, disability, gender, race, or some other characteristic, would be left to seek damages before a state agency or in state court. Many states have not waived their sovereign immunity with respect to these lawsuits or have imposed strict time deadlines on challenging administrative action. Moreover, certain federal laws do not allow suit to be brought against individual defendants, preventing use of *Young* to avoid an Eleventh Amendment defense. Therefore, upholding the states' claim of Eleventh Amendment immunity might leave injured plaintiffs without any remedy at all.

For a Federal Statute Enacted under Section 5 of the Fourteenth Amendment to Abrogate the Eleventh Amendment

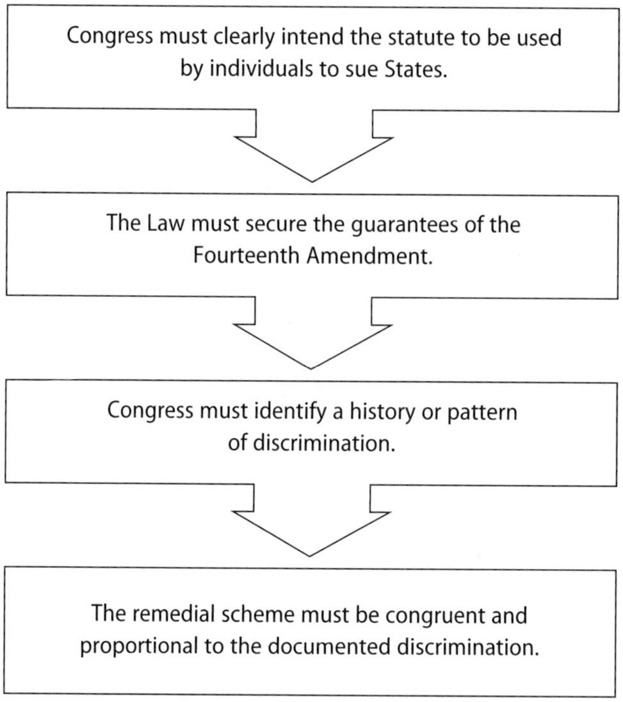

Questions to guide reading of *Kimel v. Florida Bd. of Regents*

1. Is it important to the Court's analysis that laws that discriminate on the basis of age are reviewed under a more lenient rational basis standard? Why or why not?

2. Why did the Court find it significant that, under the ADEA, states could be held liable for age discrimination even though they would not be found to have violated the equal protection clause of the Fourteenth Amendment to the Constitution?

3. Did the Court look at the legislative history with too critical an eye, i.e., did it fail to give sufficient deference to Congress's judgment? Explain your answer.
4. If the legislative history contained a stronger showing of age discrimination by states, do you think the Court would have upheld the statute under Section 5? Explain your answer.
5. Why does the Court identify other avenues of relief available to older Americans at the end of the majority opinion?

Kimel v. Florida Bd. of Regents

528 U.S. 62 (2000)

JUSTICE O'CONNOR delivered the opinion of the Court.

The Age Discrimination in Employment Act of 1967 (ADEA or Act), 81 Stat. 602, as amended, 29 U.S.C. §621 et seq. (1994 ed. and Supp. III), makes it unlawful for an employer, including a State, "to fail or refuse to hire or to discharge any individual or otherwise discriminate against any individual ... because of such individual's age." 29 U.S.C. §623(a)(1). In these cases, three sets of plaintiffs filed suit under the Act, seeking money damages for their state employers' alleged discrimination on the basis of age. In each case, the state employer moved to dismiss the suit on the basis of its Eleventh Amendment immunity.... In these cases, we are asked to consider whether the ADEA contains a clear statement of Congress' intent to abrogate the States' Eleventh Amendment immunity and, if so, whether the ADEA is a proper exercise of Congress' constitutional authority. We conclude that the ADEA does contain a clear statement of Congress' intent to abrogate the States' immunity, but that the abrogation exceeded Congress' authority under §5 of the Fourteenth Amendment.

The ADEA makes it unlawful for an employer "to fail or refuse to hire or to discharge any individual or otherwise discriminate against any individual with respect to his compensation, terms, conditions, or privileges of employment, because of such individual's age." 29 U.S.C. §623(a)(1). The Act also provides several exceptions to this broad prohibition. For example, an employer may rely on age where it "is a bona fide occupational qualification reasonably necessary to the normal operation of the particular business." §623(f)(1). The Act also permits an employer to engage in conduct otherwise prohibited by §623(a)(1) if the employer's action "is based on reasonable factors other than age," §623(f)(1), or if the employer "discharge[s] or otherwise discipline[s] an individual for good cause," §623(f)(3)....

In 1974, in a statute consisting primarily of amendments to the FLSA, Congress extended application of the ADEA's substantive requirements to the States. Fair Labor Standards Amendments of 1974 (1974 Act), §28, 88 Stat. 74. Congress accomplished that expansion in scope by a simple amendment to the definition of "employer" contained in 29 U.S.C. §630(b): "The term [employer] also means ... a State or political subdivision of a State and any agency or instrumentality of a State or a political subdivision of a State...." .... In the same 1974 Act, Congress amended 29 U.S.C.

§ 216(b), the FLSA enforcement provision incorporated by reference into the ADEA. 88 Stat. 61. Section 216(b) now permits an individual to bring a civil action "against any employer (including a public agency) in any Federal or State court of competent jurisdiction." Section 203(x) defines "[p]ublic agency" to include "the Government of a State or political subdivision thereof," and "any agency of ... a State, or a political subdivision of a State."....

To determine whether a federal statute properly subjects States to suits by individuals, we apply a "simple but stringent test: 'Congress may abrogate the States' constitutionally secured immunity from suit in federal court only by making its intention unmistakably clear in the language of the statute.' " ... We agree with petitioners that the ADEA satisfies that test. The ADEA states that its provisions "shall be enforced in accordance with the powers, remedies, and procedures provided in sections 211(b), 216 (except for subsection (a) thereof), and 217 of this title, and subsection (c) of this section." 29 U.S.C. § 626(b). Section 216(b), in turn, clearly provides for suits by individuals against States. That provision authorizes employees to maintain actions for back pay "against any employer (including a public agency) in any Federal or State court of competent jurisdiction...." Any doubt concerning the identity of the "public agency" defendant named in § 216(b) is dispelled by looking to § 203(x), which defines the term to include "the government of a State or political subdivision thereof," and "any agency of ... a State, or a political subdivision of a State." Read as a whole, the plain language of these provisions clearly demonstrates Congress' intent to subject the States to suit for money damages at the hands of individual employees....

Under our firmly established precedent then, if the ADEA rests solely on Congress' Article I commerce power, the private petitioners in today's cases cannot maintain their suits against their state employers.... Section 5 of the Fourteenth Amendment, however, does grant Congress the authority to abrogate the States' sovereign immunity. In *Fitzpatrick v. Bitzer*, 427 U.S. 445 (1976), we recognized that "the Eleventh Amendment, and the principle of state sovereignty which it embodies, are necessarily limited by the enforcement provisions of § 5 of the Fourteenth Amendment." *Id.*, at 456 (citation omitted). Since our decision in *Fitzpatrick*, we have reaffirmed the validity of that congressional power on numerous occasions....

The Fourteenth Amendment provides, in relevant part:

> "Section 1.... No State shall make or enforce any law which shall abridge the privileges or immunities of citizens of the United States; nor shall any State deprive any person of life, liberty, or property, without due process of law; nor deny to any person within its jurisdiction the equal protection of the laws."
>
> ....
>
> "Section 5. The Congress shall have power to enforce, by appropriate legislation, the provisions of this article."

As we recognized most recently in *City of Boerne v. Flores*, 521 U.S. 507, 517 (1997), § 5 is an affirmative grant of power to Congress. "It is for Congress in the first instance to 'determin[e] whether and what legislation is needed to secure the guarantees of the Fourteenth Amendment,' and its conclusions are entitled to much deference." *Id.*, at 536 (*quoting Katzenbach v. Morgan*, 384 U.S. 641, 651 (1966)). Congress' § 5 power is not confined to the enactment of legislation that merely parrots the precise wording of the Fourteenth Amendment. Rather, Congress' power "to enforce" the Amendment includes the authority both to remedy and to deter violation of rights guaranteed thereunder by prohibiting a somewhat broader swath of conduct, including that which is not itself forbidden by the Amendment's text. 521 U.S., at 518.

Nevertheless, we have also recognized that the same language that serves as the basis for the affirmative grant of congressional power also serves to limit that power. For example, Congress cannot "decree the substance of the Fourteenth Amendment's restrictions on the States.... It has been given the power 'to enforce,' not the power to determine what constitutes a constitutional violation." [*City of Boerne*], at 519 (emphases added). The ultimate interpretation and determination of the Fourteenth Amendment's substantive meaning remains the province of the Judicial Branch. *Id.*, at 536.... The line between the two is a fine one. Accordingly, recognizing that "Congress must have wide latitude in determining where [that line] lies," we held that "[t]here must be a congruence and proportionality between the injury to be prevented or remedied and the means adopted to that end." 521 U.S. at 520....

Applying the same "congruence and proportionality" test..., we conclude that the ADEA is not "appropriate legislation" under § 5 of the Fourteenth Amendment. Initially, the substantive requirements the ADEA imposes on state and local governments are disproportionate to any unconstitutional conduct that conceivably could be targeted by the Act.... Accordingly, as we recognized in [the cited Supreme Court cases], age is not a suspect classification under the Equal Protection Clause....

States may discriminate on the basis of age without offending the Fourteenth Amendment if the age classification in question is rationally related to a legitimate state interest. The rationality commanded by the Equal Protection Clause does not require States to match age distinctions and the legitimate interests they serve with razor-like precision. As we have explained, when conducting rational basis review "we will not overturn such [government action] unless the varying treatment of different groups or persons is so unrelated to the achievement of any combination of legitimate purposes that we can only conclude that the [government's] actions were irrational." ... In contrast, when a State discriminates on the basis of race or gender, we require a tighter fit between the discriminatory means and the legitimate ends they serve....

Judged against the backdrop of our equal protection jurisprudence, it is clear that the ADEA is "so out of proportion to a supposed remedial or preventive object that it cannot be understood as responsive to, or designed to prevent, unconstitutional behavior." *City of Boerne*, 521 U.S. at 532. The Act, through its broad restriction on the use of age as a discriminating factor, prohibits substantially more state employment decisions and practices than would likely be held unconstitutional under the applicable equal protection, rational basis standard. The ADEA makes unlawful, in the employment context, all "discriminat[ion] against any individual ... because of such individual's age." 29 U.S.C. § 623(a)(1)....

Petitioners stake their claim on § 623(f)(1). That section permits employers to rely on age when it "is a bona fide occupational qualification reasonably necessary to the normal operation of the particular business." Petitioner's reliance on the "bona fide occupational qualification (BFOQ) defense is misplaced....

Under the ADEA, even with its BFOQ defense, the State's use of age is prima facie unlawful.... Measured against the rational basis standard of our equal protection jurisprudence, the ADEA plainly imposes substantially higher burdens on state employers. Thus, although it is true that the existence of the BFOQ defense makes the ADEA's prohibition of age discrimination less than absolute, the Act's substantive requirements nevertheless remain at a level akin to our heightened scrutiny cases under the Equal Protection Clause.

That the ADEA prohibits very little conduct likely to be held unconstitutional, while significant, does not alone provide the answer to our § 5 inquiry. Difficult and intractable problems often require powerful remedies, and we have never held that § 5 precludes Congress from enacting reasonably prophylactic legislation. Our task is to determine whether the ADEA is in fact just such an appropriate remedy or, instead, merely an attempt to substantively redefine the States' legal obligations with respect to age discrimination. One means by which we have made such a determination in the past is by examining the legislative record containing the reasons for Congress' action....

Our examination of the ADEA's legislative record confirms that Congress' 1974 extension of the Act to the States was an unwarranted response to a perhaps inconsequential problem. Congress never identified any pattern of age discrimination by the States, much less any discrimination whatsoever that rose to the level of constitutional violation. The evidence compiled by petitioners to demonstrate such attention by Congress to age discrimination by the States falls well short of the mark. That evidence consists almost entirely of isolated sentences clipped from floor debates and legislative reports....

A review of the ADEA's legislative record as a whole, then, reveals that Congress had virtually no reason to believe that state and local governments were unconstitutionally discriminating against their employees on the basis of age. Although that lack of support is not determinative of the § 5 inquiry, ... Congress' failure to uncover any significant pattern of unconstitutional discrimination here confirms that Congress had no reason to believe that broad prophylactic legislation was necessary in this field. In light of the indiscriminate scope of the Act's substantive requirements, and the lack of evidence of widespread and unconstitutional age discrimination by the States, we hold that the ADEA is not a valid exercise of Congress' power under § 5 of the Fourteenth Amendment. The ADEA's purported abrogation of the States' sovereign immunity is accordingly invalid.

Our decision today does not signal the end of the line for employees who find themselves subject to age discrimination at the hands of their state employers. We hold only that, in the ADEA, Congress did not validly abrogate the States' sovereign immunity to suits by private individuals. State employees are protected by state age discrimination statutes, and may recover money damages from their state employers, in almost every State of the Union. Those avenues of relief remain available today, just as they were before this decision. Because the ADEA does not validly abrogate the States' sovereign immunity, however, the present suits must be dismissed. Accordingly, the judgment of the Court of Appeals is affirmed.

Most recently, in *Coleman v. Court of Appeals of Maryland*,[43] the Court held that Congress did not abrogate the states' Eleventh Amendment immunity from suits for money damages under the "self-care" provision of the Family Medical Leave Act (FMLA), 29 U.S.C. § 2612(a)(1)(d). The self-care provision requires employers to grant employees unpaid leave to allow them to recover from a serious medical condition if the employee meets other statutory prerequisites, such as not exceeding the maximum allowable annual leave under the statute. The Court found that the legislative history of the FMLA did not show that Congress enacted the provision based on a history or pattern of state employers discriminating against women who needed to take time off for self-care, including during their pregnancies. In the absence of this evidence, the Court determined that the "self-care" provision of the FMLA was not "congruent and proportional" to the type of unconstitutional behavior that would support an abrogation of the states' sovereign immunity from suit for monetary relief under Section 5 of the Fourteenth Amendment. The Court contrasted the history of the "self-care" provision with the history of the "family leave" provisions of the FMLA, which it had previously upheld as abrogating the states' Eleventh Amendment immunity based on evidence and legislative findings of gender discrimination by states. *See Nevada Dep't of Human Resources v. Hibbs*, 538 U.S. 721 (2003).

E. Can Congress Enact Laws under Its Article I Authority That Abrogate the States' Eleventh Amendment Immunity?

The Constitution gives the federal government broad and sometimes exclusive authority under Article I to enact laws in certain subject areas, such as the power to regulate interstate and foreign commerce, the power to regulate commerce with Indian Tribes, and authority over patents. When Congress enacts a law under its Article I authority, it often applies the law to the states and then expressly or indirectly provides that aggrieved parties can sue states and/or state officials for violations of the law in federal and/or state court. In addition, Congress has the power under the Spending Clause in Article I to require states to meet certain conditions in order to receive federal money. For example, Congress may require that a state agree to waive

---

43. 566 U.S. 30 (2012) (plurality opn.).

its sovereign immunity from suit if it wants to receive federal financial assistance, which can amount to hundreds of millions of dollars.

1. Commerce Clause

As the Court began to parse out the criteria for determining when legislation is appropriate under section 5, it also had to address the separate but related question of whether Congress had the authority to abrogate the states' Eleventh Amendment immunity in laws enacted under its Article I authority. Because Congress's powers under Article I are so extensive, a ruling that Article I trumps the Eleventh Amendment would significantly limit the scope of that Amendment.

In *Seminole Tribe of Fla. v. Florida*, 517 U.S. 44 (1996), the Supreme Court held that Congress did *not* have the power under Article I to supplant the states' sovereign immunity from suit. The Court wrote:

> Even when the Constitution vests in Congress complete law-making authority over a particular area, the Eleventh Amendment prevents congressional authorization of suits by private parties against unconsenting States. The Eleventh Amendment restricts the judicial power under Article III, and Article I cannot be used to circumvent the constitutional limitations placed upon federal jurisdiction.[44]

In other words, the Eleventh Amendment clarifies that the federal courts do not have authority under Article III of the Constitution to entertain lawsuits brought by private parties against states. *Seminole* reaffirmed that Congress cannot expand the federal courts' Article III authority by enacting a law under its Article I authority.[45] Although *Seminole* dealt specifically with Congress's authority to regulate trade with Indian Tribes, the lower federal courts have understood the decision to apply more generally to Congress's power under the Commerce Clause and under various other provisions in Article I, such as protection of authors' copyrights and inventors' patents.[46]

2. Spending Clause

In the mid-1980s, Congress began to enact laws that applied to states under the Spending Clause in Article I of the Constitution, U.S. Const. art. I, § 8, cl. 1. Under the Spending Clause, Congress has "broad power to set the terms on which it disperses federal money to the States,"[47] including the authority to "attach conditions on the re-

---

44. Seminole Tribe of Florida v. Florida, 517 U.S. at 72–73.

45. *Id.* at 72.

46. *See e.g.*, Close v. State of New York, 125 F.3d 31, 38 (2d Cir. 1997) (applying *Seminole* to Commerce Clause statute and concluding, "[A]fter Seminole, Congress cannot abrogate the States' Eleventh Amendment sovereign immunity pursuant to any Article I power.").

47. Arlington Cent. Sch. Dist. Bd. of Educ. v. Murphy, 548 U.S. 291, 296 (2006) (citation omitted). Under the Spending Clause, Congress has the power, among other things, to provide for the "general welfare of the United States." U.S. Const. art I, § 8, cl. 1.

ceipt of federal funds...."[48] Using this authority, Congress began conditioning the receipt of federal funds on the states' voluntary waiver of their Eleventh Amendment immunity from suit. Nothing in the Spending Clause precludes Congress from placing conditions on federal funds that go beyond what is required by the Constitution.[49] In other words, Congress cannot deprive citizens of their constitutional rights, but can require stronger civil rights protections than those guaranteed by the Constitution.

One of the first cases to address the scope of Congress's authority under the Spending Clause vis-à-vis the states was *South Dakota v. Dole*, 483 U.S. 203, 207 (1987). In that case, the Court recognized that Spending Clause inducements shift the federal-state balance. The Court, therefore, set out five requirements that must be satisfied before the legislation will be considered valid: (1) "the exercise of spending power must be in pursuit of 'the general welfare,'" (2) the conditions of funding must be imposed unambiguously, so states are cognizant of the consequences of accepting federal funds, (3) the conditions must "not be unrelated to the federal interest in particular national projects or programs" funded under the challenged legislation, (4) the legislation must not be barred by other constitutional provisions, and (5) the financial pressure created by the conditional grant of federal funds must not rise to the level of compulsion.[50]

In 1986, Congress enacted the Civil Rights Remedies Equalization Act (CRREA), 42 U.S.C. § 2000d-7 (1986), and used its Spending Clause authority as a sword to compel states to "voluntarily" waive their sovereign immunity from suit as a condition of receiving federal money. CRREA expressly conditioned a state agency's acceptance of federal funds on the state's voluntary waiver of Eleventh Amendment immunity. The Act provides that "[a] State shall not be immune under the Eleventh Amendment of the Constitution of the United States from suit in Federal court for a violation of section 504 of the Rehabilitation Act of 1973, title IX of the Educational Amendments of 1972, the Age Discrimination Act of 1975, title VI of the Civil Rights Act of 1964, or the provisions of any other Federal statute prohibiting discrimination by recipients of Federal financial assistance." The federal courts have upheld CRREA as valid Spending Clause legislation sufficient to waive the states' Eleventh Amendment immunity from suit.[51]

A recent issue that has divided the lower federal courts is whether a waiver of sovereign immunity attributable to the receipt of federal money applies to both a suit for damages and a suit for equitable relief. The cases on this issue have arisen under the Religious Land Use and Institutionalized Persons Act (RLUIPA), where Congress provided that any person may "assert a violation of this chapter as a claim or defense in a judicial proceeding and obtain *appropriate relief* against a government."[52] In *Madi-*

---

48. South Dakota v. Dole, 483 U.S. 203, 206 (1987).

49. *Id.*

50. *Id.* at 207–08, 211.

51. *See e.g.*, Barbour v. Washington Metropolitan Area Transit Auth., 374 F.3d 1161, 1164 (D.C. Cir. 2004).

52. 42 U.S.C. § 2000cc-2(a) (emphasis added).

son v. Virginia, 474 F.3d 118, 129 (4th Cir. 2006), the Fourth Circuit found that the state government could not be held liable for monetary damages under RLUIPA. The court based this conclusion on its determination that the phrase "appropriate relief" ordinarily includes injunctive and declaratory relief, but is not generally understood to include money damages.[53] The court found that any waiver of the states' sovereign immunity should be strictly construed to apply only to those claims and bases for relief to which the states expressly agree by virtue of their receipt of federal money. Because states do not lightly waive their sovereign immunity from suit for money damages, a waiver with respect to damages should not be implied but must be clearly expressed by Congress in the terms of the statute. Conversely, in *Benning v. Georgia*, 391 F.3d 1299, 1305–06 (11th Cir. 2004), the Eleventh Circuit held that RLUIPA's reference to "appropriate relief" was specific enough to constitute a waiver of sovereign immunity with respect to damages.[54]

In 2011, the Supreme Court resolved the dispute in *Sossaman v. Texas*, 563 U.S. 277, 285 (2011). In that case, the Court held that any waiver of sovereign immunity must be strictly construed and the phrase "appropriate relief" in RLUIPA "does not so clearly and unambiguously waive sovereign immunity to private suits for damages" that the Court can be certain that the states consented to be sued for monetary relief when they accepted federal funds. Based on this conclusion, the Court found that Texas had agreed only to waive its sovereign immunity with respect to suits for equitable relief by virtue of accepting federal funds for its prisons and had not agreed to be sued for money damages under RLUIPA.

F. Other Circumstances Resulting in a State Waiver of Sovereign Immunity

The courts have consistently held that states waive their sovereign immunity from suit by voluntarily appearing in federal court. For example, in *Clark v. Barnard*,[55] the State of Rhode Island brought an interpleader action to claim money being held in a fund by a federal court. Once the State obtained control of the money, it objected to any further exercise of jurisdiction by that court. The Supreme Court held that because the state had voluntarily appeared by intervening as a claimant of the fund, it waived its sovereign immunity. The Court explained that the state's sovereign immunity "is

53. *See also* Cardinal v. Metrish, 564 F.3d 794, 801 (6th Cir. 2009) (holding that RLUIPA's "appropriate relief" language does not clearly and unequivocally indicate that the waiver of sovereign immunity extends to money damages); Sossaman v. Lone Star State of Texas, 560 F.3d 316, 331 (5th Cir. 2009) (the ordinary rule of statutory construction, i.e. that a court presumes a statute affords all ordinary remedies not expressly disclaimed—does not apply when inquiring whether a state waived its sovereign immunity, and therefore damages must be "expressly provided" in the statute in order for a court to find that a state has waived immunity to such suits), *aff'd*, 563 U.S. 277 (2011).

54. *Accord* Smith v. Allen, 502 F.3d 1255, 1271 (11th Cir. 2007) (State's receipt of federal prison funds constitutes a waiver of its sovereign immunity for suits seeking money damages under RLUIPA).

55. 108 U.S. 436, 447–48 (1883).

a personal privilege which it may waive at [its] pleasure" and its appearance in the proceeding was "a voluntary submission" to the jurisdiction of the federal court.

Accordingly, when a state initiates a proceeding in federal court, whether by filing an action or claiming money in a fund as an interpleader, it waives its immunity. *See Gunther v. Atlantic Coast Line R. Co.*, 200 U.S. 273, 284 (1906) (state, by "voluntarily becom[ing] a party to a cause, and submit[ting] its rights for judicial determination," cannot escape the result of its own voluntary act by invoking the prohibitions of the Eleventh Amendment.").[56] The state's waiver, however, is generally limited by the nature of the claim asserted by the state and by the type of relief it requests. For example, a state does not consent to counterclaims on issues different than those raised in the state's complaint or to relief broader than the relief sought in the state's complaint. *See Oklahoma Tax Comm'n v. Citizen Band Potawatomi Tribe of Okla.*, 498 U.S. 505, 509–510 (1991) (Indian tribe did not waive its tribal sovereign immunity to a counterclaim for damages and prospective injunctive relief by filing a lawsuit against the state seeking to enjoin the assessment of a tax). Some courts have interpreted this principle to mean that the state's voluntary submission to the court's jurisdiction waives sovereign immunity only with respect to claims arising out of the same transaction or occurrence and that seek to reduce the relief requested by the state. According to these courts, the waiver of immunity does not extend monetarily or substantively beyond the scope of the state's claim.[57]

The courts have struggled with the question of whether a state waives its immunity when it removes a lawsuit brought against it in state court to federal court and, if the State does waive its immunity, the scope and extent of the waiver. Under 28 U.S.C. § 1441, any defendant can remove a case to federal court that could have properly been brought to that court in the first instance. However, where the state is a defendant, it does not voluntarily enter a lawsuit and the issue remains whether removal is tantamount to a voluntary submission to the federal court's jurisdiction or whether the state retains its sovereign immunity defense.

In *Lapides v. Bd. of Regents of Univ. System of Ga.*,[58] the defendants were sued under both 42 U.S.C. § 1983 and Georgia state law in state court. Under state law, the state and its agencies waived their immunity from suit in state court, but the state removed the entire case to federal court and argued that it retained its immunity from suit on both the federal and state law claims in federal court by virtue of the Eleventh Amendment.[59] The Supreme Court decided the waiver question only with respect to the pendent state law claims[60] and held that the state had "voluntarily agreed to remove

---

56. *See also* Gardner v. New Jersey, 329 U.S. 565, 574 (1947) (State waives "any immunity" it has "respecting the adjudication" of a claim that it files in federal court).

57. *See, e.g.*, United States v. Forma, 42 F.3d 759, 764–65 (2d Cir. 1994); Frederick v. United States, 386 F.2d 481, 488 (5th Cir. 1967).

58. 535 U.S. 613 (2002).

59. *Id.* at 616–617.

60. *Id.* at 616–618. The federal claims against the individual defendants were dismissed, and the remaining federal claim against the state was deemed to be invalid under 42 U.S.C. § 1983.

the case to federal court" and, as a result, had "voluntarily invoked the federal court's jurisdiction."[61] Under these circumstances, the state waived its Eleventh Amendment immunity from suit. The Court rejected the state's arguments that its waiver should not apply to suits for money damages and that the motive for the removal should be considered in determining whether the federal court had jurisdiction over the state entity.[62] The Court wrote that motives "are difficult to evaluate, while jurisdictional rules should be clear."[63]

Lapides left open the issue of whether the waiver determination should be different if (1) there is also a valid federal claim brought against the state, or (2) the state retains its sovereign immunity from suit in state court and then removes the case to federal court. Neither of these issues has been resolved by the Supreme Court.

With respect to whether the state waives its sovereign immunity if the lawsuit includes federal claims, most courts hold that removal results in waiver with respect to both federal and state law claims.[64] With respect to whether waiver applies to the removed claim if the state is immune from suit in its own courts, the Circuits are divided. Three Circuits have held that the state does not waive its sovereign immunity, while three other Circuits have concluded that removal results in a waiver even though the state is immune from suit on the removed claim in its own courts.[65]

Another issue with respect to removal is whether a state that is determined to have waived sovereign immunity also waives any substantive defenses the state may have to the underlying legal claims. In some cases, these "substantive defenses" are closely intertwined with the state's sovereign immunity defense. One example would be the defense that Congress's attempt to abrogate the state's sovereign immunity did not comply with the requirements for this abrogation under Section 5 of the Fourteenth Amendment. To date, three Circuits have concluded that the state's waiver of sovereign immunity does not waive "substantive defenses" to the underlying federal law claim, even where the defenses are closely related to the sovereign immunity defense.[66] One of those cases is *Stroud v. McIntosh*, which is set out below.

---

61. *Id.* at 620.

62. *Id.* at 621.

63. *Id.*

64. *See e.g.*, Lombardo v. Penn., Dep't of Welfare, 540 F.3d 190, 197 (3d Cir. 2008); Embury v. King, 361 F.3d 562, 564 (9th Cir. 2004); Estes v. Wyo. Dep't of Transp., 302 F.3d 1200, 1204 (10th Cir. 2002).

65. *Compare* Bergemann v. R.I. Dep't of Envtl. Mgmt., 665 F.3d 336, 341–42 (1st Cir. 2011) (removal did not result in a waiver of sovereign immunity on federal claims because state was immune from these claims in its own courts); Stewart v. North Carolina, 393 F.3d 484, 488–89 (4th Cir. 2005) (same); Watters v. Washington Metro. Area Transit Auth., 295 F.3d 36, 42 n. 13 (D.C. Cir. 2002), cert. denied, 538 U.S. 1574 (2003) (same) *with* Bd. of Regents of the Univ. of Wis. Sys. v. Phoenix Int'l Software, Inc., 653 F.3d 448, 461 (7th Cir. 2011) (state's removal results in waiver of immunity even where the state was immune from suit for the removed claims in state court); Embury v. King, 361 F.3d at 564–65 (same); Estes v. Wyo. Dep't of Transp., 302 F.3d at 1204–06.

66. *See* Stroud v. McIntosh, 722 F.3d 1294, 1302 (11th Cir. 2013), cert. denied, 571 U.S. 1131 (2014); Lombardo v. Penn. Dep't of Pub. Welfare, 540 F.3d at 198; Myers ex rel. Benzing v. Texas, 410 F.3d 236, 255 (5th Cir. 2005), cert. denied, 550 U.S. 917 (2007).

Questions to guide reading of *Stroud v. McIntosh*

1. Explain the difference between immunity from suit and immunity from liability.
2. Why would allowing a state to both remove a case to federal court and then argue immunity from suit "generate seriously unfair results?"
3. Does it make sense to separate sovereign immunity from suit and sovereign immunity from liability?

Patricia G. Stroud, Plaintiff-Appellant v. Phillip McIntosh, the Alabama Board of Pardons and Paroles, Defendants-Appellees

United States Court of Appeals, Eleventh Circuit
July 23, 2013

Before WILSON and COX, Circuit Judges, and VOORHEES, District Judge.

COX, Circuit Judge:

The principal issues we address in this appeal are (1) whether removal of this case to a federal court waived the state agency's sovereign immunity from *suit* in a federal court, and (2) whether removal of the case waived the agency's sovereign immunity from *liability* on a claim under the federal Age Discrimination in Employment Act. We conclude that removal waived the agency's immunity from suit in a federal forum but did not waive the agency's immunity from liability on this federal claim. We affirm.[67]

I. FACTS AND PROCEDURAL HISTORY

This case began in a circuit court in Montgomery County, Alabama, in December 2010, when Patricia Stroud sued her employer, the Alabama Board of Pardons and Paroles, and Phillip McIntosh, the Board's personnel director during the relevant time. Against the Board, Stroud's original complaint alleged claims under Title VII of the Civil Rights Act, 42 U.S.C. § 2000e-2, and the Alabama Age Discrimination in Employment Act (AADEA), Ala. Code §§ 25-1-20 to -29....

The Board and McIntosh removed the case to federal court, invoking the court's subject-matter jurisdiction under 28 U.S.C. § 1331. Five months after removal, Stroud amended her complaint ... and added a claim for damages under the federal Age Discrimination in Employment Act (ADEA), 29 U.S.C. §§ 621–634, against the Board.

The district court dismissed all of Stroud's federal claims other than the ADEA claim for failure to state a claim. (Immunity was not a basis for dismissal of these claims.) Importantly for this appeal, the district court held that the Board was immune from liability under the ADEA and did not waive that immunity when it removed the

---

67. The footnotes in this decision have been omitted.

case to federal court. The court entered judgment in favor of the Board on the ADEA claim and remanded the remaining state law claims against McIntosh to state court.

Stroud appeals.

II. ISSUES ON APPEAL AND CONTENTIONS OF THE PARTIES

Stroud raises a number of issues on appeal. We address only her contentions that the Board waives its immunity from suit and its immunity from liability under the ADEA when it removed the case....

III. DISCUSSION ...

B. Stroud's Contention

The ADEA, as enacted, authorized suits against states. But the Supreme Court held that Congress was without authority to abrogate states' sovereign immunity against ADEA claims. *See Kimel,* 528 U.S. at 91–92, 120 S. Ct. at 650. The Court held that the ADEA was "not a valid exercise of Congress's power under § 5 of the Fourteenth Amendment" because of "the indiscriminate scope of the Act's substantive requirements[ ] and the lack of evidence of widespread and unconstitutional age discrimination by the States." *Id.* at 91, 120 S. Ct. at 650.

Stroud recognizes *Kimel*'s holding. But she argues that the Board waived this immunity when it removed the case to federal court....

D. Our Holding ...

1.

As a preliminary matter, we agree that sovereign immunity is a divisible concept. *See Lombardo,* 540 F.3d at 198–200; *Meyers,* 410 F.3d at 252–55. The Supreme Court has repeatedly recognized that sovereign immunity is a flexible defense with multiple aspects that states can independently relinquish without affecting others. *See, e.g., Sossamon v. Texas,* 563 U.S. [277], 131 S. Ct. 1651, 1658, 179 L.Ed.2d 700 (2011) (noting that a state's waiver of sovereign immunity "in its own courts is not a waiver of its immunity from suit in federal court" and that a state can retain its "immunity to damages" even if it waives sovereign immunity against "other types of relief"); *Fed. Mar. Comm'n,* 535 U.S. at 766, 122 S. Ct. at 1877 (suggesting that sovereign immunity is an immunity "from suit" and encompasses a narrower "defense to monetary liability"); *Coll. Sav. Bank,* 527 U.S. at 676, 119 S. Ct. at 2226 (noting that a state can retain its immunity from suit in federal court even when it waives immunity in its own courts (citing *Smith v. Reeves,* 178 U.S. 436, 441–45, 20 S. Ct. 919, 921–22, 44 L. Ed. 1140 (1900))); *Atascadero State Hosp. v. Scanlon,* 473 U.S. 234, 241, 105 S. Ct. 3142, 3146–47, 87 L.Ed.2d 171 (1985) (same), *superseded by statute on other grounds,* Rehabilitation Act Amendments of 1986, Pub. L. No. 99-506, 100 Stat. 1807. And courts (including ours) have acknowledged that sovereign immunity can include immunity from suit as well as immunity from liability, depending on a state's choices in fashioning the scope of its immunity. *See, e.g., New Hampshire v. Ramsey,* 366 F.3d 1, 15 (1st Cir. 2004) ("Certainly, a state may waive its immunity from substantive liability without waiving its immunity from suit in a federal forum."); *CSX Transp.,*

Inc. v. Kissimmee Util. Auth., 153 F.3d 1283, 1286 (11th Cir. 1998) (examining Florida law and determining that Florida fashions its sovereign immunity as an immunity from liability but not from suit); *cf. Seminole Tribe of Fla. v. Florida*, 517 U.S. 44, 58, 116 S. Ct. 1114, 1124, 134 L.Ed.2d 252 (1996) (explaining that the sovereign immunity embodied by the Eleventh Amendment exists both to "preven[t] federal-court judgments that must be paid out of a State's treasury," implying an immunity from liability, and to "avoid the indignity of subjecting a State to the coercive process of judicial tribunals at the instance of private parties," implying an immunity from suit (alteration in original) (internal quotation marks omitted)).

The point that arises from these cases: a state, if it chooses, can retain immunity from liability for a particular claim even if it waives its immunity from suit in federal courts.

2.

The Board contends that *Lapides* does not apply to this case because, unlike in *Lapides*, Alabama has not waived its immunity before its own courts for ADEA claims. We agree with the Board's position that *Lapides* is distinguishable and does not *control* our result. But the first question we address is whether to accept *Lapides*'s reasoning as support for a holding that removal in this case waived the Board's immunity from a federal forum. We conclude that *Lapides*'s reasoning supports that holding.

A close reading of the opinion shows that the *Lapides* Court sought to avoid the unfairness, anomaly, and inconsistency of a state's invocation of federal jurisdiction by removal, on one hand, and on the other, its denial of federal jurisdiction by asserting immunity from federal court proceedings. The Court first mentions this potential anomaly at the beginning of its analysis:

> It would seem anomalous or inconsistent for a State both (1) to invoke federal jurisdiction, thereby contending that the "Judicial power of the United States" extends to the case at hand, and (2) to claim Eleventh Amendment immunity, thereby denying that the "Judicial power of the United States" extends to the case at hand.

Lapides, 535 U.S. at 619, 122 S. Ct. at 1643. This paradox, the Court says, "could generate seriously unfair results." *Id.* The Court notes that the voluntary-invocation principle seeks to avoid "selective use of 'immunity' to achieve litigation advantages." *Id.* at 620, 122 S. Ct. at 644. In other words, it would be unfair to allow a state to remove to a federal forum and then assert a jurisdictional immunity from that federal forum—this tactic would allow a state to essentially use removal as a jurisdictional trump card in any case initiated in a state forum that could fall under the original jurisdiction of the federal courts.

So, under *Lapides*'s reasoning, a state waives its immunity from a federal forum when it removes a case, which voluntarily invokes the jurisdiction of that federal forum. But nothing in *Lapides* suggests that a state waives any defense it would have enjoyed in state court—including immunity from liability for particular claims. *Lapides* specifies that it is addressing only immunity to a federal forum. *Id.* at 618, 122 S. Ct. at 1643 (narrowing the discussion to whether Georgia waived its "Eleventh

Amendment immunity from suit in a federal court"); *id.* at 624, 122 S.Ct. at 1646 ("[R]emoval is a form of voluntary invocation of a federal court's jurisdiction sufficient to waive the State's otherwise valid objection to *litigation of a matter ... in a federal forum.*" (emphasis added)). In fact, the opinion distinguishes this immunity against federal court proceedings from a state's "underlying sovereign immunity," *id.* at 617–18, 122 S. Ct. at 1643—implying that its discussion of immunity from federal court does not address other aspects of sovereign immunity, including a state's immunity from liability. Finally, the Court's reasoning, including its concern for the potential unfairness of a state gaining a new litigation advantage by removing, does not involve a state's immunity from liability that the state would have enjoyed had it remained in its own courts. We do not understand *Lapides* to require the state to forfeit an affirmative defense to liability simply because it changes forums. But the *Lapides* Court's reasoning supports the propositions that a state consents to federal jurisdiction over a case by removing and that it cannot then challenge that jurisdiction by asserting its immunity from a federal forum. We therefore hold that the Board waived its immunity from suit in federal court when it removed the case.

3.

That brings us to our final point. The defense of immunity from a federal forum was not the only immunity-based defense the Board had in its arsenal and asserted in the Answer. As we have established, a state can waive its forum immunity but retain other aspects of sovereign immunity, including immunity from liability for certain claims. *See Lombardo,* 540 F.3d at 198–200; *Meyers,* 410 F.3d at 252–55. Here, an arm of the state remains immune from liability for claims under the ADEA, notwithstanding its removal of the case.

The Supreme Court has made it clear that the ADEA is unconstitutional as applied to the states because Congress did not enact the law under section 5 of the Fourteenth Amendment, the only recognized constitutional basis for abrogating states' sovereign immunity. *Kimel,* 528 U.S. at 91–92, 120 S. Ct. at 650. The Board's removal of the case did not waive its constitutional objection to ADEA liability on the basis of sovereign immunity. *See Meyers,* 410 F.3d at 255 n. 27 (recognizing that, even after waiver by removal, a state may raise an objection to liability on the basis that Congress did not abrogate its sovereign immunity).

Nor has Alabama waived its immunity from ADEA claims through other means.... Alabama may assert the defense of immunity from ADEA liability in state court.... Its removal to federal court did not affect the availability of that defense. *Cf. Lombardo,* 540 F.3d at 198 ("[W]hile voluntary removal waives a State's immunity from suit in a federal forum, the removing State retains all defenses it would have enjoyed had the matter been litigated in state court, including immunity from liability."); *Meyers,* 410 F.3d at 255 ("[T]he Constitution permits and protects a state's right to relinquish its immunity from suit while retaining its immunity from liability, or vice versa...."). The Board's affirmative defense of sovereign immunity was therefore valid, and the district court correctly held that the Board did not waive that defense by removing.

IV. CONCLUSION

We conclude that the Board waived its defense of immunity from litigation in federal court when it removed to federal court, but the Board did not waive its immunity from ADEA liability. The judgment of the district court is therefore

AFFIRMED.

Index

A

L

N

P

R

S

T

U

V

W